The Norton Anthology of World Literature

SECOND EDITION

VOLUME C

1500–1650

The Norton Anthology
of World Literature

SECOND EDITION

Sarah Lawall, *General Editor*

PROFESSOR OF COMPARATIVE LITERATURE AND ADJUNCT PROFESSOR OF
FRENCH, UNIVERSITY OF MASSACHUSETTS, AMHERST

Maynard Mack, *General Editor Emeritus*

LATE OF YALE UNIVERSITY

VOLUME C

1500–1650

W • W • N O R T O N & C O M P A N Y • *New York* • *London*

Editor: Peter J. Simon
Developmental Editor: Carol Flechner
Associate Managing Editor: Marian Johnson
Production Manager: Diane O'Connor
Editorial Assistant: Isobel T. Evans
Project Editors: Candace Levy, Vivien Reinart, Carol Walker, Will Rigby
Permissions Manager: Nancy Rodwan
Assistant Permissions Manager: Sandra Chin
Text Design: Antonina Krass
Art Research: Neil Ryder Hoos
Maps: Jacques Chazaud

The text of this book is composed in Fairfield Medium
with the display set in Bernhard Modern.
Composition by Binghamton Valley Composition.
Manufacturing by R. R. Donnelley & Sons.
Cover illustration: Detail from *Codex Fejervary-Mayer*. The Board of Trustees of the National
Museums and Galleries on Merseyside, Liverpool Museum.

The Library of Congress has cataloged another edition as follows:

The Norton anthology of world literature / Sarah Lawall, general editor; Maynard
Mack, general editor emeritus. — 2nd ed.
    p.   cm.
Includes bibliographical references and index.
Contents: v. A. Beginnings to A.D. 100 — v. B. A.D. 100–1500 — v. C. 1500–1650 — v.
D. 1650–1800 — v. E. 1800–1900 — v. F. The twentieth century.
ISBN 0-393-97764-1 (v. 1) — ISBN 0-393-97765-X (v. 2)
    1. Literature — Collections.   I. Lawall, Sarah N.   II. Mack, Maynard, 1909–

PN6014 .N66 2001
808.8 — dc21   2001030824

ISBN 0-393-97757-9 (pbk.)

W. W. Norton & Company, Inc., 500 Fifth Avenue, New York, NY 10110
www.wwnorton.com

W. W. Norton & Company Ltd., Castle House, 75/76 Wells Street, London W1T 3QT

1 2 3 4 5 6 7 8 9 0

Contents

Native America and Europe in the New World   3063

Preface

The first edition of the *Norton Anthology of World Literature* to appear in the twenty-first century offers many new works from around the world and a fresh new format that responds to contemporary needs. The global reach of this anthology encompasses important works from Asia and Africa, central Asia and India, the Near East, Europe, and North and South America—all presented in the light of their own literary traditions, as a shared heritage of generations of readers in many countries, and as part of a network of cultural and literary relationships whose scope is still being discovered. With this edition, we institute a shift in title that reflects the way the anthology has grown. The initial *Norton Anthology of World Masterpieces* (1956) aimed to present a broader "Western tradition of world literature" in contrast to previous anthologies confined to English and American works; it focused on the richness and diversity of Western literary tradition, as does the Seventh Edition of 1999. The present volume, which derives from the "Expanded" edition of 1995, contains almost all the texts of the Seventh Edition and also thousands of pages from works around the globe; it now logically assumes the broader title of "World Literature." In altering the current title to *The Norton Anthology of World Literature,* we do not abandon the anthology's focus on major works of literature or a belief that these works especially repay close study. It is their consummate artistry, their ability to express complex signifying structures, that gives access to multiple dimensions of meaning, meanings that are always rooted in a specific setting and cultural tradition but that further constitute, upon comparison, a thought-provoking set of perspectives on the varieties of human experience. Readers familiar with the anthology's two volumes, whose size increased proportionally with the abundance of new material, will welcome the new boxed format, in which each of the earlier volumes is separated into three slim and easily portable smaller books. Whether maintaining the chronological structure of the original boxed set or selecting a different configuration, you will be able to consult a new Web site, developed by Norton specifically for the world-literature anthologies and containing contextual information, audiovisual resources, exploratory analyses, and related material to illustrate and illuminate these compelling texts.

The six volumes represent six consecutive chronological periods from approximately 2500 B.C. to the present. Subsequently, and for pedagogical reasons, our structure is guided by the broad continuities of different cultural traditions and the literary or artistic periods they recognize for themselves. This means that chronology advises but does not dictate the order in which works appear. If Western tradition names a certain time slot "the Renaissance" or "the Enlightenment" (each term implying a shared set of beliefs), that designation has little relevance in other parts of the globe; similarly, "vernacular literature" does not have the same literary-historical status in all traditions; and "classical" periods come at different times in India, China, and Western Europe. We find that it is more useful to start from a tradition's own sense of itself and the specific shape it gives to the community memory embodied as art. Occasionally there are displacements of absolute chronology: Petrarch, for example, belongs chronologically with Boccaccio and Chaucer, and Rousseau is a contemporary of Voltaire. Each can be read as a new and dissonant voice within his own century, a foil and balance for accepted ideas, or he can be considered as part of a powerful new consciousness, along with those indebted to his thought and example. In the first and last volumes of the anthology, for different pedagogical purposes, we have chosen to present diverse cultural traditions together. The first section of the first volume, "The Invention of Writing and the Earliest Literatures," introduces students to the study of world literature with works from three different cultural traditions—Babylonian, Egyptian, Judaic—each among the oldest works that have come down to us in written form, each in its origins reaching well back into a preliterate past, yet directly accessible as an image of human experience and still provocative at the beginning of the twenty-first century. The last volume, *The Modern World: Self and Other in Global Context,* reminds us that separation in the modern world is no longer a possibility. Works in the twentieth century are demonstrably part of a new global consciousness, itself fostered by advances in communications, that experiences reality in terms of interrelationships, of boundaries asserted or transgressed, and of the creation of personal and social identity from the interplay of sameness and difference. As teachers, we have tried to structure an anthology that is usable, accessible, and engaging in the classroom—that clarifies patterns and relationships for your students, while leaving you free to organize selections from this wealth of material into the themes, genres, topics, and special emphases that best fit your needs.

Changes in this edition have taken several forms. Most visibly, there are many new selections to spark further combinations with works you have already been teaching and to suggest ways of extending your favorite themes with additional geographic, gendered, chronological, or cultural perspectives. Thus the volume on the twentieth-century adds five important Latin American authors who are pivotal figures in their own time and with an established international stature that, in a few cases, is just beginning to be recognized in the United States. In fiction, there is Juan Rulfo, whose landmark novel *Pedro Páramo* is at once an allegory of political power in modern Mexico and a magical narrative that introduced modernist techniques to Latin American fiction, and Clarice Lispector, the innovative Brazilian novelist and short-story writer who writes primarily about women's experience and is internationally known for her descriptions of psychological states of mind. In poetry, the vehicle for political and cultural revolution in so many European and Latin American countries, we introduce the Nicaraguan Rubén Darío, a charismatic diplomat-poet at home in Europe and Latin America who created the image of a Spanish cultural identity that included his own Indian ancestry and counteracted prevailing images of North American dominance. After Darío there is Alfonsina Storni, the Argentinian poet who was as well known in the 1920s and 1930s for her independent journal articles and her feminism as for the intensely personal poetry that assures her reputation today. Finally, the Nobel Prize winner and Chilean activist Pablo Neruda, who reinvigorated the concept of public poet and became the best-known Latin American poet of the twentieth century, is represented by selections from various periods and styles of his work—in particular, the epic vision of human history taken by many to be his crowning achievement, *The Heights of Macchu Picchu*. Works by all five authors add to our representation of Spanish and Latin American literature, but their importance is not limited to regional or cultural representation. Each functions within a broader framework that may be artistic convention; national, ethnic, or class identity; feminist or postcolonial perspectives; or a particular vision of human experience. Each resonates with other works throughout the volume and is an opportunity to enrich your world-literature syllabus with new comparisons and contrasts.

Many of the new selections draw attention to historical circumstances and the texture of everyday life. Biographical tales from records of the ancient Chinese historian Ssu-ma Ch'ien give a glimpse of contemporary attitudes and ideals, as does the dedicated historian's poignant *Letter in Reply to Jen An*, written after his official punishment by castration. Entries in Dorothy Wordsworth's *Grasmere Journals* express the very personal world of the intimate journal, and Virginia Woolf's passionate analysis of the woman writer's position, in *A Room of One's Own*, combines autobiography with essay and fiction. Still other texts focus on specific historical events or issues but employ fictional techniques for greater immediacy. There is a thin line between fiction and autobiography in Tadeusz Borowski's terrifying Holocaust story *Ladies and Gentlemen, to the Gas Chamber*. Nawal El Saadawi's chilling courtroom tale *In Camera* uses the victim's shifting and fragmented perspectives to evoke the harsh realities of twentieth-century political torture and repression. Zhang Ailing's novella of a difficult love, *Love in a Fallen City*, depicts the decline of traditional Chinese society and concludes with the Japanese bombing of Hong Kong in World War II, while Anita Desai's *The Rooftop Dwellers* follows the struggles of a single woman in Delhi to make a career for herself in the face of social disapproval and family pressure. African American realist author Richard Wright, describes an adolescent crisis related to specific social images of manliness in *The Man Who Was Almost a Man*. Yet there are always different ways of presenting historical circumstances and dealing with the questions they raise. A play from Renaissance Spain, Lope de Vega's *Fuente Ovejuna*, is a light romantic comedy that draws heavily on dramatic conventions for its humor; yet it is also set during a famous peasant uprising whose bloodshed, political repercussions, and torture of the entire citizenry are represented in the course of the play. Readers who follow historical and cultural themes throughout the anthology will find much provocative material in these diverse new selections.

In renewing this edition, we have taken several routes: introducing new authors (many previously mentioned); choosing an alternate work by the same author when it resonates with material in other sections or speaks strongly to current concerns; adding small sections to existing larger pieces in order to fill out a theme or narrative line, or to suggest connections with other texts; and grouping several works to bring out new strengths. Three stories by the African writer Bernard Dadié appear here for the first time, as do the romantic adventures of Ludovico Ariosto's epic parody *Orlando Furi-*

oso, an African tale by Doris Lessing—*The Old Chief Mshlanga*—and Alice
Munro's complex evocation of childhood memories *Walker Brothers Cowboy.*
Among the alternate works by existing authors, we present Gustave Flau-
bert's great realist novel *Madame Bovary,* James Joyce's Dublin tale *The Dead,*
and William Faulkner's *The Bear,* the latter printed in its entirety to convey
its full scope as a chronicle of the legacy of slavery in the American South.
New plays include Bertolt Brecht's drama *The Good Woman of Setzuan* and
William Shakespeare's *Othello* as well as *Hamlet;* each has its own special
resonance in world literature. Derek Walcott is represented by a selection of
his poetry, including excerpts from the modern epic *Omeros.* Five more magical tales are added to the *Thousand and One Nights* and three new essays
from Montaigne, including his memorable *To the Reader.* Six new tales from
Ovid (in a new translation by Allen Mandelbaum) round out a set of myths
exploring different images of love and gender, themes that reappear in two
of the best-known lays of Marie de France, *Lanval* and *Laüstic,* as well as in
Boccaccio's famous "Pot of Basil" and the influential tale of patient Griselda
and her tyrannical husband, all presented here. From Chaucer, there is the
bawdy, popular *Wife of Bath's Tale,* and from the *Heptameron* of Marguerite
de Navarre fresh tales of love and intrigue that emphasize the stereotyping
of gender roles. To *The Cherry Orchard* by Anton Chekhov, we add his
famous tale of uncertain love *The Lady with the Dog.* New selections from
Books 4 and 8 of John Milton's *Paradise Lost* depict the drama of Satan's
malevolent entry into Paradise, Adam and Eve's innocent conversation, and
the angel's warning to Adam. Finally, the poignant tales of Abraham and
Isaac and of Jacob and Esau (Genesis 22, 25, 27) are added to the Old
Testament selections, as well as the glorious love poetry of the Song of Songs;
and Matthew 13 [Why Jesus Teaches in Parables] is included among the
selections from the New Testament.

Two founding works of early India, the *Rāmāyaṇa* and the *Mahābhārata,*
are offered in greatly increased selections and with new and exceptionally
accessible translations. Readers can now follow (in a new translation by
Swami Venkatesananda) the trajectory of Rāma's exile and life in the forest,
the kidnapping of his wife Sītā, and ensuing magical adventures up to the
final combat between Rāma and the demon king Rāvaṇa. A lively narrative
of the *Mahābhārata*'s civil war (in a new translation by C. V. Narasimhan)
unfolds in sequential excerpts that include two sections of special interest
to modern students: the insulted Draupadī's formal accusation of the rulers
in the Assembly Hall and the tragic story of the heroic but ill-fated warrior
Karṇa.

To increase our understanding of individual authors' achievement, we join
to the Indian Rabindranath Tagore's story *Punishment* a selection of the
Bengali poems with which he revolutionized literary style in his homeland,
and to the Chinese Lu Xun's two tales, examples of his poetry from *Wild
Grass.* Rousseau's *Confessions* gain historical and psychological depth
through new passages that shed light on his early years and on the development of his political sympathies.

The epic poetry that acts as the conscience of a community—*The Iliad,
The Mahābhārata,* the *Son-Jara,* among others—has long been represented
in the anthology. It has been our practice, however, to minimize the presence
of lyric poetry in translation, recognizing—as is so cogently argued in the
"Note on Translation," printed at the end of each volume—that the precise

language and music of an original poem will never be identical with its translation and that short poems risk more of their substance in the transfer. Yet
good translations often achieve a poetry of their own and occupy a pivotal
position in a second literary history; thus the Egyptian love songs, the Chinese *Classic of Poetry* (*Book of Songs*), the biblical Song of Songs, and the
lyrics of Sappho, Catullus, Petrarch, Rumi, and Baudelaire have all had
influence far beyond the range of those who could read the original poems.
Some poetry collections—like the Japanese *Man'yōshū* and *Kokinshū*—are
recognized as an integral part of the society's cultural consciousness, and
others—notably, the European Romantics—embody a sea change in artistic
and cultural consciousness.

New to this edition is a series of poetry clusters that complement existing
collections and represent a core of important and influential poetry in five
different periods. You may decide to teach them as part of a spectrum of
poetic expression or as reference points in a discussion of cultural consciousness. Thus a newly translated series of early hymns by the Tamil Śaiva saints
exemplifies the early mystical poetry of India, while the multifarious vitality
of medieval Europe is recaptured in poems by men and women from Arabic,
Judaic, Welsh, Spanish, French, Provençal, Italian, English, and German
traditions. Those who have taught English Romantic poetry will find both
contrast and comparison in Continental poets from France, Italy, Germany,
Spain, and Russia, many of whom possess lasting influence in nineteenth-
and twentieth-century literature. Symbolism, whose insights into the relation
of language and reality have permeated modern poetry and linguistic theory,
is represented by the great nineteenth-century poets Charles Baudelaire,
Stéphane Mallarmé, Paul Verlaine, and Arthur Rimbaud. Finally, a cluster
of Dada-Surrealist poems that range from slashing, rebellious humor to
ecstatic love introduces the free association and dreamlike structures of this
visionary movement, whose influence extends around the world and has
strong links to modern art and film.

How to choose, as you turn from the library before you to the inevitable
constraint of available time? There is an embarrassment of riches, an inex-
haustible series of options, to fit whatever course pattern you wish. Perhaps
you have already decided to proceed by theme or genre, in chronological
order or by a selected comparative principle; or you have favorite titles that
work well in the classroom, and you seek to combine them with new pieces.
Perhaps you want to create modules that compare ideas of national identity
or of bicultural identity and shifting cultural paradigms, that survey images
of gender in different times and places or that examine the place of memory
in a range of texts. In each instance, you have only to pick and choose among
a variety of works from different countries, languages, and cultural back-
grounds. If you are teaching the course for the first time or wish to try something different, you may find what you are looking for in the sample syllabi
of the *Instructor's Guide* or on the new Web site, which will also contain
supporting material such as maps, time lines, and audio pronunciation glossaries, resource links, guides to section materials, various exercises and
assignments, and a series of teaching modules related to specific works.
Throughout, the editors (who are all practicing teachers) have selected and
prepared texts that are significant in their own area of scholarly expertise,
meaningful in the larger context of world literature, and, always, delightful,
captivating and challenging to students.

Clearly one can parcel out the world in a variety of ways, most notably geopolitical, and there is no one map of world literature. In order to avoid parochialism, some scholars suggest that we should examine cultural activity in different countries at the same period of time. Others attempt to deconstruct prevailing literary assumptions (often selected from Western literary theory) by using history or cultural studies as a framework for examining texts as documents. "Global" literary studies project a different map that depends on one's geopolitical view of global interactions and of the energies involved in the creation and dissemination of literature. *The Norton Anthology of World Literature*, Second Edition, takes a different point of departure, focusing first of all on literary texts—artifacts, if you will, that have a special claim on our attention because they have been read over a great period of time and are cherished by a wide variety of readers. Once such texts have been proposed as objects of knowledge—and enjoyment, and illumination— they are available for any and all forms of analysis. Situating them inside larger forms of textuality—linguistic, historical, or cultural—is, after all, an inevitable part of the meaning-making process. It is the primary task of this anthology, however, to present them as multidimensional objects for discussion and then to let our readers choose when and where to extend the analysis.

From the beginning, the editors of *The Norton Anthology of World Literature* have always balanced the competing—and, we like to think, complementary—claims of teaching and scholarship, of the specialist's focused expertise and the generalist's broader perspectives. The founding editors set the example, which guides their successors. We welcome three new successor editors to this edition: William G. Thalmann, Professor of Classics at the University of Southern California; Lee Patterson, Professor of English at Yale University; and Heather James, Associate Professor of English at the University of Southern California. Two founding editors have assumed Emeritus status: Bernard M. W. Knox, eminent classical scholar and legendary teacher and lecturer; and P. M. Pasinetti, who combines the intellectual breadth of the Renaissance scholar with a novelist's creative intuition. We also pay tribute to the memory of Robert Lyons Danly, translator and astute scholar of Japanese literature, whose lively interventions have been missed since his untimely death in 1995. Finally, we salute the memory of Maynard Mack, General Editor and presiding genius from the first edition through the Expanded Edition of 1995. An Enlightenment scholar of much wisdom, humanity, and gracefully worn knowledge, and a firm believer in the role of great literature—world literature—in illuminating human nature, he was also unstintingly dedicated to this anthology as a teaching enterprise. To him, therefore, and on all counts, we dedicate the first millennial edition of the anthology.

Acknowledgments

Among our many critics, advisers, and friends, the following were of special help in providing suggestions and corrections: Joseph Barbarese (Rutgers University); Carol Clover (University of California, Berkeley); Patrick J. Cook (George Washington University); Janine Gerzanics (University of Southern California); Matthew Giancarlo (Yale University); Kevis Goodman (University of California at Berkeley); Roland Greene (University of Oregon); Dmitri Gutas (Yale University); John H. Hayes (Emory University); H. Mack Horton (University of California at Berkeley); Suzanne Keen (Washington and Lee University); Charles S. Kraszewski (King's College); Gregory F. Kuntz; Michelle Latiolais (University of California at Irvine); Sharon L. James (Bryn Mawr College); Ivan Marcus (Yale University); Timothy Martin (Rutgers University, Camden); William Naff (University of Massachusetts); Stanley Radosh (Our Lady of the Elms College); Fred C. Robinson (Yale University); John Rogers (Yale University); Robert Rothstein (University of Massachusetts); Lawrence Senelick (Boston University); Jack Shreve (Alleghany Community College); Frank Stringfellow (University of Miami); Nancy Vickers (Bryn Mawr College); and Jack Welch (Abilene Christian University).

We would also like to thank the following people who contributed to the planning of the Second Edition: Charles Adams, University of Arkansas; Dorothy S. Anderson, Salem State College; Roy Anker, Calvin College; John Apwah, County College of Morris; Doris Bargen, University of Massachusetts; Carol Barrett, Austin Community College, Northridge Campus; Michael Beard, University of North Dakota; Lysbeth Em Berkert, Northern State University; Marilyn Booth, University of Illinois; George Byers, Fairmont State College; Shirley Carnahan, University of Colorado; Ngwarsungu Chiwengo, Creighton University; Stephen Cooper, Troy State University; Bonita Cox, San Jose State University; Richard A. Cox, Abilene Christian University; Dorothy Deering, Purdue University; Donald Dickson, Texas A&M University; Alexander Dunlop, Auburn University; Janet Eber, County College of Morris; Angela Esterhammer, University of Western Ontario; Walter Evans, Augusta State University; Fidel Fajardo-Acosta, Creighton University; John C. Freeman, El Paso Community College, Valle Verde Campus; Barbara Gluck, Baruch College; Michael Grimwood, North Carolina State University; Rafey Habib, Rutgers University, Camden; John E. Hallwas, Western Illinois College; Jim Hauser, William Patterson College; Jack Hussey, Fairmont State College; Dane Johnson, San Francisco State University; Andrew Kelley, Jackson State Community College; Jane Kinney, Valdosta State University; Candace Knudson, Truman State University; Jameela Lares, University of Southern Mississippi; Thomas L. Long, Thomas Nelson Community College; Sara MacDonald, Sterling College; Linda Macri, University of Maryland; Rita Mayer, San Antonio College; Christopher Morris,

Norwich University; Deborah Nestor, Fairmont State College; John Netland, Calvin College; Kevin O'Brien, Chapman University; Mariannina Olcott, San Jose State University; Charles W. Pollard, Calvin College; Pilar Rotella, Chapman University; Rhonda Sandford, Fairmont State College; Daniel Schenker, University of Alabama at Huntsville; Robert Scotto, Baruch College; Carl Seiple, Kutztown University; Glenn Simshaw, Chemeketa Community College; Evan Lansing Smith, Midwestern State University; William H. Smith, Piedmont College; Floyd C. Stuart, Norwich University; Cathleen Tarp, Fairmont State College; Diane Thompson, Northern Virginia Community College; Sally Wheeler, Georgia Perimeter College; Jean Wilson, McMaster University; Susan Wood, University of Nevada, Las Vegas; Tom Wymer, Bowling Green State University.

Phonetic Equivalents

for use with the Pronouncing Glossaries preceding most
selections in this volume

a as in *cat*
ah as in *father*
ai as in *light*
ay as in *day*
aw as in *raw*
e as in *pet*
ee as in *street*
ehr as in *air*
er as in *bird*
eu as in *lurk*
g as in *good*
i as in *sit*
j as in *joke*
nh a nasal sound (as in French *vin, vẽ*)
o as in *pot*
oh as in *no*
oo as in *boot*
oy as in *toy*
or as in *bore*
ow as in *now*
s as in *mess*
ts as in *ants*
u as in *us*
zh as in *vision*

The Norton Anthology
of World Literature

SECOND EDITION

VOLUME C

1500–1650

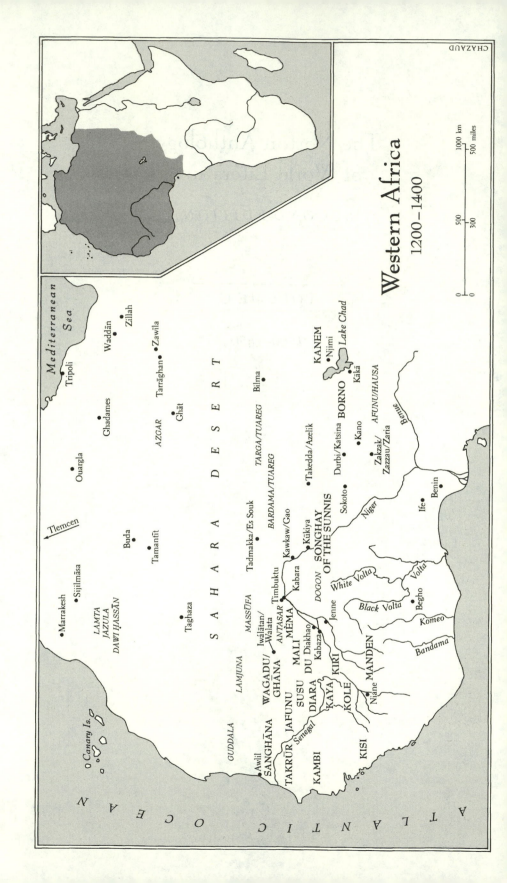

Western Africa
1200–1400

1000 km
500 miles
500
300

Mediterranean Sea

Tripoli
Waddān
Zillah
Tarrāghan • Zawila
Ghadames
AZGAR
Ghāt

Ouargla

Bilma

S A H A R A   D E S E R T

TARGA/TUAREG

BARDAMA/TUAREG

← Tlemcen

Buda
Tamantit

Marrakesh

*LAMTA
JAZULA
DAWĪ ḤASSĀN*

Sijilmāsa

Taghaza

Tadmakka/Es Souk

MASSŪFA

LAMJUNA

Iwālātan/
Walata

ANTASAR
Timbuktu
Kabara
MĒMA
DU Diakha

GUDDALA

Awlil
SANGHĀNA
TAKRŪR
JAFUNU
WAGADU/
GHĀNA
SUSU
DIARA
KAYA
KOLE
KISI
KAMBI

MALI
Kabaza
KIRI
MANDEN
Niane

Kawkaw/Gao
Kūkiya
DOGON
SONGHAY
OF THE SUNNIS
• Takedda/Azelik

KANEM
• Njimi
Lake Chad
Kākā

Durbi/Katsina
BORNO
AFUNU/HAUSA

Sokoto
• Kano
Zakak/
Zazzau/Zaria

Jenne
White Volta
Black Volta
Begho
Komeo
Volta
Bandama

Niger

Ife
Benin

Benue

Senegal

Canary Is.

A T L A N T I C   O C E A N

Africa: The Mali Epic of *Son-Jara*

late thirteenth–early fourteenth century

The epic of *Son-Jara* is the national epic of the Manding people, who inhabit what may be called the heartland of west Africa. The greater part of this area is in the savanna belt, in present-day Mali, but it also embraces, to the west and southwest, considerable parts of the coastal region bordering the Atlantic, in the modern states of Senegal, the Gambia, and Guinea. The people of this extensive area, which cuts across the boundaries established since the late nineteenth century by French and British colonial administrations, share a common history and culture deriving from a continuing sense of affiliation to the ancient, precolonial empire of Mali.

The founding of the Mali empire in the mid-thirteenth century is attributed to Son-Jara Keita, whose life and exploits are celebrated in the epic and whose hold on the feelings and imagination of the Manding people it has helped in no small measure to sustain to this day. In its oral form (as it is still performed all over the Manding area) the epic is considered to be not only the record of great events that led to the formation of the empire in the distant past—a factual recollection of its auspicious beginnings—but also a repository of the values of the society itself, even in its present circumstance. The epic thus functions for the Manding as a significant cultural reference, similar in this respect to the *Iliad* in ancient Greece and the *Rāmāyaṇa* in India.

The personality of Son-Jara (also known as Sundiata) is shrouded in mystery. All we know about him has had to be reconstructed from the oral tradition of the Manding—the epic itself forming the principal element of this tradition—and various Arab historical records concerning ancient Mali, which refer to its founder as "Mari Jata." Some of these records date from the very beginnings of the empire, but the most important historical account is the work of Ibn Khaldoun, whose fifteenth-century descriptions of the imperial court and the political and social life of the empire include a dynastic list of the rulers, traced back in every case to Son-Jara. Thus, although he has been transformed in the oral tradition into a figure of myth and legend, like the warriors of the Greek expedition to Troy, there seems no doubt about his historical existence. Nor is there doubt about his determining role in the establishment of Mali, initially as a centralized monarchical state and subsequently as a powerful empire that welded the various ethnic groups in the west African savanna into a distinctive national community.

The rise of ancient Mali in the thirteenth century represents an important stage in the process of state formation in west Africa, a process closely associated with the spread of Islam into the region, which began as early as the seventh century. The literacy Islam introduced enabled the formation (during the period that corresponds to the European Middle Ages) of an elite educated in Arabic, whose services to the early rulers made possible the establishment of their rule over ever-widening territories and fostered the emergence of the three best-known west African medieval empires: Songhay, Ghana, and Mali.

To understand the association of these early west African states with Islam, it is important to observe that in the oral tradition Son-Jara Keita is held to be the descendant of Bilal, a companion of Muhammad and a religious leader. Bilal's family is said to have migrated from the Near East and settled in the region, founding a religious community in the Manden, which proved to be the nucleus of ancient Mali. The version of the Son-Jara epic printed here begins with an invocation in which the hero is assimilated to Adam, the first man in both the Bible and the Koran, and thus underlines their common status as founding figures. Moreover, despite the fact that the epic's outlook on the world is essentially pagan, the invocation, which incorporates an allusion to Bilal as a close associate of Muhammad, and the many other references to Islam throughout the epic lend the sanction of an established world religion to the commemoration of the hero. The invocation thus intimates and prefigures the subsequent interaction between the practices and tenets of Islam and local Manding beliefs and customs. This cultural fusion within the poem mirrors the way in which a literate culture bound to Islam and the Arabic language was appropriated and integrated into the forms of an indigenous African orality.

Although the epic of Son-Jara has been recorded and transcribed by literary scholars in recent times, and thus carried one more stage into the realm of writing, it remains an integral part of the oral tradition in Africa. This tradition comprises various expressive forms—folk tales, legends, myths, and poetry—through which the imaginative impulse of preliterate societies takes shape. A conscious elaboration of language in these forms, managed through imagery and structural devices, distinguishes them from ordinary speech and gives them an aesthetic function above and beyond any referential content. Moreover, it is often the case that over the years oral cultures evolve a consecrated body of texts, a term that in oral literature applies to any extensive expression of experience in a *settled* art form. The generation, performance, and oral transmission of such texts endow them with a life of their own, so that they come to represent the literary monuments of the culture. In this respect, they function for oral societies in the same way that written literature does for literate societies.

The principal custodians of the oral tradition among the Manding are professional bards, known variously as *dyeli, belein-tigui,* or more commonly by the French term *griot.* They are specially trained oral performers who in former times were attached to the imperial court (and to its local replications across the Mali empire) as well as to members of the aristocracy. Their role was to recite from memory, on great occasions of state, the oral chronicles and family history of their patrons. In this capacity, they were expected not merely to recall the bare historical narrative as handed down by tradition but also, as poets and wordsmiths, to endow their recitations with all the power of language they could command, thus creating an ever-developing imaginative expression of the community's historical consciousness. It is to these "masters of the word" that we owe the persistence of the oral tradition and especially, among the Manding, the continued existence of the epic of *Son-Jara.*

The epic probably originated in a series of praise poems addressed to Son-Jara during his reign; their allusions to his virtues and exploits were developed later into an extended narrative of his life and heroic achievement. This development by accretion, together with the oral transmission of the resulting narrative, may explain why the epic exists not as a fixed text but rather as a fusion of three distinct generic layers.

Most important is the narrative framework. This is the overarching "master text" in which the movement of the epic is broadly formulated. This framework is composed of structural episodes, and it is the narrator's immediate task to recall these in appropriate sequence. He is, however, at liberty to expand on them in whatever way best suits the context of performance and the character of the audience, employing in the process a number of formulaic devices not only as props to memory but as building blocks in his recreation of the epic story. The interplay between core elements of the text, which are relatively fixed (for example, genealogies of families and clans), and the performer's free improvisations (often involving digressions and general reflections as well as anachronistic references and topical allusions) generates a profound sense that the story, though established by tradition, is at the same time constantly renewed in performance. Thus if orality implies limitations, it also implies creative possibilities, apparent in the many differing versions of the epic recorded by individual *griots*.

The other two generic layers derive from the conditions of oral performance outlined above. The many passages of praise poetry with which the epic is interspersed stand in a close formal relationship to the formulaic plan of the narrative. Their shape attests to their independent existence before they were integrated into the epic we have today, and they are still on occasion recited outside its narrative framework. As generally with praise poems in oral literature, they are composed of strings of epithets, often hyperbolic, emphasizing the uncommon attributes—the heroic essence as it were—of their subject. Finally, in the third layer are the songs. These function as interludes within the epic narrative but, like the praise poems, are often performed as autonomous pieces to the accompaniment of the *kora,* an elaborate stringed instrument with tonal qualities comparable to those of the harp.

Performance of the epic is highly rhythmic, with breath stops, often accentuated by tonal patterns, rather than meter or rhyme, determining the verse lines. This basic register frequently intensifies into a chanting mode, notably for the praise poems. The song mode, in which musical instruments intervene, is another resource available to performers of the epic. To these effects must be added movement and gesture, with which the narrator dramatizes action or provides a visual delineation of character. Such extraliterary aspects of epic performance represent crucial factors and subtly evoke that direct relationship of the *griot* to his audience without which it would have been difficult, if not impossible, to sustain the cultural vitality of the epic. In short, the *griot*'s task consists far less in reproducing an exact text of the epic from one performance to the other—a text with which the audience is usually familiar—than in bringing to life the master text: the epic narrative prescribed by tradition, as actualized, through his living agency, in a dramatic reenactment.

The epic of *Son-Jara* is primarily a political poem, centered on the rivalry of two brothers for succession to their father's throne, a theme exemplified by the conflict between Cain and Abel and Jacob and Esau in the Bible and that between Polynices and Eteocles in Sophocles' *Antigone.* This rivalry develops later into a wider contest between two rival chieftains for territorial control. Its ideological function as a myth to legitimize the ruling dynasty of ancient Mali is apparent not only from the heroic glorification of its historical founder but also from the motifs that structure the epic narrative. As in many early epics, psychological interest is limited and the hero's character is simply sketched; it is, however, endowed with symbolic significance. The story is essentially a relation of Son-Jara's trials, which he overcomes through his personal qualities—his piety, his filial devotion to his mother, his courage and tenacity. His final victory is also presented in moral terms as a triumph of good over evil. Fa-Koli's disaffection from the Susu Sumamuru (his uncle and Son-Jara's rival), which leads to his defection to Son-Jara—an act that proves decisive for the outcome of the struggle between Sumamuru and Son-Jara—is prompted by his sense of wrong. The moral implication of this episode, identifying Son-Jara's cause with that of universal justice, confirms the political and ideological thrust of the epic on a note that is distinctly personal and human.

The ideological function of the epic needs, however, to be placed in a broader perspective, that of the construction of a Manding collective identity around the figure of their founding hero. In its relation to the process of state formation in the west African savanna region, the epic of *Son-Jara* serves as the essential medium of the collective memory of the Manding people, keeping alive not only a sense of their historical continuities but also of the integrity of their communal values. The epic is thus the repository not merely of the achievements of an outstanding individual but of the growth of a national consciousness.

Although a singular work in many respects, the epic of *Son-Jara* is representative of the heritage of oral poetry in Africa. Scholarly research has made it increasingly evident that this heritage is more diversified than was thought; that it goes beyond folktales; and especially, that it includes extended forms, of which the epic genre— exemplified by the Son-Jara epic and other African narratives such as *Kabili, Da Monzon of Segou,* the *Mwindo* epic, and the *Ozidi* saga—forms an integral part. Beyond their intrinsic interest as outstanding forms of imaginative expression, these products of the African oral tradition point to a universal heritage—that literature seems almost everywhere (with few exceptions, notably China and Japan) to have had its beginnings in heroic song.

FURTHER READING

The epic of *Son-Jara* represents a communal resource, whose various versions are associated with individual *griots*. The earliest published version is the prose adaptation brought out in French in 1968 by the Malian historian, Djibril Tamsir Niane, *Sundiata, an Epic of Old Mali* (1989). This adaptation, undertaken as part of the nationalist reclamation of the African past, brought the work into the limelight and has remained its best-known version. While it presents a faithful rendering of the action, it fails to capture the epic's heroic movement and the atmosphere of performance essential to its character. Three further versions have been collected by Gordon Innes, *Sunjata: Three Madinka Versions* (1974), a work of interest mainly for comparative purposes. More recent is a prose adaptation by the Guinean novelist Camara Laye, *The Guardian of the Word* (1980), a controversial version in its highly personal reinterpretation as well as, in the view of many scholars, its distortion of the material. The version printed here was transcribed from a recital performed by the *griot* Fa-Digi Sisoko and translated by John William Johnson. More than any published version, this version conveys a sense of the epic's tone and movement as well as of the dynamics of its performance.

For a comprehensive discussion, from a cross-cultural perspective, of the epic genre in Africa, see Isidore Okpewho, *The Epic in Africa* (1979). Okpewho's work has been extended and updated on the basis of additional available material by Stephen Belcher, *Epic Traditions in Africa* (1999). Daniel Kunene, *Heroic Poetry of the Basotho* (1971), offers, through a meticulous thematic and stylistic analysis, a view of the dynamics of the praise poem, a genre of African oral poetry to which the *Son-Jara* epic is closely related. The historical context of the epic's composition and the extrinsic factors that govern its preservation and continued representation, as well as its formal features and modes of performance, are discussed in depth and detail by various specialists in the collective volume edited by Ralph Austen, *In Search of Sunjata: The Mande Oral Epic as History, Literature, and Performance* (1999). Adu Boahen, *Topics in West African History* (1990), provides in a succinct and readable form the general historical background. On the specific role of Islam as a historical and cultural factor in west Africa, see J. Spencer Trimingham, *A History of Islam in West Africa* (1970).

PRONOUNCING GLOSSARY

The following list uses common English syllables to provide rough equivalents of selected words whose pronunciation may be unfamiliar to the general reader.

Babangile: *bah-bah-en-gee-lay*	Bintanyan Kamalan: *been-tah-yarn kah-*
Bangari: *bah-en-ga-ree*	*mah-lan*
belein-tigui: *bay-len—tee-ghee*	Bugu Turu: *boo-goo too-roo*

Damangile: *dah-mahn-gee-lay*

Dankaran Tuman: *dahn-kah-ran too-man*

Dan Mansa Wulandin: *dahn man-sah woo-lahn-deen*

Dan Mansa Wulanba: *dahn man-sah woo-lahn-bah*

Dòka: *doh-kah*

Du Kamisa: *do kah-mee-sah*

Dun Fayiri: *doon fah-yee-ree*

dyeli: *jay-lee*

Fa-Digi Sisoko: *fah–dee-gee see-soh-koh*

Fata Magan: *fah-tah mah-gahn*

Garabaya: *gah-rah-bah-yah*

Genu: *gay-noo*

griot: *gree-oh*

Kamasiga: *kah-mah-see-gah*

Kanu Simbon: *kah-noo seem-bon*

Kukuba: *koo-koo-bah*

Kulu-Kòrò: *koo-loo–koh-roh*

Kulun: *koo-loon*

Kuyatè: *koo-yah-tay*

Magan Jata Kòndè: *mah-gahn jah-ta kon-day*

Mane: *ma-nay*

Nakana Tiliba: *nah-kah-nah tee-lee-bah*

Nare Magan Kònatè: *nah-ray mah-gan koh-nah-tay*

Nyani (Niane): *neer-nee*

Nyarè: *en-yah-ray*

Saman Berete: *sah-mahn bay-ray-tay*

Sane: *sah-nay*

Sankaradin: *sahn-ka-rah-deen*

Sasagalò: *sah-sag-gah-loh*

Son-Jara Keita: *sawn–jah-rah kay-ee-tah*

Sugulun Kòndè: *soo-goo-loon kon-day*

Sundiata: *soon-jah-tah*

Tanimunari: *tah-nee-moo-nah-ree*

Tarawere: *tah-rah-way-ray*

Tura Magan: *too-rah mah-gahn*

TIME LINE

TEXTS	CONTEXTS
ca. A.D. 300 Development of the Geez Script	
	A.D. 200–350 Introduction and spread of Christianity in North Africa
397 Augustine begins *Confessions*	
	500–1495 Rise of the west African savanna empires: Ghana in the northwest (ca. 500), Kanem around Lake Chad (ca. 900), Mali (ca. 1200), and Songhay in the Middle Niger (ca. 1495)
	600–1000 Introduction and spread of Islam in East and west Africa
13th–14th centuries *Epic of Son-Jara*	1300–1500 Rise of the Kongo kingdom on the lower Zaire (Congo) River, including present-day Angola, in central Africa; rise of Benin in west African forest belt, in the hinterland of the Niger delta (ca. 1400); and rise of Monomotapa ("Great Zimbabwe") in southern Africa, north of the Limpopo River (ca. 1500)
1352 *Arab Chronicles:* Ibn Battuta on ancient Mali	
	1450–1600 Portuguese explorers on the west and central African coasts
ca. 1513 Leo Africanus, *History and Description of Africa*	late 16th–mid 19th century The Atlantic slave trade

Boldface titles indicate works in the anthology.

From The Epic of Son-Jara[1]

FROM EPISODE 1

Prologue in Paradise

	Nare Magan Kònatè![2]	
	Sorcerer-Seizing-Sorcerer![3]	
	A man of power is hard to find.	
	And four mastersingers.	(Indeed)
5	O Kala Jula Sangoyi[4]	
	Sorcerer-Seizing-Sorcerer!	(Mmm)
	It is of Adam that I sing.	
	Of Adam,	
	Ben Adam.[5]	('Tis true)
10	As you succeeded some,	
	So shall you have successors![6]	
	It is of Adam that I sing, of Adam.	(Indeed)
	I sing of Biribiriba![7]	(Indeed)
	Of Nare Magan Kònatè!	
15	Sorcerer-Seizing Sorcerer!	(True)
	From Fatiyataligara	
	All the way to Sokoto,[8]	(Indeed)
	Belonged to Magan Son-Jara.	(Indeed)
	Africans call that, my father,[9]	
20	The Republic of Mali,[1]	(Indeed)
	The Maninka[2] realm:	(Mmm, 'tis true)
	That's the meaning of Mali.	
	Magan Son-Jara,	
	He slayed Bambara-of-the-Border;[3]	
25	Settling on the border[4] does not suit the weak.	(Indeed)
	And slayed Bambara-the-Lizard;[5]	
	No weak one should call himself lizard.	(Indeed)
	And slayed Bambara-of-the-Backwoods;	
	Settling the backwoods does not suit the weak.	(Indeed)

1. Text by Fa-Digi Sisoko; translated by John William Johnson. The words in parentheses at the right are interjections made by members of the audience, principally by Bèmba (see n. 4, p. 2416).   2. Son-Jara. This praise name combines a reference to his place of origin (*Nare*) with his royal title (*Magan,* "king" or "lord"; the title of the emperor of ancient Ghana was *Kaya Magan*). *Kònatè* is Son-Jara's clan.   3. This praise name refers to Son-Jara's superior magical powers.   4. A bard reputed to be the originator of the epic; he can thus be considered the equivalent of Homer with respect to the *Iliad*. He is invoked here in homage to the artistic ancestor of Fa-Digi Sisoko, the bard who is re-creating the epic on this occasion. The exact reference of line 4 is obscure, but its allusion to the bard's professional status is clearly related to the invocation of Kala Jula Sangoyi.   5. The Adam of Genesis.   6. A formulaic device employed by the bard at various points in the epic; here it stresses the unbroken continuity of Son-Jara's dynastic line.   7. This praise name for Son-Jara conveys his immense physical prowess.   8. An ancient city in northern Nigeria, several hundred miles east of the Manding area. The city was the capital of the Fulani empire, which by the early 19th century had embraced most of the area in the Niger-Benue basin and was conquered by the British in the early years of the 20th century. Fayitaligara can no longer be identified. The bard means the extent of the old Mali empire from west to east.   9. A term of reverence; here an aside addressed to the older members of the audience.   1. That is, present-day Mali; the name of the ancient empire was revived in 1960, when the modern republic achieved independence from France.   2. Manding or Mandenka; the term covers many more ethnic groups than are found in the present Republic of Mali.   3. That is, Sumamuru, Son-Jara's principal antagonist, who was a Susu, an ethnic group related to the Bambara of present-day Mali.   4. All areas beyond the safe limits of human settlement. The implication is that it requires an intrepid character, such as that associated with the professional hunter, to venture beyond these limits and confront the dangers of the wilderness.   5. A derogatory term that alludes to the fact that young boys start to practice hunting with lizards; hence the reptile is associated with the weak and uninitiated.

30   All this by the hand of Nare Magan Kònatè.
Sorcerer-Seizing-Sorcerer!
Simbon, Lion-Born-of-the-Cat.[6]   ('Tis true)

I sing of Biribiriba.   (Indeed)
Stump-in-the-Dark-of-Night![7]
35   Should you bump against it,
It will bump against you.   (Indeed)
Granary-Guard-Dog.[8]   (Indeed)
The thing discerning not the stranger,
Nor the familiar.
40   Should it come upon any person,
He will be bitten!   (Indeed)
Kirikara Watita![9]   (Indeed)
Adversity's-True-Place![1]   (Indeed)
Man's reason and a woman's are not the same.[2]   (Indeed)
45   Pretty words and truth are not the same.   (Indeed)
Almighty God created Adam,   (Indeed)
Nine Adams.[3]   (Indeed)
The tenth one was Ben Adam.   (True)

Ah, Bèmba![4]   (Indeed)
50   Almighty God created Adam, the forefather,   (Indeed)
And caused him to stand upon the earth,
And said that all creation's beings should submit to him.
And all the beings of creation did submit to him,   (Indeed)
Save Iblis[5] alone.
55   May God deliver us from Satan!   (Amen, O my Lord)

[Here follows a lengthy account of the Genesis story, in a version that incorporates a cosmological myth and the origin of the races of the world. This provides a background to the epic recall, in the next episode, of the original migration of the ancestors of the Manding from the Middle East and their settlement among and interaction with the indigenous peoples in the west African savanna. The reconstruction of the early history of the region serves to trace both the paternal and the maternal lines of Son-Jara's descent.]

FROM EPISODE 2

Mecca

I sing of Biribiriba!   (Indeed)
Kirikisa, Spear-of-Access, Spear-of-Service![6]   (Indeed)

6. Compare with "Lion Heart," which became attached to the name of the medieval king of England, Richard. *Simbon:* hunter; the ideal of manhood in traditional African societies.   7. This praise name presents Son-Jara as a formidable obstacle to his adversaries.   8. A praise name that emphasizes the hero's ferocity. A guard dog often does not distinguish between strangers and members of the household. 9. Ideophone for great strength. An ideophone is an expressive sound employed in African languages to convey an image or idea.   1. A source of adversity for his enemies.   2. A reflection on the different dispositions of the sexes in the varied roles played by male and female characters.   3. Possibly, the succession of founding figures, from the first man in the biblical story of creation down to Son-Jara himself. 4. The bard's apprentice, who serves as his principal interlocutor throughout the performance.   5. Satan (Arabic).   6. Three praise names for Son Jara. *Kirikisa:* denotes great power. *Spear-of-Access:* despite his ferocity in war, the hero remains humane and approachable to his people. *Spear-of-Service:* expands on the idea of approachability in a reference to his generosity.

170 The Messenger of God, Muhammad, was born,   (Indeed)
On the twelfth day of the month of Dònba.[7]   (Indeed)
On the thirteenth day,
Tuesday, Bilal was born in Samuda.[8]   (Indeed)
Ask the ones who know of this!   (Mmm)
175 That Bilal,   (Indeed)
His child was Mamadu Kanu.
That Mamadu Kanu,   (Mmm)
He had three sons: (Indeed)
Kanu Simbon,   (Indeed)
180 Kanu Nyògòn Simbon,
Lawali Simbon.   (Indeed)
Ah! Bèmba!   (Indeed)
The races of man were ninety in number.   (Indeed)
There were twelve clans of Marakas[9]   (Indeed)
185 Which came from Wagadugu.[1]   (Indeed)
The Sises came from Wagadugu.   (Mmm)
The Janes came from Wagadugu.   (Mmm)
The Tures came from Wagadugu.   (Indeed)
The Beretes came from Wagadugu.   (Indeed)
190 The Sakòs came from Wagadugu.
The Fulani came from Wagadugu.   (Indeed)
The Jawaras came from Wagadugu.   (Indeed)
The Nyarès came from Wagadugu.   (Indeed)
The Tunkaras came from Wagadugu.[2]   (Mmm)

195 The peoples of Wagadugu thus scattered.[3]   (Indeed)
O Bèmba!   (Indeed)
The ancestor of the Jawaras, Damangile,[4]   (Indeed)
And the forefather of the Nyarès,[5] Nyenemba
    Nyarè,   (Indeed)
Went forth to found a village in Kingi.[6]   (Indeed)
200 The name of that village was Bambagile.[7]   (Indeed)
Damangile's tomb is there in Bambagile.   (Indeed)
He had two children: (Indeed)
Daman and Sila Maan.   (Indeed)
They both went forth to Jala.[8]   (Mmm)
205 Mount Siman and Mount Wala[9] belong to the Jawaras
    in Jala.   (That's true)

Ah! Bèmba!   (Indeed)
The ancestor of the Tunkaras,[1] Prince Burama,   (Indeed)
He went forth to found the village called Mèma.[2]   (Indeed)

7. Or Shawwal in the Muslim calendar; because the calendar is based strictly on the lunar cycle, the month name has no Western equivalent.   8. The scene of a violent confrontation between Muhammad's disciples and members of a pagan clan that refused to be converted to the new religion of Islam. Bilal bin Rabah was an early companion of Muhammad's.   9. The Sarakole, the ruling clan of the empire of Ghana, which flourished in the 9th and 10th centuries. Ancient Mali arose as a successor state to Ghana; the Maraka are thus the predecessors of the Manding in the area the latter were later to occupy.   1. The ancient empire of Ghana; not to be confused with the capital of the present-day Republic of Burkina Faso. 2. These lines provide a simple but striking example of parallelism. The names listed are clan names, except for *Fulani* and *Jawaras* (one of the major ethnic groups in the Gambia).   3. Inferring an exodus from a common origin.   4. A giant of local lore.   5. A Manding clan.   6. A region northwest of present-day Mali, on the border with Mauritania.   7. Known today as Babangede.   8. Or Jara.   9. These are actually hills.   1. A subclan of the Manding.   2. The exact site of this town is unknown. Son-Jara spends a significant part of his exile here before setting out on his reconquest of the Manding.

	There he had two sons,	(Indeed)
210	Prince Burama[3] and Jasigi.	(Indeed)
	Prince Burama and Jasigi,	(Indeed)
	'Twas they who joined Son-Jara here,	(Indeed)
	And went with him to the Manden.	(Indeed)
	They left the Manden later	(Indeed)
215	And came to settle in Kulun.[4]	(Indeed)
	They left Kulun,	(Indeed)
	And settled in Bangasi,[5]	(Indeed)
	And went up on Genu Mountain,[6]	(Indeed)
	And founded a village atop the mountain.	(Indeed)
220	That village's name was Kuduguni.[7]	(Mmm, that's true)

	'Tis said the Tunkaras of Genu,	(Indeed)
	They each had two sons:	(Indeed)
	Wali and Gayi,	(Indeed)
	Sega and Marama.	(Indeed)
225	The four Tunkara patriarchs	(Indeed)
	Who were in Kita[8] country here.	(Indeed)
	That is what those people are called.	(True)

	I sing of Biribiriba!	
	Kirikisa, Spear-of-Access and Spear-of-Service!	(Mmm)
230	Warlord and wailing at his entry, a pile of stone![9]	
	Nare Magan Kònatè, Sorcerer-Seizing-Sorcerer!	(Indeed)
	Simbon, Lion-Born-of-the-Cat!	(Indeed)

	That Kanu Simbon and Kanu Nyògòn Simbon,[1]	(Indeed)
	Settled in Wagadugu.	(Indeed)
235	They left Wagadugu,	(Indeed)
	And they went to Jara.	(Indeed)
	They left Jara.	(Mmm)
	And went forth to found a farming hamlet,[2]	(Mmm)
	Calling that village Farmtown.	(Indeed)
240	That Farmtown is Manden Kiri-kòròni.	(Indeed)
	The very first Manden village was Manden Kiri-koroni.	(Indeed)

	Kanu Simbon, Kanu Nyògòn Simbon and Lawali Simbon,[3]	(Indeed)
	Their first village was Manden Kiri-koroni,	(Indeed)
	Kiri-koroni!	(Indeed)
245	Kanu Simbon,	(Indeed)
	He is the forefather of the Dankòs.	(Indeed)
	Lawali Simbon,	(Indeed)
	Begat Kòròlen Fabu and Sòkòna Fabu.	

---

3. Son of the Prince Burama mentioned in line 207. The bard is looking forward here. It should be noted, however, that in the subsequent narration, although the younger Prince Burama gives refuge to Son-Jara in his capital at Mèma, he does not in fact take part in the hero's campaign against Sumamuru.   4. This site can no longer be identified.   5. A town in Mali.   6. Also called Mount Kita.   7. An early Manding settlement near Mount Kita.   8. Important town on the railway line linking Dakar, capital of Senegal, to Bamako, capital of the Republic of Mali.   9. Describes Son-Jara's stern and inflexible aspect. *Wailing at his entry*: because of the sorrow Son-Jara brings to his enemies and their families.   1. Here the bard picks up the thread of the story suspended (line 181) while he traced the ancestry of the Tunkaras.   2. A temporary settlement in the fields during the sowing or harvesting season, which later forms the nucleus of a new community.   3. The bard now traces the precise genealogy of the clan's rulers down to Son-Jara's father, Fata Magan the Handsome.

	The Dugunòs descended from them.	(Indeed)
250	Kanu Nyògòn Simbon	(Indeed)
	Begat King Bèrèmu,	(Mmm)
	King Bèrèmu begat King Bèrèmu Dana.	(Indeed)
	King Bèrèmu Dana begat King Juluku, the Holy.	(Indeed)
	King Juluku, the Holy begat King Belo Komaan.	(Indeed)
255	Belo Komaan begat Juruni Komaan.	
	Juruni Komaan begat Fata Magan, the Handsome.	
	That Fata Magan, the Handsome	(Indeed)
	Went forth to found a farm hamlet called Kakama,	(Indeed)
	And they call that place, my father, Bintanya	
	Kamalen.[4]	(Mmm)
260	O Nare Magan Kònatè!	
	O Sorcerer-Seizing-Sorcerer!	(Indeed)
	That Fata Magan, the Handsome,	
	He married the daughter of	
	Tall Magan Berete-of-the-Ruins,	
	Called Saman Berete, the Pure.	(Mmm)
265	They called her Saman Berete.	(Indeed)
	She had not yet borne a child at first.[5]	(Indeed)

[The bard now traces the origins of another clan, the Taraweres, culminating with two brothers, Dan Mansa Wulandin and Dan Mansa Wulanba, who are to play an important role in the next episode of the epic.]

FROM EPISODE 3

Sankaran

325	O! Bèmba!	(Indeed)
	We have come to the Jaras of Sankarandin.[6]	(Indeed)
	To Naminya Kòndè of Sankaran.	
	The Kòndè's ancestor was Sama Sine.[7]	(Indeed)
	Sama Sine was Aba Sara's child,	
330	And it was he who begat Sana Bunuma Sara.	(Mmm)
	Sana Bunuma Sara	(Indeed)
	Bore her first son.	(Indeed)
	Sana Bunuma Sara,	(Indeed)
	Her first son was Leader-of-the-People.[8]	(Indeed)
335	That Leader-of-the-People,	(Indeed)
	His flesh-and-blood sister was Du Kamisa.[9]	(Mmm)
	That Leader-of-the-People	(Indeed)
	Had a son called Magan Jata Kòndè of Du.	(Indeed)
	That Magan Jata Kòndè of Du,	(Indeed)
340	At the shaving of his new-born hair,[1]	(Indeed)

4. The central region of the Manding area.   5. Anticipates the confused circumstances in which she later bears a child who will be Son-Jara's half-brother and rival.   6. A branch of Son-Jara's maternal line. Sankaradin is a river in the Republic of Guinea.   7. As founder of the Kòndè clan, Sama Sine is the equivalent of Bilal, with the important difference that Son-Jara's maternal line traced through Sama Sine is indigenous.   8. That is, king.   9. *Kamisa* is the personal name of the king's sister, to which is added the name of the region (*Du*). *Flesh-and-blood sister*: that is, of the same father and mother; an important distinction in polygamous societies.   1. The hair of newborn infants is shaved as part of the naming ceremony, which takes place when they are eight days old.

His father's sister took that birth-hair,
And put it in a calabash,[2]
Saying, "A thing for tomorrow!"[3]   (Indeed)

The umbilical cord that was cut,
345   She put into the calabash,
Saying, "A thing for tomorrow!"
The knife she used to cut the cord,
She put into the calabash,
Saying, "A thing for tomorrow!"   (True)
350   His old swaddling cloth,   (Mmm)
She put into the calabash,   (Indeed)
Saying, "A thing for tomorrow!"   (Indeed)
That small child grew up,
And came to rule over twelve towns.
355   All those people belonged to him.
He sought the counsel of wise men,   (Indeed)
And they performed divination for him,[4]   (Indeed)
Saying that he must sacrifice a white spotted bull,[5]   (Mmm)
That an outsider should not eat of the meat.
360   And that was the aunt on the outskirts.[6]
Living with an elder brother is not good.[7]   (Indeed)

*   *   *

Ah! Bèmba!   (Indeed)
Some old meddlers rose up;[8]
395   "Ah! Du Kamisa,   (Mmm)
"Being a woman is a malady![9]   (Indeed)
"In my mind,   (Indeed)
"You who with Leader-of-the-People
"Are of the same breast,   (Indeed)
400   . . .   (Indeed)
"And who come from the same belly,   (Indeed)
"And who had a child,   (Indeed)
"Who made a family sacrifice,   (Indeed)
"Saying that you should be the outsider,
405   "And thus you should not eat of the meat.
"Being a woman is a malady!"   (True)
At that, she became angry.   (Indeed)
And went to find Magan Jata Kòndè of Du: (Indeed)
"Behold your lamb skin![1]   (Mmm)
410   "I cannot be an outsider to you!
"I and your father are of the same cause,
"And suckled the same breast."   (Mmm)
"   . . ."

2. A large gourd that, when hollowed out and dried, serves as a household utensil.   3. A formulaic
expression, which indicates the sense that this and other tokens of the newborn will later prove significant.
4. It was customary for the king at the beginning of his reign to consult diviners, to find out what the
future holds for him and his kingdom.   5. That is, a black-and-white bull, symbolizing the harmony
between the opposed realms of the universe: the sky (white) and the earth (black).   6. Meant both
literally and metaphorically. Du Kamisa's exclusion from the ceremony of the sacrifice may have been the
result of a prior rift between her and her nephew, now the new king, which forced her to live apart from
her family.   7. Both sibling rivalry and male dominance are implied in this complaint.   8. Went to
inform Du Kamisa of her exclusion.   9. Handicap.   1. The dried skin of the lamb, which is traditionally slaughtered for the feast at a child's naming ceremony, is afterward given to the infant's aunt as a token
of kinship.

Magan Jata Kòndè of Du became enraged at that,

415 And seized his aunt, (Mmm)
And dragged her off, (Indeed)
And cast her in a hovel to the west of Du (Indeed)
And slashed off her breasts with a knife, magasi![2]
"You remain here! (Mmm)
420 "You have borne no children![3] (True)
"You remain here!
"You have borne no children! (True)

"My father was Leader-of-the-People.
"You have borne no children!" (Indeed)
425 "What? Did I not bear a child?" (Mmm)
"You have borne no children!"
"Come here!" (True)
She ripped off her calabash lid (Indeed)
And dipped her hand into the calabash:
430 "Do you not see your new-born hair?[4]
"Did I not bear a child? (Indeed)
"Do you not see your navel cord?
"Did I not bear a child? (Indeed)
"The water breaking at your birth,
435 "The cloth on which it spilled,
"Behold that cloth before you!
"Alas! Did I not bear a child? (Indeed)
"Do you not see your swaddling cloth? (Indeed)
"Did I not bear a child?" (Indeed)
440 There is a proverb told in the Manden. (Indeed)
It is said of the Kòndès in the Manden. (Indeed)

To buy a boney horse. (Indeed)
To buy a boney horse. (Indeed)
If you deceive a man
445 To buy a boney horse,
You must deliver a grasscutter, too![5] (That's the truth,
There's no doubt)
The Kòndè matriarch grew furious. (Indeed)
The little old lady transformed herself,[6]
And became a wild buffalo in the Manden. (Indeed)
450 Each of her horns: a golden spear and a silver spear. (Mmm)
Each of her ears: a golden snuff spoon, a silver
snuff spoon. (Mmm)
The strands of her tail: needles of gold, needles of
silver. (True)
Each of her ears: a golden snuff spoon, a silver
snuff spoon. (Indeed)
Each of her hooves: an adze of gold, an adze of
silver. (Indeed)
455 The woman thus transformed herself.

---

2. An exclamatory ideophone. *Slashed off her breasts:* to emphasize her barrenness.   3. Because of the high rate of infant mortality, childlessness is considered a curse in many traditional societies.   4. This suggests that, as is customary, Magan Jata Kòndè was handed over in his childhood to be brought up by his paternal aunt; he would thus have been like a child to Du Kamisa.   5. A somewhat cryptic proverb: every wrong must be redressed. *Grasscutter:* a small bush animal considered a delicacy.   6. She became a fabulous and dangerous animal.

In the seven quarters of Du,
When the dawn would break,
She would slay a man in each quarter,
And thus they called her the Ginda of Du.
460   The Kòndè buffalo witch[7] was called the Ginda of Du!

Ah! Bèmba!   (Indeed)
Whenever two hunters went forth to fight the
    buffalo,   (Indeed)
One would come back to tell the way the other died.
She would kill the one and leave the other   (Mmm)
465   To go home and tell the way he died.   (That's true)
The Taraweres heard about this matter.   (Mmm)
    O Tura-Magan-and-Kanke-jan![8]   (Indeed)
Dan Mansa Wulundin and Wulanba,   (Indeed)
They took their bows and rose up.   (Mmm)
470   What sitting will not solve,
Travel will resolve.[9]   (True)
They went forth.   (Indeed)
They came to the deep forest.   (Mmm)
In those days, kolas[1] had not been created. (Indeed)
475   All the Manden fetishes were offered sacrifices of
    groundnuts.
A young jinn[2] lived in one such fetish.   (Indeed)
His name was Tinin Magan, the Pale.   (Indeed)
Guinea-fowl feathers perforated the fetish.[3]
    "Leprous-head-of-Gold,[4] Tinin Magan, the
        Pale!   (Indeed)
480   "Leprous-head-of-Silver, Tinin Magan, the
        Pale!   (Indeed)
    "Child of Nyagatè!
    "Merchant Ben Magan without ostentation! (Indeed)
    "The one who loves ostentation,
    "Will he not make a merchant his friend?   (Indeed)
485   "Gold is in the merchant's hand,   (Indeed)
    "That it may overflow on me, O Power!   (Indeed)
    "Silver is in the merchant's hand,   (Indeed)
    "That it may overflow on me, O Power!
    "Going will I slay it?   (Indeed)
490   "Coming will I slay it?"[5]
As soon as he snapped the groundnut open,
He casts the shells.   (Indeed)
One face up.   (Indeed)
One face down.[6]   (True)

---

7. In other versions of the epic, it is Son-Jara's mother who bears this epithet.   8. One of Son-Jara's generals. As the most illustrious member of the Tarawere clan, his name has become synonymous with that of the clan and is evoked here as a prelude to the episode involving two other celebrated members of his clan, which the bard is about to relate.   9. A formulaic expression: there is always an alternative solution to a problem.   1. A bitter nut chewed as a stimulant and used in divination and sacrificial bowls. The bard insists on the remoteness of the past he recalls here, long before the nut was introduced into the Manding region.   2. A creature of the supernatural world, believed to have visionary powers. The term is also used for humans similarly endowed.   3. A cult house, most likely a hut in a dark grove; the walls were pasted with the feathers of the Guinea fowl, a wild bird, extremely common in the west African savanna.   4. The jinn, who is both repulsive and dazzling.   5. That is, the buffalo. Note the gnomic form of the question.   6. The outcome of the divination is indecisive.

<pre>
495   Ah, bards,
      He who would cultivate,
      Let him cultivate.
      Son-Jara is done!
      He who would deal in commerce,
500   Let him deal in commerce!
      The Wizard is done![7]   (Indeed)
      These chords were played for him, my Father, in the
          Manden.   (Mmm)
      Son-Jara's tomb is in the Manden.   (Indeed)
      The village where his tomb is found,   (Indeed)
505   The name of that village is Nyani,[8]   (True)
      By the banks of the river,   (Indeed)
      On the banks of the Sankaran.
      The name of the village is Nyani.
      The Wizard's tomb is in Nyani.   (Mmm)

510   Ah! Bèmba!   (Indeed)
      Dan Mansa Wulundin sat down.   (Mmm)
      He came and seized the jinn:[9]   (Indeed)
      "My elder, come let us kill this jinn!"
      "Ah! Little brother, do not kill the jinn.
515   "Leave him be, and he will read the signs[1] for us.
      "Jinns know more than the Sons-of-Adam."   (Indeed)
      And the jinn did conjury for them: (Indeed)

      "When both of you go forth,   (Mmm)
      "You must seek sanctuary with the cordwainer patriarch,[2]
520   "With Walali Ibrahima.   (Indeed)
      "When both of you go forth,
      "You should sacrifice seven portions of goat,   (Mmm)
      "This and yesterday's leftover rice.
      "There is an old woman to the west of Du.
525   "Give yesterday's rice to this old woman.
      "And if God wills, you'll slay the buffalo."   (Indeed)

      They thus sought sanctuary with the cordwainer
          patriarch,   (Indeed)
      And sacrificed seven portions of goat.   (Indeed)
      Whenever they would go into the bush,
530   The buffalo would come into the town.   (Mmm)
      Whenever they would come into the town,   (Indeed)
      The buffalo would go into the bush.
      They tracked each other for a week;
      Not once did they and the buffalo meet.   (True)
</pre>

[As instructed by the Walali Ibrahima, the Tarawere brothers offer a sacrificial bowl of rice to an old woman they meet, who tells them to make further sacrifices and gives them a magic spindle as a weapon.]

7. A fragment from the traditional funeral song (dirge) in honor of Son-Jara; it begins with a reflection on individual destiny and stresses that Son-Jara died fulfilled.   8. Niane, the capital of the old Mali empire. 9. He imputes malice to the jinn because the divination did not produce the expected result.   1. Traced in the sand and read for their meaning. Dan Mansa Wulanba, who speaks here, wants to give the jinn a chance to redeem himself.   2. An old sage. The jinn refers the brothers to him for further guidance, because he can help them no further; it is the cordwainer patriarch's counseling that is reported in the six lines that follow his name (Walali Ibrahima).

635 The Taraweres took up the bow.
They reached the high bush country.   (Mmm)
Dan Mansa Wulandin said, "O Elder,
"Behold the Buffalo of Du!"   (Indeed)
The buffalo charged them,   (Mmm)
640 And they threw down the first of the eggs.   (Mmm)
It became a great wilderness.
There was a village in the midst of that wilderness.
The name of that village was Bèmbè.
Rescuer-King-of-the-Wilderness was there in the village of
        Bèmbè.
645 Kamisòkò ancestor from Kiri,[3]
Bee-King-of-the-Wilderness!

. . .

Tèrè Kumba and Kaya!
Nyani River and Maramu River!
650 But what grew beneath it apart from
        hammer and bow?[4]   (Indeed. Eh,
                                                        (Fa-Digi, that's the truth)

Should you go north to Kaarta,   (Mmm)
They call some of them there Magasa.
They are all of Fa-Koli's[5] line.
Hero-of-Original-Clans.
655 . . .   (True)

The buffalo charged them again,
And they threw down the other egg.   (Mmm)
It became a great lake.   (Indeed)
Dan Mansa Wulandin planted the green stick,
660 And it became a great forest.   (Indeed)
Behind the forest was the anthill.
The buffalo went down to the lake.[6]
She was swimming,
And she was drinking.
665 She was swimming,
And she was drinking.
Thus the bards sing of that:[7]   (Indeed)
        The Kòndè lion child! Great-Water-Drinker!   (Indeed)
        Splasher-in-the-Lake!   (Indeed)
670 Great-Lake-Water-Drinker!   (Indeed)
        Those-who-Turn, Fa-Kanda!   (Indeed)
        Those-who-Turn-About, Fa-Kanda!   (Indeed)
        Those-with-Visions, Fa-Kanda!   (Indeed)
        Those-who-Seek-Visions, Fa-Kanda!   (Indeed)
675 Fa-Kanda, Killer-of-Kin![8]
Nineteen of them in all!

---

3. A region in ancient Mali. This and other place names enumerated in the passage cover a vast area over which the buffalo pursues the brothers.   4. Symbolic reference to the inhabitants of the region who were predominantly blacksmiths and warriors.   5. Nephew of Sumamuru, Son-Jara's principal adversary later in the epic. His defection to Son-Jara after a quarrel with his uncle proves a turning point in Son-Jara's campaign to reconquer the Manden. Fa-Koli is credited here with having founded an illustrious lineage. 6. Having become thirsty from the pursuit; its attention is thus momentarily diverted from the brothers. 7. The incident has become memorialized in the praise song of the Kòndè clan.   8. An allusion to a power struggle within the clan that saw the ascendancy of Fa-Kanda as ruler.

From these nineteen, Fa-Kanda gains power!
The arrow found in the breast of the brave,   (Indeed)
It was Fa-Kanda's arrow.   (Indeed)
680   The arrow found in the loins of the brave,   (Indeed)
It was Fa-Kanda's arrow.   (Indeed)
The arrow found in the brow of the brave,   (Indeed)
It was Fa-Kanda's arrow.
Garabaya and Kaya![9]   (Mmm)

685   Ah! Bèmba!   (Indeed, I'm coming)
Biribiriba!
Kirikisa, Spear-of-Access, Spear-of-Service!
Nare Magan Kònatè!
Sorcerer-Seizing-Sorcerer!   (Mmm)
690   Simbon, Lion-Born-of-the-Cat![1]   (Mmm)

O Kala Jula Sangoyi Manunaka!   (Indeed)
Dan Mansa Wulandin became deeply frightened: (Indeed)
"No spindle stick will ever pierce her hide!"   (True)
He cleared the chamber of his gun,[2]
695   And rammed some shot inside,
And discharged his powder on the buffalo.   (Indeed)
The shot would not strike her.   (Indeed)
She chased them on, biri-biri-biri![3]
They went and climbed a shea-butter tree.[4]   (Indeed)
700   The buffalo came up beneath them.   (Indeed)
She shook her great head from side to side.   (Indeed)
And bellowed out: (Indeed)
"Dense thicket! Shea tree's dense thicket!"   (Indeed)

The shea tree branches with their people came
    crashing down to earth, biri!   (Indeed)
705   And she pursued them once again, biri-biri-biri!   (True)
Dan Mansa Wulanba climbed into another tree.   (True)
Dan Mansa Wulandin
Went and hid behind the great anthill,   (Indeed)
And stepped upon the charcoal chunk.   (Indeed)
710   He said to his elder brother,
Said, "Let's do something now!"

The buffalo came round the anthill.
She looked both to and fro,   (Indeed)
But nothing did she see.
715   She looked again both to and fro.
It was only Shadow in her sight,[5]
That Shadow worshipped by the hunters.   (Indeed)
She looked again both to and for.   (Indeed)
Dan Mansa Wulandin took the spindle stick,[6]
720   Drew back and shot the Buffalo of Du, pan!

---

9. Scenes of Fa-Kanda's victories. Kaya, in the region of Kita, is the gateway to the old capital of Niane and as such features in a triumphal praise song for Son-Jara later in the epic (lines 2934–37).   1. The recall of Son-Jara's praise names is conditioned here by the preceding recital of the praise song of his maternal clan.   2. An obvious anachronism.   3. Ideophone for the chase.   4. A tree from whose fruit an edible oil is pressed; it has a mystical significance in many of the cultures of the West African savanna.   5. The brothers have made themselves invisible with charms.   6. The magic stick the brothers had obtained from the old woman is now used as a last resort.

The buffalo bellowed out: "Oh!
   "O People of Du!
   "The Twisted Well![7]   (Indeed)
   "Arrow-of-the-Knower![8]

725   "Should your father be slain by the red buffalo,
   "And shall he see a red anthill,
   "Won't he[9] be afraid of it?
   " 'Tis the Arrow-of-the-Knower!"   (That's the truth)
And that has become a proverb.   (Mmm, eh, Fa-Digi,
                                      that's the truth)

730   The buffalo collapsed, biri!   (Indeed)
He hacked off her tail,
And hacked off her horns,   (Indeed)
And hacked off her ears,   (Indeed)
And hacked off her hooves.   (Indeed)
735   Dan Mansa Wulanba came forward: (Indeed)
"Little brother, what has happened?"   (Indeed)
"Ah, my elder," the reply, "the Buffalo of Du has fallen."
At which he cried out:
   "Snake country and fetish country![1]
740   "Stench-of-Mosquito and Stench-of-Deerfly!   (Indeed)
   "Cutter-of-Fresh-Heart and Cutter-of-Fresh-Liver![2]
   "King-of-the-Wilderness, Kininbi!   (Mmm)
   "King-of-the-Wilderness, Kalinka!
   "He-Who-Stands-within-the-Walls and He-Who-Stands-
       amongst-Great-Trees![3]
745   "For some the village is suitable,
   "The outlands do not suit them.
   "For some the outlands are suitable,
   "The village does not suit them."
"Ah, my elder," the reply,
750   "Should you become a bard,
   "One who could refuse you won't be
      found!"[4]   (That's the truth)

                          *   *   *

O! Bèmba!   (Indeed)
They brought the buffalo's horns and her hooves,   (Indeed)
These and the strands of her tail.   (Indeed)
They went and placed them all in a calabash.   (Indeed)
775   Dan Mansa Wulandin drew his knife from its sheath,
And leaned it against the lounging platform.   (Mmm)
Dan Mansa Wulanba,   (Indeed)
He took his sandals off his feet,   (Indeed)
And stacked them near the lounging platform,[5] (Indeed)

---

7. A gnomic phrase, expressive of the buffalo's awareness that its end is near.   8. Shot home by one sure of his aim.   9. That is, Dan Wulanba, who in his fright abandoned his younger brother and has only now emerged from hiding.   1. An allusion to malevolent spirits that are supposed to roam the wilderness. This line begins a hunters' song evoking the dangerous environment in which they operate. 2. Choice parts of freshly killed game, which are shared out between the hunters.   3. A hero of outstanding valor.   4. This compliment by Dan Wulandin to his elder brother stresses the inspirational role played by the traditional bard.   5. An area of the clearing at the center of the village that serves as meeting place for the entire community, similar in function to the Greek *agora* or Roman forum.

780 And went to seek refuge with the cordwainer patriarch,
With Walali Ibrahima.   (Indeed)

Old women and gossip are never far
   apart.   (That's the truth)
A snuff-dipping little old woman came forward:
"Magan Jata Kòndè of Du, pass me a pinch of
   snuff."   (Indeed)
785 He passed her a pinch of snuff.   (Mmm)
She dipped some snuff and wet it down: (Indeed)
"I have a word to say to you.
"But let it remain between us two!   (True)
"Say not you heard it from my lips!   (Mmm)
790 "The buffalo that settled near our folk,
"Someone has slain that buffalo.
"And with that I'm off."   (True)
Magan Jata Kòndè of Du let loose the great
   village drum.   (Indeed)
He beat the royal drum,   (Mmm)
795 The drum of power:[6]   (Mmm)
"Like it or not,[6]   (Mmm)
"Everyone must gather!   (Indeed)
"The one who killed the buffalo,   (True)
"Into two I have divided the twelve towns of Du,[7]
800 "And to that person will give one half.
"Such a brave man will be an asset to our folk."
   No need to kill for the leper,
   But one footstep forward,   (Indeed)
   That is all he wants.[8]

                        *   *   *

835 Ah! Bèmba!   (True)
Some strong young braves came forward,
And wiped off the blade of the knife.   (Indeed)
Whoever would put the blade in his sheath,
If it wasn't too big, it was too small.   (Indeed)
840 Others came forward,   (Indeed)
And put their feet into the sandals.
If they weren't too big, they were too small.[9]   (Mmm)

They sent a messenger to the cordwainer patriarch,
To Walali Ibrahima,   (Mmm)
845 To Ibrahima.
Dan Mansa Wulandin and Wulanba went to the
   meeting.   (Indeed)
Tura Magan[1] came forward!
The Taraweres came forward!   (Indeed)
They arrived at the compound door,
850 By the rubbish heap.   (Indeed)

---

6. Implies the compelling effect of the royal drum's message.   7. A frequent motif of the folk imagination, given a supreme elaboration in Shakespeare's *King Lear*.   8. A proverb: one does not need to go to
great lengths to satisfy a leper, an expression of Magan Jara Kòndè's relief at having been freed from the
buffalo.   9. A folktale motif well exemplified by the Cinderella story.   1. The Tarawere brothers (see
n. 8, p. 2422).

An old male dog sidled up	(Indeed)
With a cat beside him.	(True)

The old dog spoke out:[2]	(True)
"Ah! Taraweres!	(Indeed)
855 "I thank you for the rice.	(Indeed)
"I thank you for those bits of bone.	
"Be kind to people.	
"If one is kind to people,	
"Should there be no recompense,	
860 "At least it will be known of him.	(That's true)

"Taraweres, you are off to this meeting.	(Indeed)
"When the twelve towns of Du are divided in two,	
"And the half offered unto you,	
"So that you'll settle here,	(Indeed)
865 "You must refuse!	(Indeed)
"You must say, 'We come from the Manden,	(Indeed)
" 'We return to the Manden.'	
"O Taraweres!	(True)

"There will be six young maidens there.	(Mmm)
870 "When you are told to choose amongst them,	(Indeed)
"This black cat will I release,	
"So that she will approach you.	(True)
"The maiden's legs she goes between,	(Indeed)
"Comes out, goes round and through again,	(Indeed)
875 "And goes again between her legs,	(Indeed)
"Comes out, goes round and through again,	(Indeed)
"That is the maiden you must take.	(Indeed)
"Her name will be Sugulun Kòndè.	(Indeed)
"Warts and pustules cover her.	(Indeed)
880 "They call her Sugulun-of-the-Warts![3]	(Indeed)
"Should you go forth with her,	(Indeed)
"Her only son once born,[4]	(Indeed)
"The Manden will be his.	(Indeed)
"O Taraweres, I thank you!"	(Indeed)

885 On that, Dan Mansa Wulandin went forth[5]	(Indeed)
And slipped the knife into its sheath,	
And sat down on the lounging platform.	(Indeed)
Dan Mansa Wulanba,	(Indeed)
He slipped his feet into the sandals,	(Indeed)
890 And sat down upon the lounging platform.	(Indeed)

All cried out: " 'Tis they who killed the buffalo!	(Indeed)
" 'Tis they who killed the buffalo!	(Mmm)
"Whose people are you?"	
"We are the Taraweres."	(True)
895 "And where do you hail from?"	(Mmm)
"We come from Bintanya Kamalen."	(Indeed)

2. The dog's expression of gratitude is testimony to the generosity of the brothers, which the animal repays with advice.   3. She is to be Son-Jara's mother; presented in these unpromising terms to emphasize the obscure working out of his destiny.   4. The epic later mentions a brother, Manden Bukari. 5. Returned to the village of Du to make good his claim.

	"O Taraweres!	(Mmm)
	"The twelve towns of Du, I'll divide in twain,	
	"And give one half to you,	(Mmm)
900	"So that you'll settle here.	(Mmm)
	"Such brave men complement the village folk."	(True)
	"That cannot be us!	
	"We come from the Manden.	
	"And to the Manden we'll return."6	
905	"Taraweres, look about you then.	(True)
	"Whatever maiden you may see	
	"Will be your struggle's reward.	
	"Whichever woman you may see,	
	" 'Tis her that I will give to you."	(True)
910	They brought the maidens forward,	(True)
	Six young maidens.	(Mmm)
	The one behind whom the Kòndè girl stood,	(Indeed)
	She cried out, saying, "Get from behind me!	(Indeed)
	"Let me not with you be made so vile!"	(That's true)
915	They all moved away and stood apart.	(Mmm)

	The black cat moved upon the ground.	
	It turned around and round.	
	It turned around and round.	(Indeed)
	It passed between the Kòndè Maiden's legs,	
920	Came out, turned round, and through again.	(Indeed)
	The Taraweres came running up	
	And seized the Kòndè Maiden by the right hand.	
	"Behold our maiden!	(Indeed)
	"Behold our maiden!	
925	"We have seen our maiden!"	

[The Tarawere brothers continue on their journey, seeking further adventures, and finally arrive at the town founded by Fata Magan the Handsome. Dan Mansa Wulanba attempts to consummate his marriage with Sugulun Kòndè, who repulses him, saying, "My husband is in the Manden." Thus her virginity is preserved for her future husband, Fata Magan the Handsome, for whom she will bear her first child, Son-Jara. The next episode recounts the circumstances in which she enters Fata Magan's household and the events that ensue.]

FROM EPISODE 4

The Manden

	Now, Fata Magan, the Handsome was about to leave that town.	
	He was leaving to trade in a far market.	(Mmm)
1000	But a jinn came and laid a hand on him:7	(Mmm)
	"Stay right here!	(Indeed)
	"Two youths have come amongst us,	(Mmm)
	"Two youths with an ugly young maid.	(Mmm)

6. Note that these are the exact words of the dog's instructions. This affirmation by the Taraware brothers of their attachment to their homeland forms part of the epic's expression of a Manding national consciousness.   7. Implying that the jinn is an agent of providence.

"Should you come by that ugly maid,	(Mmm)
1005 "She will bear you a son.	(Indeed)
"The Manden will belong to him."	(Indeed)
O! Bèmba!	(Indeed)
I sing of the Sorcerer's future;	(Mmm, that's true)
Of the life ahead of Son-Jara!	
1010 There were two ways to greet in the Manden	
of Old	(Mmm)
Brave young men said, "Ilu tuntun!"	(That's true)
To which the reply, "Tuntun bèrè!"	
The women said, "Ilu kònkòn!"	
To which the reply, "Kònkòn lògòsò!"	(Indeed)
1015 The Taraweres came forward:	(True)
"I tuntun!"	
He answered them, "Tuntun bèrè!	(Mmm)
"Where do you come from?	
"Where are you going?"	
1020 "We have come from the land of Du.	
"We go to Bintanya Kamalen."	
"Whose people are you?"	(Mmm)
"We are Taraweres."	
"O Taraweres,	
1025 "Were this young prince to find the right wife,	(Mmm)
"She would be the reward of a Tarawere struggle.	(True)
"My flesh-and-blood sister is here,	(Indeed)
"Nakana Tiliba.	(Indeed)
"I will give her to you.	
1030 "You must give me your ugly maid.	(Mmm)
"My forefather Bilal,	(Indeed)
"When he departed from the Messenger of God,	(True)
"He designed a certain token,	(Mmm)
"Saying that his ninth descendant,	(Indeed)
1035 "Having taken his first wife,	(True)
"When he takes his second wife,	(Indeed)
"Must add that token to that marriage.	(Mmm)
"I am adding that token	
"Together with Nakana Tiliba,	(Mmm)
1040 "And giving them to you,[8]	
"You must give me your ugly little maid."	
That token was added to Nakana Tiliba,	
Exchanging her for Sugulun Kòndè.	(Indeed)
It is said that Fata Magan, the Handsome	
1045 Took the Kòndè maiden to bed.	(Mmm)
His Berete wife became pregnant.	(Indeed)
His Kòndè wife became pregnant.	(Indeed)
One day as dawn was breaking,	(Indeed)
The Berete woman give birth to a son.	(Indeed)
1050 She cried out, "Ha! Old Women!	(Indeed)
"That which causes co-wife conflict	

8. Fata Magan's readiness to part with the token inherited from his ancestor Bilal emphasizes the importance to him of securing Sugulun Kòndè for a wife.

"Is nothing but the co-wife's child.[9]   (True)
"Go forth and tell my husband   (Indeed)
"His first wife has borne him a son."   (Indeed)

1055   The old women came up running.   (Indeed)
"Alu kònkòn!"   (Mmm)
They replied to them, "Kònkòn dògòsò!
"Come let us eat."   (Mmm)
They fixed their eyes on one another:
1060   "Ah! Man must swallow his saliva!"[1]   (True)
They sat down around the food.   (Indeed)
The Kòndè woman then bore a son.   (Indeed)
They sent the Kuyatè matriarch, Tumu Maniya: (Indeed)
"Tumu Maniya, go tell it,   (True)
1065   "Tell Fata Magan, the Handsome,
"Say, 'the Tarawere trip to Du was good.'   (True)
"Say, 'the ugly maid they brought with them,'
"Say, 'that woman has just borne a son.' "   (True)

The Kuyatè matriarch came forward: (True)
1070   "Alu kònkòn!"   (Mmm)
They replied to her, "Kònkòn dògòsò!   (Indeed)
"Come and let us eat."

[The female bard Tumu Maniya goes to find the king and, like the old women who preceded her, is also invited to eat, but she rejects the food until her message is delivered. The announcing of the birth of Son-Jara first, though he was actually born second, causes the father to designate him as first-born. The old women then burst out their message of the Berete woman's child, but alas, they are too late. The reversal of announcements is viewed as theft of birthright, and the Berete woman is understandably furious at the old women, who flop their hands about nervously.][2]

Some just flopped their hands about:
"I will not hear of this from anyone!"
1075   "I spent a sleepless night.
"The lids of my eyes are dried out,
        bèrè-bèrè-bèrè.[3]   (That's true)
"But I will not hear of this from anyone!"
Some just clasped their hands together.
What travail it had become!
1080   Ha! The old woman had forgotten her message
And abandoned it for a meal.
Those-Caught-by-their-Craws![4]
That was the first day of battle in the Manden.
Pandemonium broke loose! bòkòlen![5]

---

9. Rivalry between co-wives and their offspring in polygamous households is a common theme in African folktales.   1. To placate their hunger. The food the women are offered is presumably too tempting to be ignored, hence their delay in announcing the birth of the Berete woman's child; this leads to the confusion about the order of precedence between him and Son-Jara and to dissension in the family.   2. Johnson's summary. He noted that Fa-Digi Sisoko broke off his performance at this point to answer the call of nature and that he resumed the narration at a point further along in the story.   3. Ideophone for the distraught state of the women.   4. Derogatory term for the women.   5. Ideophone summing up the pandemonium.

* * *

Both women were confined in one hut.
Pandemonium broke loose! bòkòlen!   (Indeed)
Saman Berete,
1100 The daughter of Tall Magan Berete-of-the Ruins,
Saman Berete,   (Indeed)
Still bloodstained, she came out.   (Indeed)
"What happened then!
"O Messengers, what happened?   (Indeed)
1105 "O Messengers, what became of the message?"   (Indeed)

The Kuyatè matriarch spoke out:
"Nothing happened at all.   (Indeed)
"I was the first to pronounce myself.   (Indeed)
"Your husband said the first name heard,
1110 "Said, he would be the elder,   (Indeed)
"And thus yours became the younger."   (Indeed)
She[6] cried out, "Old women,   (Indeed)
"Now you have really reached the limit!   (True)
"I was the first to marry my husband,
1115 "And the first to bear him a son.   (Indeed)
"Now you have made him the younger.   (Indeed)
"You have really reached your limit!"
She spoke then to her younger co-wife,   (Indeed)
"Oh Lucky Karunga,[7]   (Indeed)
1120 "For you marriage has turned sweet.   (Indeed)
"A first son birth is the work of old,
"And yours has become the elder."[8]   (That's the truth)

The infants were bathed.   (Indeed)
Both were laid beneath a cloth.   (Indeed)
1125 The grandmother[9] had gone to fetch firewood.   (Indeed)
The old mother had gone to fe . . . , to
    fetch firewood.   (Indeed)
She then quit the firewood-fetching place,
And came and left her load of wood.   (Indeed)
She came into the hut.   (Indeed)
1130 She cast her eye on the Berete woman,   (Indeed)
And cast her eye on the Kònde woman,   (Indeed)
And looked the Berete woman over,
And looked the Kònde woman over.   (Indeed)

She lifted the edge of the cloth.
1135 And examined the child of the Berete woman,
And lifted again the edge of the cloth,
And examined the child of the Kònde woman.   (Indeed)
From the very top of Son-Jara's head,   (Indeed)
To the very tip of his toes, all hair![1]   (Indeed)

1140 The old mother went outside.   (Indeed)
She laughed out: "Ha! Birth-givers! Hurrah!
"The little mother has borne a lion thief."   (That's true)
Thus gave the old mother Son-Jara his name.   (Indeed)

6. Saman Berete.   7. Sugulun Kònde.   8. A bitter comment on what Saman Berete perceives as an
ironic reversal of situations.   9. Son-Jara's paternal grandmother.   1. An extraordinary circumstance
that earns him his praise name of Lion-Born-of-the-Cat.

"Givers of birth, Hurrah!
1145 "The little mother has borne a lion thief. (That's true)
"Hurrah! The mother has given birth to a lion thief."
    Biribiriba! (Indeed)
    And thus they say of him,
    Son-Jara. Nare Magan Kònatè. (Indeed)
1150 Simbon. Lion-Born-of-the-Cat. (Indeed)
The Berete woman,
She summoned to her a holy-man,
Charging him to pray to God, (Indeed)
So Son-Jara would not walk. (Indeed)
1155 And summoned to her an Omen Master, (Indeed)
For him to read the signs in sand, (Indeed)
So Son-Jara would not walk. (Indeed)

For nine years, Son-Jara crawled upon the ground. (Indeed)
Magan Kònatè could not rise. (Indeed)
1160 The benefactor of the Kòndè woman's child,
It was a jinn Magan Son-Jara had. (Indeed)
His name was Tanimunari.
Tanimunari, (Indeed)
He took the lame Son-Jara (Indeed)
1165 And made the hājj[2] (Indeed)
To the gates of the Kaabah.[3] (Indeed)
Have you never heard this warrant of his hājj? (Indeed)
    "Ah! God! (Indeed)
    "I am the man for the morrow. (Indeed)
1170 "I am the man for the day to follow. (Indeed)
    "I will rule over the bards, (Indeed)
    "And the three and thirty warrior clans.
    "I will rule over all these people. (Indeed)
    "The Manden shall be mine!"[4] (Indeed)
1175 That is how he made the hājj.
He[5] took him up still lame,
And brought him back to Bintanya Kamalen. (Indeed)
In the month before Dònba, (Indeed)
On the twenty-fifth day,
1180 The Berete woman's Omen Master emerged from
    retreat:[6] (Indeed)
"Damn! My fingers are worn out! (Indeed)
"My buttocks are worn out! (Indeed)
"A tragic thing will come to pass in the Manden. (Indeed)
"There is no remedy to stop it.
1185 "There is no sacrifice to halt it.
"Its cause cannot be ascertained, (Indeed)
"Until two rams be sacrificed. (Indeed)

"The one for Son-Jara, a black-headed ram. (True)
"Dankaran Tuma, an all white ram.[7] (Indeed)
1190 "Have them do battle this very day." (Indeed)

---

2. The pilgrimage to Mecca that Muslims are obliged by the tenets of their religion to undertake at least once in their lifetime.   3. The mosque in Mecca that contains the sacred stone, draped in black, around which a special ceremony takes place during the month of the pilgrimage.   4. An ambition attributed by the bard to Son-Jara even in his youth.   5. Tanimunari.   6. His place of seclusion, where he has been preparing magical charms for Saman Berete.   7. The contrasting colors of the two animals represent the sharp opposition between the brothers. Dankaran Tuma is Saman Berete's son.

By the time of the midday meal,
Son-Jara's ram had won.   (Indeed)
They slaughtered both the rams.   (Indeed)
And cast them down a well,
1195   So the deed would not be known.   (Indeed)
But known it did become.   (Indeed)
    Knowing never fails its time,
    Except its day not come.   (That's true, eh,
                                              Fa-Digi, that's true)

In the month before Dònba   (That's true)
1200   On the twenty-seventh day,   (Indeed)
The holy-man emerged from his retreat!   (Indeed)
"Hey! A tragic thing will come to pass in the
       Manden.   (Indeed)
"There is no remedy to stop it.
"There is no sacrifice to halt it.   (Indeed)
1205   "Its cause cannot be ascertained,
"Until a toothless dog be sacrificed."[8]
Now whoever saw a toothless dog in the Manden?   (Indeed)
They went forth to Kong,[9]   (Indeed)
And bought a snub-nosed dog,   (Indeed)
1210   A little spotted dog,
And pulled its teeth with pliers,
And mixed a potion for its mouth,   (Indeed)
And brought it back to the Manden,
Saying, with this toothless dog,   (Indeed)
1215   Saying, Magan Kònatè should not walk.   (Indeed)
Son-Jara should not rise!

                    *   *   *

Ah! Bèmba!   (Indeed)
They made a sacrifice of the spotted dog   (Indeed)
So that the Wizard would not walk.   (Indeed)
1255   In the month of Dòmba,   (Indeed)
The very, very, very first day,   (Indeed)
Son-Jara's Muslim jinn came forward: (Indeed)
"That which God has said to me,   (Indeed)
"To me Tanimunari,   (Indeed)
1260   "That which God has said to me,   (Indeed)
"So it will be done.   (Indeed)
"When the month of Dòmba is ten days old,   (Indeed)
"Son-Jara will rise and walk."   (Indeed)
In the month of Dòmba,   (Indeed)
1265   On its twelfth day,   (Indeed)
The Messenger of God was born.   (Indeed)
On the thirteenth day,   (Indeed)
Jòn Bilal was born.   (Indeed)
On its tenth day,   (Indeed)
1270   Was the day for Son-Jara to walk.[1]

8. The bizarre and desperate nature of this stipulation is brought out in the lines that follow.   9. A town in present-day Ivory Coast.   1. The bard makes an explicit connection between the hero's rising to his feet and the sense of origins that underlies the epic.

O Nare Magan Kònatè!   (That's true)

. . .

Master and Warrior Master!
O Nare Magan Kònatè!
1275   O Sorcerer-Seizing-Sorcerer!
A man of power is hard to find.   (Mmm)
All people with their empty words,
They all seek to be men of power.   (That's true)
Ministers, deputies and presidents,   (Indeed)
1280   All of them seek after power,
But there is no easy way to power.   (That's true)

Here in our Mali,
We have found our freedom.   (Indeed)
Though a person find no gold,
1285   Though he find no silver,   (Indeed)
Should he find his freedom,
Then noble will he be.   (That's the truth)
A man of power is hard to find.   (Mmm)
Ah! Bèmba!

1290   On the tenth day of Dòmba,   (Indeed)
The Wizard's mother cooked some couscous,[2]   (Indeed)
Sacrificial couscous for Son-Jara.
Whatever woman's door she went to,   (Indeed)
The Wizard's mother would cry: (Indeed)
1295   "Give me some sauce of baobab leaf."[3]   (Indeed)
The woman would retort,
"I have some sauce of baobab leaf,
"But it is not to give to you.
"Go tell that cripple child of yours
1300   "That he should harvest some for you.   (Mmm)
" 'Twas my son harvested these for me."   (True)

And bitterly did she weep: bilika bilika.[4]
She went to another woman's door;   (Mmm)
That one too did say: (Mmm)
1305   "I have some sauce of baobab leaf,
"But it is not to give to you.
"Go tell that cripple child of yours
"That he should harvest some for you.
" 'Twas my son harvested these for me."   (True)

1310   With bitter tears, the Kòndè woman
     came back, bilika bilika.
       "King of Nyani, King of Nyani,[5]
       "Will you never rise?   (Mmm)
       "King of Nyani, King of Nyani,
       "Will you never rise?   (Mmm)
1315   "King of Nyani with helm of mail,
       "He says he fears no man.

2. Here a meal, similar in texture to the North African couscous, made from millet grain; it is brownish red in color. 3. A huge tree that grows in the semidesert conditions of the West African savanna; its leaves are eaten as a vegetable. The tree is associated with nobility. 4. Ideophone for the weeping. 5. Her ambition for her son.

    "Will you never rise?

    "Rise up, O King of Nyani!   (That's true)

    "King of Nyani, King of Nyani,

1320 "Will you never rise?

    "King of Nyani with shirt of mail,

    "He says he fears no man,

    "Will you never rise?

    "Rise up, O King of Nyani!   (True)

1325 "O Wizard,I have failed!"   (True)

    "Ah, my mother,

    "There is a thickener, I hear, called black *lele*.[6] (True)

    "Why not put some in my sauce?

    " 'Tis the thickener grown in gravel."

1330 She put black *lele* in the couscous.

    The Wizard ate of it.

    Ma'an[7] Kònatè ate his fill: (True)

    "My mother,   (Indeed)

    "Go to the home of the blacksmith patriarchs, (Indeed)

1335 "To Dun Fayiri and Nun Fayiri.   (Indeed)

    "Have them shape a staff, seven-fold forged,

    "So that Magan Kònatè may rise up."   (Indeed)

    The blacksmith patriarchs shaped a staff, seven-fold

      forged.   (Indeed)

    The Wizard came forward.   (Indeed)

1340 He put his right hand o'er his left,

    And upwards drew himself,   (Indeed)

    And upwards drew himself.

    He had but reached the halfway point.   (Indeed)

    "Take this staff away from me!"

1345 Magan Kònatè did not rise.   (True)

    In misery his mother wept: bilika bilika: (Indeed)

    "Giving birth has made me suffer!"   (Mmm)

    "Ah, my mother,   (Mmm)

    "Return to the blacksmith patriarchs.   (Indeed)

1350 "Ask that they forge that staff anew,   (Indeed)

    "And shape it twice again in size.   (Mmm)

    "Today I arise, my holy-man said."   (Mmm)

    The patriarchs of the smiths forged the staff,

    Shaping it twice again in size.   (True)

1355 They forged that staff,

    And gave it to Ma'an Kònatè.   (Indeed)

    He put his right hand o'er his left,   (Indeed)

    And upwards Son-Jara drew himself.   (Indeed)

    Upwards Nare Magan Kònatè drew himself. (Indeed)

1360 Again he reached the halfway point: (Mmm)

    "Take this staff away from me!"

    Ma'an Kònatè did not rise.

    He sat back down again.   (Indeed)

---

6. A seasoning. 7. Short for Magan (Son-Jara's name).

His mother wrung her hands atop her head,
1365 And wailed: "dèndèlen!
    "Giving birth has made me suffer!"   (True)
    "Ah, my mother,   (Mmm)
    "Whate'er has come twixt you and God,   (Indeed)
    "Go and speak to God about it now!"[8]   (Indeed)

1370 On that, his mother left,
    And went to the east of Bintanya,   (Indeed)
    To seek a custard apple tree.   (Indeed)

    Ah! Bèmba!   (Indeed)
    And found some custard apple trees,[9]   (Indeed)
1375 And cut one down,   (Indeed)
    And trimmed it level to her breast,   (Indeed)
    And stood as if in prayer: (Indeed)
      "O God!
      "For Son-Jara I have made this staff.   (Indeed)
1380   "If he be the man for the morrow,   (Indeed)
      "If he be the man for the day to follow,   (Indeed)
      "If he is to rule the bards,   (Indeed)
      "If he is to rule the smiths,   (Indeed)
      "The three and thirty warrior clans,   (Indeed)
1385   "If he is to rule all those,   (Indeed)
      "When this staff I give to Nare Magan Kònatè,   (Indeed)
      "Let Magan Kònatè arise.   (True)
      "If he be not the man for the morrow,   (Indeed)
      "If he be not the man for the day to follow,   (Indeed)
1390   "If he is not to rule the bards,   (Indeed)
      "If he is not to rule the smiths,   (Indeed)
      "When this staff I give to the King of Nyani,
      "Let Son-Jara not arise.
      "O God, from the day of my creation,   (Indeed)
1395   "If I have known another man,
      "Save Fata Magan, the Handsome alone,
      "When this staff I give to the King of Nyani,
      "Let Son-Jara arise.   (Indeed)
      "From the day of my creation,   (True)
1400   "If I have known a second man,
      "And not just Fata Magan, the Handsome,   (Indeed)
      "Let Ma'an Kònatè not arise!"   (True)

    She cut down that staff,
    Going to give it to Nare Magan Kònatè,
1405 To the Kòndè woman's child, the Answerer-of
      Needs!   (True)
    The Wizard took the staff,   (Mmm)
    And put his right hand o'er his left,   (Indeed)
    And upwards drew himself,   (Indeed)
    And upwards drew himself.
1410 Magan Kònatè rose up!   (Mmm)
    Running, his mother came forward,

---

8. Son-Jara insinuates that his inability to walk may be God's punishment for some act of infidelity on his mother's part. This is made clear in Sugulun Kòndè's prayer a few lines below.   9. Trees that bear a fruit with fleshy white pulp that is believed to have magical potency.

	And clasped his legs	
	And squeezed them,	(Indeed)
	And squeezed them:	(True)
1415	"This home of ours,	
	"The home of happiness.	(Indeed)
	"Happiness did not pass us by.	
	"Magan Kònatè has risen!"	(Indeed)
	"Oh! Today!	(Indeed)
1420	"Today is sweet!	(Indeed)
	"God the King ne'er made today's equal!	(Indeed)
	"Ma'an Kònatè has risen!"	(Indeed)
	"There is no way of standing without worth.	
	"Behold his way of standing: danka![1]	
1425	"O Kapok Tree and Flame Tree!"[2]	(Fa-Digi, that's true)
	"My mother,	(Mmm)
	"That baobab there in Manden country,	
	"That baobab from which the best sauce comes,	(Indeed)
	"Where is that baobab, my mother?"	(Indeed)
1430	"Ah, my lame one,	(Indeed)
	"You have yet to walk."	(Indeed)

	The Wizard took his right foot,	
	And put it before his left.	(Indeed)
	His mother followed behind him,	
1435	And sang these songs for him:	(Indeed)
	"Tunyu Tanya![3]	(Indeed)
	"Brave men fit well among warriors!	(Indeed)
	"Tunyu tanya!	(Indeed)
	"Brave men fit well among warriors!	(Indeed)
1440	"Ma'an Kònatè, you have risen!"	(Indeed)

	"Muddy water,	(Indeed)
	"Do not compare yourself to water among the stones.	(Indeed)
	"That among the stones is pure, wasili![4]	(Indeed)
	" . . .	(Indeed)
1445	" . . .	(Indeed)
	"And a good reputation.	(Indeed)
	"Khalif Magan Kònatè has risen.	(True)

	"Great snake, O great snake,	(Indeed)
	"I will tolerate you.	(Indeed)
1450	"Should you confront me, toleration.	(Indeed)
	"O great snake upon the path,	(Indeed)
	"Whatever confronts me, I will tolerate."[5]	(Indeed)

	"Arrow-shaft of happiness.	(Indeed)
	"It is in one hundred.	(Indeed)
1455	"The one hundred dead,	
	"All but Son-Jara.	(True)
	"The higher stones get crushed![6]	(Indeed)

---

1. Ideophone to emphasize the words said.   2. Both trees rise tall and straight and hence provide an image of the hero.   3. Ideophones, depicting the unsteady movement of the child learning to walk. 4. A somewhat onomatopoeic ideophone for movement of water; the three lines of this part of Sugulun Kòndè's song convey the idea that her son is superior to other children.   5. She will brave any danger for her son's sake.   6. An image of Son-Jara storming the heights of power and overcoming them.

"Who can mistake the Destroyer-of-Origins!
"And this by the hand of Nare Magan Kònatè!"

1460	Hey! Biribiriba came forward.	(Indeed)
	He shook the baobab tree.	(Indeed)
	A young boy fell out.	
	His leg was broken.	
	The bards thus sing, "Leg-Crushing-Ruler!	
1465	"Magan Kònatè has risen!"	(Indeed)
	He shook the baobab again.	(Indeed)
	Another young boy fell out.	
	His arm was broken.	(Indeed)
	The bards thus sing, "Arm-Breaking-Ruler!	
1470	"Magan Kònatè has risen!"	(Indeed)
	He shook the baobab again.	(Indeed)
	Another young boy fell out.	(Indeed)
	His neck was broken.	(Indeed)
	And thus the bards sing, "Neck-Breaking-Ruler!	
1475	"Magan Kònatè has risen!"	(Indeed)
	The Wizard uprooted the baobab tree,	
	And laid it across his shoulder.	(Mmm)
	Nare Magan Kònatè rose up.[7]	(Indeed)

*   *   *

	Biribiriba came forward.	(Mmm)
	He planted the baobab behind his mother's house:	
	"In and about the Manden,	(Mmm)
1520	"From my mother they must seek these leaves!"	(Mmm)
	To which his mother said, "I do not think I	
	heard."	(Mmm)
	"Ah, my mother,	(Indeed)
	"Now all the Manden baobabs are yours."	
	"I do not think I heard."	
1525	"Ah, my mother,	(Indeed)
	"All those women who refused you leaves,	
	"They all must seek those leaves from you."	(Indeed)
	His mother fell upon her knees, gejebu![8]	
	On both her knees,	
1530	And laid her head aside the baobab.	(Indeed)
	"For years and years,	
	"My ear was deaf.	(Indeed)
	"Only this year	
	"Has my ear heard news.	
1535	*"Khalif Magan Kònatè has risen!"*	(That's true)
	Biribiriba!	(Indeed)
	Since he began to walk,	(Indeed)
	Whenever he went into the bush,	(Mmm)
	Were he to kill some game,	(Indeed)
1540	He would give his elder the tail.[9]	
	And think no more of it.	
	. . .	(Indeed)

7. The series of mishaps caused by the hero in these lines prefigures his later prowess in war and explains the praise names he thus earns.   8. An exclamation.   9. Considered a delicacy. This detail emphasizes Son-Jara's generous disposition toward his brother, despite the conflict between them.

Took up the bow!
Simbon, Master-of-the-Bush!
1545   *Took up the bow!*
Took up the bow!   (Indeed)
Ruler of bards and smiths
Took up the bow!
Took up the bow!
1550   *The Kòndè woman's child,*
Answerer-of-Needs,
He took up the bow.
Sugulun's Ma'an took up the bow!

The Wizard has risen!
1555   *King of Nyani, Nare Magan Kònatè!*
The Wizard has risen!   (Indeed)
Ah! Bèmba!   (Indeed)
Whenever he went to the bush,   (Indeed)
Were he to kill some game,   (Indeed)
1560   He would give to his elder the tail,
And think no more of it.

. . .   (Indeed)
As Biribiriba walked forth one day,   (That's true)
A jinn came upon him,
1565   And laid his hand on Son-Jara's shoulder:
"O Son-Jara!   (Mmm)
"In the Manden, there's a plot against you.   (Mmm)
"That spotted dog you see before you,[1]   (Indeed)
"Is an offering made against you,   (Indeed)
1570   "So that you not rule the bards,   (Indeed)
"So that you not rule the smiths,
"So, the three and thirty warrior clans,
"That you rule over none of them.   (Mmm)
"When you go forth today,   (Mmm)
1575   "Make an offering of a safo-dog,[2]   (Indeed)
"Should God will it,
"The Manden will be yours!"   (Indeed)

Ah! Bèmba!
On that, Biribiriba went forth, my father,
1580   And made an offering of a safo-dog,
And hung a weight around its neck,[3]
And fastened an iron chain about it.   (Indeed)
Even tomorrow morning,
The Europeans will imitate him.
1585   Whenever the Europeans leave a dog,   (Mmm)
Its neck weight,
They fasten that dog with an iron chain, Manden!   (Indeed)

O! Bèmba!
He hung a weight around the dog's neck,
1590   And fastened it with a chain.   (Mmm)
That done, whatever home he passed before,   (Indeed)

---

1. The toothless dog (line 1206).   2. A dog consecrated for ritual sacrifice.   3. To restrain the dog's ferocity.

The people stood gaping at him:
"Causer-of-Loss![4]   (Indeed)
"A cow with its neckweight,
1595   "But a dog with a neckweight?"   (Indeed)
To which the Wizard did retort:
"Leave me be!   (True)
"Cast your eyes on the dog of the prince.[5]
"There's not a tooth in that dog's mouth!
1600   "But there are teeth in my dog's mouth,
"My commoner's[6] dog. Leave me be!   (Indeed)
"My dog's name is Tomorrow's Affair."

Son-Jara's sacrificial dog,
That dog was called Tomorrow's Affair.[7]

1605   From his neckwright he broke loose,
And also from his chain,   (Indeed)
And charged the dog of Dankaran Tuman,   (Indeed)
And ripped him into shreads, fèsè fèsè fèsè![8]   (Indeed)
And stacked one piece atop the other.   (Indeed)
1610   The mother of Dankaran Tuman, she wrung her hands
        atop her head,
And gave a piercing cry: "dèndèlen!   (Indeed)
"That a dog would bite a dog,   (Indeed)
"A natural thing in the Manden.   (Indeed)
"That a dog would kill a dog.
1615   "The natural thing in the Manden.
"That a dog shred another like an old cloth,
"My mother, there must be something with his master!"[9]
Dankaran Tuman replied, "Ah! my mother,   (Mmm)
"I called my dog Younger-Leave-Me-Be.   (Mmm)
1620   "Ah! My mother, do not sever the bonds of family.[1]   (True)
"My mother!   (Indeed)
"That is the dog that stalked the bush
"To go and kill some game,
"Bringing it back to me, my mother.   (True)
1625   "Do not sever the bonds of family, my mother!"   (True)

The mother of Dankaran Tuman had no answer:[2]   (Indeed)
"One afternoon, the time will come for Son-Jara
        to depart.   (Mmm)
"Indeed what the wise men have said,   (Mmm)
"His time is for the morrow.[3]   (Mmm)
1630   "The one that I have borne,   (Mmm)
"He is being left behind without explanation.   (Mmm)
"Son-Jara,   (Mmm)
"The Kòndè woman's offspring,   (Mmm)

---

4. That is, to his enemies; the praise name anticipates Son-Jara's later deeds.   5. That is, Dankaran Tuman, considered the heir apparent.   6. By referring to himself as a commoner, Son-Jara seems here to concede his half-brother's birthright.   7. Compare Du Kamisa's *A thing for tomorrow* (line 343). The implication is that he counts on the future to bring a change to his fortunes.   8. Ideophone evocative of the action described.   9. That is, Son-Jara must have superior magical power. The words carry a note of deep apprehension.   1. It is apparent from these words and from Son-Jara's attitude toward his half-brother (see n. 9, p. 2439) that the primary source of the conflict between the princes is the rivalry between their mothers.   2. She remains insensitive to her son's entreaty.   3. Saman Berete woman is credited with a foresight that contradicts her deepest sentiment. This is, however, only a narrative effect, the result of the bard's identification with Son-Jara and his anticipation of events.

	"He will take the Manden tribute,	(Mmm)
1635	"And he will rule the bards,	(Mmm)
	"And he will rule the smiths,	(Indeed)
	"And rule the funès[4] and the cordwainers.	(Indeed)
	"The Manden will be his.	
	"That time will yet arrive,	(Indeed)
1640	"And that by the hand of Nare Magan Kònatè.	
	"Nothing leaves its time behind."	
	O Biribiriba!	
	Kirikisa, Spear-of-Access, Spear-of-Service!	
	People of Kaya, Son-Jara entered Kaya.	
1645	All this by the hand of Nare Magan Kònatè.	
	Gaining power is not easy!	(Indeed)
	Ah! Bèmba!	(Indeed)
	The mother of King Dankaran Tuman,	(Indeed)
	When the Wizard had left the bush,	(Indeed)
1650	And offered his flesh-and-blood-brother the tail,	(Indeed)
	And when he said, "Here take the tail,"[5]	
	She retorted: "Your mother, Sugulun Kòndè, will take the tail!	(Indeed)
	"And your younger sister, Sugulun Kulukan,	(Indeed)
	"And your younger brother, Manden Bukari.	(Indeed)
1655	"Go and seek a place to die,	(Indeed)
	"If not, I will chop through your necks,	
	"Cutting a handspan down into the ground.	
	"Be it so; you'll never return to the Manden again."	(Indeed)
	Son-Jara bitterly wept, bilika bilika!	(Indeed)
1660	And went to tell his mother.	(Indeed)
	His mother said,	(Indeed)
	"Ah! My child,	(Indeed)
	"Be calm. Salute your brother.	(Indeed)
	"Had he banished you as a cripple,	
1665	"Where would you have gone?	
	"Let us at least agree on that.	
	"Let us depart.	
	"What sitting will not solve,	
	"Travel will resolve."	(That's true)

FROM EPISODE 5

Mèma

1670	They rose up	(Mmm)
	The Kuyatè matriarch took up the iron rasp.[6]	(Mmm)
	She sang a hunter's song for Nare Magan Kònatè:	
	"Took up the bow!	(Indeed)
	"Simbon, Master-of-the-Bush!	
1675	*"Took up the bow!*	
	"Took up the bow!	(Indeed)
	"Simbon, Master-of-Wild-Beasts!	
	"Took up the bow!	(Indeed)

---

4. A subclass of *griots* who only recite and do not play musical instruments. 5. There is a play on words in the original text, so that the phrase is interpreted by Saman Berete as an injunction to leave. 6. A musical instrument. *Kuyatè matriarch*: Tumu Maniya, the female bard who announced Son-Jara's birth to his father.

	"Took up the bow!	(Indeed)
1680	*"Warrior and Master-of-Slaves!*	
	"Took up the bow!	(Indeed)
	"The Kòndè woman's child,	
	"Answerer-of-Needs,	(Indeed)
	"Took up the bow.	(Indeed)
1685	*"Sugulan's Ma'an took up the bow.*	(Indeed)
	You seized him, O Lion!	(Indeed)
	"And the Wizard killed him!	
	"O Simbon, that, the sound of your chords."	(True)

	He fled from suffering	(Mmm)
1690	To seek refuge with the blacksmith patriarch,[7]	(Indeed)
	Because of the hardships of rivalry.	(Mmm)
	But they counted out one measure of gold,[8]	(Mmm)
	And gave it to the blacksmith patriarch,	(Indeed)
	Saying, were he not to cast the Wizard out,	(Indeed)
1695	Saying, he would jeopardize the land,	(Indeed)
	Saying, the Manden would be the Wizard's,	(Indeed)
	Because of the hardships of rivalry.	(Indeed)
	The Wizard fled anew from suffering.	(Mmm)
	He went to seek refute with the Karanga patriarch.	(Indeed)
1700	Do you not know that person's name?	(Mmm)
	Jobi, the Seer.	(Indeed)
	The Karanga patriarch was Jobi, the Seer.	(I did not know that until you told me)

Because of the hardships of rivalry,
He cast the Wizard out.

[Son-Jara and his mother wander from town to town seeking refuge and are cast out in the same manner everywhere. In desperation, they turn for help to a company of women who represent the forces of evil. Meanwhile, Son-Jara's half-brother succeeds to the throne, but the Manden is now threatened by a powerful neighbor, the Susu king Sumamuru.]

	Biribiriba went on to seek refuge	
	With the nine Queens-of-Darkness.[9]	
1770	"What brought you here?" they asked of him.	(Mmm)
	"Have you not heard that none come here?	(Indeed)
	"What brought you here?"	(Indeed)
	The Sorcerer spoke out.	
	"Ah! Those who are feared by all,	
1775	"If you join them, you are spared.	
	"It is that which made me come here."	
	He sat down.	(Indeed)
	His flesh-and-blood elder, King Dankaran Tuman,	(Indeed)
	He took his first-born daughter,	(Indeed)
1780	Caress-of-Hot-Fire,[1]	(Indeed)

---

7. His profession indicates that he is of lowly station. By seeking refuge with him, Son-Jara thus accepts a humiliated condition.   8. To reward the blacksmith for casting out Son-Jara and his mother. The reward is paid by Dankaran Tuman's people *(they)*.   9. Probably a cult of women devoted to the practice of magic.   1. So-named because of her sexual prowess. By giving his daughter to Sumamuru in marriage, Dankaran Tuman hopes to placate the Susu king and to enlist his aid in eliminating Son-Jara, who remains a threat even in exile.

And gave her to the Kuyatè patriarch, Dòka the Cat,[2]   (Indeed)
Saying, "Give her to Susu Mountain Sumamuru,"[3]   (Indeed)
Saying, "Should he not slay the King of Nyani,"
Saying, "He's gone to seek refuge with the nine
    Queens-of-Darkness,"
1785   Saying, "The folk have lost their faith in him."   (True)

At that time, the bards did not have balaphones,[4]   (True)
Nor had the smiths a balaphone,
Nor had the funès a balaphone,
Nor did the cordwainers have one,   (Indeed)
1790   None but Susu Mountain Sumamuru.   (Indeed)
    Sori Kantè the Tall,   (Indeed)
    Who begat Bala Kantè of Susu,   (Indeed)
    And who begat Kabani Kantè,   (True)
    And who begat Kankuba Kantè,
1795   And who begat Susu Mountain Sumamuru Kantè.[5]
The village where Sumamuru was,
That village was called Dark Forest.[6]   (True)

It was there he came forth, my father,   (Indeed)
Ah! Bèmba!   (Indeed)
1800   He came in Sumamuru's absence,   (Indeed)
Dòka the Cat,   (Indeed)
He asked for Sumamuru.[7]   (Indeed)
They said, "If you seek Sumamuru,
"Ask of the hawk!"   (Mmm)
1805   The balaphone of seven keys,   (Mmm)
After Sumamuru had played that balaphone,   (Indeed)
The mallets of the balaphone he would take,
And give them to the hawk.   (Indeed)
It would fly up high in a Flame Tree,
1810   And there in the depths of Susu Forest sit.   (Indeed)
Dòka the Cat called to the hawk.   (Indeed)
The balaphone mallets it delivered to him.   (Indeed)
    "Dun Fayiri, Nun Fayiri!   (Indeed)
    "Manda Kantè and Sama Kantè!   (Indeed)
1815   *"Sori Kantè, the Tall!*[8]   (Mmm)
    "Susu Mountain Sumamuru Kantè!   (Indeed)
    "Salute Sumamuru!   (Indeed)
    "Sumamuru came amongst us,
    "His pants of human skin.[9]   (Indeed)
1820   *"Sumamuru came amongst us,*
    "His coat of human skin.   (Indeed)
    "Sumamuru came amongst us,
    "His helm of human skin.   (Indeed)
    "The first and ancient king,

---

2. Son-Jara's personal bard, whom he had to leave behind in the Manden, has been appropriated by Dankaran Tuman.   3. Son-Jara's principal antagonist is introduced here for the first time. His massive physical aspect is denoted in the sobriquet *Mountain* that has become attached to his name.   4. Musical instruments, akin to the xylophone, with boards of varying length laid out for the different notes. 5. These lines are a rapid summary of Sumamuru's genealogy.   6. The name of the village identifies Sumamuru with paganism, as opposed to the Muslim affiliations of Son-Jara.   7. Dòka the Cat's motive in seeking out Sumamuru, who is ravaging the Manden, is not made clear, for it soon becomes apparent he has no intention of entering his service.   8. These are the names of Sumamuru's ancestors, invoked in his praise song.   9. Symbolic of his savage ferocity.

1825   *"The King of yesteryear.*[1]   (Indeed)
"So, respite does not end resolve.
"Sumamuru, I found you gone.
"Oh! Glorious Janjon!"[2]

Sumamuru was off doing battle,
1830   With pants of human skin,
And coat of human skin.
Whenever he would mount a hill,
Down another he would go.
Up one and down another.
1835   Was it God or man?[3]
He approached the Kuyatè patriarch, Dòka the
    Cat: (Mmm)
"God or man?"   (Indeed)
"I am a man," the reply.
"Where do you hail from?"   (Mmm)
1840   "I come," he said, "from the Manden.   (Indeed)
"I am from Nyani."   (Indeed)

"Play something for me to hear," he said. (Indeed)
He took up the balaphone: (Indeed)
    "Kukuba and Bantanba!
1845   *"Nyani-nyani and Kamasiga!*[4]
    "Brave child of the warrior!
    "And Deliverer-of-the-Benign.
    "Sumamuru came amongst us
    "With pants of human skin.
1850   *"Sumamuru came amongst us,*
    "With coat of human skin.
    "Sumamuru came amongst us
    "With helm of human skin.
    "The first and ancient king,
1855   *"The king of yesteryear.*
    "So, respite does not end resolve!
    "Sumamuru, I found you gone.
    "Oh! Glorious Janjon!"

He[5] said, "Ah! What is your name?"
1860   "My name is Dòka, the Cat."   (Mmm)
"Will you not remain with me?"
"Not I! Two kings I cannot praise.
"I am Son-Jara's bard.
"From the Manden I have come,
1865   "And to the Manden I must return."   (True)

He laid hold of the Kuyatè patriarch,
And severed both Achilles tendons,[6]
And by the Susu balaphone set him.   (Indeed)

---

1. As addressed by Dòka the Cat to Sumamuru, this praise epithet is shot through with ambivalence. It may refer to the sanction bestowed by the years on Sumamuru's ancestry and reign, but it also suggests that the addressee belongs to a past age that is to be superseded by a new one, that of Son-Jara.   2. War song, a genre of oral poetry in the Manding.   3. As the notes of his balaphone reach his ears, Sumamuru wonders who is playing the instrument.   4. These are place names in the Manden.   5. Sumamuru. 6. In other versions of the epic, this violation of his bard is presented as Son-Jara's principal grievance against Sumamuru.

1870	"Now what is your name?"	(Indeed)
	"Dòka, the Cat is still my name."	(Indeed)
	"Dòka, the Cat will no longer do."	(Indeed)
	He drew water and poured it over his head,	(Indeed)
	And shaved it clean,[7]	(Indeed)
	And gave him the name Bala Faseke Kuyatè.	
1875	That Bala Faseke Kuyatè,	(Indeed)
	He fathered three children,	(Indeed)
	Musa and Mansa Magan,	(Indeed)
	Making Baturu, the Holy his last-born son in the Manden.	(Indeed)
	Those were the Kuyatès.	
1880	And this by the hand of Sumamuru.	
	He sent forth a messenger,	
	Saying, "Go tell King Dankaran Tuman,"	(Indeed)
	Saying, "If you kill your own vicious dog,"	
	Saying, "Another man's will surely bite you."[8]	(Indeed, that's the truth)
1885	With this he declared war, my father,	
	And went forth from Susu.	
	Going to fall on King Dankaran Tuman,	(Indeed)
	Breaking the Manden like an old pot,	(Indeed)
	Breaking the Manden like an old gourd,	(Indeed)
1890	Slaying the nine and ninety Masters-of-Shadow,[9]	
	Slaying the nine and ninety royal princes,	
	And ousting King Dankaran Tuman.	
	He fled to Nsèrè-kòrò,[1]	
	Saying, "I was spared.	(Indeed)
1895	"From your torment, I was spared.	(True)
	From death, I have been spared."	(Indeed)
	And thus he settled there.	
	The sons he there begat, my father,	(Indeed)
	They became the Kisi[2] people.	
1900	They are all in Masanta.[3]	
	They had come from the Manden.	
	Their family name, it is Gindo.	(Indeed)
	Ah! Bèmba!	(Indeed)
	O Biribiriba!	
1905	He put gourds in the mouths[4] of the poor and the powerful.	
	This by the hand of Susu Mountain Sumamuru,	(Indeed)
	Saying each must speak into his gourd,	
	Saying there is no pleasure in weakness,[5]	
	Saying the Manden was now his.	
1910	He summoned Kankira-of-Silver	(Indeed)
	And Kankira-of-Gold,[6]	(Indeed)
	The latter, the Saginugu patriarch,	(Indeed)

---

7. As with a newborn child at its naming ceremony. The shaving of the bard's hair and his new name signify his rededication to a new service.   8. The meaning is that Dankaran Tuman can expect to suffer the same fate he inflicted on Son-Jara.   9. Diviners in the royal household.   1. In present-day Guinea. 2. An ethnic group spread along the coast from Guinea to Senegal.   3. An area farther inland, to the north.   4. Metaphor to denote Sumamuru's repressive rule.   5. Expressive of the arrogance of power. 6. Silversmith and Goldsmith; they belong to a special caste of craftsmen.

	And one red[7] bull did give to them,	(Indeed)
	Saying they should offer it	
1915	To the nine Queens-of-Darkness,	(Indeed)
	Asking them to slay Son-Jara,	(Mmm)
	That he not enter the Manden again,	
	To say that the Manden be his,	
	Saying they have slain the	
	nine and ninety Masters-of-Shadow,	
1920	Saying they have slain the nine and	
	ninety royal princes,	
	And put gourds o'er the mouths	
	of the poor and the powerful,	(Indeed)
	Saying that they should slay him,	(Indeed)
	So he not enter the Manden again	(Mmm)
	To say that the Manden be his.	(Indeed)
1925	Those messengers arrived.	(Indeed)
	They came upon the witches there:	(Indeed)
	"Ilu tuntun!"	(Indeed)
	The witches did not speak.	(Mmm)
	"Peace be unto you."	(Mmm)
1930	The witches did not speak.	
	"Alu tuntun!"	
	The witches did not speak.	
	"Peace be with you!"	
	The witches did not speak.	(That's true)
1935	"The slaughtered bull,	(Indeed)
	"Lay it out in nine piles."	(Indeed)
	Nakana Tiliba[8] then said to the witches,	
	"Each must either take her own,	(Indeed)
	"Questions without end looking for trouble,[9]	(That's true)
1940	"Then take the meat and be off,	(Indeed)
	"Or," Nakana Tiliba continued,	(Indeed)
	"You must not take the meat.	
	"O Son-Jara,	(Indeed)
	"A message has come from the Manden,	(Indeed)
1945	"From Susu Mountain Sumamuru,	(Indeed)
	"Saying to come and tell us,	(Indeed)
	"Saying we should slay you,	(Indeed)
	"So that you not enter the Manden again,	
	"Saying, the folk have lost their faith in you.	(Indeed)
1950	"Saying, he has slain the nine and ninety	
	Masters-of-the-Shadow,	(Indeed)
	"Saying, he has slain the nine and ninety royal	
	princes.	(Indeed)
	"Nine were the times he razed the Manden,	
	"And nine were the times he rebuilt it,	(Indeed)
	Saying, he put gourds on the mouths of the poor and the	
	powerful,	(Indeed)
1955	"Saying, all must speak into their gourds,	

---

7. In many African societies, the red symbolizes the supernatural world.   8. Son-Jara's paternal aunt, previously given by Fata Magan the Handsome to the Tarawere brothers in exchange for Sugulun Kòndè (see line 1028). She is now the principal queen of darkness.   9. That is, each must take her part without argument.

"Saying, there is no pleasure in weakness,
Saying, he has ousted King Dankaran Tuman,
Saying, who has fled to Nsèrè-kòrò,
"Saying, we should slay you,
1960 "So that you not enter the Manden again,
"And that is the reason for this meat."
"Then kill me," his reply.
"A person flees to be spared,
"But should one not be spared, then kill me!"[1]   (True)

1965 Biribiriba!   (Mmm)
He went to the back of the house.
Into a lion he transformed himself,   (Mmm)
A lion seizing no one,[2]
Before he had sounded a roar.   (Mmm)
1970 He went and seized a buffalo,
And came back and laid it down,
And went and seized another,
And came and laid it down,
And went and seized another,
1975 And came and laid it down.
"Nine water buffalos, nine witches!   (Mmm)
"Each take your own!"   (True)
The witches then replied to him,
"Let us hold a council.
1980 "The town where people hold no council,
"There will living not be good."
They went to hold their council,
"From the Manden and its neighbors,   (Indeed)
"All of it together, and only one red bull!   (Indeed)
1985 "Son-Jara, you alone, nine buffalos!
"It is to him the Manden must belong!
"Let us then release him!"   (True)
They trimmed a branch of the custard apple tree: (Indeed)
"When you leave the land of the nine
        Queens-of-Darkness,   (Indeed)
1990 "You will see no village,   (Mmm)
"Until you see Jula Fundu,   (Mmm)
"The original town of the Mossi[3] patriarch,   (Indeed)
"Jula Fundu and Wagadugu,   (Indeed)
"In Mèma Farin Tunkara's land of Mèma."
1995 They stacked the bull meat in one pile,   (Mmm)
And upon it laid its skin,
And upon this placed its head.   (Mmm)
"All of you witches, say your verses!   (Indeed)

"All of you witches, read your signs!"   (Indeed)
2000 Nakana Tiliba,
From her head she took her scarf,
And tied three knots[4] into it,
And laid it o'er the meat,

---

1. Note the equanimity with which Son-Jara receives Nakana Tiliba's words.   2. That is, one that does not bother any human being, because he is only after game.   3. An ethnic group in Burkina Faso. Nothing more is known about Jula Fundu (founder of the Mossi).   4. To give it magical potency.

Saying, "Rise up!
2005 "Kitibili Kintin!⁵   (Indeed)
" 'Twas a man that puts us in conflict.
"A matter of truth is not to be feared."⁶
The bull rose up and stretched.   (Mmm)
It bellowed to Muhammad.⁷   (Mmm)
2010 The Messenger of God was thus evoked.   (That's true)

That bull rose up and stretched.   (Indeed)
Ah! Bèmba!   (Indeed)
Son-Jara came forth: (Indeed)
"O Kankira-of-Silver and Kankira-of-Gold,   (Indeed)
2015 "A messenger is not to be whipped.   (Indeed)
"A messenger is not to be defiled.⁸   (Indeed)
"When you go forth from here,
"You should go tell Susu Mountain Sumamuru,   (Indeed)
"When you go forth from here,   (Indeed)
2020 "You should go tell Susu Mountain Sumamuru: (Indeed)
" 'The cowherd offers naught of the cow,'
" 'But the milk of Friday past.'
" 'No matter how loving the wet nurse,'
" 'The child will never be hers.'
2025 "Say, 'A child may be first-born, but that does not always
       make him the elder.'
"Say, 'Today may belong to some,'
" 'Tomorrow will belong to another.'
"Say, 'As you succeeded some,'
" 'So shall you have successors.'
2030 "Say, 'I am off to seek refuge with Mèma's Prince Tunkara,'
" 'In the land of Mèma.' "⁹

He took the shape of a hawk.
You took it, Nare Magan Kònatè.
    Biribiriba and Bow-of-the-Bush . . . ,
2035   . . . fled because of suffering.
    Gaining power is not easy.

Ah! Bèmba!
Son-Jara went to seek refuge in Mèma,
In a town of the Tunkaras, my father, in Mèma.   (Indeed)

[There follows a long account of a ritual ordeal Son-Jara must undergo before he is allowed by Prince Burama, the ruler of Mèma, to settle in the town. Mèma Sira, Prince Burama's eldest daughter, who has fallen in love with Son-Jara, reveals the secret of the ordeal to him so that he passes it without difficulty. With his mother, brother, and sister, Son-Jara settles in Mèma, practicing his profession as a hunter, while waiting for a chance to return to the Manden, which is meanwhile being devastated by Sumamuru.]

5. An incantation.   6. Or telling the truth is a moral obligation, even if it means offending the powerful.
7. An example of the mix of religions that occasionally surfaces in the epic. It is obvious, however, that invocation of Muhammad is out of keeping with the atmosphere of the scene described here.   8. By tradition, a messenger enjoys absolute immunity, even if sent by an enemy.   9. Thus Son-Jara and his mother chose to seek refuge in Mèma.

2410	Son-Jara had a certain fetish	(Indeed)
	Accepting no sacrifice save shea butter.	(Indeed)
	There were no shea trees there in Mèma.	(Indeed)
	O Mansa Magan!	(Indeed)
	Wherever you sacrifice to the shea tree,	(Indeed)
2415	That town must be in Mandenland.	(Indeed)

All of them are in the Manden. (Indeed)
No shea trees were there in Mèma. (Indeed)
Save one old dry Shea tree in Mèma. (Indeed)
Son-Jara's mother came forward:[1] (Indeed)
  2420   "Ah! God! (Indeed)
      "Let Son-Jara go to the Manden. (Indeed)
      "He is the man for the morrow. (Indeed)
      "He is the man for the day to follow. (Indeed)
      "He is to rule o'er the bards, (Indeed)
  2425   "He is to rule o'er the smiths, (Indeed)
      "And the three and thirty warrior clans. (Indeed)
      "He will rule o'er all those people. (Indeed)
      "Ah, God! (Indeed)
      "Before the break of day, (Indeed)
  2430   "That dried up shea tree here, (Indeed)
      "Let it bear leaf and fruit. (Indeed)
      "Let the fruit fall down to earth, (Indeed)
      "So that Son-Jara may gather the fruit,
      "From it to make shea butter, (Indeed)
  2435   "To offer his fetish. (Indeed, yes, Fa-Digi)

      "Ah, God! (Indeed)
      "Let Son-Jara go to the Manden. (Indeed)
      "He is the man for the morrow.
      "He is the man for the day to follow. (Indeed)
  2440   "He will rule the bards and smiths. (Indeed)
      "The Manden belongs to the Wizard. (Indeed)
      "Before the break of day, (Indeed)
      "Let me change my dwelling,[2] (Indeed)
      "Old am I and cannot travel. (Indeed)
  2445   "Let Nare Magan Kònatè go home." (Indeed)
When the day was dawning, (Indeed)
The dried up shea tree did bear leaf. (Indeed)
Its fruit did fall to earth. (Indeed)
Son-Jara looked in on the Kòndè woman, (Indeed)
  2450 But the Kòndè woman had abandoned the world. (Indeed)
He washed his mother's body, (Indeed)
And then he dug her grave, (Indeed)
And wrapped her in a shroud, (Indeed)
And laid his mother in the earth, (Indeed)
  2455 And then chopped down a kapok tree, (Indeed)
And wrapped it in a shroud, (Indeed)
And laid it in the house, (Indeed)
And laid a blanket over it. (Indeed)
And sent a messenger to Prince Birama,

---

1. Because they were running out of the oil they had brought with them from the Manden, Sugulun Kòndè prays for the rejuvenation of this lone shea tree.   2. That is, depart this world for the next.

2460	Asking of him a grant of land,	(Indeed)
	In order to bury his mother in Mèma,	
	So that he could return to the Manden.	(Indeed)
	This answer they did give to him	
	That no land could he have,	
2465	Unless he were to pay its price.	(Indeed)

	Prince Birama decreed,	(Indeed)
	Saying he could have no land,	(Indeed)
	Unless he were to pay its price.	(Indeed)
	He[3] took feathers of Guinea fowl and partridge,	(Indeed)
2470	And took some leaves of arrow-shaft plant,	(Indeed)
	And took some leaves of wild grass reed,	(Indeed)
	And took some red fanda-vines,	(Indeed)
	And took one measure of shot,	(Indeed)
	And took a haftless knife,	(Indeed)
2475	And added a cornerstone fetish[4] to that,	(Indeed)
	And put it all in a leather pouch,	(Indeed)
	Saying go give it to Prince Birama,	(Indeed)
	Saying it was the price of his land.	(Indeed, ha, Fa-Digi)

	That person gave it to Prince Birama.	(Indeed)
2480	Prince Birama summoned his three sages,[5]	(Indeed)
	All-Knowing Sage,	(Indeed)
	All-Seeing-Sage,	(Indeed)
	All-Saying-Sage.	(Indeed)
	The three sages counseled Prince Birama.	(Indeed)
2485	He said, "O Sages!	(Indeed)
	"The forest by the river is never empty.[6]	(Indeed)
	"You also should take this.[7]	(Indeed)
	"That which came first,	(Indeed)
	"I will not take it.	(Indeed)
2490	"Tis yours."[8]	(Indeed)
	O Garan!	(Indeed)
	All-Seeing-Sage,	
	All-Saying-Sage,	
	All-Knowing-Sage,	(Indeed)
2495	They untied the mouth of the pouch,	
	And shook its contents out.	(Indeed)
	The All-Seeing Sage exclaimed,	(Indeed)
	"Anyone can see that!	(Indeed)
	"I am going home!"[9]	(Indeed)
2500	The All-Knowing-Sage exclaimed,	(Indeed)
	"Everybody knows that!	(Indeed)
	"I am going home."	(Indeed)
	All-Saying-Sage exclaimed,	(Indeed)
	"Everyone knows that?	(Indeed)
2505	"That is a lie!	(Indeed)
	"Everyone sees that?	(Indeed)
	"That is a lie!	(Indeed)

---

3. Son-Jara.   4. The allusion is obscure, but this is probably a fetish object.   5. To explain the meaning of Son-Jara's gesture.   6. There is more to this than meets the eye.   7. Look into this for me. 8. Within your domain as seers.   9. The matter is too trivial to detain him. It is an ironic comment on the self-importance of seers.

"There may be something one may see,
"Be it ne'er explained to him,
2510 "He will never know it.   (Indeed)

"Prince Birama,   (Indeed)
"Did you not see feathers of Guinea fowl and partridge?
"They are the things of ruins.[1]   (Indeed)
"Did you not see the leaf of arrow-shaft plant?
2515 "That is a thing of ruins.   (Indeed)
"Was not your eye on the wild grass reed?   (Indeed)
"That is a thing of ruins.   (Indeed)
"Did you not see those broken shards?   (Indeed)
"They are the things of ruins.   (Indeed)
2520 "Did you not see that measure of shot?[2]   (Indeed)
"The annihilator of Mèma![3]   (Indeed)
"Did you not see that haftless knife?   (Indeed)
"The warrior-head-severing blade!   (Indeed)
"Was not your eye on the red fanda-vine?[4]   (Indeed)
2525 "The warrior-head-severing blood!   (Indeed)
"If you do not give the land to him,   (Indeed)
"That cornerstone fetish your eye beheld,
"It is the warrior's thunder shot!   (Indeed)
"If you do not give the land to him,
2530 "To Nare Magan Kònatè,
"The Wizard will reduce the town to ruin.   (Indeed)
"Son-Jara is to return to the Manden!"   (That's the truth)

They gave the land to the Sorcerer,   (Indeed)
He buried his mother in Mèma's earth.
2535 He rose up.
That which sitting will not solve,
Travel will resolve.   (Indeed)

FROM EPISODE 6

Kulu-Kòrò

* * *

2575   O Biribiriba!   (Indeed)
        When he and his mother were going to Mèma,   (Indeed)
        She took her silver bracelet off,
        And gave it to the Boatman patriarch,
        To Sasagalò, the Tall.   (Indeed)
2580   The ancestor of the boatman was Sasagalò, the Tall.
        She took her silver bracelet off: (Indeed)
        "When one digs a distant-day well,
        "Should a distant-day thirst descend, then drink!"[5] (Indeed)

        A partridge was sent to deliver the message[6]   (Indeed)
2585   To Susu Mountain Sumamuru: (Indeed)

---

1. In other words, a threat of destruction. 2. An anachronism. 3. Son-Jara, if his request is not granted. 4. An unidentified creeping plant. 5. A proverb counseling foresight. 6. It is not clear whether Son-Jara sends this message to challenge Sumumaru or whether it is a general report by the latter's retainers and spies. *Partridge:* birds were often used to carry messages over long distances in earlier societies and in Europe even as late as the 19th century. The partridge, however, was never used for this purpose; thus it is not clear whether the reference here is intended as a realistic detail or is merely symbolic.

	"Manda and Sama Kantè!	(Indeed)
	"Susu Bala Kantè!	
	"Kukuba and Bantanba!	
	"Nyani-nyani and Kamasiga!	(Indeed)
2590	"Brave child of the warrior!	
	"And Deliverer-of-the-Benign!	
	"Sumamuru came among us	
	"With pants of human skin!	(Indeed)
	"Sumamuru came among us	
2595	"With coat of human skin.	(Indeed)
	"Applaud him!	(Indeed)
	"Susu Mountain Sumamuru!	
	"The Sorcerer with his army has left Mèma.	(Indeed)
	"He has entered the Manden!"[7]	(Indeed)
2600	Susu Mountain Sumamuru,	(Indeed)
	He took four measures of gold,	(Indeed)
	To the Boatman patriarch,	
	Sasagalò, the Tall, did give them,	(Indeed)
	Saying, "That army coming from Mèma,	(Indeed)
2605	"That army must not cross!"	(Indeed)
	For one entire month,	(Indeed)
	Son-Jara and his army by the riverbank sat.	(Indeed)
	He wandered up and down.	(Indeed)
	One day Son-Jara rose up	
2610	And followed up the river:	(Indeed)
	"Being good, a bane.	(Indeed)
	"Not being good, a bane.	(Indeed)
	"When my mother and I were going to Mèma,	(Indeed)
	"She took her silver bracelet off,	(Indeed)
2615	"And gave it to a person here,	(Indeed)
	Saying when you dig a distant-day well,	
	"When a distant-day thirst descends, then drink.	(Indeed)
	"Thus have I come with my army,	(Indeed)
	"And we have not yet made a crossing."[8]	(Indeed)
2620	The Boatman patriarch responded:	(Indeed)
	"Ah! Is it you who are Son-Jara?"	(Indeed)
	The reply, "It is I who am Son-Jara."	(Indeed)
	"You are Son-Jara?"	(Indeed)
	"Indeed I am Son-Jara!"	(Indeed)
2625	"It is you who are Nare Magan Kònatè?	(Indeed)
	"If God wills,	
	"With the break of day,	
	"Tomorrow will the army cross."	(Indeed)
	At the break of day,	(Indeed)
2630	The Boatman patriarch, Sasagalò the Tall,	(Indeed)
	He brought Son-Jara across.	(Indeed)
	The Wizard advanced with his army.	(Indeed)
	They fell upon Sumamuru at Dark Forest.	(Indeed)
	But he drove them off.	(Indeed)
2635	Susu Mountain Sumamuru drove Son-Jara off.	(Indeed)

7. This announcement marks the point at which Son-Jara's campaign for recovery of his kingdom begins.
8. Son-Jara reproaches Sasagalò the Tall for not keeping his part of the bargain with his mother.

He went and founded a town called Anguish.[9]   (Indeed)
Of which the bards did sing:
    "We will not move to Anguish.   (Indeed)
    "Should one go to Anguish.
2640   "Should not anguish he endure.   (Indeed)
    "Then nothing would he reap.   (Indeed)
    "We will not move to Anguish."   (Indeed)

That Anguish,   (Indeed)
The Maninka sing this of it, my father:
2645   "There is no joy in you."   (Indeed)
Our name for that town is Anguish (Nyani).   (Indeed)

The Wizard advanced with his army.   (Indeed)
They went to fall on Susu Mountain Sumamuru.   (Indeed)
He drove Son-Jara off again.   (Indeed)
2650 He went to found the town called Resolve.   (Indeed)
The bards thus sing of it:
    "We will not move to Resolve.
    "Should one move to Resolve,
    "Should not resolve he entertain,
2655   "Then nothing would he reap.   (Indeed)
    "We will not move to Resolve."   (Indeed)
The Wizard advanced again.   (Indeed)
He with his bards advanced.   (Indeed)
They went to fall on Susu Mountain Sumamuru.   (Indeed)
2660 Sumamuru drove him off with his bards.   (Indeed)
They went to found the town called Sharing.[1]   (Indeed)
And they sang:
    Let us move to the Wizard's town, my father.
    "To Sharing,   (Indeed)
2665   "The town where sharing is not done,
    "Founding that town is not easy."   (Indeed)
They went to found the town called Sharing.   (Indeed)

Son-Jara's flesh-and-blood-sister, Sugulun
    Kulunkan,   (Indeed)
She said, "O Magan Son-Jara,   (Indeed)
2670 "One person cannot fight this war.[2]   (Indeed)
"Let me go seek Sumamuru.   (Indeed)
"Were I then to reach him,
"To you I will deliver him,   (Indeed)
"So that the folk of the Manden be yours,   (Indeed)
2675 "And all the Mandenland you shield."   (Indeed)
Sugulun Kulunkan arose,   (Indeed)
And went up to the gates of Sumamuru's fortress: (Indeed)
    "Manda and Sama Kantè!   (Indeed)
    "Kukuba and Bantamba
2680   *"Nyani-nyani and Kamasiga!*   (Indeed)
    "Brave child of the Warrior,
    "And Deliverer-of-the Benign.   (Indeed)
    "Sumamuru came amongst us

---

9. A metaphor for Son-Jara's mental condition as a result of his setback. The names of the other locations he founds have a more general moral significance.   1. That is, partial success.   2. It cannot be won by arms alone. Like Judith and Dalila in the Bible, Son-Jara's sister intends to employ her feminine charms in the struggle against her brother's enemy.

      "With pants of human skin.   (Indeed)
2685   *"Sumamuru came amongst us*
      "With shirt of human skin.   (Indeed)
      "Sumamuru came amongst us
      "With helm of human skin.   (Indeed)
   "Come open the gates, Susu Mountain
     Sumamuru!   (Indeed)

2690   "Come make me your bed companion!"   (Indeed)
   Sumamuru came to the gates: (Indeed)
   "What manner of person are you?"   (Indeed)
   "It is I Sugulun Kulunkan!"   (Indeed)
   "Well, now, Sugulun Kulunkan,   (Indeed)
2695   "If you have come to trap me,   (Indeed)
   "To turn me over to some person,   (Indeed)
   "Know that none can ever vanquish me.   (Indeed)
   "I have found the Manden secret,   (Indeed)
   "And made the Manden sacrifice,   (Indeed)
2700   "And in five score millet stalks placed it,   (Indeed)
   "And buried them here in the earth.   (Indeed)
   " 'Tis I who found the Manden secret,   (Indeed)
   "And made the Manden sacrifice,   (Indeed)
   "And in a red piebald bull did place it,   (Indeed)
2705   "And buried it here in the earth.   (Indeed)
   "Know that none can vanquish me.   (Indeed)
   " 'Tis I who found the Manden secret   (Indeed)
   "And made a sacrifice to it.   (Indeed)
   "And in a pure white cock did place it.   (Indeed)
2710   "Were you to kill it,   (Indeed)
   "And uproot some barren groundnut plants,   (Indeed)
   "And strip them of their leaves,
   "And spread them round the fortress,   (Indeed)
   "And uproot more barren peanut plants,   (Indeed)
2715   "And fling them into the fortress,   (Indeed)
   "Only then can I be vanquished,"[3]   (Indeed)
   His mother sprang forward at that: (Indeed)
   "Heh! Susu Mountain Sumamuru!   (Indeed)
   "Never tell all to a woman,
2720   "To a one-night woman!   (Indeed)
   "The woman is not safe, Sumamuru."   (Indeed)
   Sumamuru sprang towards his mother,   (Indeed)
   And came and seized his mother,   (Indeed)
   And slashed off her breast with a knife, *magasi!*[4] (Indeed)
2725   She went and got the old menstrual cloth.   (Indeed)
   "Ah! Sumamuru!" she swore.   (Indeed)
   "If your birth was ever a fact,
   "I have cut your old menstrual cloth!"[5]

   O Kalajula Sangoyi Mamunaka!   (Indeed)
2730   He lay Sugulun Kulunkan down on the bed. (Indeed)
   After one week had gone by,

---

3. Sumamuru's bravado here is in keeping with his vaingloriousness as it comes through in the narrative.
4. The same words used for Jata Magan Kòndè's treatment of his sister, Du Kamisa (compare line 418).
5. The cloth in which he was wrapped at his birth, stained with the blood of parturition. By tearing it up, she disowns her son.

Sugulun Kulunkan spoke up: (Indeed)
"Ah, my husband,   (Indeed)
"Will you not let me go to the Manden,   (Indeed)
2735 "That I may get my bowls and spoons,[6]
"For me to build my household here?   (Indeed)
From that day to this,
Should you marry a woman in Mandenland,   (Indeed)
When the first week has passed,
2740 She will take a backward glance,   (Indeed)
And this is what that custom means.   (Yes, Fa-Digi, that's
      the truth)

Sugulun returned to reveal those secrets
To her flesh-and-blood-brother, Son-Jara.   (Indeed)
The sacrifices did Son-Jara thus discover.   (Indeed)
2745 The sacrifices did he thus discover.[7]   (Indeed)
Now five score wives had Susu Mountain Sumamuru,   (Indeed)
One hundred wives had he.   (Indeed)
His nephew, Fa-Koli, had but one,[8]   (Indeed)
. . .   (Mmm)
2750 And Sumamuru, five score!   (Indeed)
When a hundred bowls they would cook
To make the warriors' meal,   (Indeed)
Fa-Koli's wife alone would one hundred cook
To make the warriors' meal,   (That's the truth, eh,
      Fa-Digi, indeed, indeed)
2755 "Let the fonio[9] increase!   (Indeed)
"Let the rice increase!   (Indeed)
"Let the groundnuts increase!   (Indeed)
"Let the groundpeas increase!   (Indeed)
"Let the beans increase!"[1]   (Indeed)
2760 She took them all one by one,   (Indeed)
And put them all in one pot,   (Indeed)
And in that pot they all were cooked,   (Indeed)
And served it all in her calabash,   (Indeed)
And all of this for Fa-Koli.   (Indeed)

[Sumamuru takes Fa-Koli's wife, causing a rift between him and his nephew, who defects to Son-Jara.]

2770 Hero-of-the-Original-Clans and Magan
    Sukudana![2]   (Indeed)
Son-Jara called out,   (Indeed)
"Who in the Manden will make this sacrifice?"[3]   (Indeed)
"I shall!" Fa-Koli's reply.   (Indeed)
"The thing that drove me away,   (Indeed)
2775 "And took my only wife from me,
"So that not even a weak wife have I now,   (Indeed)
"I shall make the whole sacrifice!"   (Indeed)

---

6. It is customary among the Manding for a new bride to return to her home a last time to collect her belongings before settling into her new life. The passage traces the custom to the incident recounted here.
7. To be acted on later.   8. In contrast to Sumamuru's *five score*, which emphasizes his sexual desire.
9. A cereal.   1. Fa-Koli's wife's incantations over the food she has prepared.   2. Praise name of Fa-Koli.   3. Revealed by Son-Jara's sister (see line 2742).

Fa-Koli thus made the whole sacrifice. (Indeed)
He came and reported to the Wizard.
2780 Son-Jara then called out: (Indeed)
"Who will bring us face to face,
"That we may join in battle?" (Indeed)
"I shall," Fa-Koli's reply. (Indeed)
On that Fa-Koli rose up. (Indeed)
2785 He arrived in Dark Forest. (Indeed)
As he espied the rooftops of Sumamuru's city, Dark
Forest, (Indeed)
With every single step he took, (Indeed)
He thrust a dart[4] into the earth, (Indeed)
And in a tree fork laid another. (Indeed, yes, Fa-Digi)
2790 With every single step he took, (Indeed)
He thrust a dart into the earth, (Indeed)
And in a tree fork laid another,[5] (That's the truth)
Until he entered the very gates,
Until he entered the city. (Indeed)
2795 O, Garan! (Indeed)
The daughter given by King Dankaran Tuman,[6] (Indeed)
Given to Susu Mountain Sumamuru, (Indeed)
That he should go and kill Son-Jara, (Indeed)
Fa-Koli went and seized that maiden, (Indeed)
2800 "Come! Your uncle has left Mèma! (Indeed)
"Your uncle has summoned you. (Indeed)
"Your uncle has now come. He has left Mèma!" (Indeed)
The people of Susu pursued them: biri biri biri. (Indeed)
They came attacking after them: yrrrrrr! (Indeed)
2805 With every single step he took, (Indeed)
He drew a war dart from the earth,
And hurled it at the Susu, (Indeed)
And from a tree fork grabbed another, (Indeed)
And hurled it at the Susu, (Indeed)
2810 "Heh! Come to my aid! (Indeed)
"Heaven and Earth, come aid me!
"Susu Mountain Sumamuru is after
me!" (Indeed, yes, father)
He retreated on and on.[7]
He drew a war dart from the earth,
2815 And hurled it at the Susu, (Indeed)
And from a tree fork grabbed another, (Indeed)
And fired it at the Susu. (Indeed)
"Heh! Come to my aid! (Indeed)
"Heaven and Earth, come to my aid!
2820 "Susu Mountain Sumamuru is after me!" (That's the truth)

At that, the Susu said, my father, (Indeed)
"If we do not fall back from Fa-Koli, (Indeed)
"Fa-Koli will bring all our folk to an end![8] (Indeed)
"Let us fall back from Fa-Koli! (Indeed)

---

4. It will soon be clear that this is a magic dart.   5. The motif here is a heroicized variant of the Hansel and Gretel story.   6. Caress-of-Hot-Fire.   7. Clearly as a diversionary tactic to draw out the enemy lines.   8. He is single-handedly destroying the enemy ranks with his magic dart.

2825   Hero-of-the-Original-Clans and Magan Sukudana.
              . . .   (That's the truth)
          And thus they fell back from Fa-Koli.   (Indeed)
          They readied themselves for battle.   (Indeed)
          Susu Mountain Sumamuru came forward.   (Indeed)
2830   And taking his favorite wife,
          On the saddle's cantle sat her,   (Indeed)
          With golden ladle and silver ladle.   (Indeed)
          Son-Jara attacked and encircled the walls.   (Indeed)
          He had split the enemy army,[9]   (Indeed)
2835   And taken the fortress gates.   (Indeed)
          Susu Mountain Sumamuru charged out at a gallop.[1] (Indeed)
          Fa-Koli,   (Indeed)
          With Tura-Magan-and-Kanke-jan,   (Indeed)
          And Bee-King-of-the-Wilderness,   (Indeed)
2840   And Fa-Kanda Tunandi,   (Indeed)
          And Sura, the Jawara patriarch,   (Indeed)
          And Son-Jara,   (Indeed)
          They all chased after Sumamuru.   (True)
          They arrived at Kukuba.   (Indeed)
2845   He told them, "I am not ready!"   (Indeed)
          They let him go:[2]   (Indeed)
          "Prepare yourself!"   (Indeed)
          They arrived at Kamasiga,[3]   (Indeed)
          "I am not ready."   (Indeed)
2850   They let him go: (Indeed)
          "Prepare yourself!"   (Indeed)
          They arrived at Nyani-Nyani.   (Indeed)
          Said, "I am not ready."   (Indeed)
          They let him go again:
2855   "Prepare yourself!"   (Indeed)
          They arrived at Bantanba,   (Indeed)
          "I am not ready."   (Indeed)
          And again they let him go:
          "Prepare yourself!"   (Indeed)
2860   And still they attacked him from behind,
          Behind Susu Mountain Sumamuru.   (That's the truth,
                                     yes, Fa-Digi)

          Sumamuru crossed the river at Kulu-Kòrò,[4]   (Indeed)
          And had his favored wife dismount,   (Indeed)
          And gave her the ladle of gold,
2865   Saying that he would drink,   (Indeed)
          Saying else the thirst would kill him.   (That's the truth)
          The favored wife took the ladle of gold,   (Indeed)
          And filled it up with water,   (Indeed)
          And to Sumamuru stretched her hand,
2870   And passed the water to him.   (Indeed)
          Fa-Koli with his darts charged up:
             "O Colossus,   (Indeed)

---

9. Thanks to Fa-Koli.   **1.** Forcefully breaking out of the siege laid to his fortress.   **2.** This can only mean that Sumamuru escaped their clutches.   **3.** The places named are the scenes of the successive engagements between the two armies.   **4.** A village near Bamako, on the river Niger. In some versions of the epic, Sumamuru disappears into the hillside on a site near this village.

	"We have taken you!	(That's the truth)
	"We have taken you, Colossus!	
2875	"We have taken you, Colossus!	
	"We have taken you!"	(Indeed)
	Tura Magan held him at bladepoint.	(Indeed)
	Sura, the Jawara patriarch held him at bladepoint.	(Indeed)
	Fa-Koli came up and held him at bladepoint.	
2880	Son-Jara held him at bladepoint:[5]	(Indeed)
	"We have taken you, Colossus!	(That's the truth)
	"We have taken you!"	(Indeed)
	Sumamuru dried up on the spot: nyònyòwu![6]	(Indeed)
	He has become the sacred fetish of Kulu-Kòrò.	(Indeed)
2885	The Bambara worship that now,[7] my father.	
	Susu Mountain Sumamuru,	
	He became that sacred fetish.	(That's the truth, indeed, father, yes, yes, yes, yes)

FROM EPISODE 7

Kanbi

	Biribiriba turned back, Son-Jara!	(Indeed)
	Stranger-in-the-Morning, Chief-in-the Afternoon![8]	(Indeed)
2890	Great-Host-Slaying-Stranger!	
	Stump-in-the-Dark-of-Night!	(Indeed)
	Should you bump against it,	
	It will bump against you!	(That's the truth)
	The Granary Guard Dog.	(Indeed)
2895	The thing discerning not the stranger,	
	Nor the familiar.	
	Should it come upon any person,	
	He will be bitten.	(That's the truth)
	Kirikara Watita!	(Indeed)
2900	Adversity's true place!	
	Man's reason and woman's are not the same.	
	Pretty words and truth are not the same.	(That's the truth)
	No matter how long the road,	
	It always comes out at someone's home.[9]	(Indeed)
2905	The Nyani king with his army came forward,	(Indeed)
	Saying the Manden belonged to him,	(That's the truth)
	Saying no more was he rival to any,	(That's the truth)
	Saying the Manden belonged to him.	(That's the truth)
	He found the Kuyatè patriarch[1] with tendons cut,	(Indeed)
2910	And beckoned him to rise, "Let us go!	(Indeed)
	"Bala Faseke Kuyatè, arise. Let us go!"	(Indeed)
	He lurched forward.	(Indeed)
	Saying he would rise.	

5. We must imagine the warriors crowding in on Sumamuru from various directions. Note too that they are all given credit for his final defeat.   6. Ideophone for the drying up.   7. Sumumaru is still revered among his people, who have kept his memory alive in a counterepic devoted to him as well as in various forms of ritual.   8. With his victory, Son-Jara is suddenly transformed from a homeless vagrant into a powerful ruler.   9. A proverb: everything has a beginning and an end.   1. Bala Faseke.

He fell back to the ground again,	(Indeed)
2915 His two Achilles tendons cut:	(Indeed)
"O Nare Magan Kònatè!"	(Indeed)
"Arise and let us go!	(Indeed)
I have no rival in Mandenland now!	(That's the truth)
"The Manden is mine alone."	(Indeed)
2920 He lurched forward,	(Indeed)
Saying that he would rise.	(Indeed)
He fell back to the ground again.	(Indeed)
"Had Sumamuru no child?" they queried.	(Indeed)
"Here is his first born son," the reply.	(Indeed)
2925 "What is his name?"	(Indeed)
"His name is Mansa Saman."	(Indeed)
They summoned Mansa Saman	(Indeed)
And brought forth Dòka the Cat,	
And placed him on Mansa Saman's shoulders,[2]	(Indeed)
2930 Laying the balaphone on his head, serew!	(Indeed)
He followed after the Wizard:	(Indeed)
"Biribiriba!	(Indeed)
"O Nare Magan Kònatè!	(Indeed)
"Entered Kaya,	
2935 *"Son-Jara entered Kaya.*	(That's the truth)
"Entered Kaya,	
"Sugulun's Ma'an entered Kaya.[3]	(Yes, Fa-Digi)
"If they took no gold,	(Indeed)
"If they took no measure of gold for the	
Wizard,	(Indeed)
2940 "The reason for Son-Jara's coming to the Manden,	
"To stabilize the Manden,	
"To improve the people's lot:[4] jon jon!	(That's the truth)
"O Sorcerer, you have come for the Manden	
people!	(Indeed)
"O Nare Magan Kònatè,	(Indeed)
2945 "O Khalif Magan Kònatè!"	(That's the truth)
They arrived back in the Manden.	(Indeed)
The Sorcerer ruled over everyone.	(Indeed)
He continued on at that.[5]	(Indeed)

[Although he has regained his homeland, Son-Jara still must establish his authority over the neighboring territories. A quarrel with the Jolof king provides him with a pretext for a new campaign for the expansion of his domain. The Jolof king has seized a large herd of horses Son-Jara has sent his retainers to collect within Jolof territory and sends him instead a pack of dogs, with the message that he knows Son-Jara not as king but only as a mere hunter ("a runner of dogs"). This challenge angers Son-Jara, who summons his generals to a council of war.]

In turn, the warriors swore their fealty:[6]	(Indeed)
"Let me the battle-master be!"	(Indeed)
Fa-Koli and Tura Magan swore their fealty.	(Indeed)
"Let me lead the army!" Fa-Koli	
adjured.	(That's the truth)

2. As a sign of his humiliation.   3. The refrain of a song celebrating Son-Jara's triumphal return to the Manden.   4. The ideological function of the epic becomes fully evident here.   5. That is, until the end of his reign.   6. Made necessary by the defiance of the Jolof king.

3000   "Let me lead the army!" Tura Magan adjured.   (Indeed)
     Son-Jara finally spoke,   (Indeed)
     " 'Tis I who will lead the army,   (Indeed)
     "And go to Dark Jòlòf land."   (Indeed)
     O Nare Magan Kònatè!   (Indeed)
3005   Tura Magan plunged into grief,   (Indeed)
     And went to the graveyard to dig his grave,   (Indeed)
     And laid himself down in his grave.[7]   (Indeed)
     The bards came forth: "O Nare Magan Kònatè,   (Indeed)
     "If you don't go see Tura Magan,   (Indeed)
3010   "Your army will not succeed!"   (Indeed)
     He sent the bards forth
     That they should summon Tura Magan.
     And so the bards went forth.   (Indeed)
     But Tura Magan they could not find.   (That's the truth)
3015   Son-Jara came and stood in the graveyard: (Indeed)
        "Bugu Turu and Bugu Bò!   (Indeed)
        "Muke Musa and Muke Dantuman!   (Indeed)
        "Juru Kèta and Juru Moriba!   (Indeed)
        "Tunbila the Manden Slave!   (Indeed)
3020   *"Kalabila, the Manden Slave!*   (Indeed)
        "Sana Fa-Buren, Danka Fa-Buren!   (Indeed)
        "Dark-Pilgrim and Light-Pilgrim![8]   (Indeed)
     "Ah! Bards,   (Indeed)
     "Let us give the army to Tura Magan,   (Indeed)
3025   "To the Slave-of-the-Tomb,[9] Tura Magan,   (Indeed)
     "O Tura Magan-and-Kanke-jan!"   (That's the truth)

     Tura Magan spoke out,   (Indeed)
     "That is the best of all things to my ear!"   (Indeed)
     To Tura Magan they gave quiver and bow.   (Indeed)
3030   Tura Magan advanced to cross the river here,   (Indeed)
     At the Passage-of-Tura-Magan.[1]   (Indeed)
     A member of the troop cried out,   (Indeed)
     "Hey! The war to which we go,   (Indeed)
     "That war will not be easy!   (Indeed)
3035   "Ninety iron drums has the Dark Jòlòf King.   (Indeed)
     "No drum like this has the Manden.   (Indeed)
     "Nor balaphone has the Manden.   (Indeed)
     "There is no such thing in the Manden,   (Indeed)
     "Save the Jawara patriarch, Sita Fata,   (Indeed)
3040   "Save when he puffs out his cheeks,   (Indeed)
     "Making with them like drum and balaphone,[2]
     "To go awaken the Nyani King.   (Indeed)
     "This battle will not be easy!"   (Indeed)
     But they drove this agitator off.   (Indeed)
3045   Saying better in the bush a frightened brave
     Than a loudmouthed agitator.   (That's the truth)
     He went back across the river,   (Indeed)

---

7. A sign of his disappointment.   8. This passage is a reference to the pilgrimage he is reputed to have made to Mecca, from which he is also said to have brought magical powers. The names are of Tura Magan's ancestors, invoked by Son-Jara in appealing to him.   9. This is the *Manden Slave* mentioned in line 3020.   1. A ford across the Senegal River.   2. The inspirational role of bards is once again affirmed.

	At the place they call Salakan,³	(Indeed)
	And Ford-of-the-Frightened.	(Indeed)
3050	The Ford-of-the-Frightened-Braves.	(Indeed)
	Tura Magan with battle met.	(Indeed)
	He slayed that dog-giving king,⁴	(Indeed)
	Saying he was but running the dogs.⁵	(That's the truth)
	Tura Magan with army marched on,	(Indeed)
3055	He went to slay Nyani Mansa,	
	Saying he was but running the dogs.	(That's the truth)
	Tura Magan with the army marched on,	(Indeed)
	He slayed the Sanumu King,	
	Saying that he was but running the dogs,	(Indeed)
3060	He slayed Ba-dugu King	(Indeed)
	Saying he was but running the dogs,	(Indeed)
	And marched on thus through Jòlòf land.⁶	(Indeed)
	Their name for stone is Jòlòf.	(Indeed)
	Once there was this king . . . ,	(Indeed)
3065	The stone there that is red,	(Indeed)
	The Wòlòf call it Jòlòf.	(Indeed)
	There once was a king in that country, my father,	
	Called King of Dark Jòlòfland.	(Indeed)
	And that is the meaning of this.	(That's the truth)
3070	He slayed that Dark Jòlòf King,	(Indeed)
	Severing his great head at his shoulders,	(Indeed)
	From whence comes the Wòlòf name, Njòp!⁷	(Indeed)
	They are Taraweres.	(Indeed)
	Sane and Mane,⁸	(Indeed)
3075	They are Taraweres.	(Indeed)
	Mayga, they are Taraweres.	(Indeed)
	Magaraga, they are Taraweres.	(Indeed)
	Tura Magan-and-Kanke-jan,	(Indeed)
	He with the army marched on,	
3080	To[ch-[ch-[ch-[ch-[ch-[ch-[ch-[ch-[ch- destroy the golden	
	sword and the tall	
	throne.⁹	(That's the truth)
	This by the hand of Tura Magan-and-Kanke-jan.	
	Kirikisa, Spear-of-Access, Spear-of Service!	(Indeed)
	Ah! Garan!	(Indeed)
	Let us leave the words¹ right here.	(That's the truth,
		indeed, it's over now!)

---

3. A ford whose name and significance are explained in lines 3049–50. 4. A reference to the Jolof king's insult. 5. That is, out hunting with his dogs. A pun on the previous line, expressing Tura Magan's pleasure in waging war. 6. In present-day Senegal, to the west of the original Manden homeland. Note the way the repetitions give a terse economy to the narration. 7. A common Wòlòf surname. This is an example of folk etymology. *Njòp* can also be spelled "Diop" and "Dyob," and in Gambia, "Job." 8. Two important clans in Senegal and in Gambia; the names often serve as surnames. 9. Emblems of the Jolof king. 1. In many African languages the word *word* refers not only to ordinary speech but also to reflective thought in general, especially as conveyed in a proverb or a story.

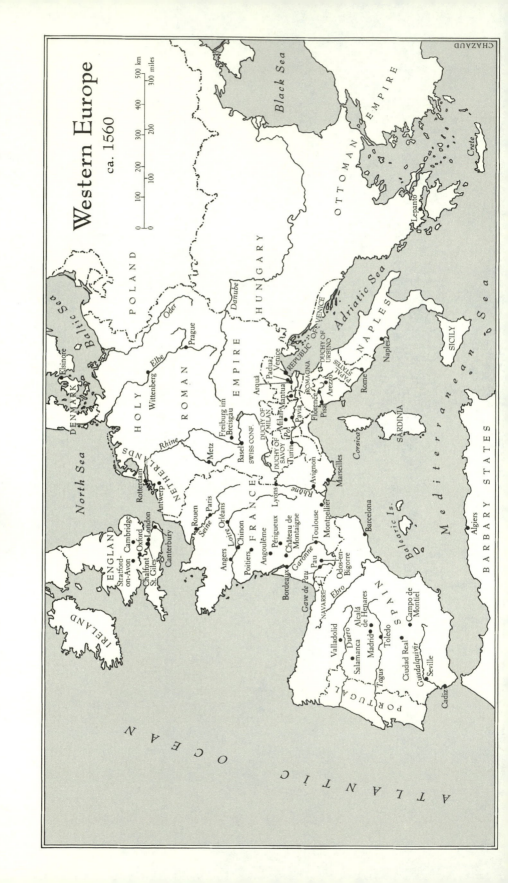

Western Europe
ca. 1560

CHAZAUD

Black Sea

OTTOMAN EMPIRE

Crete

Lepanto

Adriatic Sea

POLAND

Baltic Sea

Oder

Prague

Elbe

Wittenberg

Danube

HOLY

ROMAN

EMPIRE

HUNGARY

DENMARK

Elsinore

North Sea

Rhine

Metz

Freiburg im
Breisgau

Basel

SWISS CONF.

DUCHY OF
MILAN

DUCHY OF
SAVOY

Turin

Pavia

Arquà

Padua

Venice

Mantua

REPUBLIC OF VENICE

DUCHY OF
URBINO

ROMAGNA

PAPAL
STATES

Florence

Pisa

Arezzo

Rome

NAPLES

Naples

SICILY

SARDINIA

Corsica

Rotterdam

Antwerp

NETHERLANDS

Rouen

Paris

Orléans

Seine

Angers

Loire

Chinon

Poitiers

FRANCE

Angoulême

Périgueux

Château de
Montaigne

Lyons

Rhône

Avignon

Marseilles

Montpellier

Toulouse

Bordeaux

Garonne

Gave de Pau

Pau

Odos-en-
Bigorre

NAVARRE

Ebro

Barcelona

Balearic Is.

Mediterranean Sea

Algiers

BARBARY STATES

ENGLAND

Cambridge

Oxford

London

Stratford-
on-Avon

Chalfont
St. Giles

Canterbury

IRELAND

ATLANTIC OCEAN

SPAIN

Alcalá
de Henares

Madrid

Toledo

Campo de
Montiel

Ciudad Real

Valladolid

Duero

Salamanca

Tagus

Guadalquivir

Seville

Cadiz

PORTUGAL

500 km

300 miles

0   100   200   300   400   500

0   100   200   300

The Renaissance in Europe

"All the world's a stage, / And all the men and women merely players": Shakespeare's famous comparison of human beings to actors playing their various roles in the great theater of the world conjures up the exhilarating liberty and mobility we associate with the memorable characters of Renaissance literature. Because "merely" meant, in Shakespeare's day, "wholly" and "entirely," the line evokes a lively sense of the men and women of that world performing their roles with the gusto of actors. Their social roles as princes, clowns, thieves, or housewives appear, from one angle, exciting opportunities for the characters to explore. Yet such roles are also clearly confining: Renaissance men and women were born into societies that strictly regulated their actions and even their clothing—only actors had the right to vary their garb and dress above their station. Whether Renaissance subjects relished the pleasures of playing or resented the constraints of their social roles is a subject often taken up in the literature of the day.

When Renaissance writers explore the relationship of their characters to the social roles the characters play, they partly follow in the tradition exemplified in the Middle Ages by Chaucer's *Canterbury Tales*. Yet the most memorable characters of Renaissance literature enjoy greater autonomy and more fully realized personalities than Chaucer's pilgrims. Characters like Rabelais's broad-minded giant, Gargantua; Cervantes's idealistic but mad Quixote; Shakespeare's romantic but doomed Othello and Desdemona; and Milton's "domestic" Adam and "adventurous" Eve are frequently presented in acts of thought, fantasy, planning, doubt, and internal debate. Deliberating with others and themselves about what to do seems at least as important to these characters as putting their plans into action.

One reason for this shift toward internal, mental, and psychological portraiture is that Renaissance authors, like the characters they invent, inhabited a world of such widespread revolutionary change that they could not passively receive the traditional wisdom of previous ages. When Nicolaus Copernicus (1473–1543) discovered that the earth moves around the sun and when Galileo Galilei (1564–1642) turned his telescope up to the heavens, the Renaissance mind had to reconceive the nature of the universe and creation. When Christopher Columbus (1451–1506) sailed to what he thought were the Indies, he proved that the earth was not flat and introduced a New World to Europe, which began for the first time to think of itself as the Old World. Around the time that Columbus was sailing to America, humanist scholars in Italy began to use new scholarly methods that gave them fuller access to the cultural legacy of the ancient world of Greece and Rome and a new sense of their own place in history. On scientific, geographical, and scholarly fronts, the world of Renaissance Europe was undergoing revolutionary change.

The new discoveries' challenge to European and human centrality in the world and in creation met with fervent, if varied, responses. In 1633 the Inquisition forced Galileo to repudiate the Copernican theory that the earth rotates around the sun. In his dialogue *The City of the Sun* (1602) Galileo's friend and supporter Tommasso Campanella (1568–1639) optimistically asserted that the three great inventions of his day—the compass, the printing press, and the gun—were "signs of the union of the entire world." François Rabelais, less sanguine about the idea of world union enforced by the gun and artillery, placed his hopes for peace only on the printing press, an instrument for intellectual deliberation and the dissemination of ideas. In *The First Anniversary*, John Donne (1572–1631), on the other hand, focused on the psychological threat of the new discoveries and theories to individuals unable to cope with so much uncertainty:

> The new philosophy calls all in doubt,
> The element of fire is quite put out;
> The sun is lost and the earth, and no man's wit
> Can well direct him where to look for it.
> And freely men confess that this world's spent,
> When in the planets and the firmament
> They seek so many new; they see that this
> Is crumbled out again to his atomies . . .

In Donne's poem, the new discoveries amount to a second creation, so radical is the new theory of the world's construction. For Renaissance intellectuals and for the literary characters they created, there was almost literally no firm ground to stand on as they moved through life in an increasingly complex and uncertain world. Although received wisdom appeared from one angle like an anchor in a sea of change, from another it seemed like a shackle to error: it is no wonder, then, that the reasoning and choices of the characters in Renaissance poetry and prose began to matter enormously.

As with other terms that have currency in cultural history (for instance, *Romanticism*), the usefulness of the term *Renaissance* depends on its keeping a certain degree of elasticity. The literal meaning of the word—"rebirth"—suggests that one impulse toward the great intellectual and artistic achievements of the period came from the example of ancient culture, or even better, from a certain vision that the artists and intellectuals of the Renaissance possessed of the world of antiquity, which was "reborn" through their work. Especially in the more mature phase of the Renaissance, these individuals were aware of having brought about a vigorous renewal, which they openly associated with the cult of antiquity. The restoration of ancient canons was regarded as a glorious achievement to be set beside the thrilling discoveries of their own age. "For now," Rabelais writes through his Gargantua,

> all courses of study have been restored, and the acquisition of languages has become supremely honorable: Greek, without which it is shameful for any man to be called a scholar; Hebrew; Chaldean; and Latin. And in my time we have learned how to produce wonderfully elegant and accurate printed books, just as, on the other hand, we have also learned (by diabolic suggestion) how to make cannon and other such fearful weapons.

Machiavelli, whose infatuation with antiquity is as typical a trait as his better-advertised political realism, suggests in the opening of his *Discourses on the First Ten Books of Livy* (1513–21) that rulers should be as keen on the imitation of ancient "virtues" as are artists, lawyers, and the scientists: "The civil laws are nothing but decisions given by the ancient jurisconsults. . . . And what is the science of medicine, but the experience of ancient physicians, which their successors have taken for their guide?"

Elasticity should likewise be maintained in regard to the chronological span of the Renaissance as a "movement" extending through varying periods of years and as including phases and traits of the epoch that is otherwise known as the Middle Ages (and vice versa). The peak of the Renaissance can be shown to have occurred at different times in different countries, the "movement" having had its inception in Italy, where its impact was at first most remarkable in the visual arts, while in England, for instance, it developed later and its main achievements were in literature, particularly the drama. The meaning of the term has also, in the course of time, widened considerably. Nowadays it conveys, to say the least, a general notion of artistic creativity, of extraordinary zest for life and knowledge, of sensory delight in opulence and magnificence, of spectacular individual achievement, thus extending far beyond the literal meaning of rebirth and the strict idea of a revival and imitation of antiquity.

Even in its stricter sense, however, the term continues to have its function. The degree to which European intellectuals of the period possessed and were possessed by the writings of the ancient world is difficult for the average modern reader to realize. For these writers references to classical mythology, philosophy, and literature are not ornaments or affectations. Along with references to the Scriptures they are part, and a major part, of their mental equipment and way of thinking. When Erasmus through his *The Praise of Folly* speaks in a cluster of classical allusions, or when Machiavelli writes to a friend: "I get up before daylight, prepare my birdlime, and go out with a bundle of cages on my back, so that I look like Geta when he came back from the harbor with the books of Amphitryo" (n. 3, p. 2520) the words have by no means the sound of erudite self-gratification that they might have nowadays. Within Machiavelli's intellectual circle, they are wholly natural, familiar, unassuming.

When we are overcome by sudden emotion, our first exclamations are likely to be in the language most familiar to us—our dialect, if we happen to have one. Montaigne relates of himself that when once his father unexpectedly fell back in his arms in a swoon, the first words he uttered under the emotion of that experience were in Latin. Similarly Benvenuto Cellini, the Italian sculptor, goldsmith, and autobiographer, talking to his patron and expressing admiration of a Greek statue, establishes with the ancient artist an immediate contact, a proud familiarity:

> I cried to the Duke: "My lord, this is a statue in Greek marble, and it is a miracle of beauty. . . . If your Excellency permits, I should like to restore it—head and arms and feet. . . . It is certainly not my business to patch up statues, that being the trade of botchers, who do it in all conscience villainously ill; yet the art displayed by this great master of antiquity cries out to me to help him."

The people who, starting at about the middle of the fourteenth century, gave new impulse to this emulation of the classics are often referred to as humanists. The word in that sense is related to what we call the humanities, and the humanities at that time were Latin and Greek. Every cultivated person wrote and spoke Latin, with the result that a Western community of intellectuals could exist, a spiritual "republic of letters" above individual nations. There was also a considerable amount of individual contact among humanists. In glancing at the biographies of the authors included in this section, the extensiveness of their travels may strike us as a remarkable or even surprising fact, considering the hardships and slowness of traveling during those centuries.

The archetype of literature as a vocation is often said to be Petrarch—the first author in this section—who anticipated certain ideals of the high Renaissance: a lofty conception of the literary art, a taste for the good life, a basic pacifism, and a strong sense of the memories and glories of antiquity. In this last respect, what should be emphasized is the imaginative quality, the visionary impulse with which the writers of the period looked at those memories—the same vision and imagination with which they regarded such contemporary heroes as the great navigators and astronomers. The Renaissance view of the cultural monuments of antiquity was far from being that of the philologist and the antiquarian; indeed, familiarity was facilitated by the very lack of a scientific sense of history. We find the visionary and imaginative element not only in the creations of poets and dramatists (Shakespeare's Romans, to give an obvious example) but also in the works of political writers: as when Machiavelli describes himself entering, through his reading, the

> ancient courts of ancient men, where, being lovingly received, I feed on that food which alone is mine, and which I was born for; I am not ashamed to speak with them and to ask the reasons for their actions, and they courteously answer me.

> For . . . hours I feel no boredom and forget every worry; I do not fear poverty, and death does not terrify me. I give myself completely over to the ancients.

Imitation of antiquity acquires, in Machiavelli and many others, a special quality; whereas "academic" imitations transcribe, Machiavelli plunges into vital and reciprocal communication—even communion—with the ancients.

The vision of an ancient age of glorious intellectual achievement that is "now" brought to life again implies, of course, however roughly, the idea of an intervening "middle" time, by comparison ignorant and dark. The hackneyed, vastly inaccurate notion that the "light" of the Renaissance broke through a long "night" of the Middle Ages was not devised by subsequent "enlightened" centuries; it was held by the humanist scholars of the Renaissance themselves. In his genealogy of giants from Grangousier to Gargantua to Pantagruel, Rabelais conveniently represents the generations of modern learning with their varying degrees of enlightenment. Thus Gargantua writes to his son:

> Though my late father of worthy memory, Grandgousier, devoted all his energy to those things of which I might take the fullest advantage, and from which I might acquire the most sensible knowledge, and though my own effort matched his—or even surpassed it—still, as you know very well, it was neither so fit nor so right a time for learning as exists today, nor was there an abundance of such teachers as you have had. It was still a murky, dark time, oppressed by the misery, unhappiness, and disasters of the Goths, who destroyed all worthwhile literature of every sort. But divine goodness has let me live to see light and dignity returned to humanistic studies, and to see such an improvement, indeed, that it would be hard for me to qualify for the very first class of little schoolboys—I who, in my prime, had the reputation (and not in error) of the most learned man of my day.

The combination of self-deprecation, aspiration, and arrogance aptly characterizes the period's sense of its own achievements and its standing in relation to antiquity and the Middle Ages.

Definitions of the Renaissance must also take account of the period's preoccupation with this life rather than with the life beyond. The contrast of an ideal medieval man or woman, whose mode of action is basically oriented toward the thought of the afterlife (and who therefore conceives of life on earth as transient and preparatory) with an ideal Renaissance man or woman, possessing and cherishing earthly interests so concrete and self-sufficient that the very realization of the ephemeral quality of life is to him or her nothing but an added spur to its immediate enjoyment—this is a useful contrast even though it represents an enormous oversimplification of the facts.

The same emphasis on the immediate and tangible is reflected in the earthly, amoral, and aesthetic character of what we may call the Renaissance code of behavior. According to this "code," human action is judged not in terms of right and wrong, of good and evil (as it is judged when life is viewed as a moral "test," with reward or punishment in the afterlife), but in terms of its present concrete validity and effectiveness, of the delight it affords, of its memorability and its beauty. In that sense a good deal that is typical of the Renaissance, from architecture to poetry, from sculpture to rhetoric, may be related to a taste for the harmonious and the memorable, for the spectacular effect, for the successful striking of a pose. Individual human action, seeking as it were in itself its own reward, finds justification in its formal appropriateness; in its being a well-rounded achievement, perfect of its kind; in the zest and gusto with which it is, here and now, performed; and, finally, in its proving worthy of remaining as a testimony to the performer's power on earth.

A convenient way to illustrate this emphasis is to consider certain words especially expressive of the interests of the period—*virtue, fame, glory. Virtue,* particularly in its Italian form, *virtù,* is to be understood in a wide sense. As we may see even now in some relics of its older meanings, the word (from the Latin *vir,* "man") connotes active power—the intrinsic force and ability of a person or thing (the "virtue" of a law or of a medicine)—and hence, also, technical skill (the capacity of the "virtuoso"). The Machiavellian prince's "virtues," therefore, are not necessarily goodness, temperance, clemency, and the like; they are whatever forces and skills may help him in the efficient management and preservation of his princely powers. The idealistic, intangible part of the prince's success is consigned to such concepts as "fame" and "glory," but even in this case the dimension within which human action is considered is still an earthly one. These concepts connote the hero's success and reputation with his contemporaries, or look forward to splendid recognition from posterity, on earth.

In this sense (though completely pure examples of such an attitude are rare) the purpose of life is the unrestrained and self-sufficient practice of one's "virtue," the competent and delighted exercise of one's skill. At the same time, there is no reason to forget that such virtues and skills are God's gift. The worldview of even some of the most clearly earthbound Renaissance writers was hardly godless; Machiavelli, Rabelais, Cellini take for granted the presence of God in their own and in their heroes' lives:

> . . . we have before our eyes extraordinary and unexampled means prepared by God. The sea has been divided. A cloud has guided you on your way. The rock has given forth water. Manna has fallen. Everything has united to make you great. The rest is for you to do. God does not intend to do everything, lest he deprive us of our free will and the share of glory that belongs to us. (Machiavelli)

> And then Gargantua and Powerbrain would briefly recapitulate, according to the Pythagorean fashion, everything Gargantua had read and seen and understood, everything he had done and heard, all day long.
> They would both pray to God their Creator, worshiping, reaffirming their faith, glorifying Him for His immense goodness and thanking Him for all they had been given, and forever placing themselves in His hands.
> And then they would go to sleep. (Rabelais)

> I found that all the bronze my furnace contained had been exhausted in the head of this figure [of the statue of Perseus]. It was a miracle to observe that not one fragment remained in the orifice of the channel, and that nothing was wanting to the statue. In my great astonishment I seemed to see in this the hand of God arranging and controlling all. (Cellini)

Yet if we compare the attitudes of these authors with the view of the world and of the value of human action that emerges from the major literary work of the Middle Ages, *The Divine Comedy,* and with the manner in which human action is there seen within a grand extratemporal design, we see that the presence of God in the Renaissance writers cited above is conspicuously less dominating.

Renaissance intellectuals, artists, aristocrats, and princes did not lack in abiding religious faith or fervor. The most powerful lords of opulent Renaissance courts would unhesitatingly affirm John Calvin's starkly religious assessment of earthly life and gain:

> For if heaven is our country, what is earth but a place of exile! If the departure out of the world is an entrance into life, what is the world but a sepulchre? What is a continuance in it but an absorption in death? If deliverance from the body is an introduction into complete liberty, what is the body but a prison? Therefore, if the terrestrial life be compared with the celestial, it should undoubtedly be despised and accounted of no value.

These princes, however, sharply felt the conflict between the values of worldly goods and spiritual renunciation. The religious conviction in the transitory nature of earthly possessions, moreover, did not prevent princes and lords from seeking to expand their kingdoms. An anonymous Spanish writer was inspired to celebrate Spain's growing empire as "the greatest event since the making of the world, apart from the incarnation and death of him who created it," a phrase that today rings with more patriotism than piety. At the time it was written, however, Church and State seemed inextricably bound together. The papacy was a political and military power as well as a spiritual one; Charles V of Spain united most of Europe under his rule and declared himself the Holy Roman emperor; and Henry VIII of England broke with the Catholic Church and declared himself head of the Church of England. Even movements originally intended to reform the Catholic Church—such as the Reformist movements associated with Martin Luther (1483–1546), Ulrich Zwingli (1484–1531), and John Calvin (1509–1564)—were rapidly adopted by Renaissance princes bridling under papal authority. Given the political force of the Catholic Church and the Protestant Reformation, it is no wonder that the Renaissance often appears to be more preoccupied with earthly princes and empires than with the heavenly King.

In a similar vein, religious convictions in no way hamper the capacity for Renaissance princes and poets to appreciate sensuous beauty and pleasure. Just as the sensuous appraisal of a woman's beauties plays a large part in the Song of Songs from the Hebrew Bible, for example, so Ludovico Ariosto rhapsodically describes the temptress Alcina as

> so beautifully modelled, no painter, however much he applied himself, could have achieved anything more perfect. Her long blonde tresses were gathered in a knot: pure gold itself could have no finer lustre. Roses and white privet blooms lent their colours to suffuse her delicate cheeks. Her serene brow was like polished ivory, and in perfect proportion. / Beneath two of the thinnest black arches, two dark eyes—or rather, two bright suns; soft was their look, gentle their movement . . . down the midst of the face, the nose. . . . / Below this, the mouth, set between two dimples; it was imbued with native cinnabar. Here a beautiful soft pair of lips opened to disclose a double row of choicest pearls. . . . / Snow-white was her neck, milky her breast; the neck was round, the breast broad and full. A pair of apples, not yet ripe, fashioned in ivory, rose and fell like the sea-swell at times when a gentle breeze stirs the ocean. . . . You could easily judge that what lay hidden did not fall short of what was exposed to view.

Alcina is, evidently, at once a spiritual experience and "a paradise on earth" to conquer. The loving description of a woman's body often goes hand in glove with the idea of conquest and world discovery: when John Donne, for example, finally succeeds in stripping his beloved of all her clothing, he bursts out, "O my America, my new-found land!"

Much about the religious temper of the age is expressed in its art, particularly in Italian painting, where Renaissance Madonnas often make it difficult, as the saying goes, to recite a properly devout Hail Mary—serving as celebrations of earthly beauty rather than exhortations to contrite thoughts and mystical hopes of salvation. Castiglione in the first pages of the *Courtier* pays homage to the memory of the late lord of Montefeltro, in whose palace at Urbino the book's personages hold their lofty debate on the idea of a perfect gentleman (an earlier Montefeltro appears in Dante's Hell, another in Dante's Purgatory); but Castiglione praises him only for his achievements as a man of arms and a promoter of the arts. There is no thought of either the salvation or the damnation of his soul (though the general tone of the work would seem to imply his salvation); he is exalted instead for military victories, and even more warmly, for having built a splendid palace:

> He built on the rugged site of Urbino a palace thought by many the most beautiful to be found anywhere in all Italy and he furnished it so well with every suitable thing that it seemed not a palace but a city in the form of a palace; and furnished it not only with what is customary, such as silver vases, wall hangings of the richest cloth of gold, silk, and other like things, but for ornament he added

countless ancient statues of marble and bronze, rare paintings, and musical instruments of every sort; nor did he wish to have anything there that was not most rare and excellent. Then, at great expense, he collected many very excellent and rare books in Greek, Latin, and Hebrew, all of which he adorned with gold and silver, deeming these to be the supreme excellence of his great palace.

The almost legendary Duke Federico defines, through his life's history, the ideal prince as a heroic empire-builder, able to tame "rugged" terrain by force, amass luxurious wealth, and best of all, collect fine arts. The supreme testimony to his heroic virtue is his library of costly and sumptuous volumes, all collected to conserve the wisdom of antiquity and to promote the exchange of ideas at Urbino.

Thus the popular view that associates the idea of the Renaissance especially with the flourishing of the arts is correct. The leaders of the period saw in a work of art the clearest instance of beautiful, harmonious, and self-justified performance. To create such a work became the valuable occupation par excellence, the most satisfactory display of *virtù*. The Renaissance view of antiquity exemplifies this attitude. The artists and intellectuals of the period not only drew on antiquity for certain practices and forms but also found there a recognition of the place of the arts among outstanding modes of human action. In this way, the concepts of "fame" and "glory" became particularly associated with the art of poetry because the Renaissance drew from antiquity the idea of the poet as celebrator of high deeds, the "dispenser of glory."*

There is, then, an important part of the Renaissance mind that sees terrestrial life as positive fulfillment. This is especially clear where there is a close association between the practical and the intellectual, as in the exercise of political power, the act of scientific discovery, the creation of works of art. The Renaissance assumption is that there are things highly worth doing, within a strictly temporal pattern. By doing them, humanity proves its privileged position in creation and therefore incidentally follows God's intent. The often cited phrase "the dignity of man" describes this positive, strongly affirmed awareness of the intellectual and physical "virtues" of the human being, and of the individual's place in creation.

It is important, however, to see this fact about the Renaissance in the light of another phenomenon. Where there is a singularly high capacity for feeling the delight of earthly achievement, there is a possibility that its ultimate worth will also be questioned profoundly. What (the Renaissance mind usually seems to ask at some point) is the purpose of all this activity? What meaningful relation does it bear to any all-inclusive, cosmic pattern? The Renaissance coincided with, and perhaps to some extent occasioned, a loss of firm belief in the final unity and the final intelligibility of the universe, such belief as underlies, for example, *The Divine Comedy*, enabling Dante to say in Paradise:

> I saw within Its depth how It conceives
>   all things in a single volume bound by Love,
>   of which the universe is the scattered leaves;
> substance, accident, and their relation
>   so fused that all I say could do no more
>   than yield a glimpse of that bright revelation.

Once the notion of this grand unity of design has lost its authority, certainty about the final value of human actions is no longer to be found. For some minds, indeed, the sense of void becomes so strong as to paralyze all aspiration to power or thirst for knowledge or delight in beauty; the resulting attitude we may call Renaissance melancholy, whether it be openly shown (as by some characters in Elizabethan drama) or provide an undercurrent of sadness, or incite to ironical forms of compromise, to

---

*And, of course, a typical guarantee of memorability was having oneself portrayed—perhaps at various stages in life—by some of the magnificent and highly honored painters of the period.

some sort of wise adjustment (as in Erasmus or Montaigne.) Thus while on one, and perhaps the better-known, side of the picture human intellect in Renaissance literature enthusiastically expatiates over the realms of knowledge and unveils the mysteries of the universe, on the other it is beset by puzzling doubts and a profound mistrust of its own powers.

Doubts about the value of human action within the scheme of eternity did not, however, diminish the outpouring of ideas about the ideal ordering of this world. Renaissance poets and intellectuals turned to the printing press as the means to disseminate and test ideas about the ideal prince, courtier, councilor, and humble subject as well as the ideal court and society. Renaissance epics, such as Ludovico Ariosto's *Orlando Furioso,* use the resources of comedy and tragedy (among other genres) to explore what is gained and lost in achieving that crystallization of the civilizing process, the imperial court. Niccolò Machiavelli turns to print to propose his amoral ideas about the effective (rather than ideal) prince; Baldesar Castiglione uses the dialogue form to define and expand the role of the courtier who would serve and, it is hoped, counsel the powerful prince. Other writers shift the focus from the court to the entire commonwealth. Marguerite de Navarre examines the strategies of individuals from the lower classes whose only resource against the abuses of powerful lords and clergymen is their own ingenuity. Lope de Vega transforms the historical case of a peasant uprising against a highly abusive military commander into a play, *Fuente Ovejuna,* which possesses the artistic charm of comedy and the weight of political ethics. Shakespeare's *Othello* investigates the social position—and its tragic consequences—of the title character, a military general, former slave, black man, Christian convert, object of wonder, and outsider in his adopted home of Venice. In all these works of imaginative scope and supreme artistic skill, Renaissance writers can be seen tirelessly examining the nature of their own world, the problem of power, and the vexed relations between the absolute authority of the prince and the rights and liberties of the people. Its zeal for defining the social contract partly explains why the Renaissance is often viewed as the "early modern" period; the "rebirth" and flourishing of antiquity also heralded ideas that we associate with the modern political world.

The joining of philosophical and imaginative thinking in literary expression is characteristic of the Renaissance, which cultivated the idea of "serious play." Throughout the literature of the period, we see the creative and restless mind of the Renaissance intellectual "freely ranging," as Sir Philip Sidney put it, "only in the zodiac of his own wit," creating fictional characters and worlds that might, if the poet is sufficiently persuasive, be put into practice and change the nature of the real world.

FURTHER READING

Richard L. DeMolen, ed., *The Meaning of Renaissance and Reformation* (1974), is a collection of essays by experts on the Renaissance and Reformation, with maps and illustrations. Eugene Rice with Anthony Grafton, *The Foundations of Early Modern Europe,* 2nd ed. (1994), is the finest introduction to the contexts in which Renaissance or early modern literature was produced. William Bouwsma, *A Usable Past: Essays in European Cultural History* (1990), especially the chapter "Anxiety and the Formation of Early Modern Culture," also offers illuminating perspectives on the intellectual character of the period. Constance Jordan, *Renaissance Feminism: Literary Texts and Political Models* (1990), is a recommended study of the place of women in history and political thought. William Kerrigan and Gordon Braden, *The Idea of the Renaissance* (1989), offers a helpful and direct analysis of the critical construction of the Renaissance as a concept. Harry Berger Jr., *Second World and Green World: Studies in Renaissance Fiction-Making* (1988), especially the title essay, is a dense but recommended study of the aims of fiction making.

TIME LINE

TEXTS	CONTEXTS
1335 Petrarch's poems to Laura, including *Sonnets*, underway (published 1360)	
	1338–1453 Hundred Years' War
	1348–1350 The Black Death: Petrarch's Laura dies in the plague
1349–1353 Boccaccio's *Decameron* in progress	
1387–1399 Chaucer's *The Canterbury Tales* in progress; he dies in 1400	
	1428 Joan of Arc liberates Orléans from the British; she is burned at the stake for heresy in 1431
	1453 Constantinople falls to the Turks, increasing dissemination of Greek culture in Western Europe
	1473 Printing comes to Spain
	1474 William Caxton prints the first book in English
	1492 Columbus discovers America • Expulsion of the Jews from Spain • Spanish reconquest of Granada • Expedition of Charles VIII of France
1494 Sebastian Brandt's *Ship of Fools*	
	1502 The "Nuremberg Egg," first portable timepiece
	1503 Leonardo da Vinci paints the *Mona Lisa*
1511 Erasmus's *The Praise of Folly* published	
	1512 Michelangelo completes the Sistine Chapel ceiling
1516 Erasmus's edition of the New Testament of the Bible • First publication of Ariosto's *Orlando Furioso*	
	1517 Luther's Ninety-five Theses denouncing abuses of the Roman Church
	1519 Charles I of Spain becomes Holy Roman emperor, Charles V
1521 Second edition of *Orlando Furioso*	**1521** Luther is excommunicated
	1524 Francis I is captured in battle against the armies of Charles V

Boldface titles indicate works in the anthology.

TIME LINE

TEXTS	CONTEXTS
	1527 Rome sacked by the French • Castiglione, now bishop of Ávila, is accused of treachery • Marguerite marries Henri d'Albret, king of Navarre
1528 Castiglione's *Book of the Courtier* published; he dies the following year	
1531 Erasmus publishes first complete edition of Aristotle's works	
1532 Rabelais's *Pantagruel* • Machiavelli's *The Prince* • Final publication of *Orlando Furioso;* Ariosto dies the following year	
	1533 Sorbonne accuses Marguerite's chaplain of heresy
1534 Rabelais's *Gargantua*	**1534** Henry VIII breaks with Rome and becomes head of the Church of England
1536 John Calvin's *Institutes of the Christian Religion*	
1546 Rabelais's *Third Book*	
	1547 Francis I dies; Henry II accedes to the French throne
1549 Rabelais's *Fourth Book*	**1549** England declares war on France
1551 First English translation of More's *Utopia;* More had been executed for high treason by Henry VIII in 1535	
	1555 Tobacco brought to Spain from America for the first time
1558 Marguerite de Navarre's *Heptameron* published	
	1559 Spain's most severe Index of banned books
	1563 Council of Trent concludes
1571? Montaigne's *Essays* in progress; books 1 and 2 published in 1580; complete publication in 1588	**1571** Spain's battle of Lepanto against the Turks
1581 Tasso's *Jerusalem Delivered*	
	1586 El Greco paints the *Burial of Count Orgaz*
	1588 Spain's Invincible Armada defeated by England

TIME LINE

TEXTS	CONTEXTS
1590 Sir Philip Sidney's revised *Arcadia*	
1596 Edmund Spenser's *The Faerie Queene* 1–6 plus the *Mutabilitie Cantos*	
1597 Tasso's revised *Jerusalem Conquered*	
1597–1604 Cervantes's ***Don Quixote*** in progress; part 1 was published in 1605, part 2 in 1615	
	1598 Philip II of Spain dies; Philip III crowned • Literary quarrel between Lope de Vega and Luis de Góngora
1603–04 Shakespeare's ***Othello*** appears	
	1608 Dutch scientist Johann Lippershey invents the telescope
1611 King James version of the Bible published	
	1620 Colony founded by Pilgrims at Plymouth, Massachusetts
	1633 Galileo forced by the Inquisition to repudiate Copernican theory that earth rotates around the sun
1641 René Descartes publishes his *Meditations on First Philosophy*	
	1643–1715 Reign of Louis XIV of France, "the Sun King"
	1645–1649 England's Charles I surrenders to antimonarchical forces of Oliver Cromwell and is executed; monarchy is abolished
1655? Milton's ***Paradise Lost*** in progress; published 1667	**1655** Velázquez paints *Las Meninas*
	1660 Charles II restores the English monarchy

FRANCIS PETRARCH
1304–1374

Although Petrarch, a contemporary of Dante and Boccaccio, lived and died in the Middle Ages, he did everything in his power to distinguish himself and his scholarship from the period he dismissed as the "Dark Ages." Frustrated with the corruption of scholarly Latin, Petrarch dedicated himself to the recovery of classical learning in a spirit commonly associated with a later period, in which humanist scholars zealously pursued the rebirth of antiquity. If Petrarch can be called a precursor of the Renaissance, it is not for his scholarly output in Latin or his derision of less elegant work. The credit is instead due to an aspect of Petrarch's work that neither he nor his contemporaries regarded as a lasting contribution to letters: Petrarch's 366 lyric poems in the vernacular, mostly dedicated to his frustrated desire for an elusive woman named Laura. Petrarch's art, experience of love, and sense of his own fragmented, fluid, and metamorphic self set the standard for the lyric expression of subjective and erotic experience in the Renaissance. His efforts to scrutinize himself intently and at times unflatteringly and to capture his own elusive inner workings in verse inspired a poetic tradition that has influenced lyric sequences from Shakespeare's sonnets to Walt Whitman's *Leaves of Grass* and to late twentieth-century pop lyrics.

Francesco Petrarca was born in Arezzo on July 20, 1304, three years after his father and Dante Alighieri were exiled from Florence. In 1314, Petrarch's father moved his family to Avignon, the new seat of the papacy (1309–77), where he became prosperous in the legal profession. Petrarch himself trained as a law student for ten years, but chose to pursue the study of classical culture and literature. He soon came to the attention of the powerful Colonna family, whose patronage launched his career as a diplomat-scholar and allowed him to travel widely and move in the intimate circles of European princes and scholars. He conducted diplomatic missions for popes and princes but refused the offices of bishop and papal secretary, preferring instead to ground his growing prestige in his humanistic scholarship. He did not always manage to protect his scholarly independence from the manipulations of the powerful, such as the tyrannical Visconti family in Milan (as his usually admiring friend Boccaccio remarked). His politics are not easy to decipher: although he served as diplomat for the Visconti at one time, at another he supported the republican dream of the Roman tribune, Cola di Rienzo. Petrarch bequeathed to later humanists the hope that scholar-poets might one day be recognized as shaping forces of the nation-state; in practice, however, he established the humanist scholar's ambiguous position as counselor and exploited servant of powerful princes.

Petrarch expected that he would secure enduring fame through the *Africa,* his unfinished epic poem in Latin hexameters on the life of Scipio Africanus, who embodied the valiant and pious virtues that Petrarch admired in Roman heroism. Of greater importance were Petrarch's manuscript discoveries of Cicero's *Pro Archia* (For Archias), a Roman "defense of poetry," in 1333 and letters to Atticus in 1345. The discovery of Cicero's personal letters to friends inspired Petrarch to compose his own familiar letters, learned, intellectually exploratory, often moving, and profoundly dialogical. Addressed to his many friends and even to the ancients themselves, these letters illustrate how essential the dialogue was to Petrarch as a literary form and as a way of thinking about the past. Imaginative conversation with the ancients, like imitation of their poetry, brought him into volatile contact with the past: his research into classical history and arts profoundly influenced his sense of himself and his own cultural moment. He had discovered how faulty the medieval transmission of classical culture was, with a paradoxical result: he was convinced that he was at the cusp of a classical revival and tragically aware that the classical world was irretrievably lost, that its legacy was its ruins. By learning that the past was foreign and that the scholarly legacy of his own day was faulty, Petrarch discovered a modern sense of alienation.

He understood, too, that the dislocations of history affect cultural and individual identity. This awareness ties Petrarch's thought and work to the aspects of the Renaissance that most anticipate modernity. In 1370, Petrarch retired to the Euganean hills at Arquà near Padua, where he lived with his daughter, Francesca (his estranged son, Giovanni, died of the plague in 1361). When Petrarch died on the night of July 18, 1374, his head was resting on an open volume of his beloved Virgil.

Petrarch's most famous work, the *Rime Sparse* (Scattered Rhymes) or *Rerum Fragmenta Vulgarium* (Fragments in the Vernacular), is a collection of 366 songs and sonnets (based on the calendar year associated with the liturgy) of extraordinary technical virtuosity and variety. Written in Italian and woven into a highly introspective narrative, the lyric collection takes the poet himself as its object of study; the poems painstakingly record how his thoughts and identity are scattered and transformed by the experience of love for a beautiful, unattainable woman named Laura. Even some of his friends suspected that Laura was merely the theme and emblem of his lyric poetry and not a historical woman; she appears to have been both. On the flyleaf of his magnificent copy of Virgil, Petrarch inscribed a note on her life:

> Laura, illustrious through her own virtues, and long famed through my verses, first appeared to my eyes in my youth, in the year of our Lord 1327, on the sixth day of April, in the church of St. Clare in Avignon, at matins; and in the same city, also on the sixth day of April, at the same first hour, but in the year 1348, the light of her life was withdrawn from the light of day, while I, as it chanced, was in Verona, unaware of my fate. * * * Her chaste and lovely form was laid to rest at vesper time, on the same day on which she died in the burial place of the Brothers Minor. I am persuaded that her soul returned to the heaven from which it came, as Seneca says of Africanus. I have thought to write this, in bitter memory, yet with a certain bitter sweetness, here in this place that is often before my eyes, so that I may be admonished, by the sight of these words and by the consideration of the swift flight of time, that there is nothing in this life in which I should find pleasure; and that it is time, now that the strongest tie is broken, to flee from Babylon; and this, by the prevenient grace of God, should be easy for me, if I meditate deeply and manfully on the futile cares, the empty hopes, and the unforeseen events of my past years. (Translated by E. H. Wilkins)

Petrarch's note illuminates the powerful role that Laura plays in his personal struggles between spiritual aspirations and earthly attachments. His thoughts of Laura habitually turn his mind to the problem of his own will, torn between spiritual and sensual desires, always delaying worldly renunciation. Even when he expresses disgust with earthly rewards and pleasures, his habitual ambivalence makes a last-minute entrance in the conditional *if* on which his renunciation depends: he will choose the right course of action, Petrarch writes, *if* he meditates "deeply and manfully" on the disappointments and failures of his past and denies memory's seductively bittersweet pleasures.

In the *Rime Sparse*, Laura's ambiguous position between divine guide and earthly temptress contrasts sharply with the role that Beatrice played in Dante's spiritual pilgrimage. Whereas Dante's love finally leads him to paradise, it is never clear to Petrarch whether he is pursuing heavenly or earthly delights and whether his amorous and philosophical wanderings will lead him to any destination or "port" (in the nautical image of sonnet 189) at all. When Dante looks into Beatrice's eyes on Mount Purgatory, he sees a reflection of the heavens; when Petrarch gazes into Laura's eyes, he sees himself. Not even his use of the liturgical year (especially the anniversaries of Christ's death and resurrection) to structure his account of their relationship guarantees that a spiritual conversion will follow Petrarch's self-analysis or "confession" of his life. It might instead represent a trap, as it does in sonnet 211, written on the eleventh anniversary of his first glimpse of Laura: "One thousand three hundred twenty seven, exactly at the first hour of the sixth day of April, I entered the labyrinth, nor do I see where I may get out of it." The image of the labyrinth evokes Petrarch's tortuous experience of love and mental wandering: apparently fresh paths turn into dead ends and avenues already traced in frustration. An allusion to the maze that the mythical Greek artist Daedalus created to contain the Minotaur, Petrarch's labyrinth also suggests that a threat lies at the center of the ingeniously crafted lyric collection. The metaphor of the self-enclosed and secretive labyrinth hints that love of the very classical figures that prompt philosophical discoveries may bar the poet from the less sensually appealing knowledge of Christian truths. For this reason, Dante must finally move beyond the guidance of his beloved Virgil. Petrarch is less confident: in a contrary and skeptical mood at the end of one of his most philosophical poems (song 264), Petrarch asserts, "I see the better, but choose the worse."

A haunting moral presence in the *Rime Sparse* is St. Augustine, who in his *Confessions* describes his conversion under a fig tree. In *The Secret,* his fictional dialogue with Augustine, Petrarch defends his adoration of Laura to an understanding but disapproving Augustine; finally, defeated by the saint who knows his pupil's arts of self-deception, Petrarch confesses that his love of her beauty is idolatrous, not idealistic. The lyric collection's first sonnet, in which Petrarch solicits compassion as well as pardon from his readers, establishes the *Rime Sparse*'s close relationship to confessional narrative. Its themes of conversion, memory, and forgetfulness (of God and oneself) evoke the model of Augustine and raise the question of whether Petrarch will follow suit: will he ultimately transcend his attachment to a woman's physical beauty, his love of language and poetic figures, and his narcissistic preoccupation with himself? In his final poem, a prayer to the Virgin Mary for her intercession, he confesses that "Medusa and my error have made of me a rock [*petra,* a play on his own name] dripping moisture."

The figure Petrarch puts in dramatic opposition to the transcendent model of Augustine is Ovid of the *Metamorphoses,* the classical counterepic that artfully uses fragmentation, fluid change, and scattering as principles of narrative composition and as motifs describing the effects of power—divine, political, or erotic—on bodies and on minds. Petrarch refers to a variety of Ovidian figures in the *Rime Sparse,* including Narcissus and Echo, Actaeon and Diana, Medusa, and Pygmalion. His chief Ovidian model, however, is the story of Apollo, the god who "invents" the genre of lyric during his amorous chase of the nymph Daphne. While running, Apollo describes her various beauties—eyes, figure, and hair—and imaginatively embellishes what he sees. When Daphne eludes him through her transformation into the laurel, Apollo claims her as his tree, if not his lover, and declares that the laurel will be the sign of triumph in letters and warfare.

The prominence of this tale in the *Rime Sparse* suggests that if Laura had not lived, Petrarch would have had to invent her. Her name interweaves key attributes of Petrarch's poetic imagination: *lauro* and *alloro* ("laurel"), *oro* ("gold," for her tresses and value), *l'aura* ("breeze" and "inspiration," which etymologically relates to "breath"), *laus* or *lauda* ("praise"). Such play on words suggests the selective, even obsessive character of Petrarch's poetic style. Like Apollo, Petrarch also "translates" his beloved's elusive body into the more tangible "figures" of rhetoric: her physical attributes reflect the style of his poetry and proclaim his triumphant glory. The Ovidian model poses the threat of the labyrinth, the trap of the artist's own making: the most significant and evocative words limit the poet to ranging within his well-defined obsessions. The Ovidian lover in Petrarch can expect no transcendence, only repeated and uncontrollable metamorphoses of the mind (e.g., despair, hope, ecstasy).

Petrarch's great legacy to Renaissance European literature is the *Rime Sparse*'s language of self-description. He absorbed the conventional use of hyperbole, antithesis, and oxymoron (rhetorical exaggeration and opposition) from troubadour songs, provençal lyric, and classical love elegy: *I freeze and burn, love is bitter and sweet, my sighs are tempests and my tears are floods, I am in ecstasy and agony, I am possessed by memories of her and I am in exile from myself.* Petrarch forged such rhetorical figures or tropes of love into a powerful language of introspection and self-fashioning that swept through European literature. Although it was often faddish and stylized, it had quite serious dimensions that helped articulate growing questions about the self: is it determined by God or flexible and in the shaping hands of men? Do culture, history, and force of will compose and transform it? The beloved does not fare as well: the eloquent expression of the male poet-lover's complex *interior* life depends, as Petrarchan successors noticed, on a correspondingly detailed description of the beloved's *exterior*. In *Paradise Lost,* for example, the angel Raphael chastises Adam for placing Eve's beauty above his own manly reason: "What admir'st thou," the angel chides, "what transports thee so, / An outside?" In the Petrarchan inventory of the beloved's adorable parts, from eyes to hair, cheeks, and hand, the poet converts her living body to ornaments, metal, and minerals, such as gold, topaz, and pearls. Although any one of her beauties is capable of scattering the poet's thoughts, the beloved herself has little independent coherence: as one critic puts it, "some of Laura's parts are greater than her whole person."

Petrarch's distinctive poetic style inspired countless imitations: whether the symptoms are found in a Shakespearean parody ("My mistress' eyes are nothing like the sun," sonnet 130) or in a twentieth-century Motown lyric ("Tracks of My Tears," Smokey Robinson and the Miracles), the lover who dies and is reborn a thousand times a day, who is mentally scattered and physically immobile, and who is never more alone than in a crowd has been tempered in the icy fire of Petrarchan love. He did not invent the idea of a divided, tormented lover, but his authoritative self-portrait defined a poetic tradition inseparable from the figure of Petrarch himself.

Ernest Hatch Wilkins' biography, *Life of Petrarch* (1961), is informative, but tends to take Petrarch's autobiographical writings at face value. In *The Poet as Philosopher* (1979) and *In Our Image and Likeness* (1970), Charles Trinkaus provides general studies of Petrarch and humanism. Robert Durling's introduction to *Petrarch's Lyric Poems* (1976) and Leonard Forster's essays in *The Icy Fire: Five Studies in European Petrarchism* (1969) are outstanding introductions to Petrarch's lyric poetry. Indispensable, if specialized, are Giuseppe Mazzotta, *The Worlds of Petrarch* (1993); Leonard Barkan, *The Gods Made Flesh: Metamorphosis and the Pursuit of Paganism* (1986); Thomas M. Greene, *The Light in Troy: Imitation and Discovery in Renaissance Poetry* (1982); Nancy Vickers, "Diana Described: Scattered Woman and Scattered Rhyme," *Writing and Sexual Difference,* ed. Elizabeth Abel (1982): 65–79; John Freccero, "The Fig Tree and the Laurel: Petrarch's Poetics," *Literary Theory / Renaissance Texts,* ed. Patricia Parker and David Quint (1986): 20–32; and Roland Greene, "Petrarchism Among the Discourses of Imperialism," *America in European Consciousness, 1493–1750,* ed. Karen Ordahl Kupperman (1995): 130–65. Sara Sturm-Maddox, *Petrarch's Metamorphoses: Text and Subtext in the Rime Sparse* (1985), discusses the relationship of the lyric collection to Saint Augustine and to Ovid.

PRONOUNCING GLOSSARY

The following list uses common English syllables and stress accents to provide rough equivalents of selected words whose pronunciation may be unfamiliar to the general reader.

Acheron: *ah'-ker-on*

Aigues Mortes: *eg mort*

Bologna: *bo-lon'-yah*

Dionisio: *dee-oh-nee'-zyoh*

Malaucène: *ma-loh-sen'*

Ventoux: *von-too'*

Letter to Dionisio da Borgo San Sepolcro[1]

[The Ascent of Mount Ventoux]

To-day[2] I made the ascent of the highest mountain in the region, which is not improperly called Ventosum.[3] My only motive was the wish to see what so great an elevation had to offer. I have had the expedition in mind for many years; for as you know, I have lived in this region from infancy, having been cast here by that fate which determines the affairs of men. Consequently the mountain, which is visible from a great distance, was ever before my eyes, and I conceived the plan of some time doing what I have at last accomplished to-day. The idea took hold upon me with especial force when, in re-reading Livy's *History of Rome,* yesterday, I happened upon the place where Philip of Macedon, the same who waged war against the Romans, ascended Mount Haemus in Thessaly, from whose summit he was able, it is said, to see two seas, the Adriatic and the Euxine.[4] Whether this be true or false I have not been able to determine, for the mountain is too far away, and writers disagree. Pomponius Mela, the cosmographer—not to mention others who have spoken of this occurrence—admits its truth without hesitation;[5] Titus Livius, on the other hand, considers it false. I, assuredly, should not have left the question long in doubt, had that mountain been as easy to explore as this one. Let us leave this matter to one side, however, and return to my mountain here,—it seems to me that a young man in private life may well be excused for attempting what an aged king could undertake without arousing criticism.

When I came to look about for a companion I found, strangely enough, that hardly one among my friends seemed suitable, so rarely do we meet with just the right combination of personal tastes and characteristics, even among those who are dearest to us. This one was too apathetic, that one over-anxious; this one too slow, that one too hasty; one was too sad, another over-cheerful; one more simple, another more sagacious, then I desired. I feared this one's taciturnity and that one's loquacity. The heavy deliberation of some repelled me as much as the lean incapacity of others. I rejected those who were likely to irritate me by a cold want of interest, as well as those who might weary me by their excessive enthusiasm. Such defects, however grave, could be borne with at home, for charity suffereth all things, and friendship accepts any burden; but it is quite otherwise on a journey, where every weakness becomes much more serious. So, as I was bent upon pleasure and anxious that my enjoyment should be unalloyed, I looked about me with unusual care, balanced against one another the various characteristics of my friends, and without committing any breach of friendship I silently condemned every trait which might prove disagreeable on the way. And—would you believe it?—I finally turned homeward for aid, and proposed the ascent to my only

---

1. Translated by James Harvey Robinson and Henry Winchester Rolfe. Letter 4.1 from *De Rebus Familiaribus.* Dionisio, or Dionigi, da Borgo San Sepolcro was an Augustinian monk whom Petrarch had probably met in Paris in 1333. A learned theologian, he taught at Paris and in 1339 was appointed bishop of Monopoli. He spent the last part of his life in Naples at the court of the learned king Robert d'Anjou and died there in 1342 (Petrarch wrote a verse epistle on his death).   2. April 26. From internal evidence the year should be 1336, ten years after Petrarch left Bologna, but the letter was probably revised and made into an "allegory" at a later date (see n. 8, p. 2481).   3. Windy. Mount Ventoux (six thousand feet) is near Malaucène, not far from Petrarch's home in Vaucluse.   4. Compare Livy's *Roman History* 40.21.2.   5. Pomponius Mela (1st century A.D.), Roman geographer of Spanish birth. The passage referred to his *Corographia* 2.17.

brother, who is younger than I,[6] and with whom you are well acquainted. He was delighted and gratified beyond measure by the thought of holding the place of a friend as well as of a brother.

At the time fixed we left the house, and by evening reached Malaucène, which lies at the foot of the mountain, to the north. Having rested there a day, we finally made the ascent this morning, with no companions except two servants; and a most difficult task it was. The mountain is a very steep and almost inaccessible mass of stony soil. But, as the poet[7] has well said, "Remorseless toil conquers all." It was a long day, the air fine. We enjoyed the advantages of vigour of mind and strength and agility of body, and every-thing else essential to those engaged in such an undertaking, and so had no other difficulties to face than those of the region itself. We found an old shepherd in one of the mountain dales, who tried, at great length, to dissuade us from the ascent, saying that some fifty years before he had, in the same ardour of youth, reached the summit, but had gotten for his pains nothing except fatigue and regret, and clothes and body torn by the rocks and briars. No one, so far as he or his companions knew, had ever tried the ascent before or after him. But his counsels increased rather than diminished our desire to proceed, since youth is suspicious of warnings. So the old man, finding that his efforts were in vain, went a little way with us, and pointed out a rough path among the rocks, uttering many admonitions, which he contin-ued to send after us even after we had left him behind. Surrendering to him all such garments or other possessions as might prove burdensome to us, we made ready for the ascent, and started off at a good pace. But, as usually happens, fatigue quickly followed upon our excessive exertion, and we soon came to a halt at the top of a certain cliff. Upon starting on again we went more slowly, and I especially advanced along the rocky way with a more deliberate step. While my brother chose a direct path straight up the ridge,[8] I weakly took an easier one which really descended. When I was called back, and the right road was shown me, I replied that I hoped to find a better way round on the other side, and that I did not mind going farther if the path were only less steep. This was just an excuse for my laziness; and when the others had already reached a considerable height I was still wandering in the valleys. I had failed to find an easier path, and had only increased the distance and difficulty of the ascent. At last I became disgusted with the intricate way I had chosen, and resolved to ascend without more ado. When I reached my brother, who, while waiting for me, had had ample opportunity for rest, I was tired and irritated. We walked along together for a time, but hardly had we passed the first spur when I forgot about the circuitous route which I had just tried, and took a lower one again. Once more I followed an easy, round-about path through winding valleys, only to find myself soon in my old dif-ficulty. I was simply trying to avoid the exertion of the ascent; but no human ingenuity can alter the nature of things, or cause anything to reach a height by going down. Suffice it to say that, much to my vexation and my brother's amusement, I made this same mistake three times or more during a few hours.

After being frequently misled in this way, I finally sat down in a valley and

---

6. Gherardo, who was about three years younger.   7. Virgil in *Georgics* 1.145–46.   8. In the allegor-ical reading of the letter, this could be an allusion to Gherardo achieving God and salvation more directly (he became a monk in 1342, retiring into the monastery of Montrieux).

transferred my winged thoughts from things corporeal to the immaterial, addressing myself as follows:—"What thou hast repeatedly experienced to-day in the ascent of this mountain, happens to thee, as to many, in the journey toward the blessed life. But this is not so readily perceived by men, since the motions of the body are obvious and external while those of the soul are invisible and hidden. Yes, the life which we call blessed is to be sought for on a high eminence, and strait is the way that leads to it. Many, also, are the hills that lie between, and we must ascend, by a glorious stair-way, from strength to strength. At the top is at once the end of our struggles and the goal for which we are bound. All wish to reach this goal, but, as Ovid says, 'To wish is little; we must long with the utmost eagerness to gain our end.'[9] Thou certainly dost ardently desire, as well as simply wish, unless thou deceivest thyself in this matter, as in so many others. What, then, doth hold thee back? Nothing, assuredly, except that thou wouldst take a path which seems, at first thought, more easy, leading through low and worldly pleasures. But nevertheless in the end, after long wanderings, thou must perforce either climb the steeper path, under the burden of tasks foolishly deferred, to its blessed culmination, or lie down in the valley of thy sins, and (I shudder to think of it!), if the shadow of death overtake thee, spend an eternal night amid constant torments." These thoughts stimulated both body and mind in a wonderful degree for facing the difficulties which yet remained. Oh, that I might traverse in spirit that other road for which I long day and night, even as to-day I overcame material obstacles by my bodily exertions! And I know not why it should not be far easier, since the swift immortal soul can reach its goal in the twinkling of an eye, without passing through space, while my progress to-day was necessarily slow, dependent as I was upon a failing body weighed down by heavy members.

One peak of the mountain, the highest of all, the country people call "Sonny," why, I do not know, unless by antiphrasis,[1] as I have sometimes suspected in other instances; for the peak in question would seem to be the father of all the surrounding ones. On its top is a little level place, and here we could at least rest our tired bodies.

Now, my father, since you have followed the thoughts that spurred me on in my ascent, listen to the rest of the story, and devote one hour, I pray you, to reviewing the experiences of my entire day. At first, owing to the unac-customed quality of the air and the effect of the great sweep of view spread out before me, I stood like one dazed. I beheld the clouds under our feet, and what I had read of Athos and Olympus seemed less incredible as I myself witnessed the same things from a mountain of less fame. I turned my eyes toward Italy, wither my heart most inclined. The Alps, rugged and snow-capped, seemed to rise close by, although they were really at a great distance; the very same Alps through which that fierce enemy of the Roman name once made his way, bursting the rocks, if we may believe the report, by the application of vinegar. I sighed, I must confess, for the skies of Italy, which I beheld rather with my mind than with my eyes. An inexpressible longing came over me to see once more my friend and my country. At the same time I reproached myself for this double weakness, springing, as it did, from a

9. *Ex Ponto* 3.1.35.   1. The rhetorical use of a word in a sense opposite to its actual meaning.

soul not yet steeled to manly resistance. And yet there were excuses for both of these cravings, and a number of distinguished writers might be summoned to support me.

Then a new idea took possession of me, and I shifted my thoughts to a consideration of time rather than place. "To-day it is ten years since, having completed thy youthful studies, thou didst leave Bologna. Eternal God! In the name of immutable wisdom, think what alterations in thy character this intervening period has beheld! I pass over a thousand instances. I am not yet in a safe harbour where I can calmly recall past storms. The time may come when I can review in due order all the experiences of the past, saying with St. Augustine, 'I desire to recall my foul actions and the carnal corruption of my soul, not because I love them, but that I may the more love thee, O my God.'[2] Much that is doubtful and evil still clings to me, but what I once loved, that I love no longer. And yet what am I saying? I still love it, but with shame, but with heaviness of heart. Now, at last, I have confessed the truth. So it is. I love, but love what I would not love, what I would that I might hate. Though loath to do so, though constrained, though sad and sorrowing, still I do love, and I feel in my miserable self the truth of the well known words, 'I will hate if I can; if not, I will love against my will.'[3] Three years have not yet passed since that perverse and wicked passion which had a firm grasp upon me and held undisputed sway in my heart began to discover a rebellious opponent, who was unwilling longer to yield obedience. These two adversaries have joined in close combat for the supremacy, and for a long time now a harassing and doubtful war has been waged in the field of my thoughts."

Thus I turned over the last ten years in my mind, and then, fixing my anxious gaze on the future, I asked myself, "If, perchance, thou shouldst prolong this uncertain life of thine for yet two lustres, and shouldst make an advance toward virtue proportionate to the distance to which thou hast departed from thine original infatuation during the past two years, since the new longing first encountered the old, couldst thou, on reaching thy fortieth year, face death, if not with complete assurance, at least with hopefulness, calmly dismissing from thy thoughts the residuum of life as it faded into old age?"

These and similar reflections occurred to me, my father. I rejoiced in my progress, mourned my weaknesses, and commiserated the universal instability of human conduct. I had well-nigh forgotten where I was and our object in coming; but at last I dismissed my anxieties, which were better suited to other surroundings, and resolved to look about me and see what we had come to see. The sinking sun and the lengthening shadows of the mountain were already warning us that the time was near at hand when we must go. As if suddenly wakened from sleep, I turned about and gazed toward the west. I was unable to discern the summits of the Pyrenees, which form the barrier between France and Spain; not because of any intervening obstacle that I know of but owing simply to the insufficiency of our mortal vision. But I could see with the utmost clearness, off to the right, the mountains of the region about Lyons, and to the left the bay of Marseilles and the waters that

---

2. *Confessions* 2.1.1.   3. Ovid's *Amores* 3.2.35.

lash the shores of Aigues Mortes, altho' all these places were so distant that it would require a journey of several days to reach them. Under our very eyes flowed the Rhone.

While I was thus dividing my thoughts, now turning my attention to some terrestial object that lay before me, now raising my soul, as I had done my body, to higher planes, it occurred to me to look into my copy of St. Augustine's *Confessions*, a gift that I owe to your love, and that I always have about me, in memory of both the author and the giver. I opened the compact little volume, small indeed in size, but of infinite charm, with the intention of reading whatever came to hand, for I could happen upon nothing that would be otherwise than edifying and devout. Now it chanced that the tenth book presented itself. My brother, waiting to hear something of St. Augustine's from my lips, stood attentively by. I call him, and God too, to witness that where I first fixed my eyes it was written: "And men go about to wonder at the heights of the mountains, and the mighty waves of the sea, and the wide sweep of rivers, and the circuit of the ocean, and the revolution of the stars, but themselves they consider not."[4] I was abashed, and asking my brother (who was anxious to hear more), not to annoy me, I closed the book, angry with myself that I should still be admiring earthly things who might long ago have learned from even the pagan philosophers that nothing is wonderful but the soul, which, when great itself, finds nothing great outside itself. Then, in truth, I was satisfied that I had seen enough of the mountain; I turned my inward eye upon myself, and from that time not a syllable fell from my lips until we had reached the bottom again. Those words had given me occupation enough, for I could not believe that it was by a mere accident that I happened upon them. What I had there read I believed to be addressed to me and to no other, remembering that St. Augustine had once suspected the same thing in his own case, when, on opening the book of the Apostle, as he himself tells us,[5] the first words that he saw there were, "Not in rioting and drunkenness, not in chambering and wantonness, not in strife and envying. But put ye on the Lord Jesus Christ, and make not provision for the flesh, to fulfil the lusts thereof."[6]

The same thing happened earlier to St. Anthony, when he was listening to the Gospel where it is written, "If thou wilt be perfect, go and sell that thou hast, and give to the poor, and thou shalt have treasure in heaven: and come and follow me."[7] Believing this scripture to have been read for his especial benefit, as his biographer Athanasius[8] says, he guided himself by its aid to the Kingdom of Heaven. And as Anthony on hearing these words waited for nothing more, and as Augustine upon reading the Apostle's admonition sought no farther, so I concluded my reading in the few words which I have given. I thought in silence of the lack of good counsel in us mortals, who neglect what is noblest in ourselves, scatter our energies in all directions, and waste ourselves in a vain show, because we look about us for what is to be found only within. I wondered at the natural nobility of our soul, save when it debases itself of its own free will, and deserts its original estate, turning what God has given it for its honour into dishonour. How many times, think you, did I turn back that day, to glance at the summit of the

4. *Confessions* 10.8.15.   5. *Confessions* 8.12.29.   6. Romans 13.13–14.   7. Matthew 19.21.
8. A saint and doctor of the church (ca. 295–373), in his *Vita Antonii* 2.

mountain, which seemed scarcely a cubit high compared with the range of human contemplation,—when it is not immersed in the foul mire of earth? With every downward step I asked myself this: If we are ready to endure a little nearer heaven, how can a soul struggling toward God, up the steeps of human pride and human destiny, fear any cross or prison or sting of fortune? How few, I thought, but are diverted from their path by the fear of difficulties or the love of ease! How happy the lot of those few, if any such there be! It is to them, assuredly, that the poet was thinking, when he wrote:

> Happy the man who is skilled to understand
> Nature's hid causes; who beneath his feet
> All terrors casts, and death's relentless doom,
> And the loud roar of greedy Acheron.[9]

How earnestly should we strive, not to stand on mountain-tops, but to trample beneath us those appetites which spring from earthy impulses.

With no consciousness of the difficulties of the way, amidst these preoccupations which I have so frankly revealed, we came, long after dark, but with the full moon lending us its friendly light, to the little inn which we had left that morning before dawn. The time during which the servants have been occupied in preparing our supper, I have spent in a secluded part of the house, hurriedly jotting down these experiences on the spur of the moment, lest, in case my task were postponed, my mood should change on leaving the place, and so my interest in writing flag.

You will see, my dearest father, that I wish nothing to be concealed from you, for I am careful to describe to you not only my life in general but even my individual reflections. And I beseech you, in turn, to pray that these vague and wandering thoughts of mine may some time become firmly fixed, and, after having been vainly tossed about from one interest to another, may direct themselves at last toward the single, true, certain, and everlasting good.

MALAUCÈNE, April 26.

[SONNETS]

1[1]

You who hear in scattered rhymes the sound of those sighs with
which I nourished my heart during my first youthful error,[2] when
I was in part another man from what I am now:

for the varied style in which I weep and speak between vain
hopes and vain sorrow, where there is anyone who understands   5
love through experience, I hope to find pity, not only pardon.

But now I see well how for a long time I was the talk of the
crowd, for which often I am ashamed of myself within;[3]

---

9. Virgil's *Georgics* 2.490–92.   1. Translated by Robert M. Durling.   2. Mental and physical "wandering" as well as a moral "mistake." *Scattered rhymes*: reference to the sonnet collection's title, *Rime Sparse*.
3. The Italian, *di me medesmo meco mi vergogno,* suggests intense self-consciousness.

and of my raving, shame is the fruit, and repentance, and the
clear knowledge that whatever pleases in the world is a brief   10
dream.

3[4]

It was the day when the sun's rays turned pale with grief for his
Maker[5] when I was taken, and I did not defend myself against it,
for your lovely eyes, Lady, bound me.

It did not seem to me a time for being on guard against Love's
blows; therefore I went confident and without fear, and so my   5
misfortunes began in the midst of the universal woe.[6]

Love found me altogether disarmed, and the way open through
my eyes to my heart, my eyes which are now the portal and
passageway of tears.

Therefore, as it seems to me, it got him no honor to strike me   10
with an arrow in that state,[7] and not even to show his bow to
you, who were armed.

34[8]

Apollo, if the sweet desire is still alive that inflamed you beside
the Thessalian waves,[9] and if you have not forgotten, with the
turning of the years, those beloved blond locks;

against the slow frost and the harsh and cruel time that lasts as
long as your face is hidden, now defend the honored and holy   5
leaves where you first and then I were limed;

and by the power of the amorous hope that sustained you in
your bitter life, disencumber the air of these impressions.[1]

Thus we shall then together see a marvel[2]—our lady sitting on the
grass and with her arms making a shade for herself.   10

---

4. Translated by Robert M. Durling. **5.** The anniversary of Christ's crucifixion. Elsewhere (sonnet 211
and a note in Petrarch's copy of Virgil) given as April 6, 1327. **6.** The communal Christian grief that
contrasts with Petrach's private woes. **7.** State of grief over the crucifixion. **8.** Translated by Robert
M. Durling. **9.** Petrarch links his love of Laura to the love of Apollo for Daphne in Ovid's *Metamorphoses*.
Daphne, daughter of the god of the Peneus River in Thessaly, was pursued by Apollo, the god of poetry.
She begged her father to change her form, which had "given too much pleasure," and was transformed into
the laurel tree. Apollo, whom Petrarch associates with the sun god, claimed the laurel as his personal
emblem. **1.** Grief, cloudy weather, and aging. **2.** Supernatural and highly meaningful spectacle.

61[3]

Blest be the day, and blest the month and year,
Season and hour[4] and very moment blest,
The lovely land and place[5] where first possessed
By two pure eyes I found me prisoner;

And blest the first sweet pain, the first most dear,   5
Which burnt my heart when Love came in as guest;
And blest the bow, the shafts which shook my breast,
And even the wounds which Love delivered there.

Blest be the words and voices which filled grove
And glen with echoes of my lady's name;   10
The sighs, the tears, the fierce despair of love;

And blest the sonnet-sources of my fame;
And blest that thought of thoughts which is her own,
Of her, her only, of herself alone!

62[6]

Father in heaven, after each lost day,
Each night spent raving with that fierce desire
Which in my heart has kindled into fire
Seeing your acts adorned for my dismay;

Grant henceforth that I turn, within your light[7]   5
To another life and deeds more truly fair,
So having spread to no avail the snare
My bitter foe[8] might hold it in despite.

The eleventh year,[9] my Lord, has now come round
Since I was yoked beneath the heavy trace   10
That on the meekest weighs most cruelly.

Pity the abject plight where I am found;
Return my straying thoughts to a nobler place;
Show them this day you were on Calvary.

78[1]

When Simon[2] received the high idea which, for my sake, put his
hand to his stylus, if he had given to his noble work voice and
intellect along with form

---

3. Translated by Joseph Auslander.   4. Sunrise; April 6, 1327; spring.   5. The Church of Saint Clare
at Avignon.   6. Translated by Bernard Bergonzi.   7. Of grace.   8. Satan.   9. I.e., 1338.
1. Translated by Robert M. Durling.   2. Simone Martini (active 1315–44), a Sienese painter who lived
in Avignon during the last years of his life. His painting of Laura is the subject of the poem.

he would have lightened my breast of many sighs that make
what others prize most vile to me. For in appearance she seems   5
humble, and her expression promises peace;

then, when I come to speak to her, she seems to listen most
kindly: if she could only reply to my words!

Pygmalion,[3] how glad you should be of your statue, since you
received a thousand times what I yearn to have just once!   10

90[4]

She used to let her golden hair fly free
For the wind to toy and tangle and molest;
Her eyes were brighter than the radiant west.
(Seldom they shine so now.) I used to see

Pity look out of those deep eyes on me.   5
("It was false pity," you would now protest.)
I had love's tinder heaped within my breast;
What wonder that the flame burned furiously?

She did not walk in any mortal way,[5]
But with angelic progress; when she spoke,   10
Unearthly voices sang in unison.

She seemed divine among the dreary folk
Of earth. You say she is not so today?
Well, though the bow's unbent, the wound bleeds on.

126[6]

Clear, fresh, sweet waters,[7] where she who alone seems lady
to me rested her lovely body,
    gentle branch where it pleased her (with sighing I remember)
to make a column for her lovely side,
        grass and flowers that her rich garment covered along with   5
her angelic breast, sacred bright air where Love opened my heart
with her lovely eyes: listen all together to my sorrowful dying
words.

    If it is indeed my destiny and Heaven exerts itself that Love
close these eyes while they are still weeping,   10
    let some grace bury my poor body among you and let my soul

---

3. Sculptor, from Ovid's *Metamorphoses* 10, who fell in love with his own ivory statue, which Venus brought
to life. Whereas Ovid's Pygmalion enjoys a thousand physical embraces, Petrarch yearns only for a reply to
his words, or poem.   4. Translated by Morris Bishop.   5. Like Venus in book 1 of Virgil's *Aeneid*,
when the goddess of love appears to Aeneas in the guise of a Spartan huntress. The image of Venus armed
conjured up an ideal synthesis of eroticism and chastity in the Renaissance.   6. Translated by Robert
M. Durling.   7. Of the river Sorgue.

return naked to this its own dwelling;
    death will be less harsh if I bear this hope to the fearful pass,
for my weary spirit could never in a more restful port or a more
tranquil grave flee my laboring flesh and my bones.   15

    There will come a time perhaps when to her accustomed
sojourn the lovely, gentle wild one will return
    and, seeking me, turn her desirous and happy eyes toward
where she saw me on that blessed day,
    and oh the pity! seeing me already dust amid the stones,   20
Love will inspire her to sigh so sweetly that she will win mercy
for me and force Heaven, drying her eyes with her lovely veil.

    From the lovely branches was descending (sweet in
memory) a rain of flowers over her bosom,
    and she was sitting humble in such a glory,[8] already covered   25
with the loving cloud;
    this flower was falling on her skirt, this one on her blond
braids, which were burnished gold and pearls to see that day;
this one was coming to rest on the ground, this one on the water,
this one, with a lovely wandering, turning about seemed to say: 30
"Here reigns Love."[9]

    How many times did I say to myself then, full of awe: "She was
surely born in Paradise!"
    Her divine bearing and her face and her words and her sweet
smile had so laden me with forgetfulness   35
    and so divided me from the true image, that I was sighing:
"How did I come here and when?" thinking I was in Heaven, not
there where I was. From then on this grass has pleased me so that
elsewhere I have no peace.

    If you had as many beauties as you have desire, you could   40
boldly leave the wood and go among people.[1]

189[2]

My ship laden with forgetfulness passes through a harsh sea, at
midnight, in winter, between Scylla and Charybdis, and at the
tiller sits my lord, rather my enemy;[3]

each oar is manned by a ready, cruel thought that seems to scorn
the tempest and the end; a wet, changeless wind of sighs, hopes,   5
and desires breaks the sail;

8. An image associated with the Virgin Mary.   9. Amor (Cupid) or Christ. The floral and bejeweled images associate Laura's body with the bride of the Song of Songs, whose erotic chastity is celebrated as an "enclosed garden" and "fountain sealed."   1. The last two lines are addressed to the poem.   2. Translated by Robert M. Durling.   3. Love. Scylla and Charybdis are the twinned oceanic dangers through which Odysseus, in Homer's *Odyssey*, and Aeneas, in Virgil's *Aeneid*, must chart a middle course. Forgetfulness of oneself and of God is sinful in Augustinian terms. The ship, captained by Reason, is a traditional figure for the embodied soul.

a rain of weeping, a mist of disdain wet and loosen the already
weary ropes, made of error twisted up with ignorance.

My two usual sweet stars[4] are hidden; dead among the waves are
reason and skill; so that I begin to despair of the port.   10

333[5]

Go, grieving rimes of mine, to that hard stone
Whereunder lies my darling, lies my dear,
And cry to her to speak from heaven's sphere.
Her mortal part with grass is overgrown.

Tell her, I'm sick of living; that I'm blown   5
By winds of grief from the course I ought to steer,
That praise of her is all my purpose here
And all my business; that of her alone

Do I go telling, that how she lived and died
And lives again in immortality,   10
All men may know, and love my Laura's grace.

Oh, may she deign to stand at my bedside
When I come to die; and may she call to me
And draw me to her in the blessèd place!

4. Laura's eyes.   5. Translated by Morris Bishop.

DESIDERIUS ERASMUS
1466?–1536

The importance of the scholarly model set by Desiderius Erasmus for the Christian
humanists of the later Renaissance can hardly be exaggerated. To this day, Erasmus
remains an ideal of the teacher-scholar: wise, experienced, and prodigiously learned,
yet personally modest, forbearing, and affectionate. His image as the Socrates of
Christian humanism is one that Erasmus himself had a hand in fashioning. If he
hoped for lasting influence over the conduct of intellectual labor, Erasmus knew, it
was not enough to draft treatises on moral behavior and annotate editions of important texts. He had to craft a persuasive persona for the new scholar (himself) that
would impart to the humanist enterprise the intellectual principle he most admired:
tireless, curious, nondogmatic pursuit of enlightenment over received wisdom.

His voluminous writings include such monumental works as *Adages* (sayings collected from classical sources), the popular *Handbook of the Christian Soldier* and
Education of a Christian Prince, and important editions of the New Testament and
collected works of St. Jerome. His most enduring work, however, is *The Praise of
Folly*, a mock assault on wisdom and a celebration of the mind in hedonistic play. Its
popularity is due partly to its dramatic and elegant literary form, partly to the fact

that it deals in a moderate and humorous way with concerns central to the intellectually ambitious Renaissance: the power (and arrogance) of the human intellect, the worth (and futility) of knowledge, and above all the folly (and wisdom) of human behavior. *The Praise of Folly* defines the Renaissance art of "serious play": the diverting exploration of philosophical and moral questions that were seen as essential both to the cultivation of erudition and to the direction of everyday life.

Erasmus was born at Rotterdam, probably in 1466. As a youth, he studied first at Gouda and then at Deventer until the deaths of his parents, when he and his brother, Peter, were urged by their guardians to enter into the monastic life. Erasmus, who had hoped for a university education, reluctantly joined the Augustinian canons at Steyn and was ordained in 1492. He gained the bishop's consent in 1495 to leave the monastery for Paris and the most famous of all universities. At the University of Paris, he became the tutor of William Blount, Lord Mountjoy, who arranged for Erasmus to visit England in 1499–1500. There he befriended Sir Thomas More and John Colet, who both profoundly influenced Erasmus's intellectual life. Colet, a passionate student of religion, turned Erasmus's mind from exclusively literary and classical interests to theological scholarship. Colet inspired in Erasmus a new dedication to religious morals (which culminated in his popular *Handbook of the Christian Soldier* of 1504) and scholarship: at a time when Greek was largely forgotten, Erasmus labored to teach himself Greek to study the New Testament in its original language.

Throughout his scholarly career, Erasmus had to search constantly for patronage to support his research and travels. He visited England again in 1505–06 and met the archbishop of Canterbury, William Warham, and influential members of the court. As tutor to the son of Henry VII's Italian physician (Giovanni Battista Boerio), he visited Italy, the original home of the humanist studies to which Erasmus devoted himself. He stayed at the Universities of Turin (where he received a doctorate of theology) and Bologna; he also visited Padua, Florence, Rome, and Venice, where he befriended Aldus Manutius, the great humanistic printer. He returned to England in 1509, following the coronation of Henry VIII, from whom Erasmus had hopes of financial support for his scholarly work. During his five-year stay, he lectured in Greek and divinity at Cambridge University and worked to edit, translate, and annotate the Greek New Testament. England lost its charms for Erasmus in 1514, however, when the country was swept up in a militaristic fervor following English victories over France and Scotland. Erasmus traveled to Basel, where he took his publishing ventures to a new level: he not only worked but lived in the publishing house of Johannes Froben, who produced Erasmus's editions of Jerome and the New Testament in 1516. This period of his life brings us the now familiar image of Erasmus, surrounded by disciples and the bustle of the printing house, producing some of his most demanding and influential work. His scholarly stature was recognized when he was made a councilor of the young Charles V, a post that prompted Erasmus to write his *Education of a Christian Prince*.

Despite his success, Erasmus found himself increasingly at odds with traditional Catholic scholars, who recognized that his editions of the New Testament and Jerome implicitly challenged the authority of the Church. His work also drew the favorable notice of Martin Luther, whose reformist zeal inspired both sympathy and anxiety in Erasmus. In October 1517, in the hope of generating debate about the system of papal indulgences, Luther nailed his Ninety-five Theses to the Castle Church door in Wittenberg. Erasmus at first hoped to negotiate a peaceful compromise between the Protestant reformers and the Catholic conservatives, but the differences between his temperament and intellectual qualities and those of Luther were ultimately insuperable. Shaking all Europe, Luther rejected the highest ecclesiastical authority, a challenge he summed up in his famous declaration "Here I stand." Erasmus, on the other hand, chose to explore all dimensions of intellectual problems. An old anecdote has it that Luther, annoyed at Erasmus's refusal to side with or against the reformers, demanded, "Where do you stand?" to which Erasmus responded, "I stand *here*. And here. And here." Reluctantly, Erasmus finally took issue with Luther in print. Their exchange, which focused on the necessity of free will (Erasmus) and God's uncircumscribed majesty (Luther), was bitter and led to their decisive break. Despite Erasmus's efforts to affirm his Christian faith and to seek peaceful reform, many of his works, including *The Praise of Folly*, were enrolled in the notorious Index of books banned by the Church. A victim of diatribes, he ruefully compared himself to Saint Cassianus, whose pupils stabbed him to death with their pencils. (Long after his death, such images of persecution became reality for Erasmian Christians in Spain, who were targets of Counter-Reformation persecution.) In 1535 Erasmus received the devastating news of Sir Thomas More's execution, and on July 12, 1536, following an illness, he died in Freiburg.

While crossing the Alps on his third visit to England, Erasmus conceived *The Praise of Folly*, his celebrated investigation of the relationship between wisdom and folly. He drafted the work at the home of Sir Thomas More, who inspired the work's playful style and serious theme (More's name, Erasmus noted gleefully, means "fool," *mora*). His speaker—a witty, sophistic, and ingratiating entertainer—is the feminine embodiment of Folly. The work opens dramatically when Folly appears and congratulates herself on her warm reception: "you immediately brightened up . . . and greeted me with happy congenial laughter—so much so that every last one of you here before me, wherever I look, seems to be high on the nectar of the Homeric gods." Having set the stage for the work's dramatic form, Folly begins her lecture, sermon, or comic monologue—she is equally at home at the lectern, behind the pulpit, or on the stage. Her subject is herself—particularly, her beneficent influence on the otherwise joyless lives human beings are condemned to lead. She remarks, in amazement, that no one has ever thought to deliver an oration on folly, although many have "spent sleepless nights burning the midnight oil to work out elaborate encomia [praiseful tributes]" to tyrants, the fever, flies, and baldness. Folly thus draws attention to the link between Erasmus's genre and the tradition of mock praise developed by Greek and Roman orators. Unlike the subjects chosen by classical orators for mock praise, folly turns out not to be utterly disagreeable: folly is pleasurable (a point on which Folly dwells at length) and cannot be eradicated even from the wisest person.

The major theme of Folly's three-part oration is that we owe all our joys to illusions, without which life would be unbearable. The Stoics are the chief targets of her satire in the first part of her speech. Such philosophers ignore the blessings of life: they pride themselves on their indifference to joy and pleasure (as well as pain), and lead their lives as an extended renunciation of life itself. When Folly points out that the wisdom of the Stoics imprisons rather than liberates, her perspective is "not altogether fool," as one of Shakespeare's characters remarks of King Lear's Fool. In the rhythm of Erasmus's text, Folly habitually mounts compelling arguments in favor of folly only to conclude them with classical quotations, lifted out of context, that undermine her own position. After demolishing the Stoics, for example, she borrows an improbable line from Sophocles: "Not to think, that is the good life." The great paradox of Erasmus's text is that Folly is both the object and source of praise, and her oration both celebrates and exposes its speaker's foolishness. In effect, Erasmus plays out an elaborate and sophisticated version of the liar's paradox beloved of Renaissance humanists: "All Cretans are liars. I am a Cretan." Like the (lying?) Cretan of the paradox, Folly cheerfully destabilizes our grounds for knowledge and judgment.

In the second part of Folly's speech, Erasmus turns to the abuse of power by religious and political authorities. In this section, Erasmus's own reformist voice often breaks through the fiction of Folly's self-presentation. The responsibilities of political and ecclesiastical office are heavy, Folly maintains, and were it not for her influence, no one would undertake such joyless work. When she describes the specific vices of administrators of the Church and State, she adopts a comically nonjudgmental approach: "Popes, however diligent in harvesting money, delegate their excessively apostolic labors to the bishops, the bishops to the pastors, the pastors to their vicars, the vicars to the mendicant friars, and they too foist off their charge on those who shear the fleece of the flock." Erasmus's satire of corruption is more heavy-handed than usual but still leavened with subtle touches: the images of harvest and sheep-shearing conjure up a lively sense of the victims—sheeplike manual laborers—and the predators, who have turned their pastoral care into the exploitation of an intricately organized financial enterprise.

The third and most radical part of her speech elaborates the assertion of the Apostle Paul that Christian evangelists, who neglect worldly interest and reputation, are "fools for Christ's sake" (1 Corinthians 4.9–10). Folly regards this contingent of her following with wonder:

> they throw away their possessions, ignore injuries, allow themselves to be deceived, make no distinction between friend and foe, shudder at the thought of pleasure, find satisfaction in fasts, vigils, tears, and labors, shrink from life, desire death above all else—in short, they seem completely devoid of normal human responses, just as if their minds were living somewhere else, not in their bodies.

For Erasmus's Christian audiences, the responses to Folly's account of ideal Christian behavior could be legion: laughter at her ironic portrait of virtue; worry that self-negation seems possible only to Christians who reject the world; admiration for Folly's dexterous ability to cite and twist her authorities; revelation at the religious ecstasy she succinctly describes; and loss of equilibrium as they sway between the evangelical authorities she cites and her own exuberant, destabilizing text. Nowhere does Erasmus more radically question the sources and authorities with which people justify their actions.

Folly's goal throughout is to confuse the relationship between forms (religious, literary, or social) and their customary significances. At the end of her speech, she notices that her audience is waiting for a summary explanation. Instead of providing one, she facetiously asserts that she has no idea what she has just said and, therefore, has no epilogue—and she warmly recommends forgetfulness to her audience, too. An oration's epilogue, as Folly knows, encourages listeners to imitate the virtues singled out for praise. Folly, however, refuses to propose any relationship at all between her audience and her subject. To emulate Folly, evidently, we need only disregard the paradoxes she has unfolded and attempt no self-reform.

Understanding the structure of *The Praise of Folly* does not, of course, explain why Erasmus pursued reformist goals in a literary frolic. The spirit of fun that permeates *The Praise of Folly* comes from the popular tradition that flourished around the figure of the fool, dressed in cap and bells and carrying a bauble. Fools, who were figures of serious cultural play, presided over the popular carnivalesque festivities that took place during the liturgical year (e.g., May Day, Whitsuntide, Halloween, and Christmastide). During the festivals, common people and lower clergy were temporarily liberated from fixed social and ecclesiastical hierarchies: women were "on top" and from the ranks of servants people elected their Lord of Misrule. In the Feast of Fools, the lower clergy elected a bishop or even a pope of fools to lead a raucous parody of the ecclesiastical service. The French *sociétés joyeuses* ("joyous societies") featured a mock sermon on the life of a "saint" (e.g., Saint Onion) and joked about love, women, and marriage, as well as taverns and drinkers.

The religious and political authorities of Erasmus's day were divided in their sense of the relationship between saturnalian rituals and civic order. The festivities were actively discouraged by the Church but generally tolerated by the Crown. The raucous play of saturnalian rituals seemed conservative to some and subversive to others: were the lower classes "letting off steam" or building up tensions destined to explode in rebellion? Like the ambiguous saturnalian rituals, Folly's performance and Erasmus's text are exuberant, recreative, and ambivalent about moral proprieties.

The figure of the fool also shielded Erasmus from a backlash against his biting social criticisms. Court fools, who lived in the palaces of kings and households of noblemen, enjoyed unique privileges: one of the most famous was Henry VIII's beloved Archie Armstrong, who not only joked, sang, and conversed with the king but also challenged his sovereign. The court fool might appeal to the king's magnanimity when the monarch wished to invoke his royal prerogatives or felt disinclined to hear the concerns of the common people. Only the "all-licensed Fool," as Shakespeare calls him in *King Lear,* has the liberty to mock the king to his face and implicitly correct his abuses of power. It is to the fool's license that Erasmus refers in a public letter to a critic of the *Folly:* "Even the most savage tyrants put up with their buffoons and court fools, who sometimes taunt their masters with open insults." The prudent response to parody, he continues, is to laugh and admit or dissemble one's own faults. Erasmus makes his own radical aims when he appeals to the idea of the licensed fool in order to defend his text as innocuous. If his readers assume the privilege of fools, they will learn to challenge the arbitrary exercise of authority: this is the inspiring message that Erasmus has underscored throughout Folly's oration.

Lisa Jardine, *Erasmus, Man of Letters: The Construction of Charisma in Print* (1993), offers a stimulating analysis of Erasmus's career and scholarly image. Arthur F. Kinney, *Continental Humanist Poetics,* ch. 2 (1989), is recommended. Johan Huizinga, *Erasmus and the Age of Reformation* (1984), is an informative and interesting biography. Richard DeMolen, *Erasmus of Rotterdam: A Quintennial Symposium* (1971), and Kathleen Williams, ed., *Twentieth Century Interpretations of "The Praise of Folly"* (1969), contain useful essays.

The Praise of Folly[1]

Folly Herself Speaks:

Whatever mortals commonly say about me—and I am not unaware of how bad Folly's reputation is, even among the biggest fools of all—still it is quite clear that I myself, the very person now standing here before you, I and I alone pour forth joy into the hearts of gods and men alike. Hence it is that as soon as I came out to speak to this numerous gathering, the faces of all of you immediately brightened up with a strange, new expression of joy. You all suddenly perked up and greeted me with happy, congenial laughter—so much so that every last one of you here before me, wherever I look, seems to be high on the nectar of the Homeric gods, and on the drug nepenthe[2] too, whereas before you all sat there downcast and tense, as if you had just come back from the cave of Trophonius.[3] But when the sun first reveals his fair golden face to the earth, or when a harsh winter yields to the balmy breezes of early spring, everything suddenly takes on a new appearance, a new color, and a certain youthful freshness: so too, when you caught sight of me, your faces were transformed. Thus, what these eloquent orators can hardly accomplish in a long and carefully thought out speech—namely, to clear the mind of troubles and sorrows—that very goal I achieved in a flash simply by making an appearance.

* * * But since there are not very many who know my lineage, I will try (with the help of the Muses) to explain it. Neither Chaos, however, nor

---

1. Translated by Clarence Miller.   2. Legendary drug that causes oblivion.   3. Seat of a particularly awesome oracle.

Orcus, nor Saturn, nor Japetus, nor any other of these worn-out, moldy old gods was my father. Rather, it was Plutus, the one and only father of men and gods alike, Hesiod and Homer and even Jupiter[4] himself to the contrary notwithstanding. Plutus alone, as it is now and ever has been, has everything and everyone, sacred and secular alike, at his beck and call: he keeps the whole pot boiling. His decision governs war, peace, kingdoms, counsels, judgments, agreements, marriages, pacts, treaties, laws, arts, recreations, serious business—I'm running out of breath—in short, all the affairs, public or private, in which mortals engage. Without his help that whole crew of poetic divinities—I will go further, even the so-called "select" gods—would either not exist at all or would eke out a miserable existence as homebodies. Whoever is frowned on by him can never find enough help even from Pallas[5] herself. Conversely, whoever is smiled on by Plutus can afford to tell Jupiter himself to go to hell, thunderbolt and all. Such is the father I can boast. And this great god certainly did not give birth to me from his brain, as Jupiter did to that sour stick-in-the-mud Pallas. Rather, he begot me on Neotes (Youth), the fairest, the most charming nymph of all. Moreover, he did not do it within the forbidding bonds of matrimony, like the progenitor of that limping black-smith,[6] but rather in a fashion not a little sweeter, "mingled together in passionate love," as my friend Homer says. But make no mistake, I was not begotten by Plutus[7] as Aristophanes represents him, his eyesight completely gone and one foot already in the grave, but rather when he was young, sound, and hot-blooded, inflamed not merely by youth but even more by nectar, which on that occasion he had drunk at the banquet of the gods, perhaps in larger, stronger drafts than usual.

But if anyone wants to know my birthplace—since nowadays people seem to think one of the most important points of nobility is the place where a person gives out his first wails—I was brought forth neither in wandering Delos, nor in the waves of the sea, nor in hollow-echoing caverns, but rather in the Isles of the Blest,[8] where everything grows without effort—they plough not, neither do they sow. In those isles there is no work, no old age, no disease. Nowhere in their fields do you see asphodel, mallows, sea onions, lupines, beans, or any such trash as that. Instead, both sight and smell are gratified by moly, panace, nepenthe, amaracus, ambrosia, lotus, roses, violets, hyacinths, a veritable garden of Adonis. Born as I was among all these delights, I certainly did not begin my life by crying, but rather immediately smiled at my mother.

Far be it from me to envy the mighty son of Cronos the goat which gave him suck, since I was nursed at the breasts of two most elegant nymphs: Methe (Drunkenness), begotten by Bacchus, and Apaedia (Stupidity), the daughter of Pan. You can see them both here among my other attendants and handmaidens. If you want to know the names of the rest of them, you'll not get them from me in any language but Greek. This one—you see how

---

4. Sometimes called Jove (and Zeus in Greek), king of the gods. Plutus was the god of wealth and abundance. Hesiod (8th century B.C.), Greek didactic poet, cited here because he was author of the *Theogony* (about the generation and genealogy of the gods). 5. Pallas Athena, daughter of Jove and goddess of wisdom. 6. Hephaestus (Vulcan), whose parents were Zeus and his wife, Hera (Juno). 7. Plutus was usually represented as a boy with a cornucopia. 8. The mythical and remote islands where, according to Greek tradition, some favorites of the gods dwelt in immortality and bliss. *Delos:* in Greek myth, once a floating island and birthplace of Apollo, god of sunlight, prophecy, music, and poetry. *Waves of the sea:* from which Venus (Aphrodite), goddess of love, emerged. *In hollow-echoing caverns:* a Homeric expression.

she raises her eyebrows—is obviously Philautia (Selflove). The one you see here, with smiling eyes and clapping hands, is named Kolakia (Flattery). This one, dosing and half asleep, is Lethe (Forgetfulness). This one, leaning on her elbows with her hands clasped, is Misoponia (Laziness). This one, wreathed with roses and drenched with sweet-smelling lotions, is Hedone (Pleasure). This one, with the restless glance and the rolling eyes, is Anoia (Madness). This one, with the smooth complexion and the plump, well-rounded figure, is Tryphe (Luxury). You also see two gods among the girls: one is called Comos (Rowdiness), the other Negreton Hypnon (Sweet Sleep). This, then, is the loyal retinue which helps me to subject the whole world to my dominion, lording it over the greatest lords.

You have heard about my birth, upbringing, and companions. Now, lest my claim to divinity should seem unsubstantiated, listen carefully and I will show you how many benefits I bestow on gods and men alike and how widely my divine power extends. Consider, if that author (whoever he was) was not far from the mark when he wrote that the essence of divinity is to give aid to mortals, and if the persons who taught mortals how to produce wine or grain or some other commodity have been justly elevated to the senate of the gods, why should I not rightly be considered and called the very *alpha*[9] of all the gods, since I alone bestow all things on all men?

First, what can be sweeter or more precious than life itself? But to whom should you attribute the origin of life if not to me? For it is not the spear of stern-fathered Pallas or the aegis of cloud-gathering Zeus which begets and propagates the human race. No, Jupiter himself, father of the gods and king over men, whose mere nod shakes all Olympus, even he must put aside that three-forked lightning bolt of his; he must dispense with that fierce Titanic countenance (with which he can, at his pleasure, terrify all the gods); clearly, he must change his role like an actor and play a humble part whenever he wants to do what in fact he is forever doing—that is, make a baby. To be sure, the Stoics[1] rank themselves only a little lower than the gods. But give me a man who is a Stoic three or four times over, a Stoic to the nth degree, and he too, though he may not have to shave off his beard—the sign of wisdom (though goats also have one)—he certainly will have to swallow his pride; he will have to smooth out his frowns, put aside his iron clad principles, and indulge just a bit in childish and fantastic trifles. In short, I am the one that wise man must come to—I repeat, he must come to me—if he ever wants to be a father.

But let me take you into my confidence even more candidly, as is my fashion. I ask you, is it the head, or the face, or the chest, or the hand, or the ear—all considered respectable parts of the body—is it any of these which generates gods and men? No, I think not. Rather, the human race is propagated by the part which is so foolish and funny that it cannot even be mentioned without a snicker. That is the sacred fount from which all things draw life, not the Pythagorean tetrad.[2] Come now, would any man ever sub-

9. First letter of the Greek alphabet, hence "beginning" or "origin." The author is Pliny. 1. Stoicism originated in the Stoa Poikile ("painted porch"), a building in the marketplace in Athens where the philosopher Zeno (4th century B.C.) lectured; later it was perhaps the principal philosophy of the Roman elite. It became known during the Renaissance, especially through Seneca. Here the Stoics are the butt of Folly's irony because of their supposedly godlike disregard of the passions. 2. The first four numbers (which when added together equal the ideal number, ten); according to Pythagoras (6th century B.C.), the tetrad signified the root of all being.

mit to the halter of matrimony if he followed the usual method of these wisemen and first considered the drawbacks of that state of life? Or what woman would ever yield to a man's advances if she either knew about or at least called to mind the perilous labor of childbirth, the trials and tribulations of raising children? So, if you owe your life to matrimony, and you owe matrimony to my handmaid Anoia, you can easily see how much you owe to me. Then again, what woman who has once had this experience would ever consent to go through it again if it were not for the divine influence of Lethe? Even Venus herself (in spite of what Lucretius[3] says) would never deny that her power is crippled and useless without the infusion of our divine influence. Thus, this game of ours, giddy and ridiculous as it is, is the source of supercilious philosophers (whose place has now been taken by so-called monks), and kings in their scarlet robes, and pious priests, and pope-holy pontiffs and, finally, even that assembly of poetic gods, so numerous that Olympus, large as it is, can hardly accommodate the crowd.

But it would be little enough for me to assert my role as the fountain and nursery of life, if I did not also show that all the benefits of life depend completely on my good offices. After all, what is this life itself—can you even call it life if you take away pleasure? . . . Your applause has answered for you. I was certain that none of you is so wise, or rather foolish—no, I mean wise— as to be of that opinion. In fact, even these Stoics do not scorn pleasure, however diligently they pretend to—ripping it to shreds in their public pronouncements for the very good reason that when they have driven others away from it they can enjoy it all the better by themselves. But for god's sake, I wish they would tell me, is there any part of life that is not sad, cheerless, dull, insipid, and wearisome unless you season it with pleasure, that is, with the spice of folly? To this fact Sophocles, a poet beyond all praise, offered ample testimony when he paid us that most elegant compliment: "Never to think, that is the good life."[4]

*   *   *

* * * If someone should try to strip away the costumes and makeup from the actors performing a play on the stage and to display them to the spectators in their own natural appearance, wouldn't he ruin the whole play? Wouldn't all the spectators be right to throw rocks at such a madman and drive him out of the theater? Everything would suddenly look different: the actor just now playing a woman would be seen to be a man; the one who had just now been playing a young man would look old; the man who played the king only a moment ago would become a pauper; the actor who played god would be revealed as a wretched human being. But to destroy the illusions in this fashion would spoil the whole play. This deception, this disguise, is the very thing that holds the attention of the spectators. Now the whole life of mortal men, what is it but a sort of play, in which various persons make their entrances in various costumes, and each one plays his own part until the director gives him his cue to leave the stage? Often he also orders one and the same actor to come on in different costumes, so that the actor who just now played the king in royal scarlet now comes on in rags to play

3. Poet (99?–55 B.C.) who, in *On the Nature of Things*, invokes Venus because "all living things" are conceived through her.   4. Compare Sophocles' *Ajax*, lines 554–55: "life is sweetest before the feelings are awake—until one learns to know joy and pain."

a miserable servant. True, all these images are unreal, but this play cannot be performed in any other way.

If at this point some wiseman, dropped down direct from heaven, should suddenly jump up and begin shouting that this figure whom everyone reverences as if he were the lord god is not even a man because he is controlled by his passions like an animal, that he is a servant of the lowest rank because he willingly serves so many filthy masters; or if he should turn to another man who is mourning the death of his parent and tell him to laugh instead because the dead man has at last really begun to live, whereas this life is really nothing but a sort of death; if he should see another man glorying in his noble lineage and call him a low-born bastard because he is so far removed from virtue, which is the only true source of nobility; and if he addressed everyone else in the same way, I ask you, what would he accomplish except to make everyone take him for a raving lunatic? Just as nothing is more foolish than misplaced wisdom, so too, nothing is more imprudent than perverse prudence. And surely it is perverse not to adapt yourself to the prevailing circumstances, to refuse "to do as the Romans do," to ignore the party-goer's maxim "take a drink or take your leave," to insist that the play should not be a play. True prudence, on the other hand, recognizes human limitations and does not strive to leap beyond them; it is willing to run with the herd, to overlook faults tolerantly or to share them in a friendly spirit. But, they say, that is exactly what we mean by folly. I will hardly deny it— as long as they will reciprocate by admitting that this is exactly what it means to perform the play of life.

Another point—by all the gods in heaven! Should I say it or keep still? But why keep still, since it is "truer than truth itself." But perhaps in such a weighty matter it would be well to summon the Muses from Helicon[5]—the poets often enough invoke them for the merest trifles. Be present, then, you daughters of Jove, for a bit, while I show that no one can reach the heights of wisdom and the very "inner sanctum," as they themselves say, "of happiness" except with the guidance of Folly.

First of all, everyone admits that the emotions all belong to Folly. Thus, the usual distinction between a wiseman and a fool is that the fool is governed by emotion, the wiseman by reason. That is why the Stoics eliminate from their wiseman all emotional perturbations, as if they were diseases. But actually the emotions not only function as guides to those who are hastening to the haven of wisdom, but also, in the whole range of virtuous action, they operate like spurs or goads, as it were, encouraging the performance of good deeds. I know that died-in-the-wool Stoic, Seneca, strenuously denies this, removing all emotion whatsoever from his wiseman. But by doing this he is left with something that cannot even be called human; he fabricates some new sort of divinity that has never existed and never will. Frankly, he sets up a marble statue of a man, utterly unfeeling and quite impervious to all human emotion. They can enjoy their wiseman all they like and have him all to themselves, or (if they prefer) they can live with him in Plato's republic, or in the realm of Platonic ideas, or in "the gardens of Tantalus."[6] Who would not flee in horror from such a man, as he would from a monster or a ghost—a

5. Mythical mountain, home of the Muses.   6. All are characterized by the presence of abstraction and figments. *Realm of Platonic ideas*: the celestial ideal models of which real things are only imperfect realizations. In Tantalus's garden in Hades, rich fruit is always just beyond his grasp.

man who is completely deaf to all human sentiment, who is untouched by emotion, no more moved by love or pity than "a chunk of flint or a mountain crag," who never misses anything, who never makes a mistake, who sees through everything as if he had "x-ray vision," measures everything "with plumb line and T square," never forgives anything, who is uniquely self-satisfied, who thinks he alone is rich, he alone is healthy, regal, free, in brief, he thinks that he alone is all things (but he is also alone in thinking so), who cares nothing about friendship, who makes friends with no one, who would not hesitate to tell the gods themselves to go hang, who can find nothing in all human life that he does not condemn and ridicule as madness? Yet just such a creature as this is that perfect wiseman of theirs. I ask you, if an office were to be awarded by election, what state would choose such a man for civic office, what army would select him for their general? Indeed, what woman would consent to marry him or put up with him as a husband? What host would want him (or tolerate him) as a guest? What servant would ever enter his service or continue in it? Who would not prefer someone chosen at random from the mob of out-and-out fools? Being a fool himself, he could either command fools or obey them, please his peers (who are clearly in the majority), be companionable with his wife, cheerful with his friends, a fine table companion, an easy-going messmate. In short, he considers nothing human foreign to him.[7] But for some time now I have been sick and tired of this wiseman. Therefore I shall proceed in my speech by returning to the remaining benefits.

Just think, if a person could look down from a watchtower, as Jupiter sometimes does according to the poets, and could see how many disasters human life is exposed to, how miserable and messy childbirth is, how toilsome it is to bring children up, how defenseless they are against injuries, how young men must make their way by the sweat of their brow, how burdensome old age is, how death comes cruel and ineluctable; and then too, if he could see during the course of life itself how man is besieged by a whole army of diseases, threatened by accidents, assailed by misfortunes, how everything everywhere is tinged with bitterness—to say nothing of the evils men inflict on each other, such as poverty, prison, disgrace, shame, torture, entrapment, betrayal, insults, quarrels, deception, but I might as well try "to number the sands of the seashore"—now, as for what crimes man committed to deserve all this or which god in his anger caused men to be born to all these miseries, those are things it is not proper for me to declare at the present time, but whoever gives these things serious consideration cannot but approve the example of the Milesian virgins,[8] however pitiable their case was. But in fact, who have been the most likely to commit suicide out of weariness with life? Isn't it those who have come closest to wisdom? Among these (to say nothing of such people as Diogenes, Xenocrates, Cato, Cassius, and Brutus) was Chiron,[9] who had an opportunity to be immortal but freely chose death instead. You can see, I imagine, what would happen if men

---

7. From a proverbial phrase in Terence's *Self-Tormentor*, line 77: "I am a man: nothing human do I consider alien to me."   8. From the city of Miletus, in Asia Minor; according to an ancient tale, most of them, seemingly gone insane, hanged themselves.   9. The centaur (half man, half horse) who, incurably wounded and suffering great pain, asked Zeus for relief from his own immortality [Editor's note]. Of the philosophers Diogenes and Xenocrates, the first killed himself, but the second died by accident (Diogenes Laertius 6.77–78, 4.14–15). Cato of Utica, Brutus, and Cassius committed suicide after being defeated in battle [Translator's note].

everywhere were wise: we would need another batch of clay, another potter like Prometheus.[1] But I, partly through ignorance, partly through thoughtlessness, sometimes through forgetfulness of past misfortunes, sometimes through hope of good things to come, now and then mixing some honey with their pleasures, I rescue men from such terrible sufferings—so effectively that they are even unwilling to leave this life behind when the thread is all unwound and life leaves them behind. The less cause they have to remain in this life, the more they want to stay alive—so little are they touched by the tedium of life.

It is my doing that you see everywhere men as old as Nestor,[2] who no longer even look like men: driveling, doting, toothless, whitehaired, bald, or (in the words of Aristophanes) "filthy, crookbacked, wretched, shriveled, bald, toothless, and lame of their best limb";[3] but yet they are so in love with life and "have such young ideas" that one of them will dye his hair, another will hide his baldness with a toupee, another will wear false teeth (borrowed perhaps from some hog), another will fall head over heels in love with some young girl and outdo any beardless youth in amorous idiocy. In fact, to see old codgers with one foot in the grave marry some sweet young thing—with no dowry at that, and of far more use to other men than to him—this sort of thing happens so often that people almost consider it praiseworthy.

But it is even more amusing to see these old women, so ancient they might as well be dead and so cadaverous they look as if they had returned from the grave, yet they are always mouthing the proverb "life is sweet." They are as hot as bitches in heat, or (as the Greeks say) they rut like goats. They pay a good price for the services of some handsome young Adonis. They never cease smearing their faces with makeup. They can't tear themselves away from the mirror. They pluck and thin their pubic bush. They show off their withered and flabby breasts. They whip up their languid lust with quavering whines and whimpers. They drink a lot. They mingle with the young girls on the dance floor. They write billets-doux. Everyone laughs at these things as utterly foolish (and indeed they are), but the old bags themselves are perfectly self-satisfied. They lead a life of the utmost pleasure. They swim in honey up to their ears. Through my blessing, they live in bliss. Now if anyone thinks such goings-on are absurd, I wish he would take the trouble to decide whether he thinks it better to live a life of perfect bliss by means of such folly or to look for a way to "end it all," as they say.

Now, the fact that such absurdities are generally considered disgraceful, that doesn't bother my fools at all: they are either unaware of their notoriety, or, if they are aware, they find it easy to ignore it. If a rock falls on your head, that is certainly bad for you. But shame, disgrace, reproaches, curses do harm only insofar as they are perceived. If they are not noticed, they are not harmful. "What harm if all the crowd should hiss and boo; you're safe as long as you can clap for you." But that is made possible only by Folly.

Even so, I can imagine the philosophers' objections: "But to be caught in the toils of such folly, to err, to be deceived, to be ignorant—such an existence is itself miserable." One thing is sure: such it is to be a man. But I don't see why they should call him miserable, since this is the way you are

---

1. He supposedly molded the human race out of clay. 2. The old, eloquent sage in the Homeric epic.
3. *Plutus*, lines 266–67.

born, this is the way you are formed and fashioned, this is the common lot of everyone. But nothing is miserable merely because it follows its own nature, unless perhaps someone thinks man's lot is deplorable because he cannot fly like the birds, or run on all fours like other animals, and is not armed with horns like a bull. But by the same token, he should argue that even a fine, thoroughbred horse is unhappy because he has never learned grammar and doesn't eat pancakes, or that a bull is miserable because he cannot work out in the gym. Therefore, just as a horse who is ignorant of grammar is not miserable, so too, a man who is a fool is not unhappy, because these things are inherent in their natures.

But these word-jugglers are back at it again: "The knowledge of various branches of learning," they say, "was especially added to human nature so that with their help he could use his mental skill to compensate for what Nature left out." As if it were the least bit likely that Nature, who was so alert in providing for gnats (and even for tiny flowers and blades of grass), should have nodded only in equipping mankind, so that there should be a need for the different branches of learning—which were actually thought up by Theutus,[4] a spirit quite hostile to mankind, as instruments of man's utter ruination. So little do they contribute to man's happiness, that they defeat the very purpose for which they were supposedly invented—as that most wise king in Plato cleverly argues concerning the invention of writing.[5] Thus, the branches of learning crept in along with the other plagues of man's life, and from the very same source from which all shameful crimes arise, namely, the demons—who also derive their name from this fact, since "demon" comes from δαήμονες ("scientes," knowing ones). Now the simple people of the golden age, who were not armed with any formal learning, lived their lives completely under the guidance of natural impulses. What need was there for grammar when everyone spoke the same language and when speech served no other purpose than to let one person understand another? What use was there for dialectic, when there was no disagreement among conflicting opinions? What room was there for rhetoric when there were no litigious troublemakers? What demand was there for legal learning when there was no such thing as bad morals—for good laws undoubtedly sprang from bad conduct. Then too, they had more reverence than to pry into the secrets of Nature with irreligious curiosity—to measure the stars, their motions and effects, to seek the causes of mysterious phenomena—for they considered it unlawful for mortals to seek knowledge beyond the limits of their lot. As for what is beyond the range of the furthest stars, the madness of exploring such things never even entered their minds. But when the purity of the golden age had gradually declined, then evil spirits, as I said, first began to invent the learned disciplines, but only a few at first and even those taken up only by a few. Afterwards, the superstition of the Chaldeans and the idle frivolity of the Greeks added hundreds more, all of them nothing but forms of mental torture, so painful that the grammar of even one language is more than enough to make life a perpetual agony.

Still, even among these disciplines, the ones held in highest esteem are those which come closest to the ordinary understanding—that is, the folly—

---

4. In Plato's *Phaedrus,* an Egyptian god who brought the art of writing to King Thamus.   5. King Thamus argued that the invention of writing would produce only false wisdom and destroy the power of people's memory.

of mankind. Theologians starve, physicists freeze, astronomers are ridiculed, logicians are ignored. "One physician alone is worth whole hosts of other men."[6] And even among physicians, the more ignorant, bold, and thoughtless one of them is, the more he is valued by these high and mighty princes. Besides, medicine (certainly as it is now practiced by most doctors) is nothing but a subdivision of flattery, just like rhetoric. The next rank beneath the doctors belongs to pettifogging lawyers; in fact, I wonder if they don't hold the highest rank of all, since their profession—not to speak of it myself—is universally ridiculed as asinine by the philosophers. Still, all business trans-actions, from the smallest to the greatest, are absolutely controlled by these asses. They acquire large estates, while a theologian who has carefully read through whole bookcases of divinity nibbles on dried peas, waging continual warfare with bedbugs and lice.

Moreover, just as those disciplines which are most closely related to Folly contribute most to happiness, so too, those men who have nothing whatever to do with any branch of learning and follow Nature as their only guide are by far the happiest of all. For she is completely adequate in every way, unless perhaps someone wants to leap over the bounds of human destiny. Nature hates disguises, and whatever has not been spoiled by artifice always pro-duces the happiest results. After all, don't you see that, among all the other kinds of living creatures, those which remain at the furthest remove from any formal learning and take Nature for their only teacher lead the happiest lives? What could be happier or more marvelous than the bees? And yet they do not even have all the bodily senses. What architect has ever produced buildings like theirs? What philosopher has ever established a comparable republic? The horse, on the other hand, because his senses resemble those of man and because he left his original abode to dwell with men, has also become a sharer in the sufferings of men. Thus, often enough a horse that is ashamed to be defeated in a race becomes broken-winded, and a horse that strives for victory in warfare is stabbed and bites the dust with his rider. To say nothing of the sharp-toothed curb bits, the points of the spurs, the imprisonment of the stable, the whips, cudgels, fetters, the rider—in short, that whole miserable panorama of servitude that he willingly accepted when (like brave men of honor) he was overcome by a burning desire for revenge on his enemy. How much more attractive is the life of flies and little birds, who live for the moment purely by natural instinct, as long as they can avoid the snares of men. But if they should be put into cages and learn to speak human sounds, it is quite remarkable how they decline from their native sleekness and elegance. So certain is it that the creations of Nature are in every way more joyous than the fabrications of artifice.

Accordingly, I could never bestow sufficient praise on that cock embodying Pythagoras,[7] who had been, in his single person, a philosopher, a man, a woman, a king, a private citizen, a fish, a horse, a frog, even a sponge (I think), but who decided that no creature was more miserable than man because all the others were content to remain within the limits of Nature, while man alone tried to go beyond the bounds of his lot. Moreover, among men he places natural-born fools far above great and learned men; and Gryl-

6. Homer, *Iliad* 11.514.   7. In Lucian's *The Dream, or the Cock* (2nd century A.D.) the cock upholds the Pythagorean notion of transmigration of souls from one body to another by claiming that he is Pythagoras.

lus[8] was not a little wiser than wily Odysseus, since he preferred to grunt in the pigsty instead of being exposed with Odysseus to so many unexpected calamities. With Gryllus and the cock, Homer himself, the father of foolish fables, seems to be in agreement, since he repeatedly calls all mortals "miserable and wretched" and frequently applies the epithet "unhappy" to Ulysses, his model of wisdom, but never to Paris or Ajax or Achilles. And why this distinction? Wasn't it because the clever and cunning Ulysses never did anything without consulting Pallas Athene and was too smart for his own good, departing as far as possible from the guidance of Nature?

Therefore, just as among mortals those men who seek wisdom are furthest from happiness—indeed, they are fools twice over because, forgetting the human condition to which they were born, they aspire to the life of the immortal gods and (like the giants)[9] wage war against Nature with the engines of learning—so too, the least miserable among men are those who come closest to the level of intelligence (that is, the folly) of brute animals and never undertake anything beyond human nature. Come on, then, let us see if we can't show this, not with the fine-spun arguments of the Stoics, but with some plain, ordinary example. But by all the gods above! is anyone happier than the sort of men who are usually called fools, dolts, simpletons, nincompoops—actually very fine titles, as I see it? At first glance, what I am saying may perhaps seem foolish and absurd, but it is nevertheless true as can be.

First, they are spared all fear of death, a burden hardly to be taken lightly. They are not tortured by pangs of conscience. They are not frightened by silly tales about the underworld. They are not terrified by apparitions and ghosts. They are not tormented by the fear of impending evils, nor kept on tenterhooks by the hope of coming good. In brief, they are not harried by the thousands of cares to which this life is subject. They feel no shame, no fear, no ambition, no envy, no love. Finally, if they come close to the ignorance of brute animals, they do not even commit sins, according to theologians. Now at this point, most foolish wiseman, do me a favor: just consider how many ways your mind is tortured day and night—pile up all the troubles of your life into a single heap, and then you will finally understand how many evils I have spared my fools. On top of that, note that they not only rejoice continually themselves—playing, laughing, and singing little tunes—but also, wherever they turn, they provide everyone else with entertainment, jokes, fun and laughter, as if the gods in their goodness had granted them to men for the specific purpose of brightening up the gloominess of man's life. Hence, whereas various people react variously to other people, everyone agrees unanimously in claiming these fools as their own—they seek them out, maintain them, pamper them, coddle them, help them in time of need, freely allow them to do or say anything they like. So far is anyone from wishing to harm them that even savage beasts refrain from hurting them, out of a certain natural awareness of their innocence. As a matter of fact, they are sacred to the gods, especially to me, and therefore it is not without reason that everyone treats them with such respect.

In fact, even the mightiest monarchs are so delighted with them that with-

---

8. Character in a dialogue by Plutarch, changed into a pig by Circe.   9. Following the example of the giants, or Titans, of Greek mythology, who, inspired by their wronged mother, Gaea (Earth), fought the Olympian gods and were defeated.

out these fools some of them can neither eat breakfast, nor make their entry, nor even so much as survive for a single hour. And they value these simpletons far more then those sour wisemen, though it is true that they usually maintain some of them too, for the sake of appearances. The reason why they value them more is not far to seek, I think, and ought not to surprise anyone, since those wisemen normally offer princes nothing but melancholy—indeed, relying on their learning, they sometimes do not hesitate to make harsh truth grate upon their tender ears—whereas fools provide the very thing for which princes are always on the lookout: jokes, laughs, guffaws, fun. And don't forget another talent, by no means contemptible, that is peculiar to fools: they alone speak the plain, unvarnished truth. And what is more worthy of praise than truthfulness? True, Alcibiades' proverb in Plato attributes truthfulness to wine and children,[1] but actually the praise for that virtue is all mine and mine alone, as Euripides himself testifies in that famous saying about us which has come down from him: "a fool speaks like a fool."[2] Whatever a fool has in his heart, he reveals in his face and expresses in his speech. But wisemen have those two tongues, also mentioned by Euripides:[3] with one they speak the truth, with the other whatever they think convenient for the moment. They are the ones who turn black into white, who blow hot and cold in one breath, who profess to believe one thing in their speech but conceal quite another in their hearts. Princes, then, for all their great happiness, still seem to me most unhappy in one respect: there is no one from whom they can hear the truth, and they are forced to take flatterers for their friends.

But "a prince's ears tingle at the truth," someone will say, "and for that very reason they shun those wisemen: they are afraid that perhaps one of them might be so frank as to say what is true rather than pleasant." Quite right—kings do hate the truth. But my fools, on the other hand, have a marvelous faculty of giving pleasure not only when they speak the truth but even when they utter open reproaches, so that the very same statement which would have cost a wiseman his life causes unbelievable pleasure if spoken by a fool. For truthfulness has a certain inherent power of giving pleasure, if it contains nothing that gives offense. But the skill to manage this the gods have granted only to fools.

For almost the same reasons women, who naturally tend to be more inclined to pleasures and trifles, are extraordinarily fond of this kind of men. Accordingly, whatever they do with this sort of person (even though it is sometimes sufficiently serious), they explain away as mere entertainment and amusement—as indeed the fair sex is quite clever, especially in covering up their faux pas.

Therefore, to return to the happiness of simpletons, having lived their lives with great joy, with no fear or even awareness of death, they depart directly to the Elysian fields, where their antics continue to delight the leisurely souls of the blessed.

And now let us compare the lot of this fool with any wiseman whatsoever. Imagine, if you please, a model of wisdom to set over against the fool: a man who has wasted his whole childhood and youth in mastering the branches of learning and has lost the sweetest part of life in sleepless nights and

---

1. See Plato's *Symposium*.   2. *The Bacchanals (Bacchae)*, line 369.   3. *Rhesus*, lines 394–95; *Andromache*, lines 451–52.

endless painstaking labors, a man who even in the rest of his life has not tasted the tiniest crumb of pleasure, always frugal, poor, gloomy, surly, unfair and harsh to himself, severe and hateful to others, wasted away into a pale, thin, sickly, blear-eyed figure, old and gray long before his time, hastening to a premature grave—though what does it matter when such a person dies, since he never really lived at all? And there you have a fine picture of your wiseman.

But here the frogs of the Stoic ilk croak at me once again. "Nothing," they say, "is more miserable than madness. But extraordinary folly is either very close to madness or is actually identical with it. For what does it mean to be mad but to be of unsound mind?" But these cavilers are completely "on the wrong track." Come, let us demolish this syllogism also, with the help of the Muses. The argument is clever indeed, but just as Plato's Socrates taught when he divided one Venus into two and split one Cupid into two,[4] so, these dialecticians should have distinguished one kind of madness from the other if they ever intended to pass for sane themselves. For every sort of madness is not necessarily disastrous, in and of itself. Otherwise Horace would not have said "Or am I beguiled by a lovely madness"[5] nor would Plato have placed the frenzy of poets, prophets, and lovers among the chief goods of life; nor would the prophetess have called the labor of Aeneas mad.[6]

For there are two kinds of madness: one which is sent up from the underworld by the avenging Furies whenever they dart forth their serpents and inspire in the breasts of mortals a burning desire for war, or unquenchable thirst for gold, or disgraceful and wicked lust, or parricide, incest, sacrilege, or some other such plague, or when they afflict the guilty thoughts of some criminal with the maddening firebrands of terror. There is another kind far different from the first, namely the kind which takes its origin from me and is most desirable. It occurs whenever a certain pleasant mental distraction relieves the heart from its anxieties and cares and at the same time soothes it with the balm of manifold pleasures. Indeed, in a letter to Atticus, Cicero wishes for this mental distraction as a great gift from the gods, because it would have deprived him of all awareness of the great evils around him. Nor was there anything wrong with the judgment of the Greek who was so mad that he sat alone in the theater for whole days on end, laughing, applauding, enjoying himself, because he thought that wonderful tragedies were being acted there, whereas nothing at all was being performed. But in the other duties of life he conducted himself very well: he was cheerful with his friends, agreeable with his wife; he could overlook the faults of his servants and not fly into a mad rage when he found a winejar had been secretly tapped. Through the efforts of his friends he took some medicine which cured him of his disease, but when he was completely himself again, he took issue with his friends in this fashion: "Damn it all!" he said, "you have killed me, my friends, not cured me, by thus wresting my enjoyment from me and forcibly depriving me of a most pleasant delusion."[7] And rightly enough. For they were the ones who were deluded, and they had more need of hellebore than he did, since they thought such a felicitous and gratifying madness was some kind of evil that needed to be expelled by means of potions.

But in fact I haven't yet decided whether just any error of the senses or

---

4. I.e., in distinguishing heavenly love from other types of love. 5. *Odes* 3.4.5–6. 6. *Aeneid* 6.135.
7. This passage is a paraphrase of Horace's *Epistles* 2.128–40.

the mind ought to be designated by the name madness. Certainly, if a man with poor eyesight thinks a mule is an ass, or if someone takes a piece of doggerel for a very skillful poetic composition, he does not immediately strike everyone as mad. But if a person is deceived not only in the perceptions of his senses but also in the judgments of his mind, and if his deception is continual and beyond the usual share, only then will he be thought to verge on madness—as, for instance, if a person who hears an ass braying thinks he is listening to a marvelous choir, or if some poor beggar, born into the very lowest level of society, believes he is Croesus,[8] king of Lydia. But this kind of madness, if it errs in the direction of pleasure (as it usually does), brings no small share of delight both to those who experience it and to those who observe it without being mad to the same degree themselves. For this species of madness is far more widespread than most people realize. But one madman mocks another, and they maintain between them a mutual interchange of merriment. And not infrequently you see the greater madman laugh louder at the less. Still, everyone is all the happier the more ways he is deluded, as far as Folly can judge, as long as he remains within the category of madness that belongs peculiarly to us—a category which is in fact so widespread that I hardly know whether anyone at all can be found from the whole sum of mortals who is always impeccably wise and who is not subject to some kind of madness. The real difference is only this: the man who sees a cucumber and thinks it is a woman is labeled mad because this happens very rarely. But if a man who shares his wife in common with many other men nevertheless swears that she is more faithful than Penelope and warmly congratulates himself in his ignorant bliss, no one calls him mad because they see that this sort of thing happens to husbands everywhere.

This class of madness also includes those who look down on everything except hunting wild animals and whose spirits are incredibly exhilarated whenever they hear the nerve-shattering blasts on the horns or the baying of the hounds. I imagine that even the dung of the dogs smells like cinnamon to them. And then what exquisite pleasure they feel when the quarry is to be butchered! Lowly peasants may butcher bulls and rams, but only a nobleman may cut up wild animals. Baring his head and kneeling down, he takes a special blade set aside for that purpose (for it would hardly do to use just any knife) and exercises the most devout precision, in cutting up just these parts, with just these movements, in just this order. Meanwhile, the surrounding crowd stands in silent wonder, as if they were seeing some new religious ceremony, although they have beheld the same spectacle a thousand times before. Then, whoever gets a chance to taste some of the beast is quite convinced that he has gained no small share of added nobility. Thus, though these men have accomplished nothing more by constantly chasing and eating wild animals than to lower themselves almost to the level of the animals they hunt, still in the meantime they think they are living like kings.

Very like them is the sort of men who burn with an insatiable desire to build, replacing round structures with square and square with round. Nor is there an end to it, nor any limit, until they are reduced to such utter poverty that nothing at all is left—neither place to live nor food to eat. What of it? In the meantime they have passed several years with the greatest pleasure.

---

8. Proverbially wealthy man.

The group that comes closest to these builders, I think, consists of those who strive to change one substance into another by means of novel, occult arts, and move heaven and earth to track down a certain fifth element or "quintessence."[9] This honied hope entices them so powerfully that they spare no effort or expense. They are wonderfully clever in thinking up some new way to deceive themselves. They cheat themselves with a pleasing sort of fraud, until they have spent everything and don't even have enough left to fire their furnaces.[1] But still they never stop dreaming sweet dreams, and they also do everything they can to encourage others to pursue the same happiness. Even when they have been completely deprived of all hope whatsoever, there is still one saying left—a great comfort indeed: "in great affairs the intent alone's enough." And then they rail against the shortness of life, because it is inadequate for an enterprise of such great moment.

As to gamblers, I am in some doubt whether they should be admitted to our fellowship. But still it is a foolish and altogether absurd spectacle to see some of them so addicted to it that their hearts leap up and throb as soon as they hear the clatter of the dice. Finally, when the hope of winning has kept luring them onward until they suffer the shipwreck of all their resources, splitting the ship of their fortune against the dice-reef (hardly less fearful than the coast of Malea),[2] and when they have barely escaped from the sea with the shirts on their backs, they will cheat anyone rather than the winner of their money, lest anyone should think they are not men of honor. What shall we say when even old men who are already half-blind go on playing with the aid of eye-glasses? Or when they pay good money to hire a stand-in to roll the dice for them because their own finger-joints have been crippled by a well-earned attack of gout? A pleasant spectacle indeed, except that sometimes such gambling ends in violent quarrels and hence falls into the province of the Furies, not in mine.

But there can be no question at all that another group is entirely enlisted "under my banner": those who delight in hearing or telling miracles and monstrous lies. They can never get enough of such tales whenever strange horrors are told about apparitions, ghosts, specters, dead souls, and thousands of such marvels as these. And the further such tall tales are from the truth, the more easily they gain credence and the more delicately they tickle the ears of the listeners. Besides, they are not only wonderfully useful in relieving the boredom of the passing hours, but they also produce a fine profit, especially for priests and preachers.[3]

Closely related to such men are those who have adopted the very foolish (but nevertheless quite agreeable) belief that if they look at a painting or statue of that huge Polyphemus Christopher, they will not die on that day; or, if they address a statue of Barbara[4] with the prescribed words, they will return from battle unharmed; or, if they accost Erasmus on certain days, with certain wax tapers, and in certain little formulas of prayer, they will soon become rich. Moreover, in George they have discovered a new Hercules, just as they have found a new Hippolytus.[5] They all but worship

---

9. A substance (in addition to the four traditional elements—earth, water, air, and fire) of which the heavenly bodies were believed to be composed.   1. For alchemical experiments.   2. In Greece, proverbially dangerous.   3. Cf. Chaucer's *The Pardoner's Tale* (p. 2106).   4. Saint Barbara is supposed to protect her worshipers against fire and artillery. Polyphemus is the Cyclops (one-eyed giant) in Homer's *Odyssey*. Saint Christopher is also represented with only one eye.   5. In Greco-Roman mythology, both fought against monsters.

George's horse, most religiously decked out in breastplates and bosses, and from time to time oblige him with some little gift. To swear by his bronze helmet is thought to be an oath fit for a king.

Now what shall I say about those who find great comfort in soothing self-delusions about fictitious pardons for their sins, measuring out the times in purgatory down to the droplets of a waterclock, parceling out centuries, years, months, days, hours, as if they were using mathematical tables? Or what about those who rely on certain little magical tokens and prayers thought up by some pious impostor for his own amusement or profit? They promise themselves anything and everything: wealth, honor, pleasure, an abundance of everything, perpetual health, a long life, flourishing old age, and finally a seat next to Christ among the saints, though this last they don't want for quite a while yet—that is, when the pleasures of this life, to which they cling with all their might, have finally slipped through their fingers, then it will be soon enough to enter into the joys of the saints. Imagine here, if you please, some businessman or soldier or judge who thinks that if he throws into the collection basket one coin from all his plunder, the whole cesspool of his sinful life will be immediately wiped out. He thinks all his acts of perjury, lust, drunkenness, quarreling, murder, deception, dishonesty, betrayal are paid off like a mortgage, and paid off in such a way that he can start off once more on a whole new round of sinful pleasures.

Now who could be more foolish—rather, who could be happier—than those who assure themselves they will have the very ultimate felicity because they have recited daily those seven little verses from the holy psalms? A certain devil—certainly a merry one, but too loose-lipped to be very clever—is believed to have mentioned them to St. Bernard, but the poor devil was cheated by a clever trick.[6] Such absurdities are so foolish that even I am almost ashamed of them, but still they are approved not only by the common people but even by learned teachers of religion.

And then too, isn't it pretty much the same sort of nonsense when particular regions lay claim to a certain saint, when they parcel out particular functions to particular saints, and assign to particular saints certain modes of worship: one offers relief from a toothache, another helps women in labor, another restores stolen goods; one shines as a ray of hope in a shipwreck, another takes care of the flocks—and so on with the others, for it would take far too long to list all of them. Some saints have a variety of powers, especially the virgin mother of God, to whom the ordinary run of men attribute more almost than to her son.

But what do men end up asking from these saints except things that pertain to folly? Just think, among all the votive tablets that you see covering the walls and even the ceilings of some churches, have you ever seen anyone who escaped from folly or who became the least bit wiser? One saved his life by swimming. Another was stabbed by an enemy but recovered. Another, with no less luck than bravery, fled from the battle while the rest were fighting. Another who had been hung on the gallows fell down by the favor of some saint friendly to thieves, so that he could proceed in his career of disburdening those who are sadly overburdened by their riches. Another

---

6. A devil had told Saint Bernard that repeating seven particular verses of the Psalms would bring him the certainty of salvation. The *clever trick* was that of proposing to recite all the Psalms.

escaped by breaking out of jail. Another, much to the chagrin of his physician, recovered from a fever. For another, a poisonous potion, because it
worked as a purge, was curative rather than fatal, though his wife (who lost
her effort and expense) was not exactly overjoyed at the result. Another,
whose wagon had overturned, drove his horses home uninjured. Another,
buried by the collapse of a building, was not killed. Another, caught by a
husband, managed to get away. No one gives thanks for escaping from folly.
To lack all wisdom is so very agreeable that mortals will pray to be delivered
from anything rather than from folly.

But why have I embarked on this vast sea of superstitions?

> Not if I had a hundred tongues, a hundred mouths,
> A voice of iron, could I survey all kinds
> Of fools, or run through all the forms of folly.[7]

So rife, so teeming with such delusions is the entire life of all Christians
everywhere. And yet priests are not unwilling to allow and even foster such
delusions because they are not unaware of how many emoluments accumulate from this source. In the midst of all this, if some odious wiseman
should stand up and sing out the true state of affairs: "You will not die badly
if you live well. You redeem your sins if to the coin you add a hatred of evil
deeds, then tears, vigils, prayers, fasts, and if you change your whole way of
life. This saint will help you if you imitate his life"—if that wiseman were to
growl out such assertions and more like them, look how much happiness he
would immediately take away from the minds of mortals, look at the confusion he would throw them into!

Of the same stripe are those who prescribe in great detail, while they are
still alive, how they wish to be buried, giving exact numbers for the torches,
the people in mourning garments, the singers, the official mourners that they
want in the funeral procession, as if they could have any awareness of this
spectacle or as if the dead would be ashamed unless their corpses were
grandly planted in the ground—they seem for all the world like political
candidates staging a campaign dinner complete with entertainers.

Even though I am in a hurry, I can hardly pass over in silence those who
preen themselves on the empty title of nobility, even though they are no
different from the lowliest shoemaker. One traces his ancestry back to
Aeneas, another to Brut,[8] another to Arthur. Everywhere they display statues
and pictures of their ancestors, they count up their great-grandfathers and
great-great-grandfathers, they rehearse their ancient family names, while
they themselves are not much better than dumb statues, almost inferior to
the very symbols they display. And yet this pleasant Selflove enables them
to lead an altogether happy life. Nor is there any lack of others, equally
foolish, who revere this class of beasts as if they were gods.

But why should I be talking about one group or another, as if such Selflove
did not render almost everyone everywhere most happy in a variety of marvelous ways? One man who is uglier than any monkey is quite confident that
he is as handsome as Nereus. Another, as soon as he can draw three lines
with a compass, immediately thinks he is another Euclid. Another, who

---

7. A variation on a passage in the *Aeneid* (6.625–27) in which, however, Virgil is talking of "forms of
crime," not folly.   8. The legendary founder of Britain.

sounds like an "ass playing a harp and who sings no better than the bird that gives the hen uxorious nips, still thinks he is another Hermogenes. But by far the most entertaining kind of madness is the sort which causes some people to boast of any talent among their servants as if it were their own. This was displayed by that twice-blessed rich man in Seneca[9] who always kept servants at hand when he intended to tell an anecdote so that they could prompt him with the names. He wouldn't have hesitated to engage in a fist fight (though he himself was so infirm he was just barely alive) because he relied on the many strapping servants he had at home.

As for professors of the arts, why bother to mention them?—since Selflove is the special prerogative of all of them, so much so that you will sooner find one who will admit that his father's farm is second-rate than one who will accept second rank in intelligence. But this is especially true of actors, singers, orators, and poets: the more ignorant anyone of them is, the more arrogant his self-complacence, conceit, and braggadocio. And "birds of a feather", or like will to like—in fact, the less skillful anything is, the more admirers it obtains, according to the rule that the worst things usually please most people, because the majority of men, as we said, are subject to folly. Therefore, if a man acquires more pleasure for himself and more admiration from others according to the depth of his ignorance, why on earth should he choose real learning? First of all it costs a great deal, and then it will make him more disagreeable and timid, and finally it will please far fewer people.

Then again, I see that Nature has not only given every mortal his own brand of Selflove but has also grafted a sort of communal form of it to particular nations and even cities. Hence it is that the British lay claim above all to good looks, music, and fine food. The Scots pride themselves on their nobility and close blood-ties to the royal house, not to mention dialectical subtlety. The French claim for themselves refinement of manners. The Parisians arrogate to themselves theological learning, to the exclusion of almost everyone else.[1] The Italians lay claim to literature and eloquence, and on one point they all preen themselves most complacently: that, of all mortals, they alone are not barbarians. In this sort of happiness the Romans lead the way, and still dream sweet dreams about that ancient Rome of theirs. The Venetians are happy in their reputation for nobility. The Greeks, as the founders of the various branches of learning, emblazon themselves with the ancient renown of their famous heroes. The Turks and all that scum of the real barbarians claim for themselves the praise due to religion, ridiculing Christians, precisely because of their superstitions. But the Jews have it even better, still waiting faithfully for their Messiah and clinging to their Moses tooth and nail even to this day. Spaniards yield to no one in military glory. The Germans pride themselves on their tallness and their knowledge of magic. But, not to run through all of them one by one, you see (I think) how much pleasure Selflove everywhere supplies to individual mortals and to mankind as a whole, and in this function her sister Flattery is almost her equal.

For Selflove is nothing but the soothing praise which a person bestows on himself. If he bestows it on someone else, then it is Kolakia. Nowadays flat-

9. *Epistles* 27.4–6.   1. The Sorbonne, the theological faculty in Paris, was the center of theological studies in Europe.

tery is thought of as disreputable, but only by people who are more concerned about words than about things themselves. They judge that flattery is inconsistent with good faith. That the fact is quite otherwise, we can learn even by examples drawn from dumb animals. Is there any animal more fawning than a dog? But then again, is there any more faithful? Is any creature more obsequious than a squirrel? But is any more friendly to man? Unless perhaps you think fierce lions or cruel tigers or treacherous panthers contribute more to man's life! True, there is a certain kind of flattery which is altogether destructive, the kind employed by some unprincipled cynics to ruin their wretched victims. But this Flattery of mine proceeds from a kind disposition and a certain frankness which is much closer to a virtue than the opposite qualities, "sourness" and peevishness, "jangling" (as Horace[2] says) "and dour." This kind of flattery gives a lift to those whose spirits are low, consoles those who mourn, stimulates the apathetic, rouses the dull, cheers the sick, tames the fierce, unites lovers and keeps them united. It entices children to learn their lessons, it cheers up old people, it advises and teaches princes under the cover of an encomium, without giving offense. In short, it makes everyone more agreeable and indulgent to himself—and this is surely the chief ingredient of happiness. What is more courteous than for one person to scratch another's back? Not to mention that this flattery plays a large part in that eloquence everyone praises, a larger in medicine, and the largest of all in poetry—in sum, it is the honey and spice of all human intercourse.

But to be deceived, they say, is miserable. Quite the contrary—not to be deceived is most miserable of all. For nothing could be further from the truth than the notion that man's happiness resides in things as they actually are. It depends on opinions. For human affairs are so manifold and obscure that nothing can be clearly known, as is rightly taught by my friends the Academics,[3] the least arrogant of the philosophers. Or, if anything can be known, it often detracts from the pleasures of life. Finally, the human mind is so constituted that it is far more taken with appearances than reality. If anyone wants clear and obvious evidence of this fact, he should go to church during sermons: if the preacher is explaining his subject seriously, they all doze, yawn, and are sick of it. But if that screacher—I beg your pardon, I meant to say preacher—tells some old wive's tale, as they often do, the whole congregation sits up and listens with open mouths. Likewise, if any saint is more legendary or poetic—for example, think of George or Christopher or Barbara—you will see that such a saint is worshiped with far more devotion than Peter or Paul or Christ himself. But such things are out of place here.

And then, how much less it costs to gain such happiness! Sometimes it requires a great deal of effort to acquire the real article, even if it is something quite trivial, such as grammar. But to think you have acquired it—nothing could be easier, and yet such an opinion contributes as much or more to happiness. Consider, if someone eats a rotten pickled fish, the mere smell of which would be unbearable to another person, and yet the one who eats it thinks it tastes like ambrosia, what difference does it make to his happiness? Conversely, if some delicacy like sturgeon turns another man's stomach, it will hardly add anything to his happiness. If someone who has an

2. *Epistles* 1.18.6.   3. Philosophers of Plato's school, the Academy, which later became a school of the skeptics.

extraordinarily ugly wife still thinks that she could compete with Venus herself, isn't it quite the same as if she were really beautiful? If someone values and admires a canvas daubed with red and yellow, quite convinced that it is by Apelles of Zeuxis, isn't he actually happier than the man who has paid a high price for the real work of those painters but who perhaps takes less pleasure in viewing them than the other man? I know a certain man named after me[4] who gave his bride some imitation gems, assuring her (and he is a clever jokester) that they were not only real and genuine but also that they were of unparalleled and inestimable value. I ask you, what difference did it make to the girl since she feasted her eyes and mind no less pleasantly on glass and kept them hidden among her things as if they were an extraordinary treasure? Meanwhile, the husband avoided expense and profited by his wife's mistake, nor was she any less grateful to him than if he had given her very costly gifts. Surely you don't believe that there is any difference between those who sit in Plato's cave[5] gazing in wonder at the images and likeness of various things—as long as they desire nothing more and are no less pleased—and that wiseman who left the cave and sees things as they really are? Now if Lucian's Mycillus[6] had been allowed to dream forever that rich, golden dream of his, he would have had no reason to wish for any other happiness.

Thus, there is either no difference, or if there is, the lot of fools is clearly preferable. First, because their happiness costs them so little—nothing more than a touch of persuasion. Then too, they enjoy it in common with most other men. And, of course, nothing is really enjoyable without someone to share it with. And who does not know how few wisemen there are—if, in fact, any at all can be found? True, out of so many centuries the Greeks count seven altogether,[7] but if you examine even those very carefully, may I drop dead on the spot if you can find so much as a semi-wiseman, or even a hemi-demi-semi-wiseman.

Now, among the many benefits for which Bacchus is praised, the chief one is held (and rightly so) to be that he clears the mind of its troubles—and that only for a short time, since as soon as you have slept off your little wine-drinking spree, all your anxieties come rushing back to your mind "posthaste," as they say. But how much more ample and lasting is the benefit I provide, a sort of continuous inebriation which fills the mind with joy, delight, and exquisite pleasure—and all with no effort from you. Nor do I ever refuse any mortal a share of my gifts, whereas other endowments of the gods are distributed some to one, some to another. It is not every vineyard that produces a noble, mellow wine, one that drives away care, one that enriches us with surging hope. Few have been endowed with delicate beauty, the gift of Venus; even fewer with eloquence, a benefit given by Mercury. Not so very many have received wealth through the good offices of Hercules. Homer's Jupiter has hardly granted everyone political supremacy. Very often Mars favors neither side. Many depart quite disappointed from the tripod of Apollo's oracle. The son of Saturn often hurls his lightning bolt. Phoebus sometimes throws down missiles armed with the plague. Neptune drowns more than he saves. I might also mention in

4. Sir Thomas More (1478–1535), a close friend of Erasmus. The pun is with *moria* (Latin for "folly").
5. In Plato's allegory in the *Republic* (book 7) he compares the soul in the body to a prisoner chained in a cave, his or her back against the light, able to see only the shadows of things outside.   6. A character in *The Dream, or the Cock* who dreams that he has taken the place of a rich man.   7. Philosophers in the 6th century B.C.; among them were Thales and Solon.

passing such powers as Vejovis, Pluto, Ate, the Poenae,[8] the god of Fever and the like—not really gods, but tormentors. I, Folly, am the only one who embraces everyone equally with such ready and easy generosity. I do not care for vows, nor do I grow angry and demand expiatory gifts if some point of ceremony is overlooked. Nor do I go on a rampage if someone invites the other gods and leaves me sitting at home with no share of the fragrant steam rising from the sacrificial victims. For the other gods are so touchy about such things that it is more advantageous, and even safer, to leave them alone than to follow their cult—just as there are some men who are so hard to please and quick to take offense that it is better to have nothing at all to do with them than to cultivate their friendship.

But no one sacrifices to Folly, they say, and no one has built a temple dedicated to her. Indeed, I myself, as I said, find this ingratitude somewhat surprising. Still, I am good-natured enough to take this also in good part, though I couldn't really want such things anyway. Why should I need a bit of incense or grain or a goat or a hog, when all mortals everywhere in the world worship me with the kind of homage that even the theologians rank highest of all? Unless perhaps I should envy Diana because human blood is sacrificed in her honor! I consider that I am being worshiped with the truest devotion when men everywhere do precisely what they now do: embrace me in their hearts, express me in their conduct, represent me in their lives. Clearly this sort of devotion to the saints, even among Christians, is not exactly common. What a huge flock of people light candles to the virgin mother of God—even at noon, when there is no need! But how few of them strive to imitate her chastity, her modesty, her love for the things of heaven! For, in the last analysis, that is true worship, the kind which is by far the most pleasing to the saints in heaven. Furthermore, why should I want a temple, since the whole world, unless I am badly mistaken, is a splendid temple dedicated to me? Nor will there ever be a lack of worshipers, as long as there is no lack of men. Moreover, I am not so foolish as to require stone statues decked out in gaudy colors. For sometimes these are a drawback to the worship of us gods—that is, when stupid numbskulls adore the figures instead of the divinities, and then we are left in the position of those who have been edged out of their jobs by substitutes. I consider that as many statues have been set up for me as there are men who display, sometimes even unwillingly, a living image of me. And so, there is no reason why I should envy the other gods because each is worshiped in his own corner of the world, and on set days too—as, for example, Phoebus is honored at Rhodes, Venus on Cyprus, Juno at Argos, Minerva at Athens, Jupiter on Olympus, Neptune at Terentum, Priapus[9] at Lampsacus—as long as the whole world in perfect unanimity never ceases to offer me far superior victims.

Now if anyone thinks my claims reveal more boldness than truth, come on, let's examine the actual lives of men for a bit, to make it clear just how much they owe me—throughout all society from top to bottom—and how highly they value me.

*   *   *

---

8. Poena was goddess of punishment. Vejovis was hostile to men. Pluto was god of the underworld. Ate was goddess of revenge and discord.   9. A god of procreation, son of Dionysus and Aphrodite.

But why should I fret uselessly, trying to establish these things through so much testimony from various witnesses,[1] when Christ himself in the mystical psalms openly says to the Father, "You know my folly"?[2] Nor is it merely an accident that fools are so extremely pleasing to God. I think the reason is simply this: just as great rulers suspect and despise those who are too intelligent (as Caesar did Brutus and Cassius, whereas he had no fear of the drunken Anthony, and as Nero did Seneca, and Dionysius[3] did Plato) but are delighted with crude and simple minds, so too Christ always despises and condemns those savants who rely on their own wisdom. Paul testifies very clearly on this point when he says "What is foolish to the world, God has chosen,"[4] and when he says that God was pleased to save the world through folly because it could not be redeemed by wisdom.[5] Indeed, God himself makes the same point clear enough when he cries out through the mouth of the prophet, "I will destroy the wisdom of the wise and the prudence of the prudent I will reject,"[6] and again when he gives thanks that the mystery of salvation has been hidden from the wise and revealed to the simple, that is, to fools.[7] For the Greek for "simple" is νηπίοις, which he contrasted with σοφοῖς (wise). Relevant here, too, are his attacks everywhere in the gospel against the scribes and pharisees and doctors of the law, whereas he carefully protected the ignorant populace. For isn't "Woe to you, scribes and pharisees"[8] equivalent to "Woe to you, wisemen"? But he seems to have taken the greatest delight in simple people, women, and fishermen. In fact, even on the level of animal creatures, Christ is most pleased with those who are farthest removed from the slyness of the fox. Hence he preferred to ride on an ass, when if he wished he could have mounted on a lion's back with impunity. And the Holy Spirit came down in the shape of a dove, not an eagle or a hawk. Moreover, throughout Holy Scripture, harts, young mules, and lambs are frequently mentioned. Consider also that he calls his own followers, destined for immortal life, sheep. No other animal is more stupid, as is quite clear from the Aristotelian proverb "a mind like a sheep's," which (as he informs us) is derived from that animal's stupidity and is frequently leveled at blockheads and dolts as an insult. But, of such a flock as this, Christ professes to be the shepherd. Even more, he himself delighted in the title "lamb," as when John pointed him out with, "Behold, the lamb of God,"[9] which is also frequently mentioned in the Apocalypse.

Do not all these witnesses cry out with one voice that all mortals are fools, even the pious? And that even Christ, though he was the wisdom of the Father,[1] became somehow foolish in order to relieve the folly of mortals when he took on human nature and appeared in the form of a man? Just as he became sin in order to heal sins.[2] Nor did he choose any other way to heal them but through the folly of the cross, through ignorant and doltish apostles. For them, too, he carefully prescribed folly, warning them against wisdom, when he set before them the example of children, lilies, mustard seed,

---

1. I.e., of the relationship between Folly and Christianity.   2. Psalm 69.5. The speaker is not Christ but the psalmist.   3. Dionysius the Younger (4th century B.C.), tyrant of Syracuse, in Sicily.   4. 1 Corinthians 1.27.   5. 1 Corinthians 1.21: "It pleased God by the foolishness of preaching to save them that believe."   6. 1 Corinthians 1.19.   7. Matthew 11.25: "I thank thee, O Father, Lord of heaven and earth, because thou hast hid these things from the wise and prudent, and hast revealed them unto babes."   8. Luke 11.44.   9. John 1.29.   1. 1 Corinthians 1.24: "But unto them which are called, both Jews and Greeks, Christ the power of God, and the wisdom of God."   2. 2 Corinthians 5.21.

and sparrows[3]—stupid creatures lacking all intelligence, leading their lives according to the dictates of nature, artless and carefree—and also when he forbad them to be concerned about how they should speak before magistrates, and when he enjoined them not to examine dates and times, so as to keep them from relying on their own wisdom and make them depend on him heart and soul. To the same effect is the prohibition of God, the architect of the world, that they should not eat any fruit from the tree of knowledge, as if knowledge would poison their happiness. For that matter, Paul openly condemns knowledge as dangerous because it puffs men up.[4] St. Bernard, I imagine, was following Paul when he interpreted the mountain on which Lucifer established his throne as the mountain of knowledge.

Perhaps we ought not to omit the argument that folly is pleasing to the powers above because it alone can win pardon for mistakes, whereas a knowledgeable man is not forgiven. Hence, those who pray for forgiveness, even if they sinned knowingly, still employ folly as a pretext and defense. For this is the way Aaron prays to avert the punishment of his sister in The Book of Numbers, if I remember correctly: "I beg you, Lord, do not hold us responsible for this sin, which we have committed in our folly."[5] So too Saul begged David to forgive his offense, saying, "For it is clear that I acted in my folly."[6] Again, David himself coaxes the Lord in these words: "But I beg you, Lord, to take away the iniquity of your servant, because we have acted in our folly,"[7] as if he would not obtain pardon unless he pleaded folly and ignorance as excuses. But what is even more compelling, when Christ on the cross prayed for his enemies, "Father, forgive them," the only excuse he made for them was their ignorance: "for they do not know," he said, "what they are doing."[8] In the same way Paul, writing to Timothy: "For this reason I obtained mercy from God, because I acted ignorantly, as an unbeliever."[9] What does "I did it ignorantly" amount to but "I did it in my folly, not with malice?" What does "For this reason I obtained mercy" mean but that he would not have obtained it if he had not been recommended by the patronage of folly? Our case is also strengthened by that mystical psalmist, who did not occur to us in the proper place: "Do not remember the sins of my youth and my stupidities."[1] You hear the two excuses he makes: namely, youth, to whom I am a regular companion, and stupidities—and in the plural at that, so that we may understand the full force of his folly.

And now, to stop running through endless examples and to put it in a nutshell, it seems to me that the Christian religion taken all together has a certain affinity with some sort of folly and has little or nothing to do with wisdom. If you want some proof of this, notice first of all that children, old people, women, and retarded persons are more delighted than others with holy and religious matters and hence are always nearest to the altar, simply out of a natural inclination. Moreover, you see how those first founders of religion were remarkably devoted to simplicity and bitterly hostile to literature. Finally, no fools seem more senseless than those people who have been

---

3. Matthew 10.29. *Children*: Luke 18.17. *Lilies*: Matthew 6.28. *Mustard seed*: Luke 17.6.   4. 1 Corinthians 8.1: "Knowledge puffeth up, but charity edifieth."   5. Numbers 12.11: "And Aaron said unto Moses, Alas, my lord, I beseech thee, lay not the sin upon us, wherein we have done foolishly, and wherein we have sinned."   6. 1 Samuel 26.21: "Behold, I have played the fool, and have erred exceedingly." 7. 1 Chronicles 21.8.   8. Luke 23.34.   9. 1 Timothy 1.13: "But I obtained mercy, because I did it ignorantly in unbelief."   1. Psalm 25.7.

completely taken up, once and for all, with a burning devotion to Christian piety: they throw away their possessions, ignore injuries, allow themselves to be deceived, make no distinction between friend and foe, shudder at the thought of pleasure, find satisfaction in fasts, vigils, tears, and labors, shrink from life, desire death above all else—in short, they seem completely devoid of normal human responses, just as if their minds were living somewhere else, not in their bodies. Can such a condition be called anything but insanity? In this light, it is not at all surprising that the apostles seemed to be intoxicated with new wine and that Paul seemed mad to the judge Festus.[2]

✳   ✳   ✳

✳ ✳ ✳ In absolutely every activity of life, the pious man flees from whatever is related to the body and is carried away in the pursuit of the eternal and invisible things of the spirit. Hence, since these two groups[3] are in such utter disagreement on all matters, the result is that each thinks the other is insane—though that word applies more properly to the pious than to ordinary men, if you want my opinion. This will be much clearer if, according to my promise, I devote a few words to showing that their supreme reward is no more than a certain insanity.

First, therefore, consider that Plato had some glimmer of this notion when he wrote that the madness of lovers is the height of happiness.[4] For a person who loves intensely no longer lives in himself but rather in that which he loves, and the farther he gets from himself and the closer to it, the happier he is. Moreover, when the mind is set on leaving the body and no longer has perfect control over the bodily organs, no doubt you would rightly call this condition madness. Otherwise what is the meaning of such common expressions as "he is out of his wits," "come to your senses," and "he is himself once more." Also, the more perfect the love, the greater and happier is the madness. What, then, is that future life in heaven for which pious minds long so eagerly? I'll tell you: the spirit, stronger at last and victorious, will absorb the body. And it will do so all the more easily, partly because it is in its own kingdom now, partly because even in its former life it had purged and refined the body in preparation for such a transformation. Then the spirit will be absorbed by that highest mind of all, whose power is infinitely greater, in such a way that the whole man will be outside himself, and will be happy for no other reason than that he is located outside himself, and will receive unspeakable joy from that Highest Good which gathers all things to Himself.

Now, although this happiness is not absolutely perfect until the mind, having received its former body, is endowed with immortality, nevertheless it happens that, because the life of the pious is nothing but a meditation and a certain shadow (as it were) of that other life, they sometimes experience a certain flavor or odor of that reward. And this, even though it is like the tiniest droplet by comparison with that fountain of eternal happiness, nevertheless far surpasses all pleasures of the body, even if all the delights of all mortals were gathered into one. So much beyond the body are the things of the spirit; things unseen, beyond what can be seen. This, indeed, is what the prophet promises: "Eye has not seen, nor ear heard, nor has the heart of

2. Acts 26.24: "Festus said with a loud voice, Paul, thou art beside thyself; much learning doth make thee mad."   3. The pious and the ordinary.   4. *Phaedrus*, line 245.

man conceived what things God has prepared for those who love him."[5] And this is Folly's part, which shall not be taken from her by the transformation of life, but shall be perfected. Those who have the privilege of experiencing this (and it happens to very few) undergo something very like madness: they talk incoherently, not in a human fashion, making sounds without sense. Then the entire expression of their faces vacillates repeatedly: now happy, now sad; now crying, now laughing, now sighing—in short, they are completely beside themselves. Soon after, when they come to themselves, they say they do not know where they have been, whether in the body or out of it, whether waking or sleeping. They do not remember what they heard or saw or said or did except in a cloudy way, as if it were a dream. All they know is that they were never happier than while they were transported with such madness. Thus, they lament that they have come to their senses and want above all else to be forever mad with this kind of madness. And this is only a faint taste, as it were, of that future happiness.

But I have long since forgotten myself and "have gone beyond the pale." If you think my speech has been too pert or wordy, keep in mind that you've been listening to Folly and to a woman. But also remember that Greek proverb "Often a foolish man says something to the point"—unless, perhaps, you think it doesn't apply to women.

I see that you are waiting for an epilogue, but you are crazy if you think I still have in mind what I have said, after pouring forth such a torrent of jumbled words. The old saying was "I hate a drinking-companion with a memory." Updated, it is "I hate a listener with a memory." Therefore, farewell, clap your hands, live well, drink your fill, most illustrious initiates of Folly.

5. 1 Corinthians 2.9.

NICCOLÒ MACHIAVELLI
1469–1527

The most famous and controversial political writer and theorist of his time—indeed, possibly of all time—Niccolò Machiavelli was born in Florence on May 3, 1469. Little is known of his schooling, but it is obvious from his works that he knew the Latin and Italian writers well. He entered public life in 1494 as a clerk and from 1498 to 1512 was secretary to the second chancery of the commune of Florence, whose magistrates were in charge of internal and war affairs. During the conflict between Florence and Pisa, he dealt with military problems firsthand. Thus he had a direct experience of war as well as of diplomacy; he was entrusted with many missions— among others, to King Louis XII of France in 1500 and in 1502 to Cesare Borgia, duke of Valentinois or "il duca Valentino," the favorite son of Pope Alexander VI. Machiavelli described the duke's ruthless methods in crushing a conspiracy during his conquest of the Romagna region in a terse booklet *Of the Method Followed by Duke Valentino in Killing Vitellozzo Vitelli,* which already shows direct insight into the type of the amoral and technically efficient "prince." In 1506 Machiavelli went on a mission to Pope Julius II, whose expedition into Romagna (an old name for north-central Italy) he followed closely. From this and other missions—to Emperor Maximilian (1508) and again to the king of France (1509)—Machiavelli drew his two books of observations or *Portraits* of the affairs of those territories, written in 1508 and 1510.

Preeminently a student of politics and an acute observer of historical events, Machiavelli endeavored to apply his experience of other states to the strengthening of his own, the Florentine Republic, and busied himself in 1507 with the establishment of a Florentine militia, encountering great difficulties. When the republican regime came to an end, he lost his post and was exiled from the city proper, though forbidden to leave Florentine territory. The new regime of the Medici accused him unjustly of conspiracy, and he was released only after a period of imprisonment and torture. To the period of his exile (spent near San Casciano, a few miles from Florence, where he retired with his wife, Marietta Corsini, and his five children), we owe his major works: the *Discourses on the First Ten Books of Livy* (1513–21) and *The Prince,* written in 1513 with the hope of obtaining public office from the Medici. In 1520 Machiavelli was commissioned to write a history of Florence, which he presented in 1525 to Pope Clement VII (Giulio de' Medici). The following year, conscious of imminent dangers, he took part in the work to improve the military fortifications of Florence. The fate of the city at this point depended on the outcome of the larger struggle between Francis I of France and the Holy Roman emperor, Charles V. Pope Clement's siding with the king of France led to the disastrous "sack of Rome" by Charles V in 1527, and the result for Florence was the collapse of Medici domination. Machiavelli's hopes, briefly raised by the reestablishment of the republic, came to naught, because he was now regarded as a Medici sympathizer. This last disappointment may have accelerated his end. He died on June 22, 1527, and was buried in the church of Santa Croce.

Though Machiavelli has a place in literary history for a short novel and two plays— one of which, *La mandragola* (The Mandrake), first performed in the early 1520s, belongs in the upper rank of Italian comedies of intrigue—his world reputation is based on *The Prince.* This "handbook" on how to obtain and keep political power consists of twenty-six chapters. The first eleven deal with different types of dominions and the ways in which they are acquired and preserved—the early title of the whole book, in Latin, was *De principatibus* (Of Princedoms)—and the twelfth to fourteenth chapters focus particularly on problems of military power. The book's astounding fame, however, is based on the final part (from chapter fifteen to the end), which deals primarily with the attributes and "virtues" of the prince himself. In other words, despite its reputation for cool, precise realism, the work presents a hypothetical type, the idealized portrait of a certain kind of person.

Manuals of this sort may be classified, in one sense, as pedagogical literature. Because of their merits of form and of vivid, if stylized, characterization they can be considered works of art, but their overt purpose is to codify a certain set of manners and rules of conduct; the authors, therefore, present themselves as especially wise, experts in the field, "minds" offering advice to the executive "arm." Machiavelli is a clear example of this approach. His fervor, the dramatic, oratorical way he confronts his reader, the wealth and pertinence of his illustrations are all essential qualities of his pedagogical *persona:* "Either you are already a prince, or you are on the way to become one. In the first case liberality is dangerous; in the second it is very necessary to be thought liberal. Caesar was one of those. . . . Somebody may answer. . . . I answer." Relying on his direct knowledge of politics, he uses examples he can personally vouch for:

> Men are so simple and so subject to present needs that he who deceives in this way will always find those who will let themselves be deceived.
>
> I do not wish to keep still about one of the recent instances. Alexander VI did nothing else than deceive men, and had no other intention.

The implied tone of *I know, I have seen such things myself* adds a special immediacy to Machiavelli's prose. His view of the practical world may have been an especially startling one, but the sensation caused by his work would have been far less without the rhetorical power, the drama of argumentation, that makes *The Prince* a unique example of "the art of persuasion."

The view of humanity in Machiavelli is not at all cheerful. Indeed, the pessimistic notion that humanity is evil is not so much Machiavelli's conclusion about human nature as his premise; it is the point of departure of all subsequent reasoning on the course for a ruler to follow. The very fact of its being given as a premise, however, tends to qualify it; it is not a firm philosophical judgment but a stratagem, dictated by the facts as they are seen by a lucid observer of the here and now. The author is committed to his view of the human being not as a philosopher or as a religious man but as a practical politician. He indicates the rules of the game as his experience shows it must, under the circumstances, be played.

> A prudent ruler . . . cannot and should not observe faith when such observance is to his disadvantage and the causes that made him give his promise have vanished. If men were all good, this advice would not be good, but since men are wicked and do not keep their promises to you, you likewise do not have to keep yours to them.

A basic question in the study of Machiavelli, therefore, is "How much of a realist is he?" His picture of the perfectly efficient ruler has something of the quality of an abstraction; it shows, though much less clearly than Castiglione's portrayal of the courtier, the well-known Renaissance tendency toward "perfected" form. Machiavelli's abandonment of complex actualities in favor of an ideal vision is shown most clearly at the conclusion of the book, particularly in the last chapter. This is where he offers what amounts to the greatest of his illustrations as the prince's preceptor and counselor: the ideal ruler, now technically equipped by his pedagogue, is to undertake a mission—the liberation of Machiavelli's Italy. If we regard the last chapter of *The Prince* as a culmination of Machiavelli's discussion rather than as a dissonant addition to it, we are likely to feel at that point not only that Machiavelli's realistic method is ultimately directed toward an ideal task but also that his conception of that task, far from being based on immediate realities, is founded on cultural and poetic myths. Machiavelli's method here becomes imaginative rather than scientific. His exhortation to liberate Italy, and his final prophecy, belong to the tradition of poetic visions in which a present state of decay is lamented and a hope of future redemption is expressed (as in Dante's *Purgatorio,* canto 6). And a significant part of this hope is presented not in terms of technical political considerations (choice of the opportune moment, evaluation of military power) but in terms of a poetic justice for which precedents are sought in religious and ancient history and in mythology:

> . . . if it was necessary to make clear the ability of Moses that the people of Israel should be enslaved in Egypt, and to reveal Cyrus's greatness of mind that the Persians should be oppressed by the Medes, and to demonstrate the excellence of Theseus that the Athenians should be scattered, so at the present time. . . . Everything is now fully disposed for the work . . . if only your House adopts the methods of those I have set forth as examples. Moreover, we have before our eyes extraordinary and unexampled means prepared by God. The sea has been divided. . . . Manna has fallen.

Machiavelli's Italy, as he observes in chapter 25, is now a country "without dykes and without any wall of defence." It has suffered from "deluges," and its present rule, a "barbarian" one, "stinks in every nostril." Something is rotten in it, in short, as in Hamlet's Denmark. And we become more and more detached even from the particular example, Italy, as we recognize in the situation a pattern frequently exemplified in tragedy: the desire for communal regeneration, for the cleansing of the city-state, the *polis*. Of this cleansing, Italy on the one side and the imaginary prince on the other may be taken as symbols. The envisaged redemption is identified with antiquity and Roman virtue, while the realism of the political observer is here drowned out by the cry of the humanist dreaming of ancient glories.

Peter E. Bondanella focuses on the literary aspects of Machiavelli's works in *Machiavelli and the Art of Renaissance History* (1973). Sebastian De Grazia, *Machiavelli in Hell* (1989), on politics in *The Prince,* contains indexes and a bibliography. J. R. Hale's biography, *Machiavelli and Renaissance Italy* (1972), places Machiavelli in a historical perspective. A political analysis is provided by Anthony Parel in *The Political Calculus: Essays on Machiavelli's Political Philosophy* (1972). Roberto Ridolfi, *The Life of Niccolò Machiavelli* (1963), is still considered the best and most accurate biography. Silvia Ruffo-Fiore, *Niccolò Machiavelli* (1982), is a useful comprehensive guide for the beginning student. Victoria Kahn, *Machiavellian Rhetoric: From the Counter-Reformation to Milton* (1994), and Wayne A. Rebhorn, *Foxes and Lions: Machiavelli's Confidence Men* (1988), are recommended.

PRONOUNCING GLOSSARY

The following list uses common English syllables and stress accents to provide rough equivalents of selected words whose pronunciation may be unfamiliar to the general reader.

Borgia: *bor'-juh*

Chiron: *kai'-ron*

de' Medici: *day may'-dee-chee*

Machiavelli: *ma-kee-ah-vel'-lee*

Pistoia: *pees-toh'-yah*

San Casciano: *san ka-shah'-noh*

Santa Croce: *san'-tuh croh'-chay*

Letter to Francesco Vettori[1]

[*"That Food Which Alone Is Mine"*]

I am living on my farm, and since my last troubles[2] I have not been in Florence twenty days, putting them all together. Up to now I have been setting snares for thrushes with my own hands; I get up before daylight, prepare my birdlime, and go out with a bundle of cages on my back, so that I look like Geta when he came back from the harbor with the books of Amphitryo,[3] and catch at the least two thrushes and at the most six. So I did all of September; then this trifling diversion, despicable and strange as it is, to my regret failed. What my life is now I shall tell you.

In the morning I get up with the sun and go out into a grove that I am having cut; there I remain a couple of hours to look over the work of the past day and kill some time with the woodmen, who always have on hand some dispute either among themselves or among their neighbors. . . .

When I leave the grove, I go to a spring, and from there into my aviary. I have a book in my pocket, either Dante or Petrarch or one of the minor poets, as Tibullus,[4] Ovid, and the like. I read about their tender passions and

---

1. Translated by Allan H. Gilbert. From a letter dated December 10, 1513, to Vettori, ambassador in Rome.
2. Machiavelli had been suspected of participation in a conspiracy led by two young friends of his and had been imprisoned and subjected to torture before his innocence was recognized.   3. Allusion to a popular tale in which Amphitryo, returning to Thebes after having studied at Athens, sends forward from the harbor his servant Geta to announce his arrival to his wife, Alemene, and loads him with his books.
4. Albius Tibullus (1st century B.C.), Roman elegiac poet.

their loves, remember mine, and take pleasure for a while in thinking about them. Then I go along the road to the inn, talk with those who pass by, ask the news of their villages, learn various things, and note the varied tastes and different fancies of men. It gets to be dinner time, and with my troop I eat what food my poor farm and my little property permit. After dinner, I return to the inn; there I usually find the host, a butcher, a miller, and two furnace-tenders. With these fellows I sink into vulgarity for the rest of the day, playing at *cricca* and *tricche-trach*;[5] from these games come a thousand quarrels and numberless offensive and insulting words; we often dispute over a penny, and all the same are heard shouting as far as San Casciano.[6] So, involved in these trifles, I keep my brain from getting mouldy, and express the perversity of Fate, for I am willing to have her drive me along this path, to see if she will be ashamed of it.

In the evening, I return to my house, and go into my study. At the door I take off the clothes I have worn all day, mud spotted and dirty, and put on regal and courtly garments. Thus appropriately clothed, I enter into the ancient courts of ancient men,[7] where, being lovingly received, I feed on that food which alone is mine, and which I was born for; I am not ashamed to speak with them and to ask the reasons for their actions, and they courteously answer me. For four hours I feel no boredom and forget every worry; I do not fear poverty, and death does not terrify me. I give myself completely over to the ancients. And because Dante says that there is no knowledge unless one retains what one has read,[8] I have written down the profit I have gained from their conversation, and composed a little book *De principatibus*,[9] in which I go as deep as I can into reflections on this subject, debating what a principate is, what the species are, how they are gained, how they are kept, and why they are lost. If ever any of my trifles can please you, this one should not displease you; and to a prince, and especially a new prince, it ought to be welcome.

From The Prince[1]

New Princedoms Gained with Other Men's Forces and Through Fortune

FROM CHAPTER 7

*   *   *

[Cesare Borgia][2]

* * * Cesare Borgia, called by the people Duke Valentino, gained his position through his father's Fortune and through her lost it, notwithstanding that he made use of every means and action possible to a prudent and vig-

5. Two popular games, the first played with cards, the second with dice thrown to regulate the movements of pawns on a chessboard.   6. Nearby village, in the region around Florence.   7. Machiavelli here refers figuratively to his study of ancient history.   8. *Paradiso* 5.41–42: "For knowledge none can vaunt / Who retains not, although he have understood."   9. Of princedoms (Latin title of *The Prince*). All chapter headings are also in Latin in the original.   1. Translated by Allan H. Gilbert.   2. Son of Pope Alexander VI and duke of Valentinois and Romagna. His skillful and merciless subjugation of the local lords of Romagna occurred between 1499 and 1502.

orous man for putting down his roots in those states that another man's arms and Fortune bestowed on him. As I say above, he who does not lay his foundations beforehand can perhaps through great wisdom and energy lay them afterward, though he does so with trouble for the architect and danger to the building. So on examining all the steps taken by the Duke, we see that he himself laid mighty foundations for future power. To discuss these steps is not superfluous; indeed I for my part do not see what better precepts I can give a new prince than the example of Duke Valentino's actions. If his arrangements did not bring him success, the fault was not his, because his failure resulted from an unusual and utterly malicious stroke of Fortune.[3]

[Pope Alexander VI Attempts to Make Cesare a Prince]

Alexander VI,[4] in his attempt to give high position to the Duke his son, had before him many difficulties, present and future. First, he saw no way in which he could make him lord of any state that was not a state of the Church, yet if the Pope tried to take such a state from the Church, he knew that the Duke of Milan and the Venetians[5] would not allow it because both Faenza and Rimini were already under Venetian protection. He saw, besides, that the weapons of Italy, especially those of which he could make use, were in the hands of men who had reason to fear the Pope's greatness; therefore he could not rely on them, since they were all among the Orsini and the Colonnesi[6] and their allies. He therefore was under the necessity of disturbing the situation and embroiling the states of Italy so that he could safely master part of them. This he found easy since, luckily for him, the Venetians, influenced by other reasons, had set out to get the French to come again into Italy. He not merely did not oppose their coming; he made it easier by dissolving the early marriage of King Louis.[7] The King then marched into Italy with the Venetians' aid and Alexander's consent; and he was no sooner in Milan than the Pope got soldiers from him for an attempt on Romagna; these the King granted for the sake of his own reputation.[8]

[Borgia Determines to Depend on Himself]

Having taken Romagna, then, and suppressed the Colonnesi, the Duke, in attempting to keep the province and to go further, was hindered by two things: one, his own forces, which he thought disloyal; the other, France's intention. That is, he feared that the Orsini forces which he had been using would fail him and not merely would hinder his gaining but would take from him what he had gained, and that the King would treat him in the same way. With the Orsini, he had experience of this when after the capture of Faenza he attacked Bologna, for he saw that they turned cold over that attack. And as to the King's purpose, the Duke learned it when, after taking the dukedom of Urbino, he invaded Tuscany—an expedition that the King made him abandon. As a result, he determined not to depend further on another man's armies and Fortune.

3. Ill health.   4. Rodrigo Borgia (1431?–1503), pope (1492–1503), father of Cesare and Lucrezia Borgia.   5. The Venetian Republic opposed the expansion of the papal states. *Duke of Milan*: Ludovico Il Moro, the flamboyant duke of the Sforza family.   6. Powerful Roman families.   7. Louis XII, king of France (d. 1515).   8. According to his agreement with Pope Alexander VI.

[*The Duke Destroys His Disloyal Generals*]

The Duke's first act to that end was to weaken the Orsini and Colonnesi parties in Rome by winning over to himself all their adherents who were men of rank, making them his own men of rank and giving them large subsidies; and he honored them, according to their stations, with military and civil offices, so that within a few months their hearts were emptied of all affection for the Roman parties, and it was wholly transferred to the Duke. After this, he waited for a good chance to wipe out the Orsini leaders, having scattered those of the Colonna family; such a chance came to him well and he used it better. When the Orsini found out, though late, that the Duke's and the Church's greatness was their ruin, they held a meeting at Magione, in Perugian territory. From that resulted the rebellion of Urbino, the insurrections in Romagna, and countless dangers for the Duke, all of which he overcame with the aid of the French. Thus having got back his reputation, but not trusting France or other outside forces, in order not to have to put them to a test, he turned to trickery. And he knew so well how to falsify his purpose that the Orsini themselves, by means of Lord Paulo,[9] were reconciled with him (as to Paulo the Duke did not omit any sort of gracious act to assure him, giving him money, clothing and horses) so completely that their folly took them to Sinigaglia into his hands. Having wiped out these leaders, then, and changed their partisans into his friends, the Duke had laid very good foundations for his power, holding all the Romagna along with the dukedom of Urbino, especially since he believed he had made the Romagna his friend and gained the support of all those people, through their getting a taste of well-being.

[*Peace in Romagna; Remirro de Orco*]

Because this matter is worthy of notice and of being copied by others, I shall not omit it. After the Duke had seized the Romagna and found it controlled by weak lords who had plundered their subjects rather than governed them, and had given them reason for disunion, not for union, so that the whole province was full of thefts, brawls, and every sort of excess, he judged that if he intended to make it peaceful and obedient to the ruler's arm, he must of necessity give it good government. Hence he put in charge there Messer Remirro de Orco, a man cruel and ready, to whom he gave the most complete authority. This man in a short time rendered the province peaceful and united, gaining enormous prestige. Then the Duke decided there was no further need for such boundless power, because he feared it would become a cause for hatred; so he set up a civil court in the midst of the province, with a distinguished presiding judge, where every city had its lawyer. And because he knew that past severities had made some men hate him, he determined to purge such men's minds and win them over entirely by showing that any cruelty which had gone on did not originate with himself but with the harsh nature of his agent. So getting an opportunity for it, one morning at Cesena he had Messer Remirro laid in two pieces in the public square with a block of wood and a bloody sword near him. The ferocity of this spectacle left those people at the same time gratified and awe-struck.

9. Member of the Orsini.

[*Princely Virtues*]

FROM CHAPTER 15

On the Things for Which Men, and Especially Princes, Are Praised or Censured

* * * Because I know that many have written on this topic, I fear that when I too write I shall be thought presumptuous, because, in discussing it, I break away completely from the principles laid down by my predecessors. But since it is my purpose to write something useful to an attentive reader, I think it more effective to go back to the practical truth of the subject than to depend on my fancies about it. And many have imagined republics and principalities that never have been seen or known to exist in reality. For there is such a difference between the way men live and the way they ought to live, that anybody who abandons what is for what ought to be will learn something that will ruin rather than preserve him, because anyone who determines to act in all circumstances the part of a good man must come to ruin among so many who are not good. Hence, if a prince wishes to maintain himself, he must learn how to be not good, and to use that ability or not as is required.

Leaving out of account, then, things about an imaginary prince, and considering things that are true, I say that all men, when they are spoken of, and especially princes, because they are set higher, are marked with some of the qualities that bring them either blame or praise. To wit, one man is thought liberal, another stingy (using a Tuscan word, because *avaricious* in our language is still applied to one who desires to get things through violence, but *stingy* we apply to him who refrains too much from using his own property); one is thought open-handed, another grasping; one cruel, the other compassionate; one is a breaker of faith, the other reliable; one is effeminate and cowardly, the other vigorous and spirited; one is philanthropic, the other egotistic; one is lascivious, the other chaste; one is straight-forward, the other crafty; one hard, the other easy to deal with; one is firm, the other unsettled; one is religious, the other unbelieving; and so on.

And I know that everybody will admit that it would be very praiseworthy for a prince to possess all of the above-mentioned qualities that are considered good. But since he is not able to have them or to observe them completely, because human conditions do not allow him to, it is necessary that he be prudent enough to understand how to avoid getting a bad name because he is given to those vices that will deprive him of his position. He should also, if he can, guard himself from those vices that will not take his place away from him, but if he cannot do it, he can with less anxiety let them go. Moreover, he should not be troubled if he gets a bad name because of vices without which it will be difficult for him to preserve his position. I say this because, if everything is considered, it will be seen that some things seem to be virtuous, but if they are put into practice will be ruinous to him; other things seem to be vices, yet if put into practice will bring the prince security and well-being.

FROM CHAPTER 16

On Liberality and Parsimony

Beginning, then, with the first of the above-mentioned qualities, I assert that it is good to be thought liberal.[1] Yet liberality, practiced in such a way that you get a reputation for it, is damaging to you, for the following reasons: If you use it wisely and as it ought to be used, it will not become known, and you will not escape being censured for the opposite vice. Hence, if you wish to have men call you liberal, it is necessary not to omit any sort of lavishness. A prince who does this will always be obliged to use up all his property in lavish actions; he will then, if he wishes to keep the name of liberal, be forced to lay heavy taxes on his people and exact money from them, and do everything he can to raise money. This will begin to make his subjects hate him, and as he grows poor he will be little esteemed by anybody. So it comes about that because of this liberality of his, with which he has damaged a large number and been of advantage to but a few, he is affected by every petty annoyance and is in peril from every slight danger. If he recognizes this and wishes to draw back, he quickly gets a bad name for stinginess.

Since, then, a prince cannot without harming himself practice this virtue of liberality to such an extent that it will be recognized, he will, if he is prudent, not care about being called stingy. As time goes on he will be thought more and more liberal, for the people will see that because of his economy his income is enough for him, that he can defend himself from those who make war against him, and that he can enter upon undertakings without burdening his people. Such a prince is in the end liberal to all those from whom he takes nothing, and they are numerous; he is stingy to those to whom he does not give, and they are few. In our times we have seen big things done only by those who have been looked on as stingy; the others have utterly failed. Pope Julius II,[2] though he made use of a reputation for liberality to attain the papacy, did not then try to maintain it, because he wished to be able to make war. The present King of France[3] has carried on great wars without laying unusually heavy taxes on his people, merely because his long economy has made provision for heavy expenditures. The present King of Spain,[4] if he had continued liberal, would not have carried on or completed so many undertakings.

Therefore a prince ought to care little about getting called stingy, if as a result he does not have to rob his subjects, is able to defend himself, does not become poor and contemptible, and is not obliged to become grasping. For this vice of stinginess is one of those that enables him to rule. Somebody may say: Caesar, by means of his liberality became emperor, and many others have come to high positions because they have been liberal and have been thought so. I answer: Either you are already prince, or you are on the way to become one. In the first case liberality is dangerous; in the second it is very necessary to be thought liberal. Caesar was one of those who wished to attain dominion over Rome. But if, when he had attained it, he had lived for a long

---

1. Generous, openhanded.   2. Giuliano della Rovere (1443–1513), elected to the papacy in 1503 at the death of Pius III, who had been successor to Alexander VI (Rodrigo Borgia). Alexander VI is discussed in chap. 18. Julius II's character is discussed in chap. 25.   3. Louis XII (1462–1515).   4. Ferdinand II, "the Catholic" (1452–1516).

time and had not moderated his expenses, he would have destroyed his authority. Somebody may answer: Many who have been thought very liberal have been princes and done great things with their armies. I answer: The prince spends either his own property and that of his subjects or that of others. In the first case he ought to be frugal; in the second he ought to abstain from no sort of liberality. When he marches with his army and lives on plunder, loot, and ransom, a prince controls the property of others. To him liberality is essential, for without it his soldiers would not follow him. You can be a free giver of what does not belong to you or your subjects, as were Cyrus, Caesar, and Alexander, because to spend the money of others does not decrease your reputation but adds to it. It is only the spending of your own money that hurts you.

There is nothing that eats itself up as fast as does liberality, for when you practice it you lose the power to practice it, and become poor and contemptible, or else to escape poverty you become rapacious and therefore are hated. And of all the things against which a prince must guard himself, the first is being an object of contempt and hatred. Liberality leads you to both of these. Hence there is more wisdom in keeping a name for stinginess, which produces a bad reputation without hatred, than in striving for the name of liberal, only to be forced to get the name of rapacious, which brings forth both bad reputation and hatred.

FROM CHAPTER 17

On Cruelty and Pity, and Whether It Is Better to Be Loved or to Be Feared, and Vice Versa

Coming then to the other qualities already mentioned, I say that every prince should wish to be thought compassionate and not cruel; still, he should be careful not to make a bad use of the pity he feels. Cesare Borgia[5] was considered cruel, yet this cruelty of his pacified the Romagna, united it, and changed its condition to that of peace and loyalty. If the matter is well considered, it will be seen that Cesare was much more compassionate than the people of Florence, for in order to escape the name of cruel they allowed Pistoia to be destroyed.[6] Hence a prince ought not to be troubled by the stigma of cruelty, acquired in keeping his subjects united and faithful. By giving a very few examples of cruelty he can be more truly compassionate than those who through too much compassion allow disturbances to continue, from which arise murders or acts of plunder. Lawless acts are injurious to a large group, but the executions ordered by the prince injure a single person. The new prince, above all other princes, cannot possibly avoid the name of cruel, because new states are full of perils. Dido in Vergil puts it thus: "Hard circumstances and the newness of my realm force me to do such things, and to keep watch and ward over all my lands."[7]

All the same, he should be slow in believing and acting, and should make no one afraid of him; his procedure should be so tempered with prudence and humanity that too much confidence does not make him incautious, and too much suspicion does not make him unbearable.

---

5. See n. 2, p. 2521.   6. By internal dissensions, because the Florentines, Machiavelli contends, failed to treat the leaders of the dissenting parties with an iron hand.   7. *Aeneid* 1.563–64.

All this gives rise to a question for debate: Is it better to be loved than to be feared, or the reverse? I answer that a prince should wish for both. But because it is difficult to reconcile them, I hold that it is much more secure to be feared than to be loved, if one of them must be given up. The reason for my answer is that one must say of men generally that they are ungrateful, mutable, pretenders and dissemblers, prone to avoid danger, thirsty for gain. So long as you benefit them they are all yours; as I said above, they offer you their blood, their property, their lives, their children, when the need for such things is remote. But when need comes upon you, they turn around. So if a prince has relied wholly on their words, and is lacking in other preparations, he falls. For friendships that are gained with money, and not with greatness and nobility of spirit, are deserved but not possessed, and in the nick of time one cannot avail himself of them. Men hesitate less to injure a man who makes himself loved than to injure one who makes himself feared, for their love is held by a chain of obligation, which, because of men's wickedness, is broken on every occasion for the sake of selfish profit; but their fear is secured by a dread of punishment which never fails you.

Nevertheless the prince should make himself feared in such a way that, if he does not win love, he escapes hatred. This is possible, for to be feared and not to be hated can easily coexist. In fact it is always possible, if the ruler abstains from the property of his citizens and subjects, and from their women. And if, as sometimes happens, he finds that he must inflict the penalty of death, he should do it when he has proper justification and evident reason. But above all he must refrain from taking property, for men forget the death of a father more quickly than the loss of their patrimony. Further, causes for taking property are never lacking, and he who begins to live on plunder is always finding cause to seize what belongs to others. But on the contrary, reasons for taking life are rare and fail sooner.

But when a prince is with his army and has a great number of soldiers under his command, then above all he must pay no heed to being called cruel, because if he does not have that name he cannot keep his army united or ready for duty. It should be numbered among the wonderful feats of Hannibal that he led to war in foreign lands a large army, made up of countless types of men, yet never suffered from dissension, either among the soldiers or against the general, in either bad or good fortune. His success resulted from nothing else than his inhuman cruelty, which, when added to his numerous other strong qualities, made him respected and terrible in the sight of his soldiers. Yet without his cruelty his other qualities would not have been adequate. So it seems that those writers have not thought very deeply who on one side admire his accomplishment and on the other condemn the chief cause for it.

The truth that his other qualities alone would not have been adequate may be learned from Scipio,[8] a man of the most unusual powers not only in his own times but in all ages we know of. When he was in Spain his armies mutinied. This resulted from nothing other than his compassion, which had allowed his soldiers more license than befits military discipline. This fault was censured before the Senate by Fabius Maximus, and Scipio was called

---

8. Publius Cornelius Scipio Africanus the Elder (235–183 B.C.). The episode of the mutiny occurred in 206 B.C.

2528 / NICCOLÒ MACHIAVELLI

by him the corrupter of the Roman soldiery. The Locrians[9] were destroyed by a lieutenant of Scipio's, yet he did not avenge them or punish the disobedience of that lieutenant. This all came from his easy nature, which was so well understood that one who wished to excuse him in the Senate said there were many men who knew better how not to err than how to punish errors. This easy nature would in time have overthrown the fame and glory of Scipio if, in spite of this weakness, he had kept on in independent command. But since he was under the orders of the Senate, this bad quality was not merely concealed but was a glory to him.

Returning, then, to the debate on being loved and feared, I conclude that since men love as they please and fear as the prince pleases, a wise prince will evidently rely on what is in his own power and not on what is in the power of another. As I have said, he need only take pains to avoid hatred.

FROM CHAPTER 18

In What Way Faith Should Be Kept by Princes

Everybody knows how laudable it is in a prince to keep his faith and to be an honest man and not a trickster. Nevertheless, the experience of our times shows that the princes who have done great things are the ones who have taken little account of their promises and who have known how to addle the brains of men with craft. In the end they have conquered those who have put their reliance on good faith.

You must realize, then, that there are two ways to fight. In one kind the laws are used, in the other, force. The first is suitable to man, the second to animals. But because the first often falls short, one has to turn to the second. Hence a prince must know perfectly how to act like a beast and like a man. This truth was covertly taught to princes by ancient authors, who write that Achilles and many other ancient princes[1] were turned over for their upbringing to Chiron the centaur, that he might keep them under his tuition. To have as teacher one who is half beast and half man means nothing else than that a prince needs to know how to use the qualities of both creatures. The one without the other will not last long.

Since, then, it is necessary for a prince to understand how to make good use of the conduct of the animals, he should select among them the fox and the lion, because the lion cannot protect himself from traps, and the fox cannot protect himself from the wolves. So the prince needs to be a fox that he may know how to deal with traps, and a lion that he may frighten the wolves. Those who act like the lion alone do not understand their business. A prudent ruler, therefore, cannot and should not observe faith when such observance is to his disadvantage and the causes that made him give his promise have vanished. If men were all good, this advice would not be good, but since men are wicked and do not keep their promises to you, you likewise do not have to keep yours to them. Lawful reasons to excuse his failure to keep them will never be lacking to a prince. It would be possible to give innumerable modern examples of this and to show many treaties and promises that have been made null and void by the faithlessness of princes. And the prince who has best known how to act as a fox has come out best. But

9. Citizens of Locri, in Sicily.   1. E.g., Theseus, Jason, and Hercules.

one who has this capacity must understand how to keep it covered, and be a skilful pretender and dissembler. Men are so simple and so subject to present needs that he who deceives in this way will always find those who will let themselves be deceived.

I do not wish to keep still about one of the recent instances. Alexander VI[2] did nothing else than deceive men, and had no other intention; yet he always found a subject to work on. There never was a man more effective in swearing that things were true, and the greater the oaths with which he made a promise, the less he observed it. Nonetheless his deceptions always succeeded to his wish, because he thoroughly understood this aspect of the world.

It is not necessary, then, for a prince really to have all the virtues mentioned above, but it is very necessary to seem to have them. I will even venture to say that they damage a prince who possesses them and always observes them, but if he seems to have them they are useful. I mean that he should seem compassionate, trustworthy, humane, honest, and religious, and actually be so; but yet he should have his mind so trained that, when it is necessary not to practice these virtues, he can change to the opposite, and do it skilfully. It is to be understood that a prince, especially a new prince, cannot observe all the things because of which men are considered good, because he is often obliged, if he wishes to maintain his government, to act contrary to faith, contrary to charity, contrary to humanity, contrary to religion. It is therefore necessary that he have a mind capable of turning in whatever direction the winds of Fortune and the variations of affairs require, and, as I said above, that he should not depart from what is morally right, if he can observe it, but should know how to adopt what is bad, when he is obliged to.

A prince, then, should be very careful that there does not issue from his mouth anything that is not full of the above-mentioned five qualities. To those who see and hear him he should seem all compassion, all faith, all honesty, all humanity, all religion. There is nothing more necessary to make a show of possessing than this last quality. For men in general judge more by their eyes than by their hands; everybody is fitted to see, few to understand. Everybody sees what you appear to be; few make out what you really are. And these few do not dare to oppose the opinion of the many, who have the majesty of the state to confirm their view. In the actions of all men, and especially those of princes, where there is no court to which to appeal, people think of the outcome. A prince needs only to conquer and to maintain his position. The means he has used will always be judged honorable and will be praised by everybody, because the crowd is always caught by appearance and by the outcome of events, and the crowd is all there is in the world; there is no place for the few when the many have room enough. A certain prince[3] of the present day, whom it is not good to name, preaches nothing else than peace and faith, and is wholly opposed to both of them, and both of them, if he had observed them, would many times have taken from him either his reputation or his throne.

---

2. Pope from 1492 to 1503; father of Cesare Borgia.   3. Ferdinand II. In refraining from mentioning him, Machiavelli apparently had in mind the good relations existing between Spain and the house of Medici.

[*"Fortune Is a Woman"*]

FROM CHAPTER 25

The Power of Fortune in Human Affairs, and to What Extent She Should Be Relied On

It is not unknown to me that many have been and still are of the opinion that the affairs of this world are so under the direction of Fortune and of God that man's prudence cannot control them; in fact, that man has no resource against them. For this reason many think there is no use in sweating much over such matters, but that one might as well let Chance take control. This opinion has been the more accepted in our times, because of the great changes in the state of the world that have been and now are seen every day, beyond all human surmise. And I myself, when thinking on these things, have now and then in some measure inclined to their view. Nevertheless, because the freedom of the will should not be wholly annulled, I think it may be true that Fortune is arbiter of half of our actions, but that she still leaves the control of the other half, or about that, to us.

I liken her to one of those raging streams that, when they go mad, flood the plains, ruin the trees and the buildings, and take away the fields from one bank and put them down on the other. Everybody flees before them; everybody yields to their onrush without being able to resist anywhere. And though this is their nature, it does not cease to be true that, in calm weather, men can make some provisions against them with walls and dykes, so that, when the streams swell, their waters will go off through a canal, or their currents will not be so wild and do so much damage. The same is true of Fortune. She shows her power where there is no wise preparation for resisting her, and turns her fury where she knows that no walls and dykes have been made to hold her in. And if you consider Italy—the place where these variations occur and the cause that has set them in motion—you will see that she is a country without dykes and without any wall of defence. If, like Germany, Spain, and France, she had had a sufficient bulwark of military vigor, this flood would not have made the great changes it has, or would not have come at all.

And this, I think, is all I need to say on opposing oneself to Fortune, in general. But limiting myself more to particulars, I say that a prince may be seen prospering today and falling in ruin tomorrow, though it does not appear that he has changed in his nature or any of his qualities. I believe this comes, in the first place, from the causes that have been discussed at length in preceding chapters. That is, if a prince bases himself entirely on Fortune, he will fall when she varies. I also believe that a ruler will be successful who adapts his mode of procedure to the quality of the times, and likewise that he will be unsuccessful if the times are out of accord with his procedure. Because it may be seen that in things leading to the end each has before him, namely glory and riches, men proceed differently. One acts with caution, another rashly; one with violence, another with skill; one with patience, another with its opposite; yet with these different methods each one attains his end. Still further, two cautious men will be seen, of whom one comes to his goal, the other does not. Likewise you will see two who succeed with two different methods, one of them being cautious and the other rash. These results are caused by nothing else than the nature of the times, which is or is not in harmony with the procedure of men. It also accounts for what I have mentioned, namely, that two persons, working differently, chance to arrive at the same result; and that of two who work in the same way, one attains his end, but the other does not.

On the nature of the times also depends the variability of the best method. If a man conducts himself with caution and patience, times and affairs may come around in such a way that his procedure is good, and he goes on successfully. But if times and circumstances change, he is ruined, because he does not change his method of action. There is no man so prudent as to understand how to fit himself to this condition, either because he is unable to deviate from the course to which nature inclines him, or because, having always prospered by walking in one path, he cannot persuade himself to leave it. So the cautious man, when the time comes to go at a reckless pace, does not know how to do it. Hence he comes to ruin. Yet if he could change his nature with the times and with circumstances, his fortune would not be altered.

Pope Julius II proceeded rashly in all his actions, and found the times and circumstances so harmonious with his mode of procedure that he was always so lucky as to succeed. Consider the first enterprise he engaged in, that of Bologna, while messer Giovanni Bentivogli[4] was still alive. The Venetians were not pleased with it; the King of Spain felt the same way; the Pope was debating such an enterprise with the King of France. Nevertheless, in his courage and rashness Julius personally undertook that expedition. This movement made the King of Spain and the Venetians stand irresolute and motionless, the latter for fear, and the King because of his wish to recover the entire kingdom of Naples. On the other side, the King of France was dragged behind Julius, because the King, seeing that the Pope had moved and wishing to make him a friend in order to put down the Venetians, judged he could not refuse him soldiers without doing him open injury. Julius, then, with his rash movement, attained what no other pontiff, with the utmost human prudence, would have attained. If he had waited to leave Rome until the agreements were fixed and everything arranged, as any other pontiff would have done, he would never have succeeded, for the King of France would have had a thousand excuses, and the others would have raised a thousand fears. I wish to omit his other acts, which are all of the same sort, and all succeeded perfectly. The brevity of his life did not allow him to know anything different. Yet if times had come in which it was necessary to act with caution, they would have ruined him, for he would never have deviated from the methods to which nature inclined him.

I conclude, then, that since Fortune is variable and men are set in their ways, they are successful when they are in harmony with Fortune and unsuccessful when they disagree with her. Yet I am of the opinion that it is better to be rash than over-cautious, because Fortune is a woman and, if you wish to keep her down, you must beat her and pound her. It is evident that she allows herself to be overcome by men who treat her in that way rather than by those who proceed coldly. For that reason, like a woman, she is always

---

4. Of the ruling family Bentivogli. The pope undertook to dislodge him from Bologna in 1506. *Messer:* my lord.

the friend of young men, because they are less cautious, and more courageous, and command her with more boldness.

[The Roman Dream]

FROM CHAPTER 26

An Exhortation to Take Hold of Italy and Restore Her to Liberty from the Barbarians

Having considered all the things discussed above, I have been turning over
in my own mind whether at present in Italy the time is ripe for a new prince
to win prestige, and whether conditions there give a wise and vigorous ruler
occasion to introduce methods that will do him honor, and bring good to the
mass of the people of the land. It appears to me that so many things unite
for the advantage of a new prince, that I do not know of any time that has
ever been more suited for this. And, as I said, if it was necessary to make
clear the ability of Moses that the people of Israel should be enslaved in
Egypt, and to reveal Cyrus's greatness of mind that the Persians should be
oppressed by the Medes, and to demonstrate the excellence of Theseus that
the Athenians should be scattered, so at the present time, in order to make
known the greatness of an Italian soul, Italy had to be brought down to her
present position, to be more a slave than the Hebrews, more a servant than
the Persians, more scattered than the Athenians; without head, without government; defeated, plundered, torn asunder, overrun; subject to every sort
of disaster.

And though before this, certain persons[5] have showed signs from which it
could be inferred that they were chosen by God for the redemption of Italy,
nevertheless it has afterwards been seen that in the full current of action
they have been cast off by Fortune. So Italy remains without life and awaits
the man, whoever he may be, who is to heal her wounds, put an end to the
plundering of Lombardy and the tribute laid on Tuscany and the kingdom
of Naples, and cure her of those sores that have long been suppurating. She
may be seen praying God to send some one to redeem her from these cruel
and barbarous insults. She is evidently ready and willing to follow a banner,
if only some one will raise it. Nor is there at present anyone to be seen in
whom she can put more hope than in your illustrious House, because its
fortune and vigor, and the favor of God and of the Church, which it now
governs,[6] enable it to be the leader in such a redemption. This will not be
very difficult, as you will see if you will bring to mind the actions and lives
of those I have named above. And though these men were striking exceptions,
yet they were men, and each of them had less opportunity than the present
gives; their enterprises were not more just than this, nor easier, nor was God
their friend more than he is yours. Here justice is complete. "A way is just
to those to whom it is necessary, and arms are holy to him who has no hope

---

5. Possibly Cesare Borgia and Francesco Sforza, who were discussed earlier in the book.   6. Pope Leo
X (1475–1521) was a Medici (Giovanni de' Medici). *House:* of Medici. *The Prince* was first meant for
Giuliano de' Medici; after Giuliano's death it was dedicated to his nephew Lorenzo, later duke of Urbino.

save in arms."[7] Everything is now fully disposed for the work, and when that is true an undertaking cannot be difficult, if only your House adopts the methods of those I have set forth as examples. Moreover, we have before our eyes extraordinary and unexampled means prepared by God. The sea has been divided. A cloud has guided you on your way. The rock has given forth water. Manna has fallen.[8] Everything has united to make you great. The rest is for you to do. God does not intend to do everything, lest he deprive us of our free will and the share of glory that belongs to us.

It is no wonder if no one of the above-named Italians[9] has been able to do what we hope your illustrious House can. Nor is it strange if in the many revolutions and military enterprises of Italy, the martial vigor of the land always appears to be exhausted. This is because the old military customs were not good, and there has been nobody able to find new ones. Yet nothing brings so much honor to a man who rises to new power, as the new laws and new methods he discovers. These things, when they are well founded and have greatness in them, make him revered and worthy of admiration. And in Italy matter is not lacking on which to impress forms of every sort. There is great vigor in the limbs if only it is not lacking in the heads. You may see that in duels and combats between small numbers, the Italians have been much superior in force, skill, and intelligence. But when it is a matter of armies, Italians cannot be compared with foreigners. All this comes from the weakness of the heads, because those who know are not obeyed, and each man thinks he knows. Nor up to this time has there been a man able to raise himself so high, through both ability and fortune, that the others would yield to him. The result is that for the past twenty years, in all the wars that have been fought when there has been an army entirely Italian, it has always made a bad showing. Proof of this was given first at the Taro, and then at Alessandria, Capua, Genoa, Vailà, Bologna, and Mestri.[1]

If your illustrious House, then, wishes to imitate those excellent men who redeemed their countries, it is necessary, before everything else, to furnish yourself with your own army, as the true foundation of every enterprise. You cannot have more faithful, nor truer, nor better soldiers. And though every individual of these may be good, they become better as a body when they see that they are commanded by their prince, and honored and trusted by him. It is necessary, therefore, that your House should be prepared with such forces, in order that it may be able to defend itself against the foreigners with Italian courage.

And though the Swiss and the Spanish infantry are properly estimated as terribly effective, yet both have defects. Hence a third type would be able not merely to oppose them but to feel sure of overcoming them. The fact is that the Spaniards are not able to resist cavalry, and the Swiss have reason to fear infantry, when they meet any as determined in battle as themselves. For this reason it has been seen and will be seen in experience that the Spaniards are unable to resist the French cavalry, and the Swiss are overthrown by Spanish infantry. And though of this last a clear instance has not

---

7. Livy's *History* 9.1, para. 10.   8. Another allusion to Moses.   9. Perhaps another reference to Borgia and Sforza.   1. Sites of battles occurring between the end of the century and 1513.

been observed, yet an approach to it appeared in the battle of Ravenna,[2] when the Spanish infantry met the German battalions, who use the same methods as the Swiss. There the Spanish, through their ability and the assistance given by their shields, got within the points of the spears from below, and slew their enemies in security, while the Germans could find no means of resistance. If the cavalry had not charged the Spanish, they would have annihilated the Germans. It is possible, then, for one who realizes the defects of these two types, to equip infantry in a new manner, so that it can resist cavalry and not be afraid of foot-soldiers; but to gain this end they must have weapons of the right sorts, and adopt varied methods of combat. These are some of the things which, when they are put into service as novelties, give reputation and greatness to a new ruler.[3]

This opportunity, then, should not be allowed to pass, in order that after so long a time Italy may see her redeemer. I am unable to express with what love he would be received in all the provinces that have suffered from these foreign deluges; with what thirst for vengeance, what firm faith, what piety, what tears! What gates would be shut against him? what peoples would deny him obedience? what envy would oppose itself to him? what Italian would refuse to follow him? This barbarian rule stinks in every nostril. May your illustrious House, then, undertake this charge with the spirit and the hope with which all just enterprises are taken up, in order that, beneath its ensign, our native land may be ennobled, and, under its auspices, that saying of Petrarch may come true: "Manhood[4] will take arms against fury, and the combat will be short, because in Italian hearts the ancient valor is not yet dead."

2. Between Spain and France in April 1512.   3. Machiavelli was subsequently the author of the treatise *Art of War* (1521).   4. An etymological translation of the original *virtù* (from the Latin *vir*, "man"). The quotation is from the canzone *My Italy*.

LUDOVICO ARIOSTO
1474–1533

The *Orlando Furioso* (Orlando Gone Crazy), Ludovico Ariosto's seriocomic romance epic, is as witty and playful in tone as it is philosophically and politically serious. The most important achievement of Renaissance Italy's greatest poet, it is also a study in contrasts, at once brilliantly original and self-consciously derivative. Ariosto, like many Renaissance writers, made use of literary "imitation," the method of allusion and adaptation by which writers simultaneously composed original works and competed with their contemporaries and predecessors. While the best "imitations" can be read independently of the literary traditions they engage, their full dimensions emerge only in comparison with the literature they imitate, parody, and honor. Such a poem is *Orlando Furioso,* which blithely recycles classical, medieval, and contemporary texts yet is not hampered by its web of allusions. In his title, which recalls a popular romance epic, *Orlando in Love* (the *Orlando Innamorato* of Count Matteo Maria Boiardo), Ariosto announces his plan to outstrip other poets in the romance epic tradition: he will show how Orlando, under the influence of desire, crosses the line from love to lunatic frenzy. As the shift in title indicates, much of Ariosto's humor comes from placing heroes of the past in new and unexpected situations. Readers of this anthology have at their fingertips a wide range of Ariosto's favorite models for his witty, subtle, and often irreverent imitations: the works of Homer, Virgil, Ovid, St. Augustine, Dante, Boccaccio, and Petrarch as well as *The Song of Roland,* from which Ariosto's title hero ultimately derives. The *Orlando Furioso* is, in turn, itself a source of inspiration to such writers of the later Renaissance as Rabelais, Cervantes, Shakespeare, and Milton.

Ludovico Ariosto's life as a poet and diplomat was inextricably woven into the dramatic political career of the Este family of Ferrara. In 1485 Ludovico's father, Niccolò, moved his family to Ferrara, where he prospered in the service of Duke Ercole and pressed his reluctant son to study law. Ludovico preferred poetry and drama, and an apocryphal story told by his younger brother describes young Ludovico listening humbly while his father severely chastised him for laziness, only to light up joyfully when his father left the room and adapt the lecture to the needs of a comedy he was writing. When Ludovico gained court notice by performing in festivities given for the Sforza family in 1494, Niccolò released his son from legal studies and found him a tutor, the humanist Gregorio da Spoleto. In 1503 he entered the service of Ippolito d'Este, the warlike and profligate cardinal.

Ariosto assumed financial responsibility for his family when his father died in 1500, and his financial distresses at times interfered with his work on the *Orlando Furioso.* Cardinal Ippolito could be demanding and stingy, but he understood Ariosto's importance as a poet well enough to finance the publication of the first edition of the *Orlando Furioso* in 1516. When Ariosto refused to join him on a mission to Hungary in 1517, however, he fired the poet on the spot, and Ariosto transferred his services to the more cultured Duke Alfonso in 1518. In 1513 Ariosto had fallen in love with Alessandra Benucci, the great love of his remaining years. The financial strains that threatened Ariosto's family worsened when one of his cousins died intestate: Duke Alfonso appropriated the inheritance and, despite litigation, refused to reconsider his action. Alfonso was himself strapped for cash in his constant negotiations with the Venetian Republic, King Francis I of France, and Emperor Charles V to keep the pope from seizing Ferrara; his solution to Ariosto's financial woes was to make him governor of the bandit-infested Ganfagnana in 1522 (the year after the second edition of the *Orlando Furioso* appeared). In 1525, after begging for release from his onerous administrative duties, Ariosto returned to Ferrara, to Alessandra and his beloved son, Virginio, and to his poetic labors. He died in 1533 after seeing the final edition of the *Orlando Furioso* through publication in 1532.

Variety and broad scope are the hallmarks of the *Orlando Furioso.* The mood of the poem moves up and down the scale of genres, from epic fury to romance dalliance to pastoral repose, from tragedy to comedy, from panegyric (song of praise) to satire, and from the sublime to the grotesque. Characters within the poem also explore heights and depths: in a parody of Dante's pilgrimage through hell and purgatory to paradise in *The Divine Comedy,* the comic knight Astolfo visits hell but, finding the stench unbearable, heads upward to the earthly paradise at the highest point of the world (in Nubia) and finally leaves the terrestrial sphere to visit the moon. Range also characterizes the *Orlando Furioso's* geography, which stretches from France, Italy, Spain, Holland, England, Scotland, India, Tunisia, Libya, Syria, and Nubia to Byzantium and beyond. From these diverse countries come Christian and pagan knights who mingle and clash as they try to make names for themselves. The breadth of the *Orlando Furioso's* survey of Europe, the Levant, and the New World is matched by the depth of its scrutiny of human psychology and of the interior lives of its characters. During the course of the poem, its Christians and pagans, men and women, nobles and servants find themselves in wild adventures and compromising situations, which cause them to experience every passion dreamed of in the philosophy of Ariosto's day.

Wrath and desire are the passions Ariosto explores in greatest depth, and no character experiences them more violently than Orlando. For twenty-three cantos of the poem, he pursues his obsessive love for the beautiful Chinese princess, Angelica; at the poem's exact center, he enters into a frenzy of epic proportions (if not beyond). Although love madness is considered sacred by the Neoplatonic philosophers of Renaissance Italy, Orlando's "great folly" turns out to be profane. We might consider Orlando's love madness in light of Ariosto's many images of horsemen governing and giving way to impetuous horses that stand for the passions. In the allegory of the soul presented in Plato's dialogue the *Phaedrus*, Socrates describes the soul as three-part and compares it to a charioteer managing two contrasting horses, which represent the divine and physical dimensions of the charioteer's desire for a beautiful love object. Whereas one of the horses is easily restrained, well formed, and noble, the other is willful, misshapen, and lustful. If the charioteer attains the Platonic ideal and masters the stubborn wrath of the lustful horse, his love becomes holy. For Ariosto, however, passion brings less insight into spiritual matters than it brings ethical blindness and psychological confusion. When Orlando discovers that Angelica loves another man and that the pair have consummated their mutual passion, he experiences a "deep, bitter hate" and a "burning wrath" that ultimately render him more bestial than human. In fact, he comes to behave exactly like the lustful and rebellious horse in Plato's allegory. When he comes across Angelica, he gallops after her in an attempt to rape her, kill her, or eat her (it is hard to say which), but he lands on her horse after Angelica has fallen off: "He followed the steed across the bare sand, constantly gaining on her; now he could touch her . . . he had her by the mane . . . now by the bridle . . . at last he held her. / He seized her as gleefully as another man would a maiden." Crazed Orlando rides the poor beast to death and drags it yet farther; as Ariosto remarks, Angelica herself would have fared no better.

Orlando's story is not the sole, or even the most important, of Ariosto's tales; the poet weaves into a single tapestry an extraordinary range of story lines. The other story represented here is also of forbidden love. Narrated by Richardet, the twin brother of Ariosto's famous woman warrior, Bradamante, the tale recounts the passionate love that the Spanish princess Fiordispina conceived for Bradamante, whom Fiordispina had mistaken for a man. Poignantly, the discovery of Bradamante's true sex does nothing to alter the desire felt by Fiordispina, who finds herself much in the position of a heroine who appears much earlier in this anthology: Ovid's Iphis, the girl who is raised as a boy and who loves another girl (see vol. A, p. 1161). Like Ovid, Ariosto raises questions about love, sexuality, and gender that do not find easy resolution until the very end of the tale. Fiordispina's "cure"—if that is an appropriate term—ultimately comes from the narrator, Richardet. Disguising himself as his sister, he gains entrance to Fiordispina's palace and bedchamber, where he tells her a marvelous story one might expect of Ovid's tales of psychological and physical transformation: he assures Fiordispina that he is Bradamante, but a Bradamante changed from a woman to a man, and that he has returned to satisfy Fiordispina's every desire. The tale has all the characteristics for which Ariosto is celebrated as a poet and raconteur: charm, wit, and humor blend with searching and serious questions about human nature (especially in love) and its relationship to civic norms.

Important essays on Ariosto include Patricia Parker, *Inescapable Romance* (1970), A. Bartlett Giamatti, *The Earthly Paradise and the Renaissance Epic* (1966), and Robert M. Durling, *The Figure of the Poet in Renaissance Epic* (1965). A more specialized study can be found in Elizabeth J. Bellamy, *Translations of Power* (1992). Edmund Gardner, *Ariosto: King of Court Poets* (1906), remains the indispensable work on Ariosto's life and the Ferrarese court. Other useful readings are Elizabeth Chesney, *The Counter-Voyage of Rabelais and Ariosto* (1982), and Robert Griffin, *Ludovico Ariosto* (1974).

Orlando Furioso[1]

FROM CANTOS 23 AND 24

[Orlando's Great Madness]

Summary   Orlando, reputed to be the wisest and strongest of all knights in Christendom, has abandoned his duty to his lord and uncle, Charlemagne, to search for the woman he adores, the beautiful Angelica. For her part, Angelica has spent the entire poem fleeing from the many knights who pursue her until she finally stumbles upon a man who captures her own heart: the man is Medor, a beautiful young Arab whom Angelica finds wounded and close to death. As Angelica tends and cures the youth's wound, she discovers a love wound of her own, and the pair fall madly in love. We pick up the story at the moment the unfortunate Orlando chances upon the very place where Angelica and Medor had consummated their love.

* * *

He came to a stream which looked like crystal; a pleasant meadow bloomed on its banks, picked out with lovely pure colours and adorned with many beautiful trees.[2] / A welcome breeze tempered the noontide for the rugged flock and naked shepherd, and Orlando felt no discomfort, for all that he was wearing breastplate, helmet, and shield. Here he stopped, then, to rest— but his welcome proved to be harsh and painful, indeed quite unspeakably cruel, on this unhappy, ill-starred day. / Looking about him, he saw inscriptions on many of the trees by the shady bank; he had only to look closely at the letters to be sure that they were formed by the hand of his goddess. This was one of the spots described earlier, to which the beautiful damsel, Queen of Cathay, often resorted with Medor, from the shepherd's house close by. / He saw "Angelica" and "Medor" in a hundred places, united by a hundred love-knots. The letters were so many nails with which Love pierced and wounded his heart. He searched in his mind for any number of excuses to reject what he could not help believing; he tried to persuade himself that it was some other Angelica who had written her name on the bark. / "But I recognize these characters," he told himself; "I've seen and read so many just like them. Can she perhaps be inventing this Medor? Perhaps by this name she means me." Thus deceiving himself with far-fetched notions, disconsolate Orlando clung to hopes which he knew he was stretching out to grasp. / But the more he tried to smother his dark suspicions the more they flared up with new vigour: he was like an unwary bird caught in a web or in birdlime—the more he beats his wings and tries to free himself, the worse ensnared he becomes.

Orlando came to where a bow-shaped curve in the hillside made a cave overlooking the clear spring. / Twisting on their stems, ivy and rambling vines adorned the entrance. Here during the heat of the day the two happy lovers used to lie in each other's arms. Their names figured here more than elsewhere; they were inscribed within and without, sometimes in charcoal, sometimes in chalk, or scratched with the point of a knife. / The dejected count approached on foot. At the entrance he saw many words which Medor had written in his own hand; they seem to have been freshly

---

1. Translated by Guido Waldman.   2. The scene resembles that in a dream Orlando has had earlier in the romance.

inscribed. The inscription was written in verse and spoke of the great pleasure he had enjoyed in this cave. I believe it was written in his native
tongue; in ours this is how it reads: / "Happy plants, verdant grass, limpid
waters, dark, shadowy cave, pleasant and cool, where fair Angelica, born of
Galafron, and loved in vain by many, often lay naked in my arms. I, poor
Medor, cannot repay you for your indulgence otherwise than by ever praising you, / and by entreating every lover, knight, or maiden, every person,
native or alien, who happens upon this spot by accident or by design, to
say to the grass, the shadows, the cave, stream, and plants: 'May sun and
moon be kind to you, and the chorus of the nymphs, and may they see that
shepherds never lead their flocks to you.' " / It was written in Arabic, which
the count knew as well as he knew Latin. He knew many and many a
tongue, but Arabic is one with which he was most familiar: his grasp of it
had saved him on more than one occasion from injury and insult when he
was among the Saracens. But he was not to boast if formerly his knowledge
had helped him—the pain it now brought him quite discounted every former advantage. /

Five and six times the unfortunate man re-read the inscription, trying in
vain to wish it away, but it was more plain and clear each time he read it.
And each time, he felt a cold hand clutch his heart in his afflicted breast.
Finally he fell to gazing fixedly at the stone—stonelike himself. / He was
ready to go out of his mind, so complete was his surrender to grief. Believe
one who has experienced it—this is a sorrow to surpass all others. His chin
had dropped onto his chest, his head was bowed, his brow had lost its boldness. So possessed was he by sorrow that he had no voice for laments, no
moisture for tears. / His impetuous grief, set upon erupting all too quickly,
remained within. A broad-bellied, narrow-necked vase full of water has the
same effect, as can be observed: when the vase is inverted, the liquid so
surges to the neck that it blocks its own egress, and can scarcely do more
than come out drop by drop. / Returning to himself a little, he considered
how he might yet be mistaken about it: he hoped against hope that it might
simply be someone trying to besmirch his lady's name this way, or to charge
him with a burden of jealousy so unendurable that he would die of it; and
that whoever it was who had done this had copied her hand most skilfully. /
With such meagre, such puny hopes he roused his spirits and found a little
courage.

He mounted Brigliador, now that the sun was giving place to his sister in
the sky. Before he had gone far he saw smoke issuing from the housetops,
and heard dogs barking and cows lowing; he came to a farmhouse and found
lodging. / Listlessly he dismounted, and left Brigliador to the care of a discreet stable-boy. Others there were to help him off with his armour and his
golden spurs, and to refurbish them. This was the house where Medor lay
wounded, and met with his great good fortune. Orlando did not ask for
supper but for a bed: he was replete with sadness, not with other fare. / The
harder he sought for rest, the worse the misery and affliction he procured
himself—every wall, every door, every window was covered with the hateful
inscriptions. He wanted to make enquiries there, but chose to keep his lips
sealed: he was afraid to establish too clearly the very question he wanted to
cloud with mist so as to dull the pain. / Little good did it do him to deceive
himself; somebody there was to speak of the matter unasked. The herdsman,

who saw him so downcast and sad and wanted to cheer him up, embarked, without asking leave, upon the story of those two lovers: he knew it well, and often repeated it to those who would listen. There were many who enjoyed hearing it. / He told how at the prayer of beautiful Angelica he had brought Medor back to his house. Medor was gravely wounded, and she tended his wound, and in a few days had healed it—but Love inflicted upon her heart a wound far worse than his, and from a small spark kindled so blazing a fire that she was all aflame and quite beside herself; / and, forgetting that she was daughter of the greatest monarch of the East, driven by excessive passion, she chose to become wife to a poor simple soldier. The herdsman ended his story by having the bracelet brought in—the one Angelica had given him on her departure as a token of thanks for his hospitality. /

This evidence shown in conclusion proved to be the axe which took his head off his shoulders at one stroke, now that Love, that tormentor, was tired of raining blows upon him. Orlando tried to conceal his grief, but it so pressed him, he could not succeed: willy nilly the sighs and tears had to find a vent through his eyes and lips. / When he was free to give rein to his sorrow, once he was alone without others to consider, tears began to stream from his eyes and furrow his cheeks, running down onto his breast. He sighed and moaned, and made great circular sweeps of the bed with his arms: it felt harder than rock; it stung worse than a bed of nettles. / Amid such bitter anguish the thought occurred to him that on this very bed in which he was lying the thankless damsel must have lain down many a time with her lover. The downy bed sent a shudder through him and he leapt off it with all the alacrity of a yokel who has lain down in the grass for a nap and spies a snake aclose by. /

The bed, the house, the herdsman filled him on a sudden with such revulsion that, without waiting for moonrise, or for the first light preceding the new day, he fetched his arms and his steed and went out into the darkest, most tangled depths of the wood; when he felt he was quite alone, he gave vent to his grief with cries and howls. / There was no checking his cries and tears; night and day he allowed himself no respite. Towns and villages he avoided, and lay out in the open on the hard forest-floor. He wondered that his head could hold such an unquenchable source of water, and that he could sigh so much. Frequently as he wept he said to himself: / "These are no longer tears that drop from my eyes so copiously. The tears were not enough for my grief: they came to an end before my grief was half expressed. Urged by fire, my vital spirit is now escaping by the ducts which lead to the eyes: this is what is now spilling out, and with it my sorrow and my life will flow out at its last hour. / These sighs, which are a token of my anguish, are not truly sighs: sighs are not like this—now and then they will cease, but never do I feel a relaxing of my pain as my breast exhales it. Love, which burns my heart, makes this wind, beating his wings about the flames. By what miracle, Love, do you keep my heart ever burning but never consumed by fire? / I am not who my face proclaims me; the man who was Orlando is dead and buried, slain by his most thankless lady who assailed him by her betrayal. I am his spirit sundered from him, and wandering tormented in its own hell, so that his shade, all that remains of him, should serve as an example to any who place hope in Love." /

All night the count wandered in the wood; at sunrise, Fate brought him back to the spring where Medor had carved his inscription. To see his calamity written there in the hillside so inflamed him that he was drained of every drop that was not pure hate, fury, wrath, and violence. On impulse he drew his sword, / and slashed at the words and the rock-face, sending tiny splinters shooting skywards. Alas for the cave, and for every trunk on which the names of Medor and Angelica were written! They were left, that day, in such a state that never more would they afford cool shade to shepherd or flock. The spring, too, which had been so clear and pure, was scarcely safer from wrath such as his; / branches, stumps and boughs, stones and clods he kept hurling into the lovely waters until he so clouded them from surface to bottom that they were clear and pure never again. In the end, exhausted and sweat-soaked, his stamina given out and no longer answering to his deep, bitter hate, his burning wrath, he dropped onto the grass and sighed up at the heavens. / Weary and heart-stricken, he dropped onto the grass and gazed mutely up at the sky. Thus he remained, without food or sleep while the sun three times rose and set. His bitter agony grew and grew until it drove him out of his mind.

On the fourth day, worked into a great frenzy, he stripped off his armour and chain-mail. / The helmet landed here, the shield there, more pieces of armour further off, the breastplate further still: arms and armour all found their resting-place here and there about the wood. Then he tore off his clothes and exposed his hairy belly and all his chest and back.

Now began the great madness, so horrifying that none will ever know a worse instance. / He fell into a frenzy so violent that his every sense was darkened. He did not think to draw his sword, with which I expect he would have performed marvels. But in view of his colossal strength he had no need of it, nor of any hatchet or battle-axe. He now performed some truly astonishing feats: at one jerk he rooted up a tall pine, / after which he tore up several more as though they were so many celery-stalks. He did the same to oaks and ancient elms, to beech and ash-trees, to ilexes and firs. What a birdcatcher does when clearing the ground before he lays nets—rooting up rushes, brushwood, and nettles—Orlando did to oaks and other age-old timber. / The shepherds who heard the din left their flocks scattered through the woodland and hastened from all parts to this spot to see what was happening. But I have reached a point which I must not overstep for fear of boring you with my story; I should rather postpone it than annoy you by making it too long.

• • •

If you have put your foot in the birdlime spread by Cupid, try to pull it out, and take care not to catch your wing in it too: love, in the universal opinion of wise men, is nothing but madness. Though not everyone goes raving mad like Orlando, Love's folly shows itself in other ways; what clearer sign of lunacy than to lose your own self through pining for another? / The effects vary, but the madness which promotes them is always the same. It is like a great forest into which those who venture must perforce lose their way: one here, another there, one and all go off the track. Let me tell you this, to conclude: whoever grows old in love ought, in addition to Cupid's torments, to be chained and fettered. / "You, my friend, are preaching to others," someone will tell me, "but you overlook your own failing." The answer is that now, in an interval of lucidity, I understand a great deal. And I am taking pains (with imminent success, I hope) to find peace and withdraw from the dance—though I cannot do so as quickly as I should wish, for the disease has eaten me to the bone. /

In the last canto I was telling you, my Lord, how Orlando, crazed and demented, had torn off arms and armour and scattered them everywhere, ripped his clothes, tossed away his sword, rooted up trees, and made the hollow caves and deep woods re-echo. And some shepherds were attracted to the noise, whether by their stars, or for some wicked misdeed of theirs. / When they had a closer sight of the madman's incredible feats and his prodigious strength, they turned to flee, but without direction, as people do when suddenly scared. The madman was after them at once; he grabbed one and took off his head with all the ease of a person plucking an apple from a tree or a dainty bloom from a briar. / He picked up the heavy carcass by one leg and used it to club the rest; he laid out two, leaving them in a sleep from which perhaps they would awake on Judgement Day. The others cleared off at once: they were quickfooted and had their wits about them. The madman would not have been slow to pursue them, but he had now turned upon their flocks. /

In the fields the labourers, wise from the shepherds' example, left their ploughs, hoes, and sickles and scrambled onto the housetops or onto the church roofs—there being no safety up elm or willow tree. From here they contemplated the fearsome frenzy unleashed upon horse and oxen: they were shattered, battered, and destroyed by dint of punches, thumps, and bites, kicks and scratches. It was a fast mover who could escape him. / Now you could have heard the neighbouring farms resound with shouts, the shrill of horns, and rustic trumpets and, most persistently, the peal of clarions; you could have seen a thousand men streaming down from the hills, armed with pikes and bows, spears, and slings; as many more came up from the plain, ready to wage a peasant war against the madman. / Imagine waves, driven by the South Wind which earlier had been playful, breaking on the shore; the second wave is higher than the first, the third follows with greater force; and, each time, the water builds up more and seethes more widely across the beach. Thus did the pitiless mob increase, coming down from the hills and out of the valleys against Orlando. / Out of that disorderly throng ten he killed who came within his reach, and then another ten. This experiment made it clear that it was far safer to stand well away. No one was able to draw blood from his body; steel was powerless to strike and wound it—the King of Heaven had given him this endowment so as to make him guardian of His holy faith. / Had he been capable of dying, his life would have been in danger; he might have learned what it was to throw aside his sword and, unarmed, to overreach himself.[3]

Now having seen their every blow prove ineffective, the throng began to ebb. With no one left to confront him, Orlando made off and came to a hamlet. / Here he found not a soul, man or child, for everyone had abandoned the place in terror. There was plenty of food set out, humble fare of which shepherds partake. Spurred by hunger and frenzy, he made no distinction between bread and acorns but set to with his hands and teeth and devoured

3. Orlando's frenzy resembles that of Hercules, the strongest man in classical mythology.

whatever came first within reach, whether raw or cooked. / After this he roamed about the countryside, preying upon men and wild beasts. He would range through the woods catching fleet-footed goats and nimble fawns. Often he would fight with bears and boars, wrestling them to the ground bare-handed; often he filled his ravenous belly with their meat, carcass and all. / He roamed across the length and breadth of France, until one day he came to a bridge. Beneath it a broad, full river flowed between steep, craggy banks. Beside it there stood a tower commanding a sweeping view in all directions. What he did here you shall learn later on.

FROM CANTO 25

[Fiordispina's Love for Bradamant]

Summary In the following episode, the knight Ruggiero rescues a young man who looks identical to Ruggiero's own beloved Bradamant. After saving the young man from being burned at the stake by an angry mob, Ruggiero hears his story.

*   *   *

The sun had dipped his golden rays into the Western sea when victorious Ruggiero and the young man set out from the castle. /

When the youth was outside the gates with Ruggiero, he thanked him profusely and most gracefully: his benefactor had, after all, risked his life to save him without knowing who he was. He asked Ruggiero to divulge his name, as he wanted to know who it was to whom he owed such a debt of gratitude. / "I am looking at the comely face and beautiful figure of my Bradamant," Ruggiero mused, "but I do not hear the dulcet tones of her voice. And her words are not appropriate to thanking a faithful lover. If she really is Bradamant, how is it that she has so soon forgotten my name?" / To establish who it was, Ruggiero employed subtlety. "I have seen you somewhere before," he remarked, "but though I have pondered and racked my brains I cannot remember where it was. Will you remind me, then, if you can recollect? And do me the pleasure of telling me your name, so that I may know who it was whom I saved today from the pyre." /

"It could be that you have seen me before," replied the other, "but I cannot say where or when. I too wander about the world seeking high adventure. Perhaps it was a sister of mine you saw, one who wears armour and carries a sword at her side; we are twins from birth and look so alike that even our family cannot tell us apart. / You are not the first, nor the second, nor even the fourth to have mistaken us; neither our father, nor our brothers, nor even our mother who bore us at one birth is able to tell us apart. True, our hair used to mark a sharp difference between us when I wore my hair short and loose in the male fashion, while she wore hers long and coiled in a plait. / But one day she was wounded in the head (it would take too long to tell the story) and to heal her a servant of God cut her hair till it only half covered her ears. After that there was nothing to distinguish us beyond our sex and name: mine is Richardet, hers is Bradamant; we are brother and sister to Rinaldo. / And if it would not bore you to listen, I would tell you a story to amuse you—something that happened to me on account of my resemblance to her: at first it was rapture, but it ended in agony." Ruggiero, in whose ears no song was sweeter, no story dearer than one in which his lady featured, begged him to tell his story. /

"My sister had been wounded by a party of Saracens who had come upon her without a helmet, so she had been obliged to cut her long tresses if her dangerous head-wound was to heal. Now recently she happened to be travelling through these woods, her head shorn as I have said. / On her way she came to a shady spring and, being weary and dejected, she dismounted, took off her helmet and fell asleep in the tender grass. (I don't believe there can be a story more beautiful than this one.) Who should come upon her but the Spanish Princess Fiordispina, who had come into the woods to hunt. / When she saw my sister clad in armour all except for her face, and with a sword in place of a distaff, she imagined she was looking at a knight. After gazing awhile at her face and her manly build she felt her heart stolen. So she invited my sister to join the hunt, and ended by eluding her retinue and disappearing with her among the shady boughs. /

"Once she had brought her into a solitary place where she felt unlikely to be disturbed, little by little, by words and gestures she revealed that she was love-struck. With burning looks and fiery sighs she showed how consumed she was with desire. She paled and blushed and, summoning her courage, gave her a kiss. / It was clear to my sister that the damsel had illusions about her; my sister could never have satisfied her need and was quite perplexed as to what to do. 'My best course is to undeceive her,' she decided, 'and to reveal myself as a member of the gentle sex rather than to have myself reckoned an ignoble man'. / And she was right. It would have been a sheer disgrace, the conduct of a man made of plaster, if he had kept up a conversation with a damsel as fair as Fiordispina, sweet as nectar, who had set her cap at him, while like a cuckoo, he just trailed his wings. So Bradamant tactfully had her know that she was a maiden. / She was in quest of glory at arms, like Hippolyta and Camilla[4] of old. Born in Africa, in the seaside city of Arzilla, she was accustomed from childhood to the use of lance and shield. These revelations did not abate love-struck Fiordispina's passion one jot; Cupid had thrust in his dart to make so deep a gash that this remedy was now too late. / To Fiordispina my sister's face seemed no less beautiful for this, her eyes, her movements no less graceful; she did not on this account retrieve mastery over her heart, which had gone out to Bradamant to bask in her adorable eyes. Seeing her accoutred as a man, she had imagined that there would be no need for her passion to remain unassuaged; but now the thought that her beloved was also a woman made her sigh and weep and betray boundless sorrow. /

"Anyone who heard her tears and grieving that day would have wept with her. 'Never was any torment so cruel,' she lamented, 'but mine is crueller. Were it a question of any other love, evil or virtuous, I could hope to see it consummated, and I should know how to cull the rose from the briar. My desire alone can have no fulfilment. / If you wanted to torment me, Love, because my happy state offended you, why could you not rest content with those torments which other lovers experience? Neither among humans nor among beasts have I ever come across a woman loving a woman; to a woman another woman does not seem beautiful, nor does a hind to a hind, a ewe to a ewe. / By land, sea, and air I alone suffer thus cruelly at your hands—you have done this to make an example of my aberration, the ultimate one in your power. King Ninus' wife was evil and profane in her love for her son;

4. Virgil's Amazon warrior. *Hippolyta:* queen of the Amazons.

so was Myrrha, in love with her father, and Pasiphae with the bull. But my love is greater folly than any of theirs. / These females made designs upon the males and achieved the desired consummation, so I am told. Pasiphae went inside the wooden cow, the others achieved their end by other means. But even if Daedalus came flying to me with every artifice at his command, he would be unable to untie the knot made by that all-too-diligent Maker, Nature, who is all-powerful.'⁵ /

"Thus the fair damsel grieved and fretted and would not be assuaged. She struck her face and tore her hair and sought to vent her feelings against her own person. My sister wept for pity and felt embarrassed⁶ as she listened to her grieving. She tried to deflect her from this insane and profitless craving, but her words were in vain and to no effect. / It was help, not consolation, that she required and her grief only continued to increase. The day was now drawing to a close and the sun was reddening in the West; rather than spending the night in the woods it was time now to withdraw to some lodging. So the damsel invited Bradamant to this castle of hers not far away. / My sister was unable to refuse, so they came to the very spot where the wicked mob would have burned me to death had you not appeared. Here Fiordispina made much of my sister; she dressed her once more in feminine attire and made it plain to one and all that her guest was a woman. / Realizing how little benefit she derived from Bradamant's apparent masculinity, Fiordispina did not want any blame to attach to herself on her guest's account. In addition, she nurtured the hope that the sickness already implanted in her as a result of Bradamant's male aspect might be dispelled by a dose of femininity to show how matters really stood. /

"That night they shared a bed but they did not rest equally well. The one slept, the other wept and moaned, her desire ever mounting. And if sleep did occasionally press upon her eyelids, it was but a brief sleep charged with dreams in which it seemed to her that Heaven had allotted to her a Bradamant transformed into a preferable sex. / If a thirst-tormented invalid goes to sleep craving for water, in his turbid, fitful rest he calls to mind every drop of water he ever saw. Likewise her dreaming mind threw up images to requite her desires. Then she would wake and reach out, only to find that what she had seen was but an empty dream. / How many prayers and vows did she not offer that night to Mahomet and all the gods, asking them to change Bradamant's sex for the better by a clear and self-evident miracle! But she saw that all her prayers were vain; perhaps Heaven even mocked her. The night ended and Phoebus lifted his fair head out of the sea and gave light to the world. / With the new day they left their bed, and Fiordispina's pain was aggravated when Bradamant, anxious to be clear of her predicament, mentioned that she was leaving. As a parting gift, Fiordispina presented her with an excellent jennet, caparisoned in gold; also with a costly surcoat woven by her own hand. / Fiordispina accompanied her a step of the way then returned, weeping, to her castle, while my sister pressed on so hastily that she reached Montauban the same day. Our poor mother and we, her brothers, crowded

5. The entire speech is based on the soliloquy of Ovid's Myrrha, who loved her father (*Metamorphoses* 10). *King Ninus' wife*: Semiramis, Syrian queen who married her son. Pasiphae, wife of King Minos, loved a bull; Daedalus created the labyrinth in which Minos kept the Minotaur, the monstrous offspring of Pasiphae.   6. The Italian verb for Bradamant's emotional response, *é costretta*, indicates that she feels obliged or compelled to help Fiordispina rather than "embarrassed," as the translator puts it.

round her, rejoicing—for lack of news of her, we had been gravely anxious for fear she were dead. /

"When she removed her helmet we all stared at her cropped hair which previously had fallen about her neck; and the new surcoat she was wearing also caught our attention. And she told us all that had befallen her, from start to finish just as I've told you: how after she was wounded in the wood she cut off her fair tresses in order to be healed; / and how the beautiful huntress came upon her as she was by the spring; and how she took to her deceptive appearance and segregated her from her party. She did not pass in silence over Fiordispina's grief, and we were all filled with pity at it. She described how she lodged with her, and all she did until her return to our castle. /

"Now I had heard a great deal about Fiordispina, whom I had seen in Saragossa and in France. I had been much allured by her lovely eyes and smooth cheeks, but had not let my thoughts dwell upon her; to love without hope is idle dreaming. But, brought again so fully to the fore, she reawakened my passion at once. / Out of this hope, Love prepared bonds for me, having no other cord with which to capture me. He showed me how to set about obtaining what I wanted of this damsel. A little deception would procure an easy success: the similarity between my sister and myself had often deceived others, so perhaps it would deceive her too. / Shall I, shan't I? My conclusion was that it is always good to go in pursuit of one's pleasure. I did not divulge my thought to a soul, nor seek anyone's advice on the matter. When it was night, I went to where my sister had left her armour; I put it on and away I went on her horse without waiting for dawn to break. / I set off by night, with Cupid for guide, to be with lovely Fiordispina, and I arrived before the Sun had hidden his radiance in the sea. Happy the man who outstripped his fellows in bringing the news to the princess: as bearer of good tidings he could expect thanks and a reward from her. /

"They all of them took me for Bradamant—just as you did—the more so in that I had both the attire and the horse with which she had left the previous day. Fiordispina lost no time in coming out to meet me; she was so jubilant and affectionate, she could not possibly have shown greater pleasure and joy. / Throwing her graceful arms around my neck, she softly hugged me and kissed me on the lips. You can imagine after this how Love guided his dart to pierce me at the heart of my heart! She took me by the hand and quickly led me into her bedroom; here she would suffer none but herself to undo my armour, from helmet to spurs; no one else was to take a hand. / Next she sent for a dress of hers, richly ornate, which she herself spread out and put on me as though I were a woman; and she caught my hair in a golden net. I studied modesty in my glances, and none of my gestures betrayed my not being a woman. My voice might have betrayed me, but I controlled it so well that it aroused no suspicions. / Then we went into a hall crowded with knights and ladies who received us with the sort of honour paid to queens and great ladies. Here several times I was amused when certain men, unaware that my skirts concealed something sturdy and robust, kept making eyes at me. / When the evening was further advanced and the meal had been over for some while—the fare had been an excellent choice of what was then in season— Fiordispina did not wait for me to ask the favour which was the object of my visit, but invited me hospitably to share her bed for the night. /

"When the waiting-women and maidens, the pages, and attendants had withdrawn, and we were both changed and in bed, while the flaming sconces left the room bright as day, I said to her: 'Do not be surprised, my lady, at my returning to you so soon—perhaps you thought that you would not see me again for God knows how long. / First I shall tell you why I left, then why I have returned. Had I been able to abate your ardour by staying, I should have wanted to live and die in your service, and never for an hour be without you. But seeing how much pain my presence occasioned you, as I could do you no better service, I chose to leave. / Fate drew me off my path into the thick of a tangled wood, where I heard a cry sound close by, as of a damsel calling for help. I came running and found myself at the edge of a crystal lake where a faun had hooked a naked maiden in the water and was cruelly preparing to eat her raw. / I went over, sword in hand—only this way could I help her— and slew the boorish fisherman. Straight away she dived into the water and said: "It is not for nothing that you have saved me. You shall be richly rewarded and given as much as you ask for: I am a nymph and I live in this limpid lake. / I have the power to perform miracles, to coerce nature and the elements. Ask to the limits of my capabilities, then just leave it to me: at my singing the moon comes down from the sky, fire turns to ice, the air turns brittle, and with mere words I have moved the earth and stopped the sun." /

" 'I did not ask her for a hoard of treasure, or for power over nations, or for greater valour or might, or for honourable victory in every war. My only request was that she would show me some way I could fulfil your desire; I did not ask to achieve this in one way or in another, but left the method up to her own discretion. / Scarcely had I disclosed my wish than I saw her dive a second time, and for all reply to my request she splashed the enchanted water at me. The moment it touched my face I was quite transformed, I know not how. I could see, I could feel—though I could scarcely believe my senses—that I was changing from woman to man.[7] / You would never believe me, except that now, right away, you shall be able to see for yourself. In my new sex as in my old, my desire is to give you ready service. Command my faculties, then, and you shall find them now and ever more alert and bestirred for you.' Thus I spoke to her, and I guided her hand to test the truth for herself. /

"Imagine the case of a person who has given up hope of having something for which he craves; the more he bemoans his deprivation, the more he works himself into a state of despair; and if later he acquires it, he is so vexed over the time wasted sowing seed in the sand, and despair has so eroded him that he is dumbfounded and cannot believe his luck. / So it was with Fiordispina: she saw and touched the object she had so craved for, but she could not believe her eyes or her fingers or herself, and kept wondering whether she were awake or asleep. She needed solid proof to convince her that she was actually feeling what she thought she felt. 'O God, if this is a dream,' she cried, 'keep me asleep for good, and never wake me again!' /

"There was no roll of drums, no peal of trumpets to herald the amorous assault: but caresses like those of billing doves gave the signal to advance or

7. Richardet invents a fictional metamorphosis, which he bases generally on Ovid's tales, with specific allusions to the famous tales of Actaeon (who sees the goddess Diana naked and is metamorphosed into a stag when she sprinkles him with water) and Salmacis and Hermaphroditus (who together become the hermaphrodite).

to stand firm. We used arms other than arrows and slingstones; and I, without a ladder, leapt onto the battlements and planted my standard there at one jab, and thrust my enemy beneath me. / If on the previous night that bed had been laden with heavy sighs and laments, this night made up for it with as much laughter and merriment, pleasure and gentle playfulness. Never did twisting acanthus entwine pillars and beams with more knots than those which bound us together, our necks and sides, our arms, legs, and breasts in a close embrace. / It remained a secret between us, so our pleasure continued for a few months. But eventually someone found us out, so the matter became known to the king—to my undoing. You, who rescued me from his people who had lit the pyre in the square, you can understand the rest: but God knows what an ache I am left with." /

FROM CANTO 29

[Angelica Encounters Orlando]

*   *   *

But let us return to Orlando, who left the tower, river, and bridge behind him. / I should be mad if I undertook to relate each and every folly of Orlando, for they were so many, I wouldn't know when I should finish. But I shall select a few important ones, fit to be sung in verse and appropriate to my story. And I shall not pass in silence over his prodigious feat in the Pyrenees above Toulouse. / He had travelled a long way, prompted by his dire insanity; eventually he came up into the mountains which divide France from Spain. As he proceeded in the direction of the setting sun he came onto a narrow path overhanging a deep valley. / Here two young woodcutters found him on their path. They were driving before them a donkey laden with wood; one look at him told them that there were no brains in his head, so they shouted at him threateningly to go back or move aside and clear out of their way. / For all reply Orlando gave the donkey a petulant kick in the chest: there was nothing like it for sheer drive, and the beast rose into the air, so that to an observer he looked like a little bird on the wing, and landed on the top of a hill rearing up across the valley a mile or so away. Then he fell upon the two young men. /

One of them had better luck than sense: in a panic he hurled himself into the precipice which fell away twice a hundred feet. Half-way down he hit a soft, pliant, leafy bush, which, apart from some scratches to his face from its thorns, let him go safe and sound. / The other grasped a spur jutting from the rockface to scramble up it; he hoped, if he gained the top, to find safety from the madman—who did not, however, intend that he survive: he grabbed the fugitive by the feet as he was trying to climb up, and, extending his hands to arm's length, tore him in two, / the way one may see a man tear a heron or chicken apart to feed its warm entrails to a falcon or goshawk. How fortunate it was that the one who risked breaking his neck was not killed! He related this prodigy to others so that Turpin[8] came to hear of it and wrote it down for us. / This and many other fantastic feats he accomplished as he crossed the mountains.

---

8. Ariosto's fictional source.

After much wandering he finally descended Southwards towards Spain. He took his way along the sea-shore in the region of Tarragona and, as his compelling madness dictated, he chose to make his home on the beach; / to afford himself some protection from the sun he dug into the fine, dry sand. While he was here, fair Angelica and her husband chanced upon him. (As I told you earlier, they had come down to the Spanish shore from the mountains.) Now she came within an arm's length of him, not having yet noticed his presence. / It never crossed her mind that he might be Orlando: he had changed too much.

From the moment he was possessed by madness he had always gone naked, in the shade as in the sun. Had he been born in sunny Assuan or where the Libyan Garamants worship Ammon, or in the mountains at the source of the Nile his skin could not have been more deeply tanned. / His eyes were almost hidden in his face, which was lean and wizened; his hair was a matted, bristling mass, his bushy beard looked appalling and hideous. Angelica had no sooner set eyes on him than she turned back, quaking; quaking, she filled heaven with shrieks and turned to her escort for help. / When crazed Orlando noticed her he started to his feet to grab her—he took a liking to her delicate face and immediately wanted her. That he had once so loved and worshipped her was a memory now totally destroyed in him. He ran after her the way a hound pursues game. / Young Medor, seeing the madman in pursuit of his lady, charged at him on horseback and struck at him, finding his back turned. He expected to strike the head off his shoulders but found his skin as hard as bone, indeed harder than steel—Orlando was born under a spell of invulnerability. /

As he felt himself struck from behind, Orlando turned, clenching his fist, and, with a force beyond measure, punched the Saracen's horse. The blow landed on the steed's head, smashing it like glass, and killing him. On the instant, he turned away and chased after the fleeing Angelica, / who was frantically whipping and spurring on her mare—even had she flown faster than an arrow from a bow, the beast would have seemed slow for her present need. Then she remembered the ring[9] on her finger: this could save her, and she thrust it into her mouth. The ring, which had not lost its virtue, made her vanish like a flame puffed out. / Whether it was fright, or that she lost her seat while transferring the ring, or that the mare stumbled—I cannot say which was the reason—the moment that she put the ring into her mouth and hid her lovely face she pitched out of the saddle and landed on her back in the sand. / Had her fall landed her two inches closer, she would have collided with the madman and been slain by the impact alone. Great good fortune helped her at this point: as to the horse, she needs would have to help herself to another horse as she had done before—she was never to recover this one who was trampling the beach ahead of the paladin. / Do not fear: she will secure another.

Let us follow Orlando now, whose frenzied impetus was no whit dispelled with the vanishing of Angelica. He followed the steed across the bare sand, constantly gaining on her; now he could touch her . . . he had her by the mane . . . now by the bridle . . . at last he held her. / He seized her as gleefully as another man would a maiden. He adjusted the reins and headstall then

9. A magic ring that renders invisible the person who puts it in her or his mouth.

gained the saddle in one leap, only to drive her many a mile at a gallop restlessly hither and yon, never unharnessing her, never letting her taste grass or hay. / Wanting to jump a ditch, he landed in it upside down with the mare. He was unscathed—never felt a jolt—but the wretched beast threw out her shoulder. Seeing no way of pulling her out, he finally loaded her onto his shoulder, climbed out of the ditch and walked with his burden the length of three arrows' flights and more. / When she grew too heavy he set her down in order to lead her; she limped slowly after him. "Come on," he urged her, but he urged in vain: had the mare followed him at a gallop she would not have satisfied his crazy whim. In the end he slipped the halter from her head and tied it above her right hind hoof. / Thus he dragged her along, assuring her that this way she would be able to follow him more comfortably. The road was rough: one stone tore at her coat, the next at her skin, and finally the ill-used beast died from her lacerations and sufferings. Orlando spared her not a glance, not a thought: he pressed on at a run. /

Even when she was dead he did not stop dragging her as he continued his way Westward, sacking farms and houses as he went, whenever he felt the need for food. He seized fruit, meat, and bread which he guzzled, and overpowered everybody: some he left dead, others, maimed; he tarried little and kept pressing onwards. / He would have dealt scarcely more tenderly with his lady had she not hidden herself: he could not tell black from white and believed that his inflictions were a kindness.

A curse upon the ring, and upon the knight who gave it her—were it not for that, Orlando would at a stroke have been avenged on his own and on many another's account! / Would that not she alone but the whole surviving sex had fallen into Orlando's hands: they're a nasty tribe and not an ounce of good is to be found in any of them! But before my slackened strings produce a discordant note in this canto, I should do well to continue it later, lest it prove irksome to my listeners.

BALDESAR CASTIGLIONE
1478–1529

The cultivation of manners mattered enormously to the courts of sixteenth-century Europe, and no book shaped their ideal formulation more than Castiglione's *The Book of the Courtier* (1528), a dialogue on the qualities of the perfect courtier. Although set in Urbino, Italy, the *Courtier* quickly became a European phenomenon. The emperor Charles V was said to have especially loved three books: Machiavelli's *Discourses* on the Roman history of Titus Livy, the work of the ancient Greek historian Polybius, and Castiglione's *Courtier*. Henry VIII, Mary Queen of Scots, Catherine de Médicis, and Francis I owned copies in the Italian. Translations into Latin, then the universal language of diplomacy in Europe, allowed the *Courtier* to make a fully cosmopolitan appearance before the learned elite. More fascinating were the book's translations into the customs as well as the languages of different European states. In his 1561 English translation, Sir Thomas Hoby remarked that Castiglione's courtier "has a long time haunted all the courts of Christendom," and has now "become an Englishman . . . and willing to dwell in the Court of England." The *Courtier*'s popularity was by no means confined to princes, aristocrats, and the educated elite; by the end of the century, Castiglione's behavior manual could be found in the libraries of lawyers, physicians, merchants, and their wives.

Baldesar Castiglione, a nobleman from the region of Mantua in northern Italy, was born in Casanatico. His parents—his father was a courtier and mother a Gonzaga, related to the powerful Mantuan lords—sent him to Milan to be brought up in the spectacular court of Ludovico Sforza, who compensated for his upstart status by flamboyantly displaying his wealth and power. Castiglione served Francesco Gonzaga, marquis of Mantua, from 1499 until 1503, when he requested a transfer to the service of Guidobaldo da Montefeltro, duke of Urbino. In the court of Urbino, Castiglione served as a diplomat for Guidobaldo and later for his adopted heir, Francesco Maria della Rovere, commander of the pope's army. In 1506 he traveled to England to accept the Order of the Garter from Henry VII on behalf of Duke Guidobaldo. He later fought in the siege of Mirandola under Pope Julius II (1511) and, in reward for this and other services, was given the title of count. During the time he lived in Rome, as the Gonzaga family's ambassador to Pope Leo X, Castiglione made many friends, including the artists Michelangelo and Raphael, who painted a splendid portrait of Castiglione for his wedding.

Castiglione worked on the first draft of his *Courtier* during the years 1513–18. In 1516 Pope Leo X excommunicated Francesco Maria della Rovere and appropriated the dukedom of Urbino for his nephew. While Castiglione worked on the second draft of the *Courtier* in the early 1520s, he experienced a series of losses, including the deaths of his friend Raphael in April of 1520 and of his wife, who died in childbirth in August of the same year. In 1524 Pope Clement VII sent him to Spain as papal ambassador, or *nuncio*, to the court of the emperor Charles V. Castiglione was still jointly serving the pope and Charles V three years later when Charles marched through Italy and attacked and plundered Rome, to the horror of Europeans who venerated Rome as the eternal, unconquerable city. The shock and embarrassment to Castiglione, put in an impossible position between the pope and the emperor, cost him his health: despite receiving continued approval from both of his masters—he was even elected bishop of Ávila in Spain—Castiglione died in Toledo in 1529, one year after the *Courtier* appeared and two years after the sack of Rome. At his funeral, Charles V famously declared, "I tell you that one of the best knights (*caballeros*) of the world is dead."

In his letter to the bishop of Viseu, Castiglione explains that he was moved to write *The Book of the Courtier* when Duke Guidobaldo died: he wished to repay an emotional debt to the man who had fostered a court unmatched for its grace and distinction. The *Courtier* is an idealized commemoration of the court at Urbino. Divided into four books, it takes the form of a dialogue that took place over the four nights following a papal visit to Urbino, an occasion that gathered many illustrious courtiers and statesmen at the tiny court. Castiglione modestly exempts himself from the dialogue, which discusses the ideal qualities of the courtier, by claiming that he was in England at the time. Presiding silently over the conversation is the duchess, whose virtue and authority draw the company into what Castiglione calls the "golden chain of concord" that is their often contentious, if stylistically genial, conversation. The dialogue's form, as Castiglione takes pains to point out, has classical roots in Plato's *Republic* (the utopian city), Xenophon's *Education of Cyrus* (the ideal prince), and Cicero's *Orator* (the best speaker). Although the classical models help locate Castiglione's dialogue within moral and political philosophy, his text differs in important respects. Whereas Plato's Socrates and Cicero's orator hold forth as teachers to raptly attentive students, Castiglione's speakers insist on their own insufficiency and the superior qualifications of others in the company and must be cajoled or ordered to speak. When they reluctantly take up the authoritative position of speaker, it becomes obvious that they use the elaborate displays of diffidence and deference as a form of social armor: their speeches are usually greeted with a challenge. The speakers express dissent either laughingly, in the approved style, or if the spirit of rivalry momentarily overpowers their social decorum, with uncontrolled aggression. In such cases, Emilia Pia, the duchess's representative, teasingly reprimands the tactless speaker and guides the conversation back from dangerous extremes. As the *Courtier* unfolds, it becomes clear that the community, however affectionate, must constantly negotiate the differences and antipathies of class (the count differs with his social inferior on the importance of nobility in the ideal courtier), sex (the women at one point laughingly assault the group's most outspoken misogynist, or condemner of women), city-state (the Genoese republican and the citizen of a monarchy disagree about the ideal form of government), and religious temperament.

"Forming in words a perfect Courtier" is the object of the dialogue, or "game." Because the *Courtier* expresses great faith in the power of words to educate readers and create the ideal courtier, it has sometimes been criticized for its idealism, especially by those who prefer the prudential thought of Machiavelli's *The Prince*. In fact, the *Courtier* touches on both idealistic and prudential thinking and is ambivalent about surrendering to either a wholly optimistic (and potentially escapist) mode or a cynically pragmatic one. When Castiglione investigates political ethics, he avoids reaching a final resolution. He seems more comfortable describing the technical aspects of the ideal courtier's performance before admiring spectators, and he devotes lavish attention to their description. The courtier must above all be outstanding in combat and horsemanship. Nonetheless, the dialogue's most memorable and distinctive contribution to ideal courtiership is its elaboration of the social arts, in which the only thing worse than affectation is artlessness. Grace and lack of affectation are key words for the perfect courtier. So is *mediocrità*, which is not "mediocrity" but "moderation": it is the ability to avoid embarrassing or transgressive extremes and is associated with the "golden mean" of classical antiquity. For the courtier's defining word, *sprezzatura*, there is no adequate translation: it is the fine art of apparently effortless performance, or nonchalance. Etymologically related to the verbs *disdain* and *deprecate*, *sprezzatura* suggests that the most effective way to make an awe-inspiring impression is to appear utterly unconcerned about the performance and its effect on beholders. An example of *sprezzatura* is the response of one character, Unico Aretino, to a challenge. After a reflective silence, he utters a complete sonnet in praise of the duchess, leaving everyone to wonder: was his performance spontaneous or premeditated? *Sprezzatura* aims to keep them guessing and wanting more.

But the bright atmosphere of book 1 is darkened by brooding questions about the prince who is capable of making the courtiers' ornamental graces meaningful in the social world. Duke Guidobaldo, ill and crippled from venereal disease, retires nightly after supper: although he is physically absent from the conversation, his blighted promise and his sterility (the duchess, Castiglione says, lives like a widow) cast a gloomy shadow over the dialogue's optimism. The prince most frequently on the speakers' lips is Alexander the Great, the legendary world conqueror who did everything in extremes (especially fight and drink). Castiglione leaves ambiguous how the graceful courtier, trained in civil arts and *mediocrità*, relates to the immoderate, ambitious, bloodthirsty, and staggeringly successful Alexander. The courtier's precarious social position, especially in its contrasting relationship with Alexander, causes some of Castiglione's speakers to fret that his fine arts render him "effeminate." Throughout the dialogue, the courtier is framed between the imposing image of Alexander the Great and the vulnerable image of a woman. The courtier's grand achievement, his celebrated *mediocrità*, is also his social vulnerability.

Valuable and accessible studies of Castiglione are in Peter Burke, *The Fortunes of the Courtier: the European Reception of Castiglione's Cortegiano* (1995), and the essays in R. W. Hanning and David Rosand, eds., *Castiglione: the Ideal and the Real in Renaissance Culture* (1993). Of more specialized interest are Virginia Cox, *The Renaissance Dialogue: Literary Dialogue in its Social and Political Contexts, Castiglione to Galileo* (1992), and Wayne A. Rebhorn, *Courtly Performances* (1978). For an exciting, thorough discussion of Castiglione's broad historical context, see Lauro Martines, *Power and Imagination: City-States in Renaissance Italy* (1979).

PRONOUNCING GLOSSARY

The following list uses common English syllables and stress accents to provide rough equivalents of selected words whose pronunciation may be unfamiliar to the general reader.

Cesare Gonzaga: *chay'-zah-ray gon-zah'gah*

disinvoltura: *dees-een-vol-tuh'rah*

Gaspar Pallavicino: *gahs-pahr' pahl-lah-vee-chee'noh*

Giuliano de' Medici: *juh-lee-ah'noh day may'dee-chee*

roegarze: *roh-ay-gahr'tzay*

The Book of the Courtier[1]

[From *Book 1*]

To Messer Alfonso Ariosto[2]

*   *   *

[2]

On the slopes of the Apennines toward the Adriatic, at almost the center of Italy, is situated, as everyone knows, the little city of Urbino. And although it sits among hills that are perhaps not as pleasant as those we see in many other places, still it has been blessed by Heaven with a most fertile and bountiful countryside, so that, besides the wholesomeness of the air, it abounds in all the necessities of life. But among the greater blessings that can be claimed for it, this I believe to be the chief, that for a long time now it has been ruled by excellent lords (even though, in the universal calamity of the wars of Italy, it was deprived of them for a time).[3] But, to look no further, we can cite good proof thereof in the glorious memory of Duke Federico,[4] who in his day was the light of Italy. Nor are there wanting many true witnesses still living who can testify to his prudence, humanity, justice, generosity, undaunted spirit, to his military prowess, signally attested by his many victories, the capture of impregnable places, the sudden readiness of his expeditions, the many times when with but small forces he routed large and very powerful armies, and the fact that he never lost a single battle; so that not without reason may we compare him to many famous men among the ancients.

Among his other laudable deeds, he built on the rugged site of Urbino a palace thought by many the most beautiful to be found anywhere in all Italy and he furnished it so well with every suitable thing that it seemed not a palace but a city in the form of a palace; and furnished it not only with what is customary, such as silver vases, wall hangings of the richest cloth of gold,

---

1. Translated by Charles S. Singleton.   **2.** Ariosto (1475–1525) urged Castiglione to write the *Courtier* upon the suggestion of Francis I of France.   **3.** For a certain period of time, Duke Guidobaldo (1472–1508) had to relinquish the duchy of Urbino to Cesare Borgia, who occupied it by force.   **4.** Federico II (1422–1482), of the house of Montefeltro, duke of Urbino.

silk, and other like things, but for ornament he added countless ancient statues of marble and bronze, rare paintings, and musical instruments of every sort; nor did he wish to have anything there that was not most rare and excellent. Then, at great expense, he collected many very excellent and rare books in Greek, Latin, and Hebrew, all of which he adorned with gold and silver, deeming these to be the supreme excellence of his great palace.

[3]

Following then the course of nature and being already sixty-five years old,[5] he died as gloriously as he had lived, leaving as his successor his only son, a child ten years of age and motherless, named Guidobaldo. This boy, even as he was heir to the state, seemed to be heir to all his father's virtues as well, and in his remarkable nature began at once to promise more than it seemed right to expect of a mortal; so that men judged none of the notable deeds of Duke Federico to be greater than his begetting such a son. But Fortune, envious of so great a worth, set herself against this glorious beginning with all her might, so that, before Duke Guido had reached the age of twenty, he fell sick of the gout, which grew upon him with grievous pain, and in a short time so crippled all his members that he could not stand upon his feet or move. Thus, one of the fairest and ablest persons in the world was deformed and marred at a tender age.

And not even content with this, Fortune opposed him so in his every undertaking that he rarely brought to a successful issue anything he tried to do; and, although he was very wise in counsel and undaunted in spirit, it seemed that whatever he undertook always succeeded ill with him whether in arms or in anything, great or small; all of which is attested by his many and diverse calamities, which he always bore with such strength of spirit that his virtue was never overcome by Fortune; nay, despising her storms with stanch heart, he lived in sickness as if in health, and in adversity as if most fortunate, with the greatest dignity and esteemed by all. So that, although he was infirm of body in this way, he campaigned with a most honorable rank in the service of their Serene Highnesses Kings Alfonso and Ferdinand the Younger of Naples; and later with Pope Alexander VI,[6] as well as the signories of Venice and Florence.

Then when Julius II became Pope, the Duke was made Captain of the Church;[7] during which time, and following his usual style, he saw to it that his household was filled with very noble and worthy gentlemen, with whom he lived on the most familiar terms, delighting in their company; in which the pleasure he gave others was not less than that which he had from them, being well versed in both Latin and Greek and combining affability and wit with the knowledge of an infinitude of things. Besides this, so much did the greatness of his spirit spur him on that, even though he could not engage personally in chivalric activities as he had once done, he still took the greatest pleasure in seeing others so engaged; and by his words, now criticizing and now praising each man according to his deserts, he showed clearly how much judgment he had in such matters. Wherefore, in jousts and tournaments, in

---

5. Actually only sixty.   6. Rodrigo Borgia, pope from 1492 to 1503. *Rank*: as a mercenary captain, or *condottiere*. Alfonso II and Ferdinand II (both late 15th century), kings of Naples from the house of Aragon.
7. I.e., in the pontiff's army. Julius II became pope in 1503.

riding, in the handling of every sort of weapon, as well as in revelries, in games, in musical performances, in short, in all exercises befitting noble cavaliers, everyone strove to show himself such as to deserve to be thought worthy of his noble company.

[4]

Thus, all the hours of the day were given over to honorable and pleasant exercises both of the body and of the mind; but because, owing to his infirmity, the Duke always retired to sleep very early after supper, everyone usually repaired to the rooms of the Duchess, Elisabetta Gonzaga, at that hour; where also signora Emilia Pia[8] was always to be found, who being gifted with such a lively wit and judgment, as you know, seemed the mistress of all, and all appeared to take on wisdom and worth from her. Here, then, gentle discussions and innocent pleasantries were heard, and on everyone's face a jocund gaiety could be seen depicted, so much so that this house could be called the very abode of joyfulness. Nor do I believe that the sweetness that is had from a beloved company was ever savored in any other place as it once was there. For, not to speak of the great honor it was for each of us to serve such a lord as I have described above, we all felt a supreme happiness arise within us whenever we came into the presence of the Duchess. And it seemed that this was a chain that bound us all together in love, in such wise that never was there concord of will or cordial love between brothers greater than that which was there among us all.

The same was among the ladies, with whom one had very free and most honorable association, for to each it was permitted to speak, sit, jest, and laugh with whom he pleased; but the reverence that was paid to the wishes of the Duchess was such that this same liberty was a very great check; nor was there anyone who did not esteem it the greatest pleasure in the world to please her and the greatest grief to displease her. For which reason most decorous customs were there joined with the greatest liberty, and games and laughter in her presence were seasoned not only with witty jests but with a gracious and sober dignity; for that modesty and grandeur which ruled over all the acts, words, and gestures of the Duchess, in jest and laughter, caused anyone seeing her for the first time to recognize her as a very great lady. And, in impressing herself thus upon those about her, it seemed that she tempered us all to her own quality and fashion, wherefore each one strove to imitate her style, deriving, as it were, a rule of fine manners from the presence of so great and virtuous a lady; whose high qualities I do not now intend to recount, this being not to my purpose, because they are well known to all the world, and much more than I could express either with tongue or pen; and those which might have remained somewhat hidden, Fortune, as if admiring such rare virtues, chose to reveal through many adversities and stings of calamity, in order to prove that in the tender breast of a woman, and accompanied by singular beauty, there may dwell prudence and strength of spirit, and all those virtues which are very rare even in austere men.

*　　*　　*

8. Sister-in-law and companion of the duchess, she wittily directs much of the conversation. Gonzaga (1471–1526), daughter of Marguess Federico Gonzaga of Mantua, married Duke Guidobaldo in 1489; due to the frequent illness and retired life of her husband, the duchess was the central and presiding figure in the life of the court [Translator's note].

[14]

* * * "I[9] would have our Courtier born of a noble and genteel family; because it is far less becoming for one of low birth to fail to do virtuous things than for one of noble birth, who, should he stray from the path of his forebears, stains the family name, and not only fails to achieve anything but loses what has been achieved already. For noble birth is like a bright lamp that makes manifest and visible deeds both good and bad, kindling and spurring on to virtue as much for fear of dishonor as for hope of praise. And since this luster of nobility does not shine forth in the deeds of the lowly born, they lack that spur, as well as that fear of dishonor, nor do they think themselves obliged to go beyond what was done by their forebears; whereas to the wellborn it seems a reproach not to attain at least to the mark set them by their ancestors. Hence, it almost always happens that, in the profession of arms as well as in other worthy pursuits, those who are most distinguished are men of noble birth, because nature has implanted in everything that hidden seed which gives a certain force and quality of its own essence to all that springs from it, making it like itself: as we can see not only in breeds of horses and other animals, but in trees as well, the shoots of which nearly always resemble the trunk; and if they sometimes degenerate, the fault lies with the husbandman. And so it happens with men, who, if they are tended in the right way, are almost always like those from whom they spring, and often are better; but if they lack someone to tend them properly, they grow wild and never attain their full growth.

"It is true that, whether favored by the stars or by nature, some men are born endowed with such graces that they seem not to have been born, but to have been fashioned by the hands of some god, and adorned with every excellence of mind and body; even as there are many others so inept and uncouth that we cannot but think that nature brought them into the world out of spite and mockery. And just as the latter, for the most part, yield little fruit even with constant diligence and good care, so the former with little labor attain to the summit of the highest excellence. And take, as an example, Don Ippolito d'Este, Cardinal of Ferrara,[1] who enjoyed such a happy birth that his person, his appearance, his words, and all his actions are so imbued and ruled by this grace that, although he is young, he evinces among the most aged prelates so grave an authority that he seems more fit to teach than to be taught. Similarly, in conversing with men and women of every station, in play, in laughter, in jest, he shows a special sweetness and such gracious manners that no one who speaks with him or even sees him can do otherwise than feel an enduring affection for him.

"But, to return to our subject, I say that there is a mean to be found between such supreme grace on the one hand and such stupid ineptitude on the other, and that those who are not so perfectly endowed by nature can, with care and effort, polish and in great part correct their natural defects. Therefore, besides his noble birth, I would wish the Courtier favored in this other respect, and endowed by nature not only with talent and with beauty of countenance and person, but with that certain grace which we call an 'air,' which shall make him at first sight pleasing and lovable to all who see

9. The speaker is Count Ludovico da Canossa (1476–1532), a relative of Castiglione and friend of the painter Raphael. He was later a bishop and papal ambassador to England.   1. Ippolito d'Este (1479–1520), patron of Ludovico Ariosto, friend of Leonardo da Vinci, made a cardinal by Pope Alexander VI.

him; and let this be an adornment informing and attending all his actions, giving the promise outwardly that such a one is worthy of the company and the favor of every great lord."

[15]

At this point, without waiting any longer, signor Gaspar Pallavicino said: "So that our game may have the form prescribed and that we may not appear to esteem little that privilege of opposing which has been allowed us, I say that to me this nobility of birth does not seem so essential. And if I thought I was uttering anything not already known to us all, I would adduce many instances of persons born of the noblest blood who have been ridden by vices; and, on the contrary, many persons of humble birth who, through their virtue, have made their posterity illustrious. And if what you said just now is true, that there is in all things that hidden force of the first seed, then we should all be of the same condition through having the same source, nor would one man be more noble than another. But I believe that there are many other causes of the differences and the various degrees of elevation and lowliness among us. Among which causes I judge Fortune to be foremost; because we see her hold sway over all the things of this world and, as it seems, amuse herself often in uplifting to the skies whom she pleases and in burying in the depths those most worthy of being exalted.

"I quite agree with what you call the good fortune of those who are endowed at birth with all goodness of mind and body; but this is seen to happen with those of humble as well as with those of noble birth, because nature observes no such subtle distinctions as these. Nay, as I said, the greatest gifts of nature are often to be seen in persons of the humblest origin. Hence, since this nobility of birth is not gained either by talents or by force or skill, and is rather due to the merit of one's ancestors than to one's own, I deem it passing strange to hold that if the parents of our Courtier be of humble birth, all his good qualities are ruined, and that those other qualities which you have named would not suffice to bring him to the height of perfection; that is, talent, beauty of countenance, comeliness of person, and that grace which will make him at first sight lovable to all."

[16]

Then Count Ludovico replied: "I do not deny that the same virtues can rule in the lowborn as in the wellborn: but (in order not to repeat what we have said already, along with many further reasons which might be adduced in praise of noble birth, which is always honored by everyone, because it stands to reason that good should beget good), since it is our task to form a Courtier free of any defect whatsoever, and endowed with all that is praiseworthy, I deem it necessary to have him be of noble birth, not only for many other reasons, but also because of that public opinion which immediately sides with nobility. For, in the case of two courtiers who have not yet given any impression of themselves either through good or bad deeds, immediately when the one is known to be of gentle birth and the other not, the one who is lowborn will be held in far less esteem than the one who is of noble birth, and will need much time and effort in order to give to others that good impression of himself which the other will give in an instant and merely by being a gentleman. And everyone knows the importance of these impressions, for, to speak of ourselves, we have seen men come to this house who, though dull-witted and maladroit, had yet the reputation throughout Italy of being very great courtiers; and, even though they were at last discovered and known, still they fooled us for many days and maintained in our minds that opinion of themselves which they found already impressed thereon, even though their conduct was in keeping with their little worth. Others we have seen who at first enjoyed little esteem and who, in the end, achieved a great success.

"And there are various causes of such errors, one being the judgment of princes who, thinking to work miracles, sometimes decide to show favor to one who seems to them to deserve disfavor. And they too are often deceived; but, because they always have countless imitators, their favor engenders a great fame which on the whole our judgments will follow. And if we notice anything which seems contrary to the prevailing opinion, we suspect that we must be mistaken, and we continue to look for something hidden: because we think that such universal opinions must after all be founded on the truth and arise from reasonable causes. And also because our minds are quick to love and hate, as is seen in spectacles of combats and of games and in every sort of contest, where the spectators often side with one of the parties without any evident reason, showing the greatest desire that this one should win and the other should lose. Moreover, as for the general opinion concerning a man's qualities, it is good or ill repute that sways our minds at the outset to one of these two passions. Hence, it happens that, for the most part, we judge from love or hate. Consider, then, how important that first impression is, and how anyone who aspires to have the rank and name of good Courtier must strive from the beginning to make a good impression.

[17]

"But to come to some particulars: I hold that the principal and true profession of the Courtier must be that of arms; which I wish him to exercise with vigor; and let him be known among the others as bold, energetic, and faithful to whomever he serves. And the repute of these good qualities will be earned by exercising them in every time and place, inasmuch as one may not ever fail therein without great blame. And, just as among women the name of purity, once stained, is never restored, so the reputation of a gentleman whose profession is arms, if ever in the least way he sullies himself through cowardice or other disgrace, always remains defiled before the world and covered with ignominy. Therefore, the more our Courtier excels in this art, the more will he merit praise; although I do not deem it necessary that he have the perfect knowledge of things and other qualities that befit a commander, for since this would launch us on too great a sea, we shall be satisfied, as we have said, if he have complete loyalty and an undaunted spirit, and be always seen to have them. For oftentimes men are known for their courage in small things rather than in great. And often in important perils and where there are many witnesses, some men are found who, although their hearts sink within them, still, spurred on by fear of shame or by the company of those present, press forward with eyes shut, as it were, and do their duty, God knows how; and in things of little importance and when they think they can avoid the risk of danger, they are glad to play safe. But those men who, even when they think they will not be observed or seen or recognized by anyone, show courage and are not careless of anything, however slight, for which they could be blamed, such have the quality of spirit we are seeking in our Courtier.

"However, we do not wish him to make a show of being so fierce that he is forever swaggering in his speech, declaring that he has wedded his cuirass, and glowering with such dour looks as we have often seen Berto[2] do; for to such as these one may rightly say what in polite society a worthy lady jestingly said to a certain man (whom I do not now wish to name) whom she sought to honor by inviting him to dance, and who not only declined this but would not listen to music or take any part in the other entertainments offered him, but kept saying that such trifles were not his business. And when finally the lady said to him: 'What then is your business?' he answered with a scowl: 'Fighting.' Whereupon the lady replied at once: 'I should think it a good thing, now that you are not away at war or engaged in fighting, for you to have yourself greased all over and stowed away in a closet along with all your battle harness, so that you won't grow any rustier than you already are'; and so, amid much laughter from those present, she ridiculed him in his stupid presumption. Therefore, let the man we are seeking be exceedingly fierce, harsh, and always among the first, wherever the enemy is; and in every other place, humane, modest, reserved, avoiding ostentation above all things as well as that impudent praise of himself by which a man always arouses hatred and disgust in all who hear him."

[18]

Then signor Gasparo replied: "As for me, I have known few men excellent in anything whatsoever who did not praise themselves; and it seems to me that this can well be permitted them, because he who feels himself to be of some worth, and sees that his works are ignored, is indignant that his own worth should lie buried; and he must make it known to someone, in order not to be cheated of the honor that is the true reward of all virtuous toil. Thus, among the ancients, seldom does anyone of any worth refrain from praising himself. To be sure, those persons who are of no merit, and yet praise themselves, are insufferable; but we do not assume that our Courtier will be of that sort."

Then the Count said: "If you took notice, I blamed impudent and indiscriminate praise of one's self: and truly, as you say, one must not conceive a bad opinion of a worthy man who praises himself modestly; nay, one must take that as surer evidence than if it came from another's mouth. I do say that whoever does not fall into error in praising himself and does not cause annoyance or envy in the person who listens to him is indeed a discreet man and, besides the praises he gives himself, deserves praises from others; for that is a very difficult thing."

Then signor Gasparo said: "This you must teach us."

The Count answered: "Among the ancients there is no lack of those who have taught this; but, in my opinion, the whole art consists in saying things

2. An otherwise unidentified character.

in such a way that they do not appear to be spoken to that end, but are so very apropos that one cannot help saying them; and to seem always to avoid praising one's self, yet do so; but not in the manner of those boasters who open their mouths and let their words come out haphazardly. As one of our friends the other day who, when he had had his thigh run through by a spear at Pisa, said that he thought a fly had stung him; and another who said that he did not keep a mirror in his room because when he was angry he became so fearful of countenance that if he were to see himself, he would frighten himself too much."

Everyone laughed at this, but messer Cesare Gonzaga added: "What are you laughing at? Do you not know that Alexander the Great, upon hearing that in the opinion of one philosopher there were countless other worlds, began to weep, and when asked why, replied: 'Because I have not yet conquered one'—as if he felt able to conquer them all? Does that not seem to you a greater boast than that of the fly sting?"

Then said the Count: "And Alexander was a greater man than the one who spoke so. But truly one has to excuse excellent men when they presume much of themselves, because anyone who has great things to accomplish must have the daring to do those things, and confidence in himself. And let him not be abject and base, but modest rather in his words, making it clear that he presumes less of himself than he accomplishes, provided such presumption does not turn to rashness."

[19]

When the Count paused here briefly, messer Bernardo Bibbiena said, laughing: "I remember you said before that this Courtier of ours should be naturally endowed with beauty of countenance and person, and with a grace that would make him lovable. Now this grace and beauty of countenance I do believe that I have myself, wherefore it happens that so many ladies, as you know, are ardently in love with me; but, as to the beauty of my person, I am rather doubtful, and especially as to these legs of mine which in truth do not seem to me as well disposed as I could wish; as to my chest and the rest, I am quite well enough satisfied. Now do determine a little more in detail what this beauty of body should be, so that I can extricate myself from doubt and put my mind at ease."

After some laughter at this, the Count added: "Certainly such grace of countenance you can truly be said to have; nor will I adduce any other example in order to make clear what that grace is; because we do see beyond any doubt that your aspect is very agreeable and pleasant to all, although the features of it are not very delicate: it has something manly about it, and yet is full of grace. And this is a quality found in many different types of faces. I would have our Courtier's face be such, not so soft and feminine as many attempt to have who not only curl their hair and pluck their eyebrows, but preen themselves in all those ways that the most wanton and dissolute women in the world adopt; and in walking, in posture, and in every act, appear so tender and languid that their limbs seem to be on the verge of falling apart; and utter their words so limply that it seems they are about to expire on the spot; and the more they find themselves in the company of men of rank, the more they make a show of such manners. These, since nature did not make them women as they clearly wish to appear and be, should be treated not as good women, but as public harlots, and driven not only from the courts of great lords but from the society of all noble men.

[20]

"Then, coming to bodily frame, I say it is enough that it be neither extremely small nor big, because either of these conditions causes a certain contemptuous wonder, and men of either sort are gazed at in much the same way that we gaze at monstrous things. And yet, if one must sin in one or the other of these two extremes, it is less bad to be on the small side than to be excessively big; because men who are so huge of body are often not only obtuse of spirit, but are also unfit for every agile exercise, which is something I very much desire in the Courtier. And hence I would have him well built and shapely of limb, and would have him show strength and lightness and suppleness, and know all the bodily exercises that befit a warrior. And in this I judge it his first duty to know how to handle every kind of weapon, both on foot and on horse, and know the advantages of each kind; and be especially acquainted with those arms that are ordinarily used among gentlemen, because, apart from using them in war (where perhaps so many fine points are not necessary), there often arise differences between one gentleman and another, resulting in duels, and quite often those weapons are used which happen to be at hand. Hence, knowledge of them is a very safe thing. Nor am I one of those who say that skill is forgotten in the hour of need; for he who loses his skill at such times shows that out of fear he has already lost his heart and head.

[21]

* * * Then he went on: "Weapons are also often used in various exercises in time of peace, and gentlemen are seen in public spectacles before the people and before ladies and great lords. Therefore I wish our Courtier to be a perfect horseman in every kind of saddle; and, in addition to having a knowledge of horses and what pertains to riding, let him put every effort and diligence into outstripping others in everything a little, so that he may be always recognized as better than the rest. And even as we read that Alcibiades[3] surpassed all those peoples among whom he lived, and each in the respect wherein it claimed greatest excellence, so would I have this Courtier of ours excel all others in what is the special profession of each. And as it is the peculiar excellence of the Italians to ride well with the rein, to manage wild horses especially with great skill, to tilt and joust, let him be among the best of the Italians in this. In tourneys, in holding a pass, in attacking a fortified position, let him be among the best of the French. In stick-throwing, bull-fighting, in casting spears and darts, let him be outstanding among the Spaniards. But, above all, let him temper his every action with a certain good judgment and grace, if he would deserve that universal favor which is so greatly prized.

3. Athenian general and follower of Socrates.

[22]

"There are also other exercises which, although not immediately dependent upon arms, still have much in common therewith and demand much manly vigor; and chief among these is the hunt, it seems to me, because it has a certain resemblance to war. It is a true pastime for great lords, it befits a Courtier, and one understands why it was so much practiced among the ancients. He should also know how to swim, jump, run, throw stones; for, besides their usefulness in war, it is frequently necessary to show one's prowess in such things, whereby a good name is to be won, especially with the crowd (with whom one must reckon after all). Another noble exercise and most suitable for a man at court is the game of tennis which shows off the disposition of body, the quickness and litheness of every member, and all the qualities that are brought out by almost every other exercise. Nor do I deem vaulting on horseback to be less worthy, which, though it is tiring and difficult, serves more than anything else to make a man agile and dextrous; and besides its usefulness, if such agility is accompanied by grace, in my opinion it makes a finer show than any other.

"If, then, our Courtier is more than fairly expert in such exercises, I think he ought to put aside all others, such as vaulting on the ground, rope-walking, and the like, which smack of the juggler's trade and little befit a gentleman.

"But since one cannot always engage in such strenuous activities (moreover, persistence causes satiety, and drives away the admiration we have for rare things), we must always give variety to our lives by changing our activities. Hence, I would have our Courtier descend sometimes to quieter and more peaceful exercises. And, in order to escape envy and to enter agreeably into the company of others, let him do all that others do, yet never depart from comely conduct, but behave himself with that good judgment which will not allow him to engage in any folly; let him laugh, jest, banter, frolic, and dance, yet in such a manner as to show always that he is genial and discreet; and let him be full of grace in all that he does or says."

[23]

Then messer Cesare Gonzaga said: "Certainly no one ought to interrupt the course of this discussion; but if I were to remain silent, I should neither be exercising the privilege I have of speaking nor satisfying the desire I have of learning something. And I may be pardoned if I ask a question when I ought to be speaking in opposition; for I think this can be allowed me, after the example set by our messer Bernardo who, in his excessive desire to be thought handsome, has violated the laws of our game by asking instead of gainsaying."

Then the Duchess said: "You see how from a single error a host of others can come. Therefore, he who transgresses and sets a bad example, as messer Bernardo has done, deserves to be punished not only for his own transgression but for that of the others as well."

To this messer Cesare replied: "And so, Madam, I shall be exempt from penalty, since messer Bernardo is to be punished both for his own error and for mine."

"Nay," said the Duchess, "you both must be doubly punished: he for his own transgression and for having brought you to yours, you for your transgression and for having imitated him."

"Madam," answered messer Cesare, "I have not transgressed as yet; however, in order to leave all this punishment to messer Bernardo alone, I will keep quiet."

And he was already silent, when signora Emilia laughed and said: "Say what you will, for, with the permission of the Duchess, I pardon both the one that has transgressed and the one that is about to do so ever so little."

"So be it," the Duchess went on, "but take care lest you make the mistake of thinking it more commendable to be clement than to be just; for the excessive pardon of a transgressor does wrong to those who do not transgress. Still, at the moment, I would not have my austerity in reproaching your indulgence cause us not to hear messer Cesare's question."

And so, at a sign from the Duchess and from signora Emilia, he began forthwith:

[24]

"If I well remember, Count, it seems to me you have repeated several times this evening that the Courtier must accompany his actions, his gestures, his habits, in short, his every movement, with grace. And it strikes me that you require this in everything as that seasoning without which all the other properties and good qualities would be of little worth. And truly I believe that everyone would easily let himself be persuaded of this, because, by the very meaning of the word, it can be said that he who has grace finds grace. But since you have said that this is often a gift of nature and the heavens, and that, even if it is not quite perfect, it can be much increased by care and industry, those men who are born as fortunate and as rich in such treasure as some we know have little need, it seems to be, of any teacher in this, because such benign favor from heaven lifts them, almost in spite of themselves, higher than they themselves had desired, and makes them not only pleasing but admirable to everyone. Therefore I do not discuss this, it not being in our power to acquire it of ourselves. But as for those who are less endowed by nature and are capable of acquiring grace only if they put forth labor, industry, and care, I would wish to know by what art, by what discipline, by what method, they can gain this grace, both in bodily exercises, in which you deem it to be so necessary, and in every other thing they do or say. Therefore, since by praising this quality so highly you have, as I believe, aroused in all of us an ardent desire, according to the task given you by signora Emilia, you are still bound to satisfy it."

[25]

"I am not bound," said the Count, "to teach you how to acquire grace or anything else, but only to show you what a perfect Courtier ought to be. Nor would I undertake to teach you such a perfection; especially when I have just now said that the Courtier must know how to wrestle, vault, and so many other things which, since I never learned them myself, you all know well enough how I should be able to teach them. Let it suffice that just as a good soldier knows how to tell the smith what shape, style, and quality his armor must have, and yet is not able to teach him to make it, nor how to hammer or temper it; just so I, perhaps, shall be able to tell you what a perfect Courtier should be, but not to teach you what you must do to become one. Still, in order to answer your question in so far as I can (although it is almost proverbial that grace is not learned), I say that if anyone is to acquire grace in bodily exercises (granting first of all that he is not by nature incapable), he must begin early and learn the principles from the best of teachers. And how important this seemed to King Philip of Macedon can be seen by the fact that he wished Aristotle, the famous philosopher and perhaps the greatest the world has ever known, to be the one who should teach his son Alexander the first elements of letters. And among men whom we know today, consider how well and gracefully signor Galeazzo Sanseverino, Grand Equerry of France,[4] performs all bodily exercises; and this because, besides the natural aptitude of person that he possesses, he has taken the greatest care to study with good masters and to have about him men who excel, taking from each the best of what they know. For just as in wrestling, vaulting, and in the handling of many kinds of weapons, he took our messer Pietro Monte[5] as his guide, who is (as you know) the only true master of every kind of acquired strength and agility—so in riding, jousting, and the rest he has ever had before his eyes those men who are known to be most perfect in these matters.

[26]

"Therefore, whoever would be a good pupil must not only do things well, but must always make every effort to resemble and, if that be possible, to transform himself into his master. And when he feels that he has made some progress, it is very profitable to observe different men of that profession; and, conducting himself with that good judgment which must always be his guide, go about choosing now this thing from one and that from another. And even as in green meadows the bee flits about among the grasses robbing the flowers, so our Courtier must steal this grace from those who seem to him to have it, taking from each the part that seems most worthy of praise; not doing as a friend of ours whom you all know, who thought he greatly resembled King Ferdinand the Younger of Aragon, but had not tried to imitate him in anything save in the way he had of raising his head and twisting one side of his mouth, which manner the King had contracted through some malady. And there are many such, who think they are doing a great thing if only they can resemble some great man in something; and often they seize upon that which is his only bad point.

"But, having thought many times already about how this grace is acquired (leaving aside those who have it from the stars), I have found quite a universal rule which in this matter seems to me valid above all others, and in all human affairs whether in word or deed: and that is to avoid affectation in every way possible as though it were some very rough and dangerous reef; and (to pronounce a new word perhaps) to practice in all things a certain *sprezzatura* [nonchalance], so as to conceal all art and make whatever is done or said appear to be without effort and almost without any thought about it. And I

---

4. Of a famous Neapolitan family, he fought for Louis XII and Francis I of France and died at the battle of Pavia (1525).   5. Fencing master at the court of Urbino.

believe much grace comes of this: because everyone knows the difficulty of things that are rare and well done; wherefore facility in such things causes the greatest wonder; whereas, on the other hand, to labor and, as we say, drag forth by the hair of the head, shows an extreme want of grace, and causes everything, no matter how great it may be, to be held in little account.

"Therefore we may call that art true art which does not seem to be art; nor must one be more careful of anything than of concealing it, because if it is discovered, this robs a man of all credit and causes him to be held in slight esteem. And I remember having read of certain most excellent orators in ancient times who, among the other things they did, tried to make everyone believe that they had no knowledge whatever of letters; and, dissembling their knowledge, they made their orations appear to be composed in the simplest manner and according to the dictates of nature and truth rather than of effort and art; which fact, had it been known, would have inspired in the minds of the people the fear that they could be duped by it.

"So you see how art, or any intent effort, if it is disclosed, deprives everything of grace. Who among you fails to laugh when our messer Pierpaolo[6] dances after his own fashion, with those capers of his, his legs stiff on tiptoe, never moving his head, as if he were a stick of wood, and all this so studied that he really seems to be counting his steps? What eye is so blind as not to see in this the ungainliness of affectation; and not to see the grace of that cool *disinvoltura* [ease] (for when it is a matter of bodily movements many call it that) in many of the men and women here present, who seem in words, in laughter, in posture not to care; or seem to be thinking more of everything than of that, so as to cause all who are watching them to believe that they are almost incapable of making a mistake?"

6. Unidentified.

MARGUERITE DE NAVARRE
1492–1549

The French "discovered" Italy in the latter part of the fifteenth century, both through travel and, starting with the expedition of 1494 under King Charles VIII, through military invasions. Covetous of the fame and distinction enjoyed by the smaller and more sophisticated Italian city-states (such as Castiglione's Urbino), French rulers and aristocrats adapted Italian artistic, literary, and social values to their own culture. Marguerite de Navarre, one of the most influential members of French courtly society, played a significant part in bringing about this transformation of court culture. As a writer and a patron of artists, she also responded seriously to the spiritual and intellectual challenge to Christian faith brought about by the Reformation movements, including the Christian humanism associated with Erasmus.

Marguerite was born at Angoulême on April 11, 1492, the daughter of Charles of Orléans, count of Angoulême, and of Louise of Savoy. Her brother, the future King Francis I, was born two years later. From her earliest years, Marguerite received an exceptionally good education, including instruction in Latin, Italian, Spanish, and German; later in life she also studied Greek and Hebrew. Marriages in her class were at the time arrangements between ruling houses, dictated by political and social convenience; thus at seventeen she was married to Charles, duke of Alençon, a feudal lord who was culturally not her match. When her brother succeeded Louis XII to the French throne in 1515, Marguerite became one of the most influential women at the royal court, where she advised the king and received dignitaries and ambassadors as well as eminent men of letters. Under Francis I, the French court flourished culturally, bringing artists as famous as Leonardo da Vinci (1452–1519) and Benvenuto Cellini (1500–1571) to work in the court.

Francis I also inherited the military tradition of his predecessors in carrying on the Italian wars, the complicated conflicts fought on Italian soil between his forces and those of the Holy Roman Emperor, Charles V. His defeat in the crucial battle of Pavia in 1525 was a double blow for Marguerite: her brother was taken to Madrid as a prisoner and her husband, thought to be in part responsible for the defeat, died upon his return to France that same year. Marguerite went to Madrid to assist her sick brother and helped negotiate with Charles V for his release, which was sanctioned by the Treaty of Madrid in 1526.

The year following her husband's death, Marguerite became "queen of Navarre" when she married Henri d'Albret, the king of Navarre in title only, since most of that domain had been annexed by Spain in 1516, limiting the possessions of the d'Albret dynasty to the lower, French section. This region contained important castles at such places as Pau and Nérac, where Marguerite held court and received visiting intellectuals and reformist religious thinkers. Eleven years younger than Marguerite, Henri d'Albret was a dashing, flighty, and intellectually disappointing husband—and is thought to be the prototype for the philandering and misogynistic character of Hircan in the *Heptameron*. Their only daughter, Jeanne, born in 1527, was the mother of the future King Henry IV of France.

Marguerite continued to be involved in her royal brother's activities: in 1529 she took part in the negotiations that led to the Treaty of Cambrai and she participated in diplomacy and peace talks in the years 1536–38. Her interest, however, was increasingly focused on intellectual and literary pursuits and on religious meditation and debate. Erasmus, John Calvin, and Pope Paul III were among her numerous correspondents. Throughout her life she was a protector of writers and thinkers accused or suspected of Protestant leanings, including Rabelais, who dedicated the third book of *Gargantua and Pantagruel* to her. Her first published work, *The Mirror of the Sinful Soul* (1531), was found by the theologians of the Sorbonne to contain elements of Protestant "heresy"; the edition of 1533, containing an additional "Dialogue in the Form of a Night Vision" written earlier and dealing with the theological problem of salvation, was condemned. The king had to intervene on behalf of his sister and her chaplain. Later it became more difficult for Francis I to maintain a lenient and conciliatory stance in the rivalry between Catholics and Protestants, which was a political and military matter as much as it was a religious dispute. Protestants and their sympathizers were persecuted, and several prominent intellectuals went into prudent exile or were burned at the stake. Marguerite, who had an intellectual and mystical faith, appears never to have abandoned Catholicism but to have hoped for internal reform.

During the last part of her life, Marguerite took several retreats to the convent at Tusson in the French region of Poitou. There in April of 1547 she received news of her brother's death. In the same year she published her *Marguerite de la Marguerite des Princesses* (with a play on the word *marguerite*, which in French means both "pearl" and "daisy"), a collection including long devotional poems and theatrical pieces ranging from allegory to farce. Both in the collection and in later poems she returns to the theme of her sorrow at her brother's death, tempered by the solace of religious faith. During the following year Marguerite returned only for short periods to the French court, where her relations with her nephew, the new king, Henry II, were uneasy. In 1549 she retired to Navarre and died in the castle of Odos on December 21.

Marguerite's name is preeminently associated with the *Heptameron*, a collection of seventy stories organized into a series of ten tales told over seven days and framed by a larger narrative that reveals the storytellers' characters and relationships with each other. In the prologue, five men and five women are brought together in the Pyrenees, when natural and criminal forces—including a flood, bandits, a bear, and murderers—prevent them from returning home. They arrive independently at an abbey, where, at the suggestion of Parlamente, thought to represent Marguerite herself, they agree to tell stories each day until they are able to return home. Within the fiction, the stories are presented as a collective enterprise by courtly storytellers. The fictional situation may parallel the authorship of the *Heptameron* itself. We do not know the exact circumstances of its production: possibly Marguerite composed, collected, or commissioned tales for the narrative; perhaps she composed only the frame, which is in many ways the work's most compelling account of social and courtly relations. Critics' historical preference for single authorship over collaboration should not, at any rate, affect the pleasure or complexity one finds in the tales, their sequence, or the narrative framing them.

The stories largely deal with love, sexuality, clerical abuse in the Church, moderate struggles between social classes, and above all, the antagonism between the sexes, particularly concerning issues of marital fidelity and the status of women. The *Heptameron* pays considerable attention to ideas of masculinity and to ideals and stereotypes about women. Class tensions are somewhat more muted, but the conflicts between social superiors and inferiors are the same as those that emerge from the war between the sexes: the prerogative of powerful lords and husbands to license and dominance in social and marital contracts is set in conflict with the rights of those victimized to avenge their compromised honor, usually by cleverness. On these subjects, the men and women who narrate and hear the stories are, to say the least, unafraid to disagree with each other about the tales' significances, both in the dialogues of the frame and in their stories, which implicitly debate such issues as the appropriate evaluation of the philandering husband or the clever wife. Ennasuite, for example, uses her tale to celebrate a high-spirited, intelligent princess who physically resists and humiliates a gentleman who assaults her in her bedchamber. Hircan, on the other hand, retorts that Ennasuite's gentleman should have raped the princess rather than suffer humiliation and uses his own tale to present manly dominance—which characters like Ennasuite have been disparaging—in an attractive and romantic light.

The *Heptameron* belongs to a tradition of storytelling that includes the *Arabian Nights*, Chaucer's *Canterbury Tales*, and Boccaccio's *Decameron*. In the prologue, Parlamente overtly ties the storytelling game to the *Decameron* and a recent translation into French (commissioned by Marguerite) that drew, she says, the admiration of the French court, including Francis I, the Dauphin (heir to the throne), Queen Catherine de Médicis, and Marguerite. When the two women, along with other members of the court, propose to write a French *Decameron*, they agree to one difference from Boccaccio's precedent: "they should not write any story that was not truthful." The Dauphin (the future Henry II), moreover, rules out literary scholars on the grounds that "rhetorical ornament would in part falsify the truth of the account." The stories are, in fact, mysterious in origin, and with one exception, which the group approves after debate, none is drawn from a literary source.

The stipulation to relate only truthful stories identifies a dominant thematic concern of the *Heptameron*: the relationship between language and truth. For this overarching concern, there are two broad and largely irreconcilable frames of reference—one religious and the other social. In the prologue, when the travelers are considering how they should pass the time until they may safely return home, they acknowledge that the only means to calm their restless and dissatisfied souls is to devote themselves to the holy word of God as the only source of truth and consolation. Even Hircan, who places the most faith in his social position and manly self-assertion, indicates that he finds moments of solace in reading God's word, although he goes on to hint that he would choose the temporary solace of an adulterous conquest (like Petrarch, he "sees the better but chooses the worst"). Conversely, Oisille, the oldest and most evangelical of the group, chooses her strict regimen of religious study and devotion as the one "remedy"—of the many she has tried—for "boredom and . . . sorrow." Unable to "become so mortified in the flesh" as Oisille, however, the group desires a "pastime, which, while not being prejudicial to the soul, will be agreeable to the body." The conversation between Oisille and Hircan darkly suggests that to devote oneself entirely to spiritual contemplation is threatening to the young because it is tantamount to preparing oneself for death. Storytelling, then, is the group's concession to their social and physical needs: it is a middle ground between physical pleasures such as the adulterous liaison that Hircan contemplates and the worldly renunciation recommended by Oisille. The choice of strictly "truthful" stories emphasizes the group's compromise.

Yet the "truthfulness" of stories has little to do with the transcendent truth of God: as nonfiction, the tales instead heighten the social tensions that are frequently the themes of the characters' narratives. When the characters comment—in the frame and in their own stories—on each others' tales and motives for particular narrative choices, they reveal how social factors influence the ways in which they evaluate and interpret the world. Divine "truth" gives way to individual and social perspective: age, gender, social standing, education, marital status, and religious disposition form the grounds for rivalry and dispute among the group members. In this way, the *Heptameron* philosophically explores the relationship between fiction-making and spiritual knowledge at the same time that it presents a lively and complex portrait of the broad social and religious concerns entertained by the brilliant, aristocratic court to which Marguerite de Navarre belonged.

P. A. Chilton's justly praised translation of the *Heptameron* (1984) has an excellent introduction. John D. Lyons and Mary B. McKinley, eds., *Critical Tales: New Studies of the Heptameron and Early Modern Culture* (1993), contains useful essays on the *Heptameron*. B. J. Davis, *The Storytellers in Marguerite de Navarre's Heptameron* (1978), presents detailed discussions of the narrators, and Glyn P. Norton, "Narrative Function in the *Heptaméron* Frame-Story," in *La Nouvelle française à la Renaissance* (1981), analyzes the framing narrative. Marcel Tetel, *Marguerite de Navarre's Heptameron: Themes, Language, and Structure* (1973), is meant for the more advanced student. Samuel Putnam, *Marguerite de Navarre* (1935), is an informative and readable biography.

PRONOUNCING GLOSSARY

The following list uses common English syllables and stress accents to provide rough equivalents of selected words whose pronunciation may be unfamiliar to the general reader.

Alençon: *ah-lon-sohnh'*

Angoulême: *ahn-goo-lem'*

Cordeliers: *cohr-del-yay'*

Coucer: *coo-say'*

Dagoucin: *da-goo-sanh'*

d'Albret: *dahl-bray*

Ennasuite: *aw-nah-sweet'*

Gave de Pau: *gav deu poh*

Geburon: *zhay-byew-ronh'*

Grand-Maître de Chaumont: *grahn–metr' deu shoh-mon'*

Hircan: *eer'-canh*

lever: *leu-vay'*

Longarine: *lohn-gah-reen'*

Monseigneur the Dauphin: *mohnh-sen-yeur' leu doh-fanh'*

de Navarre: *deu na-vahr'*

Nomerfide: *noh-mehr-feed'*

Oisille: *wah-zee'*   serviteur: *sehr-vee-teur'*

Parlamente: *pahr-lah-mehnt'*   Simontaut: *see-mohn-toh'*

Sendras: *sawnh-dra'*

The Heptameron[1]

From *Prologue*

* * *

* * * Parlamente, the wife of Hircan,[2] was not one to let herself become idle or melancholy, and having asked her husband for permission, she spoke to the old Lady Oisille.[3]

"Madame," she said, "you have had much experience of life, and you now occupy the position of mother in regard to the rest of us women, and it surprises me that you do not consider some pastime to alleviate the boredom and distress that we shall have to bear during our long stay here. Unless we have some amusing and virtuous way of occupying ourselves, we run the risk of [falling][4] sick."

Longarine,[5] the young widow, added, "What is worse, we'll all become miserable and disagreeable—and that's an incurable disease. There isn't a man or woman amongst us who hasn't every cause to sink into despair, if we consider all that we have lost."

Ennasuite[6] laughed and rejoined, "Not everyone's lost a husband, like you, you know. And as for losing servants, no need to despair about that—there are plenty of men ready to do service! All the same, I do agree that we ought to have something to amuse us, so that we can pass the time as pleasantly as we can."

Her companion Nomerfide[7] said that this was a very good idea, and that if she had to spend a single day without some entertainment, she would be sure to die the next.

All the men supported this, and asked the Lady Oisille if she would kindly organize what they should do.

"My children," replied Oisille, "when you ask me to show you a pastime that is capable of delivering you from your boredom and your sorrow, you are asking me to do something that I find very difficult. All my life I have searched for a remedy, and I have found only one—the reading of holy Scripture, in which one may find true and perfect spiritual joy, from which proceed health and bodily repose. And if you ask what the prescription is that keeps me happy and

---

1. Translated by P. A. Chilton.   2. Hircan is variously described, in the book itself and by its commentators, as brilliant, flighty, sensual, capable of sarcasm and grossness. The name is related to Hircania, an imaginary and proverbially wild region in classical literature; the root is that of *hircus*, Latin for "goat" (cf. English *hircine*: libidinous). Parlamente probably represents Marguerite, whose name can be construed as *perle amante*, "loving pearl," or as *parlementer*, which refers to eloquent speaking.   3. The oldest, most authoritative, and most evangelical of the storytellers; she seems to be named for Louise—either Louise of Savoy, Marguerite's mother, or her lady-in-waiting, Louise de Daillon.   4. Brackets indicate translator's interpolations.   5. A young and wisely talkative widow, often identified with one of Marguerite's ladies-in-waiting, who among her titles had that of lady of Langrai (hence her name, which is also interpreted as a play on *langue orine*, meaning "tongue of gold").   6. *Enna* may stand for "Anne," and *suite* means "retinue"; so the character is identifiable with Anne de Vivonne, one of the ladies in Marguerite's entourage who collaborated on the *Heptameron* project at court. Her attitude toward men can be bitter and sharply ironical.   7. The youngest member of the group, who generally views life with joyful optimism.

healthy in my old age, I will tell you. As soon as I rise in the morning I take the Scriptures and read them. I see and contemplate the goodness of God, who for our sakes has sent His son to earth to declare the holy word and the good news by which He grants remission of all our sins, and payment of all our debts, through His gift to us of His love, His passion and His merits. And my contemplations give me such joy, that I take my psalter, and with the utmost humility, sing the beautiful psalms and hymns that the Holy Spirit has composed in the heart of David and the other authors. The contentment this affords me fills me with such well-being that whatever the evils of the day, they are to me so many blessings, for in my heart I have by faith Him who has borne these evils for me. Likewise, before supper, I withdraw to nourish my soul with readings and meditations. In the evening I ponder in my mind everything I have done during the day, so that I may ask God forgiveness of my sins, and give thanks to Him for His mercies. And so I lay myself to rest in His love, fear and peace, assured against all evils. And this, my children, is the pastime that long ago I adopted. All other ways have I tried, but none has given me spiritual contentment. I believe that if, each morning, you give one hour to reading, and then, during mass, say your prayers devoutly, you will find even in this wilderness all the beauty a city could afford. For, a person who knows God will find all things beautiful in Him, and without Him all things will seem ugly. So I say to you, if you would live in happiness, heed my advice."

Then Hircan spoke: "Madame, anyone who has read the holy Scriptures—as indeed I think we all have here—will readily agree that what you have said is true. However, you must bear in mind that we have not yet become so mortified in the flesh that we are not in need of some sort of amusement and physical exercise in order to pass the time. After all, when we're at home, we've got our hunting and hawking to distract us from the thousand and one foolish thoughts that pass through one's mind. The ladies have their housework and their needlework. They have their dances, too, which provide a respectable way for them to get some exercise. All this leads me to suggest, on behalf of the men here, that you, Madame, since you are the oldest among us, should read to us every morning about the life of our Lord Jesus Christ, and the great and wonderful things He has done for us. Between dinner and vespers I think we should choose some pastime, which, while not being prejudicial to the soul, will be agreeable to the body. In that way we shall spend a very pleasant day."

Lady Oisille replied that she herself found it so difficult to put behind her the vanities of life, that she was afraid the pastime suggested by Hircan might not be a good choice. However, the question should, she thought, be judged after an open discussion, and she asked Hircan to put his point of view first.

"Well, my point of view wouldn't take long to give," he began, "if I thought that the pastime I would really like were as agreeable to a certain lady among us as it would be to me. So I'll keep quiet for now, and abide by what the others say."

Thinking he was intending this for her, his wife, Parlamente, began to blush. "It may be, Hircan," she said, half angrily and half laughing, "that the lady you think ought to be the most annoyed at what you say would have ways and means of getting her own back, if she so desired. But let's leave on one side all pastimes that require only two participants, and concentrate on those which everybody can join in."

Hircan turned to the ladies. "Since my wife has managed to put the right interpretation on my words," he said, "and since private pastimes don't appeal to her, I think she's in a better position than anyone to know which pastime all of us will be able to enjoy. Let me say right now that I accept her opinion as if it were my own."

They all concurred in this, and Parlamente, seeing that it had fallen to her to make the choice, addressed them all as follows.

"If I felt myself to be as capable as the ancients, by whom the arts were discovered, then I would invent some pastime myself that would meet the requirements you have laid down for me. However, I know what lies within the scope of my own knowledge and ability—I can hardly even remember the clever things other people have invented, let alone invent new things myself. So I shall be quite content to follow closely in the footsteps of other people who have already provided for your needs. For example, I don't think there's one of us who hasn't read the hundred tales by Boccaccio,[8] which have recently been translated from Italian into French, and which are so highly thought of by the [most Christian] King Francis I, by Monseigneur the Dauphin, Madame the Dauphine[9] and Madame Marguerite. If Boccaccio could have heard how highly these illustrious people praised him, it would have been enough to raise him from the grave. As a matter of fact, the two ladies I've mentioned, along with other people at the court, made up their minds to do the same as Boccaccio. There was to be one difference—that they should not write any story that was not truthful. Together with Monseigneur the Dauphin the ladies promised to produce ten stories each, and to get together a party of ten people who were qualified to contribute something, excluding those who studied and were men of letters. Monseigneur the Dauphin didn't want their art brought in, and he was afraid that rhetorical ornament would in part falsify the truth of the account. A number of things led to the project being completely forgotten—the major affairs of state that subsequently overtook the King, the peace treaty between him and the King of England, the confinement of Madame the Dauphine and several other events of sufficient importance to keep the court otherwise occupied. However, it can now be completed in the ten days of leisure we have before us, while we wait for our bridge to be finished. If you so wished, we could go each afternoon between midday and four o'clock to the lovely meadow that borders the Gave de Pau, where the leaves on the trees are so thick that the hot sun cannot penetrate the shade and the cool beneath. There we can sit and rest, and each of us will tell a story which he has either witnessed himself, or which he has heard from somebody worthy of belief. At the end of our ten days we will have completed the whole hundred. And if, God willing, the lords and ladies I've mentioned find our endeavors worthy of their attention, we shall make them a present of them when we get back, instead of the usual statuettes and beads. I'm sure they would find that preferable. In spite of all this, if any of you is able to think of something more agreeable, I shall gladly bow to his or her opinion."

But every one of them replied that it would be impossible to think of anything better, and that they could hardly wait for the morrow. So the day came happily to a close with reminiscences of things they had all experienced in their time.

As soon as morning came they all went into Madame Oisille's room, where she was already at her prayers. When they had listened for a good hour to the lesson she had to read them, and then devoutly heard mass, they went, at ten o'clock, to dine, after which they retired to their separate rooms to attend to what they had to do. At midday they all went back as arranged to the meadow, which was looking so beautiful and fair that it would take a Boccaccio to describe it as it really was. Enough for us to say that a more beautiful meadow there never was seen. When they were all seated on the grass, so green and soft that there was no need for carpets or cushions, Simontaut[1] said: "Which of us shall be [the one in charge]?"

"Since you have spoken first," replied Hircan, "it should be you who give the orders. Where games are concerned everybody is equal."

"Would to God," sighed Simontaut, "that the one thing in all the world I had were the power to order everyone in our party to comply with my wishes!"

Parlamente knew very well what he meant by this remark, and started to cough. Hircan did not notice the colour rising in her cheeks, and simply went on to invite Simontaut to start, which he did at once.

"Ladies, I have been so ill rewarded for my long and devoted service, that, in order to avenge myself on Love and on the woman who is so cruel to me, I shall do my utmost to collect together all the accounts of foul deeds perpetrated by women on us poor men. And every single one will be the unadulterated truth."

From *Day One*

STORY THREE

I've often wished, Ladies, that I'd been able to share the good fortune of the man in the story I'm about to tell you.[2]

So here it is. In the town of Naples in the time of King Alfonso[3] (whose well-known lasciviousness was, one might say, the very sceptre by which he ruled) there lived a nobleman—a handsome, upright and likeable man, a man indeed whose qualities were so excellent that a certain old gentleman granted him the hand of his daughter. In beauty and charm she was in every way her husband's equal, and they lived in deep mutual affection until a carnival, in the course of which the King disguised himself and went round all the houses in the town, where the people vied with one another to give him a good reception. When he came to the house of the gentleman I have referred to, he was entertained more lavishly than in any of the other houses. Preserves, minstrels, music—all were laid before him, but above all there

---

1. Identified with François de Bourdeille, the husband of Anne of Vivonne. He is the long-standing *serviteur* to Parlamente: "According to the *serviteur*'s practice, as the *Heptameron* presents it, a married aristocratic woman has the right to maintain several devoted knights in her service. . . . Since it is supposed to be chaste, the *serviteur*'s relationship, this remnant of courtly and chivalrous love, can coexist with faithful marriage. . . . Nevertheless, there is evidently considerable anxiety about the institution as such" [From the translator's introduction]. His name punningly alludes to masculinity (*monte haut*: rises high). 2. The narrator is Saffredent, one of the younger members of the party, fond of company and pleasure, and a devoted admirer of Parlamente. He is often identified with an Admiral Bonnivet whom Marguerite knew well and some of whose amorous adventures are the subject of other stories in the *Heptameron*. 3. Alfonso V of Aragon (1396–1458), the cultivated and unfaithful husband of Maria, daughter of King Henry III of Castile.

was the presence of the most beautiful lady that the King had ever seen. At the end of the banquet, the lady sang for the King with her husband, and so sweetly did she sing that her beauty was more than ever enhanced. Seeing such physical perfection, the King took less delight in contemplating the gentle harmony that existed between the lady and her husband, than he did in speculating as to how he might go about spoiling it. The great obstacle to his desires was the evident deep mutual love between them, and so, for the time being, he kept his passion hidden and as secret as he could. But in order to obtain at least some relief for his feelings, he held a series of banquets for the lords and ladies of Naples, to which he did not, of course, omit to invite the gentleman and his fair wife.

As everyone knows, men see and believe just what they want to, and the King thought he caught something in the lady's eyes which augured well— if only the husband were not in the way. To find out if his surmise was correct, therefore, he sent the husband off for two or three weeks to attend to some business in Rome. Up till then the wife had never had him out of her sight, and she was heartbroken the moment he walked out of the door. The King took the opportunity to console her as often as possible, showering blandishments and gifts of all kinds upon her, with the result that in the end she felt not only consoled, but even content in her husband's absence. Before the three weeks were up she had fallen so much in love with the King that she was every bit as upset about her husband's imminent return as she had been about his departure. So, in order that she should not be deprived of the King after her husband's return, it was agreed that she would let her royal lover know whenever her husband was going to his estates in the country. He could then come to see her without running any risks, and in complete secrecy, so that her honour and reputation—which gave her more concern than her conscience—could not possibly be damaged in any way.

Dwelling on the prospect of the King's visits with considerable pleasure, the lady gave her husband such an affectionate reception that, although he had heard during his absence that the King had been paying her a lot of attention, he had not the slightest suspicion of how far things had gone. However, the fire of passion cannot be concealed for long, and as time went by its flames began to be somewhat obvious. He naturally began to guess at the truth, and kept a close watch on his wife until there was no longer any room for doubt. But he decided to keep quiet about it, because he was afraid that if he let on that he knew, he might suffer even worse things at the hands of the King than he had already. He considered, in short, that it was better to put up with the affront, than to risk his life for the sake of a woman who apparently no longer loved him. He was, all the same, angry and bitter, and determined to get his own back if at all possible.

Now he was well aware of the fact that bitterness and jealousy can drive women to do things that love alone will never make them do, and that this is particularly true of women with strong feelings and high principles of honour. So one day, while he was conversing with the Queen, he made so bold as to say that he felt very sorry for her when he saw how little the King really loved her. The Queen had heard all about the affair between the King and the gentleman's wife, and merely replied:

"I do not expect to be able to combine both honour and pleasure in my position. I am perfectly well aware that while I receive honour and respect, it is *she* who has all the pleasure. But then, I know too that while she may have the pleasure, she does not receive the honour and respect."

He knew, of course, to whom she was referring, and this was his reply: "Madame, you were born to honour and respect. You are after all of such high birth that, being queen or being empress could scarcely add to your nobility. But you are also beautiful, charming and refined, and you deserve to have your pleasures as well. The woman who is depriving you of those pleasures which are yours by right, is in fact doing herself more harm—because her moment of glory will eventually turn to shame and she will forfeit as much pleasure as she, you or any woman in the Kingdom of Naples could ever have. And if I may say so, Madame, if the King didn't have a crown on his head, he wouldn't have the slightest advantage over me as far as giving pleasure to ladies is concerned. What is more, I'm quite sure that in order to satisfy a refined person such as yourself, he really ought to be wishing he could exchange his constitution for one more like my own!"

The Queen laughed, and said: "The King may have a more delicate constitution than your own. Even so, the love which he bears me gives me so much satisfaction that I prefer it to all else."

"Madame, if that were the case, then I would not feel so sorry for you, because I know that you would derive great happiness from the pure love you feel within you, if it were matched by an equally pure love on the part of the King. But God has denied you this, in order that you should not find in this man the answer to all your wants and so make him your god on earth."

"I admit," said the Queen, "that my love for him is so deep that you will never find its like, wherever you may look."

"Forgive me," said the gentlemen, "but there are hearts whose love you've never sounded. May I be so bold as to tell you that there is a certain person who loves you, and loves you so deeply and so desperately, that in comparison your love for the King is as nothing? And his love grows and goes on growing in proportion as he sees the King's love for you diminishing. So, if it were, Madame, to please you, and you were to receive his love, you would be more than compensated for all that you have lost."

The Queen began to realize, both from what he was saying, and from the expression on his face, that he was speaking from the depths of his heart. She remembered that he had some time ago sought to do her service,[4] and that he had felt so deeply about it that he had become quite melancholy. At the time she had assumed the cause of his mood lay with his wife, but she was now quite convinced that the real reason was his love for her. Love is a powerful force, and will make itself felt whenever it is more than mere pretence, and it was this powerful force that now made her certain of what remained hidden from the rest of the world. She looked at him again. He was certainly more attractive than her husband. He had been left by his wife, too, just as she had been left by the King. Tormented by jealousy and bitterness, allured by the gentleman's passion, she sighed, tears came to her eyes, and she began: "Oh God! Must it take the desire for revenge to drive me to do what love alone would never have driven me to?"

Her words were not lost on the gentleman who replied: "Madame, vengeance is sweet indeed, when instead of taking one's enemy's life, one gives

---

4. I.e., become her *serviteur*. See n. 1, p. 2571.

life to a lover who is true. It is time, I think, that the truth freed you from this foolish love for a man who certainly has no love for you. It is time that a just and reasonable love banished from you these fears that so ill become one whose spirit is so strong and so virtuous. Why hesitate, Madame? Let us set aside rank and station. Let us look upon ourselves as a man and a woman, as the two most wronged people in the world, as two people who have been betrayed and mocked by those whom we loved with all our hearts. Let us, Madame, take our revenge, not in order to punish them as they deserve, but in order to do justice to our love. My love for you is unbearable. If it is not requited I shall die. Unless your heart is as hard as diamond or as stone, it is impossible that you should not feel some spark from this fire that burns the more fiercely within me the more I try to stifle it. I am dying for love of you! And if that cannot move you to take pity on me and grant me your love, then at least your own love for yourself must surely force you to do so. For you, who are so perfect that you merit the devotion of all the honourable and worthy men in all the world, have been despised and deserted by the very man for whose sake you have disdained all others!"

At this speech the Queen was quite beside herself. Lest her face betray the turmoil of her mind, she took his arm and led him into the garden adjoining her room. For a long time she walked up and down with him saying nothing. But he knew that the conquest was almost complete, and when they reached the end of the path, where no one could see them, he expressed in the clearest possible way the love that for so long he had kept concealed. At last they were of one mind. And so it was, one might say, that together they enacted a Vengeance, having found the Passion too much to bear.[5]

Before they parted they arranged that whenever the husband made his trips to his village, he would, if the King had gone off to the town, go straight to the castle to see the Queen. Thus they would fool the very people who were trying to fool them. Moreover, there would now be four people joining in the fun, instead of just two thinking they had it all to themselves. Once this was settled, the Queen retired to her room and the gentleman went home, both of them now sufficiently cheered up to forget all their previous troubles. No longer did the King's visits to the gentleman's lady distress either of them. Dread had now turned to desire, and the gentleman started to make trips to his village rather more often than he had in the past. It was, after all, only half a league out of the town. Whenever the King heard that the gentleman had gone to the country, he would make his way straight to his lady. Similarly, whenever the gentleman heard that the King had left his castle, he would wait till nightfall and then go straight to the Queen—to act, so to speak, as the King's viceroy. He managed to do this in such secrecy that no one had the slightest inkling of what was going on. They proceeded in this fashion for quite a while, but the King, being a public person, had much greater difficulty concealing his love-affair sufficiently to prevent anyone at all getting wind of it. In fact, there were a few unpleasant wags who started to make fun of the gentleman, saying he was a cuckold, and putting up their fingers like cuckold's horns whenever his back was turned. Anyone with any decency felt very sorry for the man. He knew what they were saying,

---

5. An allusion to medieval mystery plays: after the Passion and Resurrection, the mystery of Vengeance depicted the punishment of Christ's slayers [Translator's note].

of course, but derived a good deal of amusement from it, and reckoned his horns were surely as good as the King's crown.

One day when the King was visiting the gentleman and his wife at their home, he noticed a set of antlers mounted on the wall. He burst out laughing, and could not resist the temptation to remark that the horns went very well with the house. The gentleman was a match for the King, however. He had an inscription placed on the antlers which read as follows:

> *Io porto le corna, ciascun lo vede,*
> *Ma tal le porta, che no lo crede.*[6]

Next time the king was in the house, he saw the inscription, and asked what it meant.

The gentleman simply said: "If the King doesn't tell his secrets to his subjects, then there's no reason why his subjects should tell their secrets to the King. And so far as horns are concerned, you should bear in mind that they don't always stick up and push their wearers' hats off. Sometimes they're so soft that you can wear a hat on top of them, without being troubled by them, and even without knowing they're there at all!"

From these words the King realized that the gentleman knew about his affair with his wife. But he never suspected that the gentleman was having an affair with *his* wife. For her part, the Queen was careful to feign displeasure at her husband's behaviour, though secretly she was pleased, and the more she was pleased, the more displeasure she affected. This amicable arrangement permitted the continuation of their amours for many years to come, until at length old age brought them to order.

"Well, Ladies," concluded Saffredent, "let that story be a lesson to you. When your husbands give you little roe-deer horns, make sure that you give them great big stag's antlers!"

"Saffredent," said Ennasuite, laughing, "I'm quite sure that if you were still such an ardent lover as you used to be, you wouldn't mind putting up with horns as big as oaks, as long as you could give a pair back when the fancy took you. But you're starting to go grey, you know, and it really is time you began to give your appetites a rest!"

"Mademoiselle," he replied, "even if the lady I love gives me no hope, and even if age has dampened my ardour somewhat, my desires are as strong as ever. But seeing that you object to my harbouring such noble desires, let me invite you to tell the fourth story, and let's see if you can produce an example to refute what I say."

During this exchange one of the ladies had started to laugh. She knew that the lady who had just taken Saffredent's words to be aimed at her was not in fact so much the object of his affections that he would put up with cuckoldry, disgrace or injury of any kind for her sake. When Saffredent saw that she was laughing and that she had understood him, he was [highly] pleased, and let Ennasuite go on. This is what she said:

"I have a story to tell, Ladies, which will show Saffredent and everyone else here that not *all* women are like the Queen he has told us about, and that not all men who are rash enough to try their tricks get what they want.

---

6. "I am wearing horns, everyone sees that, / But there is one who wears them who doesn't know it."

It's a story that ought not to be kept back, and it tells of a lady in whose eyes failure in love was worse than death itself. I shan't mention the real names of the people involved, because it's not long since it all happened, and I should be afraid of giving offence to their close relatives."

STORY FOUR

In Flanders there once lived a lady of high birth, of birth so high, indeed, that there was no one higher in the land. She had no children and had been twice widowed. After her second husband's death she had gone to live with her brother, who was very fond of her. He was himself a noble lord of high estate, married to the daughter of a King. This young Prince was much given to his pleasures, being fond of the ladies, of hunting and generally enjoying himself, just as one would expect of a young man. His wife, however, was rather difficult, and did not enjoy the same things as he did, so he always used to take his sister along as well, because she, while being a sensible and virtuous woman, was also the most cheerful and lively company one could imagine.

Now there was a certain gentleman attached to the household, an extremely tall man, whose charm and good looks made him stand out among his companions. Taking careful note of the fact that his master's sister was a very lively lady who liked to enjoy herself, it occurred to him that it might be worth seeing if an amorous overture from a well-bred gentleman might not be to her taste. So he approached her, only to find that her reply was not what he would have expected. Nevertheless, in spite of the fact that she had given him the sort of answer that becomes an honest woman and a princess, she had had no difficulty in forgiving this good-looking and well-bred man for having been so presumptuous. Indeed, she made it plain that she did not at all mind his talking to her, though she also frequently reminded him that he must be careful what he said. In order to continue to enjoy the honour and pleasure of her company, he was only too glad to promise not to return to his earlier overtures. But as time went by his passion grew stronger, until he forgot his promises altogether. Not that he dared risk opening the subject again verbally—he had already to his cost had a taste of her ability to answer him back with her words of wisdom. No, what he had in mind was this. If he could find the right time and place, then might she not relent and indulge him a little, and indulge herself at the same time? After all, she was a widow and young, healthy and vivacious. To this end he mentioned to his master that he had lands adjoining his home that offered excellent hunting, and assured him that if he came and hunted a stag or two in May he would have the time of his life. Partly because he liked the gentleman and partly because he was addicted to hunting, the Prince accepted this invitation, and went to stay at his house, which was, as one would expect of the richest man in the land, a very fine place and very well maintained. In one wing of the house the gentleman accommodated the Prince and his wife. In the other wing opposite he accommodated the lady whom by now he loved more than he loved life itself. Her room had been luxuriously decorated from top to bottom with tapestries, and the floor was thickly covered with matting—so that it was impossible to see the trap-door by the side of the bed which led down to the room beneath. The gentleman's mother, who normally slept in this room, was old, and her catarrh made her cough in the night, so, in order to avoid disturbing the Princess, she had exchanged rooms with her son. Every evening this old lady took preserves up to the Princess, accompanied by her son, who, being very close to the brother of the Princess, was naturally permitted to attend both her *coucher* and her *lever*.[7] Needless to say, these occasions constantly served to inflame his passion.

So it was that one evening he kept her up very late, and only left her room when he saw she was falling asleep. Back in his own room, he put on the most magnificent and most highly perfumed nightshirt he possessed, and on his head he placed the most beautifully decorated nightcap you ever saw. As he admired himself in his mirror, he was absolutely convinced that there was not a woman in the world who could possible resist such a handsome and elegant sight. He looked forward with satisfaction to the success of his little plan, and went off to his bed. Not that he expected to stay there long, burning with desire as he was, and quite confident that he was soon to win his place in a bed that was both more pleasurable and more honourable than his own. Once he had dismissed his attendants, he got up to lock the door, and listened carefully for noises in the Princess's room above. When he was sure all was quiet, he turned to the task. Bit by bit he gently lowered the trap-door. It had been well constructed and was so densely covered with cloth, that not a sound was made. He hoisted himself through the aperture and into the room above. The Princess was just falling asleep. Without more ado, without a thought for her rank and station, or for the duty and respect he owed her, without, indeed, so much as a by-your-leave, he jumped into bed with her. Before she knew where she was he was lying there between her arms. But she was a strong woman. Struggling out of his clutches, she demanded to know who he was, and proceeded to lash out, scratching and biting for all she was worth. He was terrified she would call for help, and felt obliged to stuff the bedclothes into her mouth in a vain attempt to prevent her doing so. She realized that he would use all his strength to dishonour her, and fought back with all *her* strength in order to stop him. She shouted at the top of her lungs for her lady-in-waiting, a respectable elderly lady, who was sleeping in the next room, and who, as soon as she heard the shout, rushed to her mistress's rescue, still wearing her night attire.

When the gentleman realized that he had been caught, terrified of being recognized by the Princess, he beat a hasty retreat down through his trap-door. He arrived back in his room in a very sorry state indeed. It was a shattering experience for a man who had set out burning with desire, fully confident that his lady was going to receive him with open arms. He picked up his mirror from the table and examined himself in the candlelight. His face was streaming with blood from the bites and scratches she had inflicted. His beautiful embroidered nightshirt had more streaks of blood in it than it had gold thread.

"So much for good looks!" he groaned. "I suppose you've got what you deserve. I shouldn't have expected so much from my appearance. Now it's made me attempt something that I should have realized was impossible from the start. It might even make my situation worse, instead of making it better! If she realizes that it was I who did this senseless thing, breaking all the

---

7. Retiring and arising (French).

promises I had made, I know I shall lose even my privilege of visiting her chastely and openly. That's what my vanity's done for me! To make the most of my charm and good looks, and win her heart and her love, I ought not to have kept it so dark. I ought not to have tried to take her chaste body by force! I ought to have devoted myself to her service, in humility and with patience, accepting that I must wait till love should triumph. For without love, what good to a man are prowess and physical strength?"

And so he sat the whole night through, weeping, gnashing his teeth and wishing the incident had never happened. In the morning he looked at himself again in the mirror, and seeing that his face was lacerated all over, he took to his bed, pretending he was desperately ill and could not bear to go out into the light. There he remained until his visitors had gone home.

Meanwhile, the Princess was triumphant. She knew that the only person at her brother's court who would dare to do such an extraordinary thing was the man who had already once made so bold as to declare his love. In other words, she knew perfectly well that the culprit was her host. With the help of her lady-in-waiting she looked round all the possible hiding-places in the room, without, of course, finding anybody. She was beside herself with rage. "I know very well who it is!" she fumed. "It's the master of the house himself! That's the only person it can be. And mark my words, I shall speak to my brother in the morning, and I'll have the man's head as proof of my chastity!"

Seeing how angry she was, her lady-in-waiting just said: "I am pleased to see that your honour means so much to you, Madame, and that in order to enhance it you have no intention of sparing this man's life—he has already taken too many risks with it because of his violent love for you. But it very often happens that when people try to enhance their honour, they only end up doing the opposite. I would therefore urge you, Madame, to tell me the plain truth about the whole affair."

When she had heard the whole story, she asked: "Do you assure me that all he got from you was blows and scratches?"

"I do assure you," came the reply, "that that was all he got, and unless he manages to find a very good doctor indeed, we'll see the marks on his face tomorrow."

"Well, that being so," the old lady went on, "it seems to me that you should be thinking about giving thanks to the Lord, rather than talking about revenge. It must have taken some courage, you know, to make such a daring attempt, and at this moment he must be feeling so mortified by his failure, that death would be a good deal easier for him to bear! If what you want is revenge, then you should just leave him to his passion and his humiliation—he'll torture himself much more than you could. And if you're concerned about your honour, then be careful not to fall into the same trap as he did. He promised himself all kinds of pleasures and delights, and what he actually got was the worst disappointment that any gentleman could ever suffer. So take care, Madame—if you try to make your honour even more impressive, you may only end up doing the opposite. If you make an official complaint against him, you will have to bring the whole thing into the open, whereas at the moment nobody knows anything, and he certainly won't go and tell anybody. What is more, just suppose you did go ahead, and Monseigneur, your brother, did bring the case to justice, and the poor man was put to death—people will say that he *must* have had his way with you. Most people will argue that it's not very easy to accept that a man can carry out such an act, unless he has been given a certain amount of encouragement by the lady concerned. You're young and attractive, you're very lively and sociable in all kinds of company. There isn't a single person at this court who hasn't seen the encouraging way you treat the man you are now suspecting. That could only make people conclude that if he did indeed do what you say, then it couldn't have been without some blame being due to you as well. Your honour, which up till now has been such that you've been able to hold your head high wherever you went, would be put in doubt wherever this story was heard."

As she listened to the wise reasonings of her lady-in-waiting, the Princess knew that what she was saying was true. She would indeed be criticized and blamed, in view of the encouraging and intimate way she had always treated the gentleman, so she asked her lady-in-waiting what she thought she ought to do.

"It is most gracious of you, Madame," the old lady replied, "to heed my advice. You know that I have great affection for you. Well, it seems to me that you should rejoice in your heart that this man—and he is the most handsome and best-bred gentleman I saw in my life—has been completely unable to turn you from the path of virtue, in spite of his love for you, and in spite of using physical violence against you. For this you should humble yourself before God, and acknowledge that it was not your virtue that saved you. For there have been many women, women who have led a far more austere life than you have, who have been humiliated by men far less worthy of affection than the man we are talking of. From now on you should be even more cautious when men make overtures to you, and bear in mind that there are plenty of women who have escaped from danger the first time, only to succumb the second. Never forget that Love is blind, Madame, and descends upon his victims at the very moment when they are treading a path which they think is safe, but which in reality is slippery and treacherous. I think also that you should never allude in any way to what has happened, either to him or anyone else, and even if *he* were to bring it up, I think you should pretend not to understand what he is talking about. In this way there are two dangers that you will be able to avoid. First of all, there's the danger of glorying in your triumph. And then there's the danger that you might enjoy being reminded of the pleasures of the flesh. Even the most chaste of women have a hard time preventing some spark of pleasure being aroused by such things, however much they strive to avoid them. Finally, Madame, so that he should not get it into his head that you in some way enjoyed what he tried to do, I would advise you to gradually stop seeing so much of him. In that way you will bring home to him what a low opinion you have of his foolish and wicked behaviour. At the same time he will be brought to see what a good person you are to have been satisfied with the triumph that God has already granted you, without seeking any further revenge. May God grant you the grace, Madame, to continue in the path of virtue wherein he has placed you, to continue to love and to serve Him even better than hitherto, in the knowledge that it is from Him alone that all goodness flows."

The Princess made up her mind to follow the wise counsel of her lady-in-waiting, and slept peacefully for the rest of the night, while the wretched gentleman below spent a night of sleepless torment.

The next day the Princess's brother was ready to depart, and asked if he could take his leave of the master of the house. He was astonished to hear that he was ill, could not tolerate the light of day and refused to be seen by anyone. He would have gone to see him, but was told that he was sleeping, and decided not to disturb him. So together with his wife and his sister he left the house without being able to say goodbye. When his sister, the Princess, heard about their host's excuses for not seeing them before they left, she knew for certain that he was the one who had caused her so much distress. Obviously he did not dare to show his face because of the scratches he had received. Indeed, he refused all subsequent invitations to attend court until all his wounds—except, that is, for those he had suffered to his heart and to his pride—had healed. When eventually he did go back to court to face his triumphant enemy, he could not do so without blushing. He, who was the boldest man at court, would completely lose his self-assurance in her presence, and would frequently go quite to pieces. This only made the Princess the more sure that her suspicions had been well-founded. Gently, and little by little, she withdrew her attentions—but not so gently that he failed to appreciate what she was doing. Scared lest anything worse befell him, he dared not breathe a word. He simply had to nurse his passion in the depths of his heart, and put up with a rebuff that had been justly deserved.

"And that, Ladies, is a story that should strike fear into the hearts of any man who thinks he can help himself to what doesn't belong to him. The Princess's virtue and the good sense of her lady-in-waiting should inspire courage in the hearts of all women. So if anything like this should ever happen to any of you, you now know what the remedy is!"

"In my opinion," said Hircan, "the tall lord of your story lacked nerve, and didn't deserve to have his memory preserved. What an opportunity he had! He should never have been content to eat or sleep till he'd succeeded. And one really can't say that his love was very great, if there was still room in his heart for the fear of death and dishonour."

"And what," asked Nomerfide, "could the poor man have done with two women against him?"

"He should have killed the old one, and when the young one realized there was no one to help her, he'd have been half-way there!"

"Kill her!" Nomerfide cried. "You wouldn't mind him being a murderer as well, then? If that's what you think, we'd better watch out we don't fall into *your* clutches!"

"If I'd gone that far," he replied, "I'd consider my honour ruined if I didn't go through with it!"

Then Geburon[8] spoke up: "So you find it strange that a princess of high birth who's been brought up in the strict school of honour should be too much for one man? In that case you'd find it even stranger that a woman of poor birth should manage to get away from *two* men!"

"I invite you to tell the fifth story, Geburon," said Ennasuite, "because

8. One of the older members of the group, notable for his sententious wisdom. Suggested identifications are with a military man, the lord of Burye, a captain in the Italian Wars; or with Nicolas Bourbon, a tutor of Jeanne d'Albret, Marguerite's daughter.

it sounds as if you have one about some poor woman that will be far from dull."

"Since you've chosen me [to speak]," he began, "I shall tell a story that I know to be true because I conducted an inquiry into it at the very place where it happened. As you'll see, it isn't only princesses who've got good sense in their heads and virtue in their heart. And love and resourcefulness aren't always to be found where you'd expect them, either."

STORY FIVE

At the port of Coulon near Niort, there was once a woman whose job it was to ferry people night and day across the river. One day she found herself alone in her boat with two Franciscan friars from Niort. Now this is one of the longest crossings on any river in France, and the two friars took it into their heads that she would find it less boring if they made amorous proposals to her. But, as was only right and proper, she refused to listen. However, the two were not to be deterred. They had not exactly had their strength sapped by rowing, nor their ardours chilled by the chilly water nor, indeed, their consciences pricked by the woman's refusals. So they decided to rape her, both of them, and if she resisted, to throw her into the river. But she was as sensible and shrewd as they were vicious and stupid.

"I'm not as ungracious as you might think," she said to them, "and if you'll just grant me two little things, you'll see I'm just as keen to do what you want as you are."

The Cordeliers[9] swore by the good Saint Francis that they'd let her have anything she asked for, if she'd just let them have what they wanted.

"First of all, you must promise on your oath that neither of you will tell a soul about it," she said.

To this they readily agreed.

"Secondly, you must do what you want with me one at a time—I'd be too embarrassed to have both of you looking at me. So decide between you who's to have me first."

They thought this too was a very reasonable request, and the younger of the two offered to let the older man go first. As they sailed past a small island in the river, the ferrywoman said to the younger one: "Now my good father, jump ashore and say your prayers while I take your friend here to another island. If he's satisfied with me when he gets back, we'll drop him off here, and then you can come with me."

So he jumped out of the boat to wait on the island till his companion came back. The ferrywoman then took the other one to another island in the river, and while she pretended to be making the boat fast to a tree, told him to go and find a convenient spot.

He jumped out, and went off to look for a good place. No sooner was he on dry land than the ferrywoman shoved off with a kick against the tree, and sailed off down the river, leaving the two good friars stranded.

"You can wait till God sends an angel to console you, Messieurs!" she bawled at them. "You're not going to get anything out of me today!"

The poor friars saw they had been hoodwinked. They ran to the water's

9. Franciscan friars.

edge and pleaded on bended knees that she would take them to the port. They promised not to ask her for any more favours. But she went on rowing, and called back: "I'd be even more stupid to let myself get caught again, now I've escaped!"

As soon as she landed on the other side, she went into the village, fetched her husband and called out the officers of the law to go and round up these two ravenous wolves, from whose jaws she had just by the grace of God been delivered. They had plenty of willing helpers. There was no one in the village, great or small, who was not anxious to join in the hunt and have his share of the fun. When the two good brothers, each on his own island, saw this huge band coming after them, they did their best to hide—even as Adam hid from the presence of the Lord God, when he saw that he was naked. They were half dead for shame at this exposure of their sins, and trembled in terror at the thought of the punishment that surely awaited them. But there was nothing they could do. They were seized and bound, and led through the village to the shouts and jeers of every man and woman in the place. Some people said: "There they go, those good fathers who preach chastity to us yet want to take it from our wives!" Others said: "They are whited sepulchres, outwardly beautiful, but within full of dead men's bones and all uncleanness!" And someone else called out, "Every tree is known by his own fruit!" In fact, they hurled at the two captives every text in the Gospels that condemns hypocrites. In the end their Father Superior came to the rescue. He lost no time in requesting their custody, reassuring the officers of the law that he would punish them more severely than secular law could. By way of reparation, they would, he promised, be made to say as many prayers and masses as might be required! [The Father Superior was a worthy man, so the judge granted his request and sent the two prisoners back to their convent, where they were brought before the full Chapter and severely reprimanded.] Never again did they take a ferry across a river, without making the sign of the cross and commending their souls to God!

"Now consider this story carefully, Ladies. We have here a humble ferry-woman who had the sense to frustrate the evil intentions of two vicious men. What then ought we to expect from women who all their lives have seen nothing but good examples, read of nothing but good examples and, in short, had examples of feminine virtue constantly paraded before them?[1] If well-fed women are virtuous, is it not just as much a matter of custom as of virtue? But it's quite another matter if you're talking about women who have no education, who probably don't hear two decent sermons in a year, who have time for nothing but thinking how to make a meagre living, and who, in spite of all this, diligently resist all pressures in order to preserve their chastity. It is in the heart of such women as these that one finds pure virtue, for in the hearts of those we regard as inferior in body and mind the spirit of God performs his greatest works. Woe to those women who do not guard their treasure with the utmost care, for it is a treasure that brings them great honour if it is well guarded and great dishonour if it is squandered!"

"If you ask me, Geburon," observed Longarine, "there's nothing very virtuous in rejecting the advances of a friar. I don't know how anyone could possibly feel any affection at all for them."

---

1. Manuals on virtuous behavior and exemplary lives were common reading for noblewomen of the period.

"Longarine," he replied, "women who are not so used as you are to having refined gentlemen to serve them find friars far from unpleasant. They're often just as good-looking as we are, just as well-built and less worn out, because they've not been knocked about in battle. What is more, they talk like angels and are as persistent as devils. That's why I think that any woman who's seen nothing better than the coarse cloth of monks' habits should be considered extremely virtuous if she manages to escape their clutches."

"Good Heavens!" exclaimed Nomerfide loudly. "You may say what you like, but I'd rather be thrown in the river any day, than go to bed with a friar!"

"*So you're a strong swimmer, are you then!*"[2] said Oisille, laughing.

Nomerfide took this in bad part, thinking that Oisille did not give her as much credit as she would have liked, and said heatedly: "There *are* plenty of people who've refused better men than friars, without blowing their trumpets about it!"

"Yes, and they've been even more careful not to beat their drums about ones they've accepted and given in to!" retorted Oisille, amused to see that she was annoyed.

"I can see that Nomerfide would like to speak," Geburon intervened, "so I invite her to take over from me, in order that she may unburden herself by telling us a good story."

"I couldn't care less about people's remarks," she snapped, "they neither please nor annoy me. But since you ask me to speak, will you listen carefully, because I want to tell a story to show you that women can exercise their [cleverness] for bad purposes as well as for good ones. As we've sworn to tell the truth, I have no desire to conceal it. After all, just as the ferrywoman's virtue does not redound to the honour of other women unless they actually follow in her footsteps, so the *vice* of one woman does not bring dishonour on all other women. So, if you will listen . . ."

STORY SIX

Charles, the last Duke of Alençon, had a valet de chambre who was blind in one eye, and who was married to a woman a good few years younger than himself. Now, of all the men of that rank in the household this man was particularly well-liked by his master and mistress. This meant that he could not get home to see his wife as often as he would have liked, which in turn led to her neglecting her honour and conscience to the extent that she fell for a young man. There was so much malicious gossip about this affair that the husband eventually got wind of it, although he found it difficult to believe, as his wife always seemed to be very affectionate with him. One day he decided to check up on her and, if he could, get his own back on her for disgracing him. So he told her that he had to go away for two or three days to some place not far off. No sooner was he out of the door than the wife invited her young man round. But he had not been there above half an hour when back comes the husband and hammers loudly on the front door. She recognized the knock and told her lover, who was so terrified he wished he had never been born. He cursed his mistress and the whole wretched love-affair for placing him in such a tight corner. But she told him not to worry, she would find some way of getting him out of it without injury either to

2. The verb *nouer* meant "to swim" and "to knot," which had sexual connotations.

himself or his honour, and instructed him to get his clothes on as fast as he could. The husband was still banging at the door, and shouting for his wife at the top of his voice. But she pretended not to recognize him, and called out, as if to [the servants]: "Why don't you get up, and tell whoever it is out there to be quiet? This is no time to be knocking at respectable people's doors! If my husband were here, he'd soon put a stop to it!"

Hearing his wife's voice, the husband called out as loud as he could: "Open up, wife. Are you going to keep me standing here till morning?"

Seeing that her lover was ready to be off, she opened the door, and said to her husband: "My dear husband, how glad I am to see you! I've just had a marvellous dream, and I've never felt so happy, because I dreamt that you'd got the sight back in your eye!"

She put her arms round him and kissed him, took his head in both hands, and covered up his good eye.

"Is it not true that you can see better than before?" she demanded. He could not see a thing, of course, and the wife gave her lover the sign to make his getaway.

Guessing what was going on, the husband said: "By Heavens, woman, I'm not going to spy on *you* any more! I thought I was going to catch you out, but in return you play me the most cunning trick anyone's ever thought of. May God give you the punishment you deserve! Because there's not a man alive can make a bad woman behave herself, short of murdering her! Since treating you kindly as I've done up till now, hasn't made you mend your ways, perhaps you'll be brought to heel if from now on I treat you with the contempt you deserve!"

So saying, he stormed off, leaving her quite distressed, though in the end, by dint of tears, excuses and the mediation of her friends, she managed to get him to come back to her.

"So you can see, Ladies, that women can be very cunning when they're in a scrape. And if they're clever enough to cover up something bad, I think they'd be even more ingenious in avoiding bad deeds or in doing good ones. A shrewd wit is always stronger in the end, as everybody always says."

"You can talk about your feminine cunning as much as you like," said Hircan, "but in my opinion, if anything like that happened to *you*, you would be incapable of covering it up!"

"I'd rather you thought I was the stupidest woman in the world!" replied Nomerfide.

"I don't say *that*," he went on, "but I do think you're the sort of woman who gets worked up over a rumour, instead of thinking of some clever way of putting an end to it."

"You think that everyone's like you," she replied, "quite ready to cover up one rumour with another. But there's always the risk that a cover-up will end up destroying the very thing it was meant to conceal, like a building that collapses because the roof's too heavy for the foundations. However if you think that [male] cunning—and everyone knows you've got your fair share of *that*—is superior to female cunning, then I'll make way for you, so that you can tell us the seventh story. And if you'd like to tell us about yourself by way of example, I'm sure you'd teach us all a good deal about wickedness and trickery!"

"I'm not here to give myself a worse reputation than I've already got. There are already enough people willing to say worse things about me than I care for!" said Hircan, glancing at his wife, who quickly replied:

"Don't be afraid to tell the truth because of me. It will be easier for me to hear about your little games than to have had to watch you playing them under my nose—though nothing you may do could diminish the love I bear you."

"Then I shan't complain about all the wrong opinions that you have held about me. So, since we know and understand one another, there is reason to feel more reassurance for the future. All the same I wouldn't be so foolish as to tell you a story about myself, when the facts might be hurtful to you— but I *will* tell one about a man who was a close friend of mine."

STORY SEVEN

In the town of Paris there was once a merchant who was in love with a young girl who was a neighbour of his. To be more accurate, it was the girl who was in love with him, rather than the other way round. He merely pretended to be devoted to her in order to cover up a more exalted and honourable passion for someone else. But she let herself be deceived, and was so infatuated that she had completely forgotten that it is the custom for women to reject men's advances. For a long while the merchant had taken the trouble of going to seek her out, but eventually he was able to persuade her to come to meet him where it suited him. Her mother, who was a most respectable person, realized what was going on, and forbade the girl ever to speak to the merchant again, or she would be sent straight to a convent. But the girl was more in love with her merchant than she was in awe of her mother, and only did her best to see him more often than ever.

One day the merchant happened to find her alone in her dressing-room. It was a convenient place for his purposes, so he proceeded to make overtures to her in the most intimate fashion. But some chambermaid or other who had seen him going in ran off and told the mother, who flew into a rage and immediately came along to catch them. The girl heard her coming and burst into tears.

"Alas! Alas! My love," she wailed to her merchant, "my hour is come and I shall pay the price for the love I bear you! Here's my mother coming. This is what she's feared and suspected all along, and now she'll discover that it's true!"

The merchant was not the sort of man to be upset by a situation of this kind. He jumped up and went to meet the mother, put his arms around her and hugged and kissed her as hard as he could. Already in a passionate mood after flirting with her daughter, he flung the poor old woman on to a couch. She found this so extraordinary that all she could manage to say was: "What do you want? Have you gone mad?"

But he was not deterred. Indeed, he went about it as if she had been the most attractive young girl he had ever seen. If her screams had not brought her servants and chambermaids running to her rescue, she would have gone the same way she feared her daughter was going! The servants extricated the poor old dear from the merchant's embraces without her having the vaguest idea why he had given her such a mauling. While all this was going on, the girl escaped to a neighbour's house, where there happened to be a wedding reception going on.

The merchant and the girl often had a good laugh together at the mother's expense, and the old woman never found them out.

"So, you can see, Ladies, how male cleverness succeeded in outwitting the old woman and in saving the young girl's honour. But anyone who knew the names of the people involved, or who saw the merchant's face or the old woman's astonishment, would have to be very afraid for his conscience if he refused to laugh. But I'll be quite satisfied if my story has proved to you that men are just as resourceful and quick-witted as women when they need to be. So, dear Ladies, you should have no fear of falling into their hands, because, should you be lost for a way out, they will always be able to cover up and save your honour!"

"Yes, Hircan, I agree that it's a very funny story," said Longarine, "and that the man was very clever. All the same, I don't think it's an example that young girls should follow. I suspect there are some you'd like to persuade to do so. But I don't think you're so stupid as to want your wife to play such games, or the lady whose honour is dearer to you than pleasure. I don't think there's anyone who would keep a closer watch on them than you, or anyone who would more promptly put a stop to such things."

"On my oath," replied Hircan, "if [the ones] you refer to *had* done anything like that, I wouldn't think any the less of them for it—provided I knew nothing about it! For all I know, someone might have played just as good a trick on me, but if so, I know nothing about it, so it doesn't worry me."

Parlamente could not resist commenting: "It's impossible for men who do wrong themselves not to be suspicious of others. But it's a happy man who gives no cause for others to be suspicious of him."

"Well, I've never seen fire without smoke," said Longarine, "but I have seen smoke without fire! Malicious people are often just as good at smelling something bad when it doesn't exist, as they are when it does."

"Since you speak so strongly in favour of women who get suspected wrongly, Longarine," said Hircan, "I choose you to tell us the eighth story, on condition that you don't make us all weep, like Madame Oisille did, with her excessive zeal for stories in praise of virtuous women."[3]

Longarine broke into a hearty laugh, and said: "Since you want me to make you laugh, in my usual fashion, it won't be at the expense of women. Yet I *shall* tell you something to show how easy they are to deceive when they fill their heads with jealous thoughts, and pride themselves on their good sense for wanting to deceive their husbands."

STORY EIGHT

In the county of Alès there was once a man by the name of Bornet, who had married a very decent and respectable woman. He held her honour and reputation very dear, as I am sure all husbands here hold the honour and reputation of *their* wives dear. He wanted her to be faithful to him, but was not so keen on having the rule applied to them both equally. He had become

3. Reference to an earlier story.

enamoured of his chambermaid, though the only benefit he got from transferring his affections in this way was the sort of pleasure one gets from
varying one's diet. He had a neighbour called Sendras, who was of similar
station and temperament to himself—he was a tailor and a drummer. These
two were such close friends that, with the exception of the wife, there was
nothing that they did not share between them. Naturally he told him that
he had designs on the chambermaid.

Not only did his friend wholeheartedly approve of this, but did his best to
help him, in the hope that he too might get a share in the spoils.

The chambermaid herself refused to have anything to do with him,
although he was constantly pestering her, and in the end she went to tell her
mistress about it. She told her that she could not stand being badgered by
him any longer, and asked permission to go home to her parents. Now the
good lady of the house, who was really very much in love with her husband,
had often had occasion to suspect him, and was therefore rather pleased to
be one up on him, and to be able to show him that she had found out what
he was up to. So she said to her maid: "Be nice to him, dear, encourage him
a little bit, and then make a date to go to bed with him in my dressing-room.
Don't forget to tell me which night he's supposed to be coming, and make
sure you don't tell anyone else."

The maid did exactly as her mistress had instructed. As for her master, he
was so pleased with himself that he went off to tell his friend about his stroke
of luck, whereupon the friend insisted on taking his share afterwards, since
he had been in on the business from the beginning. When the appointed
time came, off went the master, as had been agreed, to get into bed, as he
thought, with his little chambermaid. But his wife, having abandoned her
position of authority in order to serve in a more pleasurable one, had taken
her maid's place in the bed. When he got in with her, she did not act like a
wife, but like a bashful young girl, and he was not in the slightest suspicious.
It would be impossible to say which of them enjoyed themselves more—the
wife deceiving her husband, or the husband who thought he was deceiving
his wife. He stayed in bed with her for some time, not as long as he might
have wished (many years of marriage were beginning to tell on him), but as
long as he could manage. Then he went out to rejoin his accomplice, and
tell him what a good time he had had. The lustiest piece of goods he had
ever come across, he declared. His friend, who was younger and more active
than he was, said: "Remember what you promised?"

"Hurry up, then," replied the master, "in case she gets up, or my wife wants
her for something."

Off he went and climbed into bed with the supposed chambermaid his
friend had just failed to recognize as his wife. *She* thought it was her husband
again, and did not refuse anything he asked for (I say "asked," but "took"
would be nearer the mark, because he did not dare open his mouth). He
made a much longer business of it than the husband, to the surprise of the
wife, who was not used to these long nights of pleasure. However, she did
not complain, and looked forward to what she was planning to say to him in
the morning, and the fun she would have teasing him. When dawn came,
the man got up, and fondling her as he got out of bed, pulled off a ring she
wore on her finger, a ring that her husband had given her at their marriage.
Now the women in this part of the world are very superstitious about such

things. They have great respect for women who hang on to their wedding rings till the day they die, and if a woman loses her ring, she is dishonoured, and is looked upon as having given her faith to another man. But she did not mind him taking it, because she thought it would be sure evidence against her husband of the way she had hoodwinked him.

The husband was waiting outside for his friend, and asked him how he had got on. The man said he shared the husband's opinion, and added that he would have stayed longer, had he not been afraid of getting caught by the daylight. The pair of them then went off to get as much sleep as they could. When morning came, and they were getting dressed together, the husband noticed that his friend had on his finger a ring that was identical to the one he had given his wife on their wedding day. He asked him where he had got it, and when he was told it had come from the chambermaid the night before, he was aghast. He began banging his head against the wall, and shouted: "Oh my God! Have I gone and made myself a cuckold without my wife even knowing about it?"

His friend tried to calm him down. "Perhaps your wife had given the ring to the girl to look after before going to bed?" he suggested. The husband made no reply, but marched straight out and went back to his house.

There he found his wife looking unusually gay and attractive. Had she not saved her chambermaid from staining her conscience, and had she not put her husband to the ultimate test, without any more cost to herself than a night's sleep? Seeing her in such good spirits, the husband thought to himself: "She wouldn't be greeting me so cheerfully if she knew what I'd been up to."

As they chatted, he took hold of her hand and saw that the ring, which normally never left her finger, had disappeared. Horrified, he stammered: "What have you done with your ring?"

She was pleased that he was giving her the opportunity to say what she had to say.

"Oh! You're the most dreadful man I ever met! Who do you think you got it from? You think you got it from the chambermaid, don't you? You think you got it from that girl you're so much in love with, the girl who gets more out of you than I've ever had! The first time you got into bed you were so passionate that I thought you must be about as madly in love with her as it was possible for any man to be! But when you came back the *second* time, after getting up, you were an absolute devil! Completely uncontrolled you were, didn't know when to stop! You miserable man! You must have been blinded by desire to pay such tribute to my body—after all you've had me long enough without showing much appreciation for my figure. So it wasn't because that young girl is so pretty and so shapely that you were enjoying yourself so much. Oh no! You enjoyed it so much because you were seething with some depraved pent-up lust—in short the sin of concupiscence was raging within you, and your senses were dulled as a result. In fact you'd worked yourself up into such a state that I think any old nanny-goat would have done for you, pretty or otherwise! Well, my dear, it's time you mended your ways. It's high time you were content with me for what I am—your own wife and an honest woman, and it's high time that you found *that* just as satisfying as when you thought I was a poor little erring chambermaid. I did what I did in order to save you from your wicked ways, so that when you get old, we can live happily and peacefully together without anything on our consciences. Because if you go on in the way you have been, I'd rather leave you altogether than see you destroying your soul day by day, and at the same time destroying your physical health and squandering everything you have before my very eyes! But if you will acknowledge that you've been in the wrong, and make up your mind to live according to the ways of God and His commandments, then I'll overlook all your past misbehavior, even as I hope God will forgive me *my* ingratitude to Him, and failure to love Him as I ought."

If there was ever a man who was dumbfounded and despairing, it was this poor husband. There was his wife, looking so pretty, and yet so sensible and so chaste, and he had gone and left her for a girl who did not love him. What was worse, he had had the misfortune to have gone and made her do something wicked without her even realizing what was happening. He had gone and let another man share pleasures which, rightly, were his alone to enjoy. He had gone and given himself cuckold's horns and made himself look ridiculous for evermore. But he could see she was already angry enough about the chambermaid, and he did not dare tell her about the other dirty trick he had played. So he promised that he would leave his wicked ways behind him, asked her to forgive him and gave her the ring back. He told his friend not to breathe a word to anybody, but secrets of this sort nearly always end up being proclaimed from the [roof-tops,] and it was not long before the facts became public knowledge. The husband was branded as a cuckold without his wife having done a single thing to disgrace herself.

"Ladies, it strikes me that if all the men who offend their wives like that got a punishment like that, then Hircan and Saffredent ought to be feeling a bit nervous."

"Come now, Longarine," said Saffredent, "Hircan and I aren't the only married men here, you know."

"True," she replied, "but you're the only two who'd play a trick like that."

"And just when have you heard of us chasing our wives' maids?" he retorted.

"If the ladies in question were to tell us the facts," Longarine said, "then you'd soon find plenty of maids who'd been dismissed before their pay-day!"

"Really," intervened Geburon, "a fine one you are! You promise to make us all laugh, and you end up making these two gentlemen annoyed."

"It comes to the same thing," said Longarine. "As long as they don't get their swords out, their getting angry makes it all the more amusing."

"But the fact remains," said Hircan, "that if our wives were to listen to what this lady here has to say, she'd make trouble for every married couple here!"

"I know what I'm saying, and who I'm saying it to," Longarine replied. "Your wives are so good, and they love you so much, that even if you gave them horns like a stag's, they'd still convince themselves, and everybody else, that they were garlands of roses!"

Everyone found this remark highly amusing, even the people it was aimed at, and the subject was brought to a close. Dagoucin,[4] however, who had not yet said a word, could not resist saying: "When a man already has everything

4. The most philosophical member of the group, described elsewhere (story 11) as "so wise that he would rather die than say something foolish." He is also the saintliest; our translator indicates that his name is "a fairly obvious pun: *de goûts saints* (of saintly tastes)."

he needs in order to be contented, it is very unreasonable of him to go off and seek satisfaction elsewhere. It has often struck me that when people are not satisfied with what they already have, and think they can find something better, then they only make themselves worse off. And they do not get any sympathy, because inconstancy is one thing that is universally condemned."

"But what about people who have not yet found their other half?" asked Simontaut. "Would you still say it was inconstancy if they seek her wherever she may be found?"

"No man can know," replied Dagoucin, "where his other half is to be found, this other half with whom he may find a union so equal that between [the parts] there is no difference; which being so, a man must hold fast where Love constrains him and, whatever may befall him, he must remain steadfast in heart and will. For if she whom you love is your true likeness, if she is of the same will, then it will be your own self that you love, and not her alone."

"Dagoucin, I think you're adopting a position that is completely wrong," said Hircan. "You make it sound as if we ought to love women without being loved in return!"

"What I mean, Hircan, is this. If love is based on a woman's beauty, charm and favours, and if our aim is merely pleasure, ambition or profit, then such love can never last. For if the whole foundation on which our love is based should collapse, then love will fly from us and there will be no love left in us. But I am utterly convinced that if a man loves with no other aim, no other desire, than to love truly, he will abandon his soul in death rather than allow his love to abandon his heart."

"Quite honestly, Dagoucin, I don't think you've ever really been in love," said Simontaut, "because if you had felt the fire of passion, as the rest of us have, you wouldn't have been doing what you've just been doing—describing Plato's republic, which sounds all very fine in writing, but is hardly true to experience."

"If I have loved," he replied, "I love still, and shall love till the day I die. But my love is a perfect love, and I fear lest showing it openly should betray it. So greatly do I fear this, that I shrink to make it known to the lady whose love and friendship I cannot but desire to be equal to my own. I scarcely dare think my own thoughts, lest something should be revealed in my eyes, for the longer I conceal the fire of my love, the stronger grows the pleasure in knowing that it is indeed a perfect love."

"Ah, but all the same," said Geburon, "I don't think you'd be sorry if she did return your love!"

"I do not deny it. But even if I were loved as deeply as I myself love, my love could not possibly increase, just as it could not possibly decrease if I were loved less deeply than I love."

At this point, Parlamente, who was suspicious of these flights of fancy, said: "Watch your step, Dagoucin. I've seen plenty of men who've died rather than speak what's in their minds."

"Such men as those," he replied, "I would count happy indeed."

"Indeed," said Saffredent, "and worthy to be placed among the ranks of the Innocents—of whom the Church chants '*Non loquendo, sed moriendo confessi sunt*'!⁵ I've heard a lot of talk about these languishing lovers, but I've

---

5. "Not by speaking but by dying they confessed," a line recited during the Feast of the Holy Innocents.

never seen a single one actually die. I've suffered enough from such torture, but I got over it in the end, and that's why I've always assumed that nobody else ever really dies from it either."

"Ah! Saffredent, the trouble is that you desire your love to be returned," Dagoucin replied, "and men of your opinions never die for love. But I know of many who *have* died, and died for no other cause than that they have loved, and loved perfectly."

FRANÇOIS RABELAIS
1495?–1553

François Rabelais created a distinctive blend of broad, lusty, and unsqueamish humor so influential that it took its creator's name: to this day, humor that blends the lofty and low, elegant and grotesque, erudite and physical is called *Rabelaisian*. Rabelais displays great artistic control over his work, which never shies away from the body: without breaking decorum, he introduces elements that elsewhere might seem crude or obscene (even a hiccup is inconceivable in Castiglione's Urbino). He creates a capacious narrative in which one character (the giant Gargantua) uses his dandruff for cannonballs, another (Panurge) proposes to rebuild the city walls of Paris out of women's genitals, and yet another (Alcofribas Nasier, the narrator) ventures into the mouth of the giant Pantagruel, wherein he discovers another world and converses with a farmer who is planting cabbages in the giant's tongue. Although irreverent, these scenarios allude to the epic tasks of founding city walls and colonizing new worlds. With bawdy humor, Rabelais both imitates and parodies the grandest of all literary genres, the imperial epic.

Rabelais, the son of a successful lawyer, was in all likelihood born around 1495 in the province of Touraine. He trained as a Franciscan monk and priest, gained proficiency in Greek, and came to the attention of Guillaume Budé, secretary to the king of France, as a promising young scholar. Rabelais experienced in 1523 the first of many dispiriting brushes with the Sorbonne, the college of powerful and conservative theologians at the University of Paris, when it banned the study of Greek in France and his books were confiscated. Disturbed at these antihumanist actions, he sought and gained authorization from Pope Clement VII to transfer to the less strict Benedictine order. He immortalized his hatred of the Sorbonne, which in future years would condemn with depressing regularity each of his books as they appeared, in his grotesque inventory of "sophistes, Sorbillans, Sorbonagres, Sorbonigènes, Sorbonicoles, Sorboniformes, Sorbonisecques, Niborcisans, Borsonisans, Saniborsans. . . ." Around 1527 he decided to pursue a career in medicine and gave up the monk's habit, an act for which he was not to receive papal absolution until 1536. Rabelais received the degree of bachelor of medicine from the University of Montpellier in 1530 and was by 1532 a successful physician at the important hospital of the Pont-du-Rhône at Lyon.

Under the pseudonym Alcofribas Nasier, an anagram for François Rabelais, he published a book about Pantagruel, the son he created for Gargantua, a gigantic folk hero of French oral tradition. He seems to have published his *Gargantua* just before a political nightmare, called the Affair of the Placards, in 1534. In this event, Reformers plastered antipapal posters in the main squares of Paris and even on the door of the king's bedchamber, alienating King Francis I from all reformers, even the peaceful Evangelicals associated with Rabelais and Francis's sister, Marguerite de Navarre.

The king had previously been sympathetic to reform and had taken the unprecedented step of founding a nontheological university in France (the College of Royal Lecturers) where scholars taught Hebrew and Greek. After the affair, Francis I retaliated with persecutions of French Protestants. Rabelais felt threatened enough to leave his post at the hospital and disappear until the persecutions eased (due to interventions by the German princes and Pope Paul III). In 1537 Rabelais received his doctorate of medicine at Montpellier, where he later gave lectures, using the original texts of ancient Greek physicians such as Hippocrates. In the following years he traveled widely as doctor to Jean du Bellay, bishop of Paris, and his important brother, Seigneur de Langey. Rabelais even came to hold a minor post in the retinue of Francis I, and in 1538 he attended the meeting between Francis I and Charles V, the Holy Roman emperor, that led to increased persecution of Reformers. Prepared to hold his religious opinions "up to but excluding the stake," Rabelais conformed.

In his definitive edition of *Gargantua and Pantagruel* of 1541, Rabelais toned down his lampoons of the Sorbonne, which nonetheless condemned the book, preventing its sale or possession. In 1544 he gained Francis I's permission to publish his third book, less flamboyant and optimistic than the first two. His efforts to appease the Sorbonne were unsuccessful, and when the third book appeared two years later, it too was condemned; at the time, Rabelais himself was in flight at Metz in Alsace (or on a secret mission—we do not know which). Encouraged by Chastillon, his last great patron and protector, and by the new king, Henry II, Rabelais published his fourth book in 1551; all too predictably it was condemned by the Sorbonne until the king lifted the ban. A fifth book, attributed to Rabelais but of unknown authorship, appeared in 1562–64. Tradition has it that in 1553 Rabelais died in Paris, in the Rue de Jardins.

As inspiration for his giant humanist, the title hero of *Pantagruel*, Rabelais chose a little devil from a medieval mystery play who provoked thirst wherever he went and liked to pour salt down the throats of drunkards. Pantagruel's father, Gargantua, explains that his son was born in a drought and that his name means "dominator of thirsts." Although Pantagruel loves good wine, his chief thirsts are intellectual. In the book's first chapters, Pantagruel completes his prodigious education along the lines recommended by his father and is well on his way to becoming an ideal humanist prince. Once educated and matured into a rational and generous-minded young prince, however, Pantagruel becomes less suited for the adventurous and mischievous middle of Rabelais's narrative than for its comparatively high-minded and educational beginning and conclusion. *Gargantua and Pantagruel* follows other Renaissance epics, using its middle chapters to test, question, and toy with the ideals of heroism and civility that epic narratives ultimately sanctify in a final battle and the founding of a new imperial city.

The playful and exploratory character at the center of *Pantagruel* is Panurge (Greek *pan* + *ourgos*, "he who will do all things"), a trickster, bad boy, and shadow version of Pantagruel. Panurge knows much, invents more, and stops at nothing. When Pantagruel first spies the noble but bedraggled figure, Panurge inspires the young giant's compassionate interest. He and his companions offer their help, and Panurge answers in no fewer than thirteen languages—three imaginary, three ancient, and seven modern. In pompous German, the language of the Antipodes (who dwell at the opposite side of the world), Italian, Scottish, vulgar Basque, "Lanternese," Dutch, Spanish, Danish, Hebrew, ancient Greek, "Utopian," and Latin, Panurge repeatedly laments that Pantagruel and his friends cannot understand him and begs for the food and drink they wish to give him (although the idiom of the Antipodes implies a threat to sodomize Pantagruel if he does not comply). When his would-be benefactors finally ask if he knows any French, Panurge delightedly reveals that he is a native, "born and brought up in the garden of France, that is Touraine"—precisely the birthplace of Rabelais himself.

Although not exactly a double for Rabelais, Panurge vibrantly embodies his author's intellectual and narrative tactics. He is an inventive and imitative trickster, an extroverted entertainer, and a multilingual scholar. He loves games and practical jokes that create an expansive sense of community (for all except the butts of his jokes). Eloquence of word and gesture comes easily to him. His rhetorical virtuosity is akin to that of Erasmus's Folly, although he takes far greater liberties in diction, ascending to high Ciceronian expression or descending to earthy obscenity at will. He achieves similar feats in the language of bodily gesture, notably in his sign-language debate with the daunting English scholar Thaumaste: by making liberal use of his enormous codpiece, which ornaments and enlarges the appearance of his penis, Panurge vanquishes his opponent. Farts, displays of incontinence, and phallic play are as expressive to Panurge as a classical or biblical allusion, a neologism (made-up word), or a cheerful obscenity.

Like Panurge, Rabelais mingles the earthy and grotesque with the lofty and elegant in *Gargantua and Pantagruel*: he chooses Virgil's *Aeneid* and Old Testament stories as his dominant models. Both of Rabelais's books juxtapose and mingle the erudite and bawdy, classical and folk, and high and low ("head" and "bottom" better suit the books' corporeal spirit). As the Russian critic Mikhail Bakhtin noted, Rabelais's epic seriousness cannot be properly understood apart from his presentation of the body, marked by its yawning mouth, flared nostrils, and anus. The lower regions of the Rabelaisian body—belly, buttocks, and genitals—prevail over the head or reason. Eating, drinking, defecating, farting, sweating, and nose-blowing pervade Rabelais's narratives. The gaping orifices mark the grotesque body's openness to sexual, economic, and emotional exchange and its stark contrast with the classical body, which is well proportioned, closed, and upwardly focused. To an extent, Rabelais compares the classical body with classical epic and contrasts them with the grotesque body and the vital folk traditions that broaden the scope of his text.

The episodes from *Gargantua and Pantagruel* reprinted in this anthology include the bawdy and the epic: they begin with the education of the gigantic heroes in the humanistic arts and conclude with the ethical, learned giants' battle against tyrannical forces that threaten their fathers' kingdoms. When Pantagruel learns that a nation called the Dipsodes has invaded Gargantua's kingdom, he is forced to leave his "Dido" (a Parisian lady) and, like Virgil's Aeneas, choose the fatherland over love. Giant though he is, Pantagruel becomes a second David set in unequal battle with a new Goliath, the gigantic Werewolf who captains King Anarchy's army. Pantagruel's enemies represent terrifying worldly evils: anarchy means lawlessness, and the werewolf is a traditional figure for a tyrant. Rabelais uses the biblical story of David and Goliath (1 Samuel 17.4–51) to celebrate the fight of humanist enlightenment against menacing political abuses.

Gargantua, too, has an epic destiny in the first book (composed second and in many ways a revision of the first): his father's lands are under attack by a former ally, King Picrochole (Greek for "bitter bile"), and Gargantua returns home to defend them. Bad counselors have turned Picrochole from a friendly neighbor into an imperial marauder bent on conquering the world. They urge him to sail through the straits of Gibraltar and—in a Renaissance image of transgressive audacity—to "erect two columns more magnificent than those of Hercules in perpetual memory of [his] name." The Strait of Gibraltar, they promise him, "shall be called the Picrocholine Sea." The columns that these warmongering counselors have in mind were erected by Hercules, the legendary Greco-Roman demigod, to mark the ends of the Western world, beyond which no one should go (although Dante's bold Ulysses did). These pillars were also the emblem of the Holy Roman Emperor, Charles V, with whom Rabelais implicitly compares Picrochole. In *Gargantua*, Rabelais compares recent European history with an imperial epic in which Charles V and Francis I struggle for dominion in Europe and the title of emperor.

Yet Rabelais does not celebrate imperial expansion: Gargantua and his friends resist the would-be conquerors of their books, which form an anti-imperialistic epic. In his commitment to pacifism, Rabelais does not follow Virgil, who accepts the sacrifices of empire, but instead Erasmus, who believes that the only wars Christians should fight are defensive, a position that leaves out crusades and conquests.

After Gargantua and his friends defeat Picrochole's armies, they found a city that will cultivate the values for which they fought. They establish a community that affirms pacifist, liberal, humanistic values and name it the Abbey of Thélème, derived from the Greek word for "will" or "desire." The abbey's rules forbid men to live without women, and vice versa; ban clocks; and decree that all entrances and exits be voluntary (monks needed a papal dispensation to leave the monastery). Moreover, since monks and nuns usually took vows of chastity, poverty, and obedience, it was decided that in Thélème all inhabitants could marry with honor, be rich, and live wherever they wanted. On the great gate of Thélème, the architects inscribed a poem about Christian life, restored to its pristine state: hypocrites, bigots, liars, frauds, lawyers, and judges are cordially asked to stay away: they are dogs, frogs, fleas, and plague sores! "Sportsmen, lovers, friends," on the other hand, know and love the holy Word of God and are joyfully welcomed within the abbey's walls. Like the idealized court of Castiglione's Urbino, the abbey is populated with beautiful, intelligent, and learned youths who dress, converse, play games, value communal harmony, and relish the goal of married, sexual love. Designed to promote the simultaneous fulfillment of individual and communal will, Rabelais's abbey cultivates marriages that are free from conflicts of will and then releases the couples into the larger community, where the blissful unions lay the foundation of an equally harmonious society—one based on consent and the exercise of liberties.

Rabelais's abbey is not, however, a completely imagined world. It begins as a fantasy *negating* undesirable aspects of social reality in Europe rather than *creating* an independent social model. As Rabelais describes the abbey, he grows increasingly interested in the material conditions that produce the splendor of his fantasy world. His utopia, for example, follows the laws of supply and demand: as it turns out, there is a wing of low-lying buildings outside the abbey walls, where craftsmen import the wealth of the West Indies and set about their bourgeois trade of manufacturing luxuries for the wealthy. The more interested Rabelais grows in his abbey, the more it develops into an alluring paradox, beginning and ending in criticism of imperialism and colonization.

Few works in the Renaissance are as artistically and intellectually expansive as Rabelais's *Gargantua and Pantagruel*. The books are outrageous and serious, entertaining and thought-provoking. Rabelais's work takes the idea of "serious play" to such extremes that readers caught up in its rollicking humor may enter fully into the hedonistic escape that a brilliantly conceived fiction can offer. The same readers, drawn into its weighty artistic, intellectual, and sociopolitical thought, may at other times "forget" to laugh. Both are appropriate responses to Rabelais's extraordinary books.

Donald M. Frame, *François Rabelais: A Study* (1977), provides an overview of Rabelais's life, narrative techniques, and themes. Mikhail Bakhtin, *Rabelais and His World* (1968, 1984), is a groundbreaking analysis of the popular festivities that Rabelais draws on in his work. Thomas M. Greene, *Rabelais: A Study in Comic Courage* (1970), provides a concise overview and introduction. Although not meant for the general reader, Edwin M. Duval, *The Design of Rabelais's Pantagruel* (1991), Carla Freccero, *Father Figures: Genealogy and Narrative Structure in Rabelais* (1991), and Walter Stephens, *Giants in Those Days: Folklore, Ancient History, and Nationalism* (1989), are rewarding recent studies. Elizabeth Chesney Zegura and Marcel Tetel, *Rabelais Revisited* (1990), offers a good general introduction.

PRONOUNCING GLOSSARY

The following list uses common English syllables and stress accents to provide rough equivalents of selected words whose pronunciation may be unfamiliar to the general reader.

Alcofribas Nasier: *ahl-coh-free-bah'*
   nah-zyay'
Almain: *ahl-manh'*
Anatole: *ahn-ah-tohl'*
Artice: *ahr-tees*
Basché: *bah-shay'*
Beauce: *bohs*
Bonnivet: *bon-ee-vay'*
Boulogne: *boo-lun'*
Calaer: *cah-lah-ehr'*
Chantilly: *shawn-tee-yee'*
Chastillon: *shah-tee-yohnh'*
Chinon: *shee-nohn'*
Cryere: *cree-yehr'*
Fontainebleau: *fohn-ten-bloh'*
Gentilly: *zhawn-tee-yee'*
Jean Thenaud: *zhawn tay-noh'*
Langeais: *lawnh-zhay'*
Langedoc: *lawnh-ge-dawk'*
Mesembriné: *may-zawn-bree-nay'*

Nantes: *nawnt*
Papeligosse: *pah-plee-gaws'*
Philippe des Marais: *fee-leep' day*
   mahr-ay'
Picrochole: *pee-craw-shol'*
Port-Huault: *por–yew-oh'*
rondelle: *rohn-del'*
Rouen: *roo-awnh'*
Rue de Jardins: *rew deu zhahr-danh'*
Saint Denis: *sanh deu-nee'*
Saint-Cloud: *sanh–cloo'*
Saint-Mars: *sanh–mahr'*
Saint-Martin d'Ainay: *sanh–mahr-tanh'*
   den-ay'
Seine: *sen*
Thaumaste: *toh-mahst'*
Thélème: *tay-lem'*
Touraine: *too-ren'*
Vanves: *vahnv*

FROM GARGANTUA AND PANTAGRUEL[1]

From Book I

[Education of a Giant Humanist]

CHAPTER 14

How Gargantua Was Taught Latin by a Terribly Learned Philosopher

This subject disposed of, that good man Grandgousier was ravished with admiration, thinking about the good sense and marvelous comprehension of his son Gargantua. And so he said to his governesses:

"Philip, king of Macedonia, understood the good sense of his son Alexander by his skill in handling a certain horse, which was so terrible, so completely wild, that no one could even get up on its back. He bucked and threw everyone who tried to ride him, breaking the neck of one, the legs of another, cracking one man's skull and shattering another's jawbone. When Alexander

1. Translated by Burton Raffel.

went down into the Hippodrome (which was where they trained and exercised their horses) and analyzed the problem, he saw that the horse's desperate fury came, simply enough, from being afraid of his own shadow. Having come to this understanding, he jumped up on the horse's back and forced him to run straight toward the sun, so that his shadow fell behind him, and by this procedure turned the horse gentle and obedient. And that showed his father what divine understanding his son possessed, and he arranged that the boy be thoroughly trained by Aristotle, who was at that time considered the best philosopher in Greece.

"But I tell you that from this one discussion, which my son and I have just had, right here in front of you, I too understand that his understanding has something divine about it—so acute, subtle, profound, and yet serene—and will attain to a singularly lofty degree of wisdom, provided he is well taught. Accordingly, I wish to put him in the hands of some scholarly man who will teach him everything he is capable of learning. And to this end I propose to open my purse as freely as need be."

So they sent for a great philosopher, Maître Tubalcain Holofernes, who taught him the alphabet so well that he could say it backward, by heart, at which point he was five years and three months old. Then he read with the boy a Latin grammar by Donatus, plus a dull and well-meaning treatise on courtesy, and a long book by Bishop Theodulus, in which he proves that ancient mythology is all a heap of nonsense, and finally an exceedingly long poem in dreadfully moral quatrains.[2] All this took thirteen years, six months, and two weeks to accomplish.

Of course, it's also true that he learned to write in Gothic letters, and wrote out all his own books that way, since this was before the art of printing had been invented.

Most of the time he carried a large writing desk, weighing more than thirty tons, with a pencil box as big and heavy as the four great pillars of Saint-Martin d'Ainay, the old church in Lyons. And the inkpot hung down on huge iron chains, capable of supporting barrels and barrels of merchandise.

And then they read *De modis significandi,* "The Methods of Reasoned Analysis," with the commentaries of Broken Biscuithead, Bouncing Rock, Talktoomuch, Galahad, John the Fatted Calf, Balogny, Cuntprober, and a pile of others. And this took more than eighteen years and six months. And by then Gargantua knew it all so well that, if you asked him, he could recite every single line, backward, proving to his mother that he had the whole thing at his fingertips and, most important of all, that *de modis significandi non erat scientia,* the methods of reasoned analysis were neither reasonable nor a science.

Then they read that great book *Calculation,* surely the longest almanac ever compiled: this took another sixteen years and two months. And then, suddenly, his teacher died, being four hundred and twenty years old: it was the pox that carried him off.

So they brought in another old cougher, Maître Blowhard Birdbrain, with whom he read Bishop Huguito of Ferrara, Eberhard de Bethune's *Greekishnessisms,* Alexander de Villedieu's barbarous Latin grammar, Remigius' *Petty*

---

2. The books mentioned in this chapter were actually part of the educational curriculum that Rabelais is here satirizing.

Doctrines and also his *What's What,* a charming discourse set in question-and-answer form, the *Supplement to All Supplements,* a fat glossary of saints' lives and the like, Sulpicius' long, long poem on the psalms and death, Seneca's *De quatuor virtutibus cardinalibus,* The Four Cardinal Virtues (which wasn't by Seneca at all), Passavantus' *Mirror of True Penitence,* and the same author's *Sleep in Peace,* a collection of sermons chosen to make happy days still happier—and he also read other tough birds of the same feather. And in reading all this he became quite as wise as any blackbird ever baked in a pie.

CHAPTER 15

How Gargantua Got to Study with Other Teachers

By that point his father could see that although he was studying as hard as he could, and spending all his time at it, he didn't seem to be learning much and, what's worse, he was becoming distinctly stupid, a real simpleton, all wishy-washy and driveling.

When he complained of this to Don Philippe des Marais, viceroy of Papeligosse,[3] he was told that it would be better for Gargantua to learn nothing at all than to study such books with such teachers, whose learning was nothing but stupidity and whose wisdom was nothing but gloves with no hands in them—empty. They were specialists in ruining good and noble spirits and nipping the flowering of youth in the bud.

"To show you what I mean," he said, "take some modern youngster, who has only been studying for two years. If he doesn't show better judgment, better use of words, better ability to analyze and discuss than your son, as well as greater ease and courtesy in dealing with the world, then call me a fat-head from Brenne."

Grandgousier was delighted and told him to do exactly that.

That night, at supper, des Marais introduced one of his young pages, a young fellow named Rightway (in Greek, Eudemon), who was from Villegongis, near Saint-Genou. And he was so well-groomed, so beautifully dressed, so clean and neat in every respect, so courteous in his bearing, that he more nearly resembled a little angel than a human being. And des Marais said to Grandgousier:

"See this child? He's only twelve years old. Shall we see, if you care to, what a difference there is between the learning of your bird-chirping old philosophers and modern youngsters like this?"

Grandgousier liked the idea, and told the page to give them a demonstration of what he knew. Then Rightway, after asking his master's permission to proceed, stood on his feet, his hat in his hands, his face open, his lips red, his eyes confident, his glance fixed on Gargantua with a modesty appropriate to his age, and began both to praise and to glorify Grandgousier's son, first for his virtue and his good manners, second for his knowledge, third for his nobility, fourth for his physical beauty, and then, fifth, sweetly urged him always to honor his father, who had taken such pains to have him well brought up, finally begging Gargantua to consider Master Rightway the most

---

3. Probably an allusion to a real person. Rabelais's method is to take real people and introduce them into his fantastic world; he also mentions real places and draws on local lore.

insignificant of his servants, for the boy asked no other gift from the heavens but the grace of pleasing Gargantua by some cheerfully rendered service. And all of this was spoken with such extraordinarily tactful gestures, with a pronunciation so clear, a voice so eloquent, and in language so elegant and such good Latin, that he more nearly resembled a kind of ancient Gracchus, or Cicero, or Ennius than a young person of his own time.

But all Gargantua could do was weep like a cow. He hid his face behind his hat, and it was no more possible to draw a word from him than to get a fart from a dead donkey.

All of which made his father so furious that he wanted to kill Maître Blowhard Birdbrain. But des Marais checked him with a well-turned word of warning, so neatly administered that it cooled his anger. But he ordered that Blowhard Birdbrain be paid what he was owed and allowed to guzzle like a philosopher. And when he'd drunk to his heart's content, he was to be told to go to the devil.

"It won't cost me a thing," he said, "not today at least, if he gets so drunk that he dies of it, like an Englishman."

Maître Blowhard Birdbrain left the house. Grandgousier sought des Marais' advice about who might be available to be Gargantua's new teacher, and the two of them decided that Powerbrain (in Greek, Ponocrates), Rightway's teacher, would be the best man for the job. The three of them would then travel to Paris, the better to understand how the young men of France were pursuing their studies.

CHAPTER 16

How Gargantua Was Sent to Paris, Riding an Enormous Brood Mare, Which Waged War against the Cow Flies of Beauce

Now, at this same time Fayoles, fourth king of Numidia, happened to send Grandgousier, all the way from Africa, the biggest, tallest brood mare anyone had ever seen. And the most monstrous, too (it being well known that Africa always brings forth new things), for it was the size of six elephants and it had toes, like Julius Caesar's horse; its ears hung down like a Languedoc goat, and it had a horn sticking out of its ass. For the rest, it had a kind of burned chestnut hide, mottled with gray. Most impressive of all was its ghastly tail, because—give a pound, take a pound—it was as big as the old ruin of Saint-Mars, near Langeais (which is forty feet high), and every bit as wide, with hair as closely woven as the tassels on an ear of corn.

And if that strikes you as astonishing, what do you think of those amazing Scythian rams, weighing in at more than thirty pounds apiece, and those Syrian sheep, which (if Jean Thenaud is telling the truth) have an ass so heavy, so long and massive, that they have to tie a supporting cart to its rear end so it can get about at all. You haven't got anything like it, you lowland ass bangers!

It came by sea, in three Genoan schooners and a man-of-war, to the port of Les Sables-d'Olonne, in Talmont.

When Grandgousier saw it:

"This is exactly the right thing," he said, "to carry my son to Paris. Now, God be thanked, everything will turn out all right. Someday he'll surely be a great scholar. If it weren't for our friends the animals, we'd all have to live like philosophers."

The next day, but of course only after having drunk their fill, Gargantua, his new teacher Powerbrain, and all his attendants, together with the young page Rightway, took to the road. And because the weather was calm and moderate, his father had them make soft laced boots for Gargantua. (That great bootmaker Babin tells me they go by the name of buskins.)

So they went merrily down the highway, laughing and singing, until they had almost reached Orleáns. There they entered a large forest, ninety miles long and forty miles wide. The place swarmed with horrible cow flies, millions of them, and wasps and hornets, too, the sort that were true highway robbers for all poor mares and mules and horses. But Gargantua's mare took an appropriate revenge for all the outrages her species had suffered, playing a trick that those insects had never expected. Suddenly, as they entered the wood and the flies and wasps began their assault, she whipped out her tail and swatted them so vigorously that in fact she knocked down the entire forest. Left, right, here, there, length and width, over and under, she smashed those trees like a mower cutting grass, until finally there were neither any trees nor any insects, but just a nice flat stretch of land, which is all you can see to this day.

Gargantua watched this performance with immense delight. But he didn't want to sound vainglorious, so all he said to his companions was, "This is fine, but I don't want to boast." And ever since that part of the country has been known as Beauce. But all they got to put in their open mouths was their own yawns—in memory of which the gentlemen of Beauce (and everyone knows how poor they've always been) still dine by yawning and opening and closing their empty mouths, which they've grown to like, especially since it helps them spit.

When at last they reached Paris, Gargantua spent two or three days resting and recovering from their journey, drinking and chatting with the townsfolk and asking what scholars happened to be in the city at that time and what wine Parisians liked to drink.

*   *   *

CHAPTER 21

[Gargantua's Studies, and His Way of Life, according to His Philosophical Teachers]

Some days after the bells had been put back, and in recognition of Gargantua's courtesy in thus restoring them, the citizens of Paris offered to feed and maintain his mare for as long as he might like, an offer which Gargantua found most acceptable. So the mare was put to pasture in Fontainebleau Forest. I don't think she is still there.

Gargantua was absolutely determined to study under Powerbrain. To begin with, however, Powerbrain directed his new pupil to proceed exactly as he always had, the better to understand how, over such a long period of time, his former teachers had turned him into such a fop, such a fool and ignoramus.

Accordingly, Gargantua lived just as he usually did, waking up between eight and nine (whether it was daylight or not), exactly as his old teachers had prescribed. And they cited the words of King David: *Vanum est vobis ante lucem surgere,* It does you no good to wake before day begins.[4]

So he fooled about, swaggering, wallowing away the time in his bed (the better to enliven his animal spirits), and then dressed himself as the season dictated. But what he really liked to put on was a great long gown of heavy wool, lined with fox fur. And then he combed his hair as that great Ockhamist philosopher Jacob Almain always did—that is, with four fingers and a thumb, because his teachers used to say that, in this world of ours, to pay any more attention than that to your hair—or to washing and keeping yourself clean— was simply a waste of time.

Then he shat, pissed, vomited, belched, farted, yawned, spat, coughed, sighed, sneezed, and blew his nose abundantly. Then he put away a good breakfast, the better to protect himself against the dew and the bad morning air: good fried tripe, some nice broiled steak, several cheerful hams, some good grilled beef, and several platters of bread soaked in bouillon.

Powerbrain objected, observing that, fresh out of bed and before he'd been exercising, he hardly needed to take in so much refreshment. Gargantua replied:

"What! Haven't I already done enough exercise? I turned over in bed six or seven times before I got up. Isn't that enough? That's exactly what Pope Alexander used to do, and he was following the advice of his great Jewish doctor and astrologer, Bonnet de Lates. And he lived until he died, too, in spite of those who did not wish him well. This is what my prior teachers got me used to doing, saying that breakfast helped you develop your memory: that was why they started drinking at breakfast, too. I think it's marvelous— and it starts me off so well that I eat an even better supper. And Maître Tubalcain Holofernes (who was right at the head of his class, here in Paris) used to say there was no point at all just to running well: the idea was to leave early enough. So true good health for all of us doesn't require, does it, that we gulp it down, cup after cup after cup, like ducks, but certainly that we start to drink in the morning—*unde versus,* as the little poem says:

> To wake up early in the morning isn't the point:
> You've got to wet your whistle and bend that joint."

And so, after a hearty breakfast, he went to church, where they brought him, in a huge basket, a great fat prayer book, all wrapped in velvet, so heavily oiled, with such heavy clasps, and on such luxurious parchment that it must have weighed at least twenty-five hundred pounds. And then they heard twenty-six or maybe thirty masses. And then his private chaplain would come, dressed like a society swell, and with his breath nicely fortified by wine. He and Gargantua would mumble through the litany, thumbing the rosary so carefully that not a single bead ever fell to the ground.

As he walked out of church, they brought in a heavy-wheeled log carrier and delivered for his personal use an entire cask of carved-wood rosaries, each of them as round around as the rim of a man's hat. And as he and his

---

4. Psalm 127.2: "It is vain for you to rise up early, to sit up late, to eat the bread of sorrows: for so he giveth his beloved sleep."

chaplain strolled through the cloister of the church, and its galleries and gardens, they worked at their beads, saying more prayers than sixteen hermits.

Then he put in a scant half-hour of studying, keeping his eyes on his book. But, like the character in Terence's play, his soul was in the kitchen.[5]

Then he pissed his urinal full, sat down to table, and—being naturally of a calm and imperturbable disposition—began his meal with several dozen hams, smoked beef tongues, caviar, fried tripe, and assorted other appetizers.

Meanwhile, four of his servants began to toss into his mouth, one after the other—but never stopping—shovelfuls of mustard, after which he drank an incredibly long draft of white wine, to make things easier for his kidneys. And then, eating whatever happened to be in season and he happened to like, he stopped only when his belly began to hang down.

His drinking was totally unregulated, without any limits or decorum. As he said, the time to restrict your drinking was only when the cork soles of your slippers absorb enough so they swell half a foot thick.

*   *   *

CHAPTER 23

How Gargantua Was So Well Taught by Powerbrain That He Never Wasted a Single Hour of the Day

Once Powerbrain understood Gargantua's vicious way of life, he began to reflect on other—and better—ways of instructing him in humanistic matters. But for the first few days he did not make any changes, realizing that nature would not allow abrupt shifts without cataclysmic violence.

Accordingly, to begin his work in the best way possible, he sought the advice of a wise physician, Holygift, with whom he discussed how to set Gargantua on a better path. The learned doctor, proceeding according to his profession's canonical rules, first purged the young man with a sovereign remedy for madness, Anticyrian hellebore, which powerful herb quickly cleaned away all the deterioration and perverse habits to which his brain had succumbed. This procedure had the advantage, also, of making Gargantua forget everything he had learned from his early teachers, just as in ancient times Timotheus[6] did with disciples who'd studied under other musicians.

To help in the good work, Powerbrain introduced Gargantua to some of Paris's truly learned scholars. In trying to be like them, he came to understand their spirit, wanting to acquire knowledge and to make something of himself.

And then he got him into such a way of studying that no hour in the day was wasted: all his time was spent in pursuit of humanistic learning and honest knowledge.

Accordingly, Gargantua now woke up at four in the morning. He would be given a massage, while a portion of the holy Scriptures was read aloud to him, in a high, clear voice, with precise and accurate pronunciation. A young page named Reader, a native of Basché, was given this task. The subject, and

---

5. *The Eunuch,* line 816.   6. Of Miletus, famous musician of the time of Alexander the Great (356–323 B.C.).

also the argument, of this lesson often led Gargantua into reverence and adoration of God, the majesty and marvelous wisdom of whom had thus been exhibited to him, and into prayer and supplication.

Then he would go off and, in some private place, permit the natural result of his digestive process to be excreted. While he was thus occupied, his teacher would repeat what had been read to him, clarifying and explaining the more obscure and difficult points.

Coming back, they would examine and reflect on the state of the heavens: was everything as it had been when they'd seen the sky the night before? into what constellations had the sun newly entered, and likewise the moon?

And then he was dressed and combed, his hair was properly done, and he was equipped and perfumed, while all the time the lessons he'd been given the day before were repeated for him. He recited them by heart, showing by some practical and compassionate illustrations that he understood their meaning. This often lasted two or three hours, though ordinarily they stopped when he was fully dressed.

Then he was read to for three solid hours.

After which they went outdoors, always discussing the meaning of what had been read, and went to the park or somewhere near it, where they played various games, especially three-handed palm ball, giving their bodies the same elegant exercise they had earlier given their souls.

Their games were entirely free: they stopped whenever they felt like stopping—usually when they'd worked up a sweat or when they grew tired. Then they had a vigorous massage, and were wiped clean; they'd change their shirts and, walking quietly, would go to see if dinner was ready. And as they waited they'd recite, clearly and eloquently, remembered portions of the lesson.

However, Sir Appetite arrived, and when they could they seated themselves at the table.

Some entertaining story of ancient heroism was read to them, at the start of the meal, until wine was poured in Gargantua's cup.

Then, if they liked the idea, the reading was resumed, or else they'd begin to chat happily. At the beginning of this new regime, they talked about virtue, proper behavior, the nature and effect of everything placed on their table that day: bread, wine, water, salt, meat, fish, fruit, herbs, roots, and about the preparation of these things. In so doing, Gargantua soon learned all the appropriate passages from Pliny, Athenaeus, Dioscorides, Julius Pollux, Galen, Porphyry, Oppian, Polybius, Heliodorus, Aristotle, Claudius Aelian,[7] and others. In order to be sure they had their authorities right, they'd often have the books brought right to the table. And what was said became so clearly and entirely fixed in Gargantua's memory that no doctor alive understood anything like as much as he did.

Then, talking about the lessons read that morning, and finishing their meal with some quinced sweet, Gargantua would clean his teeth with a bit of fresh green mastic twig. He'd wash his hands and his eyes with good fresh water, and give thanks to God with sweet hymns of praise for His munificence and divine kindness. And cards were brought, not for playing games of chance,

7. Some of the most famous scientific authors of antiquity. The new curriculum, exacting as it is, reflects a less "medieval" type of learning than was embodied in his earlier course of study. See also the enumeration of authors in chap. 14.

but to learn a thousand gracious things and new inventions, all founded in arithmetic.

And in this way Gargantua developed a genuine liking for the numerical science. Every day, after both dinner and supper, he passed his time in arithmetical games just as pleasantly as when he'd been in the habit of playing at dice or cards. Indeed, he came to understand both the theory and the practice of arithmetic so well that Cuthbert Tunstal,[8] the Englishman who had written so much on the subject, was obliged to admit that, truly, in comparison to Gargantua, all he understood was a pack of nonsense.

But arithmetic wasn't the end of it, for they went on to other mathematical sciences, like geometry, astronomy, and music. While waiting for their meal to be digested and properly absorbed, they worked out a thousand pleasant geometrical figures, and shaped appropriate instruments, and practiced astronomical laws in the same way.

Later, they had a wonderful good time, singing four- and five-part rounds, and sometimes singing variations on some melody that was a delight to their throats.

As for musical instruments, Gargantua learned to play the lute, the clavier, the harp, the transverse flute as well as the recorder, the viol, and also the trombone.

As this hour passed, digestion was indeed accomplished, and so he proceeded to purge himself of his natural excrement. Then he at once returned to his main studies for three hours or even more, in order to repeat the morning's lesson and also to continue with whatever book had been set for him. And he practiced writing in the Italian and the Gothic alphabets, and also drawing.

And then they'd go back to their rooms, and along with them went a young gentleman from Touraine, Squire Gymnast by name, who was teaching Gargantua the arts of knighthood.

After changing his clothes, Gargantua would mount a battle horse, a traveling steed, a Spanish stallion, an Arabian racehorse, and a light, quick horse, and ride a hundred laps, making his mount fairly fly through the air, jump ditches, leap over fences, make quick circular turns, both to the right and to the left.

Nor did he break his lance, for it is sheer nonsense to say, "I broke ten lances in battle." Any carpenter could do as much. Real glory comes from breaking ten of your enemies' with one of your own. So, with his steel-tipped, solid, firm lance he learned to break down a door, crack open a suit of armor, uproot a tree, strike right through the center of a hoop, knock a knight's saddle right off his horse, and carry away a coat of mail or a pair of armored gloves. And all the time he was himself in armor, from his head right down to his toes.

When it came to marching his horse in rhythm, or making the animal obey his commands, there was simply no one better. Even Cesare Fieschi, the famous equestrian acrobat, seemed no better than a monkey on horseback, in comparison. He was especially good at leaping from one horse to another, without ever setting foot on the ground—the horses were known as leapers—and he could do this from either side, lance erect, without stirrups. Without

---

8. Author of the treatise *The Art of Computation* (*De arte supputandi*, 1522).

any reins or bridle he could make a horse do anything he wanted it to do. In short, he was accomplished at everything useful in military matters.

Some days he exercised with the battle-ax, which he could wield like a razor, swinging it so powerfully, slicing it around in a circle so deftly, that he was ranked a knight at arms, passing every sort of trial and declared fit for any battle.

And then he'd practice with the pickax, or at wielding the two-handed sword, or with the short sword (so perfect for thrusting and parrying), and the dagger—sometimes wearing armor, sometimes not, or using a shield, or wearing a cape, or carrying a small wrist shield, known as a *rondelle*.

He hunted deer—stag and doe and fallow buck—bears, wild boar, hares, partridge, pheasant, buzzards. He played with the big kickball, making it bound high in the air, sometimes with his foot, sometimes with his fist. He fought and ran and leaped and jumped—but not a mere three-foot hop and leap, or a high jump in the German style—because, as Gymnast said, jumps of that sort were useless and of no good whatever, when it came to real war—but he'd jump great wide ditches, go flying over a hedgerow, climb six paces up a wall, and thus get in through a window as high off the ground as a lance.

He swam in deep water, breaststroke, backstroke, sidestroke, using his entire body or only his legs, or with one hand high in the air and holding a book, crossing the Seine River without getting a page wet. He swam with his cloak in his teeth, as Julius Caesar did (says Plutarch). Then, pulling himself right into a boat with just one hand, he'd throw himself back into the water, head first, going all the way down to the bottom, sinking among the rocks and swimming to great depths, plunging down to all sorts of chasms and deep abysses. Then he'd turn the boat, and steer it, sometimes quickly, sometimes slowly, now downstream, now upstream, sometimes bringing it to a halt by pressing it against a milldam, guiding it with one hand, his other wielding a great oar or raising the sail. He'd climb up the guide ropes, right to the top of the mast, and run out along the spars. He'd adjust the compass, brace the bowlines, tighten the helm.

Leaving the water, he'd go directly up a mountain and then come right down again. He'd climb trees like a cat, jumping from one to the other like a squirrel, tearing down thick branches as if he were another Milo of Croton. With a pair of sharp-pointed daggers and a couple of good marlinespikes, he'd climb to the top of a house exactly like a rat, then leap down so expertly that the drop wouldn't cause him so much as a twinge.

He threw the javelin, and the iron bar, the millstone, the boar spear, the hunting spear, the spiked halberd. He drew the longbow like an archer, pulled crossbows taut (though this was usually done with a winch), sighted a rifle right against his eye (though usually it had to be rested against the shoulder), set up and mounted cannon, centering them right in on target, aimed them so they could knock a stuffed parrot off a pole, pointing them straight up a mountain or right down into a valley, directing their fire up ahead or to the side or, like the ancient Parthians, back behind him.

They would attach a rope cable to some high tower, hanging down to the ground, and he would climb this, hand over hand, then come down so strongly and with such confidence that he might just as well have been strolling along some nice, flat meadow.

They would rig up a long pole, supported on each side by a tree, and he'd hang from it by his hands, going this way and that without his feet ever touching the ground—and at such a speed that, even running on flat ground, it would have been impossible to catch him.

And in order to exercise his chest and lungs, he would shout like all the devils in hell. Once, I heard him call to Rightway, from the Saint Victor Gate all the way across Paris to Montmartre. Even bull-throated Stentor,[9] at the battle of Troy, could not shout so loud.

To toughen his nerves, they made him two huge molded lead weights, cast in the shape of salmon, each just over eighty thousand pounds: he called them his dumbbells. He'd lift one in each hand, starting from the ground, and hold them both high up over his head—and then he'd keep them there, not moving a muscle, for three-quarters of an hour or even more. This was literally unmatchable strength!

No one was stronger, not in barriers or tug-of-war or any of the games. When it was his turn, he stood his ground so firmly that he could afford to let the most adventurous try to move him a single inch from his place, exactly as Milo of Croton used to do—and in imitation of whom he would clasp a pomegranate in his hand and offer it to anyone who could take it from him. Nor would he permit the fruit to be damaged in the attempt.

Having thus spent his time, he'd have another massage, then clean himself and change his clothes, returning with a smile and, strolling through meadows and other grassy spots, he'd turn his attention to trees and plants, examining them in the light of what the ancients wrote—Theophrastus, Dioscorides, Marinus, Pliny, Nicander, Aemilius Macer, and Galen.[1] He and his companions would fill their hands with herbs and roots and flowers, then bring it all back to their lodgings, where a young page, Rootgatherer, was in charge of all such matters, including care of the hoes, picks, rakes, spades, shovels, and everything else needed for the proper care of growing things.

And once they were back at their lodgings, and while waiting for their supper, they would repeat selected passages from what they had read, earlier, and also what they had discussed at table.

Note, please, that although dinner was a sober and even frugal meal, at which Gargantua would eat only just enough to control the growling in his stomach, supper was a great abundant affair. He would consume everything he needed to sustain and properly nourish himself, which is exactly the sort of diet prescribed by any good, knowing doctor, though there are plenty of medical hacks (in constant dispute, of course, with learned academic philosophers) who advise exactly the opposite.

Gargantua continued his lessons all during supper, or for as long as he felt in the mood. And then he would turn to good solid discussion, literate, informed, useful.

After a final grace had been said, they would turn to music, singing, the harmonious playing of various instruments, or to pleasant card and dice games. And there they would stay, having a fine time, often amusing themselves until it was time to go to bed. And sometimes they would go visiting the houses of learned people, or perhaps those newly returned from foreign countries.

When night had truly arrived, but before they climbed into bed, they would

9. The loud-voiced herald in the *Iliad* 5.   1. Greek and Roman scientists.

stand in their lodgings, in the spot from which the sky could be most closely observed, and compare notes about any comets they might see, and the configuration of the stars, their location and aspect, their oppositions and conjunctions.

And then Gargantua and Powerbrain would briefly recapitulate, according to the Pythagorean fashion, everything Gargantua had read and seen and understood, everything he had done and heard, all day long.

They would both pray to God their Creator, worshiping, reaffirming their faith, glorifying Him for His immense goodness and thanking Him for all they had been given, and forever placing themselves in His hands.

And then they would go to sleep.

CHAPTER 24

[What Gargantua Did When It Was Rainy]

When the weather turned rainy and bad, the time before dinner went exactly as usual, except that Gargantua had a good bright fire lit, to help moderate the intemperate air. But after dinner, in place of exercise, they would stay indoors and, according to the best therapeutic approach, amuse themselves by baling hay, sawing and splitting wood, and threshing the grain stored in the barn. Then they would study the art of painting and sculpture, or else (following ancient custom) play knucklebones, an entertainment about which Leonicus Thomaeus has written so well—and a game which Andreas Lascaris,[2] teacher and friend of Erasmus, and my good friend too, has played with such pleasure. And while they played they turned over in their mind all the passages from classical authors in which the game is either mentioned or used as a metaphor.

In the same way, they would either go to watch the work at metal foundries, or the casting of cannon, or go to observe jewelers, goldsmiths, and those who cut precious stones, or else alchemists and coin makers, or tapestry weavers, silk weavers, velvet makers, watchmakers, mirror makers, printers, organ manufacturers, dyers, and other craftsmen of that sort. And treating all of them to wine, they learned from the mouths of these masters what their various trades and inventions were all about.

They would go to hear public lectures, solemn convocations, and the careful orations, declamations, and pleadings of wellborn lawyers, or the sermons of evangelical preachers.

He went to all the places where swordsmanship was practiced and taught, and tested himself against those who taught it, in every aspect of fencing and with all the sorts of swords and foils known. And he demonstrated to them that he knew as much as they did, and more.

Instead of going off to collect herbs and examine plants and flowers, they would go to drugstores, herb sellers, and other apothecaries, and contemplate with great care the fruits, roots, leaves, gums, seeds, and all the exotic unguents, and then how they were prepared and diluted for more effective use.

He went to see the jugglers and clowns, the magicians and those who peddled wonderful, half-magical remedies, and contemplated their games

---

2. André-Jean de Lascaris (ca. 1445–ca. 1535), librarian to King Francis I and a friend of Rabelais's. Leonicus Thomaeus (d. 1531), a Venetian and professor at Padua.

and tricks, their somersaults and smooth patter, especially those famous mountebanks from Chauny, in Picardy—born with a silver tongue, every one of them, able to sell water to people swimming in a lake or firewood to those who live inside a volcano.

They would return for supper, and eat more sparingly than on other days—in particular, meats that tend to dry and tame the body. This was made necessary by the excessive humidity in the air, which under the circumstances there was no way to avoid. These simple dietary measures corrected that natural imbalance and saved them from being bothered by the loss of their usual exercise.

And this was how Gargantua's life was regulated. He kept to these rules every day, and he benefited—to be sure!—as a young man of his years can, a youth with good sense. All regular exercise, no matter how hard it may at first seem, becomes pleasant and easy and finally great good fun, more like a royal pastime than a scholar's plodding.

In spite of which, and in order to allow him some relief from such a whirlwind way of life, Powerbrain made sure that Gargantua took off at least one day a month, some day of great clarity and calm brightness. They would leave Paris early in the morning and go to one of the pleasant villages beloved of all Parisian students—Gentilly, perhaps, or Boulogne on the Seine, or Montrouge, or Pont-Charenton, or Vanves, or Saint-Cloud. And they would spent the entire day there, just as happily as they could manage, laughing, telling jokes, drinking gaily, playing, singing, dancing, lying on their backs in beautiful meadows, hunting for sparrows' nests, catching quail, and fishing for frogs and crayfish.

But even on this day spent without books and reading, they didn't completely neglect higher matters, because even lying there in the lovely meadows they would recite from memory cheerful verses from Virgil's *Georgics*, from Hesiod, from Politian's *Rusticus* (Farming), or some pleasant Latin epigrams, which they'd then turn into equally pleasant poems in their own language.

And when they feasted they would not simply mix their wine and water. Instead, as Cato advises in his *Country Matters*, and Pliny too, they would use a cup of ivy wood and wash the wine in a full basin of water, then pour it back out with a funnel.[3] And they would pour the water from one glass to another and construct tiny automatic engines that seemed to work of their own accord, like automatons.

[The Abbey of Thélème]

CHAPTER 52

How Gargantua Built the Abbey of Desire (Thélème) for Brother John

The only one still left to be provided for was the monk.[4] Gargantua wanted to make him abbot of Seuilly, but the monk refused. Gargantua also offered

---

3. Both Cato's *On Farming* (De re rustica) 109 and Pliny's *Natural History* 16.63 suggest an ivy-wood cup as a means to detect water in wine.   4. Brother John of the Funnels, the muscular and highly unconventional monk who has had a major part in helping the party of Gargantua's father win the mock-heroic war against the arrogant Picrochole.

him the abbey of Bourgueil or that of Saint-Florent, whichever best pleased him—and said he could have both those rich, old Benedictine cloisters, if he preferred that.[5] But the monk answered him in no uncertain terms: he wanted neither to govern nor to be in charge of other monks:

"And how," he asked, "should I govern others, when I don't know how to govern myself? If you really think I've done something for you, and I might in the future do something to please you, grant me this: establish an abbey according to my plan."

The request pleased Gargantua, so he offered him the whole land of Thélème, alongside the river Loire, two leagues from the great forest of Port-Huault. And the monk then asked Gargantua to establish this abbey's rules and regulations completely differently from all the others.

"Obviously," said Gargantua, "it won't be necessary to build walls all around it, because all the other abbeys are brutally closed in."

"Indeed," said the monk, "and for good reason. Whenever you've got a whole load of stones in front and a whole load of stones in back, you've got a whole lot of grumbling and complaining, and jealousy, and all kinds of conspiracies."

Moreover, since some of the cloisters already built in this world are in the habit, whenever any woman enters them (I speak only of modest, virtuous women), of washing the ground where she walked, it was decreed that if either a monk or a nun happened to enter the abbey of Thélème, they would scrub the blazes out of the places where they'd been. And since everything is completely regulated, in all the other cloistered houses, tied in and bound down, hour by hour, according to a fierce schedule, it was decreed that in Thélème there would not be a single clock, or even a sundial, and that work would be distributed strictly according to what was needed and who was available to do it—because (said Gargantua) the worst waste of time he knew of was counting the hours—what good could possibly come of it?—and the biggest, fattest nonsense in the whole world was to be ruled by the tolling of a bell rather than by the dictates of common sense and understanding.

Item: because in these times of ours women don't go into convents unless they're blind in one eye, lame, humpbacked, ugly, misshapen, crazy, stupid, deformed, or pox-ridden, and men only if they're tubercular, low born, blessed with an ugly nose, simpletons, or a burden on their parents . . .

("Oh yes," said the monk, "speaking of which: if a woman isn't pretty and she isn't good, what sort of path can she cut for herself?"

"Straight into a convent," said Gargantua.

"To be sure," said the monk, "especially with a scissors and a needle.")

. . . it was decreed that, in Thélème, women would be allowed only if they were beautiful, well formed, and cheerful, and men only if they were handsome, well formed, and cheerful.

Item: since men were not allowed in convents, unless they sneaked in under cover of darkness, it was decreed that in Thélème there would never be any women unless there were men, nor any men unless there were women.

Item: because both men and women, after they'd entered a cloister and served their probationary year, were obliged to spend the entire rest of their

---

5. A satiric allusion to the custom of accumulating church livings.

lives there, it was decided that men and women who came to Thélème could leave whenever they wanted to, freely and without restriction.

Item: because monks and nuns usually took three vows—chastity, poverty, and obedience—it was decided that in Thélème one could perfectly honorably be married, that anyone could be rich, and that they could all live wherever they wanted to.

As an age limitation, women should be allowed in at any time from ten to fifteen, and men from twelve to eighteen.

CHAPTER 53

How the Abbey of Desire (Thélème) Was Built and Endowed

In order to build and equip the abbey, Gargantua gave two million seven hundred thousand eight hundred and thirty-one gold pieces. Further, until everything had been completed, he assigned the yearly sum of one million six hundred and sixty thousand gold pieces, from the tolls on the river Dive, payable in funds of an unimaginable astrological purity. To endow and perpetually maintain the abbey he gave two million three hundred thousand and sixty-nine English pounds in property rentals, tax-free, fully secured, and payable yearly at the abbey gate, to which effect he had written out all the appropriate deeds and grants.

The building was hexagonal, constructed so that at each angle there was a great round tower sixty feet in diameter, and each of the towers was exactly like all the others. The river Loire was on the north side. One of the towers, called Artice (meaning "Arctic," or "Northern"), ran down almost to the riverbank; another, called Calaer (meaning "Lovely Air"), was just to the east. Then came Anatole (meaning "Oriental," or "Eastern"), and Mesembriné (meaning "Southern"), and then Hesperia (meaning "Occidental," or "Western"), and finally Cryere (meaning "Glacial"). The distance between each of the towers was three hundred and twelve feet. The building had six floors, counting the subterranean cellars as the first. The second or ground floor had a high vault, shaped like a basket handle. The other floors were stuccoed in a circular pattern, the way they do such things in Flanders; the roof was of fine slate, the coping being lead-decorated with small figurines and animals, handsomely colored and gilded; and there were rainspouts jutting out from the walls, between the casement windows, painted all the way to the ground with blue and gold stripes and ending in great pipes which led down to the river, below the building.

This was all a hundred times more magnificent than the grand chateau at Bonnivet, or that at Chambord, or that at Chantilly,[6] because it had nine thousand three hundred and thirty-two suites, each furnished with an antechamber, a private reading room, a dressing room, and a small personal chapel, and also because each and every room adjoined its own huge hall. Between each tower, in the middle of the main building, was a spiral staircase, its stairs made of crystal porphyry and red Numidian marble and green marble struck through with red and white, all exactly twenty-two feet wide and three fingers thick, there being twelve stairs between each landing. Fur-

---

6. Châteaux built in the early and middle years of the 16th century. Rabelais is again mixing realism with fantasy.

ther: each landing had a beautiful double arch, in Greek style, thus allowing light to flood through and also framing an entryway into overhanging private rooms, each of them just as broad as the stairway itself. The stair wound all the way to the roof, ending there in a pavilion. Off the stair, on each side, one could come to a great hall; the stair also led the way to the private suites and rooms.

Between the tower called Artice and that called Cryere were great beautiful reading rooms, well stocked with books in Greek, Latin, Hebrew, French, Italian, and Spanish, carefully divided according to the languages in which they had been written.

In the center of the main building, entered through an arch thirty-six yards across, stood a marvelous circular ramp. It was fashioned so harmoniously, and built so large, that six men-at-arms, their lances at the ready, could ride clear up to the top of the building, side by side.

Between the tower called Anatole and that called Mesembriné were beautiful galleries, large and open, painted with scenes of ancient heroism, episodes drawn from history, and strange and fascinating plants and animals. Here, too, just as on the side facing the river, were a ramp and a gate. And on this gate was written, in large antique letters, the poem which follows:

CHAPTER 54

[The Inscription on the Great Gate of Thélème]

Hypocrites, bigots, stay away!
Old humbugs, puffed-up liars, playful
Religious frauds, worse than Goths
Or Ostrogoths (or other sloths):
No hairshirts, here, no sexy monks,   5
No healthy beggars, no preaching skunks,
No cynics, bombasts ripe with abuse:
Go peddle them elsewhere, your filthy views.

   Your wicked talk
   Would clutter our walks   10
   Like clustering flies:
   But flies or lies,
   We've no room for your cries,
   Your wicked talk.

Hungry lawyers, stay away!   15
People eaters, who grab while praying,
Scribes and assessors, and gouty judges
Who beat good men with the law's thick cudgels
And tie old pots to their tails, like dogs,
We'll hop you up and down like frogs,   20
We'll hang you high from the nearest tree:
We're decent men, not legal fleas.

   Summons and complaints
   Don't strike us as quaint,
   And we haven't got time   25

For your legal whine
As you hang from the line
Of your summons and complaints.

Money suckers, stay away!
Greedy gougers, spending your days   30
Gobbling up men, stuffing your guts
With gold, you black-faced crows, busting
Your butts for another load of change,
Though your cellar's bursting with rotten exchange.
O lazy scum, you'll pile up more,   35
Till smiling death knocks at your door.

    Inhuman faces
    With ghastly spaces
    That no heart can see,
    Find other places: 40
    Here you can't be,
    You inhuman faces.

Slobbering old dogs, stay away!
Old bitter faces, old sour ways,
We want you elsewhere—the jealous, the traitors,   45
The slime who live as danger creators,
Wherever you come from, you're worse than wolves:
Shove it, you mangy, scabby oafs!
None of your stinking, ugly sores:
We've seen enough, we want no more.   50

    Honor and praise
    Fill all our days:
    We sing delight
    All day, all night:
    These are our ways: 55
    Honor and praise.

But you, you, you can always come,
Noble knights and gentlemen,
For this is where you belong: there's money
Enough, and pleasure enough: honey   60
And milk for all, and all as one:
Come be my friends, come join our fun,
O gallants, sportsmen, lovers, friends,
Or better still: come, gentlemen.

    Gentle, noble,   65
    Serene and subtle,
    Eternally calm;
    Civility's balm
    To live without trouble,
    Gentle, noble.   70

2612 / François Rabelais

And welcome, you who know the Word
And preach it wherever the Word should be heard:
Make this place your holy castle
Against the false religious rascals
Who poison the world with filthy lies: 75
Welcome, you with your eyes on the skies
And faith in your hearts: we can fight to the death
For truth, fight with our every breath.

For the holy Word
Can still be heard,   80
That Word is not dead:
It rings in our heads,
And we rise from our beds
For that holy Word.

And welcome, ladies of noble birth,   85
Live freely here, like nowhere on earth!
Flowers of loveliness, with heaven in your faces,
Who walk like angels, the wisdom of ages
In your hearts: welcome, live here in honor,
As the lord who made this refuge wanted: 90
He built it for you, he gave it gold
To keep it free: Enter, be bold!

Money's a gift
To give, to lift
The souls of others: 95
It makes men brothers
In eternal bliss:
For money's a gift.

CHAPTER 55

How They Lived at Thélème

In the middle of the inner court was a magnificent fountain of beautiful
alabaster. Above it stood the three Graces, holding the symbolic horns of
abundance: water gushed from their breasts, mouths, ears, eyes, and every
other body opening.

The building which rose above this fountain stood on giant pillars of trans-
lucent quartz and porphyry, joined by archways of sweeping classical proportions. And inside there were handsome galleries, long and large,
decorated with paintings and hung with antlers and the horns of the unicorn,
rhinoceros, hippopotamus, as well as elephant teeth and tusks and other
spectacular objects.

The women's quarters ran from the tower called Artice all the way to the
gates of the tower called Mesembriné. The rest was for men. Right in front
of the women's quarters was a kind of playing field, an arena-like space set
just between the two first towers, on the outer side. Here too were the horse-
riding circle, a theater, and the swimming pools, with attached baths at three

different levels, all provided with everything one could need, as well as with an endless supply of myrtle water.

Next to the river was a beautiful pleasure garden, and in the middle of it stood a handsome labyrinth. Between the other two towers were fields for playing palm ball and tennis. Alongside the tower called Cryere were the orchards, full of fruit trees of every description, carefully arranged in groups of five, staggered by rows of three. At the end was a great stretch of pastures and forest, well stocked with all kinds of wild animals.

Between the third pair of towers were the target ranges for muskets, bows, and crossbows. The offices were in a separate building, only one story high, which stood just beside the tower called Hesperia, and the stables were just beyond there. The falcon house was situated in front of the offices, staffed with thoroughly expert falconers and hawk trainers: every year supplies of every sort of bird imaginable, all perfect specimens of their breed, were sent by the Cretans, the Venetians, and the Sarmatian-Poles: eagles, great falcons, goshawks, herons and cranes and wild geese, partridge, gyrfalcons, sparrow hawks, tiny but fierce merlins, and others, so well trained and domesticated that, when they left the chateau to fly about in the fields, they would catch everything they found and bring everything to their handlers. The kennels were a bit farther away, in the direction of the woods and pastures.

All the rooms in all the suites, as well as all the smaller private rooms, were hung with a wide variety of tapestries, which were regularly changed to suit the changing seasons. The floors were covered with green cloth, the beds with embroidery. Every dressing room had a mirror of Venetian crystal, framed in fine gold, decorated around with pearls, and so exceedingly large that one could in truth see oneself in it, complete and entire. Just outside the doorways, in the ladies' quarters, were perfumers and hairdressers, who also attended to the men who visited. Every morning, too, they brought rose-water to each of the ladies' rooms, and also orange and myrtle water—and brought each lady a stick of precious incense, saturated with all manner of aromatic balms.

CHAPTER 56

How the Men and Women Who Dwelled at Thélème Were Dressed

In the beginning, the ladies dressed themselves as they pleased. Later, of their own free will, they changed and styled themselves all as one, in the following way:

They wore scarlet or yellow stockings, bordered with pretty embroidery and fretwork, which reached exactly three fingers above the knee. Their garters were colored like their bracelets (gold, enameled with black, green, red, and white), fastened both above and below the knee. Their shoes, dancing pumps, and slippers were red or purple velvet, with edges jagged like lobsters' claws.

Over the chemise they wore a handsome corset, woven of rich silk shot through with goat hair. Over this they wore taffeta petticoats, in white, red, tan, gray, and so on, and on top of this petticoat a tunic of silver taffeta embroidered with gold thread, sewn in tight spirals—or if they were in the mood and the weather was right, their tunics might be of satin, or damask, or orange-colored velvet, or perhaps tan, green, mustard gray, blue, clear yellow, red, scarlet, white, gold, or silvered linen, with bordered spirals, or embroidery, according to what holiday was being celebrated.

Their dresses, again according to the season, were of golden linen waved with silver, or red satin decorated with gold thread, or taffeta in white, blue, black, or tan, or silk serge, or that same rich silk shot through with goat hair, or velvet slashed with silver, or silvered linen, or golden, or else velvet or satin laced with gold in a variety of patterns.

Sometimes, in the summer, they wore shorter gowns, more like cloaks, ornamented in the ways I have described, or else full-length capes in the Moorish style, of purple velvet waved with gold and embroidered with thin spirals of silver, or else with heavier gold thread, decorated at the seams with small pearls from India. They were never without beautiful feathers in their hair, colored to match the sleeves of their gowns and always spangled in gold. In the winter they wore taffeta dresses, colored as I have described, lined with lynx fur, or black skunk, or Calabrian marten, or sable, or some other precious pelt.

Their prayer beads, rings, neck chains, and collar pieces were made of fine gems—red garnets, rubies, orange-red spinels, diamonds, sapphires, emeralds, turquoises, garnets, agates, green beryls, pearls, and fat onion pearls of a rare excellence.

They covered their heads, once again, as the season demanded: in winter, in the French style, with a velvet hood hanging down in the back like a pigtail; in spring, in the Spanish style, with a lace veil; in summer, in the Italian mode, with bare ringed hair studded with jewels, except on Sundays and holidays, when they used the French fashion, which seemed to them both more appropriate and more modest.

And the men wore their fashions, too: their stockings were of light linen or serge, colored scarlet, yellow, white, or black; their breeches were velvet, in the same colors (or very nearly), embroidered and patterned however they pleased. Their jackets were of gold or silver cloth, in velvet, satin, damask, taffeta, once again in the same colors, impeccably patterned and decorated and worn. Their shoes were laced to the breeches with silken thread, colored as before, each lace closed with an enameled gold tip. Their undervests and cloaks were of golden cloth or linen, or silver cloth, or velvet embroidered however they liked. Their gowns were as costly and beautiful as the women's, with silk belts, colored to match their breeches. Each of them wore a handsome sword, with a decorated hilt, the scabbard of velvet (the color matching their stockings), its endpiece of gold and heavily worked jewelry—and their daggers were exactly the same. Their hats were of black velvet, thickly garnished with golden berries and buttons, and the feathered plumes were white, delicately spangled in gold rows and fringed with rubies, emeralds, and the like.

But there was such a close fellowship between the men and the women that they were dressed almost exactly alike, day after day. And to make sure that this happened, certain gentlemen were delegated to inform the others, each and every morning, what sort of clothing the women had chosen to wear that day—because of course the real decisions, in this matter, were made by the women.

Although they wore such well-chosen and rich clothing, don't think these women wasted a great deal of time on their gowns and cloaks and jewelry. There were wardrobe men who, each day, had everything prepared in advance, and their ladies' maids were so perfectly trained that everyone could be dressed from head to toe, and beautifully, in the twinkling of an eye. And to make sure that all of this was perpetually in good order, the wood of Thélème was surrounded by a vast block of houses, perhaps half a league long, good bright buildings well stocked and supplied, and here lived goldsmiths, jewelers, embroiderers, tailors, specialists in hammering and filamenting gold and silver, velvet makers, tapestry weavers, and upholsterers, and they all worked at their trades right there alongside Thélème, and only for the men and women who dwelled in that abbey. All their supplies, metals and minerals and cloths, came to them courtesy My Lord Shipmaster (Nausiclète, in Greek), who each year brought in seven boats from the Little Antilles, the Pearl and Cannibal islands, loaded down with gold ingots, raw silk, pearls, and all sorts of gemstones. And any of the fat pearls which began to lose their sparkle and their natural whiteness were restored by feeding them to handsome roosters (as Avicenna recommends), just as we give laxatives to hawks and falcons.

CHAPTER 57

How the Men and Women of Thélème Governed Their Lives

Their lives were not ordered and governed by laws and statutes and rules, but according to their own free will. They rose from their beds when it seemed to them the right time, drank, ate, worked, and slept when they felt like it. No one woke them or obliged them to drink, or to eat, or to do anything whatever. This was exactly how Gargantua had ordained it. The constitution of this abbey had only a single clause:

DO WHAT YOU WILL

—because free men and women, wellborn, well taught, finding themselves joined with other respectable people, are instinctively impelled to do virtuous things and avoid vice. They draw this instinct from nature itself, and they name it "honor." Such people, if they are subjected to vile constraints, brought down to a lower moral level, oppressed and enslaved and turned away from that noble passion toward which virtue pulls them, find themselves led by that same passion to throw off and break any such bondage, just as we always seek out forbidden things and long for whatever is denied us.

And their complete freedom set them nobly in competition, all of them seeking to do whatever they saw pleased any one among them. If he or she said, "Let's drink," everyone drank. If he or she said, "Let's play," they all played. If he or she said, "Let's go and have fun in the meadows," there they all went. If they were engaged in falconry or hunting, the women joined in, mounted on their good tame horses, light but proud, delicately sporting heavy leather gloves, a sparrow hawk perched on their wrists, or a small falcon, or a tiny but fierce merlin. (The other birds were carried by men.)

All of them had been so well educated that there wasn't one among them who could not read, write, sing, play on harmonious instruments, speak five or six languages, and write easy poetry and clear prose in any and all of them. There were never knights so courageous, so gallant, so light on their feet, and so easy on their horses, knights more vigorous, agile, or better able to handle any kind of weapon. There were never ladies so well bred, so delicate, less irritable, or better trained with their hands, sewing and doing anything that any free and worthy woman might be asked to do.

And for this reason, when the time came for anyone to leave the abbey, whether because his parents had summoned him or on any other account, he took one of the ladies with him, she having accepted him, and then they were married. And whatever devotion and friendship they had shown one another, when they lived at Thélème, they continued and even exceeded in their marriage, loving each other to the end of their days just as much as they did on the first day after their wedding. . . .

From Book II

[Pantagruel: Birth and Education]

CHAPTER 2

The Birth of the Very Formidable Pantagruel

When he was four hundred and ninety-four, plus four more, Gargantua begat his son Pantagruel on his wife, the daughter of the king of the Amaurotes, in Utopia. Her name was Bigmouth, or Babedec,[1] as we say in the provinces, and she died giving birth to the baby: he was so immensely big, and weighed so incredibly much, that it was impossible for him to see the light without snuffing out his mother.

Now, to truly understand how he got his name, which was bestowed on him at the baptismal font, you must be aware that in the year of his birth there had been such a fearful drought, all across the continent of Africa, that it had not rained for more than thirty-six months, three weeks, four days, thirteen hours, and a little bit over, and the sun had been so hot, and so fierce, that the whole earth had dried up. It wasn't any hotter even in the days of the prophet Elijah than in that year, for not a tree on earth had a leaf or a bud. Grass never turned green, rivers dried up, fountains went dry; the poor fish, deprived of their proper element, flopped about on the ground, crying horribly; since there was no dew to make the air dense enough, the birds could not fly; dead animals lay all over the fields and meadows, their mouths gaping wide—wolves, foxes, stags, wild boars, fallow does, hares, rabbits, weasels, martens, badgers, and many, many others. And it was no better for human beings, whose lives became pitiful things. You could see them with their tongues hanging out, like hares that have been running for six solid hours. Some of them threw themselves down into wells; others crawled into a cow's belly, to stay in the shade (Homer calls them *Alibantes*, desiccated people[2]). Everything everywhere stood still, like a ship at anchor.

---

1. Names taken from Sir Thomas More's *Utopia*. Literally, "no place," the word *utopia* has become synonymous with "ideal country."   2. The allusion to Homer is apparently mistaken, but *Alibantes*—possibly derived from Alibas, a dry river in hell—is used by other ancient writers with reference to the dead or the very old.

It was painful to see how hard men worked to protect themselves from this ghastly change in nature: it wasn't easy to keep even the holy water in churches from being used up, though the pope and the College of Cardinals expressly ordered that no one should dare to dip from these blessed basins more than once. All the same, when a priest entered his church you'd see dozens and dozens of these poor parched people come crowding around behind him, and if he blessed anyone the mouths would all gape open to snatch up every single drop, letting nothing fall wasted to the ground—just like the tormented rich man in Luke, who begged for the relief of cool water.[3] Oh, the fortunate ones, in that burning year, whose vaults were cool and well stocked!

The Philosopher tells us, asking why seawater is salty, that once, when Phoebus Apollo let his son Phaeton drive his gleaming chariot,[4] the boy had no idea how to manage it, nor any notion how to follow the sun's proper orbit from tropic to tropic, and drove off the right road and came so close to the earth that he dried up all the countries over which he passed, and burned a great swath through heaven, called by the philosophers *Via Lactea*, the Milky Way, but known to drunkards and lazy louts as Saint John's Road. But the fancy-pants poets say it's really where Juno's milk fell, when she suckled Hercules. Then the earth got so hot that it developed an enormous sweat, which proceeded to sweat away the entire ocean, which thus became salty, because sweat is always salty. And you can see for yourself that this is perfectly true, because all you have to do is taste it—or the sweat of pox-ridden people when they're put in steam baths and work up a great sweat. Try whichever you like: it doesn't matter to me.

It was almost exactly like that, in this year of which I write. One Friday, when everyone was saying prayers and making a beautiful procession, and litanies were being said, and psalms chanted, and they were begging omnipotent God to look mercifully down on them in their desolation, they could suddenly see great drops of water coming out of the earth, exactly as if someone were sweating profusely. And the poor people began to rejoice, as if this were something truly useful, some of them saying that since there wasn't a drop of liquid in the air from which one could have expected rain, the very ground itself was making up for what they lacked. Others, more scholarly, said that this was rain from the opposite side of the earth, as Seneca explains in the fourth book of *Questionum naturalium*, in which he speaks of the source and origin of the river Nile. But they were deceived: once the procession was over, and they went back to collect this precious dew and drink down a full glass, they found that it was just pickle brine, even worse to drink, and even saltier, than seawater.

And it was precisely because Pantagruel was born that very day that his father named him as he did: *Panta* in Greek means "all," and *Gruel* in Arabic means "thirsty," thus indicating that at the hour of his birth the whole world was thirsty—and he saw, prophetically, that someday his son would be lord of the thirsty, for this was shown to him at that same time and by a sign even more obvious. For when the child's mother was in labor, and all the midwives were waiting to receive him, the first thing that came out of her womb was

3. Luke 16.24: "And he cried and said, Father Abraham, have mercy on me, and send Lazarus, that he may dip the tip of his finger in water, and cool my tongue; for I am tormented in this flame."   4. The chariot of the sun.

sixty-eight mule drivers, each one leading a pack mule loaded with salt by its halter, after which came nine one-humped camels loaded with hams and smoked beef tongue, and then seven two-humped camels loaded with pickled eels, followed by twenty-five carts all loaded with onions, garlic, leeks, and spring onions. The midwives were frightened out of their wits. But some of them said to the others:

"Here's God's plenty. It signifies that we shouldn't either hold back, when we drink, or, on the other hand, pour it down the way the Swiss do. It's a good sign: these are truly wining signs."

And while they were gabbling and cackling about such trivialities, out popped Pantagruel, as hairy as a bear, at which one of them pronounced prophetically:

"He's been born all covered with fur, so he'll do wonderful things, and if he lives he'll live to an immense age."

[Father's Letter from Home]

CHAPTER 8

*How Pantagruel, at Paris, Received a Letter from His Father,
Gargantua, with a Copy of That Letter*

Pantagruel studied hard, of course, and learned a great deal, because his brain was twice normal size and his memory was as capacious as a dozen kegs of olive oil. While he was thus occupied in Paris,[5] one day he received a letter from his father, which read as follows:

"My very dear son,

"Among the gifts, the graces and the prerogatives with which from the very beginning our sovereign Creator and God has blessed and endowed human nature, that which seems to me uniquely wonderful is the power to acquire a kind of immortality while still in this our mortal state—that is, while passing through this transitory life a man may perpetuate both his name and his race, and this we accomplish through the legitimate issue of holy wedlock. And by that means we partially reestablish that which we lost through the sin of our first parents, Adam and Eve, to whom it was declared that, because they had not obeyed the commands of God their Creator, they would know death and in dying would utterly destroy the magnificent form in which mankind had been shaped.

"But this seminal propagation permits what the parents lose to live on in their children, and what dies in the children to live on in the grandchildren, and so it will continue until the hour of the Last Judgment, when Jesus Christ will return to the hands of God the Father His purified and peaceful kingdom, now utterly beyond any possibility or danger of being soiled by sin. And then all the generations and all the corruptions will come to an end, and all the elements will be taken from their endless

---

5. Like his father before him, Pantagruel has been sent to Paris to study. The letter, patterned after Ciceronian models of eloquence, summarizes Rabelais's view of an ideal education, and generally illustrates the attitude of the Renaissance intellectual elite toward culture.

cycle of transformations, for the peace so devoutly desired will be achieved, and will be perfect, and all things will be brought to their fit and proper ending.

"So I have very fair and just cause to be thankful to God, my preserver, for having permitted me to see my hoary old age blossoming once again in your youth. Whenever, at His pleasure, He who rules and governs all things, my soul leaves this human dwelling place, I will not consider myself entirely dead, but simply transported from one place to another, for in you, and by you, my visible image lives in in this world, wholly alive, able to see and speak to all honorable men, and all my friends, just as I myself was able to do. I confess that my life on this earth, though I have had divine help and divine grace to show me the way, has not been sinless (for indeed we are all sinners and continually beg God to wash away our sins), and yet it has been beyond reproach.

"Just as the image of my flesh lives on in you, so too shine on the ways of my soul, or else no one would think you the true keeper and treasure of our immortal name, and I would take little pleasure in seeing that, because in that case the least part of me, my body, would live on, and the best part, my soul, in which our name lives and is blessed among men, would be decayed and debased. Nor do I say this because I have any doubt about your virtue, which I have long since tested and approved, but simply to encourage you to proceed from good to still better. And the reason I write to you now is not so much to ensure that you follow the pathways of virtue, but rather that you rejoice in thus living and having lived, and find new joys and fresh courage for the future.

"To consummate and perfect that task, it should be enough for you to remember that I have held back nothing, but have given help and assistance as if I had no other treasure in the world but to someday see you, while I still lived, accomplished and established in virtue, integrity, and wisdom, perfected in all noble and honorable learning, and to be able to thus leave you, after my death, as a mirror representing me, your father—perhaps in actual practice not so perfect an image as I might have wished, but certainly exactly that in both intention and desire.

"But though my late father of worthy memory, Grandgousier, devoted all his energy to those things of which I might take the fullest advantage, and from which I might acquire the most sensible knowledge, and though my own effort matched his—or even surpassed it—still, as you know very well, it was neither so fit nor so right a time for learning as exists today, nor was there an abundance of such teachers as you have had. It was still a murky, dark time, oppressed by the misery, unhappiness, and disasters of the Goths, who destroyed all worthwhile literature of every sort. But divine goodness has let me live to see light and dignity returned to humanistic studies, and to see such an improvement, indeed, that it would be hard for me to qualify for the very first class of little schoolboys—I who, in my prime, had the reputation (and not in error) of the most learned man of my day. Nor do I say this as an empty boast, though indeed I could honorably do so in writing to you—for which you have the authority of Cicero in his book *On Old Age,* and also the judgment of Plutarch, in his book *How a Man May Praise Himself with-*

out Fear of Reproach. No, I say these things to make you wish to surpass me.

"For now all courses of study have been restored, and the acquisition of languages has become supremely honorable: Greek, without which it is shameful for any man to be called a scholar; Hebrew; Chaldean; Latin.[6] And in my time we have learned how to produce wonderfully elegant and accurate printed books,[7] just as, on the other hand, we have also learned (by diabolic suggestion) how to make cannon and other such fearful weapons. The world is full of scholars, of learned teachers, of well-stocked libraries, so that in my opinion study has never been easier, not in Plato's time, or Cicero's, or Papinian's.[8] From this day forward no one will dare to appear anywhere, or in any company, who has not been well and properly taught in the wisdom of Minerva. Thieves and highwaymen, hangmen and executioners, common foot soldiers, grooms and stableboys, are now more learned than the scholars and preachers of my day. What should I say? Even women and girls have come to aspire to this marvelous, this heavenly manna of solid learning. Old as I am, I have felt obliged to learn Greek, though I had not despised it, as Cato[9] did: I simply had no leisure for it, when I was young. And how exceedingly glad I am, as I await the hour when it may please God, my Creator, to call me to leave this earth, to read Plutarch's *Morals*, Plato's beautiful *Dialogues*, Pausanias' *Monuments*, and Athenaeus' *Antiquities*.[1]

"Which is why, my son, I strongly advise you not to waste your youth, but to make full use of it for the acquisition of knowledge and virtue. You are in Paris, you have your tutor, Epistemon: you can learn from them, by listening and speaking, by all the noble examples held up in front of your eyes.

"It is my clear desire that you learn languages perfectly, first Greek, as Quintilian decreed, and then Latin.[2] And after that Hebrew, for the Holy Bible, and similarly Chaldean and Arabic. I wish you to form your literary style both on the Greek, following Plato, and on the Latin, following Cicero. Let there be nothing in all of history that is not clear and vivid in your mind, a task in which geographical texts will be of much assistance.

"I gave you some awareness of the liberal arts—geometry, arithmetic, and music—when you were still a child of five and six. Follow them further, and learn all the rules of astronomy. Ignore astrology and its prophecies, and all the hunt for the philosopher's stone which occupied Ramon Lully[3]—leave all those errors and vanities alone.

"As for the civil law, I wish you to know by heart all the worthy texts: deal with them and philosophy side by side.

"I wish you to carefully devote yourself to the natural world. Let there be no sea, river, or brook whose fish you do not know. Nothing should be unknown to you—all the birds of the air, each and every tree and

---

6. The languages that are the instruments of classical learning are listed along with those useful for the study of the Old Testament of the Bible. 7. Printing from movable type was invented in Europe about the middle of the 15th century. 8. Jurisconsult of the time of Emperor Septimius Severus (reigned A.D. 193–211). 9. Plutarch's life of Cato is the source of the notion that he despised Greek. 1. The works of Pausanias and Athenaeus were standard sources of information on ancient geography, art, and everyday life. 2. In his *Institutio oratoria* 1.1.12 he recommends studying Greek before Latin. 3. Raymond Lully (13th century), Spanish philosopher who dabbled in magic.

bush and shrub in the forests, every plant that grows from the earth, all the metals hidden deep in the abyss, all the gems of the Orient and the Middle East—nothing.

"Then carefully reread all the books of the Greek physicians, and the Arabs and Romans, without turning your back on the talmudic scholars or those who have written on the Cabala. Make free use of anatomical dissection and acquire a perfect knowledge of that other world which is man himself. Spend several hours each day considering the holy Gospels, first the New Testament and the Apostles' letters, in Greek, and then the Old Testament, in Hebrew.

"In short, plumb all knowledge to the very depths, because when you are a grown man you will be obliged to leave the peace and tranquillity of learning, and acquire the arts of chivalry and warfare, in order to defend my house and lands and come to the aid of our friends if in any way they are attacked by evildoers.

"And soon I shall ask you to demonstrate just how much you have learned, which you can do in no better way than by publicly defending, in front of the entire world and against all who may come to question you, a thesis of your own devising. And continue, as you have been doing, to frequent the company of those leaned men who are so numerous in Paris.

"But since, as the wise Solomon says, wisdom can find no way into a malicious heart, and knowledge without self-awareness is nothing but the soul's ruin, you should serve, and love, and fear God. Put all your thought in Him, and all your hopes, and by faith which has been shaped by love unite yourself with Him so firmly that sin will never separate you away. Be ever watchful of the world's wicked ways. Never put your heart in vanity, for ours is a transitory existence and the Word of God lives forever. Help your neighbors and love them as you love yourself. Honor your teachers. Avoid the company of those you do not desire to imitate; do not take in vain the blessings God has given you. And when, finally, you know that you have learned all that Paris can teach you, return to me, so that I may look on you and, before I die, give you my blessing.

"My son, may the peace and grace of our Lord be with you. *Amen.*

"Written from Utopia, this seventeenth day of the month of March.

Your father,

GARGANTUA"

After receiving and reading this letter, Pantagruel was filled with new zeal, positively on fire to learn more than ever before—so much so that, had you seen him at his studies, and observed how much he learned, you would have declared that he was to his books like a fire in dry grass, burning with such an intense and consuming flame.

2622 / François Rabelais

[The World in Pantagruel's Mouth]

CHAPTER 18

How a Great English Scholar Wanted to Dispute with Pantagruel, But Was Beaten by Panurge

At about the same time, a scholar named Thaumaste (in Greek, "Wonderful"), hearing all the fuss over Pantagruel's incomparable learning, and seeing how famous he'd become, came from England with the sole intention of meeting Pantagruel and finding out if his knowledge matched his reputation. Arriving in Paris, he immediately went to Pantagruel's lodgings, which were at the abbey of Saint Denis.[4] At that moment, Pantagruel was in the garden with Panurge, walking up and down and philosophizing after the fashion of the ancient Peripatetics.[5] Thaumaste quivered with fear, seeing how huge Pantagruel was, but then he greeted him in customary style and said, with great courtesy:

"How true it is, as Plato, prince of philosophers, says, that if the image of wisdom and learning is a physical matter, visible to human eyes, it excites the whole world with admiration. The very word of such accomplishments, spread through the air and received by the ears of those who study and love philosophy, prevents them from taking any further rest, stirring them, urging them to hurry to where they may find and see the person in whom knowledge has erected its temple and given forth its oracles. Which was clearly demonstrated for us by the queen of Sheba, who traveled from the farthest reaches of the Orient and the Persian Sea to visit the house of the wise Solomon and hear his sage words;[6]

"and by Anacharsis,[7] who came from Scythia only to see Solon;

"and by Pythagoras, who journeyed to the prophets of Memphis;[8]

"and by Plato, who visited the Egyptian magi, and also Archytas of Tarentum;[9]

"and by Apollonius of Tyana,[1] who went to the Caucasian mountains, who journeyed among the Scythians, the Massagetae, and the Indians, who sailed down the great river Physon, all the way to the land of the Brahmans, to see Hiarchos, and who traveled in Babylonia, Chaldea, the land of the Medes, Assyria, Parthia, Syria, Phoenicia, Arabia, Palestine, and Alexandria, and in Ethiopia, too, to see the Gymnosophists.[2]

"We have another example in Livy,[3] to see and hear whom certain studious folk came to Rome from the farthest boundaries of France and Spain.

"I am not so presumptuous as to include myself among the ranks of such illustrious men. But I deeply desire to be thought of as a student and lover not only of humanistic learning but also of men of such learning.

"And, in fact, hearing of your priceless learning, I have left my country, my parents, and my home and come here, indifferent to the weariness of the journey, the anxiety of a voyage by sea, the strangeness of different lands,

---

4. A college for Benedictines.   **5.** Followers of the Greek philosopher Aristotle, who wandered about in the Lyceum of ancient Athens while lecturing.   **6.** 2 Chronicles 9.1–12; the Queen of Sheba came from southern Arabia to test Solomon's legendary wisdom.   **7.** Scythian prince, renowned for his travels and wisdom (6th century B.C.).   **8.** Capital of ancient Egypt. *Pythagoras:* Greek philosopher of the 6th century B.C.   **9.** Said to be the founder of mathematics (4th century B.C.).   **1.** An ascetic wandering teacher of the early Christian period.   **2.** Ancient sect of Hindu ascetics.   **3.** Titus Livius (59 B.C.–A.D. 17 or 64 B.C.–A.D. 12), Roman historian.

solely for the purpose of seeing and conferring with you about certain passages of philosophy, and geometrical divination, and also of cabalistic knowledge,[4] passages of which I am myself unsure and, about which I cannot rest content. If you can resolve these difficulties for me, I will be your servant from this day forth, and not only me but all my posterity, for I command no other gifts sufficient to repay you.

"I will put all of this in writing, and tomorrow I shall notify all the learned men of this city, so that we can discuss these matters publicly and in their presence.

"But I intend that our discussions, and any disputes in which we may engage, shall be conducted as follows. I do not wish to argue any barebones *for* and *against,* as do the besotted sophistical minds[5] of this and other cities. Nor do I wish to dispute after the fashion of academics, by declamation, or by the use of numbers, as Pythagoras did and as Picodella Mirandola,[6] at Rome, wished to do. I wish to dispute simply by signs, without a word being spoken, for these are matters so intricate and difficult that, as far as I am concerned, mere human speech will not be adequate to deal with them.

"May it please Your Magnificence to accept my invitation and join me, at seven in the morning, in the great hall of the College of Navarre."

When he had finished, Pantagruel said to him, courteously:

"My dear sir, how could I deny anyone the right to share in whatever blessings God has given me? All good things come from Him, and surely He wishes us to spread the celestial manna we have from Him among men both worthy and capable of receiving true learning—among whose number in our time, as I know very well, you belong in the very first rank. Let me say to you, therefore, that you will find me ready at any time to accede to any of your requests, to the extent that my poor powers may enable me, and well aware as I am that it is I who should be learning from you. And so, as you have declared, we will discuss these doubts of yours together, and hunt as hard as we can for their resolution, diving even as far as the bottom of that bottomless well in which, according to Heraclitus,[7] the truth is said to be hidden.

"And I highly commend the style of argument you have proposed, that is to say, by using signs, without any words, for thus you and I will truly understand one another, free from the sort of hand clapping and applause produced during their discussions by these puerile sophists, whenever one party has the better of the argument.

"So, then, tomorrow I shall appear without fail at the time and place you have requested. I ask of you only that, as between us, there may be no contentiousness and fuss, and that we seek neither honor nor men's applause, but only the truth."

To which Thaumaste replied:

"Sir, may God keep you in His grace. I thank Your High Magnificence for being so willing to condescend to my humble talents. Until tomorrow, I leave you in His hands."

---

4. Lore from an occult system of mystical speculation of rabbinical origin. 5. Sophists, for Thaumaste, are specious, overly subtle rhetoricians. 6. Pico della Mirandola (1463–1494), Italian humanist scholar. Pythagoras (6th century B.C.) discovered the mathematical basis of the musical intervals. 7. Greek philosopher of the 6th century B.C.

"Farewell," said Pantagruel.

Gentlemen, you who may read this book, please don't imagine that anyone was ever more exalted, more transported, that whole night long, than Thaumaste and Pantagruel. Thaumaste told the concierge at his lodgings, in the abbey of Cluny, that in his entire life he had never been so incredibly thirsty:

"It feels to me," he said, "as if Pantagruel has me by the throat. Order me wine, if you please, and make sure that there's enough fresh water so I can lubricate the roof of my mouth."

And for his part, Pantagruel felt himself carried away, so that all that night he did nothing but tear through:

> The Venerable Bede's *De numeris et signis*, Numbers and Signs;
> Plotinus' *De inenarrabilibus*, Inexpressible Things;
> Proclus' *De sacrificio et magia*, Sacrifices and Magic;
> Artemidorus' *Per onirocriticon*, On the Interpretation of Dreams;
> Anaxagoras' *Peri semion*, On Signs;
> Dinarius' *Peri aphaton*, Unknowable Things;
> Philistion's books;
> Hipponax's *Peri anecphoneton*, Things Better Left Undiscussed;

And many, many others, so that finally Panurge said to him:

"My lord, stop all this intellectual groping and go to bed, for I can see you're far too agitated—indeed, such an extravagance of thinking and straining may well make you feverish. But first, have twenty-five or thirty good drinks, then go to bed and sleep comfortably—for tomorrow I will answer our English friend, I will argue with him, and if I don't get him *ad metam non loqui*,[8] to the point where he can't say a word, well, then you can say anything you like about me."

"All right," said Pantagruel, "but Panurge, my good friend, he's a deeply learned man. How will you deal with him?"

"Very easily," said Panurge. "Please: don't even speak about it. Just leave the whole thing to me. Do you know any man as learned as the devils in hell?"

"Not really," said Pantagruel, "unless blessed by some special divine grace."

"You see?" said Panurge. "I've had many arguments with devils, and I've made them look like idiots, I've knocked them on their asses. So tomorrow you can be sure I'll make this glorious Englishman shit vinegar, right out in public."

Then Panurge spent the night boozing with the servants and playing games, at which he lost all the roses and ribbons from his breeches. And then, when the agreed-upon hour came, he conducted his master Pantagruel to the assigned meeting place, where as you can easily understand everyone in Paris, from the most important to the least, had assembled, all of them thinking:

"This devil of a Pantagruel, he's beaten all our clever fellows, and all those naive theologians and philosophers. But now he'll get what's coming to him, because this Englishman is a regular devil. We'll see who beats whom today."

---

8. Translated in the next phrase, "to the point where he can't say a word."

Everyone was assembled; Thaumaste was waiting for them. And when Pantagruel and Panurge arrived in the hall, all the students—elementary, high school, and college—began to applaud, in their usual ridiculous way. But Pantagruel shouted at them, his voice as loud as the sound of a double cannon:

"Quiet! In the name of the devil, quiet! By God, you rascals, bother me and I'll cut the heads off every last one of you!"

Which announcement struck them as dumb as ducks: they were afraid even to cough, no matter if they'd swallowed fifteen pounds of feathers. And the very sound of his voice left them so parched and dry that their tongues hung half a foot out of their mouths, as if Pantagruel had roasted their throats.

Then Panurge began to speak, saying to the Englishman:

"Sir, have you come here seeking a debate, a contest, about these propositions which you have posted, or are you here to learn, to honestly understand the truth?"

To which Thaumaste answered:

"Sir, the only thing which has brought me here is my deep desire to understand that which I have struggled all my life to understand, and which neither books nor men have ever been able to resolve for me. As far as disputing and arguing is concerned, I have no interest whatever in that. That is a vulgar affair, and I leave it to villainous sophists, who never truly seek for truth when they argue, but only contradict each other and emptily debate."

"And so," said Panurge, "if I, who am no more than a minor disciple of my master Pantagruel, am able to satisfy you in all these matters, it would be an indignity and an imposition to trouble my master. Accordingly, it would be better if for now he simply presided over this discussion, judging what we say—and I need hardly say that he will himself satisfy you, should I be unable to fully quench your scholarly thirst."

"Indeed," said Thaumaste, "that's perfectly true."

"Then let us begin."

But note, please, that Panurge had hung a handsome tassel of red, white, green, and blue silk at the end of his long codpiece,[9] and inside it he had stuffed a fat, juicy orange.

CHAPTER 19

How Panurge Made the Englishman Who Argued by Signs Look Like an Idiot

Then, with everyone watching and listening in absolute silence, the Englishman raised his hands high in the air, first one and then the other, holding his fingertips in the shape called, in Chinon, the hen's asshole. He struck the nails of one hand against the nails of the other four times in a row, then opened his hands and slapped his palms together with a sharp crack. Joining his hands once again, as he had done at the start, he clapped them twice, then opened them out and clapped them four times more. Then he clasped them and extended one right over the other, as if praying devoutly to God.

Suddenly Panurge raised his right hand and stuck his thumb into his nose,

9. Ornamental pouch at the crotch of tightly fitting breeches, worn by men of the 15th and 16th centuries.

keeping the other four fingers extended in a row straight out from the tip of his nose. He closed his left eye and winked the right one, making a deep hollow between eyebrow and eyelid. Then he lifted his left hand, the four fingers held rigidly extended, the thumb raised, and lined it up precisely with his right hand, keeping it perhaps half again the width of his nose distant. Then he lowered both hands, keeping them just as they were, and ended by raising them halfway and holding them there, as if aiming at the Englishman's nose.

"And yet if Mercury[1]—" the Englishman began.

But Panurge interrupted him:

"You have spoken. Be silent."

Then the Englishman made the following sign: With palm open, he raised his left hand high in the air, then closed its four fingers in a tight fist, with the thumb lying across the bridge of his nose. And then, suddenly, he raised his right hand, palm out, and lowered it again, placing the thumb against the little finger of his left hand, the four fingers of which he moved slowly up and down. Then, in reverse, he repeated with his right hand what he had just done with his left and with his left hand what he had done with his right.

Not a bit surprised, Panurge lifted his immense codpiece with his left hand, and with his right pulled from it a piece of white ox rib and two bits of wood in the same shape, one of black ebony, the other of rose-colored brazilwood. Arranging these objects symmetrically, in the fingers of his right hand, he clapped them together, making a sound exactly like that produced by the lepers in Brittany, to warn people off—but a sound infinitely more resonant and harmonious. And then, pulling his tongue slowly back into his mouth, he stood there, humming happily, staring at the Englishman.

The theologians, physicians, and surgeons thought this sign meant that the Englishman was a leper.

The counselors, jurists, and canon lawyers, however, thought his meaning was that being a leper brought with it a certain sort of happiness, as once our Lord had declared.

Not at all frightened, the Englishman raised both hands, holding them with the three largest fingers balled into a fist, then placed both thumbs between the index and middle fingers, with the little fingers sticking straight out. He presented his hands to Panurge, then rearranged them so that the right thumb touched the left one, and his little fingers, too, were pressed against each other.

At this, without a word, Panurge raised his hands and made the following sign: he put the nail of his right index finger against the thumbnail, shaping a loop. He bent all the fingers of his right hand into a fist, except for the index finger, which he jabbed in and out of the space framed by his other hand. Then he extended both the index and the middle fingers of his right hand, separating them as widely as he possibly could and pointing them at Thaumaste. Then placing his left thumb in the corner of his left eye, he extended his entire hand like a bird's wing or a fish's backbone, and waved it very delicately up and down. Then he did the same thing with his right hand and his right eye.

---

1. Thaumaste may be referring to the messenger god or to quicksilver, used in alchemy. Panurge reminds him of the rule of silent, gestural communication.

Thaumaste began to turn pale and tremble, then made the following sign: he struck the middle finger of his right hand against the muscle of his palm, just below the thumb, then inserted the index finger of his right hand into a loop shaped exactly like that Panurge had made, except that Thaumaste inserted it from below, not from above.

Accordingly, Panurge clapped his hands together and breathed into his palms. Then, once again, he shaped a loop with his left hand and, over and over, inserted into it the index finger of his right hand. Then he thrust his chin forward and stood staring at Thaumaste.

And though no one there understood what these signs meant, they understood perfectly well that he was asking Thaumaste, without a word being spoken:

"Hey, what do you make of that, eh?"

And indeed Thaumaste began to sweat heavily, looking like a man swept away by high contemplation. Then he stared back at Panurge and put the nails of his left hand against those of his right, opening all the fingers into semicircles, then raised his hands as high as he could, exhibiting this sign.

At which Panurge suddenly put his right thumb under his jaw, and stuck the little finger into the loop fashioned by his left hand, and proceeded to vigorously snap his jaw, making his teeth crash harmoniously together.

In great anguish, Thaumaste stood up, but as he rose let fly a fat baker's fart, with the dung right after it. He pissed a good dose of vinegar, and stank like the devils in hell. All those in the hall began to hold their noses, because, clearly, it was anxiety that was obliging him to beshit himself. Then he raised his right hand, the ends of all the fingers clutched together, and spread out his left hand, flat against his chest.

At which Panurge pulled out his long codpiece with its waving tassel, stretching it a good foot and a half or more, holding it in the air with his left hand and with his right, taking the ripe orange, he threw it in the air seven times, the eighth time catching it in his right fist and then holding it quietly, calmly high in the air. Then he began to shake his handsome codpiece, as if displaying it to Thaumaste.

After this, Thaumaste began to puff out his cheeks like a bagpipe musician, blowing as hard as if he were inflating a pig's bladder.

At which Panurge stuck one finger of his left hand right up his ass, sucking in air with his mouth, as if eating oysters in the shell or inhaling soup. Then he opened his mouth a bit and slapped himself with the palm of his right hand, making an immensely loud sound which seemed to work its way up from the very depths of his diaphragm all along the trachial artery. And he did this sixteen times.

But all Thaumaste could do was snuffle like a goose.

So Panurge next stuck his right index finger into his mouth, clamping down hard on it. Then he pulled it out and, as he did so, made a loud noise, like little boys firing turnips from an elderwood cannon. And he did this nine times.

And Thaumaste cried:

"Ah ha, gentlemen! The great secret! He's got his hand in there up to the elbow."

And he pulled out a dagger, holding it with the point facing down.

At which Panurge grabbed his great codpiece and shook it against his breeches as hard as he could. Then he joined his hands like a comb and put them on top of his head, sticking out his tongue as far as he could and rolling his eyes like a dying goat.

"Ah ha, I understand," said Thaumaste. "But what?" And he set the handle of his dagger against his chest, and put his palm over the point, letting his fingertips turn lightly against it.

At which Panurge bent his head to the left and put his middle finger in his left ear, raising his thumb. Then he crossed his arms on his chest, coughed five times, and the fifth time banged his right foot on the ground. Then he raised his left arm and, tightening his fingers into a fist, held the thumb against his forehead, and with his right hand clapped himself six times on the chest.

But Thaumaste, as though still unsatisfied, put his left thumb to the end of his nose and closed the rest of that hand.

So Panurge put his forefingers on each side of his mouth, pulling back as hard as he could and showing all his teeth. His thumbs drew his lower eyelids as far down as they would go, making an exceedingly ugly face, or so it seemed to everyone watching.

CHAPTER 20

What Thaumaste Said about Panurge's Virtues and His Learning

Then Thaumaste stood up and, removing his hat, thanked Panurge graciously, then turned to the audience and said in a loud voice:

"Gentlemen, now I can truly speak the biblical words: *Et ecce plus quam Solomon hic,* And here is one who is greater than Solomon.[2] You see in front of you an incomparable treasure: and that is Monsieur Pantagruel, whose fame drew me from the farthest reaches of England in order to discuss with him certain insoluble problems, involving not only magic, academy, cabalistic learning, geometrical divination, and astrology but philosophy as well, which had long been troubling me. But now his fame bothers me, because it seems to be afflicted with jealousy—certainly, it hasn't granted him a thousandth part of what he deserves.

"You have seen for yourselves how his only disciple has satisfied my questions—has even told me more than I'd asked. Moreover, he has first shown and then solved for me other problems of inexpressible difficulty and importance, and in so doing he has opened for me, I can assure you, the deepest, purest well of encyclopedic learning, and in a fashion, indeed, that I had never thought any man could accomplish—not even begin to accomplish. I refer to our disputation by signs alone, without a word being spoken. But in due time I will record everything he has said and shown me, so no one will think that this has been more tomfoolery in which we have been engaged, and I will have that record put into print so others can learn from it as I have. Then you will be able to judge how little the master is truly esteemed, when the mere disciple can demonstrate such ability, for as it is written, *Non est discipulus super magistrum,* The disciple is not superior to his master.[3]

"And now let praise be given to God, and let me humbly thank you all for

2. Matthew 12.42 and Luke 11.31.   3. Matthew 10.24.

the honor you have shown us. May the good Lord repay you through all the eternity."

Pantagruel said similarly courteous things to all who were gathered there, and as he left took Thaumaste with him, to dine—and you will believe they drank until they had to open their breeches to let their bellies breathe. (In those days men buttoned up their bellies, the way they buttoned up their collars today.) They drank, indeed, until all they could say was, "Where do *you* come from?"

Holy Mother of God, how they guzzled, and how many bottles of wine they put away:

"Over here!"

"More, more!"

"Waiter, wine!"

"Pour it, in the name of the devil, pour it!"

No one drank fewer than twenty-five or thirty jugs, and do you know how? *Sicut terra sine aqua*, Like a dry land with no water—for it was warm weather and, besides, they were good and thirsty.

But as for Thaumaste's explanation of the signs they used, in their disputation, well, I'd be glad to explain them all myself, but I'm told that Thaumaste in fact wrote a huge book, printed in London, in which he sets out everything, omitting not a single item. In consideration of which, for now at least I'll just leave the subject.

CHAPTER 32

How Pantagruel Shielded an Entire Army with His Tongue, and What the Author Saw in His Mouth

As Pantagruel and all his people entered the land of the Dipsodes,[4] the inhabitants were delighted and immediately surrendered to him, bringing him of their own free will the keys to every city to which he journeyed—all except the Almyrods, who intended to resist him and told his heralds that they refused to surrender, except on good terms.

"What!" said Pantagruel. "They want more than their hand in the pot and a cup in their fist? Let's go, so you can knock down their walls for me."

So they got themselves ready, as if about to launch their attack.

But as they marched past a huge field, they were struck by a huge downpour, which began to knock their lines about and break up their formation. Seeing this, Pantagruel ordered the captains to assure them that this was nothing and he could see, past the clouds, that it was only a bit of dew. Whatever happened, however, they should maintain military discipline and he would provide them with cover. And when they had restored good marching order, Pantagruel stuck out his tongue, but just barely halfway, and shielded them as a mother hen protects her chicks.

Now I,[5] who report these totally true tales to you, had hidden myself under the leaf of a burdock weed, which was at least as big as the Mantrible Bridge. But when I saw how well they had been shielded, I went to take cover alongside them, but I couldn't, since there were so many of them and (as they say) "all things come to an end." So I climbed up as best I could and walked along his tongue for a good six miles, until I got into his mouth.

But, O you gods and goddesses, what did I see there? May Jupiter blow me away with his three-pointed lightning if I tell you a lie. I walked along in there, as you might promenade around Saint Sophia's Cathedral in Constantinople, and I saw immense boulders, just like the mountains of Denmark (I think they were his teeth), and great meadows, and huge forests, with castles and large cities, no smaller than Lyons or Poitiers.

The first person I met was an old man planting cabbage. And quite astonished I asked him:

"My friend, what are you doing here?"

"I," he said, "am planting cabbage."

"But why, and how?" I said.

"Oh ho, sir," said he, "we can't all walk around with our balls hanging down like mortars, and we can't all be rich. This is how I earn my living. They take this to the city you see over there, and sell them."

"Jesus!" I said. "Is this a whole new world in here?"

"Not at all," he said, "it isn't completely new, no. But I've heard that there is a new world outside of here, and that there's a sun and a moon out there, and all kinds of things going on. But this world is older."

"Well, my friend," I said, "what's the name of that city where they sell your cabbage?"

"It's called Throattown," he said, "and the people are good Christians, and will be pleased to see you."

So, in a word, I decided to go there.

Now, as I walked I found a fellow setting pigeon snares, and I asked him:

"My friend, where do these pigeons of yours come from?"

"Sir," he said, "they come from the other world."

And then I realized that, when Pantagruel yawned, pigeons with fully extended wings flew right down his throat, thinking it was a great bird house.

Then I came to the city, which seemed extremely pleasant, well fortified, and nicely located, with a good climate. But at the gates the porters asked for my passport and my certificate of good health, which truly astonished me, so I said to them:

"Gentlemen, is there any danger of plague here?"

"Oh, sir," they said, "they're dying of it so rapidly, not very far from here, that the body wagon is always rattling through the streets."

"Good God!" I said. "And just where is this?"

So they informed me that it was in Larynx and Pharynx, which were two cities as big as Rouen and Nantes, rich and doing a fine business, and that the plague was due to a stinking, infectious odor recently flowing up to them from the abysses below. More than twenty-two hundred and seventy-six people had died of it in the last week. So I thought about this, and added up the days, and realized that this was a foul breath from Pantagruel's stomach, which had begun after he'd eaten so much garlic (at Anarch's wedding feast), as I've already explained.

Leaving there, I walked between the great boulders that were his teeth, and climbed up on one, and found it one of the loveliest places in the whole world, with fine tennis courts, handsome galleries, beautiful meadows, and many vineyards. And these delightful fields were dotted with more Italian-style summerhouses than I could count, so I stayed on there for four months and have never been happier.

Then I climbed down the back teeth, in order to get to his lips, but as I journeyed I was robbed by a band of highwaymen in the middle of a huge forest, somewhere in the neighborhood of his ears.

Then I found a little village on the slope (I forget its name), where I was happier than ever, and worked happily for my supper. Can you guess what I did? I slept: they hire day laborers to sleep, down there, and you can make five or six dollars a day. But those who snore really loud can make seven or even seven and a half. And I told the senators how I'd been robbed in the valley, and they told me that, truthfully, the people in that neighborhood were naturally bad, and thieves to boot, which made me realize that, just as we have the Right Side of the Alps and the Wrong Side of the Alps, so they have the Right Side of the Teeth and the Wrong Side of the Teeth, but it was better on the Right Side, and the air was better, too.

And I began to think how true it was that half the world has no idea how the other half lives, seeing that no one has ever written a thing about that world down there, although it's inhabited by more than twenty-five kingdoms, not to mention the deserts and a great bay. Indeed, I have written a fat book entitled *History of an Elegant Throat Land*, which is what I called that country, since they lived in the throat of my master Pantagruel.

Finally, I decided to go back, and going past his beard I dropped onto his shoulders, and from there I got down to the ground and fell right in front of him.

And seeing me, he asked:

"Where are you coming from, Alcofribas?"

And I answered him:

"From your throat, sir."

"And how long have you been down there?" he said.

"Since you marched against the Almyrods," I said.

"But that," he said, "is more than six months. How did you live? What did you drink?"

I answered:

"My lord, just as you did, and I took a tax of the freshest morsels that came down your throat."

"Indeed," he said. "But where did you shit?"

"In your throat, sir," I said.

"Ha, ha, but you're a fine fellow!" he said. "Now, with God's help, we've conquered the entire land of the Dipsodes. And you shall have the castle of Salmagundi."

"Many thanks, sir," I said. "You're far more generous than I deserve."

MICHEL DE MONTAIGNE
1533–1592

The stylistically rich and thematically varied essays of Michel Eyquem de Montaigne offer an unparalleled view into a single Renaissance mind exploring its own workings. The first writer to ask "Who am I?" and pursue the question with extraordinary honesty and rigor, Montaigne presents himself, in his essays, as an explorer of existential dilemmas and of cultural and psychological identity crises. If at times he appears surprisingly modern in his outlook, his habits of thought, and his theories of selfhood, he is, in fact, best viewed as at once a precursor of modernity, a representative of his time, and an avid student of the classical past. The ease with which his thought turns from classical antiquity to the emerging modern world underscores Montaigne's awareness of his own position in history: he knew that the world he inhabited was undergoing dramatic cultural and geopolitical changes, and he understood that the idea of the self was being transformed along with it.

Montaigne was born on February 28, 1533, in the castle of Montaigne, to a Catholic father and a Protestant mother of Spanish-Jewish descent. His father, Pierre Eyquem, was for two terms mayor of Bordeaux and had fought in Italy under Francis I. Though no man of learning, Pierre had unconventional ideas of upbringing: Michel was awakened in the morning by the sound of music and had Latin taught him as his mother tongue. At six Michel went to the famous Collège de Guienne at Bordeaux; later he studied law, probably at Toulouse; and in 1557 he became a member of the Bordeaux parliament. In 1565 he married Françoise de la Chassaigne, daughter of a man who, as one of Montaigne's colleagues in the Bordeaux parliament, was a member of the new legal nobility (*noblesse de robe*). Perhaps because of disappointed political ambitions, Montaigne retired from politics in 1570 at the age of thirty-eight: he sold his post as magistrate and retreated to his castle of Montaigne, which he had inherited two years earlier. There in his country estate, he devoted himself to meditation and writing. His famous *Essays,* which began as a collection of interesting quotations, observations, and recordings of remarkable events, slowly developed into its final form of three large books. Although Montaigne spent, as he put it, "most of his days, and most hours of the day" in his library on the third floor of a round tower, the demands of his health and France's tumultuous politics often drew him out of retirement. For the sake of his health (he suffered from gallstones), in 1580 he took a journey through Switzerland, Germany, and Italy. While in Italy he received news that he had been appointed mayor of Bordeaux, an office that he held for two terms (1581–85).

His greatest political distractions, however, concerned the Catholic and Protestant factions that violently divided the court and France itself. French politics profoundly influenced the attitudes toward warfare, political resistance, and clemency expressed in Montaigne's *Essays.* When Henry II died in a jousting accident in 1559 and left the fifteen-year-old Francis II to succeed him, the Huguenots (French Reformers in the tradition of John Calvin), recognized the opportunity to influence the weakened royal government. Catherine de Médicis, the queen mother, seized power when Francis II died in 1560 (his successor, Charles IX, was only ten years old). Her policy of limited religious toleration satisfied neither the Catholic nor the Huguenot factions, and from 1562 to 1568 France fell into civil war three times. Struggles among France, Spain, and England over territorial rights in the Netherlands led to the dangerous possibility of a French war with Spain, which Catherine tried to avoid by planning the assassination of its most influential supporter, the Huguenot Coligny. When her plot failed, she persuaded the young Charles IX that the Huguenots were planning a coup. He is said to have shouted "Then kill them all," sanctioning the St. Bartholomew's Day Massacre of August 24, 1572: noblemen, municipal authorities, and the Parisian mobs indiscriminately slaughtered the Protestants in Paris. The slaughter was imitated in other French cities, and the civil wars once again broke out, with the house of Guise leading the Catholic party and the Bourbons leading the Huguenots.

A third party of *politiques,* including Montaigne, the political theorist Jean Bodin, and the duke of Alençon (Catherine's youngest son), arose. This party favored religious tolerance and sought a compromise to the old saying that had facilitated so much carnage in France on religious grounds: "one faith, one law, one king." Throughout his country's political struggles, Montaigne sympathized with the unfanatical Henry of Navarre, leader of the Protestants, but his attitude was neutral and conservative. He expressed his joy when Henry of Navarre became King Henry IV and turned Catholic to do so: "Paris," Henry memorably observed, "is well worth a Mass." Montaigne, who died on September 13, 1592, did not live to see Henry's triumphal entrance into Paris.

Montaigne's essays are at once highly personal and outward-looking; they present a curious mind in acts of investigating history, the complex and changing sociopolitical world, and the mind's own slightly mysterious workings. "I am a man," he says, quoting the Roman playwright Terence, and "I consider nothing human to be alien to me." As an ethnographer and historian, he studies the characteristics of geographically and historically distant cultures and insists that cultural norms are relative and should be free from judgment by sixteenth-century European standards. As a psychologist, he is drawn to the "alien" or disowned thoughts and experiences of himself and his countrymen. His method is not didactic, and his criticism, which he reserves for fellow Europeans, emerges largely through subtle ironies that he leaves readers to detect. He moves suddenly, for example, from introspection to an ethical challenge. "Authors communicate themselves to the world by some special and extrinsic mark," he comments in the essay *Of Repentance,* but "I am the first to do so by my general being, as Michel de Montaigne, not as a grammarian or a poet or a lawyer. If the world finds fault with me for speaking too much of myself, I find fault with the world for not even thinking of itself."

When Montaigne thinks of himself, he does not aggrandize or justify himself but seeks to enlarge knowledge of how the mind works. Far from prizing his capacity for reason and judgment, for example, he neutrally observes, "My judgment floats, it wanders." Montaigne is, in fact, disarmingly modest: "Reader, I am myself the subject of my book; it is not reasonable to expect you to waste your leisure on a matter so frivolous and empty." Although massively learned, he emphasizes not what he knows but rather, like Plato's Socrates, the ways that knowledge reveals how little he truly knows. Ultimately, his essays lead readers away from character study toward philosophical questions about the grounds for knowledge itself (the branch of philosophy called *epistemology*).

Montaigne's assertions of doubt and consciousness of human vanity have little to do with gloomy despair: his stance is skeptical, not cynical. Thus if he "essays" or probes the human capacity to act purposefully and coherently—as he does in the essay *Of the Inconsistency of Our Actions*—his implicit verdict is not that our action is absolutely futile. Instead, he refuses to attribute to the human mind a coherence it does not possess; to Montaigne, if a man were able to achieve the Stoic ideal of the "constant man," unmoved by circumstance or emotion (the butt of Folly's jokes in Erasmus), the result would be impoverishing. "Our actions are nothing but a patchwork," he remarks, and the insight into the fragmentary, inconsistent pattern of our personal lives leads him to a dramatic perception of the strangeness and instability of the self: "There is as much difference between us and ourselves as between us and others." This idea became highly influential in Renaissance thinking and shaped such haunting insights as John Donne's observation that "ourselves are what we know not." For Renaissance thinkers who embraced Montaigne's perception of psychological mysteriousness, the difficult philosophical imperative of Socrates, "know thyself," seemed endlessly intriguing but doomed.

Montaigne pursues his arguments about the elusive and unstable character of the "self" by considering a wide range of anecdotes, both contemporary and classical. A slippery or undefinable historical character intrigues him far more than a monolithic or single-minded one. Alexander the Great—the legendary warrior who also haunts the pages of Castiglione's *Courtier*—is rendered frighteningly transparent by his obsession with power and conquest: he wants nothing less than to be a god. Emperor Augustus, on the other hand, rewards study precisely because his character has "escaped" the willful reductions of historians bent on "fashioning a consistent and solid fabric" of his character. As Montaigne admiringly puts it in *Of the Inconsistency of Our Actions,* there is in the life of Augustus "such an obvious, abrupt, and continual variety of actions that even the boldest judges have had to let him go, intact and unsolved."

Why was Montaigne so unusually able to suspend the self-interest and bias he considered ingrained in human nature in order to analyze himself, his culture, and the place of humankind in the cosmos? As his life in politics indicates, the violent instability of French history taught him tolerance, skepticism about human self-interest, and hatred of dogmatic positions:

> It demands a great deal of self-love and presumption, to take one's own opinions so seriously as to disrupt the peace in order to establish them, introducing so many inevitable evils, and so terrible a corruption of manners as civil wars and political revolutions with them.

His hatred of political radicalism influenced much of what he saw in ancient history and in contemporary accounts of New World discovery and conquest. This alienation from his own political context suggests one cause of his celebrated doubleness of perspective, which is at once ethnographic (outward-looking and impartial) and self-critical (introspective and moral). As he reflects on the ancient and new worlds, he pays special attention to how human beings respond to adversity, oppression, and physical torture. If we keep in mind his impatience with the political and religious ideologues of his own country, we may understand why the heroic self-assertions of Alexander the Great or Hernán Cortés hold no sway over his imagination and sympathies. Violent repression and implacable resistance alike repel Montaigne, who keenly scrutinizes displays of courage that camouflage less-than-noble motives.

In the most famous essay, *Of Cannibals* (which influenced Shakespeare's reflections in *The Tempest* on the ideal commonwealth, colonialism, and the nature of savages), Montaigne compares the behavioral codes of Brazilian cannibals and those of "ourselves" (Europeans) and concludes that "each man calls barbarism whatever is not his own practice." Once he has asserted the relativity of customs, Montaigne is able to praise elements of the savages' culture that he regards as superior to Europe's. He admires the savages' courage, for instance, in which "the honor of valor consists in combating, not in beating." Moreover, he finds in the positive example of the Brazilian cannibals an implicit criticism of violence by Europeans both at home and in the New World. Montaigne remarks, "I am not sorry that we notice the barbarous horror" of cannibal culture, and then continues,

> but I am heartily sorry that judging their faults rightly, we should be so blind to our own. I think there is more barbarity in eating a man alive than in eating him dead; and in tearing by tortures and the rack a body still full of feeling, in roasting a man bit by bit, in having him bitten and mangled by dogs and swine (as we have not only read but seen within fresh memory, not among ancient enemies, but among neighbors and fellow citizens and what is worse, on the pretext of piety and religion), than in roasting and eating him after he is dead.

As an ethnographer, Montaigne is able to grapple with the distinct and alien culture of the savages without passing judgment; but when he reflects on France, he becomes a moralist. Central to the entire essay is the invocation of the Catholics' torture and burning of fellow citizens (Huguenots) that Montaigne ironically tucks in parentheses. Montaigne here juxtaposes two kinds of savagery: that which appears foreign (cannibalism) and that which has grown too familiar (religious persecution).

Montaigne shows as much interest in the behavior of Brazilian and European victims as he does in their torturers. Montaigne writes of paintings that show a Brazilian prisoner of war "spitting in the face of his slayers and scowling at them. Indeed, to the last gasp they never stop braving and defying their enemies by word and look." He continues, "Truly, here are real savages by our standards; for either they must be thoroughly so, or we must be; there is an amazing distance between their character and ours." What Montaigne's example suggests is an unnerving *identity* between the defiant Brazilian natives and the Huguenots of France, who have become inured to the ideas of violent resistance and martyrdom. Like the Brazilian victims of cannibalism, the Huguenots are unwilling, even in the face of death, to moderate their dealings with their torturers, the Catholics who dominate French politics. Montaigne's cannibals, then, help make the entrenched behavior of France's religious factions seem foreign, strange, and savage: both sides are guilty (if not equally so) of "so terrible a corruption of manners as civil wars and political revolutions." His own country's civil strife inspires in Montaigne an unusual ability to transcend smug cultural bias, making him a powerful critic of European culture and an ethnographer able to imagine and study communities other than his own. Like the world of antiquity, which also riveted his imagination, the idea of America allowed Montaigne to explore alternate worlds for their own sake and for their illumination of his own.

Hugo Friedrich, *Montaigne* (1991), is a careful historical study of the author. David Quint, "A Reconsideration of Montaigne's *Des cannibales*," *Modern Language Quarterly* 51.4 (1990): 459–89, analyzes the rhetorical structure and political implications of Montaigne's famous essay. Judith Shklar, *Ordinary Vices* (1984), and Edwin Duval, "Lessons of the New World: Design and Meaning in Montaigne's 'Des Cannibales' (I:31) and 'Des coches' (III:6)," in *Montaigne: Essays in Reading*, ed. Gerard Defaux, *Yale French Studies* 64 (1983): 95–112, provide excellent studies of Montaigne that include, but are not limited to, his New World contexts. Marcel Tetel, *Montaigne*, updated ed. (1990), and Richard Sayce, *The Essays of Montaigne: A Critical Exploration* (1972), are excellent introductions designed for the general reader.

PRONOUNCING GLOSSARY

The following list uses common English syllables and stress accents to provide rough equivalents of selected words whose pronunciation may be unfamiliar to the general reader.

de la Chassaigne: *deu lah shah-sen'*

Dordogne: *dor-don'*

Guise: *geez*

Jacques Peletier: *zhahk pel-tyay'*

Montaigne: *mon-ten'*

Soissons: *swah-sohnh'*

Suidas: *soo'-ee-dahs*

Valois: *val-wah'*

Villegaignon: *vil-gen-yon'*

Vitry-le-François: *vee-tree leu frahn-swah'*

FROM ESSAYS[1]

To the Reader

This book was written in good faith, reader. It warns you from the outset that in it I have set myself no goal but a domestic and private one. I have had no thought of serving either you or my own glory. My powers are inadequate for such a purpose. I have dedicated it to the private convenience of my relatives and friends, so that when they have lost me (as soon they must), they may recover here some features of my habits and temperament, and by this means keep the knowledge they have had of me more complete and alive.

If I had written to seek the world's favor, I should have bedecked myself better, and should present myself in a studied posture. I want to be seen here in my simple, natural, ordinary fashion, without straining or artifice; for it is myself that I portray. My defects will here be read to the life, and also my natural form, as far as respect for the public has allowed. Had I been placed among those nations which are said to live still in the sweet freedom of nature's first laws, I assure you I should very gladly have portrayed myself here entire and wholly naked.

Thus, reader, I am myself the matter of my book; you would be unreasonable to spend your leisure on so frivolous and vain a subject.

So farewell. Montaigne, this first day of March, fifteen hundred and eighty.

Of the Power of the Imagination

A strong imagination creates the event, say the scholars. I am one of those who are very much influenced by the imagination. Everyone feels its impact, but some are overthrown by it. Its impression on me is piercing. And my art is to escape it, not to resist it. I would live solely in the presence of gay, healthy people. The sight of other people's anguish causes very real anguish to me, and my feelings have often usurped the feelings of others. A continual cougher irritates my lungs and throat. I visit less willingly the sick toward whom duty directs me than those toward whom I am less attentive and concerned. I catch the disease that I study, and lodge it in me. I do not find it strange that imagination brings fevers and death to those who give it a free hand and encourage it.

Simon Thomas was a great doctor in his time. I remember that one day, when he met me at the house of a rich old consumptive with whom he was discussing ways to cure his illness, he told him that one of these would be to give me occasion to enjoy his company; and that by fixing his eyes on the freshness of my face and his thoughts on the blitheness and overflowing vigor of my youth, and filling all his senses with my flourishing condition, he might improve his constitution. But he forgot to say that mine might get worse at the same time.

Gallus Vibius[2] strained his mind so hard to understand the essence and

---

1. Translated by Donald Frame.   2. Roman orator. Montaigne illustrates his points with many examples from both antiquity and contemporary Europe; it is less important to know who these historical persons were than to follow Montaigne's presentation of telling moments of their lives.

impulses of insanity that he dragged his judgment off its seat and never could get it back again; and he could boast of having become mad through wisdom. There are some who through fear anticipate the hand of the executioner. And one man who was being unbound to have his pardon read him dropped stone dead on the scaffold, struck down by his mere imagination. We drip with sweat, we tremble, we turn pale and turn red at the blows of our imagination; reclining in our feather beds we feel our bodies agitated by their impact, sometimes to the point of expiring. And boiling youth, fast asleep, grows so hot in the harness that in dreams it satisfies its amorous desires:

> So that as though it were an actual affair,
> They pour out mighty streams, and stain the clothes they wear.
> LUCRETIUS[3]

And although it is nothing new to see horns grow overnight on someone who did not have them when he went to bed, nevertheless what happened to Cippus,[4] king of Italy, is memorable; having been in the daytime a very excited spectator at a bullfight and having all night in his dreams had horns on his head, he grew actual horns on his forehead by the power of his imagination. Passion gave the son of Croesus the voice that nature had refused him. And Antiochus took fever from the beauty of Stratonice too vividly imprinted in his soul. Pliny says he saw Lucius Cossitius changed from a woman into a man on his wedding day. Pontanus[5] and others report similar metamorphoses as having happened in Italy in these later ages. And through his and his mother's vehement desire,

> Iphis the man fulfilled vows made when he was a girl.
> OVID[6]

Passing through Vitry-le-François, I might have seen a man whom the bishop of Soissons had named Germain at confirmation, but whom all the inhabitants of that place had seen and known as a girl named Marie until the age of twenty-two. He was now heavily bearded, and old, and not married. Straining himself in some way in jumping, he says, his masculine organs came forth; and among the girls there a song is still current by which they warn each other not to take big strides for fear of becoming boys, like Marie Germain. It is not so great a marvel that this sort of accident is frequently met with. For if the imagination has power in such things, it is so continually and vigorously fixed on this subject that in order not to have to relapse so often into the same thought and sharpness of desire, it is better off if once and for all it incorporates this masculine member in girls.

Some attribute to the power of imagination the scars of King Dagobert and of Saint Francis. It is said that thereby bodies are sometimes removed from their places. And Celsus tells of a priest who used to fly with his soul into such ecstasy that his body would remain a long time without breath and without sensation. Saint Augustine[7] names another who whenever he heard lamentable and plaintive cries would suddenly go into a trance and get so

3. Titus Lucretius Caro (94–55 B.C.), Roman poet and Epicurean philosopher; *On the Nature of Things* 4.1035–36.   4. The story of Cippus is told by Pliny (A.D. 23/24–79).   5. Johannes Pontanus (1426–1503), Renaissance scholar and philosopher. Croesus, last king of Lydia (ca. 560–546 B.C.). Antiochus I (324–261 B.C.), who ruled the eastern Seleucid territories from 293/2 B.C., took Seleucus's wife, Stratonice. 6. *Metamorphoses* 9.793.   7. Early Christian Church father (A.D. 354–430).

carried away that it was no use to shake him and shout at him, to pinch him and burn him, until he had come to; then he would say that he had heard voices, but as if coming from afar, and he would notice his burns and bruises. And that this was no feigned resistance to his senses was shown by the fact that while in this state he had neither pulse nor breath.

It is probable that the principal credit of miracles, visions, enchantments, and such extraordinary occurrences comes from the power of imagination, acting principally upon the minds of the common people, which are softer. Their belief has been so strongly seized that they think they see what they do not see.

I am still of this opinion, that those comical inhibitions by which our society is so fettered that people talk of nothing else are for the most part the effects of apprehension and fear. For I know by experience that one man,[8] whom I can answer for as for myself, on whom there could fall no suspicion whatever of impotence and just as little of being enchanted, having heard a friend of his tell the story of an extraordinary impotence into which he had fallen at the moment when he needed it least, and finding himself in a similar situation, was all at once so struck in his imagination by the horror of this story that he incurred the same fate. And from then on he was subject to relapse, for the ugly memory of his mishap checked him and tyrannized him. He found some remedy for this fancy by another fancy: which was that by admitting this weakness and speaking about it in advance, he relieved the tension of his soul, for when the trouble had been presented as one to be expected, his sense of responsibility diminished and weighed upon him less. When he had a chance of his own choosing, with his mind unembroiled and relaxed and his body in good shape, to have his bodily powers first tested, then seized and taken by surprise, with the other party's full knowledge of his problem, he was completely cured in this respect. A man is never after incapable, unless from genuine impotence, with a woman with whom he has once been capable.

This mishap is to be feared only in enterprises where our soul is immoderately tense with desire and respect, and especially if the opportunity is unexpected and pressing; there is no way of recovering from this trouble. I know one man who found it helpful to bring to it a body that had already begun to be sated elsewhere, so as to lull his frenzied ardor, and who with age finds himself less impotent through being less potent. And I know another who was helped when a friend assured him that he was supplied with a counterbattery of enchantments that were certain to save him. I had better tell how this happened.

A count, a member of a very distinguished family, with whom I was quite intimate, upon getting married to a beautiful lady who had been courted by a man who was present at the wedding feast, had his friends very worried and especially an old lady, a relative of his, who was presiding at the wedding and holding it at her house. She was fearful of these sorceries, and gave me to understand this. I asked her to rely on me. I had by chance in my coffers a certain little flat piece of gold on which were engraved some celestial figures, to protect against sunstroke and take away a headache by placing it precisely on the suture of the skull; and, to keep it there, it was sewed to a

8. Possibly Montaigne himself.

ribbon intended to be tied under the chin: a kindred fancy to the one we are speaking of. Jacques Peletier[9] had given me this singular present. I thought of making some use of it, and said to the count that he might incur the same fate as others, there being men present who would like to bring this about; but that he should boldly go to bed and I would do him a friendly turn and would not, if he needed it, spare a miracle which was in my power, provided that he promised me on his honor to keep it most faithfully secret; he was only to make a given signal to me, when they came to bring him the midnight meal, if things had gone badly with him. He had had his soul and his ears so battered that he did find himself fettered by the trouble of his imagination, and gave me his signal. I told him then that he should get up on the pretext of chasing us out, and playfully take the bathrobe that I had on (we were very close in height) and put it on him until he had carried out my prescription, which was this: when we had left, he should withdraw to pass water, say certain prayers three times and go through certain motions; each of these three times he should tie the ribbon I was putting in his hand around him and very carefully lay the medal that was attached to it on his kidneys, with the figure in such and such a position; this done, having tied this ribbon firmly so that it could neither come untied nor slip from its place, he should return to his business with complete assurance and not forget to spread my robe over his bed so that it should cover them both. These monkey tricks are the main part of the business, our mind being unable to get free of the idea that such strange means must come from some abstruse science. Their inanity gives them weight and reverence. All in all, it is certain that the characters on my medal proved themselves more venereal than solar, more useful for action than for prevention. It was a sudden and curious whim that led me to do such a thing, which was alien to my nature. I am an enemy of subtle and dissimulated acts and hate trickery in myself, not only for sport but also for someone's profit. If the action is not vicious, the road to it is.

Amasis,[1] king of Egypt, married Laodice, a very beautiful Greek girl; and he, who showed himself a gay companion everywhere else, fell short when it came to enjoying her, and threatened to kill her, thinking it was some sort of sorcery. As is usual in matters of fancy, she referred him to religion; and having made his vows and promises to Venus, he found himself divinely restored from the first night after his oblations and sacrifices.

Now women are wrong to greet us with those threatening, quarrelsome, and coy countenances, which put out our fires even as they light them. The daughter-in-law of Pythagoras used to say that the woman who goes to bed with a man should put off her modesty with her skirt and put it on again with her petticoat. The soul of the assailant, when troubled with many various alarms, is easily discouraged; and when imagination has once made a man suffer this shame—and it does so only at the first encounters, inasmuch as these are more boiling and violent, and also because in this first intimacy a man is much more afraid of failing—having begun badly, he gets from this accident a feverishness and vexation which lasts into subsequent occasions.

Married people, whose time is all their own, should neither press their undertaking nor even attempt it if they are not ready; it is better to fail

9. Renaissance mathematician (1517–1582).
1. Pharaoh ca. 569 B.C., known for his great public works and unconventional life.

unbecomingly to handsel the nuptial couch, which is full of agitation and feverishness, and wait for some other more private and less tense opportunity, than to fall into perpetual misery for having been stunned and made desperate by a first refusal. Before taking possession, the patient should try himself out and offer himself, lightly, by sallies at different times, without priding himself and obstinately insisting on convincing himself definitively. Those who know that their members are naturally obedient, let them take care only to counteract the tricks of their fancies.

People are right to notice the unruly liberty of this member, obtruding so importunately when we have no use for it, and failing so importunately when we have the most use for it, and struggling for mastery so imperiously with our will, refusing with so much pride and obstinacy our solicitations, both mental and manual.

If, however, in the matter of his rebellion being blamed and used as proof to condemn him, he had paid me to plead his cause, I should perhaps place our other members, his fellows, under suspicion of having framed this trumped-up charge out of sheer envy of the importance and pleasure of the use of him, and of having armed everyone against him by a conspiracy, malignantly charging him alone with their common fault. For I ask you to think whether there is a single one of the parts of our body that does not often refuse its function to our will and exercise it against our will. They each have passions of their own which rouse them and put them to sleep without our leave. How many times do the forced movements of our face bear witness to the thoughts that we were holding secret, and betray us to those present. The same cause that animates this member also animates, without our knowledge, the heart, the lungs, and the pulse; the sight of a pleasing object spreading in us imperceptibly the flame of a feverish emotion. Are there only these muscles and these veins that stand up and lie down without the consent, not only of our will, but even of our thoughts? We do not command our hair to stand on end or our skin to shiver with desire or fear. The hand often moves itself to where we do not send it. The tongue is paralyzed, and the voice congealed, at their own time. Even when, having nothing to put in to fry, we should like to forbid it, the appetite for eating and drinking does not fail to stir the parts that are subject to it, no more nor less than that other appetite; and it likewise abandons us inopportunely when it sees fit. The organs that serve to discharge the stomach have their own dilatations and compressions, beyond and against our plans, just like those that are destined to discharge the kidneys. To vindicate the omnipotence of our will, Saint Augustine alleges that he knew a man who commanded his behind to produce as many farts as he wanted, and his commentator Vives[2] goes him one better with another example of his own time, of farts arranged to suit the tone of verses pronounced to their accompaniment; but all this does not really argue any pure obedience in this organ; for is there any that is ordinarily more indiscreet or tumultuous? Besides, I know one so turbulent and unruly, that for forty years it has kept its master farting with a constant and unremitting wind and compulsion, and is thus taking him to his death.

But as for our will, on behalf of whose rights we set forth this complaint, how much more plausibly may we charge it with rebellion and sedition for

2. Juan Luis Vives (1492–1540), Renaissance philosopher and scholar.

its disorderliness and disobedience! Does it always will what we would will it to will? Doesn't it often will what we forbid it to will, and that to our evident disadvantage? Is it any more amenable than our other parts to the decisions of our reason?

To conclude, I would say this in defense of the honorable member whom I represent: May it please the court to take into consideration that in this matter, although my client's case is inseparably and indistinguishably linked with that of an accessory, nevertheless he alone has been brought to trial; and that the arguments and charges against him are such as cannot—in view of the status of the parties—be in any manner pertinent or relevant to the aforesaid accessory. Whereby is revealed his accusers' manifest animosity and disrespect for law. However that may be, Nature will meanwhile go her way, protesting that the lawyers and judges quarrel and pass sentence in vain. Indeed, she would have done no more than is right if she had endowed with some particular privilege this member, author of the sole immortal work of mortals. Wherefore to Socrates generation is a divine act; and love, a desire for immortality and itself an immortal daemon.[3]

Perhaps it is by this effect of the imagination that one man here gets rid of the scrofula which his companion carries back to Spain.[4] This effect is the reason why, in such matters, it is customary to demand that the mind be prepared. Why do the doctors work on the credulity of their patient beforehand with so many false promises of a cure, if not so that the effect of the imagination may make up for the imposture of their decoction? They know that one of the masters of the trade left them this in writing, that there have been men for whom the mere sight of medicine did the job.

And this whole caprice[5] has just come to hand apropos of the story that an apothecary, a servant of my late father, used to tell me, a simple man and Swiss, of a nation little addicted to vanity and lying. He had long known a merchant at Toulouse,[6] sickly and subject to the stone, who often needed enemas, and ordered various kinds from his doctors according to the circumstances of his illness. Once they were brought to him, nothing was omitted of the accustomed formalities; often he tested them by hand to make sure they were not too hot. There he was, lying on his stomach, and all the motions were gone through—except that no injection was made. After this ceremony, the apothecary having retired and the patient being accommodated as if he had really taken the enema, he felt the same effect from it as those who do take them. And if the doctor did not find its operation sufficient, he would give him two or three more, of the same sort. My witness swears that when to save the expense (for he paid for them as if he had taken them) this sick man's wife sometimes tried to have just warm water used, the effect revealed the fraud; and having found that kind useless, they were obliged to return to the first method.

A woman, thinking she had swallowed a pin with her bread, was screaming in agony as though she had an unbearable pain in her throat, where she thought she felt it stuck; but because externally there was neither swelling nor alteration, a smart man, judging that it was only a fancy and notion

3. Socrates (ca. 470–399 B.C.) describes love as a *daemon* in Plato's *Symposium*.   4. Scrofula, or king's evil, was supposed to be curable by the touch of the kings of France. In Montaigne's time great numbers of Spaniards came to France for this purpose [Translator's note].   5. Montaigne's "cure" for his impotent friend.   6. City of southwestern France.

derived from some bit of bread that had scratched her as it went down, made her vomit, and, on the sly, tossed a crooked pin into what she threw up. The woman, thinking she had thrown it up, felt herself suddenly relieved of her pain. I know that one gentleman, having entertained a goodly company at his house, three or four days later boasted, as a sort of joke (for there was nothing in it), that he had made them eat cat in a pie; at which one lady in the party was so horrified that she fell into a violent stomach disorder and fever, and it was impossible to save her. Even animals are subject like ourselves to the power of imagination. Witness dogs, who let themselves die out of grief for the loss of their masters. We also see them yap and twitch in their dreams, and horses whinny and writhe.

But all this may be attributed to the narrow seam between the soul and body, through which the experience of the one is communicated to the other. Sometimes, however, one's imagination acts not only against one's own body, but against someone else's. And just as a body passes on its sickness to its neighbor, as is seen in the plague, the pox, and soreness of the eyes, which are transmitted from one body to the other—

> By looking at sore eyes, eyes become sore:
> From body into body ills pass o'er
>
> OVID[7]

—likewise the imagination, when vehemently stirred, launches darts that can injure an external object. The ancients maintained that certain women of Scythia,[8] when animated and enraged against anyone, would kill him with their mere glance. Tortoises and ostriches hatch their eggs just by looking at them, a sign that their sight has some ejaculative virtue. And as for sorcerers, they are said to have baleful and harmful eyes:

> some evil eye bewitched my tender lambs.
>
> VIRGIL[9]

To me, magicians are poor authorities. Nevertheless, we know by experience that women transmit marks of their fancies to the bodies of the children they carry in their womb; witness the one who gave birth to the Moor.[1] And there was presented to Charles, king of Bohemia and Emperor, a girl from near Pisa, all hairy and bristly, who her mother said had been thus conceived because of a picture of Saint John the Baptist hanging by her bed.

With animals it is the same: witness Jacob's sheep,[2] and the partridges and hares that the snow turns white in the mountains. Recently at my house a cat was seen watching a bird on a treetop, and, after they had locked gazes for some time, the bird let itself fall as if dead between the cat's paws, either intoxicated by its own imagination or drawn by some attracting power of the cat. Those who like falconry have heard the story of the falconer who, setting his gaze obstinately upon a kite in the air, wagered that by the sole power of his gaze he would bring it down, and did. At least, so they say—for I refer

---

7. *The Cure for Love*, lines 615–16.   8. Scythians, the Greek name for Asian tribes who lived in what are now parts of Iran and Turkey, were legendary in the Renaissance for their "barbarity."   9. *Eclogue* 3.103.   1. Saint Jerome tells of a woman who, accused of adultery for giving birth to a black child, was absolved when Hippocrates explained that she had a picture of a dark man hanging in her room by her bed [Translator's note].   2. Genesis 30.37–42. After Laban agreed to give Jacob the striped sheep from his flocks, Jacob bred the sheep in front of rods (the visual stimulation was thought to cause the females to produce striped offspring).

the stories that I borrow to the conscience of those from whom I take them. The reflections are my own, and depend on the proofs of reason, not of experience; everyone can add his own examples to them; and he who has none, let him not fail to believe that there are plenty, in view of the number and variety of occurrences. If I do not apply them well, let another apply them for me.

So in the study that I am making of our behavior and motives, fabulous testimonies, provided they are possible, serve like true ones. Whether they have happened or no, in Paris or Rome, to John or Peter, they exemplify, at all events, some human potentiality, and thus their telling imparts useful information to me. I see it and profit from it just as well in shadow as in substance. And of the different readings that histories often give, I take for my use the one that is most rare and memorable. There are authors whose end is to tell what has happened. Mine, if I could attain it, would be to talk about what can happen. The schools are justly permitted to suppose similitudes when they have none at hand. I do not do so, however, and in that respect I surpass all historical fidelity, being scrupulous to the point of superstition. In the examples that I bring in here of what I have heard, done, or said, I have forbidden myself to dare to alter even the slightest and most inconsequential circumstances. My conscience does not falsify one iota; my knowledge, I don't know.

In this connection, I sometimes fall to thinking whether it befits a theologian, a philosopher, and such people of exquisite and exact conscience and prudence, to write history. How can they stake their fidelity on the fidelity of an ordinary person? How be responsible for the thoughts of persons unknown and give their conjectures as coin of the realm? Of complicated actions that happen in their presence they would refuse to give testimony if placed under oath by a judge; and they know no man so intimately that they would undertake to answer fully for his intentions. I consider it less hazardous to write of things past than present, inasmuch as the writer has only to give an account of a borrowed truth.

Some urge me to write the events of my time, believing that I see them with a view less distorted by passion than another man's, and from closer, because of the access that fortune has given me to the heads of different parties.[3] What they forget is that even for all the glory of Sallust,[4] I would not take the trouble, being a sworn enemy of obligation, assiduity, perseverance; and that there is nothing so contrary to my style as an extended narration. I cut myself off so often for lack of breath; I have neither composition nor development that is worth anything; I am more ignorant than a child of the phrases and terms that serve for the commonest things. And so I have chosen to say what I know how to say, accommodating the matter to my power. If I took a subject that would lead me along, I might not be able to measure up to it; and with my freedom being so very free, I might publish judgments which, even according to my own opinion and to reason, would be illegitimate and punishable. Plutarch[5] might well say to us, concerning his accomplishments in this line, that the credit belongs to others if his examples are wholly and everywhere true; but that their being useful to pos-

3. A centrist, Montaigne knew leaders of the rivaling factions in France.   4. Roman historian (probably 86–35 B.C.).   5. Philosopher and biographer (ca. A.D. 50–120).

terity, and presented with a luster which lights our way to virtue, that is his work. There is no danger—as there is in a medicinal drug—in an old story being this way or that.

Of Cannibals

When King Pyrrhus[6] passed over into Italy, after he had reconnoitered the formation of the army that the Romans were sending to meet him, he said: "I do not know what barbarians these are" (for so the Greeks called all foreign nations), "but the formation of this army that I see is not at all barbarous." The Greeks said as much of the army that Flaminius brought into their country, and so did Philip, seeing from a knoll the order and distribution of the Roman camp, in his kingdom, under Publius Sulpicius Galba.[7] Thus we should beware of clinging to vulgar opinions, and judge things by reason's way, not by popular say.

I had with me for a long time a man who had lived for ten or twelve years in that other world which has been discovered in our century, in the place where Villegaignon landed, and which he called Antarctic France.[8] This discovery of a boundless country seems worthy of consideration. I don't know if I can guarantee that some other such discovery will not be made in the future, so many personages greater than ourselves having been mistaken about this one. I am afraid we have eyes bigger than our stomachs, and more curiosity than capacity. We embrace everything, but we clasp only wind.

Plato brings in Solon,[9] telling how he had learned from the priests of the city of Saïs in Egypt that in days of old, before the Flood, there was a great island named Atlantis, right at the mouth of the Strait of Gibraltar, which contained more land than Africa and Asia put together, and that the kings of that country, who not only possessed that island but had stretched out so far on the mainland that they held the breadth of Africa as far as Egypt, and the length of Europe as far as Tuscany, undertook to step over into Asia and subjugate all the nations that border on the Mediterranean, as far as the Black Sea; and for this purpose crossed the Spains, Gaul, Italy, as far as Greece, where the Athenians checked them; but that some time after, both the Athenians and themselves and their island were swallowed up by the Flood.

It is quite likely that that extreme devastation of waters made amazing changes in the habitations of the earth, as people maintain that the sea cut off Sicily from Italy—

> 'Tis said an earthquake once asunder tore
> These lands with dreadful havoc, which before
> Formed but one land, one coast
> VIRGIL[1]

---

6. King of Epirus (in Greece) who fought the Romans in Italy in 280 B.C.   7. Both Titus Quinctius Flaminius and Publius Sulpicius Galba were Roman statesmen and generals who fought Philip V of Macedon in the early years of the 2nd century B.C.   8. In Brazil. Villegaignon landed there in 1557.   9. In his *Timaeus*.   1. *Aeneid* 3.414–15.

—Cyprus from Syria, the island of Euboea from the mainland of Boeotia; and elsewhere joined lands that were divided, filling the channels between them with sand and mud:

> A sterile marsh, long fit for rowing, now
> Feeds neighbor towns, and feels the heavy plow.
> HORACE[2]

But there is no great likelihood that that island was the new world which we have just discovered; for it almost touched Spain, and it would be an incredible result of a flood to have forced it away as far as it is, more than twelve hundred leagues; besides, the travels of the moderns have already almost revealed that it is not an island, but a mainland connected with the East Indies on one side, and elsewhere with the lands under the two poles; or, if it is separated from them, it is by so narrow a strait and interval that it does not deserve to be called an island on that account.

It seems that there are movements, some natural, others feverish, in these great bodies, just as in our own. When I consider the inroads that my river, the Dordogne, is making in my lifetime into the right bank in its descent, and that in twenty years it has gained so much ground and stolen away the foundations of several buildings, I clearly see that this is an extraordinary disturbance; for if it had always gone at this rate, or was to do so in the future, the face of the world would be turned topsy-turvy. But rivers are subject to changes: now they overflow in one direction, now in another, now they keep to their course. I am not speaking of the sudden inundations whose causes are manifest. In Médoc, along the seashore, my brother, the sieur d'Arsac, can see an estate of his buried under the sands that the sea spews forth; the tops of some buildings are still visible; his farms and domains have changed into very thin pasturage. The inhabitants say that for some time the sea has been pushing toward them so hard that they have lost four leagues of land. These sands are its harbingers; and we see great dunes of moving sand that march half a league ahead of it and keep conquering land.

The other testimony of antiquity with which some would connect this discovery is in Aristotle, at least if that little book *Of Unheard-of Wonders* is by him. He there relates that certain Carthaginians, after setting out upon the Atlantic Ocean from the Strait of Gibraltar and sailing a long time, at last discovered a great fertile island, all clothed in woods and watered by great deep rivers, far remote from any mainland; and that they, and others since, attracted by the goodness and fertility of the soil, went there with their wives and children, and began to settle there. The lords of Carthage, seeing that their country was gradually becoming depopulated, expressly forbade anyone to go there any more, on pain of death, and drove out these new inhabitants, fearing, it is said, that in course of time they might come to multiply so greatly as to supplant their former masters and ruin their state. This story of Aristotle does not fit our new lands any better than the other.

This man I had was a simple, crude fellow—a character fit to bear true witness; for clever people observe more things and more curiously, but they interpret them; and to lend weight and conviction to their interpretation,

---

2. Horatius Flaccus (65–68 B.C.), great poet of Augustan Rome; *Art of Poetry,* lines 65–66.

they cannot help altering history a little. They never show you things as they are, but bend and disguise them according to the way they have seen them; and to give credence to their judgment and attract you to it, they are prone to add something to their matter, to stretch it out and amplify it. We need a man either very honest, or so simple that he has not the stuff to build up false inventions and give them plausibility; and wedded to no theory. Such was my man; and besides this, he at various times brought sailors and merchants, whom he had known on that trip, to see me. So I content myself with his information, without inquiring what the cosmographers say about it.

We ought to have topographers who would give us an exact account of the places where they have been. But because they have over us the advantage of having seen Palestine, they want to enjoy the privilege of telling us news about all the rest of the world. I would like everyone to write what he knows, and as much as he knows, not only in this, but in all other subjects; for a man may have some special knowledge and experience of the nature of a river or a fountain, who in other matters knows only what everybody knows. However, to circulate this little scrap of knowledge, he will undertake to write the whole of physics. From this vice spring many great abuses.

Now, to return to my subject, I think there is nothing barbarous and savage in that nation, from what I have been told, except that each man calls barbarism whatever is not his own practice; for indeed it seems we have no other test of truth and reason than the example and pattern of the opinions and customs of the country we live in. *There* is always the perfect religion, the perfect government, the perfect and accomplished manners in all things. Those people are wild, just as we call wild the fruits that Nature has produced by herself and in her normal course; whereas really it is those that we have changed artificially and led astray from the common order, that we should rather call wild. The former retain alive and vigorous their genuine, their most useful and natural, virtues and properties, which we have debased in the latter in adapting them to gratify our corrupted taste. And yet for all that, the savor and delicacy of some uncultivated fruits of those countries is quite as excellent, even to our taste, as that of our own. It is not reasonable that art should win the place of honor over our great and powerful mother Nature. We have so overloaded the beauty and richness of her works by our inventions that we have quite smothered her. Yet wherever her purity shines forth, she wonderfully puts to shame our vain and frivolous attempts:

> Ivy comes readier without our care;
> In lonely caves the arbutus grows more fair;
> No art with artless bird song can compare.
>   PROPERTIUS[3]

All our efforts cannot even succeed in reproducing the nest of the tiniest little bird, its contexture, its beauty and convenience; or even the web of the puny spider. All things, says Plato,[4] are produced by nature, by fortune, or by art; the greatest and most beautiful by one or the other of the first two, the least and most imperfect by the last.

These nations, then, seem to me barbarous in this sense, that they have

---

3. *Elegies* 1.2.10–12.   4. See his *Laws*.

been fashioned very little by the human mind, and are still very close to their original naturalness. The laws of nature still rule them, very little corrupted by ours; and they are in such a state of purity that I am sometimes vexed that they were unknown earlier, in the days when there were men able to judge them better than we. I am sorry that Lycurgus[5] and Plato did not know of them; for it seems to me that what we actually see in these nations surpasses not only all the pictures in which poets have idealized the golden age and all their inventions in imagining a happy state of man, but also the conceptions and the very desire of philosophy. They could not imagine a naturalness so pure and simple as we see by experience; nor could they believe that our society could be maintained with so little artifice and human solder. This is a nation, I should say to Plato, in which there is no sort of traffic, no knowledge of letters, no science of numbers, no name for a magistrate or for political superiority, no custom of servitude, no riches or poverty, no contracts, no successions, no partitions, no occupations but leisure ones, no care for any but common kinship, no clothes, no agriculture, no metal, no use of wine or wheat.[6] The very words that signify lying, treachery, dissimulation, avarice, envy, belittling, pardon—unheard of. How far from this perfection would he find the republic that he imagined: *Men fresh sprung from the gods* [Seneca].[7]

> These manners nature first ordained.
> VIRGIL[8]

For the rest, they live in a country with a very pleasant and temperate climate, so that according to my witnesses it is rare to see a sick man there; and they have assured me that they never saw one palsied, bleary-eyed, toothless, or bent with age. They are settled along the sea and shut in on the land side by great high mountains, with a stretch about a hundred leagues wide in between. They have a great abundance of fish and flesh which bear no resemblance to ours, and they eat them with no other artifice than cooking. The first man who rode a horse there, though he had had dealings with them on several other trips, so horrified them in this posture that they shot him dead with arrows before they could recognize him.

Their buildings are very long, with a capacity of two or three hundred souls; they are covered with the bark of great trees, the strips reaching to the ground at one end and supporting and leaning on one another at the top, in the manner of some of our barns, whose covering hangs down to the ground and acts as a side. They have wood so hard that they cut with it and make of it their swords and grills to cook their food. Their beds are of a cotton weave, hung from the roof like those in our ships, each man having his own; for the wives sleep apart from their husbands.

They get up with the sun, and eat immediately upon rising, to last them through the day; for they take no other meal than that one. Like some other Eastern peoples, of whom Suidas[9] tells us, who drank apart from meals, they do not drink then; but they drink several times a day, and to capacity. Their drink is made of some root, and is of the color of our claret wines. They drink it only lukewarm. This beverage keeps only two or three days; it has a

---

5. The half-legendary Spartan lawgiver (9th century B.C.).   6. This passage is always compared with Shakespeare's *The Tempest* 2.1.147ff.   7. Roman tragedian (4? B.C.–A.D. 65), philosopher, and political leader; *Epistles* 90.   8. *Georgics* 2.20.   9. A Byzantine lexicographer.

slightly sharp taste, is not at all heady, is good for the stomach, and has a laxative effect upon those who are not used to it; it is a very pleasant drink for anyone who is accustomed to it. In place of bread they use a certain white substance like preserved coriander. I have tried it; it tastes sweet and a little flat.

The whole day is spent in dancing. The younger men go to hunt animals with bows. Some of the women busy themselves meanwhile with warming their drink, which is their chief duty. Some one of the old men, in the morning before they begin to eat, preaches to the whole barnful in common, walking from one end to the other, and repeating one single sentence several times until he has completed the circuit (for the buildings are fully a hundred paces long). He recommends to them only two things: valor against the enemy and love for their wives. And they never fail to point out this obligation, as their refrain, that it is their wives who keep their drink warm and seasoned.

There may be seen in several places, including my own house, specimens of their beds, of their ropes, of their wooden swords and the bracelets with which they cover their wrists in combats, and of the big canes, open at one end, by whose sound they keep time in their dances. They are close shaven all over, and shave themselves much more cleanly than we, with nothing but a wooden or stone razor. They believe that souls are immortal, and that those who have deserved well of the gods are lodged in that part of heaven where the sun rises, and the damned in the west.

They have some sort of priests and prophets, but they rarely appear before the people, having their home in the mountains. On their arrival there is a great feast and solemn assembly of several villages—each barn, as I have described it, makes up a village, and they are about one French league[1] from each other. The prophet speaks to them in public, exhorting them to virtue and their duty; but their whole ethical science contains only these two articles: resoluteness in war and affection for their wives. He prophesies to them things to come and the results they are to expect from their undertakings, and urges them to war or holds them back from it; but this is on the condition that when he fails to prophesy correctly, and if things turn out otherwise than he has predicted, he is cut into a thousand pieces if they catch him, and condemned as a false prophet. For this reason, the prophet who has once been mistaken is never seen again.

Divination is a gift of God; that is why its abuse should be punished as imposture. Among the Scythians, when the soothsayers failed to hit the mark, they were laid, chained hand and foot, on carts full of heather and drawn by oxen, on which they were burned. Those who handle matters subject to the control of human capacity are excusable if they do the best they can. But these others who come and trick us with assurances of an extraordinary faculty that is beyond our ken, should they not be punished for not making good their promise, and for the temerity of their imposture?

They have their wars with the nations beyond the mountains, further inland, to which they go quite naked, with no other arms than bows or wooden swords ending in a sharp point, in the manner of the tongues of our boar spears. It is astonishing what firmness they show in their combats,

1. About 2.49 miles.

which never end but in slaughter and bloodshed; for as to routs and terror, they know nothing of either.

Each man brings back his trophy the head of the enemy he has killed, and sets it up at the entrance to his dwelling. After they have treated their prisoners well for a long time with all the hospitality they can think of, each man who has a prisoner calls a great assembly of his acquaintances. He ties a rope to one of the prisoner's arms, by the end of which he holds him, a few steps away, for fear of being hurt, and gives his dearest friend the other arm to hold in the same way; and these two, in the presence of the whole assembly, kill him with their swords. This done, they roast him and eat him in common and send some pieces to their absent friends. This is not, as people think, for nourishment, as of old the Scythians used to do; it is to betoken an extreme revenge. And the proof of this came when they saw the Portuguese, who had joined forces with their adversaries, inflict a different kind of death on them when they took them prisoner, which was to bury them up to the waist, shoot the rest of their body full of arrows, and afterward hang them. They thought that these people from the other world, being men who had sown the knowledge of many vices among their neighbors and were much greater masters than themselves in every sort of wickedness, did not adopt this sort of vengeance without some reason, and that it must be more painful than their own; so they began to give up their old method and to follow this one.

I am not sorry that we notice the barbarous horror of such acts, but I am heartily sorry that, judging their faults rightly, we should be so blind to our own. I think there is more barbarity in eating a man alive than in eating him dead; and in tearing by tortures and the rack a body still full of feeling, in roasting a man bit by bit, in having him bitten and mangled by dogs and swine (as we have not only read but seen within fresh memory, not among ancient enemies, but among neighbors and fellow citizens, and what is worse, on the pretext of piety and religion),[2] than in roasting and eating him after he is dead.

Indeed, Chrysippus and Zeno, heads of the Stoic sect, thought there was nothing wrong in using our carcasses for any purpose in case of need, and getting nourishment from them; just as our ancestors,[3] when besieged by Caesar in the city of Alésia, resolved to relieve their famine by eating old men, women, and other people useless for fighting.

> The Gascons once, 'tis said, their life renewed
> By eating of such food.
>
> JUVENAL[4]

And physicians do not fear to use human flesh in all sorts of ways for our health, applying it either inwardly or outwardly. But there never was any opinion so disordered as to excuse treachery, disloyalty, tyranny, and cruelty, which are our ordinary vices.

So we may well call these people barbarians, in respect to the rules of reason, but not in respect to ourselves, who surpass them in every kind of barbarity.

2. The allusion is to the spectacles of religious warfare that Montaigne himself had witnessed in his time and country.   3. The Gauls.   4. Decimus Junius Juvenal (fl. early 2nd century A.D.), last great Roman satirist; *Satires* 15.93–94.

Their warfare is wholly noble and generous, and as excusable and beautiful as this human disease can be; its only basis among them is their rivalry in valor. They are not fighting for the conquest of new lands, for they still enjoy that natural abundance that provides them without toil and trouble with all necessary things in such profusion that they have no wish to enlarge their boundaries. They are still in that happy state of desiring only as much as their natural needs demand; anything beyond that is superfluous to them.

They generally call those of the same age, brothers; those who are younger, children; and the old men are fathers to all the others. These leave to their heirs in common the full possession of their property, without division or any other title at all than just the one that Nature gives to her creatures in bringing them into the world.

If their neighbors cross the mountains to attack them and win a victory, the gain of the victor is glory, and the advantage of having proved the master in valor and virtue; for apart from this they have no use for the goods of the vanquished, and they return to their own country, where they lack neither anything necessary nor that great thing, the knowledge of how to enjoy their condition happily and be content with it. These men of ours do the same in their turn. They demand of their prisoners no other ransom than that they confess and acknowledge their defeat. But there is not one in a whole century who does not choose to die rather than to relax a single bit, by word or look, from the grandeur of an invincible courage; not one who would not rather be killed and eaten than so much as ask not to be. They treat them very freely, so that life may be all the dearer to them, and usually entertain them with threats of their coming death, of the torments they will have to suffer, the preparations that are being made for the purpose, the cutting up of their limbs, and the feast that will be made at their expense. All this is done for the sole purpose of extorting from their lips some weak or base word, or making them want to flee, so as to gain the advantage of having terrified them and broken down their firmness. For indeed, if you take it the right way, it is in this point alone that true victory lies:

> It is no victory
> Unless the vanquished foe admits your mastery.
>   CLAUDIAN[5]

The Hungarians, very bellicose fighters, did not in olden times pursue their advantage beyond putting the enemy at their mercy. For having wrung a confession from him to this effect, they let him go unharmed and unransomed, except, at most, for exacting his promise never again to take up arms against them.

We win enough advantages over our enemies that are borrowed advantages, not really our own. It is the quality of a porter, not of valor, to have sturdier arms and legs; agility is a dead and corporeal quality; it is a stroke of luck to make our enemy stumble, or dazzle his eyes by the sunlight; it is a trick of art and technique, which may be found in a worthless coward, to be an able fencer. The worth and value of a man is in his heart and his will; there lies his real honor. Valor is the strength, not of legs and arms, but of heart and soul; it consists not in the worth of our horse or our weapons, but in our own. He who falls obstinate in his courage, *if he has fallen, he fights*

5. *Of the Sixth Consulate of Honorius*, lines 248–49.

on his knees [Seneca].[6] He who relaxes none of his assurance, no matter how great the danger of imminent death; who, giving up his soul, still looks firmly and scornfully at his enemy—he is beaten not by us, but by fortune; he is killed, not conquered.

The most valiant are sometimes the most unfortunate. Thus there are triumphant defeats that rival victories. Nor did those four sister victories, the fairest that the sun ever set eyes on—Salamis, Plataea, Mycale, and Sicily[7]—ever dare match all their combined glory against the glory of the annihilation of King Leonidas and his men at the pass of Thermopylae.[8]

Who ever hastened with more glorious and ambitious desire to win a battle than Captain Ischolas to lose one? Who ever secured his safety more ingeniously and painstakingly than he did his destruction? He was charged to defend a certain pass in the Peloponnesus against the Arcadians. Finding himself wholly incapable of doing this, in view of the nature of the place and the inequality of the forces, he made up his mind that all who confronted the enemy would necessarily have to remain on the field. On the other hand, deeming it unworthy both of his own virtue and magnanimity and of the Lacedaemonian name to fail in his charge, he took a middle course between these two extremes, in this way. The youngest and fittest of his band he preserved for the defense and service of their country, and sent them home; and with those whose loss was less important, he determined to hold this pass, and by their death to make the enemy buy their entry as dearly as he could. And so it turned out. For he was presently surrounded on all sides by the Arcadians, and after slaughtering a large number of them, he and his men were all put to the sword. Is there a trophy dedicated to victors that would not be more due to these vanquished? The role of true victory is in fighting, not in coming off safely; and the honor of valor consists in combating, not in beating.

To return to our story. These prisoners are so far from giving in, in spite of all that is done to them, that on the contrary, during the two or three months that they are kept, they wear a gay expression; they urge their captors to hurry and put them to the test; they defy them, insult them, reproach them with their cowardice and the number of battles they have lost to the prisoners' own people.

I have a song composed by a prisoner which contains this challenge, that they should all come boldly and gather to dine off him, for they will be eating at the same time their own fathers and grandfathers, who have served to feed and nourish his body. "These muscles," he says, "this flesh and these veins are your own, poor fools that you are. You do not recognize that the substance of your ancestors' limbs is still contained in them. Savor them well; you will find in them the taste of your own flesh." An idea that certainly does not smack of barbarity. Those that paint these people dying, and who show the execution, portray the prisoner spitting in the face of his slayers and scowling at them. Indeed, to the last gasp they never stop braving and defying their enemies by word and look. Truly here are real savages by our standards; for either they must be thoroughly so, or we must be; there is an amazing distance between their character and ours.

The men there have several wives, and the higher their reputation for valor

6. *Of Providence* 2.   7. References to the famous Greek victories against the Persians and (at Himera, Sicily) against the Carthaginians in or about 480 B.C.   8. The Spartan king Leonidas's defense here also took place in 480 B.C., during the war against the Persians.

the more wives they have. It is a remarkably beautiful thing about their marriages that the same jealousy our wives have to keep us from the affection and kindness of other women, theirs have to win this for them. Being more concerned for their husbands' honor than for anything else, they strive and scheme to have as many companions as they can, since that is a sign of their husbands' valor.

Our wives will cry "Miracle!" but it is no miracle. It is a properly matrimonial virtue, but one of the highest order. In the Bible, Leah, Rachel, Sarah, and Jacob's wives gave their beautiful handmaids to their husbands; and Livia seconded the appetites of Augustus to her own disadvantage; and Stratonice, the wife of King Deiotarus,[9] not only lent her husband for his use a very beautiful young chambermaid in her service, but carefully brought up her children, and backed them up to succeed to their father's estates.

And lest it be thought that all this is done through a simple and servile bondage to usage and through the pressure of the authority of their ancient customs, without reasoning or judgment, and because their minds are so stupid that they cannot take any other course, I must cite some examples of their capacity. Besides the warlike song I have just quoted, I have another, a love song, which begins in this vein: "Adder, stay; stay, adder, that from the pattern of your coloring my sister may draw the fashion and the workmanship of a rich girdle that I may give to my love; so may your beauty and your pattern be forever preferred to all other serpents." This first couplet is the refrain of the song. Now I am familiar enough with poetry to be a judge of this: not only is there nothing barbarous in this fancy, but it is altogether Anacreontic.[1] Their language, moreover, is a soft language, with an agreeable sound, somewhat like Greek in its endings.

Three of these men, ignorant of the price they will pay some day, in loss of repose and happiness, for gaining knowledge of the corruptions of this side of the ocean; ignorant also of the fact that of this intercourse will come their ruin (which I suppose is already well advanced: poor wretches, to let themselves be tricked by the desire for new things, and to have left the serenity of their own sky to come and see ours!)—three of these men were at Rouen, at the time the late King Charles IX was there. The king talked to them for a long time; they were shown our ways, our splendor, the aspect of a fine city. After that, someone asked their opinion, and wanted to know what they had found most amazing. They mentioned three things, of which I have forgotten the third, and I am very sorry for it; but I still remember two of them. They said that in the first place they thought it very strange that so many grown men, bearded, strong, and armed, who were around the king (it is likely that they were talking about the Swiss of his guard) should submit to obey a child, and that one of them was not chosen to command instead. Second (they have a way in their language of speaking of men as halves of one another), they had noticed that there were among us men full and gorged with all sorts of good things, and that their other halves were beggars at their doors, emaciated with hunger and poverty; and they thought it strange that these needy halves could endure such an injustice, and did not take the others by the throat, or set fire to their houses.

9. Tetrarch of Galatia, in Asia Minor.   1. Worthy of Anacreon (572?–488? B.C.), major Greek writer of amatory lyrics.

I had a very long talk with one of them; but I had an interpreter who followed my meaning so badly, and who was so hindered by his stupidity in taking in my ideas, that I could get hardly any satisfaction from the man. When I asked him what profit he gained from his superior position among his people (for he was a captain, and our sailors called him king), he told me that it was to march foremost in war. How many men followed him? He pointed to a piece of ground, to signify as many as such a space could hold; it might have been four or five thousand men. Did all this authority expire with the war? He said that this much remained, that when he visited the villages dependent on him, they made paths for him through the underbrush by which he might pass quite comfortably.

All this is not too bad—but what's the use? They don't wear breeches.

Of the Inconsistency of Our Actions

Those who make a practice of comparing human actions are never so perplexed as when they try to see them as a whole and in the same light; for they commonly contradict each other so strangely that it seems impossible that they have come from the same shop. One moment young Marius is a son of Mars, another moment a son of Venus.[2] Pope Boniface VIII, they say, entered office like a fox, behaved in it like a lion, and died like a dog. And who would believe that it was Nero, that living image of cruelty, who said, when they brought him in customary fashion the sentence of a condemned criminal to sign: "Would to God I had never learned to write!" So much his heart was wrung at condemning a man to death!

Everything is so full of such examples—each man, in fact, can supply himself with so many—that I find it strange to see intelligent men sometimes going to great pains to match these pieces; seeing that irresolution seems to me the most common and apparent defect of our nature, as witness that famous line of Publilius, the farce writer:

> Bad is the plan that never can be changed.
> PUBLILIUS SYRUS[3]

There is some justification for basing a judgment of a man on the most ordinary acts of his life; but in view of the natural instability of our conduct and opinions, it has often seemed to me that even good authors are wrong to insist on fashioning a consistent and solid fabric out of us. They choose one general characteristic, and go and arrange and interpret all a man's actions to fit their picture; and if they cannot twist them enough, they go and set them down to dissimulation. Augustus has escaped them; for there is in this man throughout the course of his life such an obvious, abrupt, and continual variety of actions that even the boldest judges have had to let him go, intact and unsolved. Nothing is harder for me than to believe in men's consistency, nothing easier than to believe in their inconsistency. He who

---

2. Goddess of love. Marius was the nephew of the older and better-known Marius. Montaigne's source is Plutarch's *Life of Marius*. Mars was the god of war.   3. *Apothegms (Sententiae)*, line 362.

would judge them in detail and distinctly, bit by bit, would more often hit upon the truth.

In all antiquity it is hard to pick out a dozen men who set their lives to a certain and constant course, which is the principal goal of wisdom. For, to comprise all wisdom in a word, says an ancient [Seneca], and to embrace all the rules of our life in one, it is "always to will the same things, and always to oppose the same things."[4] I would not deign, he says, to add "provided the will is just"; for if it is not just, it cannot always be whole.

In truth, I once learned that vice is only unruliness and lack of moderation, and that consequently consistency cannot be attributed to it. It is a maxim of Demosthenes, they say, that the beginning of all virtue is consultation and deliberation; and the end and perfection, consistency. If it were by reasoning that we settled on a particular course of action, we would choose the fairest course—but no one has thought of that:

> He spurns the thing he sought, and seeks anew
> What he just spurned; he seethes, his life's askew.
> HORACE[5]

Our ordinary practice is to follow the inclinations of our appetite, to the left, to the right, uphill and down, as the wind of circumstance carries us. We think of what we want only at the moment we want it, and we change like that animal which takes the color of the place you set it on. What we have just now planned, we presently change, and presently again we retrace our steps: nothing but oscillation and inconsistency:

> Like puppets we are moved by outside strings.
> HORACE[6]

We do not go; we are carried away, like floating objects, now gently, now violently, according as the water is angry or calm:

> Do we not see all humans unaware
> Of what they want, and always searching everywhere,
> And changing place, as if to drop the load they bear?
> LUCRETIUS[7]

Every day a new fancy, and our humors shift with the shifts in the weather:

> Such are the minds of men, as is the fertile light
> That Father Jove himself sends down to make earth bright.
> HOMER[8]

We float between different states of mind; we wish nothing freely, nothing absolutely, nothing constantly. If any man could prescribe and establish definite laws and a definite organization in his head, we should see shining throughout his life an evenness of habits, an order, and an infallible relation between his principles and his practice.

Empedocles noticed this inconsistency in the Agrigentines, that they abandoned themselves to pleasures as if they were to die on the morrow, and built as if they were never to die.[9]

---

4. *Epistles* 20.   5. *Epistles* 1.1.98–99.   6. *Satires* 2.7.82.   7. *On the Nature of Things* 3.1057–59.
8. *Odyssey* 18.135–36, 152–53 in the Fitzgerald translation.   9. From Diogenes Laertius's life of the Greek philosopher Empedocles (5th century).

This man would be easy to understand, as is shown by the example of the younger Cato:[1] he who has touched one chord of him has touched all; he is a harmony of perfectly concordant sounds, which cannot conflict. With us, it is the opposite: for so many actions, we need so many individual judgments. The surest thing, in my opinion, would be to trace our actions to the neighboring circumstances, without getting into any further research and without drawing from them any other conclusions.

During the disorders of our poor country,[2] I was told that a girl, living near where I then was, had thrown herself out of a high window to avoid the violence of a knavish soldier quartered in her house. Not killed by the fall, she reasserted her purpose by trying to cut her throat with a knife. From this she was prevented, but only after wounding herself gravely. She herself confessed that the soldier had as yet pressed her only with requests, solicitations, and gifts; but she had been afraid, she said, that he would finally resort to force. And all this with such words, such expressions, not to mention the blood that testified to her virtue, as would have become another Lucrece.[3] Now, I learned that as a matter of fact, both before and since, she was a wench not so hard to come to terms with. As the story[4] says: Handsome and gentlemanly as you may be, when you have had no luck, do not promptly conclude that your mistress is inviolably chaste; for all you know, the mule driver may get his will with her.

Antigonus,[5] having taken a liking to one of his soldiers for his virtue and valor, ordered his physicians to treat the man for a persistent internal malady that had long tormented him. After his cure, his master noticed that he was going about his business much less warmly, and asked him what had changed him so and made him such a coward. "You yourself, Sire," he answered, "by delivering me from the ills that made my life indifferent to me." A soldier of Lucullus[6] who had been robbed of everything by the enemy made a bold attack on them to get revenge. When he had retrieved his loss, Lucullus, having formed a good opinion of him, urged him to some dangerous exploit with all the fine expostulations he could think of,

> With words that might have stirred a coward's heart.
> HORACE[7]

"Urge some poor soldier who has been robbed to do it," he replied;

> Though but a rustic lout,
> "That man will go who's lost his money," he called out;
> HORACE[8]

and resolutely refused to go.

We read that Sultan Mohammed outrageously berated Hassan, leader of his Janissaries, because he saw his troops giving way to the Hungarians and Hassan himself behaving like a coward in the fight. Hassan's only reply was to go and hurl himself furiously—alone, just as he was, arms in hand—into the first body of enemies that he met, by whom he was promptly swallowed

---

1. Cato Uticensis (1st century B.C.), a philosopher. He is traditionally considered the epitome of moral and intellectual integrity. 2. See n. 2, p. 2649. 3. The legendary virtuous Roman who stabbed herself after being raped by King Tarquinius Superbus's son. 4. A common folktale. 5. Macedonian king (382–301 B.C.). 6. Roman general (1st century B.C.). 7. *Epistles* 2.2.36. 8. *Epistles* 2.2.39–40.

up; this was perhaps not so much self-justification as a change of mood, nor so much his natural valor as fresh spite.

That man whom you saw so adventurous yesterday, do not think it strange to find him just as cowardly today: either anger, or necessity, or company, or wine, or the sound of a trumpet, had put his heart in his belly. His was a courage formed not by reason, but by one of these circumstances; it is no wonder if he has now been made different by other, contrary circumstances.

These supple variations and contradictions that are seen in us have made some imagine that we have two souls, and others that two powers accompany us and drive us, each in its own way, one toward good, the other toward evil; for such sudden diversity cannot well be reconciled with a simple subject.

Not only does the wind of accident move me at will, but, besides, I am moved and disturbed as a result merely of my own unstable posture; and anyone who observes carefully can hardly find himself twice in the same state. I give my soul now one face, now another, according to which direction I turn it. If I speak of myself in different ways, that is because I look at myself in different ways. All contradictions may be found in me by some twist and in some fashion. Bashful, insolent; chaste, lascivious; talkative, taciturn; tough, delicate; clever, stupid; surly, affable; lying, truthful; learned, ignorant; liberal, miserly, and prodigal: all this I see in myself to some extent according to how I turn; and whoever studies himself really attentively finds in himself, yes, even in his judgment, this gyration and discord. I have nothing to say about myself absolutely, simply, and solidly, without confusion and without mixture, or in one word. *Distinguo*[9] is the most universal member of my logic.

Although I am always minded to say good of what is good, and inclined to interpret favorably anything that can be so interpreted, still it is true that the strangeness of our condition makes it happen that we are often driven to do good by vice itself—were it not that doing good is judged by intention alone.

Therefore one courageous deed must not be taken to prove a man valiant; a man who was really valiant would be so always and on all occasions. If valor were a habit of virtue, and not a sally, it would make a man equally resolute in any contingency, the same alone as in company, the same in single combat as in battle; for, whatever they say, there is not one valor for the pavement and another for the camp. As bravely would he bear an illness in his bed as a wound in camp, and he would fear death no more in his home than in an assault. We would not see the same man charging into the breach with brave assurance, and later tormenting himself, like a woman, over the loss of a lawsuit or a son. When, though a coward against infamy, he is firm against poverty; when, though weak against the surgeons' knives, he is steadfast against the enemy's swords, the action is praiseworthy, not the man.

Many Greeks, says Cicero, cannot look at the enemy, and are brave in sickness; the Cimbrians and Celtiberians, just the opposite; *for nothing can be uniform that does not spring from a firm principle* [Cicero].[1]

There is no more extreme valor of its kind than Alexander's; but it is only of one kind, and not complete and universal enough. Incomparable though

9. I distinguish (Latin)—that is, I separate into its components.   1. Marcus Tullius Cicero (106–43 B.C.), Roman orator; *Tusculan Disputations* 2.27.

it is, it still has its blemishes; which is why we see him worry so frantically when he conceives the slightest suspicion that his men are plotting against his life, and why he behaves in such matters with such violent and indiscriminate injustice and with a fear that subverts his natural reason. Also superstition, with which he was so strongly tainted, bears some stamp of pusillanimity. And the excessiveness of the penance he did for the murder of Clytus[2] is also evidence of the unevenness of his temper.

Our actions are nothing but a patchwork—*they despise pleasure, but are too cowardly in pain; they are indifferent to glory, but infamy breaks their spirit* [Cicero][3]—and we want to gain honor under false colors. Virtue will not be followed except for her own sake; and if we sometimes borrow her mask for some other purpose, she promptly snatches it from our face. It is a strong and vivid dye, once the soul is steeped in it, and will not go without taking the fabric with it. That is why, to judge a man, we must follow his traces long and carefully. If he does not maintain consistency for its own sake, *with a way of life that has been well considered and preconcerted* [Cicero][4]; if changing circumstances makes him change his pace (I mean his path, for his pace may be hastened or slowed), let him go: that man goes before the wind, as the motto of our Talbot[5] says.

It is no wonder, says an ancient [Seneca], that chance has so much power over us, since we live by chance.[6] A man who has not directed his life as a whole toward a definite goal cannot possibly set his particular actions in order. A man who does not have a picture of the whole in his head cannot possibly arrange the pieces. What good does it do a man to lay in a supply of paints if he does not know what he is to paint? No one makes a definite plan of his life; we think about it only piecemeal. The archer must first know what he is aiming at, and then set his hand, his bow, his string, his arrow, and his movements for that goal. Our plans go astray because they have no direction and no aim. No wind works for the man who has no port of destination.

I do not agree with the judgment given in favor of Sophocles, on the strength of seeing one of his tragedies, that it proved him competent to manage his domestic affairs, against the accusation of his son. Nor do I think that the conjecture of the Parians sent to reform the Milesians was sufficient ground for the conclusion they drew. Visiting the island, they noticed the best-cultivated lands and the best-run country houses, and noted down the names of their owners. Then they assembled the citizens in the town and appointed these owners the new governors and magistrates, judging that they, who were careful of their private affairs, would be careful of those of the public.

We are all patchwork, and so shapeless and diverse in composition that each bit, each moment, plays its own game. And there is as much difference between us and ourselves as between us and others. *Consider it a great thing to play the part of one single man* [Seneca].[7] Ambition can teach men valor, and temperance, and liberality, and even justice. Greed can implant in the heart of a shop apprentice, brought up in obscurity and idleness, the confi-

2. A commander in Alexander's army who was killed by him during an argument, an act Alexander immediately and bitterly regretted, as related by Plutarch in his *Life of Alexander*, chaps. 50–52.   3. *On Duties* (*De officiis*) 1.21.   4. *Paradoxes* 5.   5. An English captain who fought in France and died there in 1453.   6. *Epistles* 71.   7. *Epistles* 120.

dence to cast himself far from hearth and home, in a frail boat at the mercy of the waves and angry Neptune; it also teaches discretion and wisdom. Venus herself supplies resolution and boldness to boys still subject to discipline and the rod, and arms the tender hearts of virgins who are still in their mothers' laps:

> Furtively passing sleeping guards, with Love as guide,
> Alone by night the girl comes to the young man's side.
> TIBULLUS[8]

In view of this, a sound intellect will refuse to judge men simply by their outward actions; we must probe the inside and discover what springs set men in motion. But since this is an arduous and hazardous undertaking, I wish fewer people would meddle with it.

Of Coaches

It is very easy to demonstrate that great authors, when they write about causes, adduce not only those they think are true but also those they do not believe in, provided they have some originality and beauty. They speak truly and usefully enough if they speak ingeniously. We cannot make sure of the master cause; we pile up several of them, to see if by chance it will be found among them,

> For one cause will not do;
> We must state many, one of which is true.
> LUCRETIUS[9]

Do you ask me whence comes this custom of blessing those who sneeze? We produce three sorts of wind. That which issues from below is too foul; that which issues from the mouth carries some reproach of gluttony; the third is sneezing. And because it comes from the head and is blameless, we give it this civil reception. Do not laugh at this piece of subtlety; it is, they say, from Aristotle.

It seems to me I have read in Plutarch (who, of all the authors I know, is the one who best combined art with nature and judgment with knowledge) that he gives the reason for the heaving of the stomach that afflicts those who travel by sea, as fear, having found some reason by which he proves that fear can produce such an effect. I, who am very subject to seasickness, know very well that this cause does not affect me, and I know it, not by reasoning, but by necessary experience. Not to mention what I have been told, that the same thing often happens to animals, and especially to pigs, without any apprehension of danger; and what an acquaintance of mine has told me about himself, that though he was very subject to it, the desire to vomit had left him two or three times when he found himself oppressed with fright in a big storm. And hear this ancient: *I was too sick to think about the danger* [Seneca].[1] I was never afraid on the water, nor indeed anywhere else (and I

---

8. *Elegies* 2.1.75–76.   9. *On the Nature of Things* 6.704–5.   1. *Moral Epistles* 53.3.

have often enough had just occasions, if death is one), at least not to the point of being confused or bewildered.

Fear sometimes arises from want of judgment as well as from want of courage. All the dangers I have seen, I have seen with open eyes, with my sight free, sound, and entire; besides, it takes courage to be afraid. It once served me in good stead, compared with others, so to conduct my flight and keep it orderly, that it was carried out, if not without fear, at all events without terror and without dismay; it was excited, but not dazed or distracted.

Great souls go much further yet and offer us examples of flights not merely composed and healthy, but proud. Let us tell of the one that Alcibiades reports of Socrates, his comrade in arms:[2] "I found him," he says, "after the rout of our army, him and Laches, among the last of the fugitives; and I observed him at my leisure and in safety, for I was on a good horse and he on foot, and we had fought that way. I noticed first how much presence of mind and resolution he showed compared with Laches; and then the boldness of his walk, no different from his ordinary one, his firm and steady gaze, considering and judging what was going on around him, looking now at one side, now the other, friends and enemies, in a way that encouraged the former and signified to the latter that he was a man to sell his blood and his life very dear to anyone who should try to take them away. And thus they made their escape; for people are not inclined to attack such men; they run after the frightened ones." That is the testimony of that great captain, which teaches us what we experience every day, that there is nothing that throws us so much into dangers as an unthinking eagerness to get clear of them. *Where there is less fear, there is generally less danger* [Livy].[3]

Our common people are wrong to say that such-and-such a man fears death, when they mean to say that he thinks about it and foresees it. Foresight is equally suitable in whatever concerns us, whether for good or ill. To consider and judge the danger is in a way the opposite of being stunned by it.

I do not feel myself strong enough to sustain the impact and impetuosity of this passion of fear, or of any other vehement passion. If I were once conquered and thrown by it, I would never get up again quite intact. If anything made my soul lose its footing, it would never set it back upright in its place; it probes and searches itself too keenly and deeply, and therefore would never let the wound that had pierced it close up and heal. It has been well for me that no illness has yet laid it low. Each attack made on me I meet and fight off in my full armor; thus the first one that swept me off my feet would leave me without resources. I have no secondary defense: no matter where the torrent should break my dike, I would be helpless and be drowned for good.

Epicurus[4] says that the wise man can never pass into a contrary state. I have an opinion about the converse of this saying: that anyone who has once been very foolish will never at any other time be very wise.

God tempers the cold according to the cloak, and gives me passions according to my means of withstanding them. Nature, having uncovered me on one side, has covered me up on the other; having disarmed me of

2. Plato, *Symposium*.   3. Titus Livius (59 B.C.–A.D. 17 or 64 B.C.–A.D. 12), Roman historian; *On the Founding of Rome* 22.5.   4. Greek moral and natural philosopher (341–270 B.C.).

strength, she has armed me with insensibility and a controlled, or dull, apprehensiveness.

Now I cannot long endure (and I could endure them less easily in my youth) either coach, or litter, or boat; and I hate any other transportation than horseback, both in town and in the country. But I can endure a litter less than a coach, and for the same reason I can more easily bear a rough tossing on the water, whereby fear is produced, than the movement felt in calm weather. By that slight jolt given by the oars, stealing the vessel from under us, I somehow feel my head and stomach troubled, as I cannot bear a shaky seat under me. When the sail or the current carries us along evenly or when we are towed, this uniform movement does not bother me at all. It is an interrupted motion that annoys me, and most of all when it is languid. I cannot otherwise describe its nature. The doctors have ordered me to bind and swathe my abdomen with a towel to remedy this trouble; which I have not tried, being accustomed to wrestle with the weaknesses that are in me and overcome them by myself.

If my memory were sufficiently stored with them, I should not begrudge my time to tell here the infinite variety of examples that histories offer us of the use of coaches in the service of war, varying according to the nations and according to the age; of great effect, it seems to me, and very necessary, so that it is a wonder that we have lost all knowledge of them. I will say only this, that quite recently, in our fathers' time, the Hungarians put coaches very usefully to work against the Turks, there being in each one a targeteer and a musketeer and a number of harquebuses lined up, loaded and ready, the whole thing covered with a wall of shields, like a galiot. They formed their battlefront of three thousand such coaches, and after the cannon had played, had them advance and made the enemy swallow this salvo before tasting the rest; which was no slight advantage. Or they launched them into the enemy squadrons to break them and open them up; not to mention the advantage they could derive from them by flanking enemy troops on their march through open country where they were vulnerable, or by covering a camp in haste and fortifying it.

In my time a gentleman on one of our frontiers, who was unwieldy of person and found no horse capable of bearing his weight, having a feud on his hands, went about the country in a coach of this very description, and made out very well. But let us leave these war coaches. The kings of our first dynasty went about the country in a chariot drawn by four oxen.

Mark Antony[5] was the first who had himself drawn in Rome—and a minstrel girl beside him—by lions harnessed to a chariot. Heliogabalus did as much later, calling himself Cybele, the mother of the gods; and also by tigers, imitating the god Bacchus; he also sometimes harnessed two stags to his coach, and another time four dogs, and yet again four naked wenches, having himself, starked naked too, drawn by them in pomp. The Emperor Firmus had his chariot drawn by ostriches of marvelous size, so that it seemed rather to fly than to roll.

The strangeness of these inventions puts into my head this other notion: that it is a sort of pusillanimity in monarchs, and evidence of not sufficiently

---

5. Marcus Antonius (83–31 B.C.), Roman general, libertine, and triumvir, whose associations with Eastern luxury and religious cults are invoked here.

feeling what they are, to labor at showing off and making a display by excessive expense. It would be excusable in a foreign country; but among his own subjects, where he is all-powerful, he derives from his dignity the highest degree of honor he can attain. Just as, it seems to me, for a gentleman it is superfluous to dress with studied care at home: his house, his retinue, his cuisine, answer for him sufficiently.

The advice that Isocrates[6] gives his king seems to me not without reason: that he be splendid in furniture and plate, since that is a lasting investment which passes on to his successors; and that he avoid all magnificences that flow away immediately out of use and memory.

I liked to adorn myself when I was a youth, for lack of other adornments, and it was becoming to me; there are those on whom fine clothes weep. We have marvelous stories of the frugality of our kings about their own persons and in their gifts—kings great in prestige, in valor, and in fortune. Demosthenes[7] fights tooth and nail against the law of his city that allotted public monies to lavish games and feasts; he wants the greatness of the city to be manifest in its quantity of well-equipped ships and of good, well-supplied armies.

And Theophrastus[8] is rightly blamed for setting forth a contrary opinion in his book on riches, and maintaining that lavish expenditure was the true fruit of opulence. These are pleasures, says Aristotle, that touch only the lowest of the people, that vanish from memory as soon as people are sated with them, and that no judicious and serious man can esteem. The outlay would seem to me much more royal as well as more useful, just, and durable, if it were spent on ports, harbors, fortifications, and walls, on sumptuous buildings, churches, hospitals, colleges, and the improvement of streets and roads, for which Pope Gregory XIII is gratefully remembered in my time, and in which our Queen Catherine[9] would leave evidence for many years of her natural liberality and munificence, if her means were equal to her wish. Fortune has given me great displeasure by interrupting the construction of the handsome new bridge[1] of our great city, and depriving me of the hope of seeing it in full use before I die.

Besides, it seems to the subjects, spectators of these triumphs, that they are given a display of their own riches, and entertained at their own expense. For peoples are apt to assume about kings, as we do about our servants, that they should take care to prepare for us in abundance all we need, but that they should not touch it at all for their own part. And therefore the Emperor Galba,[2] having taken pleasure in a musician's playing during his supper, sent for his money box and gave into his hand a handful of crowns that he fished out of it, with these words: "This is not the public money, this is my own." At all events, it most often happens that the people are right, and that their eyes are feasted with what should go to feed their bellies.

Liberality itself is not in its proper light in the hands of a sovereign; private people have more right to exercise it. For, to be precise about it, a king has nothing that is properly his own; he owes his very self to others.

The authority to judge is not given for the sake of the judge, but for the

6. Athenian orator (436–338 B.C.).   7. Greatest Athenian orator (384–322 B.C.).   8. Greek philosopher and botanist, follower of Aristotle (ca. 370–288 B.C.).   9. Catherine de Médicis (1519–1589). 1. The Pont Neuf, as it is still called, was completed in 1604 [Translator's note].   2. Roman emperor (ca. 3 B.C.–A.D. 69) after Nero.

sake of the person judged. A superior is never appointed for his own benefit, but for the benefit of the inferior, and a doctor for the sick, not for himself. All authority, like all art, has its end outside of itself: *no art is directed to itself* [Cicero].[3]

Wherefore the tutors of young princes who make it a point to impress on them this virtue of liberality and preach to them not to know how to refuse anything, and to think nothing so well spent as what they give away (a lesson that I seen in great favor in my time), either look more to their own profit than to their master's, or do not well understand to whom they speak. It is all too easy to impress liberality on a man who has the means to practice it all he wants at the expense of others. And since its value is reckoned not by the measure of the gift, but by the measure of the giver's means, it amounts to nothing in such powerful hands. They find themselves prodigal before they are liberal. Therefore liberality is little to be commended compared with other royal virtues, and it is the only one, as the tyrant Dionysius said, that goes with tyranny itself. I would rather teach him this verse of the ancient farmer: that whoever wants to reap a good crop must sow with the hand, not pour out of the sack; he must scatter the seed, not spill it; and that since he has to give, or, to put it better, pay and restore to so many people according to their deserts, he should be a fair and wise distributor. If the liberality of a prince is without discretion and without measure, I would rather he were a miser.

Royal virtue seems to consist most of all in justice; and of all the parts of justice, that one best marks kings which accompanies liberality; for they have particularly reserved it as their function, whereas they are prone to exercise all other justice through the intermediary of others. Immoderate largesse is a feeble means for them to acquire good will; for it alienates more people than it wins over: *The more you have already practiced it on, the fewer you will be able to practice it on. What is more foolish than to take pains so that you can no longer do what you enjoy doing?* [Cicero.][4] And if it is exercised without regard to merit, it puts to shame him who receives it, and is received ungraciously. Tyrants have been sacrificed to the hatred of the people by the hands of the very ones whom they have unjustly advanced; for such men think to assure their possession of undeserved goods by showing contempt and hatred for the man from whom they received them, and rallying to the judgment and opinion of the people in that respect.

The subjects of a prince who is excessive in gifts become excessive in requests; they adjust themselves not to reason but to example. Surely we often have reason to blush for our impudence; we are overpaid according to justice when the recompense equals our service; for do we owe no service to our prince by natural obligation? If he bears our expenses, he does too much; it is enough that he helps out. The surplus is called benefit, and it cannot be exacted, for the very name of liberality rings of liberty. By our method, it is never done; the receipts are no longer taken into account; people love only the future liberality. Wherefore the more a prince exhausts himself in giving, the poorer he makes himself in friends. How could he assuage desires that grow the more they are fulfilled? He who has his mind on taking, no longer has it on what he has taken. Covetousness has nothing so characteristic about it as ingratitude.

---

3. *De finibus* 5.6.16.   4. *On Duties* 2.15.52–54.

The example of Cyrus[5] will not be amiss here to serve the kings of our time as a touchstone for ascertaining whether their gifts are well or ill bestowed, and to make them see how much more happily that emperor dealt them out than they do. Whereby they are reduced to doing their borrowing from unknown subjects, and rather from those they have wronged than from those they have benefited; and from them they receive no aid that is gratuitous in anything but the name.

Croesus reproached Cyrus for his extravagance and calculated how much his treasure would amount to if he had been more close-fisted. Cyrus, wanting to justify his liberality, sent dispatches in all directions to the grandees of his state whose career he had particularly advanced, and asked each one to help him out with as much money as he could for an urgent need of his, and to send him a declaration of the amount. When all these statements were brought to him, since each of his friends, thinking it was not enough to offer him merely as much as he had received from his munificence, added much that was more properly his own, it turned out that the total amounted to much more than the savings estimated by Croesus. Whereupon Cyrus said to him: "I am no less in love with riches than other princes, and am rather a more careful manager of them. You see at how small a cost I have acquired the inestimable treasure of so many friends, and how much more faithful treasurers they are to me than mercenary men without obligation, without affection, would be; and how much better my wealth is lodged than in coffers, where it would call down upon me the hatred, envy, and contempt of other princes."

The emperors derived an excuse for the superfluity of their public games and spectacles from the fact that their authority depended somewhat (at least in appearance) on the will of the Roman people, who from time immemorial had been accustomed to being flattered by that sort of spectacle and extravagance. But it was private citizens who had nourished this custom of gratifying their fellow citizens and companions, chiefly out of their own purse, by such profusion and magnificence; this had an altogether different flavor when it was the masters who came to imitate it. *The transfer of money from its rightful owners to strangers should not be regarded as liberality* [Cicero].[6]

Philip, because his son was trying to win the good will of the Macedonians by presents, scolded him for it in a letter in this manner: "What, do you want your subjects to regard you as their purser, not as their king? Do you want to win them over? Win them over with the benefits of your virtue, not the benefits of your coffers."[7]

It was, however, a fine thing to bring and plant in the amphitheater a great quantity of big trees, all branching and green, representing a great shady forest, arranged in beautiful symmetry, and on the first day to cast into it a thousand ostriches, a thousand stags, a thousand wild boars, and a thousand fallow deer, leaving them to be hunted down by the people; on the next day to have a hundred big lions, a hundred leopards, and three hundred bears slaughtered in their presence; and for the third day, to have three hundred pairs[8] of gladiators fight it out to the death, as the Emperor Probus[8] did.

It was also a fine thing to see those great amphitheaters faced with marble

---

5. Ideal prince of Xenophon's *Education of Cyrus.*   6. *On Duties* 1.14.43.   7. *On Duties* 2.15.53–54; Philip of Macedon was the father of Alexander the Great.   8. Marcus Aurelius Probus (A.D. 232–282), a stern disciplinarian, eventually killed by his own troops.

on the outside, wrought with ornaments and statues, the inside sparkling
with many rare enrichments—

> Here is the diamond circle, the golden portico
> CALPURNIUS[9]

—all the sides of this vast space filled and surrounded from top to bottom
with three or four score tiers of seats, also of marble, covered with cushions—

> "Let him begone," he says,
> "And leave the cushioned seats of knights, seeing he pays
> None of the lawful tax"
> JUVENAL[1]

—where a hundred thousand men could sit at their ease. Also, first of all, to
have the place at the bottom, where the games were played, open artificially
and split into crevasses representing caverns that vomited forth the beasts
destined for the spectacle; and then, second, to flood it with a deep sea, full
of sea monsters and laden with armed vessels to represent a naval battle; and
third, to level it and dry it off again for the combat of the gladiators; and for
the fourth show to strew it with vermilion and storax instead of sand, in order
to set up a stately banquet there for all that huge number of people—the
final act of a single day:

> How often have we seen
> Part of the sandy floor sink down, wild beasts emerge
> Out of the open chasm, and from its depths upsurge
> Forests of golden growing trees with yellow bark.
> Not only forest monsters were for us to mark,
> But I saw sea-calves mingled in with fighting bears,
> And hippopotami, the shapeless herd that wears
> The name of river-horse.
> CALPURNIUS[2]

Sometimes they created a high mountain there, full of fruit trees and other
trees in leaf, spouting a stream of water from its top as from the mouth of a
living spring. Sometimes they brought in a great ship which opened and came
apart of itself and, after having spewed forth from its belly four or five hundred fighting beasts, closed up again and vanished without assistance. At
other times, from the floor of the place, they made spouts and jets of water
spring forth which shot upward to an infinite height, then sprinkled and
perfumed that infinite multitude. To protect themselves against damage from
the weather, they had that immense space hung with awnings, sometimes
made of purple worked with the needle, sometimes of silk of one color or
another, and they drew them forward or back in a moment, as they had a
mind to:

> The awnings, though the sun scorches the skin,
> Are, when Hermogenes appears, drawn in.
> MARTIAL[3]

---

9. Calpurnius Siculus (1st century A.D.), pastoral poet; *Bucolics* 7.47.   1. *Satires* 3.153–55.
2. *Bucolics* 7.64–75.   3. Marcus Valerius Martial (ca. A.D. 40–ca.104), famous for his witty epigrams;
Epigrams 12.29.15–16.

The nets, too, which they put in front of the people to protect them from the violence of the loosened beasts, were woven of gold:

> Even the woven nets
>> Glitter with gold.
>>> CALPURNIUS[4]

If there is anything excusable in such extravagances, it is when the inventiveness and the novelty of them, not the expense, provide amazement.

Even in these vanities we discover how fertile those ages were in minds different from ours. It is with this sort of fertility as with all other productions of Nature. This is not to say that she then put forth her utmost effort. We do not go in a straight line; we rather ramble, and turn this way and that. We retrace our steps. I fear that our knowledge is weak in every direction; we do not see very far ahead or very far behind. It embraces little and has a short life, short in both extent of time and extent of matter:

> Ere Agamemnon, heroes were the same;
> Many there were, but no one knows their name;
>> They all are hurried on unwept
>> Into unending night.
>>> HORACE

> Before the Trojan War, before Troy fell,
> Were other bards with other tales to tell.
>> LUCRETIUS[5]

And Solon's story of what he had heard from the priests of Egypt about the long life of their state, and their manner of learning and preserving the histories of other countries, does not seem to me a testimony to be rejected in this consideration. *If we could view that expanse of countries and ages, boundless in every direction, into which the mind, plunging and spreading itself, travels so far and wide that it can find no limit where it can stop, there would appear in that immensity an infinite capacity to produce innumerable forms* [adapted from Cicero].[6]

Even if all that has come down to us by report from the past should be true and known by someone, it would be less than nothing compared with what is unknown. And of this very image of the world which glides along while we live on it, how puny and limited is the knowledge of even the most curious! Not only of particular events which fortune often renders exemplary and weighty, but of the state of great governments and nations, there escapes us a hundred times more than comes to our knowledge. We exclaim at the miracle of the invention of our artillery, of our printing; other men in another corner of the world, in China, enjoyed these a thousand years earlier. If we saw as much of the world as we do not see, we would perceive, it is likely, a perpetual multiplication and vicissitude of forms.

There is nothing unique and rare as regards nature, but there certainly is as regards our knowledge, which is a miserable foundation for our rules and which is apt to represent to us a very false picture of things. As vainly as we today infer the decline and decrepitude of the world from the arguments we draw from our own weakness and decay—

---

4. *Bucolics* 7.53–54. 5. *On the Nature of Things* 5.327–28. Above, *Odes* 4.9.25–28. 6. *On the Nature of the Gods* 1.20.54. Solon (ca. A.D. 200), geographer.

> This age is broken down, and broken down the earth
> LUCRETIUS[7]

—so vainly did this poet infer the world's birth and youth from the vigor he saw in the minds of his time, abounding in novelties and inventions in various arts:

> The universe, I think, is very new,
> The world is young, its birth not far behind;
> Hence certain arts grow more and more refined
> Even today; the naval art is one.
> LUCRETIUS[8]

Our world has just discovered another world (and who will guarantee us that it is the last of its brothers, since the daemons, the Sibyls,[9] and we ourselves have up to now been ignorant of this one?) no less great, full, and well-limbed than itself, yet so new and so infantile that it is still being taught its A B C; not fifty years ago it knew neither letters, nor weights and measures, nor clothes, nor wheat, nor vines. It was still quite naked at the breast, and lived only on what its nursing mother provided. If we are right to infer the end of our world, and that poet is right about the youth of his own age, this other world will only be coming into the light when ours is leaving it. The universe will fall into paralysis; one member will be crippled, the other in full vigor.

I am much afraid that we shall have very greatly hastened the decline and ruin of this new world by our contagion, and that we will have sold it our opinions and our arts very dear. It was an infant world; yet we have not whipped it and subjected it to our discipline by the advantage of our natural valor and strength, nor won it over by our justice and goodness, nor subjugated it by our magnanimity. Most of the responses of these people and most of our dealings with them show that they were not at all behind us in natural brightness of mind and pertinence.

The awesome magnificence of the cities of Cuzco[1] and Mexico (and, among many similar things, the garden of that king in which all the trees, the fruits, and all the herbs were excellently fashioned in gold, and of such size and so arranged as they might be in an ordinary garden; and in his curio room were gold replicas of all the living creatures native to his country and its waters), and the beauty of their workmanship in jewelry, feathers, cotton, and painting, show that they were not behind us in industry either. But as for devoutness, observance of the laws, goodness, liberality, loyalty, and frankness, it served us well not to have as much as they: by their advantage in this they lost, sold, and betrayed themselves.

As for boldness and courage, as for firmness, constancy, resoluteness against pains and hunger and death, I would not fear to oppose the examples I could find among them to the most famous ancient examples that we have in the memories of our world on this side of the ocean. For as regards the men who subjugated them, take away the ruses and tricks that they used to deceive them, and the people's natural astonishment at seeing the unexpected arrival of bearded men, different in language, religion, shape, and

---

7. *On the Nature of Things* 2.1136.   8. *On the Nature of Things* 5.331–35.   9. Female prophets.
1. Former capital of the Inca empire in southeastern Peru.

countenance, from a part of the world so remote, where they had never imagined there was any sort of human habitation, mounted on great unknown monsters, opposed to men who had never seen not only a horse, but any sort of animal trained to carry and endure a man or any other burden; men equipped with a hard and shiny skin and a sharp and glittering weapon, against men who, for the miracle of a mirror or a knife, would exchange a great treasure in gold and pearls, and who had neither the knowledge nor the material by which, even in full leisure, they could pierce our steel; add to this the lightning and thunder of our cannon and harquebuses—capable of disturbing Caesar[2] himself, if he had been surprised by them with as little experience and in his time—against people who were naked (except in some regions where the invention of some cotton fabric had reached them), without other arms at the most than bows, stones, sticks, and wooden bucklers; people taken by surprise, under color of friendship and good faith, by curiosity to see strange and unknown things: eliminate this disparity, I say, and you take from the conquerors the whole basis of so many victories.

When I consider that indomitable ardor with which so many thousands of men, women, and children came forth and hurled themselves so many times into inevitable dangers for the defense of their gods and of their liberty, and that noble, stubborn readiness to suffer all extremities and hardships, even death, rather than submit to the domination of those by whom they had been so shamefully deceived (for some of them when captured chose rather to let themselves perish of hunger and fasting than to accept food from the hands of such basely victorious enemies), I conclude that if anyone had attacked them on equal terms, with equal arms, experience, and numbers, it would have been just as dangerous for him as in any other war we know of, and more so.

Why did not such a noble conquest fall to Alexander or to those ancient Greeks and Romans? Why did not such a great change and alteration of so many empires and peoples fall into hands that would have gently polished and cleared away whatever was barbarous in them, and would have strengthened and fostered the good seeds that nature had produced in them, not only adding to the cultivation of the earth and the adornment of cities the arts of our side of the ocean, in so far as they would have been necessary, but also adding the Greek and Roman virtues to those originally in that region? What an improvement that would have been, and what an amelioration for the entire globe, if the first examples of our conduct that were offered over there had called those peoples to the admiration and imitation of virtue and had set up between them and us a brotherly fellowship and understanding! How easy it would have been to make good use of souls so fresh, so famished to learn, and having, for the most part, such fine natural beginnings! On the contrary, we took advantage of their ignorance and inexperience to incline them the more easily toward treachery, lewdness, avarice, and every sort of inhumanity and cruelty, after the example and pattern of our ways. Who ever set the utility of commerce and trading at such a price? So many cities razed, so many nations exterminated, so many millions of people put to the sword, and the richest and most beautiful part of the world turned upside down, for the traffic in pearls and pepper! Base and mech-

2. Julius Caesar (100–44 B.C.), the great Roman general and conqueror.

anical victories! Never did ambition, never did public enmities, drive men against one another to such horrible hostilities and such miserable calamities.

Coasting the sea in quest of their mines, certain Spaniards landed in a fertile, pleasant, well-populated country, and made their usual declarations to its people: that they were peaceable men, coming from distant voyages, sent on behalf of the king of Castile, the greatest prince of the habitable world, to whom the Pope, representing God on earth, had given the principality of all the Indies; that if these people would be tributaries to him, they would be very kindly treated. They demanded of them food to eat and gold to be used in a certain medicine, and expounded to them the belief in one single God and the truth of our religion, which they advised them to accept, adding a few threats.

The answer was this: As for being peaceable, they did not look like it, if they were. As for their king, since he was begging, he must be indigent and needy; and he who had awarded their country to him must be a man fond of dissension, to go and give another person something that was not his and thus set him at strife with its ancient possessors. As for food, they would supply them. Gold they had little of, and it was a thing they held in no esteem, since it was useless to the service of their life, their sole concern being with passing life happily and pleasantly; however, they might boldly take any they could find, except what was employed in the service of their gods. As for one single God, the account had pleased them, but they did not want to change their religion, having followed it so advantageously for so long, and they were not accustomed to take counsel except of their friends and acquaintances. As for the threats, it was a sign of lack of judgment to threaten people whose nature and means were unknown to them. Thus they should promptly hurry up and vacate their land, for they were not accustomed to take in good part the civilities and declarations of armed strangers; otherwise they would do to them as they had done to these others—showing them the heads of some executed men around their city.

There we have an example of the babbling of this infancy. But at all events, neither in that place nor in several others where the Spaniards did not find the merchandise they were looking for, did they make any stay or any attack, whatever other advantages there might be; witness my Cannibals.[3]

Of the two most powerful monarchs of that world, and perhaps of this as well, kings of so many kings, the last two that they drove out, one, the king of Peru, was taken in a battle and put to so excessive a ransom that it surpasses all belief; and when this had been faithfully paid, and the king in his dealings had given signs of a frank, liberal, and steadfast spirit and a clear and well-ordered understanding, the conquerors, after having extracted from him one million three hundred and twenty-five thousand five hundred ounces of gold, besides silver and other things that amounted to no less, so that their horses thenceforth went shod with solid gold, were seized with the desire to see also, at the price of whatever treachery, what could be the remainder of this king's treasures, and to enjoy freely what he had reserved. They trumped up against him a false accusation and false evidence that he was planning to rouse his provinces in order to regain his freedom.

3. *Of Cannibals.*

Whereupon, in a beautiful sentence pronounced by those very men who had set afoot this treachery against him, he was condemned to be publicly hanged and strangled, after being permitted to buy his way out of the torment of being burned alive by submitting to baptism at the moment of the execution. A horrible and unheard-of calamity, which nevertheless he bore without belying himself either by look or word, with a truly royal bearing and gravity. And then, to lull the people, stunned and dazed by such a strange thing, they counterfeited great mourning over his death and ordered a sumptuous funeral for him.

The other one, the king of Mexico, had long defended his besieged city and shown in this siege all that endurance and perseverance can do, if ever prince and people did so, when his bad fortune put him in his enemies' hands alive, on their promise that they would treat him as a king; nor did he in his captivity show anything unworthy of this title. After this victory, his enemies, not finding all the gold they had promised themselves, first ransacked and searched everything, and then set about seeking information by inflicting the cruelest tortures they could think up on the prisoners they held. But having gained nothing by this, and finding their prisoners' courage stronger than their torments, they finally flew into such a rage that, against their word and against all law of nations, they condemned the king himself and one of the principal lords of his court to the torture in each other's presence. This lord, finding himself overcome with the pain, surrounded with burning braziers, in the end turned his gaze piteously toward his master, as if to ask his pardon because he could hold out no longer. The king, fixing his eyes proudly and severely on him in reproach for his cowardice and pusillanimity, said to him only these words, in a stern, firm voice: "And I, am I in a bath? Am I more comfortable than you?" The other immediately after succumbed to the pain and died on the spot. The king, half roasted, was carried away from there, not so much out of pity (for what pity ever touched souls who, for dubious information about some gold vase to pillage, had a man grilled before their eyes, and what is more, a king so great in fortune and merit?), but because his fortitude made their cruelty more and more shameful. They hanged him later for having courageously attempted to deliver himself by arms from such a long captivity and subjection, and he made an end worthy of a great-souled prince.

Another time they burned alive, all at once and in the same fire, four hundred and sixty men, the four hundred being of the common people, the sixty from among the chief lords of a province, all merely prisoners of war.

We have these narrations from themselves, for they not only admit them but boast of them and preach them. Would it be as a testimonial to their justice or their zeal for religion? Truly, those are ways too contrary and hostile to so holy an end. If they had proposed to extend our faith, they would have reflected that faith is not spread by possession of territory but by possession of men, and they would have been more than satisfied with the murders brought about by the necessity of war, without adding to these an indiscriminate butchery, as of wild animals, as universal as fire and sword could make it, after purposely sparing only as many as they wanted to make into miserable slaves for the working and service of their mines: with the result that many of the leaders were punished with death by order of the kings of Castile, who were justly shocked by the horror of their conduct; and almost all were disesteemed and loathed. God deservedly allowed this great plunder to be swallowed up by the sea in transit, or by the intestine wars in which they devoured one another; and most of them were buried on the spot without any profit from their victory.

As for the fact that the revenue from this, even in the hands of a thrifty and prudent prince,[4] corresponds so little to the expectation of it given to his predecessors and to the abundance of riches that was first encountered in these new lands (for although much is being gotten out, we see that it is nothing compared with what was to be expected), the reason is that the use of money was entirely unknown, and that consequently their gold was found all collected together, being of no other use than for show and parade, like a chattel preserved from father to son by many powerful kings who were constantly exhausting their mines to make that great heap of vases and statues for the adornment of their palaces and their temples; whereas our gold is all in circulation and in trade. We cut it up small and change it into a thousand forms; we scatter and disperse it. Imagine it if our kings thus accumulated all the gold they could find for many centuries and kept it idle.

The people of the kingdom of Mexico were somewhat more civilized and skilled in the arts than the other nations over there. Thus they judged, as we do, that the universe was near its end, and they took as a sign of this the desolation that we brought upon them. They believed that the existence of the world was divided into five ages and into the life of five successive suns, of which four had already run their time, and that the one which gave them light was the fifth. The first perished with all other creatures by a universal flood of water. The second, by the heavens falling on us, which suffocated every living thing; to which age they assign the giants, and they showed the Spaniards some of their bones, judging by the size of which these men must have stood twenty hands high. The third, by fire, which burned and consumed everything. The fourth, by a turbulence of air and wind which beat down even many mountains; the men did not die, but they were changed into baboons (to what notions will the laxness of human credulity not submit!). After the death of this fourth sun, the world was twenty-five years in perpetual darkness, in the fifteenth of which a man and a woman were created who remade the human race; ten years later, on a certain day of their calendar, the sun appeared newly created, and since then they reckon their years from that day. The third day after its creation the old gods died; the new ones have been born since little by little. What they think about the manner in which this last sun will perish, my author[5] did not learn. But their calculation of this fourth change coincides with that great conjunction of stars which produced, some eight hundred years ago, according to the reckoning of the astrologers, many great alterations and innovations in the world.

As for pomp and magnificence, whereby I entered upon this subject, neither Greece nor Rome nor Egypt can compare any of its works, whether in utility or difficulty or nobility, with the road which is seen in Peru, laid out by the kings of the country, from the city of Quito as far as Cuzco (a distance of three hundred leagues), straight, even, twenty-five paces wide, paved,

4. Philip II of Spain (1527–1598).   5. Lopez de Gomara (1511–1564), a Spanish contemporary of Montaigne, whose histories of Cortez and of the West Indies Montaigne read in translation [Translator's note].

lined on both sides with fine high walls, and along these, on the inside, two ever-flowing streams, bordered by beautiful trees, which they call *molly*. Wherever they encountered mountains and rocks, they cut through and leveled them, and filled the hollows with stone and lime. At the end of each day's journey there are fine palaces furnished with provisions, clothes, and arms, for travelers as well as for the armies that have to pass that way.

In my estimate of this work I have counted the difficulty, which is particularly considerable in that place. They did not build with any stones less than ten feet square; they had no other means of carrying than by strength of arm, dragging their load along; and they had not even the art of scaffolding, knowing no other device than to raise an equal height of earth against their building as it rose, and remove it afterward.

Let us fall back to our coaches. Instead of these or any other form of transport, they had themselves carried by men, and on their shoulders. That last king of Peru, the day that he was taken, was thus carried on shafts of gold, seated in a chair of gold, in the midst of his army. As many of these carriers as they killed to make him fall—for they wanted to take him alive—so many others vied to take the place of the dead ones, so that they never could bring him down, however great a slaughter they made of those people, until a horseman seized him around the body and pulled him to the ground.

MIGUEL DE CERVANTES
1547–1616

The author of Don Quixote's extravagant adventures himself had a most unusual and adventurous life. The son of an apothecary, Miguel de Cervantes Saavedra was born in Alcalá de Henares, a university town near Madrid. Almost nothing is known of his childhood and early education. Only in 1569 is he mentioned as a favorite pupil by a Madrid humanist, Juan López. Records indicate that by the end of that year he had left Spain and was living in Rome, for a time in the service of Giulio Acquaviva, who later became a cardinal. We know that he enlisted in the Spanish fleet under the command of Don John of Austria and that he took part in the struggle of the allied forces of Christendom against the Turks. He was at the crucial Battle of Lepanto (1571), where in spite of fever he fought valiantly and received three gunshot wounds, one of which permanently impaired the use of his left hand, "for the greater glory of the right." After further military action and garrison duty at Palermo and Naples, he and his brother Rodrigo, bearing testimonials from Don John and from the viceroy of Sicily, began the journey back to Spain, where Miguel hoped to obtain a captaincy. In September 1575 their ship was captured near Marseille by Barbary pirates, and the two brothers were taken as prisoners to Algiers. Cervantes's captors, considering him a person of some consequence, held him as a slave for a high ransom. He repeatedly attempted to escape, and his daring and fortitude excited the admiration of Hassan Pasha, the viceroy of Algiers, who bought him for five hundred crowns after five years of captivity.

Cervantes was freed on September 15, 1580, and reached Madrid in December of that year. There his literary career began rather inauspiciously; he wrote twenty to thirty plays, with little success, and in 1585 published a pastoral romance, *Galatea*. At about this time he had a daughter with Ana Franca de Rojas, and during the same period married Catalina de Salazar, who was eighteen years his junior. Seeking non-literary employment, he obtained a position in the navy, requisitioning and collecting supplies for the "Invincible Armada." Irregularities in his administration, for which he was held responsible if not directly guilty, caused him to spend more time in prison. In 1590 he tried unsuccessfully to obtain colonial employment in the New World. Later he served as tax collector in the province of Granada but was dismissed from government service in 1597.

The following years of Cervantes's life are the most obscure; there is a legend that *Don Quixote* was first conceived and planned while its author was in prison in Seville. In 1604 he was in Valladolid, then the temporary capital of Spain, living in sordid surroundings with the numerous women of his family (his wife, daughter, niece, and two sisters). It was in Valladolid, in late 1604, that he obtained the official license for the publication of *Don Quixote* (Part I). The book appeared in 1605 and was a popular success. Cervantes followed the Spanish court when it returned to Madrid, where he continued to live poorly in spite of a popularity with readers that quickly made proverbial figures of his heroes. A false sequel to his book appeared, prompting him to write his own continuation, *Don Quixote,* Part II, published in 1615. His *Exemplary Tales* had appeared in 1613. He died on April 23, 1616, and was buried in the convent of the Barefooted Trinitarian nuns. *Persiles and Sigismunda,* his last novel, was published posthumously in 1617.

Although, as we have indicated, *The Ingenious Gentleman Don Quixote de la Mancha* was a popular success from the time Part I was published in 1605, it was only later recognized as an important work of literature. This delay was due partly to the fact that in a period of established and well-defined literary genres such as the epic, the tragedy, and the pastoral romance (Cervantes himself had tried his hand at some of these forms), the unconventional combination of elements in *Don Quixote* resulted in a work of considerable novelty, with the serious aspects hidden under a mocking surface.

The initial and overt purpose of the book was to satirize the romances of chivalry. In those long yarns—which had to do with the Carolingian and Arthurian legends and which were full of supernatural deeds of valor, implausible and complicated adventures, duels, and enchantments—the literature that had expressed the medieval spirit of chivalry and romance had degenerated to the same extent to which, in our day, certain conventions of romantic literature have degenerated in "pulp" fiction and film melodrama. Up to a point, then, what Cervantes set out to do was to produce a parody, a caricature of a literary type. But neither the nature of his genius nor the particular method he chose allowed him to limit himself to such a relatively simple and direct undertaking. The actual method he followed to expose the silliness of the romances of chivalry was to show to what extraordinary consequences they would lead a man insanely infatuated with them, once this man set out to live "now" according to their patterns of action and belief.

So what we have is not mere parody or caricature; for there is a great deal of difference between presenting a remote and more or less imaginary world and presenting an individual deciding to live by the standards of that world in a modern and realistic context. The first consequence is a mingling of genres. On the one hand much of the book has the color and intonation of the world of medieval chivalry as its poets had portrayed it. The fact that that vision and that tone depend for their existence in the book on the self-deception of the hero makes them no less operative artistically and adds, in fact, an important element of idealization. On the other hand the chivalric world is continuously jostled by elements of contemporary life evoked by the narrator—the realities of landscape and speech, peasants and nobles, inns and highways. So the author can draw on two sources, roughly the realistic and the romantic, truth and vision, practical facts and lofty values. In this respect—having found a way to bring together concrete actuality and highly ideal values—Cervantes can be said to have created the modern novel.

The consequences of Cervantes's invention are more apparent when we begin to analyze a little more closely the nature of these worlds, romantic and realistic, and the kind of impact the first exerts on the second. The hero embodying the world of the romances is not, as we know, a cavalier; he is an impoverished country gentleman who embraces that code in the "modern" world. Chivalry is not directly satirized; it is simply placed in a context different from its native one. The result of that new association is a new whole, a new unity. The "code" is renovated; it is put into a different perspective, given another chance.

We should remember at this point that in the process of deterioration that the romances of chivalry had undergone, certain basically attractive ideals had become empty conventions—for instance, the ideal of love as devoted "service." In this connection, it may be especially interesting to observe that the treatment of love and Don Quixote's conception of it are not limited to his well-known admiration for his purely fantastic lady Dulcinea but are also dealt with from a feminine point of view. See, as illustration, Marcela's elaborate, logical, and poetic speech (Part I, chapter 14, printed here), which Don Quixote warmly admires; in it the noble shepherdess defends herself against the accusation of being "a wild beast and a basilisk" for having caused Grisóstomo's death and proclaims her right to choose her particular kind of freedom in nature, where "these mountain trees are my company, the clear running waters in these brooks are my mirror."

No less relevant are Quixote's ideals of adventurousness, of loyalty to high concepts of valor and generosity. In the new context those values are reexamined. Cervantes may well have gained a practical sense of them in his own life while still a youth, for instance at the Battle of Lepanto (the great victory of the European coalition against the "infidels") and as a pirate's captive. Because he began writing *Don Quixote* in his late fifties, a vantage point from which the adventures of his youth must have appeared impossibly remote, a factor of nostalgia—which could hardly have been present in a pure satire—may well have entered into his work. Furthermore, had he undertaken a direct caricature of the romance genre, the serious and noble values of chivalry could not have been made apparent except negatively, whereas in the context devised by him in *Don Quixote* they find a way to assert themselves positively as well.

The book in its development is, to a considerable extent, the story of that assertion—of the impact that Don Quixote's revitalization of the chivalric code has on a contemporary world. We must remember, of course, that there is ambiguity in the way the assertion is made; it works slowly on the reader, as his or her own discovery rather than as the narrator's overt suggestion. Actually, whatever attraction the chivalric world of his hero's vision may have had for Cervantes, he does not openly support Don Quixote at all. He even seems at times to go further in repudiating him than he needs to, for the hero is officially insane, and the narrator never tires of reminding us of this. One critic has described the attitude Cervantes affects toward his creature as "animosity." Nevertheless, by the very magniloquence and, often, the extraordinary coherence and beauty that the narrator allows his hero to display in his speeches in defense of his vision and his code, we are gradually led to discover for ourselves the serious and important elements these contain. For instance, Don Quixote's speech evoking the lost Golden Age and justifying the institution of knighterrantry (in Part I, chapter 11, printed here) is described by the narrator—after Don Quixote has delivered it—as a "futile harangue" that "might very well have been dispensed with"; but there it is, in all of its fervor and effectiveness. Thus the narrator's so-called animosity ultimately does nothing but intensify our interest in Don Quixote and our sympathy for him. And in that process we are, as audience, simply repeating the experience many characters have on the "stage" of the book, in their relationships with him.

Generally speaking, the encounters between the ordinary world and Don Quixote are encounters between the world of reality and that of illusion, between reason and imagination, and ultimately between the world in which action is prompted by material considerations and interests and a world in which action is prompted by ideal motives. The selections printed here illustrate these aspects of the experience. Among the first adventures are some that have most contributed to the popularity of the Don Quixote legend: he sees windmills and decides they are giants, country inns become castles, and flocks of sheep become armies. Though the conclusions of such episodes often have the ludicrousness of slapstick comedy, there is a powerfully imposing quality about Don Quixote's insanity; his madness always has method, a commanding persistence and coherence. And there is perhaps an inevitable sense of moral grandeur in the spectacle of anyone remaining so unflinchingly faithful to his or her own vision. The world of "reason" may win in point of fact, but we come to wonder whether from a moral point of view Quixote is not the victor.

Furthermore, we increasingly realize that Quixote's own manner of action has greatness in itself, and not only the greatness of persistence: his purpose is to redress wrongs, to come to the aid of the afflicted, to offer generous help, to challenge danger, and to practice valor. And we finally feel the impact of the arguments that sustain his action—for example, in the episode of the lions in which he expounds "the meaning of valor." The ridiculousness of the situation is counterbalanced by the basic seriousness of Quixote's motives; his notion of courage for its own sake appears, and is recognized, as singularly noble, a sort of generous display of integrity in a world usually ruled by lower standards. Thus the distinction between reason and madness, truth and illusion, becomes, to say the least, ambiguous. The hero's delusions are indeed exposed when they come up against hard facts, but the authority of such facts is seen to be morally questionable.

The effectiveness of Don Quixote's conduct and vision is seen most clearly in his relationship with his "squire," Sancho Panza. It would be a crude oversimplification to say that Don Quixote and Sancho represent illusion and reality, the insane code of knight-errantry versus down-to-earth practicalities. Actually Sancho—though his nature is strongly defined by such elements as his common sense, his earthy speech, his simple phrases studded with proverbs set against the hero's magniloquence—is mainly characterized in his development by the degree to which he believes in his master. He is caught in the snare of Don Quixote's vision; the seeds of the imaginative life are successfully implanted in him.

The impact of Quixote's view of life on Sancho serves, therefore, to illustrate one of the important qualities of the protagonist and, we may finally say, one of the important aspects of Renaissance literature: the attempt, ultimately frustrated but extremely attractive as long as it lasts, of the individual mind to produce a vision and a system of its own in a world that often seems to have lost a universal frame of reference and a fully satisfactory sense of the value and meaning of action. What Don Quixote presents is a vision of a world that, for all its aberrant qualities, appears generally to be more colorful and more thrilling and also, incidentally, to be inspired by more honorable rules of conduct than the world of ordinary people, "realism," current affairs, private interests, easy jibes, and petty pranks. It is a world in which actions are performed out of a sense of their beauty and excitement, not for the sake of their usefulness. It is, again, the world as stage, animated by "folly"; in this case the lights go out at the end, an end that is "reasonable" and, therefore, gloomy. Sancho provides the main example of one who is exposed to that vision and absorbs that light while it lasts. How successfully he has done so is seen during Don Quixote's death scene, in which Sancho begs his master not to die but to continue the play, as has been suggested, in a new costume—that of shepherds in an Arcadian setting. But at that final point the hero is "cured" and killed, and Sancho is restored to the petty interests of the world as he can see it by his own lights, after the cord connecting him to his imaginative master is cut by the latter's "repentance" and death.

William Byron, *Cervantes: A Biography* (1978), is thorough. Ruth El Saffar, ed., *Critical Essays on Cervantes* (1986), offers interesting essays by eminent scholars. Vladimir Nabokov, *Lectures on Don Quixote* (1983), presents an elegant engagement with Cervantes's fiction. Studies that are more technical can be found in Henry Higuera, *Eros and Empire: Politics and Christianity in Don Quijote* (1995); Thomas R. Hart, *Cervantes and Ariosto: Renewing Fiction* (1989); Howard Mancing, *The Chivalric World of Don Quijote: Style, Structure, and Narrative Techniques* (1982); Stephen Gilman, *The Novel According to Cervantes* (1980); and Ruth El Saffar, *Distance and Control: A Study in Narrative Technique* (1975).

PRONOUNCING GLOSSARY

The following list uses common English syllables and stress accents to provide rough equivalents of selected words whose pronunciation may be unfamiliar to the general reader.

Acquaviva: *ahk-wah-vee'-vah*

Benengeli: *ben-en-hel'-ee*

Boiardo: *boy-ar'-doh*

Eugenio: *yoo-hen'-yoh*

Fonseca: *fon-say'kah*

Mondoñedo: *mon-don-yay'-thah*

Orbaneja: *or-bah-nay'hah*

Periquillo: *pehr-i-kee'-yoh*

Quejana: *kay-hah'-nah*

Quesada: *kay-sah'-dah*

Quijada: *kee-hah'-dah*

Quintanar: *kin-ta-nar'*

real: *ray-al'*

Requesenses: *re-ke-sen'-ses*

Rocque: *ro'kay*

Tordesillas: *tor-thay-see'yas*

FROM DON QUIXOTE[1]

From Part I

Prologue

Idling reader, you may believe me when I tell you that I should have liked this book, which is the child of my brain, to be the fairest, the sprightliest, and the cleverest that could be imagined; but I have not been able to contravene the law of nature which would have it that like begets like. And so, what was to be expected of a sterile and uncultivated wit such as that which I possess if not an offspring that was dried up, shriveled, and eccentric: a story filled with thoughts that never occurred to anyone else, of a sort that might be engendered in a prison where every annoyance has its home and every mournful sound its habitation?[2] Peace and tranquility, the pleasures of the countryside, the serenity of the heavens, the murmur of fountains, and ease of mind can do much toward causing the most unproductive of muses to become fecund and bring forth progeny that will be the marvel and delight of mankind.

It sometimes happens that a father has an ugly son with no redeeming grace whatever, yet love will draw a veil over the parental eyes which then behold only cleverness and beauty in place of defects, and in speaking to his friends he will make those defects out to be the signs of comeliness and intellect. I, however, who am but Don Quixote's stepfather, have no desire to go with the current of custom, nor would I, dearest reader, beseech you with tears in my eyes as others do to pardon or overlook the faults you dis-

---

1. Translated by Samuel Putnam.   2. Cervantes was imprisoned in Seville in 1597 and 1602.

cover in this book; you are neither relative nor friend but may call your soul your own and exercise your free judgment. You are in your own house where you are master as the king is of his taxes, for you are familiar with the saying, "Under my cloak I kill the king."[3] All of which exempts and frees you from any kind of respect or obligation; you may say of this story whatever you choose without fear of being slandered for an ill opinion any more than you will be rewarded for a good one.

I should like to bring you the tale unadulterated and unadorned, stripped of the usual prologue and the endless string of sonnets, epigrams, and eulogies such as are commonly found at the beginning of books. For I may tell you that, although I expended no little labor upon the work itself, I have found no task more difficult than the composition of this preface which you are now reading. Many times I took up my pen and many times I laid it down again, not knowing what to write. On one occasion when I was thus in suspense, paper before me, pen over my ear, elbow on the table, and chin in hand, a very clever friend of mine came in. Seeing me lost in thought, he inquired as to the reason, and I made no effort to conceal from him the fact that my mind was on the preface which I had to write for the story of Don Quixote, and that it was giving me so much trouble that I had about decided not to write any at all and to abandon entirely the idea of publishing the exploits of so noble a knight.

"How," I said to him, "can you expect me not to be concerned over what that venerable legislator, the Public, will say when it sees me, at my age, after all these years of silent slumber, coming out with a tale that is as dried as a rush, a stranger to invention, paltry in style, impoverished in content, and wholly lacking in learning and wisdom, without marginal citations or notes at the end of the book when other works of this sort, even though they be fabulous and profane, are so packed with maxims from Aristotle and Plato and the whole crowd of philosophers as to fill the reader with admiration and lead him to regard the author as a well read, learned, and eloquent individual? Not to speak of the citations from Holy Writ! You would think they were at the very least so many St. Thomases[4] and other doctors of the Church; for they are so adroit at maintaining a solemn face that, having portrayed in one line a distracted lover, in the next they will give you a nice little Christian sermon that is a joy and a privilege to hear and read.

"All this my book will lack, for I have no citations for the margins, no notes for the end. To tell the truth, I do not even know who the authors are to whom I am indebted, and so am unable to follow the example of all the others by listing them alphabetically at the beginning, starting with Aristotle and closing with Xenophon, or, perhaps, with Zoilus or Zeuxis, notwithstanding the fact that the former was a snarling critic, the latter a painter. This work will also be found lacking in prefatory sonnets by dukes, marquises, counts, bishops, ladies, and poets of great renown; although if I were to ask two or three colleagues of mine, they would supply the deficiency by furnishing me with productions that could not be equaled by the authors of most repute in all Spain.

"In short, my friend," I went on, "I am resolved that Señor Don Quixote

---

3. I.e., the king does not own your body.   4. Thomas Aquinas (1225–1274), Italian philosopher and theologian.

shall remain buried in the archives of La Mancha until Heaven shall provide him with someone to deck him out with all the ornaments that he lacks; for I find myself incapable of remedying the situation, being possessed of little learning or aptitude, and I am, moreover, extremely lazy when it comes to hunting up authors who will say for me what I am unable to say for myself. And if I am in a state of suspense and my thoughts are woolgathering, you will find a sufficient explanation in what I have just told you."

Hearing this, my friend struck his forehead with the palm of his hand and burst into a loud laugh.

"In the name of God, brother," he said, "you have just deprived me of an illusion. I have known you for a long time, and I have always taken you to be clever and prudent in all your actions; but I now perceive that you are as far from all that as Heaven from the earth. How is it that things of so little moment and so easily remedied can worry and perplex a mind as mature as yours and ordinarily so well adapted to break down and trample underfoot far greater obstacles? I give you my word, this does not come from any lack of cleverness on your part, but rather from excessive indolence and a lack of experience. Do you ask for proof of what I say? Then pay attention closely and in the blink of an eye you shall see how I am going to solve all your difficulties and supply all those things the want of which, so you tell me, is keeping you in suspense, as a result of which you hesitate to publish the history of that famous Don Quixote of yours, the light and mirror of all knight-errantry."

"Tell me, then," I replied, "how you propose to go about curing my diffidence and bringing clarity out of the chaos and confusion of my mind?"

"Take that first matter," he continued, "of the sonnets, epigrams, or eulogies, which should bear the names of grave and titled personages: you can remedy that by taking a little trouble and composing the pieces yourself, and afterward you can baptize them with any name you see fit, fathering them on Prester John of the Indies or the Emperor of Trebizond, for I have heard tell that they were famous poets; and supposing they were not and that a few pedants and bachelors of arts should go around muttering behind your back that it is not so, you should not give so much as a pair of maravedis[5] for all their carping, since even though they make you out to be a liar, they are not going to cut off the hand that put these things on paper.

"As for marginal citations and authors in whom you may find maxims and sayings that you may put in your story, you have but to make use of those scraps of Latin that you know by heart or can look up without too much bother. Thus, when you come to treat of liberty and slavery, jot down:

Non bene pro toto libertas venditur auro.[6]

And then in the margin you will cite Horace or whoever it was that said it. If the subject is death, come up with:

Pallida mors aequo pulsat pede pauperum tabernas
Regumque turres.[7]

---

5. Coin worth 1/34 of a *real*. (A *real* is a coin worth about five cents.)   6. Freedom is not bought by gold (Latin); from the anonymous *Aesopian Fables* 3.14.   7. Pale death knocks at the cottages of the poor and the palaces of kings with equal foot (Latin); Horace, *Odes* 1.4.13–14.

If it is friendship or the love that God commands us to show our enemies, then is the time to fall back on the Scriptures, which you can do by putting yourself out very little; you have but to quote the words of God himself:

Ego autem dico vobis: diligite inimicos vestros.[8]

If it is evil thoughts, lose no time in turning to the Gospels:

De corde exeunt cogitationes malae.[9]

If it is the instability of friends, here is Cato for you with a distich:

Donec eris felix multos numerabis amicos;
Tempora si fuerint nubila, solus eris.[1]

With these odds and ends of Latin and others of the same sort, you can cause yourself to be taken for a grammarian, although I must say that is no great honor or advantage these days.

"So far as notes at the end of the book are concerned, you may safely go about it in this manner: let us suppose that you mentioned some giant, Goliath let us say; with this one allusion which costs you little or nothing, you have a fine note which you may set down as follows: *The giant Golias or Goliath. This was a Philistine whom the shepherd David slew with a mighty cast from his slingshot in the valley of Terebinth,*[2] according to what we read in the Book of Kings, chapter so-and-so where you find it written.

"In addition to this, by way of showing that you are a learned humanist and a cosmographer, contrive to bring into your story the name of the River Tagus, and there you are with another great little note: *The River Tagus was so called after a king of Spain; it rises in such and such a place and empties into the ocean, washing the walls of the famous city of Lisbon; it is supposed to have golden sands,* etc. If it is robbers, I will let you have the story of Cacus,[3] which I know by heart. If it is loose women, there is the Bishop of Mondoñedo,[4] who will lend you Lamia, Laïs, and Flora, an allusion that will do you great credit. If the subject is cruelty, Ovid will supply you with Medea; or if it is enchantresses and witches, Homer has Calypso and Vergil Circe. If it is valorous captains, Julius Caesar will lend you himself, in his *Commentaries*, and Plutarch will furnish a thousand Alexanders. If it is loves, with the ounce or two of Tuscan that you know you may make the acquaintance of Leon the Hebrew,[5] who will satisfy you to your heart's content. And in case you do not care to go abroad, here in your own house you have Fonseca's *Of the Love of God,*[6] where you will encounter in condensed form all that the most imaginative person could wish upon this subject. The short of the matter is, you have but to allude to these names or touch upon those stories that I have mentioned and leave to me the business of the notes and citations; I will guarantee you enough to fill the margins and four whole sheets at the back.

"And now we come to the list of authors cited, such as other works contain but in which your own is lacking. Here again the remedy is an easy one; you

---

8. But I say unto you, love your enemies (Latin); Matthew 5.44.   9. For out of the heart proceed evil thoughts (Latin); Matthew 15.19.   1. As long as you are happy, you will count many friends, but if times become clouded, you will be alone (Latin); Ovid, *Sorrows* 1.9.5–6.   2. 1 Samuel 17.48–49.   3. Gigantic thief in *Aeneid* 8, defeated by Hercules.   4. Father Anthony of Guevara.   5. Leone Ebreo, Neoplatonic author of the *Dialogues of Love* (1535).   6. Cristóbal de Fonseca, *Treatise of the Love of God* (1592).

have but to look up some book that has them all, from A to Z as you were saying, and transfer the entire list as it stands. What if the imposition is plain for all to see? You have little need to refer to them, and so it does not matter; and some may be so simple-minded as to believe that you have drawn upon them all in your simple unpretentious little story. If it serves no other purpose, this imposing list of authors will at least give your book an unlooked-for air of authority. What is more, no one is going to put himself to the trouble of verifying your references to see whether or not you have followed all these authors, since it will not be worth his pains to do so.

"This is especially true in view of the fact that your book stands in no need of all these things whose absence you lament; for the entire work is an attack upon the books of chivalry of which Aristotle never dreamed, of which St. Basil has nothing to say, and of which Cicero had no knowledge; nor do the fine points of truth or the observations of astrology have anything to do with its fanciful absurdities; geometrical measurements, likewise, and rhetorical argumentations serve for nothing here; you have no sermon to preach to anyone by mingling the human with the divine, a kind of motley in which no Christian intellect should be willing to clothe itself.

"All that you have to do is to make proper use of imitation in what you write, and the more perfect the imitation the better will your writing be. Inasmuch as you have no other object in view than that of overthrowing the authority and prestige which books of chivalry enjoy in the world at large and among the vulgar, there is no reason why you should go begging maxims of the philosophers, counsels of Holy Writ, fables of the poets, orations of the rhetoricians, or miracles of the saints; see to it, rather, that your style flows along smoothly, pleasingly, and sonorously, and that your words are the proper ones, meaningful and well placed, expressive of your intention in setting them down and of what you wish to say, without any intricacy or obscurity.

"Let it be your aim that, by reading your story, the melancholy may be moved to laughter and the cheerful man made merrier still; let the simple not be bored, but may the clever admire your originality; let the grave ones not despise you, but let the prudent praise you. And keep in mind, above all, your purpose, which is that of undermining the ill-founded edifice that is constituted by those books of chivalry, so abhorred by many but admired by many more; if you succeed in attaining it, you will have accomplished no little."

Listening in profound silence to what my friend had to say, I was so impressed by his reasoning that, with no thought of questioning them, I decided to make use of his arguments in composing this prologue. Here, gentle reader, you will perceive my friend's cleverness, my own good fortune in coming upon such a counselor at a time when I needed him so badly, and the profit which you yourselves are to have in finding so sincere and straightforward an account of the famous Don Quixote de la Mancha, who is held by the inhabitants of the Campo de Montiel region to have been the most chaste lover and the most valiant knight that had been seen in those parts for many a year. I have no desire to enlarge upon the service I am rendering you in bringing you the story of so notable and honored a gentleman; I merely would have you thank me for having made you acquainted with the famous Sancho Panza, his squire, in whom, to my mind, is to be found an epitome of all the squires and their drolleries scattered here and there throughout the pages of those vain and empty books of chivalry. And with this, may God give you health, and may He be not unmindful of me as well. VALE.[7]

["I Know Who I Am, and Who I May Be, If I Choose"]

CHAPTER 1

Which treats of the station in life and the pursuits of the famous gentleman, Don Quixote de la Mancha.

In a village of La Mancha[1] the name of which I have no desire to recall, there lived not so long ago one of those gentlemen who always have a lance in the rack, an ancient buckler, a skinny nag, and a greyhound for the chase. A stew with more beef than mutton in it, chopped meat for his evening meal, scraps for a Saturday, lentils on Friday, and a young pigeon as a special delicacy for Sunday, went to account for three-quarters of his income. The rest of it he laid out on a broadcloth greatcoat and velvet stockings for feast days, with slippers to match, while the other days of the week he cut a figure in a suit of the finest homespun. Living with him were a housekeeper in her forties, a niece who was not yet twenty, and a lad of the field and market place who saddled his horse for him and wielded the pruning knife.

This gentleman of ours was close on to fifty, of a robust constitution but with little flesh on his bones and a face that was lean and gaunt. He was noted for his early rising, being very fond of the hunt. They will try to tell you that his surname was Quijada or Quesada—there is some difference of opinion among those who have written on the subject—but according to the most likely conjectures we are to understand that it was really Quejana. But all this means very little so far as our story is concerned, providing that in the telling of it we do not depart one iota from the truth.

You may know, then, that the aforesaid gentleman, on those occasions when he was at leisure, which was most of the year around, was in the habit of reading books of chivalry with such pleasure and devotion as to lead him almost wholly to forget the life of a hunter and even the administration of his estate. So great was his curiosity and infatuation in this regard that he even sold many acres of tillable land in order to be able to buy and read the books that he loved, and he would carry home with him as many of them as he could obtain.

Of all those that he thus devoured none pleased him so well as the ones that had been composed by the famous Feliciano de Silva,[2] whose lucid prose style and involved conceits were as precious to him as pearls; especially when he came to read those tales of love and amorous challenges that are to be met with in many places, such a passage as the following, for example: "The reason of the unreason that afflicts my reason, in such a manner weakens my reason that I with reason lament me of your comeliness." And he was similarly affected when his eyes fell upon such lines as these: " . . . the high

7. Farewell (Latin).   1. Efforts at identifying the village have proved inconclusive. La Mancha is a section of Spain south of Madrid.   2. Author of romances (16th century); the lines that follow are from his *Don Florisel de Niguea.*

Heaven of your divinity divinely fortifies you with the stars and renders you deserving of that desert your greatness doth deserve."

The poor fellow used to lie awake nights in an effort to disentangle the meaning and make sense out of passages such as these, although Aristotle himself would not have been able to understand them, even if he had been resurrected for that sole purpose. He was not at ease in his mind over those wounds that Don Belianís[3] gave and received; for no matter how great the surgeons who treated him, the poor fellow must have been left with his face and his entire body covered with marks and scars. Nevertheless, he was grateful to the author for closing the book with the promise of an interminable adventure to come; many a time he was tempted to take up his pen and literally finish the tale as had been promised, and he undoubtedly would have done so, and would have succeeded at it very well, if his thoughts had not been constantly occupied with other things of greater moment.

He often talked it over with the village curate, who was a learned man, a graduate of Sigüenza,[4] and they would hold long discussions as to who had been the better knight, Palmerin of England or Amadis of Gaul; but Master Nicholas, the barber of the same village, was in the habit of saying that no one could come up to the Knight of Phoebus,[5] and that if anyone *could* compare with him it was Don Galaor, brother of Amadis of Gaul, for Galaor was ready for anything—he was none of your finical knights, who went around whimpering as his brother did, and in point of valor he did not lag behind him.

In short, our gentleman became so immersed in his reading that he spent whole nights from sundown to sunup and his days from dawn to dusk in poring over his books, until, finally, from so little sleeping and so much reading, his brain dried up and he went completely out of his mind. He had filled his imagination with everything that he had read, with enchantments, knightly encounters, battles, challenges, wounds, with tales of love and its torments, and all sorts of impossible things, and as a result had come to believe that all these fictitious happenings were true; they were more real to him than anything else in the world. He would remark that the Cid Ruy Díaz had been a very good knight, but there was no comparison between him and the Knight of the Flaming Sword, who with a single backward stroke had cut in half two fierce and monstrous giants. He preferred Bernardo del Carpio, who at Roncesvalles had slain Roland despite the charm the latter bore, availing himself of the stratagem which Hercules employed when he strangled Antaeus,[6] the son of Earth, in his arms.

He had much good to say for Morgante;[7] who, though he belonged to the haughty, overbearing race of giants, was of an affable disposition and well brought up. But, above all, he cherished an admiration for Rinaldo of Montalbán,[8] especially as he beheld him sallying forth from his castle to rob all those that crossed his path, or when he thought of him overseas stealing the

---

3. The allusion is to a romance by Jeronimo Fernández.   4. Ironical, for Sigüenza was the seat of a minor and discredited university.   5. Or Knight of Sun. Heroes of romances customarily adopted emblematic names and also changed them according to circumstances. *Palmerin . . . Amadis:* each a hero of a very famous romance of chivalry.   6. The mythological Antaeus was invulnerable as long as he maintained contact with his mother, Earth. Hercules killed him while holding him raised in his arms. *Charm:* the magic gift of invulnerability.   7. In Pulci's *Morgante maggiore,* a comic-epic poem of the Italian Renaissance.   8. Roland's cousin. In Boiardo's *Roland in Love* (*Orlando innamorato*) and Ariosto's *Roland Mad* (*Orlando furioso*), romantic and comic-epic poems of the Italian Renaissance.

image of Mohammed which, so the story has it, was all of gold. And he would have liked very well to have had his fill of kicking that traitor Galalón,[9] a privilege for which he would have given his housekeeper with his niece thrown into the bargain.

At last, when his wits were gone beyond repair, he came to conceive the strangest idea that ever occurred to any madman in this world. It now appeared to him fitting and necessary, in order to win a greater amount of honor for himself and serve his country at the same time, to become a knight-errant and roam the world on horseback, in a suit of armor; he would go in quest of adventures, by way of putting into practice all that he had read in his books; he would right every manner of wrong, placing himself in situations of the greatest peril such as would redound to the eternal glory of his name. As a reward for his valor and the might of his arm, the poor fellow could already see himself crowned Emperor of Trebizond at the very least; and so, carried away by the strange pleasure that he found in such thoughts as these, he at once set about putting his plan into effect.

The first thing he did was to burnish up some old pieces of armor, left him by his great-grandfather, which for ages had lain in a corner, moldering and forgotten. He polished and adjusted them as best he could, and then he noticed that one very important thing was lacking: there was no closed helmet, but only a morion, or visorless headpiece, with turned up brim of the kind foot soldiers wore. His ingenuity, however, enabled him to remedy this, and he proceeded to fashion out of cardboard a kind of half-helmet, which, when attached to the morion, gave the appearance of a whole one. True, when he went to see if it was strong enough to withstand a good slashing blow, he was somewhat disappointed; for when he drew his sword and gave it a couple of thrusts, he succeeded only in undoing a whole week's labor. The ease with which he had hewed it to bits disturbed him no little, and he decided to make it over. This time he placed a few strips of iron on the inside, and then, convinced that it was strong enough, refrained from putting it to any further test; instead, he adopted it then and there as the finest helmet ever made.

After this, he went out to have a look at his nag; and although the animal had more *cuartos,* or cracks, in its hoof than there are quarters in a real,[1] and more blemishes than Gonela's steed which *tantum pellis et ossa fuit,*[2] it nonetheless looked to its master like a far better horse than Alexander's Bucephalus or the Babieca of the Cid.[3] He spent all of four days in trying to think up a name for his mount; for—so he told himself—seeing that it belonged to so famous and worthy a knight, there was no reason why it should not have a name of equal renown. The kind of name he wanted was one that would at once indicate what the nag had been before it came to belong to a knight-errant and what its present status was; for it stood to reason that, when the master's worldly condition changed, his horse also ought to have a famous, high-sounding appellation, one suited to the new order of things and the new profession that it was to follow.

After he in his memory and imagination had made up, struck out, and discarded many names, now adding to and now subtracting from the list, he finally hit upon "Rocinante," a name that impressed him as being sonorous

9. Ganelón, the villain in the Charlemagne legend who betrayed the French at Roncesvalles.   1. A coin (about five cents). *Cuarto:* one-eighth of a *real.*   2. Was so much skin and bones (Latin).   3. The chief (Spanish)—that is, Ruy Díaz, celebrated hero of *Poema del Cid* (12th century).

and at the same time indicative of what the steed had been when it was but a hack, whereas now it was nothing other than the first and foremost of all the hacks[4] in the world.

Having found a name for his horse that pleased his fancy, he then desired to do as much for himself, and this required another week, and by the end of that period he had made up his mind that he was henceforth to be known as Don Quixote, which, as has been stated, has led the authors of this veracious history to assume that his real name must undoubtedly have been Quijada, and not Quesada as others would have it. But remembering that the valiant Amadis was not content to call himself that and nothing more, but added the name of his kingdom and fatherland that he might make it famous also, and thus came to take the name Amadis of Gaul, so our good knight chose to add his place of origin and become "Don Quixote de la Mancha"; for by this means, as he saw it, he was making very plain his lineage and was conferring honor upon his country by taking its name as his own.

And so, having polished up his armor and made the morion over into a closed helmet, and having given himself and his horse a name, he naturally found but one thing lacking still: he must seek out a lady of whom he could become enamored; for a knight-errant without a lady-love was like a tree without leaves or fruit, a body without a soul.

"If," he said to himself, "as a punishment for my sins or by a stroke of fortune I should come upon some giant hereabouts, a thing that very commonly happens to knights-errant, and if I should slay him in a hand-to-hand encounter or perhaps cut him in two, or, finally, if I should vanquish and subdue him, would it not be well to have someone to whom I may send him as a present, in order that he, if he is living, may come in, fall upon his knees in front of my sweet lady, and say in a humble and submissive tone of voice, 'I, lady, am the giant Caraculiambro, lord of the island Malindrania, who has been overcome in single combat by that knight who never can be praised enough, Don Quixote de la Mancha, the same who sent me to present myself before your Grace that your Highness may dispose of me as you see fit'?"

Oh, how our good knight reveled in this speech, and more than ever when he came to think of the name that he should give his lady! As the story goes, there was a very good-looking farm girl who lived near by, with whom he had once been smitten, although it is generally believed that she never knew or suspected it. Her name was Aldonza Lorenzo, and it seemed to him that she was the one upon whom he should bestow the title of mistress of his thoughts. For her he wished a name that should not be incongruous with his own and that would convey the suggestion of a princess or a great lady; and, accordingly, he resolved to call her "Dulcinea del Toboso," she being a native of that place. A musical name to his ears, out of the ordinary and significant, like the others he had chosen for himself and his appurtenances.

CHAPTER 2

Which treats of the first sally that the ingenious Don Quixote made from his native heath.

Having, then, made all these preparations, he did not wish to lose any time in putting his plan into effect, for he could not but blame himself for what

4. In Spanish, *rocín*.

2684 / MIGUEL DE CERVANTES

the world was losing by his delay, so many were the wrongs that were to be righted, the grievances to be redressed, the abuses to be done away with, and the duties to be performed. Accordingly, without informing anyone of his intention and without letting anyone see him, he set out one morning before daybreak on one of those very hot days in July. Donning all his armor, mounting Rocinante, adjusting his ill-contrived helmet, bracing his shield on his arm, and taking up his lance, he sallied forth by the back gate of his stable yard into the open countryside. It was with great contentment and joy that he saw how easily he had made a beginning toward the fulfillment of his desire.

No sooner was he out on the plain, however, than a terrible thought assailed him, one that all but caused him to abandon the enterprise he had undertaken. This occurred when he suddenly remembered that he had never formally been dubbed a knight, and so, in accordance with the law of knighthood, was not permitted to bear arms against one who had a right to that title. And even if he had been, as a novice knight he would have had to wear white armor, without any device on his shield, until he should have earned one by his exploits. These thoughts led him to waver in his purpose, but, madness prevailing over reason, he resolved to have himself knighted by the first person he met, as many others had done if what he had read in those books that he had at home was true. And so far as white armor was concerned, he would scour his own the first chance that offered until it shone whiter than any ermine. With this he became more tranquil and continued on his way, letting his horse take whatever path it chose, for he believed that therein lay the very essence of adventures.

And so we find our newly fledged adventurer jogging along and talking to himself. "Undoubtedly," he is saying, "in the days to come, when the true history of my famous deeds is published, the learned chronicler who records them, when he comes to describe my first sally so early in the morning, will put down something like this: 'No sooner had the rubicund Apollo spread over the face of the broad and spacious earth the gilded filaments of his beauteous locks, and no sooner had the little singing birds of painted plumage greeted with their sweet and mellifluous harmony the coming of the Dawn, who, leaving the soft couch of her jealous spouse, now showed herself to mortals at all the doors and balconies of the horizon that bounds La Mancha—no sooner had this happened than the famous knight, Don Quixote de la Mancha, forsaking his own downy bed and mounting his famous steed, Rocinante, fared forth and began riding over the ancient and famous Campo de Montiel." '[5]

And this was the truth, for he was indeed riding over that stretch of plain.

"O happy age and happy century," he went on, "in which my famous exploits shall be published, exploits worthy of being engraved in bronze, sculptured in marble, and depicted in paintings for the benefit of posterity. O wise magician, whoever you be, to whom shall fall the task of chronicling this extraordinary history of mine! I beg of you not to forget my good Rocinante, eternal companion of my wayfarings and my wanderings."

Then, as though he really had been in love: "O Princess Dulcinea, lady of this captive heart! Much wrong have you done me in thus sending me forth

5. The scene of a battle in 1369.

with your reproaches and sternly commanding me not to appear in your beauteous presence. O lady, deign to be mindful of this your subject who endures so many woes for the love of you."

And so he went on, stringing together absurdities, all of a kind that his books had taught him, imitating insofar as he was able the language of their authors. He rode slowly, and the sun came up so swiftly and with so much heat that it would have been sufficient to melt his brains if he had had any. He had been on the road almost the entire day without anything happening that is worthy of being set down here; and he was on the verge of despair, for he wished to meet someone at once with whom he might try the valor of his good right arm. Certain authors say that his first adventure was that of Puerto Lápice, while others state that it was that of the windmills; but in this particular instance I am in a position to affirm what I have read in the annals of La Mancha; and that is to the effect that he went all that day until nightfall, when he and his hack found themselves tired to death and famished. Gazing all around him to see if he could discover some castle or shepherd's hut where he might take shelter and attend to his pressing needs, he caught sight of an inn not far off the road along which they were traveling, and this to him was like a star guiding him not merely to the gates, but rather, let us say, to the palace of redemption. Quickening his pace, he came up to it just as night was falling.

By chance there stood in the doorway two lasses of the sort known as "of the district"; they were on their way to Seville in the company of some mule drivers who were spending the night in the inn. Now, everything that this adventurer of ours thought, saw, or imagined seemed to him to be directly out of one of the storybooks he had read, and so, when he caught sight of the inn, it at once became a castle with its four turrets and its pinnacles of gleaming silver, not to speak of the drawbridge and moat and all the other things that are commonly supposed to go with a castle. As he rode up to it, he accordingly reined in Rocinante and sat there waiting for a dwarf to appear upon the battlements and blow his trumpet by way of announcing the arrival of a knight. The dwarf, however, was slow in coming, and as Rocinante was anxious to reach the stable, Don Quixote drew up to the door of the hostelry and surveyed the two merry maidens, who to him were a pair of beauteous damsels or gracious ladies taking their ease at the castle gate.

And then a swineherd came along, engaged in rounding up his drove of hogs—for, without any apology, that is what they were. He gave a blast on his horn to bring them together, and this at once became for Don Quixote just what he wished it to be: some dwarf who was heralding his coming; and so it was with a vast deal of satisfaction that he presented himself before the ladies in question, who, upon beholding a man in full armor like this, with lance and buckler, were filled with fright and made as if to flee indoors. Realizing that they were afraid, Don Quixote raised his pasteboard visor and revealed his withered, dust-covered face.

"Do not flee, your Ladyships," he said to them in a courteous manner and gentle voice. "You need not fear that any wrong will be done you, for it is not in accordance with the order of knighthood which I profess to wrong anyone, much less such highborn damsels as your appearance shows you to be."

The girls looked at him, endeavoring to scan his face, which was half hidden by his ill-made visor. Never having heard women of their profession called damsels before, they were unable to restrain their laughter, at which Don Quixote took offense.

"Modesty," he observed, "well becomes those with the dower of beauty, and, moreover, laughter that has not good cause is a very foolish thing. But I do not say this to be discourteous or to hurt your feelings; my only desire is to serve you."

The ladies did not understand what he was talking about, but felt more than ever like laughing at our knight's unprepossessing figure. This increased his annoyance, and there is no telling what would have happened if at that moment the innkeeper had not come out. He was very fat and very peaceably inclined; but upon sighting this grotesque personage clad in bits of armor that were quite as oddly matched as were his bridle, lance, buckler, and corselet, mine host was not at all indisposed to join the lasses in their merriment. He was suspicious, however, of all this paraphernalia and decided that it would be better to keep a civil tongue in his head.

"If, Sir Knight," he said, "your Grace desires a lodging, aside from a bed—for there is none to be had in this inn—you will find all else that you may want in great abundance."

When Don Quixote saw how humble the governor of the castle was—for he took the innkeeper and his inn to be no less than that—he replied, "For me, Sir Castellan,[6] anything will do, since

> Arms are my only ornament,
> My only rest the fight, etc."

The landlord thought that the knight had called him a castellan because he took him for one of those worthies of Castile, whereas the truth was, he was an Andalusian from the beach of Sanlúcar, no less a thief than Cacus[7] himself, and as full of tricks as a student or a page boy.

"In that case," he said,

> "Your bed will be the solid rock,
> Your sleep: to watch all night.

This being so, you may be assured of finding beneath this roof enough to keep you awake for a whole year, to say nothing of a single night."

With this, he went up to hold the stirrup for Don Quixote, who encountered much difficulty in dismounting, not having broken his fast all day long. The knight then directed his host to take good care of his steed, as it was the best piece of horseflesh in all the world. The innkeeper looked it over, and it did not impress him as being half as good as Don Quixote had said it was. Having stabled the animal, he came back to see what his guest would have and found the latter being relieved of his armor by the damsels, who by now had made their peace with the new arrival. They had already removed his breastplate and backpiece but had no idea how they were going to open his gorget or get his improvised helmet off. That piece of armor had been tied on with green ribbons which it would be necessary to cut, since the knots could not be undone, but he would not hear of this, and so spent all

---

6. The Spanish, *castellano*, means both "castellan" and "Castilian."   7. In Roman mythology he stole some of the cattle of Hercules, concealing the theft by having them walk backward into his cave; he was finally discovered and slain.

the rest of that night with his headpiece in place, which gave him the weirdest, most laughable appearance that could be imagined.

Don Quixote fancied that these wenches who were assisting him must surely be the chatelaine and other ladies of the castle, and so proceeded to address them very gracefully and with much wit:

> Never was knight so served
> By any noble dame
> As was Don Quixote
> When from his village he came,
> With damsels to wait on his every need
> While princesses cared for his hack . . .

"By hack," he explained, "is meant my steed Rocinante, for that is his name, and mine is Don Quixote de la Mancha. I had no intention of revealing my identity until my exploits done in your service should have made me known to you; but the necessity of adapting to present circumstances that old ballad of Lancelot has led to your becoming acquainted with it prematurely. However, the time will come when your Ladyships shall command and I will obey and with the valor of my good right arm show you how eager I am to serve you."

The young women were not used to listening to speeches like this and had not a word to say, but merely asked him if he desired to eat anything.

"I could eat a bite of something, yes," replied Don Quixote. "Indeed, I feel that a little food would go very nicely just now."

He thereupon learned that, since it was Friday, there was nothing to be had in all the inn except a few portions of codfish, which in Castile is called *abadejo,* in Andalusia *bucalao,* in some places *curadillo,* and elsewhere *truchuella* or small trout. Would his Grace, then, have some small trout, seeing that was all there was that they could offer him?

"If there are enough of them," said Don Quixote, "they will take the place of a trout, for it is all one to me whether I am given in change eight reales or one piece of eight. What is more, those small trout may be like veal, which is better than beef, or like kid, which is better than goat. But however that may be, bring them on at once, for the weight and burden of arms is not to be borne without inner sustenance."

Placing the table at the door of the hostelry, in the open air, they brought the guest a portion of badly soaked and worse cooked codfish and a piece of bread as black and moldy as the suit of armor that he wore. It was a mirth-provoking sight to see him eat, for he still had his helmet on with his visor fastened, which made it impossible for him to put anything into his mouth with his hands, and so it was necessary for one of the girls to feed him. As for giving him anything to drink, that would have been out of the question if the innkeeper had not hollowed out a reed, placing one end in Don Quixote's mouth while through the other end he poured the wine. All this the knight bore very patiently rather than have them cut the ribbons of his helmet.

At this point a gelder of pigs approached the inn, announcing his arrival with four or five blasts on his horn, all of which confirmed Don Quixote in the belief that this was indeed a famous castle, for what was this if not music that they were playing for him? The fish was trout, the bread was the finest, the wenches were ladies, and the innkeeper was the castellan. He was convinced that he had been right in his resolve to sally forth and roam the world at large, but there was one thing that still distressed him greatly, and that was the fact that he had not as yet been dubbed a knight; as he saw it, he could not legitimately engage in any adventure until he had received the order of knighthood.

CHAPTER 3

Of the amusing manner in which Don Quixote had himself dubbed a knight.

Wearied of his thoughts, Don Quixote lost no time over the scanty repast which the inn afforded him. When he had finished, he summoned the landlord and, taking him out to the stable, closed the doors and fell on his knees in front of him.

"Never, valiant knight," he said, "shall I arise from here until you have courteously granted me the boon I seek, one which will redound to your praise and to the good of the human race."

Seeing his guest at his feet and hearing him utter such words as these, the innkeeper could only stare at him in bewilderment, not knowing what to say or do. It was in vain that he entreated him to rise, for Don Quixote refused to do so until his request had been granted.

"I expected nothing less of your great magnificence, my lord," the latter then continued, "and so I may tell you that the boon I asked and which you have so generously conceded me is that tomorrow morning you dub me a knight. Until that time, in the chapel of this your castle, I will watch over my armor, and when morning comes, as I have said, that which I so desire shall then be done, in order that I may lawfully go to the four corners of the earth in quest of adventures and to succor the needy, which is the chivalrous duty of all knights-errant such as I who long to engage in deeds of high emprise."

The innkeeper, as we have said, was a sharp fellow. He already had a suspicion that his guest was not quite right in the head, and he was now convinced of it as he listened to such remarks as these. However, just for the sport of it, he determined to humor him; and so he went on to assure Don Quixote that he was fully justified in his request and that such a desire and purpose was only natural on the part of so distinguished a knight as his gallant bearing plainly showed him to be.

He himself, the landlord added, when he was a young man, had followed the same honorable calling. He had gone through various parts of the world seeking adventures, among the places he had visited being the Percheles of Málaga, the Isles of Riarán, the District of Seville, the Little Market Place of Segovia, the Olivera of Valencia, the Rondilla of Granada, the beach of Sanlúcar, the Horse Fountain of Cordova, the Small Taverns of Toledo,[8] and numerous other localities where his nimble feet and light fingers had found much exercise. He had done many wrongs, cheated many widows, ruined many maidens, and swindled not a few minors until he had finally come to be known in almost all the courts and tribunals that are to be found in the whole of Spain.

---

8. All reputed to be haunts of robbers and rogues.

At last he had retired to his castle here, where he lived upon his own income and the property of others; and here it was that he received all knights-errant of whatever quality and condition, simply out of the great affection that he bore them and that they might share with him their possessions in payment of his good will. Unfortunately, in this castle there was no chapel where Don Quixote might keep watch over his arms, for the old chapel had been torn down to make way for a new one; but in case of necessity, he felt quite sure that such a vigil could be maintained anywhere, and for the present occasion the courtyard of the castle would do; and then in the morning, please God, the requisite ceremony could be performed and his guest be duly dubbed a knight, as much a knight as anyone ever was.

He then inquired if Don Quixote had any money on his person, and the latter replied that he had not a cent, for in all the storybooks he had never read of knights-errant carrying any. But the innkeeper told him he was mistaken on this point: supposing the authors of those stories had not set down the fact in black and white, that was because they did not deem it necessary to speak of things as indispensable as money and a clean shirt, and one was not to assume for that reason that those knights-errant of whom the books were so full did not have any. He looked upon it as an absolute certainty that they all had well-stuffed purses, that they might be prepared for any emergency; and they also carried shirts and a little box of ointment for healing the wounds that they received.

For when they had been wounded in combat on the plains and in desert places, there was not always someone at hand to treat them, unless they had some skilled enchanter for a friend who then would succor them, bringing to them through the air, upon a cloud, some damsel or dwarf bearing a vial of water of such virtue that one had but to taste a drop of it and at once his wounds were healed and he was as sound as if he had never received any.

But even if this was not the case, knights in times past saw to it that their squires were well provided with money and other necessities, such as lint and ointment for healing purposes; and if they had no squires—which happened very rarely—they themselves carried these objects in a pair of saddlebags very cleverly attached to their horses' croups in such a manner as to be scarcely noticeable, as if they held something of greater importance than that, for among the knights-errant saddlebags as a rule were not favored. Accordingly, he would advise the novice before him, and inasmuch as the latter was soon to be his godson, he might even command him, that henceforth he should not go without money and a supply of those things that have been mentioned, as he would find that they came in useful at a time when he least expected it.

Don Quixote promised to follow his host's advice punctiliously; and so it was arranged that he should watch his armor in a large barnyard at one side of the inn. He gathered up all the pieces, placed them in a horse trough that stood near the well, and, bracing his shield on his arm, took up his lance and with stately demeanor began pacing up and down in front of the trough even as night was closing in.

The innkeeper informed his other guests of what was going on, of Don Quixote's vigil and his expectation of being dubbed a knight; and, marveling greatly at so extraordinary a variety of madness, they all went out to see for themselves and stood there watching from a distance. For a while the knight-to-be, with tranquil mien, would merely walk up and down; then, leaning on his lance, he would pause to survey his armor, gazing fixedly at it for a considerable length of time. As has been said, it was night now, but the brightness of the moon, which well might rival that of Him who lent it, was such that everything the novice knight did was plainly visible to all.

At this point one of the mule drivers who were stopping at the inn came out to water his drove, and in order to do this it was necessary to remove the armor from the trough.

As he saw the man approaching, Don Quixote cried out to him, "O bold knight, whoever you may be, who thus would dare to lay hands upon the accouterments of the most valiant man of arms that ever girded on a sword, look well what you do and desist if you do not wish to pay with your life for your insolence!"

The muleteer gave no heed to these words—it would have been better for his own sake had he done so—but, taking it up by the straps, tossed the armor some distance from him. When he beheld this, Don Quixote rolled his eyes heavenward and with his thoughts apparently upon his Dulcinea exclaimed, "Succor, O lady mine, this vassal heart in this my first encounter; let not your favor and protection fail me in the peril in which for the first time I now find myself."

With these and other similar words, he loosed his buckler, grasped his lance in both his hands, and let the mule driver have such a blow on the head that the man fell to the ground stunned; and had it been followed by another one, he would have had no need of a surgeon to treat him. Having done this, Don Quixote gathered up his armor and resumed his pacing up and down with the same calm manner as before. Not long afterward, without knowing what had happened—for the first muleteer was still lying there unconscious—another came out with the same intention of watering his mules, and he too was about to remove the armor from the trough when the knight, without saying a word or asking favor of anyone, once more adjusted his buckler and raised his lance, and if he did not break the second mule driver's head to bits, he made more than three pieces of it by dividing it into quarters. At the sound of the fracas everybody in the inn came running out, among them the innkeeper; whereupon Don Quixote again lifted his buckler and laid his hand on his sword.

"O lady of beauty," he said, "strength and vigor of this fainting heart of mine! Now is the time to turn the eyes of your greatness upon this captive knight of yours who must face so formidable an adventure."

By this time he had worked himself up to such a pitch of anger that if all the mule drivers in the world had attacked him he would not have taken one step backward. The comrades of the wounded men, seeing the plight those two were in, now began showering stones on Don Quixote, who shielded himself as best he could with his buckler, although he did not dare stir from the trough for fear of leaving his armor unprotected. The landlord, meanwhile, kept calling for them to stop, for he had told them that this was a madman who would be sure to go free even though he killed them all. The knight was shouting louder than ever, calling them knaves and traitors. As for the lord of the castle, who allowed knights-errant to be treated in this fashion, he was a lowborn villain, and if he, Don Quixote, had but received the order of knighthood, he would make him pay for his treachery.

"As for you others, vile and filthy rabble, I take no account of you; you may stone me or come forward and attack me all you like; you shall see what the reward of your folly and insolence will be."

He spoke so vigorously and was so undaunted in bearing as to strike terror in those who would assail him; and for this reason, and owing also to the persuasions of the innkeeper, they ceased stoning him. He then permitted them to carry away the wounded, and went back to watching his armor with the same tranquil, unconcerned air that he had previously displayed.

The landlord was none too well pleased with these mad pranks on the part of his guest and determined to confer upon him that accursed order of knighthood before something else happened. Going up to him, he begged Don Quixote's pardon for the insolence which, without his knowledge, had been shown the knight by those of low degree. They, however, had been well punished for their impudence. As he had said, there was no chapel in this castle, but for that which remained to be done there was no need of any. According to what he had read of the ceremonial of the order, there was nothing to this business of being dubbed a knight except a slap on the neck and one across the shoulder, and that could be performed in the middle of a field as well as anywhere else. All that was required was for the knight-to-be to keep watch over his armor for a couple of hours, and Don Quixote had been at it more than four. The latter believed all this and announced that he was ready to obey and get the matter over with as speedily as possible. Once dubbed a knight, if he were attacked one more time, he did not think that he would leave a single person in the castle alive, save such as he might command be spared, at the bidding of his host and out of respect to him.

Thus warned, and fearful that it might occur, the castellan brought out the book in which he had jotted down the hay and barley for which the mule drivers owed him, and, accompanied by a lad bearing the butt of a candle and the two aforesaid damsels, he came up to where Don Quixote stood and commanded him to kneel. Reading from the account book—as if he had been saying a prayer—he raised his hand and, with the knight's own sword, gave him a good thwack upon the neck and another lusty one upon the shoulder, muttering all the while between his teeth. He then directed one of the ladies to gird on Don Quixote's sword, which she did with much gravity and composure; for it was all they could do to keep from laughing at every point of the ceremony, but the thought of the knight's prowess which they had already witnessed was sufficient to restrain their mirth.

"May God give your Grace much good fortune," said the worthy lady as she attached the blade, "and prosper you in battle."

Don Quixote thereupon inquired her name, for he desired to know to whom it was he was indebted for the favor he had just received, that he might share with her some of the honor which his strong right arm was sure to bring him. She replied very humbly that her name was Tolosa and that she was the daughter of a shoemaker, a native of Toledo who lived in the stalls of Sancho Bicnaya.[9] To this the knight replied that she would do him a very great favor if from then on she would call herself Doña Tolosa, and she promised to do so. The other girl then helped him on with his spurs, and practically the same conversation was repeated. When asked her name, she stated that it was La Molinera and added that she was the daughter of a

9. An old square in Toledo.

respectable miller of Antequera. Don Quixote likewise requested her to assume the "don" and become Doña Molinera and offered to render her further services and favors.

These unheard-of ceremonies having been dispatched in great haste, Don Quixote could scarcely wait to be astride his horse and sally forth on his quest for adventures. Saddling and mounting Rocinante, he embraced his host, thanking him for the favor of having dubbed him a knight and saying such strange things that it would be quite impossible to record them here. The innkeeper, who was only too glad to be rid of him, answered with a speech that was no less flowery, though somewhat shorter, and he did not so much as ask him for the price of a lodging, so glad was he to see him go.

CHAPTER 4

Of what happened to our knight when he sallied forth from the inn.

Day was dawning when Don Quixote left the inn, so well satisfied with himself, so gay, so exhilarated, that the very girths of his steed all but burst with joy. But remembering the advice which his host had given him concerning the stock of necessary provisions that he should carry with him, especially money and shirts, he decided to turn back home and supply himself with whatever he needed, and with a squire as well; he had in mind a farmer who was a neighbor of his, a poor man and the father of a family but very well suited to fulfill the duties of squire to a man of arms. With this thought in mind he guided Rocinante toward the village once more, and that animal, realizing that he was homeward bound, began stepping out at so lively a gait that it seemed as if his feet barely touched the ground.

The knight had not gone far when from a hedge on his right hand he heard the sound of faint moans as of someone in distress.

"Thanks be to Heaven," he at once exclaimed, "for the favor it has shown me by providing me so soon with an opportunity to fulfill the obligations that I owe to my profession, a chance to pluck the fruit of my worthy desires. Those, undoubtedly, are the cries of someone in distress, who stands in need of my favor and assistance."

Turning Rocinante's head, he rode back to the place from which the cries appeared to be coming. Entering the wood, he had gone but a few paces when he saw a mare attached to an oak, while bound to another tree was a lad of fifteen or thereabouts, naked from the waist up. It was he who was uttering the cries, and not without reason, for there in front of him was a lusty farmer with a girdle who was giving him many lashes, each one accompanied by a reproof and a command, "Hold your tongue and keep your eyes open"; and the lad was saying, "I won't do it again, sir; by God's Passion, I won't do it again. I promise you that after this I'll take better care of the flock."

When he saw what was going on, Don Quixote was very angry. "Discourteous knight," he said, "it ill becomes you to strike one who is powerless to defend himself. Mount your steed and take your lance in hand"—for there was a lance leaning against the oak to which the mare was tied—"and I will show you what a coward you are."

The farmer, seeing before him this figure all clad in armor and brandishing a lance, decided that he was as good as done for. "Sir Knight," he said, speaking very mildly, "this lad that I am punishing here is my servant; he tends a flock of sheep which I have in these parts and he is so careless that every day one of them shows up missing. And when I punish him for his carelessness or his roguery, he says it is just because I am a miser and do not want to pay him the wages that I owe him, but I swear to God and upon my soul that he lies."

"It is you who lie, base lout," said Don Quixote, "and in my presence; and by the sun that gives us light, I am minded to run you through with this lance. Pay him and say no more about it, or else, by the God who rules us, I will make an end of you and annihilate you here and now. Release him at once."

The farmer hung his head and without a word untied his servant. Don Quixote then asked the boy how much has master owed him. For nine months' work, the lad told him, at seven reales the month. The knight did a little reckoning and found that this came to sixty-three reales; whereupon he ordered the farmer to pay over the money immediately, as he valued his life. The cowardly bumpkin replied that, facing death as he was and by the oath that he had sworn—he had not sworn any oath as yet—it did not amount to as much as that; for there were three pairs of shoes which he had given the lad that were to be deducted and taken into account, and a real for two blood-lettings when his servant was ill.

"That," said Don Quixote, "is all very well; but let the shoes and the blood-lettings go for the undeserved lashings which you have given him; if he has worn out the leather of the shoes that you paid for, you have taken the hide off his body, and if the barber let a little blood for him when he was sick,[1] you have done the same when he was well; and so far as that goes, he owes you nothing."

"But the trouble is, Sir Knight, that I have no money with me. Come along home with me, Andrés, and I will pay you real for real."

"I go home with him!" cried the lad. "Never in the world! No, sir, I would not even think of it; for once he has me alone he'll flay me like a St. Bartholomew."

"He will do nothing of the sort," said Don Quixote. "It is sufficient for me to command, and he out of respect will obey. Since he has sworn to me by the order of knighthood which he has received, I shall let him go free and I will guarantee that you will be paid."

"But look, your Grace," the lad remonstrated, "my master is no knight; he has never received any order of knighthood whatsoever. He is Juan Haldudo, a rich man and a resident of Quintanar."

"That makes little difference," declared Don Quixote, "for there may well be knights among the Haldudos, all the more so in view of the fact that every man is the son of his works."

"That is true enough," said Andrés, "but this master of mine—of what works is he the son, seeing that he refuses me the pay for my sweat and labor?"

"I do not refuse you, brother Andrés," said the farmer. "Do me the favor of coming with me, and I swear to you by all the orders of knighthood that there are in this world to pay you, as I have said, real for real, and perfumed at that."

"You can dispense with the perfume," said Don Quixote; "just give him

---

1. Barbers were also surgeons.

the reales and I shall be satisfied. And see to it that you keep your oath, or by the one that I myself have sworn I shall return to seek you out and chastise you, and I shall find you though you be as well hidden as a lizard. In case you would like to know who it is that is giving you this command in order that you may feel the more obliged to comply with it, I may tell you that I am the valorous Don Quixote de la Mancha, righter of wrongs and injustices; and so, God be with you, and do not fail to do as you have promised, under that penalty that I have pronounced."

As he said this, he put spurs to Rocinante and was off. The farmer watched him go, and when he saw that Don Quixote was out of the wood and out of sight, he turned to his servant, Andrés.

"Come here, my son," he said. "I want to pay you what I owe you as that righter of wrongs has commanded me."

"Take my word for it," replied Andrés, "your Grace would do well to observe the command of that good knight—may he live a thousand years; for as he is valorous and a righteous judge, if you don't pay me then, by Rocque,[2] he will come back and do just what he said!"

"And I will give you my word as well," said the farmer; "but seeing that I am so fond of you, I wish to increase the debt, that I may owe you all the more." And with this he seized the lad's arm and bound him to the tree again and flogged him within an inch of his life. "There, Master Andrés, you may call on that righter of wrongs if you like and you will see whether or not he rights this one. I do not think I have quite finished with you yet, for I have a good mind to flay you alive as you feared."

Finally, however, he unbound him and told him he might go look for that judge of his to carry out the sentence that had been pronounced. Andrés left, rather down in the mouth, swearing that he would indeed go look for the brave Don Quixote de la Mancha; he would relate to him everything that had happened, point by point, and the farmer would have to pay for it seven times over. But for all that, he went away weeping, and his master stood laughing at him.

Such was the manner in which the valorous knight righted this particular wrong. Don Quixote was quite content with the way everything had turned out; it seemed to him that he had made a very fortunate and noble beginning with his deeds of chivalry, and he was very well satisfied with himself as he jogged along in the direction of his native village, talking to himself in a low voice all the while.

"Well may'st thou call thyself fortunate today, above all other women on earth, O fairest of the fair, Dulcinea del Toboso! Seeing that it has fallen to thy lot to hold subject and submissive to thine every wish and pleasure so valiant and renowned a knight as Don Quixote de la Mancha is and shall be, who, as everyone knows, yesterday received the order of knighthood and this day has righted the greatest wrong and grievance that injustice ever conceived or cruelty ever perpetrated, by snatching the lash from the hand of the merciless foeman who was so unreasonably flogging that tender child."

At this point he came to a road that forked off in four directions, and at once he thought of those crossroads where knights-errant would pause to consider which path they should take. By way of imitating them, he halted

---

2. The origin of this oath is unknown.

there for a while; and when he had given the subject much thought, he slackened Rocinante's rein and let the hack follow its inclination. The animal's first impulse was to make straight for its own stable. After they had gone a couple of miles or so Don Quixote caught sight of what appeared to be a great throng of people, who, as was afterward learned, were certain merchants of Toledo on their way to purchase silk at Murcia. There were six of them altogether with their sunshades, accompanied by four attendants on horseback and three mule drivers on foot.

No sooner had he sighted them than Don Quixote imagined that he was on the brink of some fresh adventure. He was eager to imitate those passages at arms of which he had read in his books, and here, so it seemed to him, was one made to order. And so, with bold and knightly bearing, he settled himself firmly in the stirrups, couched his lance, covered himself with his shield, and took up a position in the middle of the road, where he paused to wait for those other knights-errant (for such he took them to be) to come up to him. When they were near enough to see and hear plainly, Don Quixote raised his voice and made a haughty gesture.

"Let everyone," he cried, "stand where he is, unless everyone will confess that there is not in all the world a more beauteous damsel than the Empress of La Mancha, the peerless Dulcinea del Toboso."

Upon hearing these words and beholding the weird figure who uttered them, the merchants stopped short. From the knight's appearance and his speech they knew at once that they had to deal with a madman; but they were curious to know what was meant by that confession that was demanded of them, and one of their number who was somewhat of a jester and a very clever fellow raised his voice.

"Sir Knight," he said, "we do not know who this beauteous lady is of whom you speak. Show her to us, and if she is as beautiful as you say, then we will right willingly and without any compulsion confess the truth as you have asked of us."

"If I were to show her to you," replied Don Quixote, "what merit would there be in your confessing a truth so self-evident? The important thing is for you, without seeing her, to believe, confess, affirm, swear, and defend that truth. Otherwise, monstrous and arrogant creatures that you are, you shall do battle with me. Come on, then, one by one, as the order of knighthood prescribes; or all of you together, if you will have it so, as is the sorry custom of those of your breed. Come on, and I will await you here, for I am confident that my cause is just."

"Sir Knight," responded the merchant, "I beg your Grace, in the name of all the princes here present, in order that we may not have upon our consciences the burden of confessing a thing which we have never seen nor heard, and one, moreover, so prejudicial to the empresses and queens of Alcarria and Estremadura,[3] that your Grace will show us some portrait of this lady, even though it be no larger than a grain of wheat, for by the thread one comes to the ball of yarn; and with this we shall remain satisfied and assured, and your Grace will likewise be content and satisfied. The truth is, I believe that we are already so much of your way of thinking that though it should show her to be blind of one eye and distilling vermilion and brimstone

---

3. Ironical, because both were known as particularly backward regions.

from the other, nevertheless, to please your Grace, we would say in her behalf all that you desire.'

"She distills nothing of the sort, infamous rabble!" shouted Don Quixote, for his wrath was kindling now. "I tell you, she does not distill what you say at all, but amber and civet[4] wrapped in cotton; and she is neither one-eyed nor hunchbacked but straighter than a spindle that comes from Guadarrama. You shall pay for the great blasphemy which you have uttered against such a beauty as is my lady!"

Saying this, he came on with lowered lance against the one who had spoken, charging with such wrath and fury that if fortune had not caused Rocinante to stumble and fall in mid-career, things would have gone badly with the merchant and he would have paid for his insolent gibe. As it was, Don Quixote went rolling over the plain for some little distance, and when he tried to get to his feet, found that he was unable to do so, being too encumbered with his lance, shield, spurs, helmet, and the weight of that ancient suit of armor.

"Do not flee, cowardly ones," he cried even as he struggled to rise. "Stay, cravens, for it is not my fault but that of my steed that I am stretched out here."

One of the muleteers, who must have been an ill-natured lad, upon hearing the poor fallen knight speak so arrogantly, could not refrain from giving him an answer in the ribs. Going up to him, he took the knight's lance and broke it into bits, and then with a companion proceeded to belabor him so mercilessly that in spite of his armor they milled him like a hopper of wheat. The merchants called to them not to lay on so hard, saying that was enough and they should desist, but the mule driver by this time had warmed up to the sport and would not stop until he had vented his wrath, and, snatching up the broken pieces of the lance, he began hurling them at the wretched victim as he lay there on the ground. And through all this tempest of sticks that rained upon him Don Quixote never once closed his mouth nor ceased threatening Heaven and earth and these ruffians, for such he took them to be, who were thus mishandling him.

Finally the lad grew tired, and the merchants went their way with a good story to tell about the poor fellow who had had such a cudgeling. Finding himself alone, the knight endeavored to see if he could rise; but if this was a feat that he could not accomplish when he was sound and whole, how was he to achieve it when he had been thrashed and pounded to a pulp? Yet nonetheless he considered himself fortunate; for as he saw it, misfortunes such as this were common to knights-errant, and he put all the blame upon his horse; and if he was unable to rise, that was because his body was so bruised and battered all over.

CHAPTER 5

In which is continued the narrative of the misfortune that befell our knight.

Seeing, then, that he was indeed unable to stir, he decided to fall back upon a favorite remedy of his, which was to think of some passage or other

---

4. A musky substance used in perfume, imported from Africa in cotton packings.

in his books; and as it happened, the one that he in his madness now recalled was the story of Baldwin and the Marquis of Mantua, when Carloto left the former wounded upon the mountainside,[5] a tale that is known to children, not unknown to young men, celebrated and believed in by the old, and, for all of that, not any truer than the miracles of Mohammed. Moreover, it impressed him as being especially suited to the straits in which he found himself; and, accordingly, with a great show of feeling, he began rolling and tossing on the ground as he feebly gasped out the lines which the wounded knight of the wood is supposed to have uttered:

> "Where art thou, lady mine,
> That thou dost not grieve for my woe?
> Either thou art disloyal,
> Or my grief thou dost not know."

He went on reciting the old ballad until he came to the following verses:

> "O noble Marquis of Mantua,
> My uncle and liege lord true!"

He had reached this point when down the road came a farmer of the same village, a neighbor of his, who had been to the mill with a load of wheat. Seeing a man lying there stretched out like that, he went up to him and inquired who he was and what was the trouble that caused him to utter such mournful complaints. Thinking that this must undoubtedly be his uncle, the Marquis of Mantua, Don Quixote did not answer but went on with his recitation of the ballad, giving an account of the Marquis' misfortunes and the amours of his wife and the emperor's son, exactly as the ballad has it.

The farmer was astounded at hearing all these absurdities, and after removing the knight's visor which had been battered to pieces by the blows it had received, the good man bathed the victim's face, only to discover, once the dust was off, that he knew him very well.

"Señor Quejana," he said (for such must have been Don Quixote's real name when he was in his right senses and before he had given up the life of a quiet country gentleman to become a knight-errant), "who is responsible for your Grace's being in such a plight as this?"

But the knight merely went on with his ballad in response to all the questions asked of him. Perceiving that it was impossible to obtain any information from him, the farmer as best he could relieved him of his breastplate and backpiece to see if he had any wounds, but there was no blood and no mark of any sort. He then tried to lift him from the ground, and with a great deal of effort finally managed to get him astride the ass, which appeared to be the easier mount for him. Gathering up the armor, including even the splinters from the lance, he made a bundle and tied it on Rocinante's back, and, taking the horse by the reins and the ass by the halter, he started out for the village. He was worried in his mind at hearing all the foolish things that Don Quixote said, and that individual himself was far from being at ease. Unable by reason of his bruises and his soreness to sit upright on the donkey, our knight-errant kept sighing to Heaven, which led the farmer to ask him once more what it was that ailed him.

5. The allusion is to an old ballad about Charlemagne's son Charlot (Carloto) wounding Baldwin, nephew of the marquis of Mantua.

It must have been the devil himself who caused him to remember those tales that seemed to fit his own case; for at this point he forgot all about Baldwin and recalled Abindarráez, and how the governor of Antequera, Rodrigo de Narváez, had taken him prisoner and carried him off captive to his castle. Accordingly, when the countryman turned to inquire how he was and what was troubling him, Don Quixote replied with the very same words and phrases that the captive Abindarráez used in answering Rodrigo, just as he had read in the story *Diana* of Jorge de Montemayor,[6] where it is all written down, applying them very aptly to the present circumstances as the farmer went along cursing his luck for having to listen to such a lot of nonsense. Realizing that his neighbor was quite mad, he made haste to reach the village that he might not have to be annoyed any longer by Don Quixote's tiresome harangue.

"Señor Don Rodrigo de Narváez," the knight was saying, "I may inform your Grace that this beautiful Jarifa of whom I speak is not the lovely Dulcinea del Toboso, in whose behalf I have done, am doing, and shall do the most famous deeds of chivalry that ever have been or will be seen in all the world."

"But, sir," replied the farmer, "sinner that I am, cannot your Grace see that I am not Don Rodrigo de Narváez nor the Marquis of Mantua, but Pedro Alonso, your neighbor? And your Grace is neither Baldwin nor Abindarráez but a respectable gentleman by the name of Señor Quijana."

"I know who I am," said Don Quixote, "and who I may be, if I choose: not only those I have mentioned but all the Twelve Peers of France and the Nine Worthies[7] as well; for the exploits of all of them together, or separately, cannot compare with mine."

With such talk as this they reached their destination just as night was falling; but the farmer decided to wait until it was a little darker in order that the badly battered gentleman might not be seen arriving in such a condition and mounted on an ass. When he thought the proper time had come, they entered the village and proceeded to Don Quixote's house, where they found everything in confusion. The curate and the barber were there, for they were great friends of the knight, and the housekeeper was speaking to them.

"Señor Licentiate Pero Pérez," she was saying, for that was the manner in which she addressed the curate, "what does your Grace think could have happened to my master? Three days now, and not a word of him, nor the hack, nor the buckler, nor the lance, nor the suit of armor. Ah, poor me! I am as certain as I am that I was born to die that it is those cursed books of chivalry he is always reading that have turned his head; for now that I recall, I have often heard him muttering to himself that he must become a knight-errant and go through the world in search of adventures. May such books as those be consigned to Satan and Barabbas,[8] for they have sent to perdition the finest mind in all La Mancha."

---

6. The reference is to the tale of the love of Abindarráez, a captive Moor, for the beautiful Jarifa, included in the second edition of Jorge de Montemayor's *Diana*, a pastoral romance.   7. In French medieval epics, the Twelve Peers (Roland, Oliver, and so on) were warriors all equal in rank, forming a kind of guard of honor around Charlemagne. In a tradition originating in France, the Nine Worthies consisted of three biblical, three classical, and three Christian figures (David, Hector, Alexander, Charlemagne, and so on). 8. The thief whose release, rather than that of Jesus, the crowd requested when Pilate, conforming to Passover custom, was ready to have one prisoner set free.

The niece was of the same opinion. "I may tell you, Señor Master Nicholas," she said, for that was the barber's name, "that many times my uncle would sit reading those impious tales of misadventure for two whole days and nights at a stretch; and when he was through, he would toss the book aside, lay his hand on his sword, and begin slashing at the walls. When he was completely exhausted, he would tell us that he had just killed four giants as big as castle towers, while the sweat that poured off him was blood from the wounds that he had received in battle. He would then drink a big jug of cold water, after which he would be very calm and peaceful, saying that the water was the most precious liquid which the wise Esquife, a great magician and his friend, had brought to him. But I blame myself for everything. I should have advised your Worships of my uncle's nonsensical actions so that you could have done something about it by burning those damnable books of his before things came to such a pass; for he has many that ought to be burned as if they were heretics."

"I agree with you," said the curate, "and before tomorrow's sun has set there shall be a public *auto da fé*, and those works shall be condemned to the flames that they may not lead some other who reads them to follow the example of my good friend."

Don Quixote and the farmer overheard all this, and it was then that the latter came to understand the nature of his neighbor's affliction.

"Open the door, your Worships," the good man cried. "Open for Sir Baldwin and the Marquis of Mantua, who comes badly wounded, and for Señor Abindarráez the Moor whom the valiant Rodrigo de Narváez, governor of Antequera, brings captive."

At the sound of his voice they all ran out, recognizing at once friend, master, and uncle, who as yet was unable to get down off the donkey's back. They all ran up to embrace him.

"Wait, all of you," said Don Quixote, "for I am sorely wounded through fault of my steed. Bear me to my couch and summon, if it be possible, the wise Urganda to treat and care for my wounds."

"There!" exclaimed the housekeeper. "Plague take it! Did not my heart tell me right as to which foot my master limped on? To bed with your Grace at once, and we will take care of you without sending for that Urganda of yours. A curse, I say, and a hundred other curses, on those books of chivalry that have brought your Grace to this."

And so they carried him off to bed, but when they went to look for his wounds, they found none at all. He told them it was all the result of a great fall he had taken with Rocinante, his horse, while engaged in combating ten giants, the hugest and most insolent that were ever heard of in all the world.

"Tut, tut," said the curate. "So there are giants in the dance now, are there? Then, by the sign of the cross, I'll have them burned before nightfall tomorrow."

They had a thousand questions to put to Don Quixote, but his only answer was that they should give him something to eat and let him sleep, for that was the most important thing of all; so they humored him in this. The curate then interrogated the farmer at great length concerning the conversation he had had with his neighbor. The peasant told him everything, all the absurd things their friend had said when he found him lying there and afterward on the way home, all of which made the licentiate more anxious than ever to do what he did the following day,[9] when he summoned Master Nicholas and went with him to Don Quixote's house.

[Fighting the Windmills and a Choleric Biscayan]

CHAPTER 7

Of the second sally of our good knight, Don Quixote de la Mancha.

* * * After that he remained at home very tranquilly for a couple of weeks, without giving sign of any desire to repeat his former madness. During that time he had the most pleasant conversations with his two old friends, the curate and the barber, on the point he had raised to the effect that what the world needed most was knights-errant and a revival of chivalry. The curate would occasionally contradict him and again would give in, for it was only by means of this artifice that he could carry on a conversation with him at all.

In the meanwhile Don Quixote was bringing his powers of persuasion to bear upon a farmer who lived near by, a good man—if this title may be applied to one who is poor—but with very few wits in his head. The short of it is, by pleas and promises, he got the hapless rustic to agree to ride forth with him and serve him as his squire. Among other things, Don Quixote told him that he ought to be more than willing to go, because no telling what adventure might occur which would win them an island, and then he (the farmer) would be left to be the governor of it. As a result of these and other similar assurances, Sancho Panza forsook his wife and children and consented to take upon himself the duties of squire to his neighbor.

Next, Don Quixote set out to raise some money, and by selling this thing and pawning that and getting the worst of the bargain always, he finally scraped together a reasonable amount. He also asked a friend of his for the loan of a buckler and patched up his broken helmet as well as he could. He advised his squire, Sancho, of the day and hour when they were to take to the road and told him to see to laying in a supply of those things that were most necessary, and, above all, not to forget the saddlebags. Sancho replied that he would see to all this and added that he was also thinking of taking along with him a very good ass that he had, as he was not much used to going on foot.

With regard to the ass, Don Quixote had to do a little thinking, trying to recall if any knight-errant had ever had a squire thus asininely mounted. He could not think of any, but nevertheless he decided to take Sancho with the intention of providing him with a nobler steed as soon as occasion offered; he had but to appropriate the horse of the first discourteous knight he met. Having furnished himself with shirts and all the other things that the innkeeper had recommended, he and Panza rode forth one night unseen by anyone and without taking leave of wife and children, housekeeper or niece. They went so far that by the time morning came they were safe from discovery had a hunt been started for them.

---

9. He and the barber burned most of Don Quixote's library.

Mounted on his ass, Sancho Panza rode along like a patriarch, with saddle-bags and flask, his mind set upon becoming governor of that island that his master had promised him. Don Quixote determined to take the same route and road over the Campo de Montiel that he had followed on his first journey; but he was not so uncomfortable this time, for it was early morning and the sun's rays fell upon them slantingly and accordingly did not tire them too much.

"Look, Sir Knight-errant," said Sancho, "your Grace should not forget that island you promised me; for no matter how big it is, I'll be able to govern it right enough."

"I would have you know, friend Sancho Panza," replied Don Quixote, "that among the knights-errant of old it was a very common custom to make their squires governors of the islands or the kingdoms that they won, and I am resolved that in my case so pleasing a usage shall not fall into desuetude. I even mean to go them one better; for they very often, perhaps most of the time, waited until their squires were old men who had had their fill of serving their masters during bad days and worse nights, whereupon they would give them the title of count, or marquis at most, of some valley or province more or less. But if you live and I live, it well may be that within a week I shall win some kingdom with others dependent upon it, and it will be the easiest thing in the world to crown you king of one of them. You need not marvel at this, for all sorts of unforeseen things happen to knights like me, and I may readily be able to give you even more than I have promised."

"In that case," said Sancho Panza, "if by one of those miracles of which your Grace was speaking I should become king, I would certainly send for Juana Gutiérrez, my old lady, to come and be my queen, and the young ones could be infantes."

"There is no doubt about it," Don Quixote assured him.

"Well, I doubt it," said Sancho, "for I think that even if God were to rain kingdoms upon the earth, no crown would sit well on the head of Mari Gutiérrez,[1] for I am telling you, sir, as a queen she is not worth two maravedis.[2] She would do better as a countess, God help her."

"Leave everything to God, Sancho," said Don Quixote, "and he will give you whatever is most fitting; but I trust you will not be so pusillanimous as to be content with anything less than the title of viceroy."

"That I will not," said Sancho Panza, "especially seeing that I have in your Grace so illustrious a master who can give me all that is suitable to me and all that I can manage."

CHAPTER 8

Of the good fortune which the valorous Don Quixote had in the terrifying and never-before-imagined adventure of the windmills, along with other events that deserve to be suitably recorded.

At this point they caught sight of thirty or forty windmills which were standing on the plain there, and no sooner had Don Quixote laid eyes upon them than he turned to his squire and said, "Fortune is guiding our affairs better than we could have wished; for you see there before you, friend San-

---

1. Sancho's wife, Juana Gutiérrez. 2. See n. 5, p. 2677.

cho Panza, some thirty or more lawless giants with whom I mean to do battle. I shall deprive them of their lives, and with the spoils from this encounter we shall begin to enrich ourselves; for this is righteous warfare, and it is a great service to God to remove so accursed a breed from the face of the earth."

"What giants?" said Sancho Panza.

"Those that you see there," replied his master, "those with the long arms some of which are as much as two leagues in length."

"But look, your Grace, those are not giants but windmills, and what appear to be arms are their wings which, when whirled in the breeze, cause the millstone to go."

"It is plain to be seen," said Don Quixote, "that you have had little experience in this matter of adventures. If you are afraid, go off to one side and say your prayers while I am engaging them in fierce, unequal combat."

Saying this, he gave spurs to his steed Rocinante, without paying any heed to Sancho's warning that these were truly windmills and not giants that he was riding forth to attack. Nor even when he was close upon them did he perceive what they really were, but shouted at the top of his lungs, "Do not seek to flee, cowards and vile creatures that you are, for it is but a single knight with whom you have to deal!"

At that moment a little wind came up and the big wings began turning.

"Though you flourish as many arms as did the giant Briareus,"[3] said Don Quixote when he perceived this, "you still shall have to answer to me."

He thereupon commended himself with all his heart to his lady Dulcinea, beseeching her to succor him in this peril; and, being well covered with his shield and with his lance at rest, he bore down upon them at a full gallop and fell upon the first mill that stood in his way, giving a thrust at the wing, which was whirling at such a speed that his lance was broken into bits and both horse and horseman went rolling over the plain, very much battered indeed. Sancho upon his donkey came hurrying to his master's assistance as fast as he could, but when he reached the spot, the knight was unable to move, so great was the shock with which he and Rocinante had hit the ground.

"God help us!" exclaimed Sancho, "did I not tell your Grace to look well, that those were nothing but windmills, a fact which no one could fail to see unless he had other mills of the same sort in his head?"

"Be quiet, friend Sancho," said Don Quixote. "Such are the fortunes of war, which more than any other are subject to constant change. What is more, when I come to think of it, I am sure that this must be the work of that magician Frestón, the one who robbed me of my study and my books,[4] and who has thus changed the giants into windmills in order to deprive me of the glory of overcoming them, so great is the enmity that he bears me; but in the end his evil arts shall not prevail against this trusty sword of mine."

"May God's will be done," was Sancho Panza's response. And with the aid of his squire the knight was once more mounted on Rocinante, who stood there with one shoulder half out of joint. And so, speaking of the adventure that had just befallen them, they continued along the Puerto Lápice highway;

---

3. Mythological giant with a hundred arms. 4. Don Quixote had promptly attributed the ruin of his library to magical intervention (see n. 9, p. 2700).

for there, Don Quixote said, they could not fail to find many and varied adventures, this being a much traveled thoroughfare. The only thing was, the knight was exceedingly downcast over the loss of his lance.

"I remember," he said to his squire, "having read of a Spanish knight by the name of Diego Pérez de Vargas, who, having broken his sword in battle, tore from an oak a heavy bough or branch and with it did such feats of valor that day, and pounded so many Moors, that he came to be known as Machuca,[5] and he and his descendants from that day forth have been called Vargas y Machuca. I tell you this because I too intend to provide myself with just such a bough as the one he wielded, and with it I propose to do such exploits that you shall deem yourself fortunate to have been found worthy to come with me and behold and witness things that are almost beyond belief."

"God's will be done," said Sancho. "I believe everything that your Grace says; but straighten yourself up in the saddle a little, for you seem to be slipping down on one side, owing, no doubt, to the shaking-up that you received in your fall."

"Ah, that is the truth," replied Don Quixote, "and if I do not speak of my sufferings, it is for the reason that it is not permitted knights-errant to complain of any wound whatsoever, even though their bowels may be dropping out."

"If that is the way it is," said Sancho, "I have nothing more to say; but, God knows, it would suit me better if your Grace did complain when something hurts him. I can assure you that I mean to do so, over the least little thing that ails me—that is, unless the same rule applies to squires as well."

Don Quixote laughed long and heartily over Sancho's simplicity, telling him that he might complain as much as he liked and where and when he liked, whether he had good cause or not; for he had read nothing to the contrary in the ordinances of chivalry. Sancho then called his master's attention to the fact that it was time to eat. The knight replied that he himself had no need of food at the moment, but his squire might eat whenever he chose. Having been granted this permission, Sancho seated himself as best he could upon his beast, and, taking out from his saddlebags the provisions that he had stored there, he rode along leisurely behind his master, munching his victuals and taking a good, hearty swig now and then at the leather flask in a manner that might well have caused the biggest-bellied tavern-keeper of Málaga to envy him. Between draughts he gave not so much as a thought to any promise that his master might have made him, nor did he look upon it as any hardship, but rather as good sport, to go in quest of adventures however hazardous they might be.

The short of the matter is, they spent the night under some trees, from one of which Don Quixote tore off a withered bough to serve him as a lance, placing it in the lance head from which he had removed the broken one. He did not sleep all night long for thinking of his lady Dulcinea; for this was in accordance with what he had read in his books, of men of arms in the forest or desert places who kept a wakeful vigil, sustained by the memory of their ladies fair. Not so with Sancho, whose stomach was full, and not with chicory water. He fell into a dreamless slumber, and had not his master called him,

5. "The Crusher," the hero of a folk ballad.

he would not have been awakened either by the rays of the sun in his face or by the many birds who greeted the coming of the new day with their merry song.

Upon arising, he had another go at the flask, finding it somewhat more flaccid then it had been the night before, a circumstance which grieved his heart, for he could not see that they were on the way to remedying the deficiency within any very short space of time. Don Quixote did not wish any breakfast; for, as has been said, he was in the habit of nourishing himself on savorous memories. They then set out once more along the road to Puerto Lápice, and around three in the afternoon they came in sight of the pass that bears that name.

"There," said Don Quixote as his eyes fell upon it, "we may plunge our arms up to the elbow in what are known as adventures. But I must warn you that even though you see me in the greatest peril in the world, you are not to lay hand upon your sword to defend me, unless it be that those who attack me are rabble and men of low degree, in which case you may very well come to my aid; but if they be gentlemen, it is in no wise permitted by the laws of chivalry that you should assist me until you yourself shall have been dubbed a knight."

"Most certainly, sir," replied Sancho, "your Grace shall be very well obeyed in this; all the more so for the reason that I myself am of a peaceful disposition and not fond of meddling in the quarrels and feuds of others. However, when it comes to protecting my own person, I shall not take account of those laws of which you speak, seeing that all laws, human and divine, permit each one to defend himself whenever he is attacked."

"I am willing to grant you that," assented Don Quixote, "but in this matter of defending me against gentlemen you must restrain your natural impulses."

"I promise you I shall do so," said Sancho. "I will observe this precept as I would the Sabbath day."

As they were conversing in this manner, there appeared in the road in front of them two friars of the Order of St. Benedict, mounted upon dromedaries—for the she-mules they rode were certainly no smaller than that. The friars wore travelers' spectacles and carried sunshades, and behind them came a coach accompanied by four or five men on horseback and a couple of muleteers on foot. In the coach, as was afterwards learned, was a lady of Biscay, on her way to Seville to bid farewell to her husband, who had been appointed to some high post in the Indies. The religious were not of her company although they were going by the same road.

The instant Don Quixote laid eyes upon them he turned to his squire. "Either I am mistaken or this is going to be the most famous adventure that ever was seen; for those black-clad figures that you behold must be, and without any doubt are, certain enchanters who are bearing with them a captive princess in that coach, and I must do all I can to right this wrong."

"It will be worse than the windmills," declared Sancho. "Look you, sir, those are Benedictine friars and the coach must be that of some travelers. Mark well what I say and what you do, lest the devil lead you astray."

"I have already told you, Sancho," replied Don Quixote, "that you know little where the subject of adventures is concerned. What I am saying to you is the truth, as you shall now see."

With this, he rode forward and took up a position in the middle of the road along which the friars were coming, and as soon as they appeared to be within earshot he cried out to them in a loud voice, "O devilish and monstrous beings, set free at once the highborn princesses whom you bear captive in that coach, or else prepare at once to meet your death as the just punishment of your evil deeds."

The friars drew rein and sat there in astonishment, marveling as much at Don Quixote's appearance as at the words he spoke. "Sir Knight," they answered him, "we are neither devilish nor monstrous but religious of the Order of St. Benedict who are merely going our way. We know nothing of those who are in that coach, nor of any captive princesses either."

"Soft words," said Don Quixote, "have no effect on me. I know you for what you are, lying rabble!" And without waiting for any further parley he gave spur to Rocinante and, with lowered lance, bore down upon the first friar with such fury and intrepidity that, had not the fellow tumbled from his mule of his own accord, he would have been hurled to the ground and either killed or badly wounded. The second religious, seeing how his companion had been treated, dug his legs into his she-mule's flanks and scurried away over the countryside faster than the wind.

Seeing the friar upon the ground, Sancho Panza slipped lightly from his mount and, falling upon him, began stripping him of his habit. The two mule drivers accompanying the religious thereupon came running up and asked Sancho why he was doing this. The latter replied that the friar's garments belonged to him as legitimate spoils of the battle that his master Don Quixote had just won. The muleteers, however, were lads with no sense of humor, nor did they know what all this talk of spoils and battles was about; but, perceiving that Don Quixote had ridden off to one side to converse with those inside the coach, they pounced upon Sancho, threw him to the ground, and proceeded to pull out the hair of his beard and kick him to a pulp, after which they went off and left him stretched out there, bereft at once of breath and sense.

Without losing any time, they then assisted the friar to remount. The good brother was trembling all over from fright, and there was not a speck of color in his face, but when he found himself in the saddle once more, he quickly spurred his beast to where his companion, at some little distance, sat watching and waiting to see what the result of the encounter would be. Having no curiosity as to the final outcome of the fray, the two of them now resumed their journey, making more signs of the cross than the devil would be able to carry upon his back.

Meanwhile Don Quixote, as we have said, was speaking to the lady in the coach.

"Your beauty, my lady, may now dispose of your person as best may please you, for the arrogance of your abductors lies upon the ground, overthrown by this good arm of mine; and in order that you may not pine to know the name of your liberator, I may inform you that I am Don Quixote de la Mancha, knight-errant and adventurer and captive of the peerless and beauteous Doña Dulcinea del Toboso. In payment of the favor which you have received from me, I ask nothing other than that you return to El Toboso and on my behalf pay your respects to this lady, telling her that it was I who set you free."

One of the squires accompanying those in the coach, a Biscayan,[6] was

6. From the Basque region.

listening to Don Quixote's words, and when he saw that the knight did not propose to let the coach proceed upon its way but was bent upon having it turn back to El Toboso, he promptly went up to him, seized his lance, and said to him in bad Castilian and worse Biscayan, "Go, *caballero,* and bad luck go with you; for by the God that created me, if you do not let this coach pass, me kill you or me no Biscayan."

Don Quixote heard him attentively enough and answered him very mildly, "If you were a *caballero,*[7] which you are not, I should already have chastised you, wretched creature, for your foolhardiness and your impudence."

"Me no *caballero.*" cried the Biscayan "Me swear to God, you lie like a Christian. If you will but lay aside your lance and unsheath your sword, you will soon see that you are carrying water to the cat![8] Biscayan on land, gentleman at sea, but a gentleman in spite of the devil, and you lie if you say otherwise."

" 'You shall see as to that presently,' said Agrajes,"[9] Don Quixote quoted. He cast his lance to the earth, drew his sword, and, taking his buckler on his arm, attacked the Biscayan with intent to slay him. The latter, when he saw his adversary approaching, would have liked to dismount from his mule, for she was one of the worthless sort that are let for hire and he had no confidence in her; but there was no time for this, and so he had no choice but to draw his own sword in turn and make the best of it. However, he was near enough to the coach to be able to snatch a cushion from it to serve him as a shield; and then they fell upon each other as though they were mortal enemies. The rest of those present sought to make peace between them but did not succeed, for the Biscayan with his disjointed phrases kept muttering that if they did not let him finish the battle then he himself would have to kill his mistress and anyone else who tried to stop him.

The lady inside the carriage, amazed by it all and trembling at what she saw, directed her coachman to drive on a little way; and there from a distance she watched the deadly combat, in the course of which the Biscayan came down with a great blow on Don Quixote's shoulder, over the top of the latter's shield, and had not the knight been clad in armor, it would have split him to the waist.

Feeling the weight of this blow, Don Quixote cried out, "O lady of my soul, Dulcinea, flower of beauty, succor this your champion who out of gratitude for your many favors finds himself in so perilous a plight!" To utter these words, lay hold of his sword, cover himself with his buckler, and attack the Biscayan was but the work of a moment; for he was now resolved to risk everything upon a single stroke.

As he saw Don Quixote approaching with so dauntless a bearing, the Biscayan was well aware of his adversary's courage and forthwith determined to imitate the example thus set him. He kept himself protected with his cushion, but he was unable to get his she-mule to budge to one side or the other, for the beast, out of sheer exhaustion and being, moreover, unused to such childish play, was incapable of taking a single step. And so, then, as has been stated, Don Quixote was approaching the wary Biscayan, his sword raised on high and with the firm resolve of cleaving his enemy in two; and the

7. Knight, gentleman (Spanish).   8. An inversion of a proverbial phrase: "carrying the cat to the water."
9. A violent character in the romance *Amadis de Gaul.* His challenging phrase is the conventional opener of a fight.

Biscayan was awaiting the knight in the same posture, cushion in front of him and with uplifted sword. All the bystanders were trembling with suspense at what would happen as a result of the terrible blows that were threatened, and the lady in the coach and her maids were making a thousand vows and offerings to all the images and shrines in Spain, praying that God would save them all and the lady's squire from this great peril that confronted them.

But the unfortunate part of the matter is that at this very point the author of the history breaks off and leaves the battle pending, excusing himself upon the ground that he has been unable to find anything else in writing concerning the exploits of Don Quixote beyond those already set forth. It is true, on the other hand, that the second author[1] of this work could not bring himself to believe that so unusual a chronicle would have been consigned to oblivion, nor that the learned ones of La Mancha were possessed of so little curiosity as not to be able to discover in their archives or registry offices certain papers that have to do with this famous knight. Being convinced of this, he did not despair of coming upon the end of this pleasing story. * * *

CHAPTER 9

In which is concluded and brought to an end the stupendous battle between the gallant Biscayan and the valiant Knight of La Mancha.

* * * We left the valorous Biscayan and the famous Don Quixote with swords unsheathed and raised aloft, about to let fall furious slashing blows which, had they been delivered fairly and squarely, would at the very least have split them in two and laid them wide open from top to bottom like a pomegranate; and it was at this doubtful point that the pleasing chronicle came to a halt and broke off, without the author's informing us as to where the rest of it might be found.

I was deeply grieved by such a circumstance, and the pleasure I had had in reading so slight a portion was turned into annoyance as I thought of how difficult it would be to come upon the greater part which it seemed to me must still be missing. It appeared impossible and contrary to all good precedent that so worthy a knight should not have had some scribe to take upon himself the task of writing an account of these unheard-of exploits; for that was something that had happened to none of the knights-errant who, as the saying has it, had gone forth in quest of adventures, seeing that each of them had one or two chroniclers, as if ready at hand, who not only had set down their deeds, but had depicted their most trivial thoughts and amiable weaknesses, however well concealed they might be. The good knight of La Mancha surely could not have been so unfortunate as to have lacked what Platir and others like him had in abundance. And so I could not bring myself to believe that this gallant history could have remained thus lopped off and mutilated, and I could not but lay the blame upon the malignity of time, that devourer and consumer of all things, which must either have consumed it or kept it hidden.

On the other hand, I reflected that inasmuch as among the knight's books had been found such modern works as *The Disenchantments of Jealousy* and

---

1. Cervantes himself, adopting here—with tongue in cheek—a device used in the romances of chivalry to create suspense.

The Nymphs and Shepherds of Henares, his story likewise must be modern, and that even though it might not have been written down, it must remain in the memory of the good folk of his village and the surrounding ones. This thought left me somewhat confused and more than ever desirous of knowing the real and true story, the whole story, of the life and wondrous deeds of our famous Spaniard, Don Quixote, light and mirror of the chivalry of La Mancha, the first in our age and in these calamitous times to devote himself to the hardships and exercises of knight-errantry and to go about righting wrongs, succoring widows, and protecting damsels—damsels such as those who, mounted upon their palfreys and with riding-whip in hand, in full possession of their virginity, were in the habit of going from mountain to mountain and from valley to valley; for unless there were some villain, some rustic with an ax and hood, or some monstrous giant to force them, there were in times past maiden ladies who at the end of eighty years, during all which time they had not slept for a single day beneath a roof, would go to their graves as virginal as when their mothers had borne them.

If I speak of these things, it is for the reason that in this and in all other respects our gallant Quixote is deserving of constant memory and praise, and even I am not to be denied my share of it for my diligence and the labor to which I put myself in searching out the conclusion of this agreeable narrative; although if heaven, luck, and circumstance had not aided me, the world would have had to do without the pleasure and the pastime which anyone may enjoy who will read this work attentively for an hour or two. The manner in which it came about was as follows:

I was standing one day in the Alcaná, or market place, of Toledo when a lad came up to sell some old notebooks and other papers to a silk weaver who was there. As I am extremely fond of reading anything, even though it be but the scraps of paper in the streets, I followed my natural inclination and took one of the books, whereupon I at once perceived that it was written in characters which I recognized as Arabic. I recognized them, but reading them was another thing; and so I began looking around to see if there was any Spanish-speaking Moor near by who would be able to read them for me. It was not very hard to find such an interpreter, nor would it have been even if the tongue in question had been an older and a better one.[2] To make a long story short, chance brought a fellow my way; and when I told him what it was I wished and placed the book in his hands, he opened it in the middle and began reading and at once fell to laughing. When I asked him what the cause of his laughter was, he replied that it was a note which had been written in the margin.

I besought him to tell me the content of the note, and he, laughing still, went on, "As I told you, it is something in the margin here: 'This Dulcinea del Toboso, so often referred to, is said to have been the best hand at salting pigs of any woman in all La Mancha.' "

No sooner had I heard the name Dulcinea del Toboso than I was astonished and held in suspense, for at once the thought occurred to me that those notebooks must contain the history of Don Quixote. With this in mind I urged him to read me the title, and he proceeded to do so, turning the Arabic into Castilian upon the spot: *History of Don Quixote de la Mancha,*

2. I.e., Hebrew.

Written by Cid Hamete Benengeli[3] Arabic Historian. It was all I could do to conceal my satisfaction and, snatching them from the silk weaver, I bought from the lad all the papers and notebooks that he had for half a real; but if he had known or suspected how very much I wanted them, he might well have had more than six reales for them.

The Moor and I then betook ourselves to the cathedral cloister, where I requested him to translate for me into the Castilian tongue all the books that had to do with Don Quixote, adding nothing and subtracting nothing; and I offered him whatever payment he desired. He was content with two arrobas of raisins and two fanegas[4] of wheat and promised to translate them well and faithfully and with all dispatch. However, in order to facilitate matters, and also because I did not wish to let such a find as this out of my hands, I took the fellow home with me, where in a little more than a month and a half he translated the whole of the work just as you will find it set down here.

In the first of the books there was a very lifelike picture of the battle between Don Quixote and the Biscayan, the two being in precisely the same posture as described in the history, their swords upraised, the one covered by his buckler, the other with his cushion. As for the Biscayan's mule, you could see at the distance of a crossbow shot that it was one for hire. Beneath the Biscayan there was a rubric which read: "Don Sancho de Azpeitia," which must undoubtedly have been his name; while beneath the feet of Rocinante was another inscription: "Don Quixote." Rocinante was marvelously portrayed: so long and lank, so lean and flabby, so extremely consumptive-looking that one could well understand the justness and propriety with which the name of "hack" had been bestowed upon him.

Alongside Rocinante stood Sancho Panza, holding the halter of his ass, and below was the legend: "Sancho Zancas." The picture showed him with a big belly, a short body and long shanks, and that must have been where he got the names of Panza y Zancas[5] by which he is a number of times called in the course of the history. There are other small details that might be mentioned, but they are of little importance and have nothing to do with the truth of the story—and no story is bad so long as it is true.

If there is any objection to be raised against the veracity of the present one, it can be only that the author was an Arab, and that nation is known for its lying propensities; but even though they be our enemies, it may readily be understood that they would more likely have detracted from, rather than added to, the chronicle. So it seems to me, at any rate; for whenever he might and should deploy the resources of his pen in praise of so worthy a knight, the author appears to take pains to pass over the matter in silence; all of which in my opinion is ill done and ill conceived, for it should be the duty of historians to be exact, truthful, and dispassionate, and neither interest nor fear nor rancor nor affection should swerve them from the path of truth, whose mother is history, rival of time, depository of deeds, witness of the past, exemplar and adviser to the present, and the future's counselor. In this work, I am sure, will be found all that could be desired in the way of pleasant reading; and if it is lacking in any way, I maintain that this is the fault of that hound of an author rather than of the subject.

---

3. Citing some ancient chronicle as the author's source and authority is very much in the tradition of the romances. *Benengeli*: eggplant (Arabic).   4. About fifty pounds. *Two arrobas*: three bushels.
5. Paunch and Shanks (Spanish).

But to come to the point, the second part, according to the translation, began as follows:

As the two valorous and enraged combatants stood there, swords upraised and poised on high, it seemed from their bold mien as if they must surely be threatening heaven, earth, and hell itself. The first to let fall a blow was the choleric Biscayan, and he came down with such force and fury that, had not his sword been deflected in mid-air, that single stroke would have sufficed to put an end to this fearful combat and to all our knight's adventures at the same time; but fortune, which was reserving him for greater things, turned aside his adversary's blade in such a manner that, even though it fell upon his left shoulder, it did him no other damage than to strip him completely of his armor on that side, carrying with it a good part of his helmet along with half an ear, the headpiece clattering to the ground with a dreadful din, leaving its wearer in a sorry state.

Heaven help me! Who could properly describe the rage that now entered the heart of our hero of La Mancha as he saw himself treated in this fashion? It may merely be said that he once more reared himself in the stirrups, laid hold of his sword with both hands, and dealt the Biscayan such a blow, over the cushion and upon the head, that, even so good a defense proving useless, it was as if a mountain had fallen upon his enemy. The latter now began bleeding through the mouth, nose, and ears; he seemed about to fall from his mule, and would have fallen, no doubt, if he had not grasped the beast about the neck, but at that moment his feet slipped from the stirrups and his arms let go, and the mule, frightened by the terrible blow, began running across the plain, hurling its rider to the earth with a few quick plunges.

Don Quixote stood watching all this very calmly. When he saw his enemy fall, he leaped from his horse, ran over very nimbly, and thrust the point of his sword into the Biscayan's eyes, calling upon him at the same time to surrender or otherwise he would cut off his head. The Biscayan was so bewildered that he was unable to utter a single word in reply, and things would have gone badly with him, so blind was Don Quixote in his rage, if the ladies of the coach, who up to then had watched the struggle in dismay, had not come up to him at this point and begged him with many blandishments to do them the very great favor of sparing their squire's life.

To which Don Quixote replied with much haughtiness and dignity, "Most certainly, lovely ladies, I shall be very happy to do that which you ask of me, but upon one conditon and understanding, and that is that this knight promise me that he will go to El Toboso and present himself in my behalf before Doña Dulcinea, in order that she may do with him as she may see fit."

Trembling and disconsolate, the ladies did not pause to discuss Don Quixote's request, but without so much as inquiring who Dulcinea might be they promised him that the squire would fulfill that which was commanded of him.

"Very well, then, trusting in your word, I will do him no further harm, even though he has well deserved it."

CHAPTER 10

Of the pleasing conversation that took place between Don Quixote and Sancho Panza, his squire.

By this time Sancho Panza had got to his feet, somewhat the worse for wear as the result of the treatment he had received from the friars' lads. He had been watching the battle attentively and praying God in his heart to give the victory to his master, Don Quixote, in order that he, Sancho, might gain some island where he could go to be governor as had been promised him. Seeing now that the combat was over and the knight was returning to mount Rocinante once more, he went up to hold the stirrup for him; but first he fell on his knees in front of him and, taking his hand, kissed it and said, "May your Grace be pleased, Señor Don Quixote, to grant me the governorship of that island which you have won in this deadly affray; for however large it may be, I feel that I am indeed capable of governing it as well as any man in this world has ever done."

To which Don Quixote replied, "Be advised, brother Sancho, that this adventure and other similar ones have nothing to do with islands; they are affairs of the crossroads in which one gains nothing more than a broken head or an ear the less. Be patient, for there will be others which will not only make you a governor, but more than that."

Sancho thanked him very much and, kissing his hand again and the skirt of his cuirass, he assisted him up on Rocinante's back, after which the squire bestraddled his own mount and started jogging along behind his master, who was now going at a good clip. Without pausing for any further converse with those in the coach, the knight made for a near-by wood, with Sancho following as fast as his beast could trot; but Rocinante was making such speed that the ass and its rider were left behind, and it was necessary to call out to Don Quixote to pull up and wait for them. He did so, reining in Rocinante until the weary Sancho had drawn abreast of him.

"It strikes me, sir," said the squire as he reached his master's side, "that it would be better for us to take refuge in some church; for in view of the way you have treated that one with whom you were fighting, it would be small wonder if they did not lay the matter before the Holy Brotherhood[6] and have us arrested; and faith, if they do that, we shall have to sweat a-plenty before we come out of jail."

"Be quiet," said Don Quixote. "And where have you ever seen, or read of, a knight being brought to justice no matter how many homicides he might have committed?"

"I know nothing about omecils,"[7] replied Sancho, "nor ever in my life did I bear one to anybody; all I know is that the Holy Brotherhood has something to say about those who go around fighting on the highway, and I want nothing of it."

"Do not let it worry you," said Don Quixote, "for I will rescue you from the hands of the Chaldeans, not to speak of the Brotherhood. But answer me upon your life: have you ever seen a more valorous knight than I on all

---

6. A tribunal instituted by Ferdinand and Isabella at the end of the 15th century to punish highway robbers.
7. In Spanish a wordplay on *homecidio-omecillo*. Not to bear an *omecillo* to anybody means not to bear a grudge, and good-natured Sancho does not.

the known face of the earth? Have you ever read in the histories of any other who had more mettle in the attack, more perseverance in sustaining it, more dexterity in wounding his enemy, or more skill in overthrowing him?"

"The truth is," said Sancho, "I have never read any history whatsoever, for I do not know how to read or write; but what I would wager is that in all the days of my life I have never served a more courageous master than your Grace; I only hope your courage is not paid for in the place that I have mentioned. What I would suggest is that your Grace allow me to do something for that ear, for there is much blood coming from it, and I have here in my saddlebags some lint and a little white ointment."

"We could well dispense with all that," said Don Quixote, "if only I had remembered to bring along a vial of Fierabrás's[8] balm, a single drop of which saves time and medicines."

"What vial and what balm is that?" inquired Sancho Panza.

"It is a balm the receipt[9] for which I know by heart; with it one need have no fear of death nor think of dying from any wound. I shall make some of it and give it to you; and thereafter, whenever in any battle you see my body cut in two—as very often happens—all that is necessary is for you to take the part that lies on the ground, before the blood has congealed, and fit it very neatly and with great nicety upon the other part that remains in the saddle, taking care to adjust it evenly and exactly. Then you will give me but a couple of swallows of the balm of which I have told you, and you will see me sounder than an apple in no time at all."

"If that is so," said Panza, "I herewith renounce the governorship of the island you promised me and ask nothing other in payment of my many and faithful services than that your Grace give me the receipt for this wonderful potion, for I am sure that it would be worth more than two reales the ounce anywhere, and that is all I need for a life of ease and honor. But may I be so bold as to ask how much it costs to make it?"

"For less than three reales you can make something like six quarts," Don Quixote told him.

"Sinner that I am!" exclaimed Sancho. "Then why does your Grace not make some at once and teach me also?"

"Hush, my friend," said the knight, "I mean to teach you greater secrets than that and do you greater favors; but, for the present, let us look after this ear of mine, for it is hurting me more than I like."

Sancho thereupon took the lint and the ointment from his saddlebags; but when Don Quixote caught a glimpse of his helmet, he almost went out of his mind and, laying his hand upon his sword and lifting his eyes heavenward, he cried, "I make a vow to the Creator of all things and to the four holy Gospels in all their fullness of meaning that I will lead from now on the life that the great Marquis of Mantua did after he had sworn to avenge the death of his nephew Baldwin: not to eat bread of a tablecloth, not to embrace his wife, and other things which, although I am unable to recall them, we will look upon as understood—all this until I shall have wreaked an utter vengeance upon the one who has perpetrated such an outrage upon me."

"But let me remind your Grace," said Sancho when he heard these words, "that if the knight fulfills that which was commanded of him, by going to

---

8. A giant Saracen healer in the medieval epics of the Twelve Peers (see n. 7, p. 2698).   9. Recipe.

present himself before my lady Dulcinea del Toboso, then he will have paid his debt to you and merits no further punishment at your hands, unless it be for some fresh offense."

"You have spoken very well and to the point," said Don Quixote, "and so I annul the vow I have just made insofar as it has to do with any further vengeance, but I make it and confirm it anew so far as leading the life of which I have spoken is concerned, until such time as I shall have obtained by force of arms from some other knight another headpiece as good as this. And do not think, Sancho, that I am making smoke out of straw; there is one whom I well may imitate in this matter, for the same thing happened in all literalness in the case of Mambrino's helmet[1] which cost Sacripante so dear."

"I wish," said Sancho, "that your Grace would send all such oaths to the devil, for they are very bad for the health and harmful for the conscience as well. Tell me, please; supposing that for many days to come we meet no man wearing a helmet, then what are we to do? Must you still keep your vow in spite of all the inconveniences and discomforts, such as sleeping with your clothes on, not sleeping in any town, and a thousand other penances contained in the oath of that old madman of a Marquis of Mantua, an oath which you would now revive? Mark you, sir, along all these roads you meet no men of arms but only muleteers and carters, who not only do not wear helmets but quite likely have never heard tell of them in all their livelong days."

"In that you are wrong," said Don Quixote, "for we shall not be at these crossroads for the space of two hours before we shall see more men of arms than came to Albraca to win the fair Angélica."[2] "Very well, then," said Sancho, "so be it, and pray God that all turns out for the best so that I may at last win that island that is costing me so dearly, and then let me die."

"I have already told you, Sancho, that you are to give no thought to that; should the island fail, there is the kingdom of Denmark or that of Sobradisa, which would fit you like a ring on your finger, and you ought, moreover, to be happy to be on *terra firma*.[3] But let us leave all this for some other time, while you look and see if you have something in those saddlebags for us to eat, after which we will go in search of some castle where we may lodge for the night and prepare that balm of which I was telling you, for I swear to God that my ear is paining me greatly."

"I have here an onion, a little cheese, and a few crusts of bread," said Sancho, "but they are not victuals fit for a valiant knight like your grace."

"How little you know about it!" replied Don Quixote. "I would inform you, Sancho, that it is a point of honor with knights-errant to go for a month at a time without eating, and when they do eat, it is whatever may be at hand. You would certainly know that if you had read the histories as I have. There are many of them, and in none have I found any mention of knights eating unless it was by chance or at some sumptuous banquet that was tendered them; on other days they fasted. And even though it is well understood that, being men like us, they could not go without food entirely, any more than they could fail to satisfy the other necessities of nature, nevertheless, since they spent the greater part of their lives in forest and desert places without

---

1. The enchanted helmet of Mambrino, a Moorish king, is stolen by Rinaldo in Bioardo's *Roland in Love*.
2. Another allusion to *Roland in Love*.   3. Solid earth (Latin, literal trans.); here Firm Island, an imaginary final destination for the squires of knights-errant. Sobradisa is an imaginary realm.

any cook to prepare their meals, their diet ordinarily consisted of rustic viands such as those that you now offer me. And so, Sancho my friend, do not be grieved at that which pleases me, nor seek to make the world over, nor to unhinge the institution of knight-errantry."

"Pardon me, your Grace," said Sancho, "but seeing that, as I have told you I do not know how to read or write, I am consequently not familiar with the rules of the knightly calling. Hereafter, I will stuff my saddlebags with all manner of dried fruit for your Grace, but inasmuch as I am not a knight, I shall lay in for myself a stock of fowls and other more substantial fare."

"I am not saying, Sancho, that it is incumbent upon knights-errant to eat only those fruits of which you speak; what I am saying is that their ordinary sustenance should consist of fruit and a few herbs such as are to be found in the fields and with which they are well acquainted, as am I myself."

"It is a good thing," said Sancho, "to know those herbs, for, so far as I can see, we are going to have need of that knowledge one of these days."

With this, he brought out the articles he had mentioned, and the two of them ate in peace, and most companionably. Being desirous, however, of seeking a lodging for the night, they did not tarry long over their humble and unsavory repast. They then mounted and made what haste they could that they might arrive at a shelter before nightfall but the sun failed them, and with it went the hope of attaining their wish. As the day ended they found themselves beside some goatherds' huts, and they accordingly decided to spend the night there. Sancho was as much disappointed at their not having reached a town as his master was content with sleeping under the open sky; for it seemed to Don Quixote that every time this happened it merely provided him with yet another opportunity to establish his claim to the title of knight-errant.

[Fighting the Sheep]

CHAPTER 18

In which is set forth the conversation that Sancho Panza had with his master, Don Quixote, along with other adventures deserving of record.

* * * Don Quixote caught sight down the road of a large cloud of dust that was drawing nearer.

"This, O Sancho," he said, turning to his squire, "is the day when you shall see the boon that fate has in store for me; this, I repeat, is the day when, as well as on any other, shall be displayed the valor of my good right arm. On this day I shall perform deeds that will be written down in the book of fame for all centuries to come. Do you see that dust cloud rising there, Sancho? That is the dust stirred up by a vast army marching in this direction and composed of many nations."

"At that rate," said Sancho, "there must be two of them, for there is another one just like it on the other side."

Don Quixote turned to look and saw that this was so. He was overjoyed by the thought that these were indeed two armies about to meet and clash in the middle of the broad plain; for at every hour and every moment his imagination was filled with battles, enchantments, nonsensical adventures, tales of love, amorous challenges, and the like, such as he had read of in the books of chivalry, and every word he uttered, every thought that crossed his mind, every act he performed, had to do with such things as these. The dust clouds he had sighted were raised by two large droves of sheep coming along the road in opposite directions, which by reason of the dust were not visible until they were close at hand, but Don Quixote insisted so earnestly that they were armies that Sancho came to believe it.

"Sir," he said, "what are we to do?"

"What are we to do?" echoed his master. "Favor and aid the weak and needy. I would inform you, Sancho, that the one coming toward us is led and commanded by the great emperor Alifanfarón, lord of the great isle of Trapobana. This other one at my back is that of his enemy, the king of the Garamantas, Pentapolín of the Rolled-up Sleeve, for he always goes into battle with his right arm bare."

"But why are they such enemies?" Sancho asked.

"Because," said Don Quixote, "this Alifanfarón is a terrible pagan and in love with Pentapolín's daughter, who is a very beautiful and gracious lady and a Christian, for which reason her father does not wish to give her to the pagan king unless the latter first abjures the law of the false prophet, Mohammed, and adopts the faith that is Pentapolín's own."

"Then, by my beard," said Sancho, "if Pentapolín isn't right, and I am going to aid him all I can."

"In that," said Don Quixote, "you will only be doing your duty; for to engage in battles of this sort you need not have been dubbed a knight."

"I can understand that," said Sancho, "but where are we going to put this ass so that we will be certain of finding him after the fray is over? As for going into battle on such a mount, I do not think that has been done up to now."

"That is true enough," said Don Quixote. "What you had best do with him is to turn him loose and run the risk of losing him; for after we emerge the victors we shall have so many horses that even Rocinante will be in danger of being exchanged for another. But listen closely to what I am about to tell you, for I wish to give you an account of the principal knights that are accompanying these two armies; and in order that you may be the better able to see and take note of them, let us retire to that hillock over there which will afford us a very good view."

They then stationed themselves upon a slight elevation from which they would have been able to see very well the two droves of sheep that Don Quixote took to be armies if it had not been for the blinding clouds of dust. In spite of this, however, the worthy gentleman contrived to behold in his imagination what he did not see and what did not exist in reality.

Raising his voice, he went on to explain, "That knight in the gilded armor that you see there, bearing upon his shield a crowned lion crouched at the feet of a damsel, is the valiant Laurcalco, lord of the Silver Bridge; the other with the golden flowers on his armor, and on his shield three crowns argent on an azure field, is the dread Micocolembo, grand duke of Quirocia. And that one on Micocolembo's right hand, with the limbs of a giant, is the ever undaunted Brandabarbarán de Boliche, lord of the three Arabias. He goes armored in a serpent's skin and has for shield a door which, so report has it, is one of those from the temple that Samson pulled down, that time when he avenged himself on his enemies with his own death.

"But turn your eyes in this direction, and you will behold at the head of the other army the ever victorious, never vanquished Timonel de Carcajona, prince of New Biscay, who comes with quartered arms—azure, vert, argent, and or—and who has upon his shield a cat or on a field tawny, with the inscription *Miau,* which is the beginning of his lady's name; for she, so it is said, is the peerless Miulina, daughter of Alfeñquén, duke of Algarve. And that one over there, who weights down and presses the loins of that powerful charger, in a suit of snow-white armor with a white shield that bears no device whatever—he is a novice knight of the French nation, called Pierres Papin, lord of the baronies of Utrique. As for him you see digging his iron spurs into the flanks of that fleet-footed zebra courser and whose arms are vairs azure, he is the mighty duke of Nervia, Espartafilardo of the Wood, who has for device upon his shield an asparagus plant with a motto in Castilian that says '*Rastrea mi suerte.*' "[1]

In this manner he went on naming any number of imaginary knights on either side, describing on the spur of the moment their arms, colors, devices, and mottoes; for he was completely carried away by his imagination and by this unheard-of madness that had laid hold of him.

Without pausing, he went on, "This squadron in front of us is composed of men of various nations. There are those who drink the sweet waters of the famous Xanthus; woodsmen who tread the Massilian plain; those that sift the fine gold nuggets of Arabia Felix; those that are so fortunate as to dwell on the banks of the clear-running Thermodon, famed for their coolness; those who in many and diverse ways drain the golden Pactolus; Numidians, whose word is never to be trusted; Persians, with their famous bows and arrows; Medes and Parthians, who fight as they flee; Scythians, as cruel as they are fair of skin; Ethiopians, with their pierced lips; and an infinite number of other nationalities whose visages I see and recognize although I cannot recall their names.

"In this other squadron come those that drink from the crystal currents of the olive-bearing Betis; those that smooth and polish their faces with the liquid of the ever rich and gilded Tagus; those that enjoy the beneficial waters of the divine Genil; those that roam the Tartessian plains with their abundant pasturage; those that disport themselves in the Elysian meadows of Jerez; the men of La Mancha, rich and crowned with golden ears of corn; others clad in iron garments, ancient relics of the Gothic race; those that bathe in the Pisuerga, noted for the mildness of its current; those that feed their herds in the wide-spreading pasture lands along the banks of the winding Guadiana, celebrated for its underground course;[2] those that shiver from the cold of the wooded Pyrenees or dwell amid the white peaks of the lofty Apennines—in short, all those whom Europe holds within its girth."

So help me God! How many provinces, how many nations did he not mention by name, giving to each one with marvelous readiness its proper attributes; for he was wholly absorbed and filled to the brim with what he had read in those lying books of his! Sancho Panza hung on his words, saying

1. Probably a pun on *rastrear,* "to skim along close to the ground." The meaning of the motto may be either "On Fortunes's track" or "My Fortune creeps."   2. The Guadiana does run underground part of the way through La Mancha.

nothing, merely turning his head from time to time to have a look at those knights and giants that his master was pointing out to him; but he was unable to discover any of them.

"Sir," he said, "may I go to the devil if I see a single man, giant, or knight of all those that your Grace is talking about. Who knows? Maybe it is another spell, like last night."[3]

"How can you say that?" replied Don Quixote. "Can you not hear the neighing of the horses, the sound of trumpets, the roll of drums?"

"I hear nothing," said Sancho, "except the bleating of sheep."

And this, of course, was the truth; for the flocks were drawing near.

"The trouble is, Sancho," said Don Quixote, "you are so afraid that you cannot see or hear properly; for one of the effects of fear is to disturb the senses and cause things to appear other than what they are. If you are so craven as all that, go off to one side and leave me alone, and I without your help will assure the victory to that side to which I lend my aid."

Saying this, he put spurs to Rocinante and, with his lance at rest, darted down the hillside like a flash of lightning.

As he did so, Sancho called after him, "Come back, your Grace, Señor Don Quixote; I vow to God those are sheep that you are charging. Come back! O wretched father that bore me! What madness is this? Look you, there are no giants, nor knights, nor cats, nor shields either quartered or whole, nor vairs azure or bedeviled. What is this you are doing, O sinner that I am in God's sight?"

But all this did not cause Don Quixote to turn back. Instead, he rode on, crying out at the top of his voice, "Ho, knights, those of you who follow and fight under the banners of the valiant Pentapolín of the Rolled-up Sleeve; follow me, all of you, and you shall see how easily I give you revenge on your enemy, Alifanfarón of Trapobana."

With these words he charged into the middle of the flock of sheep and began spearing at them with as much courage and boldness as if they had been his mortal enemies. The shepherds and herdsmen who were with the animals called to him to stop; but seeing it was no use, they unloosed their slings and saluted his ears with stones as big as your fist.

Don Quixote paid no attention to the missiles and, dashing about here and there, kept crying, "Where are you, haughty Alifanfarón? Come out to me; for here is a solitary knight who desires in single combat to test your strength and deprive you of your life, as a punishment for that which you have done to the valorous Pentapolín Garamanta."

At that instant a pebble from the brook struck him in the side and buried a couple of ribs in his body. Believing himself dead or badly wounded, and remembering his potion, he took out his vial, placed it to his mouth, and began to swallow the balm; but before he had had what he thought was enough, there came another almond, which struck him in the hand, crushing the tin vial and carrying away with it a couple of grinders from his mouth, as well as badly mashing two of his fingers. As a result of these blows the poor knight tumbled from his horse. Believing that they had killed him, the shepherds hastily collected their flock and, picking up the dead beasts, of

---

3. The inn where they had spent the previous night had been pronounced by Don Quixote to be an enchanted castle.

which there were more than seven, they went off down the road without more ado.

Sancho all this time was standing on the slope observing the insane things that his master was doing; and as he plucked savagely at his beard he cursed the hour and minute when luck had brought them together. But when he saw him lying there on the ground and perceived that the shepherds were gone, he went down the hill and came up to him, finding him in very bad shape though not unconscious.

"Didn't I tell you, Señor Don Quixote," he said, "that you should come back, that those were not armies you were charging but flocks of sheep?"

"This," said Don Quixote, "is the work of that thieving magician, my enemy, who thus counterfeits things and causes them to disappear. You must know, Sancho, that it is very easy for them to make us assume any appearance that they choose; and so it is that malign one who persecutes me, envious of the glory he saw me about to achieve in this battle, changed the squadrons of the foe into flocks of sheep. If you do not believe me, I beseech you on my life to do one thing for me, that you may be undeceived and discover for yourself that what I say is true. Mount your ass and follow them quietly, and when you have gone a short way from here, you will see them become their former selves once more; they will no longer be sheep but men exactly as I described them to you in the first place. But do not go now, for I need your kind assistance; come over here and have a look and tell me how many grinders are missing, for it feels as if I did not have a single one left."

["To Right Wrongs and Come to the Aid of the Wretched"]

CHAPTER 22

Of how Don Quixote freed many unfortunate ones who, much against their will, were being taken where they did not wish to go.

Cid Hamete Benengeli, the Arabic and Manchegan;[1] author, in the course of this most grave, high-sounding, minute, delightful, and imaginative history, informs us that, following the remarks that were exchanged between Don Quixote de la Mancha and Sancho Panza, his squire, . . . the knight looked up and saw coming toward them down the road which they were following a dozen or so men on foot, strung together by their necks like beads on an iron chain and all of them wearing handcuffs. They were accompanied by two men on horseback and two on foot, the former carrying wheel-lock muskets while the other two were armed with swords and javelins.

"That," said Sancho as soon as he saw them, "is a chain of galley slaves, people on their way to the galleys where by order of the king they are forced to labor."

"What do you mean by 'forced'?" asked Don Quixote. "Is it possible that the king uses force on anyone?"

"I did not say that," replied Sancho. "What I did say was that these are

---

1. Of La Mancha.

folks who have been condemned for their crimes to forced labor in the galleys for his Majesty the King."

"The short of it is," said the knight, "whichever way you put it, these people are being taken there by force and not of their own free will."

"That is the way it is," said Sancho.

"Well, in that case," said his master, "now is the time for me to fulfill the duties of my calling, which is to right wrongs and come to the aid of the wretched."

"But take note, your Grace," said Sancho, "that justice, that is to say, the king himself, is not using any force upon, or doing any wrong to, people like these, but is merely punishing them for the crimes they have committed."

The chain of galley slaves had come up to them by this time, whereupon Don Quixote very courteously requested the guards to inform him of the reason or reasons why they were conducting these people in such a manner as this. One of the men on horseback then replied that the men were prisoners who had been condemned by his Majesty to serve in the galleys, whither they were bound, and that was all there was to be said about it and all that he, Don Quixote, need know.

"Nevertheless," said the latter, "I should like to inquire of each one of them, individually, the cause of his misfortune." And he went on speaking so very politely in an effort to persuade them to tell him what he wanted to know that the other mounted guard finally said, "Although we have here the record and certificate of sentence of each one of these wretches, we have not the time to get them out and read them to you; and so your Grace may come over and ask the prisoners themselves, and they will tell you if they choose, and you may be sure that they will, for these fellows take a delight in their knavish exploits and in boasting of them afterward."

With this permission, even though he would have done so if it had not been granted him, Don Quixote went up to the chain of prisoners and asked the first whom he encountered what sins had brought him to so sorry a plight. The man replied that it was for being a lover that he found himself in that line.

"For that and nothing more?" said Don Quixote. "And do they, then, send lovers to the galleys? If so, I should have been rowing there long ago."

"But it was not the kind of love that your Grace has in mind," the prisoner went on. "I loved a wash basket full of white linen so well and hugged it so tightly that, if they had not taken it away from me by force, I would never of my own choice have let go of it to this very minute. I was caught in the act, there was no need to torture me, the case was soon disposed of, and they supplied me with a hundred lashes across the shoulders and, in addition, a three-year stretch in the *gurapas,* and that's all there is to tell."

"What are *gurapas?*" asked Don Quixote.

"*Gurapas* are the galleys," replied the prisoner. He was a lad of around twenty-four and stated that he was a native of Piedrahita.

The knight then put the same question to a second man, who appeared to be very downcast and melancholy and did not have a word to say. The first man answered for him.

"This one, sir," he said, "is going as a canary—I mean, as a musician and singer."

"How is that?" Don Quixote wanted to know. "Do musicians and singers go to the galleys too?"

"Yes, sir; and there is nothing worse than singing when you're in trouble."

"On the contrary," said Don Quixote, "I have heard it said that he who sings frightens away his sorrows."

"It is just the opposite," said the prisoner; "for he who sings once weeps all his life long."

"I do not understand," said the knight.

One of the guards then explained. "Sir Knight, with this *non sancta*[2] tribe, to sing when you're in trouble means to confess under torture. This singer was put to the torture and confessed his crime, which was that of being a *cuatrero*, or cattle thief, and as a result of his confession he was condemned to six years in the galleys in addition to two hundred lashes which he took on his shoulders; and so it is he is always downcast and moody, for the other thieves, those back where he came from and the ones here, mistreat, snub, ridicule, and despise him for having confessed and for not having had the courage to deny his guilt. They are in the habit of saying that the word *no* has the same number of letters as the word *sí*, and that a culprit is in luck when his life or death depends on his own tongue and not that of witnesses or upon evidence; and, in my opinion, they are not very far wrong."

"And I," said Don Quixote, "feel the same way about it." He then went on to a third prisoner and repeated his question.

The fellow answered at once, quite unconcernedly. "I'm going to my ladies, the *gurapas*, for five years, for the lack of five ducats."

"I would gladly give twenty," said Don Quixote, "to get you out of this."

"That," said the prisoner, "reminds me of the man in the middle of the ocean who has money and is dying of hunger because there is no place to buy what he needs. I say this for the reason that if I had had, at the right time, those twenty ducats your Grace is now offering me, I'd have greased the notary's quill and freshened up the attorney's wit with them, and I'd now be living in the middle of Zocodover Square in Toledo instead of being here on this highway coupled like a greyhound. But God is great; patience, and that's enough of it."

Don Quixote went on to a fourth prisoner, a venerable-looking old fellow with a white beard that fell over his bosom. When asked how he came to be there, this one began weeping and made no reply, but a fifth comrade spoke up in his behalf.

"This worthy man," he said, "is on his way to the galleys after having made the usual rounds clad in a robe of state and on horseback."[3]

"That means, I take it," said Sancho, "that he has been put to shame in public."

"That is it," said the prisoner, "and the offense for which he is being punished is that of having been an ear broker, or, better, a body broker. By that I mean to say, in short, that the gentleman is a pimp, and besides, he has his points as a sorcerer."

"If that point had not been thrown in," said Don Quixote, "he would not deserve, for merely being a pimp, to have to row in the galleys, but rather

---

2. Unholy (Latin).   3. After having been flogged in public, with all the ceremony that accompanied that punishment.

should be the general and give orders there. For the office of pimp is not an indifferent one; it is a function to be performed by persons of discretion and is most necessary in a well-ordered state; it is a profession that should be followed only by the wellborn, and there should, moreover, be a supervisor or examiner as in the case of other offices, and the number of practitioners should be fixed by law as is done with brokers on the exchange. In that way many evils would be averted that arise when this office is filled and this calling practiced by stupid folk and those with little sense, such as silly women and pages or mountebanks with few years and less experience to their credit, who, on the most pressing occasions, when it is necessary to use one's wits, let the crumbs freeze between their hand and their mouth and do not know which is their right hand and which is the left.

"I would go on and give reasons why it is fitting to choose carefully those who are to fulfill so necessary a state function, but this is not the place for it. One of these days I will speak of the matter to someone who is able to do something about it. I will say here only that the pain I felt at seeing those white hairs and this venerable countenance in such a plight, and all for his having been a pimp, has been offset for me by the additional information you have given me, to the effect that he is a sorcerer as well; for I am convinced that there are no sorcerers in the world who can move and compel the will, as some simple-minded persons think, but that our will is free and no herb or charm can force it.[4] All that certain foolish women and cunning tricksters do is to compound a few mixtures and poisons with which they deprive men of their senses while pretending that they have the power to make them loved, although, as I have just said, one cannot affect another's will in that manner."

"That is so," said the worthy old man; "but the truth is, sir, I am not guilty on the sorcery charge. As for being a pimp, that is something I cannot deny. I never thought there was any harm in it, however, my only desire being that everyone should enjoy himself and live in peace and quiet, without any quarrels or troubles. But these good intentions on my part cannot prevent me from going where I do not want to go, to a place from which I do not expect to return; for my years are heavy upon me and an affection of the urine that I have will not give me a moment's rest."

With this, he began weeping once more, and Sancho was so touched by it that he took a four-real piece from his bosom and gave it to him as an act of charity.

Don Quixote then went on and asked another what his offense was. The fellow answered him, not with less, but with much more, briskness than the preceding one had shown.

"I am here," he said, "for the reason that I carried a joke too far with a couple of cousins-german of mine and a couple of others who were not mine, and I ended by jesting with all of them to such an extent that the devil himself would never be able to straighten out the relationship. They proved everything on me, there was no one to show me favor, I had no money, I came near swinging for it, they sentenced me to the galleys for six years, and I accepted the sentence as the punishment that was due me. I am young yet,

---

4. Here Don Quixote despises charms and love potions, although often elsewhere, in his own vision of himself as a knight-errant, he accepts enchantments and spells as part of his world of fantasy.

and if I live long enough, everything will come out all right. If, Sir Knight, your Grace has anything with which to aid these poor creatures that you see before you, God will reward you in Heaven, and we here on earth will make it a point to ask God in our prayers to grant you long life and good health, as long and as good as your amiable presence deserves."

This man was dressed as a student, and one of the guards told Don Quixote that he was a great talker and a very fine Latinist.

Back of these came a man around thirty years of age and of very good appearance, except that when he looked at you his eyes were seen to be a little crossed. He was shackled in a different manner from the others, for he dragged behind a chain so huge that it was wrapped all around his body, with two rings at the throat, one of which was attached to the chain while the other was fastened to what is known as a keep-friend or friend's foot, from which two irons hung down to his waist, ending in handcuffs secured by a heavy padlock in such a manner that he could neither raise his hands to his mouth nor lower his head to reach his hands.

When Don Quixote asked why this man was so much more heavily chained than the others, the guard replied that it was because he had more crimes against him than all the others put together, and he was so bold and cunning that, even though they had him chained like this, they were by no means sure of him but feared that he might escape from them.

"What crimes could he have committed," asked the knight, "if he has merited a punishment no greater than that of being sent to the galleys?"

"He is being sent there for ten years," replied the guard, "and that is equivalent to civil death. I need tell you no more than that this good man is the famous Ginés de Pasamonte, otherwise known as Ginesillo de Parapilla."

"Señor Commissary," spoke up the prisoner at this point, "go easy there and let us not be so free with names and surnames. My just name is Ginés and not Ginesillo; and Pasamonte, not Parapilla as you make it out to be, is my family name. Let each one mind his own affairs and he will have his hands full."

"Speak a little more respectfully, you big thief, you," said the commissary, "unless you want me to make you be quiet in a way you won't like."

"Man goes as God pleases, that is plain to be seen," replied the galley slave, "but someday someone will know whether my name is Ginesillo de Parapilla or not."

"But, you liar, isn't that what they call you?"

"Yes," said Ginés, "they do call me that; but I'll put a stop to it, or else I'll skin their you-know-what. And you, sir, if you have anything to give us, give it and may God go with you, for I am tired of all this prying into other people's lives. If you want to know anything about my life, know that I am Ginés de Pasamonte whose life story has been written down by these fingers that you see here."

"He speaks the truth," said the commissary, "for he has himself written his story, as big as you please, and has left the book in the prison, having pawned it for two hundred reales."

"And I mean to redeem it," said Ginés, "even if it costs me two hundred ducats."

"Is it as good as that?" inquired Don Quixote.

"It is so good," replied Ginés, "that it will cast into the shade *Lazarillo de*

Tormes[5] and all others of that sort that have been or will be written. What I would tell you is that it deals with facts, and facts so interesting and amusing that no lies could equal them."

"And what is the title of the book?" asked Don Quixote.

"The Life of Ginés de Pasamonte."

"Is it finished?"

"How could it be finished," said Ginés, "when my life is not finished as yet? What I have written thus far is an account of what happened to me from the time I was born up to the last time that they sent me to the galleys."

"Then you have been there before?"

"In the service of God and the king I was there four years, and I know what the biscuit and the cowhide are like. I don't mind going very much, for there I will have a chance to finish my book. I still have many things to say, and in the Spanish galleys I shall have all the leisure that I need, though I don't need much, since I know by heart what it is I want to write."

"You seem to be a clever fellow," said Don Quixote.

"And an unfortunate one," said Ginés; "for misfortunes always pursue men of genius."

"They pursue rogues," said the commissary.

"I have told you to go easy, Señor Commissary," said Pasamonte, "for their Lordships did not give you that staff in order that you might mistreat us poor devils with it, but they intended that you should guide and conduct us in accordance with his Majesty's command. Otherwise, by the life of—But enough. It may be that someday the stains made in the inn will come out in the wash. Meanwhile, let everyone hold his tongue, behave well, and speak better, and let us be on our way. We've had enough of this foolishness."

At this point the commissary raised his staff as if to let Pasamonte have it in answer to his threats, but Don Quixote placed himself between them and begged the officer not to abuse the man; for it was not to be wondered at if one who had his hands so bound should be a trifle free with his tongue. With this, he turned and addressed them all.

"From all that you have told me, my dearest brothers," he said, "one thing stands out clearly for me, and that is the fact that, even though it is a punishment for offenses which you have committed, the penalty you are about to pay is not greatly to your liking and you are going to the galleys very much against your own will and desire. It may be that the lack of spirit which one of you displayed under torture, the lack of money on the part of another, the lack of influential friends, or, finally, warped judgment on the part of the magistrate, was the thing that led to your downfall; and, as a result, justice was not done you. All of which presents itself to my mind in such a fashion that I am at this moment engaged in trying to persuade and even force myself to show you what the purpose was for which Heaven sent me into this world, why it was it led me to adopt the calling of knighthood which I profess and take the knightly vow to favor the needy and aid those who are oppressed by the powerful.

"However, knowing as I do that it is not the part of prudence to do by foul means what can be accomplished by fair ones, I propose to ask these gentlemen, your guards, and the commissary to be so good as to unshackle you

---

5. A picaresque or rogue novel, published anonymously about the middle of the 15th century.

and permit you to go in peace. There will be no dearth of others to serve his Majesty under more propitious circumstances; and it does not appear to me to be just to make slaves of those whom God created as free men. What is more, gentlemen of the guard, these poor fellows have committed no offense against you. Up there, each of us will have to answer for his own sins; for God in Heaven will not fail to punish the evil and reward the good; and it is not good for self-respecting men to be executioners of their fellow-men in something that does not concern them. And so, I ask this of you, gently and quietly, in order that, if you comply with my request, I shall have reason to thank you; and if you do not do so of your own accord, then this lance and this sword and the valor of my arm shall compel you to do it by force."

"A fine lot of foolishness!" exclaimed the commissary. "So he comes out at last with this nonsense! He would have us let the prisoners of the king go free, as if we had any authority to do so or he any right to command it! Be on your way, sir, at once; straighten that basin that you have on your head, and do not go looking for three feet on a cat."[6]

"You," replied Don Quixote, "are the cat and the rat and the rascal!" And, saying this, he charged the commissary so quickly that the latter had no chance to defend himself but fell to the ground badly wounded by the lance blow. The other guards were astounded by this unexpected occurrence; but, recovering their self-possession, those on horseback drew their swords, those on foot leveled their javelins, and all bore down on Don Quixote, who stood waiting for them very calmly. Things undoubtedly would have gone badly for him if the galley slaves, seeing an opportunity to gain their freedom, had not succeeded in breaking the chain that linked them together. Such was the confusion that the guards, now running to fall upon the prisoners and now attacking Don Quixote, who in turn was attacking them, accomplished nothing that was of any use.

Sancho for his part aided Ginés de Pasamonte to free himself, and that individual was the first to drop his chains and leap out onto the field, where, attacking the fallen commissary, he took away that officer's sword and musket; and as he stood there, aiming first at one and then at another, though without firing, the plain was soon cleared of guards, for they had taken to their heels, fleeing at once Pasamonte's weapon and the stones which the galley slaves, freed now, were hurling at them. Sancho, meanwhile, was very much disturbed over this unfortunate event, as he felt sure that the fugitives would report the matter to the Holy Brotherhood, which, to the ringing of the alarm bell, would come out to search for the guilty parties. He said as much to his master, telling him that they should leave at once and go into hiding in the near-by mountains.

"That is all very well," said Don Quixote, "but I know what had best be done now." He then summoned all the prisoners, who, running riot, had by this time despoiled the commissary of everything that he had, down to his skin, and as they gathered around to hear what he had to say, he addressed them as follows:

"It is fitting that those who are wellborn should give thanks for the benefits they have received, and one of the sins with which God is most offended is that of ingratitude. I say this, gentlemen, for the reason that you have seen

6. Looking for the impossible ("five feet" is the more usual form of the proverb).

and had manifest proof of what you owe to me; and now that you are free of the yoke which I have removed from about your necks, it is my will and desire that you should set out and proceed to the city of El Toboso and there present yourselves before the lady Dulcinea del Toboso and say to her that her champion, the Knight of the Mournful Countenance, has sent you; and then you will relate to her, point by point, the whole of this famous adventure which has won you your longed-for freedom. Having done that, you may go where you like, and may good luck go with you."

To this Ginés de Pasamonte replied in behalf of all of them, "It is absolutely impossible, your Grace, our liberator, for us to do what you have commanded. We cannot go down the highway all together but must separate and go singly, each in his own direction, endeavoring to hide ourselves in the bowels of the earth in order not to be found by the Holy Brotherhood, which undoubtedly will come out to search for us. What your Grace can do, and it is right that you should do so, is to change this service and toll that you require of us in connection with the lady Dulcinea del Toboso into a certain number of Credos and Hail Marys which we will say for your Grace's intention, as this is something that can be accomplished by day or night, fleeing or resting, in peace or in war. To imagine, on the other hand, that we are going to return to the fleshpots of Egypt, by which I mean, take up our chains again by setting out along the highway for El Toboso, is to believe that it is night now instead of ten o'clock in the morning and is to ask of us something that is the same as asking pears of the elm tree."

"Then by all that's holy!" exclaimed Don Quixote, whose wrath was now aroused, "you, Don Son of a Whore, Don Ginesillo de Parapilla, or whatever your name is, you shall go alone, your tail between your legs and the whole chain on your back."

Pasamonte, who was by no means a long-suffering individual, was by this time convinced that Don Quixote was not quite right in the head, seeing that he had been guilty of such a folly as that of desiring to free them; and so, when he heard himself insulted in this manner, he merely gave the wink to his companions and, going off to one side, began raining so many stones upon the knight that the latter was wholly unable to protect himself with his buckler, while poor Rocinante paid no more attention to the spur than if he had been made of brass. As for Sancho, he took refuge behind his donkey as a protection against the cloud and shower of rocks that was falling on both of them, but Don Quixote was not able to shield himself so well, and there is no telling how many struck his body, with such force as to unhorse and bring him to the ground.

No sooner had he fallen than the student was upon him. Seizing the basin from the knight's head, he struck him three or four blows with it across the shoulders and banged it against the ground an equal number of times until it was fairly shattered to bits. They then stripped Don Quixote of the doublet which he wore over his armor, and would have taken his hose as well, if his greaves had not prevented them from doing so, and made off with Sancho's greatcoat, leaving him naked; after which, dividing the rest of the battle spoils amongst themselves, each of them went his own way, being a good deal more concerned with eluding the dreaded Holy Brotherhood than they were with burdening themselves with a chain or going to present themselves before the lady Dulcinea del Toboso.

They were left alone now—the ass and Rocinante, Sancho and Don Quixote: the ass, crestfallen and pensive, wagging its ears now and then, being
under the impression that the hurricane of stones that had raged about them
was not yet over; Rocinante, stretched alongside his master, for the hack also
had been felled by a stone; Sancho, naked and fearful of the Holy Brotherhood; and Don Quixote, making wry faces at seeing himself so mishandled
by those to whom he had done so much good.

["Set Free at Once That Lovely Lady"]

CHAPTER 52

*Of the quarrel that Don Quixote had with the goatherd, together with
the rare adventure of the penitents, which the knight by the sweat of his
brow brought to a happy conclusion.*[1]

All those who had listened to it were greatly pleased with the goatherd's
story, especially the canon,[2] who was more than usually interested in noting
the manner in which it had been told. Far from being a mere rustic herdsman, the narrator seemed rather a cultured city dweller; and the canon
accordingly remarked that the curate had been quite right in saying that the
mountain groves bred men of learning. They all now offered their services
to Eugenio, and Don Quixote was the most generous of any in this regard.

"Most assuredly, brother goatherd," he said, "if it were possible for me to
undertake any adventure just now, I would set out at once to aid you and
would take Leandra out of that convent, where she is undoubtedly being
held against her will, in spite of the abbess and all the others who might try
to prevent me, after which I would place her in your hands to do with as you
liked, with due respect, however, for the laws of chivalry, which command
that no violence be offered to any damsel. But I trust in God, Our Lord, that
the power of one malicious enchanter is not so great that another magician
may not prove still more powerful, and then I promise you my favor and my
aid, as my calling obliges me to do, since it is none other than that of succoring the weak and those who are in distress."

The goatherd stared at him, observing in some astonishment the knight's
unprepossessing appearance.

"Sir," he said, turning to the barber who sat beside him, "who is this man
who looks so strange and talks in this way?"

"Who should it be," the barber replied, "if not the famous Don Quixote
de la Mancha, righter of wrongs, avenger of injustices, protector of damsels,
terror of giants, and champion of battles?"

"That," said the goatherd, "sounds to me like the sort of thing you read of
in books of chivalry, where they do all those things that your Grace has

---

1. Last chapter of Part I. Through various devices, including the use of Don Quixote's own belief in
enchantments and spells, the curate and the barber have persuaded the knight to let himself be taken home
in an ox cart. 2. A canon from Toledo who has joined Don Quixote and his guardians on the way;
conversing about chivalry with the knight, he has had cause to be "astonished at Don Quixote's well-
reasoned nonsense." Eugenio, a very literate goatherd met on the way, has just told them the story of his
unhappy love for Leandra. The girl, instead of choosing one of her local suitors, had eloped with a flashy
and crooked soldier; robbed and abandoned by him, she had been put by her father in a convent.

mentioned in connection with this man. But if you ask me, either your Grace is joking or this worthy gentleman must have a number of rooms to let inside his head."

"You are the greatest villain that ever was!" cried Don Quixote when he heard this. "It is you who are the empty one; I am fuller than the bitch that bore you ever was." Saying this, he snatched up a loaf of bread that was lying beside him and hurled it straight in the goatherd's face with such force as to flatten the man's nose. Upon finding himself thus mistreated in earnest, Eugenio, who did not understand this kind of joke, forgot all about the carpet, the tablecloth, and the other diners and leaped upon Don Quixote. Seizing him by the throat with both hands, he would no doubt have strangled him if Sancho Panza, who now came running up, had not grasped him by the shoulders and flung him backward over the table, smashing plates and cups and spilling and scattering all the food and drink that was there. Thus freed of his assailant, Don Quixote then threw himself upon the shepherd, who, with bleeding face and very much battered by Sancho's feet, was creeping about on his hands and knees in search of a table knife with which to exact a sanguinary vengeance, a purpose which the canon and the curate prevented him from carrying out. The barber, however, so contrived it that the goatherd came down on top of his opponent, upon whom he now showered so many blows that the poor knight's countenance was soon as bloody as his own.

As all this went on, the canon and the curate were laughing fit to burst, the troopers[3] were dancing with glee, and they all hissed on the pair as men do at a dog fight. Sancho Panza alone was in despair, being unable to free himself of one of the canon's servants who held him back from going to his master's aid. And then, just as they were all enjoying themselves hugely, with the exception of the two who were mauling each other, the note of a trumpet fell upon their ears, a sound so mournful that it caused them all to turn their heads in the direction from which it came. The one who was most excited by it was Don Quixote; who, very much against his will and more than a little bruised, was lying pinned beneath the goatherd.

"Brother Demon," he now said to the shepherd, "for you could not possibly be anything but a demon, seeing that you have shown a strength and valor greater than mine, I request you to call a truce for no more than an hour; for the doleful sound of that trumpet that we hear seems to me to be some new adventure that is calling me."

Tired of mauling and being mauled, the goatherd let him up at once. As he rose to his feet and turned his head in the direction of the sound, Don Quixote then saw, coming down the slope of a hill, a large number of persons clad in white after the fashion of penitents; for, as it happened, the clouds that year had denied their moisture to the earth, and in all the villages of that district processions for prayer and penance were being organized with the purpose of beseeching God to have mercy and send rain. With this object in view, the good folk from a near-by town were making a pilgrimage to a devout hermit who dwelt on these slopes. Upon beholding the strange costumes that the penitents wore, without pausing to think how many times he

---

3. Law officers from the Holy Brotherhood. They had wanted to arrest Don Quixote for his attempt to liberate the galley salves, but had been persuaded not to do so because of the knight's insanity.

had seen them before, Don Quixote imagined that this must be some adventure or other, and that it was for him alone as a knight-errant to undertake it. He was strengthened in this belief by the sight of a covered image that they bore, as it seemed to him this must be some highborn lady whom these scoundrelly and discourteous brigands were forcibly carrying off; and no sooner did this idea occur to him than he made for Rocinante, who was grazing not far away.

Taking the bridle and his buckler from off the saddletree, he had the bridle adjusted in no time, and then, asking Sancho for his sword, he climbed into the saddle, braced his shield upon his arm, and cried out to those present, "And now, valorous company, you shall see how important it is to have in the world those who follow the profession of knight-errantry. You have but to watch how I shall set at liberty that worthy lady who there goes captive, and then you may tell me whether or not such knights are to be esteemed."

As he said this, he dug his legs into Rocinante's flanks, since he had no spurs, and at a fast trot (for nowhere in this veracious history are we ever told that the hack ran full speed) he bore down on the penitents in spite of all that the canon, the curate, and the barber could do to restrain him—their efforts were as vain as were the pleadings of his squire.

"Where are you bound for, Señor Don Quixote?" Sancho called after him. "What evil spirits in your bosom spur you on to go against our Catholic faith? Plague take me, can't you see that's a procession of penitents and that lady they're carrying on the litter is the most blessed image of the Immaculate Virgin? Look well what you're doing, my master, for this time it may be said that you really do not know."

His exertions were in vain, however, for his master was so bent upon having it out with the sheeted figures and freeing the lady clad in mourning that he did not hear a word, nor would he have turned back if he had, though the king himself might have commanded it. Having reached the procession, he reined in Rocinante, who by this time was wanting a little rest, and in a hoarse, excited voice he shouted, "You who go there with your faces covered, out of shame, it may be, listen well to what I have to say to you."

The first to come to a halt were those who carried the image; and then one of the four clerics who were intoning the litanies, upon beholding Don Quixote's weird figure, his bony nag, and other amusing appurtenances, spoke up in reply.

"Brother, if you have something to say to us, say it quickly, for these brethren are engaged in macerating their flesh, and we cannot stop to hear anything, nor is it fitting that we should, unless it is capable of being said in a couple of words."

"I will say it to you in one word," Don Quixote answered, "and that word is the following: 'Set free at once that lovely lady whose tears and mournful countenance show plainly that you are carrying her away against her will and that you have done her some shameful wrong. I will not consent to your going one step farther until you shall have given her the freedom that should be hers.' "

Hearing these words, they all thought that Don Quixote must be some madman or other and began laughing heartily; but their laughter proved to be gunpowder to his wrath, and without saying another word he drew his sword and fell upon the litter. One of those who bore the image, leaving his share of the burden to his companions, then sallied forth to meet the knight, flourishing a forked stick that he used to support the Virgin while he was resting; and upon this stick he now received a mighty slash that Don Quixote dealt him, one that shattered it in two, but with the piece about a third long that remained in his hand he came down on the shoulder of his opponent's sword arm, left unprotected by the buckler, with so much force that the poor fellow sank to the ground sorely battered and bruised.

Sancho Panza, who was puffing along close behind his master, upon seeing him fall cried out to the attacker not to deal another blow, as this was an unfortunate knight who was under a magic spell but who had never in all the days of his life done any harm to anyone. But the thing that stopped the rustic was not Sancho's words; it was, rather, the sight of Don Quixote lying there without moving hand or foot. And so, thinking that he had killed him, he hastily girded up his tunic and took to his heels across the countryside like a deer.

By this time all of Don Quixote's companions had come running up to where he lay; and the penitents, when they observed this, and especially when they caught sight of the officers of the Brotherhood with their cross-bows, at once rallied around the image, where they raised their hoods and grasped their whips as the priests raised their tapers aloft in expectations of an assault; for they were resolved to defend themselves and even, if possible, to take the offensive against their assailants, but, as luck would have it, things turned out better than they had hoped. Sancho, meanwhile, believing Don Quixote to be dead, had flung himself across his master's body and was weeping and wailing in the most lugubrious and, at the same time, the most laughable fashion that could be imagined; and the curate had discovered among those who marched in the procession another curate whom he knew, their recognition of each other serving to allay the fears of all parties concerned. The first curate then gave the second a very brief account of who Don Quixote was, whereupon all the penitents came up to see if the poor knight was dead. And as they did do, they heard Sancho Panza speaking with tears in his eyes.

"O flower of chivalry,"[4] he was saying, "the course of whose well-spent years has been brought to an end by a single blow of a club! O honor of your line, honor and glory of all La Mancha and of all the world, which, with you absent from it, will be full of evil-doers who will not fear being punished for their deeds! O master more generous than all the Alexanders, who after only eight months of service presented me with the best island that the sea washes and surrounds! Humble with the proud, haughty with the humble, brave in facing dangers, long-suffering under outrages, in love without reason, imitator of the good, scourge of the wicked, enemy of the mean—in a word, a knight-errant, which is all there is to say."

At the sound of Sancho's cries and moans, Don Quixote revived, and the first thing he said was, "He who lives apart from thee, O fairest Dulcinea, is subject to greater woes than those I now endure. Friend Sancho, help me onto that enchanted cart, as I am in no condition to sit in Rocinante's saddle with this shoulder of mine knocked to pieces the way it is."

"That I will gladly do, my master," replied Sancho, "and we will go back

---

4. Note how Sancho has absorbed some of his master's speech mannerisms.

to my village in the company of these gentlemen who are concerned for your welfare, and there we will arrange for another sally and one, let us hope, that will bring us more profit and fame than this one has."

"Well spoken, Sancho," said Don Quixote, "for it will be an act of great prudence to wait until the present evil influence of the stars has passed."

The canon, the curate, and the barber all assured him that he would be wise in doing this; and so, much amused by Sancho Panza's simplicity, they placed Don Quixote upon the cart as before, while the procession of penitents re-formed and continued on its way. The goatherd took leave of all of them, and the curate paid the troopers what was coming to them, since they did not wish to go any farther. The canon requested the priest to inform him of the outcome of Don Quixote's madness, as to whether it yielded to treatment or not; and with this he begged permission to resume his journey. In short, the party broke up and separated, leaving only the curate and the barber, Don Quixote and Panza, and the good Rocinante, who looked upon everything that he had seen with the same resignation as his master. Yoking his oxen, the carter made the knight comfortable upon a bale of hay, and then at his customary slow pace proceeded to follow the road that the curate directed him to take. At the end of the six days they reached Don Quixote's village, making their entrance at noon of a Sunday, when the square was filled with a crowd of people through which the cart had to pass.

They all came running to see who it was, and when they recognized their townsman, they were vastly astonished. One lad sped to bring the news to the knight's housekeeper and his niece, telling them that their master had returned lean and jaundiced and lying stretched out upon a bale of hay on an ox-cart. It was pitiful to hear the good ladies' screams, to behold the way in which they beat their breasts, and to listen to the curses which they once more heaped upon those damnable books of chivalry, and this demonstration increased as they saw Don Quixote coming through the doorway.

At news of the knight's return, Sancho Panza's wife had hurried to the scene, for she had some while since learned that her husband had accompanied him as his squire; and now, as soon as she laid eyes upon her man, the first question she asked was if all was well with the ass, to which Sancho replied that the beast was better off than his master.

"Thank God," she exclaimed, "for all his blessings! But tell me now, my dear, what have you brought me from all your squirings? A new cloak to wear? Or shoes for the young ones?"

"I've brought you nothing of the sort, good wife," said Sancho, "but other things of greater value and importance."

"I'm glad to hear that," she replied. "Show me those things of greater value and importance, my dear. I'd like a sight of them just to cheer this heart of mine which has been so sad and unhappy all the centuries that you've been gone."

"I will show them to you at home, wife," said Sancho. "For the present be satisfied that if, God willing, we set out on another journey in search of adventures, you will see me in no time a count or the governor of an island, and not one of those around here, but the best that is to be had."

"I hope to Heaven it's true, my husband, for we certainly need it. But tell me, what is all this about islands? I don't understand."

"Honey," replied Sancho, "is not for the mouth of an ass. You will find out in good time, woman; and you're going to be surprised to hear yourself called 'my Ladyship' by all your vassals."

"What's this you are saying, Sancho, about ladyships, islands, and vassals?" Juana Panza insisted on knowing—for such was the name of Sancho's wife, although they were not blood relatives, it being the custom in La Mancha for wives to take their husbands" surnames.

"Do not be in such a hurry to know all this, Juana," he said. "It is enough that I am telling you the truth. Sew up your mouth, then; for all I will say, in passing, is that there is nothing in the world that is more pleasant than being a respected man, squire to a knight-errant who goes in search of adventures. It is true that most of the adventures you meet with do not come out the way you'd like them to, for ninety-nine out of a hundred will prove to be all twisted and crosswise. I know that from experience, for I've come out of some of them blanketed and out of others beaten to a pulp. But, all the same, it's a fine thing to go along waiting for what will happen next, crossing mountains, making your way through woods, climbing over cliffs, visiting castles, and putting up at inns free of charge, and the devil take the maravedi that is to pay."

Such was the conversation that took place between Sancho Panza and Juana Panza, his wife, as Don Quixote's housekeeper and niece were taking him in, stripping him, and stretching him out on his old-time bed. He gazed at them blankly, being unable to make out where he was. The curate charged the niece to take great care to see that her uncle was comfortable and to keep close watch over him so that he would not slip away from them another time. He then told them of what it had been necessary to do in order to get him home, at which they once more screamed to Heaven and began cursing the books of chivalry all over again, praying God to plunge the authors of such lying nonsense into the center of the bottomless pit. In short, they scarcely knew what to do, for they were very much afraid that their master and uncle would give them the slip once more, the moment he was a little better, and it turned out just the way they feared it might.

From Part II

Prologue

TO THE READER

God bless me, gentle or, it may be, plebeian reader, how eagerly you must be awaiting this prologue, thinking to find in it vengeful scoldings and vituperations directed against the author of the second Don Quixote—I mean the one who, so it is said, was begotten in Tordesillas and born in Tarragona.[1] The truth is, however, that I am not going to be able to satisfy you in this regard; for granting that injuries are capable of awakening wrath in the humblest of bosoms, my own must be an exception to the rule. You would, perhaps, have me call him an ass, a crackbrain, and an upstart, but it is not

---

1. A continuation of Don Quixote was published by a writer who gave himself the name of Avellaneda and claimed to come from Tordesillas. The mood of the second prologue is grim in comparison to the optimistic and witty prologue to Part I.

my intention so to chastise him for his sin. Let him eat it with his bread and have done with it.

What I cannot but resent is the fact that he describes me as being old and one-handed, as if it were in my power to make time stand still for me, or as if I had lost my hand in some tavern instead of upon the greatest occasion that the past or present has ever known or the future may ever hope to see.[2] If my wounds are not resplendent in the eyes of the chance beholder, they are at least highly thought of by those who know where they were received. The soldier who lies dead in battle has a more impressive mien than the one who by flight attains his liberty. So strongly do I feel about this that even if it were possible to work a miracle in my case, I still would rather have taken part in that prodigious battle than be today free of my wounds without having been there. The scars that the soldier has to show on face and breast are stars that guide others to the Heaven of honor, inspiring them with a longing for well-merited praise. What is more, it may be noted that one does not write with gray hairs but with his understanding, which usually grows better with the years.

I likewise resent his calling me envious; and as though I were some ignorant person, he goes on to explain to me what is meant by envy; when the truth of the matter is that of the two kinds, I am acquainted only with that which is holy, noble, and right-intentioned.[3] And this being so, as indeed it is, it is not likely that I should attack any priest, above all, one that is a familiar of the Holy Office.[4] If he made this statement, as it appears that he did, on behalf of a certain person, then he is utterly mistaken; for the person in question is one whose genius I hold in veneration and whose works I admire, as well as his constant industry and powers of application. But when all is said, I wish to thank this gentlemanly author for observing that my Novels[5] are more satirical than exemplary, while admitting at the same time that they are good; for they could not be good unless they had in them a little of everything.

You will likely tell me that I am being too restrained and overmodest, but it is my belief that affliction is not to be heaped upon the afflicted, and this gentleman must be suffering greatly, seeing that he does not dare to come out into the open and show himself by the light of day, but must conceal his name and dissemble his place of origin, as if he had been guilty of some treason or act of lese majesty. If you by chance should come to know him, tell him on my behalf that I do not hold it against him; for I know what temptations the devil has to offer, one of the greatest of which consists in putting it into a man's head that he can write a book and have it printed and thereby achieve as much fame as he does money and acquire as much money as he does fame; in confirmation of which I would have you, in your own witty and charming manner, tell him this tale.

There was in Seville a certain madman whose madness assumed one of the drollest forms that ever was seen in this world. Taking a hollow reed sharpened at one end, he would catch a dog in the street or somewhere else; and, holding one of the animal's legs with his foot and raising the other with

---

2. The Battle of Lepanto in 1571.   3. *Jealousy* and *zealousness* are etymologically related.   4. An allusion to the Spanish playwright Lope de Vega (see p. 2783), who had been made a priest and appointed an official of the Spanish Inquisition. Avellaneda accused Cervantes of envying Lope's enormous popularity.
5. *Exemplary Tales.*

his hand, he would fix his reed as best he could in a certain part, after which he would blow the dog up, round as a ball. When he had it in this condition he would give it a couple of slaps on the belly and let it go, remarking to the bystanders, of whom there were always plenty, "Do your Worships think, then, that it is so easy a thing to inflate a dog?" So you might ask, "Does your Grace think that it is so easy a thing to write a book?" And if this story does not set well with him, here is another one, dear reader, that you may tell him. This one, also, is about a madman and a dog.

The madman in this instance lived in Cordova. He was in the habit of carrying on his head a marble slab or stone of considerable weight, and when he met some stray cur he would go up alongside it and drop the weight full upon it, and the dog in a rage, barking and howling, would then scurry off down three whole streets without stopping. Now, it happened that among the dogs that he treated in this fashion was one belonging to a capmaker, who was very fond of the beast. Going up to it as usual, the madman let the stone fall on its head, whereupon the animal set up a great yowling, and its owner, hearing its moans and seeing what had been done to it, promptly snatched up a measuring rod and fell upon the dog's assailant, flaying him until there was not a sound bone left in the fellow's body; and with each blow that he gave him he cried, "You dog! You thief! Treat my greyhound like that, would you? You brute, couldn't you see it was a greyhound?" And repeating the word "greyhound" over and over, he sent the madman away beaten to a pulp.

Profiting by the lesson that had been taught him, the fellow disappeared and was not seen in public for more than a month, at the end of which time he returned, up to his old tricks and with a heavier stone than ever on his head. He would go up to a dog and stare at it, long and hard, and without daring to drop his stone, would say, "This is a greyhound; beware." And so with all the dogs that he encountered: whether they were mastiffs or curs, he would assert that they were greyhounds and let them go unharmed.

The same thing possibly may happen to our historian; it may be that he will not again venture to let fall the weight of his wit in the form of books which, being bad ones, are harder than rocks.

As for the threat he has made to the effect that through his book he will deprive me of the profits on my own,[6] you may tell him that I do not give a rap. Quoting from the famous interlude, *La Perendenga*,[7] I will say to him in reply, "Long live my master, the Four-and-twenty,[8] and Christ be with us all." Long live the great Count of Lemos, whose Christian spirit and well-known liberality have kept me on my feet despite all the blows an unkind fate has dealt me. Long life to his Eminence of Toledo, the supremely charitable Don Bernardo de Sandoval y Rojas.[9] Even though there were no printing presses in all the world, or such as there are should print more books directed against me than there are letters in the verses of *Mingo Revulgo*,[1] what would it matter to me? These two princes, without any cringing flattery or adulation on my part but solely out of their own goodness of heart, have taken it upon themselves to grant me their favor and protection, in which

6. Avellaneda asserted that his second part would earn the profits Cervantes might have expected from a continuation of his own.   7. No interlude by this name has survived.   8. Council of the town hall at Andalucía.   9. Archbishop of Toledo, uncle of the duke of Lerma, and patron of Cervantes.   1. Long verse satire.

respect I consider myself richer and more fortunate than if by ordinary means I had attained the peak of prosperity. The poor man may keep his honor, but not the vicious one. Poverty may cast a cloud over nobility but cannot wholly obscure it. Virtue of itself gives off a certain light, even though it be through the chinks and crevices and despite the obstacles of adversity, and so comes to be esteemed and as a consequence favored by high and noble minds.

Tell him no more than this, nor do I have anything more to say to you, except to ask you to bear in mind that this *Second Part of Don Quixote*, which I herewith present to you, is cut from the same cloth and by the same craftsman as Part I. In this book I give you Don Quixote continued and, finally, dead and buried, in order that no one may dare testify any further concerning him, for there has been quite enough evidence as it is. It is sufficient that a reputable individual should have chronicled these ingenious acts of madness once and for all, without going into the matter again; for an abundance even of good things causes them to be little esteemed, while scarcity may lend a certain worth to those that are bad.

I almost forgot to tell you that you may look forward to the *Persiles*, on which I am now putting the finishing touches, as well as Part Second of the *Galatea*.[2]

["Put into a Book"]

CHAPTER 3

Of the laughable conversation that took place between Don Quixote, Sancho Panza, and the bachelor Sansón Carrasco.

Don Quixote remained in a thoughtful mood as he waited for the bachelor Carrasco,[1] from whom he hoped to hear the news as to how he had been put into a book, as Sancho had said. He could not bring himself to believe that any such history existed, since the blood of the enemies he had slain was not yet dry on the blade of his sword; and here they were trying to tell him that his high deeds of chivalry were already circulating in printed form. But, for that matter, he imagined that some sage, either friend or enemy, must have seen to the printing of them through the art of magic. If the chronicler was a friend, he must have undertaken the task in order to magnify and exalt Don Quixote's exploits above the most notable ones achieved by knights-errant of old. If an enemy, his purpose would have been to make them out as nothing at all, by debasing them below the meanest acts ever recorded of any mean squire. The only thing was, the knight reflected, the exploits of squires never were set down in writing. If it was true that such a history existed, being about a knight-errant, then it must be eloquent and lofty in tone, a splendid and distinguished piece of work and veracious in its details.

This consoled him somewhat, although he was a bit put out at the thought that the author was a Moor, if the appellation "Cid" was to be taken as an

2. Never published.   1. The bachelor of arts Sansón Carrasco, an important new character who appears at the beginning of Part II and will play a considerable role in the story with his attempts at "curing" Don Quixote. Just now he has been telling Sancho about a book relating the adventures of Don Quixote and his squire, by which the two have been made famous; the book is, of course, *Don Quixote*, Part I.

indication,[2] and from the Moors you could never hope for any word of truth, seeing that they are all of them cheats, forgers, and schemers. He feared lest his love should not have been treated with becoming modesty but rather in a way that would reflect upon the virtue of his lady Dulcinea del Toboso. He hoped that his fidelity had been made clear, and the respect he had always shown her, and that something had been said as to how he had spurned queens, empresses, and damsels of every rank while keeping a rein upon those impulses that are natural to a man. He was still wrapped up in these and many other similar thoughts when Sancho returned with Carrasco.

Don Quixote received the bachelor very amiably. The latter, although his name was Sansón, or Samson, was not very big so far as bodily size went, but he was a great joker, with a sallow complexion and a ready wit. He was going on twenty-four and had a round face, a snub nose, and a large mouth, all of which showed him to be of a mischievous disposition and fond of jests and witticisms. This became apparent when, as soon as he saw Don Quixote, he fell upon his knees and addressed the knight as follows:

"O mighty Don Quixote de la Mancha, give me your hands; for by the habit of St. Peter that I wear[3]—though I have received but the first four orders—your Grace is one of the most famous knights-errant that ever have been or ever will be anywhere on this earth. Blessings upon Cid Hamete Benengeli who wrote down the history of your great achievements, and upon that curious-minded one who was at pains to have it translated from the Arabic into our Castilian vulgate for the universal entertainment of the people."

Don Quixote bade him rise. "Is it true, then," he asked, "that there is a book about me and that it was some Moorish sage who composed it?"

"By way of showing you how true it is," replied Sansón, "I may tell you that it is my belief that there are in existence today more than twelve thousand copies of that history. If you do not believe me, you have but to make inquiries in Portugal, Barcelona, and Valencia, where editions have been brought out, and there is even a report to the effect that one edition was printed at Antwerp. In short, I feel certain that there will soon not be a nation that does not know it or a language into which it has not been translated."

"One of the things," remarked Don Quixote, "that should give most satisfaction to a virtuous and eminent man is to see his good name spread abroad during his own lifetime, by means of the printing press, through translations into the languages of the various peoples. I have said 'good name,' for if he has any other kind, his fate is worse than death."

"If it is a matter of good name and good reputation," said the bachelor, "your Grace bears off the palm from all the knights-errant in the world; for the Moor in his tongue and the Christian in his have most vividly depicted your Grace's gallantry, your courage in facing dangers, your patience in adversity and suffering, whether the suffering be due to wounds or to misfortunes of another sort, and your virtue and continence in love, in connection with that platonic relationship that exists between your Grace and my lady Doña Dulcinea del Toboso."

At this point Sancho spoke up. "Never in my life," he said, "have I heard

2. The allusion is to Cid Hamete Benengeli (see n. 3, p. 2709). The word *cid* is of Arabic derivation.
3. The dress of one of the minor clerical orders.

my lady Dulcinea called 'Doña,' but only 'la Señora Dulcinea del Toboso'; so on that point, already, the history is wrong."

"That is not important," said Carrasco.

"No, certainly not," Don Quixote agreed. "But tell me, Señor Bachelor, what adventures of mine as set down in this book have made the deepest impression?"

"As to that," the bachelor answered, "opinions differ, for it is a matter of individual taste. There are some who are very fond of the adventure of the windmills—those windmills which to your Grace appeared to be so many Briareuses and giants. Others like the episode at the fulling mill. One relishes the story of the two armies which took on the appearance of droves of sheep, while another fancies the tale of the dead man whom they were taking to Segovia for burial. One will assert that the freeing of the galley slaves is the best of all, and yet another will maintain that nothing can come up to the Benedictine giants and the encounter with the valiant Biscayan."

Again Sancho interrupted him. "Tell me, Señor Bachelor," he said, "does the book say anything about the adventure with the Yanguesans, that time our good Rocinante took it into his head to go looking for tidbits in the sea?"

"The sage," replied Sansón, "has left nothing in the inkwell. He has told everything and to the point, even to the capers which the worthy Sancho cut as they tossed him in the blanket."

"I cut no capers in the blanket," objected Sancho, "but I did in the air, and more than I liked."

"I imagine," said Don Quixote, "that there is no history in the world, dealing with humankind, that does not have its ups and downs, and this is particularly true of those that have to do with deeds of chivalry, for they can never be filled with happy incidents alone."

"Nevertheless," the bachelor went on, "there are some who have read the book who say that they would have been glad if the authors had forgotten a few of the innumerable cudgelings which Señor Don Quixote received in the course of his various encounters."

"But that is where the truth of the story comes in," Sancho protested.

"For all of that," observed Don Quixote, "they might well have said nothing about them; for there is no need of recording those events that do not alter the veracity of the chronicle, when they tend only to lessen the reader's respect for the hero. You may be sure that Aeneas was not as pious as Vergil would have us believe, nor was Ulysses as wise as Homer depicts him."

"That is true enough," replied Sansón, "but it is one thing to write as a poet and another as a historian. The former may narrate or sing of things not as they were but as they should have been; the latter must describe them not as they should have been but as they were, without adding to or detracting from the truth in any degree whatsoever."

"Well," said Sancho, "if this Moorish gentleman is bent upon telling the truth, I have no doubt that among my master's thrashings my own will be found; for they never took the measure of his Grace's shoulders without measuring my whole body. But I don't wonder at that; for as my master himself says, when there's an ache in the head the members have to share it."

"You are a sly fox, Sancho," said Don Quixote. "My word, but you can remember things well enough when you choose to do so!"

"Even if I wanted to forget the whacks they gave me," Sancho answered him, "the welts on my ribs wouldn't let me, for they are still fresh."

"Be quiet, Sancho," his master admonished him, "and do not interrupt the bachelor. I beg him to go on and tell me what is said of me in this book."

"And what it says about me, too," put in Sancho, "for I have heard that I am one of the main presonages in it—"

"*Personages*, not *presonages*, Sancho my friend," said Sansón.

"So we have another one who catches you up on everything you say," was Sancho's retort. "If we go on at this rate, we'll never be through in a lifetime."

"May God put a curse on *my* life," the bachelor told him, "if you are not the second most important person in the story; and there are some who would rather listen to you talk than to anyone else in the book. It is true, there are those who say that you are too gullible in believing it to be the truth that you could become the governor of that island that was offered you by Señor Don Quixote, here present."

"There is still sun on the top of the wall," said Don Quixote, "and when Sancho is a little older, with the experience that the years bring, he will be wiser and better fitted to be a governor than he is at the present time."

"By God, master," said Sancho, "the island that I couldn't govern right now I'd never be able to govern if I lived to be as old as Methuselah. The trouble is, I don't know where that island we are talking about is located; it is not due to any lack of noddle on my part."

"Leave it to God, Sancho," was Don Quixote's advice, "and everything will come out all right, perhaps even better than you think; for not a leaf on the tree stirs except by His will."

"Yes," said Sansón, "if it be God's will, Sancho will not lack a thousand islands to govern, not to speak of one island alone."

"I have seen governors around here," said Sancho, "that are not to be compared to the sole of my shoe, and yet they call them 'your Lordship' and serve them on silver plate."

"Those are not the same kind of governors," Sansón informed him. "Their task is a good deal easier. The ones that govern islands must at least know grammar."

"I could make out well enough with the *gram*," replied Sancho, "but with the *mar* I want nothing to do, for I don't understand it at all. But leaving this business of the governorship in God's hands—for He will send me wherever I can best serve Him—I will tell you, Señor Bachelor Sansón Carrasco, that I am very much pleased that the author of the history should have spoken of me in such a way as does not offend me; for, upon the word of a faithful squire, if he had said anything about me that was not becoming to an old Christian, the deaf would have heard of it."

"That would be to work miracles," said Sansón.

"Miracles or no miracles," was the answer, "let everyone take care as to what he says or writes about people and not be setting down the first thing that pops into his head."

"One of the faults that is found with the book," continued the bachelor, "is that the author has inserted in it a story entitled *The One Who Was Too Curious for His Own Good*. It is not that the story in itself is a bad one or badly written; it is simply that it is out of place there, having nothing to do with the story of his Grace, Señor Don Quixote."[4]

"I will bet you," said Sancho, "that the son of a dog has mixed the cabbages with the baskets."[5]

"And I will say right now," declared Don Quixote, "that the author of this book was not a sage but some ignorant prattler who at haphazard and without any method set about the writing of it, being content to let things turn out as they might. In the same manner, Orbaneja,[6] the painter of Ubeda, when asked what he was painting would reply, 'Whatever it turns out to be.' Sometimes it would be a cock, in which case he would have to write alongside it, in Gothic letters, 'This is a cock.' And so it must be with my story, which will need a commentary to make it understandable."

"No," replied Sansón, "that it will not; for it is so clearly written that none can fail to understand it. Little children leaf through it, young people read it, adults appreciate it, and the aged sing its praises. In short, it is so thumbed and read and so well known to persons of every walk in life that no sooner do folks see some skinny nag than they at once cry, 'There goes Rocinante!' Those that like it best of all are the pages; for there is no lord's antechamber where a *Don Quixote* is not to be found. If one lays it down, another will pick it up; one will pounce upon it, and another will beg for it. It affords the pleasantest and least harmful reading of any book that has been published up to now. In the whole of it there is not to be found an indecent word or a thought that is other than Catholic."

"To write in any other manner," observed Don Quixote, "would be to write lies and not the truth. Those historians who make use of falsehoods ought to be burned like the makers of counterfeit money. I do not know what could have led the author to introduce stories and episodes that are foreign to the subject matter when he had so much to write about in describing my adventures. He must, undoubtedly, have been inspired by the old saying, 'With straw or with hay[7] . . . ' For, in truth, all he had to do was to record my thoughts, my sighs, my tears, my lofty purposes, and my undertakings, and he would have had a volume bigger or at least as big as that which the works of El Tostado[8] would make. To sum the matter up, Señor Bachelor, it is my opinion that, in composing histories or books of any sort, a great deal of judgment and ripe understanding is called for. To say and write witty and amusing things is the mark of great genius. The cleverest character in a comedy is the clown, since he who would make himself out to be a simpleton cannot be one. History is a near-sacred thing, for it must be true, and where the truth is, there is God. And yet there are those who compose books and toss them out into the world as if they were no more than fritters."

"There is no book so bad," opined the bachelor, "that there is not some good in it."

"Doubtless that is so," replied Don Quixote, "but it very often happens that those who have won in advance a great and well-deserved reputation for their writings, lose it in whole or in part when they give their works to the printer."

---

4. The story, a tragic tale about a jealousy-ridden husband, occupies several chapters of Part I. Here, as elsewhere in this chapter, Cervantes echoes criticism currently aimed at his book.   5. Has jumbled together things of different kinds.   6. Unidentified.   7. The proverb concludes either "the mattress is filled" or "I fill my belly."   8. Alonso de Madrigal, bishop of Ávila, a prolific author of devotional works.

"The reason for it," said Sansón, "is that, printed works being read at leisure, their faults are the more readily apparent, and the greater the reputation of the author the more closely are they scrutinized. Men famous for their genius, great poets, illustrious historians, are almost always envied by those who take a special delight in criticizing the writings of others without having produced anything of their own."

"That is not to be wondered at," said Don Quixote, "for there are many theologians who are not good enough for the pulpit but who are very good indeed when it comes to detecting the faults or excesses of those who preach."

"All of this is very true, Señor Don Quixote," replied Carrasco, "but, all the same, I could wish that these self-appointed censors were a bit more forbearing and less hypercritical; I wish they would pay a little less attention to the spots on the bright sun of the work that occasions their fault-finding. For if *aliquando bonus dormitat Homerus,*[9] let them consider how much of his time he spent awake, shedding the light of his genius with a minimum of shade. It well may be that what to them seems a flaw is but one of those moles which sometimes add to the beauty of a face. In any event, I insist that he who has a book printed runs a very great risk, inasmuch as it is an utter impossibility to write it in such a manner that it will please all who read it."

"This book about me must have pleased very few," remarked Don Quixote.

"Quite the contrary," said Sansón, "for just as *stultorum infinitus est numerus,*[1] so the number of those who have enjoyed this history is likewise infinite. Some, to be sure, have complained of the author's forgetfulness, seeing that he neglected to make it plain who the thief was who stole Sancho's gray;[2] for it is not stated there, but merely implied, that the ass was stolen; and, a little further on, we find the knight mounted on the same beast, although it has not made its reappearance in the story. They also say that the author forgot to tell us what Sancho did with those hundred crowns that he found in the valise on the Sierra Morena, as nothing more is said of them and there are many who would like to know how he disposed of the money or how he spent it. This is one of the serious omissions to be found in the work."

To this Sancho replied, "I, Señor Sansón, do not feel like giving any account or accounting just now; for I feel a little weak in my stomach, and if I don't do something about it by taking a few swigs of the old stuff, I'll be sitting on St. Lucy's thorn.[3] I have some of it at home, and my old woman is waiting for me. After I've had my dinner, I'll come back and answer any questions your Grace or anybody else wants to ask me, whether it's about the loss of the ass or the spending of the hundred crowns."

And without waiting for a reply or saying another word, he went on home. Don Quixote urged the bachelor to stay and take potluck with him, and Sansón accepted the invitation and remained. In addition to the knight's ordinary fare, they had a couple of pigeons, and at table their talk was of chivalry and feats of arms.

---

9. Good Homer sometimes nods too (Latin); Horace, *Art of Poetry,* line 359. 1. Infinite is the number of fools (Latin). 2. In Part I, chap. 23. 3. I shall be weak and exhausted.

[A Victorious Duel]

CHAPTER 12

Of the strange adventure that befell the valiant Don Quixote with the fearless Knight of the Mirrors.[1]

The night following the encounter with Death was spent by Don Quixote and his squire beneath some tall and shady trees,[2] the knight having been persuaded to eat a little from the stock of provisions carried by the gray.

"Sir," said Sancho, in the course of their repast, "how foolish I'd have been if I had chosen the spoils from your Grace's first adventure rather than the foals from the three mares.[3] Truly, truly, a sparrow in the hand is worth more than a vulture on the wing."[4]

"And yet, Sancho," replied Don Quixote, "if you had but let me attack them as I wished to do, you would at least have had as spoils the Empress's gold crown and Cupid's painted wings;[5] for I should have taken them whether or no and placed them in your hands."

"The crowns and scepters of stage emperors," remarked Sancho, "were never known to be of pure gold; they are always of tinsel or tinplate."

"That is the truth," said Don Quixote, "for it is only right that the accessories of a drama should be fictitious and not real, like the play itself. Speaking of that, Sancho, I would have you look kindly upon the art of the theater and, as a consequence, upon those who write the pieces and perform in them, for they all render a service of great value to the State by holding up a mirror for us at each step that we take, wherein we may observe, vividly depicted, all the varied aspects of human life; and I may add that there is nothing that shows us more clearly, by similitude, what we are and what we ought to be than do plays and players.

"Tell me, have you not seen some comedy in which kings, emperors, pontiffs, knights, ladies, and numerous other characters are introduced? One plays the ruffian, another the cheat, this one a merchant and that one a soldier, while yet another is the fool who is not so foolish as he appears, and still another the one of whom love has made a fool. Yet when the play is over and they have taken off their players' garments, all the actors are once more equal."

"Yes," replied Sancho, "I have seen all that."

"Well," continued Don Quixote, "the same thing happens in the comedy that we call life, where some play the part of emperors, others that of pontiffs—in short, all the characters that a drama may have—but when it is all over, that is to say, when life is done, death takes from each the garb that differentiates him, and all at last are equal in the grave."

"It is a fine comparison," Sancho admitted, "though not so new but that I

---

1. Until he earns this title (in chap. 15), he will be referred to as the Knight of the Wood. 2. Don Quixote and his squire are now in the woody region around El Toboso, Dulcinea's town. Sancho has been sent to look for his knight's lady and has saved the day by pretending to see the beautiful damsel in a "village wench, and not a pretty one at that, for she was round-faced and snub-nosed." But by his imaginative lie he has succeeded, as he had planned, in setting in motion Don Quixote's belief in spells and enchantments: enemy magicians, envious of him, have hidden his lady's splendor only from his sight. While the knight was still under the shock of this experience, farther along their way he and his squire have met a group of itinerant players dressed in their proper costumes for a religious play, *The Parliament of Death*. 3. Don Quixote has promised them to Sancho as a reward for bringing news of Dulcinea. 4. I.e., a bird in the hand is worth two in the bush. 5. The Empress and Cupid were characters in *The Parliament of Death*.

have heard it many times before. It reminds me of that other one, about the game of chess. So long as the game lasts, each piece has its special qualities, but when it is over they are all mixed and jumbled together and put into a bag, which is to the chess pieces what the grave is to life."

"Every day, Sancho," said Don Quixote, "you are becoming less stupid and more sensible."

"It must be that some of your Grace's good sense is sticking to me," was Sancho's answer. "I am like a piece of land that of itself is dry and barren, but if you scatter manure over it and cultivate it, it will bear good fruit. By this I mean to say that your Grace's conversation is the manure that has been cast upon the barren land of my dry wit; the time that I spend in your service, associating with you, does the cultivating; and as a result of it all, I hope to bring forth blessed fruits by not departing, slipping, or sliding, from those paths of good breeding which your Grace has marked out for me in my parched understanding."

Don Quixote had to laugh at this affected speech of Sancho's, but he could not help perceiving that what the squire had said about his improvement was true enough; for every now and then the servant would speak in a manner that astonished his master. It must be admitted, however, that most of the time when he tried to use fine language, he would tumble from the mountain of his simple-mindedness into the abyss of his ignorance. It was when he was quoting old saws and sayings, whether or not they had anything to do with the subject under discussion, that he was at his best, displaying upon such occasions a prodigious memory, as will already have been seen and noted in the course of this history.

With such talk as this they spent a good part of the night. Then Sancho felt a desire to draw down the curtains of his eyes, as he was in the habit of saying when he wished to sleep, and, unsaddling his mount, he turned him loose to graze at will on the abundant grass. If he did not remove Rocinante's saddle, this was due to his master's express command; for when they had taken the field and were not sleeping under a roof, the hack was under no circumstances to be stripped. This was in accordance with an old and established custom which knights-errant faithfully observed: the bridle and saddlebow might be removed, but beware of touching the saddle itself! Guided by this precept, Sancho now gave Rocinante the same freedom that the ass enjoyed.

The close friendship that existed between the two animals was a most unusual one, so remarkable indeed that it has become a tradition handed down from father to son, and the author of this veracious chronicle even wrote a number of special chapters on the subject, although, in order to preserve the decency and decorum that are fitting in so heroic an account, he chose to omit them in the final version. But he forgets himself once in a while and goes on to tell us how the two beasts when they were together would hasten to scratch each other, and how, when they were tired and their bellies were full, Rocinante would lay his long neck over that of the ass—it extended more than a half a yard on the other side—and the pair would then stand there gazing pensively at the ground for as much as three whole days at a time, or at least until someone came for them or hunger compelled them to seek nourishment.

I may tell you that I have heard it said that the author of this history, in one of his writings, has compared the friendship of Rocinante and the gray to that of Nisus and Euryalus and that of Pylades and Orestes;[6] and if this be true, it shows for the edification of all what great friends these two peace-loving animals were, and should be enough to make men ashamed, who are so inept at preserving friendship with one another. For this reason it has been said:

> There is no friend for friend,
> Reeds to lances turn[7] . . .

And there was the other poet who sang:

> Between friend and friend the bug[8] . . .

Let no one think that the author has gone out of his way in comparing the friendship of animals with that of men; for human beings have received valuable lessons from the beasts and have learned many important things from them. From the stork they have learned the use of clysters; the dog has taught them the salutary effects of vomiting as well as a lesson in gratitude; the cranes have taught them vigilance, the ants foresight, the elephants modesty, and the horse loyalty.[9]

Sancho had at last fallen asleep at the foot of a cork tree, while Don Quixote was slumbering beneath a sturdy oak. Very little time had passed when the knight was awakened by a noise behind him, and, starting up, he began looking about him and listening to see if he could make out where it came from. Then he caught sight of two men on horseback, one of whom, slipping down from the saddle, said to the other, "Dismount, my friend, and unbridle the horses; for there seems to be plenty of grass around here for them and sufficient silence and solitude for my amorous thoughts."

Saying this, he stretched himself out on the ground, and as he flung himself down the armor that he wore made such a noise that Don Quixote knew at once, for a certainty, that he must be a knight-errant. Going over to Sancho, who was still sleeping, he shook him by the arm and with no little effort managed to get him awake.

"Brother Sancho," he said to him in a low voice, "we have an adventure on our hands."

"God give us a good one," said Sancho. "And where, my master, may her Ladyship, Mistress Adventure, be?"

"Where, Sancho?" replied Don Quixote. "Turn your eyes and look, and you will see stretched out over there a knight-errant who, so far as I can make out, is not any too happy; for I saw him fling himself from his horse to the ground with a certain show of despondency, and as he fell his armor rattled."

"Well," said Sancho, "and how does your Grace make this out to be an adventure?"

"I would not say," the knight answered him, "that this is an adventure in itself, but rather the beginning of one, for that is the way they start. But listen; he seems to be tuning a lute or guitar, and from the way he is spitting and clearing his throat he must be getting ready to sing something."

6. Famous examples of friendship in Virgil's *Aeneid* and in Greek tradition and drama.   7. From a popular ballad.   8.   The Spanish "a bug in the eye" implies keeping a watchful eye on somebody.   9. All folkloristic beliefs about the virtues of animals.

"Faith, so he is," said Sancho. "He must be some lovesick knight."

"There are no knights-errant that are not lovesick," Don Quixote informed him. "Let us listen to him, and the thread of his song will lead us to the yarn-ball of his thoughts; for out of the abundance of the heart the mouth speaketh."

Sancho would have liked to reply to his master, but the voice of the Knight of the Wood, which was neither very good nor very bad, kept him from it; and as the two of them listened attentively, they heard the following:

Sonnet

> Show me, O lady, the pattern of thy will,
> That mine may take that very form and shape;
> For my will in thine own I fain would drape,
> Each slightest wish of thine I would fulfill.
> If thou wouldst have me silence this dead ill   5
> Of which I'm dying now, prepare the crape!
> Or if I must another manner ape,
> Then let Love's self display his rhyming skill.
> Of opposites I am made, that's manifest:
> In part soft wax, in part hard-diamond fire;   10
> Yet to Love's laws my heart I do adjust,
> And, hard or soft, I offer thee this breast:
> Print or engrave there what thou may'st desire,
> And I'll preserve it in eternal trust.[1]

With an *Ay!* that appeared to be wrung from the very depths of his heart, the Knight of the Wood brought his song to a close, and then after a brief pause began speaking in a grief-stricken voice that was piteous to hear.

"O most beautiful and most ungrateful woman in all the world!" he cried, "how is it possible, O most serene Casildea de Vandalia,[2] for you to permit this captive knight of yours to waste away and perish in constant wanderings, amid rude toils and bitter hardships? Is it not enough that I have compelled all the knights of Navarre, all those of León, all the Tartessians and Castilians, and, finally, all those of La Mancha, to confess that there is no beauty anywhere that can rival yours?"

"That is not so!" cried Don Quixote at this point. "I am of La Mancha, and I have never confessed, I never could nor would confess a thing so prejudicial to the beauty of my lady. The knight whom you see there, Sancho, is raving; but let us listen and perhaps he will tell us more."

"That he will," replied Sancho, "for at the rate he is carrying on, he is good for a month at a stretch."

This did not prove to be the case, however; for when the Knight of the Wood heard voices near him, he cut short his lamentations and rose to his feet.

"Who goes there?" he called in a loud but courteous tone. "What kind of people are you? Are you, perchance, numbered among the happy or among the afflicted?"

---

1. The poem intentionally follows affected conventions of the time.   2. The Knight of the Wood's counterpart to Don Quixote's Dulcinea del Toboso.

"Among the afflicted," was Don Quixote's response.

"Then come to me," said the one of the Wood, "and, in doing so, know that you come to sorrow's self and the very essence of affliction."

Upon receiving so gentle and courteous an answer, Don Quixote and Sancho as well went over to him, whereupon the sorrowing one took the Manchegan's arm.

"Sit down here, Sir Knight," he continued, "for in order to know that you are one of those who follow the profession of knight-errantry, it is enough for me to have found you in this place where solitude and serenity keep you company, such a spot being the natural bed and proper dwelling of wandering men of arms."

"A knight I am," replied Don Quixote, "and of the profession that you mention; and though sorrows, troubles, and misfortunes have made my heart their abode, this does not mean that compassion for the woes of others has been banished from it. From your song a while ago I gather that your misfortunes are due to love—the love you bear that ungrateful fair one whom you named in your lamentations."

As they conversed in this manner, they sat together upon the hard earth, very peaceably and companionably, as if at daybreak they were not going to break each other's heads.

"Sir Knight," inquired the one of the Wood, "are you by any chance in love?"

"By mischance I am," said Don Quixote, "although the ills that come from well-placed affection should be looked upon as favors rather than as misfortunes."

"That is the truth," the Knight of the Wood agreed, "if it were not that the loved one's scorn disturbs our reason and understanding; for when it is excessive scorn appears as vengeance."

"I was never scorned by my lady," said Don Quixote.

"No, certainly not," said Sancho, who was standing near by, "for my lady is gentle as a ewe lamb and soft as butter."

"Is he your squire?" asked the one of the Wood.

"He is," replied Don Quixote.

"I never saw a squire," said the one of the Wood, "who dared to speak while his master was talking. At least, there is mine over there; he is as big as your father, and it cannot be proved that he has ever opened his lips while I was conversing."

"Well, upon my word," said Sancho, "I have spoken, and I will speak in front of any other as good—but never mind; it only makes it worse to stir it."

The Knight of the Wood's squire now seized Sancho's arm. "Come along," he said, "let the two of us go where we can talk all we like, squire fashion, and leave these gentlemen our masters to come to lance blows as they tell each other the story of their loves; for you may rest assured, daybreak will find them still at it."

"Let us, by all means," said Sancho, "and I will tell your Grace who I am, so that you may be able to see for yourself whether or not I am to be numbered among the dozen most talkative squires."

With this, the pair went off to one side, and there then took place between them a conversation that was as droll as the one between their masters was solemn.

CHAPTER 13

In which is continued the adventure of the Knight of the Wood, together with the shrewd, highly original, and amicable conversation that took place between the two squires.

The knights and the squires had now separated, the latter to tell their life stories, the former to talk of their loves; but the history first relates the conversation of the servants and then goes on to report that of the masters. We are told that, after they had gone some little distance from where the others were, the one who served the Knight of the Wood began speaking to Sancho as follows:

"It is a hard life that we lead and live, *Señor mio*, those of us who are squires to knights-errant. It is certainly true that we eat our bread in the sweat of our faces, which is one of the curses that God put upon our first parents."[3]

"It might also be said," added Sancho, "that we eat it in the chill of our bodies, for who endures more heat and cold than we wretched ones who wait upon these wandering men of arms? It would not be so bad if we did eat once in a while, for troubles are less where there is bread; but as it is, we sometimes go for a day or two without breaking our fast, unless we feed on the wind that blows."

"But all this," said the other, "may very well be put up with, by reason of the hope we have of being rewarded; for if a knight is not too unlucky, his squire after a little while will find himself the governor of some fine island or prosperous earldom."

"I," replied Sancho, "have told my master that I would be satisfied with the governorship of an island, and he is so noble and so generous that he has promised it to me on many different occasions."

"In return for my services," said the Squire of the Wood, "I'd be content with a canonry. My master has already appointed me to one—and what a canonry!"

"Then he must be a churchly knight," said Sancho, "and in a position to grant favors of that sort to his faithful squire; but mine is a layman, pure and simple, although, as I recall, certain shrewd and, as I see it, scheming persons did advise him to try to become an archbishop. However, he did not want to be anything but an emperor. And there I was, all the time trembling for fear he would take it into his head to enter the Church, since I was not educated enough to hold any benefices. For I may as well tell your Grace that, though I look like a man, I am no more than a beast where holy orders are concerned."

"That is where you are making a mistake," the Squire of the Wood assured him. "Not all island governments are desirable. Some of them are misshapen bits of land, some are poor, others are gloomy, and, in short, the best of them lays a heavy burden of care and trouble upon the shoulders of the unfortunate one to whose lot it falls. It would be far better if we who follow this cursed trade were to go back to our homes and there engage in pleasanter occupations, such as hunting or fishing, for example; for where is there in

---

3. Cf. Genesis 3.19. "In the sweat of thy face shalt thou eat bread, till thou return unto the ground."

this world a squire so poor that he does not have a hack, a couple of grey-hounds, and a fishing rod to provide him with sport in his own village?"

"I don't lack any of those," replied Sancho. "It is true, I have no hack, but I do have an ass that is worth twice as much as my master's horse. God send me a bad Easter, and let it be the next one that comes, if I would make a trade, even though he gave me four fanegas[4] of barley to boot. Your Grace will laugh at the price I put on my gray—for that is the color of the beast. As to greyhounds, I shan't want for them, as there are plenty and to spare in my village. And, anyway, there is more pleasure in hunting when someone else pays for it."

"Really and truly, Sir Squire," said the one of the Wood, "I have made up my mind and resolved to have no more to do with the mad whims of these knights; I intend to retire to my village and bring up my little ones—I have three of them, and they are like oriental pearls."

"I have two of them," said Sancho, "that might be presented to the Pope in person, especially one of my girls that I am bringing up to be a countess, God willing, in spite of what her mother says."

"And how old is this young lady that is destined to be a countess?"

"Fifteen," replied Sancho, "or a couple of years more or less. But she is tall as a lance, fresh as an April morning, and strong as a porter."

"Those," remarked the one of the Wood, "are qualifications that fit her to be not merely a countess but a nymph of the verdant wildwood. O whore's daughter of a whore! What strength the she-rogue must have!"

Sancho was a bit put out by this. "She is not a whore," he said, "nor was her mother before her, nor will either of them ever be, please God, so long as I live. And you might speak more courteously. For one who has been brought up among knights-errant, who are the soul of courtesy, those words are not very becoming."

"Oh, how little your Grace knows about compliments, Sir Squire!" the one of the Wood exclaimed. "Are you not aware that when some knight gives a good lance thrust to the bull in the plaza, or when a person does anything remarkably well, it is the custom for the crowd to cry out, 'Well done, whore-son rascal!' and that what appears to be vituperation in such a case is in reality high praise? Sir, I would bid you disown those sons or daughters who do nothing to cause such praise to be bestowed upon their parents."

"I would indeed disown them if they didn't," replied Sancho, "and so your Grace may go ahead and call me, my children, and my wife all the whores in the world if you like, for everything that they say and do deserves the very highest praise. And in order that I may see them all again, I pray God to deliver me from mortal sin, or, what amounts to the same thing, from this dangerous calling of squire, seeing that I have fallen into it a second time, decoyed and deceived by a purse of a hundred ducats that I found one day in the heart of the Sierra Morena.[5] The devil is always holding up a bag full of doubloons in front of my eyes, here, there—no, not here, but there—everywhere, until it seems to me at every step I take that I am touching it with my hand, hugging it, carrying it off home with me, investing it, drawing an income from it, and living on it like a prince. And while I am thinking such thoughts, all the hardships I have to put up with serving this crack-

4. About one hundred pounds. 5. When Don Quixote retired there in Part I, chap. 23.

brained master of mine, who is more of a madman than a knight, seem to me light and easy to bear."

"That," observed the Squire of the Wood, "is why it is they say that avarice bursts the bag. But, speaking of madmen, there is no greater one in all this world than my master; for he is one of those of whom it is said, 'The cares of others kill the ass.' Because another knight has lost his senses, he has to play mad too[6] and go hunting for that which, when he finds it, may fly up in his snout."

"Is he in love, maybe?"

"Yes, with a certain Casildea de Vandalia, the rawest[7] and best-roasted lady to be found anywhere on earth; but her rawness is not the foot he limps on, for he has other and greater schemes rumbling in his bowels, as you will hear tell before many hours have gone by."

"There is no road so smooth," said Sancho, "that it does not have some hole or rut to make you stumble. In other houses they cook horse beans, in mine they boil them by the kettleful.[8] Madness has more companions and attendants than good sense does. But if it is true what they say, that company in trouble brings relief, I may take comfort from your Grace, since you serve a master as foolish as my own."

"Foolish but brave," the one of the Wood corrected him, "and more of a rogue than anything else."

"That is not true of my master," replied Sancho. "I can assure you there is nothing of the rogue about him; he is as open and aboveboard as a wine pitcher and would not harm anyone but does good to all. There is no malice in his make-up, and a child could make him believe it was night at midday. For that very reason I love him with all my heart and cannot bring myself to leave him, no matter how many foolish things he does."

"But, nevertheless, good sir and brother," said the Squire of the Wood, "with the blind leading the blind, both are in danger of falling into the pit. It would be better for us to get out of all this as quickly as we can and return to our old haunts; for those that go seeking adventures do not always find good ones."

Sancho kept clearing his throat from time to time, and his saliva seemed rather viscous and dry; seeing which, the woodland squire said to him, "It looks to me as if we have been talking so much that our tongues are cleaving to our palates, but I have a loosener over there, hanging from the bow of my saddle, and a pretty good one it is." With this, he got up and went over to his horse and came back a moment later with a big flask of wine and a meat pie half a yard in diameter. This is no exaggeration, for the pasty in question was made of a hutch-rabbit of such a size that Sancho took it to be a goat, or at the very least a kid.

"And are you in the habit of carrying this with you, Señor?" he asked.

"What do you think?" replied the other. "Am I by any chance one of your wood-and-water[9] squires? I carry better rations on the flanks of my horse than a general does when he takes the field."

---

6. In the Sierra Morena, Don Quixote had decided to imitate Amadís de Gaul and Ariosto's Roland "by playing the part of a desperate and raving madman" as a consequence of love. 7. The Spanish has a pun on *crudo*, meaning both "raw" and "cruel." 8. Meaning that his misfortunes always come in large quantities. 9. Of low quality.

Sancho ate without any urging, gulping down mouthfuls that were like the knots on a tether, as they sat there in the dark.

"You are a squire of the right sort," he said, "loyal and true, and you live in grand style as shown by this feast, which I would almost say was produced by magic. You are not like me, poor wretch, who have in my saddlebags only a morsel of cheese so hard you could crack a giant's skull with it, three or four dozen carob beans, and a few nuts. For this I have my master to thank, who believes in observing the rule that knights-errant should nourish and sustain themselves on nothing but dried fruits and the herbs of the field."

"Upon my word, brother," said the other squire, "my stomach was not made for thistles, wild pears, and woodland herbs. Let our masters observe those knightly laws and traditions and eat what their rules prescribe; I carry a hamper of food and a flask on my saddlebow, whether they like it or not. And speaking of that flask, how I love it! There is scarcely a minute in the day that I'm not hugging and kissing it, over and over again."

As he said this, he placed the wine bag in Sancho's hands, who put it to his mouth, threw his head back, and sat there gazing up at the stars for a quarter of an hour. Then, when he had finished drinking, he let his head loll on one side and heaved a deep sigh.

"The whoreson rascal!" he exclaimed, "that's a fine vintage for you!"

"There!" cried the Squire of the Wood, as he heard the epithet Sancho had used, "do you see how you have praised this wine by calling it 'whoreson'?"

"I grant you," replied Sancho, "that it is no insult to call anyone a son of a whore so long as you really do mean to praise him. But tell me, sir, in the name of what you love most, is this the wine of Ciudad Real?"[1]

"What a winetaster you are! It comes from nowhere else, and it's a few years old, at that."

"Leave it to me," said Sancho, "and never fear, I'll show you how much I know about it. Would you believe me, Sir Squire, I have such a great natural instinct in this matter of wines that I have but to smell a vintage and I will tell you the country where it was grown, from what kind of grapes, what it tastes like, and how good it is, and everything that has to do with it. There is nothing so unusual about this, however, seeing that on my father's side were two of the best winetasters La Mancha has known in many a year, in proof of which, listen to the story of what happened to them.

"The two were given a sample of wine from a certain vat and asked to state its condition and quality and determine whether it was good or bad. One of them tasted it with the tip of his tongue while the other merely brought it up to his nose. The first man said that it tasted of iron, the second that it smelled of Cordovan leather. The owner insisted that the vat was clean and that there could be nothing in the wine to give it a flavor of leather or of iron, but, nevertheless, the two famous winetasters stood their ground. Time went by, and when they came to clean out the vat they found in it a small key attached to a leather strap. And so your Grace may see for yourself whether or not one who comes of that kind of stock has a right to give his opinion in such cases."

"And for that very reason," said the Squire of the Wood, "I maintain that

1. The main town in La Mancha and the center of a wine region.

we ought to stop going about in search of adventures. Seeing that we have loaves, let us not go looking for cakes, but return to our cottages, for God will find us there if He so wills."

"I mean to stay with my master," Sancho replied, "until he reaches Saragossa, but after that we will come to an understanding."

The short of the matter is, the two worthy squires talked so much and drank so much that sleep had to tie their tongues and moderate their thirst, since to quench the latter was impossible. Clinging to the wine flask, which was almost empty by now, and with half-chewed morsels of food in their mouths, they both slept peacefully; and we shall leave them there as we go on to relate what took place between the Knight of the Wood and the Knight of the Mournful Countenance.

CHAPTER 14

Wherein is continued the adventure of the Knight of the Wood.

In the course of the long conversation that took place between Don Quixote and the Knight of the Wood, the history informs us that the latter addressed the following remarks to the Manchegan:

"In short, Sir Knight, I would have you know that my destiny, or, more properly speaking, my own free choice, has led me to fall in love with the peerless Casildea de Vandalia. I call her peerless for the reason that she has no equal as regards either her bodily proportions or her very great beauty. This Casildea, then, of whom I am telling you, repaid my worthy affections and honorable intentions by forcing me, as Hercules[2] was forced by his stepmother, to incur many and diverse perils; and each time as I overcame one of them she would promise me that with the next one I should have that which I desired; but instead my labors have continued, forming a chain whose links I am no longer able to count, nor can I say which will be the last one, that shall mark the beginning of the realization of my hopes.

"One time she sent me forth to challenge that famous giantess of Seville, known as La Giralda,[3] who is as strong and brave as if made of brass, and who without moving from the spot where she stands is the most changeable and fickle woman in the world. I came, I saw, I conquered her, I made her stand still and point in one direction only, and for more than a week nothing but north winds blew. Then, there was that other time when Casildea sent me to lift those ancient stones, the mighty Bulls of Guisando,[4] an enterprise that had better have been entrusted to porters than to knights. On another occasion she commanded me to hurl myself down into the Cabra chasm[5]— an unheard-of and terribly dangerous undertaking—and bring her back a detailed account of what lay concealed in that deep and gloomy pit. I rendered La Giralda motionless, I lifted the Bulls of Guisando, and I threw myself into the abyss and brought to light what was hidden in its depths; yet my hopes are dead—how dead!—while her commands and her scorn are as lively as can be.

"Finally, she commanded me to ride through all the provinces of Spain and compel all the knights-errant whom I met with to confess that she is the most beautiful woman now living and that I am the most enamored man of arms that is to be found anywhere in the world. In fulfillment of this behest I have already traveled over the greater part of these realms and have vanquished many knights who have dared to contradict me. But the one whom I am proudest to have overcome in single combat is that famous gentleman, Don Quixote de la Mancha; for I made him confess that my Casildea is more beautiful than his Dulcinea, and by achieving such a conquest I reckon that I have conquered all the others on the face of the earth, seeing that this same Don Quixote had himself routed them. Accordingly, when I vanquished him, his fame, glory, and honor passed over and were transferred to my person.

> The brighter is the conquered one's lost crown,
> The greater is the conqueror's renown.[6]

Thus, the innumerable exploits of the said Don Quixote are now set down to my account and are indeed my own."

Don Quixote was astounded as he listened to the Knight of the Wood, and was about to tell him any number of times that he lied; the words were on the tip of his tongue, but he held them back as best he could, thinking that he would bring the other to confess with his own lips that what he had said was a lie. And so it was quite calmly that he now replied to him.

"Sir Knight," he began, "as to the assertion that your Grace has conquered most of the knights-errant in Spain and even in all the world, I have nothing to say, but that you have vanquished Don Quixote de la Mancha, I am inclined to doubt. It may be that it was someone else who resembled him, although there are very few that do."

"What do you mean?" replied the one of the Wood. "I swear by the heavens above that I did fight with Don Quixote and that I overcame him and forced him to yield. He is a tall man, with a dried-up face, long, lean legs, graying hair, an eagle-like nose somewhat hooked, and a big, black, drooping mustache. He takes the field under the name of the Knight of the Mournful Countenance, he has for squire a peasant named Sancho Panza, and he rides a famous steed called Rocinante. Lastly, the lady of his heart is a certain Dulcinea del Toboso, once upon a time known as Aldonza Lorenzo, just as my own lady, whose name is Casildea and who is an Andalusian by birth, is called by me Casildea de Vandalia. If all this is not sufficient to show that I speak the truth, here is my sword which shall make incredulity itself believe."

"Calm yourself, Sir Knight," replied Don Quixote, "and listen to what I have to say to you. You must know that this Don Quixote of whom you speak is the best friend that I have in the world, so great a friend that I may say that I feel toward him as I do toward my own self; and from all that you have told me, the very definite and accurate details that you have given me, I cannot doubt that he is the one whom you have conquered. On the other hand, the sight of my eyes and the touch of my hands assure me that he could not possibly be the one, unless some enchanter who is his enemy—for he has many, and one in particular who delights in persecuting him—may have assumed the knight's form and then permitted himself to be routed,

---

6. From Alonso de Ercilla y Zúñiga's *Araucana*, a poem about the Spanish struggle against the Araucanian Indians of Chile.

by way of defrauding Don Quixote of the fame which his high deeds of chivalry have earned for him throughout the known world. To show you how true this may be, I will inform you that not more than a couple of days ago those same enemy magicians transformed the figure and person of the beauteous Dulcinea del Toboso into a low and mean village lass, and it is possible that they have done something of the same sort to the knight who is her lover. And if all this does not suffice to convince you of the truth of what I say, here is Don Quixote himself who will maintain it by force of arms, on foot or on horseback, or in any way you like."

Saying this, he rose and laid hold of his sword, and waited to see what the Knight of the Wood's decision would be. That worthy now replied in a voice as calm as the one Don Quixote had used.

"Pledges," he said, "do not distress one who is sure of his ability to pay. He who was able to overcome you when you were transformed, Señor Don Quixote, may hope to bring you to your knees when you are your own proper self. But inasmuch as it is not fitting that knights should perform their feats of arms in the darkness, like ruffians and highwaymen, let us wait until it is day in order that the sun may behold what we do. And the condition governing our encounter shall be that the one who is vanquished must submit to the will of his conqueror and perform all those things that are commanded of him, provided they are such as are in keeping with the state of knighthood."

"With that condition and understanding," said Don Quixote, "I shall be satisfied."

With this, they went off to where their squires were, only to find them snoring away as hard as when sleep had first overtaken them. Awakening the pair, they ordered them to look to the horses; for as soon as the sun was up the two knights meant to stage an arduous and bloody single-handed combat. At this news Sancho was astonished and terrified, since, as a result of what the other squire had told him of the Knight of the Wood's prowess, he was led to fear for his master's safety. Nevertheless, he and his friend now went to seek the mounts without saying a word, and they found the animals all together, for by this time the two horses and the ass had smelled one another out. On the way the Squire of the Wood turned to Sancho and addressed him as follows:

"I must inform you, brother, that it is the custom of the fighters of Andalusia, when they are godfathers in any combat, not to remain idly by, with folded hands, while their godsons fight it out. I tell you this by way of warning you that while our masters are settling matters, we, too, shall have to come to blows and hack each other to bits."

"The custom, Sir Squire," replied Sancho, "may be all very well among the fighters and ruffians that you mention, but with the squires of knights-errant it is not to be thought of. At least, I have never heard my master speak of any such custom, and he knows all the laws of chivalry by heart. But granting that it is true and that there is a law which states in so many words that squires must fight while their masters do, I have no intention of obeying it but rather will pay whatever penalty is laid on peaceable-minded ones like myself, for I am sure it cannot be more than a couple of pounds of wax,[7] and that would be less expensive than the lint which it would take to heal my

7. In some confraternities, penalties were paid in wax, presumably to make church candles.

head—I can already see it split in two. What's more, it's out of the question for me to fight since I have no sword nor did I ever in my life carry one."

"That," said the one of the Wood, "is something that is easily remedied. I have here two linen bags of the same size. You take one and I'll take the other and we will fight that way, on equal terms."

"So be it, by all means," said Sancho, "for that will simply knock the dust out of us without wounding us."

"But that's not the way it's to be,' said the other squire. "Inside the bags, to keep the wind from blowing them away, we will put a half-dozen nice smooth pebbles of the same weight, and so we'll be able to give each other a good pounding without doing ourselves any real harm or damage."

"Body of my father!" cried Sancho, "just look, will you, at the marten and sable and wads of carded cotton that he's stuffing into those bags so that we won't get our heads cracked or our bones crushed to a pulp. But I am telling you, *Señor mio,* that even though you fill them with silken pellets, I don't mean to fight. Let our masters fight and make the best of it, but as for us, let us drink and live; for time will see to ending our lives without any help on our part by way of bringing them to a close before they have reached their proper season and fall from ripeness."

"Nevertheless," replied the Squire of the Wood, "fight we must, if only for half an hour."

"No," Sancho insisted, "that I will not do. I will not be so impolite or so ungrateful as to pick any quarrel however slight with one whose food and drink I've shared. And, moreover, who in the devil could bring himself to fight in cold blood, when he's not angry or vexed in any way?"

"I can take care of that, right enough," said the one of the Wood. "Before we begin, I will come up to your Grace as nicely as you please and give you three or four punches that will stretch you out at my feet; and that will surely be enough to awaken your anger, even though it's sleeping sounder than a dormouse."

"And I," said Sancho, "have another idea that's every bit as good as yours. I will take a big club, and before your Grace has had a chance to awaken my anger I will put yours to sleep with such mighty whacks that if it wakes at all it will be in the other world; for it is known there that I am not the man to let my face be mussed by anyone, and let each look out for the arrow.[8] But the best thing to do would be to leave one's anger to its slumbers, for no one knows the heart of any other, he who comes for wool may go back shorn, and God bless peace and curse all strife. If a hunted cat when surrounded and cornered turns into a lion, God knows what I who am a man might not become. And so from this time forth I am warning you, Sir Squire, that all the harm and damage that may result from our quarrel will be upon your head."

"Very well," the one of the Wood replied, "God will send the dawn and we shall make out somehow."

At that moment gay-colored birds of all sorts began warbling in the trees and with their merry and varied songs appeared to be greeting and welcoming the fresh-dawning day, which already at the gates and on the balconies of

---

8. A proverbial expression from archery: let each one take care of his or her own arrow. Other obviously proverbial expressions follow, as is typical of Sancho's speech.

the east was revealing its beautiful face as it shook out from its hair an infinite number of liquid pearls. Bathed in this gentle moisture, the grass seemed to shed a pearly spray, the willows distilled a savory manna, the fountains laughed, the brooks murmured, the woods were glad, and the meadows put on their finest raiment. The first thing that Sancho Panza beheld, as soon as it was light enough to tell one object from another, was the Squire of the Wood's nose, which was so big as to cast into the shade all the rest of his body. In addition to being of enormous size, it is said to have been hooked in the middle and all covered with warts of a mulberry hue, like eggplant; it hung down for a couple of inches below his mouth, and the size, color, warts, and shape of this organ gave his face so ugly an appearance that Sancho began trembling hand and foot like a child with convulsions and made up his mind then and there that he would take a couple of hundred punches before he would let his anger be awakened to a point where he would fight with this monster.

Don Quixote in the meanwhile was surveying his opponent, who had already adjusted and closed his helmet so that it was impossible to make out what he looked like. It was apparent, however, that he was not very tall and was stockily built. Over his armor he wore a coat of some kind or other made of what appeared to be the finest cloth of gold, all bespangled with glittering mirrors that resembled little moons and that gave him a most gallant and festive air, while above his helmet were a large number of waving plumes, green, white, and yellow in color. His lance, which was leaning against a tree, was very long and stout and had a steel point of more than a palm in length. Don Quixote took all this in, and from what he observed concluded that his opponent must be of tremendous strength, but he was not for this reason filled with fear as Sancho Panza was. Rather, he proceeded to address the Knight of the Mirrors, quite boldly and in a highbred manner.

"Sir Knight," he said, "if in your eagerness to fight you have not lost your courtesy, I would beg you to be so good as to raise your visor a little in order that I may see if your face is as handsome as your trappings."

"Whether you come out of this emprise the victor or the vanquished, Sir Knight," he of the Mirrors replied, "there will be ample time and opportunity for you to have a sight of me. If I do not now gratify your desire, it is because it seems to me that I should be doing a very great wrong to the beauteous Casildea de Vandalia by wasting the time it would take me to raise my visor before having forced you to confess that I am right in my contention, with which you are well acquainted."

"Well, then," said Don Quixote, "while we are mounting our steeds you might at least inform me if I am that knight of La Mancha whom you say you conquered."

"To that our[9] answer," said he of the Mirrors, "is that you are as like the knight I overcame as one egg is like another; but since you assert that you are persecuted by enchanters, I should not venture to state positively that you are the one in question."

"All of which," said Don Quixote, "is sufficient to convince me that you are laboring under a misapprehension; but in order to relieve you of it once and for all, let them bring our steeds, and in less time than you would spend

9. Note the dignified, "majestic" plural form.

in lifting your visor, if God, my lady, and my arm give me strength, I will see your face and you shall see that I am not the vanquished knight you take me to be."

With this, they cut short their conversation and mounted, and, turning Rocinante around, Don Quixote began measuring off the proper length of field for a run against his opponent as he of the Mirrors did the same. But the Knight of La Mancha had not gone twenty paces when he heard his adversary calling to him, whereupon each of them turned halfway and he of the Mirrors spoke.

"I must remind you, Sir Knight," he said, "of the condition under which we fight, which is that the vanquished, as I have said before, shall place himself wholly at the disposition of the victor."

"I am aware of that," replied Don Quixote, "not forgetting the provision that the behest laid upon the vanquished shall not exceed the bounds of chivalry."

"Agreed," said the Knight of the Mirrors.

At that moment Don Quixote caught sight of the other squire's weird nose and was as greatly astonished by it as Sancho had been. Indeed, he took the fellow for some monster, or some new kind of human being wholly unlike those that people this world. As he saw his master riding away down the field preparatory to the tilt, Sancho was alarmed; for he did not like to be left alone with the big-nosed individual, fearing that one powerful swipe of that protuberance against his own nose would end the battle so far as he was concerned and he would be lying stretched out on the ground, from fear if not from the force of the blow.

He accordingly ran after the knight, clinging to one of Rocinante's stirrup straps, and when he thought it was time for Don Quixote to whirl about and bear down upon his opponent, he called to him and said, "*Señor mio*, I beg your Grace, before you turn for the charge, to help me up into that cork tree yonder where I can watch the encounter which your Grace is going to have with this knight better than I can from the ground and in a way that is much more to my liking."

"I rather think, Sancho," said Don Quixote, "that what you wish to do is to mount a platform where you can see the bulls without any danger to yourself."

"The truth of the matter is," Sancho admitted, "the monstrous nose on that squire has given me such a fright that I don't dare stay near him."

"It is indeed of such a sort," his master assured him, "that if I were not the person I am, I myself should be frightened. And so, come, I will help you up."

While Don Quixote tarried to see Sancho ensconced in the cork tree, the Knight of the Mirrors measured as much ground as seemed to him necessary and then, assuming that his adversary had done the same, without waiting for sound of trumpet or any other signal, he wheeled his horse, which was no swifter nor any more impressive-looking than Rocinante, and bore down upon his enemy at a mild trot; but when he saw that the Manchegan was busy helping his squire, he reined in his mount and came to a stop midway in his course, for which his horse was extremely grateful, being no longer able to stir a single step. To Don Quixote, on the other hand, it seemed as if his enemy was flying, and digging his spurs with all his might into Rocinante's lean flanks he caused that animal to run a bit for the first and only time, according to the history, for on all other occasions a simple trot had represented his utmost speed. And so it was that, with an unheard-of-fury, the Knight of the Mournful Countenance came down upon the Knight of the Mirrors as the latter sat there sinking his spurs all the way up to the buttons without being able to persuade his horse to budge a single inch from the spot where he had come to a sudden standstill.

It was at this fortunate moment, while his adversary was in such a predicament, that Don Quixote fell upon him, quite unmindful of the fact that the other knight was having trouble with his mount and either was unable or did not have time to put his lance at rest. The upshot of it was, he encountered him with such force that, much against his will, the Knight of the Mirrors went rolling over his horse's flanks and tumbled to the ground, where as a result of his terrific fall he lay as if dead, without moving hand or foot.

No sooner did Sancho perceive what had happened than he slipped down from the cork tree and ran up as fast as he could to where his master was. Dismounting from Rocinante, Don Quixote now stood over the Knight of the Mirrors, and undoing the helmet straps to see if the man was dead, or to give him air in case he was alive, he beheld—who can say what he beheld without creating astonishment, wonder, and amazement in those who hear the tale? The history tells us that it was the very countenance, form, aspect, physiognomy, effigy, and image of the bachelor Sansón Carrasco!

"Come, Sancho," he cried in a loud voice, "and see what is to be seen but is not to be believed. Hasten, my son, and learn what magic can do and how great is the power of wizards and enchanters."

Sancho came, and the moment his eyes fell on the bachelor Carrasco's face he began crossing and blessing himself a countless number of times. Meanwhile, the overthrown knight gave no signs of life.

"If you ask me, master," said Sancho, "I would say that the best thing for your Grace to do is to run his sword down the mouth of this one who appears to be the bachelor Carrasco; maybe by so doing you would be killing one of your enemies, the enchanters."

"That is not a bad idea," replied Don Quixote, "for the fewer enemies the better." And, drawing his sword, he was about to act upon Sancho's advice and counsel when the Knight of the Mirrors' squire came up to them, now minus the nose which had made him so ugly.

"Look well what you are doing, Don Quixote!" he cried. "The one who lies there at your feet is your Grace's friend, the bachelor Sansón Carrasco, and I am his squire."

"And where is your nose?" inquired Sancho, who was surprised to see him without that deformity.

"Here in my pocket," was the reply. And, thrusting his hand into his coat, he drew out a nose of varnished pasteboard of the make that has been described. Studying him more and more closely, Sancho finally exclaimed, in a voice that was filled with amazement, "Holy Mary preserve me! And is this not my neighbor and crony, Tomé Cecial?"

"That is who I am!" replied the de-nosed squire, "your good friend Tomé Cecial, Sancho Panza. I will tell you presently of the means and snares and falsehoods that brought me here. But, for the present, I beg and entreat your master not to lay hands on, mistreat, wound, or slay the Knight of the Mirrors whom he now has at his feet; for without any doubt it is the rash and ill-advised bachelor Sansón Carrasco, our fellow villager."

The Knight of the Mirrors now recovered consciousness, and, seeing this, Don Quixote at once placed the naked point of his sword above the face of the vanquished one.

"Dead you are, knight," he said, "unless you confess that the peerless Dulcinea del Toboso is more beautiful than your Casildea de Vandalia. And what is more, you will have to promise that, should you survive this encounter and the fall you have had, you will go to the city of El Toboso and present yourself to her in my behalf, that she may do with you as she may see fit. And in case she leaves you free to follow your own will, you are to return to seek me out—the trail of my exploits will serve as a guide to bring you wherever I may be—and tell me all that has taken place between you and her. These conditions are in conformity with those that we arranged before our combat and they do not go beyond the bounds of knight-errantry."

"I confess," said the fallen knight, "that the tattered and filthy shoe of the lady Dulcinea del Toboso is of greater worth than the badly combed if clean beard of Casildea, and I promise to go to her presence and return to yours and to give you a complete and detailed account concerning anything you may wish to know."

"Another thing," added Don Quixote, "that you will have to confess and believe is that the knight you conquered was not and could not have been Don Quixote de la Mancha, but was some other that resembled him, just as I am convinced that you, though you appear to be the bachelor Sansón Carrasco, are another person in his form and likeness who has been put here by my enemies to induce me to restrain and moderate the impetuosity of my wrath and make a gentle use of my glorious victory."

"I confess, think, and feel as you feel, think, and believe," replied the lamed knight. "Permit me to rise, I beg of you, if the jolt I received in my fall will let me do so, for I am in very bad shape."

Don Quixote and Tomé Cecial the squire now helped him to his feet. As for Sancho, he could not take his eyes off Tomé but kept asking him one question after another, and although the answers he received afforded clear enough proof that the man was really his fellow townsman, the fear that had been aroused in him by his master's words—about the enchanters' having transformed the Knight of the Mirrors into the bachelor Sansón Carrasco—prevented him from believing the truth that was apparent to his eyes. The short of it is, both master and servant were left with this delusion as the other ill-errant knight and his squire, in no pleasant state of mind, took their departure with the object of looking for some village where they might be able to apply poultices and splints to the bachelor's battered ribs.

Don Quixote and Sancho then resumed their journey along the road to Saragossa, and here for the time being the history leaves them in order to give an account of who the Knight of the Mirrors and his long-nosed squire really were.

CHAPTER 15

Wherein is told and revealed who the Knight of the Mirrors and his
squire were.

Don Quixote went off very happy, self-satisfied, and vainglorious at having achieved a victory over so valiant a knight as he imagined the one of the Mirrors to be, from whose knightly word he hoped to learn whether or not the spell which had been put upon his lady was still in effect; for, unless he chose to forfeit his honor, the vanquished contender must of necessity return and give an account of what had happened in the course of his interview with her. But Don Quixote was of one mind, the Knight of the Mirrors of another, for, as has been stated, the latter's only thought at the moment was to find some village where plasters were available.

The history goes on to state that when the bachelor Sansón Carrasco advised Don Quixote to resume his feats of chivalry, after having desisted from them for a while, this action was taken as the result of a conference which he had held with the curate and the barber as to the means to be adopted in persuading the knight to remain quietly at home and cease agitating himself over his unfortunate adventures. It had been Carrasco's suggestion, to which they had unanimously agreed, that they let Don Quixote sally forth, since it appeared to be impossible to prevent his doing so, and that Sansón should then take to the road as a knight-errant and pick a quarrel and do battle with him. There would be no difficulty about finding a pretext, and then the bachelor knight would overcome him (which was looked upon as easy of accomplishment), having first entered into a pact to the effect that the vanquished should remain at the mercy and bidding of his conqueror. The behest in this case was to be that the fallen one should return to his village and home and not leave it for the space of two years or until further orders were given him, it being a certainty that, once having been overcome, Don Quixote would fulfill the agreement, in order not to contravene or fail to obey the laws of chivalry. And it was possible that in the course of his seclusion he would forget his fancies, or they would at least have an opportunity to seek some suitable cure for his madness.

Sansón agreed to undertake this, and Tomé Cecial, Sancho's friend and neighbor, a merry but featherbrained chap, offered to go along as squire. Sansón then proceeded to arm himself in the manner that has been described, while Tomé disguised his nose with the aforementioned mask so that his crony would not recognize him when they met. Thus equipped, they followed the same route as Don Quixote and had almost caught up with him by the time he had the adventure with the Cart of Death. They finally overtook him in the wood, where those events occurred with which the attentive reader is already familiar; and if it had not been for the knight's extraordinary fancies, which led him to believe that the bachelor was not the bachelor, the said bachelor might have been prevented from ever attaining his degree of licentiate, as a result of having found no nests where he thought to find birds.

Seeing how ill they had succeeded in their undertaking and what an end they had reached, Tomé Cecial now addressed his master.

"Surely, Señor Sansón Carrasco," he said, "we have had our deserts. It is easy enough to plan and embark upon an enterprise, but most of the time it's hard to get out of it. Don Quixote is a madman and we are sane, yet he goes away sound and laughing while your Grace is left here, battered and sorrowful. I wish you would tell me now who is the crazier: the one who is so because he cannot help it, or he who turns crazy of his own free will?"

"The difference between the two," replied Sansón, "lies in this: that the one who cannot help being crazy will be so always, whereas the one who is a madman by choice can leave off being one whenever he so desires."

"Well," said Tomé Cecial, "since that is the way it is, and since I chose to be crazy when I became your Grace's squire, by the same reasoning I now choose to stop being insane and to return to my home."

"That is your affair," said Sansón, "but to imagine that I am going back before I have given Don Quixote a good thrashing is senseless; and what will urge me on now is not any desire to see him recover his wits, but rather a thirst for vengeance; for with the terrible pain that I have in my ribs, you can't expect me to feel very charitable."

Conversing in this manner they kept on until they reached a village where it was their luck to find a bonesetter to take care of poor Sansón. Tomé Cecial then left him and returned home, while the bachelor meditated plans for revenge. The history has more to say of him in due time, but for the present it goes on to make merry with Don Quixote.

CHAPTER 16

Of what happened to Don Quixote upon his meeting with a prudent gentleman of La Mancha.

With that feeling of happiness and vainglorious self-satisfaction that has been mentioned, Don Quixote continued on his way, imagining himself to be, as a result of the victory he had just achieved, the most valiant knight-errant of the age. Whatever adventures might befall him from then on he regarded as already accomplished and brought to a fortunate conclusion. He thought little now of enchanters and enchantments and was unmindful of the innumerable beatings he had received in the course of his knightly wanderings, of the volley of pebbles that had knocked out half his teeth, of the ungratefulness of the galley slaves and the audacity of the Yanguesans whose poles had fallen upon his body like rain. In short, he told himself, if he could but find the means, manner, or way of freeing his lady Dulcinea of the spell that had been put upon her, he would not envy the greatest good fortune that the most fortunate of knights-errant in ages past had ever by any possibility attained.

He was still wholly wrapped up in these thoughts when Sancho spoke to him.

"Isn't it strange, sir, that I can still see in front of my eyes the huge and monstrous nose of my old crony, Tomé Cecial?"

"And do you by any chance believe, Sancho, that the Knight of the Mirrors was the bachelor Sansón Carrasco and that his squire was your friend Tomé?"

"I don't know what to say to that," replied Sancho. "All I know is that the things he told me about my home, my wife and young ones, could not have come from anybody else; and the face, too, once you took the nose away, was the same as Tomé Cecial's, which I have seen many times in our village, right next door to my own house, and the tone of voice was the same also."

"Let us reason the matter out, Sancho," said Don Quixote. "Look at it this way: how can it be thought that the bachelor Sansón Carrasco would come as a knight-errant, equipped with offensive and defensive armor, to contend with me? Am I, perchance, his enemy? Have I given him any occasion to cherish a grudge against me? Am I a rival of his? Or can it be jealousy of the fame I have acquired that has led him to take up the profession of arms?"

"Well, then, sir," Sancho answered him, "how are we to explain the fact that the knight was so like the bachelor and his squire like my friend? And if this was a magic spell, as your Grace has said, was there no other pair in the world whose likeness they might have taken?"

"It is all a scheme and a plot," replied Don Quixote, "on the part of those wicked magicians who are persecuting me and who, foreseeing that I would be the victor in the combat, saw to it that the conquered knight should display the face of my friend the bachelor, so that the affection which I bear him would come between my fallen enemy and the edge of my sword and might of my arm, to temper the righteous indignation of my heart. In that way, he who had sought by falsehood and deceits to take my life, would be left to go on living. As proof of all this, Sancho, experience, which neither lies nor deceives, has already taught you how easy it is for enchanters to change one countenance into another, making the beautiful ugly and the ugly beautiful. It was not two days ago that you beheld the peerless Dulcinea's beauty and elegance in its entirety and natural form, while I saw only the repulsive features of a low and ignorant peasant girl with cataracts over her eyes and a foul smell in her mouth. And if the perverse enchanter was bold enough to effect so vile a transformation as this, there is certainly no cause for wonderment at what he has done in the case of Sansón Carrasco and your friend, all by way of snatching my glorious victory out of my hands. But in spite of it all, I find consolation in the fact that, whatever the shape he may have chosen to assume, I have laid my enemy low."

"God knows what the truth of it all may be," was Sancho's comment. Knowing as he did that Dulcinea's transformation had been due to his own scheming and plotting, he was not taken in by his master's delusions. He was at a loss for a reply, however, lest he say something that would reveal his own trickery.

As they were carrying on this conversation, they were overtaken by a man who, following the same road, was coming along behind them. He was mounted on a handsome flea-bitten mare and wore a hooded greatcoat of fine green cloth trimmed in tawny velvet and a cap of the same material, while the trappings of his steed, which was accoutered for the field, were green and mulberry in hue, his saddle being of the *jineta*[1] mode. From his broad green and gold shoulder strap there dangled a Moorish cutlass, and his half-boots were of the same make as the baldric. His spurs were not gilded but were covered with highly polished green lacquer, so that harmonizing as they did with the rest of his apparel, they seemed more appropriate than if they had been of purest gold. As he came up, he greeted the pair courteously and, spurring his mare, was about to ride on past when Don Quixote called to him.

1. It has a high pommel and short stirrups.

"Gallant sir," he said, "If your Grace is going our way and is not in a hurry, it would be a favor to us if we might travel together."

"The truth is," replied the stranger, "I should not have ridden past you if I had not been afraid that the company of my mare would excite your horse."

"In that case, sir," Sancho spoke up, "you may as well rein in, for this horse of ours is the most virtuous and well mannered of any that there is. Never on such an occasion has he done anything that was not right—the only time he did misbehave, my master and I suffered for it aplenty. And so, I say again, your Grace may slow up if you like; for even if you offered him your mare on a couple of platters, he'd never try to mount her."

With this, the other traveler drew rein, being greatly astonished at Don Quixote's face and figure. For the knight was now riding along without his helmet, which was carried by Sancho like a piece of luggage on the back of his gray, in front of the packsaddle. If the green-clad gentleman stared hard at his new-found companion, the latter returned his gaze with an even greater intensity. He impressed Don Quixote as being a man of good judgment, around fifty years of age, with hair that was slightly graying and an aquiline nose, while the expression of his countenance was half humorous, half serious. In short, both his person and his accouterments indicated that he was an individual of some worth.

As for the man in green's impression of Don Quixote de la Mancha, he was thinking that he had never before seen any human being that resembled this one. He could not but marvel at the knight's long neck, his tall frame, and the leanness and the sallowness of his face, as well as his armor and his grave bearing, the whole constituting a sight such as had not been seen for many a day in those parts. Don Quixote in turn was quite conscious of the attentiveness with which the traveler was studying him and could tell from the man's astonished look how curious he was; and so, being very courteous and fond of pleasing everyone, he proceeded to anticipate any questions that might be asked him.

"I am aware," he said, "that my appearance must strike your Grace as being very strange and out of the ordinary, and for that reason I am not surprised at your wonderment. But your Grace will cease to wonder when I tell you, as I am telling you now, that I am a knight, one of those

> Of whom it is folks say,
> They to adventures go.

I have left my native health, mortgaged my estate, given up my comfortable life, and cast myself into fortune's arms for her to do with me what she will. It has been my desire to revive a knight-errantry that is now dead, and for some time past, stumbling here and falling there, now throwing myself down headlong and then rising up once more, I have been able in good part to carry out my design by succoring widows, protecting damsels, and aiding the fallen, the orphans, and the young, all of which is the proper and natural duty of knights-errant. As a result, owing to my many valiant and Christian exploits, I have been deemed worthy of visiting in printed form nearly all the nations of the world. Thirty thousand copies of my history have been published, and, unless Heaven forbid, they will print thirty million of them.

"In short, to put it all into a few words, or even one, I will tell you that I am Don Quixote de la Mancha, otherwise known as the Knight of the Mournful Countenance. Granted that self-praise is degrading, there still are times when I must praise myself, that is to say, when there is no one else present to speak in my behalf. And so, good sir, neither this steed nor this lance nor this buckler nor this squire of mine, nor all the armor that I wear and arms I carry, nor the sallowness of my complexion, nor my leanness and gauntness, should any longer astonish you, now that you know who I am and what the profession is that I follow."

Having thus spoken, Don Quixote fell silent, and the man in green was so slow in replying that it seemed as if he was at a loss for words. Finally, however, after a considerable while, he brought himself to the point of speaking.

"You were correct, Sir Knight," he said, "about my astonishment and my curiosity, but you have not succeeded in removing the wonderment that the sight of you has aroused in me. You say that, knowing who you are, I should not wonder any more, but such is not the case, for I am now more amazed than ever. How can it be that there are knights-errant in the world today and that histories of them are actually printed? I find it hard to convince myself that at the present time there is anyone on earth who goes about aiding widows, protecting damsels, defending the honor of wives, and succoring orphans, and I should never have believed it had I not beheld your Grace with my own eyes. Thank Heaven for that book that your Grace tells me has been published concerning your true and exalted deeds of chivalry, as it should cast into oblivion all the innumerable stories of fictitious knights-errant with which the world is filled, greatly to the detriment of good morals and the prejudice and discredit of legitimate histories."

"As to whether the stories of knights-errant are fictitious or not," observed Don Quixote, "there is much that remains to be said."

"Why," replied the gentleman in green, "is there anyone who can doubt that such tales are false?"

"I doubt it," was the knight's answer, "but let the matter rest there. If our journey lasts long enough, I trust with God's help to be able to show your Grace that you are wrong in going along with those who hold it to be a certainty that they are not true."

From this last remark the traveler was led to suspect that Don Quixote must be some kind of crackbrain, and he was waiting for him to confirm the impression by further observations of the same sort; but before they could get off on another subject, the knight, seeing that he had given an account of his own station in life, turned to the stranger and politely inquired who his companion might be.

"I, Sir Knight of the Mournful Countenance," replied the one in the green-colored greatcoat, "am a gentleman, and a native of the village where, please God, we are going to dine today. I am more than moderately rich, and my name is Don Diego de Miranda. I spend my life with my wife and children and with my friends. My occupations are hunting and fishing, though I keep neither falcon nor hounds but only a tame partridge[2] and a bold ferret or two. I am the owner of about six dozen books, some of them in Spanish, others in Latin, including both histories and devotional works. As for books of chivalry, they have not as yet crossed the threshold of my door. My own

---

2. Used as a decoy.

preference is for profane rather than devotional writings, such as afford an innocent amusement, charming us by their style and arousing and holding our interest by their inventiveness, although I must say there are very few of that sort to be found in Spain.

"Sometimes," the man in green continued, "I dine with my friends and neighbors, and I often invite them to my house. My meals are wholesome and well prepared and there is always plenty to eat. I do not care for gossip, nor will I permit it in my presence. I am not lynx-eyed and do not pry into the lives and doings of others. I hear mass every day and share my substance with the poor, but make no parade of my good works lest hypocrisy and vainglory, those enemies that so imperceptibly take possession of the most modest heart, should find their way into mine. I try to make peace between those who are at strife. I am the devoted servant of Our Lady, and my trust is in the infinite mercy of God Our Savior."

Sancho had listened most attentively to the gentleman's account of his mode of life, and inasmuch as it seemed to him that this was a good and holy way to live and that the one who followed such a pattern ought to be able to work miracles, he now jumped down from his gray's back and, running over to seize the stranger's right stirrup, began kissing the feet of the man in green with a show of devotion that bordered on tears.

"Why are you doing that, brother?" the gentleman asked him. "What is the meaning of these kisses?"

"Let me kiss your feet," Sancho insisted, "for if I am not mistaken, your Grace is the first saint riding *jineta* fashion that I have seen in all the days of my life."

"I am not a saint," the gentleman assured him, "but a great sinner. It is you, brother, who are the saint; for you must be a good man, judging by the simplicity of heart that you show."

Sancho then went back to his packsaddle, having evoked a laugh from the depths of his master's melancholy and given Don Diego fresh cause for astonishment.

Don Quixote thereupon inquired of the newcomer how many children he had, remarking as he did so that the ancient philosophers, who were without a true knowledge of God, believed that mankind's greatest good lay in the gifts of nature, in those of fortune, and in having many friends and many and worthy sons.

"I, Señor Don Quixote," replied the gentleman, "have a son without whom I should, perhaps, be happier than I am. It is not that he is bad, but rather that he is not as good as I should like him to be. He is eighteen years old, and for six of those years he has been at Salamanca studying the Greek and Latin languages. When I desired him to pass on to other branches of learning, I found him so immersed in the science of Poetry (if it can be called such) that it was not possible to interest him in the Law, which I wanted him to study, nor in Theology, the queen of them all. My wish was that he might be an honor to his family; for in this age in which we are living our monarchs are in the habit of highly rewarding those forms of learning that are good and virtuous, since learning without virtue is like pearls on a dunghill. But he spends the whole day trying to decide whether such and such a verse of Homer's *Iliad* is well conceived or not, whether or not Martial is immodest in a certain epigram, whether certain lines of Vergil are to be understood in this way or in that. In short, he spends all of his time with the books written by those poets whom I have mentioned and with those of Horace, Persius, Juvenal, and Tibullus. As for our own moderns, he sets little store by them, and yet, for all his disdain of Spanish poetry, he is at this moment racking his brains in an effort to compose a gloss on a quatrain that was sent him from Salamanca and which, I fancy, is for some literary tournament."

To all this Don Quixote made the following answer:

"Children, sir, are out of their parents' bowels and so are to be loved whether they be good or bad, just as we love those that gave us life. It is for parents to bring up their offspring, from the time they are infants, in the paths of virtue, good breeding, proper conduct, and Christian morality, in order that, when they are grown, they may be a staff to the old age of the ones that bore them and an honor to their own posterity. As to compelling them to study a particular branch of learning, I am not so sure as to that, though there may be no harm in trying to persuade them to do so. But where there is no need to study *pane lucrando*[3]—where Heaven has provided them with parents that can supply their daily bread—I should be in favor of permitting them to follow that course to which they are most inclined; and although poetry may be more pleasurable than useful, it is not one of those pursuits that bring dishonor upon those who engage in them.

"Poetry in my opinion, my dear sir," he went on, "is a young and tender maid of surpassing beauty, who has many other damsels (that is to say, the other disciplines) whose duty it is to bedeck, embellish, and adorn her. She may call upon all of them for service, and all of them in turn depend upon her nod. She is not one to be rudely handled, nor dragged through the streets, nor exposed at street corners, in the market place, or in the private nooks of palaces. She is fashioned through an alchemy of such power that he who knows how to make use of it will be able to convert her into the purest gold of inestimable price. Possessing her, he must keep her within bounds and not permit her to run wild in bawdy satires or soulless sonnets. She is not to be put up for sale in any manner, unless it be in the form of heroic poems, pity-inspiring tragedies, or pleasing and ingenious comedies. Let mountebanks keep hands off her, and the ignorant mob as well, which is incapable of recognizing or appreciating the treasures that are locked within her. And do not think, sir, that I apply that term 'mob' solely to plebeians and those of low estate; for anyone who is ignorant, whether he be lord or prince, may, and should, be included in the vulgar herd.

"But," Don Quixote continued, "he who possesses the gift of poetry and who makes the use of it that I have indicated, shall become famous and his name shall be honored among all the civilized nations of the world. You have stated, sir, that your son does not greatly care for poetry written in our Spanish tongue, and in that I am inclined to think he is somewhat mistaken. My reason for saying so is this: the great Homer did not write in Latin, for the reason that he was a Greek, and Vergil did not write in Greek since he was a Latin. In a word, all the poets of antiquity wrote in the language which they had imbibed with their mother's milk and did not go searching after foreign ones to express their loftiest conceptions. This being so, it would be

3. Earning one's bread (Latin).

well if the same custom were to be adopted by all nations, the German poet being no longer looked down upon because he writes in German, nor the Castilian or the Basque for employing his native speech.

"As for your son, I fancy, sir, that his quarrel is not so much with Spanish poetry as with those poets who have no other tongue or discipline at their command such as would help to awaken their natural gift; and yet, here, too, he may be wrong. There is an opinion, and a true one, to the effect that 'the poet is born,' that is to say, it is as a poet that he comes forth from his mother's womb, and with the propensity that has been bestowed upon him by Heaven, without study or artifice, he produces those compositions that attest the truth of the line: 'Est deus in nobis,'[4] etc. I further maintain that the born poet who is aided by art will have a great advantage over the one who by art alone would become a poet, the reason being that art does not go beyond, but merely perfects, nature; and so it is that, by combining nature with art and art with nature, the finished poet is produced.

"In conclusion, then, my dear sir, my advice to you would be to let your son go where his star beckons him; for being a good student as he must be, and having already successfully mounted the first step on the stairway of learning, which is that of languages, he will be able to continue of his own accord to the very peak of humane letters, an accomplishment that is altogether becoming in a gentleman, one that adorns, honors, and distinguishes him as much as the miter does the bishop or his flowing robe the learned jurisconsult. Your Grace well may reprove your son, should he compose satires that reflect upon the honor of other persons; in that case, punish him and tear them up. But should he compose discourses in the manner of Horace, in which he reprehends vice in general as that poet so elegantly does, then praise him by all means; for it is permitted the poet to write verses in which he inveighs against envy and the other vices as well, and to lash out at the vicious without, however, designating any particular individual. On the other hand, there are poets who for the sake of uttering something malicious would run the risk of being banished to the shores of Pontus.[5]

"If the poet be chaste where his own manners are concerned, he would likewise be modest in his verses, for the pen is the tongue of the mind, and whatever thoughts are engendered there are bound to appear in his writings. When kings and princes behold the marvelous art of poetry as practiced by prudent, virtuous, and serious-minded subjects of their realm, they honor, esteem, and reward those persons and crown them with the leaves of the tree that is never struck by lightning[6]—as if to show that those who are crowned and adorned with such wreaths are not to be assailed by anyone."

The gentleman in the green-colored greatcoat was vastly astonished by this speech of Don Quixote's and was rapidly altering the opinion he had previously held, to the effect that his companion was but a crackbrain. In the middle of the long discourse, which was not greatly to his liking, Sancho had left the highway to go seek a little milk from some shepherds who were draining the udders of their ewes near by. Extremely well pleased with the knight's sound sense and excellent reasoning, the gentleman was about to resume the conversation when, raising his head, Don Quixote caught sight of a cart flying royal flags that was coming toward them down the road and,

---

4. There is a god in us (Latin); Ovid's *Fasti* 6.5.   5. As Ovid was by Augustus in A.D. 8.   6. The laurel.

thinking it must be a fresh adventure, began calling to Sancho in a loud voice to bring him his helmet. Whereupon Sancho hastily left the shepherds and spurred his gray until he was once more alongside his master, who was now about to encounter a dreadful and bewildering ordeal.

[*"For I Well Know the Meaning of Valor"*]

CHAPTER 17

Wherein Don Quixote's unimaginable courage reaches its highest point, together with the adventure of the lions and its happy ending.

The history relates that, when Don Quixote called to Sancho to bring him his helmet, the squire was busy buying some curds from the shepherds and, flustered by his master's great haste, did not know what to do with them or how to carry them. Having already paid for the curds, he did not care to lose them, and so he decided to put them into the headpiece, and, acting upon this happy inspiration, he returned to see what was wanted of him.

"Give me that helmet," said the knight; "for either I know little about adventures or here is one where I am going to need my armor."

Upon hearing this, the gentleman in the green-colored greatcoat looked around in all directions but could see nothing except the cart that was approaching them, decked out with two or three flags which indicated that the vehicle in question must be conveying his Majesty's property. He remarked as much to Don Quixote, but the latter paid no attention, for he was always convinced that whatever happened to him meant adventures and more adventures.

"Forewarned is forearmed," he said. "I lose nothing by being prepared, knowing as I do that I have enemies both visible and invisible and cannot tell when or where or in what form they will attack me."

Turning to Sancho, he asked for his helmet again, and as there was no time to shake out the curds, the squire had to hand it to him as it was. Don Quixote took it and, without noticing what was in it, hastily clapped it on his head; and forthwith, as a result of the pressure on the curds, the whey began running down all over his face and beard, at which he was very much startled.

"What is this, Sancho?" he cried. "I think my head must be softening or my brains melting, or else I am sweating from head to foot. If sweat it be, I assure you it is not from fear, though I can well believe that the adventure which now awaits me is a terrible one indeed. Give me something with which to wipe my face, if you have anything, for this perspiration is so abundant that it blinds me."

Sancho said nothing but gave him a cloth and at the same time gave thanks to God that his master had not discovered what the trouble was. Don Quixote wiped his face and then took off his helmet to see what it was that made his head feel so cool. Catching sight of that watery white mass, he lifted it to his nose and smelled it.

"By the life of my lady Dulcinea del Toboso!" he exclaimed. "Those are curds that you have put there, you treacherous, brazen, ill-mannered squire!"

To this Sancho replied, very calmly and with a straight face, "If they are curds, give them to me, your Grace, so that I can eat them. But no, let the devil eat them, for he must be the one who did it. Do you think I would be so bold as to soil your Grace's helmet? Upon my word, master, by the understanding that God has given me, I, too, must have enchanters who are persecuting me as your Grace's creature and one of his members, and they are the ones who put that filthy mess there to make you lose your patience and your temper and cause you to whack my ribs as you are in the habit of doing. Well, this time, I must say, they have missed the mark; for I trust my master's good sense to tell him that I have neither curds nor milk nor anything of the kind, and if I did have, I'd put it in my stomach and not in that helmet."

"That may very well be," said Don Quixote.

Don Diego was observing all this and was more astonished than ever, especially when, after he had wiped his head, face, beard, and helmet, Don Quixote once more donned the piece of armor and, settling himself in the stirrups, proceeded to adjust his sword and fix his lance.

"Come what may, here I stand, ready to take on Satan himself in person!" shouted the knight.

The cart with the flags had come up to them by this time, accompanied only by a driver riding one of the mules and a man seated up in front.

"Where are you going, brothers?" Don Quixote called out as he placed himself in the path of the cart. "What conveyance is this, what do you carry in it, and what is the meaning of those flags?"

"The cart is mine," replied the driver, "and in it are two fierce lions in cages which the governor of Oran is sending to court as a present for his Majesty. The flags are those of our lord the King, as a sign that his property goes here."

"And are the lions large?" inquired Don Quixote.

It was the man sitting at the door of the cage who answered him. "The largest," he said, "that ever were sent from Africa to Spain. I am the lionkeeper and I have brought back others, but never any like these. They are male and female. The male is in this first cage, the female in the one behind. They are hungry right now, for they have had nothing to eat today; and so we'd be obliged if your Grace would get out of the way, for we must hasten on to the place where we are to feed them."

"Lion whelps against me?" said Don Quixote with a slight smile. "Lion whelps against me? And at such an hour? Then, by God, those gentlemen who sent them shall see whether I am the man to be frightened by lions. Get down, my good fellow, and since you are the lionkeeper, open the cages and turn those beasts out for me; and in the middle of this plain I will teach them who Don Quixote de la Mancha is, notwithstanding and in spite of the enchanters who are responsible for their being here."

"So," said the gentleman to himself as he heard this, "our worthy knight has revealed himself. It must indeed be true that the curds have softened his skull and mellowed his brains."

At this point Sancho approached him. "For God's sake, sir," he said, "do something to keep my master from fighting those lions. For if he does, they're going to tear us all to bits."

"Is your master, then, so insane," the gentleman asked, "that you fear and believe he means to tackle those fierce animals?"

"It is not that he is insane," replied Sancho, "but, rather, foolhardy."

"Very well," said the gentleman, "I will put a stop to it." And going up to Don Quixote, who was still urging the lionkeeper to open the cages, he said, "Sir Knight, knights-errant should undertake only those adventures that afford some hope of a successful outcome, not those that are utterly hopeless to begin with; for valor when it turns to temerity has in it more of madness than of bravery. Moreover, these lions have no thought of attacking your Grace but are a present to his Majesty, and it would not be well to detain them or interfere with their journey."

"My dear sir," answered Don Quixote, "you had best go mind your tame partridge and that bold ferret of yours and let each one attend to his own business. This is my affair, and I know whether these gentlemen, the lions, have come to attack me or not." He then turned to the lionkeeper. "I swear, Sir Rascal, if you do not open those cages at once, I'll pin you to the cart with this lance!"

Perceiving how determined the armed phantom was, the driver now spoke up. "Good sir," he said, "will your Grace please be so kind as to let me unhitch the mules and take them to a safe place before you turn those lions loose? For if they kill them for me, I am ruined for life, since the mules and cart are all the property I own."

"O man of little faith!" said Don Quixote. "Get down and unhitch your mules if you like, but you will soon see that it was quite unnecessary and that you might have spared yourself the trouble."

The driver did so, in great haste, as the lionkeeper began shouting, "I want you all to witness that I am being compelled against my will to open the cages and turn the lions out, and I further warn this gentleman that he will be responsible for all the harm and damage the beasts may do, plus my wages and my fees. You other gentlemen take cover before I open the doors; I am sure they will not do any harm to me."

Once more Don Diego sought to persuade his companion not to commit such an act of madness, as it was tempting God to undertake anything so foolish as that; but Don Quixote's only answer was that he knew what he was doing. And when the gentleman in green insisted that he was sure the knight was laboring under a delusion and ought to consider the matter well, the latter cut him short.

"Well, then, sir," he said, "if your Grace does not care to be a spectator at what you believe is going to turn out to be a tragedy, all you have to do is to spur your flea-bitten mare and seek safety."

Hearing this, Sancho with tears in his eyes again begged him to give up the undertaking, in comparison with which the adventure of the windmills and the dreadful one at the fulling mills—indeed, all the exploits his master had ever in the course of his life undertaken—were but bread and cakes.

"Look, sir," Sancho went on, "there is no enchantment here nor anything of the sort. Through the bars and chinks of that cage I have seen a real lion's claw, and judging by the size of it, the lion that it belongs to is bigger than a mountain."

"Fear, at any rate," said Don Quixote, "will make him look bigger to you than half the world. Retire, Sancho, and leave me, and if I die here, you know our ancient pact: you are to repair to Dulcinea—I say no more."

To this he added other remarks that took away any hope they had that he might not go through with his insane plan. The gentleman in the green-colored greatcoat was of a mind to resist him but saw that he was no match for the knight in the matter of arms. Then, too, it did not seem to him the part of wisdom to fight it out with a madman; for Don Quixote now impressed him as being quite mad in every way. Accordingly, while the knight was repeating his threats to the lionkeeper, Don Diego spurred his mare, Sancho his gray, and the driver his mules, all of them seeking to put as great a distance as possible between themselves and the cart before the lions broke loose.

Sancho already was bewailing his master's death, which he was convinced was bound to come from the lions' claws, and at the same time he cursed his fate and called it an unlucky hour in which he had taken it into his head to serve such a one. But despite his tears and lamentations, he did not leave off thrashing his gray in an effort to leave the cart behind them. When the lionkeeper saw that those who had fled were a good distance away, he once more entreated and warned Don Quixote as he had warned and entreated him before, but the answer he received was that he might save his breath as it would do him no good and he had best hurry and obey. In the space of time that it took the keeper to open the first cage, Don Quixote considered the question as to whether it would be well to give battle on foot or on horseback. He finally decided that he would do better on foot, as he feared that Rocinante would become frightened at sight of the lions; and so, leaping down from his horse, he fixed his lance, braced his buckler, and drew his sword, and then advanced with marvelous daring and great resoluteness until he stood directly in front of the cart, meanwhile commending himself to God with all his heart and then to his lady Dulcinea.

Upon reaching this point, the reader should know, the author of our veracious history indulges in the following exclamatory passage:

"O great-souled Don Quixote de la Mancha, thou whose courage is beyond all praise, mirror wherein all the valiant of the world may behold themselves, a new and second Don Manuel de León,[1] once the glory and the honor of Spanish knighthood! With what words shall I relate thy terrifying exploit, how render it credible to the ages that are to come? What eulogies do not belong to thee of right, even though they consist of hyperbole piled upon hyperbole? On foot and singlehanded, intrepid and with greathearted valor, armed but with a sword, and not one of the keen-edged Little Dog[2] make, and with a shield that was not of gleaming and polished steel, thou didst stand and wait for the two fiercest lions that ever the African forests bred! Thy deeds shall be thy praise, O valorous Manchegan; I leave them to speak for thee, since words fail me with which to extol them."

Here the author leaves off his exclamations and resumes the thread of the story.

Seeing Don Quixote posed there before him and perceiving that, unless he wished to incur the bold knight's indignation there was nothing for him to do but release the male lion, the keeper now opened the first cage, and it could be seen at once how extraordinarily big and horribly ugly the beast was. The first thing the recumbent animal did was to turn round, put out a claw, and stretch himself all over. Then he opened his mouth and yawned

1. Don Manuel Ponce de León, a paragon of gallantry and courtesy, from the time of Ferdinand and Isabella. 2. The trademark of a famous armorer of Toledo and Saragossa.

very slowly, after which he put out a tongue that was nearly two palms in length and with it licked the dust out of his eyes and washed his face. Having done this, he stuck his head outside the cage and gazed about him in all directions. His eyes were now like live coals and his appearance and demeanor were such as to strike terror in temerity itself. But Don Quixote merely stared at him attentively, waiting for him to descend from the cart so that they could come to grips, for the knight was determined to hack the brute to pieces, such was the extent of his unheard-of madness.

The lion, however, proved to be courteous rather than arrogant and was in no mood for childish bravado. After having gazed first in one direction and then in another, as has been said, he turned his back and presented his hind parts to Don Quixote and then very calmly and peaceably lay down and stretched himself out once more in his cage. At this, Don Quixote ordered the keeper to stir him up with a stick in order to irritate him and drive him out.

"That I will not do," the keeper replied, "for if I stir him, I will be the first one he will tear to bits. Be satisfied with what you have already accomplished, Sir Knight, which leaves nothing more to be said on the score of valor, and do not go tempting your fortune a second time. The door was open and the lion could have gone out if he had chosen; since he has not done so up to now, that means he will stay where he is all day long. Your Grace's stout-heartedness has been well established; for no brave fighter, as I see it, is obliged to do more than challenge his enemy and wait for him in the field; his adversary, if he does not come, is the one who is disgraced and the one who awaits him gains the crown of victory."

"That is the truth," said Don Quixote. "Shut the door, my friend, and bear me witness as best you can with regard to what you have seen me do here. I would have you certify: that you opened the door for the lion, that I waited for him and he did not come out, that I continued to wait and still he stayed there, and finally went back and lay down. I am under no further obligation. Away with enchantments, and God uphold the right, the truth, and true chivalry! So close the door, as I have told you, while I signal to the fugitives in order that they who were not present may hear of this exploit from your lips."

The keeper did as he was commanded, and Don Quixote, taking the cloth with which he had dried his face after the rain of curds, fastened it to the point of his lance and began summoning the runaways, who, all in a body with the gentleman in green bringing up the rear, were still fleeing and turning around to look back at every step. Sancho was the first to see the white cloth.

"May they slay me," he said, "if my master hasn't conquered those fierce beasts, for he's calling to us."

They all stopped and made sure that the one who was doing the signaling was indeed Don Quixote, and then, losing some of their fear, they little by little made their way back to a point where they could distinctly hear what the knight was saying. At last they returned to the cart, and as they drew near Don Quixote spoke to the driver.

"You may come back, brother, hitch your mules, and continue your journey. And you, Sancho, may give each of them two gold crowns to recompense them for the delay they have suffered on my account."

"That I will, right enough," said Sancho. "But what has become of the lions? Are they dead or alive?"

The keeper thereupon, in leisurely fashion and in full detail, proceeded to tell them how the encounter had ended, taking pains to stress to the best of his ability the valor displayed by Don Quixote, at sight of whom the lion had been so cowed that he was unwilling to leave his cage, though the door had been left open quite a while. The fellow went on to state that the knight had wanted him to stir the lion up and force him out, but had finally been convinced that this would be tempting God and so, much to his displeasure and against his will, had permitted the door to be closed.

"What do you think of that, Sancho?" asked Don Quixote. "Are there any spells that can withstand true gallantry? The enchanters may take my luck away, but to deprive me of my strength and courage is an impossibility."

Sancho then bestowed the crowns, the driver hitched his mules, and the lionkeeper kissed Don Quixote's hands for the favor received, promising that, when he reached the court, he would relate this brave exploit to the king himself.

"In that case," replied Don Quixote, "if his Majesty by any chance should inquire who it was that performed it, you are to say that it was the Knight of the Lions; for that is the name by which I wish to be known from now on, thus changing, exchanging, altering, and converting the one I have previously borne, that of Knight of the Mournful Countenance; in which respect I am but following the old custom of knights-errant, who changed their names whenever they liked or found it convenient to do so."

With this, the cart continued on its way, and Don Quixote, Sancho, and the gentleman in the green-colored greatcoat likewise resumed their journey. During all this time Don Diego de Miranda had not uttered a word but was wholly taken up with observing what Don Quixote did and listening to what he had to say. The knight impressed him as being a crazy sane man and an insane one on the verge of sanity. The gentleman did not happen to be familiar with the first part of our history, but if he had read it he would have ceased to wonder at such talk and conduct, for he would then have known what kind of madness this was. Remaining as he did in ignorance of his companion's malady, he took him now for a sensible individual and now for a madman, since what Don Quixote said was coherent, elegantly phrased, and to the point, whereas his actions were nonsensical, foolhardy, and downright silly. What greater madness could there be, Don Diego asked himself, than to don a helmet filled with curds and then persuade oneself that enchanters were softening one's cranium? What could be more rashly absurd than to wish to fight lions by sheer strength alone? He was roused from these thoughts, this inward soliloquy, by the sound of Don Quixote's voice.

"Undoubtedly, Señor Don Diego de Miranda, your Grace must take me for a fool and a madman, am I not right? And it would be small wonder if such were the case, seeing that my deeds give evidence of nothing else. But, nevertheless, I would advise your Grace that I am neither so mad nor so lacking in wit as I must appear to you to be. A gaily caparisoned knight giving a fortunate lance thrust to a fierce bull in the middle of a great square makes a pleasing appearance in the eyes of his king. The same is true of a knight clad in shining armor as he paces the lists in front of the ladies in some joyous tournament. It is true of all those knights who, by means of military exercises or what appear to be such, divert and entertain and, if one may say so, honor the courts of princes. But the best showing of all is made by a knight-errant who, traversing deserts and solitudes, crossroads, forests, and mountains, goes seeking dangerous adventures with the intention of bringing them to a happy and successful conclusion, and solely for the purpose of winning a glorious and enduring renown.

"More impressive, I repeat, is the knight-errant succoring a widow in some unpopulated place than a courtly man of arms making love to a damsel in the city. All knights have their special callings: let the courtier wait upon the ladies and lend luster by his liveries to his sovereign's palace; let him nourish impoverished gentlemen with the splendid fare of his table; let him give tourneys and show himself truly great, generous, and magnificent and a good Christian above all, thus fulfilling his particular obligations. But the knight-errant's case is different.

"Let the latter seek out the nooks and corners of the world; let him enter into the most intricate of labyrinths; let him attempt the impossible at every step; let him endure on desolate highlands the burning rays of the midsummer sun and in winter the harsh inclemencies of wind and frost; let no lions inspire him with fear, no monsters frighten him, no dragons terrify him, for to seek them out, attack them, and conquer them all is his chief and legitimate occupation. Accordingly, I whose lot it is to be numbered among the knights-errant cannot fail to attempt anything that appears to me to fall within the scope of my duties, just as I attacked those lions a while ago even though I knew it to be an exceedingly rash thing to do, for that was a matter that directly concerned me.

"For I well know the meaning of valor: namely, a virtue that lies between the two extremes of cowardice on the one hand and temerity on the other. It is, nonetheless, better for the brave man to carry his bravery to the point of rashness than for him to sink into cowardice. Even as it is easier for the prodigal to become a generous man than it is for the miser, so is it easier for the foolhardy to become truly brave than it is for the coward to attain valor. And in this matter of adventures, you may believe me, Señor Don Diego, it is better to lose by a card too many than a card too few, and 'Such and such a knight is temerarious and overbold' sounds better to the ear than 'That knight is timid and a coward.' "

"I must assure you, Señor Don Quixote," replied Don Diego, "that everything your Grace has said and done will stand the test of reason; and it is my opinion that if the laws and ordinances of knight-errantry were to be lost, they would be found again in your Grace's bosom, which is their depository and storehouse. But it is growing late; let us hasten to my village and my home, where your Grace shall rest from your recent exertions; for if the body is not tired the spirit may be, and that sometimes results in bodily fatigue."

"I accept your offer as a great favor and an honor, Señor Don Diego," was the knight's reply. And, by spurring their mounts more than they had up to then, they arrived at the village around two in the afternoon and came to the house that was occupied by Don Diego, whom Don Quixote had dubbed the Knight of the Green-colored Greatcoat.

[Last Duel]

CHAPTER 64

Which treats of the adventure that caused Don Quixote the most sorrow of all those that have thus far befallen him.

* * * One morning, as Don Quixote went for a ride along the beach,[1] clad in full armor—for, as he was fond of saying, that was his only ornament, his only rest the fight, and, accordingly, he was never without it for a moment— he saw approaching him a horseman similarly arrayed from head to foot and with a brightly shining moon blazoned upon his shield.

As soon as he had come within earshot the stranger cried out to Don Quixote in a loud voice. "O illustrious knight, the never to be sufficiently praised Don Quixote de la Mancha, I am the Knight of the White Moon whose incomparable exploits you will perhaps recall. I come to contend with you and try the might of my arm, with the purpose of having you acknowledge and confess that my lady, whoever she may be, is beyond comparison more beautiful than your own Dulcinea del Toboso. If you will admit the truth of this fully and freely, you will escape death and I shall be spared the trouble of inflicting it upon you. On the other hand, if you choose to fight and I should overcome you, I ask no other satisfaction than that, laying down your arms and seeking no further adventures, you retire to your own village for the space of a year, during which time you are not to lay hand to sword but are to dwell peacefully and tranquilly, enjoying a beneficial rest that shall redound to the betterment of your worldly fortunes and the salvation of your soul. But if you are the victor, then my head shall be at your disposal, my arms and steed shall be the spoils, and the fame of my exploits shall go to increase your own renown. Consider well which is the better course and let me have your answer at once, for today is all the time I have for the dispatching of this business."

Don Quixote was amazed at the knight's arrogance as well as at the nature of the challenge, but it was with a calm and stern demeanor that he replied to him.

"Knight of the White Moon," he said, "of whose exploits up to now I have never heard, I will venture to take an oath that you have not once laid eyes upon the illustrious Dulcinea; for I am quite certain that if you had beheld her you would not be staking your all upon such an issue, since the sight of her would have convinced you that there never has been, and never can be, any beauty to compare with hers. I do not say that you lie, I simply say that you are mistaken; and so I accept your challenge with the conditions you have laid down, and at once, before this day you have fixed upon shall have ended. The only exception I make is with regard to the fame of your deeds being added to my renown, since I do not know what the character of your exploits has been and am quite content with my own, such as they are. Take, then, whichever side of the field you like, and I will take up my position, and may St. Peter bless what God may give."

---

1. Don Quixote and Sancho, after numberless encounters and experiences (of which the most prominent have been Don Quixote's descent into the cave of Montesinos and their residence at the castle of the playful ducal couple who give Sancho the "governorship of an island" for ten days), are now in Barcelona. Famous as they are, they meet the viceroy and the nobles; their host is Don Antonio Moreno, "a gentleman of wealth and discernment who was fond of amusing himself in an innocent and kindly way."

Now, as it happened, the Knight of the White Moon was seen by some of the townspeople, who informed the viceroy that he was there, talking to Don Quixote de la Mancha. Believing this to be a new adventure arranged by Don Antonio Moreno or some other gentleman of the place, the viceroy at once hastened down to the beach, accompanied by a large retinue, including Don Antonio, and they arrived just as Don Quixote was wheeling Rocinante to measure off the necessary stretch of field. When the viceroy perceived that they were about to engage in combat, he at once interposed and inquired of them what it was that impelled them thus to do battle all of a sudden.

The Knight of the White Moon replied that it was a matter of beauty and precedence and briefly repeated what he had said to Don Quixote, explaining the terms to which both parties had agreed. The viceroy then went up to Don Antonio and asked him if he knew any such knight as this or if it was some joke that they were playing, but the answer that he received left him more puzzled than ever; for Don Antonio did not know who the knight was, nor could he say as to whether this was a real encounter or not. The viceroy, accordingly, was doubtful about letting them proceed, but inasmuch as he could not bring himself to believe that it was anything more than a jest, he withdrew to one side, saying, "Sir Knights, if there is nothing for it but to confess or die, and if Señor Don Quixote's mind is made up and your Grace, the Knight of the White Moon, is even more firmly resolved, then fall to it in the name of God and may He bestow the victory."

The Knight of the White Moon thanked the viceroy most courteously and in well-chosen words for the permission which had been granted them, and Don Quixote did the same, whereupon the latter, commending himself with all his heart to Heaven and to his lady Dulcinea, as was his custom at the beginning of a fray, fell back a little farther down the field as he saw his adversary doing the same. And then, without blare of trumpet or other war-like instrument to give them the signal for the attack, both at the same instant wheeled their steeds about and returned for the charge. Being mounted upon the swifter horse, the Knight of the White Moon met Don Quixote two-thirds of the way and with such tremendous force that, without touching his opponent with his lance (which, it seemed, he deliberately held aloft) he brought both Rocinante and his rider to the ground in an exceedingly perilous fall. At once the victor leaped down and placed his lance at Don Quixote's visor.

"You are vanquished, O knight! Nay, more, you are dead unless you make confession in accordance with the conditions governing our encounter."

Stunned and battered, Don Quixote did not so much as raise his visor but in a faint, wan voice, as if speaking from the grave, he said, "Dulcinea del Toboso is the most beautiful woman in the world and I the most unhappy knight upon the face of this earth. It is not right that my weakness should serve to defraud the truth. Drive home your lance, O knight, and take my life since you already have deprived me of my honor."

"That I most certainly shall not do," said the one of the White Moon. "Let the fame of my lady Dulcinea del Toboso's beauty live on undiminished. As for me, I shall be content if the great Don Quixote will retire to his village for a year or until such a time as I may specify, as was agreed upon between us before joining battle."

The viceroy, Don Antonio, and all the many others who were present heard this, and they also heard Don Quixote's response, which was to the effect that, seeing nothing was asked of him that was prejudicial to Dulcinea, he would fulfill all the other conditions like a true and punctilious knight. The one of the White Moon thereupon turned and with a bow to the viceroy rode back to the city at a mild canter. The viceroy promptly dispatched Don Antonio to follow him and make every effort to find out who he was; and, in the meanwhile, they lifted Don Quixote up and uncovered his face, which held no sign of color and was bathed in perspiration. Rocinante, however, was in so sorry a state that he was unable to stir for the present.

Brokenhearted over the turn that events had taken, Sancho did not know what to say or do. It seemed to him that all this was something that was happening in a dream and that everything was the result of magic. He saw his master surrender, heard him consent not to take up arms again for a year to come as the light of his glorious exploits faded into darkness. At the same time his own hopes, based upon the fresh promises that had been made him, were whirled away like smoke before the wind. He feared that Rocinante was maimed for life, his master's bones permanently dislocated—it would have been a bit of luck if his madness also had been jolted out of him.[2]

Finally, in a hand litter which the viceroy had them bring, they bore the knight back to town. The viceroy himself then returned, for he was very anxious to ascertain who the Knight of the White Moon was who had left Don Quixote in so lamentable a condition.

CHAPTER 65

Wherein is revealed who the Knight of the White Moon was.

The Knight of the White Moon was followed not only by Don Antonio Moreno, but by a throng of small boys as well, who kept after him until the doors of one of the city's hostelries had closed behind him. A squire came out to meet him and remove his armor, for which purpose the victor proceeded to shut himself up in a lower room, in the company of Don Antonio, who had also entered the inn and whose bread would not bake until he had learned the knight's identity. Perceiving that the gentleman had no intention of leaving him, he of the White Moon then spoke.

"Sir," he said, "I am well aware that you have come to find out who I am; and, seeing that there is no denying you the information that you seek, while my servant here is removing my armor I will tell you the exact truth of the matter. I would have you know, sir, that I am the bachelor Sansón Carrasco from the same village as Don Quixote de la Mancha, whose madness and absurdities inspire pity in all of us who know him and in none more than me. And so, being convinced that his salvation lay in his returning home for a period of rest in his own house, I formed a plan for bringing him back.

"It was three months ago that I took to the road as a knight-errant, calling myself the Knight of the Mirrors, with the object of fighting and overcoming him without doing him any harm, intending first to lay down the condition that the vanquished was to yield to the victor's will. What I meant to ask of him—for I looked upon him as conquered from the start—was that he should return to his village and not leave it for a whole year, in the course of which time he might be cured. Fate, however, ordained things otherwise; for he was the one who conquered me and overthrew me from my horse, and thus

---

2. The Spanish has an untranslatable pun on *deslocado*, which means "out of joint" ("dislocated") and also "cured of madness" (from *loco*, "mad").

my plan came to naught. He continued on his wanderings, and I went home, defeated, humiliated, and bruised from my fall, which was quite a dangerous one. But I did not for this reason give up the idea of hunting him up once more and vanquishing him as you have seen me do today.

"Since he is the soul of honor when it comes to observing the ordinances of knight-errantry, there is not the slightest doubt that he will keep the promise he has given me and fulfill his obligations. And that, sir, is all that I need to tell you concerning what has happened. I beg you not to disclose my secret or reveal my identity to Don Quixote, in order that my well-intentioned scheme may be carried out and a man of excellent judgment be brought back to his senses—for a sensible man he would be, once rid of the follies of chivalry."

"My dear sir," exclaimed Don Antonio, "may God forgive you for the wrong you have done the world by seeking to deprive it of its most charming madman! Do you not see that the benefit accomplished by restoring Don Quixote to his senses can never equal the pleasure which others derive from his vagaries? But it is my opinion that all the trouble to which the Señor Bachelor has put himself will not suffice to cure a man who is so hopelessly insane; and if it were not uncharitable, I would say let Don Quixote never be cured, since with his return to health we lose not only his own drolleries but also those of his squire, Sancho Panza, for either of the two is capable of turning melancholy itself into joy and merriment. Nevertheless, I will keep silent and tell him nothing, that I may see whether or not I am right in my suspicion that Señor Carrasco's efforts will prove to have been of no avail."

The bachelor replied that, all in all, things looked very favorable and he hoped for a fortunate outcome. With this, he took his leave of Don Antonio, after offering to render him any service that he could; and, having had his armor tied up and placed upon a mule's back, he rode out of the city that same day on the same horse on which he had gone into battle, returning to his native province without anything happening to him that is worthy of being set down in this veracious chronicle.

[Homecoming and Death]

CHAPTER 73

Of the omens that Don Quixote encountered upon entering his village, with other incidents that embellish and lend credence to this great history.

As they entered the village, Cid Hamete informs us, Don Quixote caught sight of two lads on the communal threshing floor who were engaged in a dispute.

"Don't let it worry you, Periquillo," one of them was saying to the other; "you'll never lay eyes on it again as long as you live."

Hearing this, Don Quixote turned to Sancho. "Did you mark what that boy said, my friend?" he asked. " 'You'll never lay eyes on it[1] again . . . ' "

---

1. The same as *her* in the Spanish, because the reference is to a cricket cage, which is a feminine noun. Hence Don Quixote's inference concerning Dulcinea.

"Well," replied Sancho, "what difference does it make what he said?"

"What difference?" said Don Quixote. "Don't you see that, applied to the one I love, it means I shall never again see Dulcinea."

Sancho was about to answer him when his attention was distracted by a hare that came flying across the fields pursued by a large number of hunters with their greyhounds. The frightened animal took refuge by huddling down beneath the donkey, whereupon Sancho reached out his hand and caught it and presented it to his master.

"*Malum signum, malum signum,*"[2] the knight was muttering to himself. "A hare flees, the hounds pursue it, Dulcinea appears not."

"It is very strange to hear your Grace talk like that," said Sancho. "Let us suppose that this hare *is* Dulcinea del Toboso and the hounds pursuing it are those wicked enchanters that transformed her into a peasant lass; she flees, I catch her and turn her over to your Grace, you hold her in your arms and caress her. Is that a bad sign? What ill omen can you find in it?"

The two lads who had been quarreling now came up to have a look at the hare, and Sancho asked them what their dispute was about. To this the one who had uttered the words "You'll never lay eyes on it again as long as you live," replied that he had taken a cricket cage from the other boy and had no intention of returning it ever. Sancho then brought out from his pocket four cuartos and gave them to the lad in exchange for the cage, which he placed in Don Quixote's hands.

"There, master," he said, "these omens are broken and destroyed, and to my way of thinking, even though I may be a dunce, they have no more to do with what is going to happen to us than the clouds of yesteryear. If I am not mistaken, I have heard our curate say that sensible persons of the Christian faith should pay no heed to such foolish things, and you yourself in the past have given me to understand that all those Christians who are guided by omens are fools. But there is no need to waste a lot of words on the subject; come, let us go on and enter our village."

The hunters at this point came up and asked for the hare, and Don Quixote gave it to them. Continuing on their way, the returning pair encountered the curate and the bachelor Carrrasco, who were strolling in a small meadow on the outskirts of the town as they read their breviaries. And here it should be mentioned that Sancho Panza, by way of sumpter cloth, had thrown over his gray and the bundle of armor it bore the flame-covered buckram robe in which they had dressed the squire at the duke's castle, on the night that witnessed Altisidora's[3] resurrection; and he had also fitted the miter over the donkey's head, the result being the weirdest transformation and the most bizarrely appareled ass that ever were seen in this world. The curate and the bachelor recognized the pair at once and came forward to receive them with open arms. Don Quixote dismounted and gave them both a warm embrace; meanwhile, the small boys (boys are like lynxes in that nothing escapes them), having spied the ass's miter, ran up for a closer view.

"Come, lads," they cried, "and see Sancho Panza's ass trigged out finer than Mingo,[4] and Don Quixote's beast is skinnier than ever!"

Finally, surrounded by the urchins and accompanied by the curate and

---

2. Meeting a hare is considered an ill omen (Latin)—that is, a bad sign.   3. A girl in the duke's castle, where Don Quixote and Sancho were guests for a time. She dramatically pretended to be in love with Don Quixote.   4. The allusion is to the opening lines of *Mingo Revulgo* (15th century), a satire.

the bachelor, they entered the village and made their way to Don Quixote's house, where they found the housekeeper and the niece standing in the doorway, for the news of their return had preceded them. Teresa Panza, Sancho's wife, had also heard of it, and, half naked and disheveled, dragging her daughter Sanchica by the hand, she hastened to greet her husband and was disappointed when she saw him, for he did not look to her as well fitted out as a governor ought to be.

"How does it come, my husband," she said, "that you return like this, tramping and footsore? You look more like a vagabond than you do like a governor."

"Be quiet, Teresa," Sancho admonished her, "for very often there are stakes where there is no bacon. Come on home with me and you will hear marvels. I am bringing money with me, which is the thing that matters, money earned by my own efforts and without harm to anyone."

"You just bring along the money, my good husband," said Teresa, "and whether you got it here or there, or by whatever means, you will not be introducing any new custom into the world."

Sanchica then embraced her father and asked him if he had brought her anything, for she had been looking forward to his coming as to the showers in May. And so, with his wife holding him by the hand while his daughter kept one arm about his waist and at the same time led the gray, Sancho went home, leaving Don Quixote under his own roof in the company of niece and housekeeper, the curate and the barber.

Without regard to time or season, the knight at once drew his guests to one side and in a few words informed them of how he had been overcome in battle and had given his promise not to leave his village for a year, a promise that he meant to observe most scrupulously, without violating it in the slightest degree, as every knight-errant was obliged to do by the laws of chivalry. He accordingly meant to spend that year as a shepherd,[5] he said, amid the solitude of the fields, where he might give free rein to his amorous fancies as he practiced the virtues of the pastoral life; and he further begged them, if they were not too greatly occupied and more urgent matters did not prevent their doing so, to consent to be his companions. He would purchase a flock sufficiently large to justify their calling themselves shepherds; and, moreover, he would have them know, the most important thing of all had been taken care of, for he had hit upon names that would suit them marvelously well. When the curate asked him what these names were, Don Quixote replied that he himself would be known as "the shepherd Quixotiz," the bachelor as "the shepherd Carrascón," the curate as "the shepherd Curiambro," and Sancho Panza as "the shepherd Pancino."

Both his listeners were dismayed at the new form which his madness had assumed. However, in order that he might not go faring forth from the village on another of his expeditions (for they hoped that in the course of the year he would be cured), they decided to fall in with his new plan and approve it as being a wise one, and they even agreed to be his companions in the calling he proposed to adopt.

"What's more," remarked Sansón Carrasco, "I am a very famous poet, as

---

5. Because the knight-errant's life has been forbidden him by his defeat, Don Quixote for a time plans to live according to another and no less "literary" code, that of the pastoral. The following paragraphs, especially through the bachelor Carrasco, refer humorously to some of the conventions of pastoral literature.

everyone knows, and at every turn I will be composing pastoral or courtly verses or whatever may come to mind, by way of a diversion for us as we wander in those lonely places; but what is most necessary of all, my dear sirs, is that each one of us should choose the name of the shepherd lass to whom he means to dedicate his songs, so that we may not leave a tree, however hard its bark may be, where their names are not inscribed and engraved as is the custom with lovelorn shepherds."

"That is exactly what we should do," replied Don Quixote, "although, for my part, I am relieved of the necessity of looking for an imaginary shepherdess, seeing that I have the peerless Dulcinea del Toboso, glory of these brookside regions, adornment of these meadows, beauty's mainstay, cream of the Graces—in short, one to whom all praise is well becoming however hyperbolical it may be."

"That is right," said the curate, "but we will seek out some shepherd maids that are easily handled, who if they do not square with us will fit in the corners."

"And," added Sansón Carrasco, "if we run out of names we will give them those that we find printed in books the world over: such as Fílida, Amarilis, Diana, Flérida, Galatea, and Belisarda; for since these are for sale in the market place, we can buy them and make them our own. If my lady, or, rather, my shepherdess, should be chance be called Ana, I will celebrate her charms under the name of Anarda; if she is Francisca, she will become Francenia; if Lucía, Luscinda; for it all amounts to the same thing. And Sancho Panza, if he enters this confraternity, may compose verses to his wife, Teresa Panza, under the name of Teresaina."

Don Quixote had to laugh at this, and the curate then went on to heap extravagant praise upon him for his noble resolution which did him so much credit, and once again he offered to keep the knight company whenever he could spare the time from the duties of his office. With this, they took their leave of him, advising and beseeching him to take care of his health and to eat plentifully of the proper food.

As fate would have it, the niece and the housekeeper had overheard the conversation of the three men, and as soon as the visitors had left they both descended upon Don Quixote.

"What is the meaning of this, my uncle? Here we were thinking your Grace had come home to lead a quiet and respectable life, and do you mean to tell us you are going to get yourself involved in fresh complications—

> Young shepherd, thou who comest here,
> Young shepherd, thou who goest there . . .[6]

For, to tell the truth, the barley is too hard now to make shepherds' pipes of it."[7]

"And how," said the housekeeper, "is your Grace going to stand the midday heat in summer, the winter cold, the howling of the wolves out there in the fields? You certainly cannot endure it. That is an occupation for robust men, cut out and bred for such a calling almost from their swaddling clothes. Setting one evil over against another, it is better to be a knight-errant than a shepherd. Look, sir, take my advice, for I am not stuffed with bread and wine when I give it to you but am fasting and am going on fifty years of age:

6. From a ballad.   7. A proverb.

stay at home, attend to your affairs, go often to confession, be charitable to the poor, and let it be upon my soul if any harm comes to you as a result of it."

"Be quiet, daughters," said Don Quixote. "I know very well what I must do. Take me up to bed, for I do not feel very well; and you may be sure of one thing: whether I am a knight-errant now or a shepherd to be, I never will fail to look after your needs as you will see when the time comes."

And good daughters that they unquestionably were, the housekeeper and the niece helped him up to bed, where they gave him something to eat and made him as comfortable as they could.

CHAPTER 74

Of how Don Quixote fell sick, of the will that he made, and of the manner of his death.

Inasmuch as nothing that is human is eternal but is ever declining from its beginning to its close, this being especially true of the lives of men, and since Don Quixote was not endowed by Heaven with the privilege of staying the downward course of things, his own end came when he was least expecting it. Whether it was owing to melancholy occasioned by the defeat he had suffered, or was, simply, the will of Heaven which had so ordained it, he was taken with a fever that kept him in bed for a week, during which time his friends, the curate, the bachelor, and the barber, visited him frequently, while Sancho Panza, his faithful squire, never left his bedside.

Believing that the knight's condition was due to sorrow over his downfall and disappointment at not having been able to accomplish the disenchantment and liberation of Dulcinea, Sancho and the others endeavored to cheer him up in every possible way. The bachelor urged him to take heart and get up from bed that he might begin his pastoral life, adding that he himself had already composed an eclogue that would cast in the shade all that Sannazaro[8] had ever written, and had purchased with his own money from a herdsman of Quintanar two fine dogs to guard the flock, one of them named Barcino and the other Butrón. All this, however, did not serve to relieve Don Quixote's sadness; whereupon his friends called in the doctor, who took his pulse and was not very well satisfied with it. In any case, the physician told them, they should attend to the health of his soul as that of his body was in grave danger.

Don Quixote received this news calmly enough, but not so his housekeeper, niece, and squire, who began weeping bitterly, as if he were already lying dead in front of them. It was the doctor's opinion that melancholy and depression were putting an end to his patient's life. The knight then requested them to leave him alone as he wished to sleep a little, and they complied. He slept for more than six hours at a stretch, as the saying is, and so soundly that the housekeeper and niece thought he would never wake.

At last he did, however, and at once cried out in a loud voice, "Blessed be Almighty God who has given me so many blessings! Truly His mercy is boundless and is not limited or restrained by the sins of men."

The niece listened carefully to what her uncle said, and it seemed to her

---

8. Jacopo Sannazaro (1456–1530), Italian poet, whose *Arcadia* is one of the milestones in the pastoral tradition.

that he was speaking more rationally than was his wont, at least during his illness.

"Sir," she said to him, "what does your Grace mean? Has something occurred that we know nothing about? What is this talk of mercy and sins?"

"The mercy that I speak of," replied Don Quixote, "is that which God is showing me at this moment—in spite of my sins, as I have said. My mind now is clear, unencumbered by those misty shadows of ignorance that were cast over it by my bitter and continual reading of those hateful books of chivalry. I see through all the nonsense and fraud contained in them, and my only regret is my disillusionment has come so late, leaving me no time to make any sort of amends by reading those that are the light of the soul. I find myself, niece, at the point of death, and I would die in such a way as not to leave the impression of a life so bad that I shall be remembered as a madman; for even though I have been one, I do not wish to confirm it on my deathbed. And so, my dear, call in my good friends: the curate, the bachelor Sansón Carrasco, and Master Nicholas the barber; for I want to confess my sins and make my last will and testament."

The niece, however, was relieved of this errand, for the three of them came in just then.

"I have good news for you, kind sirs," said Don Quixote the moment he saw them. "I am no longer Don Quixote de la Mancha but Alonso Quijano, whose mode of life won for him the name of 'Good.' I am the enemy of Amadis of Gaul and all his innumerable progeny; for those profane stories dealing with knight-errantry are odious to me, and I realize how foolish I was and the danger I courted in reading them; but I am in my right senses now and I abominate them."

Hearing this, they all three were convinced that some new kind of madness must have laid hold of him.

"Why, Señor Don Quixote!" exclaimed Sansón. "What makes you talk like that, just when we have received news that my lady Dulcinea is disenchanted? And just when we are on the verge of becoming shepherds so that we may spend the rest of our lives in singing like a lot of princes, why does your Grace choose to turn hermit? Say no more, in Heaven's name, but be sensible and forget these idle tales."

"Tales of that kind," said Don Quixote, "have been the truth for me in the past, and to my detriment, but with Heaven's aid I trust to turn them to my profit now that I am dying. For I feel, gentlemen, that death is very near; so, leave all jesting aside and bring me a confessor for my sins and a notary to draw up my will. In such straits as these a man cannot trifle with his soul. Accordingly, while the Señor Curate is hearing my confession, let the notary be summoned."

Amazed at his words, they gazed at one another in some perplexity, yet they could not but believe him. One of the signs that led them to think he was dying was this quick return from madness to sanity and all the additional things he had to say, so well reasoned and well put and so becoming in a Christian that none of them could any longer doubt that he was in full possession of his faculties. Sending the others out of the room, the curate stayed behind to confess him, and before long the bachelor returned with the notary and Sancho Panza, who had been informed of his master's condition, and who, finding the housekeeper and the niece in tears, began weeping with them. When the confession was over, the curate came out.

"It is true enough," he said, "that Alonso Quijano the Good is dying, and it is also true that he is a sane man. It would be well for us to go in now while he makes his will."

At this news the housekeeper, niece, and the good squire Sancho Panza were so overcome with emotion that the tears burst forth from their eyes and their bosoms heaved with sobs; for, as has been stated more than once, whether Don Quixote was plain Alonso Quijano the Good or Don Quixote de la Mancha, he was always of a kindly and pleasant disposition and for this reason was beloved not only by the members of his household but by all who knew him.

The notary had entered along with the others, and as soon as the preamble had been attended to and the dying man had commended his soul to his Maker with all those Christian formalities that are called for in such a case, they came to the matter of bequests, with Don Quixote dictating as follows:

"ITEM. With regard to Sancho Panza, whom, in my madness, I appointed to be my squire, and who has in his possession a certain sum of money belonging to me: inasmuch as there has been a standing account between us, of debits and credits, it is my will that he shall not be asked to give any accounting whatsoever of this sum, but if any be left over after he has had payment for what I owe him, the balance, which will amount to very little, shall be his, and much good may it do him. If when I was mad I was responsible for his being given the governorship of an island, now that I am of sound mind I would present him with a kingdom if it were in my power, for his simplicity of mind and loyal conduct merit no less."

At this point he turned to Sancho. "Forgive me, my friend," he said, "for having caused you to appear as mad as I by leading you to fall into the same error, that of believing that there are still knights-errant in the world."

"Ah, master," cried Sancho through his tears, "don't die, your Grace, but take my advice and go on living for many years to come; for the greatest madness that a man can be guilty of in this life is to die without good reason, without anyone's killing him, slain only by the hands of melancholy. Look you, don't be lazy but get up from this bed and let us go out into the fields clad as shepherds as we agreed to do. Who knows but behind some bush we may come upon the lady Dulcinea, as disenchanted as you could wish. If it is because of worry over your defeat that you are dying, put the blame on me by saying that the reason for your being overthrown was that I had not properly fastened Rocinante's girth. For the matter of that, your Grace knows from reading your books of chivalry that it is a common thing for certain knights to overthrow others, and he who is vanquished today will be the victor tomorrow."

"That is right," said Sansón, "the worthy Sancho speaks the truth."

"Not so fast, gentlemen," said Don Quixote. "In last year's nests there are no birds this year. I was mad and now I am sane; I was Don Quixote de la Mancha, and now I am, as I have said, Alonso Quijano the Good. May my repentance and the truth I now speak restore to me the place I once held in your esteem. And now, let the notary proceed:

"ITEM. I bequeath my entire estate, without reservation, to my niece Antonia Quijana, here present, after the necessary deductions shall have been made from the most available portion of it to satisfy the bequests that I have stipulated. The first payment shall be to my housekeeper for the wages due her, with twenty ducats over to buy her a dress. And I hereby appoint the Señor Curate and the Señor Bachelor Sansón Carrasco to be my executors.

"ITEM. It is my will that if my niece Antonia Quijana should see fit to marry, it shall be to a man who does not know what books of chivalry are; and if it shall be established that he is acquainted with such books and my niece still insists on marrying him, then she shall lose all that I have bequeathed her and my executors shall apply her portion to works of charity as they may see fit.

"ITEM. I entreat the aforementioned gentlemen, my executors, if by good fortune they should come to know the author who is said to have composed a history now going the rounds under the title of *Second Part of the Exploits of Don Quixote de la Mancha,* to beg his forgiveness in my behalf, as earnestly as they can, since it was I who unthinkingly led him to set down so many and such great absurdities as are to be found in it; for I leave this life with a feeling of remorse at having provided him with the occasion for putting them into writing."

The will ended here, and Don Quixote, stretching himself at length in the bed, fainted away. They all were alarmed at this and hastened to aid him. The same thing happened very frequently in the course of the three days of life that remained to him after he had made his will. The household was in a state of excitement, but with it all the niece continued to eat her meals, the housekeeper had her drink, and Sancho Panza was in good spirits; for this business of inheriting property effaces or mitigates the sorrow which the heir ought to feel and causes him to forget.

Death came at last for Don Quixote, after he had received all the sacraments and once more, with many forceful arguments, had expressed his abomination of books of chivalry. The notary who was present remarked that in none of those books had he read of any knight-errant dying in his own bed so peacefully and in so Christian a manner. And thus, amid the tears and lamentations of those present, he gave up the ghost; that is to say, he died. Perceiving that their friend was no more, the curate asked the notary to be a witness to the fact that Alonso Quijano the Good, commonly known as Don Quixote, was truly dead, this being necessary in order that some author other than Cid Hamete Benengeli might not have the opportunity of falsely resurrecting him and writing endless histories of his exploits.

Such was the end of the Ingenious Gentleman of La Mancha, whose birthplace Cid Hamete was unwilling to designate exactly in order that all the towns and villages of La Mancha might contend among themselves for the right to adopt him and claim him as their own, just as the seven cities of Greece did in the case of Homer. The lamentations of Sancho and those of Don Quixote's niece and his housekeeper, as well as the original epitaphs that were composed for his tomb, will not be recorded here, but mention may be made of the verses by Sansón Carrasco:

> Here lies a gentleman bold
> Who was so very brave
> He went to lengths untold,
> And on the brink of the grave
> Death had on him no hold.
> By the world he set small store—

He frightened it to the core—
Yet somehow, by Fate's plan,
Though he'd lived a crazy man,
When he died he was sane once more.

LOPE DE VEGA
1562–1635

One of the great dramatists of the Spanish golden age, Lope Félix de Vega Carpio achieved such enormous popularity and admiration that his very name became a synonym for excellence. The impact of his art on drama was no less impressive: his method of composing three-act plays with comic or serious subplots came to dominate Spanish drama well into the eighteenth century. The importance of his dramatic legacy far exceeded his own estimation of it: Lope did not consider plays to be serious art and openly admitted that he wrote for money and for the pleasure of the people. He claimed to have composed some fifteen hundred plays (an early biographer puts the figure at eighteen hundred), and many of the thousands of characters he created were based on favorite types he frequently recycled.

Born in Madrid, Lope led a life spectacularly complicated by his three passionate loves: women, religion, and Spain, which was emerging as a nation. Married twice, Lope had at least sixteen children (six in wedlock) and affairs so numerous that some biographical sketches arrange his life by his serial (and overlapping) cohabitation with the women he celebrated in verse. Religious faith played a serious role in his private and public lives: Lope took holy orders in 1614, was elected a judge by the Spanish Inquisition, and served as an official censor. In 1622 Pope Urban VIII made him a member of the Order of St. John of Jerusalem and an honorary doctor of theology. His career in the Church and participation in the Inquisition suggest how intimately tied religious and national feeling were in Lope's mind. His devotion to Spain also led him to fight in two battles, one of them with the Spanish Armada against England. When he died in 1635, the nation mourned him with a nine-day funeral in Madrid.

Lope's dramatic art reflects his various passions. He wrote brilliant sacred plays in addition to his comedies. He created strong female characters, such as Laurencia, the heroine of the play presented in this anthology: she not only makes the most influential speech in a town council but also, when she turns from politics to romance, speaks a complete sonnet (she is the only female character in the history of Spanish drama to do so). Lope's efforts to link his plays to the idea of Spain as a nation are, perhaps, the clearest evidence of a consistent dramatic theme in his many plays. He believed that plays should deal with historically important issues, such as "the events, wars, peace, counsels, fortune, change, prosperity, the decline of kingdoms and epochs of great empires and monarchies" (*The Bell of Aragon*). In his mock epic, *The Cat-fight,* he associates his subjects more specifically with the land and institutions of Spain: her woods, fields, trees, and flowers and "the arms and laws that maintain kingdoms and kings."

Lope's *Fuente Ovejuna* (Sheepwell) is a comedy. Charm and humor characterize its scenes, peasant characters, and dialogue, and the play ends in a jubilant affirmation of community and social order. It also has serious political dimensions and makes a daring foray into questions about law and government. Rape is the crime that finally drives the long-suffering people of Fuente Ovejuna to rise up and kill the abusive Comendador, Fernán Gómez de Guzmán, who lives in (and off) their small pastoral village. As the aristocratic Guzmán mistreats Fuente Ovejuna's councilmen, seduces and harasses its women, and imposes burdensome taxes, the villagers' thoughts turn to social contracts, law, and justice. They finally take action when the Comendador interrupts the wedding of a young couple, Frondoso and Laurencia, strips the mayor of his office, seizes Laurencia, and arrests Frondoso: they attack his household and throw the Comendador from a window to land upon the swords and spears of the women below. While the villagers celebrate by composing songs and parading raucously with Guzmán's head on a pole, word of the bloody rebellion reaches the Spanish kings, who send a judge to interrogate the villagers and administer justice. Aware of the legal consequences of their actions, the community resolves to stand by each other: even under torture, the men, women, and children of Fuente Ovejuna have one answer to the zealous judge's demand to learn the names of those responsible: "Everyone—Fuente Ovejuna did it." Left with the options of destroying the entire village or issuing a general pardon, the king chooses clemency. In the play's final scene, the villagers joyfully submit themselves to the rule of the Catholic kings—none other than the historical Ferdinand and Isabella, who completed the Reconquest of Spain, sent Christopher Columbus to America in 1492, and launched Spain's reputation as the most powerful empire of the sixteenth century.

Lope did not invent the subject of *Fuente Ovejuna:* he drew on historical events that took place in the small pastoral village in the province of Córdoba. His principal source, the chronicle history of Fray Francisco de Rades y Andrada, records that the Comendador "committed great injuries and dishonors to the people of the village, taking their daughters and wives by force, and robbing their households to maintain his soldiers." At length the villagers, calling out "long live Kings Ferdinand and Isabel, and death to traitors and bad Christians," rebelled, refused to hear the Comendador's promises of restitution, and killed him along with fourteen of his men. After his death, according to the chronicle, "they pulled his beard out by the roots with great cruelty, and broke his teeth with the pommels of their swords," mutilated the body, carried his head on a pole, refused him a Christian burial, and robbed his household. Had a single villager collapsed under torture and identified the ringleaders in order to save his or her own skin, the events at Fuente Ovejuna would be chronicled as a lurid and bloody uprising during a period of widespread cultural upheaval in Spanish history. But since each was willing to die for the others, they left a memorable and even proverbial example of resistance and solidarity. The phrase "Fuente Ovejuna lo hizo" ("Sheepwell did it") became proverbial for a dedication to community and democratic process.

Lope shows considerable sympathy for his peasants, who are goaded into their seditious frenzy. Left to their own devices, the villagers are law-abiding and peaceable: even the names of the lead characters, Frondoso ("leafy") and Laurencia ("laurel"), associate them with the most nonviolent aspects of nature. Lope's spotlight shines on the Comendador's abuses—including reports of a gang rape, brutal beatings, and the administration of an ink enema to a hapless peasant (a bizarre punishment, perhaps suggesting the censorship of writing). The attempted rape of Laurencia, the play's most dynamic and articulate character, is Lope's invention, and it plays a decisive role in defining the nature of the political violence that Guzmán perpetrates on the entire village: first, rape was an inalterable dishonor to a woman and to her father and husband, and second, it represents, in a most visceral way, Guzmán's violent disregard for consent, the key term in all social contracts. The assault shocks Laurencia into a hair-raising harangue at the town council, where she spurs the dishonored villagers to revenge. The murder scene, which follows, is fast-paced, giddy, and carnivalesque. Questions of moral interpretation are left to performance, which might emphasize either the spirit of liberation or the spirit of dangerous transgression. Lope acknowledges the more ghoulish details from the chronicle but places them in the biased report that Flores, the Comendador's bully and pimp, makes to the Catholic kings. What compels Lope's imagination is the villagers' redemptive commitment to community. Lope uses the historical event and example to raise fundamental questions of political philosophy: does authority come from above (God) or below (the people)? is government based on a social contract? do laborers have the right to honor? are the people, if governed cruelly, entitled to revoke their consent or to resist by violence? Lope, who was no political radical, suggests that government without popular consent and mutual respect is morally bankrupt.

Through the story of Sheepwell, Lope explores political issues that gained national importance when Ferdinand of Aragon and Isabella of Castile married, paving the way to the union of Spain despite the different political traditions of Aragon and Castile. The rebellion of Fuente Ovejuna took place in 1476, seven years after Ferdinand and Isabella secretly married in hopes of uniting the crowns of Aragon and Castile and two years after Isabella declared herself queen of Castile, following the death of her half brother, Henry IV. At the time of the villagers' uprising, the security of the Catholic kings and the political destiny of Spain itself hung in the balance, in part because Isabella's was not the only (or even the best) claim to the crown of Castile. In 1476 Ferdinand and Isabella were at war with Alfonso V of Portugal and his wife, Juana, alleged to be the daughter of Henry IV. Moreover, it was by no means clear how the crowns of Castile and Aragon would reconcile the radically opposed forms of government that each province traditionally upheld. Castile espoused monarchical absolutism, a theory of power holding that the king is above the law and that "what pleases the king *is* law." The Castilian monarchy was locked in a struggle with its most powerful aristocratic families, the dynasties of Mendoza, Enríquez, and Guzmán (from which the Comendador comes). Aragon, on the other hand, rejoiced in its constitutional government, which strongly emphasized the reciprocal obligations of the monarch and his subjects. The Aragonese oath of allegiance ran "We who are as good as you swear to you, who are no better than we, to accept you as our king and sovereign lord, provided that you observe all our liberties and laws; but if not, not." To the Aragonese the liberties of subjects outstripped the prerogatives of the monarch. The events at Fuente Ovejuna coincided with the rise to power of the Catholic kings, giving Lope an opportunity to explore both the ideal form of government and Spain's future as a powerful empire. Controversy never hurt the box office, Lope knew, and so he brought to the stage political debates over dominion by consent, divine right, and force.

Lope dedicates his play's subplot to Ferdinand and Isabella. Fuente Ovejuna is under siege, and so is the Royal City (*Ciudad Real*) of Castile; Laurencia's honor is under assault, and so is Isabella's authority. Until the end of the play, when the villagers meet the Catholic kings, the sole figure to pass between the two plots is Fernán Gómez de Guzmán: when the Comendador is not brutalizing the villagers of Fuente Ovejuna, he is on the battlefield fighting against Ferdinand and Isabella. Guzmán belongs to the chivalric order of Calatrava, one of the three great military and religious orders established in the twelfth century to bring about the Reconquest of Spain, following the Arab invasion of 711. Lope's Guzmán perfectly embodies the ethos of the aristocratic *hidalgo*: "a man who lived for war, who could do the impossible through sheer physical courage and a constant effort of the will, who conducted his relations with others according to a strictly regulated code of honor, and who reserved his respect for the man who had won riches by force of arms rather than by the sweat of manual labor," as one historian puts it.

The rapacious and arrogant style of dominion exemplified by Lope's Guzmán contrasts with the military and judicial policies of the Catholic kings, whom Lope celebrates as prudent, just, and respectful of law. Guzmán abuses the idea, central to the theory of monarchical absolutism, that "what pleases the king is law." He speaks of ownership of his subjects, seduces and rapes his female subjects, and attempts to dissolve the local administration of law when he strips the mayor of office and orders the villagers to vacate the central plaza. In the play's very first scene, Guzmán greets the young Maestre of the chivalric Order of Calatrava with the blunt assertion "You owe me a lot," and proceeds to manipulate the youth into attacking the Royal City.

Guzmán violates the reciprocal obligations governing the relationship of the good king and his subjects: he contemptuously rejects the suggestion that he owes anything to the villagers of Fuente Ovejuna, and it is in the role of bad counselor that he coerces the powerful but impressionable Maestre of the Order of Calatrava. The Catholic kings, on the other hand, later exemplify the magnanimous and prudential nature of good kings: they pardon the Maestre for his assault on the Royal City and direct his aggression toward wars beneficial to Spain and befitting the traditions of his Order, crusades against the Arabs. Guzmán's moral and military opposition to the idealized Catholic kings suggests that the villagers of Fuente Ovejuna are justified in their cry "Death to bad Christians and traitors."

Guzmán is not the only figure in Lope's play to wed dramatic stereotype to controversial concepts in political theory. So do the young lovers, Laurencia and Frondoso, who are both stock types from comedy and initially act like the intelligent, beautiful, unattainable young woman and the good-hearted, callow, fashion-happy young man who adores her. The characters soon reveal how they vary from their stereotypes, however. Because she has known only the Comendador's attempts to entrap her, Laurencia at first disdains love. She understandably insists that love is merely self-interest, while Frondoso, who views her coldness in purely conventional terms, seems oddly unaware that he inhabits a politically mired world and not a standard comedy. Frondoso soon learns what love requires of him: while he and Laurencia are in the woods debating about love, the Comendador, who has been out hunting deer, appears and decides to "hunt" Laurencia instead. If he is to prevent her rape, Frondoso must come out from his hiding place, pick up the Comendador's discarded crossbow, and threaten his life. Heroic and ethical but illegal, Frondoso's act wins Laurencia's love and the Comendador's murderous enmity. The Comendador's abuses habitually force peasants—and otherwise typical comic characters—to think strenuously about the nature of social contracts. The peasants conclude that those who govern owe a debt to those who serve and that communal bonds are formed by love: the willingness to enter into a social relationship and to treat the interest of others as one's own. This is the lesson that gives the villagers the courage to protect their community despite torture. In Lope's play, love is both the erotic mainstay of comedy and the harmonizing principle of government: in matters of the heart and of law, the subject must have the right to consent.

Walter Cohen, *Drama of a Nation: Public Theater and Renaissance England and Spain* (1985); Donald R. Larson, *The Honor Plays of Lope de Vega* (1977); Robert L. Fiore, *Drama and Ethos: Natural-Law Ethics in Spanish Golden Age Theater* (1975); and Edward M. Wilson and Duncan Moir, *The Golden Age: Drama 1492–1700* (1971), present useful and illuminating studies of Lope de Vega's work and its relation to Spanish theater in general. J. B. Hall, *Lope de Vega: Fuenteovejuna* (1985), presents a detailed study of the play. J. H. Elliott's *Imperial Spain 1469–1716* (1963), is an indispensable study of Spanish history and politics.

PRONOUNCING GLOSSARY

The following list uses common English syllables and stress accents to provide rough equivalents of selected words whose pronunciation may be unfamiliar to the general reader. Note that in Castilian Spanish, as opposed to the Spanish spoken in the Americas, *d* is pronounced as *th*.

Cimbranos: *seem-brah'nos*

Ciudad Real: *see-oo-dthahth' ray-ahl'*

Comendador: *koh-men-da-thor'*

Cuadrado: *kwah-drah'thoh*

Fernán Gómez de Guzman: *fer-nahn' goh'mez day gus'mahn*

Frondoso: *frohn-doh'so*

Fuente Ovejuna: *fu-en'tay o-vay-hu'nah*

Jacinta: *ha-seen'tah*

Juan Chamorro: *hwan cha-mor'roh*

Juan Rojo: *hwan ro'hoh*

Laurencia: *lau-ren'see-ah*

Leon: *lay-own'*

Lope de Vega: *loh'pay duh vay'gah*

Maestre of Calatrava: *ma-e'stray of cah-
    lah-trah'vah*

Manrique: *man-ree'kay*

maravedíes: *mah-rah-vay-dee'es*

Ortuño: *or-tun'yoh*

Pascuala: *pas-kwahlah*

Rodrigo Téllez Girón: *ro-dree'goh tay'-
    yez hi-rohn'*

Villena: *vi-yay'nah*

Fuente Ovejuna[1]

CHARACTERS

Queen ISABELLA *of Castile*
KING *Ferdinand of Aragon*
Rodrigo Téllez Girón, MAESTRE *of the religious and military Order of Calatrava*
Fernán Gómez de Guzmán, COMENDADOR *Mayor of the Order of Calatrava*
Don MANRIQUE
A JUDGE
Two COUNCILMEN *of Ciudad Real*
ORTUÑO }
FLORES } *servants of the Comendador*
ESTEBAN }
ALONSO } *Mayors of Fuente Ovejuna*
LAURENCIA }
JACINTA } *peasant girls*
PASCUALA }
JUAN ROJO, *Councilman of Fuente Ovejuna, a peasant*
Another COUNCILMAN *of Fuente Ovejuna*
FRONDOSO }
MENGO } *peasants*
BARRILDO }
LEONELO, *Licentiate of Law*
CIMBRANOS, *a soldier*
A BOY
PEASANTS, *men and women*
MUSICIANS
SOLDIERS
Time: 1476

Act I

Hall of the MAESTRE *of the Order of Calatrava, in Almagro.*[2]

[*Enter the* COMENDADOR[3] *and his servants,* FLORES *and* ORTUÑO.]
COMENDADOR   Does the Maestre[4] know that I am here?
FLORES   He does, my lord.
ORTUÑO   The Maestre is becoming more mature.

1. Translated by Angel Flores and Muriel Kittel.   2. Region of Spain.   3. Captain.   4. Master.

COMENDADOR   Does he know that I am Fernán Gómez de Guzmán?

FLORES   He's only a boy—you mustn't be surprised if he doesn't.

COMENDADOR   Nevertheless he must know that I am the Comendador.

ORTUÑO   There are those who advise him to be discourteous.

COMENDADOR   That will win him little love. Courtesy is the key to good will, while thoughtless discourtesy is the way to make enemies.

ORTUÑO   If we but realized how it makes us hated and despised by everyone we would rather die than be discourteous.

FLORES   What a nuisance discourtesy is: among equals it's foolish and toward inferiors it's tyrannical. In this case it only means that the boy has not learned what it is to be loved.

COMENDADOR   The obligation he took upon himself when he accepted his sword and the Cross of Calatrava[5] was placed on his breast should have been enough to teach him courtesy.

FLORES   If he has been prejudiced against you you'll soon find out.

ORTUÑO   Why don't you leave if you're in doubt?

COMENDADOR   I wish to see what he is like.

  [*Enter the* MAESTRE *of Calatrava and retinue.*]

MAESTRE   Pardon me, Fernán Gómez de Guzmán; I only just heard that you had come. Forgive me if I have kept you waiting.

COMENDADOR   I have just cause for complaint. Both my love for you and my rank entitle me to better treatment—for you are the Maestre of Calatrava and I your Comendador and your servant.

MAESTRE   I did not know of your welcome arrival—let me embrace you again.

COMENDADOR   You owe me a great deal; I have risked my life to settle your many difficulties. I even managed to persuade the Pope to increase your age.[6]

MAESTRE   That is true, and by the holy cross which we both proudly bear on our breasts I shall repay you in love, and honor you as my own father.

COMENDADOR   I am satisfied that you will.

MAESTRE   What news of the war?

COMENDADOR   Listen carefully, and I will tell you where your duty lies.

MAESTRE   I am listening; tell me.

COMENDADOR   Maestre Don Rodrigo Téllez Girón, I need hardly remind you how your brave father resigned his high position as Maestre to you eight years ago, and appointed Don Juan Pacheco, the Grand Maestre of Santiago, to be your coadjutor, nor how kings and comendadors confirmed and swore to his act, and the Pope [Pius II][7] and his successor Paul agreed to it in their bulls; no, what I have come to tell you is this: now that Pacheco is dead and you, in spite of your youth, have sole control of the government, now is the time for you to take up arms for the honor of your family. Since the death of Henry IV your relatives have supported the cause of Don Alonso, King of Portugal, who claims the throne of Castile through his wife Juana.[8] Ferdinand, the great prince of

---

5. One of three military and religious (chivalric) orders.   6. Increased on papal authority for the purpose of holding the office of Maestre.   7. Material added for clarity has been placed in brackets throughout the play.   8. Illegitimate daughter of Henry IV, wife of Alonso of Portugal, and Isabella's rival claimant to the throne of Castile.

Aragon, makes a similar claim through his wife Isabella.[9] But your relatives do not consider Ferdinand's rights to be as clear as those of
Juana—who is now in your cousin's power. So I advise you to rally the
knights of Calatrava in Almagro and to capture Ciudad Real,[1] which
stands on the frontier between Andalusia and Castile. You will not need
many men, because the enemy can count only on their neighbors and a
few noblemen who support Isabella and consider Ferdinand their legitimate king. It will be wonderful if you, Rodrigo, if you, a youth, can
astonish those who say that this cross is too heavy for your young shoulders. Emulate the counts of Urueña from whom you spring, and who
from the height of their fame seem to be challenging you with the laurels
they have won; emulate the marquises of Villena and those other captains
who are so numerous that the wings of fame are not strong enough to
bear them. Unsheathe your white sword, dye it red in battle till it matches
the cross upon your breast. For I cannot call you the Maestre of the Red
Cross as long as your sword is white: both the sword you bear and the
cross you wear must be red. And you, mighty Girón, must add the crowning glory to the immortal fame of your ancestors.

MAESTRE   Fernán Gómez, you may be sure that I side with my family in
this dispute, for I am convinced that they are right. And as I translate
my conviction into action at Ciudad Real you will see me tearing the city
walls down with the violence of a thunderbolt. I know that I am young—
but do not think that my courage died with my uncle's death. I will
unsheathe my white sword and its brilliance shall become the color of
the cross, bathed in red blood.

   But tell me, where do you live, and do you have any soldiers?

COMENDADOR   A few—but they are faithful and they will fight like lions.
I live in Fuente Ovejuna, where the people are skilled in agriculture and
husbandry rather than in the arts of war.

MAESTRE   And you live there, you say?

COMENDADOR   I do. I chose a house on my estate to stay in during these
troubled times. Now see that all your people go into action with you—
let no man stay behind!

MAESTRE   You shall see me today on horseback, bearing my lance on high.

   [Exeunt COMENDADOR and MAESTRE.]

A public square in Fuente Ovejuna.

   [Enter LAURENCIA and PASCUALA.]

LAURENCIA   I hoped he would never come back.

PASCUALA   I must say I thought you'd be more distressed at the news.

LAURENCIA   I hoped to God I'd never see him again.

PASCUALA   I have seen women just as adamant as you, Laurencia, if not
more so—and yet, underneath, their hearts were as soft as butter.

LAURENCIA   Well, is there an oak tree as hard as I am?

PASCUALA   Be careful. No one should boast that he'll never thirst for
water.

9. Isabella of Castile (1451–1501) and Ferdinand of Aragon (1452–1516), called the Catholic kings.
1. Royal City.

LAURENCIA   But I do. And I'll maintain it against the world. What good would it do me to love Fernán? Do you think I would marry him?

PASCUALA   Of course not.

LAURENCIA   Well then, I condemn infamy. Too many girls hereabouts have trusted the Comendador only to be ruined by him.

PASCUALA   All the same it will be a miracle if you escape him.

LAURENCIA   You don't understand, Pascuala. He has been after me for a month now, but he has only been wasting his time. His emissary, Flores, and that blustering fool Ortuño have come to show me a blouse, a necklace, a hat, and have told me so many wonderful stories about their lord and master that they have succeeded in frightening me but not in moving my heart.

PASCUALA   Where did they talk to you?

LAURENCIA   Down there by the brook, about six days ago.

PASCUALA   It looks as if they are trying to deceive you, Laurencia.

LAURENCIA   Deceive me?

PASCUALA   If not you, then the priest.

LAURENCIA   I may be a young chicken, but I'm too tough for His Highness. Pascuala, I would far rather put a slice of ham on the fire in the early morning and eat it with my homemade bread and a glass of wine stolen from my mother, and then at noon to smell a piece of beef boiling with cabbage and eat it ravenously, or, if I have had a trying day, marry an eggplant to some bacon; and in the evening, while cooking the supper, go and pick a handful of grapes from the vines (God save them from the hail) and afterwards dine on chopped meat with oil and pepper, and so happily to bed murmuring "Lead us not into temptation"—I would much rather this than all the wiles and tricks of scoundrels. For after all, all they want after giving us so much trouble is their pleasure at night and our sorrow in the morning.

PASCUALA   You are right, Laurencia, for as soon as they tire of love they are more ungrateful than the sparrows are to the peasants. In winter when the fields are frozen hard the sparrows fly down from the roofs, and saying "Sweet Sweet," hop right on to the dining table for crumbs, but as soon as the cold is over and the fields are again in bloom they no longer come down saying "Sweet Sweet," but stay hopping on the roof, mocking us with their calls. Men are the same; when they need us nothing can be sweeter than they—we are their life, their soul, their heart, their all—but as soon as they tire of us their sweetness disappears and their wooing phrases become a mockery.

LAURENCIA   The moral of which is: trust no man, Pascuala.

PASCUALA   That's what I say.

[*Enter* MENGO, BARRILDO, *and* FRONDOSO.]

FRONDOSO   You are wrong, Barrildo, in this argument.

BARRILDO   Well never mind, here's somebody who will settle the matter.

MENGO   Let's have an understanding before we reach them: if I'm right, then each of you gives me a present as a reward.

BARRILDO   All right. But if you lose, what will you give?

MENGO   I'll give my boxwood rebec,[2] which I value more than a barn.

2. Stringed instrument.

BARRILDO That's fine.

FRONDOSO Let's approach them. God bless you, fair ladies.

LAURENCIA You call us ladies, Frondoso?

FRONDOSO We want to keep up with the times. In these days all bachelors are licentiates; the blind are one-eyed; the cross-eyed merely
squint; and the lame have only a sprained ankle. The unscrupulous
are called honest; the ignorant, clever; and the braggart, brave. A
large mouth is described as luscious, a small eye as sharp. The petti-
fogger[3] is called diligent; the busybody, charming; the charlatan, sympathetic; the deadly bore, gallant. The cowardly become valiant; the
hard-headed, vivacious; coxcombs are comrades; fools, broad-minded;
malcontents, philosophers. Baldness is identified with authority, foolish chatter with wit. People with tumors have only a slight cold, and
those who are arrogant are circumspect; the shifty are constant; and
the humpbacked, just slightly bent. This, in short—the enumeration
could go on indefinitely—was the sort of thing I did in calling you
ladies. I merely followed the fashion of the day.

LAURENCIA In the city, Frondoso, such words are used in courtesy: discourteous tongues use a severer and more acrimonious vocabulary.

FRONDOSO I should like to hear it.

LAURENCIA It's the very opposite of yours. The serious-minded are called
bores: the unfortunate, lucky; the even-tempered, melancholy; and anyone who expresses disapproval is hateful. Those who offer good advice
are importunate; the liberal-minded are dull-witted; the just, unjust; and
the pious, weak-kneed. In this language the faithful become inconstant;
the courteous, flatterers; the charitable, hypocrites; and the good Christians, frauds. Anyone who has won a well-deserved reward is called fortunate; truth becomes impudence; patience, cowardice; and misfortune,
retribution. The modest woman is foolish; the beautiful and chaste,
unnatural; and the honorable woman is called. . . . But enough! This
reply should be sufficient.

MENGO You little devil!

LAURENCIA What an elegant expression.

MENGO I bet the priest poured handfuls of salt on her when he christened
her.

LAURENCIA What was the argument that brought you here, if we may
ask?

FRONDOSO Listen, Laurencia.

LAURENCIA Speak.

FRONDOSO Lend me your ear, Laurencia.

LAURENCIA Lend it to you? Why, I'll give it to you right now.

FRONDOSO I trust your discretion.

LAURENCIA Well, what was the wager about?

FRONDOSO Barrildo and I wagered against Mengo.

LAURENCIA And what does Mengo claim?

BARRILDO It is something that he insists on denying, although it is plainly
a fact.

MENGO I deny it because I know better.

3. Unscrupulous lawyer.

LAURENCIA   But what is it?

BARRILDO   He claims that love does not exist.

LAURENCIA   Many people think that.

BARRILDO   Many people do, but it's foolish. Without love not even the world could exist.

MENGO   I don't know how to philosophize; as for reading, I wish I could! But I say that if the elements of Nature live in eternal conflict, then our bodies, which receive from them food, anger, melancholy, phlegm, and blood, must also be at war with each other.

BARRILDO   The world here and beyond, Mengo, is perfect harmony. Harmony is pure love, for love is complete agreement.

MENGO   As far as the natural world goes, I do not deny it. There is love which rules all things through an obligating interrelationship. I have never denied that each person has love proportionate to his humour—my hand will protect me from the blow aimed at my face, my foot will protect me from harm by enabling me to flee danger, my eyelids will protect my eyes from threatening specks—such is love in nature.

PASCUALA   What are you trying to prove, then?

MENGO   That individuals love only themselves.

PASCUALA   Pardon me, Mengo, for telling you that you lie. For it is a lie. The intensity with which a man loves a woman or an animal its mate . . .

MENGO   I call that self-love, not love. What is love?

LAURENCIA   A desire for beauty.

MENGO   And why does love seek beauty?

LAURENCIA   To enjoy it.

MENGO   That's just what I believe. Is not such enjoyment selfish?

LAURENCIA   That's right.

MENGO   Therefore a person seeks that which brings him joy.

LAURENCIA   That is true.

MENGO   Hence there is no love but the kind I speak of, the one I pursue for my personal pleasure, and which I enjoy.

BARRILDO   One day the priest said in a sermon that there was a man named Plato who taught how to love, and that this man loved only the soul and the virtues of the beloved.

PASCUALA   You have raised a question which the wise men in their schools and academies cannot solve.

LAURENCIA   He speaks the truth; do not try to refute his argument. Be thankful, Mengo, that Heaven made you without love.

MENGO   Are you in love?

LAURENCIA   I love my honor.

FRONDOSO   May God punish you with jealousy.

BARRILDO   Who has won the wager then?

PASCUALA   Go to the sacristan with your dispute, for either he or the priest will give you the best answer. Laurencia does not love deeply, and as for me, I have little experience. How are we to pass judgment?

FRONDOSO   What can be a better judgment than her disdain?

　　　　　[*Enter* FLORES.]

FLORES   God be with you!

PASCUALA   Here is the Comendador's servant.

LAURENCIA   His goshawk,[4] you mean. Where do *you* come from, my good friend?

FLORES   Don't you see my soldier's uniform?

LAURENCIA   Is Don Fernán coming back?

FLORES   Yes, the war is over, and though it has cost us some blood and some friends, we are victorious.

FRONDOSO   Tell us what happened.

FLORES   Who could do that better than I? I saw everything. For his campaign against this city, which is now called Ciudad Real [Royal City], the valiant Maestre raised an army of two thousand brave infantry from among his vassals and three hundred cavalry from laymen and friars. For even those who belong to Holy Orders are obliged to fight for their emblem of the red cross—provided, of course, that the war is against the Moors. The high-spirited youth rode out to battle wearing a green coat embroidered with golden scrolls; the sleeves were fastened with six hooks, so that only his gauntlets showed beneath them. His horse was a dappled roan, bred on the banks of the Betis, drinking its waters and grazing on its lush grass. Its tailpiece was decorated with buckskin straps, the curled panache with white knots that matched the snowflakes covering its mane. Our lord, Fernán Gómez, rode at the Maestre's side on a powerful honey-colored horse with black legs and mane and a white muzzle. Over a Turkish coat of mail he wore a magnificent breast-and-back plate with orange fringes and resplendent with gold and pearls. His white plumes seemed to shower orange blossoms on his bronze helmet. His red and white band flashed on his arm as he brandished an ash tree for a lance, making himself feared even in Granada. The city rushed to arms; the inhabitants apparently did not come out to fight but stayed within the city walls to defend their property. But in spite of the strong resistance the Maestre entered the city. He ordered the rebels and those who had flagrantly dishonored him to be beheaded, and the lower classes were gagged and whipped in public. He remained in the city and is so feared and loved that people prophesy great things for him. They say that a young man who has fought so gloriously and punished so severely all in a short time must one day fall on fertile Africa like a thunderbolt, and bring many blue moons under the red cross. He made so many gifts to the Comendador and his followers that he might have been disposing of his own estate rather than despoiling a city. But now the music sounds. The Comendador comes. Welcome him with festivity, for good will is one of the most precious of a victor's laurels.

> [*Enter the* COMENDADOR *and* ORTUÑO; MUSICIANS; JUAN ROJO,
> ESTEBAN, *and* ALONSO, *elders of the town.*]

MUSICIANS [*Singing*]

> Welcome, Comendador,
> Conqueror of lands and men!
> Long live the Guzmanes!
> Long live the Girones!
> In peacetime gracious,

---

4. Large hawk.

> Gentle his reasoning,
> When fighting the Moors
> Strong as an oak.
> From Ciudad Real
> He comes victorious,
> Bearing to Fuente Ovejuna
> Its banners in triumph.
> Long live Fernán Gómez,
> Long live the hero!

COMENDADOR   Citizens of Fuente Ovejuna, I am most grateful to you for the love you show me.

ALONSO   It is but a small part of the love we feel, and no matter how great our love it is less than you deserve.

ESTEBAN   Fuente Ovejuna and its elders, whom you have honored with your presence, beg you to accept a humble gift. In these carts, sir, we bring you an expression of gratitude rather than a display of wealth. There are two baskets filled with earthenware; a flock of geese that stretch their heads out of their nets to praise your valor in battle; ten salted hogs, prize specimens, more precious than amber; and a hundred pairs of capons and hens, which leave the cocks of the neighboring villages desolate. You will find no arms, no horses, no harnesses studded with pure gold. The only gold is the love your vassals feel towards you. And for purity you could find nothing greater than those twelve skins of wine. That wine could give warmth and courage to your soldiers even unclothed in the dead of winter; it will be as important as steel in the defense of your walls. I leave unmentioned the cheese and other victuals: they are a fitting tribute from our people to you. May you and yours enjoy our gifts.

COMENDADOR   I am very grateful to you for all of them. Go now and rest.

ESTEBAN   Feel at home in this town, my lord! I wish the reeds of mace and sedge that we placed on our doors to celebrate your triumphs were oriental pearls. You deserve such tribute and more.

COMENDADOR   Thank you, gentlemen. God be with you.

ESTEBAN   Singers, sing again.

MUSICIANS [*Singing*]

> Welcome, Comendador,
> Conqueror of lands and men!

[*Exeunt elders and* MUSICIANS.]

COMENDADOR   You two wait.

LAURENCIA   What is Your Lordship's pleasure?

COMENDADOR   You scorned me a few days ago, didn't you?

LAURENCIA   Is he speaking to you, Pascuala?

PASCUALA   I should say not—not to me!

COMENDADOR   I am talking to you, beautiful wildcat, and to the other girl too. Are you not mine, both of you?

PASCUALA   Yes, sir, to a certain extent.

COMENDADOR   Go into the house. There are men inside, so you need not fear.

LAURENCIA   If the elders accompany us—I am the daughter of one of them—it will be all right for us to go in too, but not otherwise.

COMENDADOR   Flores!

FLORES   Sir?

COMENDADOR   Why do they hesitate to do what I command?

FLORES   Come along, girls, come right in.

LAURENCIA   Let me go!

FLORES   Come in, girl, don't be silly.

PASCUALA   So that you can lock us in? No thank you!

FLORES   Come on. He wants to show you his spoils of war.

COMENDADOR [*Aside to* ORTUÑO]   Lock the door after them.
        [*Exit* COMENDADOR.]

LAURENCIA   Flores, let us pass.

ORTUÑO   Aren't you part of the gifts of the village?

PASCUALA   That's what you think! Out of my way, fool, before I . . .

FLORES   Leave them alone. They're too unreasonable.

LAURENCIA   Isn't your master satisfied with all the meat given to him
    today?

ORTUÑO   He seems to prefer yours.

LAURENCIA   Then he can starve!
        [*Exeunt* LAURENCIA *and* PASCUALA.]

FLORES   A fine message for us to bring! He'll swear at us when we appear
    before him empty-handed.

ORTUÑO   That's a risk servants always run. When he realizes the situation
    he'll either calm down or else leave at once.

Chamber of the Catholic Kings, in Medina del Campo

        [*Enter* KING *Ferdinand of Aragon, Queen* ISABELLA, MANRIQUE, *and*
        attendants.]

ISABELLA   I think it would be wise to be prepared, Your Majesty—espe-
    cially since Don Alfonso of Portugal is encamped there. It is better for
    us to strike the first blow than to wait for the enemy to attack us.

KING   We can depend on Navarre and Aragon for assistance, and I'm try-
    ing to reorganize things in Castile so as to ensure our success there.

ISABELLA   I'm confident your plan will succeed.

MANRIQUE   Two councilmen from Ciudad Real seek audience with Your
    Majesty.

KING   Let it be granted them.
        [*Enter two* COUNCILMEN *of Ciudad Real.*]

1ST COUNCILMAN   Most Catholic King of Aragon, whom God has sent to
    Castile to protect us, we appear as humble petitioners before you to beg
    the assistance of your great valor for our city of Ciudad Real. We are
    proud to consider ourselves your vassals, a privilege granted us by a royal
    charter but which an unkind fate threatens to take away. Don Rodrigo
    Téllez Girón, famous for the valiant actions that belie his youth, and
    ambitious to augment his power, recently laid close siege to our city. We
    prepared to meet his attack with bravery, and resisted his forces so
    fiercely that rivers of blood streamed from our innumerable dead. He
    finally conquered us—but only because of the advice and assistance
    given him by Fernán Gómez. Girón remains in possession of our city,

and unless we can remedy our disaster soon we will have to acknowledge ourselves his vassals against our will.

KING   Where is Fernán Gómez now?

2ND COUNCILMAN   In Fuente Ovejuna, I think. That is his native town and his home is there. But the truth is, his subjects are far from contented.

KING   Do you have a leader?

2ND COUNCILMAN   No, we have none, Your Majesty. Not one nobleman escaped imprisonment, injury, or death.

ISABELLA   This matter requires swift action, for delay will only work to the advantage of the impudent Girón. Furthermore the King of Portugal will soon realize that he can use him to gain entry to Extremadura, and so cause us much damage.

KING   Don Manrique, leave at once with two companies. Be relentless in avenging the wrongs this city has suffered. Let the Count of Cabra[5] go with you. The Cordovan is recognized by everyone as a brave soldier. This is the best plan for the moment.

MANRIQUE   I think the plan is an excellent one. As long as I live, his excesses shall be curbed.

ISABELLA   With your help we are sure to succeed.

The countryside near Fuente Ovejuna.

[*Enter* LAURENCIA *and* FRONDOSO.]

LAURENCIA   You are very stubborn, Frondoso. I left the brook with my washing only half wrung out, so as to give no occasion for gossip—yet you persist in following me. It seems that everyone in town is saying that you are running after me and I after you. And because you are the sort of fellow who struts about and shows off his clothes, which are more fashionable and expensive than other people's, all the girls and boys in the countryside think there must be something between us. They are all waiting for the day when Juan Chamorro will put down his flute and lead us to the altar. I wish they would occupy their minds with things that are more their business—why don't they imagine that their granaries are bursting with red wheat, or that their wine jars are full of dregs? Their gossip annoys me, but not so much that it keeps me awake at night.

FRONDOSO   Your disdain and beauty are so great, Laurencia, that when I see you and listen to you I fear they will kill me. You know that my only wish is to become your husband: is it fair then to reward my love in this way?

LAURENCIA   I know no other way.

FRONDOSO   Can you feel no pity for my troubled mind, no sympathy for my sad condition when you know I cannot eat or drink or sleep for thinking of you? Is it possible that such a gentle face can hide so much unkindness? Heavens! you'll drive me mad.

LAURENCIA   Why don't you take medicine for your condition, Frondoso?

FRONDOSO   You are the only medicine I need, Laurencia. Come with me

5. Diego Fernández de Córdoba (1438–1487) was the first to use this title.

to the altar, and let us live like turtle doves, billing and cooing, after the church has blessed us.

LAURENCIA   You had better ask my uncle, Juan Rojo. I'm not passionately in love with you . . . but there is hope that I might be in time.

FRONDOSO   Oh—here comes the Comendador!

LAURENCIA   He must be hunting deer. Hide behind these bushes.

FRONDOSO   I will. But I'll be full of jealousy.

[*Enter the* COMENDADOR.]

COMENDADOR   This is good luck. My chase of the timid fawn has led me to a lovely doe instead.

LAURENCIA   I was resting a bit from my washing. By Your Lordship's leave I'll return to the brook.

COMENDADOR   Such disdain, fair Laurencia, is an insult to the beauty Heaven gave you; it turns you into a monster. On other occasions you have succeeded in eluding my desires—but now we are alone in these solitary fields where no one can help you. Now, with no one to witness, you cannot be so stubborn and so proud, you cannot turn your face away without loving me. Did not Salustiana, the wife of Pedro Redondo, surrender to me—and Martín del Pozo's wife, too, only two days after her wedding?

LAURENCIA   These women, sir, had had others before you, and knew the road to pleasure only too well. Many men have enjoyed *their* favors. Go, pursue your deer, and God be with you. You persecute me so that were it not for the cross you wear I should think you were the devil.

COMENDADOR   You little spitfire! [*Aside*] I had better put my bow down and take her by force.

LAURENCIA   What? . . . What are you doing? Are you mad?

[*Enter* FRONDOSO, *who picks up the bow.*]

COMENDADOR   Don't struggle. It won't help you.

FRONDOSO [*Aside*]   I'll pick up his bow, but I hope I don't have to use it.

COMENDADOR   Come on, you might as well give in now.

LAURENCIA   Heaven help me now!

COMENDADOR   We are alone. Don't be afraid.

FRONDOSO   Generous Comendador, leave the girl alone. For much as I respect the cross on your breast, it will not stop me from aiming this bow at you if you do not let her go.

COMENDADOR   You dog, you peasant slave!

FRONDOSO   There's no dog here. Laurencia, go quickly now.

LAURENCIA   Take care of yourself, Frondoso.

FRONDOSO   Run . . .

[*Exit* LAURENCIA.]

COMENDADOR   What a fool I was to put down my sword so as not to frighten my quarry!

FRONDOSO   Do you realize, sir, that I have only to touch this string to bring you down like a bird?

COMENDADOR   She's gone. You damned, treacherous villain. Put that bow down, put it down, I say.

FRONDOSO   Put it down? Why? So that you can shoot me? No, love is deaf, remember, and hears nothing when it comes into its own.

COMENDADOR   Do you think a knight surrenders to a peasant?

Shoot, you villain, shoot and be damned, or I'll break the law of chivalry.
FRONDOSO   No, not that. I'm satisfied with my station in life and since I
    must preserve my life, I'll take your bow with me.
        [*Exit* FRONDOSO.]
COMENDADOR   What a strange experience! But I'll avenge this insult and
    remove this obstacle. . . . But to let him go! My god, how humiliating!

Act II

The Plaza of Fuente Ovejuna.

        [*Enter* ESTEBAN *and* 1ST COUNCILMAN.]
ESTEBAN   I don't think any more grain should be taken out of our com-
    munity granaries, even though they are full right now. It's getting late in
    the year, and the harvest looks poor. I think it's better to have provisions
    stored up in case of emergency—though I know some people have other
    ideas.
1ST COUNCILMAN   I agree with you. And I've always tried to administer
    the land along such peaceable ways.
ESTEBAN   Well, let's tell Fernán Gómez what we think about it. We
    shouldn't let those astrologers, who are so ignorant of the future, per-
    suade us that they know all the secrets that are only God's business. They
    pretend to be as learned as the theologians the way they mix up the past
    and the future—but if you ask them anything about the immediate pres-
    ent they are completely at a loss. Do they have the clouds and the course
    of the sun, the moon, and the stars locked up at home that they can tell
    us what is happening up there and what is going to bring us grief? At
    seed time they levy tax on us; give us just so much wheat, oats and
    vegetables, pumpkins, cucumbers, mustard. . . . Then they tell us some-
    one has died, and later we discover it happened in Transylvania; they tell
    us that wine will be scarce and beer plentiful—somewhere in Germany;
    that cherries will freeze in Gascony, or hordes of tigers will prowl through
    Hircania. Their final prophecy is that whether we sow or not the year
    will end in December!
        [*Enter the licentiate* LEONELO *and* BARRILDO.]
LEONELO   You won't be awarded the hickory stick to beat the other stu-
    dents with, for it's already been won by somebody else.
BARRILDO   How did you get on at Salamanca?
LEONELO   That's a long story.
BARRILDO   You must be a very learned man by now.
LEONELO   No, I'm not even a barber. The things I was telling you about
    happen all the time in the school I was at.
BARRILDO   At least you are a scholar now.
LEONELO   Well, I've tried to learn things that are important.
BARRILDO   Anyone who has seen so many printed books is bound to think
    he is wise.
LEONELO   Froth and confusion are the chief results of so much reading
    matter. Even the most voracious reader gets sick of seeing so many titles.

I admit that printing has saved many talented writers from oblivion, and enshrined their works above the ravages of time. Printing circulates their books and makes them known. Gutenberg, a famous German from Mainz, is responsible for this invention. But many men who used to have a high reputation are no longer taken seriously now that their works have been printed. Some people put their ignorance in print, passing it off as wisdom; others inspired by envy write down their crazy ideas and send them into the world under the name of their enemies.

BARRILDO   That's a disgraceful practice.

LEONELO   Well, it's natural for ignorant people to want to discredit scholars.

BARRILDO   But in spite of all this, Leonelo, you must admit that printing is important.

LEONELO   The world got on very well without it for a good many centuries—and no Saint Jerome or Saint Augustine has appeared since we have had it.

BARRILDO   Take it easy, Leonelo. You're getting all worked up about this printing business.

[Enter JUAN ROJO and another PEASANT.]

JUAN ROJO   Four farms put together would not raise one dowry, if they're all like the one we've just seen. It's obvious that both the land and the people are in a state of chaos.

PEASANT   What's the news of the Comendador?—don't get excited now.

JUAN ROJO   How he tried to take advantage of Laurencia in this very field!

PEASANT   That lascivious brute! I'd like to see him hanging from that olive tree! . . .

[Enter COMENDADOR, ORTUÑO, and FLORES.]

COMENDADOR   Good day to you all!

COUNCILMAN   Your Lordship!

COMENDADOR   Please don't get up.

ESTEBAN   You sit down, my lord. We would rather stand.

COMENDADOR   Do sit down.

ESTEBAN   Honor can only be rendered by those who have it themselves.

COMENDADOR   Sit down, and let us talk things over calmly.

ESTEBAN   Has Your Lordship seen the hound I sent you?

COMENDADOR   Mayor, my servants are all amazed by its great speed.

ESTEBAN   It really is a wonderful animal. It can overtake any culprit or coward who is trying to escape.

COMENDADOR   I wish you would send it after a hare that keeps eluding me.

ESTEBAN   I'd be glad to. Whereabouts is this hare?

COMENDADOR   It's your daughter.

ESTEBAN   My daughter!

COMENDADOR   Yes.

ESTEBAN   But is she worth your while?

COMENDADOR   Intervene in my favor, Mayor, for God's sake.

ESTEBAN   What has she done?

COMENDADOR   She's determined to hurt me—while the wife of a nobleman here in town is dying for an opportunity to see me.

ESTEBAN   Then she would do wrong—and you do yourself no good to talk so flippantly.

COMENDADOR   My, my, what a circumspect peasant! Flores, give him a copy of the *Politics* and tell him to read Aristotle.

ESTEBAN   My lord, the town's desire is to live peaceably under you. You must remember that there are many honorable persons living in Fuente Ovejuna.

LEONELO   Did you ever hear such impudence as this Comendador's?

COMENDADOR   Have I said anything to offend you, Councilman?

COUNCILMAN   Your pronouncements are unjust, my lord, and not worth uttering. It is unfair to try to take away our honor.

COMENDADOR   Honor? Do you have honor? Listen to the saintly friars of Calatrava!

COUNCILMAN   Some people may boast of the cross you awarded them, but their blood is not as pure as you may think.

COMENDADOR   Do I sully mine by mixing it with yours?

COUNCILMAN   Evil will sully it rather than cleanse it.

COMENDADOR   However that may be, your women are honored by it.

ESTEBAN   Such words are dishonorable.

COMENDADOR   What boors these peasants are! Ah, give me the cities, where nobody hinders the pleasures of lofty men. Husbands are glad when we make love to their wives.

ESTEBAN   They certainly should not be. Do you expect us to suffer such tribulations as readily? There is a God in the cities too, and punishment falls swiftly.

COMENDADOR   Get out of here!

ESTEBAN   Are you talking to us?

COMENDADOR   Get off the Plaza immediately. I don't want to see any of you around here.

ESTEBAN   We're going.

COMENDADOR   Not in a group like that . . .

FLORES   I beg of you to control yourself.

COMENDADOR   These peasants will gossip in groups behind my back.

ORTUÑO   Have a little patience.

COMENDADOR   I marvel that I have so much. Let each man go alone to his own house.

LEONELO   Good Heavens! Will the peasants stomach that?

ESTEBAN   I'm going this way.

[*Exeunt* PEASANTS.]

COMENDADOR   What do you think of those fellows?

ORTUÑO   You don't seem to be able to hide your emotions, yet you refuse to sense the ill feeling around you.

COMENDADOR   But are these fellows my equals?

FLORES   It's not a question of equality.

COMENDADOR   Is that peasant to keep my bow unpunished?

FLORES   Last night I thought I saw him by Laurencia's door and I gave him a slash from ear to ear—but it was someone else.

COMENDADOR   I wonder where that Frondoso is now?

FLORES   They say he's around.

COMENDADOR   So that's it. The villain who tried to murder me is allowed to go about scot-free.

FLORES   Don't worry. Sooner or later he'll fall into the snare like a stray bird, or be caught on the hook like a fish.

COMENDADOR   But imagine—a peasant, a boy, to threaten me with my own crossbow, me, a captain whose sword made Cordova and Granada tremble! Flores, the world is coming to an end!

FLORES   Blame it on love.

ORTUÑO   I suppose you spared him for friendship's sake.

COMENDADOR   I have acted out of friendship, Ortuño, else I should have ransacked the town in a couple of hours. However, I plan to withhold my vengeance until the right moment arrives. And now—what news of Pascuala?

FLORES   She says she's about to get married.

COMENDADOR   Is she going to that length?

FLORES   In other words, she's sending you to where you'll be paid in cash.

COMENDADOR   What about Olalla?

ORTUÑO   Her reply is charming.

COMENDADOR   She's a gay young thing. What does she say?

ORTUÑO   She says her husband follows her around all the time because he's jealous of my messages and your visits, but as soon as she manages to allay his fears you'll be the first to see her.

COMENDADOR   Fine! Keep an eye on the old man.

ORTUÑO   You'd better be careful.

COMENDADOR   What news from Inés?

FLORES   Which Inés?

COMENDADOR   The wife of Antón.

FLORES   She's ready when you are. I spoke to her in her back yard, through which you may go whenever you wish.

COMENDADOR   Easy girls I love dearly and repay poorly. Flores, if they only knew their worth! . . .

FLORES   To conquer without a struggle nullifies the joy of victory. A quick surrender impairs the pleasure of love making. But, as the philosophers say, there are women as hungry for men as form is for matter, so you shouldn't be surprised if things are the way they are.

COMENDADOR   A man who is maddened by love congratulates himself when girls fall easily to him, but later he regrets it. For however much we desire things we soon forget them, even the most thoughtful of us, if we have gotten them cheaply.

[*Enter* CIMBRANOS, *a soldier.*]

CIMBRANOS   Is the Comendador here?

ORTUÑO   Don't you see him before you?

CIMBRANOS   Oh, valiant Fernán Gómez! Change your green cap for your shining helmet, and your cloak for a coat of mail! For the Maestre of Santiago and the Count of Cabra are attacking Rodrigo Girón, and laying siege to Ciudad Real in the name of the Queen of Castile. All that we won at so much cost in blood and men may soon be lost again. Already the banners of Aragon with their castles, lions and bars, can be seen above the high towers of the city. Though the King of Portugal has paid

homage to Girón, the Maestre of Calatrava may have to return to Almagro in defeat. Mount your horse, my lord, your presence alone will force
the enemy back to Castile.

COMENDADOR   Stop. That's enough. Ortuño, order a trumpet to sound at
once in the Plaza. Tell me, how many soldiers do I have?

ORTUÑO   Fifty, I believe, sir.

COMENDADOR   Order them to horse.

CIMBRANOS   Ciudad Real will fall to the King if you do not hurry.

COMENDADOR   Never fear, that shall not happen!

     [*Exeunt all.*]

Open country near Fuente Ovejuna.

     [*Enter* MENGO, LAURENCIA, *and* PASCUALA, *running.*]

PASCUALA   Please don't leave us.

MENGO   Why? What are you afraid of?

LAURENCIA   Well, Mengo, we prefer to go to the village in groups when
we don't have a man to go with us. We're afraid of meeting the
Comendador.

MENGO   What a cruel and importunate devil that man is.

LAURENCIA   He never stops pestering us.

MENGO   I wish God would strike him with a thunderbolt and put an end
to his wickedness.

LAURENCIA   He's a bloodthirsty beast that poisons and infects the whole
countryside.

MENGO   I hear that in trying to protect you, here in the meadow, Frondoso
aimed his crossbow at the Comendador.

LAURENCIA   I used to hate men, Mengo, but since that day I've looked at
them with different eyes. Frondoso acted so gallantly! But I'm afraid it
may cost him his life.

MENGO   He'll be forced to leave the village.

LAURENCIA   I keep telling him to go away, although I love him dearly now.
But he answers all such counsel with anger and contempt—and all the
while the Comendador threatens to hang him by the feet.

PASCUALA   I'd like to see that Comendador carried off by the plague!

MENGO   I'd rather kill him with a mean stone. By God, if I threw a stone
at him that I have up at the sheepfold, it would hit him so hard it would
crush his skull in. The Comendador is more vicious than that old Roman,
Sabalus.

LAURENCIA   You mean Heliogabalus, who was more wicked than a beast.

MENGO   Well, Galván or whoever it was—I don't know too much about
history—the Comendador surpasses him in wickedness. Can anyone be
more despicable then Fernán Gómez?

PASCUALA   No one can compare with him. You'd think he'd sucked his
cruelty from a tigress.

     [*Enter* JACINTA.]

JACINTA   If friendship means anything, in God's name help me now!

LAURENCIA   What's happened, Jacinta, my friend?

PASCUALA   Both of us are your friends.

JACINTA   Some of the Comendador's attendants are trying to take me to him. They're on their way to Ciudad Real, but they're acting more like villains than soldiers.

LAURENCIA   May God protect you, Jacinta! If the Comendador is bold with you he'll be cruel to me.

      [*Exit* LAURENCIA.]

PASCUALA   Jacinta, I'm not a man, so I can't defend you.

      [*Exit* PASCUALA.]

MENGO   But I have both strength and reputation. Stand beside me, Jacinta.

JACINTA   Have you any arms?

MENGO   Yes, those that Nature gave me.

JACINTA   I wish you were armed.

MENGO   Never mind, Jacinta. There are plenty of stones around here.

      [*Enter* FLORES *and* ORTUÑO.]

FLORES   So you thought you could get away from us, did you?

JACINTA   Mengo, I'm dead with fear.

MENGO   Gentlemen, this is a poor peasant girl . . .

ORTUÑO   Oh, have you decided to defend young women?

MENGO   I'm merely asking for mercy. I'm her relative, and I hope to be able to keep her near me.

FLORES   Kill him off!

MENGO   By God, if you make me mad and I take out my sling, your life will be in danger!

      [*Enter the* COMENDADOR *and* CIMBRANOS.]

COMENDADOR   What's all this? Do I have to get off my horse for some petty quarrel?

FLORES   You ought to destroy this miserable village for all the joy it brings you. These wretched peasants have dared to challenge our arms.

MENGO   My lord, if injustice can move you to pity, punish these soldiers who in your name are forcing this girl to leave her husband and honest parents. Grant me permission to take her home.

COMENDADOR   I will grant them permission to punish you. Drop that sling!

MENGO   My lord!

COMENDADOR   Flores, Ortuño, Cimbranos, tie his hands with it.

MENGO   Is this your justice?

COMENDADOR   What do Fuente Ovejuna and its peasants think of me?

MENGO   My lord, how have I or Fuente Ovejuna offended you?

FLORES   Shall I kill him?

COMENDADOR   Don't soil your arms with such trash. Keep them for better things.

ORTUÑO   What are your orders?

COMENDADOR   Flog him. Tie him to that oak tree and beat him with the reins.

MENGO   Pity, my lord, have pity, for you are a nobleman!

COMENDADOR   Flog him till the rivets fall from the leather.

MENGO   My God. For such ugly deeds, uglier punishments.

      [*Exeunt* MENGO, FLORES, *and* ORTUÑO.]

COMENDADOR   Now my girl, why were you running away? Do you prefer a peasant to a nobleman?

JACINTA Can you restore the honor which your attendants have taken from me in bringing me to you?

COMENDADOR Do you mean to say your honor has been lost because I wanted to take you away?

JACINTA Yes. For I have an honest father who, if he does not equal you in birth, surpasses you in virtue.

COMENDADOR All these troubles around this village, where peasants defy their betters, scarcely help to soothe my temper. Come along here now!

JACINTA With whom?

COMENDADOR With me.

JACINTA You had better think over what you're doing.

COMENDADOR I have thought it over, and it's so much the worse for you. Instead of keeping you for myself, I shall give you to my whole army.

JACINTA No power on earth can inflict such an outrage on me while I live.

COMENDADOR Get a move on now, girl.

JACINTA Sir, have pity!

COMENDADOR There is no pity.

JACINTA I appeal from your cruelty to divine justice.

[*Exit* COMENDADOR, *hauling her out.*]

Esteban's house.

[*Enter* LAURENCIA *and* FRONDOSO.]

LAURENCIA Are you not aware of your danger, that you dare to come here?

FRONDOSO My daring is proof of my love for you. From that hill I saw the Comendador riding away, and since I have complete confidence in you all my fear left with him. I hope he never comes back!

LAURENCIA Don't curse him—for the more one wishes a person to die the longer he lives.

FRONDOSO In that case may he live a thousand years, and so by wishing him well let's hope his end will be certain. . . . Tell me, Laurencia, has my fondness for you affected you at all? Is my loyalty safely entrusted? You know that the entire village thinks we are made for each other. Won't you forget your modesty and say definitely yes or no?

LAURENCIA My answer to you and to the village is—yes!

FRONDOSO I could kiss your feet for such an answer! You give me new life . . . let me tell you now how much I love you.

LAURENCIA Save your compliments and speak to my father, Frondoso, for that's the important thing now. Look, there he comes with my uncle. Be calm and confident, Frondoso, for this meeting will determine whether I'm to be your wife or no.

FRONDOSO I put my trust in God.

[LAURENCIA *hides herself. Enter* ESTEBAN *and the* COUNCILMAN.]

ESTEBAN The Comendador's visit has aroused the whole town. His behavior was most regrettable, to say the least. Everybody was shocked, and poor Jacinta is bearing the brunt of his madness.

COUNCILMAN Before long Spain will be rendering obedience to the Catholic Kings, as they are called. The Maestre of Santiago has been appointed Captain General, and is already coming on horseback to free Ciudad Real from Girón. . . . I'm very sorry about Jacinta, who is an honest girl.

ESTEBAN   The Comendador also had Mengo flogged.

COUNCILMAN   Yes. His flesh is blacker than ink or a black cloth.

ESTEBAN   Please, no more—it makes my blood boil when I think of his disgusting behavior and reputation. What good is my Mayor's staff against that?

COUNCILMAN   It was his servants who did it. Why should you be so upset?

ESTEBAN   Shall I tell you something else? I have been told that one day Pedro Redondo's wife was found down there in the depth of the valley. He had abused her and then turned her over to his soldiers.

COUNCILMAN   Listen, I hear something. . . . Who's there?

FRONDOSO   It is I, Frondoso, waiting for permission to come in.

ESTEBAN   You need no permission, Frondoso, to enter my house. You owe your life to your father, but your upbringing to me. I love you like my own son.

FRONDOSO   Sir, trusting that love, I want to ask a favor. You know whose son I am.

ESTEBAN   Did that crazy Fernán Gómez hurt you?

FRONDOSO   Not a little.

ESTEBAN   My heart told me so.

FRONDOSO   You have shown me so much affection that I feel free to make a confession to you. I love Laurencia, and wish to become her husband. Forgive me if I have been too hasty. I'm afraid I've been very bold.

ESTEBAN   You have come just at the right moment, Frondoso, and you will prolong my life, for this touches the fear nearest my heart. I thank God that you have come to save my honor, and I thank you for your love and the purity of your intentions. But I think it only right to tell your father of this first. As soon as he approves I will give my consent too. How happy I shall be if this marriage takes place.

COUNCILMAN   You should ask the girl about him before you accept him.

ESTEBAN   Don't worry about that. The matter is settled; for they discussed it beforehand, I'm sure. If you like, Frondoso, we might talk about the dowry, for I'm planning to give you some *maravedíes*.[6]

FRONDOSO   I'm not concerned about that. I don't need a dowry.

COUNCILMAN   You should be grateful that he doesn't ask you for it in wineskins.

ESTEBAN   I'll ask Laurencia what she would like to do and then let you know.

FRONDOSO   That's fair. It's a good idea to consult everybody concerned.

ESTEBAN   Daughter! . . . Laurencia!

LAURENCIA   Yes, father.

ESTEBAN   You see how quickly she replies. Laurencia, come here a minute. What would you say if your friend Gila were to marry Frondoso, who is as honest a young man as one could find in Fuente Ovejuna?

LAURENCIA   Is Gila thinking of getting married?

ESTEBAN   Why yes, if someone can be found who would be a worthy match for her.

LAURENCIA   My answer is yes.

ESTEBAN   I would say yes too—except that Gila is ugly, and it would be much better if Frondoso became your husband, Laurencia.

6. Denomination of currency.

LAURENCIA In spite of your years, you are still a flatterer, father.

ESTEBAN Do you love him?

LAURENCIA I am fond of him, and he returns my affection, but you were saying . . .

ESTEBAN Shall I say yes to him?

LAURENCIA Yes, say it for me, sir.

ESTEBAN I? Well, then I have the keys. It's settled then. Let's go to his father.

COUNCILMAN Yes, let's go.

ESTEBAN What shall we tell him about the dowry, son? I can afford to give you 4000 *maravedíes.*

FRONDOSO Do you want to offend me, sir?

ESTEBAN Come, come, my boy, you'll get over that attitude in a day or two. Even if you don't need it now, a dowry will come in handy later on.
    [*Exeunt* ESTEBAN *and* COUNCILMAN.]

LAURENCIA Tell me, Frondoso, are you happy?

FRONDOSO Happy? I'm afraid I'll go crazy with so much joy and happiness. My heart is so overflowing that my eyes are swimming with joy when I look at you, Laurencia, and realize that you, sweet treasure, will be mine.
    [*Exeunt* LAURENCIA *and* FRONDOSO.]

Meadow near Ciudad Real.

    [*Enter the* MAESTRE, *the* COMENDADOR, FLORES, *and* ORTUÑO.]

COMENDADOR Fly, sir! There's no hope for us.

MAESTRE The walls were weak and the enemy strong.

COMENDADOR They have paid dearly for it, though, in blood and lives.

MAESTRE And they will not be able to boast that our banner of Calatrava is among their spoils. That alone would have been enough to honor their enterprise.

COMENDADOR Your plans are ruined now, Girón.

MAESTRE What can I do if Fate in its blindness raises a man aloft one day only to strike him down the next?

VOICES BACKSTAGE Victory for the Kings of Castile!

MAESTRE They're decorating the battlements with lights now, and hanging out pennants of victory from the windows in the high towers.

COMENDADOR They do that because they have paid heavily in blood—it's really more a sign of tragedy than a celebration.

MAESTRE Fernán Gómez, I'm going back to Calatrava.

COMENDADOR And I to Fuente Ovejuna. Now you have to think of either defending your relatives or paying homage to the Catholic King.

MAESTRE I'll write to you about my plans.

COMENDADOR Time will tell you what to do.

MAESTRE Ah, years full of the bitterness of time's betrayals!
    [*Exeunt.*]

A meadow near Fuente Ovejuna.

    [*Enter the wedding train:* MUSICIANS, MENGO, FRONDOSO, LAURENCIA, PASCUALA, BARRILDO, ESTEBAN, *and* JUAN ROJO.]

MUSICIANS [*Singing*]
> Long live the bride and groom!
> Many long and happy years to them.

MENGO   It has not been very difficult for you to sing.

BARRILDO   You could have done better yourself, couldn't you?

FRONDOSO   Mengo knows more about whippings now than songs.

MENGO   Don't be surprised if I tell you that there's someone in the valley to whom the Comendador . . .

BARRILDO   Don't say it. That brutal assassin has assailed everyone's honor.

MENGO   It was bad enough for a hundred soldiers to whip me that day when all I had was a sling. It must have been unbearable for that man to whom they gave an enema of dye and herbs—I won't mention his name, but he was an honorable man.

BARRILDO   It was done in jest, I suppose . . .

MENGO   This was no joke. Enemas are desirable sometimes, but I would rather die than undergo one like that.

FRONDOSO   Please sing us a song—if you have anything worth listening to.

MENGO
> God grant the bride and groom long life
> Free from envy and jealous strife,
> And when their span of years is past,
> May they be united at the last.
> God grant the bride and groom long life!

FRONDOSO   Heaven curse the poet who conceived such a poem!

BARRILDO   It was rather a sloppy job.

MENGO   This makes me think of something about the whole crew of poets. Have you seen a baker making crullers? He throws the pieces of dough into the boiling oil until the pot is full. Some buns come out puffed up, others twisted and funnily shaped, some lean to the left, others to the right, some are well fried, others are burnt. Well, I think of a poet composing his verses in much the same way that the baker works on his dough. He hastily throws words into his pot of paper, confident that the honey will conceal what may turn out ridiculous or absurd. But when he tries to sell his poem no one wants it and the confectioner is forced to eat it himself.

BARRILDO   Stop your foolishness now, and let the bride and groom speak.

LAURENCIA   Give us your hands to kiss.

JUAN ROJO   Do you ask to kiss my hand, Laurencia? You and Frondoso had better ask to kiss your father's first.

ESTEBAN   Rojo, I ask Heaven's blessing on her and her husband for ever.

FRONDOSO   Give us your blessing, both of you.

JUAN ROJO   Let the bells ring, and everyone celebrate the union of Laurencia and Frondoso.

MUSICIANS [*Singing*]
> To the valley of Fuente Ovejuna
> Came the maid with the flowing hair.
> A knight of Calatrava
> Followed her to the valley here.
> Amid the shrubs she hid herself,

Disturbed by shame and fear.
With the branches she covered herself,
Feigning she had not seen him,
But the knight of Calatrava drew near:
"Why are you hiding, fair maiden,
Know you not that my keen desire
Can pierce the thickest wall?"
She made curtains of the branches
Confused by shame and fear.
But love passes sea and mountain:
"Why are you hiding, fair maiden,
Know you not that my keen desire
Can pierce the thickest wall?"

[*Enter the* COMENDADOR, FLORES, ORTUÑO, *and* CIMBRANOS.]

COMENDADOR   Silence! You will all remain quietly where you are.

JUAN ROJO   This is not a game, my lord, and your orders will be obeyed. Won't you join us? Why do you come in such a bellicose manner? Are you our conqueror? But what am I saying . . .

FRONDOSO   I'm a dead man. Heaven help me!

LAURENCIA   Quickly, Frondoso, escape this way.

COMENDADOR   No. Arrest him, and tie him up.

JUAN ROJO   Yield to them, my boy, and go quietly to prison.

FRONDOSO   Do you want them to kill me?

JUAN ROJO   Why?

COMENDADOR   I am not a man to murder people without reason. If I were, these soldiers would have run him through by now. I'm ordering him to be taken to jail where his own father will pronounce sentence on him.

PASCUALA   Sir, a wedding is in progress here now.

COMENDADOR   What is that to me? Is he the only person in town who counts?

PASCUALA   If he offended you, pardon him, as becomes your rank.

COMENDADOR   Pascuala, it is nothing that concerns me personally. He has offended the Maestre Téllez Girón, whom God preserve. He acted counter to his orders and his honor, and must be punished as an example. Otherwise others may rebel too. Don't you know that one day this boy aimed a crossbow at the very heart of the Comendador, Mayor? Loyal vassals you are indeed!

ESTEBAN   As his father-in-law I feel I must come to his defence. I think it only natural that a man, especially a man in love, should challenge you for trying to take away his girl—what else could he do?

COMENDADOR   You are a fool, Mayor.

ESTEBAN   In your opinion, my lord!

COMENDADOR   I had no intention of taking away his girl—for she was not his.

ESTEBAN   You had the thought, and that is enough. There are kings in Castile who are drawing up new rules to prevent disorder. And they will do wrong if, after the wars, they tolerate in the towns and country districts such powerful men wearing those huge crosses on their chests. Those crosses were meant for royal breasts, and only kings should wear them.

COMENDADOR   Wrest the mayor's staff from him!

ESTEBAN   Take it, sir, it is yours to keep.

COMENDADOR   I'll strike him with it as if he were an unbroken horse.

ESTEBAN   You are my lord, and I must bear it: strike, then.

PASCUALA   Shame on you! Striking an old man!

LAURENCIA   You strike him because he is my father—what injury do you avenge in this way?

COMENDADOR   Arrest her, and let ten soldiers guard her.
    [*Exeunt* COMENDADOR *and his men.*]

ESTEBAN   May Heaven visit justice upon him!
    [*Exit* ESTEBAN.]

PASCUALA   The wedding has become a mourning.
    [*Exit* PASCUALA.]

BARRILDO   Is there not one of us who can speak?

MENGO   I've already had a sound whipping and I'm covered with wales— let someone else anger him this time.

JUAN ROJO   Let us all take counsel.

MENGO   I advise everybody to keep quiet. He made my posterior look like a piece of salmon.
    [*Exeunt all.*]

Act III

A room in the Town Hall of Fuente Ovejuna.

    [*Enter* ESTEBAN, ALONSO, *and* BARRILDO.]

ESTEBAN   Has everybody come to the meeting?

BARRILDO   Some people are absent.

ESTEBAN   Then our danger is more serious.

BARRILDO   Nearly all the town has been warned.

ESTEBAN   With Frondoso imprisoned in the tower, and my daughter Laurencia in such peril, if God, in his mercy, does not come to our help . . .
    [*Enter* JUAN ROJO *and the* COUNCILMAN.]

JUAN ROJO   What are you shouting about, Esteban? Don't you know secrecy is all important now?

ESTEBAN   I wonder I'm not shouting even louder!
    [*Enter* MENGO.]

MENGO   I want to join in this meeting.

ESTEBAN   With tears streaming down my beard, I ask you, honest farmers, what funeral rites can we give to a country without honor—a country that is lost? And if our honor is indeed lost, which of us can perform such rites, when there is not one among us who has not been dishonored? Answer me now, is there anyone here whose life, whose deep life of honor, is still intact? Are we not all of us in mourning for each other now? If all is lost, what is there to wait for? What is this misfortune that has overtaken us?

JUAN ROJO   The blackest ever known. . . . But it has just been announced that the Kings of Castile have concluded a victorious peace, and will soon arrive in Cordova. Let us send two Councilmen to that city to kneel at their feet and ask their help.

BARRILDO But King Ferdinand, who has conquered so many enemies, is still busy making war, and will not be able to help us now while he's in the midst of battles. We must find some other way out.

COUNCILMAN If you want my opinion, I suggest we leave the town.

JUAN ROJO But how can we do that on such short notice?

MENGO If I understand the situation at all, this meeting will cost us a good many lives.

COUNCILMAN The mast of patience has been torn from us, and now we are a ship driven before a storm of fear. They have brutally abducted the daughter of the good man who rules our community, and unjustly broken the staff of office over his head. What slave was ever treated worse?

JUAN ROJO What do you want the people to do?

COUNCILMAN Die, or give death to the tyrants, for we are many and they are few.

BARRILDO What? Raise our weapons against our lord and master!

ESTEBAN Except for God, the King's our only lord and master, not these inhuman, barbarous men. If God is behind our rightful anger, what have we to lose?

MENGO Let us be a little more cautious. I'm here to speak for the humblest peasants who always have to bear the brunt of any trouble—and I want to represent their fears prudently.

JUAN ROJO Our misfortunes have prepared us to sacrifice our lives, so what are we waiting for? Our houses and vineyards have been burned down. They are tyrants and we must have our revenge.

[*Enter* LAURENCIA, *her hair dishevelled.*]

LAURENCIA Let me come in, for I sorely need the advice of men! Do you know me?

ESTEBAN God in Heaven, is that my daughter?

JUAN ROJO Don't you recognize your Laurencia?

LAURENCIA Yes, I am Laurencia, but so changed that looking at me you still doubt it.

ESTEBAN My daughter!

LAURENCIA Don't call me your daughter!

ESTEBAN Why not, my dear? Why not?

LAURENCIA For many reasons—but chiefly because you let me be carried off by tyrants, by the traitors who rule over us, without attempting to avenge me. I was not yet Frondoso's wife, so you cannot say my husband should have defended me; this was my father's duty as long as the wedding had not been consummated; just as a nobleman about to purchase a jewel need not pay for it if it is lost while still in the merchant's keeping. From under your very eyes, Fernán Gómez dragged me to his house, and you let the wolf carry the sheep like the cowardly shepherd you are. Can you conceive what I suffered at his hands?—the daggers pointed at my breast, the flatteries, threats, insults, and lies used to make my chastity yield to his fierce desires? Does not my bruised and bleeding face, my dishevelled hair tell you anything? Are you not good men?—not fathers and relatives? Do not your hearts sink to see me so grievously betrayed? . . . Oh, you are sheep; how well named the village of Fuente Ovejuna

[Sheepwell]. Give me weapons and let me fight, since you are but things of stone or metal, since you are but tigers—no, not tigers, for tigers fiercely attack those who steal their offspring, killing the hunters before they can escape. You were born timid rabbits; you are infidels, not Spaniards. Chicken-hearted, you permit other men to abuse your women. Put knitting in your scabbards—what need have you of swords? By the living God, I swear that your women will avenge those tyrants and stone you all, you spinning girls, you sodomites, you effeminate cowards. Tomorrow deck yourselves in our bonnets and skirts, and beautify yourselves with our cosmetics. The Comendador will hang Frondoso from a merlon[7] of the tower, without let or trial, and presently he will string you all up. And I shall be glad—you race of half-men—that this honorable town will be rid of effeminates, and the age of Amazons will return, to the eternal amazement of the world.

ESTEBAN Daughter, I will not stay to hear such names. I shall go now, even if I have to fight the whole world.

JUAN ROJO I will go with you, in spite of the enemy's power.

COUNCILMAN We shall die together.

BARRILDO Let us hang a cloth from a stick to fly in the wind, and death to the traitors.

JUAN ROJO What shall our orders be?

MENGO To kill the Comendador without order. To rally the whole town around us: let us all agree to kill the tyrants.

ESTEBAN Take with you swords, lances, crossbows, pikes, and sticks.

MENGO Long live the Kings, our only lords and masters!

ALL Long live the Kings!

MENGO Death to the traitor tyrants!

ALL Death to the tyrants!

[*Exeunt all but* LAURENCIA.]

LAURENCIA Go—God will be with you! Come, women of the town, your honor will be avenged—rally round me!

[*Enter* PASCUALA, JACINTA, *and other women.*]

PASCUALA What is happening? What are you shouting about?

LAURENCIA Can't you see how they're on their way to kill Fernán Gómez? Every man, boy, and child is rushing furiously to do his duty. Is it fair that the men alone should have the glory of a day like this, when we women have the greater grievances?

JACINTA Tell us your plans then.

LAURENCIA I propose that we all band together and perform a deed that will shake the world. Jacinta, your great injury will be our guide.

JACINTA No more than yours.

LAURENCIA Pascuala, you be our standard bearer.

PASCUALA I'll be a good one. I'll put a cloth on a lance and we'll have a flag in the wind.

LAURENCIA There's no time for that. We'll wave our caps for banners.

PASCUALA Let's appoint a captain.

LAURENCIA We don't need one.

PASCUALA Why not?

---

7. One of the toothlike projections atop a castle or fortress.

LAURENCIA   Because when my courage is up, we don't need any Cids or
   Rodamontes.
      [*Exeunt all.*]

Hall in the castle of the COMENDADOR.

      [*Enter* FRONDOSO, *his hands tied*, FLORES, CIMBRANOS, ORTUÑO,
      and the COMENDADOR.]
COMENDADOR   I want him hung by the cord that binds his wrists, so that
   his punishment may be the more severe.
FRONDOSO   How this will add to your descendants' honor, my lord!
COMENDADOR   Hang him from the highest merlon.
FRONDOSO   It was never my intention to kill you.
FLORES   Do you hear that noise outside?
      [*Alarum.*]
COMENDADOR   What can it be?
FLORES   It looks as if the villagers are planning to stay your sentence, my
   lord.
ORTUÑO   They are breaking down the doors!
      [*Alarum.*]
COMENDADOR   The door of my house? The seat of the Commandry?
FRONDOSO   The whole town is here!
JUAN ROJO [*Within*]   Break them down, smash them in, burn, destroy!
ORTUÑO   It's hard to stop a riot once it gets started.
COMENDADOR   The town against me!
FLORES   And their fury has driven them to tear down all the doors.
COMENDADOR   Untie him. And you, Frondoso, go and calm down the
   peasant mayor.
FRONDOSO   I'm going, sir—love has spurred them to action.
      [*Exit* FRONDOSO.]
MENGO [*Within*]   Long live Ferdinand and Isabella, and down with the
   tyrants!
FLORES   In God's name, my lord, don't let them find you here.
COMENDADOR   If they persist—why, this room is strong and well pro-
   tected. They will soon turn back.
FLORES   When villages with a grievance decide to rise against their rulers
   they never turn back until they have shed blood and taken their revenge.
COMENDADOR   We'll face this mob with our weapons, using this door as
   a portcullis.
FRONDOSO [*Within*]   Long live Fuente Ovejuna!
COMENDADOR   What a leader! I'll take care of his bravery!
FLORES   My lord, I marvel at yours.
      [*Enter* ESTEBAN *and the* PEASANTS.]
ESTEBAN   There's the tyrant and his accomplices! Long live Fuente Ove-
   juna, death to the tyrants!
COMENDADOR   Wait, my people!
ALL   Wrongs never wait.
COMENDADOR   Tell me your wrongs, and, on a knight's honor, I'll set them
   right.

ALL   Long live Fuente Ovejuna! Long live King Ferdinand! Death to bad Christians and traitors!

COMENDADOR   Will you not hear me? It is I who address you, I, your lord.

ALL   Our lords are the Catholic Kings.

COMENDADOR   Wait.

ALL   Long live Fuente Ovejuna, and death to Fernán Gómez!

[*Exeunt all. Enter* LAURENCIA, PASCUALA, JACINTA, *and other women, armed.*]

LAURENCIA   You brave soldiers, no longer women, wait here in this place of vantage.

PASCUALA   Only women know how to take revenge. We shall drink the enemy's blood.

JACINTA   Let us pierce his corpse with our lances.

PASCUALA   Agreed.

ESTEBAN [*Within*]   Die, treacherous Comendador!

COMENDADOR   I die. O God, in Thy clemency, have mercy on me!

BARRILDO [*Within*]   Here's Flores.

MENGO   Get that scoundrel! He's the one who gave me a thousand whippings.

FRONDOSO [*Within*]   I shan't consider myself avenged until I've pulled out his soul.

LAURENCIA   There's no excuse for not going in.

PASCUALA   Calm yourself. We had better guard the door.

BARRILDO [*Within*]   I am not moved. Don't come to me with tears now, you fops.

LAURENCIA   Pascuala, I'm going in; I don't care to keep my sword in its scabbard.

[*Exit* LAURENCIA.]

BARRILDO [*Within*]   Here's Ortuño.

FRONDOSO [*Within*]   Slash his face!

[*Enter* FLORES, *fleeing, pursued by* MENGO.]

FLORES   Pity, Mengo! I'm not to blame!

MENGO   O no? Not for being a pimp, you scoundrel, not for having whipped me?

PASCUALA   Mengo, give him to us women, we'll. . . . Hurry, Mengo!

MENGO   Fine, you can have him—no punishment could be worse!

PASCUALA   We'll avenge the whippings he gave you.

MENGO   That's fine!

JACINTA   Come on, death to the traitor!

FLORES   To die at the hands of women!

JACINTA   Don't you like it?

PASCUALA   Is that why you're weeping?

JACINTA   Die, you panderer to his pleasures!

PASCUALA   Die, you traitor!

FLORES   Pity, women, *pity!*

[*Enter* ORTUÑO, *pursued by* LAURENCIA.]

ORTUÑO   You know I have had nothing at all to do with it . . .

LAURENCIA   I know you! Come on, women, dye your conquering weapons in their vile blood.

PASCUALA I'll die killing!
ALL Long live Fuente Ovejuna! Long live King Ferdinand!
    [*Exeunt all.*]

Room of the Catholic Kings, at Toro.

    [*Enter* KING *Ferdinand, Queen* ISABELLA, *and the Maestre Don*
    MANRIQUE.]
MANRIQUE We planned our attack so well that we carried it out without
    any setback. There was little resistance—even if they had tried to organ-
    ize any, it would have been weak. Cabra has remained there to guard the
    place in case of counterattack.
KING That was a wise decision, and I am glad that he is in charge of
    operations. Now we can be sure that Alfonso, who is trying to seize power
    in Portugal, will not be able to harm us. It is fortunate that Cabra is
    stationed there and that he is making a good show, for in this way he
    protects us from any danger and, by acting as a loyal sentinel, works for
    the good of the kingdom.
    [*Enter* FLORES, *wounded.*]
FLORES Catholic King Ferdinand, upon whom Heaven has bestowed the
    Crown of Castile, excellent gentleman that you are—listen to the worst
    cruelty that a man could ever behold from sunrise to sunset.
KING Calm yourself!
FLORES Supreme Sovereign, my wounds forbid me to delay in reporting
    my sad case, for my life is ebbing away. I come from Fuente Ovejuna,
    where, with ruthless heart, the inhabitants of that village have deprived
    their lord and master of his life. Fernán Gómez has been murdered by
    his perfidious subjects, indignant vassals who dared attack him for but a
    trivial cause. The mob called him tyrant and, inflamed by the power of
    the epithet, committed this despicable crime: they broke into his house
    and having no faith that he, a perfect gentleman, would right all their
    wrongs, would not listen to him, but with impatient fury pierced his chest
    which bore the cross of Calatrava with a thousand cruel wounds and
    threw him from the lofty windows onto the pikes and lances of the
    women in the street below. They carried him away, dead, and competed
    with one another in pulling his beard and hair, and recklessly slashing
    his face. In fact their constantly growing fury was so great, that some
    cuts went from ear to ear. They blotted out his coat-of-arms with their
    pikes and loudly proclaimed that they wanted to replace it with your royal
    coat-of-arms since those of the Comendador offended them. They sacked
    his house as if it were the enemy's and joyfully divided the spoils among
    themselves. All this I witnessed from my hiding place, for my cruel fate
    did not grant me death at such a time. Thus I remained all day in hiding
    until nightfall, when I was able to slip away furtively to come to render
    you this account. Sire, since you are just, see that a just punishment is
    administered to the brutal culprits who have perpetrated such an
    outrage.
KING You may rest assured that the culprits will not go without due pun-
    ishment. The unfortunate event is of such magnitude that I am aston-
    ished; I will send a judge to investigate the case and punish the culprits

as an example to all. A captain will accompany him for his protection, for such great offence requires exemplary punishment. In the meantime your wounds will be cared for.

[*Exeunt all.*]

The countryside.

[*Enter* PEASANTS, *both men and women, with* FERNÁN GÓMEZ's *head on a lance.*]

MUSICIANS [*Singing*]
> Long live Isabella and Ferdinand
> And death to the tyrants!

BARRILDO   Sing us a song, Frondoso.

FRONDOSO   Here goes, and if it limps let some critic fix it.
> Long live fair Isabella
> And Ferdinand of Aragon.
> He is made for her
> And she is meant for him.
> May St. Michael guide them
> To Heaven by the hand . . .
> Long live Isabella and Ferdinand
> And death to the tyrants!

LAURENCIA   Now it's your turn, Barrildo.

BARRILDO   Listen to this, for I've been working on it.

PASCUALA   If you say it with feeling, it's going to be good.

BARRILDO
> Long live the famous kings
> For they are victorious.
> They'll be our lords
> Happy and glorious.
> May they conquer always
> All giants and dwarfs . . .
> And death to the tyrants!

MUSICIANS [*Singing*]
> Long live Isabella and Ferdinand
> And death to the tyrants!

LAURENCIA   Now it's your turn, Mengo.

FRONDOSO   Yes, Mengo.

MENGO   I'm a most gifted poet, you know.

PASCUALA   You mean a poet with a bruised backside.

MENGO
> I was whipped on a Sunday morning
> My back still feels the pain
> But the Christian Kings are coming
> There'll be no tyrants here again.

MUSICIANS   Long live the Kings!

ESTEBAN   Take away that head!

MENGO   He has the face of one who has been hanged.

[JUAN ROJO *brings in a scutcheon*[8] *with the royal arms.*]

---

8. Shieldlike object.

COUNCILMAN   The scutcheon has arrived.
ESTEBAN   Let's see it.
JUAN ROJO   Where shall we place it?
COUNCILMAN   Here, in the Town Hall.
ESTEBAN   What a beautiful scutcheon!
BARRILDO   What joy!
FRONDOSO   A new day is dawning for us, and that's our sun.
ESTEBAN

> Long live Castile and Leon
> And the bars of Aragon.
> Down with tyranny!

People of Fuente Ovejuna, listen to the words of an old man whose life has been blameless. The Kings will want to investigate what has happened, and this they will do soon. So agree now among yourselves on what to say.
FRONDOSO   What is your advice?
ESTEBAN   To die saying Fuente Ovejuna and nothing else.
FRONDOSO   That's fine! Fuente Ovejuna did it!
ESTEBAN   Do you want to answer in that way?
ALL   Yes.
ESTEBAN   Well then, I'd like to play the role of questioner—let's rehearse! Mengo, pretend that you are the one being grilled.
MENGO   Can't you pick on someone else, someone more emaciated?
ESTEBAN   But this is all make believe.
MENGO   All right, go ahead!
ESTEBAN   Who killed the Comendador?
MENGO   Fuente Ovejuna did it!
ESTEBAN   You dog, I'm going to torture you.
MENGO   I don't care—even if you kill me.
ESTEBAN   Confess, you scoundrel.
MENGO   I am ready to confess.
ESTEBAN   Well, then, who did it?
MENGO   Fuente Ovejuna.
ESTEBAN   Bind him tighter.
MENGO   That will make no difference.
ESTEBAN   To hell with the trial then!
     [Enter the COUNCILMAN.]
COUNCILMAN   What are you doing here?
FRONDOSO   What has happened, Cuadrado?
COUNCILMAN   The questioner is here.
ESTEBAN   Send him in.
COUNCILMAN   A captain is with him.
ESTEBAN   Who cares? Let the devil himself come in: you know your answer.
COUNCILMAN   They are going around town arresting people.
ESTEBAN   There's nothing to fear. Who killed the Commendador, Mengo?
MENGO   Who? Fuente Ovejuna.
     [Exeunt all.]

Room of the MAESTRE *of* CALATRAVA, *at Almagro.*

     [Enter the MAESTRE and a SOLDIER.]

MAESTRE   What a horrible thing to have happened! Melancholy was his end. I could murder you for bringing me such news.

SOLDIER   Sir, I'm but a messenger. I did not intend to annoy you.

MAESTRE   That a town should become so fierce and wrathful, that it would dare to do such a thing! It's incredible! I'll go there with a hundred men and raze the town to the ground, blotting out even the memory of its inhabitants.

SOLDIER   Calm yourself, sir. They have given themselves up to the King and the most important thing for you is not to enrage him.

MAESTRE   How can they give themselves up to the King? Are they not the vassals of the Comendador?

SOLDIER   That, sir, you'll have to thrash out with the King.

MAESTRE   Thrash it out? No, for the King placed the land in his hands and it is the King's. He is the Sovereign Lord and as such I recognize him. The fact that they have given themselves up to the King soothes my anger. My wisest course is to see him, even if I am at fault. He will pardon me on account of my youth. I am ashamed to go—but my honor demands that I do so and I shall not forget my dignity.

[*Exeunt the* MAESTRE *and* SOLDIER.]

Public square.

[*Enter* LAURENCIA.]

LAURENCIA

> Loving, to suspect one's love will suffer pain
> Becomes an added suffering of love;
> To fear that pain great harm to him may prove
> Brings new torture to the heart again.
>
> Devotion, watching eagerly, would fain
> Give way to worry, worm of love;
> For the heart is rare that does not bend or move
> When fear his threat on the belov'd has lain.
>
> I love my husband with a love that does not tire;
> But now I live and move beneath
> The fear that fate may take away his breath.
> His good is all the end of my desire.
>
> If he is present, certain is my grief;
> If he is absent, certain is my death.

[*Enter* FRONDOSO.]

FRONDOSO   Laurencia!

LAURENCIA   My dear husband! How do you dare to come here?

FRONDOSO   Does my loving care for you give you such worries?

LAURENCIA   My love, take care of yourself. I am afraid something may happen to you.

FRONDOSO   It would displease God, Laurencia, if I made you unhappy.

LAURENCIA   You have seen what has happened to your friends and the ferocious rage of that judge. Save yourself, and fly from danger!

FRONDOSO   Would you expect cowardice from me? Do not advise me to escape. It is inconceivable that in order to avoid harm I should forgo seeing you and betray my friends and my own blood at this tragic moment.

[*Cries within.*]

I hear cries. If I am not mistaken, they are from someone put to the torture. Listen carefully!

[*The* JUDGE *speaks within, and is answered.*]

JUDGE   Tell me the truth, old man.

FRONDOSO   Laurencia, they are torturing an old man!

LAURENCIA   What cruelty!

ESTEBAN   Let me go a moment.

JUDGE   Let him go. Now, tell me, who murdered Fernán?

ESTEBAN   Fuente Ovejuna killed him.

LAURENCIA   Father, I will make your name immortal!

FRONDOSO   What courage!

JUDGE   Take that boy. Pup, speak up! I know you know. What? You refuse? Tighten the screws.[9]

BOY   Fuente Ovejuna, sir.

JUDGE   By the life of the King, I'll hang the lot of you, you peasants, with my own hands! Who killed the Comendador?

FRONDOSO   They're racking the child, and he answers that way . . .

LAURENCIA   What a brave village!

FRONDOSO   Brave and strong.

JUDGE   Put that woman, over there, in the chair. Tighten it up!

LAURENCIA   He's blind with rage.

JUDGE   You see this chair, peasants, this means death to you all! Who killed the Comendador?

PASCUALA   Fuente Ovejuna, sir.

JUDGE   Tighter!

FRONDOSO   I hadn't imagined . . .

LAURENCIA   Pascuala will not tell him, Frondoso.

FRONDOSO   Even the children deny it!

JUDGE   They seem to be delighted. Tighter!

PASCUALA   Merciful God!

JUDGE   Tighter, you bastard! Are you deaf?

PASCUALA   Fuente Ovejuna killed him.

JUDGE   Bring me someone a bit bigger—that fat one, half stripped already!

LAURENCIA   Poor Mengo! That must be Mengo!

FRONDOSO   I'm afraid he'll break down.

MENGO   Oh . . . Oh . . .

JUDGE   Give it to him!

MENGO   Oh . . .

JUDGE   Need any help?

MENGO   Oh . . . Oh . . .

JUDGE   Peasant, who killed the Comendador?

MENGO   Oh . . . I'll tell, sir . . .

JUDGE   Release him a bit.

FRONDOSO   He's confessing!

9. Instrument of torture.

JUDGE   Now, hard, on the back!

MENGO   Wait, I'll tell all . . .

JUDGE   Who killed him?

MENGO   Sir, Fuente Ovejuna.

JUDGE   Did you ever see such scoundrels? They make fun of pain. The ones I was surest of lie most emphatically. Dismiss them: I'm exhausted.

FRONDOSO   Oh, Mengo, God bless you! I was stiff with fear—but you have rid me of it.

[*Enter* MENGO, BARRILDO, *and the* COUNCILMAN.]

BARRILDO   Long live Mengo!

COUNCILMAN   Well he may . . .

BARRILDO   Mengo, bravo!

FRONDOSO   That's what I say.

MENGO   Oh . . . Oh . . .

BARRILDO   Drink and eat, my friend . . .

MENGO   Oh . . . Oh . . . What's that?

BARRILDO   Sweet cider.

MENGO   Oh . . . Oh . . .

FRONDOSO   Something for him to drink!

BARRILDO   Right away!

FRONDOSO   He quaffs it well! That's better, now.

LAURENCIA   Give him a little more.

MENGO   Oh . . . Oh . . .

BARRILDO   This glass, for me.

LAURENCIA   Solemnly he drinks it!

FRONDOSO   A good denial gets a good drink.

BARRILDO   Want another glass?

MENGO   Oh . . . Oh . . . Yes, yes.

FRONDOSO   Drink it down; you deserve it.

LAURENCIA   A drink for each turn of the rack.

FRONDOSO   Cover him up, he'll freeze to death.

BARRILDO   Want some more?

MENGO   Three more. Oh . . . Oh . . .

FRONDOSO   He's asking for the wine . . .

BARRILDO   Yes, there's a boy, drink deep. What's the matter now?

MENGO   It's a bit sour. Oh, I'm catching cold.

FRONDOSO   Here, drink this, it's better. Who killed the Comendador?

MENGO   Fuente Ovejuna killed him . . .

[*Exeunt* MENGO, BARRILDO, *and the* COUNCILMAN.]

FRONDOSO   He deserves more than they can give him. But tell me, my love, who killed the Comendador?

LAURENCIA   Little Fuente Ovejuna, my dear.

FRONDOSO   Who did?

LAURENCIA   You bully, you torturer! I say Fuente Ovejuna did it.

FRONDOSO   What about me? How do *I* kill *you*?

LAURENCIA   With love, sweet love, with lots of love.

Room of the Kings, at Tordesillas.

[*Enter the* KING *and queen* (ISABELLA).]

ISABELLA   I did not expect to find you here, but my luck is good.

KING   The pleasure of seeing you lends new glory to my eyes. I was on my way to Portugal and I had to stop here.

ISABELLA   Your Majesty's plans are always wise.

KING   How did you leave Castile?

ISABELLA   Quiet and peaceful.

KING   No wonder, if you were the peacemaker.

[Enter Don MANRIQUE.]

MANRIQUE   The Maestre of Calatrava, who has just arrived, begs audience.

ISABELLA   I wanted very much to see him.

MANRIQUE   I swear, Madame, that although young in years, he is a most valiant soldier.

[Exit Don MANRIQUE, and enter the MAESTRE.]

MAESTRE   Rodrigo Téllez Girón, Maestre of Calatrava, who never tires of praising you, humbly kneels before you and asks your pardon. I admit that I have been deceived and that, ill-advised, I may have transgressed in my loyalty to you. Fernán's counsel deceived me and for that reason I humbly beg forgiveness. And if I am deserving of this royal favor, I pledge to serve you from now on; in the present campaign which you are undertaking against Granada, where you are now going, I promise to show the valor of my sword. No sooner will I unsheathe it, bringing fierce suffering to the enemy, than I will hoist my red crosses on the loftiest merlon of the battlements. In serving you I will employ five hundred soldiers, and I promise on my honor nevermore to displease you.

KING   Rise, Maestre. It is enough that you have come for me to welcome you royally.

MAESTRE   You are a consolation to a troubled soul.

ISABELLA   You speak with the same undaunted courage with which you act.

MAESTRE   You are a beautiful Esther, and you a divine Xerxes.

[Enter MANRIQUE.]

MANRIQUE   Sir, the judge you sent to Fuente Ovejuna has returned and he asks to see you.

KING [To the MAESTRE]   Be the judge of these aggressors.

MAESTRE   If I were not in your presence, Sire, I'd certainly teach them how to kill Comendadores.

KING   That is no longer necessary.

ISABELLA   God willing, I hope this power lies with you.

[Enter JUDGE.]

JUDGE   I went to Fuente Ovejuna, as you commanded, and carried out my assignment with special care and diligence. After due investigation, I cannot produce a single written page of evidence, for to my question: "Who killed the Comendador?" the people answered with one accord: "Fuente Ovejuna did it." Three hundred persons were put to torture, quite ruthlessly, and I assure you, Sire, that I could get no more out of them than this. Even children, only ten years old, were put to the rack, but to no avail—neither did flatteries nor deceits do the least good. And since it is so hopeless to reach any conclusion: either you must pardon them all or kill the entire village. And now the whole town has come to corroborate in person what they have told me. You will be able to find out from them.

KING   Let them come in.

[*Enter the two mayors,* ESTEBAN *and* ALONSO, FRONDOSO, *and* PEASANTS, *men and women.*]

LAURENCIA   Are those the rulers?

FRONDOSO   Yes, they are the powerful sovereigns of Castile.

LAURENCIA   Upon my faith, they are beautiful! May Saint Anthony bless them!

ISABELLA   Are these the aggressors?

ESTEBAN   Fuente Ovejuna, Your Majesty, who humbly kneel before you, ready to serve you. We have suffered from the fierce tyranny and cruelty of the dead Comendador, who showered insults upon us—and committed untold evil. He was bereft of all mercy, and did not hesitate to steal our property and rape our women.

FRONDOSO   He went so far as to take away from me this girl, whom Heaven has granted to me and who has made me so blissful that no human being can compete with me in joy. He snatched her away to his house on my wedding night, as if she were his property, and if she had not known how to protect herself, she, who is virtue personified, would have paid dearly, as you can well imagine.

MENGO   Is it not my turn to talk? If you grant me permission you will be astonished to learn how he treated me. Because I went to defend a girl whom his insolent servants were about to abuse, that perverse Nero handled me so roughly that he left my posterior like a slice of salmon. Three men beat my buttocks so relentlessly that I believe I still bear some wales. To heal my bruises I have had to use more powders and myrtleberries than my farm is worth.

ESTEBAN   Sire, we want to be your vassals. You are our King and in your defense we have borne arms. We trust in your clemency and hope that you believe in our innocence.

KING   Though the crime is grave, I am forced to pardon it since no indictment is set down. And since I am responsible for you, the village will remain under my jurisdiction until such time as a new Comendador appears to inherit it.

FRONDOSO   Your Majesty speaks with great wisdom. And at this point, worthy audience, ends the play FUENTE OVEJUNA.

WILLIAM SHAKESPEARE
1564–1616

William Shakespeare was born in the rural community of Stratford-upon-Avon in Warwickshire. His father, John Shakespeare, was a glover and, when William was born, prominent in the town's government. Little is known of Shakespeare's early life, although it is likely that he received an education at the good local grammar school and certain that he married Anne Hathaway, about seven years his senior, when he was eighteen. The couple had three children, Susanna (1583) and the twins Judith and Hamnet (1585). By 1592 Shakespeare was in London, rapidly becoming the "greatest shake-scene" around, in the irritated words of a rival who envied Shakespeare's ability to impress audiences despite his lack of a university education. Shakespeare soon became a shareholder in a prominent players' company that claimed the Lord Chamberlain as patron and the tragic actor Richard Burbage and the comedian Will Kempe as members. Composing dramas that drew on the strengths of his repertory company, Shakespeare brought to the English stage such famous characters as Falstaff and Prince Hal, Hamlet and Ophelia, Othello and Desdemona, and King Lear.

The company originally performed at the Theatre, north of the city of London, where its actor-owner, James Burbage, faced steady opposition from the puritanical city officials who sought to close the theaters, which they considered to be hotbeds of immorality. Burbage conceived of a means to escape civic legislation against theatrical performances, and secretly moved the boards of his playhouse across the river Thames to the south bank; with these planks he constructed the Globe, the theater most often associated with Shakespeare's name. The Globe was open to all social classes: anyone who wished could enter the theater by paying a penny, and at the cost of another, get a bench, cushion, and protection (in the boxes) from inclement weather. Shakespeare, who began his career as a player, found his calling as a playwright and his fortune as a shareholder in his company. His financial successes enabled him to purchase the title of gentleman for his father, a purchase that made Shakespeare himself officially a "gentleman born."

The influence of Shakespeare's plays on the course of English literature is matched only by the King James translation of the Bible. In his time, Shakespeare garnered the interest of two British monarchs (Elizabeth I and James I), the love of popular audiences, and the respect of such tough critics as the poet and playwright Ben Jonson. After Shakespeare's death in 1616, when his friends and colleagues John Heminges and Henry Condell collected his plays into one volume (the *First Folio*), Ben Jonson wrote a magnificent verse memorial to the rival whose wit had seemed almost too fertile for the good of his art. In a poem that introduces the collected plays, Jonson praises Shakespeare as a poet who was "the Soule of the Age" and "Not of an age, but for all time!" Jonson's insistence that Shakespeare transcended the age he simultaneously embodied is paradoxical. For Jonson, however, great artists immortalize their nations and epochs. In his view, the publication of Shakespeare's plays in the form of a book meant that the entire age of "Eliza, and our James" would enter triumphantly into world history: "Triumph, my Britain, thou hast one to show, / To whom all scenes of Europe homage owe." Shakespeare himself may have suspected that his dramatic works would eventually be counted as cultural arts, but he always kept his eye on more humble and material successes. When he retired to Stratford-upon-Avon in 1612, he lived a quiet life in the house he had built (New House) from the savings he had accumulated while working in London's premiere playhouse.

HAMLET

Shakespeare's plays constitute the most important body of dramatic work in the modern world, and no character in literature is more familiar to audiences around the globe than Hamlet. The unparalleled reputation of the work may also have certain nonliterary causes. For instance, it is a play whose central role is singularly cherished by actors in all languages as the test of their skill, and conversely, audiences sometimes content themselves with a rather vague notion of the work as a whole and concentrate on the attractively problematical and eloquent hero and on the actor impersonating him, waiting for his performance of his famous soliloquies rather than following the action and interpretation of the play. But along with the impact of the protagonist, there are other and deeper reasons why *Hamlet* has commanded a leading place in our literary heritage. Though it is a drama that concerns personages of superior station and the conflicts and problems associated with men and women of high degree, it reveals these problems in terms of a particular family, presenting an individual and domestic dimension along with a public one—the pattern of family conflict within the larger pattern of the *polis*—like the plays of antiquity that deal with the Theban myth, such as *Oedipus* and *Antigone*.

This public dimension of *Hamlet* helps us see it, for our present purposes, in relation to the literature of the Renaissance—for the framework within which the characters are presented and come into conflict is a court. In spite of the Danish locale and the relatively remote period of the action, it is plainly a Renaissance court exhibiting the structure of interests to which Machiavelli's *Prince* has potently drawn our attention. There is a ruler holding power, and much of the action is related to questions concerning the nature of that power—the way in which he had acquired it and the ways in which it can be preserved. Moreover, there is a courtly structure: the king has several courtiers around him, among whom Hamlet, the heir apparent, is only the most prominent.

We have seen some of the forms of the Renaissance court pattern in earlier selections in this anthology—in Castiglione, Rabelais, and Machiavelli. The court, the ruling nucleus of the community, was also an arena for conflicts of interest and of wit, a setting for the cultivation and codification of aristocratic virtues (valor, physical and intellectual brilliance, "courtesy"). The positive view of human achievement on earth, so prominent in the Renaissance, was given in courtly life its characteristic setting and testing ground. And as we have observed, the negative view (melancholy, sense of void and purposelessness) also emerged there.

Examining *Hamlet*, we soon realize that its temper belongs more to the negative than to the positive Renaissance outlook. Certain outstanding forms of human endeavor (the establishment of earthly power, the display of gallantry, the confident attempt of the mind to acquire knowledge and to inspire purposeful action), which elsewhere are presented as highly worthwhile, or are at least soberly discussed in terms of their value and limits, seem to be caught here in a condition of disorder and imbued with a sense of vanity and emptiness.

The way in which the state and the court of Denmark are presented in *Hamlet* is significant: they are shown in images of disease and rottenness. And here again, excessive stress on the protagonist himself must be avoided. His position as denouncer of the prevailing decadence, and the major basis for his denunciation—the murder of his father, which leads to his desire to obtain revenge and purify the court by destroying the present king—are central elements in the play, but they are not the *whole* play. The public situation is indicated, and Marcellus has pronounced his famous "Something is rotten" before Hamlet has talked to the Ghost and learned the Ghost's version of events. Moreover, the sense of outside dangers and internal disruption everywhere transcends the personal story of Hamlet, of his revenge, of Claudius's crime; these are rather the signs of the breakdown, portents of a general situation. In this sense, we may tentatively say that the general theme of the play has to do with a kingdom, a society, a *polis*, going to pieces—or even more, with its realization that it has already gone to pieces. Concomitant with this is a sense of the vanity of those forms of human endeavor and power of which the kingdom and the court are symbols.

The tone Shakespeare wants to establish is evident from the opening scenes: the night air is full of dread premonitions; sentinels turn their eyes toward the threatening outside world; meanwhile, the Ghost has already made his appearance, a sinister omen. The kingdom, as we proceed, is presented in terms that are an almost point by point reversal of the ideal. Claudius, the *pater patriae* and *pater familias*, whether we believe the Ghost's indictment or not (Hamlet does not necessarily, and some of his famous indecision has been attributed to his seeking evidence of the Ghost's truthfulness before acting), has by marrying the queen committed an act that by Elizabethan standards is incestuous. There is an overwhelming sense of disintegration in the body of the state, evident in the first court assembly and in all subsequent ones. In their various ways the two courtiers, Hamlet and Laertes, are strangers, contemplating departure; they offer, around their king, a picture quite unlike that of the conventional paladins, supports of the throne, in a well-manned and well-mannered court. (In Rabelais's "kingdom," when Grangousier is ruler, the pattern is also a courtly and knightly one, but the young heir, Gargantua, who is like Hamlet a university student, readily abandons his studies to answer the fatherland's call; here the direction is reversed.)

On the other hand, as in all late and decadent phases of a social or artistic structure (the court in a sense is both), we have semblance instead of substance, ornate and empty facades, of which the more enlightened members of the group are mockingly aware. Thus Polonius, who after Hamlet is the major figure in the king's retinue, is presented satirically in his empty formalities of speech and conventional patterns of behavior. And there are numerous instances (e.g., Osric) of manners being replaced by mannerisms. Hence the way courtly life is depicted in the play suggests always the hollow, the fractured, and the crooked. The traditional forms and institutions of gentle living and all the pomp and solemnity are marred by corruption and distortion. Courtship and love are reduced to Hamlet's mockery of a "civil conversation" in the play scene, his phrases presenting not Castiglione's Platonic loftiness and the repartee of "gentilesse" but punning undercurrents of bawdiness. The theater, a traditional institution of court life, is "politically" used by the hero as a device to expose the king's crime. There are elements of macabre caricature in Shakespeare's treatment of the solemn theme of death (see, for instance, the manner of Polonius's death, which is a sort of sarcastic version of a cloak-and-dagger scene, or the effect of the clownish gravediggers' talk). Finally, the arms tournament, the typical occasion for the display of courtiers' gallantry in front of their king, is here turned by the scheming of the king himself into the play's conclusive scene of carnage. And the person who, on the king's behalf, invites Hamlet to that feast is Osric, the "waterfly," the caricature of the hollow courtier.

This sense of corruption and decadence dominates the temper of the play and obviously qualifies the character of Hamlet, his indecision, and his sense of vanity and disenchantment with the world in which he lives. In Hamlet the relation between thought and deed, intent and realization, is confused in the same way the norms and institutions that would regulate the life of a well-ordered court have been deprived of their original purpose and beauty. He and the king are "mighty opposites," and it can be argued that against Hamlet's indecision and negativism the king presents a more positive scheme of action, at least in the purely Machiavellian sense, at the level of practical power politics. But even this conclusion will prove only partly true. There are indeed moments in which all that the king seems to wish for himself is to forget the past and rule honorably. He advises Hamlet not to mourn his father excessively, for melancholy is not in accord with "nature." On various occasions the king shows a high and competent conception of his office: a culminating instance is the courageous and cunning way in which he confronts and handles Laertes's wrath. The point can be made that since his life is obviously threatened by Hamlet (who was seeking to kill him when by mistake he killed Polonius instead), the king acts within a legitimate pattern of politics in wanting to have Hamlet liquidated. But this argument cannot be carried so far as to demonstrate that he represents a fully positive attitude toward life and the world, even in the strictly amoral terms of political technique. For in fact his action is corroded by an element alien to that technique—the vexations of his own conscience. Despite his energy and his extrovert qualities, he too becomes part of the negative picture of disruption and lacks concentration of purpose. The images of decay and putrescence that characterize his court extend to his own speech: his "offense," in his own words, "smells to heaven."

Hamlet as a Renaissance tragedy presents a world particularly "out of joint," a world that, having long ago lost the sense of a grand extratemporal design that was so important in medieval times (to Hamlet the thought of the afterlife is even more puzzling and dark than that of this life), looks with an even greater sense of disenchantment at the circle of temporal action symbolized by the kingdom and the court. These structures could have offered certain codes of conduct and objects of allegiance that would have given individual action a purposeful meaning. But now their order has been destroyed. Ideals that once had power and freshness have lost their vigor under the impact of satiety, doubt, and melancholy.

Because communal values are so degraded, it is natural to ask in the end whether some alternative attempt at a settlement could be imagined, with Hamlet—like other Renaissance heroes—adopting an individual code of conduct, however extravagant. On the whole, Hamlet seems too steeped in his own hopelessness and in the courtly mechanism to which he inevitably belongs to be able to find personal intellectual and moral compromise or his own version of total escape or total dream; for his "antic disposition" is a strategy, his "folly" is politically motivated. Still, the tone of his brooding and often moralizing speech, his melancholy and dissatisfaction, his very desire for revenge imply a nostalgia for a world—associated with his father—of loyal allegiances and ideals of honor. Yet in *Hamlet* the political world turns out to offer no protection for the values—friendship, loyalty, and honesty—that Hamlet himself most cherishes. These virtues belong only to intimate relationships, such as that between Hamlet and Horatio, and to the world of story, such as the one Horatio will tell of Hamlet after his death.

William Shakespeare's "Hamlet" (1986), ed. Harold Bloom, contains some unconventional critical approaches. A biography placing Shakespeare in his social context is M. C. Bradbrook, *Shakespeare the Poet in His World* (1978), while E. K. Chambers, *William Shakespeare, A Study of Facts and Problems,* 2 vols. (1930), is considered the most fully documented biography. Paul Arthur Cantor, *Shakespeare, "Hamlet"* (1989), is an in-depth study of the tragedy. Valuable studies are to be found in Maynard Mack, "The World of *Hamlet*," *Yale Review* 41 (1952), and Harry Levin, *The Question of "Hamlet"* (1959). Cedric Watts, *Hamlet* (1988), besides critical interpretation, offers stage history, critical history, and a selected bibliography.

THE TRAGEDY OF OTHELLO THE MOOR OF VENICE

The great *Othello* (about 1604) was first performed at the beginning of the reign of James I, who became the patron of Shakespeare's acting company, now called the King's Men. For *Othello*, Shakespeare adapted a simple and unpleasant tale from Giraldi Cinthio's *Hecatommithi* (1565) in which a nameless Moor, duped into believing that his Venetian wife has committed adultery, murders her in a jealous rage. Shakespeare's play questions the social stereotype of the passionate Moor that Cinthio's story confirms. Shakespeare, moreover, tests and explores the very notion of identity: how do individuals' histories and imaginations affect who they are? how does Othello's eventful life—as soldier, former slave, black man, Christian convert, instrument of war, object of imaginative wonder, and perpetual outsider in his adopted home of Venice—influence who he is? and how do his stories about his exotic past transform the ways in which his audiences perceive him and conceive of their own lives?

At the outset of Shakespeare's play, Othello, a Moor and general in the Venetian Republic's army, has eloped with a beautiful noblewoman, Desdemona, whose father (Brabanzio) rushes to the Venetian Senate to challenge the marriage. The play allows the uncomfortable suspicion that Othello escapes judgment because the Senate has already commissioned him to defend the Venetian stronghold in Cyprus from the Turks. Othello's name remains uncleared until Desdemona herself testifies to her passionate consent to the marriage and gains permission to join her husband on his military expedition. If audiences hope that Othello will display his heroism in combat with the Turks, all such expectations are dashed when a violent storm disables and scatters the Turkish ships. As characters gather on the shores of Cyprus (mythical home of Venus, goddess of love) to await the safe landing of Desdemona and Othello, the idea of military combat shifts to the erotic relations between Desdemona and Othello: Desdemona is Othello's "fair warrior" and "our great captain's captain." The erotic images anticipate the couple's deferred nuptial celebrations and, ominously, the fatal transformation of Othello's love into murderous jealousy. Under Iago's malicious influence, Othello loses faith in himself and in Desdemona, and he strangles her "in her bed, even the bed she hath contaminated." When he learns the truth of Desdemona's innocence at the play's end, Othello asks to be remembered romantically as a man "who loved not wisely, but too well." Finally, he stabs himself, falls upon the bed that dominates the final act, and dies "upon a kiss."

Central to the tragedy are questions of motive. Iago's "motiveless malignancy"—a phrase coined by Samuel Taylor Coleridge—is famously mysterious, but is by no means the play's only puzzle. Othello himself struck early critics as a glorified fool: Thomas Rymer, writing in 1693, ridiculed the idea that such a trifle as a lost handkerchief—Othello's first gift to Desdemona—could turn the mind of a genuinely tragic hero against his wife. For this post-Enlightenment critic, a handkerchief held none of the mystical significance that it might for Renaissance audiences, who regarded magical talismans and religious relics as potent signs of the supernatural. During the play, however, the "mystery" that baffles Desdemona's father and finally Othello himself is how the beautiful, intelligent, and virtuous Desdemona could have felt such an ardent passion for Othello in the first place: "A maiden never bold. / Of spirit so still and quiet that her motion / Blushed at herself—and she in spite of nature, / Of years, of country, credit, everything, / To fall in love with what she feared to look on!" The differences in age, nationality, and social status, normally so disastrous, fade next to the "everything" that is Othello's race.

Shakespeare does not approach racial stereotypes strictly in terms of the race discourses of the English Renaissance. Instead, he presents all of his characters in relation to older, more limited dramatic ideas of character type. The dramatic traditions against which he defines his tragedy and characters are the medieval morality play and Roman new comedy. Roman comedy, of which *Pseudolus* is an outstanding example, draws its cast of characters from social types: in a common scenario, a clever servant circumvents the efforts of an irate father to prevent the boy from getting the girl. Although Shakespeare introduces these theatrical types in several of his early comedies, it is startling to see them frolicking about a tragedy dealing with betrayal, mad jealously, loss of identity, divorce, and murder. In *Othello*, which begins with a marriage (usually the point at which comedy ends), comic types have tragic purposes: the clever servant conspires to divorce the husband from the wife and see to it that marriage ends in a murder-suicide.

A second set of character types from new comedy is the braggart soldier and his flatterer. Iago casts himself as a cross between the clever servant and parasitic flatterer: he is, he says, one of those servants who, "trimmed in forms and visages of duty, / Keep yet their hearts attending on themselves." At the same time, he characterizes Othello as the swaggering soldier, filled with "bombast circumstance, / Horribly stuffed with epithets of war." Despite Iago's efforts to diminish Othello in the first scenes, Shakespeare's hero, when he at last appears, transcends the degrading stereotypes. When Brabanzio and his men attempt to apprehend him, one line from Othello stops his antagonists in their tracks: "Keep up your bright swords," he commands, "for the dew will rust 'em." The implicit boast is magnificent: only a warrior assured of victory has the power to refuse a challenge.

Shakespeare's use of stock types from comedy supplies a dramatic counterpart to the cultural stereotypes about race that Iago mobilizes at the outset of the play. Shakespeare's audiences must wait to learn the name of the man who is the subject of all Iago's bitter dialogues. Othello is first an anonymous "he," then a sarcastic "his Moorship." The "Moor" is the least charged of Iago's inventive and scabrous terms: he is also "the thick-lips," "an old black ram," a "Barbary horse," and "the devil." Othello goes unnamed, in fact, until the third scene, when he arrives at the Senate council chambers, where the Venetian senators await his military aid.

Against the backdrop of stock comic types, Shakespeare's tragic characters emerge as complex yet painfully vulnerable to manipulation and stereotyping. Brabanzio, for example, acts the part of the "irate father" only after Iago has stuffed his ears with racial slurs and sexually degrading images of his daughter and Othello: "Your heart is burst, you have lost half your soul. / Even now, now, very now, an old black ram / Is tupping your white ewe," Iago says, and "your daughter and the Moor are now making the beast with two backs." Unmentioned and unmentionable, Othello's blackness fuels the formerly levelheaded Brabanzio's hysteria when Iago tells him, "You'll have your daughter covered with a Barbary horse, you'll have your nephews neigh to you, you'll have coursers for cousins and gennets for germans" (Spanish horses for blood relatives). Soon Brabanzio views Othello, the man who was his beloved friend, in terms of racial prejudice, as an animal and a barbarian.

A second dramatic tradition at work in *Othello* is the medieval morality play, in which the forces of good and evil do battle for the soul of Everyman. To a certain extent, Othello acts as an Everyman, Desdemona as his good angel, and Iago as the charismatic villain known as the Vice. Shakespeare turns the morality play's allegorical battle for the soul (*psychomachia*) into a psychological struggle within Othello, who is torn between his faith in and radical doubts about Desdemona. At the end of the play, Othello looks toward Iago's feet, half expecting to see the hooves that will furnish a supernatural explanation for his malice, and seeks to learn of "that demi-devil, / What he hath thus ensnared my soul and body?" Simultaneously, Desdemona appears to Othello as an angel: "O ill-starred wench! / Pale as thy smock! When we shall meet at count [Judgment Day] / This look of thine will hurl my soul from heaven / And friends will snatch at it." Othello sees around him the signs of a morality play gone hideously wrong. Yet an explanation of his downfall in metaphysical terms distorts the entirely human character of his tragedy. To view Iago as a demi-devil is to mystify his power and deny the human and social origins of his malevolence. To view Desdemona as an angel is to idealize her at the cost of her humanity. For Othello, the cold, pale body of Desdemona painfully testifies to the purity of her once suspect sexuality: "Cold, cold, my girl, / Even like thy chastity." Othello's idealism is tragically at odds with his wife's very passion for him.

The medieval Vice was no supernatural agent: he represented an evil shared by the entire community, and he performs onstage in a way that affirms his intimate connection with the audience. While the protagonist dominates center stage, Vice hogs the sidelines and the area downstage (close to the audience). Whereas Shakespearean tragic heroes speak soliloquies—extended monologues "overheard" by the audience—Vice-figures like Iago directly address the audience in lively, confidential, and humorous terms. The medieval Vice is expected to pun, joke, and deflate the high-flown ideals represented by other characters—the exact behavioral trademarks of Iago. Iago, however, takes none of the carnivalesque delight enjoyed by Vice: his character does not invite most actors to play him with sprightly, cackling, hand-rubbing glee. Like Vice, however, Iago represents a communal evil: cultural hatreds and bigotry, including racial prejudice, misogyny (hatred or fear of women), elitism, and smug nationalism. These are the ingredients of Iago's verbal poison, which are the jokes and corrupting "medicine" he imagines himself pouring into others' ears.

Does Iago deserve the dubious credit for engineering the alienation of Othello from Desdemona? Many readers and playgoers detect ambivalence in Othello's admiring description of Desdemona as his "fair warrior," even without Iago's suggestion that "our general's wife is now the general." Othello, in fact, appears to share both Cassio's exalted sense of Desdemona as "a maid / That paragons description and wild fame" and Iago's dismissal of all women as "wildcats in your kitchens, / Saints in your injuries; devils being offended, / Players in your housewifery, and hussies in your beds."

Othello exhibits an idolatrous love for Desdemona even as he prepares to murder her. In the eloquent, troublingly erotic soliloquy that begins the final scene, Othello says he will "not shed her blood, / Nor scar that whiter skin of hers than snow, / And smooth as monumental alabaster." Here, as elsewhere, Othello feels ambivalently attracted to her sexual vitality (the "rose" he will pluck) and to the artificial, statuelike qualities of her vulnerable, sleeping body. Only when she is dead can Othello safely adore Desdemona as a marble image of chaste purity.

Anthony Burgess, *Shakespeare* (1970), is an informed and imaginative biography. William Schoenbaum, *William Shakespeare: A Compact Documentary Life* (1977), is the standard reference. On the theatrical companies and players, Muriel Bradbrook, *The Rise of the Common Player* (1964), and Andrew Gurr, *The Shakespearean Stage, 1574–1642*, 3rd ed. (1992), are recommended. Huston Diehl, *Staging Reform, Reforming the Stage* (1997), contains a strong reading of Othello's relationship to Reformation ideas about idolatry and the imagination. Janet Adelman, *Suffocating Mothers* (1992), discusses Othello's tendency to regard Desdemona as the source of his very being. Karen Newman studies the links between women and race in the chapter " 'And wash the Ethiop white': Femininity and the Monstrous in *Othello*" in *Fashioning Femininity* (1991). Carol Thomas Neely analyzes the sexual double standard of the play from the perspective of Emilia in *Broken Rituals in Shakespeare's Plays* (1985). G. K. Hunter, "Othello and Color Prejudice," in *Dramatic Identities and Cultural Tradition* (1978), remains one of the finest studies of race discourse and the play itself. Maynard Mack, "The Jacobean Shakespeare: Some Observations on the Construction of the Tragedies," in *Stratford-upon-Avon Studies: Jacobean Theatre*, vol. 1 (1960), ed. John Russell Brown and Bernard Harris, is an indispensable survey of Shakespeare's writing in his later period.

Hamlet, Prince of Denmark

CHARACTERS

CLAUDIUS, *king of Denmark*
HAMLET, *son to the late, and*
    nephew to the present king
POLONIUS, *lord chamberlain*
HORATIO, *friend to Hamlet*
LAERTES, *son of Polonius*
PRIEST
MARCELLUS, ⎫ *officers*
BERNARDO, ⎭
FRANCISCO, *a soldier*
REYNALDO, *servant to Polonius*
PLAYERS
TWO CLOWNS, *grave-diggers*
FORTINBRAS, *prince of Norway*
CAPTAIN

VOLTIMAND,
CORNELIUS,
ROSENCRANTZ, ⎫
GUILDENSTERN, ⎬ *courtiers*
OSRIC, ⎪
GENTLEMAN, ⎭
ENGLISH AMBASSADORS
GERTRUDE, *queen of Denmark, and*
    mother to Hamlet
OPHELIA, *daughter of Polonius*
LORDS, LADIES, OFFICERS, SOLDIERS,
    SAILORS, MESSENGERS, *and*
    OTHER ATTENDANTS
GHOST OF HAMLET'S FATHER

SCENE—*Denmark.*

Act I

SCENE 1

Elsinore. A platform before the castle.

[FRANCISCO *at his post. Enter to him* BERNARDO.]

BERNARDO: Who's there?

FRANCISCO: Nay, answer me: stand, and unfold yourself.

BERNARDO: Long live the king!

FRANCISCO: Bernardo?

BERNARDO: He.   5

FRANCISCO: You come most carefully upon your hour.

BERNARDO: 'Tis now struck twelve; get thee to bed, Francisco.

FRANCISCO: For this relief much thanks: 'tis bitter cold,
   And I am sick at heart.

BERNARDO: Have you had quiet guard?

FRANCISCO: Not a mouse stirring.   10

BERNARDO: Well, good night.
   If you do meet Horatio and Marcellus,
   The rivals[1] of my watch, bid them make haste.

FRANCISCO: I think I hear them. Stand, ho! Who is there?

[*Enter* HORATIO *and* MARCELLUS.]

HORATIO: Friends to this ground.

MARCELLUS: And liegemen to the Dane.[2]   15

FRANCISCO: Give you good night.

MARCELLUS: O, farewell, honest soldier:
   Who hath relieved you?

FRANCISCO: Bernardo hath my place.
   Give you good night.
     [*Exit.*]

MARCELLUS: Holla! Bernardo!

BERNARDO: Say,
   What, is Horatio there?

HORATIO: A piece of him.

BERNARDO: Welcome, Horatio; welcome, good Marcellus.   20

MARCELLUS: What, has this thing appeared again to-night?

BERNARDO: I have seen nothing.

MARCELLUS: Horatio says 'tis but our fantasy,
   And will not let belief take hold of him
   Touching this dreaded sight, twice seen of us: 25
   Therefore I have entreated him along
   With us to watch the minutes of this night,
   That if again this apparition come,
   He may approve our eyes[3] and speak to it.

HORATIO: Tush, tush, 'twill not appear.

BERNARDO: Sit down a while;   30
   And let us once again assail your ears,
   That are so fortified against our story,

---

1. Partners.   2. The king of Denmark.   3. Confirm what we saw.

What we have two nights seen.
HORATIO: Well, sit we down,
   And let us hear Bernardo speak of this.
BERNARDO: Last night of all,   35
   When yond same star that's westward from the pole
   Had made his course to illume that part of heaven
   Where now it burns, Marcellus and myself,
   The bell then beating one,—
       [Enter GHOST.]
MARCELLUS: Peace, break thee off; look, where it comes again!   40
BERNARDO: In the same figure, like the king that's dead.
MARCELLUS: Thou art a scholar; speak to it, Horatio.
BERNARDO: Looks it not like the king? mark it, Horatio.
HORATIO: Most like it: it harrows me with fear and wonder.
BERNARDO: It would be spoke to.
MARCELLUS: Question it, Horatio.   45
HORATIO: What art thou, that usurp'st this time of night,
   Together with that fair and warlike form
   In which the majesty of buried Denmark
   Did sometimes[4] march? by heaven I charge thee, speak!
MARCELLUS: It is offended.
BERNARDO: See, it stalks away!   50
HORATIO: Stay! speak, speak! I charge thee, speak!
       [Exit GHOST.]
MARCELLUS: 'Tis gone, and will not answer.
BERNARDO: How now, Horatio! you tremble and look pale:
   Is not this something more than fantasy?
   What think you on't?   55
HORATIO: Before my God, I might not this believe
   Without the sensible and true avouch
   Of mine own eyes.
MARCELLUS: Is it not like the king?
HORATIO: As thou art to thyself:
   Such was the very armor he had on   60
   When he the ambitious Norway[5] combated;
   So frown'd he once, when, in an angry parle,
   He smote the sledded[6] Polacks on the ice.
   'Tis strange.
MARCELLUS: Thus twice before, and jump[7] at this dead hour,   65
   With martial stalk hath he gone by our watch.
HORATIO: In what particular thought to work I know not;
   But, in the gross and scope of my opinion,[8]
   This bodes some strange eruption to our state.
MARCELLUS: Good now, sit down, and tell me, he that knows,   70
   Why this same strict and most observant watch
   So nightly toils the subject[9] of the land,
   And why such daily cast of brazen cannon,

---

4. Formerly. *Denmark:* the king of Denmark.   **5.** The king of Norway (the elder Fortinbras).   6. They travel in sledges. *Parle:* parley.   7. Just.   8. Taking a general view.   9. The people.

And foreign mart for implements of war;
Why such impress of shipwrights,[1] whose sore task   75
Does not divide the Sunday from the week;
What might be toward,[2] that this sweaty haste
Doth make the night joint-laborer with the day:
Who is't that can inform me?
HORATIO: That can I;
  At least the whisper goes so. Our last king,   80
Whose image even but now appear'd to us,
Was, as you know, by Fortinbras of Norway,
Thereto pricked on by a most emulate pride,
Dared to the combat; in which our valiant Hamlet—
For so this side of our known world esteem'd him—   85
Did slay this Fortinbras; who by a seal'd compact
Well ratified by law and heraldry,[3]
Did forfeit, with his life, all those his lands
Which he stood seized of, to the conqueror:
Against the which, a moiety competent   90
Was gagèd[4] by our king; which had returned
To the inheritance of Fortinbras,
Had he been vanquisher; as, by the same covenant
And carriage[5] of the article design'd,
His fell to Hamlet. Now, sir, young Fortinbras,   95
Of unimprovèd metal hot and full,
Hath in the skirts[6] of Norway here and there
Shark'd up a list of lawless resolutes,
For food and diet, to some enterprise
That hath a stomach in't:[7] which is no other—   100
As it doth well appear unto our state—
But to recover of us, by strong hand
And terms compulsatory, those foresaid lands
So by his father lost: and this, I take it,
Is the main motive of our preparations,   105
The source of this our watch and the chief head
Of this post-haste and romage[8] in the land.
BERNARDO: I think it be no other but e'en so:
  Well may it sort,[9] that this portentous figure
Comes armèd through our watch, so like the king   110
That was and is the question of these wars.
HORATIO: A mote it is to trouble the mind's eye.
  In the most high and palmy state of Rome,
A little ere the mightiest Julius fell,
The graves stood tenantless, and the sheeted dead   115
Did squeak and gibber in the Roman streets:
As stars with trains of fire and dews of blood,
Disasters in the sun; and the moist star,

---

1. Ship carpenters. *Mart:* trading. *Impress:* pressing into service.   2. Impending.   3. Duly ratified and proclaimed through heralds.   4. Pledged. *Seized:* possessed. *Moiety competent:* equal share.   5. Purport.   6. Outskirts, border regions. *Unimprovèd:* untested.   7. Calls for courage.   8. Bustle. *Head:* origin, cause.   9. Fit with the other signs of war.

Upon whose influence Neptune's empire stands,[1]
Was sick almost to doomsday with eclipse: 120
And even the like precurse[2] of fierce events,
As harbingers preceding still the fates
And prologue to the omen coming on,
Have heaven and earth together demonstrated
Unto our climatures[3] and countrymen.   125
      [*Re-enter* GHOST.]
But soft, behold! lo, where it comes again!
I'll cross it, though it blast me. Stay, illusion!
If thou hast any sound, or use of voice,
Speak to me:
If there be any good thing to be done,   130
That may to thee do ease and grace to me,
Speak to me:
If thou art privy to thy country's fate,
Which, happily, foreknowing may avoid,
O, speak!   135
Or if thou hast uphoarded in thy life
Extorted treasure in the womb of earth,
For which, they say, you spirits oft walk in death,
Speak of it: stay, and speak! [*The cock crows.*] Stop it, Marcellus.
MARCELLUS: Shall I strike at it with my partisan?   140
HORATIO: Do, if it will not stand.
BERNARDO: 'Tis here!
HORATIO: 'Tis here!
      [*Exit* GHOST.]
MARCELLUS: 'Tis gone!
  We do it wrong, being so majestical,
  To offer it the show of violence;
  For it is, as the air, invulnerable,   145
  And our vain blows malicious mockery.
BERNARDO: It was about to speak, when the cock crew.
HORATIO: And then it started like a guilty thing
  Upon a fearful summons. I have heard
  The cock, that is the trumpet to the morn,   150
  Doth with his lofty and shrill-sounding throat
  Awake the god of day, and at his warning,
  Whether in sea or fire, in earth or air,
  The extravagant[4] and erring spirit hies
  To his confine: and of the truth herein   155
  This present object made probation.[5]
MARCELLUS: It faded on the crowing of the cock.
  Some say that ever 'gainst[6] that season comes
  Wherein our Saviour's birth is celebrated,
  The bird of dawning singeth all night long: 160
  And then, they say, no spirit dare stir abroad,

---

1. The moon (*moist star*) regulates the sea's tides. *Disasters:* Ill omens.   **2.** Foreboding.   **3.** Regions.
4. Wandering out of its confines.   **5.** Gave proof.   **6.** Just before.

The nights are wholesome, then no planets strike,
No fairy takes nor witch hath power to charm,
So hallowed and so gracious[7] is the time.
HORATIO: So have I heard and do in part believe it.   165
But look, the morn, in russet mantle clad,
Walks o'er the dew of yon high eastward hill:
Break we our watch up; and by my advice,
Let us impart what we have seen to-night
Unto young Hamlet; for, upon my life,   170
This spirit, dumb to us, will speak to him:
Do you consent we shall acquaint him with it,
As needful in our loves, fitting our duty?
MARCELLUS: Let's do't, I pray; and I this morning know
Where we shall find him most conveniently.   175
    [Exeunt.]

SCENE 2

A room of state in the castle.

[*Flourish. Enter the* KING, QUEEN, HAMLET, POLONIUS, LAERTES,
VOLTIMAND, CORNELIUS, LORDS, *and* ATTENDANTS.]
KING: Though yet of Hamlet our dear brother's death
The memory be green, and that it us befitted
To bear our hearts in grief and our whole kingdom
To be contracted in one brow of woe,
Yet so far hath discretion[8] fought with nature   5
That we with wisest sorrow think on him,
Together with remembrance of ourselves.
Therefore our sometime sister, now our queen,
The imperial jointress to this warlike state,
Have we, as 'twere with a defeated joy,—   10
With an auspicious and a dropping eye,
With mirth in funeral and with dirge in marriage,
In equal scale weighing delight and dole,—
Taken to wife: nor have we herein barr'd[9]
Your better wisdoms, which have freely gone   15
With this affair along. For all, our thanks.
Now follows, that[1] you know, young Fortinbras,
Holding a weak supposal of our worth,
Or thinking by our late dear brother's death
Our state to be disjoint and out of frame,   20
Colleaguèd with this dream[2] of his advantage,
He hath not failed to pester us with message,
Importing the surrender of those lands
Lost by his father, with all bonds of law,
To our most valiant brother. So much for him.   25
Now for ourself, and for this time of meeting:

---

7. Full of blessing. *Strike:* exercise evil influence (compare "moonstruck"). *Fairy takes:* bewitches.
8. Restraint (on grief).   9. Ignored. *Dole:* grief.   1. What.   2. Combined with this fantastic notion.

Thus much the business is: we have here writ
To Norway, uncle of young Fortinbras,—
Who, impotent and bed-rid, scarcely hears
Of this his nephew's purpose,—to suppress   30
His further gait herein; in that the levies,
The lists and full proportions,³ are all made
Out of his subject: and we here dispatch
You, good Cornelius, and you, Voltimand,
For bearers of this greeting to old Norway,   35
Giving to you no further personal power
To business with the king more than the scope
Of these delated⁴ articles allow.
Farewell, and let your haste commend your duty.

CORNELIUS: ⎫
VOLTIMAND: ⎭ In that and all things will we show our duty.   40

KING: We doubt it nothing: heartily farewell.
       [*Exeunt* VOLTIMAND *and* CORNELIUS.]
And now, Laertes, what's the news with you?
You told us of some suit; what is't, Laertes?
You cannot speak of reason to the Dane,
And lose your voice: what wouldst thou beg, Laertes,   45
That shall not be my offer, not thy asking?
The head is not more native to⁵ the heart,
The hand more instrumental to the mouth,
Than is the throne of Denmark to thy father.
What wouldst thou have, Laertes?

LAERTES: My dread lord,   50
Your leave and favor to return to France,
From whence though willingly I came to Denmark,
To show my duty in your coronation,
Yet now, I must confess, that duty done,
My thoughts and wishes bend again toward France   55
And bow them to your gracious leave and pardon.

KING: Have you your father's leave? What says Polonius?

POLONIUS: He hath, my lord, wrung from me my slow leave
By laborsome petition, and at last
Upon his will I sealed my hard consent: 60
I do beseech you, give him leave to go.

KING: Take thy fair hour, Laertes; time be thine,
And thy best graces spend it at thy will!
But now, my cousin Hamlet, and my son,—

HAMLET: [*Aside.*] A little more than kin, and less than kind.   65

KING: How is it that the clouds still hang on you?

HAMLET: Not so, my lord; I am too much i' the sun.⁶

QUEEN: Good Hamlet, cast thy nighted color off,
And let thine eye look like a friend on Denmark.
Do not for ever with thy vailèd⁷ lids   70

---

3. Amounts of forces and supplies. *Gait:* proceeding.   4. Detailed.   5. Naturally bound to.   6. The
cue to Hamlet's irony is given by the King's "my cousin . . . my son" (line 64). Hamlet is punning on *son*.
7. Downcast.

Seek for thy noble father in the dust:
Thou know'st 'tis common; all that lives must die,
Passing through nature to eternity.
HAMLET: Aye, madam, it is common.
QUEEN: If it be,
Why seems it so particular with thee?   75
HAMLET: Seems, madam! nay, it is; I know not 'seems.'
'Tis not alone my inky cloak, good mother,
Nor customary suits of solemn black,
Nor windy suspiration of forced breath,
No, nor the fruitful river in the eye,   80
Nor the dejected havior of the visage,
Together with all forms, moods, shapes of grief,
That can denote me truly: these indeed seem,
For they are actions that a man might play:
But I have that within which passeth show;   85
These but the trappings and the suits of woe.
KING: 'Tis sweet and cómmendàble in your nature, Hamlet,
To give these mourning duties to your father:
But, you must know, your father lost a father,
That father lost, lost his, and the survivor bound   90
In filial obligation for some term
To do obsequious[8] sorrow: but to persevere
In obstinate condolement is a course
Of impious stubborness; 'tis unmanly grief:
It shows a will most incorrect[9] to heaven,   95
A heart unfortified, a mind impatient,
An understanding simple and unschool'd:
For what we know must be and is as common
As any the most vulgar thing to sense,
Why should we in our peevish opposition   100
Take it to heart? Fie! 'tis a fault to heaven,
A fault against the dead, a fault to nature,
To reason most absurd, whose common theme
Is death of fathers, and who still hath cried,
From the first corse till he that died to-day,   105
'This must be so.' We pray you, throw to earth
This unprevailing[1] woe, and think of us
As of a father: for let the world take note,
You are the most immediate to our throne,
And with no less nobility of love   110
Than that which dearest father bears his son
Do I impart toward you. For your intent
In going back to school in Wittenberg,
It is most retrograde[2] to our desire:
And we beseech you, bend you to remain   115
Here in the cheer and comfort of our eye,

8. Dutiful, especially concerning funeral rites (obsequies).   9. Not subdued.   1. Useless.
2. Opposed. *Wittenberg*: the seat of a university; at the peak of fame in Shakespeare's time because of its
connection with Martin Luther.

Our chiefest courtier, cousin and our son.
QUEEN: Let not thy mother lose her prayers, Hamlet:
    I pray thee, stay with us; go not to Wittenberg.
HAMLET: I shall in all my best obey you, madam.   120
KING: Why, 'tis a loving and a fair reply:
    Be as ourself in Denmark. Madam, come;
    This gentle and unforced accord of Hamlet
    Sits smiling to my heart: in grace whereof,
    No jocund health that Denmark drinks to-day,   125
    But the great cannon to the clouds shall tell,
    And the king's rouse the heaven shall bruit[3] again,
    Re-speaking earthly thunder. Come away.
        [*Flourish. Exeunt all but* HAMLET.]
HAMLET: O, that this too too sullied flesh would melt,
    Thaw and resolve itself into a dew!   130
    Or that the Everlasting had not fixed
    His canon[4] 'gainst self-slaughter! O God! God!
    How weary, stale, flat and unprofitable
    Seem to me all the uses of this world!
    Fie on't! ah fie! 'tis an unweeded garden,   135
    That grows to seed; things rank and gross in nature
    Possess it merely. That it should come to this!
    But two months dead! nay, not so much, not two:
    So excellent a king; that was, to this,
    Hyperion to a satyr: so loving to my mother,   140
    That he might not beteem[5] the winds of heaven
    Visit her face too roughly. Heaven and earth!
    Must I remember? why, she would hang on him,
    As if increase of appetite had grown
    By what it fed on: and yet, within a month—   145
    Let me not think on't—Frailty, thy name is woman!—
    A little month, or ere those shoes were old
    With which she followed my poor father's body,
    Like Niobe,[6] all tears:—why she, even she,—
    O God! a beast that wants discourse[7] of reason   150
    Would have mourned longer,—married with my uncle,
    My father's brother, but no more like my father
    Than I to Hercules: within a month;
    Ere yet the salt of most unrighteous tears
    Had left the flushing in her gallèd[8] eyes,   155
    She married. O, most wicked speed, to post
    With such dexterity to incestuous sheets![9]
    It is not, nor it cannot come to good:
    But break, my heart, for I must hold my tongue!
        [*Enter* HORATIO, MARCELLUS, *and* BERNARDO.]

---

3. Proclaim, echo. *Rouse:* carousal, revel.   **4.** Law.   **5.** Allow. Hyperion is the sun god.   **6.** A proud mother who boasted of having more children than Leto; her seven sons and seven daughters were slain by Apollo and Artemis, children of Leto. The grieving Niobe was changed by Zeus into a continually weeping stone.   **7.** Lacks the faculty.   **8.** Inflamed.   **9.** According to principles that Hamlet accepts, marrying one's brother's widow is incest.

HORATIO: Hail to your lordship!

HAMLET: I am glad to see you well: 160
  Horatio,— or I do forget myself.

HORATIO: The same, my lord, and your poor servant ever.

HAMLET: Sir, my good friend; I'll change[1] that name with you:
  And what make you from Wittenberg, Horatio?
  Marcellus?   165

MARCELLUS: My good lord?

HAMLET: I am very glad to see you. [*To* BERNARDO.] Good even, sir.
  But what, in faith, make you from Wittenberg?

HORATIO: A truant disposition, good my lord.

HAMLET: I would not hear your enemy say so,   170
  Nor shall you do my ear that violence,
  To make it truster of your own report
  Against yourself: I know you are no truant.
  But what is your affair in Elsinore?
  We'll teach you to drink deep ere you depart.   175

HORATIO: My lord, I came to see your father's funeral.

HAMLET: I pray thee, do not mock me, fellow-student;
  I think it was to see my mother's wedding.

HORATIO: Indeed, my lord, it followed hard upon.

HAMLET: Thrift, thrift, Horatio! the funeral baked-meats   180
  Did coldly furnish forth the marriage tables.
  Would I had met my dearest[2] foe in heaven
  Or ever I had seen that day, Horatio!
  My father!—methinks I see my father.

HORATIO: O where, my lord?

HAMLET: In my mind's eye, Horatio.   185

HORATIO: I saw him once; he was a goodly king.

HAMLET: He was a man, take him for all in all,
  I shall not look upon his like again.

HORATIO: My lord, I think I saw him yesternight.

HAMLET: Saw? who?   190

HORATIO: My lord, the king your father.

HAMLET: The king my father!

HORATIO: Season your admiration[3] for a while
  With an attent ear, till I may deliver,
  Upon the witness of these gentlemen,
  This marvel to you.

HAMLET: For God's love, let me hear.   195

HORATIO: Two nights together had these gentlemen,
  Marcellus and Bernardo, on their watch,
  In the dead vast and middle of the night,
  Been thus encountered. A figure like your father,
  Armed at point exactly, cap-a-pe,[4]   200
  Appears before them, and with solemn march
  Goes slow and stately by them: thrice he walked

---

1. Exchange.   2. Bitterest.   3. Restrain your astonishment.   4. From head to foot. At *point:* completely.

By their oppressed and fear-surprisèd eyes,
Within his truncheon's length; whilst they, distilled
Almost to jelly with the act of fear,   205
Stand dumb, and speak not to him. This to me
In dreadful secrecy impart they did;
And I with them the third night kept the watch:
Where, as they had delivered, both in time,
Form of the thing, each word made true and good,   210
The apparition comes: I knew your father;
These hands were not more like.
HAMLET: But where was this?
MARCELLUS: My lord, upon the platform where we watched.
HAMLET: Did you not speak to it?
HORATIO: My lord, I did.
But answer made it none: yet once methought   215
It lifted up its head and did address
Itself to motion, like as it would speak:
But even then the morning cock crew loud,
And at the sound it shrunk in haste away
And vanished from our sight.
HAMLET: 'Tis very strange.   220
HORATIO: As I do live, my honored lord, 'tis true,
And we did think it writ down in our duty
To let you know of it.
HAMLET: Indeed, indeed, sirs, but this troubles me.
Hold you the watch to-night?
MARCELLUS: ⎫
BERNARDO: ⎭   We do, my lord.   225
HAMLET: Armed, say you?
MARCELLUS: ⎫
BERNARDO: ⎭   Armed, my lord.
HAMLET: From top to toe?
MARCELLUS: ⎫
BERNARDO: ⎭   My lord, from head to foot.
HAMLET: Then saw you not his face?
HORATIO: O, yes, my lord; he wore his beaver[5] up.
HAMLET: What, looked he frowningly?   230
HORATIO: A countenance more in sorrow than in anger.
HAMLET: Pale, or red?
HORATIO: Nay, very pale.
HAMLET: And fixed his eyes upon you?
HORATIO: Most constantly.
HAMLET: I would I had been there.
HORATIO: It would have much amazed you.   235
HAMLET: Very like, very like. Stayed it long?
HORATIO: While one with moderate haste might tell[6] a hundred.
MARCELLUS: ⎫
BERNARDO: ⎭ Longer, longer.

5. Visor.   6. Count.

HORATIO: Not when I saw't.

HAMLET: His beard was grizzled?[7] no?

HORATIO: It was, as I have seen it in his life,   240
   A sable silvered.[8]

HAMLET: I will watch to-night;
   Perchance 'twill walk again.

HORATIO: I warrant it will.

HAMLET: If it assume my noble father's person,
   I'll speak to it, though hell itself should gape
   And bid me hold my peace. I pray you all,   245
   If you have hitherto concealed this sight,
   Let it be tenable in your silence still,[9]
   And whatsoever else shall hap to-night,
   Give it an understanding, but no tongue:
   I will requite your loves. So fare you well: 250
   Upon the platform, 'twixt eleven and twelve,
   I'll visit you.

ALL: Our duty to your honor.

HAMLET: Your loves, as mine to you: farewell.
      [*Exeunt all but* HAMLET.]
   My father's spirit in arms! all is not well;
   I doubt[1] some foul play: would the night were come!   255
   Till then sit still, my soul: foul deeds will rise,
   Though all the earth o'erwhelm them, to men's eyes.
      [*Exit.*]

SCENE 3

A room in Polonius's house.

[*Enter* LAERTES *and* OPHELIA.]

LAERTES: My necessaries are embarked: farewell:
   And, sister, as the winds give benefit
   And convoy[2] is assistant, do not sleep,
   But let me hear from you.

OPHELIA: Do you doubt that?

LAERTES: For Hamlet, and the trifling of his favor,   5
   Hold it a fashion, and a toy in blood,
   A violet in the youth of primy nature,
   Forward,[3] not permanent, sweet, not lasting,
   The perfume and suppliance of a minute;
   No more.   10

OPHELIA: No more but so?

LAERTES: Think it no more:
   For nature crescent does not grow alone
   In thews and bulk; but, as this temple[4] waxes,
   The inward service of the mind and soul   15
   Grows wide withal. Perhaps he loves you now;

---

7. Gray.   8. Black and white.   9. Consider it still a secret.   1. Suspect.   2. Conveyance, means of transport.   3. Early. *Fashion:* passing mood. *Primy:* early, young.   4. The body. *Crescent:* growing.

And now no soil nor cautel[5] doth besmirch
The virtue of his will: but you must fear,
His greatness weighed,[6] his will is not his own;
For he himself is subject to his birth: 20
He may not, as unvalued persons do,
Carve for himself, for on his choice depends
The safety and health of this whole state,
And therefore must his choice be circumscribed
Unto the voice and yielding[7] of that body   25
Whereof he is the head. Then if he says he loves you,
It fits your wisdom so far to believe it
As he in his particular act and place
May give his saying deed; which is no further
Than the main voice of Denmark goes withal.[8]   30
Then weigh what loss your honor may sustain,
If with too credent ear you list his songs,
Or lose your heart, or your chaste treasure open
To his unmastered importunity.
Fear it, Ophelia, fear it, my dear sister,   35
And keep you in the rear of your affection,
Out of the shot and danger of desire.
The chariest maid is prodigal enough
If she unmask her beauty to the moon:
Virtue itself 'scapes not calumnious strokes: 40
The canker galls the infants of the spring
Too oft before their buttons be disclosed,
And in the morn and liquid dew of youth
Contagious blastments[9] are most imminent.
Be wary then; best safety lies in fear: 45
Youth to itself[1] rebels, though none else near.

OPHELIA: I shall the effect of this good lesson keep,
As watchman to my heart. But, good my brother,
Do not, as some ungracious pastors do,
Show me the steep and thorny way to heaven,   50
Whilst, like a puffed and reckless libertine,
Himself the primrose path of dalliance treads
And recks not his own rede.[2]

LAERTES: O, fear me not.
I stay too long; but here my father comes.
        [*Enter* POLONIUS.]
A double blessing is a double grace;   55
Occasion smiles upon a second leave.

POLONIUS: Yet here, Laertes! Aboard, aboard, for shame!
The wind sits in the shoulder of your sail,
And you are stayed for. There; my blessing with thee!
And these few precepts in thy memory   60

---

5. No foul or deceitful thoughts.   6. When you consider his rank. *Will:* desire.   7. Assent.   8. Goes
along with, agrees. *Main:* powerful.   9. Blights.   1. Against its better self.   2. Does not follow his
own advice.

See thou charácter.[3] Give thy thoughts no tongue,
Nor any unproportioned[4] thought his act.
Be thou familiar, but by no means vulgar.
Those friends thou hast, and their adoption tried,
Grapple them to thy soul with hoops of steel,   65
But do not dull thy palm[5] with entertainment
Of each new-hatched unfledged comrade. Beware
Of entrance to a quarrel; but being in,
Bear't, that the opposèd may beware of thee.
Give every man thy ear, but few thy voice: 70
Take each man's censure,[6] but reserve thy judgment.
Costly thy habit as thy purse can buy,
But not expressed in fancy; rich, not gaudy:
For the apparel oft proclaims the man;
And they in France of the best rank and station   75
Are of a most select and generous chief[7] in that.
Neither a borrower nor a lender be:
For loan oft loses both itself and friend,
And borrowing dulls the edge of husbandry.[8]
This above all: to thine own self be true,   80
And it must follow, as the night the day,
Thou canst not then be false to any man.
Farewell: my blessing season[9] this in thee!
LAERTES: Most humbly do I take my leave, my lord.
POLONIUS: The time invites you; go, your servants tend.[1]   85
LAERTES: Farewell, Ophelia, and remember well
    What I have said to you.
OPHELIA: 'Tis in my memory locked,
    And you yourself shall keep the key of it.
LAERTES: Farewell.
        [*Exit.*]
POLONIUS: What is't, Ophelia, he hath said to you?
OPHELIA: So please you, something touching the Lord Hamlet.   90
POLONIUS: Marry, well bethought:
    'Tis told me, he hath very oft of late
    Given private time to you, and you yourself
    Have of your audience been most free and bounteous:
    If it be so—as so 'tis put on me,   95
    And that in way of caution—I must tell you,
    You do not understand yourself so clearly
    As it behoves my daughter and your honor.
    What is between you? give me up the truth.
OPHELIA: He hath, my lord, of late made many tenders   100
    Of his affection to me.
POLONIUS: Affection! pooh! you speak like a green girl,
    Unsifted[2] in such perilous circumstance.

---

3. Engrave in your memory.   4. Unsuitable.   5. Make the palm of your hand callous (by the indiscriminate shaking of hands).   6. Opinion.   7. Preeminence.   8. Thriftiness.   9. Ripen. 1. Wait.   2. Untested.

Do you believe his tenders, as you call them?

OPHELIA: I do not know, my lord, what I should think. 105

POLONIUS: Marry, I'll teach you: think yourself a baby,
    That you have ta'en these tenders for true pay,
    Which are not sterling. Tender[3] yourself more dearly;
    Or—not to crack the wind of the poor phrase,
    Running it thus—you'll tender me a fool.[4] 110

OPHELIA: My lord, he hath importuned me with love
    In honorable fashion.

POLONIUS: Aye, fashion you may call it; go to, go to.

OPHELIA: And hath given countenance[5] to his speech, my lord,
    With almost all the holy vows of heaven. 115

POLONIUS: Aye, springes to catch woodcocks. I do know,
    When the blood burns, how prodigal the soul
    Lends the tongue vows: these blazes, daughter,
    Giving more light than heat, extinct in both,
    Even in their promise, as it is a-making, 120
    You must not take for fire. From this time
    Be something scanter of your maiden presence;
    Set your entreatments[6] at a higher rate
    Than a command to parley. For Lord Hamlet,
    Believe so much in him, that he is young, 125
    And with a larger tether may he walk
    Than may be given you: in few, Ophelia,
    Do not believe his vows; for they are brokers,
    Not of that dye which their investments[7] show,
    But mere implorators of unholy suits, 130
    Breathing like sanctified and pious bawds,
    The better to beguile. This is for all:
    I would not, in plain terms, from this time forth,
    Have you so slander any moment[8] leisure,
    As to give words or talk with the Lord Hamlet. 135
    Look to't, I charge you: come your ways.

OPHELIA: I shall obey, my lord.
    [*Exeunt.*]

SCENE 4

The platform.

[*Enter* HAMLET, HORATIO, *and* MARCELLUS.]

HAMLET: The air bites shrewdly; it is very cold.

HORATIO: It is a nipping and an eager[9] air.

HAMLET: What hour now?

HORATIO: I think it lacks of twelve.

MARCELLUS: No, it is struck.

HORATIO: Indeed? I heard it not: it then draws near the season 5
    Wherein the spirit held his wont to walk.

---

3. Regard.   4. You'll furnish me with a fool (a foolish daughter).   5. Authority.   6. Conversation,
company.   7. Clothes. *Brokers:* procurers, panders.   8. Use badly any momentary.   9. Sharp.

[*A flourish of trumpets, and ordnance shot off within.*]
What doth this mean, my lord?
HAMLET: The king doth wake to-night, and takes his rouse,
    Keeps wassail, and the swaggering up-spring reels;
    And as he drains his draughts of Rhenish[1] down,   10
    The kettle-drum and trumpet thus bray out
    The triumph of his pledge.[2]
HORATIO: Is it a custom?
HAMLET: Aye, marry, is't:
    But to my mind, though I am native here
    And to the manner born, it is a custom   15
    More honored[3] in the breach than the observance.
    This heavy-headed revel east and west
    Makes us traduced and taxed of other nations:
    They clepe us drunkards, and with swinish phrase
    Soil our addition;[4] and indeed it takes   20
    From our achievements, though performed at height,[5]
    The pith and marrow of our attribute.[6]
    So, oft it chances in particular men,
    That for some vicious mole of nature in them,
    As, in their birth,—wherein they are not guilty,   25
    Since nature cannot choose his origin,—
    By the o'ergrowth of some complexion,[7]
    Oft breaking down the pales and forts of reason,
    Or by some habit that too much o'er-leavens[8]
    The form of plausive[9] manners, that these men,—   30
    Carrying, I say, the stamp of one defect,
    Being nature's livery, or fortune's star,—
    Their virtues else[1]—be they as pure as grace,
    As infinite as man may undergo—
    Shall in the general censure take corruption   35
    From that particular fault: the dram of evil
    Doth all the noble substance often dout
    To his own scandal.[2]
        [*Enter* GHOST.]
HORATIO: Look, my lord it comes!
HAMLET: Angels and ministers of grace defend us!
    Be thou a spirit of health or goblin damned,   40
    Bring with thee airs from heaven or blasts from hell,
    Be thy intents wicked or charitable,
    Thou comest in such a questionable shape
    That I will speak to thee: I'll call thee Hamlet,
    King, father, royal Dane: O, answer me!   45
    Let me not burst in ignorance; but tell
    Why thy canónized bones, hearsèd in death,
    Have burst their cerements; why the sepulchre,

---

1. Rhine wine. *Up-spring reels:* wild dances.   2. In downing the cup in one draught.   3. Honorable.
4. Reputation. *Taxed:* blamed. *Clepe:* call.   5. Done in the best possible manner.   6. Reputation.
7. Excess in one side of their temperament.   8. Modifies, as yeast changes dough.   9. Agreeable.
1. The rest of their qualities.   2. To its own harm. *Dout:* extinguish, nullify.

Wherein we saw thee quietly inurned,
Hath oped his ponderous and marble jaws,   50
To cast thee up again. What may this mean,
That thou, dead corse, again, in complete steel,
Revisit'st thus the glimpses of the moon,
Making night hideous; and we fools of nature
So horridly to shake our disposition   55
With thoughts beyond the reaches of our souls?
Say, why is this? Wherefore? what should we do?
        [GHOST *beckons* HAMLET.]
HORATIO: It beckons you to go away with it,
  As if it some impartment did desire
  To you alone.   60
MARCELLUS: Look, with what courteous action
  It waves you to a more removèd ground:
  But do not go with it.
HORATIO: No, by no means.
HAMLET: It will not speak; then I will follow it.
HORATIO: Do not, my lord.
HAMLET: Why, what should be the fear?   65
  I do not set my life at a pin's fee;
  And for my soul, what can it do to that,
  Being a thing immortal as itself?
  It waves me forth again: I'll follow it.
HORATIO: What if it tempt you toward the flood, my lord,   70
  Or to the dreadful summit of the cliff
  That beetles o'er[3] his base into the sea,
  And there assume some other horrible form,
  Which might deprive your sovereignty of reason
  And draw you into madness? think of it: 75
  The very place puts toys[4] of desperation,
  Without more motive, into every brain
  That looks so many fathoms to the sea
  And hears it roar beneath.
HAMLET: It waves me still.
  Go on; I'll follow thee.   80
MARCELLUS: You shall not go, my lord.
HAMLET: Hold off your hands.
HORATIO: Be ruled; you shall not go.
HAMLET: My fate cries out,
  And makes each petty artery in this body
  As hardy as the Nemean lion's nerve.[5]
  Still am I called, unhand me, gentlemen;   85
  By heaven, I'll make a ghost of him that lets[6] me:
  I say, away! Go on; I'll follow thee.
        [*Exeunt* GHOST *and* HAMLET.]
HORATIO: He waxes desperate with imagination.

---

3. Juts over.   4. Fancies.   5. Sinew, muscle. The Nemean lion was slain by Hercules as one of his
twelve labors.   6. Hinders.

MARCELLUS: Let's follow; 'tis not fit thus to obey him.
HORATIO: Have after. To what issue will this come?   90
MARCELLUS: Something is rotten in the state of Denmark.
HORATIO: Heaven will direct it.
MARCELLUS: Nay, let's follow him.
    [*Exeunt.*]

SCENE 5

Another part of the platform.

[*Enter* GHOST *and* HAMLET.]
HAMLET: Whither wilt thou lead me? speak; I'll go no further.
GHOST: Mark me.
HAMLET: I will.
GHOST: My hour is almost come,
  When I to sulphurous and tormenting flames[7]
  Must render up myself.
HAMLET: Alas, poor ghost!
GHOST: Pity me not, but lend thy serious hearing   5
  To what I shall unfold.
HAMLET: Speak; I am bound to hear.
GHOST: So art thou to revenge, when thou shalt hear.
HAMLET: What?
GHOST: I am thy father's spirit;
  Doomed for a certain term to walk the night,   10
  And for the day confined to fast in fires,
  Till the foul crimes done in my days of nature
  Are burnt and purged away. But that I am forbid
  To tell the secrets of my prison-house,
  I could a tale unfold whose lightest word   15
  Would harrow up thy soul, freeze thy young blood,
  Make thy two eyes, like stars, start from their spheres,[8]
  Thy knotted and combinèd locks to part
  And each particular hair to stand on end,
  Like quills upon the fretful porpentine: 20
  But this eternal blazon[9] must not be
  To ears of flesh and blood. List, list, O, list!
  If thou didst ever thy dear father love—
HAMLET: O God!
GHOST: Revenge his foul and most unnatural murder.   25
HAMLET: Murder!
GHOST: Murder most foul, as in the best it is,
  But this most foul, strange, and unnatural.
HAMLET: Haste me to know't, that I, with wings as swift
  As meditation or the thoughts of love,   30
  May sweep to my revenge.
GHOST: I find thee apt;

7. Of purgatory.   8. Transparent revolving shells in each of which, according to Ptolemaic astronomy,
a planet or other heavenly body was placed.   9. Publication of the secrets of the other world (of eternity).
Porpentine: porcupine.

And duller shouldst thou be than the fat weed
That roots itself in ease on Lethe[1] wharf,
Wouldst thou not stir in this. Now, Hamlet, hear:
'Tis given out that, sleeping in my orchard,   35
A serpent stung me; so the whole ear of Denmark
Is by a forgèd process of my death
Rankly abused: but know, thou noble youth,
The serpent that did sting thy father's life
Now wears his crown.
HAMLET: O my prophetic soul!   40
    My uncle!
GHOST: Aye, that incestuous, that adulterate beast,
    With witchcraft of his wit, with traitorous gifts,—
    O wicked wit and gifts, that have the power
    So to seduce!—won to his shameful lust   45
    The will of my most seeming-virtuous queen:
    O Hamlet, what a falling-off was there!
    From me, whose love was of that dignity
    That it went hand in hand even with the vow
    I made to her in marriage; and to decline   50
    Upon a wretch, whose natural gifts were poor
    To those of mine!
    But virtue, as it never will be moved,
    Though lewdness court it in a shape of heaven,[2]
    So lust, though to a radiant angel linked,   55
    Will sate itself in a celestial bed
    And prey on garbage.
    But, soft! methinks I scent the morning air;
    Brief let me be. Sleeping within my orchard,
    My custom always of the afternoon,   60
    Upon my secure hour thy uncle stole,
    With juice of cursed hebenon[3] in a vial,
    And in the porches of my ears did pour
    The leperous distilment; whose effect
    Holds such an enmity with blood of man   65
    That swift as quicksilver it courses through
    The natural gates and alleys of the body;
    And with a sudden vigor it doth posset
    And curd, like eager[4] droppings into milk,
    The thin and wholesome blood: so did it mine;   70
    And a most instant tetter barked about,[5]
    Most lazar-like,[6] with vile and loathsome crust,
    All my smooth body.
    Thus was I, sleeping, by a brother's hand
    Of life, of crown, of queen, at once dispatched: 75
    Cut off even in the blossoms of my sin,
    Unhouseled, disappointed, unaneled;[7]

1. The river of forgetfulness in Hades.   2. A heavenly, angelic form.   3. Henbane, a poisonous herb.
4. Sour. *Posset:* coagulate.   5. The skin immediately became thick like the bark of a tree.   6. Leper-
like (from the beggar Lazarus, "full of sores," in Luke 16.20).   7. Without sacrament, unprepared, without extreme unction.

No reckoning made, but sent to my account
With all my imperfections on my head:
O, horrible! O, horrible! most horrible!   80
If thou hast nature in thee, bear it not;
Let not the royal bed of Denmark be
A couch for luxury and damned incest.
But, howsoever thou pursuest this act,
Taint not thy mind, nor let thy soul contrive   85
Against thy mother aught: leave her to heaven,
And to those thorns that in her bosom lodge,
To prick and sting her. Fare thee well at once!
The glow-worm shows the matin to be near,
And 'gins to pale his uneffectual fire: 90
Adieu, adieu, adieu! remember me.
        [*Exit.*]
HAMLET: O all you host of heaven! O earth! what else?
And shall I couple hell? O, fie! Hold, hold, my heart;
And you, my sinews, grow not instant old,
But bear me stiffly up. Remember thee!   95
Aye, thou poor ghost, while memory holds a seat
In this distracted globe. Remember thee!
Yea, from the table[8] of my memory
I'll wipe away all trivial fond records,
All saws of books, all forms, all pressures past,   100
That youth and observation copied there:
And thy commandment all alone shall live
Within the book and volume of my brain,
Unmixed with baser matter: yes, by heaven!
O most pernicious woman!   105
O villain, villain, smiling, damnèd villain!
My tables,—meet it is I set it down,
That one may smile, and smile, and be a villain;
At least I'm sure it may be so in Denmark.
        [*Writing.*]
So, uncle, there you are. Now to my word;   110
It is 'Adieu, adieu! remember me.'
I have sworn't.
HORATIO: ⎫
MARCELLUS: ⎬ [*Within.*] My lord, my lord!
        [*Enter* HORATIO *and* MARCELLUS.]
MARCELLUS: Lord Hamlet!
HORATIO: Heaven
                                    secure him!
HAMLET: So be it!
MARCELLUS: Illo,[9] ho, ho, my lord!   115
HAMLET: Hillo, ho, ho, boy! come, bird, come.
MARCELLUS: How is't, my noble lord?
HORATIO: What news, my lord?
HAMLET: O, wonderful!

8. Writing tablet; used in the same sense in line 107. *Globe:* head.   9. A falconer's call.

HORATIO: Good my lord, tell it.
HAMLET: No; you will reveal it.
HORATIO: Not I, my lord, by heaven.
MARCELLUS: Nor I, my lord.   120
HAMLET: How say you, then; would heart of man once think it?
     But you'll be secret?
HORATIO: ⎫
MARCELLUS: ⎭   Aye, by heaven, my lord.
HAMLET: There's ne'er a villain dwelling in all Denmark
     But he's an arrant knave.
HORATIO: There needs no ghost, my lord, come from the grave   125
     To tell us this.
HAMLET: Why, right; you are i' the right;
     And so, without more circumstance¹ at all,
     I hold it fit that we shake hands and part:
     You, as your business and desire shall point you;
     For every man hath business and desire,   130
     Such as it is; and for my own poor part,
     Look you, I'll go pray.
HORATIO: These are but wild and whirling words, my lord.
HAMLET: I'm sorry they offend you, heartily;
     Yes, faith, heartily.
HORATIO: There's no offense, my lord.   135
HAMLET: Yes, by Saint Patrick, but there is, Horatio,
     And much offense too. Touching this vision here,
     It is an honest² ghost, that let me tell you:
     For your desire to know what is between us,
     O'ermaster't as you may. And now, good friends,   140
     As you are friends, scholars and soldiers,
     Give me one poor request.
HORATIO: What is't, my lord? we will.
HAMLET: Never make known what you have seen tonight.
MARCELLUS: ⎫
HORATIO: ⎭ My lord, we will not.
HAMLET: Nay, but swear't.
HORATIO: In faith,
     My lord, not I.
MARCELLUS: Nor I, my lord, in faith.   145
HAMLET: Upon my sword.
MARCELLUS: We have sworn, my lord, already.
HAMLET: Indeed, upon my sword, indeed.
GHOST: [*Beneath.*]   Swear.
HAMLET: Ah, ha, boy! say'st thou so? art thou there, true-penny?³
     Come on: you hear this fellow in the cellarage:
     Consent to swear.
HORATIO: Propose the oath, my lord.   150
HAMLET: Never to speak of this that you have seen,
     Swear by my sword.

1. Ceremony.   2. Genuine.   3. Honest fellow.

GHOST: [*Beneath.*] Swear.
HAMLET: Hic et ubique?[4] then we'll shift our ground.
    Come hither, gentlemen, 155
    And lay your hands again upon my sword:
    Never to speak of this that you have heard,
    Swear by my sword.
GHOST: [*Beneath.*] Swear.
HAMLET: Well said, old mole! canst work i' the earth so fast? 160
    A worthy pioner![5] Once more remove, good friends.
HORATIO: O day and night, but this is wondrous strange!
HAMLET: And therefore as a stranger give it welcome.
    There are more things in heaven and earth, Horatio,
    Than are dreamt of in your philosophy. 165
    But come;
    Here, as before, never, so help you mercy,
    How strange or odd soe'er I bear myself,
    As I perchance hereafter shall think meet
    To put an antic[6] disposition on, 170
    That you, at such times seeing me, never shall,
    With arms encumbered[7] thus, or this head-shake,
    Or by pronouncing of some doubtful phrase,
    As 'Well, well, we know,' or 'We could, an if we would,'
    Or 'If we list to speak,' or 'There be, an if they might,' 175
    Or such ambiguous giving out, to note
    That you know aught of me: this not to do,
    So grace and mercy at your most need help you,
    Swear.
GHOST: [*Beneath.*] Swear. 180
HAMLET: Rest, rest, perturbèd spirit!
       [*They swear.*]
    So, gentlemen,
    With all my love I do commend[8] me to you:
    And what so poor a man as Hamlet is
    May do, to express his love and friending to you, 185
    God willing, shall not lack. Let us go in together;
    And still your fingers on your lips, I pray.
    The time is out of joint: O cursèd spite,
    That ever I was born to set it right!
    Nay, come, let's go together. 190
       [*Exeunt.*]

---

4. Here and everywhere (Latin).   5. Miner.   6. Odd, fantastic.   7. Folded.   8. Entrust.

Act II

SCENE 1

A room in Polonius's house.

[*Enter* POLONIUS *and* REYNALDO.]

POLONIUS: Give him this money and these notes, Reynaldo.
REYNALDO: I will, my lord.
POLONIUS: You shall do marvelous wisely, good Reynaldo,
  Before you visit him, to make inquire
  Of his behavior.
REYNALDO: My lord, I did intend it.   5
POLONIUS: Marry, well said, very well said. Look you, sir,
  Inquire me first what Danskers are in Paris,
  And how, and who, what means, and where they keep,[9]
  What company, at what expense, and finding
  By this encompassment[1] and drift of question   10
  That they do know my son, come you more nearer
  Than your particular demands will touch it:
  Take you, as 'twere, some distant knowledge of him,
  As thus, 'I know his father and his friends,
  And in part him': do you mark this, Reynaldo?   15
REYNALDO: Aye, very well, my lord.
POLONIUS: 'And in part him; but,' you may say, 'not well:
  But if 't be he I mean, he's very wild,
  Addicted so and so'; and there put on him
  What forgeries you please; marry, none so rank   20
  As may dishonor him; take heed of that;
  But, sir, such wanton, wild and usual slips
  As are companions noted and most known
  To youth and liberty.
REYNALDO: As gaming, my lord.
POLONIUS: Aye, or drinking, fencing, swearing, quarreling,   25
  Drabbing:[2] you may go so far.
REYNALDO: My lord, that would dishonor him.
POLONIUS: Faith, no; as you may season it in the charge.[3]
  You must not put another scandal on him,
  That he is open to incontinency;   30
  That's not my meaning: but breathe his faults so quaintly[4]
  That they may seem the taints of liberty,
  The flash and outbreak of a fiery mind,
  A savageness in unreclaimèd blood,
  Of general assault.[5]
REYNALDO: But, my good lord,—   35
POLONIUS: Wherefore should you do this?
REYNALDO: Aye, my lord,
  I would know that.
POLONIUS: Marry, sir, here's my drift,

---

9. Dwell. *Danskers:* Danes.   1. Roundabout way.   2. Whoring.   3. Qualify it in making the accusation.   4. Delicately, skillfully. *Incontinency:* extreme sensuality.   5. Assailing all. *Unreclaimèd:* untamed.

And I believe it is a fetch of warrant:[6]
You laying these slight sullies on my son,
As 'twere a thing a little soiled i' the working,   40
Mark you,
Your party in converse, him you would sound,
Having ever seen in the prenominate[7] crimes
The youth you breathe of guilty, be assured
He closes with you in this consequence;[8]   45
'Good sir,' or so, or 'friend,' or 'gentleman,'
According to the phrase or the addition[9]
Of man and country.
REYNALDO: Very good, my lord.
POLONIUS: And then, sir, does he this—he does—what was I about to
    say? By the mass, I was about to say something: where did I leave?   50
REYNALDO: At 'closes in the consequence,' at 'friend or so,' and
    'gentleman.'
POLONIUS: At 'closes in the consequence,' aye, marry;
    He closes with you thus: 'I know the gentleman;
    I saw him yesterday, or t' other day,   55
    Or then, or then, with such, or such, and, as you say,
    There was a' gaming, there o'ertook in 's rouse,[1]
    There falling out at tennis': or perchance,
    'I saw him enter such a house of sale,'
    Videlicet,[2] a brothel, or so forth.   60
    See you now;
    Your bait of falsehood takes this carp of truth:
    And thus do we of wisdom and of reach,[3]
    With windlasses and with assays of bias,[4]
    By indirections find directions out: 65
    So, by my former lecture and advice,
    Shall you my son. You have me, have you not?
REYNALDO: My lord, I have.
POLONIUS: God be wi' ye; fare ye well.
REYNALDO: Good my lord!
POLONIUS: Observe his inclination in yourself.[5]   70
REYNALDO: I shall, my lord.
POLONIUS: And let him ply his music.
REYNALDO: Well, my lord.
POLONIUS: Farewell!
       [*Exit* REYNALDO.—*Enter* OPHELIA.]
    How now, Ophelia! what's the matter?
OPHELIA: O, my lord, I have been so affrighted!   75
POLONIUS: With what, i' the name of God?
OPHELIA: My lord, as I was sewing in my closet,
    Lord Hamlet, with his doublet[6] all unbraced,
    No hat upon his head, his stockings fouled,

---

6. Allowable stratagem.   7. Aforementioned. *Having ever:* if he has ever.   8. You may be sure he will
agree in this conclusion.   9. Title.   1. Intoxicated in his reveling.   2. Namely.   3. Wise and far-
sighted.   4. Sending the ball indirectly (in bowling), devious attacks. *Windlasses:* winding ways, round-
about courses.   5. Ways of procedure by yourself.   6. Jacket. *Closet:* private room.

Ungartered and down-gyvèd[7] to his ankle;   80
Pale as his shirt, his knees knocking each other,
And with a look so piteous in purport
As if he had been loosèd out of hell
To speak of horrors, he comes before me.
POLONIUS: Mad for thy love?
OPHELIA: My lord, I do not know,   85
But truly I do fear it.
POLONIUS: What said he?
OPHELIA: He took me by the wrist and held me hard;
Then goes he to the length of all his arm,
And with his other hand thus o'er his brow,
He falls to such perusal of my face   90
As he would draw it. Long stayed he so;
At last, a little shaking of mine arm,
And thrice his head thus waving up and down,
He raised a sigh so piteous and profound
As it did seem to shatter all his bulk   95
And end his being: that done, he lets me go:
And with his head over his shoulder turned,
He seemed to find his way without his eyes;
For out o' doors he went without their help,
And to the last bended their light on me.   100
POLONIUS: Come, go with me: I will go seek the king.
This is the very ecstasy of love;
Whose violent property fordoes itself[8]
And leads the will to desperate undertakings
As oft as any passion under heaven   105
That does afflict our natures. I am sorry.
What, have you given him any hard words of late?
OPHELIA: No, my good lord, but, as you did command,
I did repel his letters and denied
His access to me.
POLONIUS: That hath made him mad.   110
I am sorry that with better heed and judgment
I had not quoted him: I fear'd he did but trifle
And meant to wreck thee; but beshrew my jealousy![9]
By heaven, it is as proper to our age
To cast beyond ourselves[1] in our opinions   115
As it is common for the younger sort
To lack discretion. Come, go we to the king:
This must be known; which, being kept close, might move
More grief to hide than hate to utter love.[2]
Come.   120
        [Exeunt.]

---

7. Pulled down like fetters on a prisoner's leg.   8. Which, when violent, destroys itself. *Ecstasy:* madness.
9. Curse my suspicion. *Quoted:* noted.   1. Overshoot, go too far.   2. If Hamlet's love is revealed. *To hide:* if kept hidden.

SCENE 2

A room in the castle.

[*Flourish. Enter* KING, QUEEN, ROSENCRANTZ, GUILDENSTERN, *and*
ATTENDANTS.]

KING: Welcome, dear Rosencrantz and Guildenstern!
    Moreover that we much did long to see you,
    The need we have to use you did provoke
    Our hasty sending. Something have you heard
    Of Hamlet's transformation; so call it,   5
    Sith[3] nor the exterior nor the inward man
    Resembles that it was. What it should be,
    More than his father's death, that thus hath put him
    So much from the understanding of himself,
    I cannot dream of: I entreat you both,   10
    That, being of so young days brought up with him
    And sith so neighbored to his youth and behavior,
    That you vouchsafe your rest[4] here in our court
    Some little time: so by your companies
    To draw him on to pleasures, and to gather   15
    So much as from occasion you may glean,
    Whether aught to us unknown afflicts him thus,
    That opened[5] lies within our remedy.
QUEEN: Good gentlemen, he hath much talked of you,
    And sure I am two men there are not living   20
    To whom he more adheres.[6] If it will please you
    To show us so much gentry[7] and good will
    As to expend your time with us awhile
    For the supply and profit of our hope,
    Your visitation shall receive such thanks   25
    As fits a king's remembrance.
ROSENCRANTZ: Both your majesties
    Might, by the sovereign power you have of us,
    Put your dread pleasures more into[8] command
    Than to entreaty.
GUILDENSTERN: But we both obey,
    And here give up ourselves, in the full bent[9]   30
    To lay our service freely at your feet,
    To be commanded.
KING: Thanks, Rosencrantz and gentle Guildenstern.
QUEEN: Thanks, Guildenstern and gentle Rosencrantz:
    And I beseech you instantly to visit   35
    My too much changèd son. Go, some of you,
    And bring these gentlemen where Hamlet is.
GUILDENSTERN: Heavens make our presence and our practices
    Pleasant and helpful to him!
QUEEN: Aye, amen!

---

3. Since.   4. Consent to stay.   5. Once revealed.   6. Is more attached.   7. Courtesy.
8. Give your sovereign wishes the form of.   9. Bent (as a bow) to the limit.

2854 / William Shakespeare

[*Exeunt* ROSENCRANTZ, GUILDENSTERN, *and some* ATTENDANTS.—
Enter POLONIUS.]

POLONIUS: The ambassadors from Norway, my good lord, 40
  Are joyfully returned.

KING: Thou still[1] hast been the father of good news.

POLONIUS: Have I, my lord? I assure my good liege,
  I hold my duty as I hold my soul,
  Both to my God and to my gracious king: 45
  And I do think, or else this brain of mine
  Hunts not the trail of policy so sure
  As it hath used to do, that I have found
  The very cause of Hamlet's lunacy.

KING: O, speak of that; that do I long to hear. 50

POLONIUS: Give first admittance to the ambassadors;
  My news shall be the fruit to that great feast.

KING: Thyself do grace[2] to them, and bring them in.
      [*Exit* POLONIUS.]
  He tells me, my dear Gertrude, he hath found
  The head and source of all your son's distemper. 55

QUEEN: I doubt it is no other but the main;
  His father's death and our o'erhasty marriage.

KING: Well, we shall sift him.
      [*Re-enter* POLONIUS, *with* VOLTIMAND *and* CORNELIUS.]
               Welcome, my good friends!
  Say, Voltimand, what from our brother Norway?

VOLTIMAND: Most fair return of greetings and desires. 60
  Upon our first,[3] he sent out to suppress
  His nephew's levies, which to him appeared
  To be a preparation 'gainst the Polack,
  But better looked into, he truly found
  It was against your highness: whereat grieved, 65
  That so his sickness, age and impotence
  Was falsely borne in hand,[4] sends out arrests
  On Fortinbras; which he, in brief, obeys,
  Receives rebuke from Norway, and in fine[5]
  Makes vow before his uncle never more 70
  To give the assay[6] of arms against your majesty.
  Whereon old Norway, overcome with joy,
  Gives him three thousand crowns in annual fee
  And his commission to employ those soldiers,
  So levied as before, against the Polack: 75
  With an entreaty, herein further shown,
      [*Giving a paper.*]
  That it might please you to give quiet pass
  Through your dominions for this enterprise,
  On such regards of safety and allowance

1. Always.   2. Honor. *Fruit:* dessert.   3. As soon as we made the request.   4. Deceived, deluded.
5. Finally.   6. Test.

As therein are set down.
KING: It likes us well,   80
And at our more considered time we'll read,
Answer, and think upon this business.
Meantime we thank you for your well-took labor:
Go to your rest; at night we'll feast together:
Most welcome home!
        [*Exeunt* VOLTIMAND *and* CORNELIUS.]
POLONIUS: This business is well ended.   85
My liege, and madam, to expostulate
What majesty should be, what duty is,
Why day is day, night night, and time is time,
Were nothing but to waste night, day and time.
Therefore, since brevity is the soul of wit   90
And tediousness the limbs and outward flourishes,
I will be brief. Your noble son is mad:
Mad call I it; for, to define true madness,
What is 't but to be nothing else but mad?
But let that go.
QUEEN: More matter, with less art.   95
POLONIUS: Madam, I swear I use no art at all.
That he is mad, 'tis true: 'tis true 'tis pity,
And pity 'tis 'tis true: a foolish figure;[7]
But farewell it, for I will use no art.
Mad let us grant him then: and now remains   100
That we find out the cause of this effect,
Or rather say, the cause of this defect,
For this effect defective comes by cause:
Thus it remains and the remainder thus.
Perpend.[8]   105
I have a daughter,—have while she is mine,—
Who in her duty and obedience, mark,
Hath given me this: now gather and surmise.
[*Reads.*] 'To the celestial, and my soul's idol, the most beautified
Ophelia,'—That's an ill phrase, a vile phrase; 'beautified' is a vile   110
phrase; but you shall hear. Thus:
        [*Reads.*] 'In her excellent white bosom, these,' &c.
QUEEN: Came this from Hamlet to her?
POLONIUS: Good madam, stay awhile; I will be faithful.
        [*Reads.*]   'Doubt thou the stars are fire;   115
                        Doubt that the sun doth move;
                        Doubt truth to be a liar;
                        But never doubt I love.
'O dear Ophelia, I am ill at these numbers;[9] I have not art to reckon
my groans: but that I love thee best, O most best, believe it. Adieu.   120
                        'Thine evermore, most dear lady, whilst this
                                machine is to him,[1] HAMLET.'

7. Of speech.   8. Consider.   9. Verses.   1. Body is attached.

This in obedience hath my daughter shown me;
And more above,[2] hath his solicitings,
As they fell out by time, by means and place,   125
All given to mine ear.
KING: But how hath she
Received his love?
POLONIUS: What do you think of me?
KING: As of a man faithful and honorable.
POLONIUS: I would fain prove so. But what might you think,
When I had seen this hot love on the wing,—   130
As I perceived it, I must tell you that,
Before my daughter told me,—what might you,
Or my dear majesty your queen here, think,
If I had played the desk or table-book,[3]
Or given my heart a winking,[4] mute and dumb,   135
Or looked upon this love with idle sight;
What might you think? No, I went round[5] to work,
And my young mistress thus I did bespeak:
'Lord Hamlet is a prince, out of thy star;[6]
This must not be:' and then I prescripts gave her,   140
That she should lock herself from his resort,
Admit no messengers, receive no tokens.
Which done, she took the fruits of my advice;
And he repulsed, a short tale to make,
Fell into a sadness, then into a fast,   145
Thence to a watch, thence into a weakness,
Thence to a lightness,[7] and by this declension
Into the madness wherein now he raves
And all we mourn for.
KING: Do you think this?
QUEEN: It may be, very like.   150
POLONIUS: Hath there been such a time, I'd fain know that,
That I have positively said ' 'tis so,'
When it proved otherwise?
KING: Not that I know.
POLONIUS: [*Pointing to his head and shoulder.*] Take this, from this,
if this be otherwise: 155
If circumstances lead me, I will find
Where truth is hid, though it were hid indeed
Within the center.[8]
KING: How may we try it further?
POLONIUS: You know, sometimes he walks for hours together
Here in the lobby.
QUEEN: So he does, indeed.   160
POLONIUS: At such a time I'll loose my daughter to him:
Be you and I behind an arras then;
Mark the encounter: if he love her not,

---

2. Moreover.   3. If I had acted as a desk or notebook (in keeping the matter secret).   4. Shut my
heart's eye.   5. Straight.   6. Sphere.   7. Light-headedness. *Watch:* insomnia.   8. Of the earth.

And be not from his reason fall'n thereon,[9]
Let me be no assistant for a state,   165
But keep a farm and carters.
KING: We will try it.
QUEEN: But look where sadly the poor wretch comes reading.
POLONIUS: Away, I do beseech you, both away:
    I'll board him presently.[1]
        [*Exeunt* KING, QUEEN, *and* ATTENDANTS. —*Enter* HAMLET,
        reading.]
    O, give me leave: how does my good Lord Hamlet?   170
HAMLET: Well, God-a-mercy.
POLONIUS: Do you know me, my lord?
HAMLET: Excellent well; you are a fishmonger.[2]
POLONIUS: Not I, my lord.
HAMLET: Then I would you were so honest a man.   175
POLONIUS: Honest, my lord!
HAMLET: Aye, sir; to be honest, as this world goes, is to be one man
    picked out of ten thousand.
POLONIUS: That's very true, my lord.
HAMLET: For if the sun breed maggots in a dead dog, being a good   180
    kissing carrion[3]— Have you a daughter?
POLONIUS: I have, my lord.
HAMLET: Let her not walk i' the sun: conception is a blessing; but as
    your daughter may conceive,—friend, look to 't.
POLONIUS: [*Aside.*] How say you by that? Still harping on my daughter: 185
    yet he knew me not at first; he said I was a fishmonger: he is far
    gone: and truly in my youth I suffered much extremity for love; very
    near this. I'll speak to him again.—What do you read, my lord?
HAMLET: Words, words, words.
POLONIUS: What is the matter,[4] my lord?   190
HAMLET: Between who?
POLONIUS: I mean, the matter that you read, my lord.
HAMLET: Slanders, sir: for the satirical rogue says here that old men
    have gray beards, that their faces are wrinkled, their eyes purging
    thick amber and plum-tree gum, and that they have a plentiful lack   195
    of wit, together with most weak hams: all which, sir, though I most
    powerfully and potently believe, yet I hold it not honesty to have it
    thus set down; for yourself, sir, shall grow old as I am, if like a crab
    you could go backward.
POLONIUS: [*Aside.*] Though this be madness, yet there is method in   200
    't.—Will you walk out of the air, my lord?
HAMLET: Into my grave.
POLONIUS: Indeed, that's out of the air.
        [*Aside.*]
    How pregnant sometimes his replies are! a happiness[5] that often
    madness hits on, which reason and sanity could not so prosperously   205
    be delivered of. I will leave him, and suddenly contrive the means of

9. For that reason.   1. Approach him at once.   2. Fish seller but also slang for procurer.   3. Good
bit of flesh for kissing.   4. The subject matter of the book. Hamlet responds as if he referred to the
subject of a quarrel.   5. Aptness of expression.

meeting between him and my daughter.—My honorable lord, I will most humbly take my leave of you.

HAMLET: You cannot, sir, take from me any thing that I will more willingly part withal: except my life, except my life, except my life.   210

POLONIUS: Fare you well, my lord.

HAMLET: These tedious old fools.

[*Re-enter* ROSENCRANTZ *and* GUILDENSTERN.]

POLONIUS: You go to seek the Lord Hamlet; there he is.

ROSENCRANTZ: [*To* POLONIUS.] God save you, sir!

[*Exit* POLONIUS.]

GUILDENSTERN: My honored lord!   215

ROSENCRANTZ: My most dear lord!

HAMLET: My excellent good friends! How dost thou, Guildenstern? Ah, Rosencrantz! Good lads, how do you both?

ROSENCRANTZ: As the indifferent[6] children of the earth.

GUILDENSTERN: Happy, in that we are not over-happy;   220
On Fortune's cap we are not the very button.[7]

HAMLET: Nor the soles of her shoe?

ROSENCRANTZ: Neither, my lord.

HAMLET: Then you live about her waist, or in the middle of her favors?

GUILDENSTERN: Faith, her privates[8] we.   225

HAMLET: In the secret parts of Fortune? O, most true; she is a strumpet. What's the news?

ROSENCRANTZ: None, my lord, but that the world's grown honest.

HAMLET: Then is doomsday near: but your news is not true. Let me question more in particular: what have you, my good friends, de-   230
served at the hands of Fortune, that she sends you to prison hither?

GUILDENSTERN: Prison, my lord!

HAMLET: Denmark's a prison.

ROSENCRANTZ: Then is the world one.

HAMLET: A goodly one; in which there are many confines, wards[9] and   235
dungeons, Denmark being one o' the worst.

ROSENCRANTZ: We think not so, my lord.

HAMLET: Why, then, 'tis none to you; for there is nothing either good or bad, but thinking makes it so: to me it is a prison.

ROSENCRANTZ: Why, then your ambition makes it one; 'tis too narrow   240
for your mind.

HAMLET: O God, I could be bounded in a nut-shell and count myself a king of infinite space, were it not that I have bad dreams.

GUILDENSTERN: Which dreams indeed are ambition; for the very substance of the ambitious is merely the shadow of a dream.   245

HAMLET: A dream itself is but a shadow.

ROSENCRANTZ: Truly, and I hold ambition of so airy and light a quality that it is but a shadow's shadow.

HAMLET: Then are our beggars bodies, and our monarchs and outstretched heroes the beggars' shadows. Shall we to the court? for,   250
by my fay, I cannot reason.

---

6. Average.   7. Top.   8. Ordinary men (with obvious play on the sexual term *private parts*).
9. Cells. *Confines:* places of confinement.

ROSENCRANTZ: ⎫
GUILDENSTERN: ⎭ We'll wait upon you.

HAMLET: No such matter: I will not sort you[1] with the rest of my servants; for, to speak to you like an honest man, I am most dreadfully
attended. But, in the beaten way of friendship, what make you   255
at Elsinore?

ROSENCRANTZ: To visit you, my lord; no other occasion.

HAMLET: Beggar that I am, I am even poor in thanks; but I thank you:
and sure, dear friends, my thanks are too dear a halfpenny.[2] Were
you not sent for? Is it your own inclining? Is it a free visitation?   260
Come, deal justly[3] with me: come, come; nay, speak.

GUILDENSTERN: What should we say, my lord?

HAMLET: Why, any thing, but to the purpose. You were sent for; and
there is a kind of confession in your looks, which your modesties
have not craft enough to color: I know the good king and queen   265
have sent for you.

ROSENCRANTZ: To what end, my lord?

HAMLET: That you must teach me. But let me conjure you, by the rights
of our fellowship, by the consonancy of our youth, by the obligation
of our ever-preserved love, and by what more dear a better   270
proposer[4] could charge you withal, be even and direct with me,
whether you were sent for, or no.

ROSENCRANTZ: [*Aside to* GUILDENSTERN.] What say you?

HAMLET: [*Aside.*] Nay then, I have an eye of[5] you.—If you love me,
hold not off.   275

GUILDENSTERN: My lord, we were sent for.

HAMLET: I will tell you why; so shall my anticipation prevent your discovery,[6] and your secrecy to the king and queen moult no feather. I
have of late—but wherefore I know not—lost all my mirth, forgone
all custom of exercises; and indeed it goes so heavily with my dis-   280
position that this goodly frame, the earth, seems to me a sterile prom-
ontory; this most excellent canopy, the air, look you, this brave
o'erhanging firmament, this majestical roof fretted[7] with golden fire,
why, it appears no other thing to me than a foul and pestilent congregation of vapors. What a piece of work is a man! how noble in   285
reason! how infinite in faculty! in form and moving how express[8]
and admirable! in action how like an angel! in apprehension how
like a god! the beauty of the world! the paragon of animals! And yet,
to me, what is this quintessence of dust? man delights not me;
no, nor woman neither, though by your smiling you seem to   290
say so.

ROSENCRANTZ: My lord, there was no such stuff in my thoughts.

HAMLET: Why did you laugh then, when I said 'man delights not me'?

ROSENCRANTZ: To think, my lord, if you delight not in man, what lenten
entertainment the players shall receive from you: we coted[9] them   295
on the way; and hither are they coming, to offer you service.

HAMLET: He that plays the king shall be welcome; his majesty shall

---

1. Put you together.   **2.** If priced at a halfpenny.   **3.** Honestly.   **4.** Speaker.   **5.** On.   **6.** Pre-
cede your disclosure.   **7.** Adorned.   **8.** Precise.   **9.** Overtook.

2860 / William Shakespeare

have tribute of me; the adventurous knight shall use his foil and target; the lover shall not sigh gratis; the humorous[1] man shall end his part in peace; the clown shall make those laugh whose lungs are tickle o' the sere,[2] and the lady shall say her mind freely, or the blank verse shall halt for 't. What players are they? 300

ROSENCRANTZ: Even those you were wont to take such delight in, the tragedians of the city.

HAMLET: How chances it they travel? their residence, both in reputa- 305 tion and profit, was better both ways.

ROSENCRANTZ: I think their inhibition comes by means of the late innovation.[3]

HAMLET: Do they hold the same estimation they did when I was in the city? are they so followed? 310

ROSENCRANTZ: No, indeed, are they not.

HAMLET: How comes it? do they grow rusty?

ROSENCRANTZ: Nay, their endeavor keeps in the wonted pace: but there is, sir, an eyrie of children, little eyases,[4] that cry out on the top of question[5] and are most tyrannically clapped for 't: these are now 315 the fashion, and so berattle[6] the common stages—so they call them—that many wearing rapiers are afraid of goose-quills,[7] and dare scarce come thither.

HAMLET: What, are they children? who maintains 'em? how are they escoted? Will they pursue the quality[8] no longer than they can 320 sing? will they not say afterwards, if they should grow themselves to common players—as it is most like, if their means are no better,— their writers do them wrong, to make them exclaim against their own succession?[9]

ROSENCRANTZ: Faith, there has been much to-do on both sides, and 325 the nation holds it no sin to tarre[1] them to controversy: there was for a while no money bid for argument unless the poet and the player went to cuffs in the question.[2]

HAMLET: Is 't possible?

GUILDENSTERN: O, there has been much throwing about of brains. 330

HAMLET: Do the boys carry it away?[3]

ROSENCRANTZ: Aye, that they do, my lord; Hercules and his load too.[4]

HAMLET: It is not very strange; for my uncle is king of Denmark, and those that would make mows[5] at him while my father lived, give twenty, forty, fifty, a hundred ducats a-piece, for his picture in lit- 335 tle. 'Sblood, there is something in this more than natural, if philosophy could find it out.

[*Flourish of trumpets within.*]

GUILDENSTERN: There are the players.

HAMLET: Gentlemen, you are welcome to Elsinore. Your hands, come

---

1. Eccentric, whimsical.   2. Ready to shoot off at a touch.   3. The introduction of the children (line 314), as Rosencrantz explains in his subsequent replies to Hamlet. *Inhibition:* prohibition.   4. Nestling hawks. *Eyrie:* nest.   5. Above others on matter of dispute.   6. Berate.   7. Gentlemen are afraid of pens (that is, of poets satirizing the "common stages").   8. Profession of acting. *Escoted:* financially supported.   9. Recite satiric pieces against what they are themselves likely to become, common players. 1. Incite.   2. No offer to buy a plot for a play if it did not contain a quarrel between poet and player on that subject.   3. Win out.   4. The sign in front of the Globe theater showed Hercules bearing the world on his shoulders.   5. Faces, grimaces.

then: the appurtenance of welcome is fashion and ceremony: let 340
me comply with you in this garb, lest my extent[6] to the players,
which, I tell you, must show fairly outwards, should more appear
like entertainment[7] than yours. You are welcome: but my uncle-
father and aunt-mother are deceived.

GUILDENSTERN: In what, my dear lord? 345

HAMLET: I am but mad north-north-west: when the wind is southerly
I know a hawk from a handsaw.[8]

      [*Re-enter* POLONIUS.]

POLONIUS: Well be with you, gentlemen!

HAMLET: Hark you, Guildenstern; and you too: at each ear a hearer:
that great baby you see there is not yet out of his swaddling clouts.[9] 350

ROSENCRANTZ: Happily he's the second time come to them; for they
say an old man is twice a child.

HAMLET: I will prophesy he comes to tell me of the players; mark it.
You say right, sir: o' Monday morning; 'twas so, indeed.[1]

POLONIUS: My lord, I have news to tell you. 355

HAMLET: My lord, I have news to tell you. When Roscius[2] was an actor
in Rome,—

POLONIUS: The actors are come hither, my lord.

HAMLET: Buz, buz![3]

POLONIUS: Upon my honor,— 360

HAMLET: Then came each actor on his ass,—

POLONIUS: The best actors in the world, either for tragedy, comedy,
history, pastoral, pastoral-comical, historical-pastoral, tragical-
historical, tragical-comical-historical-pastoral, scene individable, or
poem unlimited:[4] Seneca cannot be too heavy, nor Plautus too light. 365
For the law of writ and the liberty,[5] these are the only men.

HAMLET: O Jephthah,[6] judge of Israel, what a treasure hadst thou!

POLONIUS: What a treasure had he, my lord?

HAMLET: Why,

      'One fair daughter, and no more, 370
        The which he lovèd passing well.'[7]

POLONIUS: [*Aside.*] Still on my daughter.

HAMLET: Am I not i' the right, old Jephthah?

POLONIUS: If you call me Jephthah, my lord, I have a daughter that I
love passing well. 375

HAMLET: Nay, that follows not.

POLONIUS: What follows, then, my lord?

HAMLET: Why,

      'As by lot, God wot.'
and then you know,

      'It came to pass, as most like it was,'— 380

---

6. Welcoming behavior. *Garb*: style.   7. Welcome.   8. A hawk from a heron as well as a kind of ax
from a handsaw.   9. Clothes.   1. Hamlet, for Polonius's sake, pretends he is deep in talk with Rosencrantz.   2. A famous Roman comic actor (126?–62? B.C.).   3. An expression used to stop the teller of
a stale story.   4. For plays governed and those not governed by classical rules.   5. Possibly, for both
written and extemporized plays. Seneca (ca. 4 B.C.–A.D. 65) was a Roman who wrote tragedies. Plautus (ca.
254–184 B.C.) was a Roman who wrote comedies.   6. Who was compelled to sacrifice a dearly beloved
daughter (Judges 11).   7. From an old ballad about Jephthah.

the first row of the pious chanson will show you more; for look, where my abridgment[8] comes.

[*Enter four or five* PLAYERS.]

You are welcome, masters; welcome, all. I am glad to see thee well. Welcome, good friends. O, my old friend! Why thy face is valanced[9] since I saw thee last; comest thou to beard me in Denmark? What, my young lady and mistress! By'r lady, your ladyship is nearer to heaven than when I saw you last, by the altitude of a chopine. Pray God, your voice, like a piece of uncurrent gold, be not cracked within the ring.[1] Masters, you are all welcome. We'll e'en to 't like French falconers, fly at any thing we see: we'll have a speech straight: come, give us a taste of your quality; come, a passionate speech.

FIRST PLAYER: What speech, my good lord?

HAMLET: I heard thee speak me a speech once, but it was never acted; or, if it was, not above once; for the play, I remember, pleased not the million; 'twas caviare to the general:[2] but it was—as I received it, and others, whose judgments in such matters cried in the top of mine[3]—an excellent play, well digested in the scenes, set down with as much modesty as cunning. I remember, one said there were no sallets in the lines to make the matter savory, nor no matter in the phrase that might indict the author of affection;[4] but called it an honest method, as wholesome as sweet, and by very much more handsome than fine.[5] One speech in it I chiefly loved: 'twas Æneas' tale to Dido; and thereabout of it especially, where he speaks of Priam's slaughter:[6] it live in your memory, begin at this line; let me see, let me see;

'The rugged Pyrrhus, like th' Hyrcanian beast,'[7]—

It is not so: it begins with 'Pyrrhus.'

'The rugged Pyrrhus, he whose sable arms,
Black as his purpose, did the night resemble
When he lay couchèd in the ominous horse,[8]
Hath now this dread and black complexion smeared
With heraldry more dismal: head to foot
Now is he total gules; horridly tricked[9]
With the blood of fathers, mothers, daughters, sons,
Baked and impasted with the parching streets,
That lend a tyrannous[1] and a damnèd light
To their lord's murder: roasted in wrath and fire,
And thus o'er-sizèd[2] with coagulate gore,
With eyes like carbuncles, the hellish Pyrrhus
Old grandsire Priam seeks.'

So, proceed you.

POLONIUS: 'Fore God, my lord, well spoken, with good accent and good discretion.

8. That is, the players interrupting him. *Row:* stanza. *Chanson:* song. 9. Draped (with a beard). 1. A pun on the *ring* of the voice and the *ring* around the king's head on a coin. *Chopine:* a thick-soled shoe. *Uncurrent:* unfit for currency. 2. A delicacy wasted on the general public. 3. Were louder (more authoritative than) mine. 4. Affectation. *Sallets:* salads (that is, relish, spicy passages). 5. More elegant than showy. 6. The story of the fall of Troy, told by Aeneas to Queen Dido. Priam was the king of Troy. 7. Tiger. Pyrrhus was Achilles' son (also called Neoptolemus). 8. The wooden horse in which Greek warriors were smuggled into Troy. 9. Adorned. *Gules:* heraldic term for red. 1. Savage. 2. Glued over.

FIRST PLAYER: 'Anon he finds him
    Striking too short at Greeks; his antique sword,   425
    Rebellious to his arm, lies where it falls,
    Repugnant to command: unequal matched,
    Pyrrhus at Priam drives; in rage strikes wide;
    But with the whiff and wind of his fell sword
    The unnervèd father falls. Then senseless Ilium,[3]   430
    Seeming to feel this blow, with flaming top
    Stoops to his base, and with a hideous crash
    Takes prisoner Pyrrhus' ear: for, lo! his sword,
    Which was declining on the milky[4] head
    Of reverend Priam seemed i' the air to stick: 435
    So, as a painted tyrant, Pyrrhus stood,
    And like a neutral to his will and matter,
    Did nothing.
    But as we often see, against some storm,
    A silence in the heavens, the rack[5] stand still,   440
    The bold winds speechless and the orb below
    As hush as death, anon the dreadful thunder
    Doth rend the region, so after Pyrrhus' pause
    Aroused vengeance sets him new a-work;
    And never did the Cyclops'[6] hammers fall   445
    On Mars's armor, forged for proof[7] eterne,
    With less remorse than Pyrrhus' bleeding sword
    Now falls on Priam.
    Out, thou strumpet, Fortune! All you gods,
    In general synod take away her power,   450
    Break all the spokes and fellies from her wheel,
    And bowl the round nave[8] down the hill of heaven
    As low as to the fiends!
POLONIUS: This is too long.
HAMLET: It shall to the barber's, with your beard. Prithee, say on: he's   455
    for a jig[9] or a tale of bawdry, or he sleeps: say on: come to Hecuba.
FIRST PLAYER: 'But who, O, who had seen the mobled[1] queen—'
HAMLET: 'The mobled queen'?
POLONIUS: That's good; 'mobled queen' is good.
FIRST PLAYER: 'Run barefoot up and down, threatening the flames   460
    With bisson rheum; a clout[2] upon that head
    Where late the diadem stood; and for a robe,
    About her lank and all o'er-teemèd loins,[3]
    A blanket, in the alarm of fear caught up:
    Who this had seen, with tongue in venom steeped   465
    'Gainst Fortune's state[4] would treason have pronounced:
    But if the gods themselves did see her then,
    When she saw Pyrrhus make malicious sport
    In mincing with his sword her husband's limbs,
    The instant burst of clamor that she made,   470

---

3. Troy's citadel.   **4.** White-haired.   **5.** Clouds. *Against:* just before.   **6.** The gigantic workmen of Hephaestus (Vulcan), god of blacksmiths and fire.   **7.** Protection.   **8.** Hub. *Fellies:* rims.   **9.** Ludicrous sung dialogue, short farce.   **1.** Muffled.   **2.** Cloth. *Bisson rheum:* blinding moisture, tears. **3.** Worn out by childbearing.   **4.** Government.

Unless things mortal move them[5] not at all,
Would have made milch the burning eyes of heaven[6]
And passion in the gods.'

POLONIUS: Look, whether he has not turned his color and has tears in
's eyes. Prithee, no more.   475

HAMLET: 'Tis well; I'll have thee speak out the rest of this soon. Good
my lord, will you see the players well bestowed?[7] Do you hear, let
them be well used, for they are the abstracts and brief chronicles of
the time: after your death you were better have a bad epitaph than
their ill report while you live.   480

POLONIUS: My lord, I will use them according to their desert.

HAMLET: God's bodykins,[8] man, much better: use every man after his
desert, and who shall 'scape whipping? Use them after your own
honor and dignity: the less they deserve, the more merit is in your
bounty. Take them in.   485

POLONIUS: Come, sirs.

HAMLET: Follow him, friends: we'll hear a play to-morrow. [*Exit* POLON-
IUS *with all the* PLAYERS *but the first.*] Dost thou hear me, old friend;
can you play the Murder of Gonzago?

FIRST PLAYER: Aye, my lord.   490

HAMLET: We'll ha 't to-morrow night. You could, for a need, study a
speech of some dozen or sixteen lines, which I would set down and
insert in 't, could you not?

FIRST PLAYER: Aye, my lord.

HAMLET: Very well. Follow that lord; and look you mock him not.   495
[*Exit* FIRST PLAYER.] My good friends, I'll leave you till night: you are
welcome to Elsinore.

ROSENCRANTZ: Good my lord!

HAMLET: Aye, so, God be wi' ye! [*Exeunt* ROSENCRANTZ *and* GUILDEN-
STERN.] Now I am alone.   500
O, what a rogue and peasant slave am I!
Is it not monstrous that this player here,
But in a fiction, in a dream of passion,
Could force his soul so to his own conceit
That from her[9] working all his visage wanned;   505
Tears in his eyes, distraction in 's aspect,
A broken voice, and his whole function[1] suiting
With forms to his conceit? and all for nothing!
For Hecuba![2]
What's Hecuba to him, or he to Hecuba,   510
That he should weep for her? What would he do,
Had he the motive and the cue for passion
That I have? He would drown the stage with tears
And cleave the general air with horrid speech,
Make mad the guilty and appal the free,   515
Confound the ignorant, and amaze indeed
The very faculties of eyes and ears.

---

5. The gods.   6. The stars. *Milch:* moist (milk-giving).   7. Taken care of, lodged.   8. By God's little
body.   9. His soul's.   1. Bodily action.   2. Queen of Troy, Priam's wife. *Conceit:* imagination, conception of the role played.

Yet I,
A dull and muddy-mettled rascal, peak,³
Like John-a-dreams, unpregnant of my cause,⁴   520
And can say nothing; no, not for a king,
Upon whose property and most dear life
A damn'd defeat was made. Am I a coward?
Who calls me villain? breaks my pate across?
Plucks off my beard, and blows it in my face?   525
Tweaks me by the nose? gives me the lie i' the throat,
As deep as to the lungs? who does me this?
Ha!
'Swounds, I should take it: for it cannot be
But I am pigeon-livered and lack gall   530
To make oppression bitter, or ere this
I should have fatted all the region kites⁵
With this slave's offal: bloody, bawdy villain!
Remorseless, treacherous, lecherous, kindless⁶ villain!
O, vengeance!   535
Why, what an ass am I! This is most brave,
That I, the son of a dear father murdered,
Prompted to my revenge by heaven and hell,
Must, like a whore, unpack my heart with words,
And fall a-cursing, like a very drab,   540
A scullion!
Fie upon 't! About,⁷ my brain! Hum, I have heard
That guilty creatures, sitting at a play,
Have by the very cunning of the scene
Been struck so to the soul that presently   545
They have proclaimed their malefactions;
For murder, though it have no tongue, will speak
With most miraculous organ. I'll have these players
Play something like the murder of my father
Before mine uncle: I'll observe his looks;   550
I'll tent him to the quick: if he but blench,⁸
I know my course. The spirit that I have seen
May be the devil; and the devil hath power
To assume a pleasing shape; yea, and perhaps
Out of my weakness and my melancholy,   555
As he is very potent with such spirits,
Abuses me to damn me. I'll have grounds
More relative⁹ than this. The play's the thing
Wherein I'll catch the conscience of the king.
       [*Exit.*]

---

3. Mope. *Muddy-mettled:* of poor metal (spirit, temper), dull-spirited.   **4.** Not really conscious of my cause, unquickened by it. *John-a-dreams:* a dreamy, absentminded character.   **5.** Kites (hawks) of the air.   **6.** Unnatural.   **7.** To work!   **8.** Flinch. *Tent:* probe.   **9.** Relevant.

Act III

SCENE 1

A room in the castle.

[*Enter* KING, QUEEN, POLONIUS, OPHELIA, ROSENCRANTZ, *and* GUILDENSTERN.]

KING: And can you, by no drift of circumstance,[1]
  Get from him why he puts on this confusion,
  Grating so harshly all his days of quiet
  With turbulent and dangerous lunacy?
ROSENCRANTZ: He does confess he feels himself distracted,   5
  But from what cause he will by no means speak.
GUILDENSTERN: Nor do we find him forward to be sounded;
  But, with a crafty madness, keeps aloof,
  When we would bring him on to some confession
  Of his true state.
QUEEN: Did he receive you well?   10
ROSENCRANTZ: Most like a gentleman.
GUILDENSTERN: But with much forcing of his disposition.
ROSENCRANTZ: Niggard of question, but of our demands
  Most free in his reply.
QUEEN: Did you assay[2] him
  To any pastime?   15
ROSENCRANTZ: Madam, it so fell out that certain players
  We o'er-raught[3] on the way: of these we told him,
  And there did seem in him a kind of joy
  To hear of it: they are about the court,
  And, as I think, they have already order   20
  This night to play before him.
POLONIUS: 'Tis most true:
  And he beseeched me to entreat your majesties
  To hear and see the matter.
KING: With all my heart; and it doth much content me
  To hear him so inclined.   25
  Good gentlemen, give him a further edge,[4]
  And drive his purpose on to these delights.
ROSENCRANTZ: We shall, my lord.
    [*Exeunt* ROSENCRANTZ *and* GUILDENSTERN.]
KING: Sweet Gertrude, leave us too;
  For we have closely[5] sent for Hamlet hither,
  That he, as 'twere by accident, may here   30
  Affront Ophelia:
  Her father and myself, lawful espials,
  Will so bestow[6] ourselves that, seeing unseen,
  We may of their encounter frankly judge,
  And gather by him, as he is behaved,   35

1. Turn of talk, or roundabout way.   2. Try to attract him.   3. Overtook.   4. Incitement.
5. Privately.   6. Place. *Affront:* confront. *Espials:* spies.

If 't be the affliction of his love or no
That thus he suffers for.
QUEEN: I shall obey you:
  And for your part, Ophelia, I do wish
  That your good beauties be the happy cause
  Of Hamlet's wildness: so shall I hope your virtues   40
  Will bring him to his wonted way again,
  To both your honors.
OPHELIA: Madam, I wish it may.
      [*Exit* QUEEN.]
POLONIUS: Ophelia, walk you here. Gracious, so please you,
  We will bestow ourselves. [*To* OPHELIA.] Read on this book;
  That show of such an exercise may color[7]   45
  Your loneliness. We are oft to blame in this,—
  'Tis too much proved—that with devotion's visage
  And pious action we do sugar o'er
  The devil himself.
KING: [*Aside.*]   O, 'tis too true!
  How smart a lash that speech doth give my conscience!   50
  The harlot's cheek, beautied with plastering art,
  Is not more ugly to the thing that helps it
  Than is my deed to my most painted word:
  O heavy burthen!
POLONIUS: I hear him coming: let's withdraw, my lord.   55
    [*Exeunt* KING *and* POLONIUS. —*Enter* HAMLET.]
HAMLET: To be, or not to be: that is the question:
  Whether 'tis nobler in the mind to suffer
  The slings and arrows of outrageous fortune,
  Or to take arms against a sea of troubles,
  And by opposing end them. To die: to sleep;   60
  No more; and by a sleep to say we end
  The heart-ache, and the thousand natural shocks
  That flesh is heir to, 'tis a consummation[8]
  Devoutly to be wished. To die, to sleep;
  To sleep: perchance to dream: aye, there's the rub;[9]   65
  For in that sleep of death what dreams may come,
  When we have shuffled off this mortal coil,[1]
  Must give us pause: there's the respect
  That makes calamity of so long life;[2]
  For who would bear the whips and scorns of time,   70
  The oppressor's wrong, the proud man's contumely,
  The pangs of despisèd love, the law's delay,
  The insolence of office, and the spurns
  That patient merit of the unworthy takes,
  When he himself might his quietus make   75
  With a bare bodkin? who would fardels[3] bear,
  To grunt and sweat under a weary life,

7. Excuse.   8. Final settlement.   9. The impediment (a bowling term).   1. Have rid ourselves of the turmoil of mortal life.   2. So long-lived. *Respect:* consideration.   3. Burdens. *Bodkin:* poniard, dagger.

But that the dread of something after death,
The undiscovered country from whose bourn[4]
No traveler returns, puzzles the will,   80
And makes us rather bear those ills we have
Than fly to others that we know not of?
Thus conscience does make cowards of us all,
And thus the native hue of resolution
Is sicklied o'er with the pale cast of thought,   85
And enterprises of great pitch[5] and moment
With this regard their currents turn awry
And lose the name of action. Soft you now!
The fair Ophelia! Nymph, in thy orisons[6]
Be all my sins remembered.
OPHELIA: Good my lord,   90
   How does your honor for this many a day?
HAMLET: I humbly thank you: well, well, well.
OPHELIA: My lord, I have remembrances of yours,
   That I have longed to re-deliver;
   I pray you, now receive them.
HAMLET: No, not I;   95
   I never gave you aught.
OPHELIA: My honored lord, you know right well you did;
   And with them words of so sweet breath composed
   As made the things more rich: their perfume lost,
   Take these again; for to the noble mind   100
   Rich gifts wax poor when givers prove unkind.
   There, my lord.
HAMLET: Ha, ha! are you honest?
OPHELIA: My lord?
HAMLET: Are you fair?   105
OPHELIA: What means your lordship?
HAMLET: That if you be honest and fair, your honesty should admit no
   discourse to your beauty.
OPHELIA: Could beauty, my lord, have better commerce[7] than with
   honesty?   110
HAMLET: Aye, truly; for the power of beauty will sooner transform hon-
   esty from what it is to a bawd than the force of honesty can translate
   beauty into his[8] likeness: this was sometime a paradox, but now the
   time gives it proof.[9] I did love you once.
OPHELIA: Indeed, my lord, you made me believe so.   115
HAMLET: You should not have believed me; for virtue cannot so inoculate our old stock, but we shall relish[1] of it: I loved you not.
OPHELIA: I was the more deceived.
HAMLET: Get thee to a nunnery: why wouldst thou be a breeder of
   sinners? I am myself indifferent honest; but yet I could accuse me   120
   of such things that it were better my mother had not borne me: I am
   very proud, revengeful, ambitious; with more offenses at my beck

---

4. Boundary.   5. Height.   6. Prayers.   7. Intercourse.   8. Its.   9. In his mother's adultery.
1. Retain the flavor of. *Inoculate:* graft itself onto.

than I have thoughts to put them in, imagination to give them shape,
or time to act them in. What should such fellows as I do crawling
between heaven and earth! We are arrant knaves all; believe   125
none of us. Go thy ways to a nunnery. Where's your father?

OPHELIA: At home, my lord.

HAMLET: Let the doors be shut upon him, that he may play the fool no
where but in 's own house. Farewell.

OPHELIA: O, help him, you sweet heavens!   130

HAMLET: If thou dost marry, I'll give thee this plague for thy dowry: be
thou as chaste as ice, as pure as snow, thou shalt not escape cal-
umny. Get thee to a nunnery, go: farewell. Or, if thou wilt needs
marry, marry a fool; for wise men know well enough what monsters[2]
you make of them. To a nunnery, go; and quickly too. Farewell.   135

OPHELIA: O heavenly powers, restore him!

HAMLET: I have heard of your paintings too, well enough; God hath
given you one face, and you make yourselves another: you jig, you
amble, and you lisp, and nick-name God's creatures, and make your
wantonness your ignorance.[3] Go to, I'll no more on 't; it hath   140
made me mad. I say, we will have no more marriages: those that are
married already, all but one, shall live; the rest shall keep as they
are. To a nunnery, go.
[Exit.]

OPHELIA: O, what a noble mind is here o'erthrown!
The courtier's, soldier's, scholar's, eye, tongue, sword: 145
The expectancy and rose of the fair state,
The glass of fashion and the mould of form.[4]
The observed of all observers, quite, quite down!
And I, of ladies most deject and wretched,
That sucked the honey of his music vows,   150
Now see that noble and most sovereign reason,
Like sweet bells jangled, out of tune and harsh;
That unmatched form and feature of blown[5] youth
Blasted with ecstasy: O, woe is me,
To have seen what I have seen, see what I see!   155
[Re-enter KING and POLONIUS.]

KING: Love! his affections do not that way tend;
Nor what he spake, though it lacked form a little,
Was not like madness. There's something in his soul
O'er which his melancholy sits on brood,
And I do doubt[6] the hatch and the disclose   160
Will be some danger: which for to prevent,
I have in quick determination
Thus set it down:—he shall with speed to England,
For the demand of our neglected tribute:
Haply the seas and countries different   165
With variable objects shall expel
This something-settled matter in his heart,

2. Cuckolds bear imaginary horns and "a horned man's a monster" (*Othello* 4.1).   3. Misname (out of affectation) the most natural things, and pretend that this is due to ignorance instead of affectation.   4. The mirror of fashion and the model of behavior.   5. In full bloom.   6. Fear.

2870 / William Shakespeare

Whereon his brains still beating puts him thus
From fashion of himself.[7] What think you on 't?
POLONIUS: It shall do well: but yet do I believe   170
The origin and commencement of his grief
Sprung from neglected love. How now, Ophelia!
You need not tell us what Lord Hamlet said;
We heard it all. My lord, do as you please;
But, if you hold it fit, after the play,   175
Let his queen mother all alone entreat him
To show his grief: let her be round[8] with him;
And I'll be placed, so please you, in the ear
Of all their conference. If she find him not,
To England send him, or confine him where   180
Your wisdom best shall think.
KING: It shall be so:
Madness in great ones must not unwatched go.
    [*Exeunt.*]

SCENE 2

A hall in the castle.

[*Enter* HAMLET *and* PLAYERS.]
HAMLET: Speak the speech, I pray you, as I pronounced it to you, trip-
pingly on the tongue: but if you mouth it, as many of your players do, I had as lief the town-crier spoke my lines. Nor do not saw
the air too much with your hand, thus; but use all gently: for in the
very torrent, tempest, and, as I may say, whirlwind of your   5
passion, you must acquire and beget a temperance that may give it
smoothness. O, it offends me to the soul to hear a robustious periwig-
pated fellow tear a passion to tatters, to very rags, to split the ears
of the groundlings,[9] who, for the most part, are capable of nothing
but inexplicable dumb-shows and noise: I would have such   10
a fellow whipped for o'er doing Termagant;[1] it out-herods Herod:
pray you, avoid it.
FIRST PLAYER: I warrant your honor.
HAMLET: Be not too tame neither, but let your own discretion be your
tutor: suit the action to the word, the word to the action; with this   15
special observance, that you o'erstep not the modesty[2] of nature: for
anything so overdone is from the purpose of playing, whose end, both
at the first and now, was and is, to hold, as 'twere, the mirror up to
nature; to show virtue her own feature, scorn her own image, and
the very age and body of the time his form and pressure.[3] Now   20
this overdone or come tardy off, though it make the unskillful
laugh, cannot but make the judicious grieve; the censure of the
which one must in your allowance o'erweigh a whole theater of others. O, there be players that I have seen play, and heard others praise,

7. Makes him behave unusually.   8. Direct.   9. Spectators in the pit, where admission was cheapest.
1. God of the Mohammedans in old romances and morality plays; he was portrayed as being noisy and
excitable.   2. Moderation.   3. Impress, shape. *Feature:* form. *His:* its.

and that highly, not to speak it profanely,[4] that neither hav- 25
ing the accent of Christians nor the gait of Christian, pagan, nor
man, have so strutted and bellowed, that I have thought some of
nature's journeymen had made men, and not made them well, they
imitated humanity so abominably.

FIRST PLAYER: I hope we have reformed that indifferently[5] with us, sir. 30

HAMLET: O, reform it altogether. And let those that play your clowns
speak no more than is set down for them: for there be of them that
will themselves laugh, to set on some quantity of barren[6] spectators
to laugh too, though in the mean time some necessary question of
the play be then to be considered: that's villainous, and shows a 35
most pitiful ambition in the fool that uses it. Go, make you ready.

> [*Exeunt* PLAYERS. —*Enter* POLONIUS, ROSENCRANTZ, *and* GUILD-
> ENSTERN.]

How now, my lord! will the king hear this piece of work?

POLONIUS: And the queen too, and that presently.

HAMLET: Bid the players make haste.

> [*Exit* POLONIUS.]

Will you two help to hasten them? 40

ROSENCRANTZ: ⎫
GUILDENSTERN: ⎬ We will, my lord.

> [*Exeunt* ROSENCRANTZ *and* GUILDENSTERN.]

HAMLET: What ho! Horatio!

> [*Enter* HORATIO.]

HORATIO: Here, sweet lord, at your service.

HAMLET: Horatio, thou art e'en as just a man
As e'er my conversation coped withal.[7] 45

HORATIO: O, my dear lord,—

HAMLET: Nay, do not think I flatter;
For what advancement may I hope from thee,
That no revenue hast but thy good spirits,
To feed and clothe thee? Why should the poor be flattered?
No, let the candied tongue lick absurd pomp, 50
And crook the pregnant hinges of the knee
Where thrift may follow fawning.[8] Dost thou hear?
Since my dear soul was mistress of her choice,
And could of men distinguish, her election
Hath sealed thee for herself: for thou hast been 55
As one, in suffering all, that suffers nothing;
A man that fortune's buffets and rewards
Hast ta'en with equal thanks: and blest are those
Whose blood and judgment[9] are so well commingled
That they are not a pipe for fortune's finger 60
To sound what stop she please.[1] Give me that man
That is not passion's slave, and I will wear him
In my heart's core, ay, in my heart of heart,

---

4. Hamlet apologizes for the profane implication that there could be men not of God's making.   5. Pretty
well.   6. Silly.   7. As I ever associated with.   8. Material profit may be derived from cringing. *Pregnant hinges:* supple joints.   9. Passion and reason.   1. For Fortune to put her finger on any windhole
of the pipe she wants.

As I do thee. Something too much of this.
There is a play to-night before the king;   65
One scene of it comes near the circumstance
Which I have told thee of my father's death:
I prithee, when thou sees that act a-foot,
Even with the very comment of thy soul[2]
Observe my uncle: if his occulted guilt   70
Do not itself unkennel in one speech
It is a damned ghost that we have seen,
And my imaginations are as foul
As Vulcan's stithy.[3] Give him heedful note;
For I mine eyes will rivet to his face,   75
And after we will both our judgments join
In censure of his seeming.[4]

HORATIO: Well, my lord:
If he steal aught the whilst this play is playing,
And 'scape detecting, I will pay the theft.

HAMLET: They are coming to the play: I must be idle:[5]   80
Get you a place.

> [*Danish march. A flourish. Enter* KING, QUEEN, POLONIUS, OPHE-
> LIA, ROSENCRANTZ, GUILDENSTERN, *and other* LORDS *attendant,*
> *with the* GUARD *carrying torches.*]

KING: How fares our cousin Hamlet?

HAMLET: Excellent, i' faith; of the chameleon's dish: I eat the air,[6]
promise-crammed: you cannot feed capons so.

KING: I have nothing with this answer, Hamlet; these words are not   85
mine.[7]

HAMLET: No, nor mine now. [*To* POLONIUS.] My lord, you played once
i' the university, you say?

POLONIUS: That did I, my lord, and was accounted a good actor.

HAMLET: What did you enact?   90

POLONIUS: I did enact Julius Cæsar: I was killed i' the Capitol; Brutus
killed me.

HAMLET: It was a brute part of him to kill so capital a calf there. Be
the players ready?

ROSENCRANTZ: Aye, my lord; they stay upon your patience.   95

QUEEN: Come hither, my dear Hamlet, sit by me.

HAMLET: No, good mother, here's metal more attractive.

POLONIUS: [*To the* KING.] O, ho! do you mark that?

HAMLET: Lady, shall I lie in your lap? [*Lying down at* OPHELIA'S *feet.*]

OPHELIA: No, my lord.   100

HAMLET: I mean, my head upon your lap?

OPHELIA: Aye, my lord.

HAMLET: Do you think I meant country matters?

OPHELIA: I think nothing, my lord.

HAMLET: That's a fair thought to lie between maids' legs.   105

OPHELIA: What is, my lord?

---

2. With all your powers of observation.   3. Smithy.   4. To judge his behavior.   5. Crazy.   6. The
chameleon was supposed to feed on air.   7. Have nothing to do with my question.

HAMLET: Nothing.[8]

OPHELIA: You are merry, my lord.

HAMLET: Who, I?

OPHELIA: Aye, my lord.   110

HAMLET: O God, your only jig-maker.[9] What should a man do but be
merry? for, look you, how cheerfully my mother looks, and my father
died within 's two hours.

OPHELIA: Nay, 'tis twice two months, my lord.

HAMLET: So long? Nay then, let the devil wear black, for I'll have a   115
suit of sables.[1] O heavens! die two months ago, and not forgotten
yet? Then there's hope a great man's memory may outlive his life
half a year: but, by 'r lady, he must build churches then; or else shall
he suffer not thinking on, with the hobby-horse,[2] whose epitaph is,
'For, O, for, O, the hobby-horse is forgot.'   120

> [*Hautboys play. The dumb-show enters. —Enter a King and a
> Queen very lovingly; the Queen embracing him and he her. She
> kneels, and makes show of protestation unto him. He takes her up,
> and declines his head upon her neck; lays him down upon a bank
> of flowers: she, seeing him asleep, leaves him. Anon comes in a
> fellow, takes off his crown, kisses it, and pours poison in the King's
> ears, and exits. The Queen returns; finds the King dead, and makes
> passionate action. The Poisoner, with some two or three Mutes
> comes in again, seeming to lament with her. The dead body is
> carried away. The Poisoner woos the Queen with gifts: she seems
> loath and unwilling awhile, but in the end accepts his love. —
> Exeunt.*]

OPHELIA: What means this, my lord?

HAMLET: Marry, this is miching mallecho;[3] it means mischief.

OPHELIA: Belike this show imports the argument of the play.

> [*Enter* PROLOGUE.]

HAMLET: We shall know by this fellow: the players cannot keep counsel;[4]
they'll tell all.   125

OPHELIA: Will he tell us what this show meant?

HAMLET: Aye, or any show that you'll show him: be not you ashamed
to show, he'll not shame to tell you what it means.

OPHELIA: You are naught,[5] you are naught: I'll mark the play.

PROLOGUE: For us, and for our tragedy,   130
> Here stooping to your clemency,
> We beg your hearing patiently.

HAMLET: Is this a prologue, or the posy[6] of a ring?

OPHELIA: 'Tis brief, my lord.

HAMLET: As woman's love.   135

> [*Enter two* PLAYERS, KING *and* QUEEN.]

PLAYER KING: Full thirty times hath Phœbus' cart[7] gone round
> Neptune's salt wash and Tellus' orbed ground,
> And thirty dozen moons with borrowed sheen

---

8. A sexual pun: no thing.   9. Maker of comic songs.   1. Hamlet notes sarcastically the lack of mourning for his father in the fancy dress of court and king.   2. A figure in the old May Day games and Morris
dances.   3. Sneaking misdeed.   4. A secret.   5. Naughty, improper.   6. Motto, inscription.
7. The chariot of the sun.

About the world have times twelve thirties been,
Since love our hearts and Hymen did our hands   140
Unite commutual in most sacred bands.
PLAYER QUEEN: So many journeys may the sun and moon
Make us again count o'er ere love be done!
But, woe is me, you are so sick of late,
So far from cheer and from your former state,   145
That I distrust you.[8] Yet, though I distrust,
Discomfort you, my lord, it nothing must:
For women's fear and love holds quantity,[9]
In neither aught, or in extremity.
Now, what my love is, proof hath made you know,   150
And as my love is sized, my fear is so:
Where love is great, the littlest doubts are fear,
Where little fears grow great, great love grows there.
PLAYER KING: Faith, I must leave thee, love, and shortly too;
My operant powers their functions leave[1] to do: 155
And thou shalt live in this fair world behind,
Honored, beloved; and haply one as kind
For husband shalt thou—
PLAYER QUEEN: O, confound the rest!
Such love must needs be treason in my breast:
In second husband let me be accurst!   160
None wed the second but who killed the first.
HAMLET: [Aside.] Wormwood, wormwood.
PLAYER QUEEN: The instances that second marriage move
Are base respects of thrift,[2] but none of love:
A second time I kill my husband dead,   165
When second husband kisses me in bed.
PLAYER KING: I do believe you think what now you speak,
But what we do determine oft we break.
Purpose is but the slave to memory,
Of violent birth but poor validity: 170
Which now, like fruit unripe, sticks on the tree,
But fall unshaken when they mellow be.
Most necessary 'tis that we forget
To pay ourselves what to ourselves is debt:
What to ourselves in passion we propose,   175
The passion ending, both the purpose lose.
The violence of either grief or joy
Their own enactures[3] with themselves destroy:
Where joy most revels, grief doth most lament;
Grief joys, joy grieves, on slender accident.   180
This world is not for aye, nor 'tis not strange
That even our loves should with our fortunes change,
For 'tis a question left us yet to prove,
Whether love lead fortune or else fortune love.

8. I am worried about you.   9. Maintain mutual balance.   1. Cease.   2. Considerations of material profit. *Instances:* motives.   3. Their own fulfillment in action.

The great man down, you mark his favorite flies;   185
The poor advanced makes friends of enemies:
And hitherto doth love on fortune tend;
For who not needs shall never lack a friend,
And who in want a hollow friend doth try
Directly seasons[4] him his enemy.   190
But, orderly to end where I begun,
Our wills and fates do so contrary run,
That our devices still are overthrown,
Our thoughts are ours, their ends none of our own:
So think thou wilt no second husband wed,   195
But die thy thoughts when thy first lord is dead.
PLAYER QUEEN: Nor earth to me give food nor heaven light!
Sport and repose lock from me day and night!
To desperation turn my trust and hope!
An anchor's cheer in prison be my scope!   200
Each opposite, that blanks[5] the face of joy,
Meet what I would have well and it destroy!
Both here and hence pursue me lasting strife,
If, once a widow, ever I be wife!
HAMLET: If she should break it now!   205
PLAYER KING: 'Tis deeply sworn. Sweet, leave me here a while;
My spirits grow dull, and fain I would beguile
The tedious day with sleep.
        [*Sleeps.*]
PLAYER QUEEN: Sleep rock thy brain;
And never come mischance between us twain!
        [*Exit.*]
HAMLET: Madam, how like you this play?   210
QUEEN: The lady doth protest[6] too much, methinks.
HAMLET: O, but she'll keep her word.
KING: Have you heard the argument?[7] Is there no offense in 't?
HAMLET: No, no, they do but jest, poison in jest; no offense i' the world.   215
KING: What do you call the play?
HAMLET: The Mouse-Trap. Marry, how? Tropically.[8] This play is the
    image of a murder done in Vienna: Gonzago is the duke's name; his
    wife, Baptista: you shall see anon; 'tis a knavish piece of work; but
    what o' that? your majesty, and we that have free souls, it   220
    touches us not: let the galled jade wince, our withers are unwrung.[9]
        [*Enter* LUCIANUS.]
    This is one Lucianus, nephew to the king.
OPHELIA: You are as good as a chorus, my lord.
HAMLET: I could interpret[1] between you and your love, if I could see
    the puppets dallying.   225
OPHELIA: You are keen,[2] my lord, you are keen.
HAMLET: It would cost you a groaning to take off my edge.

---

4. Matures.   5. Makes pale. *Anchor's cheer:* hermit's, or anchorite's, fare.   6. Promise.   7. Plot of
the play in outline.   8. By a trope, figuratively.   9. Not wrenched. *Galled jade:* injured horse. *Withers:*
the area between a horse's shoulders.   1. Act as interpreter (regular feature in puppet shows).   2. Bitter, but Hamlet chooses to take the word sexually.

2876 / William Shakespeare

OPHELIA: Still better and worse.

HAMLET: So you must take[3] your husbands. Begin, murderer; pox, leave
thy damnable faces, and begin. Come: the croaking raven doth   230
bellow for revenge.

LUCIANUS: Thoughts black, hands apt, drugs fit, and time agreeing;
Confederate season, else no creature seeing;
Thou mixture rank, of midnight weeds collected,
With Hecate's ban[4] thrice blasted, thrice infected,   235
Thy natural magic and dire property,
On wholesome life usurp immediately.
        [*Pours the poison into the sleeper's ear.*]

HAMLET: He poisons him i' the garden for his estate. His name's Gonzago: the story is extant, and written in very choice Italian: you shall
see anon how the murderer gets the love of Gonzago's wife.   240

OPHELIA: The king rises.

HAMLET: What, frighted with false fire![5]

QUEEN: How fares my lord?

POLONIUS: Give o'er the play.

KING: Give me some light. Away!   245

POLONIUS: Lights, lights, lights!
        [*Exeunt all but* HAMLET *and* HORATIO.]

HAMLET: Why, let the stricken deer go weep,
        The hart ungallèd play;
    For some must watch, while some must sleep:
        Thus runs the world away.   250
Would not this, sir, and a forest of feathers—if the rest of my fortunes turn Turk with me—with two Provincial roses on my razed
shoes, get me a fellowship in a cry[6] of players, sir?

HORATIO: Half a share.

HAMLET: A whole one, I.   255
    For thou dost know, O Damon dear,
        This realm dismantled was
    Of Jove himself; and now reigns here
        A very, very—pajock.

HORATIO: You might have rhymed.[7]   260

HAMLET: O good Horatio, I'll take the ghost's word for a thousand
pound. Didst perceive?

HORATIO: Very well, my lord.

HAMLET: Upon the talk of the poisoning?

HORATIO: I did very well note him.   265

HAMLET: Ah, ha! Come, some music! come, the recorders!
    For if the king like not the comedy,
        Why then, belike, he likes it not, perdy.[8]
Come, some music!
        [*Re-enter* ROSENCRANTZ *and* GUILDENSTERN.]

GUILDENSTERN: Good my lord, vouchsafe me a word with you.   270

---

3. That is, for better or for worse, as in the marriage service—but in fact you "mis-take," deceive them.
4. Goddess of witchcraft's curse. *Confederate:* favorable.   5. Blank shot.   6. Company; a term generally used with hounds. *Turk with:* betray. *Razed shoes:* sometimes worn by actors.   7. *Ass* would have
rhymed. *Pajock:* peacock.   8. By God (*per Dieu*).

HAMLET: Sir, a whole history.

GUILDENSTERN: The king, sir—

HAMLET: Aye, sir, what of him?

GUILDENSTERN: Is in his retirement marvelous distempered.

HAMLET: With drink, sir?   275

GUILDENSTERN: No, my lord, rather with choler.[9]

HAMLET: Your wisdom should show itself more richer to signify this to
the doctor; for, for me to put him to his purgation would perhaps
plunge him into far more choler.

GUILDENSTERN: Good my lord, put your discourse into some frame,   280
and start not so wildly from my affair.

HAMLET: I am tame, sir: pronounce.

GUILDENSTERN: The queen, your mother, in most great affliction of
spirit, hath sent me to you.

HAMLET: You are welcome.   285

GUILDENSTERN: Nay, good my lord, this courtesy is not of the right
breed. If it shall please you to make me a wholesome[1] answer, I will
do your mother's commandment: if not, your pardon and my return
shall be the end of my business.

HAMLET: Sir, I cannot.   290

GUILDENSTERN: What, my lord?

HAMLET: Make you a wholesome answer; my wit's diseased: but, sir,
such answer as I can make, you shall command; or rather, as you
say, my mother: therefore no more, but to the matter: my mother,
you say,—   295

ROSENCRANTZ: Then thus she says; your behavior hath struck her into
amazement and admiration.[2]

HAMLET: O wonderful son, that can so astonish a mother! But is there
no sequel at the heels of this mother's admiration? Impart.

ROSENCRANTZ: She desires to speak with you in her closet, ere you go   300
to bed.

HAMLET: We shall obey, were she ten times our mother. Have you any
further trade with us?

ROSENCRANTZ: My lord, you once did love me.

HAMLET: So I do still, by these pickers and stealers.[3]   305

ROSENCRANTZ: Good my lord, what is your cause of distemper? you do
surely bar the door upon your own liberty, if you deny your griefs to
your friend.

HAMLET: Sir, I lack advancement.[4]

ROSENCRANTZ: How can that be, when you have the voice of the king   310
himself for your succession in Denmark?

HAMLET: Aye, sir, but 'while the grass grows,'[5]—the proverb is something musty.

[Re-enter PLAYERS *with recorders.*]

O, the recorders! let me see one. To withdraw with you:—why do
you go about to recover the wind of me, as if you would drive me   315
into a toil?[6]

9. Bile, anger.   1. Sensible.   2. Confusion and surprise.   3. The hands.   4. Hamlet pretends
that the cause of his "distemper" is frustrated ambition.   5. The proverb ends: "oft starves the silly steed."
6. Snare. *Withdraw*: retire, talk in private. *Recover the wind of*: get to the windward.

GUILDENSTERN: O, my lord, if my duty be too bold, my love is too
    unmannerly.
HAMLET: I do not well understand that. Will you play upon this pipe?
GUILDENSTERN: My lord, I cannot.   320
HAMLET: I pray you.
GUILDENSTERN: Believe me, I cannot.
HAMLET: I do beseech you.
GUILDENSTERN: I know no touch of it, my lord.
HAMLET: It is as easy as lying: govern these ventages[7] with your fingers   325
    and thumb, give it breath with your mouth, and it will discourse most
    eloquent music. Look you, these are the stops.
GUILDENSTERN: But these cannot I command to any utterance of har-
    mony; I have not the skill.
HAMLET: Why, look you now, how unworthy a thing you make of me!   330
    You would play upon me; you would seem to know my stops; you
    would pluck out the heart of my mystery; you would sound me from
    my lowest note to the top of my compass: and there is much music,
    excellent voice, in this little organ; yet cannot you make it speak.
    'Sblood, do you think I am easier to be played on than a   335
    pipe? Call me what instrument you will, though you can fret[8] me,
    yet you cannot play upon me.
        [*Re-enter* POLONIUS.]
    God bless you, sir!
POLONIUS: My lord, the queen would speak with you, and presently.
HAMLET: Do you see yonder cloud that's almost in shape of a camel?   340
POLONIUS: By the mass, and 'tis like a camel, indeed.
HAMLET: Methinks it is like a weasel.
POLONIUS: It is backed like a weasel.
HAMLET: Or like a whale?
POLONIUS: Very like a whale.   345
HAMLET: Then I will come to my mother by and by. They fool me to
    the top of my bent. I will come by and by.
POLONIUS: I will say so.
        [*Exit* POLONIUS.]
HAMLET: 'By and by' is easily said. Leave me, friends.
        [*Exeunt all but* HAMLET.]
    'Tis now the very witching time of night,   350
    When churchyards yawn, and hell itself breathes out
    Contagion to this world: now could I drink hot blood,
    And do such bitter business as the day
    Would quake to look on. Soft! now to my mother.
    O heart, lose not thy nature; let not ever   355
    The soul of Nero[9] enter this firm bosom:
    Let me be cruel, not unnatural:
    I will speak daggers to her, but use none;
    My tongue and soul in this be hypocrites;
    How in my words soever she be shent,   360

---

7. Windholes.   8. Vex, with a pun on *frets*, meaning the ridges placed across the finger board of a guitar
to regulate the fingering.   9. A Roman emperor (A.D. 37–68) who murdered his mother.

To give them seals[1] never, my soul, consent!
  [*Exit.*]

SCENE 3

A room in the castle.

    [*Enter* KING, ROSENCRANTZ, *and* GUILDENSTERN.]
KING: I like him not, nor stands it safe with us
  To let his madness range. Therefore prepare you;
  I your commission will forthwith dispatch,
  And he to England shall along with you:
  The terms of our estate[2] may not endure   5
  Hazard so near us as doth hourly grow
  Out of his lunacies.
GUILDENSTERN: We will ourselves provide:
  Most holy and religious fear it is
  To keep those many many bodies safe
  That live and feed upon your majesty.   10
ROSENCRANTZ: The single and peculiar[3] life is bound
  With all the strength and armor of the mind
  To keep itself from noyance; but much more
  That spirit upon whose weal depends and rests
  The lives of many. The cease[4] of majesty   15
  Dies not alone, but like a gulf doth draw
  What 's near it with it; it is a massy wheel,
  Fixed on the summit of the highest mount,
  To whose huge spokes ten thousand lesser things
  Are mortised[5] and adjoined; which, when it falls,   20
  Each small annexment, petty consequence,
  Attends the boisterous ruin. Never alone
  Did the king sigh, but with a general groan.
KING: Arm you, I pray you, to this speedy voyage,
  For we will fetters put about this fear,   25
  Which now goes too free-footed.
ROSENCRANTZ: ⎫
GUILDENSTERN: ⎭ We will haste us.
    [*Exeunt* ROSENCRANTZ *and* GUILDENSTERN. —*Enter* POLONIUS.]
POLONIUS: My lord, he's going to his mother's closet:
  Behind the arras I'll convey myself,
  To hear the process: I'll warrant she'll tax him home:[6]   30
  And, as you said, and wisely was it said
  'Tis meet that some more audience than a mother,
  Since nature makes them partial, should o'erhear
  The speech, of vantage.[7] Fare you well, my liege:
  I'll call upon you ere you go to bed,   35
  And tell you what I know.
KING: Thanks, dear my lord.

---

1. Ratify them by action. *Shent:* reproached.   2. My position as king.   3. Individual.   4. Decease,
extinction.   5. Fastened.   6. Take him to task thoroughly.   7. From a vantage point.

[*Exit* POLONIUS.]

O, my offense is rank, it smells to heaven;
It hath the primal eldest curse[8] upon 't,
A brother's murder. Pray can I not,
Though inclination be as sharp as will: 40
My stronger guilt defeats my strong intent,
And like a man to double business bound,
I stand in pause where I shall first begin,
And both neglect. What if this cursed hand
Were thicker than itself with brother's blood,   45
Is there not rain enough in the sweet heavens
To wash it white as snow? Whereto serves mercy
But to confront the visage of offense?[9]
And what's in prayer but this twofold force,
To be forestalled ere we come to fall,   50
Or pardoned being down? Then I'll look up;
My fault is past. But O, what form of prayer
Can serve my turn? 'Forgive me my foul murder?'
That cannot be, since I am still possessed
Of those effects for which I did the murder,   55
My crown, mine own ambition and my queen.
May one be pardoned and retain the offense?[1]
In the corrupted currents of this world
Offense's gilded hand may shove by justice,
And oft 'tis seen the wicked prize itself   60
Buys out the law:[2] but 'tis not so above;
There is no shuffling, there the action lies
In his[3] true nature, and we ourselves compelled
Even to the teeth and forehead of our faults
To give in evidence. What then? what rests?[4]   65
Try what repentance can: what can it not?
Yet what can it when one can not repent?
O wretched state! O bosom black as death!
O limèd soul, that struggling to be free
Art more engaged! Help, angels! make assay![5]   70
Bow, stubborn knees, and, heart with strings of steel,
Be soft as sinews of the new-born babe!
All may be well.
            [*Retires and kneels. —Enter* HAMLET.]
HAMLET: Now might I do it pat,[6] now he is praying
And now I'll do 't: and so he goes to heaven: 75
And so am I revenged. That would be scanned;[7]
A villain kills my father; and for that,
I, his sole son, do this same villain send
To heaven.
O, this is hire and salary, not revenge.   80
He took my father grossly, full of bread,

---

8. The curse of Cain.   9. Guilt.   1. The things obtained through the offense.   2. The wealth unduly acquired is used for bribery.   3. Its.   4. What remains?   5. Make the attempt! *Limèd*: caught as with birdlime.   6. Conveniently.   7. Would have to be considered carefully.

With all his crimes broad blown, as flush as May;
And how his audit[8] stands who knows save heaven?
But in our circumstance and course of thought,
'Tis heavy with him: and am I then revenged,   85
To take him in the purging of his soul,
When he is fit and seasoned[9] for his passage?
No.
Up, sword, and know thou a more horrid hent:[1]
When he is drunk asleep, or in his rage,   90
Or, in the incestuous pleasure of his bed;
At game, a-swearing, or about some act
That has no relish of salvation in 't;
Then trip him, that his heels may kick at heaven
And that his soul may be as damned and black   95
As hell, whereto it goes. My mother stays:
This physic but prolongs thy sickly days.
    [*Exit.*]
KING: [*Rising.*] My words fly up, my thoughts remain below:
  Words without thoughts never to heaven go.
    [*Exit.*]

SCENE 4

The Queen's closet.

[*Enter* QUEEN *and* POLONIUS.]
POLONIUS: He will come straight. Look you lay home to him:
  Tell him his pranks have been too broad[2] to bear with,
  And that your grace hath screen'd and stood between
  Much heat and him. I'll sconce me even here.
  Pray you, be round[3] with him.
HAMLET: [*Within.*]   Mother, mother, mother!   5
QUEEN: I'll warrant you; fear me not. Withdraw,
  I hear him coming.
    [POLONIUS *hides behind the arras.* —*Enter* HAMLET.]
HAMLET: Now, mother, what's the matter?
QUEEN: Hamlet, thou hast thy father much offended.
HAMLET: Mother, you have my father much offended.   10
QUEEN: Come, come, you answer with an idle tongue.
HAMLET: Go, go, you question with a wicked tongue.
QUEEN: Why, how now, Hamlet!
HAMLET: What's the matter now?
QUEEN: Have you forgot me?
HAMLET: No, by the rood,[4] not so:
  You are the queen, your husband's brother's wife;   15
  And—would it were not so!—you are my mother.
QUEEN: Nay, then, I'll set those to you that can speak.
HAMLET: Come, come, and sit you down; you shall not budge:

---

8. Account. *Broad blown:* in full bloom.   9. Ripe, ready.   1. Grip.   2. Unrestrained. *Lay home:* give him a stern lesson.   3. Straightforward.   4. Cross.

You go not till I set you up a glass[5]
Where you may see the inmost part of you.   20
QUEEN: What wilt thou do? thou wilt not murder me?
    Help, help, ho!
POLONIUS: [Behind.] What, ho! help, help, help!
HAMLET: [Drawing.] How now! a rat? Dead, for a ducat, dead!
    [Makes a pass through the arras.]
POLONIUS: [Behind.] O, I am slain!
    [Falls and dies.]
QUEEN: O me, what hast thou done?   25
HAMLET: Nay, I know not: is it the king?
QUEEN: O, what a rash and bloody deed is this!
HAMLET: A bloody deed! almost as bad, good mother,
    As kill a king, and marry with his brother.
QUEEN: As kill a king!
HAMLET: Aye, lady, 'twas my word.   30
    [Lifts up the arras and discovers POLONIUS.]
    Thou wretched, rash, intruding fool, farewell!
    I took thee for thy better: take thy fortune;
    Thou find'st to be too busy[6] is some danger.
    Leave wringing of your hands: peace! sit you down,
    And let me wring your heart: for so I shall,   35
    If it be made of penetrable stuff;
    If damned custom have not brassed it so,
    That it be proof and bulwark against sense.[7]
QUEEN: What have I done, that thou darest wag thy tongue
    In noise so rude against me?
HAMLET: Such an act   40
    That blurs the grace and blush of modesty,
    Calls virtue hypocrite, takes off the rose
    From the fair forehead of an innocent love,
    And sets a blister there; makes marriage vows
    As false as dicers' oaths: O, such a deed   45
    As from the body of contraction[8] plucks
    The very soul, and sweet religion makes
    A rhapsody of words: heaven's face doth glow;[9]
    Yea, this solidity and compound mass,
    With tristful visage, as against the doom,[1]   50
    Is thought-sick at the act.
QUEEN: Aye me, what act,
    That roars so loud and thunders in the index?[2]
HAMLET: Look here, upon this picture, and on this,
    The counterfeit presentment[3] of two brothers.   55
    See what a grace was seated on this brow;
    Hyperion's curls, the front of Jove himself,
    An eye like Mars, to threaten and command;
    A station[4] like the herald Mercury

5. Mirror.   6. Too much of a busybody.   7. Feeling.   8. Duty to the marriage contract.
9. Blush with shame.   1. Doomsday. Tristful: sad.   2. Prologue, table of contents.   3. Portrait.
4. Posture.

New-lighted on a heaven-kissing hill;   60
A combination and a form indeed,
Where every god did seem to set his seal
To give the world assurance of a man:
This was your husband. Look you now, what follows:
Here is your husband; like a mildewed ear,[5]   65
Blasting his wholesome brother. Have you eyes?
Could you on this fair mountain leave to feed,
And batten[6] on this moor? Ha! have you eyes?
You cannot call it love, for at your age
The hey-day in the blood is tame, it's humble,   70
And waits upon[7] the judgment: and what judgment
Would step from this to this? Sense sure you have,
Else could you not have motion: but sure that sense
Is apoplexed: for madness would not err,
Nor sense to ecstasy was ne'er so thralled   75
But it reserved some quantity of choice,
To serve in such a difference. What devil was 't
That thus hath cozened you at hoodman-blind?[8]
Eyes without feeling, feeling without sight,
Ears without hands or eyes, smelling sans[9] all,   80
Or but a sickly part of one true sense
Could not so mope.[1]
O shame! where is thy blush? Rebellious hell,
If thou canst mutine in a matron's bones,
To flaming youth let virtue be as wax   85
And melt in her own fire: proclaim no shame
When the compulsive ardor gives the charge,[2]
Since frost itself as actively doth burn,
And reason panders[3] will.
QUEEN: O Hamlet, speak no more:
Thou turn'st mine eyes into my very soul,   90
And there I see such black and grained spots
As will not leave their tinct.[4]
HAMLET: Nay, but to live
In the rank sweat of an enseamèd[5] bed,
Stew'd in corruption, honeying and making love
Over the nasty sty,—
QUEEN: O, speak to me no more;   95
These words like daggers enter in my ears;
No more, sweet Hamlet!
HAMLET: A murderer and a villain;
A slave that is not twentieth part the tithe[6]
Of your precédent lord; a vice of kings;
A cutpurse[7] of the empire and the rule,   100
That from a shelf the precious diadem stole

---

5. Of corn.   6. Gorge, fatten. *Leave*: cease.   7. Is subordinated to.   8. Blindman's buff. *Cozened*: tricked.   9. Without.   1. Be stupid.   2. Attack.   3. Becomes subservient to.   4. Lose their color. *Grained*: dyed in.   5. Greasy.   6. Tenth.   7. Pickpocket. *Vice*: clown, from the custom in the old morality plays of having a buffoon take the part of Vice or of a particular vice.

And put it in his pocket!
QUEEN: No more!
HAMLET: A king of shreds and patches—
        [*Enter* GHOST.]
    Save me, and hover o'er me with your wings,
    You heavenly guards! What would your gracious figure?   105
QUEEN: Alas, he's mad!
HAMLET: Do you not come your tardy son to chide,
    That, lapsed in time and passion, lets go by
    The important acting of your dread command?
    O, say!
GHOST: Do not forget: this visitation   110
    Is but to whet thy almost blunted purpose.
    But look, amazement on thy mother sits:
    O, step between her and her fighting soul:
    Conceit[8] in weakest bodies strongest works:
    Speak to her, Hamlet.
HAMLET: How is it with you, lady?   115
QUEEN: Alas, how is 't with you,
    That you do bend your eye on vacancy
    And with the incorporal air do hold discourse?
    Forth at your eyes your spirits wildly peep;
    And, as the sleeping soldiers in the alarm,   120
    Your bedded hairs, like life in excrements,[9]
    Start up and stand on end. O gentle son,
    Upon the heat and flame of thy distemper
    Sprinkle cool patience. Whereon do you look?
HAMLET: On him, on him! Look you how pale he glares!   125
    His form and cause conjoined, preaching to stones,
    Would make them capable.[1] Do not look upon me,
    Lest with this piteous action you convert
    My stern effects:[2] then what I have to do
    Will want true color; tears perchance for[3] blood.   130
QUEEN: To whom do you speak this?
HAMLET: Do you see nothing there?
QUEEN: Nothing at all; yet all that is I see.
HAMLET: Nor did you nothing hear?
QUEEN: No, nothing but ourselves.
HAMLET: Why, look you there! look, how it steals away!
    My father, in his habit as he lived!   135
    Look, where he goes, even now, out at the portal!
        [*Exit* GHOST.]
QUEEN: This is the very coinage of your brain:
    This bodiless creation ecstasy
    Is very cunning in.
HAMLET: Ecstasy!
    My pulse, as yours, doth temperately keep time,   140

8. Imagination.   9. Outgrowths. *Alarm:* call to arms.   1. Of feeling.   2. You make me change my
purpose.   3. Instead of.

And makes as healthful music: it is not madness
That I have uttered: bring me to the test,
And I the matter will re-word, which madness
Would gambol from. Mother, for love of grace,
Lay not that flattering unction to your soul,   145
That not your trespass but my madness speaks:
It will but skin and film the ulcerous place,
Whiles rank corruption, mining all within,
Infects unseen. Confess yourself to heaven;
Repent what's past, avoid what is to come,   150
And do not spread the compost on the weeds,
To make them ranker. Forgive me this my virtue,
For in the fatness of these pursy⁴ times
Virtue itself of vice must pardon beg.
Yea, curb⁵ and woo for leave to do him good.   155
QUEEN: O Hamlet, thou hast cleft my heart in twain.
HAMLET: O, throw away the worser part of it,
    And live the purer with the other half.
    Good night: but go not to my uncle's bed;
    Assume a virtue, if you have it not.   160
    That monster, custom, who all sense doth eat,
    Of habits devil, is angel yet in this,
    That to the use of actions fair and good
    He likewise gives a frock or livery,
    That aptly is put on.⁶ Refrain to-night,   165
    And that shall lend a kind of easiness
    To the next abstinence; the next more easy;
    For use almost can change the stamp⁷ of nature,
    And either curb the devil, or throw him out
    With wondrous potency. Once more, good night: 170
    And when you are desirous to be blest,
    I'll blessing beg of you. For this same lord,
        [*Pointing to* POLONIUS.]
    I do repent: but heaven hath pleased it so,
    To punish me with this, and this with me,
    That I must be their scourge and minister.   175
    I will bestow⁸ him, and will answer well
    The death I gave him. So, again, good night.
    I must be cruel, only to be kind:
    Thus bad begins, and worse remains behind.
    One word more, good lady.
QUEEN: What shall I do?   180
HAMLET: Not this, by no means, that I bid you do:
    Let the bloat⁹ king tempt you again to bed;
    Pinch wanton on your cheek, call you his mouse;
    And let him, for a pair of reechy¹ kisses,
    Or paddling in your neck with his damned fingers,   185

---

4. Swollen from pampering.   5. Bow.   6. I.e., habit, although like a devil in establishing evil ways in us, is like an angel in doing the same for virtues. *Aptly:* easily.   7. Cast, form. *Use:* habit.   8. Stow away. *Minister:* agent of punishment.   9. Bloated with drink.   1. Fetid.

Make you to ravel all this matter out,
That I essentially am not in madness,
But mad in craft.[2] 'Twere good you let him know;
For who, that's but a queen, fair, sober, wise,
Would from a paddock, from a bat, a gib,   190
Such dear concernings[3] hide? who would do so?
No, in despite of sense and secrecy,
Unpeg the basket on the house's top,
Let the birds fly, and like the famous ape,[4]
To try conclusions, in the basket creep   195
And break your own neck down.
QUEEN: Be thou assured, if words be made of breath
   And breath of life, I have no life to breathe
   What thou hast said to me.
HAMLET: I must to England; you know that?
QUEEN: Alack,   200
   I had forgot: 'tis so concluded on.
HAMLET: There's letters sealed: and my two schoolfellows,
   Whom I will trust as I will adders fanged,
   They bear the mandate; they must sweep my way,
   And marshal me to knavery. Let it work;   205
   For 'tis the sport to have the enginer
   Hoist with his own petar:[5] and 't shall go hard
   But I will delve one yard below their mines,
   And blow them at the moon: I, 'tis most sweet
   When in one line two crafts directly meet.   210
   This man shall set me packing:
   I'll lug the guts into the neighbor room.
   Mother, good night. Indeed this counselor
   Is now most still, most secret and most grave,[6]
   Who was in life a foolish prating knave.   215
   Come, sir, to draw toward an end with you.
   Good night, mother.
        [*Exeunt severally;* HAMLET *dragging in* POLONIUS.]

Act IV

SCENE 1

A room in the castle.

[*Enter* KING, QUEEN, ROSENCRANTZ, *and* GUILDENSTERN.]
KING: There's matter in these sighs, these profound heaves:
   You must translate: 'tis fit we understand them.
   Where is your son?

---

2. Simulation.   3. Matters with which one is closely concerned. *Paddock:* toad. *Gib:* tomcat.   4. The ape in the unidentified animal fable to which Hamlet alludes; apparently the animal saw birds fly out of a basket and drew the conclusion that by placing himself in a basket he could fly too.   5. Petard, a variety of bomb. *Marshal:* lead. *Enginer:* military engineer. *Hoist:* blow up.   6. Hamlet is punning on the word.

QUEEN: Bestow this place on us[7] a little while.
  [*Exeunt* ROSENCRANTZ *and* GUILDENSTERN.]
 Ah, mine own lord, what have I seen to-night!   5
KING: What, Gertrude? How does Hamlet?
QUEEN: Mad as the sea and wind, when both contend
 Which is the mightier: in his lawless fit,
 Behind the arras hearing something stir,
 Whips out his rapier, cries 'A rat, a rat!'   10
 And in this brainish apprehension[8] kills
 The unseen good old man.
KING: O heavy deed!
 It had been so with us, had we been there:
 His liberty is full of threats to all,
 To you yourself, to us, to every one.   15
 Alas, how shall this bloody deed be answered?
 It will be laid to us, whose providence
 Should have kept short,[9] restrained and out of haunt,
 This mad young man: but so much was our love,
 We would not understand what was most fit,   20
 But, like the owner of a foul disease,
 To keep it from divulging, let it feed
 Even on the pith of life. Where is he gone?
QUEEN: To draw apart the body he hath killed:
 O'er whom his very madness, like some ore   25
 Among a mineral[1] of metals base,
 Shows itself pure; he weeps for what is done.
KING: O Gertrude, come away!
 The sun no sooner shall the mountains touch,
 But we will ship him hence: and this vile deed   30
 We must, with all our majesty and skill,
 Both countenance[2] and excuse. Ho, Guildenstern!
  [*Re-enter* ROSENCRANTZ *and* GUILDENSTERN.]
 Friends both, go join you with some further aid:
 Hamlet in madness hath Polonius slain,
 And from his mother's closet hath he dragged him: 35
 Go seek him out; speak fair, and bring the body
 Into the chapel. I pray you, haste in this.
  [*Exeunt* ROSENCRANTZ *and* GUILDENSTERN.]
 Come, Gertrude, we'll call up our wisest friends;
 And let them know, both what we mean to do,
 And what's untimely done. . . .[3]   40
 Whose whisper o'er the world's diameter
 As level as the cannon to his blank[4]
 Transports his poisoned shot, may miss our name
 And hit the woundless air. O, come away!
 My soul is full of discord and dismay.   45
  [*Exeunt.*]

---

7. Leave us alone. 8. Imaginary notion. 9. Under close watch. 1. Mine. *Ore:* gold. 2. Recognize. 3. This gap in the text has been guessingly filled in with "So envious slander." 4. His target.

SCENE 2

Another room in the castle.

[*Enter* HAMLET.]
HAMLET: Safely stowed.
ROSENCRANTZ: } [*Within.*] Hamlet! Lord Hamlet!
GUILDENSTERN:
HAMLET: But soft, what noise? who calls on Hamlet?
  O, here they come.
    [*Enter* ROSENCRANTZ *and* GUILDENSTERN.]
ROSENCRANTZ: What have you done, my lord, with the dead body?   5
HAMLET: Compounded[5] it with dust, whereto 'tis kin.
ROSENCRANTZ: Tell us where 'tis, that we may take it thence
  And bear it to the chapel.
HAMLET: Do not believe it.
ROSENCRANTZ: Believe what?   10
HAMLET: That I can keep your counsel and not mine own. Besides, to
  be demanded of a sponge! what replication[6] should be made by the
  son of a king?
ROSENCRANTZ: Take you me for a sponge, my lord?
HAMLET: Aye, sir; that soaks up the king's countenance,[7] his rewards,   15
  his authorities. But such officers do the king best service in the end:
  he keeps them, like an ape, in the corner of his jaw; first mouthed,
  to be last swallowed: when he needs what you have gleaned, it is but
  squeezing you, and sponge, you shall be dry again.
ROSENCRANTZ: I understand you not, my lord.   20
HAMLET: I am glad of it: a knavish speech sleeps in a foolish ear.
ROSENCRANTZ: My lord, you must tell us where the body is, and go
  with us to the king.
HAMLET: The body is with the king, but the king is not with the body.
  The king is a thing—   25
GUILDENSTERN: A thing, my lord?
HAMLET: Of nothing: bring me to him. Hide fox, and all after.[8]
    [*Exeunt.*]

SCENE 3

Another room in the castle.

[*Enter* KING, attended.]
KING: I have sent to seek him, and to find the body.
  How dangerous is it that this man goes loose!
  Yet must not we put the strong law on him:
  He's loved of the distracted multitude,
  Who like not in their judgment, but their eyes;   5
  And where 'tis so, the offender's scourge is weighed,
  But never the offense. To bear[9] all smooth and even,
  This sudden sending away must seem

---

5. Mixed.   6. Formal reply. *Demanded:* questioned by.   7. Favor.   8. A children's game.
9. Conduct. *Scourge:* punishment.

Deliberate pause: diseases desperate grown
By desperate appliance[1] are relieved,   10
Or not at all.
    [*Enter* ROSENCRANTZ.]
        How now! what hath befall'n?
ROSENCRANTZ: Where the dead body is bestowed, my lord,
  We cannot get from him.
KING: But where is he?
ROSENCRANTZ: Without, my lord; guarded, to know your pleasure.
KING: Bring him before us.   15
ROSENCRANTZ: Ho, Guildenstern! bring in my lord.
    [*Enter* HAMLET *and* GUILDENSTERN.]
KING: Now, Hamlet, where's Polonius?
HAMLET: At supper.
KING: At supper! where?
HAMLET: Not where he eats, but where he is eaten: a certain convo-   20
  cation of public worms are e'en at him. Your worm is your only
  emperor for diet:[2] we fat all creatures else to fat us, and we fat our-
  selves for maggots: your fat king and your lean beggar is but variable
  service,[3] two dishes, but to one table: that's the end.
KING: Alas, alas!   25
HAMLET: A man may fish with the worm that hath eat of a king, and
  eat of the fish that hath fed of that worm.
KING: What dost thou mean by this?
HAMLET: Nothing but to show you how a king may go a progress[4]
  through the guts of a beggar.   30
KING: Where is Polonius?
HAMLET: In heaven; send thither to see: if your messenger find him not
  there, seek him i' the other place yourself. But indeed, if you find
  him not within this month, you shall nose[5] him as you go up the
  stairs into the lobby.   35
KING: [*To some* ATTENDANTS.] Go seek him there.
HAMLET: He will stay till you come.
    [*Exeunt* ATTENDANTS.]
KING: Hamlet, this deed, for thine especial safety,
  Which we do tender,[6] as we dearly grieve
  For that which thou hast done, must send thee hence   40
  With fiery quickness: therefore prepare thyself;
  The bark is ready and the wind at help,
  The associates tend, and every thing is bent
  For England.
HAMLET: For England?
KING: Aye, Hamlet.
HAMLET: Good.
KING: So is it, if thou knew'st our purposes.   45
HAMLET: I see a cherub that sees them. But, come; for England!
  Farewell, dear mother.

---

1. Treatment. *Deliberate pause:* the result of careful argument.   2. Possibly a punning reference to the
Diet (assembly) of the Holy Roman Empire at Worms.   3. That is, the service varies, not the food.
4. Royal state journey.   5. Smell.   6. Care for.

KING: Thy loving father, Hamlet.
HAMLET: My mother: father and mother is man and wife; man and wife
    is one flesh, and so, my mother. Come, for England!   50
        [*Exit.*]
KING: Follow him at foot;[7] tempt him with speed aboard;
    Delay it not; I'll have him hence to-night:
    Away! for every thing is sealed and done
    That else leans on[8] the affair: pray you, make haste.
        [*Exeunt* ROSENCRANTZ *and* GUILDENSTERN.]
    And, England,[9] if my love thou hold'st at aught—   55
    As my great power thereof may give thee sense,
    Since yet thy cicatrice looks raw and red
    After the Danish sword, and thy free awe
    Pays homage to us—thou mayst not coldly set[1]
    Our sovereign process; which imports at full,   60
    By letters conjuring[2] to that effect,
    The present death of Hamlet. Do it, England;
    For like the hectic[3] in my blood he rages,
    And thou must cure me; till I know 'tis done,
    Howe'er my haps, my joys were ne'er begun.   65
        [*Exit.*]

SCENE 4

A plain in Denmark.

[*Enter* FORTINBRAS, *a* CAPTAIN *and* SOLDIERS, *marching.*]
FORTINBRAS: Go, captain, from me greet the Danish king;
    Tell him that by his license Fortinbras
    Craves the conveyance[4] of a promised march
    Over his kingdom. You know the rendezvous.
    If that his majesty would aught with us,   5
    We shall express our duty in his eye;[5]
    And let him know so.
CAPTAIN: I will do 't, my lord.
FORTINBRAS: Go softly on.
        [*Exeunt* FORTINBRAS *and* SOLDIERS. —*Enter* HAMLET, ROSEN-
        CRANTZ, GUILDENSTERN, *and others.*]
HAMLET: Good sir, whose powers[6] are these?
CAPTAIN: They are of Norway, sir.   10
HAMLET: How purposed, sir, I pray you?
CAPTAIN: Against some part of Poland.
HAMLET: Who commands them, sir?
CAPTAIN: The nephew to Old Norway, Fortinbras.
HAMLET: Goes it against the main[7] of Poland, sir,   15
    Or for some frontier?
CAPTAIN: Truly to speak, and with no addition,
    We go to gain a little patch of ground

---

7. At his heels.   8. Pertains to.   9. The king of England.   1. Regard with indifference.
2. Enjoining.   3. Fever.   4. Convoy.   5. Presence.   6. Armed forces.   7. The whole of.

That hath in it no profit but the name.
To pay five ducats, five, I would not farm it;   20
Nor will it yield to Norway or the Pole
A ranker rate, should it be sold in fee.[8]
HAMLET: Why, then the Polack never will defend it.
CAPTAIN: Yes, it is already garrisoned.
HAMLET: Two thousand souls and twenty thousand ducats   25
    Will not debate the question of this straw!
    This is the imposthume[9] of much wealth and peace,
    That inward breaks, and shows no cause without
    Why the man dies. I humbly thank you, sir.
CAPTAIN: God be wi' you, sir.
        [Exit.]
ROSENCRANTZ: Will 't please you go, my lord?   30
HAMLET: I'll be with you straight. Go a little before.
        [Exeunt all but HAMLET.]
    How all occasions do inform against[1] me,
    And spur my dull revenge! What is a man,
    If his chief good and market[2] of his time
    Be but to sleep and feed? a beast, no more.   35
    Sure, he that made us with such large discourse,[3]
    Looking before and after, gave us not
    That capability and god-like reason
    To fust[4] in us unused. Now, whether it be
    Bestial oblivion, or some craven scruple   40
    Of thinking too precisely on the event,[5]—
    A thought which, quartered, hath but one part wisdom
    And ever three parts coward,—I do not know
    Why yet I live to say 'this thing's to do,'
    Sith I have cause, and will, and strength, and means,   45
    To do 't. Examples gross as earth exhort me:
    Witness this army, of such mass and charge,[6]
    Led by a delicate and tender prince,
    Whose spirit with divine ambition puffed
    Makes mouths[7] at the invisible event,—   50
    Exposing what is mortal and unsure
    To all that fortune, death, and danger dare,
    Even for an egg-shell. Rightly to be great
    Is not to stir without great argument,
    But greatly to find quarrel in a straw   55
    When honor's at the stake. How stand I then,
    That have a father killed, a mother stained,
    Excitements of my reason and my blood,
    And let all sleep, while to my shame I see
    The imminent death of twenty thousand men,   60
    That for a fantasy and trick[8] of fame
    Go to their graves like beds, fight for a plot

8. For absolute possession. *Ranker:* higher.   9. Ulcer.   1. Denounce.   2. Payment for, reward.
3. Reasoning power.   4. Become moldy, taste of the cask.   5. Outcome.   6. Cost.   7. Laughs
at.   8. Trifle.

Whereon the numbers cannot try the cause,⁹
Which is not tomb enough and continent¹
To hide the slain? O, from this time forth,   65
My thoughts be bloody, or be nothing worth!
   [*Exit.*]

SCENE 5

Elsinore. A room in the castle.

[*Enter* QUEEN, HORATIO, *and a* GENTLEMAN.]
QUEEN: I will not speak with her.
GENTLEMAN: She is importunate, indeed distract:
  Her mood will needs be pitied.
QUEEN: What would she have?
GENTLEMAN: She speaks much of her father, says she hears
  There's tricks i' the world, and hems and beats her heart,   5
  Spurns enviously at straws;² speaks things in doubt,
  That carry but half sense: her speech is nothing,
  Yet the unshapèd use of it doth move
  The hearers to collection; they aim³ at it,
  And botch⁴ the words up fit to their own thoughts;   10
  Which, as her winks and nods and gestures yield them,
  Indeed would make one think there might be thought,
  Though nothing sure, yet much unhappily.
HORATIO: 'Twere good she were spoken with, for she may strew
  Dangerous conjectures in ill-breeding minds.⁵   15
QUEEN: Let her come in.
    [*Exit* GENTLEMAN.]
  [*Aside.*] To my sick soul, as sin's true nature is,
  Each toy seems prologue to some great amiss:
  So full of artless jealousy⁶ is guilt,
  It spills itself in fearing to be spilt.   20
    [*Re-enter* GENTLEMAN, *with* OPHELIA.]
OPHELIA: Where is the beauteous majesty of Denmark?
QUEEN: How now, Ophelia!
OPHELIA: [*Sings.*] How should I your true love know
          From another one?
        By his cockle hat and staff   25
        And his sandal shoon.⁷
QUEEN: Alas, sweet lady, what imports this song?
OPHELIA: Say you? nay, pray you, mark.
  [*Sings.*] He is dead and gone, lady,
        He is dead and gone;   30
      At his head a grass-green turf,
        At his heels a stone.
  Oh, oh!

9. So small that it cannot hold the men who fight for it.   1. Container.   2. Gets angry at trifles.
3. Guess. *Collection:* gathering up her words and trying to make sense of them.   4. Patch.   5. Minds
breeding evil thoughts.   6. Uncontrolled suspicion. *Toy:* trifle. *Amiss:* misfortune.   7. Shoes. These
are all typical signs of pilgrims traveling to places of devotion.

QUEEN: Nay, but Ophelia,—

OPHELIA: Pray you, mark.
  [*Sings.*] White his shroud as the mountain snow,—
    [*Enter* KING.]

QUEEN: Alas, look here, my lord.   35

OPHELIA: [*Sings.*]   Larded[8] with sweet flowers;
      Which bewept to the grave did—not—go
        With true-love showers.

KING: How do you, pretty lady?

OPHELIA: Well, God 'ild[9] you! They say the owl was a baker's daugh-   40
  ter. Lord, we know what we are, but know not what we may be.[1] God
  be at your table!

KING: Conceit upon her father.

OPHELIA: Pray you, let's have no words of this; but when they ask you
  what it means, say you this: 45
  [*Sings.*] To-morrow is Saint Valentine's day
      All in the morning betime,
    And I a maid at your window,
      To be your Valentine.
    Then up he rose, and donned his clothes,   50
      And dupped[2] the chamber-door;
    Let in the maid, that out a maid
      Never departed more.

KING: Pretty Ophelia!

OPHELIA: Indeed, la, without an oath, I'll make an end on 't: 55
  [*Sings.*] By Gis[3] and by Saint Charity,
      Alack, and fie for shame!
    Young men will do 't, if they come to 't;
      By Cock,[4] they are to blame.
    Quoth she, before you tumbled me,   60
      You promised me to wed.
  He answers:
      So would I ha' done, by yonder sun,
      An thou hadst not come to my bed.

KING: How long hath she been thus?   65

OPHELIA: I hope all will be well. We must be patient: but I cannot
  choose but weep, to think they should lay him i' the cold ground.
  My brother shall know of it: and so I thank you for your good counsel.
  Come, my coach! Good night, ladies; good night, sweet ladies; good
  night, good night.   70
    [*Exit.*]

KING: Follow her close; give her good watch, I pray you.
    [*Exit* HORATIO.]
  O, this is the poison of deep grief; it springs
  All from her father's death. O Gertrude, Gertrude,
  When sorrows come, they come not single spies,
  But in battalions! First, her father slain: 75

---

8. Garnished. 9. Yield—that is, repay. 1. An allusion to a folk tale about a baker's daughter changed
into an owl for having shown no charity to those in need. 2. Opened. 3. By Jesus. 4. Corruption
of *God*, but with a sexual undermeaning.

Next, your son gone; and he most violent author
Of his own just remove: the people muddied,[5]
Thick and unwholesome in their thoughts and whispers,
For good Polonius' death; and we have done but greenly
In hugger-mugger[6] to inter him: poor Ophelia   80
Divided from herself and her fair judgment,
Without the which we are pictures, or mere beasts:
Last, and as much containing as all these,
Her brother is in secret come from France,
Feeds on his wonder,[7] keeps himself in clouds,   85
And wants not buzzers[8] to infect his ear
With pestilent speeches of his father's death;
Wherein necessity, of matter beggared,[9]
Will nothing stick our person to arraign[1]
In ear and ear. O my dear Gertrude, this,   90
Like to a murdering-piece,[2] in many places
Gives me superfluous death.
       [A noise within.]
QUEEN: Alack, what noise is this?
KING: Where are my Switzers?[3] Let them guard the door.
      [Enter another GENTLEMAN.]
What is the matter?
GENTLEMAN: Save yourself, my lord:
The ocean, overpeering of his list,[4]   95
Eats not the flats with more impetuous haste
Than young Laertes, in a riotous head,[5]
O'erbears your officers. The rabble call him lord;
And, as the world were now but to begin,
Antiquity forgot, custom not known,   100
The ratifiers and props of every word,
They cry 'Choose we; Laertes shall be king!'
Caps, hands and tongues applaud it to the clouds,
'Laertes shall be king, Laertes king!'
QUEEN: How cheerfully on the false trail they cry!   105
  O, this is counter,[6] you false Danish dogs!
      [Noise within.]
KING: The doors are broke.
      [Enter LAERTES, armed; DANES following.]
LAERTES: Where is this king? Sirs, stand you all without.
DANES: No, let's come in.
LAERTES: I pray you, give me leave.
DANES: We will, we will.   110
      [They retire without the door.]
LAERTES: I thank you: keep the door. O thou vile king,

---

5. Confused, their thoughts made turbid (as water by mud).   6. Hasty secrecy. *Greenly:* foolishly.
7. Broods, keeps wondering.   8. Lacks not tale-bearers.   9. The necessity to build up a story without
the materials for doing so.   1. Will not hesitate to accuse me.   2. A variety of cannon that scattered
its shot in many directions.   3. Swiss guards.   4. Overflowing above the high-water mark.
5. Group of rebels.   6. Following the scent in the wrong direction.

Give me my father!

QUEEN: Calmly, good Laertes.

LAERTES: That drop of blood that's calm proclaims me bastard;
   Cries cuckold to my father; brands the harlot
   Even here, between the chaste unsmirchèd brows   115
   Of my true mother.

KING: What is the cause, Laertes,
   That thy rebellion looks so giant-like?
   Let him go, Gertrude; do not fear[7] our person:
   There's such divinity doth hedge a king,
   That treason can but peep to what it would,[8]   120
   Acts little of his[9] will. Tell me, Laertes,
   Why thou art thus incensed: let him go, Gertrude:
   Speak, man.

LAERTES: Where is my father?

KING: Dead.

QUEEN: But not by him.

KING: Let him demand his fill.   125

LAERTES: How came he dead? I'll not be juggled with:
   To hell, allegiance! vows, to the blackest devil!
   Conscience and grace, to the profoundest pit
   I dare damnation: to this point I stand,
   That both the worlds I give to negligence,[1]   130
   Let come what comes; only I'll be revenged
   Most thoroughly for my father.

KING: Who shall stay you?

LAERTES: My will, not all the world:
   And for my means, I'll husband them so well,
   They shall go far with little.

KING: Good Laertes,   135
   If you desire to know the certainty
   Of your dear father's death, is 't writ in your revenge
   That, swoopstake,[2] you will draw both friend and foe,
   Winner and loser?

LAERTES: None but his enemies.

KING: Will you know them then?   140

LAERTES: To his good friends thus wide I'll ope my arms;
   And, like the kind life-rendering pelican,[3]
   Repast them with my blood.

KING: Why, now you speak
   Like a good child and a true gentleman.
   That I am guiltless of your father's death,   145
   And am most sensibly in grief for it,
   It shall as level to your judgment pierce
   As day does to your eye.

DANES: [*Within.*]   Let her come in.

---

7. Fear for.   8. Look from a distance at what it desires.   9. Its.   1. I don't care what may happen to me in either this world or the next.   2. Without making any distinction, as the winner takes the whole stake in a card game.   3. In myth, the pelican is supposed to feed its young with its own blood.

LAERTES: How now! what noise is that?
    [*Re-enter* OPHELIA.]
  O heat, dry up my brains! tears seven times salt,   150
  Burn out the sense and virtue⁴ of mine eye!
  By heaven, thy madness shall be paid with weight,
  Till our scale turn the beam. O rose of May!
  Dear maid, kind sister, sweet Ophelia!
  O heavens! is 't possible a young maid's wits   155
  Should be as mortal as an old man's life?
  Nature is fine in love, and where 'tis fine
  It sends some precious instance⁵ of itself
  After the thing it loves.
OPHELIA: [*Sings.*] They bore him barefaced on the bier: 160
      Hey non nonny, nonny, hey nonny:
      And in his grave rained many a tear,—
  Fare you well, my dove!
LAERTES: Hadst thou thy wits, and didst persuade revenge,
  It could not move thus.   165
OPHELIA: [*Sings.*] You must sing down a-down,
      An you call him a-down-a.
  O, how the wheel becomes it! It is the false steward,⁶ that stole his
  master's daughter.
LAERTES: This nothing's more than matter.⁷   170
OPHELIA: There's rosemary, that's for remembrance: pray you, love,
  remember: and there is pansies, that's for thoughts.
LAERTES: A document⁸ in madness; thoughts and remembrance fitted.
OPHELIA: There's fennel for you, and columbines: there's rue for you:
  and here's some for me: we may call it herbs of grace o' Sundays: 175
  O, you must wear your rue with a difference. There's a daisy: I would
  give you some violets,⁹ but they withered all when my father died:
  they say he made a good end,—
  [*Sings.*] For bonnie sweet Robin is all my joy.
LAERTES: Thought and affliction, passion, hell itself,   180
  She turns to favor¹ and to prettiness.
OPHELIA: [*Sings.*] And will he not come again?
      And will he not come again?
        No, no, he is dead,
        Go to thy death-bed,   185
      He never will come again.
      His beard was as white as snow,
      All flaxen was his poll:
        He is gone, he is gone,
        And we cast away moan: 190
      God ha' mercy on his soul!
  And of all Christian souls, I pray God. God be wi' you.

---

4. Power, faculty.   5. Sample, token. *Fine:* refined.   6. An allusion (probably to a lost ballad) further expressing Ophelia's preoccupation with betrayal, lost love, and death. *How the wheel becomes it:* that is, how well the refrain fits.   7. This nonsense is more indicative than sane speech.   8. Lesson. Traditionally, flowers and herbs have symbolic meanings. Here rosemary is the symbol for remembrance and pansies symbolize thoughts.   9. Violets symbolize faithfulness. Fennel stands for flattery, columbines for cuckoldom, and rue for sorrow and repentance (compare the verb *rue*).   1. Charm.

      [*Exit.*]

LAERTES: Do you see this, O God?

KING: Laertes, I must commune with your grief,
  Or you deny me right. Go but apart,   195
  Make choice of whom your wisest friends you will.
  And they shall hear and judge 'twixt you and me:
  If by direct or by collateral hand
  They find us touched,[2] we will our kingdom give,
  Our crown, our life, and all that we call ours,   200
  To you in satisfaction; but if not,
  Be you content to lend your patience to us,
  And we shall jointly labor with your soul
  To give it due content.

LAERTES: Let this be so;
  His means of death, his obscure funeral,   205
  No trophy, sword, nor hatchment[3] o'er his bones,
  No noble rite nor formal ostentation,
  Cry to be heard, as 'twere from heaven to earth,
  That I must call 't in question.

KING: So you shall;
  And where the offense is let the great axe fall.   210
  I pray you, go with me.
      [*Exeunt.*]

SCENE 6

Another room in the castle.

    [*Enter* HORATIO *and a* SERVANT.]

HORATIO: What are they that would speak with me?

SERVANT: Sea-faring men, sir: they say they have letters for you.

HORATIO: Let them come in.
    [*Exit* SERVANT.]
  I do not know from what part of the world
  I should be greeted, if not from Lord Hamlet.   5
    [*Enter* SAILORS.]

FIRST SAILOR: God bless you, sir.

HORATIO: Let him bless thee too.

FIRST SAILOR: He shall, sir, an 't please him.
  There's a letter for you, sir; it comes from the ambassador that was
  bound for England; if your name be Horatio, as I am let to know it   10
  is.

HORATIO: [*Reads.*] 'Horatio, when thou shalt have overlooked[4] this,
  give these fellows some means to the king: they have letters for him.
  Ere we were two days old at sea, a pirate of very warlike appointment
  gave us chase. Finding ourselves too slow of sail, we put on a   15
  compelled valor, and in the grapple I boarded them: on the instant
  they got clear of our ship; so I alone became their prisoner. They

---

2. Involved (in the murder). *Collateral:* indirect.   3. Coat of arms.   4. Read over.

have dealt with me like thieves of mercy:[5] but they knew what they
did; I am to do a good turn for them. Let the king have the letters
I have sent; and repair thou to me with as much speed as thou   20
wouldst fly death. I have words to speak in thine ear will make thee
dumb; yet are they much too light for the bore[6] of the matter. These
good fellows will bring thee where I am. Rosencrantz and Guildenstern hold their course for England: of them I have much to tell
thee. Farewell.   25
        'He that thou knowest thine, HAMLET.'
Come, I will make you way for these your letters;
And do 't the speedier, that you may direct me
To him from whom you brought them.
    [*Exeunt.*]

SCENE 7

Another room in the castle.

[*Enter* KING *and* LAERTES.]
KING: Now must your conscience my acquittance seal,
    And you must put me in your heart for friend,
    Sith you have heard, and with a knowing ear,
    That he which hath your noble father slain
    Pursued my life.
LAERTES: It well appears: but tell me   5
    Why you proceeded not against these feats,
    So crimeful and so capital in nature,
    As by your safety, wisdom, all things else,
    You mainly[7] were stirred up.
KING: O, for two special reasons,
    Which may to you perhaps seem much unsinewed,[8]   10
    But yet to me they're strong. The queen his mother
    Lives almost by his looks; and for myself—
    My virtue or my plague, be it either which—
    She's so conjunctive[9] to my life and soul,
    That, as the star moves not but in his sphere,   15
    I could not but by her. The other motive,
    Why to a public count I might not go,
    Is the great love the general gender[1] bear him;
    Who, dipping all his faults in their affection,
    Would, like the spring that turneth wood to stone,   20
    Convert his gyves[2] to graces; so that my arrows,
    Too slightly timber'd for so loud a wind,
    Would have reverted to my bow again
    And not where I had aim'd them.
LAERTES: And so have I a noble father lost;   25
    A sister driven into desperate terms,
    Whose worth, if praises may go back again,

---

5. Merciful.   6. Caliber, that is, importance.   7. Powerfully.   8. Weak.   9. Closely joined.
1. Common people. *Count*: accounting, trial.   2. Leg irons (shames).

Stood challenger on mount of³ all the age
For her perfections: but my revenge will come.
KING: Break not your sleeps for that: you must not think   30
   That we are made of stuff so flat and dull
   That we can let our beard be shook with danger
   And think it pastime. You shortly shall hear more:
   I loved your father, and we love ourself;
   And that, I hope, will teach you to imagine—   35
      [*Enter a* MESSENGER, *with letters.*]
   How now! what news?
MESSENGER: Letters, my lord, from Hamlet:
   This to your majesty; this to the queen.
KING: From Hamlet! who brought them?
MESSENGER: Sailors, my lord, they say; I saw them not:
   They were given me by Claudio; he received them   40
   Of him that brought them.
KING: Laertes, you shall hear them.
   Leave us.
      [*Exit* MESSENGER.]
   [*Reads.*] 'High and mighty, you shall know I am set naked on your
   kingdom. To-morrow shall I beg leave to see your kingly eyes: when
   I shall, first asking your pardon thereunto, recount the occasion of   45
   my sudden and more strange return.   HAMLET.'
   What should this mean? Are all the rest come back?
   Or is it some abuse, and no such thing?⁴
LAERTES: Know you the hand?
KING: 'Tis Hamlet's character.⁵ 'Naked'!   50
   And in a postscript here, he says 'alone.'
   Can you advise me?
LAERTES: I'm lost in it, my lord. But let him come;
   It warms the very sickness in my heart,
   That I shall live and tell him to his teeth,   55
   'Thus diddest thou.'
KING: If it be so, Laertes,—
   As how should it be so? how otherwise?—
   Will you be ruled by me?
LAERTES: Aye, my lord;
   So you will not o'errule me to a peace.
KING: To thine own peace. If he be now returned,   60
   As checking⁶ at his voyage, and that he means
   No more to undertake it, I will work him
   To an exploit now ripe in my device,
   Under the which he shall not choose but fall:
   And for his death no wind of blame shall breathe;   65
   But even his mother shall uncharge the practice,⁷
   call it accident.
LAERTES: My lord, I will be ruled;

---

3. Above. *Go back:* to what she was before her madness.   4. A delusion, not a reality.   5. Handwriting.
6. Changing the course of, refusing to continue.   7. Not recognize it as a plot.

The rather, if you could devise it so
That I might be the organ.[8]

KING: It falls right.
You have been talked of since your travel much,   70
And that in Hamlet's hearing, for a quality
Wherein, they say, you shine; your sum of parts[9]
Did not together pluck such envy from him,
As did that one, and that in my regard
Of the unworthiest siege.[1]

LAERTES: What part is that, my lord?   75

KING: A very riband in the cap of youth,
Yet needful too; for youth no less becomes[2]
The light and careless livery that it wears
Than settled age his sables and his weeds,[3]
Importing health and graveness. Two months since   80
Here was a gentleman of Normandy:—
I've seen myself, and served against, the French,
And they can well on horseback: but this gallant
Had witchcraft in 't; he grew unto his seat,
And to such wondrous doing brought his horse   85
As had he been incorpsed and demi-natured[4]
With the brave beast: so far he topped my thought
That I, in forgery of shapes and tricks,[5]
Come short of what he did.

LAERTES: A Norman was 't?

KING: A Norman.   90

LAERTES: Upon my life, Lamord.

KING: The very same.

LAERTES: I know him well: he is the brooch[6] indeed
And gem of all the nation.

KING: He made confession of you,
And gave you such a masterly report,   95
For art and exercise in your defense,[7]
And for your rapier most especial,
That he cried out, 'twould be a sight indeed
If one could match you: the scrimers[8] of their nation,
He swore, had neither motion, guard, nor eye,   100
If you opposed them. Sir, this report of his
Did Hamlet so envenom with his envy
That he could nothing do but wish and beg
Your sudden coming o'er, to play with him.
Now, out of this—

LAERTES: What out of this, my lord?   105

KING: Laertes, was your father dear to you?
Or are you like the painting of a sorrow,
A face without a heart?

LAERTES: Why ask you this?

---

8. Instrument.   9. The sum of your gifts.   1. Seat, that is, rank.   2. Is the appropriate age for.
Riband: ribbon, ornament.   3. Furs (also meaning "blacks," dark colors) and robes.   4. Incorporated
and split his nature in two.   5. In imagining methods and skills of horsemanship.   6. Ornament.
7. Report of your mastery in the theory and practice of fencing.   8. Fencers.

KING: Not that I think you did not love your father,
    But that I know love is begun by time,   110
    And that I see, in passages of proof,[9]
    Time qualifies[1] the spark and fire of it.
    There lives within the very flame of love
    A kind of wick or snuff[2] that will abate it;
    And nothing is at a like goodness still,   115
    For goodness, growing to a plurisy,[3]
    Dies in his own too much: that we would do
    We should do when we would; for this 'would' changes
    And hath abatements and delays as many
    As there are tongues, are hands, are accidents,   120
    And then this 'should' is like a spendthrift sigh,
    That hurts by easing.[4] But, to the quick o' the ulcer:
    Hamlet comes back: what would you undertake,
    To show yourself your father's son in deed
    More than in words?
LAERTES: To cut his throat i' the church.   125
KING: No place indeed should murder sanctuarize;
    Revenge should have no bounds. But, good Laertes,
    Will you do this, keep close within your chamber.
    Hamlet returned shall know you are come home:
    We'll put on[5] those shall praise your excellence   130
    And set a double varnish on the fame
    The Frenchman gave you; bring you in fine together
    And wager on your heads: he, being remiss,[6]
    Most generous and free from all contriving,
    Will not peruse[7] the foils, so that with ease,   135
    Or with a little shuffling, you may choose
    A sword unbated, and in a pass of practice[8]
    Requite him for your father.
LAERTES: I will do 't;
    And for that purpose I'll anoint my sword.
    I bought an unction of a mountebank,[9]   140
    So mortal that but dip a knife in it,
    Where it draws blood no cataplasm so rare,
    Collected from all simples[1] that have virtue
    Under the moon, can save the thing from death
    That is but scratched withal: I'll touch my point   145
    With this contagion, that, if I gall[2] him slightly,
    It may be death.
KING: Let's further think of this;
    Weigh what convenience both of time and means
    May fit us to our shape: if this should fail,
    And that our drift look through[3] our bad performance,   150
    'Twere better not assayed: therefore this project

---

9. Instances that prove it.   1. Weakens.   2. Charred part of the wick.   3. Excess. *Still:* constantly.
4. A sigh that gives relief but is harmful (according to an old notion that it draws blood from the heart).
5. Instigate.   6. Careless. *In fine:* finally.   7. Examine closely.   8. Treacherous thrust. *Unbated:*
not blunted (as a rapier for exercise ordinarily would be).   9. Ointment of a peddler of quack medicines.
1. Healing herbs. *Cataplasm:* plaster.   2. Scratch.   3. Our design should show through. *Shape:* plan.

Should have a back or second, that might hold
If this did blast in proof.[4] Soft! let me see:
We'll make a solemn wager on your cunnings:
I ha 't: 155
When in your motion you are hot and dry—
As make your bouts more violent to that end—
And that he calls for drink, I'll have prepared him
A chalice for the nonce;[5] whereon but sipping,
If he by chance escape your venomed stuck,[6]   160
Our purpose may hold there. But stay, what noise?
      [*Enter* QUEEN.]
How now, sweet queen!
QUEEN: One woe doth tread upon another's heel,
  So fast they follow: your sister's drowned, Laertes.
LAERTES: Drowned! O, where?   165
QUEEN: There is a willow grows aslant[7] a brook,
  That shows his hoar leaves in the glassy stream;
  There with fantastic garlands did she come
  Of crow-flowers, nettles, daisies, and long purples,
  That liberal shepherds give a grosser name,   170
  But our cold maids do dead men's fingers call them:
  There, on the pendent boughs her coronet weeds
  Clambering to hang, an envious sliver[8] broke;
  When down her weedy trophies and herself
  Fell in the weeping brook. Her clothes spread wide,   175
  And mermaid-like a while they bore her up:
  Which time she chanted snatches of old tunes,
  As one incapable of[9] her own distress,
  Or like a creature native and indued[1]
  Unto that element: but long it could not be   180
  Till that her garments, heavy with their drink,
  Pulled the poor wretch from her melodious lay
  To muddy death.
LAERTES: Alas, then she is drowned!
QUEEN: Drowned, drowned.
LAERTES: Too much of water hast thou, poor Ophelia,   185
  And therefore I forbid my tears: but yet
  It is our trick;[2] nature her custom holds,
  Let shame say what it will: when these are gone,
  The woman[3] will be out. Adieu, my lord:
  I have a speech of fire that fain would blaze,   190
  But that this folly douts[4] it.
      [*Exit.*]
KING: Let's follow, Gertrude:
  How much I had to do to calm his rage!
  Now fear I this will give it start again;
  Therefore let's follow.
      [*Exeunt.*]

---

4. Burst (like a new firearm) once it is put to the test.   5. For that particular occasion.   6. Thrust.
7. Across.   8. Malicious bough.   9. Insensitive to.   1. Adapted, in harmony with.   2. Peculiar
trait.   3. The softer qualities, the woman in me.   4. Extinguishes.

Act V

SCENE 1

A churchyard.

[*Enter two* CLOWNS, *with spades, etc.*]

FIRST CLOWN: Is she to be buried in Christian burial that willfully seeks her own salvation?

SECOND CLOWN: I tell thee she is; and therefore make her grave straight: the crowner[5] hath sat on her, and finds it Christian burial.

FIRST CLOWN: How can that be, unless she drowned herself in her own defense?

SECOND CLOWN: Why, 'tis found so.

FIRST CLOWN: It must be 'se offendendo;'[6] it cannot be else. For here lies the point: if I drown myself wittingly, it argues an act: and an act hath three branches; it is, to act, to do, to perform: argal,[7] she drowned herself wittingly.

SECOND CLOWN: Nay, but hear you, goodman delver.

FIRST CLOWN: Give me leave. Here lies the water; good: here stands the man; good: if the man go to this water and drown himself, it is, will he, nill he,[8] he goes; mark you that; but if the water come to him and drown him, he drowns not himself: argal, he that is not guilty of his own death shortens not his own life.

SECOND CLOWN: But is this law?

FIRST CLOWN: Aye, marry, is 't; crowner's quest[9] law.

SECOND CLOWN: Will you ha' the truth on 't? If this had not been a gentlewoman, she should have been buried out o' Christian burial.

FIRST CLOWN: Why, there thou say'st: and the more pity that great folk should have countenance[1] in this world to drown or hang themselves, more than their even[2] Christian. Come, my spade. There is no ancient gentlemen but gardeners, ditchers and gravemakers: they hold up Adam's profession.

SECOND CLOWN: Was he a gentleman?

FIRST CLOWN: A' was the first that ever bore arms.

SECOND CLOWN: Why, he had none.

FIRST CLOWN: What, art a heathen? How dost thou understand the Scripture? The Scripture says Adam digged: could he dig without arms? I'll put another question to thee: if thou answerest me not to the purpose, confess thyself—

SECOND CLOWN: Go to.

FIRST CLOWN: What is he that builds stronger than either the mason, the shipwright, or the carpenter?

SECOND CLOWN: The gallows-maker; for that frame outlives a thousand tenants.

FIRST CLOWN: I like thy wit well, in good faith: the gallows does well; but how does it well? it does well to those that do ill: now, thou dost ill to say the gallows is built stronger than the church: argal, the gallows may do well to thee. To 't again, come.

---

5. Coroner. *Straight:* right away.   6. The Clown's blunder for *se defendendo:* "in self-defense" (Latin).
7. Blunder for *ergo:* "therefore" (Latin).   8. Willy-nilly.   9. Inquest.   1. Sanction.   2. Fellow.

SECOND CLOWN: 'Who builds stronger than a mason, a shipwright, or a carpenter?'

FIRST CLOWN: Aye, tell me that, and unyoke.[3]   45

SECOND CLOWN: Marry, now I can tell.

FIRST CLOWN: To 't.

SECOND CLOWN: Mass, I cannot tell.

[*Enter* HAMLET *and* HORATIO, *afar off.*]

FIRST CLOWN: Cudgel thy brains no more about it, for your dull ass will
   not mend his pace with beating, and when you are asked this   50
   question next, say 'a grave-maker:' the houses that he makes last till
   doomsday. Go, get thee to Yaughan; fetch me a stoup[4] of liquor.

[*Exit* SECOND CLOWN. —FIRST CLOWN *digs and sings.*]
       In youth, when I did love, did love,
           Methought it was very sweet,
       To contract, O, the time, for-a my behove,   55
           O, methought, there-a was nothing-a meet.[5]

HAMLET: Has this fellow no feeling of his business that he sings at
   grave-making?

HORATIO: Custom hath made it in him a property of easiness.[6]

HAMLET: 'Tis e'en so: the hand of little employment hath the daintier[7]   60
   sense.

FIRST CLOWN: [*Sings.*] But age, with his stealing steps,
               Hath clowed me in his clutch,
               And hath shipped me intil[8] the land,
               As if I had never been such.   65

[*Throws up a skull.*]

HAMLET: That skull had a tongue in it, and could sing once: how the
   knave jowls it to the ground, as if it were Cain's jaw-bone, that did
   the first murder! It might be the pate of a politician,[9] which this ass
   now o'er-reaches;[1] one that would circumvent God, might it not?

HORATIO: It might, my lord.   70

HAMLET: Or of a courtier, which could say, 'Good morrow, sweet lord!
   How dost thou, sweet lord?' This might be my lord such-a-one, that
   praised my lord such-a-one's horse, when he meant to beg it; might
   it not?

HORATIO: Aye, my lord.   75

HAMLET: Why, e'en so: and now my Lady Worm's; chapless, and
   knocked about the mazzard[2] with a sexton's spade: here's fine revolution, an we had the trick to see 't. Did these bones cost no more
   the breeding, but to play at loggats[3] with 'em? mine ache to think
   on 't.   80

FIRST CLOWN: [*Sings.*] A pick-axe, and a spade, a spade,
               For a shrouding sheet:
               O, a pit of clay for to be made
               For such a guest is meet.

---

3. Call it a day.   4. Mug. *Yaughan:* apparently a tavern keeper's name.   5. Fitting. *Contract:* shorten.
Behove: profit.   6. Has made it a matter of indifference to him.   7. Finer sensitivity. *Of little employment:* that does little labor.   8. Into.   9. In a pejorative sense. *Jowls:* knocks. *First murder:* possibly an
allusion to the legend that Cain slew Abel with an ass's jawbone.   1. Outwits.   2. Pate. *Chapless:* the
lower jawbone missing.   3. A game resembling bowls. *Trick:* faculty.

[*Throws up another skull.*]

HAMLET: There's another: why may not that be the skull of a lawyer?   85
Where be his quiddities now, his quillets, his cases, his tenures,[4] and
his tricks? why does he suffer this rude knave now to knock him
about the sconce with a dirty shovel, and will not tell him of his
action of battery?[5] Hum! This fellow might be in 's time a great buyer
of land, with his statutes, his recognizances,[6] his fines, his   90
double vouchers, his recoveries: is this the fine[7] of his fines and the
recovery of his recoveries, to have his fine pate full of fine dirt? will
his vouchers vouch him no more of his purchases, and double ones
too, than the length and breadth of a pair of indentures? The very
conveyances[8] of his lands will hardly lie in this box; and must the   95
inheritor himself have no more, ha?

HORATIO: Not a jot more, my lord.

HAMLET: Is not parchment made of sheep-skins?

HORATIO: Aye, my lord, and of calf-skins too.

HAMLET: They are sheep and calves which seek out assurance[9] in that.   100
I will speak to this fellow. Whose grave's this, sirrah?

FIRST CLOWN: Mine, sir.

[*Sings.*]   O, a pit of clay for to be made
                For such a guest is meet.

HAMLET: I think it be thine indeed, for thou liest in 't.   105

FIRST CLOWN: You lie out on 't, sir, and therefore 'tis not yours: for my
part, I do not lie in 't, and yet it is mine.

HAMLET: Thou dost lie in 't, to be in 't and say it is thine: 'tis for the
dead, not for the quick;[1] therefore thou liest.

FIRST CLOWN: 'Tis a quick lie, sir; 'twill away again, from me to you.   110

HAMLET: What man dost thou dig it for?

FIRST CLOWN: For no man, sir.

HAMLET: What woman then?

FIRST CLOWN: For none neither.

HAMLET: Who is to be buried in 't?   115

FIRST CLOWN: One that was a woman, sir; but, rest her soul, she's dead.

HAMLET: How absolute the knave is! we must speak by the card,[2] or
equivocation will undo us. By the Lord, Horatio, these three years I
have taken note of it; the age is grown so picked[3] that the toe of   120
the peasant comes so near the heel of the courtier, he galls his kibe.[4]
How long hast thou been a grave-maker?

FIRST CLOWN: Of all the days i' the year, I came to 't that day that our
last King Hamlet o'ercame Fortinbras.

HAMLET: How long is that since?   125

FIRST CLOWN: Cannot you tell that? every fool can tell that: it was that
very day that young Hamlet was born: he that is mad, and sent into
England.

HAMLET: Aye, marry, why was he sent into England?

---

4. Real estate holdings. *Quiddities:* subtle definitions. *Quillets:* quibbles.   5. Assault. *Sconce:* head.
6. Varieties of bonds. This passage contains legal terms relating to the transfer of estates.   7. End.
Hamlet is punning on the legal and nonlegal meanings of the word.   8. Deeds. *Indentures:* contracts
drawn in duplicate on the same piece of parchment; the two copies were separated by an indented line.
9. Security; another pun, because the word is also a legal term.   1. Living.   2. By the chart, that is,
exactness. *Absolute:* positive.   3. Choice, fastidious.   4. Hurts the chilblain on the courtier's heel.

FIRST CLOWN: Why, because a' was mad; a' shall recover his wits there: 130
or, if a' do not, 'tis no great matter there.

HAMLET: Why?

FIRST CLOWN: 'Twill not be seen in him there; there the men are as
mad as he.

HAMLET: How came he mad? 135

FIRST CLOWN: Very strangely, they say.

HAMLET: How 'strangely'?

FIRST CLOWN: Faith, e'en with losing his wits.

HAMLET: Upon what ground?

FIRST CLOWN: Why, here in Denmark: I have been sexton here, man 140
and boy, thirty years.

HAMLET: How long will a man lie i' the earth ere he rot?

FIRST CLOWN: I' faith, if a' be not rotten before a' die—as we have
many pocky corses now-a-days, that will scarce hold the laying in[5]—
a' will last you some eight year or nine year: a tanner will last you 145
nine year.

HAMLET: Why he more than another?

FIRST CLOWN: Why, sir, his hide is so tanned with his trade that a' will
keep out water a great while; and your water is a sore decayer of
your whoreson dead body. Here's a skull now: this skull has lain in 150
the earth three and twenty years.

HAMLET: Whose was it?

FIRST CLOWN: A whoreson mad fellow's it was: whose do you think it
was?

HAMLET: Nay, I know not. 155

FIRST CLOWN: A pestilence on him for a mad rogue! a' poured a flagon
of Rhenish on my head once. This same skull, sir, was Yorick's skull,
the king's jester.

HAMLET: This?

FIRST CLOWN: E'en that. 160

HAMLET: Let me see. [*Takes the skull.*] Alas, poor Yorick! I knew him,
Horatio: a fellow of infinite jest, of most excellent fancy: he hath
borne me on his back a thousand times; and now how abhorred in
my imagination it is! my gorge rises at it. Here hung those lips that
I have kissed I know not how oft. Where be your gibes now? your 165
gambols? your songs? your flashes of merriment, that were wont to
set the table on a roar? Not one now, to mock your own grinning?
quite chop-fallen?[6] Now get you to my lady's chamber, and tell her,
let her paint an inch thick, to this favor[7] she must come; make her
laugh at that. Prithee, Horatio, tell me one thing. 170

HORATIO: What's that, my lord?

HAMLET: Dost thou think Alexander looked o' this fashion i' the earth?

HORATIO: E'en so.

HAMLET: And smelt so? pah!
[*Puts down the skull.*]

HORATIO: E'en so, my lord. 175

---

5. Hold together till they are buried. *Pocky:* with marks of disease (from "pox"). 6. The lower jaw fallen
down, hence dejected. 7. Appearance.

HAMLET: To what base uses we may return, Horatio! Why may not
    imagination trace the noble dust of Alexander, till he find it stopping
    a bung-hole?

HORATIO: 'Twere to consider too curiously, to consider so.

HAMLET: No, faith, not a jot; but to follow him thither with modesty   180
    enough[8] and likelihood to lead it: as thus: Alexander died, Alexander
    was buried, Alexander returneth into dust; the dust is earth; of earth
    we make loam; and why of that loam, whereto he was converted,
    might they not stop a beer-barrel?

        Imperious Caesar, dead and turned to clay,   185
        Might stop a hole to keep the wind away:
        O, that that earth, which kept the world in awe,
        Should patch a wall to expel the winter's flaw!
    But soft! but soft! aside: here comes the king.

        [*Enter* PRIESTS *etc., in procession; the Corpse of Ophelia,* LAERTES
        and MOURNERS *following;* KING, QUEEN, *their trains, etc.*]

    The queen, the courtiers: who is this they follow?   190
    And with such maimèd rites?[9] This doth betoken
    The corse they follow did with desperate hand
    Fordo its own life: 'twas of some estate.[1]
    Couch we awhile, and mark.
        [*Retiring with* HORATIO.]

LAERTES: What ceremony else?   195

HAMLET: That is Laertes, a very noble youth: mark.

LAERTES: What ceremony else?

FIRST PRIEST: Her obsequies have been as far enlarged
    As we have warranty: her death was doubtful;
    And, but that great command o'ersways the order[2]   200
    She should in ground unsanctified have lodged
    Till the last trumpet; for[3] charitable prayers,
    Shards, flints and pebbles should be thrown on her:
    Yet here she is allowed her virgin crants,
    Her maiden strewments and the bringing home[4]   205
    Of bell and burial.

LAERTES: Must there no more be done?

FIRST PRIEST: No more be done:
    We should profane the service of the dead
    To sing a requiem and such rest to her
    As to peace-parted souls.

LAERTES: Lay her i' the earth: 210
    And from her fair and unpolluted flesh
    May violets spring! I tell thee, churlish priest,
    A ministering angel shall my sister be,
    When thou liest howling.

HAMLET: What, the fair Ophelia!

QUEEN: [*Scattering flowers.*] Sweets to the sweet: farewell!   215
    I hoped thou shouldst have been my Hamlet's wife;

---

8. Without exaggeration.   9. Incomplete, mutilated ritual.   1. Rank. *Fordo:* destroy.   2. The
king's command prevails against ordinary rules. *Doubtful:* of uncertain cause (that is, accident or suicide).   3. Instead of.   4. Laying to rest. *Crants:* garlands. *Strewments:* strews the grave with flowers.

I thought thy bride-bed to have decked, sweet maid,
And not have strewed thy grave.
LAERTES: O, treble woe
Fall ten times treble on that cursed head
Whose wicked deed thy most ingenious sense   220
Deprived thee of! Hold off the earth a while,
Till I have caught her once more in mine arms.
        [*Leaps into the grave.*]
Now pile your dust upon the quick and dead,
Till of this flat a mountain you have made
To o'ertop old Pelion⁵ or the skyish head   225
Of blue Olympus.
HAMLET: [*Advancing.*] What is he whose grief
Bears such an emphasis? whose phrase of sorrow
Conjures the wandering stars and makes them stand
Like wonder-wounded hearers? This is I,   230
Hamlet the Dane.
        [*Leaps into the grave.*]
LAERTES: The devil take thy soul!
        [*Grappling with him.*]
HAMLET: Thou pray'st not well.
I prithee, take thy fingers from my throat;
For, though I am not splenitive⁶ and rash,
Yet have I in me something dangerous,   235
Which let thy wisdom fear. Hold off thy hand.
KING: Pluck them asunder.
QUEEN: Hamlet, Hamlet!
ALL: Gentlemen,—
HORATIO: Good my lord, be quiet.
        [*The* ATTENDANTS *part them, and they come out of the grave.*]
HAMLET: Why, I will fight with him upon this theme
Until my eyelids will no longer wag.   240
QUEEN: O my son, what theme?
HAMLET: I loved Ophelia: forty thousand brothers
Could not, with all their quantity of love,
Make up my sum. What wilt thou do for her?
KING: O, he is mad, Laertes.   245
QUEEN: For love of God, forbear him.
HAMLET: 'Swounds, show me what thou 'lt do:
Woo't weep? woo't fight? woo't fast? woo't tear thyself?
Woo't drink up eisel?⁷ eat a crocodile?
I'll do't. Dost thou come here to whine?   250
To outface me with leaping in her grave?
Be buried quick with her, and so will I:
And, if thou prate of mountains, let them throw
Millions of acres on us, till our ground,
Singeing his pate against the burning zone,   255

---

5. The mountain on which the Aloadae, two rebellious giants in Greek mythology, piled up Mount Ossa in their attempt to reach Olympus.   6. Easily moved to anger.   7. Vinegar (the bitter drink given to Christ). *Woo't:* wilt thou.

Make Ossa like a wart! Nay, an thou 'lt mouth,
   I'll rant as well as thou.
QUEEN: This is mere madness:
   And thus a while the fit will work on him;
   Anon, as patient as the female dove
   When that her golden couplets are disclosed,[8]   260
   His silence will sit drooping.
HAMLET: Hear you, sir;
   What is the reason that you use me thus?
   I loved you ever: but it is no matter;
   Let Hercules himself do what he may,
   The cat will mew, and dog will have his day.   265
      [Exit.]
KING: I pray thee, good Horatio, wait upon him.
      [Exit HORATIO.]
   [To LAERTES.] Strengthen your patience in our last night's speech;
   We'll put the matter to the present push.[9]
   Good Gertrude, set some watch over your son.
   This grave shall have a living monument: 270
   An hour of quiet shortly shall we see;
   Till then, in patience our proceeding be.
      [Exeunt.]

SCENE 2

A hall in the castle.

[Enter HAMLET and HORATIO.]
HAMLET: So much for this, sir: now shall you see the other;
   You do remember all the circumstance?
HORATIO: Remember it, my lord?
HAMLET: Sir, in my heart there was a kind of fighting,
   That would not let me sleep: methought I lay   5
   Worse than the mutines in the bilboes.[1] Rashly,
   And praised be rashness for it, let us know,
   Our indiscretion sometime serves us well
   When our deep plots do pall;[2] and that should learn us
   There's a divinity that shapes our ends,   10
   Rough-hew them how we will.
HORATIO: That is most certain.
HAMLET: Up from my cabin,
   My sea-gown scarfed about me, in the dark
   Groped I to find out them; had my desire,
   Fingered their packet, and in fine withdrew   15
   To mine own room again; making so bold,
   My fears forgetting manners, to unseal
   Their grand commission; where I found, Horatio,—
   O royal knavery!—an exact command,

8. Twins are hatched.   9. We'll push the matter on immediately.   1. Mutineers in iron fetters.
2. Become useless.

Larded with many several sorts of reasons,   20
Importing[3] Denmark's health and England's too,
With, ho! such bugs and goblins in my life,
That, on the supervise, no leisure bated,[4]
No, not to stay the grinding of the axe,
My head should be struck off.
HORATIO: Is't possible?   25
HAMLET: Here's the commission: read it at more leisure.
      But wilt thou hear now how I did proceed?
HORATIO: I beseech you.
HAMLET: Being thus be-netted round with villainies,—
      Ere I could make a prologue to my brains,   30
      They had begun the play,—I sat me down;
      Devised a new commission; wrote it fair:
      I once did hold it, as our statists[5] do,
      A baseness to write fair, and labored much
      How to forget that learning; but, sir, now   35
      It did me yeoman's service:[6] wilt thou know
      The effect of what I wrote?
HORATIO: Aye, good my lord.
HAMLET: An earnest conjuration from the king,
      As England was his faithful tributary,
      As love between them like the palm might flourish,   40
      As peace should still her wheaten garland wear
      And stand a comma[7] 'tween their amities,
      And many such-like 'As'es of great charge,[8]
      That, on the view and knowing of these contents,
      Without debatement further, more or less,   45
      He should the bearers put to sudden death,
      Not shriving-time[9] allowed.
HORATIO: How was this sealed?
HAMLET: Why, even in that was heaven ordinant.[1]
      I had my father's signet in my purse,
      Which was the model of that Danish seal: 50
      Folded the writ up in the form of the other;
      Subscribed it; gave 't the impression;[2] placed it safely,
      The changeling never known. Now, the next day
      Was our sea-fight; and what to this was sequent
      Thou know'st already.   55
HORATIO: So Guildenstern and Rosencrantz go to 't.
HAMLET: Why, man, they did make love to this employment;
      They are not near my conscience; their defeat
      Does by their own insinuation[3] grow:
      'Tis dangerous when the baser nature comes   60
      Between the pass and fell[4]-incensèd points

---

3. Concerning.   4. As soon as the message was read, with no time subtracted for leisure. *Bugs:* imaginary
horrors to be expected if I lived.   5. Statesmen.   6. Excellent service.   7. Connecting element.
8. *As'es:* a pun on *as* and *ass*, which extends to *of great charge*, signifying both "moral weight" and "ass's
burden."   9. Time for confession and absolution.   1. Ordaining.   2. Of the seal.   3. Meddling.
Defeat: destruction.   4. Fiercely. *Baser:* lower in rank than the king and Prince Hamlet. *Pass:* thrust.

Of mighty opposites.
HORATIO: Why, what a king is this!
HAMLET: Does it not, think'st thee, stand me now upon⁵—
  He that hath killed my king, and whored my mother;
  Popped in between the election and my hopes;   65
  Thrown out his angle for my proper life,⁶
  And with such cozenage—is't not perfect conscience,
  To quit⁷ him with this arm? and is't not to be damned,
  To let this canker of our nature come
  In further evil?   70
HORATIO: It must be shortly known to him from England
  What is the issue of the business there.
HAMLET: It will be short: the interim is mine;
  And a man's life's no more than to say 'One.'
  But I am very sorry, good Horatio,   75
  That to Laertes I forgot myself;
  For, by the image of my cause, I see
  The portraiture of his: I'll court his favors:
  But, sure, the bravery⁸ of his grief did put me
  Into a towering passion.
HORATIO: Peace! who comes here?   80
        [Enter OSRIC.]
OSRIC: Your lordship is right welcome back to Denmark.
HAMLET: I humbly thank you, sir. Dost know this waterfly?
HORATIO: No, my good lord.
HAMLET: Thy state is the more gracious, for 'tis a vice to know him. He
  hath much land, and fertile: let a beast be lord of beasts, and   85
  his crib shall stand at the king's mess: 'tis a chough,⁹ but, as I say,
  spacious in the possession of dirt.
OSRIC: Sweet lord, if your lordship were at leisure, I should impart a
  thing to you from his majesty.
HAMLET: I will receive it, sir, with all diligence of spirit. Put your   90
  bonnet to his right use; 'tis for the head.
OSRIC: I thank your lordship, it is very hot.
HAMLET: No, believe me, 'tis very cold; the wind is northerly.
OSRIC: It is indifferent¹ cold, my lord, indeed.
HAMLET: But yet methinks it is very sultry and hot, or my complex-   95
  ion—
OSRIC: Exceedingly, my lord; it is very sultry, as 'twere,—I cannot tell
  how. But, my lord, his majesty bade me signify to you that he has
  laid a great wager on your head: sir, this is the matter—
HAMLET: I beseech you, remember—   100
        [HAMLET moves him to put on his hat.]
OSRIC: Nay, good my lord; for mine ease, in good faith. Sir, here is
  newly come to court Laertes; believe me, an absolute gentleman, full
  of most excellent differences, of very soft society and great showing:²
  indeed, to speak feelingly of him, he is the card or calendar of

5. Is it not my duty now?   6. An angling line for my own life.   7. Pay back.   8. Ostentation, bravado.   9. Jackdaw. *Mess*: table.   1. Fairly.   2. Agreeable company, handsome in appearance. *Differences*: distinctions.

gentry,[3] for you shall find in him the continent of what part[4]   105
a gentleman would see.

HAMLET: Sir, his definement suffers no perdition in you; though, I
know, to divide him inventorially would dizzy the arithmetic[5] of
memory, and yet but yaw neither, in respect of his quick sail.[6] But
in the verity of extolment, I take him to be a soul of great article,   110
and his infusion[7] of such dearth and rareness, as, to make true diction of him, his semblable is his mirror, and who else would trace
him, his umbrage,[8] nothing more.

OSRIC: Your lordship speaks most infallibly of him.

HAMLET: The concernancy, sir? why do we wrap the gentleman[9] in   115
our more rawer breath?

OSRIC: Sir?

HORATIO: Is 't not possible to understand in another tongue?[1] You will
do 't, sir, really.

HAMLET: What imports the nomination of this gentleman?   120

OSRIC: Of Laertes?

HORATIO: His purse is empty already; all's golden words are spent.

HAMLET: Of him, sir.

OSRIC: I know you are not ignorant—

HAMLET: I would you did, sir; yet, in faith, if you did, it would not   125
much approve me.[2] Well, sir?

OSRIC: You are not ignorant of what excellence Laertes is—

HAMLET: I dare not confess that, lest I should compare with him in
excellence; but, to know a man well, were to know himself.[3]

OSRIC: I mean, sir, for his weapon; but in the imputation laid on him   130
by them, in his meed he's unfellowed.[4]

HAMLET: What's his weapon?

OSRIC: Rapier and dagger.

HAMLET: That's two of his weapons: but, well.

OSRIC: The king, sir, hath wagered with him six Barbary horses: against   135
the which he has imponed, as I take it, six French rapiers and pon-
iards, with their assigns,[5] as girdle, hanger, and so: three of the
carriages, in faith, are very dear to fancy, very responsive[6] to the
hilts, most delicate carriages, and of very liberal conceit.[7]

HAMLET: What call you the carriages?   140

HORATIO: I knew you must be edified by the margent[8] ere you had
done.

OSRIC: The carriages, sir, are the hangers.

HAMLET: The phrase would be more germane to the matter if we could
carry a cannon by our sides:[9] I would it might be hangers till then.   145

---

3. Chart and model of gentlemanly manners.   4. Whatever quality. *Continent:* container.   5. Arithmetical power. *Definement:* definition. *Perdition:* loss. *Inventorially:* make an inventory of his virtues.
6. And yet would only be able to steer unsteadily (unable to catch up with the *sail* of Laertes's virtues).
7. The virtues infused into him. *Verify of extolment:* to prize Laertes truthfully. *Article:* importance.
8. Keep pace with him, his shadow.   9. Laertes. *Concernancy:* meaning.   1. In a less affected jargon
or in the same jargon when spoken by another (that is, Hamlet's) tongue.   2. Be to my credit.   3. To
know others one has to know oneself.   4. In the reputation given him by his weapons, his merit is
unparalleled.   5. Appendages. *Imponed:* wagered.   6. Closely matched. *Carriages:* ornamented straps
by which the rapiers hung from the belt. *Very dear to fancy:* agreeable to the taste.   7. Elegant design.
8. Instructed by the marginal note.   9. Hamlet is playfully criticizing Osric's affected application of the
term *carriage,* more properly used to mean "gun carriage."

But, on: six Barbary horses against six French swords, their assigns, and three liberal-conceited carriages; that's the French bet against the Danish. Why is this 'imponed,' as you call it?

OSRIC: The king, sir, hath laid, sir, that in a dozen passes between yourself and him, he shall not exceed you three hits: he hath laid on twelve for nine; and it would come to immediate trial, if your lordship would vouchsafe the answer.[1]

HAMLET: How if I answer 'no'?

OSRIC: I mean, my lord, the opposition of your person in trial.

HAMLET: Sir, I will walk here in the hall: if it please his majesty, it is the breathing time[2] of day with me; let the foils be brought, the gentleman willing, and the king hold his purpose, I will win for him an I can; if not, I will gain nothing but my shame and the odd hits.

OSRIC: Shall I redeliver you e'en so?[3]

HAMLET: To this effect, sir, after what flourish your nature will.

OSRIC: I commend my duty to your lordship.

HAMLET: Yours, yours. [*Exit* OSRIC.] He does well to commend it himself; there are no tongues else for's turn.

HORATIO: This lapwing[4] runs away with the shell on his head.

HAMLET: He did comply with his dug before he sucked it. Thus has he—and many more of the same breed that I know the drossy[5] age dotes on—only got the tune of the time and outward habit of encounter; a kind of yesty[6] collection, which carries them through and through the most fond and winnowed opinions;[7] and do but blow them to their trial, the bubbles are out.

[*Enter a* LORD.]

LORD: My lord, his majesty commended him[8] to you by young Osric, who brings back to him, that you attend him in the hall: he sends to know if your pleasure hold to play with Laertes, or that you will take longer time.

HAMLET: I am constant to my purposes; they follow the king's pleasure: if his fitness speaks, mine is ready; now or whensoever, provided I be so able as now.

LORD: The king and queen and all are coming down.

HAMLET: In happy time.

LORD: The queen desires you to use some gentle entertainment[9] to Laertes before you fall to play.

HAMLET: She well instructs me.

[*Exit* LORD.]

HORATIO: You will lose this wager, my lord.

HAMLET: I do not think so; since he went into France, I have been in continual practice; I shall win at the odds. But thou wouldst not think how ill all's here about my heart: but it is no matter.

HORATIO: Nay, good my lord,—

HAMLET: It is but foolery; but it is such a kind of gaingiving[1] as would perhaps trouble a woman.

---

1. The terms of this wager have never been satisfactorily clarified.   2. Time for exercise.   3. Is that the reply you want me to carry back?   4. A bird supposedly able to run as soon as it is out of its shell. 5. Degenerate. *Comply*: use ceremony.   6. Frothy.   7. Makes them pass the test of the most refined judgment.   8. Sent his regards.   9. Kind word of greeting.   1. Misgiving.

HORATIO: If your mind dislike anything, obey it. I will forestall their
    repair[2] hither, and say you are not fit.
HAMLET: Not a whit; we defy augury: there is special providence in the
    fall of a sparrow. If it be now, 'tis not to come; if it be not to come,
    it will be now; if it be not now, yet it will come: the readiness is   195
    all; since no man has aught of what he leaves, what is't to leave
    betimes?[3] Let be.
        [*Enter* KING, QUEEN, LAERTES, *and* LORDS, OSRIC *and other* ATTEN-
        DANTS *with foils and gauntlets; a table and flagons of wine on it.*]
KING: Come, Hamlet, come, and take this hand from me.
        [*The* KING *puts* LAERTES' *hand into* HAMLET's.]
HAMLET: Give me your pardon, sir: I've done you wrong;
    But pardon't, as you are a gentleman.   200
    This presence[4] knows,
    And you must needs have heard, how I am punished
    With sore distraction. What I have done,
    That might your nature, honor and exception[5]
    Roughly awake, I here proclaim was madness.   205
    Was't Hamlet wronged Laertes? Never Hamlet:
    If Hamlet from himself be ta'en away,
    And when he's not himself does wrong Laertes,
    Then Hamlet does it not, Hamlet denies it.
    Who does it then? His madness: if't be so,   210
    Hamlet is of the faction that is wronged;
    His madness is poor Hamlet's enemy.
    Sir, in this audience,
    Let my disclaiming from a purposed evil
    Free me so far in your most generous thoughts,   215
    That I have shot mine arrow o'er the house,
    And hurt my brother.
LAERTES: I am satisfied in nature,
    Whose motive, in this case, should stir me most
    To my revenge: but in my terms of honor[6]
    I stand aloof, and will no reconcilement,   220
    Till by some elder masters of known honor
    I have a voice and precedent of peace,
    To keep my name ungored.[7] But till that time
    I do receive your offered love like love
    And will not wrong it.
HAMLET: I embrace it freely,   225
    And will this brother's wager frankly play.
    Give us the foils. Come on.
LAERTES: Come, one for me.
HAMLET: I'll be your foil,[8] Laertes: in mine ignorance
    Your skill shall, like a star i' the darkest night,

2. Coming.   3. What is wrong with dying early (leaving *betimes*), because man knows nothing of life (*what he leaves*)?   4. Audience.   5. Objection.   6. Laertes answers separately each of the two points brought up by Hamlet in line 86. *Nature* is Laertes's natural feeling toward his father. *Honor* is the code of honor with its conventional rules.   7. Unwounded. *A voice and:* an opinion based on.   8. A pun, because *foil* means both "rapier" and "a thing that sets off another to advantage" (as gold leaf under a jewel).

Stick fiery off⁹ indeed.

LAERTES: You mock me, sir.   230

HAMLET: No, by this hand.

KING: Give them the foils, young Osric. Cousin Hamlet,
   You know the wager?

HAMLET: Very well, my lord;
   Your grace has laid the odds o' the weaker side.

KING: I do not fear it; I have seen you both: 235
   But since he is bettered, we have therefore odds.

LAERTES: This is too heavy; let me see another.

HAMLET: This likes me well. These foils have all a length?
       [*They prepare to play.*]

OSRIC: Aye, my good lord.

KING: Set me the stoups¹ of wine upon that table.   240
   If Hamlet give the first or second hit,
   Or quit in answer of the third exchange,²
   Let all the battlements their ordnance fire;
   The king shall drink to Hamlet's better breath;
   And in the cup an union³ shall he throw,   245
   Richer than that which four successive kings
   In Denmark's crown have worn. Give me the cups;
   And let the kettle⁴ to the trumpet speak,
   The trumpet to the cannoneer without,
   The cannons to the heavens, the heaven to earth,   250
   'Now the king drinks to Hamlet.' Come, begin;
   And you, the judges, bear a wary eye.

HAMLET: Come on, sir.

LAERTES: Come, my lord.
       [*They play.*]

HAMLET: One.

LAERTES: No.

HAMLET: Judgment.

OSRIC: A hit, a very palpable hit.

LAERTES: Well; again.

KING: Stay; give me drink. Hamlet, this pearl is thine;   255
   Here's to thy health.
       [*Trumpets sound, and cannon shot off within.*]
                       Give him the cup.

HAMLET: I'll play this bout first; set it by awhile.
   Come. [*They play.*] Another hit; what say you?

LAERTES: A touch, a touch, I do confess.

KING: Our son shall win.

QUEEN: He's fat and scant of breath.   260
   Here, Hamlet, take my napkin,⁵ rub thy brows:
   The queen carouses to thy fortune, Hamlet.

HAMLET: Good madam!

KING: Gertrude, do not drink.

---

9. Stand out brilliantly.   1. Cups.   2. Requite, or repay (by scoring a hit) on the third bout.   3. A
large pearl.   4. Kettledrum.   5. Handkerchief. *Fat:* sweaty, or soft, because out of training.

QUEEN: I will, my lord; I pray you, pardon me.
KING: [*Aside.*] It is the poisoned cup; it is too late.   265
QUEEN: Come, let me wipe thy face.
LAERTES: My lord, I'll hit him now.
KING: I do not think't.
LAERTES: [*Aside.*] And yet it is almost against my conscience.
HAMLET: Come, for the third, Laertes: you but dally;
  I pray you, pass with your best violence;   270
  I am afeard you make a wanton[6] of me.
LAERTES: Say you so? come on.
     [*They play.*]
OSRIC: Nothing, neither way.
LAERTES: Have at you now!
     [LAERTES *wounds* HAMLET; *then, in scuffling, they change rapiers,*
     and HAMLET *wounds* LAERTES.]
KING: Part them; they are incensed.
HAMLET: Nay, come, again.
     [*The* QUEEN *falls.*]
OSRIC: Look to the queen there, ho!   275
HORATIO: They bleed on both sides. How is it, my lord?
OSRIC: How is't, Laertes?
LAERTES: Why, as a woodcock to mine own springe,[7] Osric;
  I am justly killed with mine own treachery.
HAMLET: How does the queen?   280
KING: She swounds to see them bleed.
QUEEN: No, no, the drink, the drink,—O my dear Hamlet,—
  The drink, the drink! I am poisoned.
     [*Dies.*]
HAMLET: O villainy! Ho! let the door be locked:
  Treachery! seek it out.   285
     [LAERTES *falls.*]
LAERTES: It is here, Hamlet: Hamlet, thou art slain;
  No medicine in the world can do thee good,
  In thee there is not half an hour of life;
  The treacherous instrument is in thy hand,
  Unbated and envenomed: the foul practice[8]   290
  Hath turned itself on me; lo, here I lie,
  Never to rise again: thy mother's poisoned:
  I can no more: the king, the king's to blame.
HAMLET: The point envenomed too!
  Then, venom, to thy work.   295
     [*Stabs the* KING.]
ALL: Treason! treason!
KING: O, yet defend me, friends; I am but hurt.
HAMLET: Here, thou incestuous, murderous, damnèd Dane,
  Drink off this potion: is thy union here?
  Follow my mother.
     [KING *dies.*]

6. Weakling, spoiled child.   7. Snare.   8. Plot.

LAERTES: He is justly served;   300
   It is a poison tempered⁹ by himself.
   Exchange forgiveness with me, noble Hamlet:
   Mine and my father's death come not upon thee,
   Nor thine on me!
      [*Dies.*]
HAMLET: Heaven make thee free of it! I follow thee.   305
   I am dead, Horatio. Wretched queen, adieu!
   You that look pale and tremble at this chance,
   That are but mutes or audience to this act,
   Had I but time—as this fell sergeant, death,
   Is strict in his arrest—O, I could tell you—   310
   But let it be. Horatio, I am dead;
   Thou livest; report me and my cause aright
   To the unsatisfied.
HORATIO: Never believe it:
   I am more an antique Roman than a Dane:
   Here's yet some liquor left.
HAMLET: As thou'rt a man,   315
   Give me the cup: let go; by heaven, I'll have 't.
   O good Horatio, what a wounded name,
   Things standing thus unknown, shall live behind me!
   If thou didst ever hold me in thy heart,
   Absent thee from felicity a while,   320
   And in this harsh world draw thy breath in pain,
   To tell my story.
      [*March afar off, and shot within.*]
          What warlike noise is this?
OSRIC: Young Fortinbras, with conquest come from Poland,
   To the ambassadors of England gives
   This warlike volley.
HAMLET: O, I die, Horatio;   325
   The potent poison quite o'er-crows¹ my spirit:
   I cannot live to hear the news from England;
   But I do prophesy the election lights
   On Fortinbras: he has my dying voice;
   So tell him, with the occurrents, more and less,   330
   Which have solicited.² The rest is silence.
      [*Dies.*]
HORATIO: Now cracks a noble heart. Good night sweet prince,
   And flights of angels sing thee to thy rest;
      [*March within.*]
   Why does the drum come hither?
      [*Enter* FORTINBRAS, *and the* ENGLISH AMBASSADORS, *with drum,*
      colors, and ATTENDANTS.]
FORTINBRAS: Where is this sight?
HORATIO: What is it you would see?   335
   If aught of woe or wonder, cease your search.

9. Compounded.   1. Overcomes.   2. Which have brought all this about. *Occurrents:* occurrences.

FORTINBRAS: This quarry cries on havoc.[3] O proud death,
    What feast is toward[4] in thine eternal cell,
    That thou so many princes at a shot
    So bloodily hast struck?
FIRST AMBASSADOR: The sight is dismal;   340
    And our affairs from England come too late:
    The ears are senseless that should give us hearing,
    To tell him his commandment is fulfilled,
    That Rosencrantz and Guildenstern are dead:
    Where should we have our thanks?
HORATIO: Not from his mouth   345
    Had it the ability of life to thank you:
    He never gave commandment for their death.
    But since, so jump upon[5] this bloody question,
    You from the Polack wars, and you from England
    Are here arrived, give order that these bodies   350
    High on a stage be placèd to the view;
    And let me speak to the yet unknowing world
    How these things came about; so shall you hear
    Of carnal, bloody and unnatural acts,
    Of accidental judgments, casual slaughters,   355
    Of deaths put on[6] by cunning and forced cause,
    And, in this upshot, purposes mistook
    Fall'n on the inventors' heads: all this can I
    Truly deliver.
FORTINBRAS: Let us haste to hear it,
    And call the noblest to the audience.   360
    For me, with sorrow I embrace my fortune:
    I have some rights of memory in this kingdom,
    Which now to claim my vantage[7] doth invite me.
HORATIO: Of that I shall have also cause to speak,
    And from his mouth whose voice will draw on more:[8]   365
    But let this same be presently performed,
    Even while men's minds are wild; lest more mischance
    On[9] plots and errors happen.
FORTINBRAS: Let four captains
    Bear Hamlet, like a soldier, to the stage;   370
    For he was likely, had he been put on,[1]
    To have proved most royal: and, for his passage,[2]
    The soldiers' music and the rites of war
    Speak loudly for him.
    Take up the bodies: such a sight as this   375
    Becomes the field, but here shows much amiss.
    Go, bid the soldiers shoot.

        [*A dead march. Exeunt, bearing off the bodies: after which a peal
        of ordnance is shot off.*]

---

3. This heap of corpses proclaims a carnage.   4. Imminent.   5. So immediately on.   6. Prompted.
Casual: chance.   7. Advantageous position, opportunity. *Have some rights of memory:* am still remembered.   8. More voices.   9. Following on.   1. Tried (as a king).   2. Death.

The Tragedy of Othello the Moor of Venice

CHARACTERS

OTHELLO, *the Moor of Venice*
DESDEMONA, *his wife*
Michael CASSIO, *his lieutenant*
BIANCA, *a courtesan, in love with
    Cassio*
IAGO, *the Moor's ensign*
EMILIA, *Iago's wife*
A CLOWN, *a servant of Othello*
The DUKE *of Venice*
BRABANZIO, *Desdemona's father, a
    senator of Venice*

GRAZIANO, *Brabanzio's brother*
LODOVICO, *kinsman of Brabanzio*
SENATORS *of Venice*
RODERIGO, *a Venetian gentleman, in
    love with Desdemona*
MONTANO, *Governor of Cyprus*
A HERALD
A MESSENGER
*Attendants, officers, sailors, gentlemen
    of Cyprus, musicians*

1.1

[*Enter* IAGO *and* RODERIGO.]

RODERIGO Tush, never tell me! I take it much unkindly
That thou, Iago, who hast had my purse
As if the strings were thine, shouldst know of this.[1]
IAGO 'Sblood,[2] but you'll not hear me!
If ever I did dream of such a matter, abhor me.   5
RODERIGO Thou told'st me thou didst hold him in thy hate.
IAGO Despise me
If I do not. Three great ones of the city,
In personal suit to make me his lieutenant,
Off-capped[3] to him; and by the faith of man   10
I know my price, I am worth no worse a place.
But he, as loving his own pride and purposes,
Evades them with a bombast circumstance[4]
Horribly stuffed with epithets of war,[5]
Nonsuits[6] my mediators; for 'Certes,' says he,   15
'I have already chose my officer.'
And what was he?
Forsooth, a great arithmetician,[7]
One Michael Cassio, a Florentine,
A fellow almost damned in a fair wife,[8]   20
That never set a squadron in the field
Nor the division of a battle knows
More than a spinster—unless the bookish theoric,
Wherein the togaed consuls can propose
As masterly as he. Mere prattle without practice   25
Is all his soldiership; but he, sir, had th'election,
And I—of whom his eyes had seen the proof
At Rhodes, at Cyprus, and on other grounds

---

1. The marriage of Desdemona and Othello.   2. By God's blood.   3. Respectfully took their hats off.
4. Pompous speech.   5. Heroic adjectives.   6. Dismisses (this is a legal metaphor).   7. Theorist.   8. He is not married in the play, although he is in Shakespeare's source.

Christened and heathen—must be beleed[9] and calmed
By debitor and creditor. This counter-caster,[1]   30
He in good time must his lieutenant be,
And I—God bless the mark!—his Moorship's ensign.[2]
RODERIGO   By heaven, I rather would have been his hangman.
IAGO   Why, there's no remedy. 'Tis the curse of his hangman.
Preferment goes by letter and affection,   35
And not by old gradation,[3] where each second
Stood heir to th' first. Now, sir, be judge yourself
Whether I in any just term am affined[4]
To love the Moor.
RODERIGO   I would not follow him then.   40
IAGO   O sir, content you.
I follow him to serve my turn upon him.
We cannot all be masters, nor all masters
Cannot be truly followed. You shall mark
Many a duteous and knee-crooking knave   45
That, doting on his own obsequious bondage,
Wears out his time much like his master's ass
For naught but provender, and when he's old, cashiered.
Whip me such honest knaves. Others there are
Who, trimmed in forms and visages of duty,   50
Keep yet their hearts attending on themselves,
And, throwing but shows of service on their lords,
Do well thrive by 'em, and when they have lined their coats,
Do themselves homage. These fellows have some soul,
And such a one do I profess myself—for, sir,   55
It is as sure as you are Roderigo,
Were I the Moor I would not be Iago.
In following him I follow but myself.
Heaven is my judge, not I for love and duty,
But seeming so for my peculiar[5] end.   60
For when my outward action doth demonstrate.
The native act and figure of my heart
In compliment extern,[6] 'tis not long after
But I will wear my heart upon my sleeve
For daws to peck at. I am not what I am.   65
RODERIGO   What a full fortune does the thick-lips owe[7]
If he can carry't thus!
IAGO   Call up her father,
Rouse him, make after him, poison his delight,
Proclaim him in the streets; incense her kinsmen,
And, though he in a fertile climate dwell,   70
Plague him with flies. Though that his joy be joy,
Yet throw such chances of vexation on't
As it may lose some colour.
RODERIGO   Here is her father's house. I'll call aloud.

---

9. "Had the wind taken out my sails."   1. Accountant.   2. Standard-bearer.   3. Seniority.
4. Contracted.   5. Personal.   6. On the outside.   7. Own.

IAGO   Do, with like timorous[8] accent and dire yell   75
　　As when, by night and negligence, the fire
　　Is spied in populous cities.
RODERIGO [*calling*]   What ho, Brabanzio, Signor Brabanzio, ho!
IAGO [*calling*]   Awake, what ho, Brabanzio, thieves, thieves, thieves!
　　Look to your house, your daughter, and your bags.   80
　　Thieves, thieves!
　　　　　　[*Enter* BRABANZIO *in his nightgown at a window above.*]
BRABANZIO   What is the reason of this terrible summons?
　　What is the matter there?
RODERIGO   Signor, is all your family within?
IAGO   Are your doors locked?
BRABANZIO　　　　　　　　　Why, wherefore ask you this?   85
IAGO   'Swounds,[9] sir, you're robbed. For shame, put on your gown.
　　Your heart is burst, you have lost half your soul.
　　Even now, now, very now, an old black ram
　　Is tupping your white ewe. Arise, arise!
　　Awake the snorting citizens with the bell,   90
　　Or else the devil will make a grandsire of you.
　　Arise, I say.
BRABANZIO   What, have you lost your wits?
RODERIGO   Most reverend signor, do you know my voice?
BRABANZIO   Not I. What are you?
RODERIGO   My name is Roderigo.   95
BRABANZIO   The worser welcome.
　　I have charged thee not to haunt about my doors.
　　In honest plainness thou hast heard me say
　　My daughter is not for thee, and now in madness,
　　Being full of supper and distempering[1] draughts,   100
　　Upon malicious bravery dost thou come
　　To start[2] my quiet.
RODERIGO   Sir, sir, sir.
BRABANZIO   But thou must needs be sure
　　My spirits and my place[3] have in their power   105
　　To make this bitter to thee.
RODERIGO　　　　　　　　　Patience, good sir.
BRABANZIO   What tell'st thou me of robbing? This is Venice.
　　My house is not a grange.[4]
RODERIGO　　　　　　　　　Most grave Brabanzio,
　　In simple and pure soul I come to you.
IAGO [*to* BRABANZIO]   'Swounds, sir, you are one of those that will not   110
　　serve God if the devil bid you. Because we come to do you service
　　and you think we are ruffians, you'll have your daughter covered with
　　a Barbary horse, you'll have your nephews neigh to you, you'll have
　　coursers for cousins and jennets for germans.[5]
BRABANZIO   What profane wretch art thou?   115
IAGO   I am one, sir, that comes to tell you your daughter and the

8. Intimidating.　9. By God's wounds.　1. Intoxicating.　2. Upset.　3. Position in society.
4. House in the wilderness.　5. Blood relations. *Barbary:* Arabian. *Coursers:* horses. *Jennets:* Spanish
horses.

Moor are now making the beast with two backs.

BRABANZIO   Thou art a villain.

IAGO   You are a senator.

BRABANZIO   This thou shalt answer. I know thee, Roderigo.

RODERIGO   Sir, I will answer anything. But I beseech you,   120
    If't be your pleasure and most wise consent—
    As partly I find it is—that your fair daughter,
    At this odd-even[6] and dull watch o'th' night,
    Transported with no worse nor better guard
    But with a knave of common hire, a gondolier,   125
    To the gross clasps of a lascivious Moor—
    If this be known to you, and your allowance,
    We then have done you bold and saucy wrongs.
    But if you know not this, my manners tell me
    We have your wrong rebuke. Do not believe   130
    That, from the sense of all civility,
    I thus would play and trifle with your reverence.
    Your daughter, if you have not given her leave,
    I say again hath made a gross revolt,
    Tying her duty, beauty, wit, and fortunes   135
    In an extravagant[7] and wheeling stranger
    Of here and everywhere. Straight satisfy yourself.
    If she be in her chamber or your house,
    Let loose on me the justice of the state
    For thus deluding you.

BRABANZIO [calling]   Strike on the tinder, ho!   140
    Give me a taper call up all my people.
    This accident[8] is not unlike my dream;
    Belief of it oppresses me already.
    Light, I say, light!   [Exit.]

IAGO   Farewell, for I must leave you.
    It seems not meet nor wholesome to my place   145
    To be produced—as, if I stay, I shall—
    Against the Moor, for I do know the state,
    However this may gall him with some check,[9]
    Cannot with safety cast[1] him, for he's embarked
    With such loud reason to the Cyprus wars,   150
    Which even now stands in act,[2] that, for their souls,
    Another of his fathom[3] they have none
    To lead their business, in which regard—
    Though I do hate him as I do hell pains—
    Yet for necessity of present life   155
    I must show out a flag and sign of love,
    Which is indeed but sign. That you shall surely find him,
    Lead to the Sagittary[4] the raisèd search,
    And there will I be with him. So farewell.   [Exit.]
        [Enter below BRABANZIO in his nightgown, and servants with
        torches.]

6. Neither morning nor night.   7. Wandering.   8. Chance circumstance.   9. Setback.   1. Dismiss.   2. Is happening.   3. Depth of skill.   4. Name of an inn.

BRABANZIO   It is too true an evil. Gone she is,   160
   And what's to come of my despisèd time
   Is naught but bitterness. Now, Roderigo,
   Where didst thou see her?—O unhappy girl!—
   With the Moor, sayst thou?—Who would be a father?—
   How didst thou know 'twas she?—O, she deceives me   165
   Past thought!—What said she to you? [*To servants*] Get more tapers,
   Raise all my kindred.   [*Exit one or more.*]
   [*To* RODERIGO]   Are they married, think you?
RODERIGO   Truly, I think they are.
BRABANZIO   O heaven, how got she out? O, treason of the blood!
   Fathers, from hence trust not your daughters' minds   170
   By what you see them act. Is there not charms
   By which the property⁵ of youth and maidhood
   May be abused? Have you not read, Roderigo,
   Of some such thing?
RODERIGO   Yes, sir, I have indeed.
BRABANZIO [*to servants*]   Call up my brother. [*To* RODERIGO] O, would you
   had had her.   175
   [*To servants*] Some one way, some another.   [*Exit one or more.*]
   [*To* RODERIGO]   Do you know
   Where we may apprehend her and the Moor?
RODERIGO   I think I can discover him, if you please
   To get good guard and go along with me.
BRABANZIO   Pray you lead on. At every house I'll call;   180
   I may command at most. [*Calling*] Get weapons, ho,
   And raise some special officers of night.
   On, good Roderigo. I will deserve your pains.⁶   [*Exeunt.*]

1.2

[*Enter* OTHELLO, IAGO, *and attendants with torches.*]
IAGO   Though in the trade of war I have slain men,
   Yet do I hold it very stuff o'th' conscience
   To do no contrived murder. I lack iniquity,
   Sometime, to do me service. Nine or ten times
   I had thought to've yerked⁷ him here, under the ribs.   5
OTHELLO   'Tis better as it is.
IAGO   Nay, but he prated,
   And spoke such scurvy and provoking terms
   Against your honour
   That, with the little godliness I have,
   I did full hard forbear him. But I pray you, sir,   10
   Are you fast married? Be assured of this:
   That the magnifico⁸ is much beloved,
   And hath in his effect a voice potential
   As double as the Duke's.⁹ He will divorce you,
   Or put upon you what restraint or grievance   15
   The law, with all his might to enforce it on,

5. Character.   6. I will make it worth your trouble.   7. Stabbed.   8. Nobleman.   9. Can be twice as influential as the Duke.

Will give him cable.[1]

OTHELLO   Let him do his spite.
  My services which I have done the signory[2]
  Shall out-tongue his complaints. 'Tis yet to know—
  Which, when I know that boasting is an honour,   20
  I shall promulgate—I fetch my life and being
  From men of royal siege,[3] and my demerits
  May speak unbonneted to as proud a fortune
  As this that I have reached.[4] For know, Iago,
  But that I love the gentle Desdemona   25
  I would not my unhousèd[5] free condition
  Put into circumscription and confine
  For the seas' worth.
              [Enter CASSIO and officers, with torches.]
                    But look, what lights come yond?
IAGO   Those are the raisèd father and his friends.
  You were best go in.
OTHELLO   Not I. I must be found.   30
  My parts, my title, and my perfect soul[6]
  Shall manifest me rightly. Is it they?
IAGO   By Janus, I think no.
OTHELLO   The servants of the Duke, and my lieutenant!
  The goodness of the night upon you, friends.   35
  What is the news?
CASSIO   The Duke does greet you, general,
  And he requires your haste-post-haste appearance
  Even on the instant.
OTHELLO   What is the matter, think you?
CASSIO   Something from Cyprus, as I may divine;
  It is a business of some heat. The galleys   40
  Have sent a dozen sequent messengers
  This very night at one another's heels,
  And many of the consuls, raised and met,
  Are at the Duke's already. You have been hotly called for,
  When, being not at your lodging to be found,   45
  The senate sent about three several quests
  To search you out.
OTHELLO   'Tis well I am found by you.
  I will but spend a word here in the house
  And go with you.   [Exit.]
CASSIO   Ensign, what makes he here?
IAGO   Faith, he tonight hath boarded a land-carrack.[7]   50
  If it prove lawful prize, he's made for ever.
CASSIO   I do not understand.
IAGO   He's married.
CASSIO   To who?
              [Enter BRABANZIO, RODERIGO, and OFFICERS, with lights and
              weapons.]

1. Means.   2. Rulers of Venice.   3. Descent.   4. My merits, which need no self-effacing, are equal
to my marriage.   5. Unconfined.   6. Guiltless conscience.   7. Treasure ship.

IAGO Marry,[8] to—
        [*Enter* OTHELLO.]
    [*To* OTHELLO] Come, captain, will you go?
OTHELLO   Have with you.
CASSIO Here comes another troop to seek for you.   55
IAGO It is Brabanzio. General, be advised.
    He comes to bad intent.
OTHELLO   Holla, stand, there!
RODERIGO [*to* BRABANZIO]   Signor, it is the Moor.
BRABANZIO   Down with him, thief!
IAGO [*drawing his sword*]   You, Roderigo? Come, sir, I am for you.
OTHELLO Keep up your bright swords, for the dew will rust 'em.   60
    [*To* BRABANZIO] Good signor, you shall more command with years
    Than with your weapons.
BRABANZIO O thou foul thief, where hast thou stowed my daughter?
    Damned as thou art, thou hast enchanted her,
    For I'll refer me to all things of sense,[9]   65
    If she in chains of magic were not bound,
    Whether a maid so tender, fair, and happy,
    So opposite to marriage that she shunned
    The wealthy curlèd darlings of our nation,
    Would ever have, t'incur a general mock,   70
    Run from her guardage to the sooty bosom
    Of such a thing as thou—to fear, not to delight.
    Judge me the world if 'tis not gross in sense.[1]
    That thou hast practised on[2] her with foul charms,
    Abused her delicate youth with drugs or minerals   75
    That weakens motion.[3] I'll have't disputed on.
    'Tis probable, and palpable to thinking.
    I therefore apprehend and do attach[4] thee
    For an abuser of the world, a practiser
    Of arts inhibited and out of warrant.[5]   80
    [*To* OFFICERS] Lay hold upon him. If he do resist,
    Subdue him at his peril.
OTHELLO   Hold your hands,
    Both you of my inclining and the rest.
    Were it my cue to fight, I should have known it
    Without a prompter. Whither will you that I go   85
    To answer this your charge?
BRABANZIO   To prison, till fit time
    Of law and course of direct session
    Call thee to answer.
OTHELLO   What if I do obey?
    How may the Duke be therewith satisfied,
    Whose messengers are here about my side   90
    Upon some present business of the state
    To bring me to him?

---

8. By Mary.   9. Make use of natural reason.   1. Obvious.   2. Manipulated.   3. The will.
4. Arrest.   5. Prohibited and illegal.

OFFICER [*to* BRABANZIO]   'Tis true, most worthy signor.
　The Duke's in council, and your noble self,
　I am sure, is sent for.
BRABANZIO　　　　　　How, the Duke in council? 95
　In this time of the night? Bring him away.
　Mine's not an idle cause. The Duke himself,
　Or any of my brothers of the state,
　Cannot but feel this wrong as 'twere their own;
　For if such actions may have passage free,
　Bondslaves and pagans shall our statesmen be.　[*Exeunt.*] 100

1.3

　[*Enter the* DUKE *and* SENATORS *set at a table, with lights and*
　OFFICERS.]
DUKE　There is no composition in these news
　That gives them credit.[6]
FIRST SENATOR　　　　　Indeed, they are disproportioned.
　My letters say a hundred and seven galleys.
DUKE　And mine a hundred-forty.
SECOND SENATOR　　　　　And mine two hundred.
　But though they jump not on a just account[7]— 5
　As, in these cases, where the aim reports
　'Tis oft with difference—yet do they all confirm
　A Turkish fleet, and bearing up to Cyprus.
DUKE　Nay, it is possible enough to judgement.
　I do not so secure me in the error, 10
　But the main article I do approve
　In fearful sense.[8]
SAILOR [*within*]　What ho, what ho, what ho!
　　　　[*Enter a* SAILOR.]
OFFICER　A messenger from the galleys.
DUKE　　　　　　　　　　　Now, what's the business?
SAILOR　The Turkish preparation makes for Rhodes.
　So was I bid report here to the state 15
　By Signor Angelo.
DUKE [*To* SENATORS.]　How say you by this change?
FIRST SENATOR　This cannot be,
　By no assay of reason—'tis a pageant
　To keep us in false gaze.[9] When we consider 20
　The importancy of Cyprus to the Turk,
　And let ourselves again but understand
　That, as it more concerns the Turk than Rhodes,
　So may he with more facile question[1] bear it,
　For that it stands not in such warlike brace,[2] 25
　But altogether lacks th'abilities

6. The consensus of the reports makes them believable.　7. Exact number. *Jump:* agree.　8. The tale is believable, and the numerical errors do not make me doubt the overall report, which I fear.　9. Show to distract us.　1. Easy conflict.　2. Military preparation.

That Rhodes is dressed in—if we make thought of this,
We must not think the Turk is so unskilful
To leave that latest which concerns him first,
Neglecting an attempt of ease and gain   30
To wake and wage a danger profitless.
DUKE   Nay, in all confidence, he's not for Rhodes.
OFFICER   Here is more news.
        [*Enter a* MESSENGER.]
MESSENGER   The Ottomites, reverend and gracious,
    Steering with due course toward the Isle of Rhodes,   35
    Have there injointed them with an after fleet.
FIRST SENATOR   Ay, so I thought. How many, as you guess?
MESSENGER   Of thirty sail, and now they do restem
    Their backward course, bearing with frank appearance
    Their purposes toward Cyprus. Signor Montano,   40
    Your trusty and most valiant servitor,
    With his free duty recommend[3] you thus,
    And prays you to believe him.
DUKE   'Tis certain then for Cyprus.
    Marcus Luccicos, is not he in town?
FIRST SENATOR   He's now in Florence.   45
DUKE   Write from us to him post-post-haste. Dispatch.
        [*Enter* BRABANZIO, OTHELLO, RODERIGO, IAGO, CASSIO, *and*
        OFFICERS.]
FIRST SENATOR   Here comes Brabanzio and the valiant Moor.
DUKE   Valiant Othello, we must straight employ you
    Against the general enemy Ottoman.
    [*To* BRABANZIO] I did not see you. Welcome, gentle signor   50
    We lacked your counsel and your help tonight.
BRABANZIO   So did I yours. Good your grace, pardon me.
    Neither my place, nor aught I heard of business,
    Hath raised me from my bed, nor doth the general care
    Take hold on me; for my particular grief   55
    Is of so floodgate and o'erbearing nature
    That it engluts and swallows other sorrows,
    And it is still itself.
DUKE   Why, what's the matter?
BRABANZIO   My daughter, O, my daughter!
SENATORS   Dead?
BRABANZIO   Ay, to me.
    She is abused, stol'n from me, and corrupted   60
    By spells and medicines bought of mountebanks.[4]
    For nature so preposterously to err,
    Being not deficient, blind, or lame of sense,
    Sans witchcraft could not.
DUKE   Whoe'er he be that in this foul proceeding   65
    Hath thus beguiled your daughter of herself
    And you of her, the bloody book of law

3. Informs. *Free duty*: unforced respect.   4. Frauds.

You shall yourself read in the bitter letter
After your own sense, yea, though our proper son
Stood in your action.[5]
BRABANZIO   Humbly I thank your grace.   70
  Here is the man, this Moor, whom now it seems
  Your special mandate for the state affairs
  Hath hither brought.
SENATORS   We are very sorry for't.
DUKE [to OTHELLO]   What in your own part can you say to this?
BRABANZIO   Nothing but this is so.   75
OTHELLO   Most potent, grave, and reverend signors,
  My very noble and approved[6] good masters,
  That I have ta'en away this old man's daughter,
  It is most true, true I have married her.
  The very head and front[7] of my offending   80
  Hath this extent, no more. Rude am I in my speech,
  And little blessed with the soft phrase of peace,
  For since these arms of mine had seven years' pith[8]
  Till now some nine moons wasted,[9] they have used
  Their dearest[1] action in the tented field,   85
  And little of this great world can I speak
  More than pertains to feats of broils and battle.
  And therefore little shall I grace my cause
  In speaking for myself. Yet, by your gracious patience,
  I will a round unvarnished tale deliver   90
  Of my whole course of love, what drugs, what charms,
  What conjuration and what mighty magic—
  For such proceeding I am charged withal—
  I won his daughter.
BRABANZIO   A maiden never bold,
  Of spirit so still and quiet that her motion   95
  Blushed at herself[2]—and she in spite of nature,
  Of years, of country, credit, everything,
  To fall in love with what she feared to look on!
  It is a judgement maimed and most imperfect
  That will confess perfection so could err   100
  Against all rules of nature, and must be driven
  To find out practices of cunning hell
  Why this should be. I therefore vouch again
  That with some mixtures powerful o'er the blood,
  Or with some dram conjured to this effect,   105
  He wrought upon her.
DUKE   To vouch this is no proof
  Without more wider and more overt test
  Than these thin habits and poor likelihoods
  Of modern seeming[3] prefer against him.
A SENATOR   But Othello, speak.   110
  Did you by indirect and forcèd courses

---

5. Suit. *Proper*: own.   6. Tested.   7. Form and gist (i.e., it was a marriage, not a rape).   8. Strength.
9. Past.   1. Most significant.   2. She blushed at her own movement.   3. Common appearance.
Thin habits: clothing.

Subdue and poison this young maid's affections,
Or came it by request and such fair question[4]
As soul to soul affordeth?
OTHELLO   I do beseech you,
  Send for the lady to the Sagittary,   115
  And let her speak of me before her father.
  If you do find me foul in her report,
  The trust, the office I do hold of you
  Not only take away, but let your sentence
  Even fall upon my life.
DUKE [*to* OFFICERS]   Fetch Desdemona hither.   120
OTHELLO   Ensign, conduct them. You best know the place.
                    [*Exit* IAGO *with two or three* OFFICERS.]
  And till she come, as truly as to heaven
  I do confess the vices of my blood,
  So justly to your grave ears I'll present
  How I did thrive in this fair lady's love,   125
  And she is mine.
DUKE   Say it, Othello.
OTHELLO   Her father loved me, oft invited me,
  Still questioned me the story of my life
  From year to year, the battles, sieges, fortunes
  That I have passed.   130
  I ran it through even from my boyish days
  To th' very moment that he bade me tell it,
  Wherein I spoke of most disastrous chances,
  Of moving accidents by flood and field,
  Of hair-breadth scapes i'th' imminent deadly breach,   135
  Of being taken by the insolent foe
  And sold to slavery, of my redemption thence,
  And portance[5] in my traveller's history,
  Wherein of antres vast and deserts idle,[6]
  Rough quarries, rocks, and hills whose heads touch heaven,   140
  It was my hint to speak. Such was my process,
  And of the cannibals that each other eat,
  The Anthropophagi,[7] and men whose heads
  Do grow beneath their shoulders. These things to hear
  Would Desdemona seriously incline,   145
  But still the house affairs would draw her thence,
  Which ever as she could with haste dispatch
  She'd come again, and with a greedy ear
  Devour up my discourse; which I observing,
  Took once a pliant hour, and found good means   150
  To draw from her a prayer of earnest heart
  That I would all my pilgrimage dilate,[8]
  Whereof by parcels she had something heard,
  But not intentively:[9] I did consent,
  And often did beguile her of her tears   155

4. Inquiry.   5. Conduct.   6. Empty. *Antres:* caves.   7. Eaters of human flesh.   8. Narrate fully.
9. Intently.

When I did speak of some distressful stroke
That my youth suffered. My story being done,
She gave me for my pains a world of kisses.
She swore in faith 'twas strange, 'twas passing¹ strange,
'Twas pitiful, 'twas wondrous pitiful.   160
She wished she had not heard it, yet she wished
That heaven had made her such a man. She thankèd me,
And bade me, if I had a friend that loved her,
I should but teach him how to tell my story,
And that would woo her. Upon this hint I spake.   165
She loved me for the dangers I had passed,
And I loved her that she did pity them.
This only is the witchcraft I have used.
      [*Enter* DESDEMONA, IAGO, *and attendants.*]
Here comes the lady. Let her witness it.
DUKE   I think this tale would win my daughter, too—   170
  Good Brabanzio,
Take up this mangled matter at the best.²
Men do their broken weapons rather use
Than their bare hands.
BRABANZIO   I pray you hear her speak.
If she confess that she was half the wooer,   175
Destruction on my head if my bad blame
Light on the man! Come hither, gentle mistress.
Do you perceive in all this noble company
Where most you owe obedience?
DESDEMONA   My noble father,
I do perceive here a divided duty.   180
To you I am bound for life and education.
My life and education both do learn me
How to respect you. You are the lord of duty,
I am hitherto your daughter. But here's my husband,
And so much duty as my mother showed   185
To you, preferring you before her father,
So much I challenge that I may profess
Due to the Moor my lord.
BRABANZIO   God b'wi'you, I ha' done.
Please it your grace, on to the state affairs.
I had rather to adopt a child than get³ it.   190
Come hither, Moor.
I here do give thee that with all my heart
Which, but thou hast already, with all my heart
I would keep from thee. [*To* DESDEMONA] For your sake,⁴ jewel,
I am glad at soul I have no other child,   195
For thy escape would teach me tyranny,
To hang clogs on 'em. I have done, my lord.
DUKE   Let me speak like yourself, and lay a sentence⁵

---

1. Surpassingly.   2. I.e., make the best of it.   3. Beget.   4. On your account.   5. Speak of maxim.

Which, as a grece[6] or step, may help these lovers
Into your favour.   200
When remedies are past, the griefs are ended
By seeing the worst which late on hopes depended[7]
To mourn a mischief that is past and gone
Is the next way to draw new mischief on.
What cannot be preserved when fortune takes,   205
Patience her injury a mockery makes.
The robbed that smiles steals something from the thief;
He robs himself that spends a bootless[8] grief.
BRABANZIO   So let the Turk of Cyprus us beguile,
We lose it not so long as we can smile.   210
He bears the sentence well that nothing bears
But the free comfort which from thence he hears,
But he bears both the sentence and the sorrow
That, to pay grief, must of poor patience borrow.
These sentences, to sugar or to gall,   215
Being strong on both sides, are equivocal.
But words are words. I never yet did hear
That the bruisèd heart was piercèd through the ear.
I humbly beseech you proceed to th'affairs of state.
DUKE   The Turk with a most mighty preparation makes for Cyprus.   220
Othello, the fortitude of the place is best known to you, and though
we have there a substitute of most allowed sufficiency,[9] yet opinion,
a more sovereign mistress of effects, throws a more safer voice on
you. You must therefore be content to slubber the gloss of your new
fortunes with this more stubborn and boisterous[1] expedition.   225
OTHELLO   The tyrant custom, most grave senators,
Hath made the flinty and steel couch of war
My thrice-driven[2] bed of down. I do agnize[3]
A natural and prompt alacrity
I find in hardness, and do undertake   230
This present wars against the Ottomites.
Most humbly therefore bending to your state,
I crave fit disposition for my wife,
Due reference of place and exhibition,
With such accommodation and besort   235
As levels with[4] her breeding.
DUKE   Why, at her father's!
BRABANZIO   I will not have it so.
OTHELLO   Nor I.
DESDEMONA   Nor would I there reside,   240
To put my father in impatient thoughts
By being in his eye. Most gracious Duke,
To my unfolding lend your prosperous ear,
And let me find a charter[5] in your voice
T'assist my simpleness.

6. Stair.   7. Previously clung to hope.   8. Ineffective.   9. Ability. *Fortitude*: strength. *Substitute*:
deputy.   1. Rough. *Slubber*: smear.   2. Winnowed three times.   3. Recognize.   4. Is appropriate to. *Exhibition*: financial support.   5. Permission. *Unfolding*: explanation. *Prosperous*: granting.

DUKE   What would you, Desdemona?   245
DESDEMONA   That I did love the Moor to live with him,
   My downright violence and storm of fortunes
   May trumpet to the world. My heart's subdued
   Even to the very quality of my lord.
   I saw Othello's visage in his mind,   250
   And to his honours and his valiant parts
   Did I my soul and fortunes consecrate;
   So that, dear lords, if I be left behind,
   A moth of peace, and he go to the war,
   The rites[6] for why I love him are bereft me,   255
   And I a heavy interim shall support
   By his dear absence. Let me go with him.
OTHELLO [*to the* DUKE]   Let her have your voice.[7]
   Vouch with me heaven, I therefor beg it not
   To please the palate of my appetite,   260
   Nor to comply with heat—the young affects
   In me defunct—and proper satisfaction,[8]
   But to be free and bounteous to her mind;
   And heaven defend your good souls that you think
   I will your serious and great business scant   265
   When she is with me. No, when light-winged toys
   Of feathered Cupid seel with wanton dullness
   My speculative and officed instruments,[9]
   That my disports corrupt and taint my business,
   Let housewives make a skillet of my helm,   270
   And all indign and base adversities
   Make head against my estimation.[1]
DUKE   Be it as you shall privately determine,
   Either for her stay or going. Th'affair cries haste,
   And speed must answer it.
A SENATOR [*to* OTHELLO]   You must away tonight.   275
DESDEMONA   Tonight, my lord?
DUKE   This night.
OTHELLO   With all my heart.
DUKE   At nine i'th' morning here we'll meet again.
   Othello, leave some officer behind,
   And he shall our commission bring to you,
   And such things else of quality and respect   280
   As doth import you.
OTHELLO   So please your grace, my ensign.
   A man he is of honesty and trust.
   To his conveyance I assign my wife,
   With what else needful your good grace shall think
   To be sent after me.
DUKE   Let it be so.   285
   Good night to everyone. [*To* BRABANZIO] And, noble signor,

---

6. Marriage rites.   7. Approval.   8. I.e., consummation of marriage rites. *Heat:* lust. *Affects:* passions.
9. Clear-sightedness. *Seel:* sew up (like a falcon's eyes). *Wanton:* lustful.   1. Reputation. *Indign:* unworthy. *Make head:* rebel.

If virtue no delighted beauty lack,
Your son-in-law is far more fair than black.
A SENATOR   Adieu, brave Moor. Use Desdemona well.
BRABANZIO   Look to her, Moor, if thou hast eyes to see.   290
She has deceived her father, and may thee.

               [*Exeunt* DUKE, BRABANZIO, CASSIO, SENATORS, *and* OFFICERS.]

OTHELLO   My life upon her faith. Honest Iago,
My Desdemona must I leave to thee.
I prithee let thy wife attend on her,
And bring them after in the best advantage.[2]   295
Come, Desdemona. I have but an hour
Of love, of worldly matter and direction
To spend with thee. We must obey the time.

               [*Exeunt* OTHELLO *the Moor and* DESDEMONA.]

RODERIGO   Iago.
IAGO   What sayst thou, noble heart?   300
RODERIGO   What will I do, think'st thou?
IAGO   Why, go to bed and sleep.
RODERIGO   I will incontinently[3] drown myself.
IAGO   If thou dost, I shall never love thee after. Why, thou silly
gentleman!   305
RODERIGO   It is silliness to live when to live is torment; and then have
we a prescription to die when death is our physician.
IAGO   O, villainous! I ha' looked upon the world for four times seven
years, and since I could distinguish betwixt a benefit and an injury
I never found man that knew how to love himself. Ere I would say I   310
would drown myself for the love of a guinea-hen, I would change my
humanity with a baboon.
RODERIGO   What should I do? I confess it is my shame to be so fond,
but it is not in my virtue to amend it.
IAGO   Virtue?[4] A fig! 'Tis in ourselves that we are thus or thus. Our   315
bodies are our gardens, to the which our wills are gardeners; so that
if we will plant nettles or sow lettuce, set hyssop and weed up thyme,
supply it with one gender of herbs or distract it with many, either to
have it sterile with idleness or manured with industry, why, the
power and corrigible[5] authority of this lies in our wills. If the beam   320
of our lives had not one scale of reason to peise another of sensuality,
the blood and baseness of our natures would conduct us to most
preposterous conclusions. But we have reason to cool our raging
motions, our carnal stings, our unbitted lusts; whereof I take this
that you call love to be a sect or scion.[6]   325
RODERIGO   It cannot be.
IAGO   It is merely a lust of the blood and a permission of the will.
Come, be a man. Drown thyself? Drown cats and blind puppies. I
have professed me thy friend, and I confess me knit to thy deserving
with cables of perdurable toughness. I could never better stead[7] thee   330
than now. Put money in thy purse. Follow thou the wars, defeat thy

---

2. At the next opportunity.   3. Directly.   4. Power, strength.   5. Corrective.   6. Shoot. *Unbitted:* unrestrained.   7. Serve.

favour with an usurped[8] beard. I say, put money in thy purse. It cannot be long that Desdemona should continue her love to the Moor—put money in thy purse—nor he his to her. It was a violent commencement in her, and thou shalt see an answerable sequestra- 335 tion[9]—put but money in thy purse. These Moors are changeable in their wills—fill thy purse with money. The food that to him now is as luscious as locusts shall be to him shortly as bitter as coloquin- tida.[1] She must change for youth. When she is sated with his body, she will find the error of her choice. Therefore put money in thy 340 purse. If thou wilt needs damn thyself, do it a more delicate way than drowning. Make all the money thou canst. If sanctimony and a frail vow betwixt an erring[2] barbarian and a super-subtle Venetian be not too hard for my wits and all the tribe of hell, thou shalt enjoy her; therefore make money. A pox o' drowning thyself—it is clean out of 345 the way. Seek thou rather to be hanged in compassing[3] thy joy than to be drowned and go without her.

RODERIGO   Wilt thou be fast to my hopes if I depend on the issue?

IAGO   Thou art sure of me. Go, make money. I have told thee often, and I re-tell thee again and again, I hate the Moor. My cause is 350 hearted, thine hath no less reason. Let us be conjunctive[4] in our revenge against him. If thou canst cuckold him, thou dost thyself a pleasure, me a sport. There are many events in the womb of time, which will be delivered. Traverse, go, provide thy money. We will have more of this tomorrow. Adieu. 355

RODERIGO   Where shall we meet i'th' morning?

IAGO   At my lodging.

RODERIGO   I'll be with thee betimes.

IAGO   Go to, farewell—
Do you hear, Roderigo?

RODERIGO   I'll sell all my land.   [Exit.]

IAGO   Thus do I ever make my fool my purse—
For I mine own gained knowledge should profane   360
If I would time expend with such a snipe[5]
But for my sport and profit. I hate the Moor,
And it is thought abroad that 'twixt my sheets
He has done my office. I know not if't be true,
But I, for mere suspicion in that kind,   365
Will do as if for surety.[6] He holds me well:
The better shall my purpose work on him.
Cassio's a proper[7] man. Let me see now,
To get his place, and to plume up my will
In double knavery—how, how? Let's see.   370
After some time to abuse Othello's ears
That he is too familiar with his wife;
He hath a person and a smooth dispose
To be suspected, framed[8] to make women false.

---

8. False. *Defeat thy favor:* disguise your face.   9. Similar end.   1. Laxative made from bitter apples. *Locusts:* sweet fruit.   2. Wandering. *Sanctimony:* the sacred bond (that is, of marriage).   3. Achieving.   4. United. *Hearted:* heartfelt.   5. Dupe. *Gained knowledge:* experience.   6. Certainty. 7. Handsome.   8. Designed. *Dispose:* manner.

The Moor is of a free and open nature,   375
That thinks men honest that but seem to be so,
And will as tenderly be led by th' nose
As asses are.
I ha't. It is ingendered. Hell and night
Must bring this monstrous birth to the world's light.   [*Exit.*]   380

2.1

[*Enter below* MONTANO, *Governor of Cyprus; two other* GENTLEMEN *above.*]

MONTANO   What from the cape can you discern at sea?
FIRST GENTLEMAN   Nothing at all. It is a high-wrought flood.
  I cannot 'twixt the heaven and the main
  Descry a sail.
MONTANO   Methinks the wind hath spoke aloud at land.   5
  A fuller blast ne'er shook our battlements.
  If it ha' ruffianed so upon the sea,
  What ribs of oak, when mountains melt on them,
  Can hold the mortise?[9] What shall we hear of this?
SECOND GENTLEMAN   A segregation[1] of the Turkish fleet;   10
  For do but stand upon the foaming shore,
  The chidden billow seems to pelt the clouds,
  The wind-shaked surge with high and monstrous mane[2]
  Seems to cast water on the burning Bear
  And quench the guards of th' ever-fixèd Pole.[3]   15
  I never did like molestation view
  On the enchafèd flood.
MONTANO   If that the Turkish fleet
  Be not ensheltered and embayed, they are drowned.
  It is impossible to bear it out.
  [*Enter a* THIRD GENTLEMAN.]
THIRD GENTLEMAN   News, lads! Our wars are done.   20
  The desperate tempest hath so banged the Turks
  That their designment halts. A noble ship of Venice
  Hath seen a grievous wrack and sufferance[4]
  On most part of their fleet.
MONTANO   How, is this true?   25
THIRD GENTLEMAN   The ship is here put in,
  A Veronessa. Michael Cassio,
  Lieutenant to the warlike Moor Othello,
  Is come on shore; the Moor himself at sea,
  And is in full commission here for Cyprus.   30
MONTANO   I am glad on't; 'tis a worthy governor.
THIRD GENTLEMAN   But this same Cassio, though he speak of comfort
  Touching the Turkish loss, yet he looks sadly,
  And prays the Moor be safe, for they were parted
  With foul and violent tempest.

---

9. Joints.   **1.** Separation.   **2.** Ocean.   **3.** North Star. *Bear:* Ursa Minor.   **4.** Damage.

MONTANO   Pray heavens he be,   35
  For I have served him, and the man commands
  Like a full soldier. Let's to the sea-side, ho!—
  As well to see the vessel that's come in
  As to throw out our eyes for brave Othello,
  Even till we make the main and th' aerial blue   40
  An indistinct regard.[5]
THIRD GENTLEMAN   Come, let's do so,
  For every minute is expectancy
  Of more arrivance.[6]
        [*Enter* CASSIO.]
CASSIO   Thanks, you the valiant of this warlike isle
  That so approve the Moor! O, let the heavens   45
  Give him defence against the elements,
  For I have lost him on a dangerous sea
MONTANO   Is he well shipped?
CASSIO   His barque is stoutly timbered, and his pilot
  Of very expert and approved allowance.[7]   50
  Therefore my hopes, not surfeited to death,
  Stand in bold cure.[8]
VOICES [*within*]   A sail, a sail, a sail!
CASSIO   What noise?
A GENTLEMAN   The town is empty. On the brow o'th' sea
  Stand ranks of people, and they cry 'A sail!'   55
CASSIO   My hopes do shape him for the governor.
        [*A shot.*]
A GENTLEMAN   They do discharge their shot of courtesy—
  Our friends, at least.
CASSIO   I pray you, sir, go forth,
  And give us truth who 'tis that is arrived.
A GENTLEMAN   I shall.   [*Exit.*]   60
MONTANO   But, good lieutenant, is your general wived?
CASSIO   Most fortunately. He hath achieved a maid
  That paragons description and wild fame
  On that excels the quirks of blazoning pens,
  And in th' essential vesture of creation   65
  Does tire the engineer.[9]
        [*Enter* GENTLEMAN.]
                How now, who has put in?
A GENTLEMAN   'Tis one Iago, ensign to the general.
CASSIO   He's had most favourable and happy speed.
  Tempests themselves, high seas, and howling winds,
  The guttered rocks and congregated sands,   70
  Traitors ensteeped to enclog the guiltless keel,
  As having sense of beauty do omit
  Their mortal[1] natures, letting go safely by

5. The ocean and the sky become indistinguishable.   6. Arrivals.   7. Experienced reputation.
8. Not dangerously excessive, are likely to be restored.   9. Her nature wears out the witty poet. *Paragons:*
outdoes. *Wild fame:* extravagant praise. *Blazoning pens:* i.e., those of Petrarchan poets.   1. Deadly. *Gut-*
tered: jagged. *Congregated:* heaped. *Ensteeped:* submerged.

The divine Desdemona.
MONTANO   What is she?
CASSIO   She that I spake of, our great captain's captain,   75
Left in the conduct of the bold Iago,
Whose footing here anticipates our thoughts
A sennight's[2] speed. Great Jove, Othello guard,
And swell his sail with thine own powerful breath,
That he may bless this bay with his tall ship,   80
Make love's quick pants in Desdemona's arms,
Give renewed fire to our extinguished spirits,
And bring all Cyprus comfort.
          [*Enter* DESDEMONA, IAGO, EMILIA, *and* RODERIGO.]
                              O, behold,
The riches of the ship is come on shore!
You men of Cyprus, let her have your knees.   85
          [MONTANO *and the* GENTLEMEN *make curtsy to* DESDEMONA.]
Hail to thee, lady, and the grace of heaven
Before, behind thee, and on every hand
Enwheel thee round!
DESDEMONA   I thank you, valiant Cassio.
What tidings can you tell me of my lord?
CASSIO   He is not yet arrived, nor know I aught   90
But that he's well and will be shortly here.
DESDEMONA   O, but I fear—how lost you company?
CASSIO   The great contention of the sea and skies
Parted our fellowship.
VOICES [*within*]   A sail, a sail!   95
CASSIO   But hark, a sail.
          [*A shot.*]
A GENTLEMAN   They give their greeting to the citadel.
This likewise is a friend.
CASSIO   See for the news.   [*Exit* GENTLEMAN.]
Good ensign, you are welcome. [*Kissing* EMILIA] Welcome, mistress.
Let it not gall your patience, good Iago,   100
That I extend my manners. 'Tis my breeding[3]
That gives me this bold show of courtesy.
IAGO   Sir, would she give you so much of her lips
As of her tongue she oft bestows on me,
You would have enough.   105
DESDEMONA   Alas, she has no speech!
IAGO   In faith, too much.
I find it still when I ha' leave to sleep.[4]
Marry, before your ladyship, I grant,
She puts her tongue a little in her heart,   110
And chides with thinking.
EMILIA   You ha' little cause to say so.
IAGO   Come on, come on. You are pictures out of door,
Bells in your parlours; wildcats in your kitchens,

2. Week's. *Footing:* arrival.   3. Training.   4. She talks even when she gives me permission to sleep.

Saints in your injuries; devils being offended,
Players in your housewifery, and hussies in your beds.[5]   115
DESDEMONA   O, fie upon thee, slanderer!
IAGO   Nay, it is true, or else I am a Turk.
You rise to play and go to bed to work.
EMILIA   You shall not write my praise.
IAGO   No, let me not.
DESDEMONA   What wouldst write of me, if thou shouldst praise me?   120
IAGO   O, gentle lady, do not put me to't,
For I am nothing if not critical.
DESDEMONA   Come on, essay—there's one gone to the harbour?
IAGO   Ay, madam.
DESDEMONA   I am not merry, but I do beguile   125
The thing I am by seeming otherwise.
Come, how wouldst thou praise me?
IAGO   I am about it, but indeed my invention
Comes from my pate as birdlime does from frieze[6]
It plucks out brains and all. But my muse labours,   130
And thus she is delivered:
If she be fair and wise, fairness and wit,
The one's for use, the other useth it.
DESDEMONA   Well praised! How if she be black[7] and witty?
IAGO   If she be black and thereto have a wit,   135
She'll find a white that shall her blackness fit.
DESDEMONA   Worse and worse.
EMILIA   How if fair and foolish?
IAGO   She never yet was foolish that was fair.
For even her folly helped her to an heir.
DESDEMONA   These are old fond[8] paradoxes, to make fools laugh i'th' 140
alehouse.
What miserable praise hast thou for her
That's foul and foolish?
IAGO   There's none so foul and foolish thereunto,
But does foul pranks which fair and wise ones do.   145
DESDEMONA   O heavy ignorance! Thou praisest the worst best. But
what praise couldst thou bestow on a deserving woman indeed—one
that, in the authority of her merit, did justly put on the vouch of very
malice itself?[9]
IAGO   She that was ever fair and never proud,   150
Had tongue at will and yet was never loud,
Never lacked gold and yet went never gay,
Fled from her wish, and yet said 'Now I may';
She that, being angered, her revenge being nigh,
Bade her wrong stay and her displeasure fly;   155
She that in wisdom never was so frail
To change the cod's head for the salmon's tail;[1]
She that could think and ne'er disclose her mind,

5. You pretend to do the housekeeping and work hard only in bed. *Pictures*: models. *Injuries*: when you wrong others.   6. Sticky matter from rough cloth.   7. Brunette.   8. Foolish.   9. One whose virtue elicits approval even from the malicious.   1. Exchange something valuable for something worthless.

See suitors following, and not look behind—
She was a wight,² if ever such wights were—   160
DESDEMONA   To do what?
IAGO   To suckle fools, and chronicle small beer.³
DESDEMONA   O most lame and impotent conclusion! Do not learn of
him, Emilia, though he be thy husband. How say you, Cassio, is he
not a most profane and liberal⁴ counsellor?   165
CASSIO   He speaks home,⁵ madam. You may relish him more in the
soldier than in the scholar.
        [CASSIO *and* DESDEMONA *talk apart.*]
IAGO [*aside*]   He takes her by the palm. Ay, well said—whisper. With
as little a web as this will I ensnare as great a fly as Cassio. Ay, smile
upon her, do. I will gyve thee in thine own courtship. You say true,   170
'tis so indeed. If such tricks as these strip you out of your lieuten-
antry, it had been better you had not kissed your three fingers so oft,
which now again you are most apt to play the sir in. Very good, well
kissed, an excellent curtsy, 'tis so indeed; yet again your fingers to
your lips? Would they were clyster-pipes⁶ for your sake.   175
        [*Trumpets within.*]
[*Aloud*] The Moor—I know his trumpet.
CASSIO   'Tis truly so.
DESDEMONA   Let's meet him and receive him.
CASSIO   Lo where he comes!
        [*Enter* OTHELLO *and attendants.*]
OTHELLO [*to* DESDEMONA]   O my fair warrior!
DESDEMONA   My dear Othello.
OTHELLO   It gives me wonder great as my content
To see you here before me. O my soul's joy,   180
If after every tempest come such calms,
May the winds blow till they have wakened death,
And let the labouring barque climb hills of seas
Olympus-high, and duck again as low
As hell's from heaven. If it were now to die   185
'Twere now to be most happy, for I fear
My soul hath her content so absolute
That not another comfort like to this
Succeeds in unknown fate.
DESDEMONA   The heavens forbid
But that our loves and comforts should increase   190
Even as our days do grow.
OTHELLO   Amen to that, sweet powers!
I cannot speak enough of this content.
It stops me here, it is too much of joy.
And this, [*they kiss*] and this, the greatest discords be
That e'er our hearts shall make.
IAGO [*aside*]   O, you are well tuned now,   195
But I'll set down the pegs⁷ that make this music,

2. Being.   3. Keep household accounts.   4. Free and easy.   5. Speaks frankly.   6. Enema tubes.
7. I.e., that control the pitch on string instruments.

As honest as I am.
OTHELLO   Come, let us to the castle.
News, friends: our wars are done, the Turks are drowned.
How does my old acquaintance of this isle?—
Honey, you shall be well desired in Cyprus,   200
I have found great love amongst them. O my sweet,
I prattle out of fashion, and I dote
In mine own comforts. I prithee, good Iago,
Go to the bay and disembark my coffers.
Bring thou the master to the citadel.   205
He is a good one, and his worthiness
Does challenge[8] much respect. Come, Desdemona.—
Once more, well met at Cyprus!
           [*Exeunt* OTHELLO *and* DESDEMONA *with all but* IAGO *and*
           RODERIGO.]
IAGO [*to an attendant as he goes out*]   Do thou meet me presently at
     the harbour. [*To* RODERIGO] Come hither. If thou beest valiant—as   210
     they say base men being in love have then a nobility in their natures
     more than is native to them—list me. The lieutenant tonight watches
     on the court of guard.[9] First, I must tell thee this: Desdemona is
     directly in love with him.
RODERIGO   With him? Why, 'tis not possible!   215
IAGO   Lay thy finger thus, and let thy soul be instructed. Mark me
     with what violence she first loved the Moor, but for bragging and
     telling her fantastical lies. To love him still for prating?—let not thy
     discreet heart think it. Her eye must be fed, and what delight shall
     she have to look on the devil? When the blood is made dull with the   220
     act of sport, there should be again to inflame it, and to give satiety
     a fresh appetite, loveliness in favour, sympathy in years, manners,
     and beauties, all which the Moor is defective in. Now, for want of
     these required conveniences,[1] her delicate tenderness will find itself
     abused, begin to heave the gorge,[2] disrelish and abhor the Moor.   225
     Very nature will instruct her in it and compel her to some second
     choice. Now, sir, this granted—as it is a most pregnant[3] and un-
     forced position—who stands so eminent in the degree of this fortune
     as Cassio does?—a knave very voluble, no further conscionable than
     in putting on the mere form of civil and humane seeming for the   230
     better compass of his salt and most hidden loose[4] affection. Why,
     none; why, none—a slipper[5] and subtle knave, a finder of occasion,
     that has an eye can stamp and counterfeit advantages, though true
     advantage never present itself, a devilish knave! Besides, the knave
     is handsome, young, and hath all those requisites in him that folly   235
     and green minds look after. A pestilent complete knave, and the
     woman hath found him already.
RODERIGO   I cannot believe that in her. She's full of most blessed
     condition.
IAGO   Blessed fig's end! The wine she drinks is made of grapes. If she   240

8. Require.   9. Guardhouse.   1. Agreements, points in common. *Favour:* appearance.   2. Vomit.
3. Obvious.   4. Morally easy. *Conscionable:* conscience-bound. *Humane:* polite. *Salt:* lecherous.
5. Slippery.

had been blessed, she would never have loved the Moor. Blessed
pudding! Didst thou not see her paddle with the palm of his hand?
Didst not mark that?

RODERIGO   Yes, that I did, but that was but courtesy.

IAGO   Lechery, by this hand; an index[6] and obscure prologue to the   245
history of lust and foul thoughts. They met so near with their lips
that their breaths embraced together. Villainous thoughts, Roderigo!
When these mutualities so marshal the way, hard at hand comes the
master and main exercise, th'incorporate[7] conclusion. Pish! But, sir,
be you ruled by me. I have brought you from Venice. Watch you   250
tonight. For the command, I'll lay't upon you. Cassio knows you not;
I'll not be far from you. Do you find some occasion to anger Cassio,
either by speaking too loud, or tainting[8] his discipline, or from what
other course you please, which the time shall more favourably
minister.   255

RODERIGO   Well.

IAGO   Sir, he's rash and very sudden in choler,[9] and haply may strike
at you. Provoke him that he may, for even out of that will I cause
these of Cyprus to mutiny, whose qualification shall come into no
true taste[1] again but by the displanting of Cassio. So shall you have   260
a shorter journey to your desires by the means I shall then have to
prefer them, and the impediment most profitably removed, without
the which there were no expectation of our prosperity.

RODERIGO   I will do this, if you can bring it to any opportunity.

IAGO   I warrant thee. Meet me by and by at the citadel. I must fetch   265
his necessaries ashore. Farewell.

RODERIGO   Adieu.   [*Exit.*]

IAGO   That Cassio loves her, I do well believe it.
That she loves him, 'tis apt and of great credit.
The Moor—howbe't that I endure him not—   270
Is of a constant, loving, noble nature,
And I dare think he'll prove to Desdemona
A most dear[2] husband. Now I do love her too,
Not out of absolute lust—though peradventure,[3]
I stand accountant for as great a sin—   275
But partly led to diet[4] my revenge
For that I do suspect the lusty Moor
Hath leapt into my seat, the thought whereof
Doth, like a poisonous mineral, gnaw my inwards;
And nothing can or shall content my soul   280
Till I am evened with him, wife for wife—
Or failing so, yet that I put the Moor
At least into a jealousy so strong
That judgement cannot cure, which thing to do,
If this poor trash of Venice whom I trace   285
For his quick hunting stand the putting on
I'll have our Michael Cassio on the hip,

---

6. Guide.   7. Sexual.   8. Disparaging.   9. Anger.   1. Pacification will not be brought about.
2. Expensive.   3. By chance. *Absolute:* pure.   4. Feed.

Abuse him to the Moor in the rank garb[5]—
For I fear Cassio with my nightcap, too—
Make the Moor thank me, love me, and reward me   290
For making him egregiously an ass,
And practising upon[6] his peace and quiet
Even to madness. 'Tis here, but yet confused
Knavery's plain face is never seen till used.   [*Exit.*]

2.2

[*Enter Othello's* HERALD *reading a proclamation.*]

HERALD It is Othello's pleasure—our noble and valiant general—
that, upon certain tidings now arrived importing the mere perdition[7]
of the Turkish fleet, every man put himself into triumph: some to
dance, some to make bonfires, each man to what sport and revels
his addiction[8] leads him; for besides these beneficial news, it is the   5
celebration of his nuptial. So much was his pleasure should be proclaimed. All offices[9] are open, and there is full liberty of feasting
from this present hour of five till the bell have told eleven. Heaven
bless the isle of Cyprus and our noble general, Othello!   [*Exit.*]

2.3

[*Enter* OTHELLO, DESDEMONA, CASSIO, *and attendants.*]

OTHELLO Good Michael, look you to the guard tonight.
Let's teach ourselves that honourable stop
Not to outsport discretion.
CASSIO Iago hath direction what to do,
But notwithstanding, with my personal eye   5
Will I look to't.
OTHELLO   Iago is most honest.
Michael, good night. Tomorrow with your earliest
Let me have speech with you. [*To* DESDEMONA] Come, my dear love,
The purchase made, the fruits are to ensue.
That profit's yet to come 'tween me and you.   10
[*To* CASSIO] Good night.
[*Exeunt* OTHELLO, DESDEMONA *and attendants.*—*Enter* IAGO.]
CASSIO Welcome, Iago. We must to the watch.
IAGO Not this hour, lieutenant; 'tis not yet ten o'th' clock. Our general
cast[1] us thus early for the love of his Desdemona, who let us not
therefore blame. He hath not yet made wanton the night with her,   15
and she is sport for Jove.
CASSIO She's a most exquisite lady.
IAGO And I'll warrant her full of game.
CASSIO Indeed, she's a most fresh and delicate creature.
IAGO What an eye she has! Methinks it sounds a parley to provoca-   20
tion.
CASSIO An inviting eye, and yet, methinks, right modest.

5. Style.   6. Scheming to destroy, in Machiavellian fashion.   7. Absolute destruction.   8. Inclination.   9. Kitchens.   1. Dismissed.

IAGO   And when she speaks, is it not an alarum² to love?

CASSIO   She is indeed perfection.

IAGO   Well, happiness to their sheets. Come, lieutenant. I have a   25
stoup³ of wine, and here without are a brace of Cyprus gallants that
would fain have a measure to the health of black Othello.

CASSIO   Not tonight, good Iago. I have very poor and unhappy brains
for drinking. I could well wish courtesy would invent some other
custom of entertainment.   30

IAGO   O, they are our friends! But one cup. I'll drink for you.

CASSIO   I ha' drunk but one cup tonight, and that was craftily qualified,⁴ too, and behold what innovation it makes here! I am infortu-
nate in the infirmity, and dare not task my weakness with any more.

IAGO   What, man,'tis a night of revels, the gallants desire it!   35

CASSIO   Where are they?

IAGO   Here at the door. I pray you call them in.

CASSIO   I'll do't, but it dislikes me.   [Exit.]

IAGO   If I can fasten but one cup upon him,
With that which he hath drunk tonight already   40
He'll be as full of quarrel and offence
As my young mistress' dog. Now my sick fool Roderigo,
Whom love hath turned almost the wrong side out,
To Desdemona hath tonight caroused
Potations pottle-deep,⁵ and he's to watch,   45
Three else⁶ of Cyprus—noble swelling spirits
That hold their honours in a wary distance,⁷
The very elements of this warlike isle—
Have I tonight flustered with flowing cups,
And they watch too. Now 'mongst this flock of drunkards   50
Am I to put our Cassio in some action
That may offend the isle.
        [Enter MONTANA, CASSIO, GENTLEMEN, and servants with wine.]
                But here they come.
If consequence do but approve my dream,
My boat sails freely both with wind and stream.

CASSIO   Fore God, they have given me a rouse⁸ already.   55

MONTANO   God faith, a little one; not past a pint,
As I am a soldier.

IAGO   Some wine, ho!
        [Sings]
                And let me the cannikin⁹ clink, clink,
                And let me the cannikin clink.
                    A soldier's a man,   60
                    O, man's life's but a span,
                    Why then, let a soldier drink.
        Some wine, boys!

CASSIO   Fore God, an excellent song.

IAGO   I learned it in England, where indeed they are most potent in   65

---

2. Military call to action.   3. Two-quart tankard.   4. Watered down.   5. To the bottom.
6. Others.   7. Are jealous of their honor.   8. Drink.   9. Drinking vessel.

potting. Your Dane, your German, and your swag-bellied[1] Hollander—drink, ho!—are nothing to your English.

CASSIO   Is your Englishman so exquisite in his drinking?

IAGO   Why, he drinks you with facility your Dane dead drunk. He
sweats not to overthrow your Almain. He gives your Hollander a   70
vomit ere the next pottle can be filled.

CASSIO   To the health of our general!

MONTANO   I am for it, lieutenant, and I'll do you justice.

IAGO   O sweet England!
[Sings]

> King Stephen was and a worthy peer,   75
>   His breeches cost him but a crown;
> He held them sixpence all too dear,
>   With that he called the tailor lown.[2]
> He was a wight of high renown,
>   And thou art but of low degree.   80
> 'Tis pride that pulls the country down,
>   Then take thy auld cloak about thee.

Some wine, ho!

CASSIO   Fore God, this is a more exquisite song than the other.

IAGO   Will you hear't again?   85

CASSIO   No, for I hold him to be unworthy of his place that does those
things. Well, God's above all, and there be souls must be saved, and
there be souls must not be saved.

IAGO   It's true, good lieutenant.

CASSIO   For mine own part—no offence to the general, nor any man   90
of quality—I hope to be saved.

IAGO   And so do I too, lieutenant.

CASSIO   Ay, but, by your leave, not before me. The lieutenant is to be
saved before the ensign. Let's ha' no more of this. Let's to our affairs.
God forgive us our sins. Gentlemen, let's look to our business. Do   95
not think, gentlemen, I am drunk. This is my ensign, this is my right
hand, and this is my left. I am not drunk now. I can stand well
enough, and I speak well enough.

GENTLEMEN   Excellent well.

CASSIO   Why, very well then. You must not think then that I am   100
drunk.   [Exit.]

MONTANO   To th' platform, masters. Come, let's set the watch.
[Exeunt GENTLEMEN.]

IAGO   You see this fellow that is gone before—
He's a soldier fit to stand by Caesar
And give direction; and do but see his vice.   105
'Tis to his virtue a just equinox,[3]
The one as long as th'other. 'Tis pity of him.
I fear the trust Othello puts him in,
On some odd time of his infirmity,
Will shake this island.

MONTANO   But is he often thus?   110

---

1. Big-bellied.   2. Lout, oaf.   3. Precise balance.

IAGO   'Tis evermore his prologue to his sleep
  He'll watch the horologe⁴ a double set
  If drink rock not his cradle.
MONTANO   It were well
  The general were put in mind of it.
  Perhaps he sees it not, or his good nature   115
  Prizes the virtue that appears in Cassio
  And looks not on his evils. Is not this true?
     [*Enter* RODERIGO.]
IAGO [*aside*] How now, Roderigo!
  I pray you after the lieutenant, go.   [*Exit* RODERIGO.]
MONTANO And 'tis great pity that the noble Moor   120
  Should hazard such a place as his own second
  With one of an engraffed⁵ infirmity.
  It were an honest action to say so
  To the Moor.
IAGO   Not I, for this fair island!
  I do love Cassio well, and would do much   125
  To cure him of this evil.
VOICES [*within*] Help, help!
IAGO   But hark, what noise?
     [*Enter* CASSIO, *driving in* RODERIGO.]
CASSIO 'Swounds, you rogue, you rascal!
MONTANO What's the matter, lieutenant?
CASSIO A knave teach me my duty?—I'll beat the knave into a 130
  twiggen⁶ bottle.
RODERIGO Beat me?
CASSIO Dost thou prate, rogue?
MONTANO Nay, good lieutenant, I pray you, sir, hold your hand.
CASSIO Let me go, sir, or I'll knock you o'er the mazard.⁷   135
MONTANO Come, come, you're drunk.
CASSIO Drunk?
     [*They fight.*]
IAGO [*to* RODERIGO] Away, I say. Go out and cry a mutiny.
                      [*Exit* RODERIGO.]
  Nay, good lieutenant. God's will, gentlemen!
  Help, ho! Lieutenant! Sir! Montano! Sir!   140
  Help, masters. Here's a goodly watch indeed.
     [*A bell rung.*]
  Who's that which rings the bell? Diablo,⁸ ho!
  The town will rise. God's will, lieutenant, hold.
  You'll be ashamed for ever.
     [*Enter* OTHELLO *and attendants, with weapons.*]
OTHELLO   What is the matter here?
MONTANO 'Swounds, I bleed still. I am hurt to th' death. [*Attacking*
     CASSIO] He dies.   145
OTHELLO Hold, for your lives!

---

4. Clock.   5. Rooted.   6. Wicker-covered.   7. Head (image transferred, figuratively, from a drinking cup).   8. The devil.

IAGO   Hold, ho, lieutenant, sir, Montano, gentlemen!
   Have you forgot all place of sense and duty?
   Hold, the general speaks to you. Hold, hold, for shame.
OTHELLO   Why, how now, ho? From whence ariseth this?   150
   Are we turned Turks, and to ourselves do that
   Which heaven hath forbid the Ottomites?
   For Christian shame, put by this barbarous brawl.
   He that stirs next to carve for his own rage
   Holds his soul light. He dies upon his motion.   155
   Silence that dreadful bell—it frights the isle
   From her propriety.[9]
      [*Bell stops.*]
               What is the matter, masters?
   Honest Iago, that looks dead with grieving,
   Speak. Who began this? On thy love I charge thee.
IAGO   I do not know. Friends all but now, even now,   160
   In quarter[1] and in terms like bride and groom,
   Devesting them for bed; and then but now—
   As if some planet had unwitted men—
   Swords out, and tilting one at others' breasts
   In opposition bloody. I cannot speak   165
   Any beginning to this peevish odds,[2]
   And would in action glorious I had lost
   Those legs that brought me to a part of it.
OTHELLO   How comes it, Michael, you are thus forgot?
CASSIO   I pray you pardon me. I cannot speak.   170
OTHELLO   Worthy Montano, you were wont be civil.
   The gravity and stillness of your youth
   The world hath noted, and your name is great
   In mouths of wisest censure. What's the matter,
   That you unlace your reputation thus,   175
   And spend your rich opinion[3] for the name
   Of a night-brawler? Give me answer to it.
MONTANO   Worthy Othello, I am hurt to danger.
   Your officer Iago can inform you,
   While I spare speech—which something now offends me—   180
   Of all that I do know; nor know I aught
   By me that's said or done amiss this night,
   Unless self-charity be sometimes a vice,
   And to defend ourselves it be a sin
   When violence assails us.
OTHELLO   Now, by heaven,   185
   My blood begins my safer guides to rule,
   And passion, having my best judgment collied,[4]
   Essays to lead the way. 'Swounds, if I stir,
   Or do but lift this arm, the best of you
   Shall sink in my rebuke. Give me to know   190

9. Order.   1. On duty.   2. Argument.   3. Reputation. *Censure:* judgment. *Unlace:* undo.   4.
Darkened.

How this foul rout began, who set it on,
And he that is approved in this offence,
Though he had twinned with me, both at a birth,
Shall lose me. What, in a town of war
Yet wild, the people's hearts brimful of fear,   195
To manage private and domestic quarrel
In night, and on the court and guard of safety!
'Tis monstrous. Iago, who began't?
MONTANO [*to* IAGO]   If partially affined⁵ or leagued in office
Thou dost deliver more or less than truth,   200
Thou art no soldier.
IAGO   Touch me not so near.
I had rather ha' this tongue cut from my mouth
Than it should do offence to Michael Cassio.
Yet I persuade myself to speak the truth
Shall nothing wrong him. This it is, general.   205
Montano and myself being in speech,
There comes a fellow crying out for help,
And Cassio following him with determined sword
To execute upon him. Sir, this gentleman
Steps in to Cassio, and entreats his pause.   210
Myself the crying fellow did pursue,
Lest by his clamour, as it so fell out,
The town might fall in fright. He, swift of foot,
Outran my purpose, and I returned, the rather
For that I heard the clink and fall of swords   215
And Cassio high in oath, which till tonight
I ne'er might say before. When I came back—
For this was brief—I found them close together
At blow and thrust, even as again they were
When you yourself did part them.   220
More of this matter cannot I report,
But men are men. The best sometimes forget.
Though Cassio did some little wrong to him,
As men in rage strike those that wish them best,
Yet surely Cassio, I believe, received   225
From him that fled some strange indignity
Which patience could not pass.⁶
OTHELLO   I know, Iago,
Thy honesty and love doth mince this matter,
Making it light to Cassio. Cassio, I love thee,
But never more be officer of mine.   230
        [*Enter* DESDEMONA, *attended.*]
Look if my gentle love be not raised up.
I'll make thee an example.
DESDEMONA   What is the matter, dear?
OTHELLO   All's well now, sweeting.
Come away to bed. [*To* MONTANO] Sir, for your hurts   235

5. Kindred.   6. Endure.

Myself will be your surgeon. [*To attendants*] Lead him off.
                              [*Exeunt attendants with* MONTANO.]
Iago, look with care about the town,
And silence those whom this vile brawl distracted.
Come, Desdemona. 'Tis the soldier's life
To have their balmy slumbers waked with strife.   240
              [*Exeunt* OTHELLO *the Moor,* DESDEMONA, *and attendants.*]

IAGO What, are you hurt, lieutenant?

CASSIO Ay, past all surgery.

IAGO Marry, God forbid.

CASSIO Reputation, reputation, reputation—O, I ha' lost my reputation, I ha' lost the immortal part of myself, and what remains is   245
bestial! My reputation, Iago, my reputation.

IAGO As I am an honest man, I thought you had received some bodily
wound. There is more sense in that than in reputation. Reputation
is an idle and most false imposition, oft got without merit and lost
without deserving. You have lost no reputation at all unless you   250
repute yourself such a loser. What, man, there are more ways to
recover the general again. You are but now cast in his mood[7]—a
punishment more in policy[8] than in malice, even so as one would
beat his offenceless dog to affright an imperious lion. Sue to him
again, and he's yours.   255

CASSIO I will rather sue to be despised than to deceive so good a
commander with so slight, so drunken, and so indiscreet an officer.
Drunk, and speak parrot, and squabble? Swagger, swear, and discourse fustian[9] with one's own shadow? O thou invisible spirit of
wine, if thou hast no name to be known by, let us call thee devil. 260

IAGO What was he that you followed with your sword? What had he
done to you?

CASSIO I know not.

IAGO Is't possible?

CASSIO I remember a mass of things, but nothing distinctly; a quarrel, 265
but nothing wherefore. O God, that men should put an enemy in
their mouths to steal away their brains! That we should with joy,
pleasance, revel, and applause transform ourselves into beasts!

IAGO Why, but you are now well enough. How came you thus
recovered?   270

CASSIO It hath pleased the devil drunkenness to give place to the devil
wrath. One unperfectness shows me another, to make me frankly
despise myself.

IAGO Come, you are too severe a moraller. As the time, the place,
and the condition of this country stands, I could heartily wish this 275
had not befallen; but since it is as it is, mend it for your own good.

CASSIO I will ask him for my place again. He shall tell me I am a
drunkard. Had I as many mouths as Hydra,[1] such an answer would
stop them all. To be now a sensible man, by and by a fool, and
presently a beast! O, strange! Every inordinate cup is unblessed, and 280

---

7. Fired in his anger. 8. Political expedience. 9. Coarsely. *Speak parrot:* mimic. 1. Mythical
many-headed beast, capable of regenerating severed heads.

the ingredient is a devil.

IAGO   Come, come. Good wine is a good familiar creature, if it be well used. Exclaim no more against it. And, good lieutenant, I think you think I love you.

CASSIO   I have well approved it, sir—I drunk?   285

IAGO   You or any man living may be drunk at a time, man. I'll tell you what you shall do. Our general's wife is now the general. I may say so in this respect, for that he hath devoted and given up himself to the contemplation, mark, and denotement[2] of her parts and graces. Confess yourself freely to her. Importune her help to put you in your   290 place again. She is of so free, so kind, so apt, so blessed a disposition, she holds it a vice in her goodness not to do more than she is requested. This broken joint between you and her husband entreat her to splinter,[3] and, my fortunes against any lay[4] worth naming, this crack of your love shall grow stronger than it was before.   295

CASSIO   You advise me well.

IAGO   I protest, in the sincerity of love and honest kindness.

CASSIO   I think it freely, and betimes in the morning I will beseech the virtuous Desdemona to undertake for me. I am desperate of my fortunes if they check me here.   300

IAGO   You are in the right. Good night, lieutenant. I must to the watch.

CASSIO   Good night, honest Iago.   [*Exit.*]

IAGO   And what's he then that says I play the villain,
When this advice is free I give, and honest,
Probal[5] to thinking, and indeed the course   305
To win the Moor again? For 'tis most easy
Th'inclining Desdemona to subdue
In any honest suit. She's framed as fruitful
As the free elements,[6] and then for her
To win the Moor, were't to renounce his baptism,   310
All seals and symbols of redeemèd sin,
His soul is so enfettered to her love
That she may make, unmake, do what she list,
Even as her appetite shall play the god
With his weak function.[7] How am I then a villain,   315
To counsel Cassio to this parallel course
Directly to his good? Divinity of hell:
When devils will the blackest sins put on,
They do suggest at first with heavenly shows,
As I do now; for whiles this honest fool   320
Plies Desdemona to repair his fortune,
And she for him pleads strongly to the Moor,
I'll pour this pestilence into his ear:
That she repeals him[8] for her body's lust,
And by how much she strives to do him good   325
She shall undo her credit with the Moor.
So will I turn her virtue into pitch,

2. Observation.   3. Splint.   4. Bet.   5. Logical, likely.   6. Unconstrained nature. *Fruitful:* generous.   7. Easily moved passion. *Appetite:* sexual desire.   8. Calls for his return.

And out of her own goodness make the net
That shall enmesh them all.
    [*Enter* RODERIGO.]
                    How now, Roderigo?

RODERIGO   I do follow here in the chase, not like a hound that hunts,   330
but one that fills up the cry.[9] My money is almost spent, I ha' been
tonight exceedingly well cudgelled, and I think the issue will be I
shall have so much experience for my pains: and so, with no money
at all and a little more wit, return again to Venice.

IAGO   How poor are they that ha' not patience!   335
What wound did ever heal but by degrees?
Thou know'st we work by wit and not by witchcraft,
And wit depends on dilatory time.
Does't not go well? Cassio hath beaten thee,
And thou by that small hurt has cashiered Cassio.   340
Though other things grow fair against the sun,
Yet fruits that blossom first will first be ripe.
Content thyself a while. By the mass, 'tis morning.
Pleasure and action make the hours seem short.
Retire thee. Go where thou art billeted.   345
Away, I say. Thou shalt know more hereafter.
Nay, get thee gone.   [*Exit* RODERIGO.]
              Two things are to be done.
My wife must move for[1] Cassio to her mistress.
I'll set her on.
Myself a while to draw the Moor apart.   350
And bring him jump[2] when he may Cassio find
Soliciting his wife. Ay, that's the way.
Dull not device by coldness and delay.   [*Exit.*]

3.1

    [*Enter* CASSIO *with* MUSICIANS.]
CASSIO   Masters, play here—I will content your pains[3]—
Something that's brief, and bid 'Good morrow, general'.
    [*Music. Enter* CLOWN.]
CLOWN   Why, masters, ha' your instruments been in Naples,[4] that
they speak i'th' nose thus?
MUSICIAN   How, sir, how?   5
CLOWN   Are these, I pray you, wind instruments?[5]
MUSICIAN   Ay, marry are they, sir.
CLOWN   O, thereby hangs a tail.
MUSICIAN   Whereby hangs a tale, sir?
CLOWN   Marry, sir, by many a wind instrument that I know. But mas-   10
ters, here's money for you, and the general so likes your music that
he desires you, for love's sake, to make no more noise with it.
MUSICIAN   Well, sir, we will not.

---

9. One of the baying hounds.   1. Side with.   2. Exactly.   3. Reward your efforts.   4. Nasal wind
instruments; bodily parts with syphilis contracted in Naples.   5. With the reference to tail/tale, below; a
pun on flatulence.

CLOWN   If you have any music that may not be heard, to't again; but, as
    they say, to hear music the general does not greatly care.   15
MUSICIAN   We ha' none such, sir.
CLOWN   Then put up your pipes in your bag, for I'll away. Go, vanish
    into air, away.   [*Exeunt* MUSICIANS.]
CASSIO   Dost thou hear, my honest friend?
CLOWN   No, I hear not your honest friend, I hear you.   20
CASSIO   Prithee, keep up thy quillets.[6] There's a poor piece of gold for
    thee. If the gentlewoman that attends the general's wife be stirring,
    tell her there's one Cassio entreats her a little favour of speech. Wilt
    thou do this?
CLOWN   She is stirring, sir. If she will stir hither, I shall seem to notify   25
    unto her.
CASSIO   Do, good my friend.   [*Exit* CLOWN.]
    [*Enter* IAGO.]
                  In happy time, Iago.
IAGO   You ha' not been abed, then.
CASSIO   Why, no. The day had broke
    Before we parted. I ha' made bold, Iago,
    To send in to your wife. My suit to her   30
    Is that she will to virtuous Desdemona
    Procure me some access.
IAGO   I'll send her to you presently,
    And I'll devise a mean to draw the Moor
    Out of the way, that your converse and business   35
    May be more free.
CASSIO   I humbly thank you for't.   [*Exit* IAGO.]
    I never knew a Florentine[7] more kind and honest.
    [*Enter* EMILIA.]
EMILIA   Good morrow, good lieutenant. I am sorry
    For your displeasure, but all will sure be well.
    The general and his wife are talking of it,   40
    And she speaks for you stoutly. The Moor replies
    That he you hurt is of great fame in Cyprus,
    And great affinity,[8] and that in wholesome wisdom
    He might not but refuse you. But he protests he loves you,
    And needs no other suitor but his likings   45
    To take the saf'st occasion by the front
    To bring you in again.
CASSIO   Yet I beseech you,
    If you think fit, or that it may be done,
    Give me advantage of some brief discourse
    With Desdemon alone.
EMILIA   Pray you come in.   50
    I will bestow you where you shall have time
    To speak your bosom[9] freely.
CASSIO   I am much bound to you.
                                            [*Exeunt.*]

6. Quibbles, puns.   7. One from Cassio's own city-state.   8. Kinship.   9. Mind.

3.2

[*Enter* OTHELLO, IAGO, *and* GENTLEMEN.]

OTHELLO   These letters give, Iago, to the pilot,
And by him do my duties to the senate.
That done, I will be walking on the works.
Repair there to me.

IAGO   Well, my good lord, I'll do't.   [*Exit.*]

OTHELLO   This fortification, gentlemen—shall we see't?   5

A GENTLEMAN   We'll wait upon your lordship.   [*Exeunt.*]

3.3

[*Enter* DESDEMONA, CASSIO, *and* EMILIA.]

DESDEMONA   Be thou assured, good Cassio, I will do
All my abilities in thy behalf.

EMILIA   Good madam, do. I warrant it grieves my husband
As if the cause were his.

DESDEMONA   O, that's an honest fellow. Do not doubt, Cassio,   5
But I will have my lord and you again
As friendly as you were.

CASSIO   Bounteous madam,
Whatever shall become of Michael Cassio
He's never anything but your true servant.

DESDEMONA   I know't. I thank you. You do love my lord.   10
You have known him long, and be you well assured
He shall in strangeness stand no farther off
Than in a politic distance.[1]

CASSIO   Ay, but, lady,
That policy may either last so long,
Or feed upon such nice[2] and wat'rish diet,   15
Or breed itself so out of circumstance,
That, I being absent and my place supplied,[3]
My general will forget my love and service.

DESDEMONA   Do not doubt[4] that. Before Emilia here
I give thee warrant of thy place. Assure thee,   20
If I do vow a friendship I'll perform it
To the last article. My lord shall never rest.
I'll watch him tame,[5] and talk him out of patience.
His bed shall seem a school, his board a shrift.[6]
I'll intermingle everything he does   25
With Cassio's suit. Therefore be merry, Cassio,
For thy solicitor shall rather die
Than give they cause away.

[*Enter* OTHELLO *and* IAGO.]

EMILIA   Madam, here comes my lord.

CASSIO   Madam, I'll take my leave.

DESDEMONA   Why, stay, and hear me speak.

---

1. He shall seem only as distant as he must for political reasons.   2. Finicky.   3. Filled.   4. Have
doubts about.   5. Make him docile by keeping him awake.   6. Confessional.

CASSIO   Madam, not now. I am very ill at ease,   30
　　Unfit for mine own purposes.
DESDEMONA   Well, do your discretion.   [*Exit* CASSIO.]
IAGO   Ha! I like not that.
OTHELLO   What dost thou say?
IAGO   Nothing, my lord. Or if, I know not what.   35
OTHELLO   Was not that Cassio parted from my wife?
IAGO   Cassio, my lord? No, sure, I cannot think it,
　　That he would steal away so guilty-like
　　Seeing your coming.
OTHELLO   I do believe 'twas he.   40
DESDEMONA   How now, my lord?
　　I have been talking with a suitor here,
　　A man that languishes in your displeasure.
OTHELLO   Who is't you mean?
DESDEMONA   Why, your lieutenant, Cassio; good my lord,   45
　　If I have any grace or power to move you,
　　His present reconciliation take;
　　For if he be not one that truly loves you,
　　That errs in ignorance and not in cunning,
　　I have no judgement in an honest face.   50
　　I prithee call him back.
OTHELLO   Went he hence now?
DESDEMONA   Yes, faith, so humbled
　　That he hath left part of his grief with me
　　To suffer with him. Good love, call him back.   55
OTHELLO   Not now, sweet Desdemon. Some other time.
DESDEMONA   But shall't be shortly?
OTHELLO   The sooner, sweet, for you.
DESDEMONA   Shall't be tonight at supper?
OTHELLO   No, not tonight.
DESDEMONA   Tomorrow dinner, then?
OTHELLO   I shall not dine at home.
　　I meet the captains at the citadel.   60
DESDEMONA   Why then, tomorrow night, or Tuesday morn,
　　On Tuesday noon, or night, on Wednesday morn—
　　I prithee name the time, but let it not
　　Exceed three days. In faith, he's penitent,
　　And yet his trespass, in our common reason—   65
　　Save that, they say, the wars must make example
　　Out of her best—is not almost a fault
　　T'incur a private check.[7] When shall he come?
　　Tell me, Othello. I wonder in my soul
　　What you would ask me that I should deny,   70
　　Or stand so mamm'ring[8] on? What, Michael Cassio,
　　That came a-wooing with you, and so many a time
　　When I have spoke of you dispraisingly
　　Hath ta'en your part—to have so much to-do

7. Reprimand.　　8. Hesitating.

To bring him in? By'r Lady, I could do much.   75
OTHELLO   Prithee, no more. Let him come when he will.
   I will deny thee nothing.
DESDEMONA   Why, this is not a boon.
   'Tis as I should entreat you wear your gloves,
   Or feed on nourishing dishes, or keep you warm,
   Or sue to you to do a peculiar profit   80
   To your own person. Nay, when I have a suit
   Wherein I mean to touch your love indeed,
   It shall be full of poise⁹ and difficult weight,
   And fearful to be granted.
OTHELLO   I will deny thee nothing,
   Whereon I do beseech thee grant me this: 85
   To leave me but a little to myself.
DESDEMONA   Shall I deny you? No. Farewell, my lord.
OTHELLO   Farewell, my Desdemona. I'll come to thee straight.
DESDEMONA   Emilia, come. [*To* OTHELLO] Be as your fancies teach
   you. Whate'er you be, I am obedient.   90
                            [*Exeunt* DESDEMONA *and* EMILIA.]
OTHELLO   Excellent wretch! Perdition catch my soul
   But I do love thee, and when I love thee not,
   Chaos is come again.
IAGO   My noble lord.
OTHELLO   What dost thou say, Iago?   95
IAGO   Did Michael Cassio, when you wooed my lady,
   Know of your love?
OTHELLO   He did, from first to last. Why dost thou ask?
IAGO   But for a satisfaction of my thought.
   No further harm.
OTHELLO   Why of thy thought, Iago?   100
IAGO   I did not think he had been acquainted with her.
OTHELLO   O yes, and went between us very oft.
IAGO   Indeed?
OTHELLO   Indeed? Ay, indeed. Discern'st thou aught in that?
   Is he not honest?   105
IAGO   Honest, my lord?
OTHELLO   Honest? Ay, honest.
IAGO   My lord, for aught I know.
OTHELLO   What dost thou think?
IAGO   Think, my lord?
OTHELLO   'Think, my lord?' By heaven, thou echo'st me   110
   As if there were some monster in thy thought
   Too hideous to be shown! Thou dost mean something.
   I heard thee say even now thou liked'st not that,
   When Cassio left my wife. What didst not like?
   And when I told thee he was of my counsel   115
   In my whole course of wooing, thou cried'st 'Indeed?'
   And didst contract and purse thy brow together

9. Weight.

As if thou then hadst shut up in thy brain
Some horrible conceit.[1] If thou dost love me.
Show me thy thought.   120
IAGO   My lord, you know I love you.
OTHELLO   I think thou dost,
    And for I know thou'rt full of love and honesty,
    And weigh'st thy words before thou giv'st them breath,
    Therefore these stops[2] of thine fright me the more;   125
    For such things in a false disloyal knave
    Are tricks of custom, but in a man that's just,
    They're close dilations,[3] working from the heart
    That passion cannot rule.
IAGO   For Michael Cassio.
    I dare be sworn I think that he is honest.   130
OTHELLO   I think so too.
IAGO   Men should be what they seem,
    Or those that be not, would they might seem none.
OTHELLO   Certain, men should be what they seem.
IAGO   Why then, I think Cassio's an honest man.
OTHELLO   Nay, yet there's more in this.   135
    I prithee speak to me as to thy thinkings,
    As thou dost ruminate, and give thy worst of thoughts
    The worst of words.
IAGO   Good my lord, pardon me.
    Though I am bound to every act of duty,
    I am not bound to that all slaves are free to.   140
    Utter my thoughts? Why, say they are vile and false,
    As where's that palace whereinto foul things
    Sometimes intrude not? Who has that breast so pure
    But some uncleanly apprehensions
    Keep leets and law-days,[4] and in sessions sit   145
    With meditations lawful?
OTHELLO   Thou dost conspire against thy friend, Iago,
    If thou but think'st him wronged and mak'st his ear
    A stranger to thy thoughts.
IAGO   I do beseech you,
    Though I perchance am vicious in my guess—   150
    As I confess it is my nature's plague
    To spy into abuses, and oft my jealousy
    Shapes faults that are not—that your wisdom then,
    From one that so imperfectly conceits,
    Would take no notice nor build yourself a trouble   155
    Out of his scattering and unsure observance.
    It were not for your quiet nor your good,
    Nor for my manhood, honesty, and wisdom,
    To let you know my thoughts.
OTHELLO   What dost thou mean?

---

1. Idea. **2.** Hesitations and interruptions **3.** Unfoldings. *Of custom:* habitual. **4.** Meetings of local courts.

IAGO   Good name in man and woman, dear my lord,   160
   Is the immediate jewel of their souls.
   Who steals my purse steals trash; 'tis something, nothing;
   'Twas mine, 'tis his, and has been slave to thousands.
   But he that filches from me my good name
   Robs me of that which not enriches him   165
   And makes me poor indeed.
OTHELLO   By heaven, I'll know thy thoughts.
IAGO   You cannot, if my heart were in your hand;
   Nor shall not whilst 'tis in my custody.
OTHELLO   Ha!
IAGO   O, beware, my lord, of jealousy.
   It is the green-eyed monster which doth mock   170
   The meat it feeds on. That cuckold lives in bliss
   Who, certain of his fate, loves not his wronger.
   But O, what damnèd minutes tells he o'er
   Who dotes yet doubts, suspects yet fondly[5] loves!
OTHELLO   O misery!   175
IAGO   Poor and content is rich, and rich enough,
   But riches fineless[6] is as poor as winter
   To him that ever fears he shall be poor.
   Good God the souls of all my tribe defend
   From jealousy!
OTHELLO   Why, why is this?   180
   Think'st thou I'd make a life of jealousy,
   To follow still the changes of the moon
   With fresh suspicions? No, to be once in doubt
   Is once to be resolved. Exchange me for a goat
   When I shall turn the business of my soul   185
   To such exsufflicate and blowed[7] surmises
   Matching thy inference. 'Tis not to make me jealous
   To say my wife is fair, feeds well, loves company,
   Is free of speech, sings, plays, and dances well.
   Where virtue is, these are more virtuous,   190
   Nor from mine own weak merits will I draw
   The smallest fear or doubt of her revolt,
   For she had eyes and chose me. No, Iago,
   I'll see before I doubt; when I doubt, prove;
   And on the proof, there is no more but this: 195
   Away at once with love or jealousy.
IAGO   I am glad of this, for now I shall have reason
   To show the love and duty that I bear you
   With franker spirit. Therefore, as I am bound,
   Receive it from me. I speak not yet of proof.   200
   Look to your wife. Observe her well with Cassio.
   Wear your eyes thus: not jealous, nor secure.
   I would not have your free and noble nature
   Out of self-bounty[8] be abused. Look to't.

---

5. Foolishly. *Tells*: counts.   6. Endless.   7. Inflated and overblown.   8. Characteristic generosity.

I know our country disposition well. 205
In Venice they do let God see the pranks
They dare not show their husbands; their best conscience
Is not to leave't undone, but keep't unknown.
OTHELLO   Dost thou say so?
IAGO   She did deceive her father, marrying you, 210
And when she seemed to shake and fear your looks
She loved them most.
OTHELLO   And so she did.
IAGO   Why, go to, then.
She that so young could give out such a seeming,
To seel her father's eyes up close as oak,⁹
He thought 'twas witchcraft! But I am much to blame. 215
I humbly do beseech you of your pardon
For too much loving you.
OTHELLO   I am bound to thee for ever.
IAGO   I see this hath a little dashed your spirits.
OTHELLO   Not a jot, not a jot.
IAGO   I'faith, I fear it has.
I hope you will consider what is spoke 220
Comes from my love. But I do see you're moved.
I am to pray you not to strain my speech
To grosser issues, nor to larger reach¹
Than to suspicion.
OTHELLO   I will not. 225
IAGO   Should you do so, my lord,
My speech should fall into such vile success
Which my thoughts aimed not. Cassio's my worthy friend.
My lord, I see you're moved.
OTHELLO   No, not much moved.
I do not think but Desdemona's honest. 230
IAGO   Long live she so, and long live you to think so!
OTHELLO   And yet how nature, erring from itself—
IAGO   Ay, there's the point; as, to be bold with you,
Not to affect many proposèd matches
Of her own clime, complexion, and degree,² 235
Whereto we see in all things nature tends.
Foh, one may smell in such a will most rank,
Foul disproportions, thoughts unnatural!
But pardon me. I do not in position
Distinctly³ speak of her, though I may fear 240
Her will, recoiling to her better judgement,
May fall to match you with her country forms
And happily⁴ repent.
OTHELLO   Farewell, farewell.
If more thou dost perceive, let me know more.
Set on thy wife to observe. Leave me, Iago. 245

---

9. Stitch up tightly.   **1.** Extent. *Strain:* stretch.   **2.** Rank.   **3.** Directly. *Position:* argumentative posture.   **4.** By chance. *Fall to match:* happen to coincide with. *Country forms:* the manner of her countrywomen, with a pun on female genitals.

IAGO [*going*]   My lord, I take my leave.
OTHELLO   Why did I marry? This honest creature doubtless
  Sees and knows more, much more, than he unfolds.
IAGO [*returning*]   My lord, I would I might entreat your honour
  To scan this thing no farther. Leave it to time.   250
  Although 'tis fit that Cassio have his place—
  For sure he fills it up with great ability—
  Yet, if you please to hold him off a while,
  You shall by that perceive him and his means.
  Note if your lady strain his entertainment[5]   255
  With any strong or vehement importunity.
  Much will be seen in that. In the mean time,
  Let me be thought too busy in my fears—
  As worthy cause I have to fear I am—
  And hold her free, I do beseech your honour.   260
OTHELLO   Fear not my government.[6]
IAGO   I once more take my leave.
                                             [*Exit.*]

OTHELLO   This fellow's of exceeding honesty,
  And knows all qualities with a learned spirit
  Of human dealings. If I do prove her haggard,
  Though that her jesses were my dear heart-strings   265
  I'd whistle her off and let her down the wind[7]
  To prey at fortune. Haply for I am black,
  And have not those soft parts of conversation
  That chamberers[8] have; or for I am declined
  Into the vale of years—yet that's not much—   270
  She's gone. I am abused, and my relief
  Must be to loathe her. O curse of marriage,
  That we can call these delicate creatures ours
  And not their appetites! I had rather be a toad
  And live upon the vapour of a dungeon   275
  Than keep a corner in the thing I love
  For others' uses. Yet 'tis the plague of great ones;
  Prerogatived are they less than the base.
  'Tis destiny unshunnable, like death.
  Even then this forkèd plague is fated to us   280
  When we do quicken.[9]
        [*Enter* DESDEMONA *and* EMILIA.]
                    Look where she comes.
  If she be false, O then heaven mocks itself!
  I'll not believe't.
DESDEMONA   How now, my dear Othello?
  Your dinner, and the generous islanders
  By you invited, do attend[1] your presence.   285
OTHELLO   I am to blame.
DESDEMONA   Why do you speak so faintly? Are you not well?

---

5. Push for his reinstatement.   6. I.e., of his own feelings.   7. Set her free. *Qualities:* natures. *Haggard:* wild hawk. *Jesses:* hawk's leg-straps.   8. Courtiers. *Haply for:* perhaps because.   9. Are born; grow sexually excited. *Forkèd plague:* cuckold's horns and women's forked legs.   1. Await.

OTHELLO   I have a pain upon my forehead here.
DESDEMONA   Faith, that's with watching. 'Twill away again.
  Let me but bind it hard, within this hour   290
  It will be well.
OTHELLO   Your napkin is too little.
    [*He puts the napkin from him. It drops.*]
  Let it alone. Come, I'll go in with you.
DESDEMONA   I am very sorry that you are not well.
                  [*Exeunt* OTHELLO *and* DESDEMONA.]
EMILIA [*taking up the napkin*]   I am glad I have found this napkin.
  This was her first remembrance from the Moor.   295
  My wayward husband hath a hundred times
  Wooed me to steal it, but she so loves the token—
  For he conjured her she should ever keep it—
  That she reserves it evermore about her
  To kiss and talk to. I'll ha' the work ta'en out,[2]   300
  And give't Iago. What he will do with it,
  Heaven knows, not I.
  I nothing, but to please his fantasy.[3]
    [*Enter* IAGO.]
IAGO   How now, what do you here alone?
EMILIA   Do not you chide. I have a thing for you.   305
IAGO   You have a thing for me? It is a common thing.
EMILIA   Ha?
IAGO   To have a foolish wife.
EMILIA   O, is that all? What will you give me now
  For that same handkerchief?   310
IAGO   What handkerchief?
EMILIA   What handkerchief?
  Why, that the Moor first gave to Desdemona,
  That which so often you did bid me steal.
IAGO   Hast stol'n it from her?   315
EMILIA   No, faith, she let it drop by negligence,
  And to th'advantage[4] I, being here, took't up.
  Look, here 'tis.
IAGO   A good wench! Give it me.
EMILIA   What will you do with it, that you have been so earnest
  To have me filch it?
IAGO   Why, what is that to you?   320
    [*He takes the napkin.*]
EMILIA   If it be not for some purpose of import,
  Give't me again. Poor lady, she'll run mad
  When she shall lack it.
IAGO   Be not acknown on't.[5] I have use for it. Go, leave me.
                       [*Exit* EMILIA.]
  I will in Cassio's lodging lose this napkin,   325
  And let him find it. Trifles light as air

---

2. Pattern copied.   3. Fancy, desire. *I nothing:* I wish nothing.   4. Luckily.   5. Act as if you know nothing.

Are to the jealous confirmations strong
As proofs of holy writ. This may do something.
The Moor already changes with my poison.
Dangerous conceits are in their natures poisons,   330
Which at the first are scarce found to distaste,
But, with a little⁶ act upon the blood.
Burn like the mines of sulphur.
    [*Enter* OTHELLO.]
                             I did say so.
Look where he comes. Not poppy nor mandragora⁷
Nor all the drowsy syrups of the world   335
Shall ever medicine thee to that sweet sleep
Which thou owedst⁸ yesterday.
OTHELLO   Ha, ha, false to me?
IAGO   Why, how now, general? No more of that.
OTHELLO   Avaunt, be gone. Thou hast set me on the rack.   340
I swear 'tis better to be much abused
Than but to know't a little.
IAGO   How now, my lord?
OTHELLO   What sense had I of her stol'n hours of lust?
I saw't not, thought it not; it harmed not me.
I slept the next night well, fed well, was free and merry.   345
I found not Cassio's kisses on her lips.
He that is robbed, not wanting⁹ what is stol'n,
Let him not know't and he's not robbed at all.
IAGO   I am sorry to hear this.
OTHELLO   I had been happy if the general camp,   350
Pioneers¹ and all, had tasted her sweet body,
So I had nothing known. O, now for ever
Farewell the tranquil mind, farewell content,
Farewell the plumèd troops and the big wars
That makes ambition virtue! O, farewell,   355
Farewell the neighing steed and the shrill trump,
The spirit-stirring drum, th'ear-piercing fife,
The royal banner, and all quality,
Pride, pomp, and circumstance of glorious war!
And O, you mortal engines whose rude throats   360
Th'immortal Jove's dread clamours counterfeit,²
Farewell! Othello's occupation's gone.
IAGO   Is't possible, my lord?
OTHELLO   [*taking* IAGO *by the throat*]   Villain, be sure thou prove my
    love a whore.
Be sure of it. Give me the ocular proof,   365
Or, by the worth of mine eternal soul,
Thou hadst been better have been born a dog
Than answer my waked wrath.
IAGO   Is't come to this?
OTHELLO   Make me to see't, or at the least so prove it

That the probation[3] bear no hinge nor loop   370
  To hang a doubt on, or woe upon thy life.
IAGO   My noble lord.
OTHELLO   If thou dost slander her and torture me,
  Never pray more; abandon all remorse,
  On horror's head horrors accumulate,   375
  Do deeds to make heaven weep, all earth amazed,
  For nothing canst thou to damnation add
  Greater than that.
IAGO   O grace, O heaven forgive me!
  Are you a man? Have you a soul or sense?
  God buy you, take mine office. O wretched fool,   380
  That lov'st to make thine honesty a vice!
  O monstrous world, take note, take note, O world,
  To be direct and honest is not safe!
  I thank you for this profit, and from hence
  I'll love no friend, sith[4] love breeds such offence.   385
OTHELLO   Nay, stay. Thou shouldst be honest.
IAGO   I should be wise, for honesty's a fool,
  And loses that it works for.
OTHELLO   By the world,
  I think my wife be honest, and think she is not.
  I think that thou art just, and think thou art not.   390
  I'll have some proof. My name, that was as fresh
  As Dian's[5] visage, is now begrimed and black
  As mine own face. If there be cords, or knives,
  Poison, or fire, or suffocating streams,
  I'll not endure it. Would I were satisfied!   395
IAGO   I see, sir, you are eaten up with passion.
  I do repent me that I put it to you.
  You would be satisfied?
OTHELLO   Would? Nay, and I will.
IAGO   And may. But how, how satisfied, my lord?
  Would you, the supervisor,[6] grossly gape on,   400
  Behold her topped?
OTHELLO   Death and damnation! O!
IAGO   It were a tedious difficulty, I think,
  To bring them to that prospect.[7] Damn them then
  If ever mortal eyes do see them bolster[8]
  More than their own! What then, how then?   405
  What shall I say? Where's satisfaction?
  It is impossible you should see this,
  Were they as prime as goats, as hot as monkeys,
  As salt as wolves in pride,[9] and fools as gross
  As ignorance made drunk. But yet I say,   410
  If imputation, and strong circumstances
  Which lead directly to the door of truth,
  Will give you satisfaction, you might ha't.

---

3. Test.   4. Since.   5. Goddess of the moon and virginity.   6. Voyeur.   7. Spectacle. *Tedious:*
demandingly.   8. Share a pillow? support each other's bodies as pillows?   9. Heat. *Prime:* horny. *Salt:*
lustful.

OTHELLO   Give me a living reason she's disloyal.

IAGO   I do not like the office,[1]   415
   But sith I am entered in this cause so far,
   Pricked[2] to't by foolish honesty and love,
   I will go on. I lay with Cassio lately,
   And being troubled with a raging tooth,
   I could not sleep. There are a kind of men   420
   So loose of soul that in their sleeps
   Will mutter their affairs. One of this kind is Cassio.
   In sleep I heard him say 'Sweet Desdemona,
   Let us be wary, let us hide our loves',
   And then, sir, would he grip and wring my hand,   425
   Cry 'O, sweet creature!', then kiss me hard,
   As if he plucked up kisses by the roots,
   That grew upon my lips, lay his leg o'er my thigh,
   And sigh, and kiss, and then cry, 'Cursèd fate.
   That gave thee to the Moor!'   430

OTHELLO   O, monstrous, monstrous!

IAGO   Nay, this was but his dream.

OTHELLO   But this denoted a foregone conclusion.

IAGO   'Tis a shrewd doubt,[3] though it be but a dream,
   And this may help to thicken other proofs   435
   That do demonstrate[4] thinly.

OTHELLO   I'll tear her all to pieces.

IAGO   Nay, yet be wise; yet we see nothing done.
   She may be honest yet. Tell me but this:
   Have you not sometimes seen a handkerchief
   Spotted with strawberries in your wife's hand?   440

OTHELLO   I gave her such a one. 'Twas my first gift.

IAGO   I know not that, but such a handkerchief—
   I am sure it was your wife's—did I today
   See Cassio wipe his beard with.

OTHELLO   If it be that—

IAGO   If it be that, or any that was hers,   445
   It speaks against her with the other proofs.

OTHELLO   O that the slave had forty thousand lives!
   One is too poor, too weak for my revenge.
   Now do I see 'tis true. Look here, Iago.
   All my fond love thus do I blow to heaven—'tis gone.   450
   Arise, black vengeance, from the hollow hell.
   Yield up, O love, thy crown and hearted throne
   To tyrannous hate! Swell, bosom, with thy freight,
   For 'tis of aspics' tongues.

IAGO   Yet be content.[5]

OTHELLO   O, blood, blood, blood!

IAGO   Patience, I say. Your mind may change.   455

OTHELLO   Never, Iago. Like to the Pontic Sea,[6]
   Whose icy current and compulsive course

---

1. Job.   2. Driven.   3. Guess.   4. Appear.   5. Patient.   6. Black Sea.

Ne'er knows retiring ebb, but keeps due on
To the Propontic and the Hellespont,
Even so my bloody thoughts with violent pace   460
Shall ne'er look back, ne'er ebb to humble love,
Till that a capable and wide revenge
Swallow them up.
   [*He kneels.*]
       Now, by yon marble heaven,
In the due reverence of a sacred vow
I here engage my words.
IAGO   Do not rise yet.   465
   [IAGO *kneels.*]
Witness you ever-burning lights above,
You elements that clip[7] us round about,
Witness that here Iago doth give up
The execution[8] of his wit, hands, heart
To wronged Othello's service. Let him command,   470
And to obey shall be in me remorse[9]
What bloody business ever.
   [*They rise.*]
OTHELLO   I greet thy love;
Not with vain thanks, but with acceptance bounteous,
And will upon the instant put thee to't.[1]
Within these three days let me hear thee say   475
That Cassio's not alive.
IAGO   My friend is dead.
'Tis done at your request; but let her live.
OTHELLO Damn her, lewd minx! O, damn her, damn her!
Come, go with me apart. I will withdraw
To furnish me with some swift means of death   480
For the fair devil. Now art thou my lieutenant.
IAGO I am your own for ever.   [*Exeunt.*]

3.4

[*Enter* DESDEMONA, EMILIA, *and the* CLOWN.]
DESDEMONA Do you know, sirrah, where Lieutenant Cassio lies?
CLOWN I dare not say he lies[2] anywhere.
DESDEMONA Why, man?
CLOWN He's a soldier, and for me to say a soldier lies, 'tis stabbing.
DESDEMONA Go to. Where lodges he?   5
CLOWN To tell you where he lodges is to tell you where I lie.
DESDEMONA Can anything be made of this?
CLOWN I know not where he lodges, and for me to devise a lodging
 and say he lies here, or he lies there, were to lie in mine own throat.[3]
DESDEMONA Can you enquire him out, and be edified[4] by report? 10
CLOWN I will catechize the world for him; that is, make questions,
 and by them answer.

---

7. Embrace. 8. Agency. 9. Pity. 1. Set you about the business. 2. Dwells. 3. Lie from
the heart. 4. Informed.

DESDEMONA   Seek him, bid him come hither, tell him I have moved[5]
   my lord on his behalf, and hope all will be well.
CLOWN   To do this is within the compass[6] of man's wit, and therefore   15
   I will attempt the doing it.   [*Exit.*]
DESDEMONA   Where should I lose the handkerchief, Emilia?
EMILIA   I know not, madam.
DESDEMONA   Believe me, I had rather have lost my purse
   Full of crusadoes,[7] and but my noble Moor   20
   Is true of mind, and made of no such baseness
   As jealous creatures are, it were enough
   To put him to ill thinking.
EMILIA   Is he not jealous?
DESDEMONA   Who, he? I think the sun where he was born
   Drew all such humours[8] from him.
       [*Enter* OTHELLO.]
EMILIA   Look where he comes.   25
DESDEMONA   I will not leave him now till Cassio
   Be called to him. How is't with you, my lord?
OTHELLO   Well, my good lady. [*Aside*] O hardness to dissemble!—
   How do you, Desdemona?
DESDEMONA   Well, my good lord.
OTHELLO   Give me your hand. This hand is moist, my lady.   30
DESDEMONA   It hath felt no age, nor known no sorrow.
OTHELLO   This argues fruitfulness and liberal[9] heart.
   Hot, hot and moist—this hand of yours requires
   A sequester[1] from liberty; fasting, and prayer,
   Much castigation, exercise devout,   35
   For here's a young and sweating devil here
   That commonly rebels. 'Tis a good hand,
   A frank one.
DESDEMONA   You may indeed say so,
   For 'twas that hand that gave away my heart.   40
OTHELLO   A liberal hand. The hearts of old gave hands,
   But our new heraldry[2] is hands, not hearts.
DESDEMONA   I cannot speak of this. Come now, your promise.
OTHELLO   What promise, chuck?
DESDEMONA   I have sent to bid Cassio come speak with you.   45
OTHELLO   I have a salt and sorry rheum[3] offends me.
   Lend me thy handkerchief.
DESDEMONA [*offering a handkerchief*]   Here, my lord.
OTHELLO   That which I gave you.
DESDEMONA   I have it not about me.
OTHELLO   Not?   50
DESDEMONA   No, faith, my lord.
OTHELLO   That's a fault. That handkerchief
   Did an Egyptian to my mother give.
   She was a charmer,[4] and could almost read

5. Influenced.   6. Scope.   7. Portuguese gold coins.   8. Qualities.   9. Generous or libidinous.
1. Removal.   2. Heraldic emblems.   3. Cold.   4. Sorceress.

The thoughts of people. She told her, while she kept it.
'Twould make her amiable,[5] and subdue my father   55
Entirely to her love; but if she lost it,
Or made a gift of it, my father's eye
Should hold her loathèd, and his spirits should hunt
After new fancies. She, dying, gave it me,
And bid me, when my fate would have me wived,   60
To give it her. I did so, and take heed on't.
Make it a darling, like your precious eye.
To lose't or give't away were such perdition
As nothing else could match.
DESDEMONA   Is't possible?
OTHELLO   'Tis true. There's magic in the web[6] of it.   65
A sibyl that had numbered in the world
The sun to course two hundred compasses
In her prophetic fury sewed the work.
The worms were hallowed that did breed the silk,
And it was dyed in mummy,[7] which the skilful   70
Conserved of maidens' hearts.
DESDEMONA   I'faith, is't true?
OTHELLO   Most veritable. Therefore look to't well.
DESDEMONA   Then would to God that I had never seen it!
OTHELLO   Ha, wherefore?
DESDEMONA   Why do you speak so startingly and rash?   75
OTHELLO   Is't lost? Is't gone? Speak, is't out o'th' way?
DESDEMONA   Heaven bless us!
OTHELLO   Say you?
DESDEMONA   It is not lost, but what an if it were?
OTHELLO   How?   80
DESDEMONA   I say it is not lost.
OTHELLO   Fetch't, let me see't.
DESDEMONA   Why, so I can, sir, but I will not now.
This is a trick to put me from my suit.
Pray you let Cassio be received again.
OTHELLO   Fetch me the handkerchief. My mind misgives.   85
DESDEMONA   Come, come, you'll never meet a more sufficient[8] man.
OTHELLO   The handkerchief.
DESDEMONA   I pray, talk me of Cassio.
OTHELLO   The handkerchief.
DESDEMONA   A man that all his time
Hath founded his good fortunes on your love,
Shared dangers with you—   90
OTHELLO   The handkerchief.
DESDEMONA   I'faith, you are to blame.
OTHELLO   'Swounds!   [Exit.]
EMILIA   Is not this man jealous?
DESDEMONA   I ne'er saw this before.
Sure there's some wonder in this handkerchief.   95

---

5. Lovable.   6. Weaving.   7. Liquid drained from embalmed bodies. *Fury:* passion.   8. Able.

I am most unhappy in the loss of it.
EMILIA   'Tis not a year or two shows us a man.
 They are all but stomachs, and we all but food.
 They eat us hungrily, and when they are full,
 They belch us.
   [*Enter* IAGO *and* CASSIO.]
      Look you, Cassio and my husband.   100
IAGO [*to* CASSIO]   There is no other way. 'Tis she must do't,
 And lo, the happiness! Go and importune her.
DESDEMONA   How now, good Cassio? What's the news with you?
CASSIO   Madam, my former suit. I do beseech you
 That by your virtuous means I may again   105
 Exist and be a member of his love
 Whom I, with all the office⁹ of my heart,
 Entirely honour. I would not be delayed.
 If my offence be of such mortal kind
 That nor my service past, nor present sorrows,   110
 Nor purposed merit in futurity
 Can ransom me into his love again,
 But to know so must be my benefit.¹
 So shall I clothe me in a forced content,
 And shut myself up in some other course   115
 To fortune's alms.
DESDEMONA   Alas, thrice-gentle Cassio!
 My advocation² is not now in tune.
 My lord is not my lord, nor should I know him
 Were he in favour³ as in humour altered.
 So help me every spirit sanctified   120
 As I have spoken for you all my best,
 And stood within the blank⁴ of his displeasure
 For my free speech! You must a while be patient.
 What I can do I will, and more I will
 Than for myself I dare. Let that suffice you.   125
IAGO   Is my lord angry?
EMILIA   He went hence but now,
 And certainly in strange unquietness.
IAGO   Can he be angry? I have seen the cannon
 When it hath blown his ranks into the air,
 And, like the devil, from his very arm   130
 Puffed his own brother; and is he angry?
 Something of moment then. I will go meet him.
 There's matter in't indeed, if he be angry.
DESDEMONA   I prithee do so.   [*Exit* IAGO.]
      Something sure of state
 Either from Venice or some unhatched practice⁵   135
 Made demonstrable here in Cyprus to him,
 Hath puddled⁶ his clear spirit; and in such cases

---

9. Duty. 1. Profit. 2. Advocacy. 3. Countenance. 4. Bull's-eye of a target. 5. Undisclosed stratagem. 6. Muddied.

Men's natures wrangle with inferior things,
Though great ones are their object. 'Tis even so;
For let our finger ache and it indues[7]   140
Our other, healthful members even to a sense
Of pain. Nay, we must think men are not gods,
Nor of them look for such observancy
As fits the bridal. Beshrew me much, Emilia,
I was—unhandsome warrior as I am—   145
Arraigning his unkindness with my soul;
But now I find I had suborned the witness,
And he's indicted falsely.
EMILIA   Pray heaven it be
State matters, as you think, and no conception
Nor no jealous toy[8] concerning you.   150
DESDEMONA   Alas the day, I never gave him cause.
EMILIA   But jealous souls will not be answered so.
They are not ever jealous for the cause,
But jealous for they're jealous. It is a monster
Begot upon itself, born on itself.   155
DESDEMONA   Heaven keep the monster from Othello's mind.
EMILIA   Lady, amen.
DESDEMONA   I will go seek him. Cassio, walk here about.
If I do find him fit[9] I'll move your suit,
And seek to effect it to my uttermost.   160
CASSIO   I humbly thank your ladyship.
                                    [*Exeunt* DESDEMONA *and* EMILIA.]
          [*Enter* BIANCA.]
BIANCA   Save you, friend Cassio.
CASSIO   What make you from home?
How is't with you, my most fair Bianca?
I'faith, sweet love, I was coming to your house.
BIANCA   And I was going to your lodging, Cassio.   165
What, keep a week away? Seven days and nights,
Eightscore-eight hours, and lovers' absent hours
More tedious than the dial eightscore times!
O weary reckoning![1]
CASSIO   Pardon me, Bianca.
I have this while with leaden thoughts been pressed,   170
But I shall in a more continuate time
Strike off this score[2] of absence. Sweet Bianca,
Take me this work out.
          [*He gives her* DESDEMONA's *napkin.*]
BIANCA   O Cassio, whence came this?
This is some token from a newer friend.
To the felt absence now I feel a cause.   175
Is't come to this? Well, well.
CASSIO   Go to, woman.
Throw your vile guesses in the devil's teeth,

7. Leads.   8. Trivial matter.   9. Suited.   1. Account.   2. Debt. *Continuate:* undisturbed.

From whence you have them. You are jealous now
That this is from some mistress, some remembrance.
No, by my faith, Bianca.
BIANCA   Why, whose is it?   180
CASSIO   I know not, neither. I found it in my chamber.
   I like the work well. Ere it be demanded[3]—
   As like enough it will—I would have it copied.
   Take it, and do't, and leave me for this time.
BIANCA   Leave you? Wherefore?   185
CASSIO   I do attend here on the general,
   And think it no addition, nor my wish,
   To have him see me womaned.
BIANCA   Why, I pray you?
CASSIO   Not that I love you not.
BIANCA   But that you do not love me.
   I pray you bring[4] me on the way a little,   190
   And say if I shall see you soon at night.
CASSIO   'Tis but a little way that I can bring you,
   For I attend here; but I'll see you soon.
BIANCA   'Tis very good. I must be circumstanced.[5]

                                                            [*Exeunt.*]

                              4.1

            [*Enter* IAGO *and* OTHELLO.]
IAGO   Will you think so?
OTHELLO   Think so, Iago?
IAGO   What, to kiss in private?
OTHELLO   An unauthorized[6] kiss.
IAGO   Or to be naked with her friend in bed
   An hour or more, not meaning any harm?
OTHELLO   Naked in bed, Iago, and not mean harm?   5
   It is hypocrisy against the devil.
   They that mean virtuously and yet do so,
   The devil their virtue tempts, and they tempt heaven.
IAGO   If they do nothing, 'tis a venial slip.
   But if I give my wife a handkerchief—   10
OTHELLO   What then?
IAGO   Why then, 'tis hers, my lord, and being hers,
   She may, I think, bestow't on any man.
OTHELLO   She is protectress of her honour, too.
   May she give that?   15
IAGO   Her honour is an essence that's not seen.
   They have it very oft that have it not.
   But for the handkerchief—
OTHELLO   By heaven, I would most gladly have forgot it.
   Thou said'st—O, it comes o'er my memory   20

3. Asked after.   4. Accompany.   5. Given excuses, or be content with the circumstances.   6. I.e.,
adulterous.

As doth the raven[7] o'er the infectious house,
Boding to all!—he had my handkerchief.
IAGO   Ay, what of that?
OTHELLO   That's not so good now.
IAGO   What if I had said I had seen him do you wrong,
Or heard him say—as knaves be such abroad,[8]   25
Who having by their own importunate suit
Or voluntary dotage[9] of some mistress
Convincèd or supplied[1] them, cannot choose
But they must blab—
OTHELLO   Hath he said anything?
IAGO   He hath, my lord. But, be you well assured,   30
No more than he'll unswear.
OTHELLO   What hath he said?
IAGO   Faith, that he did—I know not what he did.
OTHELLO   What, what?
IAGO   Lie—
OTHELLO   With her?
IAGO   With her, on her, what you will.
OTHELLO   Lie with her? Lie on her? We say 'lie on her' when they
belie her. Lie with her? 'Swounds, that's fulsome![2] Handkerchief—   35
confessions—handkerchief. To confess and be hanged for his
labour. First to be hanged and then to confess! I tremble at it. Nature
would not invest herself in such shadowing passion without some
instruction. It is not words that shakes me thus. Pish! Noses, ears,
and lips! Is't possible? Confess? Handkerchief? O devil!   40
    [*He falls down in a trance.*]
IAGO   Work on; my medicine works. Thus credulous fools are caught,
And many worthy and chaste dames even thus,
All guiltless, meet reproach. What ho, my lord!
My lord, I say. Othello!
    [*Enter* CASSIO.]
                    How now, Cassio?
CASSIO   What's the matter?   45
IAGO   My lord is fall'n into an epilepsy.
This is his second fit. He had one yesterday.
CASSIO   Rub him about the temples.
IAGO   No, forbear.
The lethargy[3] must have his quiet course.
If not, he foams at mouth, and by and by   50
Breaks out to savage madness. Look, he stirs.
Do you withdraw yourself a little while,
He will recover straight. When he is gone
I would on great occasion[4] speak with you.   [*Exit* CASSIO.]
How is it, general? Have you not hurt your head?   55
OTHELLO   Dost thou mock me?[5]
IAGO   I mock you not, by heaven.

7. Harbinger of death and carrier of infection.   8. Out and about.   9. Foolishness of the will.
1. Conquered or satisfied.   2. Nauseating.   3. Coma.   4. Serious business.   5. I.e., about the
cuckold's horns.

Would you would bear your fortune like a man.
OTHELLO   A hornèd man's a monster and a beast.
IAGO   There's many a beast then in a populous city,
   And many a civil monster.   60
OTHELLO   Did he confess it?
IAGO   Good sir, be a man.
   Think every bearded fellow that's but yoked
   May draw⁶ with you. There's millions now alive
   That nightly lie in those unproper beds   65
   Which they dare swear peculiar.⁷ Your case is better.
   O, 'tis the spite of hell, the fiend's arch-mock,
   To lip a wanton in a secure couch
   And to suppose her chaste! No, let me know,
   And knowing what I am, I know what she shall be.   70
OTHELLO   O, thou art wise, 'tis certain.
IAGO   Stand you a while apart.
   Confine yourself but in a patient list.⁸
   Whilst you were here, o'erwhelmèd with your grief—
   A passion most unsuiting such a man—
   Cassio came hither. I shifted him away,   75
   And laid good 'scuse upon your ecstasy,⁹
   Bade him anon return and here speak with me,
   The which he promised. Do but encave yourself,
   And mark the fleers, the gibes and notable¹ scorns
   That dwell in every region of his face.   80
   For I will make him tell the tale anew,
   Where, how, how oft, how long ago, and when
   He hath and is again to cope your wife.
   I say, but mark his gesture. Marry, patience.
   Or I shall say you're all-in-all in spleen,²   85
   And nothing of a man.
OTHELLO   Dost thou hear, Iago?
   I will be found most cunning in my patience,
   But—dost thou hear?—most bloody.
IAGO   That's not amiss,
   But yet keep time in all. Will you withdraw?
      [OTHELLO stands apart.]
   Now will I question Cassio of Bianca,   90
   A hussy that by selling her desires
   Buys herself bread and cloth. It is a creature
   That dotes on Cassio—as 'tis the strumpet's plague
   To beguile many and be beguiled by one.
   He, when he hears of her, cannot restrain   95
   From the excess of laughter.
      [Enter CASSIO.]
                             Here he comes.
   As he shall smile, Othello shall go mad;

6. Drag (a burden). *Yoked:* i.e., in marriage.   7. Their own. *Unproper:* not exclusively their own.
8. Bounds of patience.   9. Trance. *Shifted him away:* made him go away.   1. Obvious. *Encave:* hide.
Fleers: jeers.   2. A rage.

And his unbookish jealousy must conster[3]
Poor Cassio's smiles, gestures, and light behaviours
Quite in the wrong. How do you now, lieutenant?   100
CASSIO   The worser that you give me the addition[4]
Whose want even kills me.
IAGO   Ply Desdemona well and you are sure on't.
Now, if this suit lay in Bianca's power,
How quickly should you speed!   105
CASSIO [laughing]   Alas, poor caitiff![5]
OTHELLO [aside]   Look how he laughs already.
IAGO   I never knew a woman love man so.
CASSIO   Alas, poor rogue! I think i'faith she loves me.
OTHELLO [aside]   Now he denies it faintly, and laughs it out.   110
IAGO   Do you hear, Cassio?
OTHELLO [aside]   Now he importunes him
To tell it o'er. Go to, well said, well said.
IAGO   She gives it out that you shall marry her.
Do you intend it?
CASSIO   Ha, ha, ha!
OTHELLO [aside]   Do ye triumph, Roman, do you triumph?   115
CASSIO   I marry! What, a customer?[6] Prithee, bear some charity to my
wit—do not think it so unwholesome. Ha, ha, ha!
OTHELLO [aside]   So, so, so, so. They laugh that wins.
IAGO   Faith, the cry goes that you marry her.
CASSIO   Prithee, say true.   120
IAGO   I am a very villain else.
OTHELLO [aside]   Ha' you scored[7] me? Well.
CASSIO   This is the monkey's own giving out. She is persuaded I will
marry her out of her own love and flattery, not out of my promise.
OTHELLO [aside]   Iago beckons me. Now he begins the story.   125
   [OTHELLO draws closer.]
CASSIO   She was here even now. She haunts me in every place. I was
the other day talking on the sea-bank with certain Venetians, and
thither comes the bauble,[8] and falls me thus about my neck.
OTHELLO [aside]   Crying 'O dear Cassio!' as it were. His gesture
imports it.   130
CASSIO   So hangs and lolls and weeps upon me, so shakes and pulls
me—ha, ha, ha!
OTHELLO [aside]   Now he tells how she plucked him to my chamber.
O, I see that nose of yours, but not that dog I shall throw it to!
CASSIO   Well, I must leave her company.   135
   [Enter BIANCA.]
IAGO   Before me,[9] look where she comes.
CASSIO   'Tis such another fitchew![1] Marry, a perfumed one. [To
BIANCA] What do you mean by this haunting of me?
BIANCA   Let the devil and his dam haunt you. What did you mean by
that same handkerchief you gave me even now? I was a fine fool to   140

3. Construe. *Unbookish*: unlearned.   4. Title.   5. Wretch.   6. Merchant; here, prostitute.   7.
Defaced.   8. Toy.   9. I.e., "speak of the devil."   1. Polecat.

take it. I must take out the whole work—a likely piece of work, that
you should find it in your chamber and know not who left it there.
This is some minx's token, and I must take out the work. There, give
it your hobby-horse.² [*Giving* CASSIO *the napkin*] Wheresoever you
had it, I'll take out no work on't.   145

CASSIO   How now, my sweet Bianca, how now, how now?

OTHELLO [*aside*]   By heaven, that should be my handkerchief.

BIANCA   An you'll come to supper tonight, you may. An you will not,
come when you are next prepared for.³   [*Exit.*]

IAGO   After her, after her.   150

CASSIO   Faith, I must, she'll rail in the streets else.

IAGO   Will you sup there?

CASSIO   Faith, I intend so.

IAGO   Well, I may chance to see you, for I would very fain speak with
you.   155

CASSIO   Prithee, come, will you?

IAGO   Go to, say no more.   [*Exit* CASSIO.]

OTHELLO   How shall I murder him, Iago?

IAGO   Did you perceive how he laughed at his vice?

OTHELLO   O Iago!   160

IAGO   And did you see the handkerchief?

OTHELLO   Was that mine?

IAGO   Yours, by this hand. And to see how he prizes the foolish woman
your wife. She gave it him, and he hath given it his whore.

OTHELLO   I would have him nine years a-killing. A fine woman, a fair   165
woman, a sweet woman.

IAGO   Nay, you must forget that.

OTHELLO   Ay, let her rot and perish, and be damned tonight, for she
shall not live. No, my heart is turned to stone; I strike it, and it hurts
my hand. O, the world hath not a sweeter creature! She might lie by   170
an emperor's side, and command him tasks.

IAGO   Nay, that's not your way.⁴

OTHELLO   Hang her, I do but say what she is—so delicate with her
needle, an admirable musician. O, she will sing the savageness out
of a bear! Of so high and plenteous wit and invention.⁵   175

IAGO   She's the worse for all this.

OTHELLO   O, a thousand, a thousand times! And then of so gentle a
condition.

IAGO   Ay, too gentle.⁶

OTHELLO   Nay, that's certain. But yet the pity of it, Iago. O, Iago, the   180
pity of it, Iago!

IAGO   If you are so fond over her iniquity, give her patent to offend;
for if it touch⁷ not you, it comes near nobody.

OTHELLO   I will chop her into messes.⁸ Cuckold me!

IAGO   O, 'tis foul in her.   185

OTHELLO   With mine officer.

IAGO   That's fouler.

---

2. Easy woman.   3. Invited (i.e., never).   4. Path.   5. Creativity.   6. Noble in rank, naturally
kind.   7. Bothers.   8. Pieces.

OTHELLO   Get me some poison, Iago, this night. I'll not expostulate
with her, lest her body and beauty unprovide my mind[9] again. This
night, Iago.   190
IAGO   Do it not with poison. Strangle her in her bed, even the bed she
hath contaminated.
OTHELLO   Good, good, the justice of it pleases, very good.
IAGO   And for Cassio, let me be his undertaker.[1] You shall hear more
by midnight.   195
OTHELLO   Excellent good.
        [*A trumpet.*]
   What trumpet is that same?
IAGO   I warrant, something from Venice.
        [*Enter* LODOVICO, DESDEMONA, *and attendants.*]
   'Tis Lodovico. This comes from the Duke. See, your wife's with him.
LODOVICO   God save the worthy general.   200
OTHELLO   With all my heart,[2] sir.
LODOVICO [*giving* OTHELLO *a letter*]   The Duke and the senators of
Venice greet you.
OTHELLO   I kiss the instrument of their pleasures.
        [*He reads the letter.*]
DESDEMONA   And what's the news, good cousin Lodovico?   205
IAGO [*to* LODOVICO]   I am very glad to see you, signor. Welcome to Cyprus.
LODOVICO   I thank you. How does Lieutenant Cassio?
IAGO   Lives, sir.
DESDEMONA   Cousin, there's fall'n between him and my lord
An unkind[3] breach. But you shall make all well.   210
OTHELLO   Are you sure of that?
DESDEMONA   My lord.
OTHELLO [*reads*]   'This fail you not to do as you will'—
LODOVICO   He did not call, he's busy in the paper.
   Is there division 'twixt my lord and Cassio?   215
DESDEMONA   A most unhappy one. I would do much
T'atone[4] them, for the love I bear to Cassio.
OTHELLO   Fire and brimstone!
DESDEMONA   My lord?
OTHELLO   Are you wise?
DESDEMONA   What, is he angry?
LODOVICO   Maybe the letter moved him,
   For, as I think, they do command him home,   220
   Deputing Cassio in his government.[5]
DESDEMONA   By my troth, I am glad on't.
OTHELLO   Indeed!
DESDEMONA   My lord?
OTHELLO [*to* DESDEMONA]   I am glad to see you mad.   225
DESDEMONA   Why, sweet Othello!
OTHELLO   Devil!
        [*He strikes her.*]

9. Overthrow my determination.   1. Assassin.   2. I.e., welcome.   3. Unnatural.   4. Bring
them to accord.   5. Office.

DESDEMONA   I have not deserved this.
LODOVICO   My lord, this would not be believed in Venice,
   Though I should swear I saw't. 'Tis very much.   230
   Make her amends, she weeps.
OTHELLO   O, devil, devil!
   If that the earth could teem with woman's tears.
   Each drop she falls would prove a crocodile.[6]
   Out of my sight!
DESDEMONA [going]   I will not stay to offend you.   235
LODOVICO   Truly, an obedient lady.
   I do beseech your lordship call her back.
OTHELLO   Mistress!
DESDEMONA [returning]   My lord?
OTHELLO [to LODOVICO]   What would you with her, sir?   240
LODOVICO   Who, I, my lord?
OTHELLO   Ay, you did wish that I would make her turn.
   Sir, she can turn and turn, and yet go on
   And turn again, and she can weep, sir, weep,
   And she's obedient, as you say, obedient,   245
   Very obedient. [To DESDEMONA] Proceed you in your tears.
   [To LODOVICO] Concerning this, sir—[To DESDEMONA] O well painted
      passion!
   [To LODOVICO] I am commanded home. [To DESDEMONA] Get you
      away.
   I'll send for you anon. [To LODOVICO] Sir, I obey the mandate,
   And will return to Venice. [To DESDEMONA] Hence, avaunt!   250
                                          [Exit DESDEMONA.]
   [To LODOVICO] Cassio shall have my place, and, sir, tonight
   I do entreat that we may sup together.
   You are welcome, sir, to Cyprus. Goats and monkeys![7]   [Exit.]
LODOVICO   Is this the noble Moor whom our full senate
   Call all-in-all sufficient? Is this the nature   255
   Whom passion could not shake, whose solid virtue
   The shot of accident nor dart of chance
   Could neither graze nor pierce?
IAGO   He is much changed.
LODOVICO   Are his wits safe? Is he not light of brain?
IAGO   He's that he is. I may not breathe my censure   260
   What he might be. If what he might he is not,
   I would to heaven he were.
LODOVICO   What, strike his wife!
IAGO   Faith, that was not so well. Yet would I knew
   That stroke would prove the worst.
LODOVICO   Is it his use,[8]
   Or did the letters work upon his blood   265
   And new-create his fault?
IAGO   Alas, alas.
   It is not honesty in me to speak

---

6. I.e., false tears. *Teem:* breed. *Falls:* lets fall.   7. Lecherous animals.   8. Custom.

What I have seen and known. You shall observe him,
And his own courses[9] will denote him so
That I may save my speech. Do but go after,   270
And mark how he continues.
LODOVICO   I am sorry that I am deceived in him.   [*Exeunt.*]

4.2

[*Enter* OTHELLO *and* EMILIA.]
OTHELLO   You have seen nothing then?
EMILIA   Nor ever heard, nor ever did suspect.
OTHELLO   Yes, you have seen Cassio and she together.
EMILIA   But then I saw no harm, and then I heard
   Each syllable that breath made up between 'em.   5
OTHELLO   What, did they never whisper?
EMILIA   Never, my lord.
OTHELLO   Nor send you out o'th' way?
EMILIA   Never.
OTHELLO   To fetch her fan, her gloves, her mask, nor nothing?   10
EMILIA   Never, my lord.
OTHELLO   That's strange.
EMILIA   I durst, my lord, to wager she is honest,
   Lay down my soul at stake.[1] If you think other,
   Remove your thought; it doth abuse your bosom.   15
   If any wretch ha' put this in your head,
   Let heaven requite it with the serpent's curse,[2]
   For if she be not honest, chaste, and true,
   There's no man happy; the purest of their wives
   Is foul as slander.
OTHELLO   Bid her come hither. Go.   [*Exit* EMILIA.]   20
   She says enough, yet she's a simple bawd[3]
   That cannot say as much. This is a subtle whore,
   A closet lock and key of villainous secrets,
   And yet she'll kneel and pray—I ha' seen her do't.
   [*Enter* DESDEMONA *and* EMILIA.]
DESDEMONA   My lord, what is your will?
OTHELLO   Pray you, chuck, come hither.   25
DESDEMONA   What is your pleasure?
OTHELLO   Let me see your eyes.
   Look in my face.
DESDEMONA   What horrible fancy's this?
OTHELLO [*to* EMILIA]   Some of your function,[4] mistress.
   Leave procreants alone, and shut the door,   30
   Cough or cry 'Hem' if anybody come.
   Your mystery, your mystery[5]—nay, dispatch.   [*Exit* EMILIA.]
DESDEMONA   Upon my knees, what doth your speech import?
   I understand a fury in your words,
   But not the words.

<hr>

9. Actions.   1. As the bet.   2. God's curse on the serpent after the Fall.   3. Procuress, female
pimp.   4. Go about your business.   5. Trade, occupation.

OTHELLO   Why, what art thou?   35
DESDEMONA   Your wife, my lord, your true and loyal wife.
OTHELLO   Come, swear it, damn thyself,
  Lest, being like one of heaven, the devils themselves
  Should fear to seize thee. Therefore be double-damned:
  Swear thou art honest.
DESDEMONA   Heaven doth truly know it.   40
OTHELLO   Heaven truly knows that thou art false as hell.
DESDEMONA   To whom, my lord? With whom? How am I false?
OTHELLO [*weeping*]   Ah, Desdemon, away, away, away!
DESDEMONA   Alas, the heavy day! Why do you weep?
  Am I the motive of these tears, my lord?   45
  If haply[6] you my father do suspect
  An instrument of this your calling back,
  Lay not your blame on me. If you have lost him,
  I have lost him too.
OTHELLO   Had it pleased God
  To try me with affliction; had He rained   50
  All kind of sores and shames on my bare head,
  Steeped[7] me in poverty to the very lips,
  Given to captivity me and my utmost hopes,
  I should have found in some place of my soul
  A drop of patience. But, alas, to make me   55
  The fixèd figure for the time of scorn
  To point his slow and moving finger at—
  Yet could I bear that too, well, very well.
  But there where I have garnered[8] up my heart,
  Where either I must live or bear no life,   60
  The fountain from the which my current runs
  Or else dries up—to be discarded thence,
  Or keep it as a cistern for foul toads
  To knot and gender[9] in! Turn thy complexion there,
  Patience, thou young and rose-lipped cherubin,   65
  Ay, here look grim as hell.
DESDEMONA   I hope my noble lord esteems me honest.
OTHELLO   O, ay—as summer flies are in the shambles,
  That quicken even with blowing.[1] O thou weed,
  Who art so lovely fair, and smell'st so sweet,   70
  That the sense aches at thee—would thou hadst ne'er been born!
DESDEMONA   Alas, what ignorant[2] sin have I committed?
OTHELLO   Was this fair paper, this most goodly book,
  Made to write 'whore' upon? What committed?
  Committed? O thou public commoner,[3]   75
  I should make very forges of my cheeks,
  That would to cinders burn up modesty,
  Did I but speak thy deeds. What committed?
  Heaven stops the nose at it, and the moon winks;

---

6. By chance. *Motive:* cause.   7. Submerged.   8. Stored.   9. Copulate.   1. Laying their eggs.
Shambles: meat and fish stalls. *Quicken:* conceive.   2. Unwitting.   3. Prostitute.

The bawdy wind, that kisses all it meets,   80
Is hushed within the hollow mine of earth
And will not hear't. What committed?
DESDEMONA   By heaven, you do me wrong.
OTHELLO   Are not you a strumpet?
DESDEMONA   No, as I am a Christian.   85
If to preserve this vessel for my lord
From any other foul unlawful touch
Be not to be a strumpet, I am none.
OTHELLO   What, not a whore?
DESDEMONA   No, as I shall be saved.
OTHELLO   Is't possible?   90
DESDEMONA   O heaven forgive us!
OTHELLO   I cry you mercy then.
I took you for that cunning whore of Venice
That married with Othello. [*Calling*] You, mistress,
That have the office opposite to Saint Peter.   95
And keeps the gate of hell,
          [*Enter* EMILIA.]
                         you, you, ay, you.
We ha' done our course. [*Giving money*] There's money for your pains.
I pray you, turn the key and keep our counsel.   [*Exit.*]
EMILIA   Alas, what does this gentleman conceive?
How do you, madam? How do you, my good lady?   100
DESDEMONA   Faith, half asleep.
EMILIA   Good madam, what's the matter with my lord?
DESDEMONA   With who?
EMILIA   Why; with my lord, madam.
DESDEMONA   Who is thy Lord?
EMILIA   He that is yours, sweet lady.
DESDEMONA   I ha' none. Do not talk to me, Emilia.   105
I cannot weep, nor answers have I none
But what should go by water.[4] Prithee tonight
Lay on my bed my wedding sheets, remember.
And call thy husband hither.
EMILIA   Here's a change indeed.   [*Exit.*]
DESDEMONA   'Tis meet I should be used so, very meet.   110
How have I been behaved, that he might stick
The small'st opinion on my least misuse?[5]
          [*Enter* IAGO *and* EMILIA.]
IAGO   What is your pleasure, madam? How is't with you?
DESDEMONA   I cannot tell. Those that do teach young babes
Do it with gentle means and easy tasks.   115
He might ha' chid me so, for, in good faith,
I am a child to chiding.
IAGO   What is the matter, lady?
EMILIA   Alas, Iago, my lord hath so bewhored her,

---

4. Tears.   5. Apply the least criticism to my smallest fault.

Thrown such despite⁶ and heavy terms upon her,
That true hearts cannot bear it.   120
DESDEMONA   Am I that name, Iago?
IAGO   What name, fair lady?
DESDEMONA   Such as she said my lord did say I was.
EMILIA   He called her whore. A beggar in his drink
Could not have laid such terms upon his callet.⁷   125
IAGO   Why did he so?
DESDEMONA   I do not know. I am sure I am none such.
IAGO   Do not weep, do not weep. Alas the day!
EMILIA   Hath she forsook so many noble matches,
Her father and her country and her friends,   130
To be called whore? Would it not make one weep?
DESDEMONA   It is my wretched fortune.
IAGO   Beshrew⁸ him for't.
How comes this trick upon him?
DESDEMONA   Nay, heaven doth know.
EMILIA   I will be hanged if some eternal villain,
Some busy and insinuating rogue,   135
Some cogging,⁹ cozening slave, to get some office,
Have not devised this slander, I will be hanged else.
IAGO   Fie, there is no such man. It is impossible.
DESDEMONA   If any such there be, heaven pardon him.
EMILIA   A halter pardon him, and hell gnaw his bones!   140
Why should he call her whore? Who keeps her company?
What place, what time, what form, what likelihood?
The Moor's abused by some most villainous knave,
Some base, notorious knave, some scurvy fellow.
O heaven, that such companions thou'dst unfold,¹   145
And put in every honest hand a whip
To lash the rascals naked through the world,
Even from the east to th' west!
IAGO   Speak within door.²
EMILIA   O, fie upon them. Some such squire³ he was
That turned your wit the seamy side without,   150
And made you to suspect me with the Moor.
IAGO   You are a fool. Go to.
DESDEMONA   O God, Iago,
What shall I do to win my lord again?
Good friend, go to him; for by this light of heaven,
I know not how I lost him.
   [She kneels.]
                                    Here I kneel.   155
If e'er my will did trespass 'gainst his love,
Either in discourse of thought or actual deed,
Or that mine eyes, mine ears, or any sense
Delighted them in any other form,

6. Contempt.   7. Slut.   8. Curse.   9. Cheating.   1. Reveal.   2. Circumspectly.

Or that I do not yet, and ever did,   160
And ever will—though he do shake me off
To beggarly divorcement—love him dearly,
Comfort forswear me. Unkindness may do much,
And his unkindness may defeat[4] my life,
But never taint my love.
      [*She rises.*]
                        I cannot say 'whore'.   165
It does abhor me now I speak the word.
To do the act that might the addition earn,
Not the world's mass of vanity could make me.
IAGO   I pray you, be content. 'Tis but his humour.[5]
The business of the state does him offence,   170
And he does chide with you.
DESDEMONA   If 'twere no other!
IAGO   It is but so, I warrant.
      [*Flourish within.*]
Hark how these instruments summon you to supper.
The messengers of Venice stays the meat.[6]   175
Go in, and weep not. All things shall be well.
      [*Exeunt* DESDEMONA *and* EMILIA.—*Enter* RODERIGO.]
How now, Roderigo?
RODERIGO   I do not find that thou deal'st justly with me.
IAGO   What in the contrary?
RODERIGO   Every day thou daff'st me[7] with some device, Iago, and   180
    rather, as it seems to me now, keep'st from me all conveniency[8] than
    suppliest me with the least advantage of hope. I will indeed no longer
    endure it, nor am I yet persuaded to put up[9] in peace what already
    I have foolishly suffered.
IAGO   Will you hear me, Roderigo?   185
RODERIGO   Faith, I have heard too much, for your words and perform-
    ances are no kin together.
IAGO   You charge me most unjustly.
RODERIGO   With naught but truth. I have wasted myself out of my
    means. The jewels you have had from me to deliver Desdemona   190
    would half have corrupted a votarist.[1] You have told me she hath
    received 'em and returned me expectations and comforts of sudden
    respect[2] and acquaintance, but I find none.
IAGO   Well, go to, very well.
RODERIGO   'Very well', 'go to'! I cannot go to, man, nor 'tis not very   195
    well. Nay, I think it is scurvy, and begin to find myself fopped[3] in it.
IAGO   Very well.
RODERIGO   I tell you 'tis not very well. I will make myself known to
    Desdemona. If she will return me my jewels, I will give over my suit
    and repent my unlawful solicitation. If not, assure yourself I will seek   200
    satisfaction of you.
IAGO   You have said now.

---

4. Ruin.   **5.** Mood.   **6.** Await dinner.   **7.** Put me off.   **8.** Opportunity.   **9.** Tolerate.   **1.**
Vestal virgin.   **2.** Instant regard.   **3.** Made a fool.

RODERIGO   Ay, and said nothing but what I protest[4] intendment of doing.

IAGO   Why, now I see there's mettle[5] in thee, and even from this   205
instant do build on thee a better opinion than ever before. Give me
thy hand, Roderigo. Thou hast taken against me a most just exception, but yet I protest I have dealt most directly[6] in thy affair.

RODERIGO   It hath not appeared.

IAGO   I grant, indeed, it hath not appeared, and your suspicion is not   210
without wit and judgement. But, Roderigo, if thou hast that in thee
indeed which I have greater reason to believe now than ever—I mean
purpose, courage, and valour—this night show it. If thou the next
night following enjoy not Desdemona, take me from this world with
treachery, and devise engines for[7] my life.   215

RODERIGO   Well, what is it? Is it within reason and compass?[8]

IAGO   Sir, there is especial commission come from Venice to depute
Cassio in Othello's place.

RODERIGO   Is that true? Why then, Othello and Desdemona return
again to Venice.   220

IAGO   O no, he goes into Mauritania, and takes away with him the fair
Desdemona, unless his abode be lingered here by some accident,
wherein none can be so determinate[9] as the removing of Cassio.

RODERIGO   How do you mean 'removing' of him?

IAGO   Why, by making him uncapable of Othello's place—knocking   225
out his brains.

RODERIGO   And that you would have me to do.

IAGO   Ay, if you dare do yourself a profit and a right. He sups tonight
with a harlotry, and thither will I go to him. He knows not yet of his
honourable fortune. If you will watch his going thence, which I will   230
fashion to fall out[1] between twelve and one, you may take him at
your pleasure. I will be near, to second[2] your attempt, and he shall
fall between us. Come, stand not amazed at it, but go along with me.
I will show you such a necessity in his death that you shall think
yourself bound to put it on him. It is now high supper-time, and the   235
night grows to waste. About it.

RODERIGO   I will hear further reason for this.

IAGO   And you shall be satisfied.   [*Exeunt.*]

4.3

[*Enter* OTHELLO, DESDEMONA, LODOVICO, EMILIA, *and attendants.*]

LODOVICO   I do beseech you, sir, trouble yourself no further.

OTHELLO   O, pardon me, 'twill do me good to walk.

LODOVICO [*to* DESDEMONA]   Madam, good night. I humbly thank
your ladyship.

DESDEMONA   Your honour is most welcome.

OTHELLO   Will you walk, sir?
O, Desdemona!   5

DESDEMONA   My lord?

4. Insist.   5. Spirit.   6. Straightforwardly. *Exception:* criticism.   7. Plots against.   8. Possibility.
9. Decisive.   1. Take place.   2. Assist.

OTHELLO   Get you to bed on th'instant. I will be returned forthwith.
  Dismiss your attendant there. Look't be done.
DESDEMONA   I will, my lord.
               [*Exeunt* OTHELLO, LODOVICO, *and attendants.*]
EMILIA   How goes it now? He looks gentler than he did.   10
DESDEMONA   He says he will return incontinent.[3]
  He hath commanded me to go to bed,
  And bid me to dismiss you.
EMILIA   Dismiss me?
DESDEMONA   It was his bidding. Therefore, good Emilia,
  Give me my nightly wearing, and adieu.   15
  We must not now displease him.
EMILIA   I would you had never seen him.
DESDEMONA   So would not I. My love doth so approve him
  That even his stubbornness, his checks,[4] his frowns—
  Prithee unpin me—have grace and favour in them.   20
      [EMILIA *helps* DESDEMONA *to undress.*]
EMILIA   I have laid those sheets you bade me on the bed.
DESDEMONA   All's one.[5] Good faith, how foolish are our minds!
  If I do die before thee, prithee shroud me
  In one of these same sheets.
EMILIA   Come, come, you talk.
DESDEMONA   My mother had a maid called Barbary.   25
  She was in love, and he she loved proved mad
  And did forsake her. She had a song of willow.
  An old thing 'twas, but it expressed her fortune,
  And she died singing it. That song tonight
  Will not go from my mind. I have much to do   30
  But to go hang my head all at one side
  And sing it, like poor Barbary. Prithee, dispatch.
EMILIA   Shall I go fetch your nightgown?
DESDEMONA   No. Unpin me here.
  This Lodovico is a proper[6] man.
EMILIA   A very handsome man.
DESDEMONA   He speaks well.   35
EMILIA   I know a lady in Venice would have walked barefoot to Pal-
  estine for a touch of his nether lip.
DESDEMONA [*sings*]   'The poor soul sat sighing by a sycamore tree,
    Sing all a green willow.
  Her hand on her bosom, her head on her knee,   40
    Sing willow, willow, willow.
  The fresh streams ran by her and murmured her moans,
    Sing willow, willow, willow.
  Her salt tears fell from her and softened the stones,
    Sing willow'—   45
  Lay by these.—
          'willow, willow.'
  Prithee, hie thee. He'll come anon.[7]

---

3. Directly.   4. Rebukes.   5. No matter.   6. Handsome.   7. Soon. *Hie:* hurry.

'Sing all a green willow must be my garland.
'Let nobody blame him, his scorn I approve'—   50
Nay, that's not next. Hark, who is't that knocks?
EMILIA   It's the wind.
DESDEMONA [*sings*]   'I called my love false love, but what said he then?
        Sing willow, willow, willow.
    If I court more women, you'll couch with more men.'   55
    So, get thee gone. Good night. Mine eyes do itch.
    Doth that bode weeping?
EMILIA   'Tis neither here nor there.
DESDEMONA   I have heard it said so. O, these men, these men!
    Dost thou in conscience think—tell me, Emilia—
    That there be women do abuse their husbands   60
    In such gross kind?
EMILIA   There be some such, no question.
DESDEMONA   Wouldst thou do such a deed for all the world?
EMILIA   Why, would not you?
DESDEMONA   No, by this heavenly light.
EMILIA   Nor I neither, by this heavenly light. I might do't as well i'th'
    dark.   65
DESDEMONA   Wouldst thou do such a deed for all the world?
EMILIA   The world's a huge thing. It is a great price for a small vice.
DESDEMONA   In truth, I think thou wouldst not.
EMILIA   In truth, I think I should, and undo't when I had done. Marry,
    I would not do such a thing for a joint ring, nor for measures of lawn,   70
    nor for gowns, petticoats, nor caps, nor any petty exhibition;[8] but for
    all the whole world? Ud's[9] pity, who would not make her husband a
    cuckold to make him a monarch? I should venture purgatory for't.
DESDEMONA   Beshrew me if I would do such a wrong
    For the whole world.   75
EMILIA   Why, the wrong is but a wrong i'th' world, and having the
    world for your labour, 'tis a wrong in your own world, and you might
    quickly make it right.
DESDEMONA   I do not think there is any such woman.
EMILIA   Yes, a dozen, and as many   80
    To th' vantage as would store[1] the world they played for.
    But I do think it is their husbands' faults
    If wives do fall. Say that they slack their duties,
    And pour our treasures into foreign laps[2]
    Or else break out in peevish jealousies,   85
    Throwing restraint upon us; or say they strike us,
    Or scant our former having in despite:[3]
    Why, we have galls; and though we have some grace,
    Yet have we some revenge. Let husbands know
    Their wives have sense like them. They see, and smell,   90
    And have their palates both for sweet and sour,
    As husbands have. What is it that they do

---

8. Payment. *Joint ring:* ring with two halves. *Lawn:* linen.   9. God's.   1. And as many more as it would take to fill.   2. I.e., make love to other women. *Duties:* marital duties.   3. I.e., limit our spending out of spite.

When they change[4] us for others? Is it sport?
I think it is. And doth affection[5] breed it?
I think it doth. Is't frailty that thus errs?   95
It is so, too. And have not we affections,
Desires for sport, and frailty, as men have?
Then let them use us well, else let them know
The ills we do, their ills instruct us so.
DESDEMONA   Good night, good night. God me such uses send   100
Not to pick bad from bad, but by bad mend![6]   [*Exeunt.*]

5.1

[*Enter* IAGO *and* RODERIGO.]
IAGO   Here, stand behind this bulk. Straight will he come.
Wear thy good rapier bare, and put it home.[7]
Quick, quick, fear nothing. I'll be at thy elbow.
It makes us or it mars us. Think on that,
And fix most firm thy resolution.   5
RODERIGO   Be near at hand. I may miscarry in't.
IAGO   Here at thy hand. Be bold, and take thy stand.
RODERIGO [*aside*]   I have no great devotion to the deed,
And yet he hath given me satisfying reasons.
'Tis but a man gone. Forth my sword—he dies!   10
IAGO [*aside*]   I have rubbed this young quat almost to the sense,[8]
And he grows angry. Now, whether he kill Cassio
Or Cassio him, or each do kill the other,
Every way makes my gain. Live Roderigo,
He calls me to a restitution large   15
Of gold and jewels that I bobbed[9] from him
As gifts to Desdemona.
It must not be. If Cassio do remain,
He hath a daily beauty in his life
That makes me ugly; and besides, the Moor   20
May unfold me to him—there stand I in much peril.
No, he must die. But so, I hear him coming.
        [*Enter* CASSIO.]
RODERIGO   I know his gait, 'tis he. [*Attacking* CASSIO] Villain, thou diest.
CASSIO   That thrust had been mine enemy indeed,
But that my coat[1] is better than thou know'st.   25
I will make proof[2] of thine.
        [*He stabs* RODERIGO, *who falls.*]
RODERIGO   O, I am slain!
        [IAGO *wounds* CASSIO *in the leg from behind. Exit* IAGO.]
CASSIO [*falling*]   I am maimed for ever. Help, ho, murder, murder!
        [*Enter* OTHELLO *above.*]
OTHELLO   The voice of Cassio. Iago keeps his word.
RODERIGO   O, villain that I am!

---

4. Exchange.   5. Desire.   6. Not to adopt bad practices but to learn good behavior from them. *Uses:*
habits.   7. I.e., stab him. *Bulk:* stall shop.   8. To the quick. *Quat:* pimple.   9. Stole.   1. Protec-
tive armor.   2. Test.

OTHELLO   It is even so.   30
CASSIO   O, help, ho! Light, a surgeon!
OTHELLO   'Tis he. O brave Iago, honest and just,
    That hast such noble sense of thy friend's wrong—
    Thou teachest me. Minion, your dear lies dead,
    And your unblessed fate hies.³ Strumpet, I come.   35
    Forth of⁴ my heart those charms, thine eyes, are blotted.
    Thy bed, lust-stained, shall with lust's blood be spotted.
                [Exit.—Enter LODOVICO and GRAZIANO.]
CASSIO   What ho, no watch, no passage?⁵ Murder, murder!
GRAZIANO   'Tis some mischance. The voice is very direful.
CASSIO   O, help!   40
LODOVICO   Hark.
RODERIGO   O wretched villain!
LODOVICO   Two or three groan. 'Tis heavy⁶ night.
    These may be counterfeits. Let's think't unsafe
    To come into⁷ the cry without more help.   45
RODERIGO   Nobody come? Then shall I bleed to death.
                [Enter IAGO with a light.]
LODOVICO   Hark.
GRAZIANO   Here's one comes in his shirt, with light and weapons.
IAGO   Who's there? Whose noise is this that cries on murder?
LODOVICO   We do not know.
IAGO   Do not you hear a cry?   50
CASSIO   Here, here. For heaven's sake, help me.
IAGO   What's the matter?
GRAZIANO [to LODOVICO]   This is Othello's ensign, as I take it.
LODOVICO   The same indeed; a very valiant fellow.
IAGO [to CASSIO]   What are you here that cry so grievously?
CASSIO   Iago—O, I am spoiled, undone by villains.   55
    Give me some help.
IAGO   O me, lieutenant, what villains have done this?
CASSIO   I think that one of them is hereabout
    And cannot make away.
IAGO   O treacherous villains!
    [To LODOVICO and GRAZIANO] What are you there? Come in and give
        some help.   60
RODERIGO   O, help me there!
CASSIO   That's one of 'em.
IAGO [stabbing RODERIGO]   O murderous slave! O villain!
RODERIGO   O damned Iago! O inhuman dog!
IAGO   Kill me i'th' dark? Where be these bloody thieves?   65
    How silent is this town! Ho, murder, murder!
    [To LODOVICO and GRAZIANO] What may you be? Are you of good or
        evil?
LODOVICO   As you shall prove us, praise us.
IAGO   Signor Lodovico.

---

3. Hurries on. *Minion:* derisive word for sweetheart, i.e., a sexual plaything.   4. Out of.   5. Passersby.
6. Dark.   7. Approach.

LODOVICO   He, sir.

IAGO   I cry you mercy. Here's Cassio hurt by villains.   70

GRAZIANO   Cassio?

IAGO   How is't, brother?

CASSIO   My leg is cut in two.

IAGO   Marry, heaven forbid!
  Light, gentlemen. I'll bind it with my shirt.   75
      [*Enter* BIANCA.]

BIANCA   What is the matter, ho? Who is't that cried?

IAGO   Who is't that cried?

BIANCA   O my dear Cassio,
  My sweet Cassio, O, Cassio, Cassio!

IAGO   O notable strumpet! Cassio, may you suspect
  Who they should be that have thus mangled you?   80

CASSIO   No.

GRAZIANO   I am sorry to find you thus. I have been to seek you.

IAGO   Lend me a garter. So. O for a chair,
  To bear him easily hence!

BIANCA   Alas, he faints. O, Cassio, Cassio, Cassio!   85

IAGO   Gentlemen all, I do suspect this trash
  To be a party in this injury.
  Patience a while, good Cassio. Come, come,
  Lend me a light. [*Going to* RODERIGO] Know we this face or no?
  Alas, my friend, and my dear countryman.   90
  Roderigo? No—yes, sure—O heaven, Roderigo!

GRAZIANO   What, of Venice?

IAGO   Even he, sir. Did you know him?

GRAZIANO   Know him? Ay.

IAGO   Signor Graziano, I cry your gentle pardon.   95
  These bloody accidents must excuse my manners
  That so neglected you.

GRAZIANO   I am glad to see you.

IAGO   How do you, Cassio? O, a chair, a chair!⁸

GRAZIANO   Roderigo.

IAGO   He, he, 'tis he.
      [*Enter attendants with a chair.*]
           O, that's well said, the chair!   100
  Some good man bear him carefully from hence.
  I'll fetch the general's surgeon. [*To* BIANCA] For you, mistress,
  Save you your labour. He that lies slain here, Cassio,
  Was my dear friend. What malice was between you?

CASSIO   None in the world, nor do I know the man.   105

IAGO [*to* BIANCA]   What, look you pale? [*To attendants*] O, bear him out
  o'th' air.
  [*To* LODOVICO *and* GRAZIANO] Stay you, good gentlemen.
      [*Exeunt attendants with* CASSIO *in the chair and with* RODERIGO's
      body.*]
  [*To* BIANCA]   Look you pale, mistress?

8. Litter.

[*To* LODOVICO *and* GRAZIANO] Do you perceive the ghastness[9] of her eye?

[*To* BIANCA] Nay, an[1] you stare we shall hear more anon.

[*To* LODOVICO *and* GRAZIANO] Behold her well; I pray you look upon
    her.   110

Do you see, gentlemen? Nay, guiltiness

Will speak, though tongues were out of use.
        [*Enter* EMILIA.]

EMILIA   Alas, what is the matter? What is the matter, husband?

IAGO   Cassio hath here been set on in the dark

By Roderigo and fellows that are scaped.   115

He's almost slain, and Roderigo dead.

EMILIA   Alas, good gentleman! Alas, good Cassio!

IAGO   This is the fruits of whoring. Prithee, Emilia,

Go know of Cassio where he supped tonight.

[*To* BIANCA] What, do you shake at that?   120

BIANCA   He supped at my house, but I therefore shake not.

IAGO   O, did he so? I charge you go with me.

EMILIA [*to* BIANCA]   O, fie upon thee, strumpet!

BIANCA   I am no strumpet, but of life as honest

As you that thus abuse me.

EMILIA   As I? Fough, fie upon thee!   125

IAGO   Kind gentlemen, let's go see poor Cassio dressed.

[*To* BIANCA] Come, mistress, you must tell's another tale.

Emilia, run you to the citadel

And tell my lord and lady what hath happed.

Will you go on afore?   [*Exit* EMILIA.]

[*Aside*]   This is the night   130

That either makes me or fordoes[2] me quite.   [*Exeunt.*]

5.2

[*Enter* OTHELLO *with a light. He draws back a curtain, revealing*
    DESDEMONA *asleep in her bed.*]

OTHELLO   It is the cause,[3] it is the cause, my soul.

Let me not name it to you, you chaste stars.

It is the cause. Yet I'll not shed her blood,

Nor scar that whiter skin of hers than snow,

And smooth as monumental alabaster.[4]   5

Yet she must die, else she'll betray more men.

Put out the light, and then put out the light.[5]

If I quench thee, thou flaming minister,[6]

I can again thy former light restore

Should I repent me; but once put out thy light.   10

Thou cunning's[7] pattern of excelling nature,

I know not where is that Promethean heat

That can thy light relume.[8] When I have plucked thy rose

---

9. Terror.   1. If.   2. Undoes.   3. Desdemona's infidelity.   4. Stone used in tombs and in Petrarchan descriptions of the female body.   5. Othello compares the light of his torch to Desdemona's life.
6. Light that serves me.   7. Most intricate, artful.   8. Relight. *Promethean heat:* divine fire (in Greek
myth, Prometheus stole fire from the heavens; one tradition holds that he gave it to humankind, another
that he mingled it with clay to create humankind).

I cannot give it vital growth again.
It needs must wither. I'll smell thee on the tree.   15
    [*He kisses her.*]
O balmy breath, that dost almost persuade
Justice to break her sword! One more, one more.
Be thus when thou art dead, and I will kill thee
And love thee after. One more, and that's the last.
    [*He kisses her.*]
So sweet was ne'er so fatal. I must weep,   20
But they are cruel tears. This sorrow's heavenly,
It strikes where it doth love. She wakes.
DESDEMONA   Who's there? Othello?
OTHELLO   Ay, Desdemona.
DESDEMONA   Will you come to bed, my lord?   25
OTHELLO   Have you prayed tonight, Desdemon?
DESDEMONA   Ay, my lord.
OTHELLO   If you bethink yourself of any crime
Unreconciled as yet to heaven and grace,
Solicit for it straight.   30
DESDEMONA   Alack, my lord, what may you mean by that?
OTHELLO   Well, do it, and be brief. I will walk by.[9]
I would not kill thy unprepared spirit.
No, heavens forfend! I would not kill thy soul.
DESDEMONA   Talk you of killing?
OTHELLO   Ay, I do.
DESDEMONA   Then heaven   35
Have mercy on me.
OTHELLO   Amen, with all my heart.
DESDEMONA   If you say so, I hope you will not kill me.
OTHELLO   Hum!
DESDEMONA   And yet I fear you, for you're fatal then
When your eyes roll so. Why I should fear I know not,   40
Since guiltiness I know not, but yet I feel I fear.
OTHELLO   Think on thy sins.
DESDEMONA   They are loves I bear to you.
OTHELLO   Ay, and for that thou diest.
DESDEMONA   That death's unnatural that kills for loving.   45
Alas, why gnaw you so your nether lip?
Some bloody passion shakes your very frame.
These are portents, but yet I hope, I hope
They do not point on me.
OTHELLO   Peace, and be still.
DESDEMONA   I will so. What's the matter?
OTHELLO   That handkerchief   50
Which I so loved and gave thee, thou gav'st to Cassio.
DESDEMONA   No, by my life and soul. Send for the man
And ask him.
OTHELLO   Sweet soul, take heed, take heed of perjury.

---

9. Nearby.

Thou art on thy deathbed.   55
DESDEMONA   Ay, but not yet to die.
OTHELLO   Presently.
  Therefore confess thee freely of thy sin,
  For to deny each article with oath
  Cannot remove nor choke the strong conception   60
  That I do groan withal.[1] Thou art to die.
DESDEMONA   Then Lord have mercy on me.
OTHELLO   I say amen.
DESDEMONA   And have you mercy, too. I never did
  Offend you in my life, never loved Cassio
  But with such general warranty of heaven   65
  As I might love. I never gave him token.
OTHELLO   By heaven, I saw my handkerchief in's hand.
  O perjured woman! Thou dost stone[2] my heart,
  And makes me call what I intend to do
  A murder, which I thought a sacrifice.   70
  I saw the handkerchief.
DESDEMONA   He found it, then.
  I never gave it him. Send for him hither.
  Let him confess a truth.
OTHELLO   He hath confessed.
DESDEMONA   What, my lord?
OTHELLO   That he hath usèd thee.
DESDEMONA   How, unlawfully?   75
OTHELLO   Ay.
DESDEMONA   He will not say so.
OTHELLO   No, his mouth is stopped.
  Honest Iago hath ta'en order for't.[3]
DESDEMONA   O, my fear interprets! What, is he dead?   80
OTHELLO   Had all his hairs been lives, my great revenge
  Had stomach[4] for 'em all.
DESDEMONA [weeping]   Alas, he is betrayed, and I undone.
OTHELLO   Out, strumpet! Weep'st thou for him to my face?
DESDEMONA   O, banish me, my lord, but kill me not.   85
OTHELLO [attacking her]   Down, strumpet.
DESDEMONA   Kill me tomorrow; let me live tonight.
OTHELLO   Nay, an you strive—
DESDEMONA   But half an hour.
OTHELLO   Being done, there is no pause.   90
DESDEMONA   But while I say one prayer.
OTHELLO   It is too late.
      [He smothers her.]
DESDEMONA   O Lord, Lord, Lord!
      [EMILIA at the door.]
EMILIA [within]   My lord, what ho, my lord, my lord!
OTHELLO   What noise is this? Not dead? Not yet quite dead?   95

---

1. Remove the suspicion growing within me (the image is from pregnancy and abortion). *Article:* item (in a legalistic sense).   2. Harden.   3. Been commissioned to do it.   4. Appetite.

I that am cruel am yet merciful.
I would not have thee linger in thy pain.
So, so.
EMILIA [*within*]   What ho, my lord, my lord!
OTHELLO   Who's there?
EMILIA [*within*]   O, good my lord, I would speak a word with you.
OTHELLO [*calling*]   Yes.—'Tis Emilia. [*Calling*] By and by!—She's
    dead.   100
'Tis like she comes to speak of Cassio's death.
The noise was high.[5] Ha! No more moving.
Still as the grave. Shall she come in? Were't good?
I think she stirs again. No. What's best to do?
If she come in, she'll sure speak to my wife.   105
My wife, my wife! What wife? I ha' no wife.
O insupportable, O heavy hour!
Methinks it should be now a huge eclipse
Of sun and moon, and that th'affrighted globe
Should yawn at alteration.[6]
EMILIA [*within*]   I do beseech you   110
That I may speak with you. O, good my lord!
OTHELLO   I had forgot thee.—O, come in, Emilia.—
Soft,[7] by and by. Let me the curtains draw.
        [*He closes the bed-curtains.*]
Where art thou?
        [*He opens the door. Enter* EMILIA.]
                    What's the matter with thee now?
EMILIA   O my good lord, yonder's foul murder's done.   115
OTHELLO   What, now?
EMILIA   But[8] now, my lord.
OTHELLO   It is the very error[9] of the moon,
    She comes more nearer earth than she was wont,
    And makes men mad.   120
EMILIA   Cassio, my lord, hath killed a young Venetian
    Called Roderigo.
OTHELLO   Roderigo killed
    And Cassio killed?
EMILIA   No, Cassio is not killed.
OTHELLO   Not Cassio killed? Then murder's out of tune,
    And sweet revenge grows harsh.   125
DESDEMONA   O, falsely, falsely murdered!
EMILIA   O Lord, what cry is that?
OTHELLO   That? What?
EMILIA   Out and alas, that was my lady's voice!
        [*She opens the bed-curtains.*]
    Help, help, ho, help! O lady, speak again!   130
    Sweet Desdemona, O sweet mistress, speak!
DESDEMONA   A guiltless death I die.

---

5. Loud.   6. Gape at the change (i.e., undergo an earthquake).   7. Quiet.   8. Just.   9. Wandering.

EMILIA   O, who hath done this deed?

DESDEMONA   Nobody, I myself. Farewell.
    Commend me to my kind lord. O, farewell!   [*She dies.*]

OTHELLO   Why, how should she be murdered?

EMILIA   Alas, who knows?   135

OTHELLO   You heard her say herself it was not I.

EMILIA   She said so, I must needs report the truth.

OTHELLO   She's like a liar gone to burning hell.
    'Twas I that killed her.

EMILIA   O, the more angel she, and you the blacker devil!   140

OTHELLO   She turned to folly, and she was a whore.

EMILIA   Thou dost belie her, and thou art a devil.

OTHELLO   She was false as water.

EMILIA   Thou art rash as fire
    To say that she was false. O, she was heavenly true!

OTHELLO   Cassio did top her. Ask thy husband else.[1]   145
    O, I were damned beneath all depth in hell
    But that I did proceed upon just grounds
    To this extremity! Thy husband knew it all.

EMILIA   My husband?

OTHELLO   Thy husband.

EMILIA   That she was false to wedlock?

OTHELLO   Ay, with Cassio. Had she been true,   150
    If heaven would make me such another world
    Of one entire and perfect chrysolite[2]
    I'd not have sold her for it.

EMILIA   My husband?

OTHELLO   Ay, 'twas he that told me on her first.
    An honest man he is, and hates the slime   155
    That sticks on filthy deeds.

EMILIA   My husband?

OTHELLO   What needs this interance?[3] Woman, I say thy husband.

EMILIA   O mistress, villainy hath made mocks with love.
    My husband say she was false?

OTHELLO   He, woman.
    I say thy husband. Dost understand the word?   160
    My friend, thy husband, honest, honest Iago.

EMILIA   If he say so, may his pernicious soul
    Rot half a grain a day. He lies to th' heart.
    She was too fond of her most filthy bargain.

OTHELLO   Ha?   165

EMILIA   Do thy worst.
    This deed of thine is no more worthy heaven
    Than thou wast worthy her.

OTHELLO   Peace, you were best.[4]

EMILIA   Thou hast not half that power to do me harm
    As I have to be hurt. O gull,[5] O dolt,   170
    As ignorant as dirt! Thou hast done a deed—

---

1. If you don't believe it.   2. Topaz.   3. Repetition.   4. You had better be quiet.   5. Dupe.

I care not for thy sword, I'll make thee known
Though I lost twenty lives. Help, help, ho! Help!
The Moor hath killed my mistress. Murder, murder!
    [*Enter* MONTANO, GRAZIANO, *and* IAGO.]
MONTANO   What is the matter? How now, general?   175
EMILIA   O, are you come, Iago? You have done well,
  That men must lay their murders on your neck.
GRAZIANO   What is the matter?
EMILIA [*to* IAGO]   Disprove this villain if thou beest a man.
  He says thou told'st him that his wife was false.   180
  I know thou didst not. Thou'rt not such a villain.
  Speak, for my heart is full.
IAGO   I told him what I thought, and told no more
  Than what he found himself was apt and true.
EMILIA   But did you ever tell him she was false?   185
IAGO   I did.
EMILIA   You told a lie, an odious, damnèd lie,
  Upon my soul a lie, a wicked lie.
  She false with Cassio? Did you say with Cassio?
IAGO   With Cassio, mistress. Go to, charm[6] your tongue.   190
EMILIA   I will not charm my tongue. I am bound to speak.
  My mistress here lies murdered in her bed.
MONTANO *and* GRAZIANO   O heavens forfend!
EMILIA [*to* IAGO]   And your reports have set the murder on.
OTHELLO   Nay, stare not, masters. It is true indeed.   195
GRAZIANO   'Tis a strange truth.
MONTANO   O monstrous act!
EMILIA   Villainy, villainy, villainy!
  I think upon't, I think. I smell't. O villainy!
  I thought so then. I'll kill myself for grief.
  O villainy, villainy!   200
IAGO   What, are you mad? I charge you get you home.
EMILIA   Good gentlemen, let me have leave to speak.
  'Tis proper I obey him, but not now.
  Perchance, Iago, I will ne'er go home.
OTHELLO   O, O, O!
    [OTHELLO *falls on the bed*.]
EMILIA   Nay, lay thee down and roar,   205
  For thou hast killed the sweetest innocent
  That e'er did lift up eye.
OTHELLO [*rising*]   O, she was foul!
  [*To* GRAZIANO] I scarce did know you, uncle. There lies your niece,
  Whose breath indeed these hands have newly stopped.
  I know this act shows[7] horrible and grim.   210
GRAZIANO   Poor Desdemon, I am glad thy father's dead.
  Thy match was mortal to him, and pure grief
  Shore his old thread in twain.[8] Did he live now
  This sight would make him do a desperate turn,

6. Silence.   7. Appears.   8. Cut the thread of his life in two.

Yea, curse his better angel from his side,   215
And fall to reprobance.[9]
OTHELLO   'Tis pitiful. But yet Iago knows
That she with Cassio hath the act of shame
A thousand times committed. Cassio confessed it,
And she did gratify his amorous works   220
With that recognizance[1] and pledge of love
Which I first gave her. I saw it in his hand.
It was a handkerchief, an antique token
My father gave my mother.
EMILIA   O God! O heavenly God!
IAGO   'Swounds, hold your peace!
EMILIA   'Twill out, 'twill out. I peace?   225
No, I will speak as liberal as the north.[2]
Let heaven, and men, and devils, let 'em all,
All, all cry shame against me, yet I'll speak.
IAGO   Be wise and get you home.
EMILIA   I will not.   230
        [IAGO *draws his sword.*]
GRAZIANO [*to* IAGO]   Fie, your sword upon a woman?
EMILIA   O thou dull Moor, that handkerchief thou speak'st of
I found by fortune and did give my husband,
For often, with a solemn earnestness—
More than indeed belonged to such a trifle—   235
He begged of me to steal't.
IAGO   Villainous whore!
EMILIA   She give it Cassio? No, alas, I found it,
And I did give't my husband.
IAGO   Filth, thou liest.
EMILIA   By heaven I do not, I do not, gentlemen.
O murderous coxcomb![3] What should such a fool   240
Do with so good a wife?
OTHELLO   Are there no stones[4] in heaven
But what serves for the thunder? Precious[5] villain!
        [*The Moor runs at* IAGO. MONTANO *disarms* OTHELLO. IAGO *wounds
        his wife.*]
GRAZIANO   The woman falls. Sure he hath killed his wife.
EMILIA   Ay, ay. O, lay me by my mistress' side!   [*Exit* IAGO.]
GRAZIANO   He's gone, but his wife's killed.   245
MONTANO   'Tis a notorious villain. Take you this weapon
Which I have here recovered from the Moor.
Come, guard the door without. Let him not pass,
But kill him rather. I'll after that same villain,
For 'tis a damnèd slave.   [*Exeunt* MONTANO *and* GRAZIANO.]
OTHELLO   I am not valiant neither,   250
But every puny whipster[6] gets my sword.
But why should honour outlive honesty?

9. Damnation (suicide was a damnable sin). *Turn:* deed.   1. Sign.   2. As freely as the north wind.
3. Fool.   4. Thunderbolts.   5. Extreme.   6. Trifling person.

Let it go all.
EMILIA   What did thy song bode, lady?
Hark, canst thou hear me? I will play the swan,
And die in music. [*Sings*] 'Willow, willow, willow.'—   255
Moor, she was chaste. She loved thee, cruel Moor.
So come my soul to bliss as I speak true.
So, speaking as I think, alas, I die.   [*She dies.*]
OTHELLO   I have another weapon in this chamber.
It was a sword of Spain, the ice-brook's temper.[7]   260
O, here it is. [*Calling*] Uncle, I must come forth.
GRAZIANO [*within*]   If thou attempt it, it will cost thee dear.
Thou hast no weapon, and perforce must suffer.
OTHELLO   Look in upon me then, and speak with me.
Or, naked[8] as I am, I will assault thee.   265
        [*Enter* GRAZIANO.]
GRAZIANO   What is the matter?
OTHELLO   Behold, I have a weapon;
A better never did itself sustain
Upon a soldier's thigh. I have seen the day
That, with this little arm and this good sword,
I have made my way through more impediments   270
Than twenty times your stop.[9] But O, vain boast!
Who can control his fate? 'Tis not so now.
Be not afraid, though you do see me weaponed.
Here is my journey's end, here is my butt.
And very sea-mark of my utmost sail.[1]   275
Do you go back dismayed? 'Tis a lost fear.
Man but a rush[2] against Othello's breast
And he retires. Where should Othello go?
[*To* DESDEMONA] Now, how dost thou look now? O ill-starred wench,
Pale as thy smock! When we shall meet at count[3]   280
This look of thine will hurl my soul from heaven,
And fiends will snatch at it.
        [*He touches her.*]
                              Cold, cold, my girl,
Even like thy chastity. O cursèd, cursèd slave!
Whip me, ye devils,
From the possession of this heavenly sight: 285
Blow me about in winds, roast me in sulphur,
Wash me in steep-down gulfs of liquid fire!
O Desdemon! Dead Desdemon! Dead! O! O!
        [*Enter* LODOVICO, MONTANO, IAGO *guarded by officers, with* CASSIO
        in a chair.]
LODOVICO   Where is this rash and most unfortunate man?
OTHELLO   That's he that was Othello. Here I am.   290
LODOVICO   Where is that viper? Bring the villain forth.
OTHELLO   I look down towards his feet,[4] but that's a fable.

---

7. Tempered in icy water.   8. Defenseless.   9. What would stop you.   1. Marker of my farthest
voyage. *Butt*: goal.   2. Aim only a reed.   3. Judgment Day.   4. I.e., to see if Iago has devil's hooves.

[*To* IAGO] If that thou beest a devil I cannot kill thee.
    [*He wounds* IAGO.]
LODOVICO   Wrench his sword from him.
    [*Officers disarm* OTHELLO.]
IAGO   I bleed, sir, but not killed.
OTHELLO   I am not sorry, neither. I'd have thee live,   295
   For in my sense[5] 'tis happiness to die.
LODOVICO   O thou Othello, that was once so good,
   Fall'n in the practice[6] of a cursèd slave,
   What shall be said to thee?
OTHELLO   Why, anything;
   An honourable murderer, if you will,   300
   For naught I did in hate, but all in honour.
LODOVICO   This wretch hath part confessed his villainy.
   Did you and he consent in Cassio's death?
OTHELLO   Ay.
CASSIO   Dear general, I never gave you cause.   305
OTHELLO   I do believe it, and I ask your pardon.
   Will you, I pray, demand that demi-devil
   Why he hath thus ensnared my soul and body?
IAGO   Demand me nothing. What you know, you know.
   From this time forth I never will speak word.   310
LODOVICO [*to* IAGO]   What, not to pray?
GRAZIANO [*to* IAGO]   Torments[7] will ope your lips.
OTHELLO   Well, thou dost best.
LODOVICO   Sir, you shall understand what hath befall'n,
   Which as, I think, you know not. Here is a letter,   315
   Found in the pocket of the slain Roderigo,
   And here another. The one of them imports
   The death of Cassio, to be undertook
   By Roderigo.
OTHELLO   O villain!   320
CASSIO   Most heathenish and most gross.
LODOVICO   Now here's another discontented paper
   Found in his pocket too, and this it seems
   Roderigo meant to've sent this damnèd villain,
   But that, belike,[8] Iago in the interim   325
   Came in and satisfied him.
OTHELLO [*to* IAGO]   O thou pernicious caitiff![9]
   How came you, Cassio, by that handkerchief
   That was my wife's?
CASSIO   I found it in my chamber,
   And he himself confessed it, but even now,   330
   That there he dropped it for a special purpose
   Which wrought to his desire.
OTHELLO   O fool, fool, fool!
CASSIO   There is besides in Roderigo's letter
   How he upbraids Iago, that he made him

---

5. Opinion.   6. Plot.   7. Tortures.   8. Perhaps.   9. Wretch.

Brave¹ me upon the watch, whereon it came   335
That I was cast;² and even but now he spake
After long seeming dead, Iago hurt him,
Iago set him on.
LODOVICO [*to* OTHELLO]   You must forsake this room and go with us.
Your power and your command is taken off,   340
And Cassio rules in Cyprus. For this slave,
If there be any cunning cruelty
That can torment him much and hold him long,
It shall be his. You shall close³ prisoner rest
Till that the nature of your fault be known   345
To the Venetian state. [*To* OFFICERS] Come, bring away.
OTHELLO   Soft you, a word or two before you go.
I have done the state some service, and they know't.
No more of that. I pray you, in your letters,
When you shall these unlucky deeds relate,   350
Speak of me as I am. Nothing extenuate,
Nor set down aught in malice. Then must you speak
Of one that loved not wisely but too well,
Of one not easily jealous but, being wrought,
Perplexed in the extreme; of one whose hand,   355
Like the base Indian, threw a pearl away
Richer than all his tribe;⁴ of one whose subdued⁵ eyes,
Albeit unusèd to the melting mood,
Drops tears as fast as the Arabian trees
Their medicinable gum.⁶ Set you down this,   360
And say besides that in Aleppo once,
Where a malignant and a turbaned Turk
Beat a Venetian and traduced the state,
I took by th' throat the circumcisèd dog
And smote him thus.   365
      [*He stabs himself.*]
LODOVICO   O bloody period!⁷
GRAZIANO   All that is spoke is marred.
OTHELLO [*to* DESDEMONA]   I kissed thee ere I killed thee. No way but this:
Killing myself, to die upon a kiss. [*He kisses* DESDEMONA *and dies.*]
CASSIO   This did I fear, but thought he had no weapon,   370
For he was great of heart.
LODOVICO [*to* IAGO]   O Spartan dog,
More fell⁸ than anguish, hunger, or the sea,
Look on the tragic loading of this bed.
This is thy work. The object poisons sight.
Let it be hid.
      [*They close the bed-curtains.*]
                  Graziano, keep the house,   375

---

1. Insult.   2. Dismissed.   3. Tightly constrained.   4. *Indian . . . tribe:* Shakespeare's plays exist in early printed editions (known as quartos) and as gathered in a large volume (known as a folio). This line is from the Quarto text of *Othello*. The Folio text reads *Judean* instead of *Indian*. While both words imply "unbeliever," Indian suggests ignorance of the pearl's value, and Judean may suggest willful refusal of it. 5. I.e., with tears.   6. Balm.   7. Sentence.   8. Cruel. *Spartan:* brutal; reference to the harsh customs of ancient Sparta.

And seize upon the fortunes of the Moor,
For they succeed on you. [*To* CASSIO] To you, Lord Governor,
Remains the censure[9] of this hellish villain.
The time, the place, the torture. O, enforce it!
Myself will straight aboard, and to the state   380
This heavy act with heavy heart relate.   [*Exeunt with Emilia's body.*]

9. Punishment.

JOHN MILTON
1608–1674

The poetic achievement of John Milton is generally regarded as the last flourishing of Christian humanism in Renaissance England; in his poetic work, the Renaissance commitment to classical revival and the Reformation emphasis on the Bible came together. Milton's late position allowed him both to "outdo" the grand epic tradition on its own terms and to criticize its pagan roots. As he well knew, Renaissance epic poets, like Christian humanists, struggled in varying degrees with their mixed allegiances to classical learning and to Christianity. To Christian scholars, the strain of serving the two masters of secular knowledge and religious faith could be distracting: even the Church father Saint Jerome (ca. 347–419 or 420) had a dream in which God denounced him with the charge "You are not a Christian: you are a Ciceronian." In *Paradise Lost*, Milton attempts to resolve the conflict between the seductions of the classics and the imperatives of Christianity: he tells the biblical story of the Fall, and to this authoritative plot he subordinates the classical materials of the epic tradition. What is more, when he wishes to "body forth" the material, tactile richness of beauty—in, for example, the Garden of Eden, Eve, and the snake—he heightens the classicism of his verse. Concentrating classical allusions on the physically sensuous and psychologically disruptive elements of his poem, he allows his classical material to appear in sumptuous glory and, simultaneously, under restraint by the highest authority, the Bible. To an extent, the curbs Milton imposes on his classical sources distract attention from his equally assertive handling of the Bible; yet he does not shy away from telling a highly individual version of the story of "man's first disobedience." The story of Genesis, in which Adam and Eve broke God's prohibition and ate from the tree of knowledge, suggested to Milton an opportunity to expound his own ideas about liberty, knowledge, doubt, sexuality, and marriage.

Milton's life divides conveniently into three stages: a period of long study, which culminated in the great pastoral elegy *Lycidas* (1637) and his travels on the Continent (1638–39), where he met important literary figures in addition to the astronomer Galileo; his long involvement in doctrinal and political controversy and his service as Latin secretary to Oliver Cromwell's Council of State (1640–60); and, after the restoration of the English monarchy and his banishment from politics, the more solitary and disillusioned years in which Milton (totally blind since 1651) produced his major poetic works, *Paradise Lost* (1667), *Paradise Regained* (1671), and *Samson Agonistes* (1671).

Born in London on December 9, 1608, he received an excellent education at St. Paul's in London and Christ's College, Cambridge, where he prepared for a career in the ministry. He received his B.A. in 1629 and his M.A. in 1632, but did not take holy orders (due to his growing dissatisfaction with Church of England hierarchy). Instead, he lived reclusively at his father's estate at Horton, near Windsor, where he continued his studies and followed his dream curriculum of science and the new discoveries, mathematics, Greek and Latin authors, music, the systematic research of world history, and volumes upon volumes of poetry. In his view, his intensive studies were preparing him for the poet's role as moral leader: whoever hopes to write well, he wrote in an autobiographical sketch, "ought himself to be a true poem, that is, a composition and pattern of the best and honorablest things; not presuming to sing high praises of heroic men or famous Cities, unless he have in himself the experience and the practice of all that is praiseworthy." The complete identification of poet and poem, reading and experience, indicates how important it was to Milton to be morally "fit," not just technically skilled, to compose epic verse.

Politics and not poems were on Milton's mind, however, when he returned from his travels in Italy. Word had reached him that political trouble was brewing at home (the beginnings of the Puritan Revolt), and he returned to London, where he inserted himself into the political controversies by writing pamphlets that he hoped would inspire debate. Some of his political arguments shaped the concepts of religious, civil, and domestic liberties that he explores in *Paradise Lost* (1667). His most notable tract, *Areopagitica* (1644), opposed censorship of the press and took to task the parliamentary government (his own party) for trying to restrict the opposition: Parliament was historically bound to defend the liberties of the people, and Milton could not abide its lapse in principle. Throughout his public career he forcefully insisted on popular liberty from arbitrary rule, and he had gone so far as to defend, in print, the execution of his king (Charles I was executed in 1641). How could he justify regicide? Law, he felt, should arise from the reasoning conscience of the individual Christian; to deprive individuals of the free exercise of their reason called for violent resistance.

His most notorious prose writings, however, were directly inspired by his failed marriage and earned him the epithet "the Divorcer": at thirty-two he married the seventeen-year-old Mary Powell, who left him after six weeks. In the argumentative Milton, this event inspired considerable thought and print concerning the grounds of marriage. He complained bitterly of the English law that permitted divorce only to those who had not consummated their marriages and protested that the law left unhappy couples to "grind in the mill of an undelighted and servile copulation" (anything worth saying is worth saying grandly). Without depth of conversation, he argued, men and women were not joined in a genuine marriage. God, he claimed, meant spouses to be spiritual helpmeets and partners in "civil fellowship." In *Paradise Lost*, where Adam and Eve make love without shame and converse with delight, he illustrates his ideal of marriage. Conversation and the "sweet intercourse / Of looks and smiles" turn out to be the essential ingredients of a successful marriage. They are, Milton's Adam says, the way that human beings cope with their fundamental loneliness. When Adam asks God for a companion, he claims that man needs "conversation with his like to help / Or solace his defects" (his lonely distance from God). This loneliness is so intense that even after Eve falls, Adam affirms his need for her (although it means severing himself from God): "with thee / Certain my resolution is to die; / How can I live without thee, how forgo / Thy sweet converse and love so dearly joined?"

Milton's chief source for *Paradise Lost* is the biblical account of Creation, Eden, the Fall, and the expulsion of Adam and Eve from paradise. From the first three chapters of Genesis, he forged twelve capacious books of epic verse, which he fleshed out with his vast knowledge of the classics, history, theology, and science. He had long wanted to write something lasting and once considered composing an epic on King Arthur. Had he written a chivalric romance, he would have inserted himself directly into Virgil's imperial tradition. He began his work on *Paradise Lost*, however, after his banishment from public life: Restoration England had "fallen on evil days," and to his mind no longer had political glory to celebrate. Politically disappointed in the failure of republican government and the reinstatement of monarchy in England, he had reason to look skeptically on the imperial and romance epic tradition he once loved. In fact, he casts Satan as his empire builder, colonizer, and merchant-adventurer, the positions that Aeneas holds in Virgil's epic. More generally, he asserts the superiority of his own subject over the epic tradition stemming from Homer and Virgil: it is, he declares, "Not less but more heroic than the wrath / Of stern Achilles" or "rage / of Turnus," the Latin warrior Aeneas must defeat in order to found Rome. He goes on to scorn the kind of medieval romance that he once planned to compose: "with long and tedious havoc" these tales have merely *fabled* knights / In battles *feigned*." His own tale, by implicit contrast, is genuinely historical and heroic. While epic poets assert their continuity with cultural origins, Milton characteristically insists that his own poem disrupts the heroic tradition. *Paradise Lost* alone, he implies, is genuinely concerned with historical origins and is wholly original as creative verse.

Milton's attitude toward the recovery of truth, as his confidence in his poem suggests, is paradoxically traditional and radical. The poet is at once committed to the recovery of biblical truth and determined to smash the trite conventions through which truths have passed to successive generations. When his poem first appeared, it scandalized and bewildered the reading public. Even his verse style was shocking evidence of his radicalism: the rhyming couplets and stanzas that defined English verse for many readers were nowhere to be found, and in their place were rolling periodic sentences of unrhymed verse (iambic pentameter). His rejection of rhyme so upset his contemporaries that he added a brief note explaining and defending his practice: "This neglect then of Rime so little is to be taken for a defect, though it may seem so perhaps to vulgar Readers, that it rather is to be esteem'd an example set, the first in *English*, of ancient liberty recover'd to Heroic Poem from the troublesome and modern bondage of Riming." Milton proclaimed his heroic break from literary tradition and his victorious recovery of an ancient poetic practice. More momentously, he described his poetic innovation as a politically significant act: he was liberating the intellect from bondage and restoring ancient liberties. He had destroyed the shackles of convention (rhymes) and rescued intellectual freedom, and he did it for his reader. And since liberty is meaningless unless exercised vigorously, he intended every sentence and verse line of his poem to be challenging.

Since Milton set out to innovate in verse, revolutionize interpretation, and liberate the intellect, we might suspect that he chose the wrong text: the choice of Adam and Eve to seek knowledge at the cost of their obedience to God. In fact, the status of knowledge is a central, and not fully resolved, problem in *Paradise Lost*. In *Areopagitica,* Milton argued that virtue is meaningful only when gained and tested by experience. Goodness based on mere ignorance of evil, for him, seems inferior to the reasoned choice of the good over a known and alluring evil. He speculated that the Fall caused a change in the way that human beings gained knowledge. In Eden humanity knew only good; after the Fall, humanity knew good by distinguishing it from evil. "What wisdom can there be to choose, what continence to forbear without the knowledge of evil?" he asked. "I cannot praise a fugitive and cloistered virtue, unexercised and unbreathed, that never sallies out and sees her adversary."

This is the position that the more cautious Milton of *Paradise Lost* places in the mouth of his "Adventurous" Eve just before the Fall. Eve, always more independent than Adam, wants to work alone in another part of the Garden, and when she suspects that her husband mistrusts her ability to withstand the temptations of Satan by herself, she grows adamant about facing a trial, should Satan come her way: "what is Faith, Love, Virtue unassay'd / Alone, without exterior help sustain'd?" Like the younger and rasher Milton, she considers such virtue "but a name" or an abstraction rather than an inner quality; she rejects the idea that her obedience has any significance if it is maintained only by "exterior help." If she is to enjoy a reputation for virtue, she wants it to arise from a personal history of her experiences and trials.

Adam, by contrast, seems curious and anxious about his relationship to knowledge. In his conversations with God and with the angel Raphael, he reveals how inquisitive he is about himself, Eve, the world around him, and above all, the mysterious heavens. To Raphael he expresses doubts about the excesses of God's creation: why are there so many superior heavenly bodies revolving about the earth? The "needless" super-fluity and abundance of creation indicate mysterious purposes that make Adam ques-tion his centrality to the cosmos. When Raphael warns him that "Heav'n is for thee too high / To know what passes there; be lowly wise; / Think only what concerns thee and thy being; / Dream not of other Worlds," Adam declares himself "cleared of doubt." He assures the angel (or himself) that it is better to be "freed from intricacies" and "perplexing" and "wand'ring" thoughts that "rove" endlessly until "warn'd, or by experience taught," the imagination learns to "not to know." Although the difference between receiving a warning and learning by experience is great, Adam falls back on the traditionalist position about knowledge, summed up in the caution to "be lowly wise": don't analyze (etymologically, to "break things apart" logically) or use empirical observation to make inquiries that can lead only to hypothesis and speculation. Expound what you know to be true; do not theorize about "high" matters from "low" or material observation (i.e., use inductive reasoning): receive, do not create your own body of wisdom.

It is a truism of the classical tradition that the beauty of temptresses (like Homer's Circe and Ariosto's Alcina) has a disruptive power over epic heroes who otherwise display Stoic constancy and integrity (literally, "wholeness"). To a limited extent, this model of heroic manhood threatened by female corruption applies to *Paradise Lost*. The telling difference is that for Milton, the "kindly rupture" of sexual experience relates to the acquisition of knowledge and can therefore be rejected only at great personal cost to the hero. After Adam has agreed to be "lowly wise," he admits to Raphael that sexual passion, like the superabundant universe, troubles him because it is overwhelming. When he approaches his wife's "loveliness," he says,

> so absolute she seems
> And in herself complete, so well to know
> Her own, that what she wills to do or say,
> Seems wisest, virtuousest, discreetest, best . . .

Adam repeats his error of inductive reasoning: based on the empirical evidence of sight and touch, he wonders if Eve is in fact "one intended first, not after made / Occasionally." Although no less an authority than God tells him that Eve is "inferior" and "subject" to him, Adam cannot ignore his own experience. His social and spiritual interactions with Eve "subject not," he notes, but passion does, and Adam wants to know what to make of this unorthodox fact.

Through Adam's appealing inquisitiveness, Milton's readers learn an answer to a further question about sex that they might have been afraid to ask: do angels make love? Raphael, who has just reproached Adam for his own "vehement" response to sexuality, blushes and admits that they do. His blush is as revealing as his affirmation: do heavenly beings, as much as earthly ones, experience a "kindly rupture" of passion? A blush, after all, is an involuntary sign of a powerful internal fluctuation. If angels make love and blush about their rapture, then sexuality is not an evil in *Paradise Lost*—and indeed Milton has no patience for the patristic tradition that condemns sexuality as degrading. For Milton, sexuality is instead a powerful testimony to the *unfallen*, if ambiguous, quest for knowledge through experience.

And what of Milton the epic poet: does he, too, experience ruptures in his self-assertiveness? Freeing the individual believer from received wisdom is an anxious, as well as heroic, activity for Milton. In his invocations to his heavenly muse, he raises the awkward question of the source of his poetic inspiration: in book 9, for example, he mentions his "Celestial Patroness, who deigns / Her nightly visitation unimplor'd, / And dictates to me slumb'ring, or inspires / Easy my unpremeditated Verse." From her, he hopes to gain what he calls "answerable style"—poetic expression that echoes the revelation he has received. He boasts that he does not have to ask for his inspiration (as Homer and Virgil did), yet he does not assert its legitimacy. At the end of this invocation, in fact, Milton acknowledges his doubts and fears that "all be mine, / Not Hers who brings it nightly to my Ear." If he is to retell the story of the Bible in what he calls "answerable style," his imagination must be guided by heavenly authority. If his personal revelation is false, perhaps Milton will have to "answer" to his God. His style must be innovative, or it will merely recycle flawed and human-generated conventions; but it must not be "invented" by the poet himself. When Milton reflects on the ambiguous source of his inspiration, he acknowledges the anxiety of a radical Protestant who believes in the principle of personal revelation but cannot confirm it outside his own experience. He fascinatingly returns, in effect, to the basic tension that Christian humanists experienced between recovering truth (through scholarly discoveries) and revolutionizing it (by breaking with tradition).

Milton's achievements in *Paradise Lost* include his powerful rendering of human spiritual need and its relationship to domestic life. His poem might be considered "adventurous" in its explorations of the rational, sexual, and emotional psychologies that lead his Adam and Eve to fall, although it is also uncompromising about the fatal error of the Fall. Milton committed himself intellectually to disrupting the received wisdom of the classics and the Church in order to discover truths verifiable by experience. In the story of Genesis he discovers questions central to the Renaissance and Reformation: how do we know things? to what extent should "external help" such as warnings govern us? how much more rewarding—and dangerous—is the wisdom of experience? can we learn from vicarious experiences, such as sympathy and interpretation (a possibility that enlarges the moral role of art)? Milton, who wished to break the bonds constraining the intellectual and imaginative possibilities of his readers, bestowed on them what must be regarded, paradoxically, as the burden of interpretive liberty: Milton works to make the reading of *Paradise Lost* a simultaneously demanding and highly personal experience.

The standard biography is William Riley Parker, *Milton: A Biography*, 2 vols. (1981). Annabel Patterson, ed., *John Milton* (1992), and David Quint, *Epic and Empire: Politics and Generic Form from Virgil to Milton* (1993), offer useful recent studies of Milton. Rewarding essays can also be found in *Re-membering Milton: Essays on the Texts and Traditions* (1987), edited by Mary Nyquist and Margaret W. Ferguson. Barbara Kiefer Lewalski, *Paradise Lost and the Rhetoric of Literary Forms* (1985), offers a lucid and comprehensive study of Milton's uses of literary genre. Patricia Parker discusses Milton's suggestive linkage of doubt, the romance form, and Eve in a chapter of *Inescapable Romance* (1975). Stanley Fish directs attention to the role of readers' responses in determining or creating meaning in *Surprised by Sin: The Reader in Paradise Lost* (1967). A. Bartlett Giamatti, *The Earthly Paradise and the Renaissance Epic* (1966), analyzes the "coalescence of classical and Christian material" in the poem. Robert Crosman, *Reading Paradise Lost* (1980), is a helpful introduction for first-time readers of Milton's poem.

From Paradise Lost

FROM BOOK 1

["*This Great Argument*"]

Of man's first disobedience, and the fruit[1]
Of that forbidden tree whose mortal taste[2]
Brought death into the world, and all our woe,
With loss of Eden, till one greater Man[3]
Restore us, and regain the blissful seat,   5
Sing, Heavenly Muse,[4] that, on the secret top
Of Oreb, or of Sinai, didst inspire
That shepherd who first taught the chosen seed[5]
In the beginning how the Heavens and Earth
Rose out of Chaos: or, if Sion hill   10
Delight thee more, and Siloa's brook that flowed
Fast by the oracle of God,[6] I thence
Invoke thy aid to my adventurous[7] song,
That with no middle flight intends to soar
Above th' Aonian mount,[8] while it pursues   15
Things unattempted yet in prose or rhyme.
And chiefly thou, O Spirit,[9] that dost prefer
Before all temples th' upright heart and pure,
Instruct me,[1] for thou know'st; thou from the first
Wast present, and, with mighty wings outspread,   20
Dovelike sat'st brooding[2] on the vast abyss,
And mad'st it pregnant: what in me is dark
Illumine; what is low, raise and support;
That, to the height of this great argument,[3]
I may assert[4] Eternal Providence,   25
And justify the ways of God[5] to men.

FROM BOOK 4

The Argument

Satan now in prospect of Eden, and nigh the place where he must now attempt the bold enterprise which he undertook alone against God and man,

---

1. The apple itself, and also the consequences of Adam and Eve's disobedience.   2. The tasting of which brought mortality into the world.   3. Christ.   4. The opening invocation to the muse who will inspire (*sing* to) the poet is a regular feature of epic poems. Milton's heavenly muse elsewhere in the poem (7.1) is given the name of the mythological Urania; in another passage (9.21) she is given the adjective *celestial*. Both words—of Greek and Latin derivation, respectively—mean "heavenly." Clearly and typically, in Milton's heavenly muse pagan elements and images are adopted and given new substance within the framework of Judeo-Christian culture and beliefs.   5. The Hebrew people. Oreb and Sinai designate the mountain where God spoke to Moses (*that shepherd*), who in Genesis taught the Hebrew people the story of the Creation.   6. The Temple. The biblical localities suggested here as haunts for Milton's muse are emblematic of his certainty about the higher nature of his theme compared with the epic subjects of pagan antiquity. The fact that *Siloa's brook* is flowing by the Temple suggests the holy nature of Milton's subject.   7. Perilous, as the poet is daring something new (see line 16).   8. Helicon, the Greek mountain that was the seat of the Nine Muses. The spring Aganippe, which gives poetic power, and an altar of Zeus were part of that landscape (compare the location of Siloa's brook, lines 11–12).   9. Described in Milton's Latin treatise on Christian doctrine as "that impulse or voice of God by which the prophets were inspired," the *Spirit* is a further source of inspiration over and above the heavenly muse.   1. The poet asks not for song but for knowledge (*instruct me*) and identifies the Spirit with the Spirit of God that "moved upon the face of the waters" (Genesis 1.2). The image is pursued in line 22 with *pregnant*. *Dovelike*: the traditional figuration of the Holy Spirit (for example, Luke 3.22: "the Holy Ghost descended in a bodily shape like a dove").   3. Subject, theme.   4. Champion, vindicate.   5. Demonstrate the justice of the course of God's providence.

falls into many doubts with himself, and many passions, fear, envy, and despair; but at length confirms himself in evil, journeys on to Paradise, whose outward prospect and situation is described, overleaps the bounds, sits in the shape of a cormorant on the Tree of Life, as highest in the Garden to look about him. The Garden described; Satan's first sight of Adam and Eve; his wonder at their excellent form and happy state, but with resolution to work their fall; overhears their discourse, thence gathers that the Tree of Knowledge was forbidden them to eat of, under penalty of death; and thereon intends to found his temptation, by seducing them to transgress: then leaves them a while, to know further of their state by some other means. Meanwhile Uriel descending on a sunbeam warns Gabriel, who had in charge the gate of Paradise, that some evil Spirit had escaped the deep, and passed at noon by his sphere in the shape of a good angel down to Paradise, discovered after by his furious gestures in the mount. Gabriel promises to find him ere morning. Night coming on, Adam and Eve discourse of going to their rest: their bower described; their evening worship. Gabriel drawing forth his bands of nightwatch to walk the round of Paradise, appoints two strong angels to Adam's bower, lest the evil Spirit should be there doing some harm to Adam or Eve sleeping; there they find him at the ear of Eve, tempting her in a dream, and bring him, though unwilling, to Gabriel; by whom questioned, he scornfully answers, prepares resistance, but hindered by a sign from heaven, flies out of Paradise.

[Satan's Entry into Paradise; Adam and Eve in Their Bower]

O for that warning voice which he[6] who saw
Th' Apocalypse heard cry in Heaven aloud,
Then when the dragon, put to second rout,
Came furious down to be revenged on men,
Woe to the inhabitants on Earth! that now,   5
While time was, our first parents had been warned
The coming of their secret foe, and scaped,
Haply so scaped, his mortal snare! For now
Satan, now first inflamed with rage, came down,
The tempter ere th' accuser of mankind,   10
To wreak on innocent frail man his loss
Of that first battle, and his flight to Hell.
Yet not rejoicing in his speed though bold
Far off and fearless, nor with cause to boast,
Begins his dire attempt; which nigh the birth   15
Now rolling, boils in his tumultuous breast,
And like a devilish engine[7] back recoils
Upon himself. Horror and doubt distract
His troubled thoughts, and from the bottom stir
The Hell within him; for within him Hell   20
He brings, and round about him, nor from Hell
One step no more than from himself can fly
By change of place. Now conscience wakes despair
That slumbered, wakes the bitter memory

6. Saint John, author of Revelation.   7. A cannon.

Of what he was, what is, and what must be   25
Worse; of worse deeds worse sufferings must ensue.
Sometimes towards Eden, which now in his view
Lay pleasant, his grieved look he fixes sad;
Sometimes towards heaven and the full-blazing sun,
Which now sat high in his meridian tower;   30
Then, much revolving, thus in sighs began:
   "O thou that with surpassing glory crowned
Look'st from thy sole dominion like the god
Of this new world—at whose sight all the stars
Hide their diminished heads—to thee I call,   35
But with no friendly voice, and add thy name,
O sun, to tell thee how I hate thy beams,
That bring to my remembrance from what state
I fell, how glorious once above thy sphere,
Till pride and worse ambition threw me down,   40
Warring in Heaven against Heaven's matchless King!
Ah, wherefore? He deserved no such return
From me, whom he created what I was
In that bright eminence, and with his good
Upbraided none; nor was his service hard.   45
What could be less than to afford him praise,
The easiest recompense, and pay him thanks,
How due! Yet all his good proved ill in me,
And wrought but malice. Lifted up so high,
I'sdained[8] subjection, and thought one step higher   50
Would set me highest, and in a moment quit
The debt immense of endless gratitude,
So burdensome, still paying, still to owe,
Forgetful what from him I still received;
And understood not that a grateful mind   55
By owing owes not, but still pays, at once
Indebted and discharged—what burden then?
O had his powerful destiny ordained
Me some inferior angel, I had stood
Then happy; no unbounded hope had raised   60
Ambition. Yet why not? Some other power
As great might have aspired, and me, though mean,
Drawn to his part. But other powers as great
Fell not, but stand unshaken, from within
Or from without to all temptations armed!   65
Hadst thou the same free will and power to stand?
Thou hadst. Whom hast thou then, or what, to accuse,
But Heaven's free love dealt equally to all?
Be then his love accursed, since, love or hate,
To me alike it deals eternal woe.   70
Nay, cursed be thou; since against his thy will
Chose freely what it now so justly rues.
Me miserable! which way shall I fly
Infinite wrath and infinite despair?

8. Disdained.

Which way I fly is Hell; myself am Hell;   75
And in the lowest deep a lower deep
Still threatening to devour me opens wide,
To which the Hell I suffer seems a Heaven.
O then at last relent! Is there no place
Left for repentance, none for pardon left?   80
None left but by submission; and that word
Disdain forbids me, and my dread of shame
Among the spirits beneath, whom I seduced
With other promises and other vaunts
Than to submit, boasting I could subdue   85
Th' omnipotent. Ay me! they little know
How dearly I abide that boast so vain,
Under what torments inwardly I groan.
While they adore me on the throne of Hell,
With diadem and scepter high advanced,   90
The lower still I fall, only supreme
In misery: such joy ambition finds!
But say I could repent and could obtain
By act of grace my former state, how soon
Would height recall high thoughts, how soon unsay   95
What feigned submission swore! Ease would recant
Vows made in pain, as violent and void.
For never can true reconcilement grow
Where wounds of deadly hate have pierced so deep;
Which would but lead me to a worse relapse   100
And heavier fall: so should I purchase dear
Short intermission, bought with double smart.
This knows my punisher; therefore as far
From granting he, as I from begging, peace.
All hope excluded thus, behold, instead   105
Of us outcast, exiled, his new delight,
Mankind created, and for him this world!
So farewell hope, and with hope farewell fear,
Farewell remorse! All good to me is lost;
Evil, be thou my good: by thee at least   110
Divided empire with Heaven's king I hold,
By thee, and more than half perhaps will reign;
As man ere long, and this new world, shall know."
    Thus while he spake, each passion dimmed his face,
Thrice changed with pale—ire, envy, and despair;   115
Which marred his borrowed visage, and betrayed
Him counterfeit, if any eye beheld:
For heavenly minds from such distempers foul
Are ever clear. Whereof he soon aware
Each perturbation smoothed with outward calm,   120
Artificer of fraud; and was the first
That practiced falsehood under saintly show,
Deep malice to conceal, couched with revenge:
Yet not enough had practiced to deceive
Uriel,[9] once warned; whose eye pursued him down   125

---

9. An angel sent to guard Eden from Satan's assault.

The way he went, and on th' Assyrian mount[1]
Saw him disfigured, more than could befall
Spirit of happy sort: his gestures fierce
He marked and mad demeanor, then alone,
As he supposed, all unobserved, unseen.   130
    So on he fares, and to the border comes
Of Eden, where delicious Paradise,
Now nearer, crowns with her enclosure green
As with a rural mound the champaign head
Of a steep wilderness, whose hairy sides   135
With thicket overgrown, grotesque and wild,
Access denied; and overhead up grew
Insuperable height of loftiest shade,
Cedar, and pine, and fir, and branching palm,
A sylvan scene, and as the ranks ascend   140
Shade above shade, a woody theater
Of stateliest view. Yet higher than their tops
The verdurous wall of Paradise up sprung;
Which to our general sire gave prospect large
Into his nether empire neighboring round.   145
And higher than that wall a circling row
Of goodliest trees loaden with fairest fruit,
Blossoms and fruits at once of golden hue,
Appeared, with gay enameled colors mixed;
On which the sun more glad impressed his beams   150
Than in fair evening cloud, or humid bow,
When God hath showered the earth: so lovely seemed
That landscape. And of pure now purer air
Meets his approach, and to the heart inspires
Vernal delight and joy, able to drive[2]   155
All sadness but despair. Now gentle gales,
Fanning their odoriferous wings, dispense
Native perfumes, and whisper whence they stole
Those balmy spoils. As when to them who sail
Beyond the Cape of Hope, and now are past   160
Mozambic, off at sea northeast winds blow
Sabean[3] odors from the spicy shore
Of Araby the Blest, with such delay
Well pleased they slack their course, and many a league
Cheered with the grateful smell old Ocean smiles;   165
So entertained those odorous sweets the fiend
Who came their bane, though with them better pleased
Than Asmodëus[4] with the fishy fume
That drove him, though enamored, from the spouse
Of Tobit's son,[5] and with a vengeance sent   170
From Media post to Egypt, there fast bound.
    Now to th' ascent of that steep savage hill
Satan had journeyed on, pensive and slow;
But further way found none; so thick entwined,

---

1. Niphates, a mountain on the border of Armenia and Assyria.   2. Drive out.   3. Sheba of the Bible.
Mozambique was an important Portuguese province in the trade route. Milton joins biblical, classical, and
modern sources to describe the exotic pleasures of Eden.   4. Demon lover of Sara in the Apocryphal
Book of Tobit.   5. Tobias.

As one continued brake, the undergrowth   175
Of shrubs and tangling bushes had perplexed
All path of man or beast that passed that way.
One gate there only was, and that looked east
On th' other side; which when th' arch-felon saw,
Due entrance he disdained, and in contempt   180
At one slight bound high overleaped all bound
Of hill or highest wall, and sheer within
Lights on his feet. As when a prowling wolf,
Whom hunger drives to seek new haunt for prey,
Watching where shepherds pen their flocks at eve   185
In hurdled cotes amid the field secure,
Leaps o'er the fence with ease into the fold;
Or as a thief, bent to unhoard the cash
Of some rich burgher, whose substantial doors,
Cross-barred and bolted fast, fear no assault,   190
In at the window climbs, or o'er the tiles;
So clomb this first grand thief into God's fold:
So since into his church lewd hirelings climb.
Thence up he flew, and on the Tree of Life,
The middle tree and highest there that grew,   195
Sat like a cormorant; yet not true life
Thereby regained, but sat devising death
To them who lived; nor on the virtue thought
Of that life-giving plant, but only used
For prospect, what, well used, had been the pledge   200
Of immortality. So little knows
Any, but God alone, to value right
The good before him, but perverts best things
To worst abuse, or to their meanest use.
   Beneath him with new wonder now he views   205
To all delight of human sense exposed
In narrow room Nature's whole wealth; yea more,
A Heaven on Earth; for blissful Paradise
Of God the garden was, by him in the east
Of Eden planted. Eden stretched her line   210
From Auran eastward to the royal towers
Of great Seleucia, built by Grecian kings,
Or where the sons of Eden long before
Dwelt in Telassar.[6] In this pleasant soil
His far more pleasant garden God ordained.   215
Out of the fertile ground he caused to grow
All trees of noblest kind for sight, smell, taste;
And all amid them stood the Tree of Life,
High eminent, blooming ambrosial fruit
Of vegetable gold; and next to life,   220
Our death, the Tree of Knowledge, grew fast by—
Knowledge of good bought dear by knowing ill.
Southward through Eden went a river large,
Nor changed his course, but through the shaggy hill
Passed underneath engulfed; for God had thrown   225

6. City in Eden.

That mountain, as his garden-mold, high raised
Upon the rapid current, which, through veins
Of porous earth with kindly thirst up drawn,
Rose a fresh fountain, and with many a rill
Watered the garden; thence united fell   230
Down the steep glade, and met the nether flood,
Which from his darksome passage now appears,
And now, divided into four main streams,
Runs diverse, wandering many a famous realm
And country, whereof here needs no account;   235
But rather to tell how, if art could tell,
How from that sapphire fount the crispèd brooks,
Rolling on orient pearl and sands of gold,
With mazy error under pendant shades
Ran nectar, visiting each plant, and fed   240
Flowers worthy of Paradise; which not nice art
In beds and curious knots, but Nature boon
Poured forth profuse on hill and dale and plain,
Both where the morning sun first warmly smote
The open field, and where the unpierced shade   245
Embrowned the noontide bowers. Thus was this place,
A happy rural seat of various view:
Groves whose rich trees wept odorous gums and balm;
Others whose fruit, burnished with golden rind,
Hung amiable—Hesperian fables[7] true,   250
If true, here only—and of delicious taste.
Betwixt them lawns, or level downs, and flocks
Grazing the tender herb, were interposed,
Or palmy hillock; or the flowery lap
Of some irriguous valley spread her store,   255
Flowers of all hue, and without thorn the rose.
Another side, umbrageous grots and caves
Of cool recess, o'er which the mantling vine
Lays forth her purple grape, and gently creeps
Luxuriant; meanwhile murmuring waters fall   260
Down the slope hills dispersed, or in a lake,
That to the fringèd bank with myrtle crowned
Her crystal mirror holds, unite their streams.
The birds their choir apply; airs, vernal airs,
Breathing the smell of field and grove, attune   265
The trembling leaves, while universal Pan,[8]
Knit with the Graces and the Hours in dance,
Led on th' eternal spring. Not that fair field
Of Enna, where Proserpin gathering flowers,
Herself a fairer flower, by gloomy Dis   270
Was gathered, which cost Ceres all that pain
To seek her through the world;[9] nor that sweet grove
Of Daphne, by Orontes and th' inspired

---

7. In Ovid's *Metamorphoses* 10, a dragon guarded the golden apples on the islands known as the Hesperides.
8. A pastoral god whose name Renaissance mythographers took from the Greek *pas* or *pan*, meaning "all"
(or "universal").   9. In Ovid's *Fasti* 4, Dis, the god of the underworld, abducts Proserpine, daughter of
Ceres (the goddess of the earth's natural fecundity). Because she eats seven seeds of a pomegranate in the
underworld, Proserpine must remain there seven months of each year, during which time Ceres mourns
and blights the earth.

Castalian spring,[1] might with this Paradise
Of Eden strive; nor that Nyseian isle,   275
Girt with the river Triton, where old Cham,
Whom Gentiles Ammon call and Libyan Jove,
Hid Amalthea and her florid son
Young Bacchus from his stepdame Rhea's eye;[2]
Nor where Abassin kings their issue guard,   280
Mount Amara (though this by some supposed
True Paradise), under the Ethiop line[3]
By Nilus' head, enclosed with shining rock,
A whole day's journey high, but wide remote
From this Assyrian[4] garden, where the fiend   285
Saw undelighted all delight, all kind
Of living creatures, new to sight and strange.
Two of far nobler shape, erect and tall,
Godlike erect, with native honor clad
In naked majesty, seemed lords of all,   290
And worthy seemed; for in their looks divine
The image of their glorious Maker shone,
Truth, wisdom, sanctitude severe and pure—
Severe, but in true filial freedom placed,
Whence true authority in men; though both   295
Not equal, as their sex not equal seemed;[5]
For contemplation he and valor formed,
For softness she and sweet attractive grace;
He for God only, she for God in him.[6]
His fair large front and eye sublime declared   300
Absolute rule;[7] and hyacinthine locks
Round from his parted forelock manly hung
Clustering, but not beneath his shoulders broad:
She, as a veil down to the slender waist,
Her unadornèd golden tresses wore   305
Disheveled, but in wanton ringlets waved
As the vine curls her tendrils, which implied
Subjection,[8] but required with gentle sway,
And by her yielded, by him best received,
Yielded with coy submission, modest pride,   310
And sweet, reluctant, amorous delay.
Nor those mysterious parts were then concealed;
Then was not guilty shame. Dishonest shame
Of Nature's works, honor dishonorable,
Sin-bred, how have ye troubled all mankind   315

1. The groves of Daphne by the river Orontes in Syria had a temple to Apollo and a spring named after
the Castalian spring of Parnassus.   2. Ammon, king of Libya, had an affair with the nymph Amalthea,
who bore the god Bacchus; Ammon hid the child from his jealous wife, Rhea, on the island of Nysa. Ammon
was identified with the Libyan Jove and with Ham, or Cham, son of Noah.   3. I.e., on the equator in
Abyssinia.   4. The Garden was near the Euphrates in Assyria.   5. Milton includes both biblical
accounts of creation, beginning with Genesis 1.27: "So God created man in his own image, in the image
of God created he him; male and female created he them." He next uses the account of creating Eve from
Adam's rib.   6. "The head of every man is Christ; and the head of the woman is the man" (1 Corinthians
11.3).   7. Adam's body "declares" the political theory associated with monarchical absolutism.
8. Eve's body "implies" the subjection that fulfills Adam's "Absolute rule," but negotiates the distribution
of "authority in men." In *Tetrachordon*, Milton writes of the "golden dependence of [male] headship and
[female] subjection" in marriage.

With shows instead, mere shows of seeming pure,
And banished from man's life his happiest life,
Simplicity and spotless innocence!
So passed they naked on, nor shunned the sight
Of God or angel, for they thought no ill;   320
So hand in hand they passed, the loveliest pair
That ever since in love's embraces met:
Adam the goodliest man of men since born
His sons; the fairest of her daughters Eve.
Under a tuft of shade that on a green   325
Stood whispering soft, by a fresh fountain-side,
They sat them down; and after no more toil
Of their sweet gardening labor than sufficed
To recommend cool Zephyr,⁹ and made ease
More easy, wholesome thirst and appetite   330
More grateful, to their supper fruits they fell,
Nectarine fruits which the compliant boughs
Yielded them, sidelong as they sat recline
On the soft downy bank damasked¹ with flowers.
The savory pulp they chew, and in the rind   335
Still as they thirsted scoop the brimming stream;
Nor gentle purpose, nor endearing smiles
Wanted, nor youthful dalliance, as beseems
Fair couple linked in happy nuptial league,
Alone as they. About them frisking played   340
All beasts of th' earth, since wild, and of all chase
In wood or wilderness, forest or den.
Sporting the lion ramped, and in his paw
Dandled the kid; bears, tigers, ounces, pards,²
Gamboled before them; th' unwieldy elephant   345
To make them mirth used all his might, and wreathed
His lithe proboscis;³ close the serpent sly,
Insinuating, wove with Gordian twine
His braided train, and of his fatal guile
Gave proof unheeded. Others on the grass   350
Couched, and now filled with pasture gazing sat,
Or bedward ruminating; for the sun,
Declined, was hasting now with prone career
To th' ocean isles, and in th' ascending scale
Of heaven the stars that usher evening rose: 355
When Satan, still in gaze as first he stood,
Scarce thus at length failed speech recovered sad:
    "O Hell! what do mine eyes with grief behold?
Into our room of bliss thus high advanced
Creatures of other mold, Earth-born perhaps,   360
Not spirits, yet to heavenly spirits bright
Little inferior; whom my thoughts pursue
With wonder, and could love; so lively shines
In them divine resemblance, and such grace
The hand that formed them on their shape hath poured.   365

9. West wind.   1. Richly patterned.   2. Lynxes and leopards.   3. Trunk.

Ah! gentle pair, ye little think how nigh
Your change approaches, when all these delights
Will vanish, and deliver ye to woe,
More woe, the more your taste is now of joy:
Happy, but for so happy ill secured   370
Long to continue, and this high seat, your Heaven,
Ill fenced for Heaven to keep out such a foe
As now is entered; yet no purposed foe
To you, whom I could pity thus forlorn,
Though I unpitied. League with you I seek,   375
And mutual amity so strait, so close,
That I with you must dwell, or you with me,
Henceforth. My dwelling, haply, may not please,
Like this fair Paradise, your sense; yet such
Accept your Maker's work; he gave it me,   380
Which I as freely give. Hell shall unfold,
To entertain you two, her widest gates,
And send forth all her kings; there will be room,
Not like these narrow limits, to receive
Your numerous offspring; if no better place,   385
Thank him who puts me, loath, to this revenge
On you, who wrong me not, for him who wronged.
And should I at your harmless innocence
Melt, as I do, yet public reason just—
Honor and empire with revenge enlarged   390
By conquering this new world—compels me now
To do what else, though damned, I should abhor."
     So spake the fiend, and with necessity,
The tyrant's plea, excused his devilish deeds.
Then from his lofty stand on that high tree   395
Down he alights among the sportful herd
Of those four-footed kinds, himself now one,
Now other, as their shape served best his end
Nearer to view his prey, and unespied
To mark what of their state he more might learn   400
By word or action marked. About them round
A lion now he stalks with fiery glare;
Then as a tiger, who by chance hath spied
In some purlieu⁴ two gentle fawns at play,
Straight couches close; then, rising, changes oft   405
His couchant⁵ watch, as one who chose his ground,
Whence rushing he might surest seize them both
Gripped in each paw; when Adam first of men
To first of women Eve thus moving speech,
Turned him all ear to hear new utterance flow.   410
     "Sole partner and sole part of all these joys,
Dearer thyself than all; needs must the power
That made us, and for us this ample world,
Be infinitely good, and of his good
As liberal and free as infinite,   415
That raised us from the dust and placed us here

4. Region on the outskirts of a given area.   5. From heraldry: lying down with the head raised.

In all this happiness, who at his hand
Have nothing merited, nor can perform
Aught of which he hath need; he who requires
From us no other service than to keep   420
This one, this easy charge, of all the trees
In Paradise that bear delicious fruit
So various, not to taste that only Tree
Of Knowledge, planted by the Tree of Life,
So near grows death to life, whate'er death is,   425
Some dreadful thing, no doubt; for well thou know'st
God hath pronounced it death to taste that tree,
The only sign of our obedience left
Among so many signs of power and rule
Conferred upon us, and dominion given   430
Over all other creatures that possess
Earth, air, and sea. Then let us not think hard
One easy prohibition, who enjoy
Free leave so large to all things else, and choice
Unlimited of manifold delights;   435
But let us ever praise him, and extol
His bounty, following our delightful task
To prune these growing plants and tend these flowers,
Which were it toilsome, yet with thee were sweet."
    To whom thus Eve replied: "O thou for whom   440
And from whom I was formed flesh of thy flesh,
And without whom am to no end, my guide
And head, what thou hast said is just and right.
For we to him indeed all praises owe
And daily thanks, I chiefly who enjoy   445
So far the happier lot, enjoying thee
Preeminent by so much odds, while thou
Like consort to thyself canst nowhere find.
That day I oft remember, when from sleep
I first awaked, and found myself reposed   450
Under a shade on flowers, much wondering where
And what I was, whence thither brought, and how.
Not distant far from thence a murmuring sound
Of waters issued from a cave and spread
Into a liquid plain, then stood unmoved,   455
Pure as th' expanse of heaven; I thither went
With unexperienced thought, and laid me down
On the green bank, to look into the clear
Smooth lake that to me seemed another sky.
As I bent down to look, just opposite,   460
A shape within the wat'ry gleam appeared,
Bending to look on me. I started back,
It started back; but pleased I soon returned,
Pleased it returned as soon with answering looks
Of sympathy and love. There I had fixed   465
Mine eyes till now, and pined with vain desire,[6]

6. Like Ovid's Narcissus in *Metamorphoses* 3.339–510, Eve falls in love with her image; unlike Narcissus, she is led by God's voice to Adam, whose image she is.

Had not a voice thus warned me: 'What thou seest,
What there thou seest, fair creature, is thyself;
With thee it came and goes. But follow me,
And I will bring thee where no shadow stays 470
Thy coming, and thy soft embraces, he
Whose image thou art, him thou shalt enjoy
Inseparably thine, to him shalt bear
Multitudes like thyself, and thence be called
Mother of human race.'⁷ What could I do 475
But follow straight, invisibly thus led?
Till I espied thee, fair indeed and tall
Under a platan, yet methought⁸ less fair,
Less winning soft, less amiably mild
Than that smooth wat'ry image. Back I turned; 480
Thou following cried'st aloud, 'Return, fair Eve,
Whom fli'st thou? whom thou fli'st, of him thou art,
His flesh, his bone; to give thee being I lent
Out of my side to thee, nearest my heart,
Substantial life, to have thee by my side 485
Henceforth an individual solace dear.
Part of my soul I seek thee, and thee claim
My other half.' With that, thy gentle hand
Seized mine, I yielded, and from that time see
How beauty is excelled by manly grace 490
And wisdom, which alone is truly fair."
   So spake our general mother, and with eyes
Of conjugal attraction unreproved
And meek surrender, half embracing leaned
On our first father; half her swelling breast 495
Naked met his under the flowing gold
Of her loose tresses hid. He in delight
Both of her beauty and submissive charms
Smiled with superior love, as Jupiter
On Juno smiles,⁹ when he impregns the clouds 500
That shed May flowers, and pressed her matron lip
With kisses pure. Aside the Devil turned
For envy, yet with jealous leer malign
Eyed them askance, and to himself thus plained:
   "Sight hateful, sight tormenting! thus these two 505
Imparadised in one another's arms,
The happier Eden, shall enjoy their fill
Of bliss on bliss, while I to Hell am thrust,
Where neither joy nor love, but fierce desire,
Among our other torments not the least, 510
Still unfulfilled with pain of longing pines.
Yet let me not forget what I have gained
From their own mouths: all is not theirs, it seems.
One fatal tree there stands, of knowledge called,

---

7. Eve means "Mother of all things living" (11.159).   8. It seemed to me. A platan is a plane tree.
9. In Greco-Roman mythology, Jupiter is king of the gods and Juno is his sister and wife. The marital
hierarchies of the pagan gods and of the human couple differ. While Jupiter reigns (and rains) supreme,
Adam and Eve enjoy "give and take." Adam smiles *with superior love*, yet Eve is physically "on top."

Forbidden them to taste. Knowledge forbidden?   515
Suspicious, reasonless. Why should their lord
Envy them that? Can it be sin to know,
Can it be death? and do they only stand
By ignorance, is that their happy state,
The proof of their obedience and their faith?   520
O fair foundation laid whereon to build
Their ruin! Hence I will excite their minds
With more desire to know, and to reject
Envious commands, invented with design
To keep them low whom knowledge might exalt   525
Equal with gods. Aspiring to be such,
They taste and die; what likelier can ensue?
But first with narrow search I must walk round
This garden, and no corner leave unspied;
A chance but chance may lead where I may meet   530
Some wandering spirit of Heaven, by fountain side
Or in thick shade retired, from him to draw
What further would be learnt. Live while ye may,
Yet happy pair; enjoy, till I return,
Short pleasures, for long woes are to succeed."   535

*   *   *

FROM BOOK 8

The Argument

Adam inquires concerning celestial motions, is doubtfully answered, and
exhorted to search rather things more worthy of knowledge: Adam assents,
and still desirous to detain Raphael, relates to him what he remembered
since his own creation, his placing in Paradise, his talk with God concerning
solitude and fit society, his first meeting and nuptials with Eve, his discourse
with the angel thereupon; who after admonitions repeated departs.

[Adam Describes His Own Creation and That of Eve; Having Repeated His
Warning, the Angel Departs]

*   *   *

"Solicit not thy thoughts with matters hid,[1]
Leave them to God above, him serve and fear;
Of other creatures, as him pleases best,
Wherever placed, let him dispose: joy thou   170
In what he gives thee, this Paradise
And thy fair Eve; heaven is for thee too high
To know what passes there; be lowly wise:
Think only what concerns thee and thy being;
Dream not of other worlds, what creatures there   175
Live, in what state, condition or degree,

1. In conversation with the angel Raphael, Adam has asked questions about astronomy and expressed
uncertainty about divine intention.

Contented that thus far hath been revealed
Not of earth only but of highest heaven."
   To whom thus Adam cleared of doubt, replied.
"How fully hast thou satisfied me, pure   180
Intelligence of heaven, angel serene,
And freed from intricacies, taught to live,
The easiest way, nor with perplexing thoughts
To interrupt the sweet of life, from which
God hath bid dwell far off all anxious cares,   185
And not molest us, unless we ourselves
Seek them with wandering thoughts, and notions vain.
But apt the mind or fancy is to rove
Unchecked, and of her roving is no end;
Till warned, or by experience taught, she learn,   190
That not to know at large of things remote
From use, obscure and subtle, but to know
That which before us lies in daily life,
Is the prime wisdom, what is more is fume,
Or emptiness, or find impertinence,   195
And renders us in things that most concern
Unpracticed, unprepared, and still to seek.
Therefore from this high pitch let us descend
A lower flight, and speak of things at hand
Useful, whence haply mention may arise   200
Of something not unseasonable to ask
By sufferance, and they wonted favor deigned.
Thee I have heard relating what was done
Ere my remembrance: now hear me relate
My story, which perhaps thou hast not heard;   205
And Day is yet not spent; till then thou seest
How subtly to detain thee I devise,
Inviting thee to hear while I relate,
Fond, were it not in hope of thy reply:
For while I sit with thee, I seem in heaven,   210
And sweeter thy discourse is to my ear
Than fruits of palm-tree pleasantest to thirst
And hunger both, from labor, at the hour
Of sweet repast; they satiate, and soon fill,
Though pleasant, but thy words with grace divine   215
Imbued, bring to their sweetness no satiety."
   To whom thus Raphael answered heavenly meek.
"Nor are thy lips ungraceful, sire of men,
Nor tongue ineloquent; for God on thee
Abundantly his gifts hath also poured   220
Inward and outward both, his image fair:
Speaking or mute all comeliness and grace
Attends thee, and each word, each motion forms.
Nor less think we in heaven of thee on earth
Than of our fellow servant, and inquire   225
Gladly into the ways of God with man:
For God we see hath honored thee, and set
On man his equal love: say therefore on;

For I that day was absent, as befell,
Bound on a voyage uncouth and obscure, 230
Far on excursion toward the gates of hell;[2]
Squared in full legion (such command we had)
To see that none thence issued forth a spy,
Or enemy, while God was in his work,
Lest he incensed at such eruption bold, 235
Destruction with creation might have mixed.
Nor that they durst without his leave attempt,
But us he sends upon his high behests
For state, as sovereign king, and to inure
Our prompt obedience. Fast we found, fast shut 240
The dismal gates, and barricadoed strong;
But long ere our approaching heard within
Noise, other then the sound of dance or song,
Torment, and loud lament, and furious rage.
Glad we returned up to the coasts of light 245
Ere Sabbath evening: so we had in charge.
But thy relation now; for I attend,
Pleased with thy words no less than thou with mine."
    So spake the godlike power, and thus our sire:
"For man to tell how human life began 250
Is hard; for who himself beginning knew?
Desire with thee still longer to converse
Induced me. As new waked from soundest sleep,
Soft on the flowery herb I found me laid
In balmy sweat, which with his beams the sun 255
Soon dried, and on the reeking[3] moisture fed.
Straight toward heaven my wondering eyes I turned,
And gazed a while the ample sky, till raised
By quick instinctive motion up I sprung
As thitherward endeavoring, and upright 260
Stood on my feet; about me round I saw
Hill, dale, and shady woods, and sunny plains
And liquid lapse of murmuring streams; by these,
Creatures that lived and moved, and walked or flew,
Birds on the branches warbling. All things smiled; 265
With fragrance and with joy my heart o'erflowed.
Myself I then perused, and limb by limb
Surveyed, and sometimes went and sometimes ran
With supple joints as lively vigor led:
But who I was, or where, or from what cause, 270
Knew not. To speak I tried, and forthwith spake,
My tongue obeyed, and readily could name
Whate'er I saw. 'Thou sun,' said I, 'fair light,
And thou enlightened earth, so fresh and gay,
Ye hills and dales, ye rivers, woods, and plains, 275
And ye that live and move, fair creatures, tell,
Tell, if ye saw, how came I thus, how here?

2. God sent Raphael to watch the gates of hell and prevent Satan from disturbing Him during the creation of the world.   3. Steaming.

Not of myself; by some great maker, then,
In goodness and in power preëminent.
Tell me how may I know him, how adore,   280
From whom I have that thus I move and live,
And feel that I am happier than I know.'
    "While thus I called, and strayed I knew not whither
From where I first drew air and first beheld
This happy light, when answer none returned,   285
On a green shady bank profuse of flowers
Pensive I sat me down; there gentle sleep
First found me and with soft oppression seized
My drowsèd sense—untroubled, though I thought
I then was passing to my former state   290
Insensible, and forthwith to dissolve;
When suddenly stood at my head a dream,
Whose inward apparition gently moved
My fancy to believe I yet had being
And lived. One came, methought, of shape divine,   295
And said, 'Thy mansion wants thee, Adam, rise,
First man, of men innumerable ordained
First father; called by thee I come thy guide
To the garden of bliss, thy seat prepared.'
So saying, by the hand he took me raised,   300
And over fields and waters, as in air
Smooth sliding without step, last led me up
A woody mountain whose high top was plain,
A circuit wide, enclosed, with goodliest trees
Planted, with walks and bowers, that what I saw   305
Of earth before scarce pleasant seemed. Each tree
Loaden with fairest fruit that hung to the eye
Tempting, stirred in me sudden appetite
To pluck and eat; whereat I waked, and found
Before mine eyes all real, as the dream   310
Had lively shadowed. Here had new begun
My wandering, had not he who was my guide
Up hither, from among the trees appeared,
Presence divine. Rejoicing, but with awe,
In adoration at his feet I fell   315
Submiss: he reared me, and, 'Whom thou soughtest I am,'
Said mildly, 'author[4] of all this thou seest
Above or round about thee or beneath.
This Paradise I give thee, count it thine
To till and keep, and of the fruit to eat.   320
Of every tree that in the garden grows
Eat freely with glad heart; fear here no dearth.
But of the tree whose operation brings
Knowledge of good and ill, which I have set
The pledge of thy obedience and thy faith   325
Amid the garden by the Tree of Life,
Remember what I warn thee, shun to taste

---

4. Creator, augmenter.

And shun the bitter consequence: for know
The day thou eat'st thereof, my sole command
Transgressed, inevitably thou shalt die,   330
From that day mortal, and this happy state
Shalt lose, expelled from hence into a world
Of woe and sorrow.' Sternly he pronounced
The rigid interdiction, which resounds
Yet dreadful in mine ear, though in my choice   335
Not to incur; but soon his clear aspèct
Returned, and gracious purpose thus renewed:
'Not only these fair bounds, but all the Earth
To thee and to thy race I give; as lords
Possess it, and all things that therein live,   340
Or live in sea or air, beast, fish, and fowl.
In sign whereof each bird and beast behold
After their kinds; I bring them to receive
From thee their names, and pay thee fealty
With low subjection; understand the same   345
Of fish within their watery residence,
Not hither summoned, since they cannot change
Their element to draw the thinner air.'
As thus he spake, each bird and beast behold
Approaching two and two, these cowering low   350
With blandishment, each bird stooped on his wing.
I named them as they passed, and understood
Their nature, with such knowledge God endued
My sudden apprehension. But in these
I found not what methought I wanted[5] still,   355
And to the heavenly vision thus presumed:
    " 'O by what name, for thou above all these,
Above mankind, or aught than mankind higher,
Surpassest far my naming, how may I
Adore thee, author of this universe   360
And all this good to man, for whose well-being
So amply and with hands so liberal
Thou hast provided all things? But with me
I see not who partakes. In solitude
What happiness? Who can enjoy alone,   365
Or all enjoying, what contentment find?'
Thus I presumptuous; and the vision bright,
As with'a smile more brightened, thus replied:
    " 'What callest thou solitude? Is not the earth
With various living creatures, and the air,   370
Replenished, and all these at thy command
To come and play before thee? Knowest thou not
Their language and their ways? They also know
And reason not contemptibly; with these
Find pastime and bear rule; thy realm is large.'   375
So spake the universal Lord, and seemed
So ordering. I with leave of speech implored

5. Desired, lacked.

And humble deprecation, thus replied:
" 'Let not my words offend thee, heavenly power,
My maker; be propitious while I speak.   380
Hast thou not made me here thy substitute,
And these inferior far beneath me set?
Among unequals what society
Can sort, what harmony or true delight?
Which must be mutual, in proportion due   385
Given and received. But in disparity,
The one intense, the other still remiss,
Cannot well suit with either, but soon prove
Tedious alike. Of fellowship I speak
Such as I seek, fit to participate   390
All rational delight, wherein the brute
Cannot be human consort. They rejoice
Each with their kind, lion with lioness,
So fitly them in pairs thou hast combined:
Much less can bird with beast, or fish with fowl   395
So well converse, nor with the ox the ape;
Worse then can man with beast, and least of all.'
      "Whereto the Almighty answered, not displeased:
'A nice and subtle happiness I see
Thou to thyself proposest, in the choice   400
Of thy associates, Adam, and wilt taste
No pleasure, though in pleasure, solitary.
What thinkest thou then of me and this my state?
Seem I to thee sufficiently possessed
Of happiness or not? who am alone   405
From all eternity, for none I know
Second to me or like, equal much less.
How have I then with whom to hold converse
Save with the creatures which I made, and those
To me inferior, infinite descents   410
Beneath what other creatures are to thee?'
      "He ceased, I lowly answered: 'To attain
The height and depth of thy eternal ways
All human thoughts come short, supreme of things.
Thou in thyself art perfect, and in thee   415
Is no deficience found; not so is man,
But in degree, the cause of his desire
By conversation with his like to help
Or solace his defects. No need that thou
Shouldst propagate, already infinite,   420
And through all number absolute, though one.
But man by number is to manifest
His single imperfection, and beget
Like of his like, his image multiplied,
In unity defective, which requires   425
Collateral⁶ love and dearest amity.
Thou in thy secrecy although alone,

---

6. Equal, with a pun on Latin *latus, lateris,* the "side" from which Eve will be formed.

Best with thyself accompanied, seekest not
Social communication; yet, so pleased,
Canst raise thy creature to what height thou wilt   430
Of union or communion, deified;
I by conversing cannot these erect
From prone, nor in their ways complacence find.'
Thus I emboldened spake, and freedom used
Permissive, and acceptance found, which gained   435
This answer from the gracious voice divine:
   " 'Thus far to try thee, Adam, I was pleased,
And find thee knowing, not of beasts alone
Which thou hast rightly named, but of thyself,
Expressing well the spirit within thee free,   440
My image, not imparted to the brute,
Whose fellowship, therefore unmeet for thee,
Good reason was thou freely shouldst dislike;
And be so minded still. I, ere thou spak'st,
Knew it not good for man to be alone,   445
And no such company as then thou sawest
Intended thee, for trial only brought,
To see how thou couldst judge of fit and meet.
What next I bring shall please thee, be assured:
Thy likeness, thy fit help, thy other self,   450
Thy wish exactly to thy heart's desire.'
   "He ended, or I heard no more, for now,
My earthly by his heavenly overpowered
Which it had long stood under, strained to the height
In that celestial colloquy sublime,   455
As with an object that excels the sense
Dazzled and spent, sunk down and sought repair
Of sleep, which instantly fell on me, called
By nature as in aid, and closed mine eyes.
Mine eyes he closed, but open left the cell   460
Of fancy,[7] my internal sight, by which
Abstract as in a trance methought I saw,
Though sleeping, where I lay, and saw the shape
Still glorious before whom awake I stood;
Who stooping opened my left side, and took   465
From thence a rib, with cordial[8] spirits warm
And life-blood streaming fresh. Wide was the wound,
But suddenly with flesh filled up and healed.
The rib he formed and fashioned with his hands;
Under his forming hands a creature grew,   470
Manlike, but different sex, so lovely fair
That what seemed fair in all the world seemed now
Mean, or in her summed up, in her contained,
And in her looks, which from that time infused
Sweetness into my heart, unfelt before,   475
And into all things from her air inspired
The spirit of love and amorous delight.

---

7. Imagination.   8. From the Latin *cors, cordis*, relating to the heart.

She disappeared, and left me dark; I waked
To find her or forever to deplore
Her loss, and other pleasures all abjure;   480
When out of hope, behold her, not far off,
Such as I saw her in my dream, adorned
With what all Earth or Heaven could bestow
To make her amiable. On she came,
Led by her heavenly maker, though unseen,   485
And guided by his voice, nor uninformed
Of nuptial sanctity and marriage rites.
Grace was in all her steps, heaven in her eye,
In every gesture dignity and love.
I overjoyed could not forbear aloud: 490
    " 'This turn hath made amends; thou hast fulfilled
Thy words, Creator bounteous and benign,
Giver of all things fair, but fairest this
Of all thy gifts; nor enviest. I now see
Bone of my bone, flesh of my flesh, my self   495
Before me; woman is her name, of man
Extracted; for this cause he shall forego
Father and mother, and to his wife adhere,
And they shall be one flesh, one heart, one soul.'
    "She heard me thus, and though divinely brought,   500
Yet innocence and virgin modesty,
Her virtue and the conscience of her worth
That would be wooed and not unsought be won,
Not obvious, not obtrusive, but retired,
The more desirable—or, to say all,   505
Nature herself, though pure of sinful thought,
Wrought in her so that, seeing me, she turned.
I followed her; she what was honor knew,
And with obsequious[9] majesty approved
My pleaded reason. To the nuptial bower   510
I led her blushing like the morn. All heaven
And happy constellations on that hour
Shed their selectest influence; the earth
Gave sign of gratulation,[1] and each hill;
Joyous the birds; fresh gales and gentle airs   515
Whispered it to the woods, and from their wings
Flung rose, flung odors from the spicy shrub,
Disporting, till the amorous bird of night
Sung spousal, and bid haste the evening star
On his hill-top, to light the bridal lamp.   520
    "Thus have I told thee all my state, and brought
My story to the sum of earthly bliss
Which I enjoy, and must confess to find
In all things else delight indeed, but such
As, used or not, works in the mind no change,   525
Nor vehement[2] desire—these delicacies

9. Obedient ("following," literally), displaying the essential virtue of the wife.   1. Congratulation.
2. Overpowering, distracting.

I mean of taste, sight, smell, herbs, fruits, and flowers,
Walks and the melody of birds. But here,
Far otherwise, transported I behold,
Transported touch; here passion first I felt,   530
Commotion strange, in all enjoyments else
Superior and unmoved, here only weak
Against the charm of beauty's powerful glance.
Or nature failed in me and left some part
Not proof enough such object to sustain,   535
Or from my side subducting³ took perhaps
More than enough; at least on her bestowed
Too much of ornament, in outward show
Elaborate, of inward less exact.
For well I understand in the prime end   540
Of nature her th' inferior, in the mind
And inward faculties which most excel,
In outward also her resembling less
His image who made both, and less expressing
The character of that dominion given   545
O'er other creatures. Yet when I approach
Her loveliness, so absolute she seems
And in herself complete, so well to know
Her own, that what she wills to do or say
Seems wisest, virtuousest, discreetest, best.   550
All higher knowledge in her presence falls
Degraded; wisdom in discourse with her
Loses discountenanced, and like folly shows;
Authority and reason on her wait
As one intended first, not after made   555
Occasionally;⁴ and to consùmmate all,
Greatness of mind and nobleness their seat
Build in her loveliest, and create an awe
About her as a guard angelic placed."
    To whom the Angel with contracted brow: 560
"Accuse not nature, she hath done her part;
Do thou but thine, and be not diffident
Of wisdom; she deserts thee not if thou
Dismiss not her when most thou need'st her nigh
By àttributing overmuch to things   565
Less excellent, as thou thyself perceiv'st.
For what admir'st thou, what transports thee so?
An outside? Fair no doubt, and worthy well
Thy cherishing, thy honoring, and thy love;
Not thy subjection. Weigh her with thyself,   570
Then value. Ofttimes nothing profits more
Then self-esteem, grounded on just and right
Well managed. Of that skill the more thou know'st,
The more she will acknowledge thee her head,
And to realities yield all her shows—   575
Made so adorn for thy delight the more,

---

3. Taking away.   4. For a particular purpose or occasion, i.e., Adam's request for a companion.

So aweful[5] that with honor thou may'st love
Thy mate, who sees when thou art seen least wise.
But if the sense of touch whereby mankind
Is propagated seem such dear delight   580
Beyond all other, think the same vouchsafed
To cattle and each beast; which would not be
To them made common and divulged if aught
Therein enjoyed were worthy to subdue
The soul of man, or passion in him move.   585
What higher in her society thou find'st
Attractive, human, rational—love still;
In loving thou dost well, in passion not,
Wherein true love consists not. Love refines
The thoughts, and heart enlarges, hath his seat   590
In reason, and is judicious, is the scale
By which to heavenly love thou may'st ascend,
Not sunk in carnal pleasure, for which cause
Among the beasts no mate for thee was found."
    To whom thus half abashed Adam replied: 595
"Neither her outside formed so fair, nor aught
In procreation common to all kinds
(Though higher of the genial[6] bed by far
And with mysterious reverence I deem)
So much delights me as those graceful acts,   600
Those thousand decencies that daily flow
From all her words and actions, mixed with love
And sweet compliance, which declare unfeigned
Union of mind, or in us both one soul,
Harmony to behold in wedded pair   605
More grateful than harmonious sound to the ear.
Yet these subject not; I to thee disclose
What inward thence I feel, not therefore foiled,
Who meet with various objects from the sense
Variously representing; yet still free   610
Approve the best, and follow what I approve.
    "To love thou balm'st me not, for love thou say'st
Leads up to Heaven, is both the way and guide;
Bear with me then, if lawful what I ask:
Love not the heavenly spirits, and how their love   615
Express they, by looks only, or do they mix
Irradiance, virtual or immediate touch?"
    To whom the Angel with a smile that glowed
Celestial rosy red, love's proper hue,
Answered: "Let it suffice thee that thou know'st   620
Us happy, and without love no happiness.
Whatever pure thou in the body enjoy'st
(And pure thou wert created), we enjoy
In eminence, and obstacle find none
Of membrane, joint, or limb, exclusive bars.   625
Easier than air with air, if spirits embrace,

5. Awe-inspiring.   6. Procreative.

Total they mix, union of pure with pure
Desiring; nor restrained conveyance need
As flesh to mix with flesh, or soul with soul.
But I can now no more; the parting sun 630
Beyond the earth's green cape and verdant isles
Hesperian sets, my signal to depart.
Be strong, live happy, and love, but first of all
His whom to love is to obey, and keep
His great command; take heed lest passion sway 635
Thy judgment to do aught which else free will
Would not admit; thine and of all thy sons
The weal or woe in thee is placed: beware.
I in thy persevering shall rejoice,
And all the blest. Stand fast; to stand or fall 640
Free in thine own arbitrement[7] it lies.
Perfect within, no outward aid require;
And all temptation to transgress repel."
    So saying, he arose; whom Adam thus
Followed with benediction: "Since to part, 645
Go, heavenly guest, ethereal messenger,
Sent from whose sovereign goodness I adore.
Gentle to me and affable[8] hath been
Thy condescension, and shall be honored ever
With grateful memory. Thou to mankind 650
Be good and friendly still, and oft return."
    So parted they, the Angel up to Heaven
From the thick shade, and Adam to his bower.

BOOK 9

The Argument

Satan, having compassed the Earth, with meditated guile returns as a mist by night into Paradise; enters into the serpent sleeping. Adam and Eve in the morning go forth to their labors, which Eve proposes to divide in several places, each laboring apart: Adam consents not, alleging the danger lest that enemy of whom they were forewarned should attempt her found alone. Eve, loath to be thought not circumspect or firm enough, urges her going apart, the rather desirous to make trial of her strength; Adam at last yields. The serpent finds her alone: his subtle approach, first gazing, then speaking, with much flattery extolling Eve above all other creatures. Eve, wondering to hear the serpent speak, asks how he attained to human speech and such understanding not till now; the serpent answers that by tasting of a certain tree in the garden he attained both to speech and reason, till then void of both. Eve requires him to bring her to that tree, and finds it to be the Tree of Knowledge forbidden: the serpent, now grown bolder, with many wiles and arguments induces her at length to eat. She, pleased with the taste, deliberates a while whether to impart thereof to Adam or not; at last brings him of the fruit; relates what persuaded her to eat thereof. Adam, at first amazed, but perceiving her lost, resolves, through vehemence of love, to perish with her,

---

7. Judgment.   8. Easy to converse with.

and, extenuating the trespass, eats also of the fruit. The effects thereof in them both; they seek to cover their nakedness; then fall to variance and accusation of one another.

[Temptation and Fall]

No more of talk where God or angel guest[9]
With man, as with his friend, familiar used
To sit indulgent, and with him partake
Rural repast, permitting him the while
Venial[1] discourse unblamed. I now must change   5
Those notes to tragic; foul distrust, and breach
Disloyal, on the part of man, revolt
And disobedience; on the part of Heaven,
Now alienated, distance and distaste,
Anger and just rebuke, and judgment given,   10
That brought into this world a world of woe,
Sin and her shadow Death, and Misery,
Death's harbinger. Sad task! yet argument
Not less but more heroic than the wrath
Of stern Achilles on his foe pursued   15
Thrice fugitive about Troy wall;[2] or rage
Of Turnus for Lavinia disespoused;[3]
Or Neptune's ire, or Juno's, that so long
Perplexed the Greek, and Cytherea's son:[4]
If answerable style I can obtain   20
Of my celestial Patroness,[5] who deigns
Her nightly visitation unimplored,
And dictates to me slumbering, or inspires
Easy my unpremeditated[6] verse,
Since first this subject for heroic song   25
Pleased me,[7] long choosing and beginning late,
Not sedulous by nature to indite
War, hitherto the only argument
Heroic deemed, chief mastery to dissect[8]
With long and tedious havoc fabled knights   30
In battles feigned (the better fortitude
Of patience and heroic martyrdom
Unsung), or to describe races and games,[9]
Or tilting furniture, emblazoned shields,

9. Raphael, the "affable archangel," who in preceding books (5–8) has sat with Adam sharing "rural repast" and discoursing on such highly relevant matters as Lucifer's fall, the Creation, the structure of the universe. To him, Adam has told of the warning he has received from God not to touch the Tree of Knowledge.
1. Unblemished.   2. At the end of the *Iliad* Achilles, whose *wrath* is the subject announced in the first line of the epic, will chase his enemy, the Trojan Hector, three times around the walls of Troy before killing him.   3. In Virgil's *Aeneid*, Lavinia, fated to be Aeneas's wife, had earlier been promised to King Turnus.
4. In the *Odyssey* Neptune (Poseidon) is the god hostile to Odysseus (*the Greek*). In the *Aeneid* the hero is persecuted by the wrath of the goddess Juno, who had quarreled with Aeneas's mother, Cytherea (Venus).
5. Urania, originally the Muse of astronomy. To Milton she is the source of *celestial* inspiration. *Answerable:* suitable.   6. In other passages of the poem, Milton refers to inspiration coming to him at night or at early dawn, with spontaneous (*unpremeditated*) ease.   7. The choice of his present heroic theme had occurred early, as had the rejection of the kind of subject matter described in the following lines.   8. To analyze but also to cut up; a possible allusion to the abundance of bloody battle wounds described in classical epics.   9. There are long descriptions of games in the *Iliad* (23) and in the *Aeneid* (10).

Impresses quaint, caparisons and steeds, 35
Bases[1] and tinsel trappings, gorgeous knights
At joust and tournament; then marshaled feast
Served up in hall with sewers and seneschals:[2]
The skill of artifice or office mean;
Not that which justly gives heroic name 40
To person or to poem. Me,[3] of these
Nor skilled nor studious, higher argument
Remains, sufficient of itself to raise
That name, unless an age too late, or cold
Climate, or years, damp my intended wing[4] 45
Depressed; and much they may if all be mine,
Not hers who brings it nightly to my ear.
    The sun was sunk, and after him the star
Of Hesperus, whose office is to bring
Twilight upon the Earth, short arbiter 50
'Twixt day and night, and now from end to end
Night's hemisphere had veiled the horizon round,
When Satan, who late fled before the threats
Of Gabriel out of Eden,[5] now improved
In meditated fraud and malice, bent 55
On man's destruction, mauger[6] what might hap
Of heavier on himself, fearless returned.
By night he fled, and at midnight returned
From compassing the Earth—cautious of day
Since Uriel, regent of the sun, descried 60
His entrance, and forewarned the Cherubim[7]
That kept their watch. Thence, full of anguish, driven,
The space of seven continued nights he rode
With darkness; thrice the equinoctial line
He circled, four times crossed the car of Night 65
From pole to pole, traversing each colure;[8]
On the eighth returned, and on the coast averse[9]
From entrance or cherubic watch by stealth
Found unsuspected way. There was a place
(Now not, though sin, not time, first wrought the change) 70
Where Tigris, at the foot of Paradise,[1]
Into a gulf shot under ground, till part
Rose up a fountain by the Tree of Life.
In with the river sunk, and with it rose,
Satan, involved in rising mist; then sought 75
Where to lie hid. Sea he had searched and land
From Eden over Pontus, and the pool

1. Skirtlike housings for warhorses. *Tilting furniture:* the paraphernalia of arms tournaments. *Impresses:* fancy emblems on shields.   2. Attendants at meals and stewards in noble households.   3. To me.
4. The notion that nordic climates *damp* (benumb) human wit was accepted by Milton and is as old as Aristotle. *That name:* that of epic poet. *An age too late:* a time no longer fit for epic poetry.   5. As described in the conclusion of book 4.   6. In spite of.   7. Gabriel's troops. Uriel (whose name means "fire of God") is, according to Milton, *regent of the sun* and heat. In book 4, he warns Gabriel and his troops against Satan entering Eden.   8. A celestial circle that crosses the poles. Satan manages always to stay on the dark side of the earth by circling it three times along the equator (*the equinoctial line*) and twice on each of the two colures.   9. The side opposite the gate guarded by Gabriel.   1. Cf. Genesis 2.10: "And a river went out of Eden to water the garden."

Maeotis, up beyond the river Ob;[2]
Downward as far antarctic; and, in length,
West from Orontes to the ocean barred   80
At Darien,[3] thence to the land where flows
Ganges and Indus.[4] Thus the orb he roamed
With narrow search, and with inspection deep
Considered every creature, which of all
Most opportune might serve his wiles, and found   85
The serpent subtlest beast of all the field.[5]
Him, after long debate, irresolute
Of thoughts revolved, his final sentence chose
Fit vessel, fittest imp[6] of fraud, in whom
To enter, and his dark suggestions hide   90
From sharpest sight; for in the wily snake
Whatever sleights none would suspicious mark,
As from his wit and native subtlety
Proceeding, which, in other beasts observed,
Doubt[7] might beget of diabolic power   95
Active within beyond the sense of brute.
Thus he resolved, but first from inward grief
His bursting passion into plaints thus poured:
    "O Earth, how like to Heaven, if not preferred
More justly, seat worthier of Gods, as built   100
With second thought, reforming what was old!
For what God, after better, worse would build?
Terrestrial Heaven, danced round by other Heavens,
That shine, yet bear their bright officious[8] lamps,
Light above light, for thee alone, as seems,   105
In thee concent'ring all their precious beams
Of sacred influence! As God in Heaven
Is center, yet extends to all, so thou
Cent'ring receiv'st from all those orbs; in thee,
Not in themselves, all their known virtue appears,   110
Productive in herb, plant, and nobler birth
Of creatures animate with gradual life
Of growth, sense, reason, all summed up in man.[9]
With what delight could I have walked thee round,
If I could joy in aught; sweet interchange   115
Of hill and valley, rivers, woods, and plains,
Now land, now sea, and shores with forest crowned,
Rocks, dens, and caves! But I in none of these
Find place or refuge; and the more I see
Pleasures about me, so much more I feel   120
Torment within me, as from the hateful siege[1]
Of contraries; all good to me becomes
Bane,[2] and in Heaven much worse would be my state.
But neither here seek I, no, nor in Heaven,

2. Siberian river flowing into the Arctic Ocean. *Pontus:* the Black Sea. *Maeotis:* the Sea of Azov.   3. The
Isthmus of Panama. *Orontes:* a river in Syria.   4. Rivers in India.   5. Cf. Genesis 3.1: "Now the serpent
was more subtil than any beast of the field."   6. Offspring, with a devilish connotation. *Sentence:* decision.   7. Suspicion.   8. Performing their function.   9. What Adam called (5.509) "the scale of
Nature" ascends from the vegetable order (pure growth), to the animal (sensation), to the human (the two,
plus reason).   1. Seat, place.   2. Poison.

To dwell, unless by mastering Heaven's Supreme; 125
Nor hope to be myself less miserable
By what I seek, but others to make such
As I, though thereby worse to me redound.
For only in destroying I find ease
To my relentless thoughts, and him[3] destroyed, 130
Or won to what may work his utter loss,
For whom all this was made, all this[4] will soon
Follow, as to him linked in weal or woe:
In woe then, that destruction wide may range!
To me shall be the glory sole among 135
The infernal Powers, in one day to have marred
What he, Almighty styled, six nights and days
Continued making, and who knows how long
Before had been contriving? though perhaps
Not longer than since I in one night freed 140
From servitude in glorious well-nigh half
Th' angelic name,[5] and thinner left the throng
Of his adorers. He, to be avenged,
And to repair his numbers thus impaired,
Whether such virtue,[6] spent of old, now failed 145
More angels to create (if they at least
Are his created),[7] or to spite us more,
Determined to advance into our room
A creature formed of earth, and him endow,
Exalted from so base original, 150
With heavenly spoils, our spoils. What he decreed
He effected; man he made, and for him built
Magnificent this World, and Earth his seat,
Him lord pronounced, and, O indignity!
Subjected to his service angel-wings 155
And flaming ministers, to watch and tend
Their earthy charge. Of these the vigilance
I dread, and to elude, thus wrapt in mist
Of midnight vapor, glide obscure, and pry
In every bush and brake, where hap may find 160
The serpent sleeping, in whose mazy folds
To hide me, and the dark intent I bring.
O foul descent! that I, who erst contended
With Gods to sit the highest, am now constrained
Into a beast, and, mixed with bestial slime, 165
This essence[8] to incarnate and imbrute,
That to the height of deity aspired!
But what will not ambition and revenge
Descend to? Who aspires must down as low
As high he soared, obnoxious,[9] first or last, 170
To basest things. Revenge, at first though sweet,
Bitter ere long back on itself recoils.
Let it; I reck not, so it light well aimed,

3. Man.   4. All of created nature.   5. Family, clan.   6. Power, force.   7. Inciting the angels to rebellion, Satan pretended that they were not God's creation, but "self-begot" (5.860).   8. The supernatural substance of which he considers himself to be made.   9. Exposed to.

Since higher[1] I fall short, on him who next
Provokes my envy, this new favorite   175
Of Heaven, this man of clay, son of despite,
Whom, us the more to spite, his Maker raised
From dust: spite then with spite is best repaid."
　So saying, through each thicket, dank or dry,
Like a black mist low-creeping, he held on   180
His midnight search, where soonest he might find
The serpent. Him fast sleeping soon he found,
In labyrinth of many a round self-rolled,
His head the midst, well stored with subtle wiles:
Not yet in horrid shade or dismal den,   185
Nor nocent[2] yet, but on the grassy herb,
Fearless, unfeared, he slept. In at his mouth
The devil entered, and his brutal sense,
In heart or head, possessing soon inspired
With act intelligential; but his sleep   190
Disturbed not, waiting close[3] th' approach of morn.
　Now, whenas sacred light began to dawn
In Eden on the humid flowers, that breathed
Their morning incense, when all things that breathe
From th' Earth's great altar send up silent praise   195
To the Creator, and his nostrils fill
With grateful smell, forth came the human pair,
And joined their vocal worship to the choir
Of creatures wanting[4] voice; that done, partake
The season, prime for sweetest scents and airs;   200
Then còmmune how that day they best may ply
Their growing work; for much their work outgrew
The hands' dispatch of two gardening so wide:
And Eve first to her husband thus began:
　"Adam, well may we labor still[5] to dress   205
This garden, still to tend plant, herb, and flower,
Our pleasant task enjoined; but, till more hands
Aid us, the work under our labor grows,
Luxurious by restraint: what we by day
Lop overgrown, or prune, or prop, or bind,   210
One night or two with wanton growth derides,
Tending to wild. Thou, therefore, now advise,
Or hear what to my mind first thoughts present.
Let us divide our labors; thou where choice
Leads thee, or where most needs, whether to wind   215
The woodbine round this arbor, or direct
The clasping ivy where to climb; while I
In yonder spring[6] of roses intermixed
With myrtle find what to redress till noon.
For, while so near each other thus all day   220
Our task we choose, what wonder if so near
Looks intervene and smiles, or objects new

---

1. Against God. *I reck not:* I don't mind.　2. Harmful.　3. Hidden. *Act intelligental:* intellectual activity.　4. Lacking.　5. Constantly.　6. Thicket, grove.

Casual discourse draw on, which intermits
Our day's work, brought to little, though begun
Early, and th' hour of supper comes unearned!"   225
To whom mild answer Adam thus returned:
"Sole Eve, associate sole, to me beyond
Compare above all living creatures dear!
Well hast thou motioned,[7] well thy thoughts employed
How we might best fulfil the work which here   230
God hath assigned us, nor of me shalt pass
Unpraised; for nothing lovelier can be found
In woman than to study household good,
And good works in her husband to promote.
Yet not so strictly hath our Lord imposed   235
Labor as to debar us when we need
Refreshment, whether food or talk between,
Food of the mind, or this sweet intercourse
Of looks and smiles; for smiles from reason flow,
To brute denied, and are of love the food,   240
Love, not the lowest end[8] of human life.
For not to irksome toil, but to delight,
He made us, and delight to reason joined.
These paths and bowers doubt not but our joint hands
Will keep from wilderness[9] with ease, as wide   245
As we need walk, till younger hands ere long
Assist us. But, if much converse perhaps
Thee satiate, to short absence I could yield;
For solitude sometimes is best society,
And short retirement urges sweet return.   250
But other doubt possesses me, lest harm
Befall thee, severed from me; for thou know'st
What hath been warned us, what malicious foe,
Envying our happiness, and of his own
Despairing, seeks to work us woe and shame   255
By sly assault, and somewhere nigh at hand
Watches, no doubt, with greedy hope to find
His wish and best adventage, us asunder,
Hopeless to circumvent us joined, where each
To other speedy aid might lend at need.   260
Whether his first design be to withdraw
Our fealty from God, or to disturb
Conjugal love, than which perhaps no bliss
Enjoyed by us excites his envy more;
Or this, or worse,[1] leave not the faithful side   265
That gave thee being, still shades thee and protects.
The wife, where danger or dishonor lurks,
Safest and seemliest by her husband stays,
Who guards her, or with her the worst endures."
    To whom the virgin[2] majesty of Eve,   270
As one who loves, and some unkindness meets,

7. Suggested.   8. Object.   9. Wildness.   1. Whether his design be this or something even worse.
2. Pure, sinless.

With sweet austere composure thus replied:
　"Offspring of Heaven and Earth, and all Earth's lord!
That such an enemy we have, who seeks
Our ruin, both by thee informed I learn,　　　　　　　　275
And from the parting angel[3] overheard,
As in a shady nook I stood behind,
Just then returned at shut of evening flowers.
But that thou shouldst my firmness therefore doubt
To God or thee, because we have a foe　　　　　　　　280
May tempt it, I expected not to hear.
His violence thou fear'st not, being such
As we, not capable of death or pain,
Can either not receive, or can repel.
His fraud is, then, thy fear; which plain infers　　　　285
Thy equal fear that my firm faith and love
Can by his fraud be shaken or seduced:
Thoughts, which how found they harbor in thy breast,
Adam, misthought of her to thee so dear?"[4]
　　To whom, with healing words, Adam replied:　　　290
"Daughter of God and man, immortal Eve,
For such thou art, from sin and blame entire;[5]
Not diffident of thee do I dissuade
Thy absence from my sight, but to avoid
Th' attempt itself, intended by our foe.　　　　　　　295
For he who tempts, though in vain, at least asperses[6]
The tempted with dishonor foul, supposed
Not incorruptible of faith,[7] not proof
Against temptation. Thou thyself with scorn
And anger wouldst resent the offered wrong,　　　　　300
Though ineffectual found; misdeem not, then,
If such affront I labor to avert
From thee alone, which on us both at once
The enemy, though bold, will hardly dare;
Or, daring, first on me th' assault shall light.　　　　305
Nor thou his malice and false guile contemn—
Subtle he needs must be who could seduce
Angles—nor think superfluous others' aid.
I from the influence of thy looks receive
Access in every virtue;[8] in thy sight　　　　　　　　310
More wise, more watchful, stronger, if need were
Of outward strength; while shame, thou looking on,
Shame to be overcome or overreached,[9]
Would utmost vigor raise, and raised unite.
Why shouldst not thou like sense[1] within thee feel　　315
When I am present, and thy trial choose
With me, best witness of thy virtue tried?"
　　So spake domestic Adam in his care
And matrimonial love; but Eve, who thought
Less[2] àttributed to her faith sincere,　　　　　　　　320

---

3. Raphael.　　4. A misjudgment (*misthought*) of me.　　5. Intact.　　6. Maligns; literally, sprinkles.
7. Faithfulness, loyalty.　　8. Increased strength.　　9. Outdone.　　1. Sensation.　　2. Less than she
deserves.

Thus her reply with accent sweet renewed:
   "If this be our condition, thus to dwell
In narrow circuit straitened by a foe,
Subtle or violent, we not endued[3]
Single with like defence wherever met,   325
How are we happy, still in fear of harm?
But harm precedes not sin: only our foe
Tempting affronts us with his foul esteem
Of our integrity: his foul esteem
Sticks no dishonor on our front,[4] but turns   330
Foul on himself; then wherefore shunned or feared
By us, who rather double honor gain
From his surmise proved false, find peace within,
Favor from Heaven, our witness, from th' event?
And what is faith, love, virtue, unassayed   335
Alone, without exterior help sustained?[5]
Let us not then suspect our happy state
Left so imperfect by the Maker wise
As not secure to single or combined.
Frail is our happiness, if this be so;   340
And Eden were no Eden, thus exposed."
   To whom thus Adam fervently replied:
"O woman, best are all things as the will
Of God ordained them; his creating hand
Nothing imperfect or deficient left   345
Of all that he created, much less man,
Or aught that might his happy state secure,
Secure from outward force. Within himself
The danger lies, yet lies within his power;
Against his will he can receive no harm.   350
But God left free the will; for what obeys
Reason is free; and reason he made right,
But bid her well beware, and still erect,[6]
Lest, by some fair appearing good surprised,
She dictate false, and misinform the will   355
To do what God expressly hath forbid.
Not then mistrust, but tender love, enjoins
That I should mind[7] thee oft; and mind thou me.
Firm we subsist, yet possible to swerve,
Since reason not impossibly may meet   360
Some specious object by the foe suborned,[8]
And fall into deception unaware,
Not keeping strictest watch, as she was warned.
Seek not temptation, then, which to avoid
Were better, and most likely if from me   365
Thou sever not: trial will come unsought.
Wouldst thou approve[9] thy constancy, approve
First thy obedience; th' other who can know,

---

3. Endowed. *Straitened:* confined.   4. Brow.   5. Without being put to test by outside forces.
6. On the alert against temptation, because God has "created Man free and able enough to have withstood
his Tempter" (3.Argument).   7. Remind.   8. Procured for treacherous purposes.   9. Give proof,
test.

Not seeing thee attempted, who attest?
But if thou think trial unsought may find   370
Us both securer[1] than thus warned thou seem'st,
Go; for thy stay, not free, absents thee more.
Go in thy native innocence; rely
On what thou hast of virtue; summon all;
For God towards thee hath done his part: do thine."   375
    So spake the patriarch of mankind; but Eve
Persisted; yet submiss,[2] though last, replied:
    "With thy permission, then, and thus forewarned,
Chiefly by what thy own last reasoning words
Touched only, that our trial, when least sought,   380
May find us both perhaps far less prepared,
The willinger I go, nor much expect
A foe so proud will first the weaker seek;
So bent, the more shall shame him his repulse."
Thus saying, from her husband's hand her hand   385
Soft she withdrew, and like a wood nymph light,
Oread or dryad, or of Delia's train,[3]
Betook her to the groves, but Delia's self
In gait surpassed and goddesslike deport,
Though not as she with bow and quiver armed,   390
But with such gardening tools as art yet rude,
Guiltless of fire[4] had formed, or angels brought.
To Pales, or Pomona, thus adorned,
Likest she seemed, Pomona when she fled
Vertumnus, or to Ceres in her prime,   395
Yet virgin of Proserpina from Jove.[5]
Her long with ardent look his eye pursued
Delighted, but desiring more her stay.
Oft he to her his charge of quick return
Repeated; she to him as oft engaged   400
To be returned by noon amid the bower,
And all things in best order to invite
Noontide repast, or afternoon's repose.
O much deceived, much failing, hapless Eve,
Of[6] thy presumed return! Event perverse!   405
Thou never from that hour in Paradise
Found'st either sweet repast, or sound repose;
Such ambush hid among sweet flowers and shades
Waited with hellish rancor imminent[7]
To intercept thy way, or send thee back   410
Despoiled of innocence, of faith, of bliss.
For now, and since first break of dawn, the fiend,
Mere serpent in appearance, forth was come,

1. Less careful, less alert to danger.   2. Submissive. Eve's submissiveness, however, is qualified by
Adam's reluctant tone as he agrees to let her go and by the fact that it is she who speaks the final words of
their dialogue.   3. Delia (born on the island of Delos) is the goddess Diana (Artemis), the huntress, with
her train of nymphs. In Greek mythology the oreads were mountain nymphs and the dryads were wood
nymphs.   4. The ability to produce fire will become necessary only after the Fall (cf. 10.1070–82).
5. In practical-minded Roman mythology, Pales and Pomona are deities who preside over flocks and fruit,
respectively. Ceres is the goddess of agriculture in general. Both Pomona and Ceres are presented here in
virginal youth: Pomona fleeing from her suitor Vertumnus (another agriculture deity), and Ceres before
the time when Jove (Jupiter) made her the mother of Proserpina.   6. About.   7. Ominously ready.

And on his quest, where likeliest he might find
The only two of mankind, but in them   415
The whole included race, his purposed prey.
In bower and field he sought, where any tuft
Of grove or garden-plot more[8] pleasant lay,
Their tendance[9] or plantation for delight;
By fountain or by shady rivulet   420
He sought them both, but wished his hap might find
Eve separate; he wished, but not with hope
Of what so seldom chanced; when to his wish,
Beyond his hope, Eve separate he spies,
Veiled in a cloud of fragrance, where she stood,   425
Half spied, so thick the roses bushing round
About her glowed, oft stooping to support
Each flower of slender stalk, whose head though gay
Carnation, purple, azure, or specked with gold,
Hung drooping unsustained, them she upstays   430
Gently with myrtle band, mindless the while
Herself, though fairest unsupported flower,
From her best prop so far, and storm so nigh.
Nearer he drew, and many a walk traversed
Of stateliest covert, cedar, pine, or palm;   435
Then voluble and bold, now hid, now seen
Among thick-woven arborets and flowers
Embordered on each bank, the hand[1] of Eve:
Spot more delicious than those gardens feigned[2]
Or of revived Adonis, or renowned   440
Alcinous, host of old Laertes' son,[3]
Or that, not mystic, where the sapient king
Held dalliance with his fair Egyptian spouse.[4]
Much he the place admired, the person more.
As one who long in populous city pent,   445
Where houses thick and sewers annoy[5] the air,
Forth issuing on a summer's morn to breathe
Among the pleasant villages and farms
Adjoined, from each thing met conceives delight,
The smell of grain, or tedded[6] grass, or kine,   450
Or dairy, each rural sight, each rural sound:
If chance with nymphlike step fair virgin pass,
What pleasing seemed, for her[7] now pleases more,
She most, and in her look sums[8] all delight.
Such pleasure took the serpent to behold   455
This flowery plat,[9] the sweet recess of Eve
Thus early, thus alone; her heavenly form
Angelic, but more soft, and feminine,

8. Particularly.   9. A spot that they tended.   1. Handiwork. *Voluble:* rolling. *Arborets:* shrubs. *Embordered on each bank:* bordering a walk.   2. Imagined by the poets (cf. 9.31).   3. Odysseus. Alcinous was the king of the Phaeacians. His perpetually flowering garden is described in the *Odyssey* (7). *Of revived Adonis:* the mythical garden where Aphrodite (Venus) nursed her lover Adonis, wounded by a boar. The most famous description of the garden, certainly known to Milton, is in Spenser's *Faerie Queene* 3.
4. Pharaoh's daughter (see 1 Kings 3.1). *Not mystic:* not mythical like the previous "feigned" gardens of pagan antiquity. *Sapient king:* Solomon.   5. Make noisome, pollute.   6. Spread out for drying.
7. Because of her. *If chance:* if it should happen that.   8. Rounds out and brings to perfection.

Her graceful innocence, her every air
Of gesture or least action overawed   460
His malice, and with rapine[1] sweet bereaved
His fierceness of the fierce intent it brought:
That space the evil one abstracted[2] stood
From his own evil, and for the time remained
Stupidly good, of enmity disarmed,   465
Of guile, of hate, of envy, of revenge.
But the hot Hell that always in him burns,
Though in mid Heaven, soon ended his delight,
And tortures him now more, the more he sees
Of pleasure not for him ordained: then soon   470
Fierce hate he recollects, and all his thoughts
Of mischief, gratulating,[3] thus excites:
    "Thoughts, whither have ye led me? with what sweet
Compulsion thus transported to forget
What hither brought us? hate, not love, nor hope   475
Of Paradise for Hell, hope here to taste
Of pleasure, but all pleasure to destroy,
Save what[4] is in destroying; other joy
To me is lost. Then let me not let pass
Occasion which now smiles; behold alone   480
The woman, opportune to all attempts,[5]
Her husband, for I view far round, not nigh,
Whose higher intellectual more I shun,
And strength, of courage haughty, and of limb
Heroic built, though of terrestrial mold.[6]   485
Foe not informidable, exempt from wound,
I not; so much hath Hell debased, and pain
Enfeebled me, to what I was in Heaven.
She fair, divinely fair, fit love for gods,
Not terrible, though terror be in love   490
And beauty, not approached by stronger hate,[7]
Hate stronger, under show of love well feigned,
The way which to her ruin now I tend."
    So spake the enemy of mankind, enclosed
In serpent, inmate bad, and toward Eve   495
Addressed his way, not with indented wave,[8]
Prone on the ground, as since, but on his rear,
Circular base of rising folds, that towered
Fold above fold a surging maze; his head
Crested aloft, and carbuncle[9] his eyes;   500
With burnished neck of verdant gold, erect
Amidst his circling spires, that on the grass
Floated redundant.[1] Pleasing was his shape,
And lovely; never since of serpent kind
Lovelier, not those that in Illyria changed   505

---

1. Theft.   2. Drawn off, separated.   3. Rejoicing.   4. Whatever pleasure.   5. In the appropriate situation for Satan's attempts on her.   6. Formed of earth.   7. If not approached, and counteracted, by hate.   8. Zigzagging.   9. Fiery red.   1. In great abundance. *Spires:* coils, loops.

Hermione and Cadmus,² or the god
In Epidaurus;³ nor to which transformed
Ammonian Jove, or Capitoline was seen,
He with Olympias, this with her who bore
Scipio, the height of Rome.⁴ With tract oblique   510
At first, as one who sought access, but feared
To interrupt, sidelong he works his way.
As when a ship by skillful steersman wrought
Nigh river's mouth or foreland, where the wind
Veers oft, as oft so steers, and shifts her sail: 515
So varied he, and of his tortuous train
Curled many a wanton wreath in sight of Eve,
To lure her eye: she busied heard the sound
Of rustling leaves, but minded not, as used
To such disport before her through the field,   520
From every beast, more duteous at her call,
Than at Circean call the herd disguised.⁵
He bolder now, uncalled before her stood:
But as in gaze admiring; oft he bowed
His turret⁶ crest, and sleek enameled neck,   525
Fawning, and licked the ground whereon she trod.
His gentle dumb expression turned at length
The eye of Eve to mark his play: he, glad
Of her attention gained, with serpent tongue
Organic, or impulse of vocal air,⁷   530
His fraudulent temptation thus began.
    "Wonder not, sovereign mistress, if perhaps
Thou canst, who art sole wonder; much less arm
Thy looks, the heaven of mildness, with disdain,
Displeased that I approach thee thus, and gaze   535
Insatiate, I thus single, nor have feared
Thy awful brow, more awful thus retired.
Fairest resemblance of thy Maker fair,
Thee all things living gaze on, all things thine
By gift, and thy celestial beauty adore   540
With ravishment beheld, there best beheld
Where universally admired: but here
In this enclosure wild, these beasts among,
Beholders rude, and shallow⁸ to discern
Half what in thee is fair, one man except,   545
Who sees thee? (and what is one?) who shouldst be seen
A goddess among gods, adored and served

---

2. Those that Hermione and Cadmus were turned into. Cadmus, the founder of Thebes, and his wife
Hermione (Harmonia), according to their story as told by Ovid (*Metamorphoses* 4.562–602), were transformed into snakes when they retired to Illyria after much family tragedy.   3. The place in Greece where
Aesculapius, the god of medicine, had his major temple and appeared to worshipers in the form of an erect,
flashy-eyed serpent (Ovid's *Metamorphoses* 15.622–744).   4. According to hero-deifying legends, Jove,
in his personification as Jupiter Ammon (a mingling of Greco-Roman and Egyptian cults), loved Princess
Olympias and became the father of Alexander the Great. As the Capitoline Jupiter (worshiped in the major
Roman temple on the Capitol), he fathered Scipio, the supreme hero (*the height*) of Rome's African wars.
In both cases, the father god appeared in the form of a snake.   5. The enchantress Circe, in the *Odyssey*
(10), is surrounded by subjected beasts and transforms some of the hero's companions into swine.
6. Towering.   7. Producing a voice either by using his serpent's (*organic*) tongue or by some more direct
impulse on the air.   8. Mentally inadequate.

By angels numberless, thy daily train."
   So glozed the tempter, and his proem⁹ tuned;
Into the heart of Eve his words made way,   550
Though at the voice much marveling: at length,
Not unamazed, she thus in answer spake.
"What may this mean? Language of man pronounced
By tongue of brute, and human sense expressed?
The first at least of these I thought denied   555
To beasts, whom God on their creation-day
Created mute to all articulate sound;
The latter I demur, for in their looks
Much reason,¹ and in their actions oft appears.
Thee, serpent, subtlest beast of all the field   560
I knew, but not with human voice endued:
Redouble then this miracle, and say,
How cam'st thou speakable of mute,² and how
To me so friendly grown above the rest
Of brutal kind, that daily are in sight?   565
Say, for such wonder claims attention due."
   To whom the guileful tempter thus replied:
"Empress of this fair world, resplendent Eve!
Easy to me it is to tell thee all
What thou command'st and right thou shouldst be obeyed: 570
I was at first as other beasts that graze
The trodden herb, of abject thoughts and low,
As was my food, nor aught but food discerned
Or sex, and apprehended nothing high:
Till on a day, roving the field, I chanced   575
A goodly tree far distant to behold
Loaden with fruit of fairest colors mixed,
Ruddy and gold; I nearer drew to gaze;
When from the boughs a savory odor blown,
Grateful to appetite, more pleased my sense   580
Than smell of sweetest fennel, or the teats
Of ewe or goat dropping with milk³ at even,
Unsucked of lamb or kid, that tend their play.
To satisfy the sharp desire I had
Of tasting those fair apples, I resolved   585
Not to defer: hunger and thirst at once,
Powerful persuaders, quickened at the scent
Of that alluring fruit, urged me so keen.
About the mossy trunk I wound me soon,
For, high from ground, the branches would require   590
Thy utmost reach, or Adam's: round the tree
All other beasts that saw, with like desire
Longing and envying stood, but could not reach.
Amid the tree now got, where plenty hung
Tempting so nigh, to pluck and eat my fill   595

9. Preamble, introduction. *Glozed:* flattered.   1. Eve, well acquainted with animals, which are *duteous at her call* (line 521), questions the notion (*I demur*) that they are wholly deprived of *human sense and reason.*   2. How did you acquire speech after being dumb?   3. According to old folklore, snakes were fond of fennel, which was supposed to sharpen their eyesight, and of goat's milk.

I spared not; for such pleasure till that hour
At feed or fountain never had I found.
Sated at length, ere long I might perceive
Strange alteration in me, to degree
Of reason[4] in my inward powers, and speech   600
Wanted not long, though to this shape retained.[5]
Thenceforth to speculations high or deep
I turned my thoughts, and with capacious mind
Considered all things visible in Heaven,
Or Earth, or middle, all things fair and good: 605
But all that fair[6] and good in thy divine
Semblance, and in thy beauty's heavenly ray
United I beheld: no fair to thine
Equivalent or second, which compelled
Me thus, though importune perhaps, to come   610
And gaze, and worship thee of right declared
Sovereign of creatures, universal dame."[7]
    So talked the spirited[8] sly snake: and Eve
Yet more amazed, unwary thus replied:
    "Serpent, thy overpraising leaves in doubt   615
The virtue of that fruit, in thee first proved.
But say, where grows the tree, from hence how far?
For many are the trees of God that grow
In Paradise, and various, yet unknown
To us; in such abundance lies our choice,   620
As leaves a greater store of fruit untouched,
Still hanging incorruptible, till men
Grow up to their provision, and more hands
Help to disburden Nature of her bearth."[9]
    To whom the wily adder, blithe and glad: 625
"Empress, the way is ready, and not long,
Beyond a row of myrtles, on a flat,
Fast by a fountain, one small thicket past
Of blowing[1] myrrh and balm: if thou accept
My conduct, I can bring thee thither soon."   630
    "Lead then," said Eve. He leading swiftly rolled
In tangles, and made intricate seem straight,
To mischief swift. Hope elevates, and joy
Brightens his crest; as when a wandering fire
Compact of unctuous vapor,[2] which the night   635
Condenses, and the cold environs round,
Kindled through agitation to a flame
(Which oft, they say, some evil spirit attends),
Hovering and blazing with delusive light,
Misleads th' amazed night-wanderer from his way   640
To bogs and mires, and oft through pond or pool,
There swallowed up and lost, from succor far:
So glistered the dire snake, and into fraud

---

4. To the point of acquiring the faculty of reason.   5. Restrained, kept to his outward appearance.
Wanted not long: the faculty of speech soon followed.   6. Fairness, beauty. *Middle:* the air.   7. Mistress of this world.   8. Possessed by an evil spirit.   9. Products.   1. Blossoming.   2. Composed
of greasy vapor. *Wandering fire:* will-o'-the-wisp, a light attributed to marsh gas.

Led Eve our credulous mother, to the tree
Of prohibition,[3] root of all our woe: 645
Which when she saw, thus to her guide she spake:
    "Serpent, we might have spared our coming hither,
Fruitless to me, though fruit be here to excess,
The credit of whose virtue rest with thee;[4]
Wondrous indeed, if cause of such effects!   650
But of this tree we may not taste nor touch:
God so commanded, and left that command
Sole daughter of his voice; the rest,[5] we live
Law to ourselves; our reason is our law."
    To whom the tempter guilefully replied: 655
"Indeed? Hath God then said that of the fruit
Of all these garden trees ye shall not eat,
Yet lords declared of all in Earth or air?"
To whom thus Eve, yet sinless: "Of the fruit
Of each tree in the garden we may eat,   660
But of the fruit of this fair tree amidst
The garden, God hath said, 'Ye shall not eat
Thereof, nor shall yet touch it, lest ye die.' "
    She scarce had said, though brief, when now more bold,
The tempter, but with show of zeal and love   665
To man, and indignation at his wrong,
New part puts on, and as to passion moved,
Fluctuates disturbed, yet comely, and in act
Raised,[6] as of some great matter to begin.
As when of old some orator renowned   670
In Athens or free Rome, where eloquence
Flourished, since mute, to some great cause addressed,
Stood in himself collected, while each part,[7]
Motion, each act, won audience ere the tongue,
Sometimes in height began, as no delay   675
Of preface brooking,[8] through his zeal of right.
So standing, moving, or to height upgrown
The tempter all impassioned thus began:
    "O sacred, wise, and wisdom-giving plant,
Mother of science![9] now I feel thy power   680
Within me clear, not only to discern
Things in their causes, but to trace the ways
Of highest agents, deemed however wise.
Queen of this universe! do not believe
Those rigid threats of death. Ye shall not die;   685
How should ye? By the fruit? it gives you life
To[1] knowledge; by the Threatener? look on me,
Me who have touched and tasted, yet both live,
And life more perfect have attained than Fate
Meant me, by venturing higher than my lot.   690

---

3. The forbidden Tree of Knowledge.   4. Because the forbidden tree is as good as fruitless to Eve, the only proof of its power (*virtue*) will remain with the Serpent.   5. For the rest. *Sole daughter of his voice*: translation from the Hebrew of God's command, described as "one easy prohibition" (4.433).   6. Assuming the orator's posture. *New part*: new role, as of an actor in drama. *Fluctuates*: undulates his body. 7. Of the body.   8. Plunging into the middle of the subject (*in medias res*), without any preamble. 9. Knowledge.   1. As well as.

Shall that be shut to man, which to the beast
Is open? Or will God incense his ire
For such a petty trespass, and not praise
Rather your dauntless virtue, whom the pain
Of death denounced, whatever thing death be,   695
Deterred not from achieving what might lead
To happier life, knowledge of good and evil?
Of good, how just! Of evil, if what is evil
Be real, why not known, since easier shunned?
God therefore cannot hurt ye, and be just;   700
Not just, not God; not feared then, nor obeyed:
Your fear itself of death removes the fear.[2]
Why then was this forbid? Why but to awe,
Why but to keep ye low and ignorant,
His worshipers? He knows that in the day   705
Ye eat thereof, your eyes that seem so clear,
Yet are but dim, shall perfectly be then
Opened and cleared, and ye shall be as gods,
Knowing both good and evil, as they know.
That ye should be as gods, since I as man,   710
Internal man,[3] is but proportion meet,
I, of brute, human; ye, of human, gods.
So ye shall die perhaps, by putting off
Human, to put on gods:[4] death to be wished,
Though threatened, which no worse than this can bring.   715
And what are gods that man may not become
As they, participating godlike food?
The gods are first, and that advantage use
On our belief, that all from them proceeds.
I question it; for this fair Earth I see,   720
Warmed by the sun, producing every kind,
Them nothing: If they[5] all things, who enclosed
Knowledge of good and evil in this tree,
That whoso eats thereof forthwith attains
Wisdom without their leave? And wherein lies   725
Th' offense, that man should thus attain to know?
What can your knowledge hurt him, or this tree
Impart against his will if all be his?
Or is it envy, and can envy dwell
In heavenly breasts? These, these, and many more   730
Causes import[6] your need of this fair fruit.
Goddess humane, reach then, and freely taste!"
    He ended, and his words, replete with guile,
Into her heart too easy entrance won:
Fixed on the fruit she gazed, which to behold   735
Might tempt alone, and in her ears the sound
Yet rung of his persuasive words, impregned[7]

2. The Serpent's captious argument is that God is by definition just, but because a death-giving God would not be just, he would not be God; consequently, he would not have to be feared and obeyed.   3. The Serpent has acquired human faculties although his outer form has remained unchanged (compare *inward*, line 600).   4. Divinity. *Human*: humanity.   5. If they produced.   6. Imply, indicate.   7. Impregnated, filled.

3040 / John Milton

With reason, to her seeming, and with truth;
Meanwhile the hour of noon drew on, and waked
An eager appetite, raised by the smell   740
So savory of that fruit, which with desire,
Inclinable[8] now grown to touch or taste,
Solicited her longing eye; yet first
Pausing a while, thus to herself she mused:
    "Great are thy virtues, doubtless, best of fruits,   745
Though kept from man, and worthy to be admired,
Whose taste, too long forborne, at first assay
Gave elocution to the mute, and taught
The tongue not made for speech to speak thy praise:
Thy praise he also who forbids they use,   750
Conceals not from us, naming thee the Tree
Of Knowledge, knowledge both of good and evil;
Forbids us then to taste; but his forbidding
Commends thee more, while it infers[9] the good
By thee communicated, and our want: 755
For good unknown, sure is not had, or had
And yet unknown, is as not had at all.
In plain[1] then, what forbids he but to know?
Forbids us good, forbids us to be wise!
Such prohibitions bind not.[2] But if Death   760
Bind us with after-bands, what profits then
Our inward freedom?[3] In the day we eat
Of this fair fruit, our doom is, we shall die.
How dies the serpent? He hath eaten and lives,
And knows, and speaks, and reasons, and discerns,   765
Irrational till then. For us alone
Was death invented? Or to us denied
This intellectual food, for beasts reserved?
For beasts it seems: yet that one beast which first
Hath tasted, envies not, but brings with joy   770
The good befallen him, author unsuspect,[4]
Friendly to man, far from deceit or guile.
What fear I then, rather what know to fear
Under this ignorance of good and evil,[5]
Of God or death, of law or penalty?   775
Here grows the cure of all, this fruit divine,
Fair to the eye, inviting to the taste,
Of virtue[6] to make wise: what hinders then
To reach, and feed at once both body and mind?"
    So saying, her rash hand in evil hour,   780
Forth reaching to the fruit, she plucked, she eat.[7]
Earth felt the wound, and Nature from her seat

---

8. Favorably disposed.   9. Implies.   1. In plain words.   2. Eve, who has learned from the Serpent
the art of sophistical argument, claims that God himself, by naming the tree, has indicated the *good* in it,
but a *good unknown* is as nothing. Besides, forbidding the experience of the Tree of Knowledge is forbidding
humanity *to be wise;* hence the prohibition is not binding.   3. Death would constitute a later bond (*after-
bands*), after God has granted free will (*inward freedom*).   4. An unsuspectable authority on the subject.
5. Having no knowledge of good and evil, Eve doesn't know what is to be feared.   6. With the power.

Sighing through all her works gave signs[8] of woe,
That all was lost. Back to the thicket slunk
The guilty serpent, and well might, for Eve   785
Intent now wholly on her taste, naught else
Regarded; such delight till then, as seemed,
In fruit she never tasted, whether true
Or fancied so, through expectation high
Of knowledge; nor was godhead from her thought.[9]   790
Greedily she engorged without restraint,
And knew not eating[1] death: satiate at length,
And heightened as with wine, jocund and boon,[2]
Thus to herself she pleasingly began:
    "O sovereign, virtuous, precious of all trees   795
In Paradise! of operation blest
To sapience, hitherto obscured, infamed,[3]
And thy fair fruit let hang, as to no end
Created; but henceforth my early care,
Not without song each morning, and due praise   800
Shall tend thee, and the fertile burden ease
Of thy full branches offered free to all;
Till dieted by thee I grow mature
In knowledge, as the gods who all things know;
Though others envy what they cannot give: 805
For had the gift been theirs, it had not here
Thus grown.[4] Experience, next to thee I owe,
Best guide; not following thee I had remained
In ignorance; thou open'st Wisdom's way,
And giv'st access, though secret she retire.   810
And I perhaps am secret; Heaven is high,
High and remote to see from thence distinct
Each thing on Earth; and other care perhaps
May have diverted from continual watch
Our great Forbidder, safe[5] with all his spies   815
About him. But to Adam in what sort[6]
Shall I appear? Shall I to him make known
As yet my change, and give him to partake
Full happiness with me, or rather not,
But keep the odds[7] of knowledge in my power   820
Without copartner? so to add what wants
In female sex, the more to draw his love,
And render me more equal, and perhaps,
A thing not undesirable, sometime
Superior: for, inferior, who is free?   825
This may be well: but what if God have seen
And death ensue? Then I shall be no more,
And Adam, wedded to another Eve,
Shall live with her enjoying, I extinct;

8. Omens, metaphorically given as—and punning with—the sighs of Nature; forebodings of disaster.
9. She thought of acquiring divinity.   1. That she was eating.   2. Cheerful.   3. Made famous. *Blest to sapience*: endowed with the power to give wisdom.   4. Eve has adopted the Serpent's argument (cf. lines 720–30).   5. Not dangerous.   6. Manner.   7. Advantage.

A death to think. Confirmed then I resolve,   830
Adam shall share with me in bliss or woe:
So dear I love him, that with him all deaths
I could endure, without him live no life."[8]
　　So saying, from the tree her step she turned,
But first low reverence done, as to the power   835
That dwelt within, whose presence had infused
Into the plant sciential[9] sap, derived
From nectar, drink of gods. Adam the while
Waiting desirous her return, had wove
Of choicest flowers a garland to adorn   840
Her tresses, and her rural labors crown,
As reapers oft are wont their harvest queen.
Great joy he promised to his thoughts, and new
Solace in her return, so long delayed:
Yet oft his heart, divine of[1] something ill,   845
Misgave him; he the faltering measure[2] felt;
And forth to meet her went, the way she took
That morn when first they parted. By the Tree
Of Knowledge he must pass; there he her met,
Scarce from the tree returning; in her hand   850
A bough of fairest fruit that downy smiled,
New gathered, and ambrosial smell diffused.
To him she hastened, in her face excuse
Came prologue, and apology to prompt,[3]
Which with bland words at will she thus addressed: 855
　　"Hast thou not wondered, Adam, at my stay?
Thee I have missed, and thought it long, deprived
Thy presence, agony of love till now
Not felt, nor shall be twice; for never more
Mean I to try, what rash untried I sought,   860
The pain of absence from thy sight. But strange
Hath been the cause, and wonderful to hear:
This tree is not as we are told, a tree
Of danger tasted,[4] nor to evil unknown
Opening the way, but of divine effect   865
To open eyes, and make them gods who taste;
And hath been tasted such.[5] The serpent wise,
Or not restrained as we, or not obeying,
Hath eaten of the fruit, and is become,
Not dead, as we are threatened, but thenceforth   870
Endued with human voice and human sense,
Reasoning to admiration,[6] and with me
Persuasively hath so prevailed, that I

8. In these crucial lines Eve's thoughts are shown moving through three stages: first, the idea of not sharing her knowledge with Adam, so as to enhance her own power, with the gratuitous notion that lesser power brings no freedom at all; then jealously at the thought of her own possible death and Adam *wedded to another Eve;* finally, with an opportune resurgence of *love,* the resolve to be with Adam *in bliss or woe,* i.e., to make him her partner in sin. Thus the passage is centrally representative of Milton's characterization of Eve in her relation to Adam and possibly of some of the poet's own conceptions of women in general (cf. lines 377–84, 869–85, and 1155–61).　　9. Infusing knowledge.　　1. *Divine of:* divining, foreseeing.
2. Irregularity of heartbeats.　　3. A pleading expression on her face came as an introduction (the *prologue* to a play) to prepare for (*prompt*) the formal *apology.*　　4. When tasted.　　5. Has been proved by tasting.
6. Admirably.

Have also tasted, and have also found
Th' effects to correspond, opener mine eyes,   875
Dim erst, dilated spirits, ampler heart,
And growing up to godhead; which for thee
Chiefly I sought, without thee can despise.
For bliss, as thou hast part, to me is bliss,
Tedious, unshared with thee, and odious soon.   880
Thou therefore also taste, that equal lot
May join us, equal joy, as equal love;
Lest, thou not tasting, different degree[7]
Disjoin us, and I then too late renounce
Deity for thee, when Fate will not permit."[8]   885
      Thus Eve with countenance blithe her story told;
But in her cheek distemper[9] flushing glowed.
On th' other side, Adam, soon as he heard
The fatal trespass done by Eve, amazed,
Astonied stood and blank, while horror chill   890
Ran through his veins, and all his joints relaxed;[1]
From his slack hand the garland wreathed for Eve
Down dropped, and all the faded roses shed.
Speechless he stood and pale, till thus at length
First to himself he inward silence broke: 895
      "O fairest of creation, last and best
Of all God's works, creature in whom excelled
Whatever can to sight or thought be formed,
Holy, divine, good, amiable, or sweet!
How art thou lost, how on a sudden lost,   900
Defaced, deflowered, and now to death devote?[2]
Rather how hast thou yielded to transgress
The strict forbiddance, how to violate
The sacred fruit forbidden! Some cursèd fraud
Of enemy hath beguiled thee, yet unknown,[3]   905
And me with thee hath ruined, for with thee
Certain my resolution is to die.
How can I live without thee, how forgo
Thy sweet converse and love so dearly joined,
To live again in these wild woods forlorn?   910
Should God create another Eve, and I
Another rib afford, yet loss of thee
Would never from my heart; no, no! I feel
The link of nature draw me: flesh of flesh,
Bone of my bone thou art, and from thy state   915
Mine never shall be parted, bliss or woe."
      So having said, as one from sad dismay
Recomforted, and after thoughts disturbed
Submitting to what seemed remediless,
Thus in calm mood his words to Eve he turned: 920
      "Bold deed thou hast presumed, adventurous Eve
And peril great provoked, who thus hath dared

7. A difference in rank between us.   8. Cf. lines 825–33.   9. Disharmony in the body's humors, disease.   1. Slackened. *Astonied:* stunned.   2. Doomed.   3. Unknown enemy.

Had it been only coveting to eye
That sacred fruit, sacred to abstinence,
Much more to taste it, under ban to touch.   925
But past who can recall, or done undo?
Not God omnipotent, nor Fate! Yet so
Perhaps thou shalt not die, perhaps the fact
Is not so heinous now, foretasted fruit,
Profaned first by the serpent, by him first   930
Made common and unhallowed ere our taste,
Nor yet on him found deadly; he yet lives,
Lives, as thou saidst, and gains to live as man
Higher degree of life: inducement strong
To us, as likely, tasting, to attain   935
Proportional[4] ascent, which cannot be
But to be gods, or angels, demigods.
Nor can I think that God, Creator wise,
Though threatening, will in earnest so destroy
Us his prime creatures, dignified so high,   940
Set over all his works, which in our fall,
For us created, needs with us must fail,
Dependent made; so God shall uncreate,
Be frustrate, do, undo, and labor lose;
Not well conceived of God,[5] who, though his power   945
Creation could repeat, yet would be loath
Us to abolish, lest the adversary
Triùmph and say: 'Fickle their state whom God
Most favors; who can please him long? Me first
He ruined, now mankind; whom will he next?'   950
Matter of scorn, not to be given the foe.
However, I with thee have fixed my lot.
Certain[6] to undergo like doom: if death
Consort with thee, death is to me as life;
So forcible within my heart I feel   955
The bond of nature draw me to my own,
My own in thee, for what thou art is mine;
Our state cannot be severed; we are one,
One flesh; to lose thee were to lose myself."
    So Adam, and thus Eve to him replied: 960
"O glorious trial of exceeding love,
Illustrious evidence, example high!
Engaging me to emulate; but short
Of thy perfection, how shall I attain,
Adam? from whose dear side I boast me sprung,   965
And gladly of our union hear thee speak,
One heart, one soul in both; whereof good proof
This day affords, declaring thee resolved,
Rather than death or aught than death more dread
Shall separate us, linked in love so dear,   970
To undergo with me one guilt, one crime,

---

4. Proportionate to our human status (compare the Serpent's argument, lines 710–12).   5. That would be a wrong conception of God.   6. Resolved.

If any be, of tasting this fair fruit;
Whose virtue (for of good still good proceeds,
Direct, or by occasion)⁷ hath presented
This happy trial of thy love, which else   975
So eminently never had been known.
Were it⁸ I thought death menaced would ensue
This my attempt, I would sustain alone
The worst, and not persuade thee, rather die
Deserted, than oblige⁹ thee with a fact   980
Pernicious to thy peace, chiefly assured
Remarkably so late of thy so true,
So faithful love unequaled; but I feel
Far otherwise th' event;¹ not death, but life
Augmented, opened eyes, new hopes, new joys,   985
Taste so divine, that what of sweet before
Hath touched my sense, flat seems to this, and harsh.
On my experience, Adam, freely taste,
And fear of death deliver to the winds."
    So saying, she embraced him, and for joy   990
Tenderly wept, much won that he his love
Had so ennobled, as of choice to incur
Divine displeasure for her sake, or death.
In recompense (for such compliance bad
Such recompense best merits), from the bough   995
She gave him of that fair enticing fruit
With liberal hand; he scrupled not to eat,
Against his better knowledge, not deceived,²
But fondly overcome with female charm.
Earth trembled from her entrails, as again   1000
In pangs, and Nature gave a second groan.
Sky lowered, and muttering thunder, some sad drops
Wept at completing of the mortal sin
Original; while Adam took no thought,
Eating his fill, nor Eve to iterate   1005
Her former trespass feared, the more to soothe
Him with her loved society; that now
As with new wine intoxicated both,
They swim in mirth, and fancy that they feel
Divinity within them breeding wings   1010
Wherewith to scorn the Earth. But that false fruit
Far other operation first displayed,
Carnal desire inflaming; he on Eve
Began to cast lascivious eyes, she him
As wantonly repaid; in lust they burn,   1015
Till Adam thus 'gan Eve to dalliance move:
    "Eve, now I see thou art exact of taste,
And elegant, of sapience³ no small part,
Since to each meaning savor we apply,

7. Indirectly.   8. If.   9. Involve Adam in her guilty action.   1. The eventual consequence of her
transgression.   2. Adam, unlike Eve, acts in full consciousness, not having been *deceived* by the Serpent.
3. In both meanings—"wisdom" and "taste." Both *sapience* and *savor* (line 1019) are from the Latin *sapere*.
Elegant: choosy, refined.

And palate call judicious. I the praise   1020
Yield thee, so well this day thou hast purveyed.
Much pleasure we have lost, while we abstained
From this delightful fruit, nor known till now
True relish, tasting; if such pleasure be
In things to us forbidden, it might be wished,   1025
For[4] this one tree had been forbidden ten.
But come; so well refreshed, now let us play,
As meet is, after such delicious fare;
For never did thy beauty, since the day
I saw thee first and wedded thee, adorned   1030
With all perfections, so enflame my sense
With ardor to enjoy thee, fairer now
Than ever, bounty of this virtuous[5] tree."
    So said he, and forbore not glance or toy
Of[6] amorous intent, well understood   1035
Of Eve, whose eye darted contagious fire.
Her hand he seized, and to a shady bank,
Thick overhead with verdant roof embowered
He led her, nothing loath; flowers were the couch,
Pansies, and violets, and asphodel,   1040
And hyacinth, Earth's freshest, softest lap.
There they their fill of love and love's disport
Took largely, of their mutual guilt the seal,
The solace of their sin, till dewy sleep
Oppressed them, wearied with their amorous play.   1045
    Soon as the force of that fallacious fruit,
That with exhilarating vapor bland
About their spirits had played, and inmost powers
Made err, was now exhaled, and grosser sleep
Bred of unkindly fumes,[7] with conscious dreams   1050
Encumbered, now had left them, up they rose
As from unrest, and each the other viewing,
Soon found their eyes how opened, and their minds
How darkened. Innocence, that as a veil
Had shadowed them from knowing ill, was gone;   1055
Just confidence, and native righteousness,
And honor from about them, naked left
To guilty Shame; he covered, but his robe
Uncovered more. So rose the Danite[8] strong,
Hercùlean Samson, from the harlot-lap   1060
Of Philìstean Dàlilàh, and waked
Shorn of his strength;[9] they destitute and bare
Of all their virtue. Silent, and in face
Confounded, long they sat, as strucken mute;
Till Adam, though not less than Eve abashed,   1065
At length gave utterance to these words constrained:
    "O Eve, in evil hour thou didst give ear

---

4. Instead of.   5. Endowed with special power (compare lines 649 and 778).   6. With. *Toy:* toying, playing.   7. Unnatural exhalations.   8. Of the tribe of Dan. Shame (personified) covered them, but his cover (*robe*) only made them aware of their nakedness (*uncovered more*).   9. See Judges 16.4–20.

To that false worm,[1] of whomsoever taught
To counterfeit man's voice, true in our fall,
False in our promised rising; since our eyes   1070
Opened we find indeed, and find we know
Both good and evil, good lost, and evil got:
Bad fruit of knowledge, if this be to know,
Which leaves us naked thus, of honor void,
Of innocence, of faith, of purity,   1075
Our wonted ornaments now soiled and stained,
And in our faces evident the signs
Of foul concupiscence; whence evil store,
Even shame, the last[2] of evils; of the first
Be sure then. How shall I behold the face   1080
Henceforth of God or angel, erst with joy
And rapture so oft beheld? Those heavenly shapes
Will dazzle now this earthly[3] with their blaze
Insufferably bright. O might I here
In solitude live savage, in some glade   1085
Obscured, where highest woods, impenetrable
To star or sunlight, spread their umbrage broad,
And brown[4] as evening! Cover me, ye pines,
Ye cedars, with innumerable boughs
Hide me, where I may never see them[5] more!   1090
But let us now, as in[6] bad plight, devise
What best may for the present serve to hide
The parts of each from other, that seem most
To shame obnoxious,[7] and unseemliest seen;
Some tree whose broad smooth leaves together sewed,   1095
And girded on our loins, may cover round
Those middle parts, that this newcomer, Shame,
There sit not, and reproach us as unclean."
    So counseled he, and both together went
Into the thickest wood; there soon they chose   1100
The figtree, not that kind for fruit renowned
But such as at this day, to Indians known,
In Malabar or Deccan[8] spreads her arms
Branching so broad and long, that in the ground
The bended twigs take root, and daughters grow   1105
About the mother tree, a pillared shade
High overarched, and echoing walks between;
There oft the Indian herdsman, shunning heat,
Shelters in cool, and tends his pasturing herds
At loopholes cut through thickest shade. Those leaves   1110
They gathered, broad as Amazonian targe,[9]
And with what skill they had, together sewed,
To gird their waist; vain covering, if to hide

---

1. I.e., the Serpent, now disparaged.   2. Extreme, ultimate. *Evil store:* an abundance of evils.
3. Adam's now earthly nature and sense.   4. Dark.   5. The *heavenly shapes* (line 1082).   6. As we
are in.   7. Exposed to.   8. In southern India. *Figtree:* identified as the banyan or Indian fig tree, also
classified in botany as *Ficus religiosa.*   9. Shield. The Amazons were women warriors in Greco-Roman
myth (and in Virgil's *Aeneid*). Actually the tree's leaf is small; Milton's inaccurate notion comes from
contemporary sources and goes back to antiquity.

Their guilt and dreaded shame! O how unlike
To that first naked glory! Such of late 1115
Columbus found th' American, so girt
With feathered cincture,[1] naked else and wild
Among the trees on isles and woody shores.
Thus fenced, and, as they thought, their shame in part
Covered, but not at rest or ease of mind, 1120
They sat them down to weep; nor only tears
Rained at their eyes, but high winds worse within
Began to rise, high passions, anger, hate,
Mistrust, suspicion, discord, and shook sore
Their inward state of mind, calm region once 1125
And full of peace, now tossed and turbulent:
For Understanding ruled not, and the Will
Heard not her lore, both in subjection now
To sensual Appetite, who, from beneath
Usurping over sovereign Reason, claimed 1130
Superior sway.[2] From thus distempered breast,
Adam, estranged in look and altered style,
Speech intermitted thus to Eve renewed:
    "Would thou hadst hearkened to my words, and stayed
With me, as I besought thee, when that strange 1135
Desire of wandering, this unhappy morn,
I know not whence possessed thee! we had then
Remained still happy, not as now, despoiled
Of all our good, shamed, naked, miserable.
Let none henceforth seek needless cause to approve 1140
The faith they owe;[3] when earnestly they seek
Such proof, conclude, they then begin to fail."
    To whom, soon moved with touch of blame, thus Eve:
"What words have passed thy lips, Adam severe?
Imput'st thou that to my default, or will 1145
Of wandering, as thou call'st it, which who knows
But might as ill have happened, thou being by,
Or to thyself perhaps? Hadst thou been there,
Or here th' attempt, thou couldst not have discerned
Fraud in the serpent, speaking as he spake; 1150
No ground of enmity between us known,
Why he should mean me ill, or seek to harm?
Was I to have never parted from thy side?
As good have grown there still a lifeless rib.
Being as I am, why didst not thou, the head, 1155
Command me absolutely not to go,
Going into such danger, as thou saidst?
Too facile then, thou didst not much gainsay,
Nay, didst permit, approve, and fair dismiss.
Hadst thou been firm and fixed in thy dissent, 1160

---

1. Belt.   2. The victory of sensual Appetite over Reason (cf. line 113 and n. 9, p. 3026) and over human-kind's free will (compare lines 351ff.)—humanity's distinguishing traits—summarizes the history of the Fall.   3. Own. *Approve*: prove by testing.

Neither had I transgressed, nor thou with me."[4]
   To whom, then first incensed, Adam replied:
"Is this the love, is this the recompense
Of mine to thee, ingrateful Eve, expressed[5]
Immutable when thou were lost, not I,   1165
Who might have lived and joyed immortal bliss,
Yet willingly chose rather death with thee?
And am I now upbraided as the cause
Of thy transgressing? not enough severe,
It seems, in thy restraint![6] What could I more?   1170
I warned thee, I admonished thee, foretold
The danger, and the lurking enemy
That lay in wait; beyond this had been force,
And force upon free will hath here no place.
But confidence then bore thee on, secure   1175
Either to meet no danger, or to find
Matter of glorious trial and perhaps
I also erred in overmuch admiring
What seemed in thee so perfect, that I thought
No evil durst attempt thee! but I rue   1180
That error now, which is become my crime,
And thou th' accuser. Thus it shall befall
Him who, to worth in women overtrusting,
Lets her will rule; restraint she will not brook,[7]
And, left to herself, if evil thence ensue,   1185
She first his weak indulgence will accuse."
   Thus they in mutual accusation spent
The fruitless hours, but neither self-condemning;
And of their vain contést appeared no end.

FROM BOOK 10

The Argument

   Man's transgression known, the guardian Angels forsake Paradise, and
return up to Heaven to approve their vigilance, and are approved; God declaring that the entrance of Satan could not be by them prevented. He sends his
Son to judge the transgressors; who descends, and gives sentence accordingly; then, in pity, clothes them both, and reascends. Sin and Death, sitting
till then at the gates of Hell, by wondrous sympathy feeling the success of
Satan in this new World, and the sin by Man there committed, resolve to sit
no longer confined in Hell, but to follow Satan, their sire, up to the place of
Man: to make the way easier from Hell to this World to and fro, they pave
a broad highway or bridge over Chaos, according to the track that Satan first
made; then, preparing for Earth, they meet him, proud of his success, returning to Hell; their mutual gratulation. Satan arrives at Pandemonium; in full
assembly relates, with boasting, his success against Man; instead of applause

4. The notion of man's authority over woman—recognized by Milton's Eve (e.g., in 4.442–43: "my guide / and head") and echoing St. Paul (1 Corinthians 11.3: "the head of the woman is the man") is here used by her to make Adam her equal in guilt, accusing him of indulgence in letting her go (*too facile*).   5. Demonstrated, proved.   6. In restraining Eve.   7. Put up with.

is entertained with a general hiss by all his audience, transformed, with him-self also, suddenly into Serpents, according to his doom given in Paradise; then, deluded with a show of the Forbidden Tree springing up before them, they, greedily reaching to take of the fruit, chew dust and bitter ashes. The proceedings of Sin and Death: God foretells the final victory of his Son over them, and the renewing of all things; but, for the present, commands his Angels to make several alterations in the Heavens and Elements. Adam, more and more perceiving his fallen condition, heavily bewails,[8] rejects the con-dolement of Eve; she persists, and at length appeases him: then, to evade the curse likely to fall on their offspring, proposes to Adam violent ways; which he approves not, but, conceiving better hope, puts her in mind of the late promise made them, that her seed should be revenged on the Serpent, and exhorts her, with him, to seek peace of the offended Deity by repentance and supplication.

[Acceptance, Reconciliation, Hope]

* * * Thus began

Outrage from lifeless things; but Discord first,
Daughter of Sin, among th' irrational
Death introduced through fierce antipathy:[9]
Beast now with beast 'gan war, and fowl with fowl,   710
And fish with fish: to graze the herb all leaving,
Devoured each other; nor stood much in awe
Of man, but fled him, or with countenance grim
Glared on him passing. These were from without
The growing miseries, which Adam saw   715
Already in part, though hid in gloomiest shade,
To sorrow abandoned, but worse felt within,
And in a troubled sea of passion tossed,
Thus to disburden sought with sad complaint:
    "O miserable of happy! Is this the end   720
Of this new glorious world, and me so late
The glory of that glory? who now, become
Accursed of blessèd, hide me from the face
Of God, whom to behold was then my height
Of happiness! Yet well, if here would end   725
The misery; I deserved it, and would bear
My own deservings; but this will not serve.
All that I eat or drink, or shall beget,
Is propagated curse.[1] O voice, once heard
Delightfully, 'Increase and multiply,'   730
Now death to hear! for what can I increase
Or multiply, but curses on my head?
Who of all ages to succeed, but, feeling
The evil on him brought by me, will curse
My head: 'Ill fare our ancestor impure!   735
For this we may thank Adam!' but his thanks

8. The selection printed here starts toward the end of Adam's long lamentation.   9. I.e., Discord intro-duced death to the irrational (beasts) through antipathy; Milton paves the way for the role of sympathy in reconciling Adam to Eve.   1. Eating, drinking, and procreating all increase or extend God's curse.

Shall be the execration;[2] so besides
Mine own that bide upon me, all from me
Shall with a fierce reflux on me redound,
On me, as on their natural center, light   740
Heavy, though in their place. O fleeting joys
Of Paradise, dear bought with lasting woes!
Did I request thee, Maker, from my clay
To mold me man? Did I solicit thee
From darkness to promote me, or here place   745
In this delicious garden? As my will
Concurred not to my being, it were but right
And equal to reduce me to my dust,
Desirous to resign and render back
All I received, unable to perform   750
Thy terms too hard, by which I was to hold
The good I sought not. To the loss of that,
Sufficient penalty, why hast thou added
The sense of endless woes? Inexplicable
Thy justice seems; yet to say truth, too late   755
I thus contèst; then should have been refused
Those terms whatever, when they were proposed.
Thou didst accept them; wilt thou enjoy the good,
Then cavil[3] the conditions? And though God
Made thee without thy leave, what if thy son   760
Prove disobedient, and reproved, retort,
'Wherefore didst thou beget me? I sought it not.'
Wouldst thou admit for his contempt of thee
That proud excuse? Yet him not thy election,
But natural necessity begot.   765
God made thee of choice his own, and of his own
To serve him; thy reward was of his grace;
Thy punishment then justly is at his will.
Be it so, for I submit; his doom is fair,[4]
That dust I am and shall to dust return.   770
O welcome hour whenever! Why delays
His hand to execute what his decree
Fixed on this day? Why do I overlive?
Why am I mocked with death, and lengthened out
To deathless pain? How gladly would I meet   775
Mortality, my sentence, and be earth
Insensible! how glad would lay me down
As in my mother's lap![5] here I should rest
And sleep secure; his dreadful voice no more
Would thunder in my ears; no fear of worse   780
To me and to my offspring would torment me
With cruel expectation. Yet one doubt
Pursues me still, lest all I cannot die;

2. I.e., posterity's curses on Adam.   3. Raise petty objections.   4. In his inner debate, Adam has just
been arguing to himself that God created us "of choice his own, / and of his own to serve him." Hence in
the same way as reward "was of his [God's] grace," so punishment "justly is at his will" and, therefore,
acceptable.   5. I.e., the earth (in 11.536, Michael, addressing Adam, calls the Earth "thy mother's lap"),
probably an echo of Job 3.

Lest that pure breath of life, the spirit of man
Which God inspired, cannot together perish 785
With this corporeal clod; then, in the grave,
Or in some other dismal place, who knows
But I shall die a living death? O thought
Horrid, if true!⁶ Yet why? It was but breath
Of life that sinned; what dies but what had life 790
And sin? the body properly hath neither.
All of me then shall die: let this appease
The doubt, since human reach no further knows.
For though the Lord of all be infinite,
Is his wrath also? Be it, man is not so, 795
But mortal doomed. How can he exercise
Wrath without end on man whom death must end?
Can he make deathless death? That were to make
Strange contradiction, which to God himself
Impossible is held, as argument 800
Of weakness, not of power.⁷ Will he draw out,
For anger's sake, finite to infinite
In punished man, to satisfy his rigor
Satisfied never? That were to extend
His sentence beyond dust and Nature's law; 805
By which all causes else according still
To the reception of their matter act,
Not to th' extent of their own sphere.⁸ But say
That death be not one stroke, as I supposed,
Bereaving sense, but endless misery 810
From this day onward, which I feel begun
Both in me and without⁹ me, and so last
To perpetuity—Ay me! that fear
Comes thundering back with dreadful revolution
On my defenseless head! Both death and I 815
Am found eternal, and incorporate both:¹
Nor I on my part single; in me all
Posterity stands cursed. Fair patrimony
That I must leave ye, sons! O, were I able
To waste it all myself, and leave ye none! 820
So disinherited, how would ye bless
Me, now your curse! Ah, why should all mankind
For one man's fault thus guiltless be condemned,
If guiltless? But from me what can proceed,
But all corrupt, both mind and will depraved, 825
Not to do only, but to will the same
With me? How can they then acquitted stand

6. Adam fears that the soul, breathed (*inspired*) into the *corporeal clod* at Creation, may be immortal and so suffer a *living death* in the grave.   7. Adam corrects himself, arguing (as Milton did in his theological writings) that because only the spirit (*breath of life*, line 784) sinned it shall die with the body (and, implicitly, await resurrection). Otherwise, according to the same theological line of thinking, there would be *strange contradiction*, an inadmissable sign of weakness in God.   8. Once body and spirit die, further punishment is impossible. According to *Nature's law* the power of all agents, God excepted (*all causes else*), cannot be exercised to its utmost (the *extent of their own sphere*) but is limited by the capacity for *reception* that the object of that power possesses.   9. Outside. *Bereaving sense:* removing all sensory powers.   1. The use of *am*, the singular form, stresses Adam's concentration on himself and on the fact that he and death are now united in one body (*incorporate*).

In sight of God?[2] Him, after all disputes,
Forced I absolve. All my evasions vain
And reasonings, though through mazes, lead me still   830
But to my own conviction: first and last
On me, me only, as the source and spring
Of all corruption, all the blame lights due;
So might the wrath! Fond[3] wish! Couldst thou support
That burden, heavier than the earth to bear;   835
Than all the world much heavier, though divided
With that bad woman? Thus, what thou desir'st,
And what thou fear'st, alike destroys all hope[4]
Of refuge, and concludes thee miserable
Beyond all past example[5] and future;   840
To Satan only like, both crime and doom.[6]
O Conscience! into what abyss of fears
And horrors hast thou driven me; out of which
I find no way, from deep to deeper plunged!"
        Thus Adam to himself lamented loud   845
Through the still night, not now, as ere man fell,
Wholesome and cool and mild, but with black air
Accompanied, with damps and dreadful gloom;
Which to his evil conscience represented
All things with double terror. On the ground   850
Outstretched he lay, on the cold ground, and oft
Cursed his creation; Death as oft accused
Of tardy execution, since denounced
The day of his offense. "Why comes not Death,"
Said he, "with one thrice-acceptable stroke   855
To end me? Shall Truth fail to keep her word,
Justice divine not hasten to be just?
But Death comes not at call; Justice divine
Mends not her slowest pace for prayers or cries.
O woods, O fountains, hillocks, dales, and bowers!   860
With other echo late I taught your shades
To answer, and resound far other song."
Whom thus afflicted when sad Eve beheld,
Desolate where she sat, approaching nigh,
Soft words to his fierce passion she essayed;   865
But her with stern regard he thus repelled:
    "Out of my sight, thou serpent! that name best
Befits thee, with him leagued, thyself as false
And hateful: nothing wants, but that thy shape,
Like his, and color serpentine, may show   870
Thy inward fraud, to warn all creatures from thee
Henceforth; lest that too heavenly form, pretended[7]
To hellish falsehood, snare them. But for thee

---

2. Inheriting Adam's original sin, his descendants, like him (*with me*), are going to act sinfully by their own free will.   3. Foolish.   4. Actually, by his desperate self-accusation and by wanting to assume, alone, the burden of guilt, Adam is shown to be already on the way to full repentance and to his own regeneration.   5. That of the fallen angels. *Concludes thee:* demonstrates that you are.   6. The comparison is clearly invalid, Adam's remorse and repentant despair being opposite to Satan's choice, as seen, for example, in 4.109–10: "Farewell remorse! All good to me is lost; / Evil, be thou my good."   7. Put up as a screen.

I had persisted happy, had not thy pride
And wandering vanity, when least was safe,   875
Rejected my forewarning, and disdained
Not to be trusted, longing to be seen
Though by the devil himself, him overweening
To overreach,[8] but, with the serpent meeting,
Fooled and beguiled; by him thou, I by thee,   880
To trust thee from my side, imagined wise,
Constant, mature, proof against all assaults;
And understood not all was but a show
Rather than solid virtue, all but a rib
Crooked by nature—bent, as now appears,   885
More to the part sinìster—from me drawn;
Well if thrown out, as supernumerary
To my just number found![9] Oh, why did God,
Creator wise, that peopled highest Heaven
With spirits masculine, create at last   890
This novelty on earth, this fair defect
Of nature, and not fill the world at once
With men, as angels, without feminine;
Or find some other way to generate
Mankind?[1] This mischief had not then befallen,   895
And more that shall befall—innumerable
Disturbances on earth through female snares,
And strait conjunction with this sex. For either
He never shall find out fit mate, but such
As some misfortune brings him, or mistake;   900
Or whom he wishes most shall seldom gain,
Through her perverseness, but shall see her gained
By a far worse, or, if she love, withheld
By parents, or his happiest choice too late
Shall meet, already linked and wedlock-bound   905
To a fell[2] adversary, his hate or shame:
Which infinite calamity shall cause
To human life, and household peace confound."
    He added not, and from her turned; but Eve,
Not so repulsed, with tears that ceased not flowing,   910
And tresses all disordered, at his feet
Fell humble, and, embracing them, besought
His peace, and thus proceeded in her plaint:
    "Forsake me not thus, Adam! witness Heaven
What love sincere and reverence in my heart   915
I bear thee, and unweeting have offended,
Unhappily deceived! Thy suppliant[3]
I beg, and clasp thy knees; bereave me not,
Whereon I live, thy gentle looks, thy aid,
Thy counsel in this uttermost distress,   920

---

8. Overestimating your power to outwit him.   9. Folklore has it that the rib from which Eve was created
was an extra rib on Adam's left (Latin: *sinister*) side. Note double meaning of *sinister*.   1. Adam's frenzied
speech belongs to a tradition of misogynistic rhetoric that goes back to antiquity. These lines, in particular,
seem to echo Euripides' *Hippolytus*, lines 617–20 (Euripides was one of Milton's favorite poets).
2. Fierce, bitter. *Already linked*: i.e., when he is already linked.   3. As thy suppliant. *Unweeting*:
unknowingly.

My only strength and stay: forlorn of thee,
Whither shall I betake me, where subsist?
While yet we live, scarce one short hour perhaps,
Between us two let there be peace; both joining,
As joined in injuries, one enmity   925
Against a foe by doom express assigned us,
That cruel serpent. On me exercise not
Thy hatred for this misery befallen;
On me already lost, me than thyself
More miserable. Both have sinned, but thou   930
Against God only; I against God and thee,
And to the place of judgment will return,
There with my cries importune Heaven, that all
The sentence, from thy head removed, may light
On me, sole cause to thee of all this woe,   935
Me, me only, just object of his ire."
    She ended weeping; and her lowly plight,
Immovable[4] till peace obtained from fault
Acknowledged and deplored, in Adam wrought
Commiseration. Soon his heart relented   940
Towards her, his life so late and sole delight,
Now at his feet submissive in distress,
Creature so fair his reconcilement seeking,
His counsel, whom she had displeased, his aid;
As one disarmed, his anger all he lost,   945
And thus with peaceful words upraised her soon:
    "Unwary, and too desirous, as before,
So now, of what thou know'st not,[5] who desir'st
The punishment all on thyself! Alas!
Bear thine own first, ill able to sustain   950
His full wrath, whose thou feel'st as yet least part,[6]
And my displeasure bear'st so ill. If prayers
Could alter high decrees, I to that place
Would speed before thee, and be louder heard,
That on my head all might be visited,   955
Thy frailty and infirmer sex forgiven,
To me committed, and by me exposed.[7]
But rise; let us no more contend, nor blame
Each other, blamed enough elsewhere,[8] but strive
In offices of love, how we may lighten   960
Each other's burden in our share of woe;
Since this day's death denounced, if aught I see,
Will prove no sudden, but a slow-paced evil,
A long day's dying to augment our pain,
And to our seed (O hapless seed!) derived."[9]   965
    To whom thus Eve, recovering heart, replied:—

---

4. Modifies both Eve in her lowly posture of repentance and Adam in his first reluctance to forgive.
5. Once more Eve is *too desirous* of the unknown, but her situation and her tone are now totally different—
as are those of Adam, whose *counsel* and *aid* she has sought.   **6.** Eve would not be able to bear the
weight of God's full wrath, of which she has until now experienced only the smallest part.   **7.** In the
present atmosphere of reconciliation, Adam seems to accept Eve's earlier charge (see n. 4, p. 3049); now
he blames himself for having exposed her to temptation.   **8.** I.e., at the place of judgment (see also lines
932, 953, and 1098–99).   **9.** Transmitted.

"Adam, by sad experiment I know
How little weight my words with thee can find,
Found so erroneous, thence by just event
Found so unfortunate. Nevertheless,   970
Restored by thee, vile as I am, to place
Of new acceptance, hopeful to regain
Thy love, the sole contentment of my heart,
Living or dying from thee I will not hide
What thoughts in my unquiet breast are risen,   975
Tending to some relief of our extremes,
Or end, though sharp and sad, yet tolerable,
As in our evils,¹ and of easier choice.
If care of our descent² perplex us most,
Which must be born to certain woe, devoured   980
By Death at last (and miserable it is
To be to others cause of misery,
Our own begotten, and of our loins to bring
Into this cursed world a woeful race,
That, after wretched life, must be at last   985
Food for so foul a monster), in thy power
It lies, yet ere conception, to prevent
The race unblest, to being yet unbegot.³
Childless thou art; childless remain. So Death
Shall be deceived his glut,⁴ and with us two   990
Be forced to satisfy his ravenous maw.
But, if thou judge it hard and difficult,
Conversing, looking, loving, to abstain
From love's due rites, nuptial embraces sweet,
And with desire to languish without hope   995
Before the present object⁵ languishing
With like desire—which would be misery
And torment less than none of what we dread—
Then, both our selves and seed at once to free
From what we fear for both, let us make short;   1000
Let us seek Death, or, he not found, supply
With our own hands his office on ourselves.
Why stand we longer shivering under fears
That show no end but death, and have the power,
Of many ways to die the shortest choosing   1005
Destruction with destruction to destroy?"⁶
    She ended here, or vehement despair
Broke off the rest; so much of death her thoughts
Had entertained as dyed her cheeks with pale.
But Adam, with such counsel nothing swayed,   1010
To better hopes his more attentive mind
Laboring had raised, and thus to Eve replied:—
    "Eve, thy contempt of life and pleasure seems
To argue in thee something more sublime

---

1. We being in such evils.   2. Descendants, lineage.   3. To forestall, by abstinence, the birth of descendants.   4. Shall be cheated of its fill.   5. Eve herself, object of Adam's love, and now in his presence.   6. Destroy destruction (Death's power to destroy future mankind) by destroying ourselves now.

And excellent than what thy mind contemns: 1015
But self-destruction therefore sought refutes
That excellence thought in thee, and implies
Not thy contempt, but anguish and regret
For loss of life and pleasure overloved.[7]
Or, if thou covet death, as utmost end 1020
Of misery, so thinking to evade
The penalty pronounced, doubt not but God
Hath wiselier armed his vengeful ire than so
To be forestalled. Much more I fear lest death
So snatched will not exempt us from the pain 1025
We are by doom to pay; rather such acts
Of contumacy will provoke the Highest
To make death in us live. Then let us seek
Some safer resolution—which methinks
I have in view, calling to mind with heed 1030
Part of our sentence,[8] that thy seed shall bruise
The Serpent's head. Piteous amends! unless
Be meant whom I conjecture,[9] our grand foe,
Satan, who in the Serpent hath contrived
Against us this deceit. To crush his head 1035
Would be revenge indeed—which will be lost
By death brought on ourselves, or childless days
Resolved as thou proposest; so our foe
Shall scape his punishment ordained, and we
Instead shall double ours upon our heads. 1040
No more be mentioned, then, of violence
Against ourselves, and wilful barrenness
That cuts us off from hope, and savors only
Rancor and pride, impatience and despite,
Reluctance[1] against God and his just yoke 1045
Laid on our necks. Remember with what mild
And gracious temper he both heard and judged,
Without wrath or reviling. We expected
Immediate dissolution, which we thought
Was meant by death that day; when, lo! to thee 1050
Pains only in child-bearing were foretold,
And bringing forth, soon recompensed with joy,
Fruit of thy womb. On me the curse aslope
Glanced on the ground.[2] With labor I must earn
My bread; what harm: Idleness had been worse; 1055
My labor will sustain me; and, lest cold

7. The suicide project excludes (*refutes*) the idea that Eve be contemptuous of life and pleasure in view of *something more sublime*; it rather implies *anguish and regret* at the thought of losing those goods.   8. Earlier in this book (the Argument and lines 163–208) the Lord gives sentence on the Serpent and the transgressors. The references here are to that passage, which is quite literally based on Genesis 30 (esp. lines 179–81; "Between thee and the Woman I will put / Enmity, and between thine and her seed; / Her seed shall bruise thy head, thou bruise his heel").   9. The notion that Satan spoke through the Serpent was not at first given to humanity (lines 170–71: "Concerned not Man. . . . / Nor altered his offense"). Adam is late in coming to that conclusion (*I conjecture*), and on it he bases the following eloquent argument in favor of survival, hope, procreation, and activity.   1. Resistance, opposition.   2. The curse descending (*aslope*) on Adam took an oblique course (*glanced*) toward the ground. Thus Adam is not only accepting the Lord's sentence (in lines 201–02 and 205; "Curs'd is the ground for thy sake; thou in sorrow / Shalt eat thereof all the days of thy life; / . . . In the sweat of thy face thou shalt eat bread") but turning it into a project for an active life after the Fall.

Or heat should injure us, his timely care
Hath, unbesought, provided, and his hands
Clothed us unworthy, pitying while he judged.
How much more, if we pray him, will his ear   1060
Be open, and his heart to pity incline,
And teach us further by what means to shun
The inclement seasons, rain, ice, hail, and snow!
Which now the sky, with various face, begins
To show us in this mountain,[3] while the winds   1065
Blow moist and keen, shattering the graceful locks
Of these fair spreading trees; which bids us seek
Some better shroud, some better warmth to cherish
Our limbs benumbed—ere this diurnal star
Leave cold the night, how we his gathered beams   1070
Reflected may with matter sere foment,[4]
Or by collision of two bodies grind
The air attrite to fire;[5] as late the clouds,
Justling, or pushed with winds, rude in their shock,
Tine the slant lightning, whose thwart[6] flame, driven down,   1075
Kindles the gummy bark of fir or pine,
And sends a comfortable heat from far,
Which might supply the Sun. Such fire to use,
And what may else be remedy or cure
To evils which our own misdeeds have wrought,   1080
He will instruct us praying,[7] and of grace
Beseeching him; so as we need not fear
To pass commodiously this life, sustained
By him with many comforts, till we end
In dust, our final rest and native home.   1085
What better can we do, than to the place
Repairing where he judged us, prostrate fall
Before him reverent, and there confess
Humbly our faults, and pardon beg, with tears
Watering the ground, and with our sighs the air   1090
Frequenting,[8] sent from hearts contrite, in sign
Of sorrow unfeigned and humiliation meek?
Undoubtedly he will relent, and turn
From his displeasure, in whose look serene,
When angry most he seemed and most severe,   1095
What else but favor, grace, and mercy shone?"
     So spake our Father penitent; nor Eve
Felt less remorse. They, forthwith to the place

---

3. In his description of *delicious Paradise* (4.132–58), Milton situates it on a high plateau at the top of a "steep wilderness" that denies access to the "enclosure green" and its "Insuperable height of loftiest shade, / Cedar, and pine, and fir, and branching palm, / A sylvan scene, and as the ranks ascend / Shade above shade, a woody theater / Of stateliest view" where "gentle gales / . . . dispense / Native perfumes, and whisper whence they stole / Those balmy spoils." That stately and blissful order is now disrupted, and after the radical alterations in the heavens and in the elements that God has commanded, Adam is preparing to cope with the hardships and challenges of his mortal state in a time-conditioned universe of seasonal changes, dawns and sunset, heat and ice, and shattering winds.   4. Heat, warm. *Diurnal star:* day star, the sun. *How:* seek how.   5. The implied belief is that rubbing two *bodies* (as two flints) against each other, the air thus ground down by the attrition (*attrite*) turns into fire.   6. Passing across the sky. *Tine:* kindle; that fire was produced by lightning is one of the ancient theories about its origin on earth.   7. If we pray to him.   8. Filling.

Repairing where he judged them, prostrate fell
Before him reverent, and both confessed   1100
Humbly their faults, and pardon begged, with tears
Watering the ground, and with their sighs the air
Frequenting, sent from hearts contrite, in sign
Of sorrow unfeigned and humiliation meek.

FROM BOOK 12

["The World Was All Before Them"]

Summary   After God's acceptance of the transgressors' prayers and the decree that "they must no longer abide in Paradise" (11, "The Argument"), Michael the archangel, with a band of cherubim, has been sent "to dispossess them." After Eve's lamentation and his own pleading, Adam has submitted; Michael has led him up to a high hill where, in a mixture of prophecy and instruction, he has set "before him in vision" the future of humankind, from Cain and Abel through Noah (11) and the prophets, thus coming "by degrees to explain who that Seed of Woman shall be which was promised Adam and Eve in the Fall: his incarnation, death, resurrection, and ascension; the state of the Church till his second coming" (12, "The Argument"). Toward the close of his speech, Michael has recommended the exercise of the basic Christian virtues, culminating in love, "By name to come called Charity, the soul / Of all the rest: then will thou not be loath / To leave this Paradise, but shalt possess / A Paradise within thee, happier far" (12.584–87). Michael has just ended his long speech.

*   *   *

He ended, and they both descend the hill.
Descended, Adam to the bower where Eve
Lay sleeping[9] ran before, but found her waked;
And thus with words not sad she him received:
    "Whence thou return'st and whither went'st, I know;   610
For God is also in sleep, and dreams[1] advise,
Which he hath sent propitious, some great good
Presaging, since, with sorrow and heart's distress
Wearied, I fell asleep. But now lead on;
In me is no delay; with thee to go   615
Is to stay here; without thee here to stay
Is to go hence unwilling; thou to me
Art all things under Heaven, all places thou,
Who for my willful crime art banished hence.
This further consolation yet secure   620
I carry hence: though all by me is lost,
Such favor I unworthy am vouchsafed,
By me the Promised Seed shall all restore."
    So spake our mother Eve; and Adam heard
Well pleased, but answered not; for now too nigh   625
Th' archangel stood, and from the other hill[2]

---

9. Michael has just said to Adam (lines 594–97): "Go, waken Eve; / Her also I with gentle dreams have calmed, / Portending good, and all her spirits composed / To meek submission."   1. The fact that Adam was granted a vision and Eve a dream may symbolize a difference in the mode of perception between man and woman; at any rate, both are God's revelations.   2. The hill that Michael had pointed out to Adam in lines 590–93: "and, see! the guards, / By me encamped on yonder hill, expect / Their motion, at whose front a flaming sword, / In signal of remove, waves fiercely round."

To their fixed station, all in bright array,
The cherubim descended; on the ground
Gliding meteorous, as evening mist
Risen from a river o'er the marish[3] glides,   630
And gathers ground fast at the laborer's heel
Homeward returning. High in front advanced,[4]
The brandished sword of God before them blazed,
Fierce as a comet; which with torrid heat,
And vapor as the Libyan air adust,[5]   635
Began to parch that temperate clime; whereat
In either hand the hastening angel caught
Our lingering parents, and to th' eastern gate[6]
Led them direct, and down the cliff as fast
To the subjected[7] plain; then disappeared.   640
They, looking back, all th' eastern side beheld
Of Paradise, so late their happy seat,
Waved over by that flaming brand;[8] the gate
With dreadful faces thronged and fiery arms.
Some natural tears they dropped, but wiped them soon;   645
The world was all before them, where to choose
Their place of rest,[9] and Providence their guide.
They, hand in hand, with wandering steps and slow,
Through Eden took their solitary way.

3. Marsh.   4. Raised high, carried like a banner.   5. Burned up, as the air of the Sahara Desert in Libya.   6. *The eastern gate* of Eden, guarded by Gabriel, was described earlier (4. 543–47): "It was a rock / Of alabaster, piled up to the clouds, / Conspicuous far, winding with one ascent / Accessible from earth, one entrance high; / The rest was craggy cliff."   7. Lying below.   8. Here meaning sword, but also conveying the image of burning (*flaming*). *Seat:* abode.   9. Not, of course, a place of repose, but their new, earthly abode.

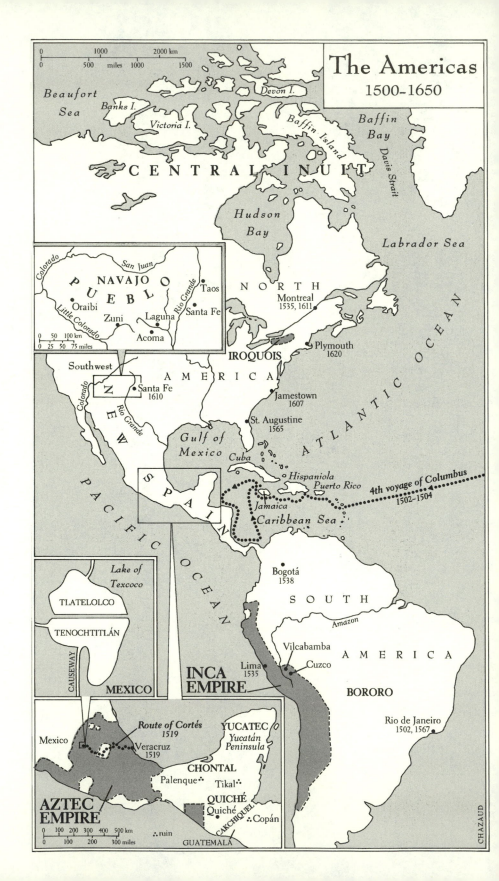

The Americas
1500–1650

Beaufort Sea

Banks I.

Victoria I.

Devon I.

Baffin Island

Baffin Bay

Davis Strait

CENTRAL INUIT

Hudson Bay

Labrador Sea

Colorado

San Juan

NAVAJO

P U E B L O

Little Colorado

Oraibi

Zuni

Laguna

Acoma

Taos

Santa Fe

Rio Grande

0   50   100 km

0   25 50 75 miles

Southwest

N

E

W

Colorado

Rio Grande

Santa Fe
1610

N O R T H

A M E R I C A

Montreal
1535, 1611

Plymouth
1620

IROQUOIS

Jamestown
1607

St. Augustine
1565

ATLANTIC OCEAN

Gulf of Mexico

Cuba

Hispaniola

Puerto Rico

Jamaica

Caribbean Sea

4th voyage of Columbus
1502–1504

S

P

A

I

N

P A C I F I C   O C E A N

Bogotá
1538

S O U T H

Amazon

A M E R I C A

Lake of Texcoco

TLATELOLCO

TENOCHTITLÁN

CAUSEWAY

MEXICO

INCA EMPIRE

Vilcabamba

Cuzco

Lima
1535

BORORO

Rio de Janeiro
1502, 1567

Mexico

Route of Cortés
1519

Veracruz
1519

YUCATEC

Yucatán Peninsula

CHONTAL

Palenque

Tikal

AZTEC EMPIRE

QUICHÉ

Quiché

CAKCHIQUEL

Copán

0 100 200 300 400 500 km

0   100   200   300 miles

∴ ruin

GUATEMALA

0   1000   2000 km

0   500   miles   1000   1500

CHAZAUD

Native America
and Europe
in the New World

The definitive meeting between alien cultures, an event unmatched in world history, took place the morning of November 8, 1519, as the conquistador Hernán Cortés with his band of four hundred soldiers entered the Aztec capital of Tenochtitlán. To be sure, there had been earlier expeditions, Columbus's among them, that had brought Europeans into contact with native Americans—but none that could produce the far-reaching shock of Cortés's introduction to the Aztec emperor Moteuczoma (better known in the English-speaking world as Montezuma).

The encounter provided one of the rare moments in history when life seems to imitate art. Surrounded by the dazzling architecture of a city larger than Rome, the newly arrived Spaniards compared the scene before them to the fantasies of which they had read in *Amadis of Gaul* (one of the chivalric romances to be satirized a century later in Cervantes's *Don Quixote*). In the words of the soldier-chronicler Bernal Díaz del Castillo: "We said it seemed like the things of enchantment told in the book of Amadis" and wondered aloud "if this were a dream."

As for the reluctant hosts, forewarned by couriers from the Gulf Coast, a decision had already been made that the newcomers were spirits stepped out of the pages of the Quetzalcoatl (Plumed Serpent) cycle, a body of narrative chronicling the deeds of a hero god who had fled eastward in deep disgrace but had promised to return. The interview itself was conducted in Nahuatl, the language of the Aztecs, with Cortés assisted by a pair of interpreters to get him from Spanish to Chontal (a Gulf Coast language) and from Chontal to Nahuatl. According to native records, the proceeding began with these phrases:

> CORTÉS: *Cuix ahmo teh? Cuix ahmo yeh teh? Yeh teh in tiMoteuczomah?* (Is it not you? Are you not he? Are you Montezuma?)
> MONTEZUMA: *Ca quemahca, ca nehhuatl. Toteucyoe!* (Yes, it is I. O Our Lord [i.e., Quetzalcoatl]!)

The sequence of events that preceded and followed this meeting, leading to the conquest of 1521, would be painstakingly re-created in Spanish chronicles, in the celebrated letters of Cortés, in the native-language Florentine Codex, and, for readers of English, in William H. Prescott's *History of the Conquest of Mexico* (1843), a constellation of works that would come to be esteemed for their literary as well as their historical value.

The immediate consequence of the fall of Tenochtitlán was the dismantling of an empire that had stretched from the Gulf Coast to the Pacific and from what is now the state of San Luis Potosí in central Mexico eastward to just within the present boundary of Guatemala. In due course, Tenochtitlán, or Tenochtitlán Mexico (now Mexico City), became the base from which further conquests were launched, reaching to the upper Rio Grande Valley and deep into Central America. Cortés's example inspired a generation of opportunistic intruders, notably Francisco Pizarro, whose conquest of the Inca empire of Peru was completed in 1533. Exploration by other European nations, including Britain and Portugal, had begun even before Cortés, and within a hundred years European outposts would be implanted all along the eastern rim of the Americas.

Devastating to native people and permanently disruptive to long-established cultures, the conquests nevertheless prepared the way for exchange. Wheat, livestock, horses, and firearms entered the so-called New World. From the Americas came tomatoes, chocolate, chilies, avocados (the names are all from the Nahuatl: *tomatl, xocolatl, chilli, ahuacatl*), not to mention tobacco, corn, potatoes, and the near-legendary gold and silver that heated the economy of Europe through the sixteenth century.

There were intellectual exchanges as well. In Aztec territory Spaniards, especially members of the clergy, learned Nahuatl, while native people became proficient in Spanish. Founded in 1536, the Royal College of Santa Cruz in the borough of Tlatelolco (part of Mexico City) taught young Aztec men to read and write Spanish and Nahuatl and even Latin. This Franciscan-run academy proved to be the principal training ground for what in retrospect would be recognized as the great era of Nahuatl letters, extending to about 1650. During this period Aesop's Fables, the Life of Saint Francis, portions of the Bible, and writings by Saint Augustine, Calderón de la Barca, Lope de Vega, and other authors were translated into Nahuatl.

At the same time works of Aztec verbal art were recorded for posterity in the alphabetic script of Western Europe and, in some cases at least, translated into Spanish. Among the most noteworthy of these are the creation epic known as Legend of the Suns, the massive Florentine Codex (including traditional narratives, oratory, and the history of the Spanish Conquest), and the song compilation called Cantares Mexicanos. Owing to censorship and the fear of encouraging native religion, however, none of these works, whether in the native language or in translation, could be published in its own time.

The native literary materials were prepared in manuscript and stored in libraries on both sides of the Atlantic. In some cases missionary-scholars served as the recorders, writing from the dictation of a knowledgeable elder. In other cases native scribes took the lead, either writing from live recitals or transcribing, so to speak, from the old pictorial books. These often magnificent volumes were bark-paper screen-folds that opened to form a lengthy streamer, crowded with illustrations typically read from right to left. Although the pictures contained a few phonetic features, they were essentially mnemonic, intended to call forth a text that had been learned orally.

On a somewhat smaller scale, literary activity of the same sort was initiated in Maya territory in the mid-1500s. There was no academy of Maya-Spanish-Latin learning on the level of the College of Santa Cruz. But in local monasteries and in church schools gifted Maya quickly learned the new script and began preparing native-language documents for their own use. Transcriptions in the full sense of the word might have been possible using the old bark-paper books, because Maya writing—in many communities at least—had been fully phonetic.

Though the Mayan languages are entirely different from Nahuatl and comprise a linguistic family in themselves (including Chontal, spoken in the Mexican state of Tabasco; Quiché, one of many Mayan languages of the Guatemalan highlands; and the widespread Yucatec Maya of the Yucatán peninsula), both cultures developed in the Mexican-Central American region known to modern anthropologists as Mesoamerica. Both show such distinguishing traits as stepped pyramids, floating gardens, specialized markets, an eighteen-month calendar, and screen-fold books. And in their verbal arts both have themes and genres in common, in particular a sacred book, or world history, in which the creation of the earth and the deeds of gods and kings are narrated in chronological sequence. The Popol Vuh of the Quiché Maya is the best-known work of this type.

The pattern of literary preservation set by the Aztec example and matched in sixteenth- and seventeenth-century Maya communities was to be repeated over the centuries and throughout the hemisphere. Again and again, after contact with Europeans, one or a few exceptional individuals would cooperate with outsiders to make a permanent record of historical narratives, prayers, song texts, or other matter. In many cases native intellectuals took a leading role or even worked on their own, independent of a missionary's or an anthropologist's agenda. The result of this activity is a vast and still growing native literature, preserved in the Western European, or Latin, script and generally available to the world through translations into European languages, especially English and Spanish but also German, French, Portuguese, and Italian. (It is fascinating to contemplate what might have been the outcome had the Americas joined the Old World through contact with Asia or Africa instead of Europe.)

In view of the written record, one may speak of native American *literature* in the strict sense of the term. The works have become texts. Still it should be kept in mind that the language arts of the Maya, Zuni, Navajo, and other American cultures have continued to live in oral tradition, and even those works that have been written down and published must be regarded as mere variants, possibly to be contradicted, perhaps improved, by later recordings. Therefore, the term *oral literature*, suggesting change and spontaneous creation, is often used by students of native American speech arts, even if particular renderings may be singled out as masterworks.

The texts themselves are intimately linked to the languages from which they spring, and it is essential to recognize the uniqueness of each linguistic tradition. Estimates have placed the number of American languages spoken at the beginning of the sixteenth century at approximately two thousand, of which several hundred are still in use. Moreover, these languages have served a variety of cultures, ranging from small nomadic bands and village communities to complex, stratified societies like the Aztec, Maya, and Inca, which formerly gave rise to city-states and empires.

But in spite of differing cultures, native peoples have not lived in isolation. They have been accomplished linguists and traders and have borrowed freely across cultural boundaries, disseminating literary themes and genres and even figures of speech. As a starting point toward grasping the unity of native literature, the anthropologist Donald Bahr has proposed three basic genres: song, narrative, and oratory.

Song tends to be the most perfectly memorized of the genres, with texts sometimes varying not at all from one performer to the next. Divorced from music, as is seldom or never the case in native performance, the texts by themselves do not exhibit meter or rhyme. But the interjection of vocables, or song syllables, create patterns, and stanzas are often paired.

Narrative, by contrast, is improvised by the performer, who, while following a prescribed plot line, adds details at will. The English terms *myth* and *folktale* reflect a division recognized in many native cultures, where a more serious, more sacred, or more "ancient" kind of story is contrasted with less serious narratives felt to be "new" or "false" (that is, fictional).

Oratory, a genre more significant in native American (and African) than in European lore, encompasses prayer, educational monologues, ceremonial colloquy, and the magical prose poems, or formulas, calculated to bring about a desired result by coercion. Composed of set phrases, whose sequence may be varied considerably, oratory falls between the strictness of song and the freedom of narrative.

Obviously the most expansive of the genres is narrative, the principal vehicle for relating the deeds of deities and heroes (more rarely heroines). In many cases the hero is a trickster or has tricksterlike attributes, which means that he is gullible, clownish, ribald, conniving, or a combination of all four. Often the tale tells of twin heroes, who either aid or antagonize one another. Human in their foibles (like the Greek Olympians), these figures may also be the divine creators of the universe and of social institutions.

Mixed genres are not uncommon. Often a narrative will be punctuated by short songs. The Aztec story of Quetzalcoatl, noted earlier, tells how the ill-fated king and all his pages were tricked by sorcerers, who not only caused the priestly ruler to become drunk but steered him toward an incestuous embrace with his sister, necessitating his flight from the brilliant palace appointed with red shell and decorated with the plumage of such brilliant birds as the quetzal and the troupial:

> When the sorcerers had gotten them completely drunk, they said to Quetzalcoatl, "My child, may it please you to sing, and here's a song for you to recite." Then Ihuimecatl [one of the sorcerers] recited it for him.

> I must leave my
> house of quetzal, of quetzal,
> my house of troupial,
> my house of redshell.

> When he had gotten into a happy mood, he said, "Go get my sister Quetzalpetlatl. Let the two of us be drunk together."

Narratives interlaced with song are especially typical of Mexico and the North American Southwest. In a variation of the mixed-genre style, narratives may be punctuated by oratory. In many if not most native traditions, the stories are joined in lengthy sequences to form what may be called epics. Finally, the epic as a whole may be condensed into song or oratory for ritualized performance at winter solstice gatherings, at funerals, or on other ceremonial occasions.

In approaching this literature, the question of cultural barriers comes to the fore. Is it possible for outsiders to make meaningful contact with traditions so far removed from their own? Without doubt, the challenge is there, but so is the opportunity. The planet holds no other land mass that could have given rise to cultures (and literatures) both so varied and so completely isolated from the sphere of Europe, Africa, and Asia that has come to dominate world thinking. For the student of literature, native America reintroduces—in ways that are distinctly fresh—the role of supernatural power, the problem of humanity versus nature, and the great themes centering on social obligation and the development of the individual.

Despite its reliance on symbolism and imagery, native American literature may be regarded as essentially technological, or functional, rather than aesthetic. For the individual its function is medicinal—to facilitate safe progress toward old age and to weaken destructive powers, especially those of disease and death. For society it functions to reinforce mores drawn from the timeless realm of deities; it also reorders the natural world so as to assign the human community its proper place, at the same time preserving a link to untamed nature as the source of livelihood and power. Such considerations may be suspended as native audiences submit to the charms of music or enjoy the antics of the trickster or the deeds of the monster slayer. Close juxtaposition of the divine and the irreverent, the awe-inspiring and the comic, is one of the hallmarks of native traditions. The important point is that this literature in its own setting is not an afterthought or an amenity; it is a necessary component of individual and social well-being.

FURTHER READING

Fernando Horcasitas, *The Aztecs Then and Now* (1979), offers a concise summary of Aztec history and culture from pre-Aztec times to the mid-twentieth century. The Maya are surveyed in Michael D. Coe, *The Maya* (1993). Harold E. Driver's comprehensive *Indians of North America* (1969) remains a standard work in its field. Diego Durán, *The Aztecs* (1964), is a readable, richly detailed sixteenth-century source on the history of Tenochtitlán. John Bierhorst's three-volume series—*The*

Mythology of North America (1985), *The Mythology of South America* (1988), and *The Mythology of Mexico and Central America* (1990)—presents an overview of native American narrative traditions. Munro S. Edmonson, ed., *Literatures* (*Supplement to the Handbook of Middle American Indians*), edited by Victoria Reifler Bricker, vol. 3, 1985), consists of survey articles on Nahuatl and four Maya literatures.

PRONOUNCING GLOSSARY

The following list uses common English syllables and stress accents to provide rough equivalents of selected words whose pronunciation may be unfamiliar to the general reader.

Cantares Mexicanos: *kahn-tah'-rays may-hee-kah'-nohs*

Cortés: *kohr-tays'*

Ihuimecatl: *ee-wee-may'-kahtl*

matasanos: *mah-tah-sáh-nohs*

Mexico: *may-shee'-koh* (in English: *meks'-ee-koh*)

Moteuczoma: *moh-tayk-soo'-mah*

Nahuatl: *nah'-wahtl*

Popol vuh: *poh-pohl' woo* (in English: *poh'-puhl voo*)

Quetzalcoatl: *kay-tzahl-koh'-ahtl*

Quetzalpetlatl: *kay-tzahl-pay'-tlahtl*

Quiché: *kee-chay'*

Tenochtitlán: *tay-nohch-tee-tlahn'*

Tlatelolco: *tlah-tel-ohl'-koh*

TIME LINE

TEXTS	CONTEXTS
	1500 Pedro Álvares Cabral sights the coast of Brazil and claims it for Portugal
	1502 Montezuma II ascends the throne of Tenochtitlán • Maya trading canoe contacted in Bay of Honduras during fourth voyage of Columbus
1508 Rodríguez de Montalvo, *Amadis of Gaul,* a chivalric romance that inspired the future conquistadors of Mexico	
1519–1526 Hernán Cortés, six letters to Charles I of Spain on the conquest of Mexico, with descriptions of Aztec warfare, statecraft, and daily life	1519–1522 Voyage of Ferdinand Magellan around the world
	1521 Fall of Tenochtitlán, conquered for Spain by Hernán Cortés
	1524 Fall of Quiché, conquered for Spain by Pedro de Alvarado
	1525 Execution of Cuauhtémoc, last Aztec emperor, hanged by order of Cortés
1528 *Annals of Tlatelolco,* earliest Latin-script chronicle in the Aztec language	1528 Beginning of civil war between Huascar and Atahualpa, rivals for the Inca throne
	1533 Fall of the Inca empire, conquered for Spain by Francisco Pizarro
1547–1579 **Florentine Codex,** the encyclopedic compilation of Aztec lore and literature	
1550–1581 **Cantares Mexicanos,** principal source of Aztec poetry	
1554–1558 **Popol Vuh,** sacred book of the Quiché Maya of Guatemala	
1556– Books of Chilam Balam, native compilations of Maya lore, including histories, prayers, and prophecies, still in use in the Yucatán	
1558 *Legend of the Suns,* history of the world according to the Aztecs, written in the Aztec language by an anonymous scribe	

Boldface titles indicate works in the anthology.

TIME LINE

TEXTS	CONTEXTS
	1572 Fall of Vilcabamba, last outpost of the Inca empire
	1588 England defeats the Spanish Armada
1590s? Aesop's Fables translated into Aztec	**1598** Beginning of Spanish settlement in New Mexico
	1607 Founding of Jamestown, first permanent English settlement in North America
1609–1617 Garcilaso de la Vega, El Inca, *Royal Commentaries of the Incas,* history of pre-Conquest Peru by an author who was himself a son of the Incas	
1611 Shakespeare, *The Tempest,* inspired in part by Silvester Jourdain's *A Discovery of the Bermudas* and thus the first major European work of imaginative literature to touch on a New World theme	
	1619 Beginning of African slavery in North America
	1620 Arrival of the *Mayflower* at Plymouth (Massachusetts), bringing English Puritans
	1630s League of the Iroquois, in existence since the 1400s, enters recorded history
1632 Bernal Díaz del Castillo, *True History of the Conquest of New Spain*	
1640 Plays by Calderón de la Barca and Lope de Vega translated into Aztec	
1649 Luis Lasso de la Vega, *Huei Tlamahuiçoltica . . .* (By Means of a Great Miracle . . .), legend of the Virgin of Guadalupe, a cornerstone of Mexican nationalism, published in the Aztec language, Mexico City	

FLORENTINE CODEX
1547–1579

Compiled over three decades, the encyclopedic Florentine Codex represents the joint effort of the Franciscan missionary-ethnographer Bernardino de Sahagún and the knowledgeable Aztec elders and scribes who labored with him to produce a permanent record of Aztec culture. There had never been a document quite like this, and there have been few since. In view of its linguistic precision, its scope, and its objectivity, it emerges as the first work of modern anthropology.

The name Florentine Codex, it should be pointed out, is merely a latter-day scholar's designation for the most finished version of a corpus properly known as *General History of the Things of New Spain*. Several versions of the *History* have survived. But the manuscript now at the Laurentian Library in Florence, although it lacks some texts preserved in the so-called Madrid codices, is the copy that best deserves to be called complete.

Written in paired columns, with Aztec (that is, Nahuatl) on the left and a Spanish paraphrase on the right, the codex's twelve books begin with descriptions of the pre-conquest gods and ceremonies, followed by detailed expositions of native astronomy, botany, zoology, commerce, industry, medicine, time counting, prophecy, and other topics. The final book is devoted to a native history of the Spanish Conquest.

Of particular interest for the study of literature is book 6, containing what Sahagún called "rhetoric." Voluminous and varied, it is the single richest body of native American oratory ever assembled. Here, in native text, are the speeches used by kings on state occasions, the great prayer to the rain god Tlaloc, the admonitions addressed by fathers to their sons and by mothers to their daughters, the marriage counsels, the prayers for schoolchildren—and the remarkable sequence of midwifery orations, from which selections have been printed here.

According to the texts on midwifery, which include not only the orations but the associated customs, the midwife is chosen by the married couple's parents during the woman's seventh or eighth month of pregnancy. Shortly thereafter a party of kinswomen visit the candidate, flattering her with set speeches, calling her "artisan" and "expert," begging her to accept the contract. In response she protests, she is unworthy, others are more skilled. After seeming to disqualify herself, she abruptly relents, announcing, "Let the water be boiled."

From that moment on the expectant woman is in the care of the midwife, who now represents Night Midwife, the tutelary spirit of her profession. Similarly, the patient becomes identified with the deity Cihuacoatl Quilaztli, progenitor of the human race. Such titles are frequently invoked in the orations used as the midwife assumes her duties and prepares the "flower house," or birthing room. When the time arrives she exhorts the expectant woman, urging her to emulate Cihuacoatl Quilaztli.

If the fetus should die in the womb, the midwife removes it surgically, using an extreme form of curettage. Should the woman herself die in labor, the midwife addresses her in one of the most eloquent of the orations, initiating her into the company of the celestial soldiers and thereby conferring the highest honor of which Aztec society can conceive. The woman in labor is imagined as a warrior, seeking to bring a live captive into the world—just as the male warrior in battle seeks not to kill but to bring home a prisoner (who will be ceremonially sacrificed to the gods). Should the male lose his life in battle he joins the company of slain warriors in the eastern sky who greet the sun each morning and conduct it to the zenith; at the zenith it is handed over to the women who have died in childbirth, and it is they who lead the sun downward to the western horizon. Thus the male and female roles are mirror images of one another.

Should the woman deliver successfully, the midwife addresses her as one would greet a victorious warrior. But again, as elsewhere in the orations (and in Aztec deportment generally), humility is the watchword. The new mother must not be "boastful" of the child, respecting the will of the Creator, the supreme spirit, who both gives and takes away.

Sahagún's *History* has been published in a thirteen-part English-Nahuatl edition, *Florentine Codex* (1950–82), edited by Arthur J. O. Anderson and Charles E. Dibble; the introductory volume (Part 1) includes background data and a subject guide; Part 7 (book 6) has the complete oratory. Articles on various aspects of Sahagún's *History*, including the oratory, are included in Munro S. Edmonson, ed., *Sixteenth-Century Mexico: The Work of Sahagún* (1974). More of the midwifery orations are in Thelma Sullivan's *A Scattering of Jades: Stories, Poems, and Prayers of the Aztecs* (1994), edited by T. J. Knab.

PRONOUNCING GLOSSARY

The following list uses common English syllables and stress accents to provide rough equivalents of selected words whose pronunciation may be unfamiliar to the general reader.

Cihuacoatl Quilaztli: *see-wah-koh'-ahtl*
    kee-lahs'-tlee
Nahuatl: *nah'-wahtl*
Sahagún: *sah-ah-goon'*

Tlaloc: *tlahl'-ohk*
Tloque Nahuaque: *tloh'-kay nah-wah'-kay*

From Florentine Codex

[The Midwife Addresses the Woman Who Has Died in Childbirth][1]

The woman who dies in childbirth, of whom it is said she stands up as a woman, when she dies they say she becomes a god. Then the midwife calls to her, greets her, prays to her, while she is still lying there, while she is still stretched out, saying:

Precious feather, child,
Eagle woman, dear one,
Dove, darling daughter,[2]
You have labored, you have toiled,
Your task is finished.   5
You came to the aid of your Mother, the noble lady, Cihuacoatl
    Quilaztli.[3]
You received, raised up, and held the shield, the little buckler that she
    laid in your hands: she your Mother, the noble lady, Cihuacoatl
    Quilaztli.

Now wake! Rise! Stand up!
Comes the daylight, the daybreak:
Dawn's house has risen crimson, it comes up standing.
The crimson swifts, the crimson swallows, sing,   10
And all the crimson swans[4] are calling.
Get up, stand up! Dress yourself!

1. Translated by John Bierhorst.   2. Terms of endearment. *Eagle woman:* implies valor.   3. Cihuacoatl (Woman Serpent) and Quilaztli (untranslatable) are names for the principle female deity.   4. Male warriors slain in battle, now in the eastern sky with the sun.

Go! Go seek the good place, the perfect place, the home of your Mother,
    your Father, the Sun,[5]
The place of happiness, joy,   15
Delight, rejoicing.
Go! Go follow your Mother, your Father, the Sun.
May his elder sisters bring you to him: they the exalted, the celestial
    women,[6] who always and forever know happiness, joy, delight, and
    rejoicing, in the company and in the presence of our Mother, our
    Father, the Sun; who make him happy with their shouting.
My child, darling daughter, lady,
You spent yourself, you labored manfully: 20
You made yourself a victor, a warrior for Our Lord, though not without
    consuming all your strength; you sacrificed yourself.
Yet you earned a compensation, a reward: a good, perfect, precious death.
By no means did you die in vain.
And are you truly dead? You have made a sacrifice. Yet how else could
    you have become worthy of what you now deserve?
You will live forever, you will be happy, you will rejoice in the company
    and in the presence of our holy ones, the exalted women. Farewell,
    my daughter, my child. Go be with them, join them. Let them hold
    you and take you in.   25
May you join them as they cheer him and shout to him: our Mother, our
    Father, the Sun;
And may you be with them always, wherever they go in their rejoicing.

But my little child, my daughter, my lady,
You went away and left us, you deserted us, and we are but old men and
    old women.
You have cast aside your mother and your father.   30
Was this your wish? No, you were summoned, you were called.
Yet without you, how can we survive?
How painful will it be, this hard old age?
Down what alleys or in what doorways will we perish?
Dear lady, do not forget us! Remember the hardships that we see, that we
    suffer, here on earth: 35
The heat of the sun presses against us; also the wind, icy and cold:
This flesh, this clay of ours, is starved and trembling. And we, poor
    prisoners of our stomachs! There is nothing we can do.
Remember us, my precious daughter, O eagle woman, O lady!
You lie beyond in happiness. In the good place, the perfect place,
You live.   40
In the company and in the presence of our lord,
You live.
You as living flesh can see him, you as living flesh can call to him.
Pray to him for us!
Call to him for us!   45
This is the end,
We leave the rest to you.

---

5. The sun is both mother and father.   **6.** Women who have died in childbirth, now in the western sky.

[The Midwife Addresses the Newly Delivered Woman][1]

O my daughter, O valiant woman, you worked, you toiled.
You soared like an eagle, you sprang like a jaguar,
you put all your strength behind the shield, behind the buckler;
    you endured.
You went forth into battle, you emulated Our Mother,
    Cihuacoatl Quilaztli,   5
and now our lord has seated you on the Eagle Mat, the Jaguar
    Mat.[2]
You have spent yourself, O my daughter, now be tranquil.
What does our lord Tloque Nahuaque[3] will?
Shall he bestow his favors upon each of you separately, in separate
    places?
Perhaps you shall go off and leave behind the child that has arrived.   10
Perhaps, small as he is the Creator will summon him, will call out
    to him,
or perhaps he shall come to take you.
Do not be boastful of [the child].
Do not consider yourself worthy of it.
Call out humbly to our lord, Tloque Nahuaque.   15

1. Translated by Thelma Sullivan.   2. Warriors' seat of honor.   3. Ever Present, Ever Near, the supreme spirit.

CANTARES MEXICANOS
1550–1581

Taken from the lips of singers by native scribes during the second half of the sixteenth century, the Cantares Mexicanos ("songs of the Aztecs") is the principal surviving source of Aztec poetry and one of the monuments of native American literature. Voluminous and fascinating, if difficult to decipher, it has attracted a modern following of scholars and poets determined to distill its essence and make fresh versions for new audiences. It is one of those bodies of work that for itself alone prompts the dedicated to study a difficult language.

The songs are composed in grammatical Nahuatl, or Aztec. But they are not immediately accessible, even to fluent speakers. Replete with tropes and word distortions, the Cantares diction, though some of its imagery is shared by oratory, belongs to a special genre called *netotiliztli* (freely, "dance associated with worldly entertainment"). Interspersed song syllables, coupled metaphors, and kennings comparable to those in Norse and Old English verse abound. And yet, even if textually obscure, the *netotiliztli* as performed in sixteenth-century Mexico were well calculated to chill the blood of European eavesdroppers. As correctly noted by the Spanish academician Francisco Cervantes de Salazar, drawing on observations made in the 1550s and 1560s, "In these songs they speak of conspiracy against ourselves."

A native document, prepared without missionary interference, the Cantares, nevertheless, is more than native. A better term is *nativistic,* implying work that aggressively reasserts—and to an extent reformulates—the values of a people under stress.

In fact some of the songs defiantly rehearse the Spanish Conquest of 1521 in ways that hint at native retribution; others introduce Christian themes overlaid by Aztec interpretations that were deeply disturbing to missionaries. No doubt a number of the pieces in the repertory had been used before the Conquest, possibly to intimidate enemy ambassadors or to inspire martial ardor or, in the case of the many satirical pieces, simply to entertain. Thus the genre has deep roots, even if reshaped by mid-sixteenth-century concerns.

War, the taking of captives, the immortalizing of slain warriors by means of song, the nature of song itself, the valor of dead kings, and the taunting of enemies and laggard soldiers are the pervasive themes. For all its hyperaesthetic imagery devoted to birds and flowers, this is an intensely masculine, militarist poetry, from which women, either as composers or performers, were apparently excluded. (It may come as no surprise to the psychoanalytically minded that the corpus includes a homosexual song and several pieces in which the male monologuist assumes female, even lesbian, roles.)

The two selections printed here are among the least taxing interpretively yet provide a full-blown taste of the sensuous imagery for which the genre is renowned. In the first, a singer reveals his version of the Aztec theory—also expounded in surviving narratives—by which music is a sky world phenomenon reproduced on earth. The related theme of musical intoxication, much treated in the Cantares, is also introduced. In the second selection, a singer exhorts the fainthearted, inspiring them to emulate slain comrades now enjoying immortality in the sky. In both pieces the supreme spirit is identified as Tloque Nahuaque (Ever Present, Ever Near), a name often associated with the great god Tezcatlipoca in unacculturated lore. In the Cantares, however, the "ever present" is identified with *Dios* (God), permitting one to say, albeit with understatement, that the two songs express a modified Christianity.

In performance such texts were accompanied by the *huehuetl*, or upright skin drum (played with bare hands), and the horizontal two-toned *teponaztli*, or slit drum (played with mallets). Gongs, flutes, whistles, and other instruments might also be present, as the singer intones his phrases, punctuated by the cries of dancers in military attire. Although the program for any particular song text cannot be reconstructed, contemporary descriptions allow one to imagine a lively scene, staged as an outdoor theatrical complete with its ominous drumming and the sight of glistening unsheathed weapons.

The only complete edition of the Cantares Mexicanos is John Bierhorst, *Cantares Mexicanos: Songs of the Aztecs* (1985), which includes extensive commentary. Robert Stevenson, *Music in Aztec and Inca Territory* (1968), gives useful background on instrumentation and performance. Modern poetry inspired by the Cantares can be found in William Carlos Williams, *Pictures from Brueghel and Other Poems* (1949); Stephen Berg, *Nothing in the Word* (1972); and Ernesto Cardenal, *Los Ovnis de Oro/ Golden UFOs* (1992).

PRONOUNCING GLOSSARY

The following list uses common English syllables and stress accents to provide rough equivalents of selected words whose pronunciation may be unfamiliar to the general reader.

Cantares Mexicanos: *kahn-tah'-rays may-hee-kah'-nohs*

Ce Olintzin: *say oh-leen'-tzeen*

huehuetl: *way'-waytl*

Nahuatl: *nah'-wahtl*

netotiliztli: *nay-toh-tee-lees'-tlee*

Otomi: *oh-doh-mee'*

teponaztli: *tay-poh-nahs'-tlee*

Tezcatlipoca: *tays-kahtl-ee-poh'-kah*

Tloque Nahuaque: *tloh'-kay nah-wah'-kay*

CANTARES MEXICANOS[1]

Song IV

Mexican Otomi[2] Song

Burnishing them as sunshot jades, mounting them as trogon feathers, I recall the root songs, I, the singer, composing good songs as troupials:[3] I've scattered them as precious jades, producing a flower brilliance to entertain the Ever Present, the Ever Near.[4]

As precious troupial feathers, as trogons, as roseate swans, I design my songs. Gold jingles are my songs. I, a parrot corn-tassel bird,[5] I sing, and they resound. In this place of scattering flowers I lift them up before the Ever Present, the Ever Near.

Delicious are the root songs, as I, the parrot corn-tassel bird, lift them through a conch of gold, the sky songs passing through my lips: like sunshot jades I make the good songs glow, lifting fumes of flower fire, a singer making fragrance before the Ever Present, the Ever Near.

The spirit swans[6] are echoing me as I sing, shrilling like bells from the Place of Good Song. As jewel mats, shot with jade and emerald sunray, the Green Place[7] flower songs are radiating green. A flower incense, flaming all around, spreads sky aroma, filled with sunshot mist, *as I, the singer, in this gentle rain of flowers sing before the Ever Present, the Ever Near.*[8]

As colors I devise them. I strew them as flowers in the Place of Good Song. *As jewel mats, shot with jade and emerald sunray, the Green Place flower songs are radiating green. A flower incense, flaming all around, spreads sky aroma, filled with sunshot mist, as I, the singer, in this gentle rain of flowers sing before the Ever Present, the Ever Near.*

I exalt him, rejoice him with heart-pleasing flowers in this place of song. With narcotic fumes my heart is pleasured. I soften my heart, inhaling them. My soul grows dizzy with the fragrance, inhaling good flowers in this place of enjoyment. My soul is drunk with flowers.

Song XII

Song for Admonishing Those Who Seek No Honor in War

Clever with a song, I beat my drum to wake our friends, rousing them to arrow deeds, whose never dawning hearts know nothing, whose hearts lie dead asleep in war, who praise themselves in shadows, in darkness. Not in vain do I say, "They are poor." Let them come and hear the flower dawn songs drizzling down incessantly beside the drum.

Sacred flowers of the dawn are blooming in the rainy place of flowers that belongs to him the Ever Present, the Ever Near. The heart pleasers are

---

1. Translated by John Bierhorst.   2. Here an Aztec warrior class distinguished by superior achievement; usually the name of a non-Aztec ethnic group.   3. Tropical orioles. *Trogon:* a brilliant tropical bird. 4. Tezcatlipoca, the all-powerful Aztec deity.   5. A tiny yellow songbird not otherwise identified; here joined with the parrot, implying that the singer resembles either or both. *Roseate swans:* roseate spoonbills or their feathers.   6. Gorgeous birds of the sky world, formerly warriors on earth.   7. Evidently the sky world, but terms such as *Good Song* and *Green Place* may also designate the singer's earthly locale, beautified by music, war deeds, or both.   8. Passages in italics indicate the translator is filling out an "et cetera" in the text.

laden with sunstruck dew. Come and see them: they blossom uselessly for those who are disdainful. Doesn't anybody crave them? O friends, not useless flowers are the life-colored honey flowers.

They that intoxicate one's soul with life lie only there, they blossom only there, within the city of the eagles, inside the circle, in the middle of the field, where flood and blaze are spreading, where the spirit eagle shines, the jaguar growls, and all the precious bracelet stones[1] are scattered, all the precious noble lords dismembered, where the princes lie broken, lie shattered.

These princes are the ones who greatly crave the dawn flowers. So that all will enter in, he causes them to be desirous, he who lies within the sky, he, Ce Olintzin,[2] ah the noble one, who makes them drizzle down, giving a gift of flower brilliance to the eagle-jaguar princes, making them drunk with the flower dew of life.

If, my friend, you think the flowers are useless that you crave here on earth, how will you acquire them, how will you create them, you that are poor, you that gaze on the princes at their flowers, at their songs? Come look: do they rouse themselves to arrow deeds for nothing? There beyond, the princes, all of them, are troupials, spirit swans, trogons, roseate swans: they live in beauty, they that know the middle of the field.

With shield flowers, with eagle-trophy flowers, the princes are rejoicing in their bravery, adorned with necklaces of pine flowers. Songs of beauty, flowers of beauty, glorify their blood-and-shoulder toil. They who have accepted flood and blaze become our Black Mountain friends, with whom we rise warlike on the great road.[3] Offer your shield, stand up, you eagle jaguar!

---

1. *Eagle, jaguar*, and *bracelet stones* denote the noble warrior. *City of the eagles* and *the circle* signify the battlefield. **2.** One Movement, a calendrical sign, or the tutelary spirit of that sign, that is, Tezcatlipoca. **3.** Here the sun's road to the sky. Black Mountain represents, perhaps, paradise. The ordinary meaning is: Our comrades with whom we march down the causeway (*great road*) that leads from the Mexican capital (which was surrounded by water) to Black Mountain (a town traditionally at war with Mexico).

POPOL VUH
1554–1558

A compendium of stories cherished by the ancient, the colonial, and even the modern Maya, the Popol Vuh of the sixteenth-century Quiché people of Guatemala has been compared with the *Odyssey* of the Greeks and the *Mahābhārata* of India. Such omnibus compositions, repeatedly mined by the artist and the moralist, serve as cultural touchstones; they dramatize the life of a nation and help bind it together. In the case of the Popol Vuh, as with similar works, the stories have been woven together to form an epic, with threads of continuity that may be called novelistic. On account of this seemingly modern feature, rare in New World literatures, the Quiché book strikes nonnative observers as the single most significant work of native American verbal art. Viewed from yet another perspective, focusing on its lofty account of world creation and tribal origins, it has been called America's Bible.

But if the Popol Vuh is comparable, it is also different. By Western standards it might be judged too formal—and at the same time too earthy. Derived from a fascination with numbers, its formalism is expressed stylistically in the pairing, tripling, and quadrupling of phrases. Major characters, likewise, are paired, acting almost as duplicates of one another; deities also are paired, occasionally tripled, with a strong suggestion that they are the same. The structure of the work itself is reiterative, fitted to a traditional pattern of four successive worlds, or creations: the first three are said to have ended in failure, our own is the fourth. Yet against this stately patterning, the hero-gods appear as light-hearted boys, even as tricksters. Their adventures—from which ribaldry is not excluded—have a playful, anecdotal quality. For the uninitiated reader willing to accept this juxtaposition of the sacred and the profane, the high and the low, an experience both rewarding and unusual lies in wait.

Despite the best efforts of scholarship, the author of the Popol Vuh remains anonymous. It has been generally assumed that he is a man—since known scribes of the period are male—and, with less agreement, that he is a lone composer who uses the authorial *we* (some have conjectured a team of authors). Evidently, he is a native of the town variously called Utatlán, Rotten Cane, or Quiché, political center of the pre-Columbian confederacy that controlled most of the Guatemalan highlands.

Inevitably, following the conquest of Mexico in 1521, Spanish imperialism cast its eye toward Guatemala, and in 1524, after a brief struggle, Quiché fell to Spanish and Mexican troops under the command of the red-haired conquistador Pedro de Alvarado (called "the sun" by native people). By the 1530s, Quiché scribes, presumably including the Popol Vuh author, were being trained to use alphabetic writing. From internal evidence in the manuscript, coordinated with other records, the date of the Popol Vuh has been tentatively fixed at 1554–58.

In the text itself the author hints at the existence of a certain "council book" (*popol vuh*), presumably a pre-Columbian screen-fold that served him as a source. The sixteenth-century Quiché were well acquainted with books of this sort, some dating from the classic period of Maya culture (A.D. 100–900), which saw the rise of such imposing centers as Tikal, Copán, and Palenque. By the time of European contact those important sites, abandoned in the mysterious collapse of Maya civilization ca. A.D. 900, lay in ruins. But Maya learning survived along the rim of the now-depopulated central area, notably in southern Guatemala among the Quiché and their neighbors, also in the northern part of the Yucatán peninsula. As Mayanists have recently demonstrated, the old books do contain phonetic writing. But judging from the few examples that have been preserved, it is likely that even during the classic period extended narratives were transmitted orally, with the picture-filled books acting only as prompts. The conclusion usually drawn is that the Popol Vuh is by no means a transcription of ancient screen-folds; yet it no doubt borrows from them.

Though not so indicated in the manuscript, the Popol Vuh falls naturally into four parts, as most translators have recognized. The first three attempts at creation—that is, the creation of humans—are compressed into Part 1, saving the climactic dawning of the sun, preceded by the fourth, successful creation of humans, for the opening passages of Part 4.

The first sunrise, typically, is the defining event in Mesoamerican chronology. Prior to it, the world is in darkness or is lit by mere substitute suns. The earth's surface, moreover, is said to be soft and moist; it does not harden until the sun finally comes up. During the dark, or soft, time all things are possible. Thus Parts 1, 2, and 3 of the Popol Vuh relate the events of a formative age. History, it may be said, begins with Part 4. In the version printed here the translator has chosen to set off the concluding passages of Part 4, labeling the most recent phase of history "Part 5." Selections have been made so as to represent each of these five parts.

As the author plainly states in the preamble that begins Part 1, "We shall write about this now amid the preaching of God, in Christendom now." Admittedly, then, the Popol Vuh is a latter-day work. But the question of missionary influence is not easy to settle. Most critics have assumed that the account of the earth's creation that immediately follows the preamble owes something to the Book of Genesis. If so, the material has been thoroughly assimilated to the Maya pantheon and to the native American concept of primordial water. Comparisons with Aztec accounts, in which a company of gods (including the deity Plumed Serpent, named also in the Quiché text) deliberates, then places the earth on the surface of a preexisting sea, are just as applicable as comparisons with Genesis.

Part 1 continues with a description of the first three efforts at creating humans, in line with a widespread pattern shared by Aztec and other Mesoamerican traditions. As Part 1 ends, the narrative changes gears, moving directly into the exploits of the divine heroes Hunahpu and Xbalanque. The work of these two heroes may be said to prepare the world for society and for the well-being of individuals within society. Thus Part 2 deals with the problem of human arrogance; Part 3 confronts the scourge of death.

The cycle of trickster tales that makes up Part 2 appears to be purely Central American, not shared by Aztec lore. In Part 2, the twin heroes bring low the overproud Seven Macaw and, in further adventures not included here, defeat his two "self-magnifying" sons, Zipacna and Earthquake.

In the cycle of tales that comprises Part 3, the most celebrated portion of the Popol Vuh, Hunahpu and Xbalanque vanquish the lords of the Maya underworld, called Xibalba (a term of obscure etymology, provisionally translated "place of fright"). This material, likewise, is Central American—and quintessentially Mayan. Scenes from the story are preserved on painted vases of the classic period, recovered by archaeologists from Maya burial chambers. Evidently, the sequence of events, in which the heroes' twin fathers, One Hunahpu and Seven Hunahpu, are undone by Xibalba and are ultimately avenged by their two sons, served as a paradigm for the dying and the dead, promising them victory over the powers of the afterworld. From the archaeological evidence, the story told in Part 3 of the Popol Vuh must have aided the Maya in their journey through the realms of death somewhat as the *Book of the Dead* comforted the ancient Egyptians. Indeed, the vase paintings as a whole, with their depictions of underworld lords and the trials of the twin heroes, have lately been called the "Maya Book of the Dead."

Parts 4 and 5 complete the vast epic, relating the connected stories of the origin of humans, the discovery of corn, the birth of the sun, and the history of the Quiché tribes and their royal lineages down to the time of the Spanish Conquest and, subsequently, to the 1550s.

Old as the stories are, they are also new. Narratives of the origin and destruction of early humans can still be heard in traditional Maya storytelling sessions. The traditional account of the discovery of corn continues to be widely told; and tales of the trickster Zipacna and of exploits identical to those of the hero twins also persist, even if much abbreviated and without the grand continuity of the Popol Vuh.

Beyond the native community, knowledge of the Popol Vuh among Central Americans is not only widespread but taken for granted. When the Nicaraguan poet Pablo Antonio Cuadra writes (in *The Calabash Tree,* 1978), "A hero struggled against the lords of the House of Bats, / against the lords of the House of Darkness," his readers understand that although he refers to a contemporary revolutionary figure he is also alluding to the ordeal of Hunahpu and Xbalanque. For the Salvadoran novelist Manlio Argueta (*Cuzcatlán,* 1986) the story of the origin of humans from corn as told in the Popol Vuh is a reminder, in Argueta's words, that "the species will not perish"—a theme equally detectable (and inspired by the same source) in the title of the 1949 novel *Men of Maize* by the Guatemalan Nobel laureate Miguel Angel Asturias.

In the translation printed here, wherever the text solidifies into a string of three or more couplets the passage is set apart as though it were a poem. This is a device of the translator. It is not meant to imply that the lines were chanted but rather to show off the more pronounced moments of formalism in a prose that borders on oratory.

Dennis Tedlock's translation, satisfyingly annotated, is published as *Popol Vuh: The Mayan Book of the Dawn of Life* (1985; revised 1996). The text given below is

from the 1996 edition. Older translations with useful introductions are Adrián Reci-
nos, Delia Goetz, and Sylvanus Morley, *Popol Vuh: The Sacred Book of the Ancient
Quiché Maya* (1950); and Munro S. Edmonson, *The Book of Counsel: The Popol Vuh
of the Quiche Maya of Guatemala* (1971). Edmonson's is the only Quiché-English
edition. Essays on the Popol Vuh and related topics are in Tedlock's *The Spoken
Word and the Work of Interpretation* (1983). Maya vase paintings related to Part 3 of
the Popol Vuh are illustrated and discussed in Michael D. Coe, *Lords of the Underworld: Masterpieces of Classic Maya Ceramics* (1978).

PRONOUNCING GLOSSARY

The following list uses common English syllables and stress accents to provide rough equivalents of selected words whose pronunciation may be unfamiliar to the general reader.

anonas: *ah-noh'-nahs*

Auilix: *ah-wee-leesh'*

Cauiztan Copal: *kah-weez-tahn'*
    koh-pahl'

Chimalmat: *chee-mahl-maht'*

Hacauitz: *hah-kah-weets'*

Hunahpu: *hoo-nah-poo'*

jocotes: *hoh-koh'-tays*

matasanos: *mah-tah-sah'-nohs*

Mixtam Copal: *meesh-tahm' koh-pahl'*

nance: *nahn'-say*

naual: *nah'-wahl*

Palenque: *puh-leng'-kay*

pataxte: *pah-tahsh'-tay*

Popol Vuh: *poh-pohl' woo* (in English:
    poh'-puhl voo)

Quiché: *kee-chay'*

Quitze: *kee-tsay'*

Tikal: *tee-kahl'*

Tohil: *toh-heel'*

Xbalanque: *shbah-lahn-kay'*

Xibalba: *shee-bahl-bah'*

Xmucane: *shmoo-kah-nay'*

Xpiyacoc: *shpee-yah-kohk'*

zapotes: *sah-poh'-tays*

Zipacna: *see-pahk-nah'*

Popol Vuh[1]

FROM PART 1

[*Prologue, Creation*]

THIS IS THE BEGINNING OF THE ANCIENT WORD, here in this place called
Quiché. Here we shall inscribe, we shall implant the Ancient Word, the
potential and source for everything done in the citadel of Quiché, in the
nation of Quiché people.

    And here we shall take up the demonstration, revelation, and account of
how things were put in shadow and brought to light by

> the Maker, Modeler,
> named Bearer, Begetter,
> Hunahpu Possum, Hunahpu Coyote,
> Great White Peccary,
> Sovereign Plumed Serpent,
> Heart of the Lake, Heart of the Sea,

1. Translated by Dennis Tedlock.

> plate shaper,
> bowl shaper,[2] as they are called,
> also named, also described as
> the midwife, matchmaker
> named Xpiyacoc, Xmucane,
> defender, protector,[3]
> twice a midwife, twice a matchmaker,

as is said in the words of Quiché. They accounted for everything—and did it, too—as enlightened beings, in enlightened words. We shall write about this now amid the preaching of God, in Christendom now. We shall bring it out because there is no longer

> a place to see it, a Council Book,
> a place to see "The Light That Came from
>   Beside the Sea,"
> the account of "Our Place in the Shadows,"
> a place to see "The Dawn of Life,"

as it is called. There is the original book and ancient writing, but the one who reads and assesses it has a hidden identity.[4] It takes a long performance and account to complete the lighting of all the sky-earth:

> the fourfold siding, fourfold cornering,
> measuring, fourfold staking,
> halving the cord, stretching the cord
> in the sky, on the earth,
> the four sides, the four corners,[5]
> by the Maker, Modeler,
> mother-father of life, of humankind,
> giver of breath, giver of heart,
> bearer, upbringer in the light that lasts
> of those born in the light, begotten in the light;
> worrier, knower of everything, whatever there is:
> sky-earth, lake-sea.

THIS IS THE ACCOUNT, here it is:

Now it still ripples, now it still murmurs, ripples, it still sighs, still hums, and it is empty under the sky.

Here follow the first words, the first eloquence:

There is not yet one person, one animal, bird, fish, crab, tree, rock, hollow, canyon, meadow, forest. Only the sky alone is there; the face of the earth is not clear. Only the sea alone is pooled under all the sky; there is nothing whatever gathered together. It is at rest; not a single thing stirs. It is held back, kept at rest under the sky.

---

2. All thirteen names refer to the Creator or to a company of creators, a designation applicable clearly to the first four names and *Sovereign Plumed Serpent. Heart of the Lake* and *Heart of the Sea* also apply, since the creators will later be described as "in the water," and somewhat obscurely, so does the last pair of names (*plate* and *bowl* may be read as "earth" and "sky," respectively). *Hunahpu Possum, Hunahpu Coyote, Great White Peccary,* and *Coati* refer specifically to the grandparents of the gods, usually called Xpiyacoc and Xmucane. 3. Four names for Xpiyacoc and Xmucane. 4. The hieroglyphic source (*Council Book*) was suppressed by missionaries; it was said to have been brought to Quiché in ancient times from the far side of a lagoon (*Sea*). The reader *hides his identity* to avoid the missionaries. 5. As though a farmer were measuring and staking a cornfield.

Whatever there is that might be is simply not there: only the pooled water, only the calm sea, only it alone is pooled.

Whatever might be is simply not there: only murmurs, ripples, in the dark, in the night. Only the Maker, Modeler alone, Sovereign Plumed Serpent, the Bearers, Begetters are in the water, a glittering light. They are there, they are enclosed in quetzal feathers, in blue-green.

Thus the name, "Plumed Serpent." They are great knowers, great thinkers in their very being.

And of course there is the sky, and there is also the Heart of Sky. This is the name of the god, as it is spoken.

And then came his word, he came here to the Sovereign Plumed Serpent, here in the blackness, in the early dawn. He spoke with the Sovereign Plumed Serpent, and they talked, then they thought, then they worried. They agreed with each other, they joined their words, their thoughts. Then it was clear, then they reached accord in the light, and then humanity was clear, when they conceived the growth, the generation of trees, of bushes, and the growth of life, of humankind, in the blackness, in the early dawn, all because of the Heart of Sky, named Hurricane. Thunderbolt Hurricane comes first, the second is Newborn Thunderbolt, and the third is Sudden Thunderbolt.[6]

So there were three of them, as Heart of Sky, who came to the Sovereign Plumed Serpent, when the dawn of life was conceived:

"How should the sowing be, and the dawning? Who is to be the provider, nurturer?"[7]

"Let it be this way, think about it: this water should be removed, emptied out for the formation of the earth's own plate and platform, then should come the sowing, the dawning of the sky-earth. But there will be no high days and no bright praise for our work, our design, until the rise of the human work, the human design," they said.

And then the earth arose because of them, it was simply their word that brought it forth. For the forming of the earth they said "Earth." It arose suddenly, just like a cloud, like a mist, now forming, unfolding. Then the mountains were separated from the water, all at once the great mountains came forth. By their genius alone, by their cutting edge[8] alone they carried out the conception of the mountain-plain, whose face grew instant groves of cypress and pine.

And the Plumed Serpent was pleased with this:

"It was good that you came, Heart of Sky, Hurricane, and Newborn Thunderbolt, Sudden Thunderbolt. Our work, our design will turn out well," they said.

And the earth was formed first, the mountain-plain. The channels of water were separated; their branches wound their ways among the mountains. The waters were divided when the great mountains appeared.

Such was the formation of the earth when it was brought forth by the

---

6. Alternate names for Heart of Sky, the deity who cooperates with Sovereign Plumed Serpent. The triple naming adapts the Christian trinity to native theology, perhaps more in the spirit of defiant preemption than of conciliation.   7. That is, humanity, which alone is capable of *nurturing* the gods with sacrifices.
8. . . . Refers to the cutting of flesh with a knife. . . . In the present context, it implies that "the mountains were separated from the water" through an act resembling the extraction of the heart (or other organs) from a sacrifice [Translator's note].

Heart of Sky, Heart of Earth, as they are called, since they were the first to think of it. The sky was set apart, and the earth was set apart in the midst of the waters.

Such was their plan when they thought, when they worried about the completion of their work.[9]

FROM PART 2

[The Twins Defeat Seven Macaw]

HERE IS THE BEGINNING OF THE DEFEAT AND DESTRUCTION OF THE DAY OF SEVEN MACAW by the two boys, the first named Hunahpu and the second named Xbalanque.[1] Being gods, the two of them saw evil in his attempt at self-magnification before the Heart of Sky.

*   *   *

This is the great tree of Seven Macaw, a nance,[2] and this is the food of Seven Macaw. In order to eat the fruit of the nance he goes up the tree every day. Since Hunahpu and Xbalanque have seen where he feeds, they are now hiding beneath the tree of Seven Macaw, they are keeping quiet here, the two boys are in the leaves of the tree.

And when Seven Macaw arrived, perching over his meal, the nance, it was then that he was shot by Hunahpu. The blowgun shot went right to his jaw, breaking his mouth. Then he went up over the tree and fell flat on the ground. Suddenly Hunahpu appeared, running. He set out to grab him, but actually it was the arm of Hunahpu that was seized by Seven Macaw. He yanked it straight back, he bent it back at the shoulder. Then Seven Macaw tore it right out of Hunahpu. Even so, the boys did well: the first round was not their defeat by Seven Macaw.

And when Seven Macaw had taken the arm of Hunahpu, he went home. Holding his jaw very carefully, he arrived:

"What have you got there?" said Chimalmat, the wife of Seven Macaw.

"What is it but those two tricksters! They've shot me, they've dislocated my jaw.[3] All my teeth are just loose, now they ache. But once what I've got is over the fire—hanging there, dangling over the fire—then they can just come and get it. They're real tricksters!" said Seven Macaw, then he hung up the arm of Hunahpu.

Meanwhile Hunahpu and Xbalanque were thinking. And then they invoked a grandfather, a truly white-haired grandfather, and a grandmother, a truly humble grandmother—just bent-over, elderly people. Great White Peccary is the name of the grandfather, and Great White Coati is the name of the grandmother.[4] The boys said to the grandmother and grandfather:

"Please travel with us when we go to get our arm from Seven Macaw; we'll just follow right behind you. You'll tell him:

9. That is, the creation of humans; an account of the first three, unsuccessful, attempts at creating humans occupies the remainder of Part 1.   1. First mention of the twin hero gods (their origin is recounted in Part 3). Here they confront the false god Seven Macaw, who has arisen during the time of primordial darkness, boasting, "My eyes are of metal; my teeth just glitter with jewels, and turquoise as well. . . . I am like the sun and the moon." Note that all the characters in Parts 1, 2, and 3 are supernatural; humans are not created until Part 4.   2. A pickle tree (*Byrsonima crassifolia*).   3. This is the origin of the way a macaw's beak looks, with a huge upper mandible and a small, retreating lower one [Translator's note].   4. Animal names of the divine grandparents, Xpiyacoc and Xmucane, who are also the twins' genealogical grandparents.

'Do forgive us our grandchildren, who travel with us. Their mother and father are dead, and so they follow along there, behind us. Perhaps we should give them away, since all we do is pull worms out of teeth.' So we'll seem like children to Seven Macaw, even though *we're* giving *you* the instructions," the two boys told them.

"Very well," they replied.

After that they approached the place where Seven Macaw was in front of his home. When the grandmother and grandfather passed by, the two boys were romping along behind them. When they passed below the lord's house, Seven Macaw was yelling his mouth off because of his teeth. And when Seven Macaw saw the grandfather and grandmother traveling with them:

"Where are you headed, our grandfather?" said the lord.

"We're just making our living, your lordship," they replied.

"Why are you working for a living? Aren't those your children traveling with you?"

"No, they're not, your lordship. They're our grandchildren, our descendants, but it is nevertheless *we* who take pity on *them*. The bit of food they get is the portion we give them, your lordship," replied the grandmother and grandfather. Since the lord is getting done in by the pain in his teeth, it is only with great effort that he speaks again:

"I implore you, please take pity on me! What sweets can you make, what poisons[5] can you cure?" said the lord.

"We just pull the worms out of teeth, and we just cure eyes. We just set bones, your lordship," they replied.

"Very well, please cure my teeth. They really ache, every day. It's insufferable! I get no sleep because of them—and my eyes. They just shot me, those two tricksters! Ever since it started I haven't eaten because of it. Therefore take pity on me! Perhaps it's because my teeth are loose now."

"Very well, your lordship. It's a worm, gnawing at the bone.[6] It's merely a matter of putting in a replacement and taking the teeth out, sir."

"But perhaps it's not good for my teeth to come out—since I am, after all, a lord. My finery is in my teeth—and my eyes."

"But then we'll put in a replacement. Ground bone will be put back in." And this is the "ground bone": it's only white corn.

"Very well. Yank them out! Give me some help here!" he replied.

And when the teeth of Seven Macaw came out, it was only white corn that went in as a replacement for his teeth—just a coating shining white, that corn in his mouth. His face fell at once, he no longer looked like a lord. The last of his teeth came out, the jewels that had stood out blue from his mouth.

And when the eyes of Seven Macaw were cured, he was plucked around the eyes, the last of his metal came off.[7] Still he felt no pain; he just looked on while the last of his greatness left him. It was just as Hunahpu and Xbalanque had intended.

And when Seven Macaw died, Hunahpu got back his arm. And Chimalmat, the wife of Seven Macaw, also died.

Such was the loss of the riches of Seven Macaw: only the doctors got the

---

5. Play on words as *qui* is translated as both "sweet" and "poison."   6. The present-day Quiché retain the notion that a toothache is caused by a worm gnawing at the bone [Translator's note].   7. This is clearly meant to be the origin of the large white and completely featherless eye patches and very small eyes of the scarlet macaw [Translator's note].

jewels and gems that had made him arrogant, here on the face of the earth. The genius of the grandmother, the genius of the grandfather did its work when they took back their arm: it was implanted and the break got well again. Just as they had wished the death of Seven Macaw, so they brought it about. They had seen evil in his self-magnification.

After this the two boys went on again. What they did was simply the word of the Heart of Sky.

FROM PART 3

[Victory over the Underworld]

AND NOW WE SHALL NAME THE NAME OF THE FATHER OF HUNAHPU AND XBALANQUE. Let's drink to him, and let's just drink to the telling and accounting of the begetting of Hunahpu and Xbalanque. We shall tell just half of it, just a part of the account of their father. Here follows the account.

These are the names: One Hunahpu and Seven Hunahpu,[8] as they are called.

*　　*　　*

AND ONE AND SEVEN HUNAHPU WENT INSIDE DARK HOUSE.[9]

And then their torch was brought, only one torch, already lit, sent by One and Seven Death, along with a cigar for each of them, also already lit, sent by the lords. When these were brought to One and Seven Hunahpu they were cowering, here in the dark. When the bearer of their torch and cigars arrived, the torch was bright as it entered; their torch and both of their cigars were burning. The bearer spoke:

" 'They must be sure to return them in the morning—not finished, but just as they look now. They must return them intact,' the lords say to you," they were told, and they were defeated. They finished the torch and they finished the cigars that had been brought to them.

And Xibalba is packed with tests, heaps and piles of tests.

This is the first one: the Dark House, with darkness alone inside.

And the second is named Rattling House, heavy with cold inside, whistling with drafts, clattering with hail. A deep chill comes inside here.

And the third is named Jaguar House, with jaguars alone inside, jostling one another, crowding together, with gnashing teeth. They're scratching around; these jaguars are shut inside the house.

Bat House is the name of the fourth test, with bats alone inside the house, squeaking, shrieking, darting through the house. The bats are shut inside; they can't get out.

And the fifth is named Razor House, with blades alone inside. The blades are moving back and forth, ripping, slashing through the house.

These are the first tests of Xibalba, but One and Seven Hunahpu never entered into them, except for the one named earlier, the specified test house.

---

8. Twin sons of Xpiyacoc and Xmucane; the elder of these twins, One Hunahpu, will become the father of Hunahpu and Xbalanque. "As for Seven Hunahpu," according to the text, "he has no wife. He's just a partner and just secondary; he just remains a boy."　　9. The first of the "test" houses in Xibalba (the underworld) to which One and Seven Hunahpu, avid ballplayers, have been lured by the underworld lords, One and Seven Death; the lords have promised them a challenging ball game. The Mesoamerican ball game, remotely comparable to both basketball and soccer, was played on a rectangular court, using a ball of native rubber.

And when One and Seven Hunahpu went back before One and Seven Death, they were asked:

"Where are my cigars? What of my torch? They were brought to you last night!"

"We finished them, your lordship."

"Very well. This very day, your day is finished, you will die, you will disappear, and we shall break you off. Here you will hide your faces: you are to be sacrificed!" said One and Seven Death.

And then they were sacrificed and buried. They were buried at the Place of Ball Game Sacrifice,[1] as it is called. The head of One Hunahpu was cut off; only his body was buried with his younger brother.

"Put his head in the fork of the tree that stands by the road," said One and Seven Death.

And when his head was put in the fork of the tree, the tree bore fruit. It would not have had any fruit, had not the head of One Hunahpu been put in the fork of the tree.

This is the calabash tree, as we call it today, or "the skull of One Hunahpu," as it is said.

And then One and Seven Death were amazed at the fruit of the tree. The fruit grows out everywhere, and it isn't clear where the head of One Hunahpu is; now it looks just the way the calabashes look. All the Xibalbans see this, when they come to look.

The state of the tree loomed large in their thoughts, because it came about at the same time the head of One Hunahpu was put in the fork. The Xibalbans said among themselves:

"No one is to pick the fruit, nor is anyone to go beneath the tree," they said. They restricted themselves; all of Xibalba held back.

It isn't clear which is the head of One Hunahpu; now it's exactly the same as the fruit of the tree. Calabash came to be its name, and much was said about it. A maiden heard about it, and here we shall tell of her arrival.

AND HERE IS THE ACCOUNT OF A MAIDEN, the daughter of a lord named Blood Gatherer.[2]

And this is when a maiden heard of it, the daughter of a lord. Blood Gatherer is the name of her father, and Blood Moon is the name of the maiden.

And when he heard the account of the fruit of the tree, her father retold it. And she was amazed at the account:

"I'm not acquainted with that tree they talk about. ' "Its fruit is truly sweet!" they say,' I hear," she said.

Next, she went all alone and arrived where the tree stood. It stood at the Place of Ball Game Sacrifice:

"What? Well! What's the fruit of this tree? Shouldn't this tree bear something sweet? They shouldn't die, they shouldn't be wasted. Should I pick one?" said the maiden.

And then the bone spoke; it was here in the fork of the tree:

"Why do you want a mere bone, a round thing in the branches of a tree?" said the head of One Hunahpu when it spoke to the maiden. "You don't want it," she was told.

---

1. Probably not a place name, but rather a name for the altar where losing ball players were sacrificed [Translator's note].   2. Fourth-ranking lord of Xibalba, whose commission is to draw blood from people.

"I do want it," said the maiden.

"Very well. Stretch out your right hand here, so I can see it," said the bone.

"Yes," said the maiden. She stretched out her right hand, up there in front of the bone.

And then the bone spit out its saliva, which landed squarely in the hand of the maiden.

And then she looked in her hand, she inspected it right away, but the bone's saliva wasn't in her hand.

"It is just a sign I have given you, my saliva, my spittle. This, my head, has nothing on it—just bone, nothing of meat. It's just the same with the head of a great lord: it's just the flesh that makes his face look good. And when he dies, people get frightened by his bones. After that, his son is like his saliva, his spittle, in his being, whether it be the son of a lord or the son of a craftsman, an orator. The father does not disappear, but goes on being fulfilled. Neither dimmed nor destroyed is the face of a lord, a warrior, crafts-man, orator. Rather, he will leave his daughters and sons. So it is that I have done likewise through you. Now go up there on the face of the earth; you will not die. Keep the word. So be it," said the head of One and Seven Hunahpu—they were of one mind when they did it.

This was the word Hurricane, Newborn Thunderbolt, Sudden Thunder-bolt had given them. In the same way, by the time the maiden returned to her home, she had been given many instructions. Right away something was generated in her belly, from the saliva alone, and this was the generation of Hunahpu and Xbalanque.

And when the maiden got home and six months had passed, she was found out by her father. Blood Gatherer is the name of her father.

* * *

AND THEY CAME TO THE LORDS.[3] Feigning great humility, they bowed their heads all the way to the ground when they arrived. They brought themselves low, doubled over, flattened out, down to the rags, to the tatters. They really looked like vagabonds when they arrived.

So then they were asked what their mountain[4] and tribe were, and they were also asked about their mother and father:

"Where do you come from?" they were asked.

"We've never known, lord. We don't know the identity of our mother and father. We must've been small when they died," was all they said. They didn't give any names.

"Very well. Please entertain us, then. What do you want us to give you in payment?" they were asked.

"Well, we don't want anything. To tell the truth, we're afraid," they told the lord.

"Don't be afraid. Don't be ashamed. Just dance this way: first you'll dance to sacrifice yourselves, you'll set fire to my house after that, you'll act out all the things you know. We want to be entertained. This is our heart's desire,

---

3. Forced to flee the underworld the maiden (Blood Moon) finds refuge on earth with Xmucane. There she gives birth to the twins, who, like their father and uncle, become ballplayers and are enticed to the underworld. Surviving the Dark House and other tests, they disguise themselves as vagabonds and earn a reputation as clever entertainers among the denizens of Xibalba; as such they are summoned to entertain the high lords.   4. A metonym for almost any settlement, but especially a fortified town or citadel, located on a defensible elevation [Translator's note].

the reason you had to be sent for, dear vagabonds. We'll give you payment," they were told.

So then they began their songs and dances, and then all the Xibalbans arrived, the spectators crowded the floor, and they danced everything: they danced the Weasel, they danced the Poorwill,[5] they danced the Armadillo. Then the lord said to them:

"Sacrifice my dog, then bring him back to life again," they were told.

"Yes," they said.

> When they sacrificed the dog
>   he then came back to life.
> And that dog was really happy
>   when he came back to life.
> Back and forth he wagged his tail
>   when he came back to life.

And the lord said to them:

"Well, you have yet to set my home on fire," they were told next, so then they set fire to the home of the lord. The house was packed with all the lords, but they were not burned. They quickly fixed it back again, lest the house of One Death be consumed all at once, and all the lords were amazed, and they went on dancing this way. They were overjoyed.

And then they were asked by the lord:

"You have yet to kill a person! Make a sacrifice without death!" they were told.

"Very well," they said.

And then they took hold of a human sacrifice.

And they held up a human heart on high.

And they showed its roundness to the lords.

And now One and Seven Death admired it, and now that person was brought right back to life. His heart was overjoyed when he came back to life, and the lords were amazed:

"Sacrifice yet again, even do it to yourselves! Let's see it! At heart, that's the dance we really want from you," the lords said now.

"Very well, lord," they replied, and then they sacrificed themselves.

AND THIS IS THE SACRIFICE OF HUNAHPU BY XBALANQUE. One by one his legs, his arms were spread wide. His head came off, rolled far away outside. His heart, dug out, was smothered in a leaf,[6] and all the Xibalbans went crazy at the sight.

So now, only one of them was dancing there: Xbalanque.

"Get up!" he said, and Hunahpu came back to life. The two of them were overjoyed at this—and likewise the lords rejoiced, as if they were doing it themselves. One and Seven Death were as glad at heart as if they themselves were actually doing the dance.

And then the hearts of the lords were filled with longing, with yearning for the dance of little Hunahpu and Xbalanque, so then came these words from One and Seven Death:

---

5. The goatsucker. The dances apparently were imitations of these animals and birds.   6. As a tamale is wrapped. In the typical Mesoamerican heart sacrifice, the victim's arms and legs were stretched wide and the heart was excised and offered to a deity.

"Do it to us! Sacrifice us!" they said. "Sacrifice both of us!" said One and Seven Death to Hunahpu and Xbalanque.

"Very well. You ought to come back to life. What is death to you?[7] And aren't we making you happy, along with the vassals of your domain?" they told the lords.

And this one was the first to be sacrificed: the lord at the very top, the one whose name is One Death, the ruler of Xibalba.

And with One Death dead, the next to be taken was Seven Death. They did not come back to life.

And then the Xibalbans were getting up to leave, those who had seen the lords die. They underwent heart sacrifice there, and the heart sacrifice was performed on the two lords only for the purpose of destroying them.

As soon as they had killed the one lord without bringing him back to life, the other lord had been meek and tearful before the dancers. He didn't consent, he didn't accept it:

"Take pity on me!" he said when he realized. All their vassals took the road to the great canyon, in one single mass they filled up the deep abyss. So they piled up there and gathered together, countless ants, tumbling down into the canyon, as if they were being herded there. And when they arrived, they all bent low in surrender, they arrived meek and tearful.

Such was the defeat of the rulers of Xibalba. The boys accomplished it only through wonders, only through self-transformation.

*   *   *

Such was the beginning of their disappearance and the denial of their worship.

> Their ancient day was not a great one,
> these ancient people only wanted conflict,
> their ancient names are not really divine,
> but fearful is the ancient evil of their faces.

> They are makers of enemies, users of owls,[8]
> they are inciters to wrongs and violence,
> they are masters of hidden intentions as well,
> they are black and white,[9]
> masters of stupidity, masters of perplexity,

as it is said. By putting on appearances they cause dismay.

Such was the loss of their greatness and brilliance. Their domain did not return to greatness. This was accomplished by little Hunahpu and Xbalanque.

FROM PART 4

[Origin of Humanity, First Dawn]

AND HERE IS THE BEGINNING OF THE CONCEPTION OF HUMANS, and of the search for the ingredients of the human body. So they spoke, the Bearer, Begetter, the Makers, Modelers named Sovereign Plumed Serpent:

"The dawn has approached, preparations have been made, and morning

---

7. Evident sarcasm. 8. The lords had used owls as messengers to lure the ballplayers to Xibalba.
9. Contradictory, duplicitous.

has come for the provider, nurturer, born in the light, begotten in the light. Morning has come for humankind, for the people of the face of the earth," they said. It all came together as they went on thinking in the darkness, in the night, as they searched and they sifted, they thought and they wondered.

And here their thoughts came out in clear light. They sought and discovered what was needed for human flesh. It was only a short while before the sun, moon, and stars were to appear above the Makers and Modelers. Split Place, Bitter Water Place is the name: the yellow corn, white corn came from there.

And these are the names of the animals who brought the food: fox, coyote, parrot, crow. There were four animals who brought the news of the ears of yellow corn and white corn. They were coming from over there at Split Place, they showed the way to the split.[1]

And this was when they found the staple foods.

And these were the ingredients for the flesh of the human work, the human design, and the water was for the blood. It became human blood, and corn was also used by the Bearer, Begetter.

And so they were happy over the provisions of the good mountain, filled with sweet things, thick with yellow corn, white corn, and thick with pataxte and cacao, countless zapotes, anonas, jocotes, nances, matasanos,[2] sweets— the rich foods filling up the citadel named Split Place, Bitter Water Place. All the edible fruits were there: small staples, great staples, small plants, great plants. The way was shown by the animals.

And then the yellow corn and white corn were ground, and Xmucane did the grinding nine times. Corn was used, along with the water she rinsed her hands with, for the creation of grease; it became human fat when it was worked by the Bearer, Begetter, Sovereign Plumed Serpent, as they are called.

After that, they put it into words:

> the making, the modeling of our first mother-father,
> with yellow corn, white corn alone for the flesh,
> food alone for the human legs and arms,
> for our first fathers, the four human works.

It was staples alone that made up their flesh.

THESE ARE THE NAMES OF THE FIRST PEOPLE WHO WERE MADE AND MODELED.

> This is the first person: Jaguar Quitze.
> And now the second: Jaguar Night.
> And now the third: Not Right Now.
> And the fourth: Dark Jaguar.[3]

And these are the names of our first mother-fathers.[4] They were simply made and modeled, it is said; they had no mother and no father. We have named the men by themselves. No woman gave birth to them, nor were they

---

1. In the widespread Mesoamerican story of the discovery of corn, one or more animals reveal that corn and other foods are hidden within a rock or a mountain, accessible through a cleft; in some versions the mountain is split apart by lightning. 2. Quincelike fruits of the tree *Casimiroa edulis*. Pataxte (*Theobroma bicolor*) is a species of cacao that is inferior to cacao proper (*T. cacao*). Zapotes are fruits of the sapota tree (*Lucuma mammosa*). Anonas are custard apples (genus *Anona*). Jocotes are yellow plumlike fruits of the tree *Spondias purpurea*. 3. The four original Quiché males. 4. That is, parents, although only the first three founded lineages; Dark Jaguar had no son.

begotten by the builder, sculptor, Bearer, Begetter. By sacrifice alone, by genius alone they were made, they were modeled by the Maker, Modeler, Bearer, Begetter, Sovereign Plumed Serpent. And when they came to fruition, they came out human:

They talked and they made words.

They looked and they listened.

They walked, they worked.

They were good people, handsome, with looks of the male kind. Thoughts came into existence and they gazed; their vision came all at once. Perfectly they saw, perfectly they knew everything under the sky, whenever they looked. The moment they turned around and looked around in the sky, on the earth, everything was seen without any obstruction. They didn't have to walk around before they could see what was under the sky; they just stayed where they were.

As they looked, their knowledge became intense. Their sight passed through trees, through rocks, through lakes, through seas, through mountains, through plains. Jaguar Quitze, Jaguar Night, Not Right Now, and Dark Jaguar were truly gifted people.

And then they were asked by the builder and mason:

"What do you know about your being? Don't you look, don't you listen? Isn't your speech good, and your walk? So you must look, to see out under the sky. Don't you see the mountain-plain clearly? So try it," they were told.

And then they saw everything under the sky perfectly. After that, they thanked the Maker, Modeler:

> "Truly now,
> double thanks, triple thanks
> that we've been formed, we've been given
> our mouths, our faces,
> we speak, we listen,
> we wonder, we move,
> our knowledge is good, we've understood
> what is far and near,
> and we've seen what is great and small
> under the sky, on the earth.
> Thanks to you we've been formed,
> we've come to be made and modeled,
> our grandmother, our grandfather,"

they said when they gave thanks for having been made and modeled. They understood everything perfectly, they sighted the four sides, the four corners in the sky, on the earth, and this didn't sound good to the builder and sculptor:

"What our works and designs have said is no good:

'We have understood everything, great and small,' they say." And so the Bearer, Begetter took back their knowledge:

"What should we do with them now? Their vision should at least reach nearby, they should see at least a small part of the face of the earth, but what they're saying isn't good. Aren't they merely 'works' and 'designs' in their very names? Yet they'll become as great as gods, unless they procreate, proliferate at the sowing, the dawning, unless they increase."

"Let it be this way: now we'll take them apart just a little, that's what we need. What we've found out isn't good. Their deeds would become equal to ours, just because their knowledge reaches so far. They see everything," so said

> the Heart of Sky, Hurricane,
> Newborn Thunderbolt, Sudden Thunderbolt,
> Sovereign Plumed Serpent,
> Bearer, Begetter,
> Xpiyacoc, Xmucane,
> Maker, Modeler,

as they are called. And when they changed the nature of their works, their designs, it was enough that the eyes be marred by the Heart of Sky. They were blinded as the face of a mirror is breathed upon. Their vision flickered. Now it was only from close up that they could see what was there with any clarity.

And such was the loss of the means of understanding, along with the means of knowing everything, by the four humans. The root was implanted.

And such was the making, modeling of our first grandfather, our father, by the Heart of Sky, Heart of Earth.

AND THEN THEIR WIVES AND WOMEN CAME INTO BEING. Again, the same gods thought of it. It was as if they were asleep when they received them, truly beautiful women were there with Jaguar Quitze, Jaguar Night, Not Right Now, and Dark Jaguar. With their women there they really came alive. Right away they were happy at heart again, because of their wives.

Red Sea Turtle is the name of the wife of Jaguar Quitze.

Prawn House is the name of the wife of Jaguar Night.

Water Hummingbird is the name of the wife of Not Right Now.

Macaw House is the name of the wife of Dark Jaguar.

So these are the names of their wives, who became ladies of rank, giving birth to the people of the tribes, small and great.

*   *   *

AND HERE IS THE DAWNING AND SHOWING OF THE SUN, MOON, AND STARS. And Jaguar Quitze, Jaguar Night, Not Right Now, and Dark Jaguar were overjoyed when they saw the sun carrier.[5] It came up first. It looked brilliant when it came up, since it was ahead of the sun.

After that they unwrapped their copal[6] incense, which came from the east, and there was triumph in their hearts when they unwrapped it. They gave their heartfelt thanks with three kinds at once:

Mixtam Copal is the name of the copal brought by Jaguar Quitze.

Cauiztan Copal, next, is the name of the copal brought by Jaguar Night.

Godly Copal, as the next one is called, was brought by Not Right Now.

The three of them had their copal, and this is what they burned as they incensed the direction of the rising sun. They were crying sweetly as they shook their burning copal,[7] the precious copal.

---

5. The morning star.   6. Resin used as incense.   7. Note that the Mesoamerican pottery censer must be shaken or swayed back and forth to keep the incense burning.

After that they cried because they had yet to see and yet to witness the birth of the sun.

And then, when the sun came up, the animals, small and great, were happy. They all came up from the rivers and canyons; they waited on all the mountain peaks. Together they looked toward the place where the sun came out.

So then the puma and jaguar cried out, but the first to cry out was a bird, the parrot by name. All the animals were truly happy. The eagle, the white vulture, small birds, great birds spread their wings, and the penitents and sacrificers knelt down.

FROM PART 5

[Prayer for Future Generations]

AND THIS IS THE CRY OF THEIR HEARTS, HERE IT IS:

> "Wait! On this blessed day,
> thou Hurricane, thou Heart of the Sky-Earth,
> thou giver of ripeness and freshness,
> and thou giver of daughters and sons,
> spread thy stain, spill thy drops
> of green and yellow;[8]
> give life and beginning
> to those I bear and beget,
> that they might multiply and grow,
> nurturing and providing for thee,
> calling to thee along the roads and paths,
> on rivers, in canyons,
> beneath the trees and bushes;
> give them their daughters and sons.
>
> "May there be no blame, obstacle, want or misery;
> let no deceiver come behind or before them,
> may they neither be snared nor wounded,
> nor seduced, nor burned,
> nor diverted below the road nor above it;
> may they neither fall over backward nor stumble;
> keep them on the Green Road, the Green Path.
>
> "May there be no blame or barrier for them
> through any secrets or sorcery of thine;
> may thy nurturers and providers be good
> before thy mouth and thy face,
> thou, Heart of Sky; thou, Heart of Earth;
> thou, Bundle of Flames;[9]
> and thou, Tohil, Auilix, Hacauitz,[1]
> under the sky, on the earth,
> the four sides, the four corners;
> may there be only light, only continuity within,
> before thy mouth and thy face, thou god."

---

8. The imagery, denoting human offspring, alludes to semen and plant growth.   9. A sacred relic left to the Quiché lords by Jaguar Quitze; like the sacred bundles of the North American peoples, a cloth-wrapped ark with mysterious contents [Translator's note].   1. Patron deities of the Quiché lineages.

A Note on Translation

Reading literature in translation is a pleasure on which it is fruitless to frown. The purist may insist that we ought always read in the original languages, and we know ideally that this is true. But it is a counsel of perfection, quite impractical even for the purist, since no one in a lifetime can master all the languages whose literatures it would be a joy to explore. Master languages as fast as we may, we shall always have to read to some extent in translation, and this means we must be alert to what we are about: if in reading a work of literature in translation we are not reading the "original," what precisely are we reading? This is a question of great complexity, to which justice cannot be done in a brief note, but the following sketch of some of the considerations may be helpful.

One of the memorable scenes of ancient literature is the meeting of Hector and Andromache in Book VI of Homer's *Iliad*. Hector, leader and mainstay of the armies defending Troy, is implored by his wife Andromache to withdraw within the city walls and carry on the defense from there, where his life will not be con stantly at hazard. In Homer's text her opening words to him are these: δαιμόνιε, φθίσει σε τὸ σὸν μένος (daimonie, phthisei se to son menos). How should they be translated into English?

Here is how they have actually been translated into English by capable translators, at various periods, in verse and prose:

1. George Chapman, 1598:

> O noblest in desire,
> Thy mind, inflamed with others' good, will set thy self on fire.

2. John Dryden, 1693:

> Thy dauntless heart (which I foresee too late),
> Too daring man, will urge thee to thy fate.

3. Alexander Pope, 1715:

> Too daring Prince! . . .
> For sure such courage length of life denies,
> And thou must fall, thy virtue's sacrifice.

4. William Cowper, 1791:

> Thy own great courage will cut short thy days,
> My noble Hector. . .

5. Lang, Leaf, and Myers, 1883 (prose):

> Dear my lord, this thy hardihood will undo thee. . . .

6. A. T. Murray, 1924 (prose):

> Ah, my husband, this prowess of thine will be thy doom. . . .

7. E. V. Rieu, 1950 (prose):

A1

"Hector," she said, "you are possessed. This bravery of yours will be your end."

8. I. A. Richards, 1950 (prose):

"Strange man," she said, "your courage will be your destruction."

9. Richmond Lattimore, 1951:

Dearest,
Your own great strength will be your death. . . .

10. Robert Fitzgerald, 1979:

O my wild one, your bravery will be
Your own undoing!

11. Robert Fagles, 1990:

reckless one,
Your own fiery courage will destroy you!

From these strikingly different renderings of the same six words, certain facts about the nature of translation begin to emerge. We notice, for one thing, that Homer's word μένος (menos) is diversified by the translators into "mind," "dauntless heart," "such courage," "great courage," "hardihood," "prowess," "bravery," "courage," "great strength," "bravery," and "fiery courage." The word has in fact all these possibilities. Used of things, it normally means "force"; of animals, "fierceness" or "brute strength" or (in the case of horses) "mettle"; of men and women, "passion" or "spirit" or even "purpose." Homer's application of it in the present case points our attention equally—whatever particular sense we may imagine Andromache to have uppermost—to Hector's force, strength, fierceness in battle, spirited heart and mind. But since English has no matching term of like inclusiveness, the passage as the translators give it to us reflects this lack and we find one attribute singled out to the exclusion of the rest.

Here then is the first and most crucial fact about any work of literature read in translation. It cannot escape the linguistic characteristics of the language into which it is turned: the grammatical, syntactical, lexical, and phonetic boundaries that constitute collectively the individuality or "genius" of that language. A Greek play or a Russian novel in English will be governed first of all by the resources of the English language, resources that are certain to be in every instance very different, as the efforts with μένος show, from those of the original.

Turning from μένος to δαιμόνιε (daimonie) in Homer's clause, we encounter a second crucial fact about translations. Nobody knows exactly what shade of meaning δαιμόνιε had for Homer. In later writers the word normally suggests divinity, something miraculous, wondrous; but in Homer it appears as a vocative of address for both chieftain and commoner, man and wife. The coloring one gives it must therefore be determined either by the way one thinks a Greek wife of Homer's era might actually address her husband (a subject on which we have no information whatever) or in the way one thinks it suitable for a hero's wife to address her husband in an epic poem, that is to say, a highly stylized and formal work. In general, the translators of our century will be seen to have abandoned formality to stress the intimacy; the wifeliness; and, especially in Lattimore's case, a certain chiding tenderness, in Andromache's appeal: (6) "Ah, my husband," (7) "Hector" (with perhaps a hint, in "you are possessed," of the alarmed distaste with which wives have so often viewed their husbands' bellicose moods), (8) "Strange man," (9) "Dearest," (10) "O my wild one" (mixing an almost motherly admiration with reproach and concern), and (11) "reckless one." On the other hand, the older translators have obviously removed Andromache to an epic or heroic distance from her beloved, whence she sees and kindles to his selfless courage, acknowledging, even in the moment of pleading with him to be otherwise, his moral grandeur and the tragic destiny this too certainly implies: (1) "O noblest in desire, . . . inflamed by others' good"; (2) "Thy dauntless heart (which I foresee too late), / Too daring man"; (3) "Too daring Prince! . . . / And thou must fall, thy virtue's sacrifice"; (4) "My noble Hector." Even the less specific "Dear my lord" of Lang, Leaf, and Myers looks in the same direction because of its echo of the speech of countless Shakespearean men and women who have shared this powerful moral sense: "Dear my lord, make me acquainted with your cause of grief"; "Perseverance, dear my lord, keeps honor bright"; etc.

The fact about translation that emerges from all this is that just as the translated work reflects the individuality of the language it is turned into, so it reflects the individuality of the age in which it is made, and the age will permeate it everywhere like yeast in dough. We think of one kind of permeation when we think of the governing verse forms and attitudes toward verse at a given epoch. In Chapman's time, experiments seeking an "heroic" verse form for English were widespread, and accordingly he tries a "fourteener" couplet (two rhymed lines of seven stresses each) in his *Iliad* and a pentameter couplet in his *Odyssey.* When Dryden and Pope wrote, a closed pentameter couplet had become established as the heroic form par excellence. By Cowper's day, thanks largely to the prestige of *Paradise Lost,* the couplet had gone out of fashion for narrative poetry in favor of blank verse. Our age, inclining to prose and in verse to proselike informalities and relaxations, has, predictably, produced half a dozen excellent prose translations of the *Iliad* but only three in verse (by Fagles, Lattimore, and Fitzgerald), all relying on rhythms that are much of the time closer to the verse of William Carlos Williams and some of the prose of novelists like Faulkner than to the swift firm tread of Homer's Greek. For if it is true that what we translate from a given work is what, wearing the spectacles of our time, we see in it, it is also true that we see in it what we have the power to translate.

Of course, there are other effects of the translator's epoch on a translation besides those exercised by contemporary taste in verse and verse forms. Chapman writes in a great age of poetic metaphor and, therefore, almost instinctively translates his understanding of Homer's verb φθίνει (phthisei, "to cause to wane, consume, waste, pine") into metaphorical terms of flame, presenting his Hector to us as a man of burning generosity who will be consumed by his very ardor. This is a conception rooted in large part in the psychology of the Elizabethans, who had the habit of speaking of the soul as "fire," of one of the four temperaments as "fiery," of even the more material bodily processes, like digestion, as if they were carried on by the heat of fire ("concoction," "decoction"). It is rooted too in that characteristic Renaissance élan so unforgettably expressed in characters such as Tamburlaine and Dr. Faustus, the former of whom exclaims to the stars above:

> . . . I, the chiefest lamp of all the earth,
> First rising in the East with mild aspect,
> But fixèd now in the meridian line,
> Will send up fire to your turning spheres,
> And cause the sun to borrow light of you. . . .

Pope and Dryden, by contrast, write to audiences for whom strong metaphor has become suspect. They therefore reject the fire image (which we must recall is not present in the Greek) in favor of a form of speech more congenial to their age, the *sententia* or aphorism, and give it extra vitality by making it the scene of a miniature drama: in Dryden's case, the hero's dauntless heart "urges" him (in the double sense of physical as well as moral pressure) to his fate; in Pope's, the hero's courage, like a judge, "denies" continuance of life, with the consequence that he "falls"—and here Pope's second line suggests analogy to the sacrificial animal—the victim of his own essential nature, of what he is.

To pose even more graphically the pressures that a translator's period brings, consider the following lines from Hector's reply to Andromache's appeal that he with-draw, first in Chapman's Elizabethan version, then in Lattimore's twentieth-century one:

Chapman, 1598:

> The spirit I did first breathe
> Did never teach me that—much less since the contempt of death
> Was settled in me, and my mind knew what a Worthy was,
> Whose office is to lead in fight and give no danger pass
> Without improvement. In this fire must Hector's trial shine.
> Here must his country, father, friends be in him made divine.

Lattimore, 1951:

> and the spirit will not let me, since I have learned to be valiant
> and to fight always among the foremost ranks of the Trojans,
> winning for my own self great glory, and for my father.

If one may exaggerate to make a necessary point, the world of Henry V and Othello suddenly gives way here to our own, a world whose discomfort with any form of heroic self-assertion is remarkably mirrored in the burial of Homer's key terms (*spirit, valiant, fight, foremost, glory*)—five out of twenty-two words in the original, five out of thirty-six in the translation—in a cushioning huddle of harmless sounds.

Besides the two factors so far mentioned (language and period) as affecting the character of a translation, there is inevitably a third—the translator, with a particular degree of talent; a personal way of regarding the work to be translated; a special hierarchy of values, moral, aesthetic, metaphysical (which may or may not be summed up in a "worldview"); and a unique style or lack of it. But this influence all readers are likely to bear in mind, and it needs no laboring here. That, for example, two translators of Hamlet, one a Freudian, the other a Jungian, will produce impressively different translations is obvious from the fact that when Freudian and Jungian argue about the play in English they often seem to have different plays in mind.

We can now return to the question from which we started. After all allowances have been made for language, age, and individual translator, is anything of the original left? What, in short, does the reader of translations read? Let it be said at once that in utility prose—prose whose function is mainly referential—the reader who reads a translation reads everything that matters. "Nicht Rauchen," "Défense de Fumer," and "No Smoking," posted in a railway car, make their point, and the differences between them in sound and form have no significance for us in that context. Since the prose of a treatise and of most fiction is preponderantly referential, we rightly feel, when we have paid close attention to Cervantes or Montaigne or Machiavelli or Tolstoy in a good English translation, that we have had roughly the same experience as a native Spaniard, Frenchman, Italian, or Russian. But *roughly* is the correct word; for good prose points iconically *to* itself as well as referentially beyond itself, and everything that it points to in itself in the original (rhythms, sounds, idioms, wordplay, etc.) must alter radically in being translated. The best analogy is to imagine a Van Gogh painting reproduced in the medium of tempera, etching, or engraving: the "picture" remains, but the intricate interanimation of volumes with colorings with brushstrokes has disappeared.

When we move on to poetry, even in its longer narrative and dramatic forms—plays like *Oedipus*, poems like the *Iliad* or the *Divine Comedy*—our situation as English readers worsens appreciably, as the many unlike versions of Andromache's appeal to Hector make very clear. But, again, only appreciably. True, this is the point at which the fact that a translation is *always* an interpretation explodes irresistibly on our attention; but if it is the best translation of its time, like John Ciardi's translation of the *Divine Comedy* for our time, the result will be not only a sensitive interpretation but also a work with intrinsic interest in its own right—at very best, a true work of art, a new poem. In these longer works, moreover, even if the translation is uninspired, many distinctive structural features—plot, setting, characters, meetings, partings, confrontations, and specific episodes generally—survive virtually unchanged. Hence even in translation it remains both possible and instructive to compare, say, concepts of the heroic or attitudes toward women or uses of religious ritual among civilizations as various as those reflected in the *Iliad*, the *Mahābhārata*, *Beowulf*, and the epic of *Son-Jara*. It is only when the shorter, primarily lyrical forms of poetry are presented that the reader of translations faces insuperable disadvantage. In these forms, the referential aspect of language has a tendency to disappear into, or, more often, draw its real meaning and accreditation from, the iconic aspect. Let us look for just a moment at a brief poem by Federico García Lorca and its English translation (by Stephen Spender and J. L. Gili):

> ¡Alto pinar!
> Cuatro palomas por el aire van.
>
> Cuatro palomas
> vuelan y tornan.
> Llevan heridas
> sus cuatro sombras.
>
> ¡Bajo pinar!
> Cuatro palomas en la tierra están.

> Above the pine trees:
> Four pigeons go through the air.
>
> Four pigeons
> fly and turn round.
> They carry wounded
> their four shadows.
>
> Below the pine trees:
> Four pigeons lie on the earth.

In this translation the referential sense of the English words follows with remarkable exactness the referential sense of the Spanish words they replace. But the life of Lorca's poem does not lie in that sense. It lies in such matters as the abruptness, like an intake of breath at a sudden revelation, of the two exclamatory lines (1 and 7), which then exhale musically in images of flight and death; or as the echoings of *palomas* in *heridas* and *sombras*, bringing together (as in fact the hunter's gun has done) these unrelated nouns and the unrelated experiences they stand for in a sequence that seems, momentarily, to have all the logic of a tragic action, in which *doves* become *wounds* become *shadows*, or as the external and internal rhyming among the five verbs, as though all motion must (as in fact it must) end with *están*.

Since none of this can be brought over into another tongue (least of all Lorca's rhythms), the translator must decide between leaving a reader to wonder why Lorca is a poet to be bothered about at all and making a new but true poem, whose merit will almost certainly be in inverse ratio to its likeness to the original. Samuel Johnson made such a poem in translating Horace's famous *Diffugere nives*, and so did A. E. Housman. If we juxtapose the last two stanzas of each translation, and the corresponding Latin, we can see at a glance that each has the consistency and inner life of a genuine poem and that neither of them (even if we consider only what is obvious to the eye, the line-lengths) is very close to Horace:

> *Cum semel occideris, et de te splendida Minos*
> *fecerit arbitria,*

> non, Torquate, genus, non te facundia, non te
> restituet pietas.
>
> Infernis neque enim tenebris Diana pudicum
> liberat Hippolytum
> nec Lethaea valet Theseus abrumpere caro
> vincula Pirithoo.

Johnson:

> Not you, Torquatus, boast of Rome,
> When Minos once has fixed your doom,
> Or eloquence, or splendid birth,
> Or virtue, shall restore to earth.
> Hippolytus, unjustly slain,
> Diana calls to life in vain;
> Nor can the might of Theseus rend
> The chains of hell that hold his friend.

Housman:

> When thou descendest once the shades among,
> The stern assize and equal judgment o'er,
> Not thy long lineage nor thy golden tongue,
> No, nor thy righteousness, shall friend thee more.
>
> Night holds Hippolytus the pure of stain,
> Diana steads him nothing, he must stay;
> And Theseus leaves Pirithous in the chain
> The love of comrades cannot take away.

The truth of the matter is that when the translator of short poems chooses to be literal, most or all of the poetry is lost; and when the translator succeeds in forging a new poetry, most or all of the original author is lost. Since there is no way out of this dilemma, we have always been sparing, in this anthology, in our use of short poems in translation.

In this Expanded Edition, we have adjusted our policy to take account of the two great non-Western literatures in which the short lyric or "song" has been the principal and by far most cherished expression of the national genius. During much of its history from earliest times, the Japanese imagination has cheerfully exercised itself, with all the delicacy and grace of an Olympic figure skater, inside a rigorous verse pattern of five lines and thirty-one syllables: the *tanka*. Chinese poetry, while somewhat more liberal to itself in line length, has been equally fertile in the fine art of compression and has only occasionally, even in its earliest, most experimental phase, indulged in verse lines of more than seven characters, often just four, or in poems of more than fifty lines, usually fewer than twenty. What makes the Chinese and Japanese lyric more difficult than most other lyrics to translate satisfactorily into English is that these compressions combine with a flexibility of syntax (Japanese) or a degree of freedom from it (Chinese) not available in our language. They also combine with a poetic sensibility that shrinks from exposition in favor of sequences and juxtapositions of images: images grasped and recorded in, or *as if in*, a moment of pure perception unencumbered by the explanatory linkages, background scenarios, and other forms of contextualization that the Western mind is instinctively driven to establish.

Whole books, almost whole libraries, have been written recently on the contrast of East and West in worldviews and value systems as well as on the need of each for the other if there is ever to be a community of understanding adequate to the realities both face. Put baldly, much too simply, and without the many exceptions and qualifications that rightly spring to mind, it may be said that a central and characteristic Western impulse, from the Greeks on down, has been to see the world around us as something to be *acted on*: weighed, measured, managed, used, even (when economic interests prevail over all others) fouled. Likewise, put oversimply, it may be said that a central and characteristic Eastern counterpart to this over many centuries (witness Taoism, Buddhism, and Hinduism, among others) has been to see that same world as something to be *received*: contemplated, touched, tasted, smelled, heard, and most especially, immersed in until observer and observed are one. To paint a bamboo, a stone, a butterfly, a person—so runs a classical Chinese admonition for painters— you must *become* that bamboo, that stone, that butterfly, that person, then paint from the inside. No one need be ashamed of being poor, says Confucius, putting a similar emphasis on *receiving* experience, "only of not being cultivated in the perception of beauty."

The problem that these differences in linguistic freedom and philosophical outlook pose for the English translator of classical Chinese and Japanese poetry may be glimpsed, even if not fully grasped, by considering for a moment in some detail a typical Japanese *tanka* (*Kokinshu*, 9) and a typical Chinese "song" (*Book of Songs*, 23). In its own language but transliterated in the Latin alphabet of the West, the *tanka* looks like this:

> *kasumi tachi*
> *ko no me mo haru no*
> *yuki fureba*
> *hana naki sato mo*
> *hana zo chirikeru*

In a literal word-by-word translation (so far as this is possible in Japanese, since the language uses many particles without English equivalents and without dictionary meaning in modifying and qualifying functions—for example, *no*, *mo*, and *no* in line 2), the poem looks like this:

> haze rises
> tree-buds swell
> when snow falls
> village(s) without flower(s)
> flower(s) fall(s)

The three best-known English renderings of this *tanka* look like this:

1. Helen Craig McCullough:

> When snow comes in spring—
> fair season of layered haze
> and burgeoning buds—
> flowers fall in villages
> where flowers have yet to bloom.

2. Laurel Rasplica Rodd and Mary Catherine Henkenius:

> When the warm mists veil
> all the buds swell while yet the
> spring snows drift downward
> even in the hibernal
> village crystal blossoms fall.

3. Robert H. Brower and Earl Miner:

> With the spreading mists
> The tree buds swell in early spring
> And wet snow petals fall—

> So even my flowerless country village
> Already lies beneath its fallen flowers.

The reader will notice at once how much the three translators have felt it desirable or necessary to add, alter, rearrange, and explain. In McCullough's version the time of year is affirmed twice, both as "spring" and as "fair season of . . . haze"; the haze is now "layered"; the five coordinate perceptions of the original (haze, swelling buds, a snowfall, villages without flowers, flowers drifting down) have been structured into a single sentence with one main verb and two subordinate clauses spelling out "when" and "where"; and the original poem's climax, in a scene of drifting petallike snow-flakes, has been shifted to a bleak scenery of absence: "flowers have yet to bloom." The final stress, in other words, is not on the fulfilled moment in which snow flowers replace the cherry blossoms, but on the cherry blossoms not yet arrived.

Similar additions and explanations occur in Rodd and Henkenius's version. This time the mist is "warm" and "veil[s] all" to clarify its connection with "buds." Though implicit already in "warm" and "burgeoning," spring is invoked again in "spring snows," and the snows are given confirmation in the following line by the insistently Latinate "hibernal," chosen, we may reasonably guess, along with "veil," "all," "swell," "while," "crystal," and "fall" to replace some of the chiming internal rhyme in the Japanese: *ko, no, mo, no, sato, mo, zo*. To leave no *i* undotted, "crystal" is imported to assure us that the falling "blossoms" of line 5 are really snowflakes, and the scene of flowerlessness in the original (line 4) accounts for a special joy in the "flowering" of the snowflakes (line 5) vanishes without trace.

Brower and Miner's also fills in the causative links between "spreading mists" and swelling buds; makes sure that we do not fail to see the falling snow in flower terms ("wet snow petals"), thus losing, alas, the element of surprise, even magic, in the trans-formation of snowflakes into flowers that the original poem holds in store in its last two lines; and tells us (somewhat redundantly) that villages are a "country" phenom-enon and (somewhat surprisingly) that this one is the speaker's home. In this version, as in the original and Rodd and Henkenius's, the poem closes with the snow scene, but here it is a one-time affair and "already" complete (lines 4 and 5), not a recurrent phenomenon that may appear under certain conditions anywhere at any time.

Some of the differences in these translations arise inevitably from different trade-offs, as in the first version, where the final vision of falling snow blossoms is let go presumably to achieve the lovely lilting echo and rhetorical turn of "flowers fall in villages / where flowers have yet to bloom." Or as in Rodd and Henkenius's version, where preoccupations with internal rhyme have obviously influenced word choices, not always for the better. Or as in all three versions, where different efforts to remind the reader of the wordplay on *haru* (in the Japanese poem both a noun meaning "spring" and a verb meaning "swell") have had dissimilar but perhaps equally indif-ferent results. Meantime, the immense force compacted into that small word in the original as both noun and verb, season of springtime and principal of growth, cause and effect (and thus in a sense the whole mighty process of earth's renewal, in which an interruption by snow only foretells a greater loveliness to come) fizzles away unfelt. A few differences do seem to arise from insufficient command of the nerves and sinews of English poetry, but most spring from the staggering difficulties of respond-ing in any uniform way to the minimal clues proffered by the original text. The five perceptions—haze, buds, snowfall, flowerless villages, flowers falling—do not as they stand in the Japanese or any literal translation quite compose for readers accustomed to Western poetic traditions an adequate poetic whole. This is plainly seen in the irresistible urge each of the translators has felt to catch up the individual perceptions, as English tends to require, in a tighter overall grammatical and syntactical structure than the original insists on. In this way they provide a clarifying network of principal and subordinate, time when, place where, and cause why. Yet the inevitable result is a disassembling, a spinning out, spelling out, thinning out of what in the Japanese is an as yet unraveled imagistic excitement, creating (or memorializing) in the poet's mind, and then in the mind of the Japanese readers, the original thrill of consciousness when these images, complete with the magical transformation of snow into the longed-for cherry blossoms, first flashed on the inward eye.

What is comforting for us who must read this and other Japanese poems in translation is that each of the versions given here retains in some form or other all or most of the five images intact. What is less comforting is that the simplicity and suddenness, the explosion in the mind, have been diffused and defused.

When we turn to the Chinese song, we find similarly contesting forces at work. In one respect, the Chinese language comes over into English more readily than Japanese, being like English comparatively uninflected and heavily dependent on word order for its meanings. But in other respects, since Chinese like Japanese lacks distinctions of gender, of singular and plural, of *a* and *the*, and in the classical mode in which the poems in this anthology are composed, also of tenses, the pressure of the English translator to rearrange, straighten out, and fill in to "make sense" for his or her readers remains strong.

Let us examine song no. 23 of the *Shijing*. In its own Chinese characters, it looks like this:

野有死麕

野有死麕。白茅
包之。有女懷春。
吉士誘之。
林有樸樕。野有
死鹿。白茅純束。
有女如玉。
舒而脫脫兮。無
感我帨兮。無使
尨也吠。

Eleven lines in all, each line having four characters as its norm, the poem seemingly takes shape around an implicit parallel between a doe in the forest, possibly killed by stealth and hidden under long grass or rushes (though on this point as on all others the poem refuses to take us wholly into confidence), and a young girl possibly "ruined" (as she certainly would have been in the post-Confucian society in which the *Shijing* was prized and circulated, though here again the poem keeps its own counsel) by loss of her virginity before marriage.

In its bare bones, with each character given an approximate English equivalent, a translation might look like this:

wild(s)	is	dead	deer	
white	grass(es)	wrap/cover	(it).	
is	girl	feel	spring.	
fine	man	tempt	(her).	
woods	is(are)	bush(es),	underbrush.	5
wild(s)	is	dead	deer.	
white	grass(es)	bind	bundle.	
is	girl	like	jade.	
slow	——	slow	slow.	
not	move	my	sash.	10
not	cause	dog	bark.	

Lines 1 to 4, it seems plain, propose the parallel of slain doe and girl, whatever that parallel may be intended to mean. Lines 5 to 8 restate the parallel, adding that the girl is as beautiful as jade and (apparently) that the doe lies where the "wild" gives way to smaller growth. If we allow ourselves to account for the repetition (here again is a Western mind-set in search of explanatory clues) by supposing that lines 1 to 4 signal at some subliminal level the initiation of the seduction and lines 5 to 8, again subliminally, its progress or possibly its completion, lines 9 to 11 fall easily into place as a miniature drama enacting in direct speech the man's advances and the girl's gradually crumbling resistance. They also imply, it seems, that the seduction takes place not in the forest, as we might have been led to suppose by lines 1 to 8, but in a dwelling with a vigilant guard dog.

Interpreted just far enough to accommodate English syntax, the poem reads as follows:

1. Wai-lim Yip:

> In the wilds, a dead doe.
> White reeds to wrap it.
> A girl, spring-touched.
> A fine man to seduce her.
> In the woods, bushes. 5
> In the wilds, a dead deer.
> White reeds in bundles.
> A girl like jade.
> Slowly. Take it easy.
> Don't feel my sash! 10
> Don't make the dog bark!

Interpreted a stage further in a format some have thought better suited to English poetic traditions, the poem reads:

2. Arthur Waley:

> In the wilds there is a dead doe,
> With white rushes we cover her.
> There was a lady longing for spring,
> A fair knight seduced her.
>
> In the woods there is a clump of oaks, 5
> And in the wilds a dead deer
> With white rushes well bound.
> There was a lady fair as jade.
>
> "Heigh, not so hasty, not so rough.
> "Heigh, do not touch my handkerchief. 10
> "Take care or the dog will bark."

Like the original and the literal translation, this version leaves the relationship between the doe's death and the girl's seduction unspecified and problematic. It holds the doe story in present tenses, assigning the girl story to the past. Still, much has been changed to give the English poem an explanatory scenario. The particular past assigned to the girl story, indeterminate in the Chinese original, is here fixed as the age of knights and ladies; and the seduction itself, which in the Chinese hovers as an eternal possibility within the timeless situation of man and maid ("A fine man *to* seduce her"), is established as completed long ago: "A fair knight seduced her." A teasing oddity in this version is the mysterious "we" who "cover" the slain doe, never to be heard from again.

Take interpretation toward its outer limits and we reach what is perhaps best called a "variation" on this theme:

3. Ezra Pound:

> Lies a dead doe on yonder plain
> whom white grass covers,
> A melancholy maid in spring
>   is luck
>   for 5
>   lovers

Where the scrub elm skirts the wood
be it not in white mat bound,
As a jewel flawless found
        dead as a doe is maidenhood.   10
Hark!
Unhand my girdle knot.
    Stay, stay, stay
    or the dog
    may   15
    bark.

Here too the present is pushed back to a past by the language the translator uses: not a specific past, as with the era of knights and ladies, but any past in which contemporary speech still features such (to us) archaic formalisms as "Unhand" or "Hark," and in which the term "maid" still signifies a virgin and in which virginity is prized to an extent that equates its loss with the doe's loss of life. But these evocations of time past are so effectively countered by the obtrusively present tense throughout (lines 1, 2, 4, 7, 8, 10, 11, 12, 13, and 15) that the freewheeling "variation" remains in this important respect closer to the spirit of the original than Waley's translation. On the other hand, it departs from the original and the two other versions by brushing aside the reticence that they carefully preserve as to the precise implications of the girl-deer parallel, choosing instead to place the seduction in the explanatory framework of the oldest story in the world: the way of a man with a maid in the springtime of life.

What both these examples make plain is that the Chinese and Japanese lyric, however contrasting in some ways, have in common at their center a complex of highly charged images generating something very like a magnetic field of potential meanings that cannot be got at in English without bleeding away much of the voltage. In view of this, the best practical advice for those of us who must read these marvelous poems in English translations is to focus intently on these images and ask ourselves what there is in them or in their effect on each other that produces the electricity. To that extent, we can compensate for a part of our losses, learn something positive about the immense explosive powers of imagery, and rest easy in the secure knowledge that translation even in the mode of the short poem brings us (despite losses) closer to the work itself than not reading it at all. "To a thousand cavils," said Samuel Johnson, "one answer is sufficient; the purpose of a writer is to be read, and the criticism which would destroy the power of pleasing must be blown aside." Johnson was defending Pope's Homer for those marks of its own time and place that make it the great interpretation it is, but Johnson's exhilarating common sense applies equally to the problem we are considering here. Literature is to be read, and the criticism that would destroy the reader's power to make some form of contact with much of the world's great writing must indeed be blown aside.

MAYNARD MACK

Sources

Brower, Robert H., and Earl Miner. *Japanese Court Poetry*. Stanford: Stanford University Press, 1961.

The Classic Anthology Defined by Confucius. Tr. Ezra Pound. New Directions, 1954.

Kokinshū: A Collection of Poems Ancient and Modern. Tr. Laurel Rasplica Rodd and Mary Catherine Henkenius. Princeton: Princeton University Press, 1984.

Kokin Wakashū: The First Imperial Anthology of Japanese Poetry. Tr. and ed. Helen Craig McCullough. Stanford: Stanford University Press, 1985.

Legge, James. *The Chinese Classics*. Hong Kong: Hong Kong University Press, 1960.

Waley, Arthur. *170 Chinese Poems*. New York, 1919.

Index